The 1995-96 Official PFA

FOOTBALLI

FACTFI

The Facts & Figures on over 2,000 Professional Players
EDITED BY BARRY J. HUGMAN

Alan Shearer, the 1995 P.F.A. "Player Of The Year"

Stanley Paul
LONDON

First published 1995

1 3 5 7 9 10 8 6 4 2

© Barry Hugman, 1995

Barry Hugman has asserted his right under
the Copyright, Designs and Patent Act, 1988
to be identified as the author of this work

First published in the United Kingdom in 1995 by
Stanley Paul
Random House, 20 Vauxhall Bridge Road, London SW1V 2SA

Random House Australia (Pty) Limited
20 Alfred Street, Milsons Point, Sydney,
New South Wales 2061, Australia

Random House New Zealand Limited
18 Poland Road, Glenfield
Auckland 10, New Zealand

Random House South Africa (Pty) Limited
PO Box 337, Bergvlei, South Africa

Random House UK Limited Reg. No. 954009

A CIP catalogue record for this book
is available from the British Library

ISBN 0091808545

Title page photo: Neal Simpson (Empics Sports Photo Agency)

Typeset and designed by Typecast (Artwork & Design),
West Country Marketing, 8 Mudford Road, Yeovil, Somerset BA21 4AA

Printed in Great Britain by BPC Paulton Books Limited

Acknowledgements

A tremendous amount of hard work has gone into this unique publication, with a great deal of help being diligently provided by many people, and I would like to record my gratitude as best I can within these pages.

Firstly, I must thank the Professional Footballers' Association for their great support and endorsement of the product. **Gordon Taylor**, the Chief Executive, has always been supportive of my work ever since I published *Football League Players' Records*, the listing in some fair detail of every player who had played League football since the last war. In this instance, I am most grateful to **Brian Marwood**, the former Arsenal and England star, and now a PFA executive, who has co-ordinated these pages with me and literally proof-read every player profile. Also, the book could not have been completed without the financial backing of Windsor Insurance Brokers Limited, through their Sports Division's Managing Director, **Jonathan Ticehurst**.

As in previous publications, **Michael Featherstone** (Assistant Editor) has been at my side throughout the intensive work load. A keen sporting statistician, he works in the accounts department of a large public company and first became interested in the sport many years ago when collecting statistical information appertaining to players.

The FA Premier League and the Football League have always been most helpful providing information for past people I have been involved in and this year was no exception. In helping to make this work complete, my thanks go to **Mike Foster** and **Neil Harrison** and **Sheila Murphy** and **Debbie Birch**, respectively.

International appearances at varying levels, even if current, are always difficult to track down with so many games during a season these days and help in this area is forthcoming from **David Barber** (English FA), **Kitty Barlers** (FA of Ireland), **Malcolm Brodie** (Belfast Telegraph), **Marion Nelson** (Scottish FA), and **Ceri Stennett** (Official FAW statistician).

For details provided on players, I have listed below, in alphabetical order, the names of the "team", without whose help this book would not have been possible to produce. I thank every one of them for all the hard work they put in.

Audrey Adams *(Watford):* Producer and statistician for BBC Radio Sport and a Watford supporter since the days of Cliff Holton, Audrey is also the club statistician for the *Endsleigh League Directory*.

Steve Adamson *(Scarborough):* Previously the club programme editor for eight years, and a lifelong supporter, Steve possesses a massive collection of "Boro" statistics going back to 1879.

Denise Allibone *(Aston Villa):* In her own words, Denise is a mad, crazy Villa supporter, who follows them up-and-down the country without fail. Her only previous football work was to help me with the club's profiles required for the *Premier League: The Players* publication.

Geoff Allman *(Walsall):* A university lecturer by trade, he saw his first ever game in February 1944; Walsall versus "Wolves". Has written for Walsall's programme for the last 27 seasons and, at one time or another, has provided articles for more than half of the clubs currently in the Premiership and Football League. Geoff is also a Methodist local preacher and press officer.

Lawrence Appleby *(Hereford United):* In supporting Hereford for 25 years, for the past 15 he has collected stats and club history and has provided the data for the *Endsleigh League Directory*. Currently writing two club histories in between attending over 200 matches at all levels in 1994-95. Our thanks also go to **John Layton** (manager) and **Simon Shakeshaft** (physio) for assisting on the player profiles.

Stuart Basson *(Chesterfield):* The founding editor of the *Crooked Spireite* publication and a former contributor to the club programme, Stuart would welcome any enquiries on Chesterfield.

Ian Bates *(Bradford):* Has followed City since 1951 and refereed in amateur football up until last season. A member of the AFS, this is the first publication that Ian has been involved in.

David Batters *(York City):* A supporter since 1948, he is club historian, a contributor to the programme and author of *York City: The Complete Record 1922-1990*. Also commentates on matches at York Hospital.

Harry Berry *(Blackburn Rovers):* Author of the club centenary history, *A Century of Soccer* and other books on Rovers, and co-author of the *Preston North End* history, along with several books on athletics.

Peter Bishop *(Tranmere Rovers):* The club's programme editor and historian for ten years, Peter is the author of the *"A-Z of Tranmere"*, the first book ever published on Rovers. Has also contributed to many other books.

Simon Bowden *(Barnet):* As Sports Editor of the *Barnet Advertiser*, he has followed the club home and away for the past two seasons. I am especially grateful to Simon, as he stepped into the breach at the 11th hour.

Peter Bower and **Ken Craig** *(Colchester United):* The former, a lifelong fan since the mid-1950s, worked with Ken to produce the input for the enclosed. The latter currently edits a monthly newsletter for all United fans living away from the area called *U's from 'Ome.*

Eddie Brennan *(Sunderland):* A regular at Roker since 1976 (aged nine) and currently the club statistician for the *Endsleigh League Directory*.

Stuart Brennan *(Stockport County):* As sports editor of the *Stockport Express* newspaper from 1989 to 1994, he covered the club's fortunes both home and away and was a programme contributor. Also County's statistician for the *Endsleigh League Directory*.

Jonathan Brewer *(Plymouth Argyle):* Currently the Argyle statistician for the *Endsleigh League Directory*, Jonathan also writes articles for the *Pasty News*, a publication run by the London branch of the Supporters' Club.

Jim Brown *(Coventry City):* The club's official statistician and contributor to the programme, he also pens a column for the local newspaper answering readers' queries.

Derek Buckle *(Southampton):* A member of the AFS (Association of Football Statisticians) and a "Saints" fan for 35 years. Formerly the club contributor to the *Rothmans Yearbook*.

Trevor Bugg *(Hull City):* Is a contributor to City's innovative matchday programme and also a committee member of the club's fund-raising "Put a Tiger in your Team Appeal".

Simon Case *(Wimbledon):* Other football publications Simon has voluntarily compiled statistics and text for, include the *Endsleigh League Directory (1992-1996)* and the *FA Carling Premiership: The Players (1993-1994)*.

Graham Caton *(Bournemouth):* Along with **Janey Orchard**, Graham was introduced by another member of the team, and did well in helping rein in all the information required on the "Cherries'" players.

Wallace Chadwick *(Burnley):* A supporter for over 30 years, he has seen all the extremes in the period from the great days of the '60s, including the Championship of all four divisions and a narrow escape from relegation to the Conference. Wallace is a regular contributor to the "Clarets'" programme.

Dennis Chapman *(Manchester City):* Now retired, Dennis has followed City since 1937-38. Has worked on several publications, including the *FA Carling Premier League: The Players* and the *Endsleigh League Directory*. Possesses possibly the largest collection of City programmes, the earliest being 1902-03.

Paul Clayton *(Charlton Athletic):* Writes in the club's matchday programme and various other publications connected with the club. A Charlton season ticket-holder, despite living in Wiltshire, and a member of the AFS, Paul also compiles the statistics for the *Endsleigh League Directory*.

Grant Coleby *(Exeter City):* A member of the Exeter City Supporters Club and the AFS, this is the first publication he has worked on and proved to be a valued member of the team.

Eddie Collins *(Nottingham Forest):* A Forest supporter since 1956, and a member of the Associated Football Statisticians, this is the first publication he has been involved in.

David Copping *(Barnsley):* The writer of the past meetings column in the Barnsley programme for the last six seasons, he also commentated live hospital broadcasts from Oakwell between 1978 and 1991 and has since narrated for the club videos.

Frank Coumbe *(Brentford):* Has seen every "Bees'" first team match since 1977. A contributor to the Brentford matchday magazine for many years, and the club statistician for the *Endsleigh League*

Directory for the past 11 years, Frank has also written for other club's magazines.

Mike Davage *(Norwich City)*: Author of the ultimate who's who, *Glorious Canaries*, and co-author of *Canary Citizens*. Presently involved in the seventh volume of the *Norwich City handbook* and is a regular contributor to local and national TV, radio and newspapers. As a contributor to over 60 books, Mike is currently working with Jim Creasy on a 1919-1939 supplemental book to the author's *Football League Players' Records, 1946-1992*.

Gareth Davies *(Wrexham)*: Assists in the much acclaimed club programme, the editor of which, **Geraint Parry**, also helped on heights and weights, etc, for this publication. Gareth has written and published the *Coast of Soccer Memories*, the centenary history of the *North Wales Coast FA (1995)*, and co-authored with Ian Garland the *Who's Who of Welsh International Soccer Players (1991)*. Also heavily involved in *Wrexham, A Complete Record 1872-1992*, written by Peter Jones. Currently researching *Wrexham FC's Who's Who* at the moment, he still finds time to compile the club section for the *Endsleigh League Directory* and to help me with the names of all current players who have won Welsh Cup winners' medals.

David Downs *(Reading)*: Teaches in a local primary school and works part-time for Reading FC at their Centre of Excellence. The official historian and statistician for the club, David is the author of *"Biscuits & Royals"*, the history of Reading.

Dave Drage *(Birmingham City)*: A City supporter since 1966, he has contributed to the *Endsleigh League Directory* every year since its inception. Has also contributed to the *History of Birmingham City (1989)* and the *Who's Who of Birmingham City (1991)*. Is on the committee of the recently formed "Blues'" Collectors and Historical Society.

Mark Evans *(Leeds United)*: Has supported United for the last 27 years and describes his association with the club as one of the loves of his life. The Leeds' statistician for Tony Williams' *Endsleigh League Directory* for nearly seven years, he was also involved in my two editions of the *FA Carling Premiership: The Players*.

Colin Faiers *(Cambridge United)*: A 36-year-old chartered accountant, Colin, a fan for over 25 years, is the recognised club statistician and currently writes the historical features for the programme. Planned for 1995-96 are pen-portraits on all the 250+ players who have appeared in the Football League.

Harold Finch *(Crewe Alexandra)*: The club's historian and a supporter for over 60 years, Harold has been the programme editor for more than 40 of them. A one club man, he has travelled extensively to watch them play.

Paul Gilligan *(Doncaster Rovers)*: A keen follower of Rovers for over 30 years, Paul has written three books on the club and is a regular contributor in the matchday programme. Also the official club photographer.

Dave Goody *(Southend United)*: United historian, statistician and collector, he co-authored *Southend United: The Official History of the Blues* and is a regular contributor to the programme.

Frank Grande *(Northampton Town)*: Author of *The Cobblers, A History of Northampton Town FC* and a *Who's Who* on the club. Has contributed a regular column to the club programme for the past 15 seasons.

Roy Grant *(Oxford United)*: Assistant Secretary at Oxford. As the club programme editor and statistician, he also handles the Clubline telephone service. Contributes to the *Endsleigh League Directory* and, in the past, the *Official Football League Yearbook*.

Paul Greenlees *(Bury)*: Has been going to Gigg Lane since the late '60s following a family tradition dating back to 1910. On matchday he can be found on the television gantry where he provides the commentary for the club's video. Collects Bury memorabilia and is always on the lookout for unusual items.

Don Hales *(Leyton Orient and Luton Town)*: A management consultant in financial services, Don has contributed to *World Soccer, Team Talk* and the *Endsleigh Directory*, as well as compiling the obituary column for the AFS. In compiling the Orient and Luton information, Don was assisted by life-long "O's" fan, **David Randlesome**, a chartered accountant, and his son, **Daniel Hales**, currently studying for his A-levels, respectively.

Roger Harrison *(Blackpool)*: Lifelong supporter who has seen the "Pool" play every other League side both home and away. Joint programme editor and club statistician, Roger also contributes to other publications, including the *Endsleigh League Directory*.

Ron Hockings *(Chelsea)*: Has now published four books involving the history of Chelsea, European and South American Cups. *The Nations of Europe*, currently available in two volumes, includes every line-up for all the European countries' matches up until 1993, with volume three envisaged being ready early in 1997. Ron is currently working on *90 Years of the "Blues"*, the statistical history of Chelsea, and would welcome any contributions.

Mike Jay *(Bristol Rovers)*: Apart from helping out on other publications, notably the *Endsleigh League Directory*, Mike has had two books of his own published on Bristol Rovers, namely *The Complete Record (1883-1987)* and *Pirates in Profile, A Who's Who of the Players 1920-1995*.

Alan Jenkins *(Cardiff City)*: Lifelong Cardiff fan who formerly produced statistics for the *Rothmans Yearbook*, but now provides the service for the *Endsleigh League Directory*. Publishes a regular music magazine and is involved in various other publications.

Colin Jones *(Swansea City)*: A fan since the early 1960s and a contributor to the club programme during the last four years. Played non-league football, also later being involved in training and coaching.

Gordon Lawton *(Oldham Athletic)*: Employed as the Public Relations Officer at the club and Athletic's official photographer. Other publications contributed to, include *Carling Premiership: The Players, Rothmans Yearbook, Endsleigh League Directory* and *News of the World* annual.

Geoffrey Lea *(Wigan Athletic)*: The club statistician for the *Endsleigh League Directory*, Geoffrey has been following the "Latics" for over 20 years and is a major contributor to the matchday programme that won the "Third Division Programme of the Year" in 1993-94. Also assists with the match commentary on the Clubcall.

Richard Lindsay *(Millwall)*: Author of *Millwall: The Complete Record 1895-1991*, and currently in the process of helping establish the Millwall FC Museum at the New Den. If any fans or ex-players feel they can help, please ring 0171 232 1222. Further assistance came from **Deano Standing**.

John Lovis *(Torquay United)*: A supporter since 1955, and a regular contributor to the club programme, he is also United's statistician for the *Endsleigh League Directory*.

Steve McGhee *(Derby County)*: A collector of Derby memorabilia and a fan since 1969. Earlier involved in a bi-monthly historical magazine on County, he currently compiles the club section for the *Endsleigh League Directory*.

Peter Macey *(Portsmouth)*: A contributor to the "Pompey" matchday programme, Peter also supplies the club input for the *Endsleigh League Directory* and is yet another member of the AFS.

John Maguire *(Manchester United)*: A member of the AFS for many years, and a qualified FA coach, John has recently completed four booklets entitled *"The Dream Double"* and is currently working on others sports related topics.

Simon Marland *(Bolton Wanderers)*: Club historian, statistician, and editor of Wanderers' matchday programme, he is also the author of *Bolton Wanderers: A Complete Record* and *One Hundred Years at Burnden Park, 1895-1995*.

John Martin *(Chester City)*: Club statistician for both the *Rothmans Yearbook* and *Endsleigh League Directory*, he also contributes for various other publications. Was City's programme editor for ten years up until 1993-94, winning the "Third Division Programme of the Year" award that same season.

Wade Martin *(Stoke City)*: For many years a major contributor to the club programme, as well as writing *A Potters Tale* and the *Master Potters'* series of books.

Tony Matthews *(West Bromwich Albion)*: Official statistician and curator of Albion, his publications include, the *complete records of Aston Villa, Birmingham City, WBA, "Wolves", Walsall* and *Stoke City*. Has also compiled *Who's Whos* on the first four clubs listed above, plus Manchester United and currently contributes to eight programmes.

Ian Mills *(Notts County)*: Saw his first County game in 1959-60 when his grandfather took him and has been hooked ever since, missing just one game since 1970. Ian, who can be reached at the club shop, runs the matchday programme sales at Meadow Lane.

Ian Nannestad *(Lincoln City)*: A past contributor to the "Imps'" programme and co-author of the *Who's Who of Lincoln City, 1892-1994*, publication.

John Northcutt (*West Ham United*): Has supported the "Hammers" since 1959 and is the co-author of West Ham books, *The Complete Record* and the *Illustrated History*. A regular contributor to the club programme and the club adviser to the *Endsleigh League Directory*.

Michael Norton (*Scunthorpe United*): Former matchday club programme editor and now a contributor, Michael is also the "Irons'" statistician for the *Endsleigh League Directory*. Is an avid collector of programmes and memorabilia.

Janey Orchard and Richard Hayhoe (*Tottenham Hotspur*): Introduced by a member of the "team", this was the first time Janey, aided by Richard, had done anything of this nature. However, it all came right in the end and a big "thank you" is in order.

Brian Pead (*Liverpool*): Author of three editions of *Liverpool, A Complete Record*, *Liverpool: Champion of Champions* (1990) and *Ee Aye Addio - We've Won the Cup* (1993), Brian was the statistician for the *Rush for Glory* video and has contributed to many publications, including the *Footballer* magazine and the *Endsleigh League Directory*.

Steve Peart and Dave Finch (*Wycombe Wanderers*): A former programme editor of the club and a supporter for over 20 years, Steve put together the player profiles, while the club statistics were supplied by Dave, the official Wycombe statistician.

Steve Phillips (*Rochdale*): A "Dale" fan of 30 years standing, he is the club's official statistician and author of *The Survivors: The Story of Rochdale AFC*.

Paul Plowman (*Swindon Town*): Football historian, statistician and freelance journalist.

Mike Purkiss (*Crystal Palace*): Having supported Palace since 1950 and produced stats on them since 1960, Mike is the author of the *Complete History of Crystal Palace, 1905-1989*, the club statistician for the *Endsleigh League Directory* and contributed to *Premier League: The Players*.

Mike Renshaw (*Sheffield Wednesday*): Has followed Wednesday for 40 years and is a great supporter of European soccer. Currently produces the club section for the *Endsleigh League Directory*.

Mick Robinson (*Peterborough United*): Another lifelong fan, for a number of years Mick has contributed to the club programme and was the joint editor of the *Official Peterborough History*. Also the club statistician for the *Endsleigh League Directory*.

Phil Sherwin (*Port Vale*): As Vale's statistician, Phil works on a number of other publications and has contributed to the club programme for 14 years. A fan since 1968, he follows them home and away.

Andy Shute (*Queens Park Rangers*): Life-long QPR supporter and compiler of the QPR and Tottenham details for the *Endsleigh League Directory*.

Derrick Slasor (*Middlesbrough*): First saw the "Boro" play in December 1946 and, as Managing Director of Trapezium Transport Services, is well known in the area for sponsoring various club activities.

Mike Slater (*Wolverhampton Wanderers*): Having seen the majority of "Wolves'" matches since 1965, Mike both wrote and published a book in 1988 on the club history called *"Molineux Memories"*, selling all 3,600 copies over two years. Since 1990, he has compiled and read out the questions for the *"Brain of Wolves'"* quiz.

Gordon Small (*Hartlepool United*): Has supported United since October 1965, experiencing two promotions, two relegations, six re-elections and several close calls. Is the statistician for the *Endsleigh League Directory*.

Dave Smith (*Leicester City*): A regular columnist in the programme, co-author of *Fossils & Foxes* and the forthcoming *Foxes Alphabet* to be published in October 1995, he assists with several other club handbooks.

Gerry Somerton (*Rotherham United*): Deputy Sports Editor of the *Rotherham Advertiser* and part-time sports reporter for the New Hallam FM local commercial radio station. Author of the *Official History of Rotherham United*, due to be published in November 1995.

Richard Stead (*Huddersfield Town*): Has supported his hometown team, Huddersfield, since the early '70s and, despite living in Manchester these days, continues to do so. Also contributes to the *Endsleigh League Directory*.

David Steele (*Carlisle United*): A regular contributor to the club programme for several years now, his current interest is in tracking down ex-United players.

Pete Stevenson (*Mansfield Town*): Club statistician for the *Endsleigh League Directory* and a member of the AFS, Pete has followed the "Stags" for over 40 years.

David Stewart (*Newcastle United*): Has supported United since 1963 and is the club contributor for the *Endsleigh League Directory* and produced work for the final edition of the *FA Carling Premier League: The Players*.

Richard Stocken (*Shrewsbury Town*): A supporter of 37 years and a collector of club programmes and memorabilia, Richard is an annual contributor to the *Endsleigh League Directory* and other publications.

Richard Swift (*Everton*): The Everton statistician for both the *FA Carling Premier League: The Players* and the *Endsleigh League Directory*, Richard is an enthusiastic Everton and Sheffield Wednesday supporter.

Alan Tait (*Scottish clubs*): A regular contributor to Tony Brown's ultimate *Scottish League* book and a compiler of statistics appertaining to that country, Alan is currently working on a project, probably five years down the road, that will give line-ups for all Scottish League matches since 1890.

Chris Thompson (*Arsenal*): Born in Greenwich the week before Charlton won the FA Cup, Chris has held season tickets for both the Valley and Highbury. Publications worked on, include *FA Carling Premiership: The Players* and, currently, the *Endsleigh Directory*.

David Ticehurst (*Brighton & Hove Albion*): Author of *Brighton & Hove Albion, A Portrait in Old Picture Postcards*, Secretary of the Football Postcard Collector's Club and a member of the AFS.

Andrew Treherne (*Sheffield United*): Contributor to the *Endsleigh League Directory*, *The Premier League: The Players* and *Sheffield United: The first Hundred Years*. Also a member of the AFS.

Les Triggs (*Grimsby Town*): First became involved with the statistical side of the club when asked to assist with Town's centenary exhibition in 1978. A retired librarian, Les, who first saw the "Mariners" in a wartime League match, is the co-author of the Grimsby Town volume in the *Complete Record* series and has been club statistician to the *Endsleigh League Directory* since its inception.

Roger Triggs (*Gillingham*): Has written three books on the club, *Gillingham FC - A Chronology 1893-1984*, *Priestfield Profiles 1950-1988* and the centenery publication, *Home of the Shouting Men*, which he co-authored with Andy Bradley. Also a feature writer in the programme since 1975.

Dennis Turner (*Fulham*): Former editor of the club programme and author of *Fulham: A Complete Record*, he has contributed to many magazines and compiles the club section for the *Endsleigh League Directory*.

Frank Tweddle (*Darlington*): The club's official historian and statistician, Frank is the author of *Darlington's Centenary History* and the programme editor since 1975. Also a contributor for various other publications, including the *Endsleigh League Directory*.

Paul Voller (*Ipswich Town*): A Town supporter since 1963-64, Paul works at the ground on matchdays and is a member of the Supporters' Management Committee. Other publications worked on include the *FA Carling Premier League: The Players* and the *Endsleigh League Directory*.

Tony Woodburn and Martin Atherton (*Preston North End*): Tony, who started watching the club in the late '60s and is a member of the AFS, the 92 club and the Scottish 38 club, provided the statistics, while Martin, who has now completed 30 years as a supporter and has seen North End on 50 other grounds, produced the player profiles.

David Woods (*Bristol City*): A life member of the AFS, and a member of the 92 club, David has been watching City on a regular basis since 1958. Has also written two books on his favourite team.

Finally, on the production side of the book, all the photo's were supplied by Neal Simpson and his team at Empics Photo Agency, 26 Musters Road, West Bridgford, Nottingham NG2 7PL. Tel: (0115) 945 5885. As in previous books of mine, they have been more than helpful and, in this case, nobody could have done more to make this publication a viable proposition in the bookshops. Last, but not least, my thanks go to Jean Bastin, of Typecast (Artwork & Design), for her patience and diligent work on the typesetting and design, which went far beyond the call of normal duty and was much appreciated.

Forewords

When Barry Hugman, one of football's finest statisticians and the author of the unique *Football League Players' Records*, approached us with the idea of establishing the Footballers' Factfile, we were more than pleased to endorse the project. This is a work based on statistics and profiles for every professional footballer who played in England and Wales during the 1994-95 season.

The publication has been sponsored by Windsor Insurance Brokers, who play an important role with regard to the protection of players against injury.

I hope the PFA Footballers' Factfile annual becomes a familiar sight on the desks of every football enthusiast, administrator, and commentator of our great game for years to come.

Gordon Taylor, Chief Executive of the Professional Footballers' Association.

The Windsor Insurance Group has been closely involved with professional football for over 20 years. Every registered contract professional player, all of whom appear in this book are, or have been at some time, insured for injury and sickness through the Premier League and Football League Basic Scheme that we arrange.

Additionally, the great majority of players in this book are able to look to a securer future once their playing days are over, by virtue of the Players' Cash Benefit Scheme and the Retirement Income Scheme that was set up jointly with the Football League and the Professional Footballers Association in the mid-1980s.

It is, with this background, that Windsor are only too delighted to be able to support and lend our name as sponsors to this excellent publication.

It is a unique and easy to follow guide and will offer invaluable assistance not only to the administrators of the game and football experts, but will also prove to be a necessity for all genuine lovers and followers of English football.

Probably never before has football enjoyed such high a profile and following – across the generations and both sexes. To everyone who is fortunate enough to obtain a copy of the PFA Footballers' Factfile, I am confident that you will come to regard it as the definitive authority on those currently playing the game. It is also a most enjoyable read.

Jonathan Ticehurst, Managing Director of the Sports Division, Windsor Insurance Brokers

Editorial Introduction

This book, the first of its kind to be published in this country and one that I have longed to be involved in for many years, portrays the statistical career record of every FA Carling Premiership and Endsleigh League player who made an appearance in 1994-95, whether it be in League football, the Football League (Coca Cola) Cup, FA Cup (Sponsored by Littlewoods Pools), Charity Shield, European Cup, European Cup Winners' Cup, UEFA Cup, (Allbright Bitter) Welsh Cup, Anglo-Italian Cup, Auto Windscreen Trophy, or in the Play-Offs. In short, all first class matches. It goes beyond mere statistics, however, with a write-up on all of the 2,280 players involved and also records faithfully last season's playing records separately by club.

The work falls into two sections, both inter-relating. Firstly, the main core, PFA Footballers' Factfile: A-Z (pages 9-242), and secondly, FA Carling Premiership and Endsleigh League Clubs: Summary of Appearances and Goals for 1994-95 (pages 243-256). Below is an explanation on how to follow the PFA Footballers' Factfile.

As the title suggests all players are listed in alphabetical order and are shown by Surnames first, followed by full Christian names, with the one the player is commonly known by shown in **bold**. Any abbreviation or pseudonym is bracketed.

Birthplace/date: you will note that several players, who would be predominately classified as British, were born in places like Germany and India, for example. In my book, Football League Players' Records (last edition: 1992), which covered every man who had played League football since the war, has, in the past, used the family domicile as a more realistic "birthplace". But, for our purposes here, I have reverted to that which has been officially recorded.

Height and Weight: Listed in feet and inches, and stones and pounds, respectively. It must be remembered that a player's weight can frequently change and, on that basis, the recorded data should be used as a guide only, especially as they would have been weighed several times during the season.

Club Honours: Those shown, cover careers from the Conference and FA Trophy upwards. For abbreviations, read:- EC (European Cup), ESC (European Super Cup), ECWC (European Cup Winners' Cup). English Honours: FAC (FA Cup), FLC (Football League Cup), CS (Charity Shield), FMC (Full Members Cup, which takes in the Simod and Zenith Data sponsorships), AMC (Associated Members Cup – Freight Rover, Sherpa Van, Leyland DAF, Autoglass and Auto Windscreen), AIC (Anglo-Italian Cup), GMVC (GM Vauxhall Conference), FAT (FA Trophy), FAYC (FA Youth Cup). Scottish Honours: SPD (Scottish Premier Division), S Div 1/2 (Scottish Leagues), SC (Scottish Cup), SLC (Scottish League Cup). Welsh Honours: WC (Welsh Cup).

International Honours: For abbreviations, read:- E (England), NI (Northern Ireland), S (Scotland), W (Wales) and Ei (Republic of Ireland). Under 21 through to full internationals give total appearances (inclusive of subs), while schoolboy (U16s and U18s) representatives are just listed, as are players from countries outside of Britain. This we will try and remedy in future annuals. The cut-off date used for appearances was 13 June, the end of the home countries' international programme.

Player Descriptions: Gives position and playing strengths and, in keeping the work topical, a few words on how their season went in 1994-95. This takes into account, in a positive fashion, key performances, along with value to the team, injuries, honours, and other points of interest, etc. To allow for play-off imput to be included, and the publication date to be maintained, the cut-off date used was 31 May and anything additional to that has been shown as stop press.

Career Records: Full appearances, plus substitutes and goals, are given for all Premiership and Endsleigh League games and, if a player who is in the book has played in any of the senior Scottish Leagues, his appearances with the club in question will also be recorded. Other information given, includes the origination of players (clubs in the non-leagues, junior football, or from abroad), registered signing dates, transfer fees, and a breakdown of matches by P/FL (Premiership and Football League), PL (Premier League), FL (Football League), FLC (Football League Cup), FAC (FA Cup), and Others. As mentioned in the first paragraph, other matches will take in the Welsh Cup, play-offs, Anglo-Italian Cup, Auto Windscreen Shield, Charity Shield, and any major European competition. All of these matches are lumped together for reasons of saving space. Finally, regarding transfer fees, these are the figures that have been reported in newspapers and magazines and should only be used as a guide to a player's valuation. Scottish appearances for players on loan to P/FL clubs in 1994-95 are shown at the point of transfer and do not include games following their return to Scotland. The cut-off date used for this part of the book was 20 May, as to fall into line with the retained lists for the Premiership and Football League.

Displayed in a similar fashion that has been popularised by cricket publications down the years, the playing statistics recorded within these pages are depicted as such:- Appearances + substitutes/goals.

Although the PFA Footballers' Factfile is not written in "tongue-in-cheek" fashion, there is more than enough information to satisfy the most serious of "fantasy football" buffs.

I wish you an enjoyable read and do hope you find the book enlightening, and one that gives you a better understanding of some of the players you do not see every week.

Barry J. Hugman, Editor, PFA Footballers' Factfile

PFA Footballers' Factfile : A-Z

ABBOTT Gregory (Greg) Stephen
Born: Coventry, 14 December 1963
Height: 5'9" Weight: 10.7
Club Honours: Div 3 '85
As Hull's captain, "Abbo" is a leader by example. The midfielder is a tough tackler and an accurate predominantly right-footed passer who regularly advances into goal-scoring positions. His valuable experience was lost for the majority of 1994-95 as appearances were severely restricted by suspension and injuries to his groin and knee (cartilage).
Coventry C (From apprentice on 5/1/82)
Bradford C (Free on 10/9/82) FL 256+25/38 FLC 22+3/6 FAC 15+1/3 Others 19+2/5
Halifax T (£25,000 on 22/7/91) FL 24+4/1 FLC 2 FAC 2 Others 2 (Free to Guisley on 18/9/92)
Hull C (Free on 14/12/92) FL 89+4/9 FLC 3/1 FAC 2+1 Others 4+2/2

ABLETT Gary Ian
Born: Liverpool, 19 November 1965
Height: 6'0" Weight: 11.4
Club Honours: Div 1 '88, '90; CS '88, '90; FAC '89, '95
International Honours: E: B-1; U21-1
Primarily a central defender, Gary can play anywhere across Everton's back four. Very comfortable in possession, he provides precise passes and rarely gives the ball away, clearing his lines both quickly and effectively. He is also known for his one-twos, which allow him to move forward into advanced positions and cross the ball accurately. Played in virtually all of the club's games last season, often covering at left-back when required. Managed to avoid injury and was a crucial cog in the "Blues'" FA Cup Final victory over Manchester United.
Liverpool (From apprentice on 19/11/83) FL 103+6/1 FLC 10+1 FAC 16+2 Others 9
Derby Co (Loaned on 25/1/85) FL 3+3 Others 2
Hull C (Loaned on 10/9/86) FL 5
Everton (£750,000 on 14/1/92) F/PL 115/5 FLC 11 FAC 9

Gary Ablett   Neal Simpson
(Empics Sports Photo Agency)

ABRAHAMS Paul
Born: Colchester, 31 October 1973
Height: 5'8" Weight: 10.6
Striker. A product of the Colchester youth policy, Paul missed the whole of 1993-94 through injury, but re-discovered his goal touch last season, including a purple patch of four in a week during November. He seemed to lose favour following the change of managers and moved on to Brentford, where he lent his goals to the "Bees'" promotion challenge.
Colchester U (From trainee on 11/8/92) FL 30+25/8 FLC 2+3 FAC 4/2 Others 3/2
Brentford (£30,000 on 9/3/95) FL 7+3/3 Others 1

ADAMS Darren Stephen
Born: Bromley, 12 January 1974
Height: 5'7" Weight: 10.7
A young Cardiff striker who made his debut in 1993-94, Darren had very few opportunities to shine last season. Playing in a struggling side was not a help, either.
Cardiff C (Free from Danson Furnace on 21/1/94) FL 13+7/1 Others 2+1

ADAMS Kieran Charles
Born: Cambridge, 20 October 1977
Height: 5'11" Weight: 11.6
Part of Barnet's fledgling youth side, he was the first YTS player to break into the full side late last season. With good touch, this midfielder will challenge for a regular place in 1995-96.
Barnet (Trainee) FL 2+2

ADAMS Michael (Micky) Richard
Born: Sheffield, 8 November 1961
Height: 5'6" Weight: 11.11
International Honours E: Yth
An experienced left-sided defender, or midfielder, Micky is now part of the coaching set-up at Fulham. Although injuries restricted his appearances in 1994-95, he was still top-scorer, with all his 12 goals coming from penalties or free-kicks.
Gillingham (From apprentice on 1/11/79) FL 85+7/5 FLC 5 FAC 6
Coventry C (£75,000 on 19/7/83) FL 85+5/9 FLC 9/1 FAC 7 Others 2
Leeds U (£110,000 on 23/1/87) FL 72+1/2 FLC 4 FAC 6/1 Others 6
Southampton (£250,000 on 14/3/89) F/PL 141+3/7 FLC 16 FAC 8 Others 6
Stoke C (Free on 24/3/94) FL 10/3
Fulham (Free on 14/7/94) FL 18+3/7 FLC 1 FAC 2/4 Others 2/1

ADAMS Neil James
Born: Stoke, 23 November 1965
Height: 5'8" Weight: 10.8
Club Honours: CS '86; Div 1 '87, Div 2 '91
International Honours: E: U21-1
A right-winger with the pace and ability to run at defenders or cross the early ball, Neil was John Deehan's first signing for Norwich and featured in the first 21 games last season, as the club rose to a top six position. Scored crucial goals against Newcastle and Coventry, before drifting out of the side as

Daryl Sutch was preferred. From then on, the management team, unable to choose between the two men, played them periodically.
Stoke C (Signed on 1/7/85) FL 31+1/4 FLC 3 FAC 1 Others 3
Everton (£150,000 on 7/7/86) FL 17+3 FLC 4+1/1 Others 5+1
Oldham Ath (Loaned on 11/1/89) FL 9
Oldham Ath (£100,000 on 21/6/89) F/PL 93+36/23 FLC 13+2/1 FAC 10+2/2 Others 1+1
Norwich C (£250,000 on 17/2/94) PL 34+13/3 FLC 6/1 FAC 3

ADAMS Tony Alexander
Born: Romford, 10 October 1966
Height: 6'3" Weight: 13.11
Club Honours: Div 1 '89, '91; FLC '87, '93; FAC '93; ECWC '94
International Honours: E: 35; B-4; U21-5; Yth
Much coveted Arsenal and England central defender who captains both club and country, and a former PFA "Young Player of the Year" (1987), Tony's "never-say-die" attitude was sorely missed when sidelined by injury last season. Exceptional in the air in both boxes and a commanding presence at any level, he can be relied upon to get his share of the goals when the side has its back to the wall. Also specialises in knocking good early balls behind opposing defences. As skipper of the side that won the European Cup Winners Cup in 1993-94, the club went mighty close to winning it again in 1994-95, just failing to an exceptional long-range goal.
Arsenal (From apprentice on 30/1/84) F/PL 343+3/23 FLC 48+1/3 FAC 29+1/5 Others 28/3

ADCOCK Anthony (Tony) Charles
Born: Bethnal Green, 27 February 1963
Height: 5'10" Weight: 11.9
An experienced goalscorer with two good feet and a respectable strike-rate, Tony was signed by Luton prior to the start of 1994-95 to provide extra competition up-front. As it happened, a series of injuries just about wiped out the season for him, with just a handful of substitute outings around Christmas and the New Year to his name, and he was freed during the summer.
Colchester U (From apprentice on 31/3/81) FL 192+18/98 FLC 16+1/5 FAC 12+2/3 Others 9/6
Manchester C (£75,000 on 1/6/87) FL 12+3/5 FLC 2+1/1 FAC 2 Others 2/3
Northampton T (£85,000 on 25/1/88) FL 72/30 FLC 6/3 FAC 1 Others 4/1
Bradford C (£190,000 on 6/10/89) FL 33+5/6 FLC 1 FAC 0+1 Others 2
Northampton T (£75,000 on 11/1/91) FL 34+1/10 FLC 1 FAC 1/1 Others 2/1
Peterborough U (£35,000 on 30/12/91) FL 107+4/35 FLC 8+1/3 FAC 5/1 Others 3+2
Luton T (£20,000 on 4/8/94) FL 0+2 FAC 0+1

ADEBOLA David Adeolu (Dele)
Born: Lagos, Nigeria, 23 June 1975
Height: 6'3" Weight: 12.8
Although born in Nigeria, Dele has spent most of his life in Liverpool, playing for the

City's schoolboys before coming to Crewe. Having graduated through the club's YT scheme, he is proving to be a real prospect in his role as striker, being deceptively fast with a powerful shot in his left-foot and a real handful for defenders.
Crewe Alex (From trainee on 21/6/93) FL 25+12/7 FLC 1+1 FAC 1 Others 4/2

ADEKOLA David Adeolu
Born: Nigeria, 18 May 1968
Height: 5'11" Weight: 12.2
International Honours: Nigeria

Very direct right-winger who uses his pace to go past defenders, the former Nigerian international signed for Wigan on a monthly basis from Bournemouth last season, having been earlier freed by Bury. After six appearances, mainly as a substitute, he was released without being offered a contract, spending trial periods with Hereford and Halifax, before ending the season with Bath.
Bury (Signed on 15/1/93) FL 21+14/12 FLC 0+1 FAC 1 Others 4/2
Exeter C (Loaned on 18/2/94) FL 1+2/1
Bournemouth (Free on 29/9/94) FLC 0+1
Wigan Ath (Free on 14/10/94) FL 1+3 FAC 0+1 Others 0+1
Hereford U (Free on 2/2/95)

AGANA Patrick Anthony (Tony)
Born: Bromley, 2 October 1963
Height: 6'0" Weight: 12.0
Club Honours: AIC '95
International Honours: E: SP-1

Having enjoyed a prolific goalscoring partnership with Brian Deane at Sheffield Wednesday, Tony came to Notts County in 1991-92, but has yet to achieve that kind of strike-rate. Still scores valuable goals, including the winner against Ascoli in the Anglo-Italian Cup Final at Wembley in 1994-95. Although held back by niggling injuries last season, he continued to show the ability to hold the ball up well for his team-mates.
Watford (£35,000 from Weymouth on 13/8/87) FL 12+3/1 FLC 1+1/2 FAC 2 Others 1
Sheffield U (£45,000 on 19/2/88) FL 105+13/42 FLC 12/3 FAC 14/5 Others 4+1/1
Leeds U (Loaned on 27/2/92) FL 1+1
Notts Co (£750,000 on 12/11/91) FL 77+16/10 FLC 5+1/2 FAC 5/1 Others 11+1/3

AGNEW Paul
Born: Lisburn, 15 August 1965
Height: 5'9" Weight: 10.12
International Honours: NI: U23-1; Yth; Sch

A left-sided defender and strong tackler who loves going forward, he was somewhat eclipsed by the emergence of some talented young defenders from Grimsby's youth scheme and towards the end of 1994-95 he left to join former "Mariner's" boss, Alan Buckley, at WBA. With the number three slot causing concern, he slotted in perfectly at Albion and eventually took over the captaincy from the injured Paul Mardon.
Grimsby T (£4,000 from Cliftonville on 15/2/84) FL 219+23/3 FLC 17+1 FAC 23+1 Others 12+2
West Bromwich A (£65,000 on 23/2/95) FL 14/1

AGNEW Stephen (Steve) Mark
Born: Shipley, 9 November 1965
Height: 5'9" Weight: 10.6

Central midfielder who signed for Sunderland last January, having led Leicester to promotion in 1993-94. Quickly established himself at Roker in a midfield which had been lacking in invention, with a series of impressive displays. Opened his scoring account with an important winner at Southend in February and captained the side at Barnsley in the absence of Kevin Ball and Gary Bennett.
Barnsley (From apprentice on 10/11/83) FL 186+8/29 FLC 13/3 FAC 20/4 Others 6+1
Blackburn Rov (£700,000 on 25/6/91) FL 2 FLC 2
Portsmouth (Loaned on 21/11/92) FL 3+2 Others 2
Leicester C (£250,000 on 9/2/93) F/PL 52+4/4 FLC 4+1 FAC 2 Others 2
Sunderland (£250,000 on 11/1/95) FL 16/2

AINSLEY Jason
Born: Stockton, 13 July 1970
Height: 6'0" Weight: 12.8

Attacking Hartlepool midfielder who had a mixed introduction to the Endsleigh League in 1994-95, after several years at Spennymoor. Making a slow start, but improving under David McCreery, he was later transfer-listed at his own request, feeling he was not being given enough opportunities. In February, he joined West Australian side, Inglewood Kiev, with Hartlepool retaining his registration.
Hartlepool U (£12,000 from Spennymoor U on 19/7/94) FL 14+1/1 FLC 2 FAC 1 Others 2

AINSWORTH Gareth
Born: Blackburn, 10 May 1973
Height: 5'9" Weight: 11.9

A great favourite with the Preston crowd, Gareth's season was unfortunately punctuated by a series of injuries. Always gives 100 per-cent effort on the right wing, combining pace with a powerful shot and good tackling back, he is young enough to put 1994-95 behind him.
Preston NE (Signed from Northwich Vic on 21/1/92) FL 2+3 Others 1/1
Cambridge U (Free on 17/8/92) FL 1+3/1 FLC 0+1
Preston NE (Free on 23/12/92) FL 76+4/12 FLC 3 FAC 3+1 Others 8+1/1

AIZLEWOOD Mark
Born: Newport, 1 October 1959
Height: 6'1" Weight 13.12
Club Honours: Div 2 '82
International Honours: W: 39; U21-2; Sch

1994-95 was a strange season for Mark. When playing well in the centre of the Cardiff defence, he was dropped by manager, Eddie May, but after it became clear that a consortium were interested in taking over, the club wanted him as second in command to whoever they chose as the new manager. Later, he took on the role of coach under Terry Yorath, before being freed during the summer.
Newport Co (From apprentice on 1/10/77) FL 35+3/1 FAC 2
Luton T (£50,000 on 1/4/78) FL 90+8/3 FLC 7/1 FAC 5
Charlton Ath (£50,000 on 4/11/82) FL 152/9 FLC 10/1 FAC 6/1 Others 2
Leeds U (£200,000 on 5/2/87) FL 65+5/3 FLC 3 FAC 1 Others 7/1
Bradford C (£200,000 on 16/8/89) FL 39/1 FLC 1 FAC 2

Bristol C (£125,000 on 8/8/90) FL 99+2/3 FLC 8 FAC 5+1 Others 2+1
Cardiff C (Free on 15/10/93) FL 39/4 FLC 1 FAC 6+1 Others 10/1

AKINBIYI Adeola (Ade) Peter
Born: Hackney, 10 October 1974
Height: 6'1" Weight: 12.0

Striker with good balance and quick feet who twists and turns on chances around the box. In the Norwich side at the beginning of last season, but frequently substituted, Ade spent a beneficial loan spell at Brighton, scoring four goals in seven games, before returning to Carrow Road. The Albion fans loved his somersault ritual performed after each goal. Unable to hit the target for City in 1994-95, 11 reserve strikes, including three doubles, merely confirmed he has an eye for a goal and he should show to advantage in the First Division this coming season.
Norwich C (From trainee on 5/2/93) PL 6+9 FLC 0+1 FAC 1+2 Others 0+1
Hereford U (Loaned on 21/1/94) FL 3+1/2
Brighton & Hove A (Loaned on 24/11/94) FL 7/4

Philippe Albert　　　Tony Marshall
(Empics Sports Photo Agency)

ALBERT Philippe
Born: Bouillon, Belgium, 10 August 1967
Height: 6'3" Weight: 13.7
International Honours: Belgium

Philippe's season ended last December, when he suffered serious cruciate ligament damage to his right-knee while training. He had joined Newcastle from Belgian Champions, Anderlecht, after starring for his country in the 1994 World Cup. A tall and very capable defender, he soon became a firm favourite with the supporters, being more than comfortable when pushing forward into midfield and attack, due to his skill on the ball and heading ability. Highlights of his season, included scoring the vital first goal eight minutes from time in the 2-0 Coca Cola defeat of Manchester United, and twice in the 3-1 home win over Leicester.
Newcastle U (£2,650,000 from Anderlecht on 10/8/94) PL 17/2 FLC 4/1 Others 4

ALDRIDGE John William
Born: Liverpool, 18 September 1958
Height: 5'11" Weight: 11.4
Club Honours: WC '80; Div 2 '85, Div 1 '88; FLC '86; CS '88; FAC '89
International Honours: Ei: 64

Tranmere's captain and goalscoring inspiration may now be approaching the twilight of his career, but with 24 League goals to his credit and a "Golden Boot" award as the First Division's top-scorer in 1994-95, his powers show no sign of diminishing just yet. Scorer of two hat-tricks and four against Barnsley during the season, "Aldo" also reached the personal landmark of 400 goals, despite missing three months of the season due to an ankle injury which required an operation. His season was further highlighted when he was elected to the PFA award winning First Division team.
Newport Co (£3,500 from South Liverpool on 2/5/79) FL 159+11/69 FLC 11/5 FAC 12+1/7 Others 4/2
Oxford U (£78,000 on 21/3/84) FL 111+3/72 FLC 17/14 FAC 5/2 Others 5/2
Liverpool (£750,000 on 27/1/87) FL 69+14/50 FLC 7+1/3 FAC 12/8 Others 1/2 (£1,000,000 to Real Sociedad on 1/9/89)
Tranmere Rov (£250,000 on 11/7/91) FL 137+3/88 FLC 18/18 FAC 6+1/4 Others 18/10

John Aldridge   Tony Marshall
(Empics Sports Photo Agency)

ALDRIDGE Martin James
Born: Northampton, 6 December 1974
Height: 5'11" Weight: 11.4

A goal poacher, rather than an out-and-out striker, pacy, and hard to knock off the ball, Martin scored nine goals in 21 starts for Northampton last season.
Northampton T (From trainee on 27/8/93) FL 50+20/17 FLC 1+2 FAC 1+1/1 Others 5/4

ALEXANDER Graham
Born: Coventry, 10 October 1971
Height: 5'10" Weight: 11.10

A right-sided midfield player with a good turn of speed, who likes taking on defenders,

he packs an explosive shot in both feet, either on the run or from set-pieces, as proved by many spectacular, long-range strikes for Scunthorpe. Only slightly built, but an aggressive competitor, Graham has attracted enquiries from bigger clubs.
Scunthorpe U (From trainee on 20/3/90) FL 149+10/18 FLC 11+1/2 FAC 12/1 Others 13+2/3

ALEXANDER Keith
Born: Nottingham, 14 November 1958
Height: 6'4" Weight: 12.7

Striker. At the age of 37, and Mansfield's youth team coach, Keith appeared as a substitute for the club in several matches last season, scoring two goals against Crewe in the Auto Windscreen Shield.
Grimsby T (£11,500 from Barnet on 11/7/88) FL 64+19/26 FLC 4+2/1 FAC 8/1 Others 4+1/1
Stockport Co (£8,500 on 10/9/90) FL 9+2 FAC 1 Others 0+1
Lincoln C (£7,000 on 12/12/90) FL 26+19/4 FLC 1+4 FAC 1 Others 1
Mansfield T (Free on 26/8/94) FL 0+2 Others 0+1/2

ALEXANDER Timothy (Tim) Mark
Born: Chertsey, 29 March 1974
Height: 6'0" Weight: 12.2

A gritty and determined player who gave his all for Barnet in every game. During his spell at the club, Tim filled in at full-back, centre-half, and in midfield, before being released midway through last season. Later played for Woking.
Barnet (Free from Wimbledon juniors on 6/8/92) FL 29+7 FLC 3+2 FAC 2+2 Others 2+1

Bradley Allen   Tony Marshall
(Empics Sports Photo Agency)

ALLEN Bradley James
Born: Romford, 13 September 1971
Height: 5'7" Weight: 10.0
International Honours: E: U21-8; Yth

A very disappointing last season for Bradley, injuries having kept him out of the QPR side for most of the time. And just as he was regaining his place in the first team squad, a hernia operation was needed, which ruled him out of the latter part of the season.

Still managed to score three goals in just three starts for the first team and will be hoping for better luck in 1995-96, where his skill and vision will be invaluable.
Queens Park R (From juniors on 30/9/88) F/PL 51+22/26 FLC 5+2/5 FAC 1+2 Others 1

ALLEN Christopher (Chris) Anthony
Born: Oxford, 18 November 1972
Height: 5'11" Weight: 12.2
International Honours: E: U21-2

Oxford left-winger who, on his day, is a provider of goals and a winner of many penalties due to his pace and mazy running. Although his two goals last season were a disappointing return, ironically, he scored for the Endsleigh League against the Italian select in February, prior to making his international debut for England in the Toulon U21 tournament this summer.
Oxford U (From trainee on 14/5/91) FL 97+29/9 FLC 7+2/2 FAC 4+3/1 Others 4+3

ALLEN Leighton Gary
Born: Brighton, 22 January 1973
Height: 6'0" Weight: 11.8

A forward released by Wimbledon in the summer of 1994, Leighton was one of many trialists at Colchester in the early part of last season. However, unlike most, he did make the first-team (two subs' appearances) but was not offered terms. Two weeks earlier he had been at Gillingham on a similar basis.
Wimbledon (From trainee on 2/7/92)
Gillingham (Free on 16/8/94)
Colchester U (Free on 31/8/94) FL 0+2

ALLEN Malcolm
Born: Caernarfon, 21 March 1967
Height: 5'8" Weight: 11.2
International Honours: W: 14; B-1; Yth

A Newcastle player who can operate up-front or in midfield, Malcolm is both skilful and tricky, and has a good scoring record. Sidelined for almost all of 1994-95, following a cruciate ligament injury, he came back to first team action as a sub on 3 May at St James' against Tottenham. If fully fit, he will certainly be a candidate for one of the forward positions in 1995-96.
Watford (From apprentice on 23/3/85) FL 27+12/5 FLC 4+1/2 FAC 6+8/6
Aston Villa (Loaned on 3/9/87) FL 4
Norwich C (£175,000 on 12/8/88) FL 24+11/8 FLC 0+3 FAC 5/7 Others 2+1
Millwall (£400,000 on 20/3/90) FL 64+17/24 FLC 7/2 FAC 0+1 Others 1
Newcastle U (£300,000 on 13/8/93) PL 9+1/5 FLC 3/2

ALLEN Martin James
Born: Reading, 14 August 1965
Height: 5'10" Weight: 11.0
International Honours: E: U21-2; Yth

West Ham midfielder who loves to be in the thick of the action and is affectionately known as "Mad Dog" by the fans. Early on last season he scored vital goals in the victories over Chelsea and Southampton, before suffering a punctured lung in a challenge with Graham Hyde at Sheffield Wednesday in November, and being out of the side until the New Year. Martin comes from a footballing family, his father Dennis played for Charlton, Reading and Bournemouth, uncle Les for Chelsea, "Spurs" and QPR, and three cousins, Clive, Paul and Bradley, are currently involved in the game.

Queens Park R (From apprentice on 27/5/83) FL 128+8/16 FLC 15+3/1 FAC 9/1 Others 2/1
West Ham U (£675,000 on 24/8/89) F/PL 160+27/24 FLC 15+3/5 FAC 14/4 Others 10

ALLEN Paul Kevin

Born: Aveley, 28 August 1962
Height: 5'7" Weight: 10.10
Club Honours: FAC '80, '91; CS '91
International Honours: E: B; U21-3; Yth (UEFAYC '80)

After playing in midfield in 12 of Southampton's opening 13 games last season, before losing his place, he spent the rest of the season on loan at Luton and Stoke. At Luton, his hard-tackling and accurate crossing promised much, but he did not stay long enough to make a real contribution, while the signs are that he will move to Stoke, having been there since January.

West Ham U (From apprentice on 29/8/79) FL 149+3/6 FLC 20+4/2 FAC 15+3/3 Others 2+1
Tottenham H (£400,000 on 19/6/85) F/PL 276+16/23 FLC 42+2/4 FAC 26+1/1 Others 12+2
Southampton (£550,000 on 16/9/93) PL 40+3/1 FLC 4 FAC 2
Luton T (Loaned on 9/12/94) FL 4
Stoke C (Loaned on 20/1/95) FL 17/1 Others 2

ALLISON Neil James

Born: Hull, 20 October 1973
Height: 6'2" Weight: 11.10

Gary Hobson and Rob Dewhurst's dominance at the heart of Hull's back four meant that Neil's involvement was minimal until the swap to a five man backline last January. Noticeably increasing his strength, the right-footed "Spanner" used his aerial advantage to good effect.

Hull C (From trainee on 13/7/92) FL 51+9/1 FLC 6 FAC 2 Others 3+1

ALLISON Wayne

Born: Huddersfield, 16 October 1968
Height: 6'1" Weight: 13.5

Bristol City's leading scorer for the past two seasons, Wayne has all the attributes to be a top-class striker, combining aerial ability and good movement off the ball, with great enthusiasm and endeavour. Would have been even more effective in a side that did not have its back to the wall throughout the campaign.

Halifax T (From trainee on 6/7/87) FL 74+10/23 FLC 3/2 FAC 4+1/2 Others 8+1/3
Watford (£250,000 on 26/7/89) FL 6+1
Bristol C (£300,000 on 9/8/90) FL 149+46/48 FLC 4+5/2 FAC 12+1/5 Others 6+2/2

ALLON Joseph (Joe) Ball

Born: Gateshead, 12 November 1966
Height: 5'11" Weight: 12.2
Club Honours: FAYC '85
International Honours: E: Yth

A striker who was far from a regular at Port Vale last season, but had the knack of scoring when he did play. The dressing room joker, who celebrates goals in a variety

of bizarre fashions, he comes alive in the penalty area when there is a sniff of a chance.

Newcastle U (From trainee on 16/11/84) FL 9/2 FLC 1
Swansea C (Free on 6/8/87) FL 27+7/11 FLC 2 FAC 2 Others 2/1
Hartlepool U (Free on 29/11/88) FL 112/50 FLC 5/2 FAC 6+1/5 Others 7/2
Chelsea (£250,000 on 14/8/91) FL 3+11/2 FLC 0+2 Others 1+1/1
Port Vale (Loaned on 27/2/92) FL 2+4
Brentford (£275,000 on 19/11/92) FL 38+7/19 FLC 2 FAC 2/2 Others 7/7
Southend U (Loaned on 16/9/93) FL 2+1
Port Vale (Signed on 24/3/94) FL 13+10/9 FLC 0+1 FAC 2/1

ALLPRESS Timothy (Tim) John

Born: Hitchin, 21 January 1971
Height: 6'1" Weight: 12.7

A regular reserve defender, who spent most of last season on the Colchester bench waiting his chance, he was released in March and joined non-league Hitchin.

Luton T (From trainee on 1/7/89) FL 1 Others 2 (Free to Bayer Uerdingen in 1993 close season)
Preston NE (Loaned on 30/10/91) FL 7+2 FAC 2 Others 1
Colchester U (Free on 16/8/93) FL 24+10 FLC 2+1 Others 1

ALSFORD Julian

Born: Poole, 24 December 1972
Height: 6'2" Weight: 13.7

Chester central defender. Signed from Watford during the 1994 close season, Julian is particularly good in the air and can also play at right-back.

Watford (From trainee on 30/4/91) FL 9+4/1 FLC 1 Others 2
Chester C (Free on 11/8/94) FL 32+3/1 FLC 1 FAC 2 Others 2

AMMANN Michael (Mike) Anton

Born: California, USA, 8 February 1971
Height: 6'2" Weight: 13.2

American goalkeeper signed in the 1994 close season, who made his Charlton debut earlier than expected when he replaced the injured Mike Salmon after 16 minutes of the second game of 1994-95. Although still learning, he is generally regarded as the best long-term prospect at the club, having steadily improved throughout the season despite a fractured wrist sustained in training during February that put him out of contention for six weeks.

Charlton Ath (Free from LA Cobras on 20/7/94) FL 18+1

AMOKACHI Daniel Owofen

Born: Groko, Nigeria, 30 December 1972
Height: 5'10" Weight: 13.0
Club Honours: FAC '95
International Honours: Nigeria

Very quick Nigerian international forward who uses his pace to unsettle defences and is at his best when running onto through passes. Combining good first touch with excellent natural skill, he accelerates well from a standing start, causing panic when racing goalbound to unleash terrific shots with either foot. Following his transfer from Belgium last August, he was unable to gain a regular first team position at Everton, but towards the end of the season he eagerly

took his chance, stepping up from the bench to score numerous important goals, the most notable being a hat-trick in the FA Cup semi-final. Came on for Anders Limpar to be presented with an FA Cup winners' medal, following the victory over Manchester United.

Everton (£3,000,000 from FC Bruges on 27/8/94) PL 17+1/4 FLC 2 FAC 0+2/2

Daniel Amokachi   Neal Simpson
(Empics Sports Photo Agency)

AMPADU Patrick Kwame

Born: Bradford, 20 December 1970
Height: 5'10" Weight: 11.10
Club Honours: AMC '94
International Honours: Ei: U21-4; Yth

"Paddy" excelled on the left-side of the Swansea midfield last season with his aggressive, attacking style of play. Always on the look out for goalscoring opportunities, he also showed his ability at scoring from dead ball situations and stood out with his measured passes and general distribution of the ball. Made the occasional appearance for the "Swans" at left-back.

Arsenal (From trainee on 19/11/88) FL 0+2
Plymouth Arg (Loaned on 31/10/90) FL 6/1 Others 1
West Bromwich A (£50,000 on 24/6/91) FL 27+22/4 FLC 6+1 FAC 1 Others 5/1
Swansea C (£15,000 on 16/2/94) FL 47+10/6 FLC 3+1 FAC 3/1 Others 9/1

ANDERSON Colin Russell

Born: Newcastle, 26 April 1962
Height: 5'8" Weight: 10.8

Solid left-footed defender, who likes to get forward whenever possible, injuries restricted the amount of appearances he made in 1994-95, his first season at Exeter.

Burnley (From apprentice on 29/4/80) FL 3+3
Torquay U (Free on 18/9/82) FL 107+2/11 FLC 5 FAC 7/1 Others 3
West Bromwich A (£20,000 on 27/3/85) FL 131+9/10 FLC 5+2 FAC 2/2 Others 2+1
Walsall (Free on 22/8/91) FL 25+1/2 FAC 2 Others 4
Hereford U (Free on 13/8/92) FL 67+3/1 FLC 4+1 FAC 2+2 Others 5
Exeter C (Free on 14/7/94) FL 21/1 FLC 1

ANDERSON Vivian (Viv) Alexander

Born: Nottingham, 29 August 1956
Height: 6'1" Weight: 12.9
Club Honours: ASC '77; Div 1 '78; EC '79, '80; ESC '79; FLC '78; CS '78

International Honours: E: 30; B-7; U21-1

Viv made club history when he turned out for Middlesbrough's first team against WBA at the Hawthorns on "All Fools Day", 1 April 1995, crowning a brilliant performance as the oldest debutant for the "Boro". Winning the first of his 30 international caps at full-back in 1978, he still exudes absolute fitness and whenever injuries to squad members have indicated that his services may be required, has frequently played in midweek reserve team games to prepare himself. His forté now is that of behind the scenes tactician and dug-out guru, but he is always more than ready to answer the call to arms, whenever it is made. Viv has just concluded the first season of a brilliant managerial partnership with old team-mate, Bryan Robson, culminating fittingly in winning promotion to the Premiership as Champions of the Endsleigh First Division.

Nottingham F (From apprentice on 1/8/74) FL 323+5/15 FLC 39/5 FAC 23+1/1 Others 33
Arsenal (£250,000 on 3/8/84) FL 120/9 FLC 18/3 FAC 12/3
Manchester U (£250,000 on 9/7/87) FL 50+4/2 FLC 6+1/1 FAC 7/1 Others 2
Sheffield Wed (Free on 10/1/91) F/PL 60+10/8 FLC 9/1 FAC 8+2/2 Others 5/2
Barnsley (Free on 1/7/93) FL 20/3 FLC 2
Middlesbrough (Free on 23/7/94) FL 2

ANDERTON Darren Robert
Born: Southampton, 3 March 1972
Height: 6'0" Weight: 11.7
International Honours: E: 9; U21-7; Yth

Darren's superb skill and athleticism in midfield continued to improve last season, earning him a regular full international place, while linking up with Tottenham team-mate, Teddy Sheringham, to produce some exciting football. His ability to dominate the middle of the field and deliver long balls and corners into opponents' 18 yard boxes, created many of the club's goals, as well as producing some breathtaking moves when joining up with Jurgen Klinsmann and Sheringham. He also continued to demonstrate his great ability to score goals, as well as being instrumental in their build-up, the one at Southampton in the FA Cup fifth round replay at the Dell, being particularly satisfying, as it silenced the crowd who had never let him forget his early days at Portsmouth, Southampton's neighbours and arch-rivals. A regular England international and widely recognised as one of the best crossers of the ball in the English game.

Portsmouth (From trainee on 5/2/90) FL 53+9/7 FLC 3+2/1 FAC 7+1/5 Others 2
Tottenham H (£1,750,000 on 3/6/92) PL 104+4/17 FLC 9/2 FAC 13+1/2

ANDRADE Jose Manuel
Born: Portugal, 1 June 1970
Height: 6'0" Weight: 11.2

Having signed for Stoke with only minutes to spare on deadline day, he scored within seconds of a behind closed doors friendly and quickly progressed into the first team squad as a striker. Good in the air, Zay Angola, as he is known, became an instant hit with a goal on his full home debut, before being unfortunate to break a leg at Swindon on Easter Monday. Now back home recuperating, the fans would like to see him signed on a permanent basis when fully recovered.

Stoke C (Loaned from Academica on 23/3/95) FL 2+2/1

ANDREWS Ian Edmund
Born: Nottingham, 1 December 1964
Height: 6'2" Weight: 12.2
International Honours: E: U21-1; Yth

Signed from Southampton last September, after "Saints" bought Bruce Grobbelaar, Ian made his debut for Bournemouth against Northampton in the Coca Cola Cup and quickly settled in, his command of the area and his agility giving the defence the confidence it needed. Produced many outstanding displays for the "Cherries" in helping them stay in the Second Division.

Leicester C (From apprentice on 6/12/82) FL 126 FLC 6 FAC 7
Swindon T (Loaned on 1/1/84) FL 1
Glasgow Celtic (£300,000 on 26/7/88) SL 5 SLC 2 Others 1
Leeds U (Loaned on 15/12/88) FL 1
Southampton (£200,000 on 22/12/89) F/PL 10 Others 1
Bournemouth (£20,000 on 5/9/94) FL 38 FLC 3 FAC 2 Others 2

Daren Anderton

Neil Simpson
(Empics Sports Photo Agency)

ANDREWS Philip (Phil)
Born: Andover, 14 September 1976
Height: 5'11" Weight: 11.0
A promising young Brighton striker who showed some neat touches on his few appearances, via the subs-bench. Looked lively and came close to opening his goal count for the first team. Still a trainee.
Brighton & Hove A (Trainee) FL 1+9 FLC 0+1 FAC 0+1 Others 0+1

ANGELL Brett Ashley
Born: Marlborough, 20 August 1968
Height: 6'2" Weight: 13.0
Arrived at Sunderland from Everton on transfer deadline day, becoming Mick Buxton's final signing for the club. A bustling centre-forward, Brett had not enjoyed the best of times at Goodison and was clearly short of match sharpness when he joined, but his displays lacked nothing in effort as Sunderland fought against relegation. Next term will hopefully see him back to his scoring best.
Portsmouth (From trainee on 1/8/86)
Derby Co (£40,000 from Cheltenham T on 19/2/88)
Stockport Co (£33,000 on 20/10/88) FL 60+10/28 FLC 3 FAC 3/1 Others 8/4
Southend U (£100,000 on 2/8/90) FL 109+6/47 FLC 7+1/4 FAC 3/2 Others 9+1/10
Everton (£500,000 on 17/1/94) PL 16+4/1 FLC 0+1
Sunderland (£600,000 on 23/3/95) FL 8

ANGUS Terence (Terry) Norman
Born: Coventry, 14 January 1966
Height: 6'0" Weight: 13.9
Terry proved his versatility when he switched from his usual central defensive role to full-back last season. A natural left-sided player with total commitment, he is a great favourite with the Fulham supporters.
Northampton T (£15,000 from VS Rugby on 22/8/90) FL 115+1/6 FLC 7 FAC 5+1 Others 9
Fulham (Free on 12/7/93) FL 49+10/2 FLC 1+1 FAC 1/1 Others 7

ANNON Darren Carlton
Born: London, 17 February 1972
Height: 5'8" Weight: 10.11
Tricky winger who can operate down either flank. A regular in the Brentford side last December and January, turning in a number of impressive performances, he lost his place when Paul Stephenson returned from injury and was unfortunate not to get back.
Brentford (£20,000 from Carshalton on 8/3/94) FL 14+5/2 FAC 1/1 Others 1+1/1

ANNON Richard
Born: Leeds, 4 December 1968
Height: 5'8" Weight: 10.0
Not the tallest of players to have occupied both full-back slots for Crewe in recent years, but he more than made up for that with his speed off the mark. And, although opportunities were limited during his time at the club, Richard always acquitted himself well, making one appearance in the Coca Cola Cup last August, before being released a month later.
Doncaster Rov (Free from Leeds U juniors on 21/10/87)
Crewe Alex (£6,000 from Guisley on 15/5/92) FL 17+2/1 FLC 2 FAC 1+1 Others 1

ANSAH Andrew (Andy)
Born: Lewisham, 19 March 1969
Height: 5'10" Weight: 11.1
Lightly built, but tricky forward, who missed much of the early part of Southend's 1994-95 season due to a contractual dispute, which saw him loaned out to Brentford, Andy's willingness to run at defenders and take them on, allied to his ability to cross well with either foot, made him a formidable opponent. A lack of inches does not prevent him being good in the air and his workrate can never be questioned. Missed the final part of last season, following a knee operation.
Brentford (Free from Dorking on 21/3/89) FL 3+5/2 FLC 0+1
Southend U (Free on 29/3/90) FL 141+12/33 FLC 7+2 FAC 4 Others 6+2/5
Brentford (Loaned on 4/11/94) FL 2+1/1 Others 2/1

ANTHONY Graham John
Born: South Shields, 9 August 1975
Height: 5'8" Weight: 9.7
Young Sheffield United midfield player who has worked his way through the ranks to earn a professional contract. Made his first team debut last season in the Anglo-Italian Cup against Ancona, and his FL debut as a 12-minute substitute against Burnley. Will continue to gain experience through the reserves.
Sheffield U (From trainee on 7/7/93) FL 0+1 Others 2

ANTHROBUS Stephen (Steve) Anthony
Born: Lewisham, 10 November 1968
Height: 6'2" Weight: 12.13
Wimbledon winger who is very strong physically and difficult to knock off the ball. Useful in the air, especially at the far post, surprisingly, for the second season running, he failed to play for the "Dons" in 1994-95, his only first team football coming in a loan spell at Chester last September.
Millwall (From juniors on 4/8/86) FL 19+2/4 FLC 3 Others 1
Wimbledon (£150,000 on 16/2/90) F/PL 27+1 FLC 1 FAC 2
Peterborough U (Loaned on 21/1/94) FL 2
Chester C (Loaned on 26/8/94) FL 7

APPLEBY Matthew Wilfred
Born: Middlesbrough, 16 April 1972
Height: 5'10" Weight: 11.0
Versatile Darlington defender signed in the 1994 close season from Newcastle after being on loan for two months in 1993-94, "Matty" operated mainly at right-back, with a few games in midfield, scoring twice (one a penalty).
Newcastle U (From trainee on 4/5/90) F/PL 18+2 FLC 2+1 FAC 2 Others 2+2
Darlington (Loaned on 25/11/93) FL 10/1 Others 1
Darlington (Signed on 15/6/94) FL 35+1/1 FLC 2 FAC 1 Others 3/1

ARCHDEACON Owen Duncan
Born: Greenock, 4 March 1966
Height: 5'7" Weight: 11.0
Club Honours: SPD '86
International Honours: S: U21-1; Yth
A succession of injuries made 1994-95 a season to forget for Owen. Achilles injuries

to both ankles restricted his appearances for Barnsley in midfield to a bare minimum and, after recovering, he damaged a thigh in his first full match in March and his season was over.
Glasgow Celtic (From Gourock U on 20/8/82) SL 38+38/7 SLC 1+4/1 SC 3+1 Others 1+3
Barnsley (£80,000 on 7/7/89) FL 186+9/20 FLC 12+1/2 FAC 12+1/2 Others 9+1/4

ARCHER Lee
Born: Bristol, 6 November 1972
Height: 5'9" Weight 11.4
A fast raiding, left-winger who provided many accurate crosses for a good number of Bristol Rovers' goals last season. Another product of the club's successful youth development policy, Lee has grown in confidence since establishing himself in the first team.
Bristol Rov (From trainee on 18/7/91) FL 73+13/12 FLC 5 FAC 4+1/1 Others 7+2

ARDLEY Neil Christopher
Born: Epsom, 1 September 1972
Height: 5'11" Weight: 11.9
International Honours: E: U21-3
After starting 1994-95 on the Wimbledon bench, Neil was selected for the next six matches, mainly on the right of midfield. A strong tackler, who is not easily beaten, and a good passer of the ball, he was in-and-out for the rest of the season, despite scoring in the club's 4-3 classic win over Aston Villa in November.
Wimbledon (From trainee on 29/7/91) F/PL 55+10/6 FLC 8+2/2 FAC 8

ARMSTRONG Alun
Born: Gateshead, 22 February 1975
Height: 6'1" Weight: 11.13
Striker who made an immediate impact for Stockport after signing from Newcastle last summer. Scored on his debut against Cardiff and netted seven times in his first 15 games, showing great promise, and is already a favourite with the Edgeley Park fans.
Newcastle U (From trainee on 1/10/93)
Stockport Co (£50,000 on 23/6/94) FL 40+5/14 FLC 3/1 FAC 0+1 Others 2

ARMSTRONG Steven Craig
Born: South Shields, 23 May 1975
Height: 5'11" Weight: 12.4
Left-back who had his initial taste of first team football with Burnley, while on loan from Nottingham Forest last December. Showed a willingness to go forward, but defensive inexperience was evident and he returned to the City Ground before his time was up.
Nottingham F (From trainee on 2/6/92)
Burnley (Loaned on 29/12/94) FL 4

ARMSTRONG Christopher (Chris) Peter
Born: Newcastle, 19 June 1971
Height: 6'0" Weight: 11.0
Club Honours: Div 1 '94
International Honours: E: B-1
Crystal Palace striker who has made excellent progress since joining the club and has become one of the most sought after players in the country. Tall, strong and pacy, Chris started last season, having signed a

new four year contract, scoring in the heavy defeat at the hands of Liverpool, but unable to find the net again until November. Cup games gave both him and the side a change of fortune as he struck ten in eleven games, with two at "Wolves" being outstanding volleys. Following an injury, and a well publicised off the field problem, he came back strongly to play well in the losing FA Cup semi-final games against Manchester United and to score in each of the last three PL matches. Had the chance at the end of an up-and-down season to choose between joining up with the Republic of Ireland squad or Nigeria. Stop Press: A summer signing for Tottenham in a move reported to be worth £4,500,000.

Wrexham (Free from Llay Welfare on 3/3/89) FL 40+20/13 FLC 2+1 FAC 0+1 Others 5+1/3
Millwall (£50,000 on 16/8/91) FL 11+17/5 FLC 3+1/2 FAC 0+1 Others 0+1
Crystal Palace (£1,000,000 on 1/9/92) F/PL 118/45 FLC 8/6 FAC 8/5 Others 2/1

ARMSTRONG Gordon Ian
Born: Newcastle, 15 July 1967
Height: 6'0" Weight: 11.10
Club Honours: Div 3 '88
Long-serving Sunderland left-sided midfielder, who was awarded a testimonial prior to the start of last season against Bobby Robson's Porto, he endured a frustrating term due to a succession of niggling injuries. A handy goalscorer from midfield in previous years, Gordon's two early goals at Carlisle in the FA Cup replay, helped to secure a lucrative home-tie against Tottenham in round four.

Sunderland (From apprentice on 10/7/85) FL 331+17/50 FLC 25+3/3 FAC 19/4 Others 18+1/4

ARNOLD Ian
Born: Durham, 4 July 1972
Height: 5'9" Weight: 11.0
A Carlisle forward who made a handful of appearances early last season, but could not command a regular place. Joined Kettering in December for £10,000.

Middlesbrough (From trainee on 24/1/90) FL 0+3 Others 0+1
Carlisle U (Free on 14/8/92) FL 34+13/11 FLC 0+4 FAC 2+3/4 Others 6+1/2

ARNOTT Andrew (Andy) John
Born: Chatham, 18 October 1973
Height: 6'1" Weight: 12.0
Started last season in a striker's role at Gillingham but, having turned in some impressive displays for the reserves at centre-back he is now regarded as a defender who is equally at home at full-back. Cool under pressure, Andy looks to have a bright future in his new position.

Gillingham (From trainee on 13/5/91) FL 50+22/12 FLC 2+3 FAC 10+2/1 Others 3+1

ASABA Carl
Born: London, 28 January 1973
Height: 6'2" Weight: 13.0
A bustling Brentford centre-forward who scored on his only first team appearance last season against Gillingham in the AWS before going on loan to Colchester. In his stint with the Essex club, Carl played 12 FL games and struck two goals before returning.

Brentford (Free from Dulwich Hamlet on 9/8/94) Others 1/1
Colchester U (Loaned on 16/2/95) FL 9+3/2

ASHBEE Ian
Born: Birmingham, 6 September 1976
Height: 6'1" Weight: 12.10
International Honours: E: Yth
Beginning last season as Derby's youth team skipper and apprentice professional, his steady displays as a central defender led to promotion in the reserves. Predominantly left-footed, Ian was rewarded with a full contract in November and further progress ensured a FL debut towards the end of the campaign.

Derby Co (From trainee on 9/11/94) FL 1

ASHBY Barry John
Born: Brent, 21 November 1970
Height: 6'2" Weight: 13.2
Club Honours: FAYC '89
Composed Brentford central defender who is good in the air and on the ground. Formed an excellent defensive partnership with Jamie Bates in 1994-95 as the "Bees" only fell at the play-off stage.

Watford (From trainee on 1/12/88) FL 101+13/3 FLC 6 FAC 4 Others 2+1
Brentford (Signed on 22/3/94) FL 48/2 FLC 3 FAC 2 Others 5

ASHCROFT Lee
Born: Preston, 7 September 1972
Height: 5'10" Weight: 11.2
International Honours: E: U21-1
A fast and tricky WBA winger who prefers to play wide on the left, but can also figure on the opposite flank. Perhaps too elaborate and over-anxious at times, he packs an explosive right-foot shot and has also headed some vital goals when choosing to arrive unnoticed inside the area. His finest goal of the last campaign was undoubtedly the sixth minute header in the local derby against "Wolves" at The Hawthorns in mid-March, where he also set up Bob Taylor's goal in Albion's 2-0 win.

Preston NE (From trainee on 16/7/91) FL 78+13/13 FLC 3 FAC 5 Others 6+2/1
West Bromwich A (£250,000 on 1/8/93) FL 53+6/13 FLC 2+1 FAC 3/1 Others 5+1

ASHLEY Kevin Mark
Born: Birmingham, 31 December 1968
Height: 5'7" Weight: 11.10
Diminutive full-back who is consistent and reliable and never over-elaborates, Kevin joined Peterborough from "Wolves" prior to the start of last season. Unfortunately, he was restricted to limited appearances due to injury.

Birmingham C (From apprentice on 7/1/87) FL 56+1/1 FLC 5 FAC 3 Others 1+1
Wolverhampton W (£500,000 on 13/9/90) FL 87+1/1 FLC 5 FAC 1+1 Others 4
Peterborough U (Free on 10/8/94) FL 27 FLC 2 FAC 2

ASPIN Neil
Born: Gateshead, 12 April 1965
Height: 6'0" Weight: 12.6
Club Honours: AMC '93
Solid Port Vale defender who gave everything and had one of the best seasons of his career in 1994-95. A leg injury ruled him out of the first 12 games, but he

returned first at right-back and then as a central defender to cover for injury in that department. That was where he stayed and his "never-say-die" attitude made him a big favourite with the fans, particularly when he ventured into opposition territory.

Leeds U (From apprentice on 6/10/82) FL 203+4/5 FLC 9/1 FAC 17 Others 11
Port Vale (£200,000 on 28/7/89) FL 235+2/2 FLC 12 FAC 16 Others 15

ASPINALL Brendan James
Born: South Africa, 22 July 1975
Height: 6'0" Weight: 12.4
Mansfield central defender who, after appearing in the first 11 matches last season, lost his place to new signing, Mark Peters. Although inexperienced, he never let the side down and scored a spectacular goal against Halifax in the FA Cup, prior to being released at the end of 1994-95.

Mansfield T (Signed on 20/7/94) FL 13+7 FLC 3 FAC 2+1/1 Others 2

ASPINALL Warren
Born: Wigan, 13 September 1967
Height: 5'9" Weight: 11.12
Club Honours: AMC '85
International Honours: E: Yth
Signed from Portsmouth in 1993-94, Warren began last season in Bournemouth's midfield, before moving up-front where he scored four goals in 14 appearances. After losing his place, following the arrival of Steve Jones and Steve Robinson, he finished the season on loan at Carlisle.

Wigan Ath (From apprentice on 31/8/85) FL 39+12/22 FLC 1 FAC 2+3/2 Others 3+5/4
Everton (£150,000 on 5/5/86) FL 0+7 FLC 0+1 Others 0+2
Aston Villa (£300,000 on 19/2/87) FL 40+4/14 FLC 4/2 FAC 1+1
Portsmouth (£315,000 on 26/8/88) FL 97+35/21 FLC 8+3/3 FAC 4+5/2 Others 6+1/2
Bournemouth (Loaned on 27/8/93) FL 4+2/1
Swansea C (Loaned on 14/10/93) FL 5 Others 1
Bournemouth (£20,000 on 31/12/93) FL 26+1/8 FLC 4 FAC 1 Others 1
Carlisle U (Loaned on 8/3/95) FL 6+1/1

ATHERTON Peter
Born: Orrell, 6 April 1970
Height: 5'11" Weight: 12.3
International Honours: E: U21-1; Sch
Following his 1994 close season move to Sheffield Wednesday as the club's replacement for Roland Nilsson, Peter settled in very well and was greatly appreciated by the fans who voted him their "Player of the Year". Strong tackling, mobile, and positionally sound, he has made the right-back spot his own and has even helped out in central defence on occasion. Has also started to find his attacking boots with powerful right-wing runs and crosses. All-in-all, an excellent aquisition for Wednesday.

Wigan Ath (From trainee on 12/2/88) FL 145+4/1 FLC 8 FAC 7 Others 12+1
Coventry C (£300,000 on 23/8/91) F/PL 113+1 FLC 4 FAC 2
Sheffield Wed (£800,000 on 1/6/94) PL 41/1 FLC 4 FAC 3

ATKIN Paul Anthony
Born: Nottingham, 3 September 1969
Height: 6'0" Weight: 12.4
International Honours: E: Yth; Sch

15

Composed and reliable York central defender who rarely gets ruffled. A good clubman, he also played on occasion in midfield when called upon last season.

Notts Co (From trainee on 6/7/87)
Bury (Signed on 22/3/89) FL 14+7/1 Others 2+1
York C (Free on 1/7/91) FL 100+12/3 FLC 3+1 FAC 6 Others 8+1

ATKINS Mark Nigel
Born: Doncaster, 14 August 1968
Height: 6'0" Weight: 12.5
Club Honours: PL '95
International Honours: E: Sch

Kenny Dalglish's ultimate choice to replace the injured David Batty in midfield last season was the long-serving Mark. The Blackburn manager knew he was getting a man who played the system perfectly, closing down space, getting goalside of his opponent, and defending the last third of the field. Six PL goals were an added bonus, and a Premiership medal was a dream reward for one of the club's lesser known players.

Scunthorpe U (From juniors on 9/7/86) FL 45+5/2 FLC 3+1 FAC 5 Others 6+1
Blackburn Rov (£45,000 on 16/6/88) F/PL 224+29/35 FLC 20+2/4 FAC 11+3 Others 16+1/1

ATKINSON Brian
Born: Darlington, 19 January 1971
Height: 5'10" Weight: 11.6
International Honours: E: U21-6

Tough-tackling Sunderland midfielder who, most significantly, was immediately restored to the side by new manager, Peter Reid, last April. Highly rated by many Sunderland fans, not only for his combative style, but also his undoubted ability on the ball, he suffered a succession of injuries last season, including a punctured lung. Has represented England at U21 level and, at 24, still has time on his side to fully realise his potential.

Sunderland (From trainee on 21/7/89) FL 114+20/4 FLC 5+2 FAC 13/2 Others 2+3

ATKINSON Dalian Robert
Born: Shrewsbury, 21 March 1968
Height: 5'11" Weight: 11.7
Club Honours: FLC '94
International Honours: E: B-1

Powerful Aston Villa striker who is extremely quick and commits defenders when running straight at them. Also good in the air, Dalian had a difficult time of it in 1994-95, apart from an excellent spell in November when he scored five goals in six games. Unable to attain full fitness earlier in the season, on coming back and struggling to regain his form, he suffered a number of further injuries picked up either in training or reserve matches, that made it difficult for him to maintain a regular place in the side. 1995-96 cannot come quick enough for the big man.

Ipswich T (From apprentice on 4/6/85) FL 49+11/18 FLC 5+1/3 Others 2+1
Sheffield Wed (£450,000 on 16/6/89) FL 38/10 FLC 3/3 FAC 2/1 Others 2/1 (£1,700,000 to Real Sociedad on 1/8/90)
Aston Villa (£1,600,000 on 11/7/91) F/PL 79+8/23 FLC 15/11 FAC 4 Others 8/2

ATKINSON Graeme
Born: Hull, 11 November 1971
Height: 5'8" Weight: 10.5

Equally at home on either flank, in attack or defence, Graeme scored on his Preston debut at Hartlepool. Signed from Hull last season, he became a valuable squad member, but has yet to show his best form from a regular position.

Hull C (From trainee on 6/5/90) FL 129+20/23 FLC 6+3/2 FAC 4+1/1 Others 9
Preston NE (Signed on 7/10/94) FL 8+7/1

AUNGER Geoffrey (Geoff) Edward
Born: Red Deer, Canada, 4 February 1968
Height: 5'8" Weight: 11.10
International Honours: Canada

Released by Luton in July 1994, he joined non-league Sudbury Town before having a trial with Chester last December, making five appearances, four of them from the subs' bench. A forward player with good pace, he left City at the end of January.

Luton T (Free from Vancouver 86ers on 6/9/93) FL 5/1
Chester C (Free from Sudbury T on 16/12/94) FL 1+4

AUSTIN Dean Barry
Born: Hemel Hempstead, 26 April 1970
Height: 5'11" Weight: 12.4

Made only three appearances during Ossie Ardiles' reign at White Hart Lane, but was brought back into the side to strengthen a leaky defence when Gerry Francis took over last season. A right-back, whose speed and commitment in tackles helped Tottenham to address the weaknesses in defence and achieve six consecutive clean sheets beginning away at Everton in December, and continuing until the 2-1 victory over West Ham in January, Dean was a member of the side that reached the FA Cup semi-finals before losing out to Everton.

Southend U (£12,000 from St Albans C on 22/3/90) FL 76/2 FLC 4/1 FAC 2 Others 7
Tottenham H (£375,000 on 4/6/92) PL 76+5 FLC 4+2 FAC 11+1

AUSTIN Kevin Levi
Born: London, 12 February 1973
Height: 5'9" Weight: 10.12

Defender in his second season with Orient, who made the left-back his own last season, missing games only through injury or suspension. A strong tackler who likes to come forward, he can expect to play in a higher grade if he continues his rate of development.

Leyton Orient (Free from Saffron Walden on 19/8/93) FL 69/2 FLC 2 FAC 5 Others 6

AWFORD Andrew (Andy) Terence
Born: Worcester, 14 July 1972
Height: 5'10" Weight: 12.0
International Honours: E: U21-4; Yth

Skilful Portsmouth defender whose understanding of the game allows him time and space to play the ball. For Andy, 1994-95 was a non-event as he suffered a double fracture to his right shin, breaking both his tibia and fibula half way down the bones, an injury which put him out of the game for the whole season. He will be hoping 1995-96

offers a fresh start and better luck.

Portsmouth (From trainee on 24/7/89) FL 138+8 FLC 16+1 FAC 10 Others 12

AYRTON Matthew Robert
Born: Rotherham, 16 December 1976
Height: 5'10" Weight: 11.0

Still a Rotherham trainee, Matthew features wide on the right, where he has a great turn of speed, coupled with good crossing ability. However, he was restricted to just one game in the Auto Windscreens Shield last season.

Rotherham U (Trainee) Others 1

BABB Philip (Phil) Andrew
Born: Lambeth, 30 November 1970
Height: 6'0" Weight: 12.3
Club Honours: FLC '95
International Honours: Ei:16; B-1

After impressing in the 1994 World Cup Finals with the Republic of Ireland side, Phil came back to star for Coventry, before being signed by Liverpool last September. Found it difficult at first, but gradually settled in, and his marvellous timing in the tackle allowed "Reds'" fans to think of the elegant Mark Lawrenson. A mainly defensive utility player, who has pace and strength, allied to great vision, there is nothing he likes better than getting up with the attack to deliver quality crosses to the front men.

Millwall (From trainee on 25/4/89)
Bradford C (Free on 10/8/90) FL 73+7/14 FLC 5+1 FAC 3 Others 3+1
Coventry C (£500,000 on 21/7/92) PL 70+7/3 FLC 5/1 FAC 2
Liverpool (£3,600,000 on 1/9/94) PL 33+1 FLC 7 FAC 6

BADDELEY Lee Matthew
Born: Cardiff, 12 July 1974
Height: 6'1" Weight: 12.7

Although starting 1994-95 out of the Cardiff first team, Lee was recalled and quickly established himself as the lynchpin at the centre of the defence, where he gave some typically polished performances.

Cardiff C (From trainee on 13/8/91) FL 81+13/1 FLC 0+2 FAC 7 Others 20

BAILEY Danny Stephen
Born: Leyton, 21 May 1964
Height: 5'8" Weight: 12.7
Club Honours: Div 4 '90

Wholehearted ball-winning midfield player who, although an infrequent scorer, hits spectacular goals. Popular with the fans, and in his second spell at Exeter, Danny was freed at the end of 1994-95.

Bournemouth (Apprentice) FL 1+1
Torquay U (Free from Walthamstow Ave on 1/3/84) FL 1
Exeter C (Free from Wealdstone, via Grays Ath, Harringey Bor and Kingsbury T, on 1/8/89) FL 63+1/2 FLC 8 FAC 7/1 Others 4+1/1
Reading (£50,000 on 26/12/90) FL 49+1/2 FAC 3
Fulham (Loaned on 29/7/92) FL 2+1
Exeter C (Free on 7/12/92) FL 70+5/2 FLC 6 FAC 5/1 Others 12/1

BAILEY Dennis Lincoln
Born: Lambeth, 13 November 1965
Height: 5'10" Weight: 11.6

QPR striker, or winger, who is quick off the mark and loves to run at defences.

Unfortunate not to make an appearance in the first team last season, he did, however, have a successful spell on loan at Brentford.

Fulham (Free from Barking on 8/11/86)
Crystal Palace (£10,000 from Farnborough T on 2/12/87) FL 0+5/1
Bristol Rov (Loaned on 27/2/89) FL 17/9 Others 1+1/1
Birmingham C (£80,000 on 3/8/89) FL 65+10/23 FLC 6/2 FAC 6 Others 3+3
Bristol Rov (Loaned on 28/3/91) FL 6/1
Queens Park R (£175,000 on 2/7/91) FL 32+7/10 FLC 5/3 FAC 1+1 Others 1
Charlton Ath (Loaned on 29/10/93) FL 0+4 Others 2
Watford (Loaned on 24/3/94) FL 2+6/4
Brentford (Loaned on 26/1/95) FL 6/3

BAIRD Ian James
Born: Rotherham, 1 April 1964
Height: 6'0" Weight: 12.9
Club Honours: Div 2 '90
International Honours: E: Sch
Bristol City forward with a career record of over a 100 first team goals. Has done well to come back after suffering a punctured lung, and there were times in 1994-95 that he looked to be getting back to his best form. As competitive as ever, at his best he can hold the ball up well for others and take on the best of defences.

Southampton (From apprentice on 5/4/82) FL 20+2/5 FLC 1+1
Cardiff C (Loaned on 1/11/80) FL 12/6
Newcastle U (Loaned on 1/12/86) FL 4+1/1
Leeds U (£75,000 on 10/3/85) FL 84+1/33 FLC 4 FAC 5/4 Others 7
Portsmouth (£285,000 on 12/8/87) FL 20/1 FLC 1 FAC 1
Leeds U (£120,000 on 4/3/88) FL 76+1/17 FLC 5/1 FAC 3/2 Others 6
Middlesbrough (£500,000 on 29/1/90) FL 60+3/19 FLC 5+1 FAC 3/1 Others 4/1
Heart of Midlothian (£400,000 on 31/7/91) SL 64/15 SLC 5/2 SC 7/1 Others 3/1
Bristol C (£295,000 on 6/7/93) FL 44+12/11 FLC 3 FAC 2/1 Others 1

BAKER Clive Edward
Born: West Runton, 14 March 1959
Height: 5'9" Weight: 11.0
Ipswich goalkeeper who makes up for his lack of height with agility and shot-stopping abilities. The regular understudy to Craig Forrest, Clive was troubled by knee problems last season, his first appearance coming in the FA Cup defeat at Wrexham. Unfortunate against Arsenal, his best performance was probably in the home game with West Ham, when he kept his side in the match with some stunning saves.

Norwich C (From juniors on 29/7/77) FL 14 FAC 2
Barnsley (Free on 7/8/84) FL 291 FLC 15 FAC 23 Others 8
Coventry C (Free on 23/8/91) FLC 1
Ipswich T (Free on 20/8/92) PL 47+1 FLC 8 FAC 10

BAKER David Paul
Born: Newcastle, 5 January 1963
Height: 6'1" Weight: 12.10
Signed from Gillingham last October, when he and his family became unsettled in the south, Paul scored on his full FL debut for York at home against Huddersfield. An experienced striker, having begun his career as a centre-half, he added both height and power to the City attack and finished second top-scorer with 14 goals.

Southampton (£4,000 from Bishop Auckland on 1/7/94)
Carlisle U (Free on 2/7/85) FL 66+5/11 FLC 4/1 FAC 3 Others 2+1
Hartlepool U (Free on 31/7/87) FL 192+5/67 FLC 12/4 FAC 16/6 Others 16/5
Motherwell (£77,500 on 1/8/92) SL 5+4/1 SLC 1
Gillingham (£40,000 on 7/1/93) FL 58+4/16 FAC 5/1 Others 2
York C (£15,000 on 1/10/94) FL 25+5/13 FAC 2 Others 1+1/1

BALDRY Simon
Born: Huddersfield, 12 February 1976
Height: 5'10" Weight: 11.0
A home-grown Huddersfield product who played at the start of last season, but then found it difficult to establish himself in the first team, Simon impressed on the right-hand side of midfield. Very fast and a good passer of the ball.

Huddersfield T (From trainee on 14/7/94) FL 18+3/2 FLC 2 Others 1+2/1

BALL Kevin Anthony
Born: Hastings, 12 November 1964
Height: 5'9" Weight: 11.6
Sunderland club captain, who can operate in midfield or, more regularly, at centre-back. Very popular with supporters for his aggressive style of leadership on the field, although this approach at times lands him in trouble with referees, Kevin is a very good reader of the game and his presence in the Sunderland midfield adds vital stability to this area.

Portsmouth (Free from Coventry C juniors on 6/10/82) FL 96+9/4 FLC 8+1 FAC 8 Others 6
Sunderland (£350,000 on 16/7/90) FL 185+2/9 FLC 11/2 FAC 14 Others 4/1

BALMER Stuart Murray
Born: Falkirk, 20 June 1969
Height: 6'1" Weight: 12.4
Right-sided Charlton defender who can play at right-back or in central defence, Stuart is good in the air and distributes the ball well. Out of favour in the early part of last season, when returning to the side in February he put in some splendid performances alongside Richard Rufus in central defence and made the place his own. Appointed team captain towards the end of 1994-95.

Glasgow Celtic (From juniors in 1987)
Charlton Ath (£120,000 on 24/8/90) FL 130+17/5 FLC 6 FAC 6 Others 9+1

BAMBER John David (Dave)
Born: St Helens, 1 February 1959
Height: 6'3" Weight: 13.10
An experienced striker who played only four games for Blackpool in 1994-95, due to an injury which threatened his career, he was freed at the end of the season.

Blackpool (Free from Manchester University on 20/9/79) FL 81+5/29 FLC 6/5 FAC 7+1/2
Coventry C (£50,000 on 9/6/83) FL 18+1/3 FLC 2/1 FAC 0+1
Walsall (£20,000 on 22/3/84) FL 17+3/7 FLC 3
Portsmouth (£20,000 on 19/12/84) FL 4/1
Swindon T (£12,500 on 22/11/85) FL 103+3/31 FLC 10/7 FAC 6/5 Others 15/4
Watford (£105,000 on 28/6/88) FL 16+2/3 FLC 2/1 Others 2
Stoke C (£190,000 on 21/12/88) FL 43/8 FLC 2 FAC 3/2 Others 1/1

Hull C (£130,000 on 1/2/90) FL 25+3/5 FLC 2
Blackpool (£25,000 on 29/11/90) FL 111+2/61 FLC 8+1/9 FAC 3/1 Others 12/2

BANGER Nicholas (Nicky) Lee
Born: Southampton, 25 February 1971
Height: 5'9" Weight: 11.6
Signed from Southampton last November, having already impressed Oldham manager, Joe Royle, during a five match spell on loan at the club, Nicky is a winger who can cause defenders problems with quick darting runs. Opened his "Latics'" scoring account with a terrific double salvo against Sheffield United.

Southampton (From trainee on 25/4/89) F/PL 18+37/8 FLC 2+2/3 FAC 0+2 Others 1
Oldham Ath (£250,000 on 4/10/94) FL 20+8/3 FLC 2 FAC 1

BANKS Ian Frederick
Born: Mexborough, 9 January 1961
Height: 5'9" Weight: 11.13
Vastly experienced player who captained Darlington for most of last season, his strong tackling and accurate passing out of the centre of defence was a stabilising influence on the team and an inspiration to younger players. Surprisingly freed during the summer.

Barnsley (From apprentice on 11/1/79) FL 158+6/37 FLC 19/3 FAC 11/1
Leicester C (£100,000 on 1/6/83) FL 78+15/14 FLC 3+1/1 FAC 6
Huddersfield T (£45,000 on 19/9/86) FL 78/17 FLC 4/1 FAC 4 Others 1
Bradford C (£180,000 on 21/7/88) FL 26+4/3 FLC 5/3 FAC 1 Others 1
West Bromwich A (£100,000 on 24/3/89) FL 2+2
Barnsley (£100,000 on 2/8/89) FL 87+9/7 FLC 6 FAC 5+1 Others 4+1/4
Rotherham U (Free on 30/7/92) FL 76/8 FLC 8/2 FAC 6 Others 3
Darlington (Free on 8/8/94) FL 39/1 FLC 2 FAC 2 Others 3

BANKS Steven
Born: Hillingdon, 9 February 1972
Height: 5'11" Weight: 13.2
Signed from West Ham, this young Gillingham 'keeper gained a regular first team place in September 1994 and has not looked back since. Impressed with his coolness under pressure and looks likely to go on to higher things.

West Ham U (From trainee on 24/3/90) Others 1
Gillingham (Free on 25/3/93) FL 67 FAC 7 Others 2

BANNISTER Gary
Born: Warrington, 22 July 1960
Height: 5'8" Weight: 11.3
International Honours: E: U21-1
An intelligent and creative midfield player who signed for Lincoln last September, following a brief spell in Hong Kong, his experience proved an asset to the team and he scored some vital goals including the winner at Hull in the FA Cup. Freed during the summer.

Coventry C (From apprentice on 10/5/78) FL 17+5/3 FLC 2 FAC 2
Sheffield Wed (£100,000 on 3/8/81) FL 117+1/55 FLC 13/6 FAC 12/4
Queens Park R (£200,000 on 13/8/84) FL 136/56 FLC 23/9 FAC 9/1 Others 4/6
Coventry C (£300,000 on 10/3/88) FL 39+4/11 FLC 5/2

West Bromwich A (£250,000 on 9/3/90) FL 62+10/18 FLC 3+1/1 FAC 1+1 Others 2+1/1
Oxford U (Loaned on 19/3/92) FL 7+3/2
Nottingham F (Free on 1/8/92) FL 27+4/8 FLC 2+1/1 FAC 3/1
Stoke C (Free on 21/5/93) FL 10+5/2 FAC 2 Others 0+1
Lincoln C (Free from Hong Kong R on 14/9/94) FL 25+4/7 FLC 2 FAC 1+1/1 Others 1

Ian Baraclough   Barrington Coombes
(Empics Sports Photo Agency)

BARACLOUGH Ian Robert
Born: Leicester, 4 December 1970
Height: 6'1" Weight: 12.0
International Honours: E: Yth

Mansfield left-back who had a fine season in 1994-95 and played occasionally on the left-hand side of midfield. An enthusiastic player who loves to get forward, and who is also the club's dead-ball specialist, he scored a remarkable goal against Hereford from fully 40 yards out.
Leicester C (From trainee on 15/12/88) FAC 1 Others 0+1
Wigan Ath (Loaned on 22/3/90) FL 8+1/2
Grimsby T (Loaned on 21/12/90) FL 2+3
Grimsby T (Free on 13/8/91) FL 1
Lincoln C (Free on 21/8/92) FL 68+5/10 FLC 7/1 FAC 4 Others 7
Mansfield T (Free on 6/6/94) FL 36/3 FLC 5 FAC 4 Others 3

BARBER Frederick (Fred)
Born: Ferryhill, 26 August 1963
Height: 5'10" Weight: 12.10

Very experienced goalkeeper, although on the small side, he was signed by Luton from Peterborough at the start of 1994-95 as cover for Juergen Sommer. However, unable to get a game at Kenilworth Road, Fred was loaned back to his old club in December and performed well before unfortunately suffering a broken collar bone.
Darlington (From apprentice on 27/8/81) FL 135 FLC 9 FAC 12 Others 7
Everton (£50,000 on 8/4/86)
Walsall (£100,000 on 20/10/86) FL 153 FLC 9 FAC 12 Others 15
Peterborough U (Loaned on 16/10/89) FL 6
Chester C (Loaned on 18/10/90) FL 3
Blackpool (Loaned on 29/11/90) FL 2
Chester C (Loaned on 28/3/91) FL 5
Peterborough U (£25,000 on 15/8/91) FL 63 FLC 8 FAC 5 Others 10

Chesterfield (Loaned on 1/2/93) Others 2
Colchester U (Loaned 19/3/93) FL 10
Luton T (£25,000 on 12/8/94)
Peterborough U (Loaned on 23/12/94) FL 5

BARBER Philip (Phil) Andrew
Born: Tring, 10 June 1965
Height: 5'11" Weight: 12.6

Left-sided Millwall midfielder who can attack or defend whatever the occasion demands. With a proliferation of similar players at the club in 1994-95, Phil's services were not required and he had a spell on loan at Plymouth in December, before returning to the Den and reserve team football. Stop Press: Signed for Bristol on a free transfer during the summer.
Crystal Palace (£7,500 from Aylesbury U on 14/2/84) FL 207+27/35 FLC 13+6/3 FAC 14/1 Others 19+2/2
Millwall (£100,000 on 25/7/91) FL 104+6/12 FLC 7 FAC 2 Others 2+1
Plymouth Arg (Loaned on 23/12/94) FL 4 FAC 1

BARDSLEY David John
Born: Manchester, 11 September 1964
Height: 5'10" Weight: 10.0
International Honours: E: 2; Yth

A superb attacking defender, David supports the QPR forwards very well and is an excellent crosser of the ball, leading to many goals. His performances have been consistently of high quality, and he was very unfortunate not to have been called up into the England squad, though a few minor injuries kept him out of the first team during mid-season.
Blackpool (From apprentice on 5/11/82) FL 45 FLC 2/1 FAC 2
Watford (£150,000 on 23/11/83) FL 97+3/7 FLC 6/1 FAC 13+1/1 Others 1
Oxford U (£265,000 on 18/9/87) FL 74/7 FLC 12 FAC 5 Others 3
Queens Park R (£500,000 on 15/9/89) F/PL 212/4 FLC 18/1 FAC 18 Others 3/1

BARFOOT Stuart John
Born: Southampton, 10 December 1975
Height: 5'11" Weight: 11.0

A right-back who made his debut for Bournemouth when coming on as a substitute against Chelsea in the Coca Cola Cup-tie last October, he made two further appearances as a substitute, before moving to Torquay as a non-contract player in March.
Bournemouth (From trainee on 14/7/94) FL 0+2 FLC 0+1
Torquay U (Free on 23/3/95)

BARKER Simon
Born: Farnworth, 4 November 1964
Height: 5'9" Weight: 11.0
Club Honours: FMC '87
International Honours: E: U21-4

Having trained pre-season with Swindon, after failing to sign a new contract with QPR, the two clubs could not agree a fee, which turned out to be good news for Rangers as he was without doubt one of their best players last season. Benefited greatly under the guidance of new manager, Ray Wilkins, and showed a superb attitude in the centre of midfield, whilst scoring four League goals, including a brave 87th minute

header to earn a 1-1 draw against Nottingham Forest in February. Between mid-December and the end of the season, QPR lost just seven games, coincidentally, five of which Simon was missing, thus proving his value to the team.
Blackburn Rov (From apprentice on 6/11/82) FL 180+2/35 FLC 11/4 FAC 12 Others 8/2
Queens Park R (£400,000 on 20/7/88) F/PL 200+21/21 FLC 21+2/5 FAC 20+1/3 Others 7

BARLOW Andrew (Andy) John
Born: Oldham, 24 November 1965
Height: 5'9" Weight: 11.1
Club Honours: Div 2 '91

Oldham left-back who is always prepared to support the attack, and a great striker of the ball, Andy also spells danger with his long-throws. Unfortunate to pick up a serious knee injury in only the second game of last season, he tried to play through the "pain barrier" in the reserves but, ultimately, an operation was inevitable. Freed in May, having been granted a testimonial, after serving the club for 13 years.
Oldham Ath (From juniors on 31/7/84) F/PL 245+16/5 FLC 22 FAC 19 Others 6
Bradford C (Loaned on 1/11/93) FL 2

BARLOW Martin David
Born: Barnstaple, 26 June 1971
Height: 5'7" Weight: 10.3

A converted central midfielder who is predominantly right-footed, he is also capable of playing as a right-winger. Is a player with plenty of tenacity, who is always willing to battle hard for Plymouth, and his consistency made him an automatic choice in 1994-95.
Plymouth Arg (From trainee on 1/7/89) FL 127+25/9 FLC 6+1/2 FAC 7 Others 8+1

BARLOW Stuart
Born: Liverpool, 16 July 1968
Height: 5'10" Weight: 11.0

Everton centre-forward with a good turn of speed, who likes to hold the ball up and allow others to feed from his service. In addition to his team play, he manages to poach crucial goals, especially from set-pieces. Unfortunately, due to the number of strikers at the club, Stuart only made nine starts during 1994-95.
Everton (Free from Sherwood Park on 6/6/90) F/PL 24+44/10 FLC 3+4/1 FAC 4+3/2
Rotherham U (Loaned on 10/1/92) Others 0+1

BARMBY Nicholas (Nick) Jonathan
Born: Hull, 11 February 1974
Height: 5'6" Weight: 11.3
International Honours: E: 2 B-1; U21-3; Yth; Sch

This skilful Tottenham striker, played in a midfield role throughout last season and produced the flair and teamwork that resulted in him being capped by England. Scored his first goal of 1994-95 in the opening game against Sheffield Wednesday, showing great ability to create and produce individual efforts, as well as being a dedicated team player. Also, his forward thinking and great vision created many openings for his colleagues, Jurgen Klinsmann and Teddy Sheringham, with his

Nick Barmby

Steve Morton
(Empics Sports Photo Agency)

consistency and enthusiasm for the game being among his greatest attributes. A tantalising hope for England's International success, Nicky will undoubtedly continue to prosper in the Premier League this season.

Tottenham H (From trainee on 9/4/91) PL 81+6/20 FLC 7+1/2 FAC 12+1/5

BARNARD Darren Sean
Born: Rintein, Germany, 30 November 1971
Height: 5'10" Weight: 11.0
International Honours: E: Sch

Predominately a winger, Darren has the ability to go past defenders and is an excellent crosser of the ball. Although failing to make an appearance at Chelsea last season, he was loaned out to Reading in November following an injury to their striker, Stuart Lovell, and had a four match spell before returning to Stamford Bridge and reserve team football.

Chelsea (£50,000 from Wokingham T on 25/7/90) F/PL 18+11/2 FLC 1+1 FAC 1+1
Reading (Loaned on 18/11/94) FL 3+1

BARNES David
Born: Paddington, 16 November 1961
Height: 5'10" Weight: 11.4

International Honours: E: Yth (UEFAYC '80)

Experienced Watford left-back, who knows just when to make a tackle and, who is now with his sixth club, he was handicapped by persistent stomach problems in 1994-95, following a hernia operation, but caught the eye on his occasional appearances, especially when going forward.

Coventry C (From apprentice on 31/5/79) FL 9 FAC 4
Ipswich T (Free on 12/4/82) FL 16+1
Wolverhampton W (£35,000 on 3/10/84) FL 86+2/4 FLC 7 FAC 6 Others 6
Aldershot (£25,000 on 22/8/87) FL 68+1/1 FLC 2 FAC 2+2 Others 4
Sheffield U (£50,000 on 11/7/89) F/PL 82/1 FLC 6 FAC 14 Others 4
Watford (£50,000 on 14/1/94) FL 6 FAC 1+1

BARNES John Charles
Born: Jamaica, 7 September 1963
Height: 5'11" Weight: 11.10
Club Honours: FAYC '82; Div 1 '88, '90; FAC '89; CS '88, '89, '90; FLC '95
International Honours: E: 78; U21-3

The PFA "Player of the Year" in 1988, John is one of the most skilful players produced in this country over the last decade and can play in any position up-front, although more frequently used on the left-side where his stronger foot can take him past defenders as if they do not exist. Still a regular in Terry Venables' England side, after a period where his form suffered as captain of Liverpool, he was back to his best in 1994-95. Although his defensive duties meant that he was not able to get forward as much as he used to, his overall contribution to the team was of a greater depth.

Watford (Free from Sudbury Court on 14/7/81) FL 232+1/65 FLC 21/7 FAC 31/11 Others 7
Liverpool (£900,000 on 19/6/87) F/PL 240+3/77 FLC 20/3 FAC 42/16 Others 5/2

BARNES Paul Lance
Born: Leicester, 16 November 1967
Height: 5'10" Weight: 10.6

Leading York scorer for the third successive season, Paul is a very skilful striker who, at his best, is a fine leader of the attack with ability to hold the ball up. The subject of much transfer talk, he missed most of the second half of last season owing to a troublesome calf injury. Hit two hat-tricks during the course of the campaign.

Notts Co (From apprentice on 16/11/85) FL 36+17/14 FAC 0+1 Others 4+6/5
Stoke C (£30,000 on 23/3/90) FL 10+14/3 FLC 0+2 Others 3+1/2
Chesterfield (Loaned on 8/11/90) FL 1 FAC 1/1
York C (£50,000 on 15/7/92) FL 117+1/61 FLC 5 FAC 4 Others 11/2

BARNES Richard Ian
Born: Wrexham, 6 September 1975
Height: 5'10" Weight: 11.6

Taken on by Wrexham as a midfielder, he was later moved to a wide position, before making his first team debut last April at right-back. Richard is currently a non-contract player at the club.

Wrexham (From trainee on 31/5/94) FL 0+1

BARNESS Anthony
Born: Lewisham, 25 March 1973
Height: 5'10" Weight: 10.12

Young Chelsea left-back with two good feet, who can pass both long and short to turn defence into attack. Showed he could also play on the other flank when deputising for the injured Steve Clarke last season, and impressed when running the length of the pitch to cross a ball that Paul Furlong headed on to Dennis Wise for "Blues'" only goal in a 3-1 defeat at Arsenal in October. Reads the game well and with experience could become a regular.

Charlton Ath (From trainee on 6/3/91) FL 21+6/1 FLC 2 FAC 3 Others 1+1/1
Chelsea (£350,000 on 8/9/92) PL 12+2 FLC 1 Others 2+1
Middlesbrough (Loaned on 12/8/93) Others 1

BARNETT David (Dave) Kwame
Born: Birmingham, 16 April 1967
Height: 6'1" Weight: 12.8
Club Honours: AMC '95; Div 2 '95

Dave's Birmingham career did not get off to the best of starts, but following an injury to Chris Whyte he grasped the opportunity to forge a solid central central defensive partnership with Liam Daish in 1994-95. Picked up winners medals from the Auto Windscreen win over Carlisle at Wembley, and another following the club's promotion back to the First Division. Unfortunately, he was unable to finish the season after suffering an achilles tendon injury against Brentford and will be out of action for some while yet.

Colchester U (Signed from Windsor & Eton on 25/8/88) FL 19+1 FLC 2 FAC 3+2 Others 3 (Freed in June 1988)
West Bromwich A (Free from Edmonton Oilers on 13/10/89)
Walsall (Free on 17/7/90) FL 4+1 FLC 2 (Free to Kidderminster Hrs on 1/10/90)
Barnet (£10,000 on 29/2/92) FL 58+1/3 FLC 5 FAC 3 Others 5
Birmingham C (£150,000 on 20/12/93) FL 39+1 FLC 1 FAC 5 Others 8

BARNETT Gary Lloyd
Born: Stratford, 11 March 1963
Height: 5'9" Weight: 9.13
Club Honours: Div 3 '84

An experienced midfielder who maintained a place in the Orient squad throughout 1994-95, although he frequently found himself coming on as a sub, rather than making the starting line-up. A steady and reliable player, Gary can attack with pace and possesses a strong shot. Freed during the summer.

Coventry C (From apprentice on 22/1/81)
Oxford U (Free on 7/7/82) FL 37+8/9 FLC 6+2/1 FAC 5 Others 1
Wimbledon (Loaned on 24/2/83) FL 5/1
Fulham (Loaned on 19/12/84) FL 0+2/1
Fulham (£20,000 on 12/9/85) FL 167+13/30 FLC 17/3 FAC 8+1/1 Others 8+2/1
Huddersfield T (£30,000 on 20/7/90) FL 92+8/11 FLC 11/3 FAC 10/2 Others 7+2/1
Leyton Orient (Signed on 20/8/93) FL 47+16/7 FLC 3 FAC 4 Others 5+2/1

BARNHOUSE David John
Born: Swansea, 19 March 1975
Height: 5'9" Weight: 10.9
International Honours: W: U21-1

A versatile, tough-tackling defender, capable of playing in any defensive position, David impressed when called into first team

action with Swansea last season, especially in the FA Cup-tie against Middlesbrough at the Vetch Field. Also capped for the Welsh U21 side against Moldova.

Swansea C (From trainee on 8/7/93) FL 6+2 FAC 1 Others 2

BARR William (Billy) Joseph
Born: Halifax, 21 January 1969
Height: 5'11" Weight: 10.8

Left his home town to join Crewe during the 1994 close season and enjoyed an excellent first term at Crewe. Developing all the time, and often to be found in a defensive midfield role, he is adaptable and popular with everyone at the club.

Halifax T (From trainee on 6/7/87) FL 178+18/13 FLC 8+1/2 FAC 11+1/2 Others 14+3
Crewe Alex (Free on 17/6/94) FL 29+5/2 FLC 2 Others 6

BARRAS Anthony (Tony)
Born: Billingham, 29 March 1971
Height: 6'0" Weight: 12.3

Created a good impression in 1994-95, his first season at York, having moved from Stockport during the summer. A generally commanding figure in the heart of the City defence, he missed a number of games mid-term due to injury.

Hartlepool U (From trainee on 6/7/89) FL 9+3 FLC 2 FAC 1 Others 1
Stockport Co (Free on 23/7/90) FL 94+5/5 FLC 2 FAC 7 Others 19+1
Rotherham U (Loaned on 25/2/94) FL 5/1
York C (Signed on 18/7/94) FL 27+4/1 FLC 2 FAC 2 Others 2

BARRATT Anthony (Tony)
Born: Salford, 18 October 1965
Height: 5'7" Weight: 10.3

York utility player who missed the first six months of last season owing to a serious groin injury. During the closing weeks of the campaign, he made a few appearances, mainly at full-back, before being freed during the summer.

Grimsby T (Free from Billingham T on 16/8/85) FL 20+2 FLC 3 FAC 1 Others 2 (Freed during 1986 close season)
Hartlepool U (£1,000 from Billingham T on 4/12/86) FL 93+5/4 FLC 4 FAC 8 Others 6
York C (Signed on 23/3/89) FL 116+31/10 FLC 5 FAC 3+3 Others 8

BARRETT Earl Delisser
Born: Rochdale, 28 April 1967
Height: 5'10" Weight: 11.2
Club Honours: Div 2 '91; FLC '94
International Honours: E: 3; B-4; U21-4

Versatile Everton defender who can play as a centre-back or in a right-back role with an added ability to act as a man-to-man marker. Also makes good use of both feet to outwit forwards and often falls back on his lightening speed to move the ball out of defence. Joined the club from Aston Villa last January, shortly after Joe Royle took the helm, slotting into the back four and proving to be an invaluable addition to the squad, creating increased competition for places, while turning in steady performances. Cup-tied with Villa, Earl missed out on Everton's FA Cup Final win over Manchester United.

Manchester C (From trainee on 26/4/85) FL 2+1 FLC 1

Chester C (Loaned on 1/3/86) FL 12
Oldham Ath (£35,000 on 24/11/87) FL 181+2/7 FLC 20/1 FAC 14/1 Others 4
Aston Villa (£1,700,000 on 25/2/92) F/PL 118+1/1 FLC 15/1 FAC 9 Others 7
Everton (£1,700,000 on 30/1/95) PL 17

BARRETT Michael John
Born: Exeter, 20 October 1963
Height: 5'10" Weight: 12.5

Plucked from local non-league soccer, Mike made four appearances as a non-contract player for Exeter last Christmas when injuries and suspension forced the regular goalkeepers to force his inclusion.

Exeter C (Signed from Crediton on 16/12/94) FL 4

BARRETT Scott
Born: Ilkeston, 2 April 1963
Height: 6'0" Weight: 13.8
Club Honours: GMVC '92; FAT '92

An experienced goalkeeper, he lost his Gillingham first team place to Steve Banks in September 1994 and had to sit on the subs' bench from then on. Freed during the summer.

Wolverhampton W (Signed from Ilkeston T on 27/9/84) FL 30 FLC 1 FAC 1 Others 3
Stoke C (£10,000 on 24/7/87) FL 51 FLC 2 FAC 3 Others 4
Colchester U (Loaned on 10/1/90) FL 13
Stockport Co (Loaned on 22/3/90) FL 10 Others 2
Gillingham (Free on 14/8/92) FL 51 FLC 7 FAC 4 Others 4

Dean Barrick Tony Marshall
(Empics Sports Photo Agency)

BARRICK Dean
Born: Hemsworth, 30 September 1969
Height: 5'9" Weight: 11.9

Signed for Cambridge from Rotherham in August 1993. A left-sided player, playing as an attacking full-back, he only missed two games and was a key member of the defence last season.

Sheffield Wed (From trainee on 7/5/88) FL 11/2
Rotherham U (£50,000 on 14/2/91) FL 96+3/7 FLC 6 FAC 8 Others 5/1
Cambridge U (£50,000 on 11/8/93) FL 88/2 FLC 6/1 FAC 7/1 Others 6

BARRON Michael James
Born: Chester le Street, 22 December 1974
Height: 5'11" Weight: 11.9
Strong-tackling, determined young Middlesbrough defender with three first team appearances to his credit last season. As an all-rounder who displays sound defensive qualities, he is quick and very good in the air, and normally plays on the right-side of central defence, although preferring full-back. Shows much perception when hitting long balls over the heads of opposing defenders.
Middlesbrough (From trainee on 2/2/93) FL 1+1 FLC 1 Others 2+1

BARROW Lee Alexander
Born: Belper, 1 May 1973
Height: 5'11" Weight: 13.0
A highly successful campaign for Lee. Starting last season in central defence in place of the suspended Darren Moore, his pace and clever interceptions made him a permanent Torquay fixture.
Notts Co (From trainee on 9/7/91)
Scarborough (Free on 3/8/92) FL 11 FLC 2 Others 1
Torquay U (Free on 18/2/93) FL 74+1/5 FLC 5 FAC 6 Others 3

BARRY George
Born: London, 19 September 1967
Height: 5'8" Weight: 11.10
Signed as a non-contract defender, as resource starved Leyton Orient saw their squad depleted through injuries and transfers last season, he made an impressive debut in a 0-0 draw at Cambridge. Acquitted himself well in subsequent matches.
Leyton Orient (Free from Fisher on 16/3/95) FL 5+1

BARTLEY Carl Alexander
Born: Lambeth, 6 October 1976
Height: 6'3" Weight: 13.5
A tall, well-built teenager and still a YTS player, who scored regularly for Fulham's juniors, Carl is on the verge of the first team, making his debut last September and being given one further outing.
Fulham (Trainee) FL 1 FLC 1

BARTON Warren Dean
Born: Stoke Newington, 19 March 1969
Height: 6'0" Weight: 11.0
International Honours: E: 3; B-2
In showing excellent form throughout 1994-95, Warren was once again Wimbledon's most consistent player. His performances, whether at right-back or on the right-side of midfield, were full of skill, pace, and drive, and his raids up the flank often ended with excellent crosses that could be converted into goals. It was this ability that saw him capped by England and playing in the now infamous friendly against Eire, his debut lasting just 27 minutes. Stop Press: Signed by Newcastle during the summer for a fee of £4,000,000.
Maidstone U (£10,000 from Leytonstone on 28/7/89) FL 41+1 FLC 0+2 FAC 3/1 Others 7
Wimbledon (£300,000 on 7/6/90) F/PL 178+2/10 FLC 16/1 FAC 11 Others 2

Warren Barton Neal Simpson
(Empics Sports Photo Agency)

BARTRAM Vincent (Vince) Lee
Born: Birmingham, 7 August 1968
Height: 6'2" Weight: 13.4
A 1994 summer signing from Bournemouth as cover for David Seaman in the Arsenal goal, with the latter injured, Vince had two runs in the side last season and showed himself to be a sound and competent 'keeper. Making 11 starts in all, he gave a superb performance up at Newcastle, where only a goal right out of the top bracket from Peter Beardsley denied the "Gunners" a point.
Wolverhampton W (From juniors on 17/8/85) FL 5 FLC 2 FAC 3
Blackpool (Loaned on 27/10/89) FL 9 Others 2
Bournemouth (£65,000 on 24/7/91) FL 132 FLC 10 FAC 14 Others 6
Arsenal (£400,000 on 10/8/94) PL 11 FLC 0+1

BART-WILLIAMS Christopher (Chris) Gerald
Born: Sierra Leone, 16 June 1974
Height: 5'10" Weight: 11.0
International Honours: E: B-1; U21-14; Yth
A vital member of the England U21 side, he is thought to be on the verge of the full England set-up. His cause was not helped by him being played wide on both the left and right flanks for Sheffield Wednesday last season, rather than in his favoured centre of midfield position. At his best, he is a lovely touch player, good with both feet, and an eye for an opening. Yet to sign a new contract for Wednesday.
Leyton Orient (From trainee on 18/7/91) FL 34+2/2 FLC 4 Others 2
Sheffield Wed (£275,000 on 21/11/91) F/PL 95+29/16 FLC 10+6/4 FAC 9+3/2 Others 1+3/2

BASHAM Michael (Mike)
Born: Barking, 27 September 1973
Height: 6'2" Weight: 12.8
Club Honours: AMC '94
International Honours: E: Yth; Sch

1994-95 saw Michael impress in the middle of the Swansea defence with his strong tackling and excellent ball distribution. Unfortunately, in February, the former "Hammer" picked up a thigh injury which forced him to miss the rest of the season.
West Ham U (From trainee on 3/7/92)
Colchester U (Loaned on 18/11/93) FL 1
Swansea C (Free on 24/3/94) FL 18 FAC 5 Others 8

BASS Jonathan (Jon) David
Born: Bristol, 1 January 1976
Height: 6'0" Weight: 12.2
Young Birmingham right-back who made his first team debut in 1994-95 against Blackburn in the Coca Cola Cup. Very steady and cool under pressure, Jon showed up well against Jason Wilcox and, although the rest of his season was spent in the reserves, he could well be in contention for a regular place in 1995-96.
Birmingham C (From juniors on 27/6/94) FLC 1

BATES James (Jamie) Alan
Born: Croydon, 24 February 1968
Height: 6'1" Weight: 13.0
Club Honours: Div 3 '92
A commanding centre-half and captain, Jamie's ninth season for Brentford was clearly his best. Heading, tackling, distribution, and leadership, were all strengths in defence, where he combined well with Barry Ashby. Failed to convert in the play-off penalty shoot-out against Huddersfield, an unlucky conclusion to a marvellous campaign.
Brentford (From trainee on 1/6/87) FL 259+20/10 FLC 21+3/2 FAC 7+1/1 Others 32/1

BATTERSBY Anthony (Tony)
Born: Doncaster, 30 August 1975
Height: 6'0" Weight: 12.7
Second year Sheffield United professional and an outstanding prospect as a striker. His only first team appearances came in the Anglo-Italian Cup last season, but he spent a month on loan at Southend in April to gain further experience.
Sheffield U (From trainee on 5/7/93) FL 2+1/1
Southend U (Loaned on 23/3/95) FL 6+2/1

David Batty Neal Simpson
(Empics Sports Photo Agency)

BATTY David
Born: Leeds, 2 December 1968
Height: 5'7" Weight: 10.7
Club Honours: Div 2 '90, Div 1 '92
International Honours: E: 17; B-5; U21-7; Yth

Last season was a frustrating one for this great little midfield competitor, having ended 1993-94 with an operation to cure a split bone in his foot. Initially, surgery was not successful, and it took two further attempts to get him back on the field of play for Blackburn with just six games left. It was only in the final game at Liverpool that he began to take control of the midfield, with quick passes and keeping play moving at the right tempo. Although Rovers lost that game, with Manchester United unable to win at West Ham, the title went to Ewood for the first time since 1913-14. Unfortunately, David did not play enough games to warrant a medal.

Leeds U (From trainee on 3/8/87) F/PL 201+10/4 FLC 17 FAC 12 Others 17
Blackburn Rov (£2,750,000 on 26/10/93) PL 30+1 FLC 2 FAC 4

BAYES Ashley John
Born: Lincoln, 19 April 1972
Height: 6'1" Weight: 12.9
International Honours: E: Yth

Torquay goalkeeper who is improving all the time, with shot-stopping his speciality, Ashley is enthusiastic and a great crowd favourite.

Brentford (From trainee on 5/7/90) FL 4 FLC 5 FAC 2 Others 1
Torquay U (Free on 13/8/93) FL 69 FLC 3 FAC 6 Others 4

BAYLISS David (Dave) Anthony
Born: Liverpool, 8 June 1976
Height: 5'8" Weight: 11.0

Rochdale trainee central defender who made his FL debut in place of the suspended Paul Butler against Barnet last March and filled the breach admirably.

Rochdale (Trainee) FL 1

BAZELEY Darren Shaun
Born: Northampton, 5 October 1972
Height: 5'10" Weight" 10.9
International Honours: E: U21-1

Versatile performer who started the season with Watford as an adventurous full-back, before becoming a successful emergency striker and scoring a polished hat-trick at Southend.

Watford (From trainee on 6/5/91) FL 64+38/12 FLC 7+3/1 FAC 5+1 Others 3+1

BEADLE Peter Clifford
Born: Lambeth, 13 May 1972
Height: 6'1" Weight: 11.12

Signed by Tottenham in 1992, after being the subject of much speculation, he failed to make a single appearance in over three years before moving to Watford last September. A tall, orthodox centre-forward, Peter finally got a run in the "Hornets'" first team at the very end of the season, after making regular appearances as substitute.

Gillingham (From trainee on 5/5/90) FL 42+25/14

FLC 2+4/2 FAC 1+1 Others 1
Tottenham H (£300,000 on 4/6/92)
Bournemouth (Loaned on 25/3/93) FL 9/2
Southend U (Loaned on 4/3/94) FL 8/1
Watford (Signed on 12/9/94) FL 9+11/1

Peter Beagrie   Paul Marriott
(Empics Sports Photo Agency)

BEAGRIE Peter Sydney
Born: Middlesbrough, 28 November 1965
Height: 5'8" Weight: 9.10
International Honours: E: B-2; U21-2

Following on from 1993-94, Peter fitted in well with Manchester City's attacking policy last season, keeping wide on the left-wing, starting deep and taking defenders on and always looking to get a shot in with his favoured left-foot. However, seemingly a touch jaded after the New Year, he was later found to have been playing with a hairline fracture of the shin. Has an excellent rapport with the crowd, who long for him to score in order for him to celebrate with a double back somersault.

Middlesbrough (From juniors on 10/9/83) FL 24+9/2 FLC 1 Others 1+1
Sheffield U (£35,000 on 16/8/86) FL 81+3/11 FLC 5 FAC 5 Others 4
Stoke C (£210,000 on 29/6/88) FL 54/7 FLC 4 FAC 3/1
Everton (£750,000 on 2/11/89) F/PL 88+26/11 FLC 7+2/3 FAC 7+2 Others 5+1/1
Sunderland (Loaned on 26/9/91) FL 5/1
Manchester C (£1,100,000 on 24/3/94) F/PL 42+5/3 FLC 6/1 FAC 4/1

BEARD Mark
Born: Roehampton, 8 October 1974
Height: 5'10" Weight: 10.12

A right-back with the ability to play in midfield, Mark is a tenacious ball-winner who never flinches from a tackle. Scored the opening Millwall goal at Highbury in the 2-0 FA Cup replay last season, when he found himself space in the penalty area to

fire home. Was out injured for a while after breaking a wrist.

Millwall (From trainee on 18/3/93) FL 32+13/2 FLC 3+1 FAC 4/1

Mark Beard   Steve Morton
(Empics Sports Photo Agency)

BEARDSLEY Peter Andrew
Born: Newcastle, 18 January 1961
Height: 5'8" Weight: 11.7
Club Honours: Div 1 '88, '90; FAC '89; CS '88, '89, '90
International Honours: E: 57; B-2

Peter is the perfect role model for any youngster to follow, showing terrific enthusiasm and perfect behaviour on and off the field and this, coupled with his tremendous ability, is what has kept him at the top for so long. Highlights last season, include being a regular for the full England side and scoring some important goals for Newcastle, many of which can only be described as stunning. Missed 11 games, due to the fractured left-cheekbone he sustained in the opening match of 1994-95 at Leicester and hamstring trouble. Currently the club's penalty taker, he scored his 100th goal for them against "Spurs".

Carlisle U (Free from Wallsend BC on 9/8/79) FL 93+11/22 FLC 6+1 FAC 15/7 (£275,000 to Vancouver Whitecaps on 1/4/82)
Manchester U (£300,000 on 9/9/82) FLC 1 (Free to Vancouver Whitecaps on 1/3/83)
Newcastle U (£150,000 on 23/9/83) FL 146+1/61 FLC 10 FAC 6 Others 1
Liverpool (£1,900,000 on 24/7/87) FL 120+11/46 FLC 13+1/1 FAC 22+3/11 Others 5/1
Everton (£1,000,000 on 5/8/91) F/LP 81/25 FLC 8/5 FAC 4/1 Others 2/1
Newcastle U (£1,400,000 on 16/7/93) PL 69/34 FLC 6/1 FAC 8/2 Others 4/2

BEARDSMORE Russell Peter
Born: Wigan, 28 September 1968
Height: 5'6" Weight 9.0
Club Honours: ESC '91
International Honours: E: U21-5

A former England U21 international, Russell played in midfield and in the back four for Bournemouth last season and even

Peter Beardsley

Steve Morton
(Empics Sports Photo Agency)

looked comfortable at full-back. Quick to support the front players, he is especially dangerous when attacking down either wing.

Manchester U (From apprentice on 2/10/86) FL 30+26/4 FLC 3+1 FAC 4+4 Others 2+5
Blackburn Rov (Loaned on 19/12/91) FL 1+1
Bournemouth (Free on 29/6/93) FL 58+9/3 FLC 7/1 FAC 4 Others 2

BEASANT David (Dave) John
Born: Willesden, 20 March 1959
Height: 6'3" Weight: 13.0
Club Honours: Div 4 '83, Div 2 '89; FAC '88; FMC '90
International Honours: E: 2; B-7

To have two eccentric goalkeepers in one club would seem to be excessive. However, Dave did not let Southampton down last season when called upon, usually at very short notice, to deputise for the absent Bruce Grobbelaar. Came on as a sub after only three minutes against Everton to keep a clean sheet and, when recalled to the side at a crucial stage of the season, he gave several confident displays.

Wimbledon (£1,000 from Edgware T on 7/8/79) FL 340 FLC 21 FAC 27 Others 3
Newcastle U (£800,000 on 13/6/88) FL 20 FLC 2 FAC 2 Others 1
Chelsea (£725,000 on 14/1/89) F/PL 133 FLC 11 FAC 5 Others 8
Grimsby T (Loaned on 24/10/92) FL 6
Wolverhampton W (Loaned on 12/1/93) FL 4 FAC 1
Southampton (£300,000 on 4/11/93) PL 37+1 FAC 2

BEASLEY Andrew (Andy)
Born: Sedgley, 5 February 1964
Height: 6'2" Weight: 12.2

Following Chris Marples' broken leg last January, thoughts of a goalkeeping crisis at Chesterfield were banished by some fine performances from Andy. A good shot-stopper, with keen anticipation, his strong presence in the box and unquestioned bravery were his greatest strengths. Unfortunately, having set up the first goal in the second-leg of the Third Division play-offs against Mansfield, he was injured and had to miss the final.

Luton T (From apprentice on 23/2/82)
Mansfield T (Free on 6/7/84) FL 94 FLC 5 FAC 3 Others 7
Peterborough U (Loaned on 28/7/86) FL 7 FLC 3
Scarborough (Loaned on 1/3/88) FL 4
Bristol Rov (Loaned on 25/3/93) FL 1
Doncaster Rov (Free on 30/7/93) FL 37 FLC 2 FAC 1 Others 2
Chesterfield (Free on 12/8/94) FL 20+1 FLC 1 Others 5

BEAUCHAMP Joseph (Joey) Daniel
Born: Oxford, 13 March 1971
Height: 5'10" Weight: 11.10
International Honours: E: Yth

A £1 million signing by West Ham in June 1994, he was unable to adapt to life with the East London club and quickly moved back closer to his Oxford roots. The midfielder, who looks happier playing wide on either flank, joined Swindon just a few days into last season, with central defender Adrian Whitbread going in the opposite direction.

Oxford U (From trainee on 16/5/89) FL 117+7/20

FLC 6+1/2 FAC 8/3 Others 5+1
Swansea C (Loaned on 30/10/91) FL 5/2 Others 1
West Ham U (£1,000,000 on 22/6/94)
Swindon T (£850,000 on 18/8/94) FL 38+4/3 FLC 7+1 FAC 2 Others 4

BEAUMONT Christopher (Chris) Paul
Born: Sheffield, 5 December 1965
Height: 5'11" Weight: 11.7

The longest serving player on Stockport's books, Chris has turned out as a right-back, midfielder, winger and central striker, showing an adaptability which has made him a regular and useful member of the squad for the past six years.

Rochdale (Free from Denaby U on 21/7/88) FL 31+3/7 FLC 0+1/1 FAC 2/1 Others 2
Stockport Co (£8,000 on 21/7/89) FL 200+15/39 FLC 9+3/3 FAC 11/2 Others 32+2/7

BECKFORD Darren Richard
Born: Manchester, 12 May 1967
Height: 6'1" Weight: 13.6
International Honours: E: Yth; Sch

Oldham striker with good skills for a big lad and dangerous in the air. After suffering niggling knee and back injuries throughout last season, Darren's appearances were restricted to just five from the subs' bench and he spent much of the time languishing in the reserves. Is the elder brother of Jason.

Manchester C (From apprentice on 21/8/84) FL 7+4 FLC 0+1
Bury (Loaned on 10/10/85) FL 12/5
Port Vale (£15,000 on 26/3/87) FL 169+9/72 FLC 12/3 FAC 14/4 Others 9+1/3
Norwich C (£925,000 on 14/6/91) F/PL 32+6/8 FLC 3+2/3 FAC 4+1/1 Others 1/1
Oldham Ath (£300,000 on 25/3/93) P/FL 19+13/9 FLC 2/1 FAC 5+3/3

BECKFORD Jason Neil
Born: Manchester, 14 February 1970
Height: 5'9" Weight: 12.13
International Honours: E: Yth; Sch

Out of contract at Stoke, Jason signed for Millwall just before last Christmas and made an instant impact when setting up Richard Cadette with a pinpoint cross. A wide right-footed midfield/flank player with plenty of ball skills, after just three games a hamstring injury forced him out. Joined Northampton at the end of the season.

Manchester C (From trainee on 18/8/87) FL 8+12/1 FLC 1+4/1
Blackburn Rov (Loaned on 14/3/91) 3+1
Port Vale (Loaned on 26/9/91) FL 4+1/1
Birmingham C (£50,000 on 2/1/92) FL 5+2/2 Others 1
Bury (Loaned on 24/4/94) FL 3
Stoke C (Free on 10/8/94) FL 2+2 Others 1
Millwall (Free on 15/12/94) FL 6+3
Northampton T (Signed on 15/5/95)

BECKHAM David Robert
Born: Leytonstone, 2 May 1975
Height: 5'11" Weight: 10.9
Club Honours: FAYC '92
International Honours: E: U21-2; Yth

Young Manchester United midfield player, who possesses excellent vision and can turn defence into attack with a superb range of passes. Also known for his tremendous workrate, David had a wonderful introduction to the Old Trafford stage in 1994-95, when he scored an outstanding goal and

set up another for Roy Keane in United's European Cup match against Galatasaray. Looks to have an excellent future.

Manchester U (From trainee on 29/1/93) PL 2+2 FLC 3+1 FAC 1+1 Others 1/1
Preston NE (Loaned on 28/2/95) FL 4+1/2

BEDROSSIAN Ara
Born: Cyprus, 2 June 1967
Height: 5'9" Weight: 10.0
International Honours: Cyprus

A talented midfield player, who left Fulham during last season to return to Cyprus, his neat control and subtle passing skills at times looked out of place in the lower reaches of the Endsleigh League.

Fulham (Free from AP Limassol on 25/3/93) FL 34+8/1 FLC 0+1 FAC 1 Others 1

BEECH Christopher (Chris) Stephen
Born: Blackpool, 16 September 1974
Height: 5'11" Weight: 11.4

A local lad and a regular member of the Blackpool squad, he normally plays in midfield, but can also be used as a sweeper. Likes to get into forward positions, from where he scored a great goal against Brighton last season.

Blackpool (From trainee on 9/7/93) FL 50+14/4 FLC 3+3 FAC 1 Others 2

BEESLEY Paul
Born: Liverpool, 21 July 1965
Height: 6'1" Weight: 11.5

Dependable Sheffield United central defender who has never failed to give 100 per cent, Paul suffered a knee ligament injury at the start of last season, which meant a period out of the side. Played several games at left-back on his return, and captained the side on several occasions in the absence of Brian Gayle.

Wigan Ath (Free from Marine on 22/9/84) FL 153+2/3 FLC 13 FAC 6 Others 11
Leyton Orient (£175,000 on 20/10/89) FL 32/1 FAC 1 Others 2/1
Sheffield U (£300,000 on 10/7/90) F/PL 162+6/7 FLC 12+1 FAC 9+2/1 Others 3/1

BEESTON Carl Frederick
Born: Stoke, 30 June 1967
Height: 5'9" Weight: 10.9
Club Honours: Div 2 '93
International Honours: E: U21-1

After an 18 month battle against a serious ankle injury, Carl re-emerged in 1994-95 in excellent shape, assisting Stoke to its best run of form in an indifferent season. Sadly, further injuries have taken the edge off the comeback, but he has proved once again that when fit he is an outstanding central midfield player, who combines playmaking skills with ruthless tackling.

Stoke C (From apprentice on 1/7/85) FL 194+8/13 FLC 12/1 FAC 7+1/1 Others 15/2

BELL Michael (Mickey)
Born: Newcastle, 15 November 1971
Height: 5'10" Weight: 11.4

Forceful and exciting two-footed Wycombe player who, since his transfer from Northampton in October 1994, admirably replaced the departed left-winger, Steve Guppy. Scored a number of important goals last season, usually from the edge of the penalty area with fiercely driven shots.

Northampton T (From trainee on 1/7/90) FL 133+20/10 FLC 7+1 FAC 5/1 Others 9+2/1
Wycombe W (£55,000 on 21/10/94) FL 31/3 FAC 3/2 Others 1

BELLAMY Gary
Born: Worksop, 4 July 1962
Height: 6'2" Weight: 11.5
Club Honours: Div 4 '85, '88, Div 3 '89; AMC '88; WC '92

Highly experienced defender, who can also play in a central midfield role, Gary played a major part in shoring up Orient's defence in 1994-95, a season when injury and lack of firepower doomed the cash starved Londoners to a perpetual fight for survival. His contribution to the side was recognised in March when he was appointed skipper after Ian Hendon's temporary move to Birmingham.

Chesterfield (From apprentice on 25/6/80) FL 181+3/7 FLC 12 FAC 7/1 Others 4/1
Wolverhampton W (£17,000 on 21/7/87) FL 133+3/9 FLC 9 FAC 3 Others 16
Cardiff C (Loaned on 18/3/92) FL 9
Leyton Orient (£30,000 on 10/9/92) FL 97+3/5 FLC 1 FAC 6 Others 12

BELLOTTI Ross Christopher
Born: Pembury, 15 May 1978
Height: 6'0" Weight: 11.5

A regular in the Exeter youth team, Ross made his debut at 16 against Scarborough last season when called into action as a substitute goalkeeper. Still a YTS, he is one for the future.

Exeter C (Trainee) FL 1+1 FAC 0+1

BENALI Francis (Franny) Vincent
Born: Southampton, 30 December 1968
Height: 5'9" Weight: 11.0

Although Franny's rugged no-nonsense style has earned him over 40 disciplinary points, three suspensions and an appearance before the FA Committee, he is something of a cult figure at Southampton. Often asked to man mark the opposition's star player last season, a role to which he is well suited, he virtually never advanced over the halfway line, even for corners.

Southampton (From apprentice on 5/1/87) F/PL 151+22 FLC 13+6 FAC 17 Others 3+1

BENJAMIN Ian Tracey
Born: Nottingham, 11 December 1961
Height: 5'11" Weight: 13.1
Club Honours: Div 4 '87
International Honours: E: Yth

The much travelled centre-forward made Wigan Athletic his 11th Football League club when he arrived last September from Brentford. However, injuries unfortunately restricted his appearances to just 12 League starts, with six goals to his credit.

Sheffield U (From apprentice on 26/5/79) FL 4+1/3 FLC 1
West Bromwich A (£100,000 on 31/8/79) FL 1+1
Notts Co (Free on 5/2/82)
Peterborough U (Free on 12/8/82) FL 77+3/14 FLC 7+1/1 FAC 5
Northampton T (Free on 20/8/84) FL 147+3/59 FLC 12/2 FAC 9/3 Others 9/5
Cambridge U (Free on 29/10/87) FL 20+5/2 FAC 2/1

Chester C (Free on 28/7/88) FL 18+4/2 FLC 2 FAC 2/1 Others 2/1
Exeter C (Free on 2/2/89) FL 30+2/4 FLC 2/1 FAC 4+1 Others 4/1
Southend U (Free on 2/3/90) FL 122/33 FLC 8/1 FAC 2 Others 7/4
Luton T (£50,000 on 20/11/92) FL 7+6/2 FLC 2 FAC 2
Brentford (Signed on 24/9/93) FL 13+2/2 FLC 0+1 FAC 1 Others 2
Wigan Ath (Free on 30/9/94) FL 12+5/6 FAC 0+1 Others 0+1

BENN Wayne
Born: Pontefract, 7 August 1976
Height: 5'10" Weight: 11.0

A promising Bradford youngster who can play at full-back or in midfield, Wayne made 12 starts in 1994-95.

Bradford C (From trainee on 1/6/94) FL 8+2 FLC 3 Others 1+1

BENNETT Frank
Born: Birmingham, 3 January 1969
Height: 5'7" Weight: 11.8

Speedy Southampton striker with strength and pace. Yet to make his mark at the club, Frankie made just one subs' appearance in the Coca Cola Cup last season, being mainly confined to reserve team football. A player whose speed takes him into good scoring positions and, who many supporters would like to see more of regularly, 1995 could be his year.

Southampton (£7,500 from Halesowen T on 24/2/93) PL 0+8/1 FLC 1+1 FAC 0+1

BENNETT Gary Ernest
Born: Manchester, 4 December 1961
Height: 6'1" Weight: 12.1
Club Honours: Div 3 '88

A central defender who has been with Sunderland since 1984, he was in-and-out of the side last term, before being restored as a first choice by Peter Reid and rewarding the new boss with some excellent performances. Good in the air, a strong tackler, and still pacy at 33, Gary has been a tremendous club servant, something that is borne out by his popularity on the terraces.

Manchester C (Free from Ashton U on 8/9/79)
Cardiff C (Free on 16/9/81) FL 85+2/11 FLC 6/1 FAC 3
Sunderland (£65,000 on 26/7/84) FL 362+7/23 FLC 34+1/1 FAC 17+1 Others 21/1

BENNETT Gary Michael
Born: Liverpool, 20 September 1963
Height: 5'11" Weight: 12.0
Club Honours: AMC '85; WC '95

Must be the "Free Transfer" bargain of all time! Wrexham manager, Brian Flynn, moved Gary into a striker role after he had played on the right-side of midfield at Chester and former clubs, which transformed him into a prolific goalscorer overnight. Signed in the 1992 close season, "Benno" had scored 100 goals in all competitions by the end of February 1995 (2½ seasons), which prompted unsuccessful enquiries by Birmingham and Tranmere in their quest for honours. Ever dangerous, he makes things happen with his ability to run at defences, a tactic that often produces penalties. Elected by his fellow profes-

sionals to the PFA Second Division team at the Awards Night.

Wigan Ath (Free from Kirby T on 9/10/84) FL 10+10/3 FAC 1 Others 3+1/1
Chester C (Free on 22/8/85) FL 109+17/36 FLC 6+4/1 FAC 8+1/5 Others 10/5
Southend U (Signed on 11/11/88) FL 36+6/6 FLC 4/4 FAC 1 Others 2+1
Chester C (£20,000 on 1/3/90) FL 71+9/15 FLC 8/2 FAC 5/1 Others 4+1/1
Wrexham (Free on 12/8/92) FL 120+1/77 FLC 17/9 FAC 7/3 Others 9/9

BENNETT Ian Michael
Born: Worksop, 10 October 1970
Height: 6'0" Weight: 12.0
Club Honours: Div 2 '95; AMC '95

Signed from Peterborough in December 1993, Ian followed a long line of Birmingham goalkeeping heroes, being ever-present in 1994-95, while winning a Second Division Championship medal as well as an Auto Windscreen winners' medal, following the Wembley victory over Carlisle. Possessing superb agility and positional sense, he is one of the most highly rated 'keepers outside of the Premiership. Set up a club record of nine successive clean sheets last season and was one of four City players recognised by their fellow professionals as being the best in the division at the PFA Awards dinner.

Newcastle U (Free from Queens Park R juniors on 20/3/89)
Peterborough U (Free on 22/3/91) FL 72 FLC 10 FAC 3 Others 4
Birmingham C (£325,000 on 17/12/93) FL 68 FLC 4 FAC 6 Others 7

Ian Bennett   Tony Marshall
(Empics Sports Photo Agency)

BENNETT Michael (Mickey) Richard
Born: Camberwell, 27 July 1969
Height: 5'11" Weight: 11.3
International Honours: E: Yth

Now in his second spell at Charlton, Mickey is a right-sided midfielder who can also play at right-back. Strong and deceptively fast for his build, he is an excellent crosser of the ball, possesses a strong shot, and is also good in the air. Had a disappointing time in 1994-95, never really establishing himself in the team, despite his unquestioned ability, and joined Millwall on a free transfer after the season had ended.

Charlton Ath (From apprentice on 27/4/87) FL 24+11/2 FLC 4 FAC 1 Others 6+1
Wimbledon (£250,000 on 9/1/90) FL 12+6/2 FLC 1+1 FAC 0+1 Others 1+1
Brentford (£60,000 on 14/7/92) FL 40+6/4 FLC 4+1 FAC 1 Others 6+1
Charlton Ath (Free on 24/3/94) FL 19+1/1 FAC 1

BENNETT Thomas (Tom) McNeill
Born: Falkirk, 12 December 1969
Height: 5'11" Weight: 11.8

A steady, rather than spectacular midfield player, he did not appear in any of Wolverhampton's League games until last December, playing in front of the centre-backs at Millwall. In February he was praised on "Match of the Day" for his FA Cup fifth round display against Leicester's Mark Draper, but was unfortunate to sustain a swollen knee in the quarter-final replay at home to Crystal Palace. Stop Press: Signed by Stockport for £75,000 during the summer.

Aston Villa (From apprentice on 16/12/87)
Wolverhampton W (Free on 5/7/88) FL 103+12/2 FLC 7 FAC 5+2 Others 3+1

BENT Junior Antony
Born: Huddersfield, 1 March 1970
Height: 5'5" Weight: 10.6

Had his best ever season at Bristol City in 1994-95, since arriving in March 1990, when playing 40 FL games and scoring six goals, finishing along with Ian Baird as joint runner-up in the goalscoring charts to Wayne Allison. Extremely popular amongst the junior supporters as their "Player of the Year", there is no doubt that with his great turn of speed he has the potential to become even more effective. Recognised as a midfielder, Junior is probably at his best playing in a wide role.

Huddersfield T (From trainee on 9/12/87) FL 25+11/6 FLC 1 FAC 3+1/1 Others 4
Burnley (Loaned on 30/11/89) FL 7+2/3
Bristol C (£30,000 on 22/3/90) FL 92+27/15 FLC 5+1 FAC 9+3/2 Others 2+2
Stoke C (Loaned on 26/3/92) FL 1

BERESFORD David
Born: Middlesbrough, 11 November 1976
Height: 5'7" Weight: 11.4
International Honours: E: Yth

A young player who has yet to start a game for Oldham, David came off the bench twice last season to add to a previous subs' appearance. Another product of Billy Urmson's youth team, of whom great things are expected this coming season, David is an exciting left-winger with electrifying pace, who came through the FA School of Excellence.

Oldham Ath (From trainee on 22/7/94) P/FL 0+3

BERESFORD John
Born: Sheffield, 4 September 1966
Height: 5'6" Weight: 10.12
Club Honours: Div 1 '93
International Honours: E: B-2; Yth; Sch

Had had a very consistent 1994-95 for Newcastle at left-back, being sound and competitive in defence, and also pressing forward at every opportunity, where his

quick one-two's, close to the penalty area, created numerous problems for defenders. Highlights of the season include an England "B" appearance against Eire and a goal in the FAC victory over Manchester City, where his shot, cum centre, sailed into the roof of the net leaving Andy Dibble stranded. There have also been one or two lows, namely, being sidelined due to suspension and having two separate spells out of the team with hamstring trouble, the last instance forcing him to leave the field in the vital FAC tie against Everton, which ended in a 1-0 defeat.

Manchester C (From apprentice on 16/9/83)
Barnsley (Free on 4/8/86) FL 79+9/5 FLC 5+2/2 FAC 5/1
Portsmouth (£300,000 on 23/3/89) FL 102+5/8 FLC 12/2 FAC 11 Others 2
Newcastle U (£650,000 on 2/7/92) F/PL 109/1 FLC 12 FAC 11/1 Others 6

BERESFORD Marlon
Born: Lincoln, 2 September 1969
Height: 6'1" Weight: 12.6

Highly-rated Burnley goalkeeper, often rumoured to be the target of bigger clubs, Marlon is an excellent shot-stopper and one of the best in the business when facing penalties. Sent off twice for "professional fouls", he had a brief spell as second choice 'keeper towards the end of last season.

Sheffield Wed (From trainee on 23/9/87)
Bury (Loaned on 25/8/89) FL 1
Northampton T (Loaned on 27/9/90) FL 13 Others 2
Crewe Alex (Loaned on 28/2/91) FL 3
Northampton T (Loaned on 15/8/91) FL 15
Burnley (£95,000 on 28/8/92) FL 130 FLC 8 FAC 13 Others 7

BERG Henning
Born: Norway, 1 September 1969
Height: 6'0" Weight: 11.9
Club Honours: PL '95
International Honours: Norway

Of all the Blackburn heroes last season, no-one was more undersung than Henning. A right-back with good skills, who likes to get forward, the Norwegian international was a calming influence throughout the campaign, whether he was in his favoured full-back position, or at centre-back. One of the great stand-up tacklers, and seldom off his feet, his great balance allowed him to miss the first tackle with one foot, only to recover the ball with the other. And, as a shrewd reader of the game, he frequently dropped into the centre to make the extra man. Missed just two PL matches on his way to a Championship medal, also winning the Norwegian "Player of the Year" award.

Blackburn Rov (£400,000 from Lillestrom on 26/1/93) PL 80+5/2 FLC 9 FAC 6 Others 3

BERGSSON Gudni
Born: Iceland, 21 July 1965
Height: 6'1" Weight: 12.3
Club Honours: CS '91
International Honours: Iceland

Icelandic international captain. Gudni joined Bolton last March after a trial period, making just a couple of reserve appearances, before a first team call-up at Wembley saw him come on as substitute in the Coca Cola

Cup Final against Liverpool. Since then, only International duty has kept him out of the side, where he has proved to be capable at both full-back and centre-half. A member of the side that reached the Premiership, via the play-offs.

Tottenham H (£100,000 from Valur on 15/12/88) F/PL 51+20/2 FLC 4+2 FAC 2+2 Others 5+1
Bolton W (£65,000 on 21/3/95) FL 8 FLC 0+1 Others 3

BERKLEY Austin James
Born: Dartford, 28 January 1973
Height: 5'9" Weight: 10.10

Midfielder who, despite some impressive performances in Swindon's Combination side and the Anglo-Italian Cup, has, in three seasons, seen only 21 minutes of League football - as a substitute against Charlton last September. Released on a free transfer at the end of 1994-95.

Gillingham (From trainee on 13/5/91) FL 0+3 Others 0+3
Swindon T (Free on 16/5/92) FL 0+1 FLC 0+1 Others 3+1/1

BERNAL Andrew (Andy)
Born: Canberra, Australia, 16 May 1966
Height: 5'10" Weight: 12.5
International Honours: Australia

Tough-tackling Reading right-back, into his second spell of English football last season, having previously played for Ipswich. A current Australian international, Andy can also play at centre-back and make exciting runs forward. His confidence and reliability in defence contributed greatly to "Royals'" place in the play-offs.

Ipswich T (Free from Sporting Gijon on 24/9/87) FL 4+5 Others 0+2
Reading (£30,000 from Sydney Olympic on 26/7/94) FL 33 FLC 3 FAC 1 Others 3

BERNARD Paul Robert
Born: Edinburgh, 30 December 1972
Height: 5'9" Weight: 11.8
International Honours: S: 2; U21-15

Another success for Oldham's youth policy. A very positive midfielder with two good feet, passing ability, and physical toughness, Paul was yet another long-term injury case at the club last season. Starting with a back problem, he made a handful of appearances in November, before having an operation and being out for a further 25 games. Came back in style, however, being selected for the Scottish tour of Japan in May and gaining his first full cap.

Oldham Ath (From trainee on 16/7/91) F/PL 88+7/17 FLC 10+1/2 FAC 11/1 Others 0+1

BERRY Gregory (Greg) John
Born: Grays, 5 March 1971
Height: 5'11" Weight: 12.0

Left-footed midfielder who plays wide, Greg was drafted into the Millwall number nine shirt and scored both goals in the 2-0 Coca Cola Cup win at Nottingham Forest in 1994-95. A pre-season ankle injury has restricted his challenge for a first team place.

Leyton Orient (£2,000 from East Thurrock on 3/7/89) FL 68+12/14 FLC 6/3 FAC 8+2/2 Others 5+3/1
Wimbledon (£250,000 on 17/8/92) PL 6+1/1 FAC 0+1

Millwall (£200,000 on 24/3/94) FL 9+10/1 FLC 1/2 Others 1/1

BETTS Simon Richard
Born: Middlesbrough, 3 March 1973
Height: 5'7" Weight: 11.4
A full-back in his third season with Colchester, Simon recovered well from a "Gazza type" facial injury in pre-season 1994-95, and has not missed a game since. Equally at home on either flank, he caused great relief when successfully scoring from the penalty spot in March after his colleagues had missed five previous attempts.
Ipswich T (From trainee on 2/7/91)
Wrexham (Free on 13/8/92)
Scarborough (Free on 3/11/92)
Colchester U (Free on 11/12/92) FL 88+3/3 FLC 1 FAC 5+1 Others 4

BIBBO Salvatore (Sal)
Born: Basingstoke, 24 August 1974
Height: 6'2" Weight: 13.0
Young and agile Sheffield United goalkeeper. On the bench on eight occasions last season, he made his first team debut in the Anglo-Italian Cup. Has strong competition for a first team spot with Alan Kelly, Simon Tracey and Billy Mercer on United's books and spent a month on loan at Chesterfield, as cover, to gain experience.
Sheffield U (Free from Crawley T on 18/8/93) Others 2
Chesterfield (Loaned on 10/2/95) FL 0+1

BIGGINS Wayne
Born: Sheffield, 20 November 1961
Height: 5'11" Weight: 11.0
Club Honours: AMC '92
A prolific goalscorer in his first spell at Stoke, he was unable to match his previous strike record on his return from Scotland. On his day, a leading target man in this standard of football, good in the air and strong for his build, he failed to retain his first team place in 1994-95, before having a successful loan spell at Luton. However, hopes that this could become permanent were dashed in deadline week and he was released at the end of the season.
Lincoln C (From apprentice on 22/11/79) FL 8/1 (Free to Kings Lynn during 1981 close season)
Burnley (£7,500 from Matlock on 4/2/84) FL 78/29 FLC 6/1 FAC 3/1 Others 7/5
Norwich C (£40,000 on 17/10/85) FL 66+13/16 FLC 6/2 FAC 4 Others 6+2/3
Manchester C (£150,000 on 15/7/88) FL 29+3/9 FLC 4/1 FAC 2
Stoke C (£250,000 on 10/8/89) FL 120+2/46 FLC 10/2 FAC 6 Others 10/5
Barnsley (£200,000 on 2/10/92) FL 44+3/16 FAC 3+1
Glasgow Celtic (Signed on 25/11/93) SL 4+5 SC 0+1
Stoke C (£125,000 on 24/3/94) FL 18+9/6 FLC 1+1 Others 3+1/2
Luton T (Loaned on 20/1/95) FL 6+1/1 FAC 2/1

BILLING Peter Graham
Born: Liverpool, 24 October 1964
Height: 6'1" Weight: 13.11
Club Honours: AMC '93
Dependable Port Vale central defender who spent virtually the whole of last season in the reserves. A squad player who is good in

the air, he had, ironically, just made one of his rare first team appearances when he was forced to drop due to suspension, having picked up a number of bookings in the reserves. Freed during the summer.
Everton (Free from South Liverpool on 15/1/86) FL 1 Others 4
Crewe Alex (£12,000 on 23/12/86) FL 83+5/1 FLC 1+1 FAC 5 Others 9
Coventry C (£120,000 on 28/6/89) F/PL 51+7/1 FLC 9+1 FAC 7 Others 2
Port Vale (£35,000 on 26/2/93) FL 23+3 FLC 1 Others 3+2

BILLY Christopher (Chris) Anthony
Born: Huddersfield, 2 January 1973
Height: 5'11" Weight: 11.8
A home-grown Huddersfield product, Chris originally started out as a midfielder before making a claim for the right-back spot and, although impressing, many believe his most natural position is on the right of midfield. Scored the deciding goal in the play-off final last season.
Huddersfield T (From trainee on 1/7/91) FL 76+18/4 FLC 8+2 FAC 5 Others 15+2/2

BIMSON Stuart James
Born: Liverpool, 29 September 1969
Height: 5'11" Weight: 11.12
Joined Bury last February from non-league Macclesfield and immediately made the left-back spot his own. A strong-tackling, defender, who linked well with David Pugh down the left-flank, his season was ended at Deepdale in the play-offs, when a leg injury deprived him of an almost certain Wembley place.
Bury (£12,500 from Macclesfield T on 6/2/95) FL 19 Others 2

BIRCH Paul
Born: Birmingham, 20 November 1962
Height: 5'6" Weight: 10.9
Club Honours: FAYC '80; ESC '82
Plays on the right side of the Wolverhampton midfield and did well against WBA last August with a typical bustling display. Paul had made 12 full appearances by the end of November, scoring with two low drives against Nottingham Forest and Bolton, before suffering tendonitis in the knee. Quickly returning as a sub at Reading, only to pull a hamstring, he played twice in January, but was hurt again and was out of team action until April.
Aston Villa (From apprentice on 15/7/80) FL 153+20/16 FLC 21+4/5 FAC 9+5/3 Others 5+2/1
Wolverhampton W (£400,000 on 1/2/91) FL 123+12/15 FLC 9/3 FAC 2+1 Others 8+1/1

BIRD Anthony
Born: Cardiff, 1 September 1974
Height: 5'10" Weight: 10.7
International Honours: W: U21-7
Striker. Despite making some lively contributions earlier on last season, he languished in Cardiff's reserves for most of Terry Yorath's managerial reign at the club. Later made the most of his chances in the fight against relegation.
Cardiff C (From trainee on 4/8/93) FL 35+28/9 FLC 5/1 FAC 4/1 Others 11+3/3

BISHOP Charles (Charlie) Darren
Born: Nottingham, 16 February 1968
Height: 6'0" Weight: 12.11
Charlie started last season with Barnsley in possession of a central defensive position. However, a period of indifferent form and the introduction of the fit again Steve Davis meant a spell in the reserves, where a knee injury put paid to any thoughts of a return.
Watford (Free from Stoke C juniors on 17/4/86)
Bury (Free on 10/8/87) FL 104+10/6 FLC 5 FAC 4/1 Others 12+1
Barnsley (£50,000 on 24/7/91) FL 112+5/1 FLC 8+1 FAC 9 Others 5

BISHOP Edward (Eddie) Michael
Born: Liverpool, 28 November 1962
Height: 5'10" Weight: 12.6
Club Honours: AMC '90
Left-sided Chester midfield player with good passing skills, who likes to get forward. Scored the only goal in the final home game of last season, prior to being released.
Tranmere Rov (Signed from Northwich Vic on 17/3/88) FL 46+30/19 FLC 8+3/3 FAC 2+2 Others 2+4
Chester C (£70,000 on 28/12/90) FL 93+16/23 FLC 10/1 FAC 3+3 Others 3+2
Crewe Alex (Loaned on 19/3/92) FL 3

BISHOP Ian William
Born: Liverpool, 29 May 1965
Height: 5'9" Weight: 10.12
International Honours: E: B-1
West Ham midfielder whose stylish play catches the eye, his brilliant passing has made many goals. Not known for his goalscoring exploits, Ian was delighted to stab home a half-volley in the 3-1 victory over Nottingham Forest last December and, at the same time, he also improved his tackling, which gave the team extra bite in midfield. This was apparent in the crucial game with Blackburn when he came in for some fierce tackling, but still remained calm and in control of his game.
Everton (From apprentice on 24/5/83) FL 0+1
Crewe Alex (Loaned on 22/3/84) FL 4
Carlisle U (£15,000 on 11/10/84) FL 131+1/14 FLC 8/1 FAC 5/1 Others 4
Bournemouth (£35,000 on 14/7/88) FL 44/2 FLC 4 FAC 5 Others 4
Manchester C (£465,000 on 2/8/89) FL 18+1/2 FLC 4/1 Others 1
West Ham U (£500,000 on 28/12/89) F/PL 176+11/10 FLC 13 FAC 17+1/3 Others 4+1/1

BISSETT Nicholas (Nicky)
Born: Fulham, 5 April 1964
Height: 6'2" Weight: 12.10
His cruel luck with injuries continued when his season came to a premature end after being stretchered off against Bournemouth last November with cruciate knee ligament damage. Up to that stage, right-footed Nicky's performances were typically solid and reliable in the middle of the Brighton defence with his strength being in the air. Also had seven wholehearted games at right-back, although clearly preferring his more usual central defensive position. Released during the summer.
Brighton & Hove A (£125,000 from Barnet on 8/9/88) FL 94+3/9 FLC 11 FAC 6 Others 10

BJORNEBY Stig-Inge
Born: Norway, 11 December 1969
Height: 5'10" Weight: 11.9
Club Honours: FLC '95
International Honours: Norway

After a lengthy spell in the Liverpool first team, Stig has proved himself to be a useful attacking left-back, somewhat in the mould of Alan Kennedy and, at times, his penetrating crosses have led to Liverpool scoring some useful goals. His sound positional sense made him one of the better defenders in the Premiership during 1994-95.

Liverpool (£600,000 from Rosenborg on 18/12/92) PL 48+3 FLC 7 FAC 7+2

BLACK Anthony
Born: Barrow, 15 July 1969
Height: 5'9" Weight: 10.0

An old fashioned right-winger who arrived at Wigan near the end of last season from Unibond League side, Bamber Bridge, for whom he had scored 16 goals. Made an impressive debut for the "Latics", winning the "Man of the Match" award with his lightening speed down the flank.

Wigan Ath (£12,500 from Bamber Bridge on 22/3/95) FL 9

BLACK Kingsley Terence
Born: Luton, 22 June 1968
Height: 5'8" Weight: 10.11
Club Honours: FLC '88; FMC '92
International Honours: NI: 30; B; U21-1

Left or right-winger, and a player with lovely skills and control, who can create chances from either flank with super crosses. A current Northern Ireland international, and a Nottingham Forest regular at the start of 1994-95, he went down with a virus in October and, unable to get his place back in the side from Ian Woan, spent the last couple of months of the season on loan at Sheffield United.

Luton T (From juniors on 7/7/86) FL 123+4/26 FLC 16+2/1 FAC 5+1/2 Others 3+2/1
Nottingham F (£1,500,000 on 2/9/91) F/PL 79+17/14 FLC 19+1/5 FAC 4 Others 4+2/1
Sheffield U (Loaned on 2/3/95) FL 8+3/2

BLACKMORE Clayton Graham
Born: Neath, 23 September 1964
Height: 5'8" Weight: 11.12
Club Honours: FAC '90; CS '90; ECWC '91; ESC '91; PL '93; Div 1 '95
International Honours: W: 38; U21-3; Yth; Sch

Former team-mate of the Middlesbrough player-manager, Bryan Robson, at Manchester United, he was snapped up on a "free" during the 1994 close season. Clayton had no hesitation in enlisting his services for the club's promotion push to the Premier, being equally at home in defence or midfield, where his vast experience was a major factor in the club's enormously successful season. On the opening day of last season, he was one of five "Boro" players making debuts against Burnley. Winner of a First Division Championship medal at the end of 1994-95.

Manchester U (From apprentice on 28/9/82) F/PL 150+36/19 FLC 23+2/3 FAC 15+6/1 Others 19/4
Middlesbrough (Free on 11/7/94) FL 26+4/2 FLC 1 Others 1

Clayton Blackmore   Barry Coombs
(Empics Sports Photo Agency)

BLACKSTONE Ian Kenneth
Born: Harrogate, 7 August 1964
Height: 6'0" Weight: 13.2

Experienced striker who joined Scarborough from York in the summer of 1994. Capable of operating in a wide role, or central striking position, Ian suffered a bad knee ligament injury which disrupted his season, and he left in March for a spell in Hong Kong.

York C (Signed from Harrogate RI on 9/9/90) FL 107+22/37 FLC 3+1/1 FAC 3+1/2 Others 11/2
Scarborough (Signed on 12/8/94) FL 11+2 FLC 4/2 FAC 0+2

BLACKWELL Kevin Patrick
Born: Luton, 21 December 1958
Height: 5'11" Weight: 12.10
Club Honours: GMVC '87

Second choice Huddersfield goalkeeper, who also doubles up as the youth team coach and has proved to be an able deputy for Steve Francis, Kevin has also played for the then Town manager, Neil Warnock, at Scarborough, Notts County and Torquay. Although a good man to have on the bench, he was freed at the end of last season.

Scarborough (Signed from Barnet on 1/11/86) FL 44 FLC 11 FAC 2 Others 2
Notts Co (£15,000 on 8/11/89)
Torquay U (Free on 15/1/93) FL 18 Others 2
Huddersfield T (Free on 5/8/93) FL 3+2 FLC 0+1 FAC 1 Others 3

BLADES Paul Andrew
Born: Peterborough, 5 January 1965
Height: 6'0" Weight: 11.0
Club Honours: Div 2 '87
International Honours: E: Yth

Wolverhampton central defender who tackles well, he stepped in to replace Neil Emblen in the second match of last season, but was briefly dropped in September. Returning for a 16 game run, only to make way for John De Wolf, Paul soon came in at

right-back, where he remained in-and-out of the side.

Derby Co (From apprentice on 29/12/82) FL 157+9/1 FLC 9+3 FAC 12 Others 8+2
Norwich C (£700,000 on 18/7/90) FL 47 FLC 8 FAC 2 Others 5
Wolverhampton W (£325,000 on 14/8/92) FL 103+4/2 FLC 4+1 FAC 9/1 Others 6

BLAKE Mark Antony
Born: Nottingham, 16 December 1970
Height: 5'11" Weight: 12.7
International Honours: E: U21-9; Yth; Sch

A one-time Leicester record signing, he was initially used as a midfield foil to the man who took over that mantle, Mark Draper. Occasionally played as an emergency fullback, on either flank, to cover injuries or suspensions, Mark usually performed with credit, but found it hard to hold a regular place after Mark McGhee had signed Garry Parker.

Aston Villa (From trainee on 1/7/89) FL 26+5/2 FLC 1+1 FAC 2 Others 2
Wolverhampton W (Loaned on 17/1/91) FL 2
Portsmouth (£400,000 on 5/8/93) FL 15 Others 4+1
Leicester C (£360,000 on 24/3/94) F/PL 34+5/4 FLC 2 Others 3

BLAKE Mark Christopher
Born: Portsmouth, 19 December 1967
Height: 6'1" Weight: 12.8
International Honours: E: Yth

A rugged central defender, Mark joined Fulham at the beginning of last season and immediately established himself in the team, impressing with his power in the air and pace and ability to get forward for set-pieces.

Southampton (From apprentice on 23/12/85) FL 18/2 FLC 2 FAC 3 Others 1+2
Colchester U (Loaned on 5/9/89) FL 4/1
Shrewsbury T (£100,000 on 22/3/90) FL 142/3 FLC 12 FAC 9 Others 12
Fulham (Free on 16/9/94) FL 34+1/3 FLC 2/1 FAC 4/1 Others 3

BLAKE Nathan Alexander
Born: Cardiff, 27 January 1972
Height: 5'11" Weight: 12.8
Club Honours: WC '92, '93; Div 3 '93
International Honours: W: 4; B-1; U21-5

A converted striker, Nathan made an explosive entrance at Sheffield United at the end of the 1993-94 Premier League campaign. He continued to gain favour with the United fans and finished 1994-95 as leading scorer at the club with 18 goals. Many of them came after strong runs past defenders, followed by a rocket-like shot into the net. Scored his first international goal for Wales against Moldova last October.

Cardiff C (Free from Chelsea juniors on 20/8/90) FL 113+18/35 FLC 6+2 FAC 10/4 Others 13+2/1
Sheffield U (£300,000 on 17/2/94) P/FL 35+12/22 FLC 2+1/1 FAC 1 Others 1

BLAKE Robert James
Born: Middlesbrough, 4 March 1976
Height: 5'11" Weight: 12.0

Young local player who came through Darlington's youth and reserve ranks to force his way into the forward line last

season, where his darting runs were unlucky not to be rewarded with a goal or two.
Darlington (From trainee on 1/7/94) FL 3+6

BLISSETT Gary Paul
Born: Manchester, 29 June 1964
Height: 6'0" Weight: 12.7
Club Honours: Div 3 '92
Struggled with injuries and form throughout 1994-95 and, even when fit, found it difficult to gain a Wimbledon first team place due to competition up front from players like Dean Holdsworth, Mick Harford, Efan Ekoku and Jon Goodman. A strong centre-forward, who is good on the ball with a nice touch, he was only to make a handful of appearances, with three consecutive starts at the end of November, being his longest spell.
Crewe Alex (Signed from Altrincham on 23/8/83) FL 112+10/39 FLC 9/3 FAC 4 Others 6+1/4
Brentford (£60,000 on 26/3/87) FL 220+13/79 FLC 16+3/9 FAC 14/7 Others 23+2/10
Wimbledon (£350,000 on 23/7/93) PL 10+17/3 FLC 1+2 FAC 1+2

BLOUNT Mark
Born: Derby, 5 January 1974
Height: 5'10" Weight: 12.0
Signed as a full-back from Gresley Rovers, he was converted to a central defender by Sheffield United and made his debut in the Anglo-Italian Cup last season, followed by assured FL appearances as cover for injuries. He is the first player at the Lane to be bought solely by contributions from the "Blades' Revival Fund".
Sheffield U (£12,500 from Gresley Rov on 11/2/94) FL 4+1 Others 2

BODEN Christopher (Chris) Desmond
Born: Wolverhampton, 13 October 1973
Height: 5'9" Weight: 11.0
Signed from Aston Villa towards last March's transfer deadline as cover for the Derby defence, he took over from Shane Nicholson at the tail-end of the season and was excellent in the 5-0 win over Tranmere. A left-sided player, he prefers full-back, but is quite competent in a midfield role if needed.
Aston Villa (From trainee on 3/12/91) PL 0+1
Barnsley (Loaned on 15/10/93) FL 4
Derby Co (£150,000 on 24/3/95) FL 4+2

BODIN Paul John
Born: Cardiff, 13 September 1964
Height: 5'10" Weight: 10.11
International Honours: W: 23; U21-1; Yth
Missed the second half of last season, after suffering a back injury in January which required surgery. The campaign had begun so well for the Welsh international full-back when he was appointed Swindon captain, and in making a successful comeback in the reserves in the final week, Paul will be raring to go in 1995-96.
Newport Co (Free from Chelsea juniors on 28/1/82)
Cardiff C (Free on 1/8/82) FL 68+7/4 FLC 11 FAC 4 (Free to Bath C during 1985 close season)
Newport Co (£15,000 on 27/1/88) FL 6/1
Swindon T (£30,000 on 7/3/88) FL 87+6/9 FLC 12 FAC 6 Others 8/1
Crystal Palace (£550,000 on 20/3/91) FL 8+1 FLC 1
Newcastle U (Loaned on 5/12/91) FL 6

Swindon T (£225,000 on 10/1/92) F/PL 108+5/26 FLC 10 FAC 6 Others 7/1

BODLEY Michael (Mick) John
Born: Hayes, 14 September 1967
Height: 5'11" Weight: 12.0
Club Honours: GMVC '91
Southend central defender, Mick, had one of the most up-and-down seasons imaginable in 1994-95. Told he was no longer required by manager, Peter Taylor, he had loan spells with Gillingham and Birmingham, before new manager, Steve Thompson, installed him in tandem with Andy Edwards at the heart of the defence. It was a masterstroke and he became one of the reasons Southend avoided the drop. Strong in the air, and very safe on the ground, he will be one that the club will build their team around this season.
Chelsea (From apprentice on 17/9/85) FL 6/1 FLC 1 Others 1
Northampton T (£50,000 on 12/1/89) FL 20 Others 2
Barnet (£15,000 on 1/10/89) FL 69/3 FLC 2 FAC 10 Others 9
Southend U (Free on 15/7/93) FL 28/1 FLC 1 FAC 1 Others 3
Gillingham (Loaned on 23/11/94) FL 6+1 Others 1
Birmingham C (Loaned on 23/1/95) FL 3

BOERE Jeroen Willem
Born: Arnhem, Holland, 18 November 1967
Height: 6'3" Weight: 13.5
Striker. The big Dutchman hit the headlines with two goals when West Ham were trailing 2-0 at Leeds last December. He also scored a vital equaliser in the last minute at Ipswich in April to earn the "Hammers" a valuable point. Throughout last season, his height and strength took the pressure off Tony Cottee, who enjoyed playing alongside him. Unfortunately, a broken nose in the exciting win over the Champions elect, Blackburn, and then a knee injury, forced him to miss the last two games of the campaign.
West Ham U (£250,000 from Go Ahead Eagles on 22/9/93) PL 15+9/7 FLC 1+1/1 FAC 2
Portsmouth (Loaned on 24/3/94) FL 4+1
West Bromwich A (Loaned on 8/9/94) FL 5

BOGIE Ian
Born: Newcastle, 6 December 1967
Height: 5'7" Weight: 10.2
Midfielder with outstanding ball control and good passing ability who joined Port Vale on deadline day from Leyton Orient, he scored on his full debut against one of his old clubs, Millwall. Soon settled into a central role vacated by the injured Ray Walker, playing his part in the club's climb from the relegation zone. Currently the team's penalty taker.
Newcastle U (From apprentice on 18/12/85) FL 7+7 FLC 0+1 FAC 1+2 Others 3/1
Preston NE (Signed on 9/2/89) FL 67+12/12 FLC 3+1 FAC 3 Others 4+1
Millwall (£145,000 on 16/8/91) FL 44+7/1 FLC 1 FAC 2 Others 3
Leyton Orient (Signed on 14/10/93) FL 62+3/5 FLC 2 FAC 2 Others 8+1
Port Vale (£50,000 on 23/3/95) FL 7+2/2

BOHINEN Lars
Born: Vadso, Norway, 8 September 1966
Height: 5'11" Weight: 12.2
International Honours: Norway
Fair haired Norwegian international who joined Nottingham Forest at the end of 1993 after a protracted transfer saga was finally resolved, he soon impressed with his silky skills. Playing on the left or centre of midfield in 1994-95, and in his first season of Premiership football, Lars proved to be not only creative, but also a scorer of great individual goals. All-in-all, an excellent first full season for the Scandinavian.
Nottingham F (£450,000 from Young Boys of Berne on 5/11/93) F/PL 52+5/7 FLC 6+1 FAC 2/1

Lars Bohinen   Steve Morton
(Empics Sports Photo Agency)

BOLAND William (Willie) John
Born: Ennis, Ireland, 6 August 1975
Height: 5'9" Weight: 11.2
International Honours: Ei: U21-5; Yth
Outstanding Coventry youngster, and a product of club's youth scheme, Willie is a skilful midfielder who rarely wastes the ball. Made the scapegoat for early last season defeats, but given an opportunity by new manager, Ron Atkinson, at Villa Park, he responded with an excellent performance. A great prospect who is highly rated by the club's management.
Coventry C (From juniors on 4/11/92) PL 33+7 FLC 4

BOLT Daniel (Danny) Anthony
Born: Wandsworth, 5 February 1976
Height: 5'7" Weight: 11.8
A young left-sided midfield player who came through Fulham's junior sides, Danny impressed with his touch, control, and passing skills when making the breakthrough at the end of last season.
Fulham (From trainee on 15/7/94) FL 2

BOLTON Nigel Alan
Born: Bishop Auckland, 14 January 1975
Height: 6'0" Weight: 12.5
Signed from Northern League side, Shildon, after impressing in a pre-season friendly, Nigel, a centre-forward with a history of goalscoring, had little chance to shine at Darlington in 1994-95. Making just two appearances, he was released during the summer.
Darlington (Signed from Shildon on 30/8/94) FL 1+1

BONNER Mark
Born: Ormskirk, 7 June 1974
Height: 5'10" Weight: 11.0
A young midfielder, Mark did not figure in the Blackpool squad as much as usual last season because of injury, but he is a skilful player who looks to have a good future in the game.
Blackpool (From trainee on 18/6/92) FL 58+17/7 FLC 6+2 FAC 4 Others 3+3

BOOTH Andrew David
Born: Huddersfield, 6 December 1973
Height: 6'0" Weight: 10.8
International Honours: E: U21-2
Another home-grown Huddersfield striker, Andy shot to prominence in 1994-95 on an avalanche of goals, and proved to be a superb header of the ball. Has already been called up for the England U21's and, although valued at over £2 million by the club, they will have a struggle on their hands to keep him. Scored in the play-off final, his 30th of the season, and was instrumental to Town's promotion to the First Division. Along with Tom Cowan, he was elected for the PFA Award winning Second Division team.
Huddersfield T (From trainee on 1/7/92) FL 66+14/38 FLC 6+1 FAC 4/1 Others 12+1/4

BOOTHROYD Adrian Neil
Born: Bradford, 8 February 1971
Height: 5'7" Weight: 11.0
Mansfield right-back. Played consistently well in 1994-95 through the early and mid-season matches, but later missed a few games through suspension.
Huddersfield T (From trainee on 1/7/89) FL 9+1
Bristol Rov (£30,000 on 20/6/90) FL 10+6 FLC 1 FAC 0+1
Heart of Midlothian (Free on 19/11/92) SL 0+4 SC 0+2/2
Mansfield T (Free on 9/12/93) FL 57+2/1 FLC 5 FAC 4 Others 4

BOOTY Martyn James
Born: Kirby Muxloe, 30 May 1971
Height: 5'8" Weight: 11.2
Since being released by Coventry and moving to Crewe, Martyn has made the number two spot his own. Had it not been for a slight injury, he would have been an ever-present last season. Is a capable right-back who also enjoys excursions up the flank whenever possible.
Coventry C (From trainee on 30/5/89) FL 4+1 FLC 2 FAC 2
Crewe Alex (Free on 7/10/93) FL 74+1/3 FLC 2 FAC 5 Others 11

BORROWS Brian
Born: Liverpool, 20 December 1960
Height: 5'10" Weight: 10.12
International Honours: E: B-1
Started his tenth season with Coventry as first choice right-back in 1994-95, but suffered a hamstring injury early on and struggled to displace Ally Pickering. Returned to right-back after the Palace debacle and later moved to centre-back, when injuries and suspensions necessitated. Played superbly in the unaccustomed role and had a great game against Alan Shearer in March, before being suspended on reaching 21 points. Recorded 350 League games for the club during 1994-95 and, if he maintains that level of consistency, will play many more.
Everton (From juniors on 23/4/80) FL 27 FLC 2
Bolton W (£10,000 on 24/3/83) FL 95 FLC 7 FAC 4 Others 4
Coventry C (£80,000 on 6/6/85) F/PL 359+6/11 FLC 35/1 FAC 22/1 Others 10+1
Bristol C (Loaned on 17/9/93) FL 6

BOSNICH Mark John
Born: Sydney, Australia, 13 January 1972
Height: 6'2" Weight: 13.7
Club Honours: FLC '94
International Honours: Australia
Very agile and decisive Aston Villa goalkeeper who is not afraid to come out for crosses. Due to the back-pass ruling, his kicking (left-footed) has improved and, although he missed a few games in 1994-95 due to a combination of illness and injury, including a freak accident in training which saw him pick up a medial ligament problem, Mark had a consistent season. Is a definite showman who likes to make his presence felt.

Mark Bosnich

Neal Simpson
(Empics Sports Photo Agency)

Manchester U (Free from Sydney Croatia on 5/6/89) Fl 3
Aston Villa (Free on 28/2/92) F/PL 76 FLC 10+1 FAC 5 Others 2

Steve Bould (left) with Tony Adams
Steve Morton   (Empics Sports Photo Agency)

BOULD Stephen (Steve) Andrew
Born: Stoke, 16 November 1962
Height: 6'2" Weight: 13.11
Club Honours: Div 1 '89, '91; ECWC '94
International Honours: E: 2; B-1

Steve had a relatively injury free season in 1994-95, in making 43 starts for Arsenal. A reliable centre-back who is always likely to pop up with important goals, he is particularly dangerous at set-pieces and corners and has made the near post flick-on his trademark. Scored two goals against Sampdoria at Highbury in the European Cup Winners Cup semi-final-leg during a five minute spell, only to miss the final through suspension. Never afraid to come out of defence with the ball looking to make the right pass.
Stoke C (From apprentice on 15/11/80) FL 179+4/6 FLC 13/1 FAC 10 Others 5
Torquay U (Loaned on 19/10/82) FL 9 FAC 2
Arsenal (£390,000 on 13/6/88) F/PL 184+8/5 FLC 22 FAC 17 Others 13+3/2

BOUND Matthew Terence
Born: Melksham, 9 November 1972
Height: 6'2" Weight: 12.0

Big, powerful central defender who came from Southampton early last season after Stockport scouts had gone to watch another player! Still inexperienced, he has not yet pinned down a regular place at Stockport.
Southampton (From trainee on 3/5/91) F/PL 2+3
Hull C (Loaned on 27/8/93) FL 7/1
Stockport Co (£100,000 on 27/10/94) FL 14 FAC 1 Others 2/1

BOWDEN Jonathan (Jon) Lee
Born: Stockport, 21 January 1963
Height: 6'0" Weight: 11.7

A terrific pro and a favourite with the Rochdale fans, he is equally happy in midfield, defence or at centre-forward. Greatly missed, when struck down by a series of injuries which restricted him to a handful of League appearances last season,

he was freed during the summer.
Oldham Ath (From juniors on 22/1/80) FL 73+9/5 FLC 5 FAC 4/1
Port Vale (£10,000 on 6/9/85) FL 64+6/7 FLC 3+1 FAC 5+1 Others 6
Wrexham (£12,500 on 6/8/87) FL 137+10/20 FLC 12 FAC 3+1/1 Others 14/3
Rochdale (£10,000 on 18/9/91) FL 73+33/17 FLC 2+1 FAC 8/1 Others 5

BOWEN Jason Peter
Born: Merthyr Tydfil, 24 August 1972
Height: 5'6" Weight: 9.0
Club Honours: AMC '94
International Honours: W: 1; U21-5; Yth

Capped by Wales in the friendly against Estonia in 1994, much was expected from Jason last season in the Second Division with Swansea. With top clubs watching his progress, his season was interrupted continually by ankle ligament problems, a factor which prevented him displaying his usual sharpness in front of goal.
Swansea C (From trainee on 1/7/90) FL 93+31/26 FLC 6+1/2 FAC 9+2/1 Others 15+3/8

BOWEN Mark Rosslyn
Born: Neath, 7 December 1963
Height: 5'8" Weight: 11.6
International Honours: W: 32; U21-3; Yth; Sch

Now the most capped Norwich player, Mark is a sound left-back, who surprisingly favours his right foot, and is extremely dangerous when joining up with the attack. Made his 300th appearance for City in 1994-95, but his attack mindedness was later curtailed in the interests of trying to tighten up the defence as the club was faced with relegation. Amazingly, only ten men in Norwich's history have scored more Premiership/First Division goals than Mark.
Tottenham H (From apprentice on 1/12/81) FL 14+3/2 FLC 3 Others 0+1
Norwich C (£97,000 on 23/7/87) F/PL 285+4/22 FLC 28/1 FAC 29/1 Others 17/1

Mark Bowen   Neal Simpson
(Empics Sports Photo Agency)

BOWLING Ian
Born: Sheffield, 27 July 1965
Height: 6'3" Weight: 14.8

A giant of a man who is very brave, he would certainly have been the regular Bradford 'keeper but for the form of Paul Tomlinson. Released at the end of 1994-95 after making six starts during the season.
Lincoln C (Free from Gainsborough Trinity on 23/10/88) FL 59 FLC 3 FAC 2 Others 4
Hartlepool U (Loaned on 17/8/89) FL 1
Bradford C (Loaned on 25/3/93) FL 7
Bradford C (£27,500 on 28/7/93) FL 29 FLC 2 FAC 2+1 Others 1

BOWRY Robert (Bobby)
Born: Hampstead, 19 May 1971
Height: 5'8" Weight: 10.0
Club Honours: Div 1 '94

Promising young Crystal Palace midfielder who was signed from non-league soccer in 1992. Had a steady run in the side last season up to Christmas, but found the heavy grounds hard going and was rested. Stop Press: Having recently signed a new contract, this slim, skilful player was surprisingly signed by Millwall during the summer.
Queens Park R (Signed on 8/8/90)
Crystal Palace (Free from Carshalton on 4/4/92) F/PL 36+14/1 FLC 10 FAC 1

BOWYER Lee David
Born: London, 3 January 1977
Height: 5'9" Weight: 9.11
International Honours: E: Yth

Young Charlton midfield player who joined the professional ranks a year earlier than usual from the youth team, he made his debut in the Coca Cola Cup against Swindon and his FL debut the following week in the home game with Watford. Kept his place for the next four games but made only one further appearance in 1994-95. Very comfortable on the ball, with good distribution, Lee should mature into a classy player.
Charlton Ath (From trainee on 13/4/94) FL 5 FLC 0+1

Gary Brabin   Matthew Ashton
(Empics Sports Photo Agency)

BRABIN Gary
Born: Liverpool, 9 December 1970
Height: 5'11" Weight: 14.8

Highly competitive midfield player who joined Doncaster from non-league football during the 1994 close season, his value to the club was blighted by his disappointing record of four dismissals and six bookings. Still managed better than a goal every four games, though.
Stockport Co (From trainee on 14/12/89) FL 1+1 Others 1+1
Doncaster Rov (£45,000 from Runcorn on 26/7/94) FL 27+1/8 FLC 2 FAC 1 Others 2

BRACE Deryn Paul John
Born: Haverfordwest, 15 March 1975
Height: 5'7" Weight: 10.6
Club Honours: WC '95
International Honours: W: U21-5; Yth

Tenacious little player, full of industry, who likes to get forward and delivers well into the box. A regular in the Welsh U21 side managed by his Wrexham boss, he could well make the right-back slot his own in 1995-96, especially if Barry Jones takes up a central defensive position on a permanent basis.
Norwich C (From trainee on 6/7/93)
Wrexham (Free on 28/4/94) FL 11+4 FAC 1 Others 4

BRACEWELL Paul William
Born: Heswall, 19 July 1962
Height: 5'8" Weight: 10.9
Club Honours: CS '84, '85; ECWC '85; Div 1 '85, '93
International Honours: E: 3; U21-13 (UEFAC '84)

Paul's season started last December, after being sidelined with a serious pelvic injury. Just to be able to play for Newcastle again was a huge relief to Paul and his family, because complications were feared with the injury, which thankfully proved unfounded. A very brave player, and natural leader on the field, his main job is to win the ball in midfield, but he also has good control and passing ability as well. Stop Press: Always involved in the game, he signed for Sunderland on a free transfer during the summer and will double-up as manager, Peter Reid's assistant.
Stoke C (From apprentice on 6/2/80) FL 123+6/5 FLC 6 FAC 6/1
Sunderland (£250,000 on 1/7/83) FL 38/4 FLC 4 FAC 2
Everton (£425,000 on 25/5/84) FL 95/7 FLC 11/2 FAC 19+2 Others 17+2/1
Sunderland (£250,000 on 23/8/89) FL 112+1/2 FLC 9 FAC 10 Others 6
Newcastle U (£250,000 on 16/6/92) F/PL 64+9/3 FLC 3+1/1 FAC 6+2 Others 2

BRACEY Lee Michael Ian
Born: Barking, 11 September 1968
Height: 6'1" Weight: 12.8
Club Honours: WC '89

As understudy to Bury's regular goalkeeper, Gary Kelly, Lee made only five starts last season as the club went close to climbing out of the Third Division. However, when called upon, he performed well.
West Ham U (From trainee on 6/7/87)
Swansea C (Free on 27/8/88) FL 99 FLC 8 FAC 11 Others 10

Halifax T (£47,500 on 17/10/91) FL 73 FLC 2 FAC 1 Others 2
Bury (£20,000 on 23/8/93) FL 44+2 FLC 1 FAC 2 Others 1

BRADLEY Darren Michael
Born: Birmingham, 24 November 1965
Height: 5'11" Weight: 11.10
International Honours: E: Yth

An aggressive, wholehearted WBA midfield player who is good on the ball and who passes long and accurate. Was troubled by injury during the course of 1994-95 and that, combined with loss of form and suspension, meant that he was an absentee from Albion's first team duty for some time. Freed during the summer.
Aston Villa (From apprentice on 19/12/83) FL 16+4 FLC 3
West Bromwich A (Signed on 14/3/86) FL 236+18/9 FLC 13/1 FAC 10/2 Others 11/1

BRADLEY Russell
Born: Birmingham, 28 March 1966
Height: 6'2" Weight: 12.5
Club Honours: WC '90

Scunthorpe's club captain, he is unspectacular but nonetheless a solid and effective performer at the centre of defence. A strong tackler, who is good in the air, he missed several games last season due to a delayed hernia operation.
Nottingham F (Signed from Dudley T on 20/5/88)
Hereford U (Loaned on 13/11/88) FL 12/1 FAC 1 Others 3
Hereford U (£15,000 on 26/7/89) FL 75+2/3 FLC 7 Others 5+1
Halifax T (£45,000 on 6/9/91) FL 54+2/3 FLC 2 FAC 3 Others 4
Scunthorpe U (Free on 30/6/93) FL 58+1/3 FLC 2 FAC 7 Others 6

BRADSHAW Carl
Born: Sheffield, 2 October 1968
Height: 6'0" Weight: 11.0
International Honours: E: Yth

A Norwich 1994 close season signing from Sheffield United, Carl played his 250th senior game against Manchester United in 1994-95, having made his FL debut back in 1986-87. City missed his "hard but fair" defensive approach and foraging right-flank runs from full-back, following his mid-December torn thigh muscle injury. Out for eight weeks, the solid looking defensive team that had comprised himself, Jon Newsome, John Polston and Mark Bowen, were clearly unsettled, something Norwich never quite recovered from.
Sheffield Wed (From apprentice on 23/8/86) FL 16+16/4 FLC 2+2 FAC 6+1/3 Others 1
Barnsley (Loaned on 23/8/86) FL 6/1
Manchester C (£50,000 on 30/9/88) FL 1+4 FLC 0+1 Others 0+1
Sheffield U (£50,000 on 7/9/89) F/PL 122+25/8 FLC 10+1/2 FAC 12+1/3 Others 4
Norwich C (£500,000 on 28/7/94) PL 25+1/1 FLC 2/1 FAC 1

BRADSHAW Darren Shaun
Born: Sheffield, 19 March 1967
Height: 5'10" Weight: 11.3
International Honours: E: Yth

Started last season at Peterborough, having a spell on loan at Plymouth before signing for Blackpool in October. Began his "Pool"

career in midfield, but was later moved into defence where his confidence and skill on the ball gave the club a lift.
Chesterfield (On trial from Matlock T on 12/8/87) FL 18 FLC 2
York C (Free from Matlock T on 14/11/87) FL 58+1/3 FLC 2 FAC 2 Others 3
Newcastle U (£10,000 on 16/8/89) FL 32+6 FLC 3 FAC 2+1 Others 3
Peterborough U (Free on 13/8/92) FL 70+3/1 FLC 7/1 FAC 4 Others 2
Plymouth Arg (Loaned on 18/8/94) FL 5+1/1 FLC 1
Blackpool (£35,000 on 20/10/94) FL 26/1 FAC 1 Others 1

BRADY Matthew John
Born: London, 27 October 1977
Height: 5'9" Weight: 10.4

Made his debut for Barnet, while still a trainee, three minutes from the end of the final game of last season. As a striker, he scored lots of goals for the youth team in 1994-95.
Barnet (Trainee) FL 0+1

BRAMMER David
Born: Bromborough, 28 February 1975
Height: 5'8" Weight: 11.0

Strong-tackling player on the perimeter of the Wrexham first team, he is more of a "deep lying" central midfielder and packs a powerful shot when in sight of goal. Has not developed as quickly as hoped for in 1994-95, but has time on his side.
Wrexham (From trainee on 2/7/93) FL 30+8/3 FLC 3 FAC 1 Others 3+2

BRANAGAN Keith Graham
Born: Fulham, 10 July 1966
Height: 6'0" Weight: 13.2
International Honours: Ei: B-1

Keith regained his fitness to become Bolton's number one 'keeper again during 1994-95, being recognised at international level for the first time when Jack Charlton selected him for Ireland's "B" international against England at Anfield. His most memorable saves of the term came in injury time of the Coca Cola Cup fifth round-tie against Norwich at Burnden Park and in the play-off final at Wembley when he saved Stuart Lovell's penalty. That last save was crucial, and was the turning point of a game that ultimately saw Wanderers gain promotion to the Premiership.
Cambridge U (From juniors on 4/8/83) FL 110 FLC 12 FAC 6 Others 6
Millwall (£100,000 on 25/3/88) FL 46 FLC 1 FAC 5 Others 1
Brentford (Loaned on 24/11/89) FL 2 Others 1
Gillingham (Loaned on 1/10/91) FL 1
Bolton W (Free on 3/7/92) FL 99 FLC 16 FAC 8 Others 6

BRANCH Graham
Born: Liverpool, 12 February 1972
Height: 6'2" Weight: 12.2

A jet-paced Tranmere winger who can both make and take chances, he had to take a back seat for most of last season due to the form of Pat Nevin and John Morrissey. Made only one League substitute appearance, plus one full outing in the Anglo-Italian Cup, and has yet to realise his full potential.

Tranmere Rov (Free from Heswall on 2/7/91) FL 6+15 FLC 0+2 FAC 0+1 Others 2+1
Bury (Loaned on 20/11/92) FL 3+1/1 Others 1

BRANNAN Gerard (Ged) Daniel
Born: Prescot, 15 January 1972
Height: 6'0" Weight: 12.3

Having received rave notices in 1993-94 as a goalscoring midfielder, Ged found goals much harder to come by during 1994-95. In consequence, he was switched back to his original left-back position and, on occasions, omitted from the side. A powerful right-sided player with strength, determination, and no little skill, he is regarded as one of Tranmere's top young prospects.
Tranmere Rov (From trainee on 3/7/90) FL 152+8/14 FLC 19/3 FAC 8+1 Others 26+1/1

BRASS Christopher (Chris) Paul
Born: Easington, 24 July 1975
Height: 5'10" Weight: 11.8

A product of Burnley's youth side, normally a right-back, but capable of playing on either flank, his first few appearances in the side last season showed promise, with speed, sureness in the tackle, and no lack of confidence. Also had a spell on loan at Torquay.
Burnley (From trainee on 8/7/93) FL 2+3
Torquay U (Loaned on 14/10/94) FL 7 FAC 2 Others 1

BRAZIL Derek Michael
Born: Dublin, 14 December 1968
Height: 5'11" Weight: 10.6
Club Honours: Div 3 '93; WC '93
International Honours: Ei: B-2; U23-1; U21-7; Yth

Cardiff central defender who can also play equally well in either full-back positions. Consistent throughout 1994-95, despite carrying an injury in January, he was a mainstay of the defence, especially in marshalling the players around him.
Manchester U (Free from Rivermount BC on 12/3/86) FL 0+2
Oldham Ath (Loaned on 20/1190) FL 1 Others 1
Swansea C (Loaned on 12/9/91) FL 12/1 FLC 2 Others 2
Cardiff C (£85,000 on 26/8/92) FL 90+5/1 FLC 6 FAC 8 Others 12+3/1

BRAZIL Gary Nicholas
Born: Tunbridge Wells, 19 September 1962
Height: 5'11" Weight: 10.2

An experienced Fulham striker, who relies more on skill and pace than physical strength, Gary was switched from the centre to wide on the left, providing support rather than being at the heart of the attack last season. This role did not seem to make full use of his finely developed predatory instincts.
Sheffield U (Free from Crystal Palace juniors on 11/8/80) FL 39+23/9 FLC 4+1 FAC 4+5/1 Others 1+1
Port Vale (Loaned on 24/8/84) FL 6/3
Preston NE (£12,500 on 15/2/85) FL 163+3/58 FLC 13/6 FAC 10/3 Others 13/5
Newcastle U (Signed on 9/2/89) FL 7+16/2 FLC 1+1/1 FAC 0+1 Others 0+1
Fulham (£110,000 on 6/9/90) FL 190+6/46 FLC 10/3 FAC 7/5 Others 14/3

BREAKER Timothy (Tim) Sean
Born: Bicester, 2 July 1965
Height: 6'0" Weight: 12.6
Club Honours: FLC '88
International Honours: E: U21-2

West Ham right-back who loves to go forward at every opportunity. Tim was in outstanding form last season and it was a big blow when he was missing for two months, following a cartilage operation in October. A tireless worker, who crosses the ball well, he laid on goals for Tony Cottee against Aston Villa, Manchester City and Wimbledon.
Luton T (From apprentice on 15/5/83) FL 204+6/3 FLC 22+2 FAC 21 Others 7
West Ham U (£600,000 on 12/10/90) F/PL 168+2/8 FLC 11 FAC 22 Others 7

BRECKIN Ian
Born: Rotherham, 24 February 1975
Height: 6'1" Weight: 12.9

A strong defender who has come into the Rotherham side and forged himself a regular place at the heart of the defence and he is particularly good in the air, having got on the scoresheet on a couple of occasions from set-pieces in 1994-95. Should be one of the players who will prove to be a key factor for the future.
Rotherham U (From trainee on 1/11/93) FL 51/2 FLC 1 FAC 3 Others 3

BREEN Gary Patrick
Born: Hendon, 12 December 1973
Height: 6'1" Weight: 12.0
International Honours: E: U21-6

Very useful central defender, who can also play in midfield, Gary has the potential to go on to bigger things as his displays for the Eire U21 side have shown. Having signed for Peterborough during the 1994 close season, it was not long before leading club managers were giving him the once over and being suitably impressed.
Maidstone U (Free from Charlton Ath juniors on 6/3/91) FL 19
Gillingham (Free on 2/7/92) FL 45+6 FLC 4 FAC 5 Others 1
Peterborough U (£70,000 on 5/8/94) FL 43+1/1 FLC 2 FAC 2 Others 3/1

BRENNAN Mark Robert
Born: Rossendale, 4 October 1965
Height: 5'10" Weight: 11.1
International Honours: E: U21-6; Yth

Very skilful Oldham midfielder with a superb left-foot and good vision, who specialises in providing chances for others. Made a disappointing start to 1994-95 but, following the appointment of a new manager, Graeme Sharp, he was immediately installed on the left-flank to add balance and width to the side. Was an ever-present from then on.
Ipswich T (From apprentice on 7/4/83) FL 165+3/19 FLC 21+1/2 FAC 12/3 Others 11/1
Middlesbrough (£375,000 on 27/7/88) FL 61+4/6 FLC 6 FAC 4 Others 8/1
Manchester C (£500,000 on 25/7/90) FL 25+4/6 FLC 4/1 FAC 1 Others 2
Oldham Ath (£200,000 on 24/11/92) P/FL 59+6/4 FLC 5+1 FAC 4

BRESSINGTON Graham
Born: Eton, 8 July 1966
Height: 6'0" Weight: 12.0

An exceptionally strong, laid back and cool Southend defender, who also played in midfield, Graham's 1994-95 season was punctuated by a number of injuries and, due to the competitive nature of his game coupled with the new FA rules, several suspensions. Missing the final part of the season, following a knee operation, he was freed during the summer.
Lincoln C (£10,000 from Wycombe W on 23/11/87) FL 136+5/7 FLC 10/2 FAC 6 Others 6
Southend U (£25,000 on 9/7/93) FL 45+2/5 FLC 2 FAC 1 Others 5

BREVETT Rufus Emanuel
Born: Derby, 24 September 1969
Height: 5'8" Weight: 11.0

Very fast QPR defender who is equally at home in the midfield, he played in five consecutive games early last season as left-back and wide midfield but, apart from a couple of appearances as substitute, did not start another game until January. Was then used again in a variety of roles, particularly as a specific man marker, a job he does superbly. Too good a player to be left out permanently.
Doncaster Rov (From trainee on 8/7/88) FL 106+3/3 FLC 4 FAC 4 Others 10+1
Queens Park R (£250,000 on 15/2/91) F/PL 51+8 FLC 2+1 FAC 2

BRIEN Anthony (Tony) James
Born: Dublin, 10 February 1969
Height: 5'11" Weight: 11.9

A central defender who was a regular at Rotherham until he lost his place last season, due to suspension, he only managed to play a handful more games before being freed during the summer.
Leicester C (From apprentice on 13/2/87) FL 12+4/1 FLC 1 FAC 1 Others 3
Chesterfield (£90,000 on 16/12/88) FL 201+3/8 FLC 14 FAC 7 Others 14
Rotherham U (Signed on 8/10/93) FL 41+2/2 FLC 2 FAC 4 Others 6

BRIGGS Gary
Born: Leeds, 21 June 1959
Height: 6'3" Weight: 12.10
Club Honours: Div 3 '84, Div 2 '85; FLC '88

A strong and experienced defender, he only played two games for Blackpool last season due to injury and was freed during the summer.
Middlesbrough (From apprentice on 1/5/77)
Oxford U (£12,500 on 7/1/78) FL 418+2/18 FLC 49/3 FAC 24 Others 8/1
Blackpool (Free on 27/6/89) FL 137/4 FLC 20/2 FAC 7 Others 13

BRIGHT Mark Abraham
Born: Stoke, 6 June 1962
Height: 6'0" Weight: 11.0
Club Honours: FMC '91

1994-95 was not as good a season for the experienced Sheffield Wednesday striker as in previous campaigns, although he re-mained the club's leading goalscorer. Mark suffered mainly because he never had a regular striking partner. Still, however, a much proven attacker, at his best he is very fast with great touch and able to control the ball with all parts of his body; head, chest, thighs and feet.

Port Vale (Free from Leek T on 15/10/81) FL 18+11/10 FLC 1+1 FAC 0+1/1 Others 2
Leicester C (£33,000 on 19/7/84) FL 26+16/6 FLC 3+1 FAC 1
Crystal Palace (£75,000 on 13/11/86) F/PL 224+3/92 FLC 22/11 FAC 13+1/2 Others 23/9
Sheffield Wed (£1,375,000 on 11/9/92) PL 97+10/41 FLC 17/8 FAC 13/7

Mark Bright　　　Tony Marshall
(Empics Sports Photo Agency)

BRIGHTWELL David John
Born: Lutterworth, 7 January 1971
Height: 6'2" Weight: 12.7

Manchester City player who shows promise, David is more at home in the centre of the defence, utilising his aerial ability, but due to injuries last season he was often called upon to play in the left-back position. Scored a face-saving equaliser at Notts County in the FA Cup, thus giving City another bite at the cherry.

Manchester C (From juniors on 11/4/88) F/PL 35+8/1 FLC 2+1 FAC 5+2/1
Chester C (Loaned on 22/3/91) FL 6

BRIGHTWELL Ian Robert
Born: Lutterworth, 9 April 1968
Height: 5'10" Weight: 11.7
International Honours: E: U21-4; Yth; Sch

Finally recovered from an injury which dogged him in 1993-94, Ian was very consistent for Manchester City last season, adapting well, both in defence and midfield. An ideal clubman, who can slot into a number of positions and a resolute tackler who can distribute well, Ian had outstanding games against Andy Cole, Ian Rush and Alan Shearer, all in the space of a week.

Manchester C (From juniors on 7/5/86) F/PL 204+30/16 FLC 24+2 FAC 13+4/1 Others 4+3

BRISCOE Lee Stephen
Born: Pontefract, 30 September 1975
Height: 5'10" Weight: 10.9

A fine young left-sided Sheffield Wednesday prospect, Lee started to make the breakthrough he had been looking for in 1994-95. An important member of the reserves, although left-back would appear to be his position, he is equally effective in

midfield. Either way, next season could see him come to the fore.

Sheffield Wed (From trainee on 22/5/94) PL 6+1

Jason Brissett　　　Barrington Coombes
(Empics Sports Photo Agency)

BRISSETT Jason Curtis
Born: Wanstead, 7 September 1974
Height: 5'11" Weight: 12.7

A free transfer from Peterborough last December, Jason made his Bournemouth debut against Bristol Rovers on Boxing Day. As a winger, using his speed and strength to great effect, he showed he could take defenders on and deliver telling crosses. Can play on either flank, although primarily left-sided.

Peterborough U (Free from Arsenal juniors on 14/6/93) FL 27+8 FLC 5+1/1 FAC 2+1/1 Others 3+1/1
Bournemouth (Free on 23/12/94) FL 24+1

BROCK Kevin Stanley
Born: Bicester, 9 September 1962
Height: 5'9" Weight: 10.12
Club Honours: Div 3 '84, Div 2 '85; FLC '86
International Honours: E: U21-4 (EUFAC '84); Sch

An experienced midfielder who played just one match for Stockport in 1994-95, he left last November after failing to find a regular place in the side and joined Stevenage Borough in the Conference, before moving on to Yeovil.

Oxford U (From apprentice on 1/9/79) FL 229+16/26 FLC 30+2/5 FAC 17+1/1 Others 3
Queens Park R (£260,000 on 13/8/87) FL 38+2/2 FLC 6 FAC 4/1 Others 1
Newcastle U (£300,000 on 8/12/88) FL 135+10/14 FLC 7/1 FAC 11/1 Others 8+1/1
Cardiff C (Loaned on 25/2/94) FL 14/2
Stockport Co (Free on 26/9/94) FLC 1

BRODIE Stephen (Steve) Eric
Born: Sunderland, 14 January 1973
Height: 5'7" Weight: 10.6

Diminutive young striker who has still to

start a first team game for Sunderland, Steve has been a prolific goalscorer at reserve level and it is hoped he will make the jump to the senior stage permanent in time. Very quick, with good feet, 1995-96 might be his season.

Sunderland (From trainee on 1/7/91) FL 1+11

BROOKS Shaun
Born: London, 9 October 1962
Height: 5'7" Weight: 11.0
International Honours: E: Yth; Sch

Six weeks after coming back into League football with Bournemouth as a non-contract player last October, this skilful midfielder returned to Leyton Orient on a monthly contract after a seven year absence. A first class distributor of the ball with an eye for goal, his return to the club was spoilt by a calf injury which restricted his appearances. However he scored the winning goal - a fierce shot from 35 yards - against Shrewsbury in the AWS Southern semi-final, thereby setting up a money spinning clash with Birmingham.

Crystal Palace (From apprentice on 16/10/79) FL 47+7/4 FLC 5+1/1 FAC 5
Leyton Orient (Free on 17/10/83) FL 140+8/26 FLC 10/1 FAC 12/4 Others 7+3/1
Bournemouth (£20,000 on 22/6/87) FL 114+14/13 FLC 12 FAC 4+1/1 Others 3
Bournemouth (Free from Dorchester T on 6/10/94) FL 1
Leyton Orient (Free on 18/11/94) FL 8+1 FAC 0+1 Others 3/1

BROUGH John Robert
Born: Ilkeston, 8 January 1973
Height: 6'0" Weight: 12.6

Signed last October from Telford, John proved he could play anywhere for Hereford, and did just that. A very strong tackler, and both confident on the ground and in the air, he always gave 100 per-cent no matter what the position.

Notts Co (From trainee on 9/7/91)
Shrewsbury T (Free on 6/7/92) FL 7+9/1 FLC 1+1 FAC 1 Others 1
Hereford U (Free from Telford on 4/11/94) FL 16+2/1 Others 0+2

BROWN Grant Ashley
Born: Sunderland, 19 November 1969
Height: 6'0" Weight: 11.12

Solidly built defender who had his most consistent spell in Lincoln's colours to date, linking up well with Colin Greenall in 1994-95 to form an effective central defensive partnership.

Leicester C (From trainee on 1/7/88) FL 14 FLC 2
Lincoln C (£60,000 on 20/8/89) FL 220/11 FLC 13/1 FAC 9 Others 14/1

BROWN Ian O'Neal
Born: Ipswich, 11 September 1965
Height: 5'10" Weight: 11.5

Fast, direct winger who signed for Northampton in 1994-95, having earlier been on loan from Bristol City, he prefers to play wide on the right, and take on his man. Freed at the end of the season.

Bristol C (Signed from Chelmsford C on 7/5/93) FL 5+7/1 FLC 0+2 Others 2
Colchester U (Loaned on 22/3/94) FL 4/1
Northampton T (Signed on 23/12/94) FL 23/4

BROWN Jonathan (Jon)
Born: Barnsley, 8 September 1966
Height: 5'10" Weight: 11.3
At home in Exeter's defence or midfield in 1994-95, and the club's longest serving player having joined in 1990, Jon started 38 games, before being released at the end of the season.
Exeter C (£1,500 from Denaby U on 1/7/90) FL 149+15/2 FLC 8+1 FAC 12+1/1 Others 17/1

BROWN Kenneth (Kenny) James
Born: Upminster, 11 July 1967
Height: 5'8" Weight: 11.6
An experienced full-back, and comfortable on both flanks, when called he comes into the West Ham side and plays well, although yet to gain a regular place. Always looking to go forward, he scored from a header to clinch the FA Cup-tie victory at Wycombe last January.
Norwich C (From juniors on 10/7/85) FL 24+1 Others 3
Plymouth Arg (Free on 10/8/88) FL 126/4 FLC 9 FAC 6 Others 3
West Ham U (£175,000 on 2/8/91) F/PL 52+8/5 FLC 2+1 FAC 7+2/1 Others 2+2

BROWN Linton James
Born: Hull, 12 April 1968
Height: 5'9" Weight: 11.0
Linton's electrifying pace makes him a threat to any defence and he now has the composure to turn chances into goals. Forms a formidable striking partnership for Hull with Dean Windass. A bubbly character, "Browny", who favours his right-foot and prefers a central role but can also be used wide, was brought to the club by funds raised by the supporters. Forced out for the last 11 games of 1994-95 with a pelvic problem.
Halifax T (Free from Guisley on 18/12/92) FL 3
Hull C (Free on 8/1/93) FL 90+8/24 FLC 4 FAC 3/1 Others 2

BROWN Michael (Mickey) Antony
Born: Birmingham, 8 February 1968
Height: 5'9" Weight: 10.12
Club Honours: Div 3 '94
A very fast right-winger who likes to take on defenders and a pinpoint crosser of the ball, Micky is traditionally a provider rather than scorer. Early 1994-95 injury problems at Shrewsbury resulted in a cartilage operation and, after recovering, he moved on to Preston where further injuries prevented his Deepdale debut.
Shrewsbury T (From apprentice on 11/2/86) FL 174+16/9 FLC 17/2 FAC 10/1 Others 11
Bolton W (£100,000 on 15/8/91) FL 27+6/3 FLC 0+1 FAC 3 Others 2
Shrewsbury T (£25,000 on 23/12/92) FL 66+1/11 FLC 8/1 FAC 3 Others 2
Preston NE (£75,000 on 30/11/94)

BROWN Philip (Phil)
Born: South Shields, 30 May 1957
Height: 5'11" Weight: 11.6
Club Honours: AMC '89
Very experienced Blackpool signing from Bolton during the 1994 close season, Phil started at right-back and was appointed captain. Likes to attack, scoring five goals in

his first 11 games, before losing his place last January when Gary Rowett came on loan.
Hartlepool U (Signed on 7/7/78) FL 210+7/8 FLC 12 FAC 11 Others 3/1
Halifax T (Free on 30/7/85) FL 135/19 FLC 6/1 FAC 8/1 Others 9
Bolton W (£17,000 on 23/6/88) FL 254+4/14 FLC 25/1 FAC 23/1 Others 28/1
Blackpool (Free on 25/7/94) FL 28+3/5 FLC 2/1 FAC 1 Others 2

BROWN Richard Anthony
Born: Nottingham, 13 January 1967
Height: 5'10" Weight: 11.2
Released by Blackburn last March, he signed a one month contract for Stockport, playing just one game at right-back, before being substituted and subsequently leaving.
Sheffield Wed (£10,000 from Ilkeston T on 8/1/85)
Blackburn Rov (£15,000 from Kettering, via Ilkeston T, Grantham and Boston U, on 26/9/90) F/PL 26+2 FLC 1+1 FAC 2 Others 1
Maidstone U (Loaned on 21/2/91) FL 3
Stockport Co (Free on 3/3/95) FL 1

BROWN Steven (Steve) Byron
Born: Brighton, 13 May 1972
Height: 6'1" Weight: 12.0
Firmly established in the Charlton side, Steve had a good season in 1994-95, mainly at right-back, although playing several games in midfield and one in central defence. Likes to get forward, with a very strong right-foot, he is often used in set pieces for his shooting power. Also the club's penalty taker.
Charlton Ath (From trainee on 3/7/90) FL 60+2/3 FLC 2 FAC 7 Others 2

BROWN Steven (Steve) Ferold
Born: Northampton, 6 July 1966
Height: 6'1" Weight: 11.4
Skilful left-footed Wycombe midfielder who improved dramatically throughout 1994-95. Filled the problem left-back spot early on, but his pacy runs from midfield, combined with some gritty tackling, earned him the choice as supporters' "Player of the Season".
Northampton T (From juniors on 11/8/83) FL 14+1/3 (Free to Irthlingborough T in December 1985)
Northampton T (Free on 21/7/89) FL 145+13/19 FLC 10/1 FAC 12/2 Others 10+1/1
Wycombe W (Signed on 9/2/94) FL 46+3/2 FLC 1+1 FAC 3 Others 1+1

BROWN Steven (Steve) Robert
Born: Southend, 6 December 1973
Height: 6'0" Weight: 12.7
As a young forward, who arrived at Colchester in September 1993 amid a barrage of goals, he found them harder to come by last season, although he managed eight before losing his place under the new manager. Moved on to Gillingham in exchange for Robbie Reinelt and, happily re-discovered his goal touch there, scoring inside three minutes on his debut against Bury.
Southend U (From trainee on 10/7/92) FL 10/2 FAC 0+1 Others 1
Scunthorpe U (Free on 5/7/93)
Colchester U (Free on 27/8/93) FL 56+6/17 FLC

2 FAC 5/1 Others 4/1
Gillingham (Signed on 22/3/95) FL 8/1

BROWNING Marcus Trevor
Born: Bristol, 22 April 1971
Height: 6'1" Weight: 12.10
A contractual dispute which was eventually settled early last season clearly unsettled Marcus, but his ball winning qualities and promptings from Bristol Rovers' midfield improved as the campaign progressed. A very fit player, the heavy grounds during the wet winter brought out the best in him.
Bristol Rov (From trainee on 1/7/89) FL 83+20/7 FLC 1+3 FAC 7/1 Others 6+5/2
Hereford U (Loaned on 18/9/92) FL 7/5

BROWNRIGG Andrew (Andy) David
Born: Sheffield, 2 August 1976
Height: 6'0" Weight: 11.10
International Honours: S: Yth
Signed by Norwich from Hereford last March as a long term investment, it would surprise a few shrewd judges in the game if the lad did not make it. Initially a YTS, Andrew, who only turned pro at the beginning of 1995, quickly showed what a good prospect he was in central defence. Winning everything in the air, and excellent on the ground, he dominated the nine games he played in before his transfer. Yet to play for the "Canaries", his debut should not be long in coming.
Hereford U (From trainee on 3/1/95) FL 8 Others 1
Norwich C (£100,000 on 9/3/95)

Steve Bruce
Neal Simpson
(Empics Sports Photo Agency)

BRUCE Stephen (Steve) Roger
Born: Corbridge, 31 December 1960
Height: 6'0" Weight: 12.6
Club Honours: Div 2 '86, PL '93, '94; FLC '85, '92; FAC '90, '94; CS '90, '93, '94; ECWC '91; ESC '91;
International Honours: E: B-1; Yth
As Manchester United's captain, Steve is a consistent central defender, who is good in the air and excellent in the tackle. A natural competitor, he often scores important goals from corners and set-plays. Last season, his first team future at Old Trafford appeared to be in some doubt, following the signing of

David May from Blackburn but, once the campaign began, he was an immovable force in the centre of defence. His partnership with Gary Pallister is still one of the strongest in the Premiership, and his eye for a goal gave United some vital results. Although he now accepts that an England call is unlikely, his influence at Old Trafford remains as strong as ever.

Gillingham (From apprentice on 27/10/78) FL 203+2/29 FLC 15/6 FAC 14/1
Norwich C (£125,000 on 24/8/84) FL 141/14 FLC 20/5 FAC 9/1 Others 10
Manchester U (£800,000 on 18/12/87) F/PL 279/35 FLC 31+1/6 FAC 36/3 Others 30+9/7

BRYAN Marvin Lee
Born: Paddington, 2 August 1975
Height: 6'0" Weight: 12.7

QPR outside-right who is both quick and strong and always looking to run past defenders and cross, he performed consistently well for the reserves last season. Yet to play for the first team, Marvin was loaned out to Doncaster for his initial taste of League football, scoring one goal in five appearances.

Queens Park R (From trainee on 17/8/92)
Doncaster Rov (Loaned on 8/12/94) FL 5/1

BRYANT Matthew (Matt)
Born: Bristol, 21 September 1970
Height: 6'1" Weight: 12.4

Even though Bristol City were relegated at the end of 1994-95, it had been an outstanding season on a playing front for Matt. Apart from doing his central defensive duties without qualm, he even found time to notch three goals and was a popular choice as the fans' "Player of the Year". Will relish the challenge of getting the side back to the First Division.

Bristol C (From trainee on 1/7/89) FL 170+1/7 FLC 7 FAC 10 Others 6
Walsall (Loaned on 24/8/90) FL 13 FLC 4

Ian Bryson   Laurence Griffiths
(Empics Sports Photo Agency)

BRYSON James Ian Cook
Born: Kilmarnock, 26 November 1962
Height: 5'11" Weight: 11.11

Two-footed midfielder, or forward, Ian has established himself at Preston playing just in front of the defence, from where he distributes the ball, or starts his surging runs forward. Regular penalty taker and free-kick specialist around the penalty area for the club last season.

Kilmarnock (Signed from Hurlford in 1981) SL 194+21/40 SLC 12+7/1 SC 14+2/3
Sheffield U (£40,000 on 24/8/88) F/PL 138+17/36 FLC 11+2/1 FAC 18+4/4 Others 7/3
Barnsley (£20,000 on 12/8/93) FL 16/3 FLC 2/1 Others 2
Preston NE (£42,500 on 29/11/93) FL 65+1/7 FLC 1+1 FAC 4+1 Others 7/1

BUCKLE Paul John
Born: Hatfield, 16 December 1970
Height: 5'8" Weight: 10.8
Club Honours: Div 3 '92

Midfielder who came through a disappointing mid-season in 1994-95 to demonstrate that he is the best passer of the ball at Torquay.

Brentford (From trainee on 1/7/89) FL 42+15/1 FLC 5+1 FAC 3+1 Others 6+5
Torquay U (Free on 3/2/94) FL 46+2/5 FLC 4 FAC 3 Others 1

BULL Garry William
Born: Tipton, 12 June 1966
Height: 5'8" Weight: 11.7
Club Honours: GMVC '91

Younger brother of the more famous Steve, and also a goalscorer, although not quite in the same vein, Garry came to Nottingham Forest in the 1993 close season after being deemed to be a free agent. A poacher of goals, he is most effective when playing off a target man. With Stan Collymore a regular up-front for Forest, he has had few chances to shine and was loaned out to Birmingham for two months last September, but in his one game in the Premiership in 1994-95 he scored the only goal of the game against Crystal Palace.

Southampton (Signed from Paget R on 15/10/86)
Cambridge U (Signed on 29/3/88) FL 13+6/4 FLC 0+1 Others 0+2
Barnet (£2,000 on 1/3/89) FL 83/37 FLC 4/4 FAC 11/3 Others 8/2
Nottingham F (Free on 21/7/93) F/PL 4+8/1 FLC 2 FAC 0+3
Birmingham C (Loaned on 12/9/94) FL 10/6 Others 2/1

BULL Stephen (Steve) George
Born: Tipton, 28 March 1965
Height: 5'11" Weight: 11.4
Club Honours: Div 4 '88, Div 3 '89; AMC '88
International Honours: E: 13; B-5; U21-5

An aggressive centre-forward, Steve has the most important ingredients which make a goalscorer. His promising pre-season was disrupted by injury and he lasted only ten minutes of Wolverhampton's opening match of 1994-95, though he did find time to make the winner. He was back within a month and the goal he lashed in at Stoke was like the "Bully" of old. Against Luton he was substituted for the first time and his 15 match spell ended as a heel injury kept him out for almost a month again. Struggled on with injections in December, before

succumbing to an achilles tendon operation that kept him absent for almost two months. Came back to captain the side for the first time in 1994-95 at Southend, his late winner being the 200th goal of his League career.

West Bromwich A (Free from Tipton T on 24/8/85) FL 2+2/2 FLC 2/1 Others 1+2
Wolverhampton W (£35,000 on 21/11/86) FL 341/201 FLC 19/13 FAC 12/5 Others 31+1/32

Steve Bull   Neal Simpson
(Empics Sports Photo Agency)

BULLIMORE Wayne Alan
Born: Sutton in Ashfield, 12 September 1970
Height: 5'9" Weight: 10.6
International Honours: E: Sch

A skilful, left-footed midfield player with good ball control, he was elected by his fellow professionals to the award winning PFA Third Division team at the end of last season. Being small and lightweight, his delightful skills have brought him some classic goals for Scunthorpe.

Manchester U (From trainee on 16/9/88)
Barnsley (Free on 9/3/91) FL 27+8/1 FLC 2+1 FAC 1+1
Stockport Co (Free on 11/10/93)
Scunthorpe U (Free on 19/11/93) 51+2/9 FLC 2/1 FAC 5/1 Others 3/1

BULLOCK Darren John
Born: Worcester, 12 February 1969
Height: 5'8" Weight: 12.4

Another signing from non-league soccer, Darren is an uncompromising Huddersfield midfielder who gives very little away and is a ferocious tackler. Previously on the transfer list, he looks to be staying with the club after playing in all three of the play-off games that ultimately saw Town gain promotion to the First Division.

Huddersfield T (£55,000 from Nuneaton Borough on 19/11/93) FL 59/9 FLC 3 FAC 2/1 Others 9/1

BULLOCK Martin John
Born: Derby, 5 March 1975
Height: 5'5" Weight: 10.7

One of the finds of last season. An attacking

midfield player, he forced his way into the Barnsley team after a series of fine displays in the reserves, making the position in the hole behind the front two his own. Likes to run with the ball and his ability to beat defenders put fear into the opposition. The sky's the limit for this talented youngster.

Barnsley (£15,000 from Eastwood T on 4/9/93) FL 17+12 FAC 0+1 Others 1

BURGESS Daryl
Born: Birmingham, 24 January 1971
Height: 5'11" Weight: 12.3

Strong-tackling defender, able to play at right-back or at centre-half, he has good pace, strong heading ability, and a solid tackle. Was plagued by injury during the first half of 1994-95, but on regaining full fitness was immediately installed into WBA's back division, occupying the right-back berth where he was totally committed.

West Bromwich A (From trainee on 1/7/89) FL 173+5/5 FLC 8+2/1 FAC 6 Others 8

BURGESS David (Dave) John
Born: Liverpool, 20 January 1960
Height: 5'10" Weight: 11.5

An experienced Carlisle defender, Dave had a spell on loan at Hartlepool early in 1994-95, playing in 13 matches before returning to Brunton Park. Still unable to get his number two shirt back from Joe Joyce and not being called upon for first team duty all season, he was released during the summer.

Tranmere Rov (Signed on 4/8/81) FL 217+1/1 FLC 16 FAC 15 Others 11
Grimsby T (Signed on 20/8/86) FL 66+3 FLC 6 FAC 4 Others 3
Blackpool (£30,000 on 7/7/88) FL 101/1 FLC 12 FAC 7/1 Others 13
Carlisle U (Loaned on 26/3/93) FL 6
Carlisle U (£5,000 on 9/6/93) FL 36+4/1 FLC 2 FAC 4 Others 5+2
Hartlepool U (Loaned on 15/9/94) FL 11 FLC 2

BURKE David Ian
Born: Liverpool, 6 August 1960
Height: 5'10" Weight: 11.6
International Honours: E: Yth

Joined Blackpool during the 1994 close season, two days after his former Bolton team-mate, Phil Brown. A steady performer, he was the regular left-back until making way for Scott Darton last January.

Bolton W (From apprentice on 25/8/77) FL 65+4/1 FLC 5 FAC 1+1
Huddersfield T (Free on 16/6/81) FL 189/3 FLC 19 FAC 15
Crystal Palace (£78,000 on 9/10/87) FL 80+1 FLC 4 FAC 3 Others 9
Bolton W (£60,000 on 27/7/90) FL 104+2 FLC 11+1 FAC 13/1 Others 7
Blackpool (Free on 27/7/94) FL 23 FLC 2 FAC 1 Others 2

BURKE Mark Stephen
Born: Solihull, 12 February 1969
Height: 5'10" Weight: 11.8
International Honours: E: Yth

Skilful right-sided midfield player who was virtually a permanent substitute at Port Vale until a dislocated shoulder ended his season last Christmas. His 15 appearances from the bench equalled a club record and he scored a couple of important goals when coming

on, both late winners against Barnsley and Millwall. Freed during the summer.

Aston Villa (From trainee on 16/2/87) FL 5+2 Others 0+1
Middlesbrough (£50,000 on 23/12/87) FL 32+25/6 FLC 3 FAC 2+1 Others 2+1
Darlington (Loaned on 3/10/90) FL 5/1
Wolverhampton W (£15,000 on 14/3/91) FL 53+15/11 FLC 3/2 FAC 2 Others 2+2/1
Luton T (Loaned on 4/3/94) FL 2+1 FAC 0+1
Port Vale (Free on 16/8/94) FL 4+11/2 FLC 1+2 FAC 0+2

BURLEY Craig William
Born: Irvine, 24 September 1971
Height: 5'10" Weight: 11.7
International Honours: S: 3; U21-7; Yth; Sch

Nephew of George, the man currently in charge at Ipswich, Chelsea's Craig, who had been unable to play until November due to a pre-season injury, was rewarded for his good displays in 1994-95 with selection for the full Scottish side against Japan in May, thus being capped at every level. A midfielder with great vision and long-range shooting ability, he scored the equaliser against his uncle's team in January, just four minutes after coming on the pitch in the 84th minute. And he had a goal disallowed in the same period!

Chelsea (From trainee on 1/9/89) F/PL 43+17/5 FLC 3 FAC 9+2/3 Others 3

BURLEY George Elder
Born: Cumnock, 3 June 1956
Height: 5'10" Weight: 11.0
Club Honours: FAC '78; EUFAC '81
International Honours: S: 11; U23-2; Yth; Sch

George, who joined Colchester as player-manager from Scottish football in the summer of 1994, was well down the road to becoming a Layer Road legend as United rocketed up the League, before he left to take over at Ipswich. Unfortunately, Colchester never really recovered from his departure on Christmas Eve and failed to gain promotion, while Ipswich were relegated from the Premiership.

Ipswich T (From apprentice on 6/6/73) FL 394/6 FLC 35 FAC 43/4 Others 27/1
Sunderland (£50,000 on 26/9/85) FL 54 FLC 2 FAC 5/1 Others 5/1
Gillingham (Free on 21/7/88) FL 46/2 FLC 3 FAC 2 Others 3
Motherwell (Free during 1989 close season) SL 54 SLC 5/1 SC 2
Ayr U (Free on 9/1/91) SL 66+1 SLC 3 SC 8 Others 2
Falkirk (Free in January 1994) SL 1
Motherwell (Free in February 1994) SL 3+2
Colchester U (Free on 3/8/94) FL 5+2 FLC 0+1 Others 0+1

BURNDRED John Nigel
Born: Stoke, 23 March 1968
Height: 5'8" Weight: 10.6

Nippy striker who was taken on trial as a non-contract player by Port Vale for the remaining three months of last season and made his debut in the final game against Notts County. A self confessed Vale fan, he scored over 40 goals for the local non-league side, Knypersley Victoria.

Port Vale (Free from Knypersley Victoria on 21/2/95) FL 1

BURNETT Wayne
Born: Lambeth, 4 September 1971
Height: 6'0" Weight: 12.6
International Honours: E: Yth

A very talented central midfielder who has plenty of flair, skill and passing ability, he drifted in-and-out of the Plymouth team in 1994-95, following the return of the two Steves, Castle and McCall.

Leyton Orient (From trainee on 13/11/89) FL 34+6 FLC 3+1/1 FAC 3+1 Others 4
Blackburn Rov (£90,000 on 19/8/92)
Plymouth Arg (Signed on 9/8/93) FL 55+9/3 FLC 1 FAC 3 Others 4+1

BURNHAM Jason John
Born: Mansfield, 8 May 1973
Height: 5'10" Weight: 13.3

Chester left-back who likes to join up with the attack where he crossed the ball to good effect in 1994-95. Joined the club from Northampton during the 1994 close season.

Northampton T (From trainee on 23/7/91) FL 79+9/2 FLC 4+2 FAC 6 Others 8
Chester C (Free on 29/7/94) FL 22+2 FLC 2 FAC 1 Others 2

BURNS Christopher (Chris)
Born: Manchester, 9 November 1967
Height: 6'0" Weight: 12.0

Midfielder who likes to play in the middle of the park and spray the ball about. Freed by Portsmouth last November, he had a short spell as a non-contract player with Swansea, before signing for Northampton.

Portsmouth (£25,000 from Cheltenham T on 15/3/91) FL 78+12/9 FLC 7+2/2 FAC 7 Others 9+1/1
Swansea C (Loaned on 17/12/93) FL 4 Others 1/1
Bournemouth (Loaned on 11/3/94) FL 13+1/1
Swansea C (Free on 25/11/94) FL 3+2 FAC 0+1
Northampton T (Free on 13/1/95) FL 16+1/2

BURRIDGE John
Born: Workington, 3 December 1951
Height: 5'11" Weight: 13.3
Club Honours: FLC '77; Div 2 '79; SLC '91

An amazing 43-year-old goalkeeper who played in the Premiership in 1994-95 for Manchester City when Tony Coton was indisposed. John is not the oldest player to have appeared for City, Billy Meredith holds that record, but he is surely the oldest debutant. Signed from Dumbarton last October, and ahead of Martyn Margetson as second choice 'keeper, after coming on for the injured Coton against Newcastle and maintaining a clean sheet in a 1-1 draw, he played out the remaining three games of the season prior to being listed in the summer.

Workington (From apprentice on 2/1/70) FL 27 FLC 1 FAC 4
Blackpool (£10,000 on 1/4/71) FL 134 FLC 10 FAC 4 Others 17
Aston Villa (£100,000 on 1/9/75) FL 65 FLC 9 FAC 6
Southend U (Loaned on 20/1/78) FL 6
Crystal Palace (£65,000 on 9/3/78) FL 88 FLC 7 FAC 7
Queens Park R (£200,000 on 19/12/80) FL 39 FLC 4 FAC 2
Wolverhampton W (£75,000 on 26/8/82) FL 74 FLC 2 FAC 5
Derby Co (Loaned on 21/9/84) FL 6 FLC 2
Sheffield U (£10,000 on 26/10/84) FL 109 FLC 6 FAC 6 Others 4

Southampton (£30,000 on 11/8/87) FL 62 FLC 7 FAC 4 Others 2
Newcastle U (£25,000 on 3/10/89) FL 67 FLC 4 FAC 7 Others 5
Hibernian (Free during 1991 close season) SL 65 SLC 5 SC 5 Others 2
Newcastle U (Free on 13/8/93)
Scarborough (Free on 29/10/93) FL 3 Others 1
Lincoln C (Free on 24/12/93) FL 4
Aberdeen (Free in March 1994) SL 3 SC 1
Dumbarton (Free in October 1994) SL 3
Manchester C (Free on 15/12/94) PL 3+1

John Burridge   Paul Marriott
(Empics Sports Photo Agency)

BURROWS David
Born: Dudley, 25 October 1968
Height: 5'10" Weight: 11.8
Club Honours: CS '89 '90; Div 1 '90; FAC '92
International Honours: E: B-3; U21-7
Started last season as a West Ham player, before moving, first to Everton in September, and then to Coventry in March, just 23 games later. A hard-tackling left-back who can also play in central defence if required, David is always on the look-out for shooting opportunities when getting down down the flank. Signed by Ron Atkinson to help in Coventry's relegation struggle, his experience and skill had an immediate impact on the side as he quickly built up a good understanding with Peter Ndlovu. Looks to be an excellent signing for the "Sky Blues".
West Bromwich A (From apprentice on 8/11/86) FL 37+9/1 FLC 3+1 FAC 2 Others 1
Liverpool (£550,000 on 20/10/88) F/PL 135+11/3 FLC 16 FAC 16+1 Others 14
West Ham U (Signed on 17/9/93) PL 29/1 FLC 3/1 FAC 3
Everton (Signed on 6/9/94) PL 19 FLC 2 FAC 2
Coventry C (£1,100,000 on 2/3/95) PL 11

BURTON Deon John
Born: Reading, 25 October 1976
Height: 5'8" Weight: 11.9
A striker with no little skill and a finishing ability, after making his Portsmouth first team debut in 1993-94, Deon continued his good form at youth and reserve team levels, while getting only fleeting opportunities in the first team last season. As a first year

professional, he helped the youth team to the third round of the FA Youth Cup and to the semi-finals of the Southern Junior Floodlit Cup.
Portsmouth (From trainee on 15/2/94) FL 6+3/2 FLC 0+1

BURTON Nicholas (Nicky) John
Born: Bury, 10 February 1975
Height: 5'11" Weight: 11.12
A Torquay central defender who has been tremendously unlucky with a number of quite serious injuries, he was transferred to non-league, Yeovil, at the end of last season.
Torquay U (Free from Portsmouth juniors on 13/8/93) FL 14+2/2 FLC 2 FAC 0+1 Others 2

BUSHELL Stephen (Steve) Paul
Born: Manchester, 28 December 1972
Height: 5'7" Weight: 10.5
Another York player who missed most of last season through injury, Steve is a skilful and tireless midfield dynamo. His absence was keenly felt, not only for his ability, but also for an infectious enthusiasm which runs through the side.
York C (From trainee on 25/2/91) FL 73+7/5 FLC 2 FAC 2 Others 6/1

BUSST David John
Born: Birmingham, 30 June 1967
Height: 6'1" Weight: 12.10
With Peter Atherton and Phil Babb sold, David took the opportunity handed to him to make the Coventry centre-half position his own and, until his injury against Forest on Boxing Day, was an ever-present in 1994-95. Excellent in the air and improving on the ground, he scored two good headed goals against Wimbledon and West Ham. Unfortunately, a groin injury kept him out for the rest of the season and his big test will come in 1995-96.
Coventry C (Free from Moor Green on 14/1/92) F/PL 32+1/2 FLC 3+1 FAC 0+1

BUTLER Philip Anthony (Tony)
Born: Stockport, 28 September 1972
Height: 6'2" Weight: 12.0
Central defender. An outstanding prospect, Tony has made nearly 150 first team appearances since turning professional with Gillingham and is a dominant force in the air.
Gillingham (From trainee on 13/5/91) FL 108+4/3 FLC 10 FAC 11 Others 3+1

BUTLER John Edward
Born: Liverpool, 7 February 1962
Height: 5'11" Weight: 11.7
Club Honours: AMC '92; Div 2 '93
Another excellent season at Stoke for the always committed John Butler in 1994-95, he was asked to play in a number of various positions and coped well. In his element as a positive overlapping full-back, he also turned out at centre-back and in midfield.
Wigan Ath (Free from Prescot Cables on 15/1/82) FL 238+7/15 FLC 17+1 FAC 20+1/2 Others 18
Stoke C (£75,000 on 23/12/88) FL 258+4/7 FLC 19 FAC 11 Others 26+1/2

BUTLER Lee Simon
Born: Sheffield, 30 May 1966
Height: 6'2" Weight: 13.0

Lee's 1994-95 season was one of patience, having lost out in the goalkeeping selection stakes to David Watson. Had to wait until November to make his first appearance and while in the team Barnsley enjoyed a fine run. However, once Watson was fit, he returned to the bench.
Lincoln C (Free from Haworth Colliery on 16/6/86) FL 30 FLC 1 FAC 1
Aston Villa (£100,000 on 21/8/87) FL 8 Others 2
Hull C (Loaned on 18/3/91) FL 4
Barnsley (£165,000 on 22/7/91) FL 117 FLC 5 FAC 9 Others 4

BUTLER Martin Neil
Born: Wordsley, 15 September 1974
Height: 5'10" Weight: 11.3
A lively young Walsall striker, who scored three goals in the final month of 1993-94 and who is equally happy on the left-flank or in the centre. Only played 13 games for the club last season, but netted twice in the first round FA Cup win over Rochdale.
Walsall (From trainee on 24/5/93) FL 10+13/3 FLC 0+1 FAC 1+2/2 Others 1

BUTLER Paul John
Born: Manchester, 2 November 1972
Height: 6'2" Weight: 13.0
Central defender who blossomed into a mainstay of the Rochdale side last season, forming an excellent partnership with Peter Valentine, which led to the club conceding only five goals in 12 league games after the New Year. And, as "Dale's" longest (continuously) currently serving player, he was voted "Player of the Year".
Rochdale (From trainee on 5/7/91) FL 113+7/7 FLC 6+1 FAC 3+2 Others 9+1

BUTLER Peter James
Born: Halifax, 27 August 1966
Height: 5'9" Weight: 11.1
A general midfielder, who is both a good tackler and passer of the ball, Peter joined Notts County from Premier League side, West Ham, last October. Came straight into the team and played 24 consecutive games before being stretchered off with a leg injury against Stoke in the semi-final of the Anglo-Italian Cup. Happily recovered, he came back for three of the last four matches.
Huddersfield T (From apprentice on 21/8/84) FL 0+5
Cambridge U (Loaned on 24/1/86) FL 14/1 Others 1
Bury (Free on 8/7/86) FL 9+2 FLC 2/1 FAC 1
Cambridge U (Free on 10/12/86) FL 55/9 FLC 4 FAC 2 Others 2
Southend U (£75,000 on 12/2/88) FL 135+7/9 FLC 12/1 FAC 2 Others 11/2
Huddersfield T (Loaned on 24/3/92) FL 7
West Ham U (£125,000 on 12/8/92) F/PL 70/3 FLC 4 FAC 3 Others 1
Notts Co (£350,000 on 4/10/94) FL 20 FLC 2 FAC 2 Others 3

BUTLER Stephen (Steve)
Born: Birmingham, 27 January 1962
Height: 6'2" Weight: 13.6
Club Honours: GMVC '89
International Honours: E: SP-3
After scoring 21 goals for Cambridge in the 1993-94 season, including two hat-tricks and five in one game, the goals continued to

flow from this experienced centre-forward who, together with Carlo Corazzin, formed one of the most deadly strike pairings in the division.
Brentford (Free from Windsor & Eton on 19/12/84) FL 18+3/3 Others 2
Maidstone U (Free on 1/8/86) FL 76/41 FLC 4/3 FAC 18/7 Others 10/4
Watford (£150,000 on 28/3/91) FL 40+22/9 FLC 4+3 FAC 1 Others 2+1
Bournemouth (Loaned on 18/12/92) FL 1
Cambridge U (£75,000 on 23/12/92) FL 91+2/41 FLC 4+1 FAC 5/4 Others 3

BUTT Nicholas (Nicky)
Born: Manchester, 21 January 1975
Height: 5'10" Weight: 11.0
Club Honours: FAYC '92
International Honours: E: U21; Yth (UEFA Yth '93); Sch
A central midfielder with excellent communication skills, Nicky often pops up to score important goals from vital positions. In 1994-95, he yet again belied his years to give Manchester United a series of solid midfield performances, and was one of the great successes of the "Reds'" shortlived European Cup campaign, gaining valuable experience in opposing players like Romario, Hagi and Stoichkov. Appears to have a wonderful future ahead of him.
Manchester U (From trainee on 29/1/93) PL 11+13/1 FLC 3 FAC 3+2 Others 5+1

BUTTERS Guy
Born: Hillingdon, 30 October 1969
Height: 6'3" Weight: 13.0
International Honours: E: U21-3
Uncompromising defender, solid in the tackle, good in the air, and with a strong left-foot, Guy had a disappointing start to last season, being left out until December, during which time he had a period on loan at Oxford. On his return, the team started to improve and tightened up defensively, with Guy building a good understanding with Kit Symons and Jon Gittens in the absence of Andy Awford at the back.
Tottenham H (From trainee on 5/8/88) FL 34+1/1 FLC 2+1 FAC 1
Southend U (Loaned on 13/1/90) FL 16/3 Others 2
Portsmouth (£375,000 on 28/9/90) FL 104+6/4 FLC 11+1/1 FAC 6 Others 7+2
Oxford U (Loaned on 4/11/94) FL 3/1 Others 1

BYNG David Graeme
Born: Coventry, 9 July 1977
Height: 6'1" Weight: 11.10
A second year Torquay YTS, and one for the future, David has an excellent build for a striker and has well earned a full contract.
Torquay U (Trainee) FL 8+2/3 FLC 0+1

BYRNE John Frederick
Born: Manchester, 1 February 1961
Height: 6'0" Weight: 12.4
Club Honours: Div 4 '84
International Honours: Ei: 23
A popular forward who rejoined Brighton towards the end of last February, after being allowed to leave Oxford due to personal problems. Made an early impression with his fine control and deft touches, as well as scoring some valuable goals. Nicknamed "Budgie".
York C (From apprentice on 31/1/79) FL 167+8/55 FLC 10+2/5 FAC 10+1/3 Others 1
Queens Park R (£115,000 on 30/10/84) FL 108+18/30 FLC 12+1/4 FAC 7+2/2 Others 1 (£175,000 to Le Havre in May 1988)
Brighton & Hove A (£120,000 on 1/9/90) FL 47+4/14 FLC 2/2 FAC 2/2 Others 2+1
Sunderland (£225,000 on 23/10/91) FL 33/8 FLC 2 FAC 8/7
Millwall (£250,000 on 28/10/92) FL 12+5/1
Brighton & Hove A (Loaned on 25/3/93) FL 5+2/2
Oxford U (£50,000 on 1/11/93) FL 52+3/17 FLC 4 FAC 5/2 Others 2
Brighton & Hove A (Free on 24/2/95) FL 14/4

BYRNE Paul Peter
Born: Dublin, 30 June 1972
Height: 5'11" Weight: 13.0
International Honours: Ei: Yth
On loan from Glasgow Celtic last season, he was used in a midfield role where he turned in some useful performances for Brighton and scored a great goal from 40 yards at Rotherham. Returned home after the Hull game on 8 April.
Oxford U (From trainee on 4/7/89) FL 4+2 (Free to Bangor in September 1991)
Glasgow Celtic (Signed on 26/5/93) SL 24+5/3 SLC 1 SC 1
Brighton & Hove A (Loaned on 10/3/95) FL 8/1

BYRNE Raymond (Ray)
Born: Newry, 4 July 1972
Height: 6'1" Weight: 11.2
Clever midfield player with excellent ball control, his potential was spotted while playing in Ireland and he signed for Forest along with Roy Keane. Joined Northampton prior to the start of last season, but was soon released.
Nottingham F (Free from Newry on 22/2/91)
Northampton T (Free on 8/8/94) FL 2 FLC 1

BYRNE Wesley John
Born: Dublin, 9 February 1977
Height: 5'10" Weight: 11.6
International Honours: Ei: Yth; Sch
Right-back. Another strong-tackling Middlesbrough youngster, whose greatest asset is his tremendous speed from a standing start. Strong and fearless in the tackle and accurate in the pass, he shows up well on the overlap.
Middlesbrough (From trainee on 24/2/94) Others 1

CADETTE Richard Raymond
Born: Hammersmith, 21 March 1965
Height: 5'8" Weight: 11.7
Club Honours: B&QC '94
Pacy Millwall striker with a gift for turning defenders, Richard is right-footed with good close ball control. Signed after a spell on loan from Falkirk, a knee injury and subsequent operation have sidelined him since last February. Scored three times in his first four games, the highlight being the late winner against his old club, Sheffield United, at the Den.
Leyton Orient (Free from Wembley on 25/8/84) FL 19+2/4 FLC 4 FAC 1/1 Others 2
Southend U (Free on 15/8/85) FL 90/49 FLC 5+1/1 FAC 4/5 Others 5/1
Sheffield U (£130,000 on 20/7/87) FL 26+2/7 FLC 1 FAC 2 Others 2
Brentford (£80,000 on 22/7/88) FL 67+20/20

FLC 10+3/6 FAC 9/1 Others 14/4
Bournemouth (Loaned on 22/3/90) FL 4+4/1
Falkirk (Signed on 9/1/92) SL 74+10/29 SLC 3+1/4 SC 5+1/1 Others 4/6
Millwall (£135,000 on 13/10/94) FL 12+4/4 FLC 2/1 FAC 1

CAESAR Gus Cassius
Born: Tottenham, 5 March 1966
Height: 6'0" Weight: 12.7
International Honours: E: U21-3
A free transfer signing in the summer of 1994, Gus was a regular in the Colchester back four all last season. Having added his experience to what was otherwise at times a very young defence, he even treated the fans to a rare goal at Easter!
Arsenal (From apprentice on 10/2/84) FL 27+17 FLC 2+3 FAC 0+1
Queens Park R (Loaned on 28/11/90) FL 5
Cambridge U (Free on 31/7/91)
Bristol C (Free on 6/9/91) FL 9+1 FLC 1 FAC 1 Others 1
Airdrie (Free on 30/1/92) SL 57/1 SLC 3 SC 5+1 Others 1
Colchester U (Free on 11/8/94) FL 39/1 FLC 2 FAC 4 Others 2

CAHILL Oliver (Ollie) Francis
Born: Clonmell, 29 September, 1975
Height: 5'10" Weight: 11.2
Ball playing left-winger, not fast but tricky who likes to take on his man. Spotted in Ireland by Northampton's youth team coach, he signed last September after a trial.
Northampton T (Signed from Clonmel on 2/9/94) FL 5+3/1 Others 1+2

CAIG Antony (Tony)
Born: Whitehaven, 11 April 1974
Height: 6'1" Weight: 12.0
Club Honours: Div 3 '95
Having become Carlisle's first choice goalkeeper only midway through the previous campaign, 1994-95 was his first full season of League football. Yet his achievement of playing at Wembley in the AWS Final and helping set a new club record for the fewest goals conceded in a season is the stuff of which dreams are made. An excellent shot-stopper, he has worked hard on other areas of his game under the guidance of coach, Mervyn Day. Won a Third Division Championship medal.
Carlisle U (From trainee on 10/7/92) FL 61 FLC 4 FAC 6 Others 13

CALDERWOOD Colin
Born: Stranraer, 20 January 1965
Height: 6'0" Weight: 12.0
Club Honours: Div 4 '86
International Honours: S: 5
Began last season in midfield for Tottenham, a position in which he never really developed. The appointment of Gerry Francis in mid-November, however, saw him take up his favoured position in central defence, where his consistency and strength began to tighten up a disorganised defence. His work-rate and great ability in the air kept him his place alongside Sol Campbell for the rest of the season. Clinched a goal to earn Tottenham a draw away at Nottingham Forest in March, a game that saw a frenzy of action in the last ten minutes, and further

consistent performances earned him a call-up to the Scottish International side in March, where he made his debut in the European Championships against Russia.

Mansfield T (Signed on 19/3/82) FL 97+3/1 FLC 4 FAC 6/1 Others 7
Swindon T (£30,000 on 1/7/85) FL 328+2/20 FLC 35 FAC 17/1 Others 32
Tottenham H (£1,250,000 on 22/7/93) PL 61+1/2 FLC 6 FAC 9

CALVERT Mark Robert
Born: Consett, 11 September 1970
Height: 5'9" Weight: 11.8

Consistent and inspirational Scarborough midfield player, and a former team captain. His outstanding form towards the end of last season was a major factor in "Boro's" successful bid to avoid bottom position in the Football League.

Hull C (From trainee on 1/7/89) FL 24+6/1 FLC 1+1 Others 2+1
Scarborough (Free on 4/8/93) FL 68+4/5 FLC 6 FAC 2+1 Others 3+1/1

CAME Mark Raymond
Born: Exeter, 14 September 1961
Height: 6'0" Weight: 13.0

Exeter team captain and a leader by example, Mark is an asset at corners and wins most things in the air. Last season, his first at the club, having been signed from Chester during the summer of 1994, he forged a good defensive partnership with Jon Richardson and helped his young team-mate mature considerably.

Bolton W (Signed from Winsford U on 28/4/84) FL 188+7/7 FLC 15+4/2 FAC 16+2 Others 27/2
Chester C (Signed on 4/12/92) FL 47/1 FLC 2 FAC 3 Others 6/1
Exeter C (Free on 14/7/94) FL 32/1 FLC 2 FAC 1 Others 1

CAMPBELL David (Dave) Anthony
Born: Londonderry, 2 June 1965
Height: 5'9" Weight: 10.9
International Honours: NI: 10

A former Northern Ireland international midfielder, David was released by Burnley during the 1994 close season, signing on a monthly contract for Wigan. After leaving Springfield Park, he joined Cambridge as a non-contract player, but his first game for the club ended prematurely, a broken leg sidelining him.

Nottingham F (From apprentice on 1/6/83) FL 35+6/3 FLC 4/2 FAC 0+1
Notts Co (Loaned on 12/2/87) FL 18/2
Charlton Ath (£75,000 on 9/10/87) FL 26+4/1 FLC 3 FAC 1+1 Others 2
Plymouth Arg (Loaned on 9/3/89) FL 1
Bradford C (£75,000 on 17/3/89) FL 27+8/4 FLC 2 FAC 0+1 Others 0+1 (Free to Derry C on 14/12/90)
Rotherham U (Free on 11/11/92) FL 0+1 Others 1
West Bromwich A (Free on 10/2/93)
Burnley (Free on 19/3/93) FL 7+1
Lincoln C (Loaned on 7/2/94) FL 2+2/1 Others 1
Wigan Ath (Free on 29/7/94) FL 7 FLC 4
Cambridge U (Free on 27/1/95) FL 1

CAMBELL Jamie
Born: Birmingham, 21 October 1972
Height: 6'1" Weight: 11.3

A utility player who, in the past, has been used by Luton as a striker, in midfield, and

in defence. However, there was no place for him with the "Hatters" last season and he had a spell on loan at Mansfield in November, prior to seeing out the campaign on a similar basis at Cambridge. Freed during the summer, this hard-working player should have no difficulty finding a suitable club.

Luton T (From trainee on 1/7/91) FL 10+26/1 FLC 1+1 FAC 1+3 Others 1+2
Mansfield T (Loaned on 25/11/94) FL 3/1 FAC 2
Cambridge U (Loaned on 10/3/95) FL 12

CAMPBELL Kevin Joseph
Born: Lambeth, 4 February 1970
Height: 6'0" Weight: 13.1
Club Honours: FAYC '88; FLC '93; FAC '93; ECWC '94
International Honours: E: B-1; U21-4

More effective in the role of central striker, he was yet another Arsenal player whose season ended prematurely, due to injury, in 1994-95. With the build of a pro boxer, terrific pace, two useful feet, and good in the air, Kevin still has every chance to reach the very top of the tree if he gets an extended run in the side. Can set up others as well as scoring himself.

Arsenal (From trainee on 11/2/88) F/PL 124+42/46 FLC 14+10/6 FAC 13+6/2 Others 15+4/5
Leyton Orient (Loaned on 16/1/89) FL 16/9
Leicester C (Loaned on 8/11/89) FL 11/5 Others 1/1

CAMPBELL Sulzeer (Sol) Jeremiah
Born: Newham, 18 September 1974
Height: 6'1" Weight: 12.10
International Honours: E: B-1; U21-9; Yth (UEFA Yth '93); Sch

Sol, whose natural position is in midfield, was Tottenham's first choice in central defence for all but one game between the beginning of last season and up until injury struck in March. His great awareness and ability to make surging forward runs, were frequently the source of attacks resulting in goals. Among the most memorable was the run which produced an own goal by former "Spurs'" player, Neil Ruddock, at Anfield in November to give the club a much deserved 1-1 draw. Throughout the season, he demonstrated his athleticism and displayed creative skills in the middle of the field, his consistency earning him a call-up for the full England squad for the game against the Republic of Ireland in Dublin.

Tottenham H (From trainee on 23/9/92) PL 66+9/1 FLC 8/1 FAC 4+2

CANHAM Anthony (Tony)
Born: Leeds, 8 June 1960
Height: 5'7" Weight: 11.0

Experienced York campaigner who has been at the club over ten years. During last season he made his 400th senior appearance - only the sixth player in York's history to reach this milestone. Tony, a skilful ball player who on his day can trouble the best of defences, was surprisingly released during the summer.

York C (Free from Harrogate RI on 16/1/85) FL 309+38/57 FLC 18/2 FAC 20/6 Others 24+4/4

CANTONA Eric
Born: Marseille, France, 24 May 1966
Height: 6'1" Weight: 13.7
Club Honours: French Div 1 '90; French Cup '89, '90; Div 1 '92; PL '93, '94; CS '93, '94; FAC '94
International Honours: France

The PFA "Player of the Year" in 1994, he is an exceptionally gifted Manchester United striker, who has an excellent "football" brain, and is very quick off the mark, with a repertoire of skills that leaves defenders standing. He is also capable of scoring spectacular goals. Eric's mid-season ban, following the well documented controversial incident at Crystal Palace last January, robbed United of their leading scorer and most inspirational player. Before the ban, his early season performances had been of the highest order, and the "Reds" clearly missed his subtle flicks, deft touches, and remarkable vision. Although most of his 14 goals had the hallmark of class, his brilliant lob against Sheffield United in the FA Cup was the most memorable. Meanwhile, Eric, unavailable for first team action until October, has already pledged his support to United, despite overtures from Inter Milan and a host of other European clubs, and signed a new three year contract in April.

Leeds U (£900,000 from Nimes on 6/2/92) F/PL 18+10/9 FLC 1 Others 6/5
Manchester U (£1,200,000 on 27/11/92) PL 76+1/39 FLC 5/1 FAC 7/5 Others 8/3

CAPLETON Melvyn (Mel) David
Born: London, 24 October 1973
Height: 6'0" Weight: 12.8

Signed before the 1993-94 season got underway, he finally made his Blackpool debut at Chester last November when coming on for the injured Lee Martin. "Man of the Match" on his full debut, a week later, he was dropped following the 7-1 defeat at Birmingham. A lively personality, and popular with the fans.

Southend U (From trainee on 1/7/92)
Blackpool (Free on 1/8/93) FL 8+2

CARBON Matthew (Matt)
Born: Nottingham, 8 June 1975
Height: 6'2" Weight: 12.4

Fine young Lincoln prospect who switched from a midfield/defensive role to striker last season and scored some excellent goals, including a 30 yard lob over the Darlington 'keeper in a 3-1 victory. A left-footed player, his good ball control skills and an ability to "hang" in the air when reaching for crosses, make him reminiscent of the young Mick Harford.

Lincoln C (From trainee on 13/4/93) FL 40+3/7 FLC 3/1 FAC 3 Others 2+2

CAREY Alan William
Born: Greenwich, 21 August 1975
Height: 5'7" Weight: 10.2

Graduate of Reading's youth scheme, having been recommended by the club's scout in Tipperary. A regular scorer in youth football, first team opportunities have been limited by the excellent form of other

Eric Cantona

Neal Simpson
(Empics Sports Photo Agency)

strikers. Alan did well in his two substitute appearances last season and although loaned out to Weymouth for a while, may well be a name for the future.

Reading (From trainee on 20/7/94) FL 0+3

CAREY Brian Patrick
Born: Cork, 31 May 1968
Height: 6'3" Weight: 13.9
International Honours: Ei: 7; U21-1

Right-footed Leicester central defender, Brian was unlucky to be shown the red card in his seasonal debut at Wimbledon in 1994-95. Regained a first team place in March to plug a leaking defence and retained it in a five man back-line until the end of the season.

Manchester U (£100,000 from Cork C on 2/9/89)
Wrexham (Loaned on 17/1/91) FL 3
Wrexham (Loaned on 24/12/91) FL 13/1 FAC 3 Others 3

Leicester C (£250,000 on 16/7/93) F/PL 35+4 FLC 1 FAC 0+1 Others 4

CARMICHAEL Matthew (Matt)
Born: Singapore, 13 May 1964
Height: 6'2" Weight: 11.7

Arriving at Preston last March, former squaddie, Matt, scored twice on his debut against Bury. A good finisher, who is strong on the ball and in the air, he is an ideal tall target man and can also play at both full-back and centre-half. Apart from appearing for Scunthorpe in 1994-95, he spent a period on loan at Barnet, before coming to Deepdale and being freed at the end of the season.

Lincoln C (Free from Basingstoke T on 8/8/89) FL 113+20/18 FLC 9+1/1 FAC 4+1 Others 7+1/2
Scunthorpe U (Free on 16/7/93) FL 51+11/20 FLC 1+1 FAC 4+3/2 Others 5/5
Barnet (Loaned on 23/9/94) FL 2+1
Preston NE (Free on 10/3/95) FL 7+3/3

CARPENTER Richard
Born: Sheerness, 30 September 1972
Height: 6'0" Weight: 13.0

Former captain of Gillingham's youth team, he has a sweet right-foot which he puts to good use at free-kicks from his midfield position. Richard missed six weeks of last season during the early part of 1995 through a knee injury.

Gillingham (From trainee on 13/5/91) FL 99+10/4 FLC 2+1 FAC 9 Others 5/1

CARR Darren John
Born: Bristol, 4 September 1968
Height: 6'2" Weight: 13.0

This giant of a man suffered early problems last season in the post-World Cup referees' clampdown, but then emerged as a commanding figure at the heart of Chesterfield's defence. Overwhelmingly strong in the air, and in the tackle, Darren was voted the supporters' "Player of the Year" as the club reached the Second Division, via the play-offs.

Bristol Rov (From trainee on 20/8/86) FL 26+4 FLC 2+2 FAC 3 Others 2
Newport Co (£3,000 on 30/10/87) FL 9
Sheffield U (£8,000 on 10/3/88) FL 12+1/1 FLC 1 FAC 3+1 Others 1
Crewe Alex (£35,000 on 18/9/90) FL 96+8/5 FLC 8 FAC 12/2 Others 10
Chesterfield (£30,000 on 21/7/93) FL 63/3 FLC 7 FAC 3 Others 7

CARR Franz Alexander
Born: Preston, 24 September 1966
Height: 5'7" Weight: 10.12
Club Honours: FMC '89; FLC '90
International Honours: E: U21-9; Yth

Tricky right-sided wide player. Began last season out of favour at Sheffield United, his only appearance coming in the Anglo-Italian Cup in Piacenza, where a stunning goal earned a permanent move to Leicester, following a spell on loan. Shone in a City victory over Southampton, before linking up with former manager, Brian Little, at Aston Villa, in a deal that took Garry Parker in the opposite direction.

Blackburn Rov (From apprentice on 30/7/84)
Nottingham F (£100,000 on 2/8/84) FL 122+9/17 FLC 16+2/5 FAC 4 Others 5+2/1
Sheffield Wed (Loaned on 22/12/89) FL 9+3 FAC 2
West Ham U (Loaned on 11/3/91) FL 1+2
Newcastle U (£250,000 on 13/6/91) FL 20+5/3 FLC 2+2 Others 3+1
Sheffield U (£120,000 on 12/1/93) P/FL 18/4 FAC 4 Others 1/1
Leicester C (£100,000 on 8/9/94) PL 12+1/1
Aston Villa (£250,000 on 10/2/95) PL 0+2

CARRAGHER Matthew
Born: Liverpool, 14 January 1976
Height: 5'9" Weight: 10.7

A product of Wigan's youth policy, the attacking right-back only missed one League match throughout last season, attracting the attention of several Premier League clubs. In his first full season as a professional, his performances were rewarded when winning the club's "Young Player of the Year" award for the second year running.

Wigan Ath (From trainee on 25/11/93) FL 68+5 FLC 3/1 FAC 6/2 Others 5+1

41

CARROLL David (Dave) Francis
Born: Paisley, 20 September 1966
Height: 6'0" Weight: 12.0
Club Honours: FAT '91, '93; GMVC '93
International Honours: E: Sch
Two-footed right-winger who can play anywhere in midfield or attack, he is perhaps the most skilful player at Wycombe, with excellent close ball control, dangerous with free-kicks and corners, and the scorer of several important goals last season. His 339 first team appearances have taken him into the top 20 all-time appearances for the club.
Wycombe W (£6,000 from Ruislip Manor in 1988 close season) FL 82/12 FLC 6 FAC 15/3 Others 8/3

Martin Carruthers   Barrington Coombs
(Empics Sports Photo Agency)

CARRUTHERS Martin George
Born: Nottingham, 7 August 1972
Height: 5'11" Weight: 11.9
Into his second season at Stoke, he clearly worked hard in 1994-95 at developing the physical strength necessary to maintain a position in a First Division attack. As a pacy, left-footed striker with a high workrate and commitment, who is still trying hard to achieve the potential Lou Macari saw in him when he snapped him up from Aston Villa, he is intent on going all the way. His former manager, Ron Atkinson has been heard to comment that every time he sees Carruthers play he realises how Macari "stole" him!
Aston Villa (From trainee on 4/7/90) F/PL 2+2 FAC 0+1 Others 0+1
Hull C (Loaned on 31/10/92) FL 13/6 Others 3
Stoke C (£300,000 on 5/7/93) FL 50+16/10 FLC 4+2/1 FAC 2+1 Others 8+3/6

CARSLEY Lee Kevin
Born: Birmingham, 28 February 1974
Height: 5'11" Weight: 11.11
Versatile and energetic Derby midfielder who made quick progress from the youth team to first eleven in a matter of months last season. Scored twice in his first three games during September and, on the verge of a Republic of Ireland U21 cap, he received a knee ligament injury against Bolton in February. Can also play

effectively as a defender.
Derby Co (From trainee on 6/7/92) FL 22+1/2 FLC 3+1 FAC 1 Others 3

CARTER Darren (Danny) Stephen
Born: Hackney, 29 June 1969
Height: 5'11" Weight: 11.12
A tricky right-winger, or midfielder, with the ability to take on defenders and cross with accuracy, Danny's season was ruined by uncertainty. Omitted from the Orient side at the start of 1994-95, due to failure to sign a new contract, he was only recalled when results went against the club. He then missed the middle of the campaign through an ankle injury and despite the interest of a host of clubs, including Luton and Southend, he remained at Brisbane Road.
Leyton Orient (Signed from Billericay T on 4/7/88) FL 168+20/22 FLC 13+3/2 FAC 10/3 Others 17+2/1

CARTER James (Jimmy) William Charles
Born: Hammersmith, 9 November 1965
Height: 5'10" Weight: 10.4
Club Honours: Div 2 '88
A tricky Arsenal right-winger with a good turn of pace, Jimmy has the ability to knock balls past the full-back to get in telling crosses. With opportunities still limited at the club, he was loaned out to Oxford last December, making three FL starts, before returning to Highbury. Released at the end of 1994-95.
Crystal Palace (From apprentice on 15/11/83)
Queens Park R (Free on 30/9/85)
Millwall (£15,000 on 12/3/87) FL 99+11/10 FLC 6+1 FAC 6+1/2 Others 5+1
Liverpool (£800,000 on 10/1/91) FL 2+3 FAC 2 Others 0+1
Arsenal (£500,000 on 8/10/91) F/PL 18+7/2 FLC 1 FAC 2+1
Oxford U (Loaned on 23/3/94) FL 5
Oxford U (Loaned on 23/12/94) FL 3+1

Mark Carter   Barrington Coombs
(Empics Sports Photo Agency)

CARTER Mark Colin
Born: Liverpool, 17 December 1960
Height: 5'9" Weight: 11.6
International Honours: E: SP-11

A prolific scorer for Bury, Mark was yet again savaged by injury. Scored 11 times in the opening 14 games, before a serious knee problem halted his progress and, while he re-appeared in December, it was soon apparent that the trouble had not cleared up. Following further treatment, he was back in time for the play-offs, but was unable to influence the scorelines.
Barnet (£40,000 from Runcorn on 20/2/91) FL 62+20/30 FLC 5/2 FAC 4+1/6 Others 7+2/8
Bury (£6,000 on 10/9/93) FL 57+5/34 FLC 2/1 FAC 3 Others 8+1

CARTER Timothy (Tim) Douglas
Born: Bristol, 5 October 1967
Height: 6'2" Weight: 13.11
International Honours: E: Yth
Competent understudy to Kasey Keller at Millwall, his appearances between the posts in 1994-95 were restricted to a mere handful, and he was released at the end of the season.
Bristol Rov (From apprentice on 8/10/85) FL 47 FLC 2 FAC 2 Others 2
Newport Co (Loaned on 14/12/87) FL 1
Sunderland (£50,000 on 24/12/87) FL 37 FLC 9 Others 4
Carlisle U (Loaned on 18/3/88) FL 4
Bristol C (Loaned on 15/9/88) FL 3
Birmingham C (Loaned on 21/11/91) FL 2 FLC 1
Hartlepool U (Free on 1/8/92) FL 18 FLC 4 FAC 1 Others 2
Millwall (Free on 6/1/94) FL 4 FLC 0+1

CARTWRIGHT Lee
Born: Rawtenstall, 19 September 1972
Height: 5'8" Weight: 10.8
Midfield dynamo, much of whose work goes unnoticed, Lee is Preston's longest serving player. Makes strong runs at pace in support of the attack, is a strong tackler, good passer of the ball, and a tight marker.
Preston NE (From trainee on 30/7/91) FL 138+18/10 FLC 6/1 FAC 11 Others 9+2

Jimmy Case   Neal Simpson
(Empics Sports Photo Agency)

CASE James (Jimmy) Robert
Born: Liverpool, 18 May 1954
Height: 5'9" Weight: 12.5
Club Honours: Div 1 '76, '77, '79, '80; ESC '77; EC '77, '78, '81; FLC '81
International Honours: E: U23-1

Early outings usually found Jimmy in a central midfield role, encouraging the younger players around him and using the ball as effectively as ever. However, the Brighton coach was frustratingly out of action for much of the season with injury and his vast experience was sorely missed. A nerve problem in the right buttock kept him sidelined for two months before Christmas and a brief re-appearance was followed by another lengthy absence caused by an Achilles heel injury. The highlight of the season was his benefit match at the Goldstone on 17 October against Liverpool. A wonderful 15,645 crowd turned out to pay tribute to a popular and respected player. Released during the summer.

Liverpool (Signed from South Liverpool on 1/5/73) FL 170+16/23 FLC 21+1/3 FAC 20+1/7 Others 28+3/13
Brighton & Hove A (£350,000 on 19/8/81) FL 124+3/10 FLC 8 FAC 13+1/5
Southampton (£30,000 on 20/3/85) FL 213+2/10 FLC 34/2 FAC 15/1 Others 7/1
Bournemouth (Free on 25/7/91) FL 38+2/1 FLC 3 FAC 5 Others 2/1
Halifax T (Free on 16/5/92) FL 17+4/2 FLC 1 FAC 1
Wrexham (Free on 26/2/93) FL 1+3
Darlington (Free on 22/10/93) FL 1 (Free to Sittingbourne in December 1993)
Brighton & Hove A (Free on 30/12/93) FL 30 FLC 2

CASKEY Darren Mark
Born: Basildon, 21 August 1974
Height: 5'8" Weight: 11.9
International Honours: E: Yth (UEFAYC '93); Sch
A natural midfielder, Darren made his first appearances of 1994-95 for Tottenham as a substitute for Jurgen Klinsmann, after the German had been knocked out by the knee of Aston Villa goalkeeper, Mark Bosnich, last January. Caskey's skills lie in his commitment, strong-tackling, and general enthusiasm for the game.
Tottenham H (From trainee on 6/3/92) PL 17+12/4 FLC 3+1/1 FAC 3+1

CASPER Christopher (Chris) Martin
Born: Burnley, 28 April 1975
Height: 5'11" Weight: 10.9
Club Honours: FAYC '92
International Honours: E: U21-1; Yth (EUFAC '93)
The son of former Burnley striker, Frank, Chris is a promising Manchester United central defender, who possesses excellent passing skills, reads the game well and likes to come from the back to set up effective counter-attacks. Showed excellent promise when making his first team debut against Port Vale in the Coca Cola Cup last season, and built on that with an England U21 appearance during the summer.
Manchester U (From trainee on 3/2/93) FLC 1

CASTLE Stephen (Steve) Charles
Born: Barking, 17 May 1966
Height: 5'11" Weight: 12.5
Plymouth's captain missed most of last season through jaundice and it is probably no coincidence that the club's position reflected this. A wholehearted midfielder who scores plenty of goals and an inspirational leader, he is mainly left-footed, with the ability to produce spectacular goals from dead-ball situations.
Leyton Orient (From apprentice on 18/5/84) FL 232+11/55 FLC 15+1/5 FAC 23+1/6 Others 18+2
Plymouth Arg (£195,000 on 30/6/92) FL 98+3/35 FLC 5/1 FAC 8/2 Others 6/1

CASTLEDINE Gary John
Born: Dumfries, 27 March 1970
Height: 5'8" Weight: 11.4
Left-footed Mansfield midfield player with excellent ball control and dribbling skills, he made four starts for the club last season. Released from his contract in March, Gary had trials with Birmingham before joining Telford.
Mansfield T (Signed from Shirebrook Colliery on 1/2/91) FL 43+23/3 FLC 8+1 FAC 1 Others 5+1

CASTLEDINE Stewart Mark
Born: Wandsworth, 22 January 1973
Height: 6'1" Weight: 12.13
Started 1994-95 in the centre of Wimbledon's midfield, scoring the goal that earned the club a point against Coventry on the opening day of the season. Playing the next three games, but appearing only once more before falling out of contention, Stewart is an aggressive player with good workrate, who has vision, and can also pass the ball well.
Wimbledon (From trainee on 2/7/91) F/PL 8+3/2

CAWLEY Peter
Born: Walton on Thames, 15 September 1965
Height: 6'4" Weight: 16.0
A much-travelled "Gentle Giant" who plays at the heart of Colchester's defence, Peter was again enjoying an excellent season until hit with hamstring problems last Spring. His presence was then missed in the unsuccessful play-off run-in. Incidentally, his return from a pre-season injury had coincided with Colchester's stunning climb from bottom of the League in August to a promotion challenge by Christmas.
Wimbledon (Signed from Chertsey T on 26/1/87) FL 1 Others 1
Bristol Rov (Loaned on 26/2/87) 9+1
Fulham (Loaned on 14/12/88) FL 3+2
Bristol Rov (Free on 17/7/89) FL 1+2
Southend U (Free on 6/7/90) FL 6+1/1 FLC 1 FAC 1 Others 1
Exeter C (Free on 22/11/90) FL 7
Barnet (Free on 8/11/91) FL 3
Colchester U (Free on 9/10/92) FL 81+2/6 FAC 7 Others 4

CECERE Michele (Mike) Joseph
Born: Chester, 4 January 1968
Height: 6'0" Weight: 11.4
Although troubled by injuries last season, Mike finished 1994-95 as Exeter's top-scorer. Likes nothing better than running onto balls from midfield and finishing superbly. Watch out for his goal tally next season when fully fit.
Oldham Ath (From apprentice on 17/1/86) FL 35+17/8 FLC 4+1 FAC 1+2/1 Others 2+1/1
Huddersfield T (£100,000 on 11/11/88) FL 50+4/8 FLC 4/1 FAC 7+1/3 Others 5/1
Stockport Co (Loaned on 22/3/90) FL 0+1
Walsall (£25,000 on 23/8/90) FL 92+20/32 FLC 10+1 FAC 4+2 Others 12/2
Exeter C (Signed on 13/1/94) FL 29+1/11 FLC 2/1 FAC 1/1 Others 3/2

CHALK Martyn Peter Glyn
Born: Louth, 30 August 1969
Height: 5'6" Weight: 10.0
Small, tricky winger whose skill and eye for the odd goal made him an early favourite at Stockport last season. Since then, he has faded in-and-out of the first team.
Derby Co (£10,000 from Louth U on 23/1/90) FL 4+3/1 FAC 3/1 Others 0+1
Stockport Co (£40,000 on 30/6/94) FL 24+9/6 FLC 3/1 FAC 1 Others 1+1

CHAMBERLAIN Alec Francis Roy
Born: March, 20 June 1964
Height: 6'2" Weight: 11.11
Goalkeeper. Alec was unlucky to lose his first team place at Sunderland last season, following the defeat by Tottenham in the FA Cup and joined Liverpool on loan in March, collecting a Coca Cola Cup winners' medal as a non-playing substitute. Has had to endure criticism at times, but has turned in several match winning displays and has an impressive collection of clean sheets to his name.
Ipswich T (Free from Ramsey T on 27/7/81)
Colchester U (Free on 3/8/82) FL 188 FLC 11 FAC 10 Others 12
Everton (£80,000 on 28/7/87)
Tranmere Rov (Loaned on 1/11/87) FL 15
Luton T (£150,000 on 27/7/88) FL 138 FLC 7 FAC 7 Others 7
Sunderland (Free on 8/7/93) FL 60+1 FLC 5 FAC 6 Others 1

CHAMBERLAIN Mark Valentine
Born: Stoke, 19 November 1961
Height: 5'9" Weight" 10.7
International Honours: E: 8; U21-4 (UEFA U21 '84); Sch
Made his first appearance for Brighton when coming on as substitute against Plymouth at the Goldstone and scoring in a 1-1 draw. Favouring the right flank, and proving to be a good crosser of the ball, after an encouraging start he lost his place due to an Achilles injury and never quite regained his form after coming back. Released during the summer.
Port Vale (From apprentice on 1/5/79) FL 90+6/17 FLC 4 FAC 10/2
Stoke C (£135,000 on 24/8/82) FL 110+2/17 FLC 9 FAC 4/1
Sheffield Wed (£300,000 on 13/9/85) FL 32+34/8 FLC 5+2/1 FAC 1+1/1 Others 2+1
Portsmouth (£200,000 on 2/8/88) FL 143+24/20 FLC 11+2/1 FAC 7+1/1 Others 9+1
Brighton & Hove A (Free on 20/8/94) FL 12+7/2 FLC 3/1 FAC 1 Others 1

CHAMBERS Leroy Dean
Born: Sheffield, 25 October 1972
Height: 5'11" Weight: 12.0
Chester forward with a good turn of speed who joined the club during the 1994 close season. Playing mainly in a central attacking role, Leroy made his FL debut on 13 August 1994 against Bradford, starting nine times in all.
Sheffield Wed (From trainee on 13/6/91)
Chester C (Free on 12/8/94) FL 6+7/1 FLC 1/1 Others 2

CHANDLER Dean Andrew Robert
Born: London, 6 May 1976
Height: 6'2" Weight: 11.10

Tall central defender who made his debut for Charlton in the final game of last season at Reading and scored. A strong tackler, and good in the air, Dean likes to get forward for set-pieces and could well break into the side on a regular basis in 1995-96.

Charlton Ath (From trainee on 13/4/94) FL 1/1

CHANNING Justin Andrew
Born: Reading, 19 November 1968
Height: 5'10" Weight: 11.7
International Honours: E: Yth

Another transfer signing from Queens Park Rangers three seasons ago, he is a hard-working, ball-winning Bristol Rovers' midfielder who distributes well. Justin has a powerful shot and is a versatile footballer who can play at full-back, in midfield, or as a winger. Known for his ability to take accurate and dangerous runs.

Queens Park R (From apprentice on 27/8/86) F/PL 42+13/5 FLC 4+1 FAC 2 Others 5
Bristol Rov (£250,000 on 24/10/92) FL 86+8/10 FLC 3 FAC 4 Others 6+1

CHAPMAN Daniel (Danny) Graham
Born: Deptford, 21 November 1974
Height: 5'11" Weight: 13.6

Right-footed Millwall midfielder who graduated from the youth team last season and is very strong in the tackle. Unfortunately, his progress was restricted by a thigh injury and he was released during the summer.

Millwall (From trainee on 18/3/93) FL 4+8 FLC 0+1

CHAPMAN Gary Anthony
Born: Leeds, 1 May 1964
Height: 5'8" Weight: 11.0

A busy Darlington forward who always gives 100 per-cent effort in chasing and harrying for the ball, he had little luck in front of goal last season, with only two strikes, starting as substitute nearly as many times as making full appearances. Freed during the summer.

Bradford C (Free from Frickley Ath on 27/9/88) FL 2+3 FLC 0+1
Notts Co (£15,000 on 13/9/89) FL 13+12/4 Others 2+1
Mansfield T (Loaned on 4/10/90) FL 6
Exeter C (£10,000 on 5/9/91) FL 20+4/5 FLC 0+1 FAC 4 Others 2
Torquay U (Free on 19/2/93) FL 6+2
Darlington (Free on 9/8/93) FL 57+17/9 FLC 2+1 FAC 2 Others 4

CHAPMAN Ian Russell
Born: Brighton, 31 May 1970
Height: 5'9" Weight: 12.5

Ian had a great season for Brighton, either at left-back or on the left-side of midfield. Tenacious and committed, he likes to get forward and provided some excellent left foot crosses and scored a cracking goal in Albion's 2-1 reverse at Brentford.

Brighton & Hove A (From trainee on 5/6/87) FL 229+16/11 FLC 17+1 FAC 10+2/2 Others 8+4

CHAPMAN Lee Roy
Born: Lincoln, 5 February 1959
Height: 6'2" Weight: 13.0
Club Honours: FLC '89; FMC '89; Div 2 '90, Div 1 '92
International Honours: E: B-1; U21-1

Traditional centre-forward with great aerial ability, and a player who gets in front of defenders to great advantage, Lee came to Ipswich from West Ham last January, in the hope that his goals would prevent the club being relegated. Had his best game on his debut against Chelsea when coming on as a substitute and creating both goals. The son of a former pro, Roy, he still wins most aerial balls and scored his only goal against Southampton, with his head. Was also on loan to Southend during the season.

Stoke C (From juniors on 22/6/78) FL 95+4/34 FLC 5/3 FAC 3/1
Plymouth Arg (Loaned on 5/12/78) FL 3+1
Arsenal (£500,000 on 25/8/82) FL 15+8/4 FLC 0+2 FAC 0+1 Others 2/2
Sunderland (£200,000 on 29/12/83) FL 14+1/3 FAC 2/1
Sheffield Wed (£100,000 on 24/8/84) FL 147+2/63 FLC 17/6 FAC 17+1/10 Others 2+1 (£350,000 to Niort on 1/6/88)
Nottingham F (£350,000 on 17/10/88) FL 48/15 FLC 12/6 FAC 5/3 Others 6/3
Leeds U (£400,000 on 11/1/90) F/PL 133+4/62 FLC 15/10 FAC 11/4 Others 10/4
Portsmouth (£250,000 on 11/8/93) FL 5/2 Others 1
West Ham (£250,000 on 16/9/93) PL 33+7/7 FLC 4+1/2 FAC 6/2
Southend U (Loaned on 13/1/95) FL 1/1
Ipswich T (£70,000 on 19/1/95) PL 9+7/1

CHAPPLE Philip (Phil) Richard
Born: Norwich, 26 November 1966
Height: 6'2" Weight: 12.7
Club Honours: Div 3 '91

Tall right-footed Charlton central defender who is good in the air and a strong tackler, Phil likes to get forward for corners and set pieces, and gets his fair share of goals. Lost his place in the side early in 1995 and found it difficult to regain, due to the impressive form of Richard Rufus and Stuart Balmer.

Norwich C (From apprentice on 10/7/85)
Cambridge U (Signed on 29/3/88) FL 183+4/19 FLC 11/2 FAC 23/1 Others 17
Charlton Ath (£100,000 on 13/8/94) FL 61+4/7 FLC 4 FAC 5 Others 5

CHAPPLE Shaun Ronald
Born: Swansea, 14 February 1973
Height: 5'11" Weight: 12.3
International Honours: W: U21-10

After struggling to get a place in the Swansea squad in the early part of last season, Shaun had a successful loan period with Konica League of Wales side, Barry Town. When he did get his opportunity in the first team he showed some excellent touches in midfield and also earned good reviews when representing Wales at U21 level against Bulgaria and West Germany.

Swansea C (From trainee on 15/7/91) FL 44+19/7 FLC 2+1/1 FAC 7+2 Others 8+2/1

CHARLERY Kenneth (Kenny)
Born: Stepney, 28 November 1964
Height: 6'1" Weight: 13.3

Striker. Led Peterborough by example in 1994-95, being the leading scorer and netting some fine individual goals on the way. Now in his second spell at the club, it is difficult to imagine them being without him.

Maidstone U (£35,000 from Beckton on 1/3/89) FL 41+18/11 FLC 1+3/1 FAC 0+3 Others 5+4

Peterborough U (£20,000 on 28/3/91) FL 45+6/19 FLC 10/5 FAC 3/1 Others 11/7
Watford (£350,000 on 16/10/92) FL 45+3/13 FLC 3 FAC 1+1
Peterborough U (£150,000 on 16/12/93) FL 70/24 FLC 2 FAC 2+1/3 Others 2/1

CHARLES Gary Andrew
Born: Newham, 13 April 1970
Height: 5'9" Weight: 11.2
Club Honours: FMC '92
International Honours: E: 2; U21-6

A stylish right-back with great pace and good balance, Gary likes to push forward down the flank to link up with the attack and get in crosses. Signed from Derby last February, following the departure of Earl Barrett to Everton, he featured regularly in an Aston Villa side that were forced to battle its way out of the Premiership relegation zone.

Nottingham F (From trainee on 7/11/87) F/PL 54+2/1 FLC 9 FAC 8+2/1 Others 4+2
Leicester C (Loaned on 16/3/89) FL 5+3
Derby Co (£750,000 on 29/7/93) FL 61/3 FLC 5+1 FAC 1 Others 9
Aston Villa (Signed on 6/1/95) PL 14+2

CHARLES Stephen (Steve)
Born: Sheffield, 10 May 1960
Height: 5'9" Weight: 10.7
Club Honours: Div 4 '82; WC '86

Scarborough captain and the club's senior professional in 1994-95, Steve is a veteran of over 500 League games and more than 100 goals from midfield, including many from the penalty spot. Although a splendid example to the club's younger players, and immensely popular with the fans, at the age of 35, he was given a free transfer at the end of last season.

Sheffield U (Free from Sheffield University on 16/1/80) FL 112+11/10 FLC 12/1 FAC 9+1/1 Others 3/1
Wrexham (£10,000 on 2/11/84) FL 111+2/37 FLC 8 FAC 4+1/1 Others 11+1/5
Mansfield T (£15,000 on 3/8/87) FL 231+6/36 FLC 16/1 FAC 12/4 Others 12+1/4
Scunthorpe U (Loaned on 20/11/92) FL 4 Others 2
Scarborough (Signed on 26/2/93) FL 93/15 FLC 5/1 FAC 7 Others 4/1

CHARLTON Simon Thomas
Born: Huddersfield, 25 October 1971
Height: 5'7" Weight: 11.1
International Honours: E: Sch

After appearing in the first dozen games of last season, Simon lost his Southampton slot through injury and it was not until April that suspensions enabled him to regain a regular place at left-back. A natural left-footer, he brought a good measure of stability to that side of the defence and gave some solid performances, which indicate the loss of Jeff Kenna may not be so severely felt as initially feared.

Huddersfield T (From trainee on 1/7/89) FL 121+3/1 FLC 9/1 FAC 10 Others 14
Southampton (£250,000 on 8/6/93) PL 54+4/2 FLC 3+1 FAC 4

CHEESEWRIGHT John Anthony
Born: Romford, 12 January 1973
Height: 6'0" Weight: 14.0

Goalkeeper. Regular first choice for Colchester throughout the first half of last season, but then contracted a mystery virus which affected his balance and vision, causing him to miss the last 20 games. Freed during the summer.

Southend U (Free from Tottenham H juniors on 28/3/91)
Birmingham C (Free on 28/11/91) FL 1 Others 1 (Free to Kingsbury T on 7/1/94)
Colchester U (£10,000 from Braintree T, via Redbridge, F and Cohb Ramblers, on 13/1/94) FL 40 FLC 1 FAC 3 Others 2

CHEETHAM Michael Martin
Born: Amsterdam, Holland, 30 June 1967
Height: 5'10" Weight: 12.2
Club Honours: Div 3 '91

Experienced winger who joined Colchester on the 1995 transfer deadline day, having been unable to command a regular place in the Chesterfield first team, he added width and pace to the attack as well as posing a goal threat.

Ipswich T (Free from Basingstoke T on 10/10/88) FL 1+3 Others 0+1
Cambridge U (£50,000 on 11/10/89) FL 123+9/22 FLC 8+1/1 FAC 17/1 Others 12+1/3
Chesterfield (Free on 15/7/94) FL 5 FLC 2/1 Others 0+1
Colchester U (Free on 23/3/95) FL 8+1/1

CHENERY Benjamin (Ben) Roger
Born: Ipswich, 28 January 1977
Height: 6'1" Weight: 11.5

A reserve Luton defender who is equally at home at right-back or in central defence, he had a testing debut last January away to Bristol Rovers in the FA Cup. After a shaky start, he regained his composure and played a part in a 1-0 victory. February saw mixed fortunes, with an injury sidelining him from first team contention. However, on reaching his 18th birthday he was awarded a full contract and should get more opportunities next season.

Luton T (From trainee on 3/3/95) FAC 1

Steve Cherry   Phil O'Brien
(Empics Sports Photo Agency)

CHERRY Steven (Steve) Reginald
Born: Nottingham, 5 August 1960
Height: 6'1" Weight: 13.0
Club Honours: AIC '95
International Honours: E: Yth

Consistent Notts County goalkeeper, who has been an excellent last line of defence for the club since joining them early in 1989. Has played well over 300 games during that period and has proved to be brave, good on crosses, and a 'keeper capable of saving more than his share of penalties. As last season ended, Steve was out of contract and being granted a free transfer.

Derby Co (From apprentice on 22/3/78) FL 77 FLC 5 FAC 8
Port Vale (Loaned on 26/11/80) FL 4 FAC 4
Walsall (£25,000 on 10/8/84) FL 71 FLC 10 FAC 7 Others 6
Plymouth Arg (£17,000 on 23/10/86) FL 73 FLC 4 FAC 5 Others 1
Chesterfield (Loaned on 1/12/88) FL 10 Others 3
Notts Co (£70,000 on 16/2/89) FL 266 FLC 17 FAC 14 Others 31

CHETTLE Stephen (Steve)
Born: Nottingham, 27 September 1968
Height: 6'1" Weight: 13.3
Club Honours: FMC '89, '92; FLC '90
International Honours: E: U21-12

A good, reliable Nottingham Forest centre-back who is comfortable on the ball and capable of making great interceptions, amazingly Steve is the only local-born player in the current side. In the club's first Premiership season, he formed an excellent partnership with Colin Cooper, which was one of the foundations the club built their success on. Consistent to a fault, he just gets on with the job at hand.

Nottingham F (From apprentice on 28/8/86) F/PL 243+13/7 FLC 36+3/1 FAC 24+1 Others 13+2/1

CHILDS Gary Paul Colin
Born: Birmingham, 19 April 1964
Height: 5'6" Weight: 10.9
International Honours: E: Yth

A clever, quick-thinking and creative footballer at home in midfield or up-front. He is one of Grimsby's major play makers. His ability to take on and beat defenders, and to put telling crosses into the box, fit in perfectly with the creative footballing style that the club have adopted over recent years. Not a prolific goal scorer, but can be relied on for a few each season.

West Bromwich A (From apprentice on 13/2/82) FL 2+1
Walsall (£15,000 on 7/10/83) FL 120+11/17 FLC 14+2/2 FAC 9+1/2 Others 7/2
Birmingham C (£50,000 on 8/7/87) FL 39+16/2 FLC 0+2 FAC 3 Others 2
Grimsby T (Free on 20/7/89) FL 152+19/22 FLC 13/1 FAC 9 Others 7+2

CHIVERS Gary Paul Stephen
Born: Stockwell, 15 May 1960
Height: 5'11" Weight: 13.1

A defender with a huge amount of FL experience, Gary started seven games as a non-contract player for Bournemouth in 1994-95, plus one substitute appearance. Able to play right across the back four if required, he was used mainly at left-back last season.

Chelsea (From apprentice on 7/8/78) FL 128+5/4 FLC 8 FAC 8
Swansea C (Free on 1/8/83) FL 10
Queens Park R (Free on 15/2/84) FL 58+2 FLC 6 FAC 2 Others 1
Watford (Free on 10/9/87) FL 14 FLC 1 FAC 4
Brighton & Hove A (Signed on 18/3/88) FL 215+2/14 FLC 12 FAC 12 Others 11/2
Bournemouth (Signed on 1/11/93) FL 29+2/2 FAC 4 Others 1+2

CLARIDGE Stephen (Steve) Edward
Born: Portsmouth, 10 April 1966
Height: 5'11" Weight: 11.8
Club Honours: Div 3 '91, Div 2 '95; AMC '95

Probably the most recognisable member of the Birmingham side, Steve has proved to be a tremendous team man who never stops working. Not only that, his goalscoring record in 1994-95 was pretty impressive too, as he became the first man since Trevor Francis to score 20 FL goals in a season. After winning a Second Division Championship medal and an Auto Windscreen winners' medal, he was deservedly voted the fans' "Player of the Year".

Bournemouth (Signed from Fareham on 30/11/84) FL 3+4/1 Others 1 (£10,000 to Weymouth in October 1985)
Crystal Palace (Signed on 11/10/88)
Aldershot (£14,000 on 13/10/88) FL 58+4/19 FLC 2+1 FAC 6/1 Others 5/2
Cambridge U (£75,000 on 8/2/90) FL 56+23/28 FLC 2+4/2 FAC 1 Others 6+3/1
Luton T (£160,000 on 17/7/92) FL 15+1/2 FLC 2/3 Others 2/1
Cambridge U (£195,000 on 20/11/92) FL 53/18 FLC 4/3 FAC 4 Others 3
Birmingham C (£350,000 on 7/1/94) FL 58+2/27 FLC 3/1 FAC 5 Others 7/4

Steve Claridge   Neal Simpson
(Empics Sports Photo Agency)

CLARK Anthony John
Born: London, 7 April 1977
Height: 5'7" Weight: 10.7
Quick, two-footed forward who made an impressive debut for Wycombe in the final game of last season, after some excellent performances for the reserves. Anthony, an associated schoolboy, is now the youngest player to represent the club in a first class game.
Wycombe W (Ass Schoolboy) FL 1

CLARK Howard William
Born: Coventry, 19 September 1968
Height: 5'11" Weight: 11.1
Consistent and reliable Hereford right-back, who can also play in deep midfield and who is always dangerous at free-kicks. Unfortunate with a number of minor injuries during 1994-95, Howard was put on the free transfer list at the end of the season.
Coventry C (From apprentice on 22/9/86) FL 9+11/1 FLC 1 FAC 0+1 Others 0+1
Darlington (Loaned on 19/9/91) FL 5
Shrewsbury T (Free on 16/12/91) FL 51+5 FAC 2 Others 3
Hereford U (Free on 15/7/93) FL 52+3/6 FLC 7 FAC 2 Others 4

CLARK John Brown
Born: Edinburgh, 22 September 1964
Height: 6'0" Weight: 13.1
International Honours: S: Yth
Tough, determined full-back with a strong defensive clearance and the ability to play anywhere in defence or midfield. Signed by Stoke at the beginning of 1994, John was transferred to Falkirk last September for £100,000 after just 18 games, when he and his family failed to settle in the district.
Dundee U (From juniors on 27/7/81) SL 195+47/19 SLC 13+9/6 SC 22+13/3 Others 20+5/8
Stoke C (£150,000 on 10/2/94) FL 17 Others 1/1

CLARK Lee Robert
Born: Wallsend, 27 October 1972
Height: 5'8" Weight: 11.7
Club Honours: Div 1 '93
International Honours: E: U21-8; Yth
Did not become available for Newcastle selection until the end of last September, when he finally regained fitness after a serious foot injury, which required a bone graft. Having spent the rest of the season mostly as a substitute, Lee, with great reluctance, turned down a new contract and made himself available for transfer. A busy and skilful midfield player, he has good vision when on the ball and can deliver accurate passes. Highlight of his season was, undoubtedly, when scoring the winning goal in the 2-1 FAC replay win at Blackburn.
Newcastle U (From trainee on 9/12/89) F/PL 122+20/19 FLC 13 FAC 11/2 Others 5+2/1

CLARK Simon
Born: Boston, 12 March 1967
Height: 6'1" Weight: 12.6
A promising Peterborough recruit from non-league soccer in 1993-94, Simon has proved to be both a tough tackler and versatile, turning out last season in a number of positions, including full-back, central defence, and occasionally in midfield.
Peterborough U (Free from Stevenage Borough on 25/5/94) FL 33 FLC 2 FAC 2 Others 0+1

CLARK William (Billy) Raymond
Born: Christchurch, 19 May 1967
Height: 6'0" Weight: 12.3
Bristol Rovers' longest serving player and a reliable central defender, Billy scored a very important winning goal in injury time against Leyton Orient to help the club reach the play-offs last season. Good in the air, and a fine man-to-man marker, consistency should be his middle name.
Bournemouth (From apprentice on 25/9/84) FL 4
Bristol Rov (Signed on 16/10/87) FL 171+11/11 FLC 7+1 FAC 8+1 Others 13+2/1

CLARKE Adrian James
Born: Cambridge, 28 September 1974
Height: 5'10" Weight: 11.0
International Honours: E: Yth; Sch
Young Arsenal striker who can also play wide on either flank where he is clever on the ball and an excellent crosser. Having made good progress since coming to Highbury as a schoolboy international, Adrian made his debut last December when coming off the bench for the final 15 minutes against QPR. Definitely one for the future.
Arsenal (From trainee on 6/7/93) PL 0+1

CLARKE Andrew (Andy) Weston
Born: Islington, 22 July 1967
Height: 5'10" Weight: 11.7
Club Honours: GMVC '91
International Honours: E: SP-2
Used mainly as a substitute at Wimbledon in 1994-95, and making only a handful of starts, Andy had previously been used to good effect up-front, or as a goalscoring winger, combining great pace with two good feet. A player who is always looking for shooting positions, he scored valuable goals last season against Newcastle and Liverpool.
Wimbledon (£250,000 from Barnet on 21/2/91) F/PL 60+67/14 FLC 9+5/2 FAC 7+1/1

CLARKE Christopher (Chris) John
Born: Barnsley, 1 May 1974
Height: 6'1" Weight: 12.10
A young goalkeeper signed by Rochdale during last summer, he had a brilliant start to his FL career, only to suffer a serious head injury against Blackpool. Re-appeared after four months out and was soon back to his best.
Bolton W (From trainee on 13/7/92)
Rochdale (Free on 4/7/94) FL 24 FLC 2 Others 3

CLARKE Dean Brian
Born: Hereford, 28 July 1977
Height: 5'9" Weight: 10.10
Defender. Still a trainee, Dean, who made his Hereford debut from the bench in the final game of 1993-94, as a 16-year-old, started three times last season. Tries hard and always gives every effort, he looks to have a bright future.
Hereford U (Trainee) FL 3+3 FLC 0+1

Matt Clark   Barrington Coombs
(Empics Sports Photo Agency)

CLARKE Matthew (Matt) John
Born: Sheffield, 3 November 1973
Height: 6'3" Weight: 11.7
A goalkeeper with enormous potential, he was Rotherham's key figure in 1994-95, with his ability to stop shots and cut out crosses with consummate ease. Matt, who has frequently attracted the attention of several clubs, was put on stand-by for the England U21 squad which played Italy.
Rotherham U (From trainee on 28/7/92) FL 83+1 FAC 3 Others 3

CLARKE Stephen (Steve)
Born: Saltcoats, 29 August 1963
Height: 5'9" Weight: 11.10
Club Honours: Div 2 '89
International Honours: S: 6; B-3; U21-8; Yth
Still of international standard, Chelsea's "Player of the Year" for 1993-94, was again beset by injuries last season. At his best, Steve is an excellent right-back, with good positional sense, and not afraid to make a tackle. His other forte is in starting-up quick counter attacks with good interceptions and long balls played into the "channels". Chelsea fans will be praying for him to have an injury free 1995-96.
St Mirren (Free from Beith Juniors in 1981) SL 151/6 SLC 21 SC 19/1 Others 6
Chelsea (£422,000 on 19/1/87) F/PL 247+4/6 FLC 16/1 FAC 20/1 Others 21/1

CLARKE Timothy (Tim) Joseph
Born: Stourbridge, 19 September 1968
Height: 6'3" Weight: 13.7
An imposing custodian who made his Shrewsbury debut at York last September, but had to wait until March for an extended run which began with three clean sheets in a run of four unbeaten games. Tim looks at ease with high crosses and has a very strong clearance.

Coventry C (£25,000 from Halesowen T on 22/10/90)
Huddersfield T (£15,000 on 22/7/91) FL 70 FLC 7 FAC 6 Others 8
Rochdale (Loaned on 12/2/93) FL 2
Shrewsbury T (Signed on 21/10/93) FL 15+1

CLARKE Wayne
Born: Wolverhampton, 28 February 1961
Height: 6'0" Weight: 11.8
Club Honours: CS '87; Div 3 '94
International Honours: E: Yth; Sch

Vastly experienced Shrewsbury striker, who is a deadly finisher with undoubted skills on the ball, Wayne had a disappointing time of it since last November, due to a number of injury interruptions and having to play a little deep. Nevertheless, he still netted 12 times to show his lethal streak. Freed at the end of the season.
Wolverhampton W (From apprentice on 13/3/78) FL 129+19/30 FLC 8+2/2 FAC 9+2/1 Others 0+1
Birmingham C (£80,000 on 24/8/84) FL 92/38 FLC 6/4 FAC 5 Others 2/1
Everton (£300,000 on 6/3/87) FL 46+11/18 FLC 3+3/1 FAC 2+8 Others 3/3
Leicester C (£500,000 on 27/7/89) FL 10+1/1 FLC 1/1
Manchester C (£500,000 on 12/1/90) FL 7+14/2 FAC 1 Others 1
Shrewsbury T (Loaned on 17/10/90) FL 7/6 Others 1
Stoke C (Loaned on 7/3/91) FL 9/3
Wolverhampton W (Loaned on 26/9/91) FL 1
Walsall (Free on 30/7/92) FL 39/21 FLC 4/1 FAC 1 Others 3+1/2
Shrewsbury T (Free on 13/8/93) FL 53+6/22 FLC 44+1/1 FAC 2 Others 2

CLARKSON Ian Stewart
Born: Solihull, 4 December 1970
Weight: 5'11" Weight: 12.0
Club Honours: AMC '91

After a lengthy spell with Stoke reserves, Ian re-emerged in the first team last December and played some of the best football during his spell at the Victoria Ground. Principally an attacking right-back, he is also noted for his tackling abilities which he showed off to advantage in the Coca Cola Cup game at Anfield.
Birmingham C (From trainee on 15/12/88) FL 125+11 FLC 12 FAC 5+1 Others 17+1
Stoke C (£40,000 on 13/9/93) FL 29+3 FLC 3 FAC 3 Others 4+2

CLARKSON Philip (Phil) Ian
Born: Garstang, 13 November 1968
Height: 5'10" Weight: 10.8

Happily recovered from a broken leg which kept him out of football for over a year. Millmoor was the scene of Phil's comeback in November 1994 and since then he has been utilised by Crewe as a striker, a midfielder, and a wide player. Not the tallest of men, but has excellent heading ability.
Crewe Alex (£22,500 from Fleetwood T on 15/10/91) FL 75+18/27 FLC 6+1/1 FAC 3+1/2 Others 6+6/1

CLAYTON Gary
Born: Sheffield, 2 February 1963
Height: 5'10" Weight: 11.7
International Honours: E: SP-1

A utility player, Gary rarely featured for Huddersfield in FL games last season and

tended to make his appearances in cup competitions, especially the Auto Windscreen Shield in place of regular first teamers who were rested. Prefers to play in midfield, but is a reliable performer whatever the position.
Doncaster Rov (Signed from Burton A on 23/8/86) FL 34+4/5 FLC 2 FAC 3 Others 2
Cambridge U (£10,000 on 2/7/87) FL 166+13/17 FLC 17+1/3 FAC 9 Others 7/2
Peterborough U (Loaned on 25/1/91) FL 4
Huddersfield T (£20,000 on 18/2/94) FL 15+4/1 FAC 0+1 Others 4/2

CLIFFORD Mark Robert
Born: Nottingham, 11 September 1977
Height: 5'10" Weight: 10.5

Still a trainee, Mark appeared in Mansfield's final League match of last season at right-back and looked to be a useful prospect.
Mansfield T (Trainee) FL 1

CLODE Mark James
Born: Plymouth, 24 February 1973
Height: 5'10" Weight: 10.10
Club Honours: AMC '94

A former midfield player, Mark's attacking bursts from the left-back position during his first season at Swansea, culminated in him signing a three year contract at the end of 1993-94. Following a two month period on the sidelines with a shin injury, he regained his first team place last season and showed excellent attacking form, coupled to tigerish tackling.
Plymouth Arg (From trainee on 30/3/91)
Swansea C (Free on 23/7/93) FL 59+2/2 FLC 6 FAC 3 Others 7

CLOUGH Nigel Howard
Born: Sunderland, 19 March 1966
Height: 5'9" Weight: 11.8
Club Honours: FLC '89, '90; FMC '89, '92
International Honours: E: 14; B-3; U21-15

Famous as the son of Brian, and a good player in his own right, as witnessed by his international appearances, 1994-95 was a season of disappointment. Failed to obtain a regular first team place at Liverpool and, although there was talk of him moving to other clubs, at the time of writing he appears content to fight for a regular place. A deep-lying centre-forward, Nigel creates goals as well as scoring them and, on his day, his subtle touches and penetrating passes can damage any defence in the country.
Nottingham F (Free from Heanor T on 15/9/84) F/PL 307+4/101 FLC 46/22 FAC 28/6 Others 11+3/1
Liverpool (£2,275,000 on 7/6/93) PL 28+9/7 FLC 3/2 FAC 2

COADY Lewis
Born: Liverpool, 20 September 1976
Height: 6'1" Weight: 11.1

Still a trainee, Lewis made his Wrexham debut last April. A left-sided midfielder and very composed, he seemed to have time on the ball and looks like one for the future, having been offered pro terms for 1995-96.
Wrexham (Trainee) FL 2

COATES Jonathan Simon
Born: Swansea, 27 June 1975
Height: 5'8" Weight: 10.4

Jonathan struggled to break into the Swansea first team last season, making just a couple of appearances as a substitute. However, as a tricky left-winger, he made a telling contribution in the club's reserve side as they pressed for the Combination Second Division Championship.
Swansea C (From trainee on 8/7/93) FL 0+9/1

COCKERILL Glenn
Born: Grimsby, 25 August 1955
Height: 6'0" Weight: 12.4

Aggressive, committed, bustling central midfielder, Glenn had to fight hard last season in an Orient team that struggled to score goals. Two suspensions and injury caused him to miss several matches during the term, but his ball-winning capacity linked well with the delicate skills of Ian Bogie to form one of the best midfields in the division. Sent off in the FA Cup against Bristol Rovers, his enthusiasm at times over-ruled his judgement, but his long passes and accurate shooting resulted, directly or indirectly, to a high proportion of Orient's meagre goal total. Briefly acted as player-manager until the appointment of Pat Holland.
Lincoln C (Free from Louth U on 1/11/76) FL 65+6/10 FLC 2 FAC 2
Swindon T (£11,000 on 6/12/79) FL 23+3/1 FLC 3
Lincoln C (£40,000 on 12/8/81) FL 114+1/25 FLC 16/1 FAC 7 Others 1
Sheffield U (£125,000 on 23/3/84) FL 62/10 FLC 2 FAC 2
Southampton (£225,000 on 17/10/85) F/PL 272+15/32 FLC 35+2/5 FAC 20+2/2 Others 12
Leyton Orient (Free on 10/12/93) FL 51+1/2 FLC 2/1 FAC 2 Others 9

CODNER Robert George
Born: Walthamstow, 23 January 1965
Height: 5'11" Weight: 11.8
International Honours: E: SP-1

Brighton midfield player with plenty of talent, who, on his day, can be a match winner with incisive passes and penetrating forward runs. Scored a memorable goal at Plymouth last season when a poor clearance from the 'keeper was thumped back over his head and into the net from over 40 yards and netted another 13 minutes later as Brighton ran out 3-0 winners. Released during the summer.
Leicester C (Free from Tottenham H juniors on 17/9/83)
Brighton & Hove A (£125,000 from Barnet, via Dagenham, on 8/9/88) FL 257+9/39 FLC 18+2/1 FAC 11+1/4 Others 16+1/3

COLCOMBE Scott
Born: West Bromwich, 15 December 1971
Height: 5'5" Weight: 10.6

Torquay midfield player who can be used in a number of roles, but still suffering the effects of a bad knee injury sustained in April 1994. Scott made a comeback last January, prior to being released at the end of the season.
West Bromwich A (From trainee on 5/7/90)
Torquay U (Free on 14/8/91) FL 78+11/1 FLC 8+1 FAC 4+1/1 Others 5

COLDICOTT Stacy
Born: Redditch, 29 April 1974
Height: 5'8" Weight: 11.2

Promising right-back or midfield player, determined and competitive, who loves to overlap when occupying the former position. Has never been a regular in the first team, but is still a vital member of WBA's senior squad.
West Bromwich A (From trainee on 4/3/92) FL 23+7 FLC 3+1 FAC 1+1 Others 4+1

COLE Andrew (Andy) Alexander
Born: Nottingham, 15 October 1971
Height: 5'10" Weight: 11.2
Club Honours: Div 1 '93
International Honours: E: 1; B-1; U21-8; Yth, Sch

The PFA "Young Player of the Year" in 1994, Andy is a tremendous striker who has the ability to turn defenders in the box. His exceptional pace makes him a constant threat on the ground, and he is equally as dangerous in the air. Last season began in spectacular fashion, with him scoring prolifically as Newcastle stormed to the top of the Premiership. But when a long-standing injury put him on the sidelines, Newcastle's form nosedived and Andy's career dramatically changed. His record busting transfer to Manchester United was the biggest sensation of the year, but in true style he soon began to deliver the goods. A fine opportunist strike against Manchester City at Maine Road endeared him to the United faithful, then he scored five against Ipswich Town at Old Trafford to establish a new club record. His much awaited England debut came in March against Uruguay at Wembley, when only the crossbar prevented him from making it a night to remember.
Arsenal (From trainee on 18/10/89) FL 0+1 Others 0+1
Fulham (Loaned on 5/9/91) FL 13/3 Others 2/1
Bristol C (£500,000 on 12/3/92) FL 41/20 FLC 3/4 FAC 4/1
Newcastle U (£1,750,000 on 12/3/93) F/PL 69+1/55 FLC 7/8 FAC 4/1 Others 3/4
Manchester U (£6,000,000 on 12/1/95) PL 17+1/12

Andy Cole   Neal Simpson
(Empics Sports Photo Agency)

COLEMAN Christopher (Chris)
Born: Swansea, 10 June 1970
Height: 6'2" Weight: 12.10
Club Honours: WC '89, '91; Div 1 '94
International Honours: W:4; U21-10; Yth; Sch

Had another outstanding season with Crystal Palace and Wales and, with Richard Shaw, formed a good partnership. A left-back, or centre-half, who is a natural athlete and who has the perfect build for a defender, Chris cleared many crosses with great accuracy and constantly found John Salako with long left-footed passes. Unfortunately, injury caused him to miss the last four games in which nine goals were conceded.
Swansea C (From from Manchester C juniors on 1/9/87) FL 159+1/2 FLC 8 FAC 13/1 Others 15
Crystal Palace (£275,000 on 19/7/91) F/PL 126+11/13 FLC 20+2/2 FAC 8/1 Others 2

COLEMAN Simon
Born: Worksop, 13 March 1968
Height: 6'0" Weight: 10.8

Signed from Sheffield Wednesday last October, he settled well in the middle of Bolton's defence, chipping in with some important goals, before tragedy struck in February during Bolton's 2-1 reverse at Derby. Simon unfortunately broke his leg in a challenge with Marco Gabbiadini, an injury which will keep him out of the game until late in 1995.
Mansfield T (From juniors on 29/7/85) FL 96/7 FLC 9 FAC 7 Others 7/1
Middlesbrough (£400,000 on 26/9/89) FL 51+4/2 FAC 5 Others 10/1
Derby Co (£300,000 on 15/8/91) FL 62+8/2 FLC 5+1 FAC 5 Others 12
Sheffield Wed (£250,000 on 20/1/94) PL 11+5/1 FLC 3 FAC 2
Bolton W (£350,000 on 5/10/94) FL 22/4 FLC 4 FAC 1

COLKIN Lee
Born: Nuneaton, 15 July 1974
Height: 5'11" Weight: 11.1

Left-sided defender or midfielder, with an aggressive style of play that wins him many supporters. Broke into the Northampton first team in 1993-94, but missed part of last season with a facial injury that saw him make his comeback in a "Gazza type" mask.
Northampton T (From trainee on 31/8/92) FL 59+10/2 FLC 3 FAC 1 Others 1

COLLETT Andrew (Andy) Alfred
Born: Stockton, 28 October 1973
Height: 5'11" Weight: 12.0

Enjoyed a one month loan spell with Bristol Rovers last October when deputising for the club's injured goalkeeper, Brian Parkin, and impressed enough to make the move permanent in March. A confident and competent young man, Andy had limited first team opportunities at Middlesbrough, but will hope to provide a strong challenge for the number one spot at Twerton Park this coming season.
Middlesbrough (From trainee on 6/3/92) PL 2 Others 3
Bristol Rov (£10,000 on 18/10/94) FL 4 Others 1

COLLIER Daniel (Danny) Joseph
Born: Eccles, 15 January 1974
Height: 6'1" Weight: 10.5

His education in football started in Wolverhampton where, unable to get a regular place, he was recommended to Crewe. Had some first team experience in 1994-95, but was mainly used as an understudy for the central defensive role. Still young, Danny will improve with experience.
Wolverhampton W (From trainee on 7/7/92)
Crewe Alex (Free on 15/6/94) FL 3+2 FLC 1 Others 0+2

COLLIER Darren James
Born: Stockton, 1 December 1967
Height: 5'11" Weight: 11.9

Reserve Darlington goalkeeper, Darren made only two appearances in 1994-95, following an injury to first choice Mike Pollitt, after being ever-present the season before. Freed during the summer.
Middlesbrough (Signed on 27/3/86)
Blackburn Rov (Free on 24/12/87) FL 27 FLC 3 Others 1
Darlington (Signed on 28/7/93) FL 44 FLC 2 FAC 1 Others 3

COLLINS David Dennis
Born: Dublin, 30 October 1971
Height: 6'0" Weight: 12.10
International Honours: Ei: U21-6

Honest and reliable, David was used by Oxford mainly in the reserve team during 1994-95, but can play both at centre-back and in midfield. Released at the end of last season.
Liverpool (From trainee on 3/11/88)
Wigan Ath (Loaned on 9/1/92) FL 9
Oxford U (Free on 30/7/92) FL 33+9 FAC 4 Others 3+1

COLLINS Simon
Born: Pontefract, 16 December 1973
Height: 5'9" Weight: 10.5

A homegrown Huddersfield product who was on the fringe of first team selection throughout last season, and making just three starts, Simon, who can play right across midfield, showed good vision when called upon. Likes to get forward and trouble 'keepers from the edge of the box.
Huddersfield T (From trainee on 1/7/92) FL 3+3 FLC 0+1 Others 1+3

COLLINS Wayne Anthony
Born: Manchester, 4 March 1969
Height: 6'0" Weight: 12.0

Wayne, who came straight from non-league football into the Crewe League side at the start of 1993-94, is a pacy midfielder. Showed that he had an eye for a goal by finishing as the club's leading FL scorer last season. Normally plays on the right-side.
Crewe Alex (£10,000 from Winsford U on 29/7/93) FL 65+10/14 FLC 2 FAC 4+1 Others 10/1

COLLYMORE Stanley (Stan) Victor
Born: Stone, 22 January 1971
Height: 6'4" Weight: 13.1
International Honours: E: 2

Made a sensational start to the Premiership programme with Nottingham Forest and, at one stage towards the end of last season, scored six goals in six games. A strong player, who is good in the air, it was his great pace and surging runs that really frightened many a defence as he fully justified his price-tag. Struck up a brilliant attacking partnership with the Dutch newcomer, Bryan Roy, which proved, on its day, to be one of the highspots of football in general. Stop Press: Having made his England debut on 3 June against Japan in the Umbro Cup, a few weeks later, Stan smashed the British transfer record when reported as being in the process of signing for Liverpool for a fee of £8.5 million.

Wolverhampton W (From trainee on 13/7/89)
Crystal Palace (£100,000 from Stafford R on 4/1/91) FL 4+16/1 FLC 2+3/1
Southend U (£100,000 on 20/11/92) FL 30/15 FAC 3/3
Nottingham F (£2,000,000 on 5/7/93) F/PL 64+1/41 FLC 9/2 FAC 2/1 Others 2/1

Stan Collymore   Tony Marshall
          (Empics Sports Photo Agency)

COMYN Andrew (Andy) John
Born: Wakefield, 2 August 1968
Height: 6'1" Weight: 11.12

Plymouth central defender whose form has suffered from the plight of his team, whom he captained for a period in Steve Castle's absence. Has played at the highest level and is sure to reproduce the form that got him recognised. A very clean player, he rarely attracts the attention of the referee.

Manchester U (From juniors on 5/8/86)
Aston Villa (£34,000 from Alvechurch on 22/8/89) FL 12+3 FLC 2+1 FAC 2 Others 1
Derby Co (£200,000 on 8/8/91) FL 59+4/1 FLC 7 FAC 3+1/1 Others 9/2
Plymouth Arg (£200,000 on 1/8/93) FL 76/5 FLC 4 FAC 7 Others 6

CONNELLY Sean Patrick
Born: Sheffield, 26 June 1970
Height: 5'10" Weight: 11.10

Stockport defender picked up from non-league football, he doubles up as the club's assistant physio after recently passing his exams. A very promising young player, who reads the game well and can play at right-back or in a more central role.

Stockport Co (Free from Hallam on 12/8/92) FL 74+4 FLC 4 FAC 2+1 Others 8

CONNOLLY David James
Born: London, 6 June 1977
Height: 5'8" Weight: 11.4

A local boy, David was plunged into premature first team action with Watford last season because of injuries and held the ball up well as a lone striker. Small, but skilful, he signed pro forms last November.

Watford (From trainee on 15/11/94) FL 0+2 FAC 1+1

CONNOLLY Karl Andrew
Born: Prescot, 9 February 1970
Height: 5'11" Weight: 11.2
Club Honours: WC '95

A skilful, penetrating, wide left-sided midfielder with an excellent work-rate and very good in the air who, when on song, makes mazy runs through opposition defences, leaving them in his wake. Very left-footed, he can be just as effective in a central forward position where he tends to be more involved and strikes a ball well. Often the "Jewel" in the side, Wrexham will do well to hang on to him.

Wrexham (Free from Napoli, in local Sunday League, on 8/5/91) FL 156+6/29 FLC 12/21 FAC 12/3 Others 19+1/3

CONNOR James Richard
Born: Twickenham, 22 August 1974
Height: 6'0" Weight: 12.9

Another youth team graduate at Millwall, James proved to be a talented right-footed midfield player, with flair and his debut last season marks him down as one for the future. Unfortunately dislocated his shoulder, before a hamstring, calf strain and finally a further collar bone injury ruled him out.

Millwall (From trainee on 21/11/92) FL 1

Mike Conroy   Barrington Coombs
          (Empics Sports Photo Agency)

CONROY Michael (Mike) Kevin
Born: Glasgow, 31 December 1965
Height: 6'0" Weight: 11.0
Club Honours: Div 4 '92

One of Preston's many forwards troubled by injury, resulting in a disrupted season in 1994-95, Mike still showed his undoubted class in front of goal, especially on the near post with both foot and head. Is also a good crosser from the wings.

Clydebank (Free from Coventry C juniors in 1984) SL 92+22/38 SLC 4+1 SC 5+2
St Mirren (Signed in Dec 1987) SL 9+1/1 SC 0+1
Reading (£50,000 on 28/9/88) FL 65+15/7 FLC 3+2 FAC 8+2/1 Others 2+2
Burnley (£35,000 on 16/7/91) FL 76+1/30 FLC 4/1 FAC 9+1/4 Others 7+1/4
Preston NE (£85,000 on 20/8/93) FL 50+7/22 FLC 2+1 FAC 7/2 Others 2+3

CONWAY Paul James
Born: London, 17 April 1970
Height: 6'1" Weight: 12.6
Club Honours: Div 3 '95
International Honours: USA: U21

Injury delayed his first appearance in Carlisle's midfield until last October, but he made an early input with four goals in his first six matches, including a brilliant solo effort against Barnet. A good striker of the ball, his creative play added an extra dimension to the side. Having missed several games in the spring with a hernia operation, he returned to feature prominently in the AWS Final and win a Third Division Championship medal.

Carlisle U (Signed on 29/10/93) FL 40+2/10 FAC 4/2 Others 9/1

COOK Andrew (Andy) Charles
Born: Romsey, 10 August 1969
Height: 5'9" Weight: 12.0

Andy made a surprise return to first team duty with Swansea last April at Huddersfield, 12 months after he had suffered a broken leg at Hartlepool and, after recovering from a hernia operation in the 1994 close season. Unfortunately, just two appearances later, he encountered further groin problems that forced him to miss the rest of the campaign. An exciting, attacking full-back, he has also played in midfield since joining the "Swans" from Exeter.

Southampton (From apprentice on 6/7/87) FL 11+5/1 FLC 4 FAC 1 Others 1
Exeter C (£50,000 on 13/9/91) FL 70/1 FLC 2 FAC 7/1 Others 6/1
Swansea C (£125,000 on 23/7/93) FL 24+5 FLC 2 FAC 2 Others 7+1/2

COOK Mitchell (Mitch) Christopher
Born: Scarborough, 15 October 1961
Height: 6'0" Weight: 12.3
Club Honours: GMVC '87

Much travelled defender who was signed last November from Blackpool to add experience to the Hartlepool side, he proved a strong left-footed player, with his accurate kicks being a feature of set-piece play. Released at the end of the season, he has been appointed player-manager of Guiseley.

Darlington (Signed from Scarborough on 13/8/84) FL 34/4 FLC 1 FAC 6 Others 3
Middlesbrough (Signed on 13/9/85) FL 3+3 Others 1+1

Scarborough (Free on 1/8/86) FL 61+20/10 FLC 6+2/4 FAC 3/1 Others 7+1
Halifax T (£25,000 on 2/8/89) FL 52+2/2 FLC 7/1 Others 5/2
Scarborough (Loaned on 1/10/90) FL 9/1 FAC 1
Darlington (Free on 26/3/91) FL 35+1/3 FLC 2/1 FAC 2
Blackpool (Signed on 26/3/92) FL 66+2 FLC 6 FAC 1 Others 5
Hartlepool U (Free on 18/11/94) FL 22+2

COOK Paul Anthony
Born: Liverpool, 22 February 1967
Height: 5'11" Weight: 10.10
Paul, a skilful left-sided midfield player, joined Coventry on the eve of last season from "Wolves" and made his debut as a substitute against Wimbledon on the opening day. His excellent control and good passing ability was something that City's midfield had lacked for some time and his corners created a number of goals. Scored at QPR and followed up with two penalties, but missed spot-kicks at Hillsborough and Selhurst Park.
Wigan Ath (Signed from Marine on 20/7/84) FL 77+6/14 FLC 4 FAC 6+1 Others 5+1/1
Norwich C (£73,000 on 23/5/88) FL 3+3 Others 1+1
Wolverhampton W (£250,000 on 1/11/89) FL 191+2/19 FLC 7/1 FAC 5+2 Others 6+1/1
Coventry C (£600,000 on 18/8/94) FL 33+1/3 FLC 3 FAC 3

COOKSEY Scott Andrew
Born: Birmingham, 24 June 1972
Height: 6'3" Weight: 13.10
Young Peterborough goalie who has yet to fulfil his expected potential, Scott was loaned out to GMVC clubs, Welling and Stalybridge, last season.
Derby Co (From trainee on 25/7/90)
Shrewsbury T (Free on 7/2/91)
Peterborough U (£25,000 from Bromsgrove Rov on 30/12/93) FL 15 FLC 2 FAC 2 Others 1

COOPER Colin Terence
Born: Sedgefield, 28 February 1967
Height: 5'11" Weight: 11.5
International Honours: E: 2; U21-8
Tough-tackling, no-nonsense Nottingham Forest central defender, who can also play at right-back, Colin formed an excellent no-frills partnership with Steve Chettle last season. Virtually an ever-present, he wasted no time in adapting to life in the Premiership, not only impressing with his defensive displays, but also in the opponents' penalty area where he was a "dab hand" at set-pieces. Called up to the England squad, he made his debut against Sweden in the Umbro Cup on 8 June 1995.
Middlesbrough (From juniors on 17/7/84) FL 183+5/6 FLC 18 FAC 13 Others 19+1/2
Millwall (£300,000 on 25/7/91) FL 77/6 FLC 6 FAC 2 Others 2
Nottingham F (£1,700,000 on 21/6/93) F/PL 71+1/8 FLC 8/1 FAC 3/1

COOPER David Barry Ernest
Born: Hatfield, 7 March 1973
Height: 6'0" Weight: 12.0
An attack minded Exeter defender, Dave made his first appearance of last season for 17 months at home against Hartlepool after suffering a broken leg and was freed during the summer.

Exeter C (Free from Luton T juniors on 6/8/91) FL 39+9 FLC 4 FAC 1 Others 5+1

COOPER Gary
Born: Hammersmith, 20 November 1965
Height: 5'8" Weight: 11.3
Club Honours: Div 2 '95; AMC '95
International Honours: E: Yth; Sch
The unsung hero of Birmingham's great run of success in 1994-95, at one stage Gary thought he was on his way out, but came back into the side just before Christmas and never looked back. Performing consistently at left-back and in midfield, when required, he was a member of the side that won the Auto Windscreen Shield and later capped a memorable season with a Second Division Championship medal.
Queens Park R (From apprentice on 2/6/83) FL 1 FLC 1+1 Others 0+1 (Free to Fisher Ath in February 1986)
Brentford (Loaned on 1/9/85) FL 9+1
Maidstone U (Signed on 1/3/89) FL 53+7/7 FLC 3 FAC 3+1 Others 10/1
Peterborough U (£20,000 on 28/3/91) FL 83+5/10 FLC 12/1 FAC 5/2 Others 9/1
Birmingham C (Free on 17/12/93) FL 42+2/2 FLC 1 FAC 4+1/1 Others 4+1

COOPER Geoffrey (Geoff) Victor
Born: Kingston, 27 December 1960
Height: 5'10" Weight: 11.0
A Barnet stalwart, he made just one appearance last season, on the left-hand side of midfield, before announcing his retirement from the game and emigrating to New Zealand, following a short spell as the club's community officer.
Brighton & Hove A (Signed from Bognor Regis on 30/12/87) FL 2+5 FAC 1 Others 0+1
Barnet (Free during 1989 close season) FL 30+1/1 FLC 2 FAC 1 Others 5
Wycombe W (Free on 26/7/93)
Barnet (Free on 10/8/93) FL 25+12/3 FLC 4 FAC 0+1 Others 2

COOPER Kevin Lee
Born: Derby, 8 February 1975
Height: 5'6" Weight: 10.7
Speedy left-winger and a regular in the Derby reserve side, Kevin made his first team debut as a substitute in the AIC game against Udinese last November. Can also play at left-back, if required.
Derby Co (From trainee on 2/7/93) FL 0+1 Others 0+1

COOPER Mark David
Born: Watford, 5 April 1967
Height: 6'1" Weight: 13.0
A Ray Clemence signing from Leyton Orient prior to the start of 1994-95, he was bought to score goals for Barnet and did. Responsible for leading the line, the big centre-forward enjoyed a good start and finish to his first season at Underhill.
Cambridge U (From apprentice on 16/10/84) FL 62+9/17 FLC 7/3 FAC 4 Others 2
Tottenham H (Signed on 2/4/87)
Shrewsbury T (Loaned on 10/9/87) FL 6/2
Gillingham (£105,000 on 9/10/87) FL 38+11/11 FLC 2+1 FAC 3+1 Others 4
Leyton Orient (Signed on 2/2/89) FL 117+33/45 FLC 6/2 FAC 8+2/4 Others 10+2/4
Barnet (Free on 13/7/94) FL 32+2/11 FLC 2+1/2 FAC 2/2 Others 1/1

COOPER Mark Nicholas
Born: Wakefield, 18 December 1968
Height: 5'8" Weight" 11.4
Club Honours: Div 4 '90
Midfield hustler and deadly with free-kicks around the box, Mark, now in his second spell at Exeter, chips in with his quota of goals. Has been used as a stand-in forward and loves to volley.
Bristol C (From trainee on 10/9/87)
Exeter C (Free on 3/10/89) FL 46+4/12 FLC 4+1 FAC 3+1/1 Others 5
Southend U (Loaned on 22/3/90) FL 4+1
Birmingham C (Signed on 5/9/91) FL 30+9/4 FAC 2 Others 3/1
Fulham (£40,000 on 21/11/92) FL 10+4 FLC 2 Others 3
Huddersfield T (Loaned on 25/3/93) FL 10/4
Wycombe W (Free on 10/1/94) FL 0+2/1
Exeter C (Free on 11/2/94) FL 52+9/14 FLC 1 FAC 2 Others 4/1

COOPER Stephen (Steve) Brian
Born: Birmingham, 22 June 1964
Height: 6'1" Weight: 11.10
Played in York's opening 11 games last season, before being transferred to Airdrie for £60,000 on 30 September. A dangerous striker, who is very good in the air, Steve's goals helped his new club to the Scottish Cup Final.
Birmingham C (Signed from Moor Green on 10/11/83)
Halifax T (Loaned on 23/12/83) FL 7/1
Newport Co (Free on 28/9/84) FL 38/11 FAC 5 Others 5
Plymouth Arg (Free on 9/8/85) FL 58+15/15 FLC 2+3 FAC 5+1/3 Others 0+1
Barnsley (£100,000 on 28/7/88) FL 62+15/13 FLC 5/1 FAC 9/3 Others 1
Tranmere Rov (£100,000 on 13/12/90) FL 16+16/3 FLC 0+1 FAC 3+1 Others 6+3/3
Peterborough U (Loaned on 26/3/92) FL 2+7 Others 0+4/1
Wigan Ath (Loaned on 24/12/92) FL 4 Others 2
York C (£35,000 on 3/8/93) FL 37+1/6 FLC 4/1 FAC 1 Others 2+1

CORAZZIN Giancarlo (Carlo) Michele
Born: Canada, 25 December 1971
Height: 5'9" Weight: 12.7
International Honours: Canada
A live-wire forward who scored ten goals for Cambridge in 1993-94, Carlo followed that up with a further 20 last season, in becoming the club's leading scorer. His good form also saw him selected for the Canadian national team, making him only the third United player to win a full cap.
Cambridge U (£20,000 from Vancouver 86ers on 10/12/93) FL 73+1/29 FLC 2 FAC 4 Others 3/2

CORDEN Simon Wayne
Born: Leek, 1 November 1975
Height: 5'9" Weight: 10.6
Tricky left-winger from Port Vale's junior ranks, who impressed enough to be given his chance as a sub in the final game of last season. Has a bright future.
Port Vale (From trainee on 20/9/94) FL 0+1

CORK Alan Graham
Born: Derby, 4 March 1959
Height: 6'0" Weight: 12.0
Club Honours: FAC '88

A very experienced striker who has scored over 150 goals in a career dating back to 1977, and now in the veteran stage, he was used by Fulham as a non-contract player in 1994-95, mainly as cover.

Derby Co (From juniors on 2/7/77)
Lincoln C (Loaned on 14/9/77) FL 5
Wimbledon (Free on 9/2/78) FL 352+78/145 FLC 29+7/14 FAC 30+7/8 Others 3+4/1
Sheffield U (Free on 9/3/92) F/PL 25+29/7 FLC 2+2 FAC 5+1/2
Fulham (Free on 12/8/94) FL 11+4/3 FLC 3 FAC 4/1

CORNFORTH John Michael
Born: Whitley Bay, 7 October 1967
Height: 6'1" Weight: 12.11
Club Honours: Div 3 '88; AMC '94
International Honours: W: 2

A talented Swansea midfielder who stood out last season from the usual aggressive, physical midfielders of the Second Division. Despite a calf strain and suspension, which forced him to miss a number of games, John was also a regular inclusion in the Welsh squad and collected his first cap as a second-half substitute in Bulgaria. Named by his fellow professionals at the PFA Awards Night as being the Second Division's best player in his position.

Sunderland (From apprentice on 11/10/85) FL 21+11/2 FLC 0+1 Others 1+3
Doncaster Rov (Loaned on 6/11/86) FL 6+1/3 Others 2
Shrewsbury T (Loaned on 23/11/89) FL 3 Others 2
Lincoln C (Loaned on 11/1/90) FL 9/1
Swansea C (£50,000 on 2/8/91) FL 130+2/14 FLC 12 FAC 11/1 Others 19/1

Tony Coton   Paul Marriott
(Empics Sports Photo Agency)

COTON Anthony (Tony) Philip
Born: Tamworth, 19 May 1961
Height: 6'2" Weight: 13.7
International Honours: E: B-1

Made a brilliant start to 1994-95 with a series of great saves that gave Manchester City a useful start, before injuring his shoulder at Leeds in October. Two weeks later, not 100 per-cent fit, he came on as the substitute goalie at QPR after Andy Dibble had been sent off and somehow held out. Sidelined for almost five months with the shoulder problem and a concurrent back injury, Tony finished the season in style as a cornerstone of the club's winning battle against relegation. Definitely in the top rung of English goalkeepers.

Birmingham C (Free from Mile Oak Rov on 13/10/78) FL 94 FLC 10 FAC 10
Watford (£300,000 on 27/9/84) FL 233 FLC 18 FAC 32 Others 8
Manchester C (£1,000,000 on 20/7/90) F/PL 162+1 FLC 16 FAC 12 Others 3

Tony Cottee   Steve Morton
(Empics Sports Photo Agency)

COTTEE Anthony (Tony) Richard
Born: West Ham, 11 July 1965
Height: 5'8" Weight: 11.5
International Honours: E: 7; U21-8; Yth

The PFA "Young Player of the Year" for 1986 and a very experienced striker, Tony returned home to West Ham last September from Everton and soon began scoring the goals which helped keep the "Hammers" in the Premiership. His pace and skill was always recognised by the fans, but his all-round team play was an added bonus. Scored a brilliant hat-trick against Manchester City in December and was no doubt delighted with two that counted against his old Everton team-mates in February. Having notched his 100th League goal for the club at Leicester, he finished the season as "Hammers'" top goalscorer and deservedly gained the runners-up award in the "Hammer of the Year" competition.

Unfortunately, he missed the final five games of the season due to a calf injury.

West Ham U (From apprentice on 1/9/82) FL 203+9/92 FLC 19/14 FAC 24/11 Others 1/1
Everton (£2,300,000 on 2/8/88) F/PL 161+23/72 FLC 19+4/11 FAC 15+6/4 Others 11+2/12
West Ham U (Signed on 7/9/94) PL 31/12 FLC 3/1 FAC 2/1

COTTERELL Leo Spencer
Born: Cambridge, 2 September 1974
Height: 5'9" Weight: 10.0
International Honours: E: Yth; Sch

As a promising young Ipswich right-back, Leo made his PL debut as a substitute at Southampton last season. Still awaiting his first full game, having made two other appearances from the bench, he gets forward well and shows much enthusiasm.

Ipswich T (From trainee on 1/7/93) PL 0+2 FLC 0+1

COTTERILL Stephen (Steve) John
Born: Cheltenham, 20 July 1964
Height: 6'1" Weight: 12.5

Striker. After finishing 1993-94 as Bournemouth's top-scorer with 15 goals, Steve made ten appearances and scored three goals at the beginning of last season, before suffering a knee injury that kept him out of the side for the rest of the campaign. Hopefully, he will be back to full fitness for the start of 1995-96.

Wimbledon (£30,000 from Burton A on 27/2/89) F/PL 10+7/6 FLC 2 FAC 1/1 Others 1+1
Brighton & Hove A (Loaned on 13/8/92) FL 11/4
Bournemouth (£80,000 on 14/8/93) FL 44+1/15 FLC 6/2 FAC 2+1/1 Others 1

COUGHLIN Russell James
Born: Swansea, 15 February 1960
Height: 5'8" Weight: 11.12
Club Honours: WC '91

Playmaker who can create something out of nothing, Russell made plenty of goals for Exeter last season, but was unfortunately hit by injuries and was one of eight players freed during the summer.

Manchester C (From apprentice on 3/3/78)
Blackburn Rov (£40,000 on 26/3/79) FL 22+2 FLC 1+1
Carlisle U (£20,000 on 30/10/80) FL 114+16/13 FLC 5+1/1 FAC 12
Plymouth Arg (£20,000 on 25/7/84) FL 128+3/18 FLC 8/2 FAC 8/1 Others 5/1
Blackpool (£75,000 on 11/12/87) FL 100+2/8 FLC 9/1 FAC 13 Others 10/1
Shrewsbury T (Loaned on 11/9/90) FL 4+1 FLC 1
Swansea C (£30,000 on 17/10/90) FL 99+2/2 FLC 4+1 FAC 8 Others 10+1
Exeter C (Signed on 12/7/93) FL 58+2 FLC 4 FAC 5 Others 4

COUSINS Jason Michael
Born: Hayes, 4 October 1970
Height: 5'11" Weight: 12.4
Club Honours: GMVC '93; FAT '93

Made the Wycombe right-back spot very much his own in 1994-95 and is appreciated by the supporters for his commitment and tough-tackling style of play.

Brentford (From trainee on 13/7/89) FL 20+1 Others 2+2
Wycombe W (Free on 1/7/91) FL 78/3 FLC 6/1 FAC 11 Others 10

COUZENS Andrew (Andy)
Born: Shipley, 4 June 1975
Height: 5'10" Weight: 11.11
Club Honours: FAYC '93
International Honours: E: U21-1

Another member of the 1993 FAYC winners to break into the Leeds' side, Andy made his debut last season when coming on for the injured Lucas Radebe against Coventry at Elland Road. A right-back, who likes getting forward and a good passer of the ball, he kept his place for the following game at Manchester United, and rounded 1994-95 off when selected by England for the last two matches of the Toulon U21 tournament during the summer.
Leeds U (From trainee on 5/3/93) PL 2+2

COWAN Thomas (Tom)
Born: Bellshill, 28 August 1969
Height: 5'8" Weight: 10.8

An uncompromising left-back, originally on loan from Sheffield United at the end of 1993-94, the proceeds from the Autoglass Trophy final were used to make his move to Huddersfield permanent. Naturally two-footed and a very good passer, both long and short, he was elected to last season's PFA Division Two side.
Clyde (Free from Netherdale BC in 1988-89) SL 16/2 SC 2
Glasgow R (Signed in February 1989) SL 8+4 SC 0+1 Others 2
Sheffield U (£350,000 on 1/8/91) F/PL 45 FLC 5 FAC 2 Others 1
Stoke C (Loaned on 1/10/93) FL 14 FLC 1 Others 3
Huddersfield T (£150,000 on 24/3/94) FL 47/2 FLC 4 FAC 2 Others 6

Gordon Cowans   Matthew Ashton
(Empics Sports Photo Agency)

COWANS Gordon Sidney
Born: Cornforth, 27 October 1958
Height: 5'7" Weight: 10.6
Club Honours: FLC '77; Div 1 '81; CS '81; EC '82; ESC '82
International Honours: E: 10; B-2; U21-5; Yth

A veteran midfield player, he still has good passing ability and vision and proved a bargain signing from Derby last December, when Wolverhampton badly needed some-

one who could put a foot on the ball. Damaged knee ligaments at WBA saw him missing for a while, though he was not out for too long.
Aston Villa (From apprentice on 1/9/76) FL 276+10/42 FLC 23+4/5 FAC 19+1/3 Others 23+1/2 (£500,000 to Bari on 1/7/85)
Aston Villa (£250,000 on 13/7/88) FL 114+3/7 FLC 15 FAC 9 Others 11+1
Blackburn Rov (£200,000 on 28/11/91) F/PL 49+1/2 FLC 4 FAC 5/1 Others 3
Aston Villa (Free on 5/7/93) PL 9+2 FLC 2 Others 4
Derby Co (£80,000 on 3/2/94) FL 36 FLC 3 Others 5+1/1
Wolverhampton W (£20,000 on 19/12/94) FL 21 FAC 5/1 Others 2

COX Ian Gary
Born: Croydon, 25 March 1971
Height: 6'0" Weight: 12.2
Tall Crystal Palace right-wing forward who possesses a fine burst of speed. After the heavy defeat at the hands of Liverpool last season, Ian was given his first taste of PL soccer with a sub appearance at Norwich, later making his full debut against QPR. An outstanding prospect, he was a surprise choice for the FA Cup replay at Wolverhampton at right-back.
Crystal Palace (£35,000 from Carshalton on 8/3/94) PL 1+10 FAC 1+1

Neil Cox   Neal Simpson
(Empics Sports Photo Agency)

COX Neil James
Born: Scunthorpe, 8 October 1971
Height: 6'0" Weight: 13.2
Club Honours: FLC '94; Div 1 '95
International Honours: E: U21-6

A record signing when "Robbo" brought him to Middlesbrough in the 1994 close season, he was the club's first £1 million player. Freely tipped as future occupant of England's right-back berth, Neil is a determined defender who is quick, strong and has a good "football" brain. Elected by his fellow pro's to the PFA Award winning First Division team, Neil followed it up with a First Division Championship medal.

Scunthorpe U (From trainee on 20/3/90) FL 17/1 FAC 4 Others 4+1
Aston Villa (£400,000 on 12/2/91) F/PL 26+16/3 FLC 5+2 FAC 4+2/1 Others 2
Middlesbrough (£1,000,000 on 19/7/94) FL 39+1/1 FLC 2+1 Others 2

COX Paul Richard
Born: Nottingham, 6 January 1972
Height: 5'11" Weight: 11.12

Notts County central defender who has spent most of his time at the club as a squad member, deputising when called upon and never letting them down. Out of contract at the end of last season, Paul was given a free transfer. Earlier, last December, he was on loan at Hull for a handful of FL games.
Notts Co (From trainee on 16/8/89) FL 39+5/1 FLC 3/1 FAC 1+1 Others 2+1
Hull C (Loaned on 16/12/94) FL 5/1

COYLE Owen Columba
Born: Glasgow, 14 July 1966
Height: 5'9" Weight: 10.5
International Honours: Ei: 1; B-4; U21-2

An Irish international, Owen failed to become a regular in the Bolton side during 1994-95, due to the form of both John McGinlay and Mixu Paatelainen. However, when he was called upon he did deliver the goals, two coming against Grimsby at Burnden Park, in what was his first full game of the term and, of course, a vital one in the play-off final, that ultimately saw the club reach the Premiership. Was the leading goalgetter in the Pontins' Central League Championship winning side, hitting the net 23 times in 22 games.
Dumbarton (Signed from Renfrew YM in 1985) SL 85+18/36 SLC 4 SC 2
Clydebank (Signed on 1/8/88) SL 63/33 SLC 2 SC 3/1
Airdrie (£175,000 on 1/2/90) SL 116+7/50 SLC 6/2 SC 9+1/1 Others 4
Bolton W (£250,000 on 30/6/93) FL 33+16/12 FLC 5+2/1 FAC 8/5 Others 7+1/5

COYNE Daniel (Danny)
Born: Prestatyn, 27 August 1973
Height: 5'11" Weight: 12.7
International Honours: W: U21-10; Yth; Sch

Regarded by no less than Neville Southall as Wales' future 'keeper, Danny played the first four games of last season for Tranmere as a replacement for the suspended Eric Nixon, and kept his place briefly. Returned to the side for the second-leg of the play-offs against Reading, again in place of Nixon. Athletic and brave, he kicks splendidly and has obviously benefited from the international experience he has gained with Wales.
Tranmere Rov (From trainee on 8/5/92) FL 10+1 Others 2

CRADDOCK Jody Darryl
Born: Bromsgrove, 25 July 1975
Height: 6'0" Weight: 11.13

After making his debut for Cambridge in 1993-94, last season saw this promising young right-footed central defender become a fixture in the first team, with performances that drew attention from a number of Premier League sides.
Cambridge U (Free from Christchurch on 13/8/93) FL 57+1 FLC 2/1 FAC 3 Others 3

CRANSON Ian
Born: Easington, 2 July 1964
Height: 5'11" Weight: 12.4
Club Honours: AMC '92; Div 2 '93
International Honours: E: U21-5

Still Stoke's record signing, he has become the defensive pivot the club had searched for for a long time. A succession of knee injuries disrupted his time at Sheffield and also his first two seasons at Stoke as cruciate ligament damage took its toll. However, he missed only nine games in 1994-95 and his consistency was excellent. Strong in the air and a sound tackler, he has also captained the side on occasions.

Ipswich T (From apprentice on 5/7/82) FL 130+1/5 FLC 15 FAC 11+1 Others 7
Sheffield Wed (£450,000 on 24/3/88) FL 29+1 FLC 2 FAC 2 Others 1
Stoke C (£450,000 on 25/7/89) FL 191+2/8 FLC 16/1 FAC 13/1 Others 26/1

Gerry Creaney   Matthew Ashton
(Empics Sports Photo Agency)

CREANEY Gerard (Gerry) Thomas
Born: Coatbridge, 13 April 1970
Height: 5'11" Weight: 12.7
International Honours: S: U21-11

Skilful Portsmouth striker with tremendous self-confidence who holds the ball up well, and has good strike-rate. 1994-95 was a fine season for Gerry who was rewarded for his excellent form with a call-up to the full Scotland squad. Despite often having to play up-front on his own, he scored a goal in almost every other game and has made the transition to English football quite easily.

Glasgow Celtic (From juniors on 15/5/87) SL 85+28/36 SLC 9+1/7 SC 9/8 Others 6+3/3
Portsmouth (£500,000 on 25/1/94) FL 57/29 FLC 5/3 FAC 2/1

CREASER Glyn Robert
Born: London, 1 September 1959
Height: 6'4" Weight: 14.10
Club Honours: FAT '91; GMVC '93

Wycombe club captain who made his League debut in 1993-94 at the age of 34, Glyn never let the side down with his more infrequent appearances last season. Seldom beaten in aerial battles, he is an inspiring leader.

Wycombe W (£15,000 from Barnet in September 1988) FL 17+2/2 FLC 2 FAC 10+1/2 Others 7+1/2

CRICHTON Paul Andrew
Born: Pontefract, 3 October 1968
Height: 6'0" Weight: 12.1

A goalkeeper with great anticipation and quick reactions who was remarkably released on a free transfer by Doncaster at the end of 1992-93, Paul has proved one of Grimsby's bargains of the '90s. Initially signed as cover for Rhys Wilmot, he took advantage of an injury to the latter to claim his first team place and has appeared in all senior League and cup games over the last two seasons, until rested to give deputy, Jason Pearcey, First Division experience in the final three matches of 1994-95. Voted the supporters' "Player of the Year" for 1993-94 he is arguably the club's best 'keeper since the legendary George Tweedy.

Nottingham F (From juniors on 23/5/86)
Notts Co (Loaned on 19/9/86) FL 5
Darlington (Loaned on 30/1/87) FL 5
Peterborough U (Loaned on 27/3/87) FL 4
Darlington (Loaned on 28/9/87) FL 3 FLC 1 Others 1
Swindon T (Loaned on 24/12/87) FL 4
Rotherham U (Loaned on 9/3/88) FL 6
Torquay U (Loaned on 25/8/88) FL 13 FLC 2
Peterborough U (Signed on 3/11/88) FL 47 FAC 5 Others 3
Doncaster Rov (Free on 25/8/90) FL 77 FLC 5 FAC 3 Others 5
Grimsby T (Free on 9/7/93) FL 89 FLC 5 FAC 3 Others 2

Paul Critchton   Barrington Coombs
(Empics Sports Photo Agency)

CROCKER Marcus Alan
Born: Plymouth, 8 October 1974
Height: 5'10" Weight: 11.5

A young striker, who is to be released by Plymouth at the end of the season, he spent a period on loan with Bath City and impressed. Has plenty of speed and is likely to get another chance at League football.

Plymouth Arg (From trainee on 8/6/93) FL 4+6 Others 0+1

CROFT Gary
Born: Burton on Trent, 17 February 1974
Height: 5'9" Weight: 10.8
International Honours: E: U21-3

A two-footed player, nominally a defender, but with the versatility to play almost anywhere, Gary is one of the pick of the young men to emerge from Grimsby's youth scheme. Equally at home on either side of defence, he is a strong tackler who loves carrying the ball and taking on the opposing defence. Having had the misfortune to miss a League representative game last season due to suspension, he made up for that disappointment when selected by England for the Toulon U21 tournament this summer.

Grimsby T (From trainee on 7/7/92) FL 103+10/2 FLC 5 FAC 3+2/1 Others 3

Ian Crook   Paul Marriott
(Empics Sports Photo Agency)

CROOK Ian Stuart
Born: Romford, 18 January 1963
Height: 5'8" Weight: 10.6
International Honours: E: B-1

Talented Norwich midfielder with silky passing skills. Played in the first 31 games in 1994-95, before a two match suspension sidelined him. With the club lacking goals on all fronts, not least from midfield, Ian tried desperately to redress the balance but, despite hitting the woodwork against Nottingham Forest in April, all he had to show for his efforts was a long-range shot that counted at Grimsby in the FA Cup. However, with a testimonial year on the horizon, he will be an integral part of City's drive to regain their Premiership place at the first attempt.

Tottenham H (From apprentice on 1/8/80) FL 10+10/1 FLC 1 FAC 0+1 Others 1+1
Norwich C (£80,000 on 13/6/86) F/PL 254+22/14 FLC 25+5/3 FAC 18+4/1 Others 16+1/1

CROSBY Andrew (Andy) Keith
Born: Rotherham, 3 March 1973
Height: 6'2" Weight: 13.0

Strong no-nonsense central defender who is commanding in the air and firm in the tackle, despite regularly coming forward for corners and free-kicks, Andy is still looking for his first goal in a Darlington shirt in over 60 appearances.

Doncaster Rov (Free from Leeds U juniors on 4/7/91) FL 41+10 FLC 1+1 FAC 2 Others 4+1/1
Darlington (Free on 10/12/93) FL 60 FLC 2 FAC 2 Others 2

CROSBY Gary
Born: Sleaford, 8 May 1964
Height: 5'7" Weight: 9.13
Club Honours: FLC '90; FMC '92

Left-winger. Initially struggled to establish himself in the Huddersfield first team in 1994-95 but, after starting to reproduce some of his best form, he suffered a cruel injury in dislocating his elbow. Although this ruled him out for the latter part of the season he was back in time for the play-offs. At his best, Gary is extremely quick off the mark and gets in super early crosses.

Lincoln C (Free from Lincoln U on 23/8/86) FL 6+1 FLC 2 (Free to Grantham in November 1986)
Nottingham F (£20,000 on 21/12/87) F/PL 139+13/12 FLC 29+1/6 FAC 18+3/3 Others 10+1/4
Grimsby T (Loaned on 23/8/93) FL 2+1
Huddersfield T (Free on 27/9/94) FL 16+3/4 FLC 1 FAC 1 Others 5+2/1

CROSS Jonathan Neil
Born: Wallasey, 2 March 1975
Height: 5'10" Weight: 11.4

This talented young Wrexham prospect, who plays on the right-hand side of midfield, was tipped a few years ago as having a big future in the game. Although his progress has slowed a little, he is fast and excellent on the ball, difficult to shake off when in possession, has a powerful shot, and is also effective up-front.

Wrexham (From trainee on 15/11/92) FL 75+17/10 FLC 4+2/1 FAC 4+1/1 Others 7+4/1

CROSS Nicholas (Nicky) Jeremy
Born: Birmingham, 7 February 1961
Height: 5'9" Weight: 11.2
Club Honours: AMC '93

Coming to Hereford during the 1994 close season, having been released by Port Vale, Nicky showed the ability to hold the ball up, allied to good vision. A dogged battler, with an excellent workrate, he played just behind the forwards.

West Bromwich A (From apprentice on 12/2/79) FL 68+37/15 FLC 6+2/2 FAC 5/1 Others 0+1
Walsall (£48,000 on 15/8/85) FL 107+2/45 FLC 10/2 FAC 12+1/3 Others 6+1/1

Leicester C (£65,000 on 21/1/88) FL 54+4/15 FLC 3+2/1 FAC 1 Others 1
Port Vale (£125,000 on 28/6/89) FL 120+24/39 FLC 2+4 FAC 12/1 Others 12+1/2
Hereford U (Free on 13/7/94) FL 24+4/6 FLC 4 FAC 2 Others 2+1/1

CROSS Paul
Born: Barnsley, 31 October 1965
Height: 5'8" Weight: 10.0

Started last season as Darlington club captain, but suffered a serious knee injury in October and has not played since. His steadying influence and overlapping from left-back was sorely missed. Freed during the summer.

Barnsley (From apprentice on 1/11/83) FL 115+4 FLC 8 FAC 11+1 Others 3+1
Preston NE (Loaned on 26/9/91) FL 5 Others 1
Hartlepool U (£20,000 on 24/1/92) FL 73+1/1 FLC 8 FAC 4 Others 5
Darlington (Signed on 18/11/93) FL 39/2 FLC 2/1 Others 1

CROSS Ryan
Born: Plymouth, 11 October 1972
Height: 6'0" Weight: 11.8

One of four players to have played at right-back last season for Bury, Ryan proved to be defensively sound but, with the manager calling for a more attacking format, he stood down.

Plymouth Arg (From trainee on 30/3/91) FL 18+1 FLC 2 Others 1
Hartlepool U (£75,000 on 11/6/92) FL 49+1/2 FLC 8 FAC 5 Others 5
Bury (Signed on 7/12/93) FL 27+2 FLC 2 FAC 4 Others 1

CROSSLEY Mark Geoffrey
Born: Barnsley, 16 June 1969
Height: 6'0" Weight: 15.0
International Honours: E: U21-3

A goalkeeper who stands up well and presents as little target as possible, Mark is at his best in one-to-one situations. With Nottingham Forest as a pro for over eight years, he has continued to improve, following a faltering start, to the point where he is now one of the top 'keepers in the country. Ever-present last season and one of the reasons why Forest gave such a good account of themselves in the Premiership.

Nottingham F (From trainee on 2/7/87) F/PL 199+1 FLC 29 FAC 22 Others 10

CROSSLEY Matthew (Matt) John William
Born: Basingstoke, 18 March 1968
Height: 6'2" Weight: 13.4
Club Honours: FAT '91, '93; GMVC '93

Had an outstanding season for Wycombe in 1994-95 at centre-half, where he was rarely beaten in the air, or on the ground, thanks to his deceptive pace and fine anticipation.

Wycombe W (Signed from Overton U in 1987-88) FL 74+1/2 FLC 4 FAC 14 Others 9

CULLING Gary
Born: Braintree, 6 April 1972
Height: 5'10" Weight: 11.4

Young right-back who Colchester signed from Braintree after a successful trial spell prior to 1994-95, he started off in the first team but quickly lost his place. Released in March 1995, Gary returned to non-league level.

Colchester U (£5,000 from Braintree T on 11/8/94) FL 2 FLC 1

CULVERHOUSE Ian Brett
Born: Bishops Stortford, 22 September 1964
Height: 5'10" Weight: 11.2
Club Honours: Div 2 '86
International Honours: E: Yth

Experienced defender signed from Norwich City last December, and Steve McMahon's first capture as manager, Ian looked set to give some added stability to Swindon's back-line, but sadly his season was over by the beginning of March. A persistent ankle problem became too troublesome and he was restricted to just a dozen games.

Tottenham H (From apprentice on 24/9/82) FL 1+1
Norwich C (£50,000 on 8/10/85) F/PL 295+1/1 FLC 23 FAC 28 Others 22/1
Swindon T (£250,000 on 9/12/94) FL 9 FLC 1 FAC 2

CUNNINGHAM Kenneth (Ken) Edward
Born: Dublin, 28 June 1971
Height: 6'0" Weight: 11.8
International Honours: Ei: B-2; U21-4

Part of the £1,250,000 deal that took both him and Jon Goodman to Wimbledon from Millwall last November, Ken is a consistent right-back who can also fill in on the other flank with ease, if required. Since arriving at Selhurst Park, he has hardly put a foot wrong, shown good use of the ball, worked the overlap well, and become an automatic choice. Has also played in a three man central defence on occasion.

Millwall (Signed from Tolka Rov on 18/9/89) FL 132+4/1 FLC 10 FAC 1 Others 5+1/1
Wimbledon (Signed on 9/11/94) PL 28 FAC 4

Ken Cunningham   Neal Simpson
(Empics Sports Photo Agency)

Keith Curle

Paul Marriott
(Empics Sports Photo Agency)

Consistent as ever in the centre of the defence, Keith held Manchester City together through difficult times in 1994-95. Injured against Arsenal, he showed his resilience when staying on the field after both subs had been used and throughout the season he would be continually dogged by hamstring problems. Gave a masterful performance at Maine Road against Leeds, when spraying passes about and roaming forward on occasions. Also, an addition to his repertoire, was in picking the right opportunity of going forward, trading passes with the front men, and finishing with a shot on goal. It would be difficult to imagine City without him.

Bristol Rov (From apprentice on 20/11/81) FL 21+11/4 FLC 3 FAC 1
Torquay U (£5,000 on 4/11/83) FL 16/5 FAC 1/1 Others 1
Bristol C (£10,000 on 3/3/84) FL 113+8/1 FLC 7+1 FAC 5 Others 14/1
Reading (£150,000 on 23/10/87) FL 40 FLC 8 Others 5
Wimbledon (£500,000 on 21/10/88) FL 91+2/3 FLC 7 FAC 5 Others 6/1
Manchester C (£2,500,000 on 14/8/91) F/PL 139/11 FLC 15/1 FAC 9 Others 1

CURRAN Christopher (Chris)
Born: Birmingham, 17 September 1971
Height: 5'11" Weight: 11.9
Central defender and Torquay captain, and a man who leads by example, suspension and injury caused him to miss a number of key games in 1994-95.

Torquay U (From trainee on 13/7/90) FL 127+6/3 FLC 12 FAC 5 Others 8

CURRIE Darren Paul
Born: Hampstead, 29 November 1974
Height: 5'9" Weight: 11.7
A left-winger with the ability to go past defenders and cross with either foot, Darren had two spells at Shrewsbury in 1994-95, while on loan from West Ham. Always giving Town total commitment, and scoring a fine goal on his debut, his runs down the line made him very popular with the crowd before he returned to Upton Park.

West Ham U (From trainee on 2/7/93)
Shrewsbury T (Loaned on 5/9/94) FL 10+2/2
Shrewsbury T (Loaned on 3/2/95) FL 5

CURRIE David Norman
Born: Stockton, 27 November 1962
Height: 6'0" Weight: 11.13
Club Honours: Div 2 '91, Div 3 '95
After a slow start at Carlisle, David soon established himself as the orchestrator of the side and fulcrum of many of the attacks. His touch and passing skill, coupled with the ability to deliver wicked left-footed crosses and corners, posed many problems for opposing defences and led to a number of goals. He also scored himself and a 35 yard effort against Rochdale was voted "Goal of the Season". Won a Third Division Championship medal.

Middlesbrough (Signed on 5/2/82) FL 94+19/31 FLC 6/1 FAC 5+1 Others 2
Darlington (Free on 17/6/86) FL 76/33 FLC 6 FAC 3 Others 5/3
Barnsley (£150,000 on 26/2/88) FL 80/30 FLC 3/1 FAC 5/4 Others 1

CUNNINGTON Shaun Gary
Born: Bourne, 4 January 1966
Height: 5'9" Weight: 11.0
Club Honours: WC '86
Strong-running Sunderland midfielder, whose season in 1994-95 was ruined by a succession of leg injuries, he is at his best in a wide-right position and can weigh-in with his share of goals.

Wrexham (From juniors on 11/1/84) FL 196+3/12 FLC 13 FAC 9/1 Others 21/2
Grimsby T (£55,000 on 19/2/88) FL 182/13 FLC 11 FAC 11/3 Others 9
Sunderland (£650,000 on 17/7/92) FL 52+6/8 FLC 3 FAC 2/1 Others 2

CURETON Jamie
Born: Bristol, 28 August 1975
Height: 5'8" Weight: 10.0
International Honours: E: Yth

Extremely quick around the box, and always looking for the chance to score, at the end of last season, Jamie had netted 126 goals in 180 games for Norwich at all levels. Having arrived in the senior team earlier, he struck an outstanding goal in the March "derby" match against Ipswich, helping to end the club's depressing sequence of 11 Premiership games without a victory and also scored against Chelsea, Arsenal and Manchester City. With a little more weight he will be a handful for any defender.

Norwich C (From trainee on 5/2/93) PL 9+8/4 FLC 0+1 FAC 0+2

CURLE Keith
Born: Bristol, 14 November 1963
Height: 6'0" Weight: 12.0
Club Honours: AMC '86; FMC '88
International Honours: E: 3; B-4

Nottingham F (£750,000 on 19/1/90) FL 4+4/1
Oldham Ath (£460,000 on 23/8/90) FL 17+14/3 FLC 2+1/2 FAC 1 Others 0+1
Barnsley (£250,000 on 5/9/91) FL 53+22/12 FLC 2+1 FAC 4+1 Others 1+1/1
Rotherham U (Loaned on 15/10/92) FL 5/2
Huddersfield T (Loaned on 10/1/94) FL 7/1 Others 1
Carlisle U (Free on 18/7/94) FL 38/4 FLC 3+1 FAC 3/1 Others 7/4

CURTIS Robert (Robbie) Anthony
Born: Shirebrook, 21 May 1972
Height: 6'0" Weight: 13.0

Signed from Boston during the 1994 close season as cover to the central defenders, Robbie made several appearances for Northampton last season, and played with a no-nonsense style of safety first. Unfortunate to miss a large chunk of the campaign through injury, he was released during the summer.

Northampton T (Free from Boston U on 19/6/94) FL 13 FLC 2 Others 1+1

CURTIS Thomas (Tommy) David
Born: Exeter, 1 March 1973
Height: 5'8" Weight: 11.4

A regular in the middle of Chesterfield's midfield with some typically tigerish performances last season, he excels at denying others space, while opening play up with a cultured short-passing game that belies his comparative inexperience. Tom's emergence is all the more remarkable for the fact that he is a full-time student at Loughborough University. Missed very few games in the clubs run to the Second Division, via the play-offs.

Derby Co (From juniors on 1/7/91)
Chesterfield (Free on 12/8/93) FL 74+2/5 FLC 8+1 FAC 3 Others 5

CUSACK Nicholas (Nicky) John
Born: Maltby, 24 December 1965
Height: 6'0" Weight: 11.13

After an impressive two month loan period at Fulham, Nicky was transferred from Oxford in December 1994. Full of running, and strong in the air, he built up a good understanding with both Rory Hamill and Gary Brazil and brought a cohesion to the front line that was previously missing.

Leicester C (Signed from Alvechurch on 18/6/87) FL 5+11/1 FAC 0+1 Others 1+1
Peterborough U (£40,000 on 29/7/88) FL 44/10 FLC 4/1 FAC 4/1 Others 2
Motherwell (£100,000 on 2/8/89) SL 68+9/17 SLC 5/4 SC 3+1/2 Others 1+1/1
Darlington (£95,000 on 24/1/92) FL 21/6
Oxford U (£95,000 on 16/7/92) FL 48+13/10 FLC 3/2 FAC 4+2/1 Others 2+1
Wycombe W (Loaned on 24/3/94) FL 2+2
Fulham (Free on 4/11/94) FL 26+1/7 FAC 2 Others 2/1

DAISH Liam Sean
Born: Portsmouth, 23 September 1968
Height: 6'2" Weight: 13.5
Club Honours: Div 3 '91, B-1; Div 2 '95; AMC '95
International Honours: Ei: 1; U21-5

Barry Fry once said of Liam that if ever a double decker bus came along he would herd it away. This epitomised the whole-hearted defender and Birmingham captain,

who was a great inspiration to the whole team in 1994-95, while forming a solid central defensive partnership with Dave Barnett. Dangerous at set-pieces, he scored a number of vital goals during the promotion push, none more so than in the key game against Brentford. In leading the club to the Second Division title and the Auto Windscreen Shield victory, his qualities were recognised by Jack Charlton, who recalled him to the Republic of Ireland squad, and by his fellow professionals, who voted him into the PFA Award winning Second Division team.

Portsmouth (From apprentice on 29/9/86) FL 1 Others 1+1
Cambridge U (Free on 11/7/88) FL 138+1/4 FLC 11 FAC 17 Others 15/3
Birmingham C (£50,000 on 10/1/94) FL 56/3 FLC 3/1 FAC 5 Others 7

Liam Daish   Barry Coombs
(Empics Sports Photo Agency)

DAKIN Simon Mark
Born: Nottingham, 30 November 1974
Height: 5'9" Weight: 11.2

It was thought that Simon was mainly competing for the Hull right-back berth in 1994-95 until an impressive late term stint at centre-back. Earlier, he had struggled to establish a regular place following an early season injury. Had a terrible accident during the summer when falling 60 feet down a lift shaft, but escaped with broken ribs.

Hull C (Free from Derby Co juniors on 24/3/94) FL 27+3/1 FLC 1+1 FAC 1 Others 1

DALE Carl
Born: Colwyn Bay, 24 April 1966
Height: 5'8" Weight: 10.7
Club Honours: WC '92, '93; Div 3 '93

Played in the shadow of fellow Cardiff striker, Phil Stant, for much of last season but, following his departure, Carl struck up a rich goalscoring seam until knee ligament trouble meant he missed six crucial matches. Scored on his return, however.

Chester C (£12,000 from Bangor C on 19/5/88) FL 106+10/41 FLC 7+1 FAC 9/5 Others 6/2
Cardiff C (£100,000 on 19/8/91) FL 100+11/38 FLC 5+1/2 FAC 4 Others 14+1/13

DALEY Anthony (Tony) Mark
Born: Birmingham, 18 October 1967
Height: 5'8" Weight: 10.8
Club Honours: FLC '94
International Honours: E: 7; B-1; Yth

A winger famed for acceleration and fast shooting, Tony was a big money Wolverhampton signing from Villa in the summer of 1994, but suffered a pre-season setback when his cartilage went. The fans waited until October, before he was brought on as a sub against Millwall, but within seconds he was limping. Completed the match, but those 13 minutes were his entire season as he now had a cruciate problem and required reconstructive surgery to his left-knee.

Aston Villa (From apprentice on 31/5/85) F/PL 189+44/31 FLC 22+2/4 FAC 15+1/2 Others 15+2/1
Wolverhampton W (£1,250,000 on 6/6/94) FL 0+1

DALEY Philip (Phil)
Born: Liverpool, 12 April 1967
Height: 6'2" Weight: 12.9

Strong and powerful Lincoln striker capable of holding the ball up well. Unfortunately, a knee injury suffered against Darlington at the turn of the year, necessitated a cartilage operation and led to a lengthy absence.

Wigan Ath (Signed from Newtown on 12/10/89) FL 152+9/39 FLC 16/1 FAC 11+1 Others 15/6
Lincoln C (£40,000 on 1/8/94) FL 19+1/4 FLC 2+1 FAC 1 Others 2+1/1

DALLI Jean
Born: Enfield, 13 August 1976
Height: 5'9" Weight: 10.10

A young left-back who worked his way through the Colchester youth ranks and made his debut in the opening game of last season, Jean was unfortunate to have further chances restricted by a long-term injury. Currently on the club's books as a non-contract player.

Colchester U (From juniors on 12/8/94) FL 1

DALTON Paul
Born: Middlesbrough, 25 April 1967
Height: 5'11" Weight: 12.0

An extremely talented winger who can play on either side of the pitch, he is pre-dominantly left-footed and has the ability to embarrass any defender at this level, with his exceptional close control. Absent for the majority of last season with a back problem. Plymouth have missed his ability to create and score goals and at dead-ball situations.

Manchester U (£35,000 from Brandon U on 3/5/87)
Hartlepool U (£20,000 on 4/3/89) FL 140+11/37 FLC 10/2 FAC 7/1 Others 9/3
Plymouth Arg (£275,000 on 11/6/92) FL 93+5/25 FLC 5/2 FAC 7/5 Others 6

DANIEL Raymond (Ray) Christopher
Born: Luton, 10 December 1964
Height: 5'8" Weight: 12.2
International Honours: E: Yth

Left-sided, hard-tackling Portsmouth full-back who had a real season of ups-and-downs. Having asked to go on the transfer list under Jim Smith, and following a loan

period at Notts County, he decided to come off it after discussions with new manager, Terry Fenwick. Left out in the cold for most of the season, he regained his place in December as the fortunes of the team changed, but was then hit by injury early in 1995 and was once again sidelined. Freed during the summer.
Luton T (From apprentice on 7/9/82) FL 14+8/4 FLC 2 FAC 5+1
Gillingham (Loaned on 1/9/83) FL 5
Hull C (Free on 30/6/86) FL 55+3/3 FLC 1 FAC 1+1 Others 0+1
Cardiff C (£40,000 on 22/8/89) FL 56/1 FLC 5 FAC 5 Others 1
Portsmouth (£80,000 on 9/11/90) FL 91+9/4 FLC 7+2 FAC 6 Others 6+1/1
Notts Co (Loaned on 28/10/94) FL 5 Others 1

DANIELS Scott Charles
Born: Benfleet, 22 November 1969
Height: 6'1" Weight: 11.9
A central defender, who can also play at full-back or in midfield, he was taken off after a few minutes of his Northampton debut with an injury, forcing him to miss six weeks of the season. Signed from Exeter last January, he was released during the summer.
Colchester U (From trainee on 1/7/88) FL 64+9 FLC 2 FAC 10 Others 4+1
Exeter C (£50,000 on 16/8/91) FL 114+3/7 FLC 7 FAC 10+1 Others 15/1
Northampton T (Free on 30/1/95) FL 5+3

DANZEY Michael (Mick) James
Born: Widnes, 8 February 1971
Height: 6'1" Weight: 12.0
Released by Cambridge at the end of the 1993-94 season, Mick returned to the club as a non-contract player, which included a spell on loan at Aylesbury. A left-footed defensive player, he was normally used in a utility role.
Nottingham F (From trainee on 20/5/89)
Chester C (Loaned on 27/2/90) FL 0+2
Peterborough U (Free on 30/1/91) FL 0+1
Cambridge U (Signed from St Albans C on 23/10/92) FL 18+9/3 FLC 4+1/1 FAC 0+2 Others 1+2
Scunthorpe U (Loaned on 4/2/94) FL 3/1

DARBY Duane Anthony
Born: Birmingham, 17 October 1973
Height: 5'11" Weight: 11.2
Torquay striker who had a disappointing season in 1994-95, but is still the best finisher at Torquay. Continues to have a bright future ahead of him.
Torquay U (From trainee on 3/7/92) FL 60+48/26 FLC 4+3/1 FAC 1+4 Others 5+3/2

DARBY Julian Timothy
Born: Bolton, 3 October 1967
Height: 6'0" Weight: 11.4
Club Honours: AMC '89
International Honours: E: Sch
Hard-working Coventry midfielder/utility player, who was almost ever-present under Phil Neal, but replaced by Kevin Richardson as soon as Ron Atkinson arrived last season. His strength in getting into the opponent's penalty area was rarely displayed and, subsequently, he scored only one goal in 35 games.
Bolton W (From trainee on 22/7/86) FL

258+12/36 FLC 25/8 FAC 19/3 Others 31+1/5
Coventry C (£150,000 on 28/10/93) PL 52+3/5 FLC 3/1 FAC 2+2

DARTON Scott Richard
Born: Ipswich, 27 March 1975
Height: 5'11" Weight: 11.3
A young left-back with good technique, having come in for a lot of criticism from Albion fans early in 1994-95, he had a spell on loan at Blackpool before signing permanently. Since arriving at Bloomfield Road, Scott has performed impressively and, at 20-years-of-age, looks certain to make steady progress.
West Bromwich A (From trainee on 28/10/92) FL 15 FLC 1 Others 5/1
Blackpool (£7,500 on 20/1/95) FL 18

DAUGHTRY Paul William
Born: Oldham, 14 February 1973
Height: 5'6" Weight: 10.5
Right-sided Hartlepool midfielder who was signed last November from Droylsden after unsuccessful trials with Gillingham and York. Although a hard worker, the club's lack of finances meant he was only on a month-to-month contract, before being released in April to join Swedish side, Moron Bollklubbe.
Stockport Co (Free from Buxton on 19/1/94)
Hartlepool U (Free from Droylsden on 25/11/94) FL 14+1

D'AURIA David Alan
Born: Swansea, 26 March 1970
Height: 5'8" Weight: 11.0
Club Honours: WC '94
International Honours: W: Yth; Sch
David was the "find" of last season for Scarborough, being signed from Welsh non-league soccer and making an immediate impact in scoring some priceless goals from an attacking midfield role. Won the supporters' "Player of the Year" award.
Swansea C (From trainee on 2/8/88) FL 27+18/6 FLC 2+2 FAC 1 Others 4 (Free transfer to Merthyr Tydfil during 1991 close season)
Scarborough (Signed on 22/8/94) FL 31+3/7 FLC 1+2 FAC 3+1 Others 1

DAVENPORT Peter
Born: Birkenhead, 24 March 1961
Height: 5'11" Weight: 11.3
International Honours: E: 1; B-1
Much travelled striker, who still knows where the goal is, although more of a maker than taker these days, Peter came to Stockport last season as a deadline day signing, having spent nearly two seasons in Scottish football. Scored his first goal for County a month later in the 2-0 home win against Brighton.
Nottingham F (Free from Camel Laird on 5/1/82) FL 114+4/54 FLC 10/1 FAC 7+1/1 Others 10+1/2
Manchester U (£750,000 on 12/3/86) FL 73+19/22 FLC 8+2/4 FAC 2+2
Middlesbrough (£750,000 on 3/11/88) FL 53+6/7 FLC 2 FAC 4 Others 7+1/1
Sunderland (£350,000 on 19/7/90) FL 72+27/15 FLC 5+2/1 FAC 9+1/1 Others 14+1
Airdrie (Free during 1993 close season) SL 35+3/9 SLC 3/1 SC 3+2
St Johnstone (Free on 16/8/94) SL 12+10/4 SLC 3 SC 0+1 Others 2/1
Stockport Co (on 23/3/95) FL 3+3/1

Simon Davey   Tony Marshall
(Empics Sports Photo Agency)

DAVEY Simon
Born: Swansea, 1 October 1970
Height: 5'10" Weight: 11.2
Club Honours: Div 3 '95
Right-sided Preston midfielder, signed from Carlisle in a surprise deal last season, Simon is a tough tackler, powerful going forward, with an eye for goal, and an excellent passer and dead-ball specialist, who adds fire to midfield at both ends of the field.
Swansea C (From trainee on 3/7/89) FL 37+12/4 FLC 1 FAC 1+2/1 Others 2+3
Carlisle U (Free on 5/8/92) FL 105/18 FLC 10/1 FAC 7/2 Others 15/2
Preston NE (£125,000 on 22/2/95) FL 13/3 Others 2

DAVIDSON Craig Lee
Born: Romford, 2 May 1974
Height: 5'9" Weight: 11.8
An all-action, combative midfielder who was on the fringe of Southend's First Division squad in 1994-95, after coming on for the last eight minutes of the losing Coca Cola Cup game at Watford in September. However, he failed to break-through and was freed at the end of the season.
Southend U (From trainee on 6/7/93) FLC 0+1

DAVIDSON Ross James
Born: Chertsey, 13 November 1973
Height: 5'8" Weight: 11.6
Having earned a contract from his trial period in the summer of 1993, Ross was another of the Sheffield United youngsters to play in the Anglo-Italian Cup last season. Made his FL debut in the final match of 1994-95 at right-back, giving an assured performance.
Sheffield U (Signed from Walton & Hersham on 5/6/93) FL 1 Others 2

DAVIES Gareth Melville
Born: Hereford, 11 December 1973
Height: 5'10" Weight: 11.3

International Honours: W: U21-7

Hereford central defender. Now a regular at Welsh U21 level, Gareth is a strong and forceful tackler, who can also play in midfield, from where he likes to push forward. Always giving 100 per-cent, he is a centre-forward's nightmare.

Hereford U (From trainee on 10/4/92) FL 91+4/2 FLC 5+2 FAC 4 Others 5

DAVIES Kevin Cyril
Born: Sheffield, 26 March 1977
Height: 6'2" Weight: 12.6
International Honours: E: Yth

A remarkable young talent, Kevin operates on the right-hand side of Chesterfield's forward line and contributed some vital goals to the play-off campaign in 1994-95. Still only 18, he possesses fine, close control and plays without fear of failure, being supremely confident for one so young.

Chesterfield (From trainee on 18/4/94) FL 57+8/15 FLC 4+1/1 FAC 1 Others 5+2/1

DAVIES Michael (Mike) John
Born: Stretford, 19 January 1966
Height: 5'9" Weight: 11.10

As Blackpool's longest serving player, and the regular right-back until suffering a serious injury in January 1994, he only started one game last season because of continuing fitness problems and was freed during the summer.

Blackpool (From apprentice on 19/1/84) FL 276+34/16 FLC 23+1/1 FAC 15+6 Others 23+6/2

DAVIES Simon Ithel
Born: Winsford, 23 April 1974
Height: 5'11" Weight: 11.8
Club Honours: FAYC '92

Skilful Manchester United midfield player who possesses superb skills on the ball. Simon made a great impression on Alan Ball, when on loan at Exeter City in 1993-94, but made a bigger name for himself at Old Trafford when he scored a wonderful goal against Galatasaray in the European Cup last season. A former Youth team captain, he is another with a bright future.

Manchester U (From trainee on 6/7/92) PL 3+2 FLC 3 Others 2/1
Exeter C (Loaned on 17/12/93) FL 5+1/1 FAC 1

DAVIES William (Will)
Born: Derby, 27 September 1975
Height: 6'2" Weight: 13.4

Another of the Derby players to come through the youth side, the young central defender's outstanding form in the reserves brought him promotion to the first team squad last October at Piacenza in the AIC. Injuries led to him playing up-front in the next League game against Watford, where he had the misfortune to dislocate his shoulder. Returned as an occasional squad member later in the season.

Derby Co (From trainee on 12/7/94) FL 1+1 Others 0+1

DAVIS Arron Spencer
Born: Wanstead, 11 February 1972
Height: 5'7" Weight: 11.0

A former Torquay professional, now with

Dorchester, he had a brief trial at Colchester last August in an attempt to plug the gap at left-back and looked reasonable, although not retained.

Torquay U (From trainee on 17/8/91) FL 20+4 FLC 2+1 Others 1
Colchester U (Free from Dorchester T on 18/8/94) FL 4 FLC 1

DAVIS Darren John
Born: Sutton in Ashfield, 5 February 1967
Height: 6'0" Weight: 11.0
International Honours: E: Yth

Uncompromising Scarborough central defender who, unfortunately, struggled with niggling injuries last season. Although outstanding in the club's two FA Cup clashes with First Division Watford, and is a wholehearted player who always gave 100 per-cent, Darren was freed at the end of 1994-95.

Notts Co (From apprentice on 5/2/85) FL 90+2/1 FLC 6 FAC 6/1 Others 7
Lincoln C (Signed on 25/8/88) FL 97+5/4 FLC 8/1 FAC 4/1 Others 6/1
Maidstone U (£27,500 on 28/3/91) FL 31/2 FLC 2 FAC 2 Others 1 (Free to Frickley Ath during 1992 close season)
Scarborough (Free on 1/8/93) FL 46+2/3 FLC 2+1 FAC 6 Others 4/1

DAVIS Kelvin Geoffrey
Born: Bedford, 29 September 1976
Height: 6'1" Weight: 13.2
International Honours: E: Yth

Having made his Luton first team debut in the final match of 1993-94, this goalkeeping prodigy had to wait until the home derby with Watford last March for his next chance. Standing in for Juergen Sommer, he took it in style, even making a penalty save and subsequently retained his place, with the American international on the bench. Earlier, Kelvin had enjoyed a successful loan spell at Torquay, had been a reserve for the Endsleigh U21 side in Italy and had played for the England Youth team, before being called up to join England's U21 squad at the end of the season. Clearly, at 18-years-of-age, he is an outstanding prospect.

Luton T (From trainee on 1/7/94) FL 10
Torquay U (Loaned on 16/9/94) FL 2 FLC 1 Others 1

DAVIS Michael (Mike) Vernon
Born: Bristol, 19 October 1974
Height: 6'0" Weight: 12.0

Despite scoring on his Bristol Rovers' FL debut at Millwall two seasons ago, the young striker has failed to add to that tally of goals at first team level. Due to the tremendous competition for forward places, Mike made just two subs' appearances for Rovers last season, having been loaned out to Hereford earlier.

Bristol Rov (Free from Yate T on 26/4/93) FL 2+11/1 Others 0+1
Hereford U (Loaned on 19/8/94) FL 1

DAVIS Paul Vincent
Born: Dulwich, 9 December 1961
Height: 5'10" Weight: 10.13
Club Honours: FLC '87, '93; Div 1 '89, '91; FAC '93; ECWC '94
International Honours: E: B-1; U21-11

The longest serving Arsenal player of last year's squad, Paul turned pro back in the 1979 close season. At his best, a silky, cultured midfielder with a super left-foot, and a player who always appeared to have plenty of time on the ball. Still reckoned by many to be the club's number one playmaker, with his good vision and precise passing, he scored at Nottingham Forest last December when making a rare first team appearance, before being given a free transfer at the end of the season.

Arsenal (From apprentice on 11/7/79) F/PL 331+20/30 FLC 47+5/4 FAC 22+5/3 Others 19+1/1

DAVIS Stephen (Steve) Mark
Born: Hexham, 30 October 1968
Height: 6'2" Weight: 12.8
Club Honours: Div 4 '92

Took over as Burnley's captain at the start of last term and had his best season at the club. A commanding central defender, Steve was often the man to ease a crisis situation at the back, and was equally impressive on surging runs forward or in his positional sense at set-pieces. In a campaign when the club seemed unable to find a successful strike partner-ship, he was joint leading scorer for a spell and, although his form was less consistent in the second half, Burnley will do well to retain his services.

Southampton (From trainee on 6/7/87) FL 5+1
Burnley (Loaned on 21/11/89) FL 7+2
Notts Co (Loaned on 28/3/91) FL 0+2
Burnley (£60,000 on 17/8/91) FL 162/22 FLC 10/2 FAC 18/1 Others 13

DAVIS Steven (Steve) Peter
Born: Birmingham, 26 July 1965
Height: 6'0" Weight: 12.7
International Honours: E: Yth

After three injury wrecked seasons, Steve finally showed the Barnsley public his true form in 1994-95. His calming influence and ability to read the game brought about a definite tightening up in the centre of the defence. He also proved a handful in attack from set pieces.

Crewe Alex (Free from Stoke C juniors on 17/8/83) FL 140+5/1 FLC 10 FAC 3 Others 7+1
Burnley (£15,000 on 3/10/87) FL 147/11 FLC 7 FAC 9 Others 19/1
Barnsley (£180,000 on 26/7/91) FL 52+4/2 FLC 2 FAC 1

DAVISON Aidan John
Born: Sedgefield, 11 May 1968
Height: 6'1" Weight: 13.12

A capable understudy to Keith Branagan in Bolton's goal, Aidan did not get his first chance of 1994-95 until last February, when Branagan was sent off in a 1-1 draw at Notts County. Davison was then sent off himself in a 1-1 draw at Stoke, which opened the door for the evergreen Peter Shilton to take over as the substitute 'keeper.

Notts Co (Signed from Billingham Synthonia on 25/3/88) FL 1
Bury (£6,000 on 7/10/89)
Millwall (Free on 14/8/91) FL 34 FLC 3 FAC 3 Others 2
Bolton W (£25,000 on 26/7/93) FL 33+2 FAC 8 Others 4

DAVISON Robert (Bobby)
Born: South Shields, 17 July 1959
Height: 5'9" Weight: 11.9
Club Honours: Div 2 '87, '90

Joined Rotherham from Sheffield United in the early part of last season and quickly became a valuable asset, with his experience showing through. He also demonstrated that he still has the goalscoring knack that has been a feature of his play for many years.
Huddersfield T (£1,000 from Seaham Colliery on 2/7/80) FL 1+1
Halifax T (£20,000 on 28/8/81) FL 63/29 FLC 4/4 FAC 2
Derby Co (£90,000 on 2/12/82) FL 203+3/83 FLC 18/6 FAC 11/7 Others 4/2
Leeds U (£350,000 on 27/11/87) FL 79+12/31 FLC 4/1 FAC 2+4/1 Others 7+2/3
Derby Co (Loaned on 19/9/91) FL 10/8
Leicester C (£50,000 on 12/8/92) FL 21+4/6 FLC 3/1 Others 3/2
Sheffield U (Loaned on 6/3/92) FL 6+5/4
Sheffield U (Free on 4/11/93) P/FL 9+3/1 FLC 2/1 Others 2
Rotherham U (Free on 14/10/94) FL 19+2/4 FAC 2/3 Others 2

DAWE Simon
Born: Plymouth, 16 March 1977
Height: 5'11" Weight: 11.0

A young midfielder, who was promoted to the Plymouth first team in the absence of more experienced colleagues, he made his debut at home to Brighton while still a trainee.
Plymouth Arg (Trainee) FL 3+1

DAWES Ian Robert
Born: Croydon, 22 February 1963
Height: 5'10" Weight: 11.10
Club Honours: Div 2 '83
International Honours: E: Sch

One of Millwall's longest serving players, consistently putting in faultless performances at either right or left-back. Equally adept whether defending or assisting the attack, 1994-95 for Ian was decimated by an ongoing knee problem.
Queens Park R (From apprentice on 24/12/80) FL 229/3 FLC 28/1 FAC 8 Others 5
Millwall (£150,000 on 26/8/88) FL 119+6/5 FLC 17+1 FAC 16 Others 8+1

DAWS Anthony (Tony)
Born: Sheffield, 10 September 1966
Height: 5'8" Weight: 11.10
International Honours: E: Yth; Sch

Nippy Lincoln striker who on occasion last season suffered severely at the hands of opposition defenders. Has excellent ball control and creates chances by finding good positions in the box.
Notts Co (From apprentice on 18/9/84) FL 6+2/1
Sheffield U (Free on 21/8/86) FL 7+4/3 FAC 1 Others 0+1
Scunthorpe U (Free on 2/7/87) FL 166+17/63 FLC 15+1/4 FAC 9/2 Others 23+1/3
Grimsby T (£50,000 on 25/3/93) FL 14+2/1 FLC 2 Others 1+1/1
Lincoln C (£50,000 on 15/2/94) FL 34+6/10 FAC 1+1 Others 1

DAWS Nicholas (Nick) John
Born: Manchester, 15 March 1970
Height: 5'11" Weight: 13.2

Midfield powerhouse and Bury's anchorman, Nick's ability to reach the area with his long throw-ins created many chances for the side throughout last season.
Bury (£10,000 from Altrincham on 13/8/92) FL 98+9/4 FLC 6+1 FAC 9 Others 10+2

DEANE Brian Christopher
Born: Leeds, 7 February 1968
Height: 6'3" Weight: 12.7
International Honours: E: 3; B-3

Had a much improved season at Leeds in 1994-95, without getting the goals he merited. Began at centre-forward, but eventually operated in a more withdrawn left-sided position, using his power in the air to create chances for others. Quick off the mark, brave and powerful, Brian always gives his all and is immensely popular with the supporters. It also showed he was appreciated by the club when Howard Wilkinson rejected a pre-deadline bid of £2,300,000 from Everton.
Doncaster Rov (From juniors on 14/12/85) FL 59+7/12 FLC 3 FAC 2+1/1 Others 2+2
Sheffield U (£30,000 on 19/7/88) F/PL 197+82 FLC 16/11 FAC 23+1/11 Others 2/2
Leeds U (£2,900,000 on 14/7/93) PL 74+2/20 FLC 3+1 FAC 6/2

Brian Deane   Neal Simpson
(Empics Sports Photo Agency)

DEARDEN Kevin Charles
Born: Luton, 8 March 1970
Height: 5'11" Weight: 12.8

Good shot-stopping goalkeeper. Another excellent season for Kevin at Brentford, where he proved to be extremely reliable, in keeping 25 clean sheets during 1994-95. Apart from his ability between the posts, his early use of the ball makes him vital to the club's cause.
Tottenham H (From trainee on 5/8/88) PL 0+1 FLC 1
Cambridge U (Loaned on 9/3/89) FL 15
Hartlepool U (Loaned on 31/8/89) FL 10
Swindon T (Loaned on 23/3/90) FL 1
Peterborough U (Loaned on 24/8/90) FL 7
Hull C (Loaned on 10/1/91) FL 3
Rochdale (Loaned on 16/8/91) FL 2
Birmingham C (Loaned on 19/3/92) FL 12
Brentford (Free on 30/9/93) FL 78 FLC 4 FAC 4 Others 9

Kevin Dearden   Paul Marriott
(Empics Sports Photo Agency)

DEARY John Steele
Born: Ormskirk, 18 October 1962
Height: 5'10" Weight: 12.4
Club Honours: Div 4 '92

The sale of John to Rochdale last January was one of Burnley's most unpopular decisions of 1994-95. A battling midfielder with an eye for goal, he seemed to have found a new maturity and was frequently the focal point of the side, before losing his place to Jamie Hoyland. Marked his debut at Rochdale by scoring the winning goal against Hartlepool.
Blackpool (From apprentice on 13/3/80) FL 285+18/43 FLC 20/5 FAC 16+2/4 Others 14/1
Burnley (£30,000 on 18/7/89) FL 209+6/23 FLC 13+3/1 FAC 20+1/2 Others 21/1
Rochdale (£25,000 on 30/1/95) FL 17/1 Others 3

DEEGAN Mark
Born: Liverpool, 12 November 1971
Height: 6'0" Weight: 11.7
International Honours: W: SP

Joined Oxford last August from Holywell Town and was the regular back-up 'keeper for Phil Whitehead in 1994-95, making five appearances. Although showing promise, Mark was released during the summer.
Oxford U (Free from Holywell T on 24/8/94) FL 2 Others 3

DE FREITAS Fabian
Born: Paramaribo, 28 July 1972
Height: 6'1" Weight: 12.9

Forward. As Bolton's record signing from FC Vollendam, just before the start of last season, Fabian found the pace of the English game difficult at first, but settled down to show that his own pace was not in question, causing many a defence problems in his few FL appearances. He saved the best till last, however, hitting two goals to double his tally in the play-off final, in a game that saw the club reach the Premiership with a 4-3 victory over Reading.
Bolton W (£400,000 from Vollendam on 19/8/94) FL 7+6/2 FLC 0+3 Others 0+2/2

DELAP Rory John
Born: Sutton Coldfield, 6 July 1976
Height: 6'0" Weight: 11.13

Forward. A product of Carlisle's youth ranks who made two full appearances near the end of last season as injuries took their toll of regular players. Possesses a notable long-throw.

Carlisle U (From trainee on 18/7/94) FL 2+3 Others 0+1

DEMPSEY Mark Anthony
Born: Dublin, 10 December 1972
Height: 5'7" Weight: 10.9
Left-winger who signed for Orient, having been released by Gillingham, in the 1994 close season, he impressed at the start with his crossing ability and accurate left-footed shooting. Often asked to play a wing-back role, his confidence seemed to ebb away as the club's season deteriorated, but in a new set-up he could come good again in 1995-96.
Gillingham (From trainee on 9/8/90) FL 27+21/2 FLC 0+1 FAC 5 Others 6
Leyton Orient (Free on 4/7/94) FL 43/1 FLC 2 FAC 1+1 Others 5/1

Mark Dempsey   Matthew Ashton
(Empics Sports Photo Agency)

DENNIS John Anthony (Tony)
Born: Maidenhead, 1 December 1963
Height: 5'8" Weight: 13.0
Club Honours: Div 3 '91
Another free transfer signing in the 1994 close season, Tony gave added bite to the Colchester midfield. A tireless worker and ball-winner, his goal at Scarborough in early September lifted the "U's" from the bottom of the table to a really successful run up until Christmas.
Plymouth Arg (From apprentice on 3/12/81) FL 7+2 FLC 1/1 FAC 0+1
Exeter C (Free on 15/8/83) FL 3+1 FLC 1 (Free to Bideford on 1/10/83)

Cambridge U (£15,000 from Slough T, via Taunton, on 22/2/89) FL 89+22/10 FLC 6+2 FAC 2+4 Others 7+2/1
Chesterfield (£20,000 on 15/6/93) FL 4+6 FLC 2 Others 2
Colchester U (Free on 10/8/94) FL 32+1/2 FLC 2 FAC 1+3 Others 2

DENNISON Robert
Born: Banbridge, 30 April 1963
Height: 5'7" Weight: 11.0
Club Honours: AMC '88; Div 4 '88, Div 3 '89
International Honours: NI: 17; B
A left-winger who is able to make goals with accurate crosses, he found himself virtually out of the picture for Wolverhampton last season, despite Tony Daley's injury and departures of other left-sided players. However, when Steve Froggatt was hurt in December, Robbie came in and got off to a good start, and at Barnsley he began and finished a move that gave "Wolves" a 16 second lead. Scored four goals in his first six games of the season and played 21 in succession.
West Bromwich A (£40,000 from Glenavon on 13/9/85) FL 9+7/1 FLC 1 FAC 2 Others 1
Wolverhampton W (£20,000 on 13/3/87) FL 255+24/39 FLC 12+3/3 FAC 15+2/2 Others 24+2/4

DESOUZA Miquel Juan
Born: Newham, 11 February 1970
Height: 5'11" Weight: 13.8
Speedy striker who made a dramatic debut for Wycombe, scoring two goals at Chester last January, after signing from Birmingham. Having netted six goals in six games, a training injury ruled him out until the final game of the season. Had a spell earlier in the season on loan at Bury.
Charlton Ath (Signed from Clapton on 4/7/89)
Bristol C (Free on 1/8/90)
Birmingham C (£25,000 from Dagenham & Redbridge, via Yeovil T, Dorchester T and Bashley, on 1/2/94) FL 5+10 FLC 2 Others 1
Bury (Loaned on 25/11/94) FL 2+1
Wycombe W (£100,000 on 27/1/95) FL 6+1/6

DEVLIN Paul John
Born: Birmingham, 14 April 1972
Height: 5'9" Weight: 10.10
Club Honours: AIC '95
Notts County right-winger who can also play at centre-forward. Good at getting past the full-back to get crosses in, Paul is also direct and proved his all-round value to the team by top-scoring with 12 goals last season. Missed both the beginning and end of 1994-95, through injury and internal problems, respectively, but is too good a player to languish on the sidelines and will be back as good as new.
Notts Co (£40,000 from Stafford R on 22/2/92) FL 106+9/19 FLC 9+1/1 FAC 5/1 Others 14+1/4

DEWHURST Robert (Rob) Matthew
Born: Keighley, 10 September 1971
Height: 6'3" Weight: 12.0
The authoritative cornerstone of Hull's defence, Rob came to manager Terry Dolan's attention as a youngster at Bradford. An assured tackler, his power in the air also supplements the attack in set-piece situa-

tions as does a thunderous left-foot shot. A memorable blockbuster earned the club an excellent win at Brentford last season.
Blackburn Rov (From trainee on 15/10/90) FL 13 FLC 2 Others 1
Darlington (Loaned on 20/12/91) FL 11/1 Others 1
Huddersfield T (Loaned on 2/10/92) FL 7
Hull C (Free on 5/11/93) FL 68/10 FLC 2 FAC 3 Others 3

DE WOLF John
Born: Schiedam, Holland, 10 December 1962
Height: 6'2" Weight: 14.3
International Honours: Holland
This big, long-haired, bearded central defender had the leadership qualities Wolverhampton sought, and he was quickly made captain after Feyenoord surprisingly sold him last December. Struggled to adapt to the pace of the British game at first, but once he settled down he looked a class player. A cool penalty against Sheffield United completed a great recovery as "Wolves" hit two in the last two minutes to draw. Scored from the spot again at Port Vale to complete the first hat-trick of his career, but when he fell awkwardly against Sunderland and damaged his cartilage in March, his season was over.
Wolverhampton W (£600,000 from Feyenoord on 6/12/94) FL 13/4 FAC 4

DIBBLE Andrew (Andy) Gerald
Born: Cwmbran, 8 May 1965
Height: 6'2" Weight: 13.7
Club Honours: FLC '88
International Honours: W: 3; U21-3; Yth; Sch
Given a run in Manchester City's goal in 1994-95, due to Tony Coton's injury, Andy again proved to be a goalkeeper of the highest standing, even allowing for the odd lapse of concentration. Sent off at QPR and Newcastle, the TV camera later showed his tackle on Les Ferdinand appear to have been fair, but against United, he delayed clearing a back-pass, only for Keith Gillespie to round him and score. On the other side of the coin, however, he saved two penalties in the space of six days at Liverpool and Newcastle. A valuable clubman for City, Andy could easily claim a regular first team place elsewhere.
Cardiff C (From apprentice on 27/8/82) FL 62 FLC 4 FAC 4
Luton T (£125,000 on 16/7/84) FL 30 FLC 4 FAC 1 Others 1
Sunderland (Loaned on 21/2/86) FL 12
Huddersfield T (Loaned on 26/3/87) FL 5
Manchester C (£240,000 on 1/7/88) F/PL 101+2 FLC 12 FAC 8+1 Others 2
Aberdeen (Loaned on 20/10/90) SL 5
Middlesbrough (Loaned on 20/2/91) FL 19 Others 2
Bolton W (Loaned on 6/6/91) FL 13 Others 1
West Bromwich A (Loaned on 27/2/92) FL 9

DICHIO Daniele (Danny) Salvatore Ernest
Born: Hammersmith, 19 October 1974
Height: 6'2" Weight: 11.0
International Honours: E: Sch
Very good in the air, and a player who utilises his team-mates well, Danny made his debut for QPR against Manchester City in last season's Coca Cola Cup. Having

scored on his League debut four days later against Aston Villa at Loftus Road, he made way for the returning Les Ferdinand in the next game. The following weekend he appeared as substitute in the away game at Newcastle, and scored again. Played a handful of games later in the season as a replacement for Ferdinand and formed an excellent partnership with Bradley Allen in the reserves.

Queens Park R (From trainee on 17/5/93) PL 4+5/3 FLC 1 FAC 1
Barnet (Loaned on 24/3/94) FL 9/2

DICKINS Matthew (Matt) James
Born: Sheffield, 3 September 1970
Height: 6'4" Weight: 14.0
Tall and agile goalkeeper who moved to Stockport last season after failing to establish himself at Blackburn, he is currently engaged in a terrific tussle for the number one jersey with Neil Edwards. Matt also had a loan period at Rochdale in 1994-95 and initially came to County as a temporary transfer, before signing on a permanent basis last March.

Sheffield U (From trainee on 1/7/89)
Lincoln C (Free on 27/2/91) FL 27 FLC 1 FAC 1 Others 2
Blackburn Rov (£250,000 on 27/3/92) FL 1
Blackpool (Loaned on 22/1/93) FL 19
Lincoln C (Loaned on 19/11/93) Others 1
Rochdale (Loaned on 14/10/94) FL 4 Others 1
Stockport Co (Signed on 13/2/95) FL 11+1

DICKOV Paul
Born: Livingston, 1 November 1972
Height: 5'6" Weight: 11.5
Club Honours: ECWC '94
International Honours: S: U21-5; Yth; Sch
A short and tenacious Scottish striker, who looks to be in the David Speedie mould, Paul, who prior to last season had only made one start for Arsenal, finally got a run in the side when standing in for the suspended Ian Wright. Is a real competitor, and skilful with it.

Arsenal (From trainee on 28/12/90) PL 5+8/2 FLC 2+2/3
Luton T (Loaned on 8/10/93) FL 8+7/1
Brighton & Hove A (Loaned on 23/3/94) FL 8/5

DICKS Julian Andrew
Born: Bristol, 8 August 1968
Height: 5'7" Weight: 11.7
International Honours: E: B-2; U21-4
A tough-tackling left-back, who is also good in the air, and the fans' favourite, Julian was welcomed back to Upton Park last October from Liverpool. Has a ferocious left-foot shot and scored a spectacular goal from a free-kick at Nottingham Forest, along with vital penalties in home wins over Leicester and Wimbledon. Having greatly improved his temperament, his "fighting spirit" inspired a late West Ham revival in avoiding relegation.

Birmingham C (From apprentice on 12/4/86) FL 83+6/1 FLC 5+1 FAC 5 Others 2
West Ham U (£300,000 on 25/3/88) FL 159/29 FLC 19/5 FAC 14/2 Others 11/4
Liverpool (£1,500,000 on 17/9/93) PL 24/3 FLC 3 FAC 1
West Ham U (£1,000,000 on 20/10/94) PL 29/5 FLC 2 FAC 2

Julian Dicks — Steve Morton
(Empics Sports Photo Agency)

DIGBY Fraser Charles
Born: Sheffield, 23 April 1967
Height: 6'1" Weight: 12.12
International Honours: E: U21-5; Yth; Sch
Former England U21 'keeper who was once again a consistent performer between the posts in 1994-95, missing only a dozen games and taking his appearance tally for Swindon to close on 400. Due for a testimonial next year, Fraser may yet not reap his reward for being the club's longest serving professional, having failed to agree terms for 1995-96 at the time of going to press.

Manchester U (From apprentice on 25/4/85)
Swindon T (£32,000 on 25/9/86) F/PL 323 FLC 30 FAC 13 Others 30+1

Fraser Digby — Neal Simpson
(Empics Sports Photo Agency)

DIGWEED Perry Michael
Born: Westminster, 26 October 1959
Height: 6'0" Weight: 11.4
A very experienced goalkeeper, he had limited opportunities at Watford, thanks to the consistency of Kevin Miller, but proved a reliable second string throughout 1994-95. Freed during the summer.

Fulham (From apprentice on 5/8/77) FL 15

Brighton & Hove A (£150,000 on 15/1/81) FL 179 FLC 5 FAC 9 Others 8
Chelsea (Loaned on 2/2/88) FL 3
Wimbledon (Free on 18/3/93)
Watford (Free on 17/12/93) FL 28+1 FLC 1 FAC 1

DINNING Anthony (Tony)
Born: Wallsend, 12 April 1975
Height: 6'2" Weight: 12.11
Stockport defender picked up from Newcastle in the summer of 1994 as "one for the future", he quickly claimed a regular first-team place last season with some mature and commanding performances.

Newcastle U (From trainee on 1/10/93)
Stockport Co (Free on 23/6/94) FL 38+2/1 FLC 2 FAC 0+1 Others 2/1

DIXON Benjamin (Ben) Marcus
Born: Lincoln, 16 September 1974
Height: 6'1" Weight: 11.0
Made the switch from Lincoln's midfield to left-back last season. In doing so, his play showed greater confidence and maturity and he was rewarded with an extended run in the first team during the second half of the campaign.

Lincoln C (From trainee on 4/11/92) FL 23+8 FAC 0+1 Others 2+1

DIXON Kerry Michael
Born: Luton, 24 July 1961
Height: 6'0" Weight: 13.10
Club Honours: Div 2 '84, '89; FMC '90
International Honours: E: 8; U21-1
As a former international player nearing the end of his career, and lacking the pace of his earlier years, Kerry is still a dangerous striker and a supplier of chances for team-mates. Although in-and-out of the Luton side, as he battled with Dwight Marshall and John Hartson for a first team spot, he scored several fine goals, including chipping the Barnsley goalie from 30 yards in January, and several fine headers. He also remains a good passer and an excellent crosser of the ball. Left Luton just before the transfer deadline, bound for Millwall, and scored a goal on his debut in the win over Tranmere.

Tottenham H (From apprentice on 1/7/78)
Reading (£20,000 from Dunstable on 22/7/80) FL 110+6/51 FLC 6+1 FAC 2+1
Chelsea (£175,000 on 4/8/83) FL 331+4/147 FLC 40+1/24 FAC 18+2/8 Others 25/12
Southampton (£575,000 on 19/7/92) PL 8+1/2 FLC 2 FAC 1
Luton T (Free on 19/2/93) FL 66+9/19 FLC 2 FAC 7+2 Others 2/1
Millwall (£5,000 on 23/3/95) FL 9/4

DIXON Lee Michael
Born: Manchester, 17 March 1964
Height: 5'9" Weight: 11.8
Club Honours: Div 1 '89, '91; FAC '93; ECWC '94
International Honours: E: 21; B-4
Quick, attack minded Arsenal and England right-back who had an injury free season in missing just three PL matches in 1994-95, Lee was again at his best in going forward to get in excellent crosses and scored a rare goal against Norwich. A strong character, whose defensive qualities have improved over the years, his coolness under pressure sees him always willing to take penalties in

shoot-out situations and he was certainly up to it in the European Cup Winners Cup match in Genoa. Has also captained the club on occasions.

Burnley (From juniors on 21/7/82) FL 4 FLC 1
Chester C (Free on 16/2/84) FL 56+1/1 FLC 2 FAC 1 Others 3
Bury (Free on 15/7/85) FL 45/5 FLC 4 FAC 8/1 Others 1
Stoke C (£40,000 on 18/7/86) FL 71/5 FLC 6 FAC 7 Others 4
Arsenal (£400,000 on 29/1/88) F/PL 251+3/16 FLC 32 FAC 26/1 Others 28

Lee Dixon   Steve Morton
                          (Empics Sports Photo Agency)

DOBBIN James (Jim)
Born: Dunfermline, 17 September 1963
Height: 5'9" Weight: 10.7
International Honours: S: Yth

A right-sided midfielder who is an intelligent, quick-thinking, and accurate passer. Also has a devastating long-range shot which has created many a goal out of nothing for Grimsby and makes him invaluable in dead-ball situations.

Glasgow Celtic (Free from Whitburn BC on 9/10/80) SL 1+1 SLC 4/1
Motherwell (Loaned on 1/2/84) SL 1+1
Doncaster Rov (£25,000 on 19/3/84) FL 56+8/13 FLC 5/1 FAC 2 Others 3
Barnsley (£35,000 on 19/9/86) FL 116+13/12 FLC 3+1 FAC 11 Others 4/1
Grimsby T (£200,000 on 15/7/91) FL 133+5/18 FLC 11/3 FAC 6/1 Others 5/1

DOBSON Anthony (Tony) John
Born: Coventry, 5 February 1969
Height: 6'1" Weight: 13.6
Club Honours: FAYC '87
International Honours: E: U21-4

A left-sided defender, who can play in the centre or at full-back, Tony started most of his games for Portsmouth at centre-back last season, partnering Kit Symons and Jon Gittens. However, after playing in 17 games, he was left out of the side and, immediately

prior to Christmas, went on loan to Oxford.

Coventry C (From apprentice on 7/7/86) FL 51+3/1 FLC 5+3 Others 0+1
Blackburn Rov (£300,000 on 17/1/91) F/PL 36+5 FLC 5 FAC 2 Others 1
Portsmouth (£150,000 on 22/9/93) FL 37+1/2 FLC 5 FAC 1+1 Others 4/1
Oxford U (Loaned on 15/12/94) FL 5

DODD Jason Robert
Born: Bath, 2 November 1970
Height: 5'10" Weight: 11.10
International Honours: E: U21-8

The sale of Jeff Kenna to Blackburn last season gave Jason the opportunity to regain the Southampton right-back position he lost while recovering from an ankle injury. An excellent crosser of the ball, he also has a good shot and scored a couple of goals when playing in midfield for a short spell earlier in the campaign and is a more than useful player to have on your side.

Southampton (£50,000 from Bath C on 15/3/89) F/PL 119+16/3 FLC 18+1 FAC 16 Others 5

DOHERTY Neil
Born: Barrow, 21 February 1969
Height: 5'8" Weight: 10.9

Another early Barry Fry signing from non-league soccer, Neil made 12 appearances, eight of them from the subs' bench, for Birmingham last season. Seen mainly on the left-wing, he has yet to settle into the full-time game and needs more time.

Watford (From trainee on 5/3/87)
Birmingham C (£40,000 from Barrow on 9/2/94) FL 15+6/1 FLC 1 FAC 0+1 Others 0+2

DOLBY Christopher (Chris) John
Born: Dewsbury, 4 September 1974
Height: 5'8" Weight: 9.12

A left-footed midfielder, or forward, with a talent for dead-ball situations, Chris was used only on four occasions for Rotherham last season, starting twice, before being released during the summer.

Rotherham U (From trainee on 5/8/93) FL 0+3 FAC 1 Others 2

DOLING Stuart James
Born: Newport, IOW, 28 October 1972
Height: 5'6" Weight: 11.6
International Honours: E: Yth

Skilful Portsmouth midfielder with good passing ability and tenacious in the tackle. A disappointing 1994-95 for Stuart, but he announced his first appearance of last season with a 25 yard equaliser against Sunderland in February. Certain to be given more opportunities to impress.

Portsmouth (From trainee on 25/6/90) FL 20+17/4 FLC 4+3 FAC 1 Others 4+3/1

DOMINGUEZ Jose Manuel Martins
Born: Lisbon, Portugal, 16 February 1974
Height: 5'3" Weight: 10.0
Club Honours: Div 2 '95
International Honours: Portugal U21

Little Jose has proved an instant favourite with the Birmingham fans since his arrival from Portugal, his scintillating skills and wing play on the left-flank, showing him to be a cut above the average. Deservedly capped at U21 level by his country, a series

of niggling injuries restricted his appearances last season, but not enough to stop him winning a Second Division Championship medal.

Birmingham C (£180,000 from Benfica on 9/3/94) FL 15+20/3 FLC 1+2 FAC 2+1 Others 2+2/1

DONALDSON O'Neill McKay
Born: Birmingham, 24 November 1969
Height: 6'0" Weight: 11.4

Freed by Shrewsbury during the 1994 close season, he signed for Doncaster and was in the process of having a successful trial with Mansfield when, out of the blue, he was offered the chance of signing for Sheffield Wednesday. Needless to say, he took it. A regular in the reserves, where he plays as a pacy striker, to date O'Neill has made just one brief appearance, something he will be aiming to build on in 1995-96.

Shrewsbury T (Free from Hinckley T on 13/11/91) FL 15+13/4 Others 3
Doncaster Rov (Free on 10/8/94) FL 7+2/2 FLC 2 Others 0+1
Mansfield T (Loaned on 23/12/94) FL 4/6 FAC 1/1
Sheffield Wed (£50,000 on 9/1/95) PL 0+1

DONOVAN Kevin
Born: Halifax, 17 December 1971
Height: 5'8" Weight: 11.0

Thoughtful and determined WBA midfield player - nicknamed Jason - who enjoys a role wide on the right from where he loves to drive forward, often running at defenders before checking and either crossing for his fellow strikers or laying the ball back. Possesses a cracking right-foot shot and was a key figure in several vital games for Albion in 1994-95, scoring and making some important goals, including a winner against Luton and the clincher at Grimsby in March.

Huddersfield T (From trainee on 11/10/89) FL 11+9/1 FLC 1+1 FAC 1/2 Others 4
Halifax T (Loaned on 13/2/92) FL 6
West Bromwich A (£70,000 on 1/10/92) FL 94+8/19 FLC 5/3 FAC 6+1/3 Others 9+1/4

DONOWA Brian Louis (Louie)
Born: Ipswich, 24 September 1964
Height: 5'9" Weight: 12.2
Club Honours: FAYC '83; FLC '85; Div 2 '95; AMC '95
International Honours: E: U21-3

Forward. Amazingly, Louie is one of Birmingham's longest serving players, having been at St Andrews since August 1991. Prior to Barry Fry's arrival, his early "Blues'" career was dogged by inconsistency and he had spells on loan at Burnley and Shrewsbury, before finally showing the form that everybody knew he was capable of in 1994-95. Using his devastating pace down both flanks to great effect and scoring some spectacular goals in the process, he picked up a Second Division Championship medal to go with the one he collected at Wembley, following the 1-0 win over Carlisle in the Auto Windscreen final.

Norwich C (From apprentice on 28/9/82) FL 56+6/11 FLC 13+2/3 FAC 1+2/1 (£400,000 to Real Deportivo on 1/2/86)
Stoke C (Loaned on 23/12/85) FL 4/1 FAC 0+1

Ipswich T (Free from Willem 11 on 14/8/89) FL 17+6/1 FLC 0+2 FAC 2 Others 2+1/1
Bristol C (£55,000 on 10/8/90) FL 11+13/3 FLC 1 FAC 0+1
Birmingham C (£60,000 on 30/8/91) FL 73+26/18 FLC 12+1 FAC 7/1 Others 8+3/1
Burnley (Loaned on 15/1/93) FL 4 Others 2
Shrewsbury T (Loaned on 27/1/94) FL 4

DOOLAN John
Born: Liverpool, 10 November 1968
Height: 5'9" Weight: 10.12

A versatile Wigan performer who can play at full-back or in midfield, John's career has been plagued by injuries over the last two seasons. Returning to League action last January, however, he scored the only goal of the game and his first for the club, against Colchester.
Wigan Ath (Free from Knowsley U on 18/3/92) FL 27+8/1 FLC 4 Others 2

DOOLAN John
Born: Liverpool, 7 May 1974
Height: 5'11" Weight: 12.4

Signed from Everton at the beginning of last season, this right-footed utility player appeared for Mansfield as a central defender, at full-back (right and left), and in central midfield, showing endless enthusiasm and commitment.
Everton (From trainee on 1/6/92)
Mansfield T (Free on 2/9/94) FL 21+3/1 FLC 2 FAC 2 Others 1+1

DORIGO Anthony (Tony) Robert
Born: Australia, 31 December 1965
Height: 5'8" Weight: 10.7
Club Honours: Div 2 '89, Div 1 '92; FMC '90; CS '92
International Honours: E: 15; B-7; U21-11

1994-95 saw him suffer the longest sequence of setbacks since joining Leeds, as pre-season knee damage, followed by hamstring problems at the end of October, forced him to miss much of the season. Once back in action, however, and at full fitness, Tony began to show the qualities he is well known for. A very quick and stylish left-back, who tackles and covers well behind the central defenders, he confidently combines defensive and attacking duties and, with Garry Kelly on the other flank, the club possesses the fastest pair of full-backs in the Premiership.
Aston Villa (From apprentice on 19/7/83) FL 106+5/1 FLC 14+1 FAC 7 Others 2
Chelsea (£475,000 on 3/7/87) FL 146/11 FLC 14 FAC 4 Others 16/1
Leeds U (£1,300,000 on 6/6/91) F/PL 136/4 FLC 8+1 FAC 9 Others 7/1

DOW Andrew (Andy) James
Born: Dundee, 7 February 1973
Height: 5'9" Weight: 10.7
International Honours: S: U21-3

Chelsea left-back who can also play the left-hand side of midfield. Not an out-and-out defender, Andy would rather come out of defence with the ball, looking to make a pass, rather than just clear his lines. Failed to make an appearance in the Premiership last season and had a spell on loan at Bradford in October, playing five times, before returning to Stamford Bridge.

Dundee (From Sporting Club 85 on 10/11/90) SL 8+10/1 SC 1
Chelsea (£250,000 on 15/7/93) PL 13+1 FLC 2 FAC 1
Bradford C (Loaned on 14/10/94) FL 5

DOWELL Wayne Anthony
Born: Durham, 28 December 1973
Height: 5'10" Weight: 11.2

Chris Vinnicombe's broken jaw seemed to have given Wayne his first team opportunity for Burnley in 1994-95, but the bad luck that seemed to attach itself to the number three shirt, saw him pick up a knee ligament injury in the abandoned Boxing Day game against Port Vale. A youth team graduate, he had, in his few appearances, looked a more than capable stand-in at left-back.
Burnley (From trainee on 27/3/93) FL 5 FLC 1 FAC 2

Iain Dowie Steve Morton
(Empics Sports Photo Agency)

DOWIE Iain
Born: Hatfield, 9 January 1965
Height: 6'1" Weight: 12.12
International Honours: NI: 32; U21-1

An experienced Northern Ireland international striker, Ian was linked with Crystal Palace right from the beginning of last season, the move finally coming to fruition in January, a month after he had netted the winner for Southampton reserves against the men from Selhurst Park. Scored important goals in wins over Ipswich, Sheffield Wednesday and at QPR in the Premiership, and the first in the FA Cup semi-final draw with Manchester United. The big blond, who is an excellent header of the ball, and a good target man, also scored his country's only goal in the 1-1 draw against the Republic in Dublin.
Luton T (£30,000 from Hendon on 14/12/88) FL 53+13/16 FLC 3+1 FAC 1+2 Others 5/4
Fulham (Loaned on 13/9/89) FL 5/1
West Ham U (£480,000 on 22/3/91) FL 12/4
Southampton (£500,000 on 3/9/91) F/PL 115+7/30 FLC 8+3/1 FAC 6/1 Others 4
Crystal Palace (£400,000 on 13/1/95) PL 15/4 FAC 6/4

DOWNING Keith Gordon
Born: Oldbury, 23 July 1965
Height: 5'8" Weight: 11.0

Club Honours: Div 4 '88, Div 3 '89; AMC '88

A fiercely competitive midfield destroyer, he was signed by Joe Jordan when Stoke took over his contract from Birmingham at the beginning of last season without the payment of a fee. Keith had two extended spells in the first team, his bite in the tackle enabling the side to build a platform in midfield, prior to being released during the summer.
Notts Co (Free from Mile Oak Rov on 16/5/84) FL 23/1
Wolverhampton W (Free on 6/8/87) FL 169+22/8 FLC 9+3 FAC 7/2 Others 15+3/1
Birmingham C (Free on 22/7/93) FL 1 FLC 1
Stoke C (Free on 9/8/94) FL 16 FLC 2 FAC 1 Others 3+2

DOWNS Gregory (Greg)
Born: Nottingham, 13 December 1958
Height: 5'9" Weight: 10.7
Club Honours: FAC '87

Longstanding, experienced left-back, with nearly 20 years in the game. Greg, as Hereford's player-manager, made four appearances in 1994-95, before leaving the club in September. Later played for non-league sides, Kettering and Merthyr.
Norwich C (From apprentice on 1/12/76) FL 162+7/7 FLC 16 FAC 20/1
Torquay U (Loaned on 29/11/77) FL 1/1
Coventry C (£40,000 on 16/7/85) FL 142+4/4 FLC 19+1/2 FAC 9/1 Others 7
Birmingham C ((Free on 2/8/90) FL 16+1 FLC 2/1 FAC 2 Others 2
Hereford U (Free on 18/7/91) FL 105+3/2 FLC 9 FAC 10 Others 7

DOYLE Stephen (Steve) Charles
Born: Neath, 2 June 1958
Height: 5'9" Weight: 11.1
Club Honours: Div 3 '88
International Honours: W: U21-3

By far Rochdale's most experienced player, Steve, who celebrated 20 years since his FL debut, appeared more often as an emergency defender than in his usual midfield role last season. And, following long spells on the injured list, he joined Chorley as player-coach last April.
Preston NE (From apprentice on 1/6/75) FL 178+19/8 FLC 16+1 FAC 11+1/1
Huddersfield T (Free on 3/9/82) FL 158+3/6 FLC 15 FAC 11
Sunderland (£57,500 on 18/9/86) FL 99+1/2 FLC 4 FAC 5 Others 6
Hull C (£75,000 on 14/8/89) FL 47/2 FLC 5 FAC 1 Others 1
Rochdale (£5,000 on 22/11/90) FL 115+6/1 FLC 8 FAC 4 Others 7

DOZZELL Jason Alvin Winans
Born: Ipswich, 9 December 1967
Height: 6'2" Weight: 12.0
Club Honours: Div 2 '92
International Honours: E: U21-9; Yth

Tottenham midfield player who is good in the air and whose first touch on the ground gives him both time and space and the opportunity to run at defenders. With tremendous competition for midfield places at the club, Jason had a disappointing time in 1994-95, making just eight starts. However, his ability to defend or attack, and score excellent goals, was shown to good effect in the reserves, where he starred regularly last season. Too good a player not to be playing regular first team football, he is bound to come again.

Ipswich T (From apprentice on 20/12/84) F/PL 312+20/52 FLC 29+1/3 FAC 22/12 Others 22/4
Tottenham H (£1,900,000 on 1/8/93) PL 34+5/8 FLC 6 FAC 2/1

DRAPER Mark Andrew
Born: Long Eaton, 11 November 1970
Height: 5'10" Weight: 11.0
International Honours: E: U21-3

Right-footed midfielder and record 1994 summer signing from Notts County, Mark continually turned in class performances, despite Leicester's struggles. Outstanding in the home win over Tottenham and away defeat at Newcastle, he was used in a more advanced midfield role after Mark McGhee's arrival, from where he improved his striking rate. Constantly linked with several big clubs throughout the season and the subject of a failed £3 million bid from former manager, Brian Little, on transfer deadline day, he was troubled by a niggling hamstring late in the season.

Notts Co (From trainee on 12/12/88) FL 206+16/40 FLC 14+1/2 FAC 10/2 Others 21+2/5
Leicester C (£1,250,000 on 22/7/94) PL 39/5 FLC 2 FAC 2

DREYER John Paul
Born: Alnwick, 11 June 1963
Height: 6'1" Weight: 11.6

An astute signing by Joe Jordan in the summer of 1994, his first team spot in the heart of the Stoke defence was lost following a nightmare performance against old club, Luton. An experienced left-sided defender, John played all along the back four, turning in some reliable performances, before being loaned to Bolton on transfer deadline day in order to aid the Lancashire club with their promotion ambitions.

Oxford U (Signed from Wallingford on 8/1/85) FL 57+3/2 FLC 10+1 FAC 2 Others 3
Torquay U (Loaned on 13/12/85) FL 5
Fulham (Loaned on 27/3/88) FL 12/2
Luton T (£140,000 on 27/6/88) FL 212+2/13 FLC 13+1/1 FAC 14 Others 8/1
Stoke C (Free on 15/7/94) FL 16+2/2 FLC 2 Others 3
Bolton W (Loaned on 23/3/95) FL 1+1 Others 1+1

DRUCE Mark Andrew
Born: Oxford, 3 March 1974
Height: 5'11" Weight: 11.11

Enigmatic Oxford striker who struggled for any consistency early on last season, but in the New Year rose to the task and kept out Paul Moody for a while. Showed signs that goals were coming but, unfortunately, ruptured an Achilles tendon and spent a lengthy spell out of action. Has good pace, although not a prolific scorer.

Oxford U (From trainee on 3/12/91) FL 17+27/4 FLC 1+3 Others 2+1

DRYDEN Richard Andrew
Born: Stroud, 14 June 1969
Height: 6'0" Weight: 12.0
Club Honours: Div 4 '90

Signed from Birmingham last December, Richard eventually came into the centre of Bristol City's defence alongside Matt Bryant and Mark Shail. At times it looked as though the middle of the field was overmanned and, in consequence, it took some time for him to find his feet. A centre-half of the old school, once settled, he proved to be a no-nonsense defender who cleared his lines most effectively.

Bristol Rov (From trainee on 14/7/87) FL 12+1 FLC 2+1 FAC 0+2 Others 2
Exeter C (Loaned on 22/9/88) FL 6
Exeter C (Signed on 8/3/89) FL 86/13 FLC 7/2 FAC 2 Others 4
Notts Co (£250,000 on 9/8/91) FL 30+1/1 FLC 1+1 FAC 2+1 Others 2
Plymouth Arg (Loaned on 18/11/92) FL 5 Others 1
Birmingham C (£165,000 on 19/3/93) FL 48 FLC 5 FAC 1
Bristol C (£140,000 on 16/12/94) FL 15+4/1 FAC 0+1

DRYSDALE Jason
Born: Bristol, 17 November 1970
Height: 5'10" Weight: 12.0
Club Honours: FAYC '89
International Honours: E: Yth

Left-back. Having joined Newcastle from Watford, prior to the start of last season, he later became Swindon's only transfer deadline newcomer, after not settling on Tyneside. Jason, whose father Brian played over 300 games for local rivals, Bristol City, was brought in to plug the gap left by the long-term injury to Paul Bodin. However, he soon became a casualty himself, hobbling out of the County Ground on crutches, following his debut against Charlton, and taking no further part in the action.

Watford (From trainee on 8/9/88) FL 135+10/11 FLC 8+1/2 FAC 2 Others 4
Newcastle U (£425,000 on 2/8/94)
Swindon T (£340,000 on 23/3/95) FL 1

Dion Dublin
Paul Marriott
(Empics Sports Photo Agency)

DUBLIN Dion
Born: Leicester, 22 April 1969
Height: 6'1" Weight: 12.4
Club Honours: Div 3 '91

The big striker was hailed as the buy of the season after joining Coventry from Manchester United early last season, scoring ten goals in his first 13 games. Suffered a bad groin injury at Upton Park in November and was out for six League matches, none of which were won. His overall contribution to City's play should not be under estimated, with him frequently back helping his defence, something that may have detracted from his goalscoring potential.

Norwich C (From trainee on 24/3/88)
Cambridge U (Free on 2/8/88) FL 133+23/52 FLC 8+2/5 FAC 21/11 Others 14+1/5
Manchester U (£1,000,000 on 7/8/92) PL 4+8/2 FLC 1+1/1 FAC 1+1 Others 0+1
Coventry C (£2,000,000 on 9/9/94) PL 31/13 FLC 3/2 FAC 4/1

DUBLIN Keith Barry
Born: High Wycombe, 29 January 1966
Height: 6'0" Weight: 12.10
International Honours: E: Yth

It was the intention of Southend manager, Peter Taylor, to build the defence around Keith, when he signed from Watford prior to the start of 1994-95. In his defensive role, he proved capable in the air, speedy and safe on the ground; his first thought is always to clear any danger with haste. He was later used as a makeshift striker by new manager, Steve Thompson, when the side had injury and suspension problems, and finished the season at right-back.

Chelsea (From apprentice on 28/1/84) FL 50+1 FLC 6 FAC 5 Others 5+1
Brighton & Hove A (£3,500 on 14/8/87) FL 132/5 FLC 5 FAC 7/1 Others 7
Watford (£275,000 on 17/7/90) FL 165+3/2 FLC 12 FAC 4 Others 6
Southend U (Signed on 21/7/94) FL 40/2 FLC 2 FAC 1

DUFFY Christopher (Chris) John
Born: Manchester, 31 October 1973
Height: 5'10" Weight: 11.7

From previous manager, Kenny Swain's old club, Crewe, his Wigan appearances last season were restricted to five as a substitute. A fast, attacking winger, Chris joined Vauxhall Conference side, Northwich Victoria, last February, after a loan spell with the Cheshire club.

Crewe Alex (From trainee on 29/7/92)
Wigan Ath (Free on 29/7/93) FL 15+16/1 FLC 1+1 FAC 2/1 Others 1+1

DUMITRESCU Ilie
Born: Bucharest, Romania, 6 January 1969
Height: 5'9" Weight: 10.7
International Honours: Romania

A talented Romanian international midfielder who signed for Tottenham after starring for his country in the World Cup Finals. With great ability to control the ball close to his feet and to turn opponents with flowing movement, he scored his first goal in England at Ipswich last August. Settled into Premiership football well, and his pace often proved a great advantage, especially when up against very physical sides like Leicester and Wimbledon. Illie, a natural attacking player, found the two goals he scored in the defeat by Manchester City (2-5) to be one of his last opportunities to add any more to his tally and later lost his place at Tottenham, as new manager, Gerry

Francis, began to concentrate more on keeping goals out. With David Howells and Nick Barmby finding form under the new management, he found it difficult to regain his position and, in December, went on loan to Seville for the remainder of the season, a transfer that was eventually made permanent.

Tottenham H (£2,600,000 from Steau Bucharest on 3/8/94) PL 11+2/4 FLC 2/1

DUNFORD Neil
Born: Rochdale, 18 July 1967
Height: 6'0" Weight: 12.7

Local "brickie" and Rochdale's reserve team goalkeeper, he had a brilliant FL debut against Doncaster, saving a penalty and helping "Dale" to a 2-0 win. A non-contract player, Neil is no longer with the club.

Rochdale (Signed on 18/9/93) FL 2 FAC 1

DUNGEY James Andrew
Born: Plymouth, 7 February 1978
Height: 5'8" Weight: 10.1

This extremely talented young Plymouth goalkeeper, who is still a trainee, made his league debut when replacing Alan Nicholls as substitute at Stockport last season, and kept a clean sheet. A player with a big future.

Plymouth Arg (Trainee) FL 3+1

DUNN Iain George
Born: Howden, 1 April 1970
Height: 5'10" Weight: 11.7
International Honours: E: Sch

An enigmatic Huddersfield player who at times can be quite brilliant, Iain is a scorer of quality goals, rather than quantity, and when he hits the back of the net it is usually memorable. Making history when becoming the first player to settle a cup-tie in sudden death extra-time, he is most comfortable up-front on the left-hand side.

York C (From juniors on 7/7/88) FL 46+31/11 FLC 3+1 FAC 3+1 Others 1+3
Chesterfield (Free on 14/8/91) FL 8+5/1
Scarborough (Free on 27/8/92)
Peterborough U (Free on 29/9/92) Others 0+1
Scarborough (Free on 9/10/92)
Huddersfield T (Free from Goole T on 4/12/92) FL 58+43/14 FLC 5+2/3 FAC 6+2/3 Others 11+7/9

Joseph Dunne   Barry Coombs
(Empics Sports Photo Agency)

DUNNE Joseph (Joe) John
Born: Dublin, 25 May 1973
Height: 5'9" Weight: 11.6
International Honours: Ei: U21-1; Yth

Although regarded as a full-back, he played a number of games towards the end of last season in a midfield role and it was from that position that he scored his first senior goal for Gillingham in April in a 1-1 draw at Preston, after more than 100 appearances. Mixes 100 per-cent commitment with a typical Irish humour.

Gillingham (From trainee on 9/8/90) FL 107+6/1 FLC 6 FAC 5 Others 3+1

DUNPHY Nicholas (Nick) Owen
Born: Sutton Coldfield, 3 August 1974
Height: 6'0" Weight: 12.0

A 1994 close season Peterborough signing from non-league circles, Nick acquitted himself well in 1994-95 as a right-back who can also play at centre-half. Very composed, he is capable of both clearing his lines well, or coming out with the ball, and has a good level of fitness that will stand him in good stead.

Peterborough U (Free from Hednesford T on 26/8/94) FL 0+2

DUNPHY Sean
Born: Maltby, 5 November 1970
Height: 6'3" Weight: 13.5

A solid central defender who was unable to win a first team place at Lincoln last season, Sean was loaned to Scarborough and played regularly between August and November, before being released by the "Imps" in February 1995. At non-league Kettering briefly, he moved on to Halifax in March.

Barnsley (From trainee on 19/6/89) FL 5+1
Lincoln C (£30,000 on 12/7/90) FL 48+5/2 FLC 5+1/1 FAC 2 Others 1
Doncaster Rov (Loaned on 15/10/93) FL 1 Others 1
Scarborough (Loaned on 26/8/94) FL 10 FLC 2

DURKAN Kieran John
Born: Chester, 1 December 1973
Height: 5'11" Weight: 12.0
Club Honours: WC '95
International Honours: Ei: U21-2

Another of the promising youngsters developed by Wrexham's excellent youth policy under the watchful eye of Cliff Sear, Mike Buxton and Brian Prandle. The best crosser of a ball at the club and a strong looking right-footer, he tasted a fair slice of glory in the third round FA Cup-tie at home against Ipswich last season, giving the "Robins" the lead with a superb volley and continued in that vein with the opening goal at Old Trafford in the fourth round. Now a Republic of Ireland U21 International.

Wrexham (From trainee on 16/7/92) FL 37+5/3 FLC 2 FAC 3+1/2 Others 14/1

DURNIN John Paul
Born: Bootle, 18 August 1965
Height: 5'10" Weight: 11.10

Bustling Portsmouth midfielder/forward, who is tough in the tackle, John had a season plagued by injuries and, apart from a couple of appearances as a sub in late 1994, it was not until February that he managed to find a place on the bench. He regained his place in

the team when the squad was depleted by injuries and suspensions in late March and celebrated with a series of good performances.

Liverpool (Free from Waterloo Dock on 29/3/86) FLC 1+1
West Bromwich A (Loaned on 20/10/88) FL 5/2
Oxford U (£225,000 on 10/2/89) FL 140+21/44 FLC 7/1 FAC 7/1 Others 4+1/1
Portsmouth (£200,000 on 15/7/93) FL 31+13/8 FLC 7+1/2 FAC 1+1 Others 4+2

DURRANT Iain
Born: Glasgow, 29 October 1966
Height: 5'10" Weight: 11.0
Club Honours: SPD '87, '88, '92, '93; SLC '87, '88, '93, '94; SC '92
International Honours: S: 11; U21-4; Yth

Glasgow Ranger's central midfielder who acts as a playmaker, picking up the ball and spraying perfectly weighted passes, Iain possesses a good footballing brain and is adept at keeping possession with simple, but effective, play. Loaned to Everton early last October, he made four PL starts and provided much amunition for the strikers, before returning to Scotland following his clubs' reluctance to release him.

Glasgow R (Signed from Glasgow U on 27/7/84) SL 166+26/22 SLC 31/8 SC 8+2/3 Others 24+2/7
Everton (Loaned on 3/10/94) PL 4+1

DUXBURY Lee Edward
Born: Keighley, 7 October 1969
Height: 5'10" Weight: 11.6

Signed from local rivals, Bradford, last December for a Huddersfield record fee, Lee joined old team-mates, Lee Sinnott, signed in the same deal, and Paul Reid. Took a time to get used to Town's style of play on the left-hand side of midfield, but, once scttlcd, he showed good form in the "engine room", impressing with his distribution.

Bradford C (From trainee on 4/7/88) FL 204+5/25 FLC 18+1/3 FAC 11 Others 13
Rochdale (Loaned on 18/1/90) FL 9+1 FAC 1
Huddersfield T (£250,000 on 23/12/94) FL 26/2 Others 3

DYCHE Sean Mark
Born: Kettering, 28 June 1971
Height: 6'0" Weight: 11.7

Originally a midfielder, Sean's strong-tackling and teasing crosses made him a natural for an attacking right-back role. Sadly, a string of injuries hampered his progress at Chesterfield in 1994-95 but, with his distinctive ginger hair and broad grin, he clearly enjoys the game and is as valuable a personality as he is a player.

Nottingham F (From trainee on 20/5/89)
Chesterfield (Free on 1/2/90) FL 144+10/8 FLC 5 FAC 5 Others 13

DYER Alexander (Alex) Constantine
Born: Forest Gate, 14 November 1965
Height: 5'10" Weight: 12.0

Cool, calm and collected, Alex likes time on the ball and is a very skilful player. Although naturally a forward, he spent a large part of last season at left-back, using the experience to good effect in Oxford's cause.

Blackpool (Free from Watford Juniors on 20/10/83) FL 101+7/19 FLC 8+1/1 FAC 4+1 Others 7/1

Hull C (£37,000 on 13/2/87) FL 59+1/14 FLC 2 FAC 4/1
Crystal Palace (£250,000 on 11/11/88) FL 16+1/2 FLC 3+1 FAC 1+1 Others 3+1/3
Charlton Ath (£100,000 on 30/11/90) FL 60+18/13 FLC 2+1 FAC 1/1 Others 3+1
Oxford U (Free on 26/7/93) FL 62+14/6 FLC 4/1 FAC 5/1 Others 5

DYER Bruce Antonio
Born: Ilford, 13 April 1975
Height: 6'0" Weight: 10.9
International Honours: E: U21-6
A skilful, young attacking Crystal Palace winger, who, after a marvellous U21 tournament for England in the summer of 1994, started last season in the Premiership as a sub. Only made nine first team starts in all, scoring just one PL goal at Manchester City, before requesting a transfer in March, following a steady diet of reserve football. Still an excellent prospect.
Watford (From trainee on 19/4/93) FL 29+2/6 FLC 4/2 FAC 1 Others 2/1
Crystal Palace (£1,100,000 on 10/3/94) F/PL 9+18/1 FLC 1+2/1 FAC 1+2

Bruce Dyer — Steve Morton (Empics Sports Photo Agency)

DYKSTRA Sieb
Born: Kerkrade, Holland, 20 October 1966
Height: 6'5" Weight: 14.7
A pre-season signing from Motherwell, he had to wait until October to make his QPR debut at Norwich and was then on the wrong end of a 2-4 scoreline. His home debut, three days later, was in the Coca Cola Cup against Manchester City. This time the score was 3-4. Although losing his place just after Christmas, Sieb will be hoping to return to the first team where his obvious abilities could also be valuable to the Dutch national team.

Motherwell (From Roda JC on 14/8/91) SL 80 SLC 3 SC 4
Queens Park R (£250,000 on 22/7/94) PL 11 FLC 1

DYSON Jonathan (Jon) Paul
Born: Mirfield, 23 March 1972
Height: 6'1" Weight: 12.0
A home-grown Huddersfield product who originally combined playing for Town with obtaining a degree, Jon has proved to be very versatile. Spent most of last season at centre-half, but also played a number of games at right-back.
Huddersfield T (From juniors on 29//12/90) FL 57+8/2 FLC 9 FAC 3 Others 7+4

EADEN Nicholas (Nicky) Jeremy
Born: Sheffield, 12 December 1972
Height: 5'10" Weight: 11.3
Nicky's season started slowly in 1994-95, but after being left out on a couple of occasions, he came back to be an integral part of Barnsley's promotion challenge. His crossing skills as a right-back, cum winger, caused many defences problems and a high proportion of the club's goals came from these. If he continued to improve at his current rate, he has the ability to play at the top level.
Barnsley (From juniors on 4/6/91) FL 81+3/3 FLC 3+1 FAC 5 Others 2

EADIE Darren Malcolm
Born: Chippenham, 10 June 1975
Height: 5'8" Weight: 10.6
International Honours: E: U21-2; Yth
Left-winger with great pace who, when on form, can produce electrifying runs that cause constant danger to defenders, especially those of the back-pedalling variety. A regular selection for Norwich after the first six games of 1994-95, he scored against Notts County in the Coca Cola Cup after just 42 seconds. Unfortunately, for both him and City, a pulled hamstring ruled him out of the final crucial matches of the season.
Norwich C (From trainee on 5/2/93) PL 31+10/5 FLC 9/1 FAC 4/1 Others 1+1

EARLE Robert (Robbie) Gerald
Born: Newcastle under Lyme, 27 January 1965
Height: 5'9" Weight: 10.10
A talented central midfielder, with an eye for a goal, Robbie had a most frustrating time of it in 1994-95, being absent for much of the season through injury. Not available until late December, Wimbledon also severely missed his pacy attacking play. Back in the side, things went well for the first three months of 1995, before he was crocked again. Apart from the odd game, that was it as far as Robbie was concerned and he will now be praying for an injury free 1995-96.
Port Vale (From juniors on 5/7/82) FL 284+10/77 FLC 21+2/4 FAC 20+1/4 Others 18+1/5
Wimbledon (£775,000 on 19/7/91) F/PL 133/30 FLC 12/3 FAC 14/2 Others 1/1

EBBRELL John Keith
Born: Bromborough, 1 October 1969
Height: 5'7" Weight: 10.0
International Honours: E: B-1; U21-14; Yth; Sch

Everton midfield anchorman who tends to play just in front of the back four and helps the team to gel as a unit. With good vision, John is able to get the ball out down the channels accurately, has a high workrate and the knack of getting his foot in to break up a move. Dogged with numerous injuries in the second half of 1994-95, his chances of holding down a regular place were blighted and he missed out on the final stages of the club's great FA Cup run.
Everton (From trainee on 7/11/86) F/PL 176+9/9 FLC 16/1 FAC 16/2 Others 6+2/1

John Ebbrell — Neal Simpson (Empics Sports Photo Agency)

EBDON Marcus
Born: Pontypool, 17 October 1970
Height: 5'8" Weight: 12.4
International Honours: W: U21-2; Yth
Ball playing Peterborough midfielder who, on his day, can run the game. Apart from his intricate play, Marcus is a great striker of the ball and a free-kick specialist to boot.
Everton (From trainee on 16/8/89)
Peterborough U (Free on 15/7/91) FL 85+3/12 FLC 9+1 FAC 6+1 Others 9+1

ECKHARDT Jeffrey (Jeff) Edward
Born: Sheffield, 7 October 1965
Height: 6'0" Weight: 11.7
A hard-working and versatile Stockport player who has impressed both in midfield and defence, he was also, on occasion, pressed into service as a centre-forward. Strong and fearless in the tackle, Jeff unfortunately missed the final two months of 1994-95 through injury.
Sheffield U (From juniors on 23/8/84) FL 73+1/2 FLC 7 FAC 2 Others 5
Fulham (£50,000 on 20/11/87) FL 245+4/25 FLC 13 FAC 5+1 Others 15/3
Stockport Co (£50,000 on 21/7/94) FL 26+1/1 FLC 4 FAC 1 Others 1

EDESON Matthew Kirk
Born: Hull, 11 August 1976
Height: 5'10" Weight: 11.0
A stockily built forward who favours his right-side, when making his debut as a sub

at Fulham in October 1992, Matthew became Hull's youngest-ever player. Although a regular in the reserves, there have been few first team opportunities since and, following three appearances from the bench in 1994-95, he was released at the end of the season.

Hull C (From trainee on 7/7/94) FL 0+5 Others 0+1

EDGHILL Richard Arlon
Born: Oldham, 23 September 1974
Height: 5'8" Weight: 10.6
International Honours: E: B-1; U21-3
Manchester City right-back, with a style similar to Terry Phelan, Richard has a strong physique, is hard-running and overlaps well with the club's wingmen. Made an impressive start to 1994-95, before picking up an injured knee at Ipswich which necessitated various treatments to eradicate the problem. Returned at Tottenham in mid-April and quickly showed that he was back to full fitness. Highly rated and happy to be called up by Terry Venables for an England get-together.

Manchester C (From trainee on 15/7/92) PL 36 FLC 7 FAC 1

EDINBURGH Justin Charles
Born: Brentwood, 18 December 1969
Height: 5'9" Weight: 11.6
Club Honours: FAC '91; CS '91
Justin was another member of the Tottenham side whose performances greatly improved under the Gerry Francis regime last season. A full-back with tremendous enthusiasm to join the attack, which saw him make the occasional appearance in midfield, his form from late January was instrumental to a "Spurs'" side that was defeated only twice between 23 November and 22 March. Understandably gaining in confidence, he showed versatility, paired with a good left foot and a willingness to link up with the attack.

Southend U (From trainee on 5/8/88) FL 36+1 FLC 2+1 FAC 2 Others 4+1/1
Tottenham H (£150,000 on 30/7/90) F/PL 120+7/1 FLC 14+3 FAC 17 Others 3

EDMONDSON Darren Stephen
Born: Coniston, 4 November 1971
Height: 6'0" Weight: 12.2
Club Honours: Div 3 '95
One of the longest serving players at Carlisle, despite being only 23-years-old. Now returned to full fitness, after missing much of the previous term, he normally played right-back where his pace and tackling ability could be used to full advantage. A positive and committed footballer who makes penetrating forward runs when opportunity permits, Darren won a Third Division Championship medal.

Carlisle U (From trainee on 17/7/90) FL 146+6/7 FLC 11/3 FAC 12/1 Others 17

EDWARDS Alistair Martin
Born: Whyalia, Australia, 21 June 1968
Height: 6'1" Weight: 12.6
International Honours: Australia
Signed from Malaysian club, Selangor, during last winter, he was thrown in at the deep end at Millwall owing to their injury crisis and had exceptional games against Arsenal and Chelsea in the FA Cup. A groin strain halted a very promising re-start in English football for this extremely fast, left-footed striker, but that will not hold him back.

Brighton & Hove A (Free from Sydney Olympic on 29/11/89) FL 1
Millwall (Free from Selangor on 15/12/94) FL 3+1 FAC 3+1

EDWARDS Andrew (Andy) David
Born: Epping, 17 September 1971
Height: 6'2" Weight: 12.7
Mr Dependable, "Eagle" spent the whole of 1994-95 quietly going about his defensive duties at Southend, as is his trademark. Exceptionally good in the air, he has out-played more illustrious opponents than himself on many occasions. Quick on the ground, and able to use both feet equally well, Andy's knack of making saving tackles came into use on more than one occasion during a difficult season.

Southend U (From trainee on 14/12/89) FL 141+6/5 FLC 5 FAC 4 Others 9/2

EDWARDS Christian (Chris) Nicholas Howells
Born: Caerphilly, 23 November 1975
Height: 6'3" Weight: 11.9
A 19-year-old defender who was given his chance in the Swansea first team last season when Frank Burrows adopted a triple central defensive formation in away matches, his first team outings also brought him a call-up to the Wales U21 squad for the matches against Bulgaria and West Germany.

Swansea C (From trainee on 20/7/94) FL 9 Others 1+1

EDWARDS Michael (Mike)
Born: Bebington, 11 September 1974
Height: 6'0" Weight: 11.10
Tenacious young Tranmere midfielder who graduated through the club's youth scheme, making his debut in the Anglo-Italian Cup last September, he went on to feature in eight matches, starting five of them. A good passer, Michael strikes the ball cleanly and gets forward into goalscoring positions.

Tranmere Rov (From trainee on 5/7/93) FL 2+1 FLC 0+2 Others 3

EDWARDS Neil Ryan
Born: Aberdare, 5 December 1970
Height: 5'10" Weight: 11.10
International Honours: W: U21-1; Yth
A goalkeeper who makes up for his small stature with great agility and bravery, he eventually regained his place in the Stockport team last season after a shoulder operation in the summer of 1994. Faces a strong challenge from Matt Dickens in 1995-96.

Leeds U (From trainee on 10/3/89) Others 1
Stockport Co (£5,000 on 3/9/91) FL 118+1 FLC 6 FAC 7 Others 27

EDWARDS Paul
Born: Liverpool, 22 February 1965
Height: 5'11" Weight: 11.5
Club Honours: Div 3 '94
Shrewsbury goalkeeper, who excels on reflex saves and shows his best on low shots, Paul also has a fairly good record on penalty stops. A little unsure with high crosses on occasion, he surrendered the jersey to Tim Clarke last March.

Crewe Alex (Free from Leek T on 24/8/88) FL 29 FLC 4 FAC 3 Others 4
Shrewsbury T (Free on 6/8/92) FL 115 FLC 10 FAC 7 Others 7

EDWARDS Paul Ronald
Born: Birkenhead, 25 December 1963
Height: 5'11" Weight: 12.2
Club Honours: FLC '85
Usually a left-back, who played very well at times for WBA during the first half of 1994-95 when he was drafted to a more central defensive position alongside Paul Mardon, he has a fine left-foot. Lost his place in the side following the arrival of Paul Agnew from Grimsby and, soon after, suffered a niggling injury which sidelined him for almost two months.

Crewe Alex (Free from Altrincham on 12/1/88) FL 82+4/6 FLC 6 FAC 8 Others 7+1/1
Coventry C (£350,000 on 16/3/90) FL 32+4 FLC 6 FAC 2 Others 2
Wolverhampton W (£100,000 on 13/8/92) FL 43+3 FLC 2 FAC 2 Others 1
West Bromwich A (£80,000 on 19/1/94) FL 35 FLC 1 FAC 2

EDWARDS Robert (Rob)
Born: Manchester, 23 February 1970
Height: 5'8" Weight: 11.7
Almost the veteran of the Crewe side, Rob is usually to be found in one of the front positions, and can score equally well with head or feet. Has been unfortunate during the last couple of seasons with injuries, but is still a good competitor.

Crewe Alex (From trainee on 11/7/88) FL 81+42/29 FLC 5/1 FAC 8+5/3 Others 7+8/4

EDWARDS Robert William
Born: Kendal, 1 July 1973
Height: 6'0" Weight: 11.10
International Honours: W: U21-7; Yth
Started last season on the left-side of midfield for Bristol City with a flourish, incisive when winning the ball and intelligent in its distribution, before poor team performances in general began to effect his play. Much is expected of him in the coming season as the team looks to go back to Division One at the first time of asking.

Carlisle U (From trainee on 10/4/90) FL 48/5 FLC 4 FAC 1 Others 2+1
Bristol C (£135,000 on 27/3/91) FL 86+20/3 FLC 6+1/1 FAC 8+1 Others 5+1/1

EDWORTHY Marc
Born: Barnstaple, 24 December 1972
Height: 5'7" Weight: 9.8
A versatile player, who has turned out in defence and midfield for Plymouth, he improved throughout last season to command a regular place, keeping out more experienced colleagues. Has plenty of pace and is probably most at home in central defence. Scored his first League goal at Stockport and has plenty more to look forward to.

Plymouth Arg (From trainee on 30/3/91) FL 52+17/1 FLC 5+2 FAC 5+2 Others 2+2

EHIOGU Ugochuku (Ugo)
Born: Hackney, 3 November 1972
Height: 6'1" Weight: 12.0
International Honours: E: B-1; U21-15

One of the most improved defenders in the Premiership, Aston Villa's Ugo has good pace, is strong in the air, reads the game well and can be used as a man-to-man marker when the occasion warrants. Also dangerous at set-pieces, he was very consistent in 1994-95, missing games only through suspension and, although never playing, he was delighted to be called-up for the full England squad. If he continues in the same vein his chance could come soon.

West Bromwich A (From trainee on 13/7/89) FL 0+2
Aston Villa (£40,000 on 12/7/91) F/PL 57+11/3 FLC 4+1 FAC 2+2 Others 5/1

EKELUND Ronald (Ronnie) Michael
Born: Denmark, 21 August 1972
Height: 5'11" Weight: 12.8
International Honours: Denmark

Signed from Barcelona after protracted negotiations, Ronnie made his Southampton debut last September. His goalscoring and all-round skilful play made him an instant favourite with the supporters, who felt the club had found a player to share the load with Matt Le Tissier. He also made his debut for Denmark, but a back injury led to his making just one brief appearance as a sub after the New Year and, an apparent refusal to have an operation, led to his being released last March.

Southampton (£500,000 from Barcelona on 15/9/94) PL 15+2/5 FLC 2+1

Efan Ekoku   Tony Marshall
(Empics Sports Photo Agency)

EKOKU Efangwu (Efan) Goziem
Born: Manchester, 8 June 1967
Height: 6'1" Weight: 12.0
International Honours: Nigeria

In a surprise switch from Norwich to Wimbledon last October, Efan became the "Don's" record signing, scoring his first goal for his new club, ironically, against his old one. Settling in well up-front, his strength, pace, and direct running, giving Wimbledon a good edge in attack, Efan hit nine goals in 23 starts, before picking up an ankle injury in February that limited his appearances for the rest of the season.

Bournemouth (£100,000 from Sutton U on 11/5/90) FL 43+19/21 FLC 0+2 FAC 5+2/2 Others 3+1/2
Norwich C (£500,000 on 26/3/93) PL 26+11/15 FLC 3/1 FAC 1+1 Others 3/1
Wimbledon (£900,000 on 14/10/94) PL 24/9 FAC 3

ELAD Diodene Efon
Born: Hillingdon, 5 September 1970
Height: 5'10" Weight: 12.0

Started 1994-95 as a non-contract player with Cambridge, having arrived during the close season from Northampton, before moving to Mansfield in a similar capacity. As an attacking wide player who can play on either side, Efon showed terrific pace and strength on the ball in two subs' appearances at Town, but, unable to agree terms, he moved on last March.

Northampton T (Free from Cologne on 17/1/94) FL 8+2
Cambridge U (Free on 29/7/94) FL 2+1 FLC 0+1
Mansfield T (Free on 3/2/95) FL 0+2

ELI Roger
Born: Bradford, 11 September 1965
Height: 5'10" Weight: 11.4
Club Honours: Div 4 '92

Forward. Released by Burnley during the 1994 close season, having failed to get on the team sheet in 1993-94 due to a knee problem, Roger arrived at Scunthorpe, via Hong Kong, last February and made just two subs' appearances as a non-contract player before moving on soon after.

Leeds U (From apprentice on 15/9/83) FL 1+1
Wolverhampton W (Signed on 17/1/86) FL 16+2 FLC 1+1 Others 1
Cambridge U (Free on 10/8/87)
Crewe Alex (Free on 9/9/87) FL 20+7/1 FAC 1 Others 2/1 (Free to Pontefract during 1988 close season)
York C (Free on 3/11/88) FL 3+1/1 FAC 1 Others 1
Bury (Free on 14/12/88) FL 0+2
Burnley (Free on 18/7/89) FL 70+29/20 FLC 4+2 FAC 7+5/5 Others 14/6 (Free to Hong Kong during the 1994 close season)
Scunthorpe U (Free on 16/2/95) FL 0+2

ELKINS Gary
Born: Wallingford, 4 May 1966
Height: 5'9" Weight: 11.13
International Honours: E: Yth

Attacking Wimbledon left-back who can also play in midfield, Gary has an excellent left-foot and a whole range of passing skills and is, above all, determined. Held down a first team slot in 1994-95 until mid-season, when, with competition for midfield places high, he missed out on occasion. Came back into the side against Manchester United in March and then scored a goal in the 2-0 defeat of Manchester City.

Fulham (From apprentice on 3/12/83) FL 100+4/2 FLC 6 FAC 2+2 Others 7+1
Exeter C (Loaned on 23/12/89) FL 5
Wimbledon (£20,000 on 20/8/90) F/PL 93+7/3 FLC 7 FAC 7/1 Others 1+1

ELLIOTT Anthony (Tony) Robert
Born: Nuneaton, 30 November 1969
Height: 6'0" Weight: 12.12
Club Honours: WC '90
International Honours: E: Yth; Sch

Goalkeeper. Spent most of last season on Carlisle's bench, but kept clean sheets in two of his three full appearances. In the third game he crowned an outstanding display with a brilliant penalty save at Chesterfield to clinch a Carlisle win. A very competent 'keeper who could easily be first choice elsewhere.

Birmingham C (From apprentice on 3/12/86) FLC 1
Hereford U (Free on 22/12/88) FL 75 FLC 5 FAC 6 Others 9
Huddersfield T (Free on 29/7/92) FL 15 FLC 2 FAC 3 Others 3
Carlisle U (Free on 28/6/93) FL 8+1 FLC 1 Others 2

ELLIOTT Matthew Stephen
Born: Wandsworth, 1 November 1968
Height: 6'3" Weight: 13.6

Commanding centre-back, who also likes to get the ball down and play, Matthew can dominate in the air and is also a valuable asset at set-pieces, with a good amount of goals coming from that area. Took over as Oxford's captain, following the injury to Mike Ford, and was a virtual ever-present (missing just one game) last season. Matt is one of the club's most prized assets and is a key member of the side.

Charlton Ath (£5,000 from Epsom & Ewell on 9/9/88) FLC 1
Torquay U (£10,000 on 23/3/89) FL 123+1/5 FLC 9/2 FAC 9/2 Others 16/1
Scunthorpe U (£50,000 on 26/3/92) FL 61/8 FLC 6 FAC 2 Others 8
Oxford U (£150,000 on 5/11/93) FL 67/10 FLC 4 FAC 5/2 Others 3

ELLIOTT Robert (Robbie) James
Born: Newcastle, 25 December 1973
Height: 5'10" Weight: 11.6
International Honours: E: Yth

A promising left-back with good tackling and passing ability, who is also capable of playing in midfield. Unfortunately, his career has been dogged by injury, last season being no different, with him being sidelined for four months following a stress fracture of the shin and later tearing his medial ligaments. Highlight of the season must be his first ever goal for Newcastle, a left-foot shot after coming on as substitute in the 3-1 win at Leicester. If he is given a run without injuries, Robbie is young and talented enough to make his mark in the game. Hopes to be fit in time for 1995-96.

Newcastle U (From trainee on 3/4/91) F/PL 37+7/2 FLC 1 FAC 5+1 Others 1

ELLIS Anthony (Tony) Joseph
Born: Salford, 20 October 1964
Height: 5'11" Weight: 11.0

A proven goalscorer, he signed for Blackpool during the 1994 close season and started where he left off at Preston, in scoring spectacular goals.

Oldham Ath (Free from Northwich Victoria on 22/8/86) FL 5+3 FLC 1 FAC 1
Preston NE (£23,000 on 16/10/87) FL 80+6/27 FLC 3 FAC 5 Others 11+1/5

Stoke C (£250,000 on 20/12/89) FL 66+11/19 FLC 5+1/1 FAC 1+4 Others 3+2
Preston NE (£140,000 on 14/8/92) FL 70+2/48 FLC 4/2 FAC 6/3 Others 6/3
Blackpool (£165,000 on 25/7/94) FL 40/18 FLC 2/1 FAC 1 Others 1

Tony Ellis   Matthew Ashton
(Empics Sports Photo Agency)

ELLIS Kevin Edward
Born: Tiptree, 11 May 1977
Height: 5'10" Weight: 11.5
Left-back. As a promising Ipswich young-ster, Kevin made his debut at Arsenal last Easter, but picked up an injury and was substituted with just ten minutes remaining. A good prospect, he is still a trainee.
Ipswich T (Trainee) PL 1

EMBERSON Carl Wayne
Born: Epsom, 13 July 1973
Height: 6'2" Weight: 14.7
Signed from Millwall during the 1994 close season, after an impressive three months on loan at Layer Road in 1992-93, he had to wait for his chance, but has been a regular in Colchester's goal since last January. Solid, big and strong, Carl looks to have a good future in the game.
Millwall (From trainee on 4/5/91) Others 1
Colchester U (Loaned on 17/12/92) FL 13
Colchester U (£25,000 on 6/7/94) FL 19+1 FLC 1 FAC 1

EMBLEN Neil Robert
Born: Bromley, 19 June 1971
Height: 6'2" Weight: 13.3
Despite his limited experience with Millwall, Neil came to Wolverhampton during the 1994 close season in order to solve their long-standing centre-half weakness. Made a nervy debut and was briefly rested, before endearing himself to the crowd with a fine display in midfield against WBA, His attacking style and strong running helped him get three goals in four League games, including a cracking drive against Tranmere, but he was injured in September. Whenever he was regaining his sharpness he seemed to suffer another knock, the latest being damaged medial

ligaments against Barnsley in April.
Millwall (£175,000 from Sittingbourne on 8/11/93) FL 12 Others 1
Wolverhampton W (£600,000 on 14/7/94) FL 23+4/7 FLC 1+1 FAC 3+2 Others 2+1

EMBLETON Daniel (Danny) Charles
Born: Liverpool, 27 March 1975
Height: 5'11" Weight: 12.7
Useful young goalkeeper with a calm temperament and safe pair of hands, Danny spent two years at Liverpool before linking up with Walsall in August 1994. On the subs' bench for 11 games, he acquitted himself well when keeping a clean sheet in the second half of his debut game at Hereford, after Trevor Wood had been sent off. Released during the 1995 close season.
Liverpool (From trainee on 21/8/91)
Walsall (Free on 22/8/94) FL 0+1

EMENALO Michael
Born: Aba, Nigeria, 12 August 1966
Height: 5'11" Weight: 11.4
Club Honours: AIC '95
International Honours: Nigeria
Defender who looks better when going forward. After playing for Nigeria in the 1994 World Cup, Michael came to Notts County, following trials with Molenbeek, having previously played in Germany. Introduced to English football at left-back, he was later moved up alongside Devon White in the attack.
Notts Co (Free from Molenbeek on 18/8/94) FL 7 Others 3+1

EMERSON Dean
Born: Salford, 27 December 1962
Height: 5'8" Weight: 10.8
Having joined Preston from Stockport early last season, this experienced midfielder, who, in his prime had been an aggressive tackler and good passer of the ball, never really had the chance to show his abilities through a lack of first team games and moved on to Chorley in March.
Stockport Co (Signed on 12/2/82) FL 156/7 FLC 10/3 FAC 3 Others 3/1
Rotherham U (£30,000 on 4/7/85) FL 55/8 FLC 6/1 FAC 4 Others 3/1
Coventry C (£100,000 on 16/10/86) FL 98+16 FLC 4+4 FAC 6 Others 3+1
Hartlepool U (Free on 16/5/92) FL 44+1/1 FLC 7 FAC 3 Others 4+1
Stockport Co (Signed on 18/11/93) FL 8+3 FLC 2/1 FAC 1
Preston NE (Free on 2/11/94) FL 1+1 FAC 0+2

ENGLISH Anthony (Tony) Karl
Born: Luton, 19 October 1966
Height: 6'0" Weight: 12.10
Club Honours: GMVC '92; FAT '92
International Honours: E: Yth
As Colchester club captain, he enjoyed a deserved Testimonial season in 1994-95 after ten years service at Layer Road. A versatile performer, Tony has appeared in every position (including goalkeeper) in his time at the club and last season played at centre-back, in midfield and in both full-back berths.
Colchester U (Free from Coventry C juniors on 24/12/84) FL 325+5/42 FLC 14/1 FAC 28/2 Others 19+1

ESTEVES Rui Manuel Guerreiro Nolme
Born: Lisbon, Portugal, 30 January 1967
Height: 6'0" Weight: 12.0
Coming on loan to Birmingham from Benfica last March, Rui made just one appearance in the AWS area final at Orient, before being substituted and spending the rest of the season in the reserves, acclimatising to English conditions. A skilful midfielder, he has yet to sign on a permanent basis.
Birmingham C (On loan from Benfica on 10/3/95) Others 1

EVANS David Andrew
Born: Aberystwyth, 25 November 1975
Height: 6'1" Weight: 12.1
Striker. First year Cardiff pro who made his debut as a sub in the final match of 1993-94 and put together another 15 first team appearances last season, five of them as a starter . With a lot of enthusiasm added to his natural game, he looked a good prospect at times and could stake a regular claim for a place in 1995-96.
Cardiff C (From trainee on 19/12/94) FL 4+9 Others 1+2

EVANS Michael (Mickey) James
Born: Plymouth, 11 January 1973
Height: 6'0" Weight: 11.5
A lack of consistency made him a regular substitute for Plymouth last term, but he has the ability to score tremendous goals from his favoured centre-forward position. Can also play on the wide right.
Plymouth Arg (From trainee on 30/3/91) FL 56+29/14 FLC 4 FAC 4+2 Others 2/1

EVANS Paul Simon
Born: Oswestry, 1 September 1974
Height: 5'6" Weight: 10.8
Club Honours: Div 3 '94
International Honours: W: U21-2
Very busy, strong-tackling midfielder, who shows maturity beyond his years, he secured a regular Shrewsbury place last November and used his bullet like shooting ability to strike some important goals in tight matches that earned welcome points. A tireless worker, his reward came in the shape of a Welsh U21 debut as substitute against Germany in April.
Shrewsbury T (From trainee on 2/7/93) FL 42+9/5 FLC 5+1/1 FAC 1+1 Others 2

EVANS Terence (Terry)
Born: Pontypridd, 8 January 1976
Height: 5'8" Weight: 10.7
International Honours: W: U21-3
Another young Cardiff prospect who plays in defence, predominantly at right-back, Terry gave a number of encouraging displays last season and was rewarded with three Welsh U21 caps. If his current rate of progress is maintained, he should become one of the cornerstones that the club build on.
Cardiff C (From trainee on 8/7/94) FL 11+1 FLC 2 FAC 1 Others 2+1

EVANS Terence (Terry) William
Born: Hammersmith, 12 April 1965
Height: 6'5" Weight: 15.7
Club Honours: Div 3 '92

A giant in every sense of the word, completely dominant in the air and an inspiring Wycombe team captain, Terry was revered by the supporters for his whole-hearted displays at centre-half in 1994-95.
Brentford (£5,000 from Hillingdon Borough on 22/7/85) FL 228+1/23 FLC 15+1/4 FAC 17/2 Others 23/1
Wycombe W (£40,000 on 26/8/93) FL 64+2/11 FLC 4/1 FAC 6 Others 4/1

EVANS Duncan Wayne
Born: Welshpool, 25 August 1971
Height: 5'10" Weight: 12.0
Splendidly consistent Walsall defender with a fine temperament and strength in the tackle, who plays mainly on the right-flank. Lost his place for a short spell after injuring a foot at Chesterfield last September, but battled back to be ever-present from February onwards during the run-in to promotion.
Walsall (Free from Welshpool on 13/8/93) FL 77 FLC 5+1 FAC 8 Others 3

EVERSHAM Paul Jonathan
Born: Hereford, 28 January 1975
Height: 5'9" Weight: 11.7
A Hereford youngster who had made his debut for the club the previous year, Paul had a few games both in defence and midfield in 1994-95, without being able to establish himself, and was freed at the end of the season.
Hereford U (From trainee on 15/7/93) FL 6+7/1 Others 1

EYRE John Robert
Born: Hull, 9 October 1974
Height: 5'11" Weight: 11.3
Young Oldham centre-forward who can also play on the wide right if required. Fast and skilful and, having ended 1993-94 as the reserve side's top-scorer, he was sent on loan to Scunthorpe last December in order to gain experience, and scored eight goals in nine games. Returned to register his first for the "Latics" at Barnsley, a goal which, incidentally, ended the "Tykes'" promotion hopes. A very bright future is predicted for him.
Oldham Ath (From trainee on 16/7/93) P/FL 4+6/1 FLC 0+2
Scunthorpe U (Loaned on 15/12/94) FL 9/8

EYRES David
Born: Liverpool, 26 February 1964
Height: 5'10" Weight: 11.0
Scorer of 27 goals for Burnley in 1993-94, David's ability to cut in from the left and shoot from distance was still his trademark last season. His campaign started late as a result of an ankle injury, and he was switched to left-back, following injuries to Chris Vinnicombe and Wayne Dowell, being occasionally employed as a central striker.
Blackpool (£10,000 from Rhyl on 15/8/89) FL 147+11/38 FLC 11+1/1 FAC 11/2 Others 13+2/4
Burnley (£90,000 on 29/7/93) FL 83+1/27 FLC 6/3 FAC 9/6 Others 5/2

FAIRCLOUGH Courtney (Chris) Huw
Born: Nottingham, 12 April 1964
Height: 5'11" Weight: 11.2
Club Honours: Div 2 '90, Div 1 '92; CS '92

International Honours: E: B-1; U21-7
An experienced central defender, apart from making a single appearance, Chris was unable to break into the Leeds' first team last season and was placed on the transfer list in November. Unfortunately, he suffered a groin injury at the same time, which kept him out of action for quite a while and, at the time of going to press, is still with the club.
Nottingham F (From apprentice on 12/10/81) FL 102+5/1 FLC 9+1/1 FAC 6 Others 9+2
Tottenham H (£387,000 on 3/7/87) FL 60/5 FLC 7 FAC 3
Leeds U (£500,000 on 23/3/89) FL 187+6/21 FLC 17+2/2 FAC 14+1 Others 14

FAIRCLOUGH Wayne Ricks
Born: Nottingham, 27 April 1968
Height: 5'10" Weight: 12.0
At home in the centre of Chesterfield's defence or midfield, having arrived on a free transfer from Mansfield during the 1994 close season, Wayne proved to be a cool reader of the game who took more time on the ball than the average Third Division player, but somehow seemed to find it. His opportunities were restricted simply by the strength of competition at the club.
Notts Co (From apprentice on 28/4/86) FL 39+32 FLC 1+2 FAC 3 Others 10+3
Mansfield T (£80,000 on 5/3/90) FL 131+10/12 FLC 5 FAC 4+1/1 Others 10
Chesterfield (Free on 23/6/94) FL 12+1 FLC 3 FAC 2 Others 3

FARNWORTH Simon
Born: Chorley, 28 October 1963
Height: 5'11" Weight: 11.0
International Honours: E: Sch
In his second season at Wigan, the vastly experienced goalkeeper celebrated his 100th consecutive first team appearance for the club at Walsall last April. His consistent performances were rewarded with the offer of a new contract.
Bolton W (From apprentice on 5/9/81) FL 113 FLC 11 FAC 6 Others 8
Stockport Co (Loaned on 11/9/86) FL 10 FLC 2
Tranmere Rov (Loaned on 9/1/87) FL 7
Bury (Free on 12/3/87) FL 105 FLC 11 FAC 3 Others 5
Preston NE (Free on 1/7/90) FL 81 FLC 6 FAC 3 Others 7
Wigan Ath (Free on 27/7/93) FL 83 FLC 6 FAC 6 Others 6

FARRELL Andrew (Andy) James
Born: Colchester, 7 October 1965
Height: 5'11" Weight: 11.0
Club Honours: Div 4 '92
A versatile Wigan performer who never lets the side down whether playing in defence or in midfield, he became Graham Barrow's first cash signing when joining the club from Burnley last September. An experienced campaigner, Andy celebrated his 350th Football League start at Bury on 26 December.
Colchester U (From apprentice on 21/9/83) FL 98+1/5/7 FLC 5 FAC 8 Others 6
Burnley (£13,000 on 7/8/87) FL 237+20/19 FLC 17+4/1 FAC 19+2 Others 27+3/3
Wigan Ath (£20,000 on 22/9/94) FL 30+1 FLC 1 FAC 2 Others 4/1

FARRELL David (Dave) William
Born: Birmingham, 11 November 1971
Height: 5'11" Weight: 11.9
Aston Villa reserve left-winger with good pace and an excellent crosser of the ball. Still finding his way in the game, having originally come from non-league football, Dave struggled hard to gain a place in the side, making just two starts, both in the Coca Cola Cup. However, he is a promising player who just needs a few more games under his belt.
Aston Villa (£45,000 from Redditch U on 6/1/92) F/PL 5+1 FLC 2
Scunthorpe U (Loaned on 25/1/93) Others 2

FARRELL Sean Paul
Born: Watford, 28 February 1969
Height: 6'0" Weight: 13.7
Plagued by injury in 1994-95, Peterborough's big money signing, and an experienced midfielder, Sean will be looking to live up to expectations in 1995-96.
Luton T (From apprentice on 5/3/87) FL 14+11/1 FAC 2+1/1 Others 1+2/2
Colchester U (Loaned on 1/3/88) FL 4+5/1
Northampton T (Loaned on 13/9/91) FL 4/1
Fulham (£100,000 on 19/12/91) FL 93+1/31 FLC 5+1/3 FAC 2/3 Others 8/1
Peterborough U (£120,000 on 5/8/94) FL 25+8/8 FLC 2 FAC 1 Others 1

FARRELLY Gareth
Born: Dublin, 28 August 1975
Height: 6'1" Weight: 12.4
International Honours: Ei: U21-2
Aston Villa central midfielder, who enjoys the passing game, Gareth had a spell on loan last season with Rotherham. Selected for the Republic of Ireland U21 squad, playing twice, he showed impressive form during the closing weeks of the campaign.
Aston Villa (From trainee on 21/1/92)
Rotherham U (Loaned on 21/3/95) FL 9+1/2

FARRINGTON Mark Anthony
Born: Liverpool, 15 June 1965
Height: 5'10" Weight: 11.12
An experienced midfielder, having arrived back from playing on the continent last October, Mark spent a few weeks at Hereford where he made a substitute appearance as a non-contract player, before going his own way.
Norwich C (Free from Everton juniors on 19/5/83) FL 11+3/2 FLC 1 FAC 3
Cambridge U (Loaned on 28/3/85) FL 10/1
Cardiff C (Free on 19/7/85) FL 24+7/3 FLC 2/1 Others 1
Brighton & Hove A (£100,000 from Feyenoord on 24/8/91) FL 15+13/4 FLC 0+2 Others 3
Hereford U (Signed on 7/10/94) FL 0+1

FASHANU John
Born: Kensington, 18 September 1962
Height: 6'1" Weight: 11.2
Club Honours: FAC '88
International Honours: E: 2
Signed by Aston Villa from Wimbledon prior to the start of 1994-95, John commenced the season not quite match fit, then faced the rest of the campaign dogged by ill-luck. The problems continued with an achilles tendon injury ruling him out of contention for places between September

and December and, on returning, he picked up some dental work. Four games later, a career threatening knee ligament injury suffered against Manchester United, saw him stretchered off and not featuring again during the campaign. At his best, he is a great target man who can hold the ball up until support is forthcoming, and is both dangerous and brave in the air.

Norwich C (Free from Cambridge U juniors on 23/10/79) FL 6+1/1
Crystal Palace (Loaned on 23/8/83) FL 1 FLC 1
Lincoln C (Free on 23/9/83) FL 31+5/10 FLC 2 FAC 2+1 Others 1
Millwall (£55,000 on 30/11/84) FL 50/12 FLC 4/2 FAC 9/4 Others 2/1
Wimbledon (£125,000 on 27/3/86) F/PL 271+5/107 FLC 21+2/9 FAC 27/11 Others 5/2
Aston Villa (£1,350,000 on 4/8/94) PL 11+2/3 FAC 2 Others 1

John Fashanu   Neal Simpson
(Empics Sports Photo Agency)

FEAR Peter Stanley
Born: Sutton, 10 September 1973
Height: 5'10" Weight: 11.7
International Honours: E: U21-3
Very talented Wimbledon central midfielder who found chances in the first team hard to come by in 1994-95 after his successes of the previous season. A player capable of creating opportunities for others with good passing ability and clever footwork, Peter can also play in defence.
Wimbledon (From trainee on 2/7/92) PL 33+8/2 FLC 3+2 FAC 2

FELGATE David Wynne
Born: Blaenau, Ffestiniog, 4 March 1960
Height: 6'1" Weight: 15.0
Club Honours: AMC '89
International Honours: W: 1; Sch
A vastly experienced Welsh international goalkeeper, Peter again produced some tremendous saves for Chester last season. Organises his defence well and has become a firm favourite with the fans.
Bolton W (From juniors on 1/8/78)
Rochdale (Loaned on 7/10/78) FL 35
Crewe Alex (Loaned on 27/9/79) FL 12
Rochdale (Loaned on 9/3/80) FL 12
Lincoln C (£25,000 on 5/9/80) FL 198 FLC 16 FAC 10 Others 2

Cardiff C (Loaned on 1/12/84) FL 4
Grimsby T (£27,000 on 23/2/85) FL 36 FLC 2 FAC 1
Bolton W (Loaned on 14/2/86) FL 15 Others 4
Bolton W (£15,000 on 17/2/87) FL 223 FLC 14 FAC 17 Others 27
Bury (Free on 17/7/93)
Wolverhampton W (Free on 12/8/93)
Chester C (Free on 1/10/93) FL 71+1 FLC 2 FAC 6 Others 5

David Felgate   Matthew Ashton
(Empics Sports Photo Agency)

FENSOME Andrew (Andy) Brian
Born: Northampton, 18 February 1969
Height: 5'7" Weight: 10.10
Club Honours: Div 3 '91
Right-footed Andrew was Preston's most improved player last season and, as the regular right-back, he increasingly overlapped as the season progressed. Sound in defence, and a long-throw specialist, he was ever-present in all competitions.
Norwich C (From apprentice on 16/2/87)
Cambridge U (Free from Bury T on 21/11/89) FL 122+4/1 FLC 11 FAC 17+2 Others 9+1
Preston NE (Signed on 8/10/93 FL 73/1 FLC 2/1 FAC 7 Others 9

FENTON Graham Anthony
Born: Wallsend, 22 May 1974
Height: 5'10" Weight: 11.9
Club Honours: FLC '94
International Honours: E: U21-1
An attacking, hard-working Aston Villa midfielder with pace, and a real prospect, Graham struggled to find a place in a struggling side last season, most of his appearances being made from the subs' bench. However, his high spot came in November when he received his first England U21 cap for the game against the Republic of Ireland.
Aston Villa (From trainee on 13/2/92) PL 16+13/3 FLC 2+3
West Bromwich A (Loaned on 10/1/94) FL 7/3

FENWICK Terence (Terry) William
Born: Seaham, 17 November 1959
Height: 5'10" Weight: 10.11
Club Honours: FAYC '77, '78; Div 2 '79, '83; CS '91
International Honours: E: 20; U21-11 (UEFA) '82); Yth

Former England central defender. Played in the opening two games of last season for Swindon, before falling foul of manager, John Gorman, following an on-field scuffle with a team-mate. When Gorman was relieved of his position in November, Terry was tipped as a possible replacement, but, unsuccessful, his contract was cancelled at the end of December. It was ironic that he should return to the County Ground in April as the manager of Portsmouth to seal Swindon's relegation fate.
Crystal Palace (From apprentice on 1/12/76) FL 62+8 FLC 4+1 FAC 7/1
Queens Park R (£110,000 on 17/12/80) FL 256/33 FLC 28+1/6 FAC 18/6 Others 5
Tottenham H (£550,000 on 31/12/87) FL 90+3/8 FLC 14/2 FAC 7 Others 5
Leicester C (Loaned on 25/10/90) FL 8/1 Others 1
Swindon T (Free on 6/9/93) F/PL 25+3 FLC 3 FAC 2

FERDINAND Leslie (Les)
Born: Acton, 18 December 1966
Height: 5'11" Weight: 13.5
Club Honours: Turkish Cup '89 (During loan spell in 1988-89 with Besiktas)
International Honours: E: 7
For the third consecutive season, Les was QPR's leading goalscorer, amidst a time full of speculation surrounding his future at the club. Among his goals, were strikes against Manchester United at Loftus Road, and Wimbledon at Selhurst Park, both worthy "Goal of the Season" contenders. A constant threat in the air, especially from set-pieces, his overall finishing has certainly improved, and only injury prevented him from adding considerably to his England caps. Stop Press: Signed by Newcastle for £6 million.
Queens Park R (£15,000 from Hayes on 12/3/87) F/PL 152+11/80 FLC 11+2/7 FAC 6+1/3 Others 1
Brentford (Loaned on 24/3/88) FL 3

FEREDAY Wayne
Born: Warley, 16 June 1963
Height: 5'9" Weight: 11.8
International Honours: E: U21-5
Cardiff utility player, who played in a variety of positions last season, he was perhaps best when running from deep positions. As the campaign wore on, his skill and workrate were a constant source of inspiration for younger players. Surprisingly freed during the summer.
Queens Park R (From apprentice on 3/9/80) FL 167+30/21 FLC 23+3/3 FAC 11+3 Others 6/1
Newcastle (£300,000 on 8/6/89) FL 27+6 FLC 3+1 FAC 1 Others 1+2
Bournemouth (Signed on 30/11/90) FL 20+3 FLC 0+2 FAC 2+1/1 Others 0+2
West Bromwich A (£60,000 on 12/12/91) FL 39+9/3 FLC 1 FAC 0+1 Others 3
Cardiff C (Free on 11/3/94) FL 41+1/2 FLC 1 Others 4

FERGUSON Darren
Born: Glasgow, 9 February 1972
Height: 5'10" Weight: 10.9
Club Honours: PL '93
International Honours: S: U21-5; Yth
A neat Wolverhampton midfielder, and son of Manchester United manager, Alex, Darren was involved in the first 30 matches and was booked six times, despite not being a really physical player. Dropped in favour of Gordon Cowans, he was not used again

until coming on as a sub in April.
Manchester U (From trainee on 11/7/90) F/PL 20+7 FLC 2+1
Wolverhampton W (£250,000 on 13/1/94) FL 34+4 FLC 3 FAC 4 Others 4

FERGUSON Derek

Born: Glasgow, 31 July 1967
Height: 5'8" Weight: 10.11
Club Honours: SL '87, '89; SLC '87, '88, '89
International Honours: S: 2; U21-5; Yth; Sch

Sunderland's Scottish international midfielder is a busy player whose undoubted passing ability has won him many fans at Roker, although a record of only one goal in two years is not to his satisfaction. Turned in particularly impressive displays last season when playing alongside Steve Agnew.
Glasgow R (Signed from Gartcosh U on 1/8/83) SL 92+19/7 SLC 6+4/1 SC 8 Others 11+2/1
Dundee (Loaned on 1/1/90) SL 4
Heart of Midlothian (Signed on 1/8/90) SL 99+4/4 SLC 8 SC 0+3 Others 3+2
Sunderland (£750,000 on 29/7/93) FL 64 FLC 3 FAC 6/1 Others 2

FERGUSON Duncan

Born: Stirling, 27 December 1971
Height: 6'4" Weight: 14.6
Club Honours: SL '94; SLC '94; FAC '95
International Honours: S: 5; B; U21-7

Everton target man who puts his large frame to good use, especially to flick balls on with great accuracy. Seldomly beaten in the air, another integral part of his game is to hold the ball up, enabling the "Blues" to progress forward. A quality all-round striker, he is lethal in the penalty area and scores many of his goals from corners, where his predatory instincts cause defenders constant problems. Moved from Rangers for £4 million last December, having been at Everton on loan since October, and became an instant hero with his commitment to the cause and an impressive goal ratio. Disciplinary problems have unfortunately dogged his short career, but under manager, Joe Royle, there is no reason why he should not put all of his former problems behind him. Won an FA Cup winners' medal when coming on as a sub in the 1-0 victory over Manchester United.
Dundee U (Signed from Carse Thistle on 1/2/90) SL 75+2/28 SLC 2+1/2 SC 8/6
Glasgow R (£4,000,000 on 20/7/93) SL 35/5 SLC 1+1 SC 0+3 Others 1
Everton (£4,400,000 on 4/10/94) PL 22+1/7 FLC 1 FAC 3+1/1

FERNANDES Tamer Hasan

Born: Paddington, 7 December 1974
Height: 6'3" Weight: 13.7
International Honours: E: Yth

Tall goalkeeper and reserve to Kevin Dearden, he performed well as the deputy, particularly at Cambridge and Bournemouth, in keeping Brentford on course during 1994-95.
Brentford (From trainee on 12/7/93) FL 3+2 Others 0+1

FERNEY Martin John

Born: Lambeth, 8 November 1971
Height: 5'11" Weight: 12.4

A product of Fulham's youth policy, Martin is an all-action midfield player, fast, energetic and totally committed. However, having been very unlucky with a series of injuries and, although making six starts in 1994-95, he was freed at the end of last season.
Fulham (From trainee on 11/7/90) FL 49+11/1 FLC 6 FAC 1+1 Others 4+2

FERRETT Christopher (Chris) Andrew

Born: Poole, 10 February 1977
Height: 6'0" Weight: 11.10

A young Bournemouth defender, and still a trainee, Chris made his debut as a substitute against Shrewsbury last October, his only appearance for the club to date.
Bournemouth (Trainee) FL 0+1

FETTIS Alan William

Born: Belfast, 1 February 1971
Height: 6'1" Weight: 11.4
International Honours: NI: 10; B-2

Alan has now joined the long list of outstanding Hull goalkeepers. The Northern Ireland international is an excellent shot-stopper and possessor of superb reflexes and, with growing strength and confidence, he is becoming more dominant from crosses and in taking charge of his area. A nagging thumb injury gave the likeable Irishman a frustrating autumn and early winter period which, nonetheless, also gave him a permanent place in the game's record books. Having been asked to appear as an outfield sub, he promptly scored in the defeat of leaders, Oxford, amid unprecedented scenes at Boothferry Park and eclipsed that with another goal at Blackpool with the last kick of 1994-95.
Hull C (£50,000 from Ards on 14/8/91) FL 127+1/2 FLC 7 FAC 5 Others 6

FEUER Anthony (Tony) Ian

Born: Las Vegas, USA, 20 May 1970
Height: 6'5" Weight: 15.7

Giant American goalie who joined West Ham at the back-end of 1993-94. Used as the first team substitute 'keeper until Les Sealey became a "Hammer" last November, Tony played 21 games in the reserve side, before being loaned out to Peterborough in February. Saw out the remainder of the season at London Road and acquitted himself well in 16 Second Division matches.
West Ham U (£70,000 on 23/3/94)
Peterborough U (Loaned on 20/2/95) FL 16

FEWINGS Paul John

Born: Hull, 18 February 1978
Height: 5'11" Weight: 11.7

With nine goals in just 13 games for the Hull junior side, and still a first year YTS, Paul received a first team call at the end of last season. Introduced at Crewe, the speedy left-footed forward enjoyed a tremendous debut and is one to watch out for.
Hull C (Trainee) FL 0+2

FICKLING Ashley

Born: Sheffield, 15 November 1972
Height: 5'10" Weight: 11.0
International Honours: E: Sch

Versatile central defender or full-back, who made appearances for Sheffield United in the Coca Cola Cup and the Anglo-Italian Cup last season, before requesting a transfer and moving to Grimsby on deadline day.
Sheffield U (From juniors on 26/7/91) FLC 2+1 Others 3
Darlington (Loaned on 26/11/92) FL 14 Others 1
Darlington (Loaned on 12/8/93) FL 1 FLC 1
Grimsby T (Free on 23/3/95) FL 1

FILAN John Richard

Born: Sydney, Australia, 8 February 1970
Height: 5'11" Weight: 12.10
International Honours: Australia: U21

Regular first team 'keeper for Cambridge until injured last November, John was loaned to Nottingham Forest at the end of December, without getting off the bench, before transferring to Coventry in March. With two appearances behind him at City he is relatively young as goalies go and can be considered a prospect.
Cambridge U (£40,000 from Budapest St George on 12/3/93) FL 68 FLC 6 FAC 3 Others 3
Coventry C (£300,000 on 2/3/95) PL 2

FINLAY Darren Jonathan

Born: Belfast, 19 December 1973
Height: 5'4" Weight: 10.0
International Honours: NI: B-1; U21; Yth

An energetic young Doncaster midfielder, who was signed from QPR during the 1994 close season, Darren was sent off at Hereford on the opening day of 1994-95. Following that, appearances were few and far between and, although he played for Northern Ireland at "B" International level during 1995, he was released at the end of the season.
Queens Park R (From trainee on 15/5/92)
Doncaster Rov (Free on 6/7/94) FL 6+2/1 FLC 1+1 Others 0+1

FINNIGAN Anthony (Tony)

Born: Wimbledon, 17 October 1962
Height: 6'0" Weight: 12.0
International Honours: E: Yth

Although he made his Fulham debut in November 1994 as a non-contract player, Tony had previously been at the Cottage in the early 1980s, without ever making the first team. On his return, however, he showed skill and composure in the back four, where he was used primarily as cover.
Fulham (From apprentice on 3/11/80)
Crystal Palace (Free from Corinthian Casuals on 5/2/85) FL 94+11/10 FLC 7+1 FAC 2+1 Others 2
Blackburn Rov (£45,000 on 29/7/88) FL 21+14 FLC 3 FAC 5/1 Others 3/1
Hull C (£30,000 on 3/8/90) FL 15+3/1 FLC 2+1
Swindon T (Free on 18/3/91) FL 2+1
Brentford (Free on 17/1/92) FL 3 Others 1
Barnet (Signed on 28/9/93) FL 5+1/1 FLC 0+1
Fulham (Free from Enfield on 30/9/94) FL 7+4 FAC 1 Others 1

FISHER Neil John

Born: St Helens, 7 November 1970
Height: 5'10" Weight: 10.9

Midfielder. All of Neil's Bolton appearances during 1994-95 came in the early part of the season and, after being substituted in a 1-1 draw at Port Vale, he failed to figure again.
Stop Press: Signed for Chester on a free transfer during the summer.

Bolton W (From trainee on 12/7/89) FL 17+7/1 FLC 4 FAC 1

FISHLOCK Murray Edward
Born: Marlborough, 23 September 1973
Height: 5'8" Weight: 10.8
Picked up from non-league football last September, Murray, a determined battler, fought Kevin Lloyd all the way for Hereford's left-back spot, before being slowed down by a number of injuries. Not downhearted, he will come again.
Hereford U (Free from Trowbridge on 30/9/94) FL 2+2 FLC 1 Others 2

FITZGERALD Gary Michael
Born: Hampstead, 27 October 1976
Height: 6'1" Weight: 12.4
A young Watford defender, who only turned professional last November, he made a premature first team debut at the age of 18 because of injuries.
Watford (From trainee on 15/11/94) FL 1

FITZGERALD Scott Brian
Born: Westminster, 13 August 1969
Height: 6'0" Weight: 12.12
International Honours: Ei: B-1; U21-2
Tough and commanding Wimbledon centre-back who was ever-present until losing his place last October, despite having some good performances under his belt from earlier in the season. Came back in December for three matches, however, as a replacement for the suspended Alan Reeves, before making way for Chris Perry. Failed to make further appearances, due to injuries and hefty competition for places.
Wimbledon (From trainee on 13/7/89) F/PL 93+9/1 FLC 13 FAC 5 Others 1

Jan-Aage Fjortoft   Neal Simpson
(Empics Sports Photo Agency)

FJORTOFT Jan-Aage
Born: Aaesund, Norway, 10 January 1967
Height: 6'0" Weight: 12.8
International Honours: Norway
In becoming Middlesbrough's record signing on transfer deadline day, last March, quality striker Jan was already leading goal-scorer in the First Division when he joined

the club on a three year contract from Swindon. His deft touches and ball control, allied to his intelligent reading of the game, ensured that his team-mates were constantly brought into play, sharing with him the responsibility for scoring goals and keeping opposing defenders under extreme pressure. Like three more of his team-mates, he was elected to the PFA Award winning First Division team.
Swindon T (£500,000 from Rapid Vienna on 29/7/93) P/FL 62+10/27 FLC 9/9 FAC 3+1/2 Others 1+1
Middlesbrough (£1,300,000 on 31/3/95) FL 8/3

FLAHAVAN Aaron Adam
Born: Southampton, 15 December 1975
Height: 6'1" Weight: 12.4
A goalkeeper with good reflexes, Aaron entered the Portsmouth first team fray last season when coming on for 20 minutes in an FA Cup-tie with Leicester City, after Alan Knight had been sent off.
Portsmouth (From trainee on 15/2/94) FAC 0+1

FLATTS Mark Michael
Born: Islington, 14 October 1972
Height: 5'6" Weight: 9.8
International Honours: E: Yth; Sch
Wide midfield player who is still on the periphery of the Arsenal first team. A wingman with pace, two good feet, and a tackler to boot, Mark impressed on trial at Bristol City last March. Although only making four appearances for the "Gunners" during the season, two of them from the bench, he still has the skill to become a big name.
Arsenal (From trainee on 28/12/90) PL 9+7 FLC 1 FAC 0+1
Cambridge U (Loaned on 14/10/93) FL 5/1
Brighton & Hove A (Loaned on 31/12/93) FL 9+1/1
Bristol C (Loaned on 23/3/95) FL 4+2

FLECK Robert
Born: Glasgow, 11 August 1965
Height: 5'7" Weight: 10.8
Club Honours: SPD '87; SLC '87, '88
International Honours: S: 4; U21-6; Yth
In three seasons at Chelsea this once highly coveted striker has played only 35 full Premier League games and scored just three times, failing to make a single appearance in 1994-95. A stocky, bustling forward, who is quick and aggressive, at his best, he is capable of unsettling defenders and delivering goals (at Norwich he scored 66 in 196 appearances), Last season, loaned to struggling First Division side, Bristol City, Robert played well in his ten matches, being highly thought of at Ashton Gate, and it was only his price tag that stopped a permanent transfer.
Glasgow R (Free from Possil YM in 1983) SL 61+24/29 SLC 3+5/2 SC 1+1 Others 3+4/3
Partick Thistle (Loaned in November 1983) SL 1+1/1
Norwich C (£580,000 on 17/12/87) FL 130+13/40 FLC 13/11 FAC 16+2/11 Others 7/4
Chelsea (£2,100,000 on 13/8/92) PL 35+5/3 FLC 7/1 FAC 1
Bolton W (Loaned on 17/12/93) FL 6+1/1 Others 1
Bristol C (Loaned on 12/1/95) FL 10/1

FLEMING Craig
Born: Halifax, 6 October 1971
Height: 6'0" Weight: 11.7
Another of Joe Royle's master buys for Oldham, and recognised at one time by none other than Alex Ferguson as the best man-to-man marker in the English game, Craig is strong in the tackle and very much the "Norman Hunter" of the '90s. A right-back who can also play in the centre of defence, he made just five appearances in 1994-95 due to a hernia problem but, following two operations, has now been pronounced fit and is raring to go.
Halifax T (From trainee on 21/3/90) FL 56+1 FLC 4 FAC 3 Others 3+2
Oldham Ath (£80,000 on 15/8/91) F/PL 93+5/1 FLC 7+1 FAC 10 Others 1

FLEMING Curtis
Born: Manchester, 8 October 1968
Height: 5'11" Weight: 12.8
Club Honours: Div 1 '95
International Honours: Ei: B-1; U23-1; U21-5; Yth
Brilliant Middlesbrough defender who occupied the left-back position with absolute authority last season, Curtis is renowned for his strong tackling and in coming away from the most difficult situations to set up counter attacks. Another reason why "Boro" have taken automatic entry to the Premiership, he is popular with all the fans, and a special favourite of the Holgate end.
Middlesbrough (£50,000 from St Patricks on 16/8/91) F/PL 101+12 FLC 7+2 FAC 7 Others 7+1

FLEMING Gary James
Born: Londonderry, 17 February 1967
Height: 5'9" Weight: 11.1
International Honours: NI-31
A regular selection for Northern Ireland, Gary was an ever-present for Barnsley in 1994-95 after moving to a sweeper role, He also developed into a class player in that position and his ability to read the game means he deals with situations before they develop. At home, especially, he will also come out of defence with the ball when the situation allows and pass accurately.
Nottingham F (From apprentice on 19/11/84) FL 71+3 FLC 5+1 FAC 2+1 Others 0+1
Manchester C (£150,000 on 17/8/89) FL 13+1 FLC 4 Others 1
Notts Co (Loaned on 8/3/90) FL 3 Others 1
Barnsley (£85,000 on 23/3/90) FL 234+2 FLC 14 FAC 12 Others 6

FLEMING Paul
Born: Halifax, 6 September 1967
Height: 5'7" Weight: 11.8
Speedy full-back who made a couple of appearances for Mansfield last season whilst engaged on a week-to-week basis. Later had a trial with Scarborough, before joining Halifax in the Vauxhall Conference.
Halifax T (From apprentice on 10/9/85) FL 135+4/1 FLC 7+1 FAC 7/1 Others 13+1
Mansfield T (£10,000 on 4/7/91) FL 65+3 FLC 2+1 FAC 2 Others 6

FLEMING Terence (Terry) Maurice
Born: Marston Green, 5 January 1973
Height: 5'9" Weight: 10.9

A Preston 1994 close season signing, he became a good squad member who was able to provide cover at full-back or on the wing, but unable to secure a regular place until late last season. Very fast and popular with the fans, Terry lacked the consistency needed for an early breakthrough.

Coventry C (From trainee on 2/7/91) F/PL 8+5 FLC 0+1
Northampton T (Free on 3/8/93) FL 26+5/1 FLC 2 FAC 0+1 Others 0+1
Preston NE (Free on 18/7/94) FL 20+7/2 FLC 2 FAC 0+1 Others 3+1

Terry Fleming　　　　　Barry Coombs
(Empics Sports Photo Agency)

FLETCHER Steven (Steve) Mark
Born: Hartlepool, 26 June 1972
Height: 6'0" Weight: 12.1

Last season was the best so far in a Bournemouth shirt for Steve in scoring six goals and becoming the fans' choice as "Player of the Year". Very strong in the air, he always gave 100 per-cent and struck up a good partnership with fellow striker, Steve Jones.

Hartlepool U (From trainee on 23/8/90) FL 19+13/4 FLC 0+2/1 FAC 1+2 Others 2
Bournemouth (£30,000 on 28/7/92) FL 97+10/16 FLC 10/1 FAC 2 Others 2

FLITCROFT David John
Born: Bolton, 14 January 1974
Height: 5'11" Weight: 13.5

Brother of Manchester City's Gary, David is a strong Chester midfielder who can also play wide on the right. Made 25 appearances, plus 12 of the sub variety in 1994-95.

Preston NE (From trainee on 2/5/92) FL 4+4/2 FLC 0+1 Others 0+1
Lincoln C (Loaned on 17/9/93) FL 2 FLC 0+1
Chester C (Free on 9/12/93) FL 24+16/1 FLC 1 FAC 2 Others 2

FLITCROFT Garry William
Born: Bolton, 6 November 1972
Height: 5'10" Weight: 11.0
International Honours: E: U21-5; Yth; Sch

An excellent Manchester City midfield prospect, he had a very good season in 1994-95 and most of the few goals that he

scored came at a crucial time and changed the outcome of the match. Is now maturing well, both in physique and skilful play, and was given the added bonus of captaining the side on occasion. Very conscientious, he is always willing to listen and learn from his more experienced team-mates and further honours cannot be far away.

Manchester C (From trainee on 2/7/91) PL 84+6/13 FLC 10+1 FAC 10/1
Bury (Loaned on 5/3/92) FL 12

Garry Flitcroft　　　　　Paul Marriott
(Empics Sports Photo Agency)

Jostein Flo　　　　　Tony Marshall
(Empics Sports Photo Agency)

FLO Jostein
Born: Eid, Norway, 3 October 1964
Height: 6'4" Weight: 13.12
International Honours: Norway

Following a successful 1994 World Cup USA, Jostein struggled to recover his form. A sending-off in the first home game of last season led to early problems, probably not helped by him being played as a central striker at Sheffield United and as a midfielder for his country. Continued to retain his place in the Norwegian squad, however, and came strongly towards the end of the campaign with some powerful displays for both club and country.

Sheffield U (£400,000 from Songdal on 10/8/93) P/FL 57+8/15 FLC 3/2 FAC 1+1

FLOUNDERS Andrew (Andy) John
Born: Hull, 13 December 1963
Height: 5'11" Weight: 11.6

Prolific scorer in the lower divisions, with both Scunthorpe and Rochdale, he was manager John Barnwell's last signing for Northampton (December 1994) before he left. Released at the end of last season.

Hull C (From apprentice on 24/12/81) FL 126+33/54 FLC 6+2/3 FAC 10+3/4 Others 6+3/2
Scunthorpe U (£30,000 on 5/3/87) FL 186+10/87 FLC 14/6 FAC 11+2/3 Others 19/4
Rochdale (Free on 9/8/91) FL 82+3/31 FLC 8+1/1 FAC 6/1 Others 4
Rotherham U (Loaned on 7/2/93) FL 6/2
Carlisle U (Loaned on 30/10/93) FL 6+2/1 Others 2/1
Northampton T (Free from Halifax T on 21/12/94) FL 2

FLOWERS Timothy (Tim) David
Born: Kenilworth, 3 February 1967
Height: 6'2" Weight: 14.0
Club Honours: PL '95
International Honours: E: 7; U21-3; Yth

Blackburn and England goalkeeper. Showed his supreme temperament last season when spending long spells under-employed, but still retaining the concentration needed when being called upon. Quick to get down to the low shot, and spotting any sudden change of direction, his performances in crucial PL games against Arsenal, Norwich and, above all, Newcastle, contributed heavily to maintaining the club's momentum. Capped several times in 1994-95, the only downside of a glorious campaign, which saw him win a Championship medal, was in breaking a toe at Leeds and being despatched from the field of play after just two minutes. One of six Blackburn players elected to the PFA "PL Team of the Year".

Wolverhampton W (From apprentice on 28/8/84) FL 63 FLC 5 FAC 2 Others 2
Southampton (£70,000 on 13/6/86) F/PL 192 FLC 26 FAC 16 Others 8
Swindon T (Loaned on 23/3/87) FL 2
Swindon T (Loaned on 13/11/87) FL 5
Blackburn Rov (£2,400,000 on 4/11/93) PL 68 FLC 4 FAC 6 Others 3

FLYNN Michael (Mike) Anthony
Born: Oldham, 23 February 1969
Height: 6'0" Weight: 11.0
International Honours: E: Yth

Stockport defender who was the team's captain and inspiration last season, yet again showed the uncompromising approach and "never-say-die" attitude that had made him the fans' "Player of the Year" for 1993-94. Tough and determined, both on the ground and in the air, it is difficult to imagine a County side without him.

Oldham Ath (From apprentice on 7/2/87) FL 37+3/1 FLC 1+1/1 FAC 1 Others 2
Norwich C (£100,000 on 22/12/88)
Preston NE (£125,000 on 4/12/89) FL 134+2/7 FLC 6 FAC 6+1/1 Others 13
Stockport Co (£125,000 on 25/3/93) FL 98+1/3 FLC 6 FAC 5 Others 12

FLYNN Sean Michael
Born: Birmingham, 13 March 1968
Height: 5'8" Weight: 11.8

Coventry striker, cum midfield player, who has the skills required at Premier League level to go with a "never-say-die" attitude. Scored some vital goals last season, including an excellent header at home to Liverpool and two against Leicester, and was often a focal point for City's attacks when getting on the end of long diagonal balls into the penalty area. Away from home, he looked comfortable in the holding role on the right-hand side of midfield, covering the overlapping full-back, before injuring an ankle against QPR and missing the end of the campaign.
Coventry C (£20,000 from Halesowen T on 3/12/91) F/PL 90+7/9 FLC 5/1 FAC 3

FOLEY Stephen (Steve)
Born: Liverpool, 4 October 1962
Height: 5'7" Weight: 10.12
Club Honours: AMC '92; Div 2 '93

Hard-tackling Lincoln midfield player, who suffered firstly at the hands of referees and later with injuries, causing him to be absent for lengthy spells during last season, prior to being released in April.
Liverpool (From apprentice on 2/9/80)
Fulham (Loaned on 16/12/83) FL 2+1
Grimsby T (Free on 20/8/84) FL 31/2 FLC 6/2 FAC 3/1
Sheffield U (Free on 20/8/85) FL 56+10/14 FLC 5/3 FAC 5/1 Others 2+1
Swindon T (£40,000 on 24/6/87) FL 142+9/23 FLC 14+2/1 FAC 10/2 Others 12+1/3
Stoke C (£50,000 on 16/1/92) FL 106+1/10 FLC 8 FAC 6 Others 14/3
Lincoln C (Free on 14/7/94) FL 15+1 FLC 1 FAC 2 Others 2

FOOT Daniel (Danny) Francis
Born: Edmonton, 6 September 1975
Height: 5'10" Weight: 12.3

Not offered pro terms by "Spurs", after spending two years as a trainee at White Hart Lane, Danny joined Southend prior to the start of 1994-95 and two appearances in their midfield gave the fans a brief indication of his all-action style and excellent stamina.
Southend U (Free from Tottenham H juniors on 2/8/94) FL 2+1

FORAN Mark James
Born: Aldershot, 30 October 1973
Height: 6'4" Weight: 13.12

Tall Sheffield United central defender who spent a period on loan last season at Rotherham United to gain valuable experience. Following a substitute appearance in the Anglo-Italian Cup, he finally made his United FL debut against Stockport in place of the injured Brian Gayle, marking the giant Kevin Francis. Later played four FL games, scoring his first League goal with a fine header against "Wolves".
Millwall (From trainee on 3/11/90)
Sheffield U (£25,000 on 28/8/93) FL 4/1 FLC 1 Others 0+1
Rotherham U (Loaned on 26/8/94) FL 3

FORBES Steven Dudley
Born: London, 24 December 1975
Height: 6'2" Weight: 12.6

Another non-league signing for Millwall from Sittingbourne, during the summer of 1994, Steven proved to be a play anywhere youngster who could operate in defence or midfield with equal ease. Made excellent progress to come off the bench during the final game of the season.
Millwall (£45,000 from Sittingbourne on 11/7/94) FL 0+1

FORD Anthony (Tony)
Born: Grimsby, 14 May 1959
Height: 5'9" Weight: 12.2
Club Honours: Div 3 '80; FLGC '82
International Honours: E: B-2

The Scunthorpe player-coach, who settled into the team at right-back after joining from Grimsby during the 1994 close season, he is a steady, experienced performer who makes up for lost speed in the twilight of his career by sound positional sense. Being an ex-winger, he can still take up good overlapping positions.
Grimsby T (From apprentice on 1/5/77) FL 321+34/54 FLC 31+3/4 FAC 15+4/2 Others 2
Sunderland (Loaned on 27/3/86) FL 8+1/1
Stoke C (£35,000 on 8/7/86) FL 112/13 FLC 8 FAC 9 Others 6/1
West Bromwich A (£145,000 on 24/3/89) FL 114/14 FLC 7 FAC 4/1 Others 2+1
Grimsby T (£50,000 on 21/11/91) FL 59+9/3 FLC 1 FAC 3
Bradford C (Loaned on 16/9/93) FL 5 FLC 2
Scunthorpe U (Free on 2/8/94) FL 38/2 FLC 2 FAC 4 Others 1

FORD Jonathan (Jon) Steven
Born: Birmingham, 12 April 1968
Height: 6'0" Weight: 12.0
Club Honours: AMC '94

1994-95 turned out to be Jon's most consistent season for Swansea since arriving from non-league, Cradley Town. Equally at home at left-back, or in midfield, he was ever-present in defence, playing alongside three different central defenders. A feature of his game are strong, attacking runs down the left-hand side from defence, plus an ability to score vital goals from set pieces.
Swansea C (£5,000 from Cradley T on 19/8/91) FL 145+15/7 FLC 12+1 FAC 8+5/2 Others 15+5

FORD Michael (Mike) Paul
Born: Bristol, 9 February 1966
Height: 6'0" Weight: 11.6
Club Honours: WC '88

Mike is equally at home at centre-back, or left-back, and featured in both positions for Oxford in 1994-95. Missed over half the season with an achilles injury and, indeed, his seven years at the Manor Ground has cost him lots of appearances with a string of

Tim Flowers

Neal Simpson
(Empics Sports Photo Agency)

injuries. A creative player, and a real motivator of team-mates, and the crowd, he likes to get forward for a few goals. Was captain until his latest injury.

Leicester C (From apprentice on 11/2/84)
Cardiff C (Free from Devizes T on 19/9/84) FL 144+1/13 FLC 6 FAC 9 Others 7
Oxford U (£150,000 on 10/6/88) FL 166+15/10 FLC 13+1/1 FAC 5+1 Others 5/1

FORD Robert (Bobby) John
Born: Bristol, 22 September 1974
Height: 5'8" Weight: 11.0
International Honours: E: Yth

Young, creative Oxford midfield player, who looks to have a successful career ahead of him, Bobby was called up for the Endsleigh League side in 1994-95 (non-playing substitute). Able to take players on and beat them, he is also a good crosser of the ball. Scored his first goals last season and is certainly one for the future.

Oxford U (From trainee on 6/10/92) FL 32+5/2 FLC 0+1 FAC 3 Others 4/1

FORD Stuart Trevor
Born: Sheffield, 20 July 1971
Height: 6'1" Weight: 11.12

Very capable Scarborough 'keeper, now in his second spell with the club. Was unfortunately blighted by injuries in 1994-95, and towards the end of the campaign joined Halifax Town on loan, before being released on a free transfer in the summer.

Rotherham U (From trainee on 1/7/89) FL 5
Scarborough (Free on 26/3/92) FL 28 FLC 3 FAC 1 Others 3
Bury (Free on 23/7/93)
Doncaster Rov (Free on 16/8/93)
Scarborough (Free on 4/7/94) FL 6

FOREMAN Darren
Born: Southampton, 12 February 1968
Height: 5'11" Weight: 11.2
International Honours: E: Sch

Nicknamed "Deadly Darren" by the Scarborough supporters, he is the club's record goalscorer with 31 goals in 1992-93. Unfortunately, he never fully recovered from a broken leg suffered at the end of that campaign, and, although making 12 starts in 1994-95, he was released prior to the season ending.

Barnsley (Free from Fareham on 5/9/86) FL 33+14/8 FLC 2+1 FAC 2+3 Others 1
Crewe Alex (£80,000 on 8/3/90) FL 19+4/4 FLC 1+2
Scarborough (Free on 8/3/91) FL 77+20/35 FLC 12+1/4 FAC 1 Others 4+1/2

FOREMAN Matthew
Born: Newcastle, 15 February 1975
Height: 6'0" Weight: 12.1

Another of the crop of second year Sheffield United professionals who made appearances in the Anglo-Italian Cup last season, Matthew came in at full-back for one start and a couple from the bench. A versatile player who can also play in midfield, he has been retained for 1995-96 and is currently in New Zealand.

Sheffield U (From trainee on 5/7/93) Others 1+2

FORMBY Kevin
Born: Ormskirk, 22 July 1971
Height: 5'11" Weight: 12.0

Although signed as a forward at the end of 1993-94, the former Royal Marine made the Rochdale left-back spot his own for most of last season.

Rochdale (Free from Burscough on 24/3/94) FL 29+4 FLC 2 FAC 1 Others 7

FORREST Craig Lorne
Born: Vancouver, Canada, 20 September 1967
Height: 6'4" Weight: 14.4
Club Honours: Div 2 '92
International Honours: Canada

Ipswich goalkeeper who is an excellent shot-stopper, and is very quick off his line to collect balls played in behind defenders. Performed consistently last season, despite conceding the most goals in the Premier Division and saved the club from heavier defeats on numerous occasions. Had an outstanding game at Tottenham, making brilliant saves from Jurgen Klinsman and was voted "Player of the Year" by the supporters, a tribute to his consistency.

Ipswich T (From apprentice on 31/8/85) F/PL 236 FLC 13 FAC 10 Others 11
Colchester U (Loaned on 1/3/88) FL 11

FORRESTER Jamie Mark
Born: Bradford, 1 November 1974
Height: 5'6" Weight: 10.4
Club Honours: FAYC '93
International Honours: E: Yth (UEFAYC '93); Sch

With such a wealth of talent jockeying for forward positions at Leeds, Jamie failed to make a first team appearance at the club last season, playing his football in two loan spells at Southend and Grimsby, respectively. A small, compact striker with good control, and the ability to turn defenders around the box, and still only 20-years-old, with added weight he would be sure to make his mark in the game.

Leeds U (£60,000 from Auxere on 20/10/92) PL 7+2 FAC 1+1/2
Southend U (Loaned on 1/9/94) FL 3+2
Grimsby T (Loaned on 10/3/95) FL 7+2/1

FORSTER Nicholas (Nicky) Michael
Born: Caterham, 8 September 1973
Height: 5'10" Weight: 11.5
International Honours: E: U21-3

A striker with electrifying pace, fast turns and a good shot, Nicky scored 26 goals in his first season for Brentford, including a hat-trick at Chester. And, as the only ever-present "Bee" in Endsleigh League matches, he combined well with strike partner, Robert Taylor. Undoubtedly, the most exciting prospect at Griffin Park for many years, he has already been capped by England at U21 level in 1994-95, as well as being recognised by his fellow professionals when it came to the PFA Division Two team award.

Gillingham (Signed from Horley T on 22/5/92) FL 54+13/24 FLC 3+2 FAC 6/2
Brentford (£100,000 on 17/6/94) FL 46/24 FLC 4 FAC 2 Others 4+1/2

FORSYTH Michael (Mike) Eric
Born: Liverpool, 20 March 1966
Height: 5'11" Weight: 12.2
Club Honours: Div 2 '87

International Honours: E: B-1; U21-1; Yth

Signed from Derby last February, having given the club almost ten years of excellent service, Michael slotted into Notts County's left-back spot, before being used in central defence. Out of the side for the remaining seven games of the season, his initial displays showed him to be a good tackler, who could also go forward to deliver timely crosses when required.

West Bromwich A (From apprentice on 16/11/83) FL 28+1 FLC 1 FAC 2 Others 1
Derby Co (£25,000 on 28/3/86) FL 323+2/8 FLC 36/1 FAC 15+1 Others 29/1
Notts Co (£200,000 on 23/2/95) FL 7

FOSTER Adrian Michael
Born: Kidderminster, 19 March 1971
Height: 5'9" Weight: 11.0

Signed from Torquay on the eve of last season, this hard-working Gillingham striker missed all of September and October through a foot injury. Took a few months to get back into action, but showed real form towards the end of the campaign.

West Bromwich A (From trainee on 20/7/89) FL 13+14/2 FLC 1+3 FAC 0+2
Torquay U (Free on 3/7/92) FL 55+20/24 FLC 5+1/3 FAC 3/1 Others 4+3
Gillingham (£60,000 on 11/8/94) FL 27+2/8 FLC 2 FAC 3 Others 1

FOSTER Colin John
Born: Chidlehurst, 16 July 1964
Height: 6'4" Weight: 14.1

A central defender who has effectively partnered some of the best in the business, including Des Walker and Alvin Martin, he is now the lynchpin of the Watford defence. With excellent feet for a big man, and always looking to find the right pass, Colin made good use of his height at both ends of the field and along with David Holdsworth and Keith Millen, formed a formidable back three.

Leyton Orient (From apprentice on 4/2/82) FL 173+1/10 FLC 12 FAC 19/5 Others 5/1
Nottingham F (Signed on 4/3/87) FL 68+4/5 FLC 8/1 FAC 5 Others 2
West Ham U (Signed on 22/9/89) F/PL 88+5/5 FLC 5 FAC 9/1 Others 2+2
Notts Co (Loaned on 10/1/94) FL 9 Others 2
Watford (£100,000 on 23/3/94) FL 40/3 FLC 3/1 FAC 5

FOSTER John Colin
Born: Manchester, 19 September 1973
Height: 5'11" Weight: 11.2
International Honours: E: Sch

Naturally a right-back, he can play in a number of defensive positions, being both robust and a good passer of the ball. Started his first full game of last season at Newcastle in the Coca Cola Cup replay and excelled in a hard fought Manchester City victory, before going back to the reserves. Came back into contention for the end of season run-in and contributed to important wins over Liverpool and Blackburn that averted relegation. Continues to show great skill when playing out of defence to create forward play.

Manchester C (From trainee on 15/7/92) PL 10+3 FLC 1+1 FAC 2+1

FOSTER Stephen (Steve) Brian
Born: Portsmouth, 24 September 1957
Height: 6'1" Weight: 14.0
Club Honours: FLC '88
International Honours: E: 3; U21-1

Brighton central defender of vast experience, who is still producing fine performances and remains dominant in the air and strong in the tackle. As club captain, he is much respected, always advising and encouraging the younger players, Steve was greatly missed when out for two months with a fractured cheekbone.

Portsmouth (From apprentice on 1/10/75) FL 101+8/6 FLC 10 FAC 8/2
Brighton & Hove A (£150,000 on 6/7/79) FL 171+1/6 FLC 13/2 FAC 16
Aston Villa (£200,000 on 3/3/84) FL 15/3 FLC 2
Luton T (£150,000 on 29/11/84) FL 163/11 FLC 20/1 FAC 27/2 Others 2
Oxford U (£175,000 on 13/7/89) FL 95/9 FLC 9/2 FAC 5 Others 4/1
Brighton & Hove A (Free on 14/8/92) FL 107/6 FLC 9 FAC 2 Others 3

FOSTER Wayne Paul
Born: Leigh, 11 September 1963
Height: 5'10" Weight: 11.11
International Honours: E: Yth

A strong forward signed on loan from Hearts last October, Wayne scored on his Hartlepool debut and briefly formed a useful partnership with Keith Houchen. After one month, however, he opted for a return to Scotland to try and win back his first team place.

Bolton W (From apprentice on 6/8/81) FL 92+13/13 FLC 3+2/1 FAC 6/3 Others 2+2
Preston NE (Free on 2/7/85) FL 25+6/3 FLC 3 FAC 1/1 Others 1+1
Heart of Midlothian (Free on 11/8/86) SL 115+44/12 SLC 5+6/1 SC 8+9/5 Others 8+2/4
Hartlepool U (Loaned on 14/10/94) FL 4/1 Others 2

FOWLER Jason Kenneth
Born: Bristol, 20 August 1974
Height: 6'0" Weight: 11.12

Bristol City left-sided midfield player. A local lad, Jason held his place in the side on merit early last season and it is expected that he will be in regular contention for a first team spot in 1995-96. Looks a good bet for the future.

Bristol C (From trainee on 8/7/93) FL 10+5 FLC 0+1 Others 1+1

FOWLER John Anthony
Born: Preston, 27 October 1974
Height: 5'10" Weight: 12.3

Young central midfield player on the fringe of the Cambridge first team, he had a few opportunities early on last season before being in-and-out of the side.

Cambridge U (From trainee on 18/4/92) FL 30+9 FLC 2+4/1 FAC 4+1 Others 3+1
Preston NE (Loaned on 19/2/93) FL 5+1

FOWLER Robert (Robbie) Bernard
Born: Liverpool, 9 April 1975
Height: 5'8" Weight: 11.8
Club Honours: FLC '95
International Honours: E: B-1; U21-6; Yth (UEFAYC '93)

Robbie really progressed last season as an ever-present, putting himself into the position of Liverpool's top-scorer. In the mould of Ian Rush, he possesses a powerful shot and makes space for himself. Also has the ability to run onto the ball and bury it in the back of the net with consummate ease and, like his mentor, he can also create goals for his team-mates. Recognised by his fellow professionals when winning the PFA's "Young Player of the Year" award in 1994-95.

Liverpool (From trainee on 23/4/92) FL 69+1/37 FLC 13/10 FAC 8/2

FOX Mark Stephen
Born: Basingstoke, 17 November 1975
Height: 5'11" Weight: 10.9

Promising Brighton youngster who was given several outings in midfield last term as part of his learning process and scored his first ever league goal with a good diving header in Albion's 3-0 victory at Leyton Orient. Even appeared on the team sheet as substitute goalkeeper during an injury crisis, but fortunately was not needed! Elder brother of Simon.

Brighton & Hove A (From trainee on 21/7/94) FL 8+13/1 Others 1

FOX Peter David
Born: Scunthorpe, 5 July 1957
Height: 5'11" Weight: 12.4
Club Honours: AMC '92; Div 2 '93

Reserve team boss and first choice 'keeper, "Mr Reliable", Peter, is an excellent shot-stopper who saved Exeter on more than one occasion last season. Now 38-years-old, and a pro for 20 years, he was recognised as "Player of the Year" prior to being freed during the summer.

Sheffield Wed (From apprentice on 1/6/75) FL 49 FAC 3
Barnsley (Loaned on 22/12/77) FL 1 FLC 1
Stoke C (£15,000 on 4/3/78) FL 409 FLC 32 FAC 22 Others 14
Exeter C (Free on 15/7/93) FL 56+1 FLC 5 FAC 5 Others 2

Ruel Fox

Steve Morton
(Empics Sports Photo Agency)

FOX Ruel Adrian
Born: Ipswich, 14 January 1968
Height: 5'6" Weight: 10.0
International Honours: E: B-2

Very popular with the Newcastle supporters, with his excellent close control, dribbling skills and pace, creating excitement on the terraces, as well as being a constant threat to the opposition. Plays mostly at outside-right, but can also perform on the left. Has the ability to deliver accurate crosses from either wing, which frequently create goalscoring opportunities for the team. Surprisingly for a man of his size, he is dangerous in the air, having scored in the 2-1 home win against Nottingham Forest when he headed a deep cross past Mark Crossley, as well as netting in the 4-2 defeat at "Spurs". Also represented England "B" against Eire.

Norwich C (From apprentice on 20/1/86) F/PL 148+24/12 FLC 13+3/3 FAC 11+4 Others 12+4
Newcastle U (£2,250,000 on 2/2/94) PL 54/12 FLC 2/1 FAC 5 Others 4/1

FOX Simon Mark
Born: Basingstoke, 28 August 1977
Height: 5'11" Weight: 10.2

Younger brother of Mark, he is another player of potential being given valuable first team experience at Brighton. A forward, he made a promising full debut at York last March. Still a trainee.

Brighton & Hove A (Trainee) FL 1+2

FOYLE Martin John
Born: Salisbury, 2 May 1963
Height: 5'10" Weight: 11.2
Club Honours: AMC '93

As Port Vale's leading goalscorer, Martin had an excellent season in 1994-95. A central striker, who only missed a handful of games through injury, he operated with three different partners whilst notching 20 goals himself. Good in the air for his height, his main highlights included a hat-trick in the FA Cup against Hartlepool and the winner in the local derby at Stoke. Won the "Player of the Year" award.

Southampton (From apprentice on 13/8/80) FL 6+6/1 FLC 0+2/2
Aldershot (£10,000 on 3/8/84) FL 98/35 FLC 10/5 FAC 8/5 Others 6
Oxford U (£140,000 on 26/3/87) FL 120+6/36 FLC 16/4 FAC 5/3 Others 3+1/1
Port Vale (£375,000 on 25/6/91) FL 129+9/49 FLC 12/6 FAC 9+1/7 Others 11+1/5

FRAIN David
Born: Sheffield, 11 October 1962
Height: 5'8" Weight: 10.8

A cultured midfielder, whose six-year stay at Stockport ended last March when he left the country to play in Hong Kong, he is now back in England with Conference side, Stalybridge Celtic. Earlier in 1994-95, David had a loan spell at Mansfield.

Sheffield U (Signed from Dronfield on 7/9/85) FL 35+9/5 FLC 3+2 Others 2
Rochdale (Free on 18/7/88) FL 42/12 FLC 2 FAC 2/1 Others 2
Stockport Co (£50,000 on 21/7/89) FL 176+11/12 FLC 11 FAC 9+3/1 Others 34/1
Mansfield T (Loaned on 2/9/94) FL 4+2 FLC 1

FRAIN John William
Born: Birmingham, 8 October 1968
Height: 5'9" Weight: 11.9
Club Honours: AMC '91

A loyal Birmingham player, John is at home in either full-back positions, or midfield, and never gives anything less than 100 per-cent. Proud to represent his local club, he takes a well deserved testimonial this coming season, but unfortunately missed much of 1994-95 due to injury and illness, making just ten starts.

Birmingham C (From apprentice on 10/10/86) FL 242+8/23 FLC 22/1 FAC 10 Others 20/2

FRANCIS John Andrew
Born: Dewsbury, 21 November 1963
Height: 5'8" Weight: 11.2
Club Honours: Div 4 '92

Injured at Wembley in the 1994 play-offs, John's 1994-95 was restricted to a few appearances as a substitute. Burnley had no real replacement for their speediest player, a man always capable of threatening any defence. After three knee operations, he was still a long way from fitness at the end of the season.

Halifax T (On trial from Emley on 8/2/85) FL 1+3 Others 2
Sheffield U (£10,000 from Emley on 15/9/88) FL 14+28/6 FLC 0+2 FAC 0+1 Others 3+2/1
Burnley (£90,000 on 24/1/90) FL 99+2/26 FLC 6 FAC 8 Others 11+1/4
Cambridge U (£95,000 on 13/8/92) FL 15+14/3 FLC 2+2/1 Others 0+1
Burnley (£70,000 on 25/3/93) FL 40+14/8 FLC 3+1/1 FAC 4+1 Others 4+1/2

FRANCIS Kevin Michael
Born: Birmingham, 6 December 1967
Height: 6'7" Weight: 15.8
Club Honours: Div 2 '95; AMC '95

The tallest player in the League football, Kevin finally got to play for the side he supported as a youngster, when leaving Stockport for Birmingham last January. Having already scored 13 for County, he kicked off in the same vein, netting nine in 18 games and, after breaking his Wembley "duck" following the 1-0 defeat of Carlisle in the Auto Windscreen Shield, he won a Second Division Championship medal as City finished three points clear of their nearest rivals, Reading. Unfortunate to fall foul of the club's injury jinx, he will be out of action until October.

Derby Co (Free from Mile Oak Rov on 2/2/89) FL 0+10 FLC 1+2 FAC 1+2/1 Others 0+1
Stockport Co (£45,000 on 21/2/91) FL 147+5/88 FLC 12/5 FAC 9/6 Others 25/18
Birmingham C (£800,000 on 20/1/95) FL 15/8 Others 3/1

FRANCIS Stephen (Steve) Stuart
Born: Billericay, 29 May 1964
Height: 5'11" Weight: 11.5
Club Honours: FMC '86, '88
International Honours: E: Yth

First choice Huddersfield goalkeeper who continues to impress with outstanding saves. In 1993-94 he was Town's "Player of the Year", having appeared in every game and only a thigh injury last season prevented him from repeating the feat.

Chelsea (From apprentice on 28/4/82) FL 71 FLC 6 FAC 10 Others 1
Reading (£20,000 on 27/2/87) FL 216 FLC 15 FAC 15 Others 13
Huddersfield T (£150,000 on 1/8/93) FL 89 FLC 8 FAC 4 Others 12

FREEDMAN Douglas (Dougie) Alan
Born: Glasgow, 21 January 1974
Height: 5'9" Weight: 11.2
International Honours: S: U21-7; Sch

Freed by QPR during the summer of 1994, Dougie finished the campaign as both Barnet's and the Third Division's highest scorer, and ever-present. Quick, with good touch and vision, he earned a Scottish U21 call-up as the goals flew in from every angle and with either foot. One of the finds of the season, with many big clubs casting envious eyes in his direction, he was elected by his fellow professionals to the PFA Award winning Third Division side.

Queens Park R (From trainee on 15/5/92)
Barnet (Free on 26/7/94) FL 42/24 FLC 4/5 FAC 2 Others 2

FREEMAN Darren Barry Andduet
Born: Brighton, 22 August 1973
Height: 5'11" Weight: 13.0

After signing for Gillingham, and looking to secure a regular place in the side following an impressive trial period last January, this fleet-footed winger unluckily tore a cartilage which ended his season at the club, almost before it had started.

Gillingham (Free from Worthing on 31/1/95) FL 0+2

FREESTONE Christopher (Chris) Mark
Born: Nottingham, 4 September 1971
Height: 5'11" Weight: 11.7

Speedy young striker with a keen eye for goal, Chris joined Middlesbrough last December from non-league, Arnold Town. As an opportunist, he has impressed all at the club with his exceptional speed and ability to score goals.

Middlesbrough (£10,000 from Arnold T on 2/12/94) FL 0+1

FREESTONE Roger
Born: Newport, 19 August 1968
Height: 6'3" Weight: 14.6
Club Honours: Div 2 '89; AMC '94
International Honours: W: U21-1

A call-up to the Welsh International squad last April against West Germany, forced Roger to miss his first FL appearance for Swansea since signing from Chelsea in September 1991, although he had earlier been used as a second-half substitute at Blackpool. An excellent shot-stopper, he was recognised last season as one of the most consistent goalkeepers outside the First Division, with 19 clean sheets claimed in FL matches.

Newport Co (From trainee on 2/4/86 FL 13 Others 1
Chelsea (£95,000 on 10/3/87) FL 42 FLC 2 FAC 3 Others 6
Swansea C (Loaned on 29/9/89) FL 14 Others 1
Hereford U (Loaned on 9/3/90) FL 8
Swansea C (£45,000 on 5/9/91) FL 178+1 FLC 12 FAC 15 Others 24

Steve Froggatt Neal Simpson
(Empics Sports Photo Agency)

FROGGATT Stephen (Steve) Junior
Born: Lincoln, 9 March 1973
Height: 5'10" Weight: 11.0
International Honours: E: U21-2

A pacy left-winger with a useful centre, Steve scored quickly on his Wolverhampton debut, having been signed from Aston Villa during the 1994 close season, and his bright start continued with some fine attacking form. Played as a sort of advanced left-back at Millwall and in most games until the visit to Reading. Suffered a bad injury to his ankle which took over two months to establish the need for surgery, before an infection ironically caused the operation to be delayed further.
Aston Villa (From trainee on 26/1/91) F/PL 30+5/2 FLC 1+1 FAC 5+2/1
Wolverhampton W (£1,000,000 on 11/7/94) FL 20/2 FLC 3/1 Others 2

FRY Christopher (Chris) David
Born: Cardiff, 23 October 1969
Height: 5'10" Weight: 10.2
International Honours: W: Sch

Lightweight winger who has been in-and-out of the Colchester team since joining from Hereford in December 1993, he popped up with a number of goals last season. Possibly the best crosser of a ball at the club, and a player who always gives his all for the cause.
Cardiff C (From trainee on 3/8/88) FL 22+33/1 FLC 1+2 FAC 0+2 Others 0+2
Hereford U (Free on 2/8/91) FL 76+14/10 FLC 6+2 FAC 8+2/1 Others 6+1
Colchester U (Signed on 24/10/93) FL 36+14/8 FLC 1 FAC 1+1 Others 0+1

FUCHS Uwe
Born: Kaiserslautern, Germany, 23 July 1966
Height: 6'2" Weight: 14.1
Club Honours: Div 1 '95

Strong-running striker, and a loan signing from Germany in order to bolster Middlesbrough's promotion challenge, he became the darling of the Holgate end, who were all bitterly disappointed when he didn't appear on "Robbo's" retained list. "Oovay" did the job that he was engaged to do in great style, scoring some memorable goals along the way.
Middlesbrough (Loaned from Kaiserslautern on 27/1/95) FL 13+2/9

FUNNELL Simon Paul
Born: Brighton, 8 August 1974
Height: 6'0" Weight: 12.8

A young Brighton forward who never made the expected breakthrough to a regular first team place. After only three brief appearances as substitute early in the season, he was loaned out to local Unijet County League side, Shoreham, last January, prior to being released.
Brighton & Hove A (From trainee on 2/7/92) FL 14+14/2 FLC 3+2 FAC 0+1 Others 0+2

FURLONG Carl David
Born: Liverpool, 18 October 1976
Height: 5'11" Weight: 12.6

A second year trainee, who scored on his Football League debut for Wigan at Scarborough in 1993-94, Carl is a forward with terrific pace and goalscoring awareness. Looks to have a promising future in the game.
Wigan Ath (Trainee) FL 1+2/1 FAC 0+1

FURLONG Paul Anthony
Born: Wood Green, 1 October 1968
Height: 6'0" Weight: 11.8
Club Honours: FAT '88
International Honours: E: SP-5

Strong, hard-running striker who came to Chelsea from Watford during the 1994 close season. Throughout 1994-95, Paul continued to make progress and the experience of playing in Europe, where he scored seven goals, lifted him considerably. Provides the team with much endeavour and commitment up-front, something typified in Bruges when he converted a seemingly lost cause into the winning goal that saw the "Blues" reach the European Cup Winners Cup semi-final stage.
Coventry C (£130,000 from Enfield on 31/7/91) FL 27+10/4 FLC 4/1 FAC 1+1 Others 1
Watford (£250,000 on 24/7/92) FL 79/37 FLC 7/4 FAC 2 Others 4
Chelsea (£2,300,000 on 26/5/94) PL 30+6/10 FLC 2 FAC 1 Others 7/3

FURNELL Andrew (Andy) Paul
Born: Peterborough, 13 February 1977
Height: 5'10" Weight: 12.5
International Honours: E: Yth

Skilful Peterborough youngster who can play up-front or in midfield, he turned pro last season, having come through the club's junior ranks. Yet to be given the chance his undoubted ability deserves, Andy has the potential to be a very fine player, indeed.
Peterborough U (From trainee on 31/12/94) FL 9+9/1 FLC 1 FAC 1

FUTCHER Paul
Born: Chester, 25 September 1956
Height: 6'0" Weight: 12.3

International Honours: E: U21-11

Right-footed central defender who was signed from the obscurity of Halifax reserves, his career underwent somewhat of a revival at Blundell Park. Although in his mid-30s, his ability to read a game and his anticipation, made him the pivot of the defence for four seasons, while his constructive distribution created many an attacking opportunity. Voted supporters' "Player of the Year" in two successive seasons, his presence alongside Grimsby's talented young defenders has proved invaluable in the development of their game. Passed over as successor to Alan Buckley for the managerial chair, he parted company with the club shortly after Brian Law's appointment last March.
Chester C (From apprentice on 1/1/74) FL 20 FAC 1
Luton T (£100,000 on 1/6/74) FL 131/1 FLC 4 FAC 6
Manchester C (£350,000 on 2/6/78) FL 36+1 FLC 3+1 FAC 3 Others 2
Oldham Ath (£150,000 on 1/8/80) FL 98/1 FLC 10 FAC 3
Derby Co (£44,000 on 28/1/83) FL 35 FLC 1 FAC 4
Barnsley (£30,000 on 22/3/84) FL 229+1 FLC 13 FAC 20 Others 4
Halifax T (Free on 24/7/90) FL 15 FLC 4 FAC 3
Grimsby T (£10,000 on 17/1/91) FL 131+1 FLC 9 FAC 6 Others 3

Marco Gabbiadini Neal Simpson
(Empics Sports Photo Agency)

GABBIADINI Marco
Born: Nottingham, 20 January 1968
Height: 5'10" Weight: 12.4
Club Honours: Div 3 '88
International Honours: E: B-1; FL-1; U21-2; Yth

A lively and energetic Derby striker, Marco had a mixed season in 1994-95. After being sent off in a pre-season friendly in Norway and receiving a three match suspension, he regained his place in the side only to suffer a knee cartilage injury in training. On his return, he formed a fruitful partnership with

Tommy Johnson until the latter's transfer to Villa, before teaming up with new signing, Lee Mills. His bustling style makes him a handful for opposing defenders and a favourite with the home fans.

York C (From apprentice on 5/9/85) FL 42+18/14 FLC 4+3/1 Others 4/3
Sunderland (£80,000 on 23/9/87) FL 155+2/74 FLC 14/9 FAC 5 Others 9/4
Crystal Palace (£1,800,000 on 1/10/91) FL 15/5 FLC 6/1 FAC 1 Others 3/1
Derby Co (£1,000,000 on 31/1/92) FL 125+10/39 FLC 9/6 FAC 7/2 Others 16+1/8

GAGE Kevin William
Born: Chiswick, 21 April 1964
Height: 5'10" Weight: 12.11
Club Honours: Div 4 '83
International Honours: E: Yth

Kevin produced yet another season of consistency at right-back for Sheffield United in 1994-95, having made the position his own following the transfer of Carl Bradshaw to Norwich, and his whole-hearted approach deservedly won him the "Player of the Season" award. Once again scoring some stunning goals, including two at Luton in the team's 6-3 win, he also captained the side in the absence of skipper, Brian Gayle.

Wimbledon (From apprentice on 4/1/82) FL 135+33/15 FLC 7+2/1 FAC 8+3/1 Others 0+1
Aston Villa (£100,000 on 17/7/87) FL 113+2/8 FLC 13/3 FAC 9/1 Others 8
Sheffield U (£150,000 on 15/11/91) F/PL 105+5/7 FLC 6 FAC 10+2 Others 1

GALE Shaun Michael
Born: Reading, 8 October 1969
Height: 6'0" Weight: 11.6

Signed by Barnet during the 1994 close season, having been freed by Portsmouth, Shaun showed himself to be a full-back who could play down both flanks if required. Suffered a bad injury in October, but returned to the side four months later and finished the campaign in a good vein of form.

Portsmouth (From trainee on 12/7/88) FL 2+1 Others 0+1
Barnet (Free on 13/7/94) FL 25+2/2 FLC 4 Others 1

GALE Anthony (Tony) Peter
Born: Westminster, 19 November 1959
Height: 6'1" Weight: 12.4
Club Honours: PL '95
International Honours: E: U21-1; Yth

Released by West Ham during the 1994 close season, and in training with Barnet, the 35-year-old was plucked from relative obscurity to replace the recently transferred, David May, in the centre of Blackburn's defence, for the Charity Shield game at Wembley. Played his part early in the campaign, with impeccable timing and shrewd use of the ball, before being replaced by the younger Ian Pearce. Although Tony was hardly involved after the turn of the year and was given a free transfer during the summer, with the club winning the PL title, his 15 games entitled him to a Championship medal, something he would not have thought possible 12 months ago.

Fulham (From apprentice on 5/8/77) FL 277/19 FLC 22/2 FAC 16

West Ham U (£200,000 on 1/8/84) F/PL 293+7/5 FLC 28+2/1 FAC 29/1 Others 9
Blackburn Rov (Free on 11/8/94) PL 15 FLC 2 Others 3

GALLACHER Kevin William
Born: Clydebank, 23 November 1966
Height: 5'8" Weight: 10.10
International Honours: S: 19; B-2; U21-7; Yth

An excellent player to have in your side, Blackburn's Kevin started last season recovering from a horrendous triple fracture of a leg, before re-appearing in the New Year. Having progressed through the reserves, he was thrown into the vital Crystal Palace game, and scored what proved to be the winning goal, but unfortunately ended the day with his leg back in plaster after it was broken in the same spot. A winger, cum striker, with great pace, always looking to hit the early cross, and composed in the box, he will be sad to have missed out on a Championship medal.

Dundee U (Signed from Duntocher BC in 1983) SL 118+13/27 SLC 13/5 SC 20+3/5 Others 15+6/3
Coventry C (£900,000 on 29/1/90) F/PL 99+1/28 FLC 11/7 FAC 4 Others 2
Blackburn Rov (£1,500,000 on 22/3/93) PL 37+3/13 FLC 4 FAC 4/1

GALLAGHER Thomas (Tommy) Duncan
Born: Nottingham, 25 August 1974
Height: 5'10" Weight: 11.8
Club Honours: AIC '95

An out-and-out full-back, preferring the right-hand side of the pitch, Tommy is relatively inexperienced, having started for Notts County just 25 times in the last two seasons. A hard tackler, who can also go down the line to cross, he could establish himself in the first team in 1995-96.

Notts Co (From trainee on 1/6/92) FL 20 Others 5+2

GALLEN Kevin Andrew
Born: Chiswick, 21 September 1975
Height: 6'0" Weight: 12.3
International Honours: E: U21-3; Yth (EUFAC '93); Sch

An excellent prospect, Kevin made his PL debut for QPR at Old Trafford on the opening day of last season and made a great impression, being unlucky to have a goal ruled out. Scored the winner on his home debut four days later in the 3-2 victory over Sheffield Wednesday, but after making one more start he was then used as a substitute in the next eight games. Recalled to the starting line-up at Norwich, he again scored, following that up with a goal after just 14 seconds against Manchester City. Remaining in the team for the rest of the season, forming a formidable partnership with Les Ferdinand and scoring 12 goals, in March he made his debut for the England U21's against Ireland in Dublin.

Queens Park R (From trainee on 22/9/92) PL 31+6/10 FLC 1+1/1 FAC 4/1

GALLIMORE Anthony (Tony) Mark
Born: Crewe, 21 February 1972
Height: 5'11" Weight: 11.3
Club Honours: Div 3 '95

A solid and cultured Carlisle defender, whose performances led to his being elected to the PFA Third Division side last season, Tony likes to overlap down the wing, where possible, and was often featured in attacks. Early on, he was nominated as Carlisle's penalty-taker, a duty he carried out with coolness and aplomb. Has attracted considerable attention from clubs at a much higher level, in winning a Third Division Championship medal.

Stoke C (From trainee on 11/7/90) FL 6+5
Carlisle U (Loaned on 3/10/91) FL 8
Carlisle U (Loaned on 26/2/92) FL 8
Carlisle U (£15,000 on 25/3/93) FL 88/7 FLC 6/1 FAC 7 Others 17/1

GALLOWAY Michael (Mike)
Born: Oswestry, 30 May 1965
Height: 5'11" Weight: 11.7
International Honours: S: 1; U21-2; Yth

A loan signing from Celtic, to add steel to the Leicester midfield area last season, his pin-point right-wing crosses brought reward in the thriller at the Villa. Had hoped for permanent deal after the first month, but had to settle for extension to loan with a view to a summer move, before a hamstring injury jeopardised the deal.

Mansfield T (Signed on 8/9/83) FL 39+15/3 FLC 1+1 FAC 1 Others 1
Halifax T (Signed on 21/2/86) FL 79/5 FLC 4 FAC 3 Others 4
Heart of Midlothian (£60,000 on 18/11/87) SL 52+4/8 SLC 3 SC 6/1 Others 8/5
Glasgow Celtic (£500,000 on 16/6/89) SL 103+22/8 SLC 13+2 SC 7+4 Others 9/2
Leicester C (Loaned on 3/2/95) PL 4+1 FAC 1

GALLOWAY Michael (Mick) Anthony
Born: Nottingham, 13 October 1974
Height: 5'11" Weight: 11.5

Pronounced as Notts County's "Reserve Team Player of the Year" by the fans at the end of last season, Mick had earlier been given a first team debut as a sub at Luton, before starting the remaining six games in the number 11 shirt. Is an attacking left-sided midfielder, cum forward, and a proven goalscorer in reserve football.

Notts Co (From trainee on 15/6/93) FL 6+1

GANNON James (Jim) Paul
Born: Southwark, 7 September 1968
Height: 6'2" Weight: 13.0

One of Stockport's longest serving players, he has worn almost every shirt, having played at right-back, in all midfield positions, on the wing and at centre forward, although favouring the role of central defender. The most versatile player at the club and still going strong in 1994-95.

Sheffield U (Signed from Dundalk on 27/4/89)
Halifax T (Loaned on 22/2/90) FL 2
Stockport Co (£40,000 on 7/3/90) FL 211+6/46 FLC 13/1 FAC 9/1 Others 31+2/8
Notts Co (Loaned on 14/1/94) FL 2

GANNON John Spencer
Born: Wimbledon, 18 December 1966
Height: 5'9" Weight: 11.10

A gritty Sheffield United midfielder and dead-ball kicker, John started 1994-95 on crutches following a close season operation on his achilles tendon. His first appearance did not come until September, when he scored a late equaliser in the Anglo-Italian Cup match against Piacenza with a diving header, and further injuries during the campaign limited his total to just 12 FL starts. Put in a transfer request in November, due to the lack of first team football, but later regained his place until his season ended with a minor cartilage operation, after being injured at Oldham.

Wimbledon (From apprentice on 19/12/84) FL 13+3/2 FLC 1+1 Others 1
Crewe Alex (Loaned on 19/12/86) FL 14+1 Others 1
Sheffield U (Free on 23/2/89) F/PL 15+12/6 FLC 13+1 FAC 13 Others 6/1
Middlesbrough (Loaned on 5/11/93) FL 6+1 Others 2

GARDINER Mark Christopher
Born: Cirencester, 25 December 1966
Height: 5'11" Weight: 12.3

Long-serving Crewe player who has proved to be most versatile, having occupied numerous positions in the side, both in defence and attack. Good in dead-ball situations, Mark made just nine starts in 1994-95, and had a spell on loan at Chester in March, prior to being released at the end of the season.

Swindon T (From apprentice on 1/10/84) FL 7+3/1 FAC 0+2/1
Torquay U (Free on 6/2/87) FL 37+12/4 FLC 3+1 FAC 1+1/1 Others 1+1
Crewe Alex (Free on 22/8/88) FL 179+14/33 FLC 13+3/3 FAC 18+1/5 Others 17+3/1
Chester C (Loaned on 3/3/95) FL 2+1

GARLAND Peter John
Born: Croydon, 20 January 1971
Height: 5'9" Weight: 12.0
International Honours: E: Yth

Right-sided Charlton midfield player who was out for most of last season suffering firstly a groin strain and then a pelvic problem, before spending a month on loan at Wycombe in a bid to regain full fitness. A competitive player, he likes to shoot from long distance and can score spectacular goals. When fully fit should prove an asset to the team.

Tottenham H (From trainee on 1/7/89) FL 0+1
Newcastle U (£35,000 on 24/3/92) FL 0+2 Others 0+1
Charlton Ath (Signed on 18/12/92) FL 37+13/2 FLC 3 FAC 2 Others 4+1/1
Wycombe W (Loaned on 18/3/95) FL 5

GARNER Simon
Born: Boston, 23 November 1959
Height: 5'9" Weight: 12.11
Club Honours: FMC '87

Top-scorer last season, and very much a legend at Wycombe, his close ball control, guile and quick-thinking forward play, opened up many a defence. Given a free transfer at the end of 1994-95, despite featuring in nearly every game and being the first ever Wanderer to score a first class hat-trick in the FA Cup, something he did at Hitchin.

Blackburn Rov (From apprentice on 5/7/78) FL 455+29/168 FLC 32+2/11 FAC 24+5/7 Others 17+1/6

West Bromwich A (£30,000 on 6/8/92) FL 25+8/8 FLC 3 FAC 3 Others 4+2/1
Wycombe W (Free on 4/2/94) FL 45+8/12 FLC 2 FAC 3/3 Others 5/4

Simon Garner   Barrington Coombs
(Empics Sports Photo Agency)

GARNETT Shaun Maurice
Born: Wallasey, 22 November 1969
Height: 6'3" Weight: 13.4
Club Honours: AMC '90

As Tranmere's first choice centre-half, he relishes physical battle with a centre-forward. Tall, combative and, with a good turn of pace, Shaun was sent off at Barnsley, only for the referee to later quash the offence in the view of video evidence. Strong in the air, he scored his one goal of last season with a thumping header at Sunderland, giving Rovers a 1-0 win.

Tranmere Rov (From trainee on 15/6/88) FL 59+1/4 FLC 8/1 FAC 1 Others 10+2
Chester C (Loaned on 1/10/92) FL 9
Preston NE (Loaned on 11/12/92) FL 10/2 Others 1
Wigan Ath (Loaned on 26/2/93) FL 47/2 FLC 4 FAC 2 Others 5

GARRETT Scott
Born: Gateshead, 9 January 1974
Height: 5'10" Weight: 11.3

Young defender who made just one appearance as a substitute for Hartlepool last season, playing only a minute of first team football. Due to financial cutbacks he was released in mid-season and was later reported to be training with Gateshead.

Hartlepool U (From trainee on 7/5/92) FL 14+1

GARVEY Stephen (Steve) Hugh
Born: Stalybridge, 22 November 1973
Height: 5'9" Weight: 10.9
International Honours: E: Yth

Another Mancunian at Crewe, Steve plays mainly in one of the wide positions, either left or right, despite being a right-footed player. Had a good run-in last season and, although not high on the scoring lists, still made a useful contribution.

Crewe Alex (From trainee on 25/10/91) FL 33+17/4 FLC 4+4/2 FAC 2+1/1 Others 5

GAUDINO Maurizio
Born: Brule, Germany, 12 December 1966
Height: 6'0" Weight: 12.2

Arrived at Manchester City last December on loan until the end of the season, having not trained seriously for a month and was put straight into the side at Newcastle. Following a fairly tough baptism, Maurizio was suitably rested, but once fully fit he came back in a free role up-front, scoring a brilliant goal against Chelsea. With his crowd pleasing arrogance and swagger, his play was at times a delight to watch and he looked a very good player, indeed. Also scored a magnificent headed winner against Liverpool from fully 15 yards.

Manchester C (Loaned from Eintracht Frankfurt on 19/12/94) PL 17+3/3 FLC 1+1 FAC 3/1

GAUGHAN Steven (Steve) Edward
Born: Doncaster, 14 April 1970
Height: 5'11" Weight: 11.2

"Stan", as he is known at Darlington, is the club's second longest serving player, and his strong-running from midfield, and ability to hold off a challenge, have resulted in some spectacular goals from outside the box.

Doncaster Rov (Free from Hatfield Main Colliery on 21/1/88) FL 42+25/3 FLC 2+2 FAC 4+1 Others 5+1
Sunderland (Free on 1/7/90)
Darlington (£10,000 on 21/1/92) FL 125+5/12 FLC 6 FAC 4 Others 5+1

GAVIN Mark Wilson
Born: Bailleston, 10 December 1963
Height: 5'8" Weight: 10.7

A tricky left-winger who was a main source of Exeter's goals last season, Mark loves to take on defenders and is a good crosser of the ball. One of the first names on the teamsheet.

Leeds U (From apprentice on 24/12/81) FL 20+10/3 FLC 4+1/1 FAC 0+1
Hartlepool U (Loaned on 29/3/85) FL 7
Carlisle U (Free on 4/7/85) FL 12+1/1 FLC 2/1 Others 1
BBolton W (Free on 27/3/86) FL 48+1/3 FLC 1 FAC 5/1 Others 10/1
Rochdale (Signed on 14/8/87) FL 23/6 FLC 3 FAC 1 Others 2
Heart of Midlothian (£30,000 on 3/2/88) SL 5+4
Bristol C (£30,000 on 4/10/88) FL 62+7/6 FLC 8 FAC 13/1 Others 6/1
Watford (Signed on 9/8/90) FL 8+5
Bristol C (£60,000 on 6/12/91) FL 34+7/2 FLC 0+1 FAC 4 Others 4
Exeter C (Signed on 11/2/94) FL 49/2 FLC 2 FAC 2 Others 3

GAVIN Patrick (Pat) John
Born: Hammersmith, 5 June 1967
Height: 6'0" Weight: 12.8

A big, powerful striker, and an excellent header of the ball, Pat was Wigan's second highest scorer in 1993-94. However, injuries restricted him to just a handful of appearances and he has been given a free transfer.

Gillingham (Free from Hanwell T on 9/3/89) FL 13/7
Leicester C (Free on 16/6/89) FL 1+2
Gillingham (Loaned on 1/9/89) FL 18+16/1 FAC 0+2 Others 2+1
Peterborough U (£15,000 on 29/3/91) FL 18+5/5 FLC 4+2/4 Others 3+1/1

Northampton T (Free on 26/2/93) FL 13+1/4
Wigan Ath (Free on 29/7/93) FL 37+5/8 FLC 6/3
FAC 3+1/1 Others 2

GAYLE Brian Wilbert
Born: Kingston, 6 March 1965
Height: 6'1" Weight: 12.7

Sheffield United club skipper and centre-back. Despite being hardly able to train during the week, he hardly missed a game in 1994-95 until his dodgy knees finally gave out, necessitating an operation. At his best, he is a quick and aggressive player who defends well and is good in the air, and it was no great surprise that his absence coincided with the team's slide out of play-off contention. As if his problems were not enough, he managed to score own goals in both games against Luton, and at both ends in the game at Bristol City!
Wimbledon (From apprentice on 31/10/84) FL 76+7/3 FLC 7/1 FAC 8/1 Others 2
Manchester C (£325,000 on 6/7/88) FL 55/3 FLC 8 FAC 2 Others 1
Ipswich T (£330,000 on 19/1/90) FL 58/4 FLC 3 FAC 0+1
Sheffield U (£750,000 on 17/9/91) F/PL 112/9 FLC 9 FAC 10/1 Others 1/1

GAYLE John
Born: Bromsgrove, 30 July 1964
Height: 6'4" Weight: 13.1
Club Honours: AMC '91

Signed from Coventry in the 1994 close season, his Burnley debut showed that he was capable of skilful play but, following endless speculation, he signed for Stoke after just four months at Turf Moor. Appearing to be a short-term signing to assist the club in their efforts to reach the Anglo-Italian Cup Final, John played only four games in the League.
Wimbledon (£30,000 from Bromsgrove on 1/3/89) FL 17+3/2 FLC 3
Birmingham C (£175,000 on 21/11/90) FL 39+5/10 FAC 2 Others 8+1/4
Walsall (Loaned on 20/8/93) FL 4/1
Coventry C (£100,000 on 13/9/93) PL 3 FLC 1+2
Burnley (£70,000 on 17/8/94) FL 7+7/3 FLC 1+1/1 FAC 1+1/1
Stoke C (£70,000 on 23/1/95) FL 1+3 Others 2

Marcus Gayle　　　　　Neal Simpson
(Empics Sports Photo Agency)

GAYLE Marcus Anthony
Born: Hammersmith, 27 September 1970
Height: 6'1" Weight: 12.9
Club Honours: Div 3 '92
International Honours: E: Yth

A tricky player with two good feet and crossing ability, Marcus played in 14 of Wimbledon's first 16 matches last season, scoring two goals from the left-wing, before an injury kept him out until February. Coming back into the squad, he figured, one way or another, in the rest of the 1994-95 programme without ever setting the team alight. Can only be better for the experience.
Brentford (From trainee on 6/7/89) FL 118+38/22 FLC 6+3 FAC 6+2/2 Others 14+6/2
Wimbledon (£250,000 on 24/3/94) PL 32+1/2 FLC 2/1

GAYLE Mark Samuel Roye
Born: Bromsgrove, 21 October 1969
Height: 6'2" Weight: 12.3

Mark has had to work hard to firstly claim and then reclaim the goalkeeping jersey at Crewe. However, since his last recall he has shown a lot of added confidence and that, allied to his natural ability, helped the team to do well in 1994-95.
Leicester C (From trainee on 1/7/88)
Blackpool (Free on 15/8/89) FLC 1 (Free to Worcester C in July 1990)
Walsall (£15,000 on 8/5/91) FL 74+1 FLC 8 FAC 1 Others 8
Crewe Alex (£35,000 on 21/12/93) FL 32+1 Others 4

GEE Philip (Phil) John
Born: Pelsall, 19 December 1964
Height: 6'0" Weight: 10.0
Club Honours: Div 2 '87

Right-footed forward. Scored a last-gasp equaliser from bench against QPR to earn Leicester's first Premiership point last season. Also netted in the home game with Villa, amidst a vitriolic welcome for ex-manager, Brian Little. Found it hard to win regular place and was loaned to Plymouth, before a £75,000 permanent move fell through when the "Pilgrims" could not raise the cash.
Derby Co (£5,000 from Gresley Rov on 2/9/85) FL 107+17/26 FLC 11+2/3 FAC 6+1/2 Others 7+1
Leicester C (Signed on 11/3/92) P/FL 34+17/9 FLC 2+3 Others 5+1/4
Plymouth Arg (Loaned on 27/1/95) FL 6

GEMMILL Scot
Born: Paisley, 2 January 1971
Height: 5'11" Weight: 11.0
International Honours: S: 3; U21-4

Son of former Nottingham Forest favourite, Archie, Scot followed in his father's footsteps in coming to the City Ground as a trainee back in 1988. A good all-round midfield player, with vision and stamina in abundance, he is always looking to play one-twos around the box and packs a fair shot. Started 1994-95 in good form until losing his place through a hernia injury, and then illness and, on getting back into the side towards the end of the season, celebrated by winning the first of three full caps for Scotland.

Scot Gemmill　　　　　Neal Simpson
(Empics Sports Photo Agency)

Nottingham F (From trainee on 5/1/90) F/PL 123+3/18 FLC 21+1/3 FAC 10/1 Others 7/4

GERRARD Paul William
Born: Heywood, 20 January 1973
Height: 6'2" Weight: 12.3
International Honours: E: U21-17

England's current U21 goalkeeper, with a record of 12 clean sheets in 17 inter-nationals, Paul missed just five of Oldham's FL games in 1994-95, having been the club's first choice for over two years. Now fully recovered from a bad knee injury in 1993, he is both brave, cuts a commanding figure, and kicks hard and long. Also has a brilliant attitude.
Oldham Ath (From trainee on 2/11/91) P/FL 82+1 FLC 5 FAC 4

GIBBS Nigel James
Born: St Albans, 20 November 1965
Height: 5'7" Weight: 11.11
Club Honours: FAYC '82
International Honours: E: U21-5; Yth

Returned to first team action with Watford last season after more than two years out of the game with a career-threatening knee injury. The composure on the ball and positional awareness were still there as he felt his way back into the side in 14 starts.
Watford (From apprentice on 23/11/83) FL 277+5/3 FLC 15/2 FAC 30+1 Others 13

GIBBS Paul Derek
Born: Gorleston, 26 October 1972
Height: 5'10" Weight: 11.3

Goalscoring hero of Diss' FA Vase success in 1994, Paul took the plunge into pro football last March and quickly filled Colchester's problem area of left-back/left-side of midfield. Has also become the club's dead-ball expert and will continue to im-prove, especially when attaining maximum fitness.
Colchester U (Signed from Diss T on 6/3/95) FL 8+1

Ryan Giggs

Neal Simpson
(Empics Sports Photo Agency)

GIBSON Colin John
Born: Bridport, 6 April 1960
Height: 5'8" Weight: 11.2
Club Honours: Div 1 '81; ESC '82
International Honours: E: B-1; U21-1

Stylish left-flank defender who can also play in midfield. An exciting exponent of the overlap and packing a powerful shot, Colin joined Walsall last September from Blackpool, having been freed by Leicester. Linking up again with manager, Chris Nicholl, he was a key member of the club's promotion side and a fine influence on the younger players.
Aston Villa (From apprentice on 13/4/78) FL 181+4/10 FLC 26/4 FAC 12/1 Others 14+1/2
Manchester U (£275,000 on 29/11/85) FL 74+5/9 FLC 7 FAC 8+1 Others 2/1
Port Vale (Loaned on 27/9/90) FL 5+1/2
Leicester C (£100,000 on 21/12/90) FL 50+9/4 FLC 4 FAC 1+1 Others 7+1
Blackpool (Free on 12/8/94) FL 1+1 FLC 2
Walsall (Free on 2/9/94) FL 31+2 FAC 5 Others 2/1

GIBSON Terence (Terry) Bradley
Born: Walthamstow, 23 December 1962
Height: 5'5" Weight: 10.0
Club Honours: FAC '88
International Honours: E: Yth; (UEFAYC '80); Sch

Became Barnet's youth team coach at the start of last season and battled back from injury to play a handful of games, mostly as a sub. Showed he could still brighten up a game, before injury finally beat him, and forced him to retire at the end of the campaign.
Tottenham H (From apprentice on 30/1/80) FL 16+2/4 FLC 1/1 FAC 5/1 Others 0+2/1
Coventry C (£100,000 on 24/8/83) FL 97+1/43 FLC 7/3 FAC 6/5 Others 2/1
Manchester U (£650,000 on 31/1/86) FL 14+9/1 FLC 0+2 FAC 1+1
Wimbledon (£200,000 on 27/8/87) FL 80+6/22 FLC 12/6 FAC 10/2 Others 8/1
Swindon T (Loaned on 26/3/92) FL 8+1/1
Peterborough U (Free on 10/12/93) FL 1
Barnet (Free on 12/2/94) FL 24+8/5

GIGGS Ryan Joseph
Born: Cardiff, 29 November 1973
Height: 5'11" Weight: 10.9
Club Honours: ESC '91; FAYC '92; FLC '92; PL '93, '94; CS '93, '94; FAC '94
International Honours: W: 13; U21-1; Yth. E: Sch

The PFA "Young Player of the Year" in 1992 and 1993, Ryan is a left-winger with lovely skills who delights in taking defenders on. Possesses a beautiful left-foot shot, which he uses to full effect at set-plays, and is also capable of scoring spectacular goals. His early form for Manchester United in 1994-95 was severely disrupted by a niggling calf strain that robbed him of his blistering pace. However, once recovered, he played a key role in United's continuing search for honours. Although his goal-tally was down on previous campaigns, he provided the necessary armoury from the left-flank with his customary mazy dribbles and penetrating crosses. His ability to handle intense media pressure off the field is admirable, and has largely unaffected his play on it. A regular for the Welsh side.

Manchester U (From trainee on 1/12/90) F/PL 134+14/28 FLC 14+4/6 FAC 17+2/4 Others 11+1/2

GILBERT David (Dave) James
Born: Lincoln, 22 June 1963
Height: 5'4" Weight: 10.4
Club Honours: Div 4 '87

Left-sided midfielder, and a highly skilled ball player, who is able to take on, beat the opposing defence, and create havoc in the box. An accurate crosser of the ball and a tireless worker, he is one of Grimsby's most entertaining players to watch.

Lincoln C (From apprentice on 29/6/81) FL 15+15/1 FLC 5 FAC 3
Scunthorpe U (Free on 18/8/82) FL 1 FLC 1 (Free to Boston U in 1982-83)
Northampton T (Signed on 30/6/86) FL 120/21 FLC 10/2 FAC 6/3 Others 9/1
Grimsby T (£55,000 on 23/3/89) FL 259/41 FLC 18/4 FAC 11/2 Others 9

Dave Gilbert   Laurence Griffiths
(Empics Sports Photo Agency)

GILCHRIST Philip Alexander
Born: Stockton on Tees, 25 August 1973
Height: 5'11" Weight: 11.12

Signed just before last March's transfer deadline from Hartlepool, Phil settled well into the heart of the Oxford defence. Good in the air, he is a left-sided defender who also possesses a good long-throw. Scored the only goal of his career in his third game (v Chester) and looks set for a long run in the side during 1995-96.

Nottingham F (From trainee on 5/12/90)
Middlesbrough (Free on 10/1/92)
Hartlepool U (Free on 27/11/92) FL 77+5 FLC 4+1 FAC 4 Others 5
Oxford U (£100,000 on 17/2/95) FL 18/1

GILKES Michael Earl
Born: Hackney, 20 July 1965
Height: 5'8" Weight: 10.10
Club Honours: FMC '88; Div 3 '86, Div 2 '94

Reading's longest-serving player, Michael continues to excite crowds with his incredible pace and ability to go past defenders. A hero of the club's losing play-off final against Bolton last season, he has now played at Wembley twice and, while having had loan spells with Chelsea and Southampton in the past, still harbours hopes of playing in the Premier with the "Royals". Turned out at full-back, in midfield and as a striker during 1994-95.

Reading (Free from Leicester C juniors on 10/7/84) FL 285+32/42 FLC 22+4/6 FAC 28+2/1 Others 26+2/2
Chelsea (Loaned on 28/1/92) FL 0+1 Others 0+1
Southampton (Loaned on 4/3/92) FL 4+2

Mike Gilkes   Neal Simpson
(Empics Sports Photo Agency)

GILLESPIE Gary Thomson
Born: Stirling, 5 July 1960
Height: 6'2" Weight: 12.7
Club Honours: Div 1 '86, '88, '90
International Honours: S: 13; U21-8

The experienced defender returned to Coventry last season, ten years after moving to Liverpool. Joining as a free agent, having been released by Celtic, injury restricted his appearances and he started only two League games; at Leicester where he was controversially sent off and at Hillsborough where City lost 1-5. He subsequently signed a three year contract as a player-coach, with the intention of helping the youth players, but was never fit enough to be considered for first team football after the New Year. From rare glimpses, Gary has lost none of his poise and ability to read the game.

Falkirk (From juniors in 1977-78) SL 22 SLC 2 SC 1
Coventry C (£75,000 on 10/3/78) FL 171+1/6 FLC 16 FAC 13
Liverpool (£325,000 on 8/7/83) FL 152+4/14 FLC 22/2 FAC 21+2 Others 8+2
Glasgow Celtic (£925,000 on 15/8/91) SL 67+2/2 SLC 3 SC 4 Others 6
Coventry C (Free on 23/8/94) PL 2+1 FLC 1

GILLESPIE Keith Robert
Born: Bangor, 18 February 1975
Height: 5'10" Weight: 10.11
Club Honours: FAYC '92
International Honours: NI: 8; U21; Yth

Keith joined Newcastle practically un-noticed, being valued at £1 million in the deal that took Andy Cole to Manchester United last January. It did not take him long to make his mark though. A right-winger, Keith has tremendous pace, which coupled to good close control and dribbling skills, make him a defenders nightmare, especially with his ability to deliver accurate crosses. Highlights of his season, include his two goals in the 3-1 victory over Manchester City in the FAC fifth round-tie at St James Park, where after chasing a long ball out of defence he blocked 'keeper Andy Dibble's attempted clearance and headed the loose ball into the empty net. He then got his second when he stole in after the defender hesitated. Recently won his fourth cap for Northern Ireland in the 1-1 draw against Eire, in which he made the equalising goal with a right-wing cross. A terrific prospect.

Manchester U (From trainee on 3/2/93) PL 3+6/1 FLC 3 FAC 1+1/1
Wigan Ath (Loaned on 3/9/93) FL 8/4 Others 2
Newcastle U (£1,000,000 on 12/1/95) PL 15+2/2 FAC 3/2

GITTENS Jonathan (Jon) Antoni
Born: Mossley, 22 January 1964
Height: 5'11" Weight: 12.10

A steady and reliable defender, Jon produced yet another consistent season in 1994-95. There was nothing spectacular, but his partnership with Kit Symons at the back held together Portsmouth's defence. One low, however, was his sending off against Leicester in the FA Cup, a game "Pompey" lost 1-0, after finishing with nine men.

Southampton (£10,000 from Paget R on 16/10/85) FL 18 FLC 4 FAC 1
Swindon T (£40,000 on 22/7/87) FL 124+2/6 FLC 15+1 FAC 9 Others 13+1/1
Southampton (£400,000 on 28/3/91) FL 16+3 FLC 4 Others 1
Middlesbrough (Loaned on 19/2/92) FL 9+3/1
Middlesbrough (£200,000 on 27/7/92) PL 13 FLC 0+1 FAC 1
Portsmouth (Free on 9/8/93) FL 67+1/1 FLC 10 FAC 2 Others 3/1

GLASS James (Jimmy) Robert
Born: Epsom, 1 August 1973
Height: 6'1" Weight: 11.10

Goalkeeper. A product of the Crystal Palace youth programme, but yet to make his debut for the club, he had a spell on loan at Portsmouth last season, playing three times. An excellent shot-stopper, who is also reliable on crosses, Jimmy is now third choice at Palace behind Nigel Martyn and Rhys Wilmot.

Crystal Palace (From trainee on 4/7/91)
Portsmouth (Loaned on 10/2/95) FL 3

GLEGHORN Nigel William
Born: Seaham, 12 August 1962
Height: 6'0" Weight: 12.3
Club Honours: AMC '91; Div 2 '93

Continued to make the left-sided midfield position his own in 1994-95, his third season at Stoke, captaining the side in Vince Overson's absence. Possesser of a fine left-foot, which has contributed to many set-piece goals, he is good in the air and has built a strong partnership with Lee Sandford down the left flank.

Ipswich T (Free from Seaham RS on 30/8/85) FL 54+12/11 FLC 3+2 FAC 3+1 Others 7+2/2
Manchester C (£47,500 on 4/8/88) FL 27+7/7 FLC 2+1/2 FAC 0+1/1 Others 1/1
Birmingham C (£175,000 on 9/9/89) FL 142/33 FLC 13/5 FAC 7/3 Others 14/2
Stoke C (£100,000 on 24/10/92) FL 116+4/17 FLC 7/2 FAC 8 Others 17/3

Dean Glover   Neal Simpson
(Empics Sports Photo Agency)

GLOVER Dean Victor
Born: Birmingham, 29 December 1963
Height: 5'10" Weight: 11.2
Club Honours: AMC '93

Central defender who began last season for Port Vale in fine form before being sent off against Sheffield United, he returned to the side after suspension but then suffered a combination of back and ankle injuries that led to the recruitment of Kevin Scott on loan. Although regaining full fitness, Dean had to wait three months before coming back into the team in April.
Aston Villa (From apprentice on 30/12/81) FL 25+3 FLC 7/1 FAC 3 Others 1
Sheffield U (Loaned on 17/10/86) FL 5
Middlesbrough (Signed on 17/6/87) FL 44+6/5 FLC 4 FAC 5 Others 7/2
Port Vale (£200,000 on 3/2/89) FL 266+1/12 FLC 18 FAC 16/1 Others 20/3

GLOVER Edward Lee
Born: Kettering, 24 April 1970
Height: 5'10" Weight: 12.1
Club Honours: FMC '92
International Honours: S; U21-3; Yth

Started last season in explosive style for Port Vale with six goals in the first 11 games, but a barren spell saw him relegated to the bench before being left out altogether. A skilful player who can operate in midfield, or up-front, he holds the ball up well but only made a handful of appearances in the second part of the campaign.
Nottingham F (From apprentice on 2/5/87) F/PL 61+15/9 FLC 6+5/2 FAC 8+2/1 Others 4+1/1
Leicester C (Loaned on 14/9/89) FL 3+2/1
Barnsley (Loaned on 18/1/90) FL 8 FAC 4

Luton T (Loaned on 2/9/91) FL 1
Port Vale (£200,000 on 2/8/94) FL 21+7/4 FLC 4/3 FAC 0+2

GOATER Leonard Shaun
Born: Hamilton, Bermuda, 25 February 1970
Height: 5'11" Weight: 11.4
International Honours: Bermuda

Striker. Shaun really came into his own last season with his best ever haul of goals, which have come mainly from his ability to turn defenders and his speed over a short distance. His new found confidence led him to becoming Rotherham's regular penalty taker, with great success.
Manchester U (From juniors on 8/5/89)
Rotherham U (Free on 25/10/89) FL 125+40/52 FLC 9+4/1 FAC 11+3/5 Others 7+5/4
Notts Co (Loaned on 12/11/93) FL 1

GONZAQUE Michael Alexander Granville
Born: Canning Town, 27 March 1975
Height: 6'1" Weight: 12.5

A very tall centre-half, Michael was signed by Hereford on a free transfer from Southend during the 1994 close season. Made three starts for the club but, unable to dislodge the regular pairing, he was released last February.
Southend U (From trainee on 6/7/93)
Hereford U (Free on 5/8/94) FL 2+1 Others 1

GOODACRE Samuel (Sam) David
Born: Chesterfield, 1 December 1970
Height: 5'7" Weight: 11.0
International Honours: E; Sch

Nippy Scunthorpe attacker who knows where the goal is and shields the ball well for the right lay-off. On the small side, Sam suffered from persistent injuries last season, making just three starts, before being freed during the summer.
Sheffield Wed (From trainee on 1/7/89)
Scunthorpe U (Free on 4/7/91) FL 24+20/12 FLC 2+3 FAC 1+1/2 Others 3/1

GOODEN Ty Michael
Born: Canvey Island, 23 October 1972
Height: 5'8" Weight: 12.6

A wide player who looked set for a bright future, following his debut towards the end of Swindon's Premiership season, he had to wait nine months before being given a further chance to prove his worth. Following Jan Fjortoft's departure to Middlesbrough last March, Ty was switched to a central striking role and seemed to relish the challenge.
Swindon T (Free from Wycombe W on 17/9/93) P/FL 15+5/2 FLC 1 Others 0+1

GOODING Michael (Mick) Charles
Born: Newcastle, 12 April 1959
Height: 5'9" Weight: 10.7
Club Honours: Div 3 '81, '89, Div 2 '94

A very experienced Reading midfield player, who can also perform at full-back, and an inspiration to players around him with his determination and non-stop running, Mick was appointed as joint player-manager with Jimmy Quinn last December. However, despite the additional duties he continued to lead the team by example and was instrumental in getting

them to the Wembley First Division play-off final. A neat, tidy passer of the ball, he is noted for his consistency.
Rotherham U (Signed from Bishop Auckland on 18/7/79) FL 90+12/10 FLC 9/3 FAC 3
Chesterfield (Signed on 24/12/82) FL 12
Rotherham U (Signed on 9/9/83) FL 149+7/33 FLC 18/3 FAC 13/4 Others 7
Peterborough U (£18,000 on 13/8/87) FL 47/21 FLC 8/2 FAC 1/2 Others 4/2
Wolverhampton W (£85,000 on 20/9/88) FL 43+1/4 FLC 4 Others 5+1/1
Reading (£65,000 on 26/12/89) FL 226+5/23 FLC 13 FAC 14+1/2 Others 16/2

Don Goodman   Steve Morton
(Empics Sports Photo Agency)

GOODMAN Donald (Don) Ralph
Born: Leeds, 9 May 1966
Height: 5'10" Weight: 11.7
Club Honours: Div 3 '85

A strong forward, who is at his best on the right-hand side of the attack, Don moved to Wolverhampton from Sunderland last December. Soon won the fans over with some gritty displays and scored the deciding goal in the penalty shoot-out with Sheffield Wednesday. Good in the air, he gives non-stop effort for 90 minutes.
Bradford C (Free from Collingham on 10/7/84) FL 65+5/14 FLC 5+1/2 FAC 2+3/4 Others 4+1/2
West Bromwich A (£50,000 on 27/3/87) FL 140+18/60 FLC 11/1 FAC 7/1 Others 5/1
Sunderland (£900,000 on 6/12/91) FL 112+4/40 FLC 9/1 FAC 3/1 Others 4/2
Wolverhampton W (£1,100,000 on 6/12/94) FL 24/3 FAC 5+1 Others 2

GOODMAN Jonathan (Jon)
Born: Walthamstow, 2 June 1971
Height: 5'11" Weight: 12.3

Was Millwall's leading scorer when signing for Wimbledon, along with Ken Cunningham, last November. Apart from a spell out injured, Jon, a fleet-footed, hard running, never-say-die kind of player, has made a permanent place for himself in the Premier League side, his best spell coming with a three goal burst in two games against Leicester and Chelsea. All-in-all, he has fitted in well to Wimbledon's forward structure.

Millwall (£50,000 from Bromley on 20/8/90) FL 97+12/35 FLC 5+4/2 FAC 5+1 Others 3
Wimbledon (Signed on 9/11/94) PL 13+6/4 FAC 0+1

Jon Goodman   Neal Simpson
                    (Empics Sports Photo Agency)

GOODRIDGE Gregory Ronald St Clair
Born: Barbados, 10 February 1975
Height: 5'6" Weight: 10.0
International Honours: Barbados

Flying Torquay winger who started last season as he finished the previous one, running full-backs ragged. His form fell away from mid-term, but he still has the pace and skill to make it big in English football.
Torquay U (Free from Lambada on 24/3/94) FL 32+6/4 FLC 4/1 FAC 2+1 Others 3+1/1

GOODWIN Shaun
Born: Rogherham, 14 June 1969
Height: 5'8" Weight: 10.11
Club Honours: Div 4 '89

A home-bred Rotherham player who was in his best form for some time when his season came to an abrupt halt at the end of last October, following a foot injury which needed several operations and left him very frustrated. His best position is running at defenders from midfield and he was revelling in that role when injury struck.
Rotherham U (From trainee on 1/7/87) FL 218+15/30 FLC 13+7/1 FAC 16+1/3 Others 15+2/1

GORDON Dale Andrew
Born: Great Yarmouth, 9 January 1967
Height: 5'10" Weight: 11.8
Club Honours: SC '92; SPD '92, '93; SLC '93
International Honours: E: B-2; U21-4; Yth; Sch

West Ham right-winger with skill and pace and the ability to score goals. Very experienced, Dale spent another frustrating season in 1994-95 with the "Hammers", trying to overcome a long-term injury. Limited to just eight reserve matches, he was loaned out to Peterborough in March,

scoring once in six games. Will be looking for a good start to 1995-96.
Norwich C (From apprentice on 17/1/84) FL 194+12/31 FLC 21/3 FAC 19/6 Others 14+2/3
Glasgow R (£1,200,000 on 8/11/91) SL 41+4/6 SLC 1+1/1 SC 6+1/1 Others 1
West Ham U (£750,000 on 20/7/93) PL 8/1 FLC 1
Peterborough U (Loaned on 23/3/95) FL 6/1

GORDON Dean Dwight
Born: Croydon, 10 February 1973
Height: 6'0" Weight: 11.5
Club Honours: Div 1 '94
International Honours: E: U21-10

The England U21 international defender had another fine season for Crystal Palace in 1994-95, supporting John Salako down the wing, and causing many problems for opponents with his runs and crosses. A player who can perform equally well, either on the left-wing, at left-back, or in the centre of defence, Dean is a strong tackler and adept at hitting long balls behind defenders. Scored a last minute goal against Lincoln in the FA Cup to force extra-time, following which, the club won the match and went on to the semi-finals.
Crystal Palace (From trainee on 4/7/91) F/PL 85+15/7 FLC 10+3/2 FAC 6+1/1 Others 2+1

GORE Ian George
Born: Prescot, 10 January 1968
Height: 5'11" Weight: 12.4

An experienced Blackpool defender, who only started five games last season due to injury and subsequent signings, he went on loan to non-league Chorley in March 1995, before being released during the summer.
Birmingham C (From trainee on 1/5/86)
Blackpool (Free from Southport on 21/1/88) FL 196+4 FLC 15+1 FAC 11 Others 20+2

GOSS Jeremy
Born: Cyprus, 11 May 1965
Height: 5'9" Weight: 10.9
Club Honours: FAYC '83
International Honours: W: 7

Non-stop defensive midfield player, who also has an eye for the goal, he completed his 13th year at Norwich last season. Out of action following a hernia operation, having recovered earlier from back and pelvic injuries, the club missed his fighting qualities. His longest spell in the side was for the first eight games, while his missing 13 matches towards the season's end was of no help to City's cause in avoiding relegation. A regular for both club and country when fit.
Norwich C (From juniors on 23/3/83) F/PL 146+26/13 FLC 14+3/3 FAC 13+4 Others 15/6

GOUCK Andrew (Andy) Scott
Born: Blackpool, 8 June 1972
Height: 5'9" Weight: 11.2

A local Blackpool lad, and one who thrives on midfield "battles", he also likes to get forward when the opportunity presents itself. Although he played in the majority of first team games last season, he achieved the unusual feat of scoring a hat-trick of penalties in a reserve match.
Blackpool (From trainee on 4/7/90) FL 113+19/21 FLC 7+3 FAC 3 Others 7/3

GOULD Jonathan (Jon) Alan
Born: Paddington, 18 July 1968
Height: 6'1" Weight: 12.6

Goalkeeping son of Bobby Gould, who lost his Coventry place to Steve Ogrizovic after his father's departure, but waited patiently for his chance. Renowned for his excellent reflexes and shot-stopping ability, Jon came into the side last March at Southampton, with "Oggy" injured, and made several outstanding saves and had another good game at Villa Park. He made a mistake at home to Blackburn which resulted in Alan Shearer equalising and was dropped after another at Leeds. When playing in the first team, he was rumoured to be on the verge of the Scotland squad.
Halifax T (Free from Clevedon T on 18/7/90) FL 32 FLC 2 FAC 5 Others 5
West Bromwich A (Free on 30/1/92)
Coventry C (Free on 15/7/92) PL 25

GOURLAY Archibald (Archie) Murdoch
Born: Greenock, 29 June 1969
Height: 5'10" Weight: 11.7

Trialist who joined Hartlepool in the 1994 close season, after spending a similar spell with Preston. A lightweight midfielder, he made just one appearance as a non-contract substitute, before being released.
Morton (From juniors in 1985) SL 2
Newcastle U (Signed on 25/3/88) FL 2+1 FLC 0+2
Morton (Loaned on 5/1/90) SL 4 SLC 1
Motherwell (Signed on 31/3/92) SL 0+3
Preston NE (Free on 22/7/94)
Hartlepool U (Free on 9/9/94) FL 0+1

GRAHAM Deniol William
Born: Cannock, 4 October 1969
Height: 5'10" Weight: 10.7
International Honours: W: U21-1; Yth

Originally one of "Fergie's Fledglings", he arrived at Stockport in June 1994, via Barnsley, after failing to make the grade at Old Trafford. A striker, Deniol was unable to secure a regular place in the side and was freed at the end of last season.
Manchester U (From trainee on 8/10/87) FL 1+1 FLC 0+1 FAC 0+1/1
Barnsley (£50,000 on 8/8/91) FL 18+20/2 FLC 1+3
Preston NE (Loaned on 24/10/92) FL 8 FAC 2/1 Others 1
Carlisle U (Loaned on 29/11/93) FL 2/1 Other 1
Stockport Co (Free on 30/6/94) FL 5+6/2

GRAHAM James (Jimmy)
Born: Glasgow, 5 November 1969
Height: 6'0" Weight: 11.8

The balding left-back soon became a cult hero in his first season with Hull. Having worked under Terry Dolan at Bradford and Rochdale, Jimmy can be a fierce tackler, yet a calming influence when the pressure is on. His enthusiastic approach also means he's not afraid to join the attack.
Bradford C (From trainee on 12/9/88) FL 6+1
Rochdale (Loaned on 3/11/89) FL 11 FAC 4 Others 3
Rochdale (£15,000 on 9/7/90) FL 120+6/1 FLC 13+1 FAC 8 Others 6/1
Hull C (Free on 5/8/94) FL 39 FLC 2 FAC 1 Others 2

GRAHAM Richard Ean
Born: Dewsbury, 28 November 1974
Height: 6'2" Weight: 12.1
Skilful Oldham central midfielder with good vision and touch, and a player who is extremely comfortable on the ball, Richard came into his own last season when holding down a regular place in the side and impressing enough to be chosen for the Endsleigh League XI that met Italy's Series "B" select. Showing plenty of character for one so young, without doubt, he could become one of the big names of the future.
Oldham Ath (From trainee on 16/7/93) PL 33+4/2 FLC 4 FAC 2

GRAINGER Martin Robert
Born: Enfield, 23 August 1972
Height: 5'11" Weight: 12.0
Brentford left-back whose style is a cross between Julian Dicks and Stuart Pearce. Had a fine season in 1994-95, not only defending, but attacking on the overlap as well. Free-kick and penalty expert (six out of six), with a good long-throw, his whole-hearted performances made him a crowd favourite.
Colchester U (From trainee on 28/7/92) FL 37+9/7 FLC 3 FAC 3+2 Others 3/1
Brentford (£60,000 on 21/10/93) FL 67+1/9 FLC 2 FAC 4/1 Others 5/2

GRANT Anthony (Tony) James
Born: Liverpool, 14 November 1974
Height: 5'10" Weight: 10.2
Talented young Everton player who likes to spray passes about from midfield. Skilful, with good vision and touch, Tony was the mainstay of the reserve side last season, before being given a first team start in a 3-2 win at QPR in March. Also made four subs' appearances and could have a good future.
Everton (From trainee on 8/7/93) PL 1+4

GRANT Kim Tyrone
Born: Ghana, 25 September 1972
Height: 5'10" Weight: 10.12
Predominantly right-footed, hard-working Charlton striker who has been unable to command a regular place in the side, despite some impressive performances in the reserve team. Kim's scoring record last season, however, was reasonably good, his best game probably being the 2-2 draw at Derby where he struck both goals.
Charlton Ath (From trainee on 6/3/91) FL 54+39/11 FLC 2+5 FAC 6+4/3 Others 5+2/1

GRANVILLE Daniel (Danny) Patrick
Born: Islington, 19 January 1975
Height: 5'11" Weight: 12.5
Left-footed player operating in midfield, or at full-back, Danny is yet another product of the Cambridge youth team. Can also get forward to score.
Cambridge U (From trainee on 19/5/93) FL 21+6/7 FLC 1 FAC 0+1 Others 1+2

GRAY Andrew (Andy)
Born: Southampton, 25 October 1973
Height: 5'6" Weight: 10.10
Neat, lively striker signed from Reading, where he was unable to break into the first team. Scored on his full Orient debut last August against Hull, but generally struggled to make an impact in a team that found goals hard to come by. A number of injuries held his progress back and he has yet to fulfill his early promise.
Reading (From trainee on 3/7/92) FL 8+9/3 0+1/1 Others 1+1
Leyton Orient (Free on 20/7/94) FL 13+12/3 FLC 0+2 FAC 1/1 Others 0+1

GRAY Ian James
Born: Manchester, 25 February 1975
Height: 6'2" Weight: 12.0
Promising young Oldham goalkeeper who sits behind Paul Gerrard and Jon Hallworth in the pecking order and has yet to make his first team debut for the club, Ian joined Rochdale on loan last November in order to gain experience. Made so great an impression, conceding only one goal in his last five FL games, that Athletic refused to consider selling him when his three months was up.
Oldham Ath (From trainee on 16/7/93)
Rochdale (Loaned on 18/11/94) FL 12 Others 3

GRAY Kevin John
Born: Sheffield, 7 January 1972
Height: 6'0" Weight: 13.0
Signed from Mansfield during the 1994 close season, he struggled to establish himself in Huddersfield's first team, being restricted to appearances as a result of injury or suspensions to players. As a former captain of his previous club, and an experienced player for one so young, Kevin filled in admirably in the centre of the defence when required.
Mansfield T (From trainee on 1/7/90) FL 129+12/3 FLC 7/1 FAC 6+1 Others 12+2/2
Huddersfield T (£20,000 on 18/7/94) FL 5 Others 3

GRAY Martin David
Born: Stockton on Tees, 17 August 1971
Height: 5'9" Weight: 10.11
Sunderland player who is equally effective at right-back or in midfield, he began last season as a first choice in defence, but was unluckily injured. Martin's main strengths are his willingness to compete and tackle in midfield and is a useful player to have on the substitutes' bench.
Sunderland (From trainee on 1/2/90) FL 42+15/1 FLC 5+1 FAC 0+2 Others 3+1
Aldershot (Loaned on 9/1/91) FL 3+2 Others 1

GRAY Michael
Born: Sunderland, 3 August 1974
Height: 5'7" Weight: 10.8
Left-sided midfielder who has also operated at left-back for Sunderland, Michael found his first team opportunities last season limited, due to the emergence of Martin Smith. Quick and skilful, and still only 20, he has time yet to establish himself as a regular first teamer.
Sunderland (From trainee on 1/7/92) FL 49+16/3 FLC 2+3 FAC 1+1

GRAY Philip (Phil)
Born: Belfast, 2 October 1968
Height: 5'10" Weight: 11.7
International Honours: NI: 14; U23-1
A current Northern Ireland international striker, Phil has been top-scorer at Sunderland for the last two seasons. An inventive player, who creates chances for others, his partnership with Don Goodman never really scaled the heights that were expected and Phil spent most of 1994-95 partnering a number of strikers up-front. Scorer of some spectacular goals, perhaps the best last season was the lob over a number of defenders on the goal line at Carlisle.
Tottenham H (From apprentice on 21/8/86) FL 4+5 FAC 0+1
Barnsley (Loaned on 17/1/90) FL 3 FAC 1
Fulham (Loaned on 8/11/90) FL 3 Others 2/1
Luton T (£275,000 on 16/8/91) FL 54+5/22 FLC 4/3 FAC 2/1 Others 2
Sunderland (£800,000 on 19/7/93) FL 80+3/26 FLC 5/4 FAC 6/2 Others 2

Phil Gray Barrington Coombs
(Empics Sports Photo Agency)

GRAYSON Neil
Born: York, 1 November 1964
Height: 5'10" Weight: 12.4
A hard-working striker, or midfield player, who enjoys going wide and cutting inside, took time to settle at Northampton, after signing from Boston during the 1994 close season, but is now a crowd favourite.
Doncaster Rov (Free from Rowntree Mackintosh on 22/3/90) FL 21+8/6 FAC 1+1 Others 2+1/1
York C (Free on 28/3/91) FL 0+1
Chesterfield (Free on 16/8/91) FL 9+6 FLC 2 FAC 1 Others 1
Northampton T (Free from Boston U, via Gateshead, on 19/6/94) FL 34+4/8 FLC 2 FAC 1 Others 3/2

GRAYSON Simon Nicholas
Born: Ripon, 16 December 1969
Height: 5'11" Weight: 12.10
The 1994 Leicester "Player of the Season", Simon held the regular right-back spot throughout 1993-94, but found it hard to make the same impact at the higher level last season. Had been City's Wembley skipper and continued in that role under Brian Little. With less opportunities to surge forward this year as team was spending more time defending, he was occasionally drafted into midfield to cover injuries.

Leeds U (From trainee on 13/6/88) FL 2 Others 1+1
Leicester C (£50,000 on 13/3/92) F/PL 100+11/2 FLC 6+1 FAC 4 Others 10+1

GRAYSTON Neil James
Born: Keighley, 25 November 1975
Height: 5'8" Weight: 10.9
Another promising young Bradford defender who made four appearances in 1994-95, Neil plays regularly for the reserves. However, he is sure to be knocking on the door before too long.
Bradford C (From trainee on 27/5/94) FL 5 Others 1

GREEN Richard Edward
Born: Wolverhampton, 22 November 1967
Height: 6'0" Weight: 13.12
As Gillingham club captain and centre-half, Richard missed only a handful of games last season. Does good work in the opponents' penalty box, where his flick-ons from corners and throws result in numerous goals.
Shrewsbury T (From trainee on 19/7/86) FL 120+5/5 FLC 11/1 FAC 5 Others 5/1
Swindon T (Free on 25/10/90)
Gillingham (Free on 6/3/92) FL 126+1/12 FLC 7 FAC 9+1/1 Others 4

GREEN Scott Paul
Born: Walsall, 15 January 1970
Height: 5'10" Weight: 12.5
Forced his way into Bolton's first team last October in the right-back position, having been converted from a midfielder, cum forward, and scored his only goal of the term in his first appearance, when coming on as a substitute at Port Vale. Not frightened of overlapping, and possessing a good engine, Scott lost his place in the side briefly, following the arrival of Gudni Bergsson. However, he battled back to produce his best form of the season in the play-off games, that ultimately saw the club attain Premiership status.
Derby Co (From trainee on 20/7/88)
Bolton W (£50,000 on 17/3/90) FL 133+44/21 FLC 16+1/1 FAC 16+2/2 Others 16+4/1

GREENALL Colin Anthony
Born: Billinge, 30 December 1963
Height: 5'11" Weight: 11.10
International Honours: E: Yth
A central defender whose experience brought much needed stability to Lincoln's defence in 1994-95, he was appointed club captain and performed consistently well throughout the campaign.
Blackpool (From apprentice on 17/1/81) FL 179+4/9 FLC 12/2 FAC 9 Others 2
Gillingham (£40,000 on 10/9/86) FL 62/4 FLC 3/1 FAC 6/1 Others 9/2
Oxford U (£285,000 on 15/2/88) FL 67/2 FLC 4 FAC 1 Others 2
Bury (Loaned on 4/1/90) FL 3 Other 1
Bury (£125,000 on 16/7/90) FL 66+2/5 FLC 3 FAC 1 Others 8/1
Preston NE (£50,000 on 27/3/92) FL 29/1
Chester (Free on 13/8/93) FL 42/1 FLC 2 FAC 4/1 Others 4
Lincoln C (Free on 27/7/94) FL 39/3 FLC 4 FAC 3/1 Others 2

GREENE David Michael
Born: Luton, 26 October 1973
Height: 6'2" Weight: 11.10
International Honours: Ei: U21-11
A reliable centre-back, who continues to make steady progress at Luton, and whose chance for a regular place may come when the veteran Trevor Peake gives way, he started last season, but dropped out as the side took shape, with ever-present Peake and Marvin Johnson as the central defenders. Continued to play for the Republic of Ireland U21 side and as 1994-95 drew to a close he got a further chance at Kenilworth Road in the left-back spot.
Luton T (From juniors on 3/9/91) FL 18+1 FLC 2 FAC 1 Others 0+1

GREGAN Sean Matthew
Born: Guisborough, 29 March 1974
Height: 6'2" Weight: 12.5
Although still only 21, Sean is the longest serving player at Darlington and made his debut in December 1991. A product of the club's youth team, he has developed into a very strong central defender who has now appeared in over a 100 first team games.
Darlington (From trainee on 20/1/91) FL 75+7/4 FLC 3 FAC 4 Others 5+1

GREGORY David Spencer
Born: Sudbury, 23 January 1970
Height: 5'11" Weight: 11.10
A right-sided Ipswich player who can perform in midfield, or up-front, and the regular penalty taker for the reserves, David made just one subs' appearance last season and had a month on loan at Hereford early in the New Year.
Ipswich T (From trainee on 31/3/87) F/PL 16+16/2 FLC 3+2 FAC 1 Others 3+2/4
Hereford U (Loaned on 9/1/95) FL 2 Others 1

GREGORY John Graham
Born: Hounslow, 16 May 1977
Height: 6'0" Weight: 14.0
A young Fulham trainee 'keeper who is good on crosses and a shot-stopper, John made his FL debut from the subs' bench after Lee Harrison had been sent off in the home fixture against Hartlepool last April, and maintained a clean sheet in a 1-0 win. Still a YTS, he is due to be released at the end of July, due to the club's goalkeeping strength in depth.
Fulham (Trainee) FL 0+1

GREGORY Neil Richard
Born: Ndola, Zambia, 7 October 1972
Height: 5'11" Weight: 11.0
A hard-running central striker who scores regularly for Ipswich's reserves, Neil made his full debut against Wimbledon last season, during which he led the line well and hit the bar with a great right-foot shot. Was on loan at Scunthorpe in the latter stages of the campaign.
Ipswich T (From trainee on 21/2/92) PL 1+2
Chesterfield (Loaned on 3/2/94) FL 2+1/1
Scunthorpe U (Loaned on 6/3/95) FL 10/7

GRIDELET Philip (Phil) Raymond
Born: Hendon, 30 April 1967
Height: 5'11" Weight: 12.0

International Honours: E: SP-4
Phil's greatest qualities, his 100 per-cent commitment and "never-say-die" attitude, coupled with new rules which did not favour competitive players, caused him a few problems with suspensions early on last season. And, when the Southend manager, Peter Taylor, complained that the mid-fielders were not scoring sufficient goals, Phil responded with two in four matches, including one in the 1-0 away victory at Middlesbrough, and endeared himself to the Southend fans who enjoyed his all-action style and good passing.
Barnsley (£175,000 from Barnet on 21/1/90) FL 3+3 FAC 1 Others 1
Rotherham U (Loaned on 5/3/93) FL 9
Southend U (Free on 25/9/93) FL 47+11/4 FAC 1 Others 4/1

GRIFFITH Cohen
Born: Georgetown, Guyana, 26 December 1962
Height: 5'10" Weight: 11.7
Club Honours: WC '92, '93; Div 3 '93
Tireless Cardiff left-sided forward, who can sometimes be prone to exerting a lot of energy to little effect, his running became more effective as last season wore on. Freed during the summer.
Cardiff C (£70,000 from Kettering T on 5/10/89) FL 205+29/38 FLC 9/5 FAC 14+2 Others 21+2/4

GRIFFITHS Bryan Kenneth
Born: St Helens, 20 January 1965
Height: 5'5" Weight: 11.2
Striker. Announced his decision to retire from the game last February, after returning from a spell on loan at Scarborough, and a week later signed for non-league, Telford. Earlier in the season, however, he played 18 first team matches for Blackpool.
Wigan Ath (Signed from St Helens on 2/11/88) FL 176+13/44 FLC 12+2/2 FAC 11+2/6 Others 20+1/6
Blackpool (Signed on 23/7/93) FL 54+3/17 FLC 8 FAC 2 Others 3
Scarborough (Loaned on 5/12/94) FL 5/1

GRIFFITHS Carl Brian
Born: Welshpool, 16 July 1971
Height: 5'9" Weight: 10.6
International Honours: W: U21-2; Yth
A young player with a wealth of experience, albeit in the lower Leagues, he made only the odd appearance for Manchester City in 1994-95. Following the arrival of more seasoned strikers, Carl had very little scope, but he is obviously being groomed for the future and has shown much promise in the reserves, proving that he has not lost the goal touch.
Shrewsbury T (From trainee on 26/9/88) FL 110+33/54 FLC 7+4/3 FAC 6/2 Others 7+3/3
Manchester C (£500,000 on 29/10/93) PL 11+7/4 FLC 0+1 FAC 2

GRIFFITHS Gareth John
Born: Winsford, 10 April 1970
Height: 6'4" Weight: 14.0
Tall Port Vale central defender who per-formed well in the first half of last season until suffering a groin strain, cum hernia, at Christmas. At first he was only expected to

miss three weeks, but complications set in and it was April before he was fully fit again. Good in the air, he has a promising future.

Port Vale (Signed from Rhyl on 8/2/93) FL 23+1/2 FLC 3 FAC 2/1

Bruce Grobbelaar   Barry Coombs
(Empics Sports Photo Agency)

GROBBELAAR Bruce David
Born: Durban, South Africa, 6 October 1957
Height: 6'1" Weight: 12.0
Club Honours: Div 1 '82, '83, '84, '86, '88, '90; FLC '82, '83, '84, '90; FAC '86, '89, '92; CS '82, '86, '88, '89; EC '84
International Honours: Zimbabwe

If ever a player proved his strength of character, it must have been Bruce Grobbelaar this past season. Arriving at Southampton on a free transfer from Liverpool, he started 1994-95 in good form, using his vast experience in goal to bolster a young defence. He even managed some excursion to the left-back position where, said his manager, "he drops his left shoulder . . . and the pit of my stomach". Came October after only three minutes of the home game against Everton, a collision with Francis Benali left Bruce with a serious facial injury. Returned after missing only two games wearing a mask to protect the injury. He continued in good form until mid-March when the strain stemming from much publicised events appeared to tell, and he was replaced by Dave Beasant for the crucial remaining games.

Crewe Alex (On trial from Vancouver Whitecaps on 18/12/79) FL 24/1
Liverpool (£250,000 from Vancouver Whitecaps on 12/3/81) F/PL 440 FLC 70 FAC 62 Others 56
Stoke C (Loaned on 17/3/93) FL 4
Southampton (Free on 11/8/94) PL 30 FLC 3 FAC 5

GROVES Paul
Born: Derby, 28 February 1966
Height: 5'11" Weight: 11.5

Grimsby's most expensive signing, Paul is a right-footed midfield ball-winner, and a provider of accurate service to the strikers. Telling runs into the box also enable him to get amongst the goals himself. He is the club's most consistent player, having the remarkable record of appearing in every FL and cup game over the past three seasons.

Leicester C (£12,000 from Burton A on 18/4/88) FL 7+9/1 FLC 1/1 FAC 0+1 Others 0+1
Lincoln C (Loaned on 20/8/89) FL 8/1 FLC 2
Blackpool (£60,000 on 25/1/90) FL 106+1/21 FLC 6/1 FAC 9/4 Others 13/3
Grimsby T (£150,000 on 12/8/92) FL 137+1/33 FLC 8+1/2 FAC 7/1 Others 4/1

GUENTCHEV Bontcho Lubomisov
Born: Tchoshevo, Bulgaria, 7 July 1964
Height: 5'10" Weight: 11.7
International Honours: Bulgaria

A very skilful player with good passing ability with either foot, who is better suited playing wide rather than as an out-and-out striker leading the line, Bontcho returned to Ipswich full of enthusiasm following his participation in the 1994 USA World Cup, where he had helped Bulgaria reach the semi-finals (he scored the vital goal in a penalty shoot-out with Mexico). In-and-out of the side last season, his best game was at QPR early on when he forced a defender to concede an own goal, scored the second himself, but missed a penalty. Not with the club this coming season as he did not make the required number of appearances to earn an extension to his work permit.

Ipswich T (£250,000 from Sporting Lisbon on 29/12/92) PL 39+22/6 FLC 6 FAC 6+2/5

GUNN Bryan James
Born: Thurso, 22 December 1963
Height: 6'2" Weight: 12.5
International Honours: S: 6; B-3; U21-9; Yth; Sch

The loss of this most consistent of goalkeepers, the victim of a fluke injury at Nottingham Forest last December, was a major blow to Norwich in their unsuccessful attempts to stave off relegation from the Premiership. A broken lower leg and fractured ankle ended a run of 25 consecutive games, with only 21 goals conceded, and strenuous attempts made for his early return were defeated by his inability to kick any distance from dead-ball situations. Good on crosses, Bryan gives the side an air of confidence and will be a vital cornerstone of City's plans to bounce back into the Premiership.

Aberdeen (Signed from Invergordon BC in 1980) SL 15 SLC 4 SC 1 Others 1
Norwich C (£150,000 on 23/10/86) F/PL 304 FLC 29 FAC 24 Others 22

GUPPY Stephen (Steve)
Born: Winchester, 29 March 1969
Height: 5'11" Weight: 10.10
Club Honours: FAT '91, '93; GMVC '93
International Honours: E: SP-1

Left-winger who made an immediate impact by making two goals on his Port Vale debut

against Millwall, following a move from Newcastle last November. An excellent crosser of the ball, he featured more prominently in home games and scored the winning goal against WBA with his head. The only time he was left out of the side was when a back five policy was adopted. At Newcastle, Steve had been unable to get into the side, apart from one subs' appearance, following his 1994 close season transfer from Wycombe.

Wycombe W (Signed in 1989-90) FL 41/8 FLC 4 FAC 8/2 Others 10
Newcastle U (£150,000 on 2/8/94) FLC 0+1
Port Vale (£225,000 on 25/11/94) FL 25+2/2 FAC 1

GURNEY Andrew (Andy) Robert
Born: Bristol 25 January 1974
Height: 5'11" Weight: 12.0

Another local-born player who has graduated from the Bristol Rovers' YTS academy. Naturally right-footed, Andy took over the left-back position after Lee Maddison was injured in the first match of last season and only lost his place in March following a one match ban. His powerful shooting from distance makes him a real threat and his first goal against Peterborough is hopefully the first of many in what promises to be a long and successful career.

Bristol Rov (From trainee on 10/7/92) FL 37+4/1 FLC 1 FAC 4 Others 7

HAALAND Alf-Inge Rasdal
Born: Stavanger, Norway, 23 November 1972
Height: 5'10" Weight: 12.12
International Honours: Norway

A Norwegian international who joined Nottingham Forest halfway through 1993-94, a month or so after his countryman, Lars Bohinen, he came good last season. Able to play at right-back, or in the centre of his defence, Alf proved a revelation in central midfield, before making way for Bohinen in the New Year. Good aerial ability and ball-winning, coupled to creativity, are among his strengths.

Nottingham F (Signed from Young Boys of Berne on 25/1/94) F/PL 21+2/1 FLC 0+4 FAC 1

HACKETT Gary Stuart
Born: Stourbridge, 11 October 1962
Height: 5'8" Weight: 11.6
Club Honours: WC '84

Pacy left-sided winger who joined Chester from Peterborough in September 1994, despite being a wide player, he packs a tremendous shot and is not afraid to have a go from well outside the area. Released at the end of the season.

Shrewsbury T (£5,000 from Bromsgrove Rov on 21/7/83) FL 142+8/17 FLC 15/2 FAC 6/1 Others 2+1
Aberdeen (£80,000 on 16/7/87) SL 6+9 SLC 1+2 SC 2 Others 0+2
Stoke C (£110,000 on 11/3/88) FL 64+9/7 FLC 3+1 FAC 3+1 Others 3
West Bromwich A (£70,000 on 1/3/90) FL 26+18/3 FLC 0+2/1 FAC 0+1 Others 4
Peterborough U (£40,000 on 3/9/93) FL 18+4/1 FLC 5/1 Others 0+1
Chester C (Free on 31/8/94) FL 30+5/5 FAC 2 Others 2

HACKETT Warren James
Born: Plaistow, 16 December 1971
Height: 5'9" Weight: 10.7
Club Honours: FAYC '90

An undoubted success in his first campaign at Doncaster, this classy full-back who had been signed from Leyton Orient during the previous summer, missed only three League games in 1994-95, fitting smoothly into Rovers' back four, which looked sound and compact, until the season's end.

Leyton Orient (Free from Tottenham H juniors on 3/7/90) FL 74+2/3 FLC 4 FAC 8/2 Others 7
Doncaster Rov (Free on 26/7/94) FL 39/2 FLC 2 FAC 1 Others 3

HADLEY Stewart
Born: Dudley, 30 December 1973
Height: 6'0" Weight: 13.2

Speedy Mansfield forward who, due to his strength, aggression, and powerful running, caused panic in opposition defences last season. Scored several outstanding goals during the campaign, although mainly used as a substitute during the latter part.

Derby Co (Free from Halesowen T on 6/7/92)
Mansfield T (Signed on 9/2/94) FL 42+11/19 FLC 3+2 FAC 3/1 Others 3/1

Paul Hague   Matthew Ashton
(Empics Sports Photo Agency)

HAGUE Paul
Born: Shotley Bridge, 16 September 1972
Height: 6'2" Weight: 12.6

A September 1994 signing from Gillingham, Paul had a dramatic start to his career at Orient, being sent off in his first match (AWS v Colchester) and scoring his first ever League goal in his second (Div 2 v Oxford). Both games were lost and he then found himself in-and-out of the side. A tall, rather awkward looking centre-back, he is still developing his game and could soon emerge as a regular.

Gillingham (From trainee on 13/5/91) FL 8+1 Others 4
Leyton Orient (Signed on 12/9/94) FL 17+1/1 Others 2+1

HAILS Julian
Born: Lincoln, 20 November 1967
Height: 5'10" Weight: 11.1

Lightly built midfield player who joined Southend midway through the 1994-95 season, having being released by Fulham. Quite nippy and willing to attack and defend, Julian's wholehearted efforts got him quickly accepted by the home fans. His ability to play in midfield, or to be used as a wide striker, being of great use to the club during their injury-hit final third of the season. Is a very direct footballer who likes to take defenders on in one-to-one situations.

Fulham (Signed from Hemel Hempstead on 29/8/90) FL 99+10/12 FLC 5+1 FAC 2 Others 8+1/1
Southend U (Free on 2/12/94) FL 20+6/2

HALL Gareth David
Born: Croydon, 12 March 1969
Height: 5'8" Weight: 12.0
Club Honours: Div 2 '89, FMC '90
International Honours: W: 9; U21-1

Played very few games for Chelsea last season but, when called up, he could always be relied on to give a solid performance, none more so than in the 0-0 draw at Manchester United. Can fill in for a number of positions, although being most comfortable at right-back where he can get forward well in support of the attack. Also has good long-range shooting ability.

Chelsea (From apprentice on 25/4/86) F/PL 115+16/3 FLC 12+1 FAC 6 Others 10+4/1

HALL Derek Robert
Born: Ashton under Lyme, 5 January 1965
Height: 5'8" Weight: 12.3

Highly experienced midfield man who signed for Rochdale in the 1994 close season. However, after a few early season games, injuries affected his form and he was unable to regain a first team place.

Coventry C (From apprentice on 8/10/82) FL 1
Torquay U (Free on 23/3/84) FL 55/6 FLC 2 FAC 2 Others 3/1
Swindon T (Free on 29/7/85) FL 9+1 FLC 2 FAC 1+1
Southend U (Free on 21/8/86) FL 120+3/15 FLC 13/1 FAC 6/2 Others 8/1
Halifax T (Free on 25/7/89) FL 48+1/4 FLC 5/1 FAC 2 Others 5/1
Hereford U (Free on 18/7/91) FL 98+5/18 FLC 8/2 FAC 11/1 Others 9/1
Rochdale (£10,000 on 8/8/94) FL 5+4/1 FLC 1+1 Others 1+2

HALL Leigh
Born: Hereford, 10 June 1975
Height: 5'11" Weight: 11.7

A Hereford non-contract signing last March, he had a baptism of fire in his FL debut, when coming into central defence as a sub in the 83rd minute at Hartlepool with his side already 3-0 down. Incidentally, the final score was 4-0.

Hereford U (Signed on 23/3/95) FL 0+1

HALL Marcus Thomas
Born: Coventry, 24 March 1976
Height: 6'1" Weight: 12.2

Outstanding young Coventry defender who came through the club's youth scheme and made his debut last season as a substitute at home to "Spurs" on New Years Eve, and looked good. Can play at left-back or in central defence and excellent reports from the reserves bode well for his future.

Coventry C (From trainee on 1/7/94) PL 2+3

HALL Paul Anthony
Born: Manchester, 3 July 1972
Height: 5'7" Weight: 11.0

Right-sided Portsmouth winger with good close control. Started off on the wing, but as the results got worse he was left out of the side. Not a player to languish in the reserves, he regained his place in February, on the suspension of Darryl Powell, and partnered Gerry Creaney well up-front.

Torquay U (From trainee on 9/7/90) FL 77+16/1 FLC 7 FAC 4+1/2 Others 5+1/1
Portsmouth (£70,000 on 25/3/93) FL 46+25/9 FLC 4+2/1 FAC 0+1 Others 6+2/2

Richard Hall   Paul Marriott
(Empics Sports Photo Agency)

HALL Richard Anthony
Born: Ipswich, 14 March 1972
Height: 6'2" Weight: 13.1
International Honours: E: U21-11; Yth

Southampton central defender, who is strong in the air and a solid tackler, Richard was back to his best in 1994-95, after being absent for most of the previous season with a serious ankle injury. Scored some useful goals, mainly from corners by Matt Le Tissier and was greatly missed when suspended for the Tottenham FA Cup replay. Called up to the England squad get-together after some excellent performances at the climax of the season, he can only get better.

Scunthorpe U (From trainee on 20/3/90) FL 22/3 FLC 2 FAC 3 Others 4
Southampton (£200,000 on 13/2/91) F/PL 89+7/11 FLC 7+1 FAC 10/2 Others 3

HALL Wayne
Born: Rotherham, 25 October 1968
Height: 5'8" Weight: 10.2

Having virtually been an ever-present for York in the previous four seasons, Wayne's form in 1994-95 proved a little inconsistent and he lost his senior place for a time. Returned to the side in his former position on the left-wing, before being restored to the left-back berth during the closing weeks.

Darlington (From trainee on 19/12/88)
York C (Free from Hatfield Main Colliery on 15/3/89) FL 224+12/8 FLC 10+1 FAC 9+1/1 Others 17/1

HALLE Gunnar
Born: Oslo, Norway, 11 August 1965
Height: 5'11" Weight: 11.2
Club Honours: Div 2 '91
International Honours: Norway

A player who can adapt to any position, although favouring the wide right, Gunnar recently became only the fourth man to reach 50 appearances for Norway, while missing only six games for Oldham last season. An excellent passer, very quick, and a fitness fanatic, he loves getting forward and has become a big favourite at Boundary Park.
Oldham Ath (£280,000 from Lillestrom on 15/2/91) F/PL 130+6/11 FLC 9/1 FAC 5/2

HALLIDAY Stephen William
Born: Sunderland, 3 May 1976
Height: 5'10" Weight: 11.2

Fast, skilful forward, whose attacking play earned him regular first team opportunities at Hartlepool last season. Initially not a goalscoring success, all that changed in the last game of the campaign when he scored a hat-trick, just days after his 19th birthday. A great prospect, Stephen has attracted interest from many clubs.
Hartlepool U (From trainee on 5/7/94) FL 26+13/5 FLC 2+1 FAC 1 Others 1+1

HALLWORTH Jonathan (Jon) Geoffrey
Born: Stockport, 26 October 1965
Height: 6'1" Weight: 12.12
Club Honours: Div 2 '91

Confident Oldham goalkeeper who presents a commanding figure and comes off his line quickly for crosses, Jon lost his place in the Oldham side to Paul Gerrard after suffering an arm injury at Old Trafford in 1993-94. Called upon just seven times last season, he is a good man to have in reserve with over 200 League games under his belt.
Ipswich T (From apprentice on 26/5/83) FL 45 FLC 4 FAC 1 Others 6
Bristol Rov (Loaned on 1/1/85) FL 2 Others 1
Oldham Ath (£75,000 on 3/2/89) F/PL 157+2 FLC 18 FAC 20 Others 1

HAMILL Rory
Born: Coleraine, 4 May 1976
Height: 5'8" Weight: 12.3
International Honours: NI: B-1

An exciting Fulham striker, who broke through towards the end of 1994, Rory is young and raw, but shows tremendous enthusiasm. Fast, direct, and aggressive, his great potential was rewarded with a call-up for the Northern Ireland "B" side that played Scotland in February.
Fulham (Free from Southampton juniors on 18/11/94) FL 18+5/5 FAC 0+2/2 Others 0+1

HAMILTON Derrick (Des) Vivian
Born: Bradford, 15 August 1976
Height: 5'11" Weight: 11.10

Big and strong, Des, as he is known at Bradford, can play either in defence or midfield. Always gives 100 per-cent and is an exciting player who loves to run at the

opposing defences. Started in 26 matches last season.
Bradford C (From trainee on 1/6/94) FL 25+7/2 FLC 1 FAC 1 Others 1

HAMILTON Ian Richard
Born: Stevenage, 14 December 1967
Height: 5'9" Weight: 11.3

A purposeful WBA midfielder with a strong right-foot shot, Ian likes to come from deep positions and had a fairly good 1994-95, creating several opportunities for his colleagues, as well as scoring a few important goals himself. Has practically been an ever-present throughout his three campaigns at The Hawthorns.
Southampton (From apprentice on 24/12/85)
Cambridge U (Signed on 29/3/88) FL 23+1/1 FLC 1 FAC 2 Others 2
Scunthorpe U (Signed on 23/12/88) FL 139+6/18 FLC 6 FAC 6+1 Others 14/3
West Bromwich A (£160,000 on 19/6/92) FL 122+1/14 FLC 6 FAC 7/1 Others 9+2/3

HAMLET Alan Graham
Born: Watford, 30 September 1977
Height: 5'11" Weight: 11.3

Another one of Terry Gibson's Barnet youth team squad, this leggy full-back gained some important FL experience last season, when stepping in to fill gaps. Still a trainee, he should figure more as he puts on weight and fills out.
Barnet (Trainee) FL 3

HAMMOND Nicholas (Nicky) David
Born: Hornchurch, 7 September 1967
Height: 6'0" Weight: 11.13

Has been challenging Fraser Digby for the goalkeeper's jersey at Swindon for the past eight years and has only once made more appearances than his rival. 1995 began brightly for Nicky, with a run of ten games, but he was then once again consigned to the subs' bench. Earlier, he became the first Town 'keeper in more than 30 years to finish a game in an outfield role, when playing as an emergency striker in an Anglo-Italian Cup-tie in Venice!
Arsenal (From apprentice on 12/7/85)
Bristol Rov (Loaned on 23/8/86) FL 3
Swindon T (Free on 1/7/87) F/PL 65+2 FLC 11 FAC 10 Others 6

HAMON Christopher (Chris) Anthony
Born: Jersey, 27 April 1970
Height: 6'1" Weight: 13.7

Tall striker who had to wait until the latter stages of last season, before adding to his one previous full League appearance for Swindon. Promptly grabbed his first goal, netting after only eight minutes against Notts County, but was unsuccessful in his quest for further honours and was made available for transfer at the end of the campaign.
Swindon T (Free from St Peters on 8/7/92) F/PL 3+5/1 FAC 0+1 Others 0+2/1

HANCOX Richard
Born: Wolverhampton, 4 October 1968
Height: 5'10" Weight: 13.0

A Torquay striker, Richard started last season with a bang, including a magnificent hat-trick against Cardiff, but found the

going much harder later in the campaign.
Torquay U (Free from Stourbridge Swifts on 18/3/93) FL 35+11/9 FLC 4/3 FAC 1+3/1 Others 2

HANDYSIDE Peter David
Born: Dumfries, 31 July 1974
Height: 6'1" Weight: 13.0
International Honours: S: U21-5

A right-footed central defender, Peter is a very highly rated graduate of Grimsby's youth scheme and his game has developed rapidly through his playing alongside veteran, Paul Futcher. Strong, both in the air and on the ground, and an effective distributor of the ball from defence, only injury prevented him gaining his second full Scottish U21 cap against Russia last March.
Grimsby T (From trainee on 21/11/92) FL 56+3 FLC 3 FAC 3 Others 4

HANSEN Vergard
Born: Dramen, Norway, 8 August 1969
Height: 6'1" Weight: 12.12

On loan from Norwegian side, Stromgodset, Vergard slotted into the Bristol City line up at right-back last November as if he had been there for ever and, after giving many fine displays, was eventually signed on a permanent basis. Won many admirers at Ashton Gate and, all in all, he looks to be a fine acquisition.
Bristol C (£105,000 from Stromgodset on 18/11/94) FL 29 FAC 3

HARDING Paul John
Born: Mitcham, 6 March 1964
Height: 5'10" Weight: 12.5
Club Honours: FAT '88

Having played a number of games in Birmingham's midfield in 1993-94, due to increased competition for places since the arrival of Mark Ward and Peter Shearer, he only started eight games last season. Unfortunately, injuries have further hampered his progress.
Notts Co (£60,000 from Barnet on 28/9/90) FL 45+9/1 FLC 1 FAC 6 Others 7+1/2
Southend U (Loaned on 26/8/93) FL 2+3 Others 2
Watford (Loaned on 2/11/93) FL 1+1
Birmingham C (£50,000 on 3/12/93) FL 19+3 FLC 3 FAC 1/1

HARDY Philip (Phil)
Born: Chester, 9 April 1973
Height: 5'8" Weight: 11.2
Club Honours: WC '95
International Honours: Ei: U21-7

Phil seems to have been around at Wrexham for years, although still only 21. A reliable, strong-tackling left-back, with good distribution, he has a good understanding with Karl Connolly. His quick tackling and no-nonsense play has won him the captaincy of the Republic of Ireland U21 side, and he seems destined to achieve further honours, hopefully with Wrexham.
Wrexham (From trainee on 24/11/90) FL 176 FLC 13 FAC 13 Others 26

HARDYMAN Paul George
Born: Portsmouth, 11 March 1964
Height: 5'8" Weight: 11.12
International Honours: E: U21-2

A versatile Bristol Rovers' player, Paul has

91

a strong left-foot and is a fine passer of the ball. Last season his experience was used to good effect to bring on the young professionals in the club's reserve side, before releasing him in June.
Portsmouth (Free from Waterford on 8/7/83) FL 113+4/3 FLC 5 FAC 6 Others 8/1
Sunderland (£130,000 on 25/7/89) FL 101+5/9 FLC 11/2 FAC 8+1/1 Others 3
Bristol Rov (£160,000 on 3/8/92) FL 54+13/5 FLC 3 FAC 3+1 Others 3/1

HARE Matthew
Born: Barnstaple, 26 December 1976
Height: 6'1" Weight: 12.0
Defender. A product of the youth set up, and still a trainee, Matthew made his Exeter debut against Plymouth in the AWS last season. Will be looking for more opportunities in 1995-96.
Exeter C (Trainee) Others 1

Mick Harford   Steve Morton
(Empics Sports Photo Agency)

HARFORD Michael (Mick) Gordon
Born: Sunderland, 12 February 1959
Height: 6'2" Weight: 12.9
Club Honours: FLC '88
International Honours: E: 2; B-1
One of the great target men of the last decade, Mick had a very good first season for Wimbledon in 1994-95, having been signed from Coventry last August. Scored a more than useful eight goals in 16 starts from August to January and, although being mainly used as a sub from then on, with his strength in the air and vast experience, he continued to trouble Premiership defences throughout the rest of the campaign.
Lincoln C (Free from Lambton Street BC on 6/7/77) FL 109+6/41 FLC 8/5 FAC 3
Newcastle U (£180,000 on 24/12/80) FL 18+1/4
Bristol C (£160,000 on 24/8/81) FL 30/11 FLC 5/1 FAC 5/2
Birmingham C (£100,000 on 26/3/82) FL 92/25 FLC 10/6 FAC 7/2
Luton T (£250,000 on 13/12/84) FL 135+4/57 FLC 16/10 FAC 27/11 Others 4/3

Derby Co (£450,000 on 18/1/90) FL 58/15 FLC 7/3 FAC 1 Others 2
Luton T (£325,000 on 12/9/91) FL 29/12 FLC 1 Others 1
Chelsea (£300,000 on 13/8/92) PL 27+1/9 FLC 5/2 FAC 1
Sunderland (£250,000 on 18/3/93) FL 10+1/2
Coventry C (£200,000 on 12/7/93) PL 0+1/1
Wimbledon (£50,000 on 18/8/94) PL 17+10/6 FLC 2+1/1 FAC 2+2/1

HARFORD Paul Raymond Thomas
Born: Chelmsford, 21 October 1974
Height: 6'4" Weight: 14.0
The son of Blackburn's assistant manager, Ray, Paul was Kenny Swain's last Wigan signing when he arrived on a month's loan from Ewood Park. A midfield player, who has a lovely touch for such a big lad, he had another loan spell at Shrewsbury, before returning to Rovers.
Blackburn Rov (Free from Arsenal juniors on 24/8/93)
Wigan Ath (Loaned on 2/9/94) FL 3
Shrewsbury T (Loaned on 15/12/94) FL 3+3

HARGREAVES Christian (Chris)
Born: Cleethorpes, 12 May 1972
Height: 5'11" Weight: 11.0
Another "Put a Tiger in your Team" appeal signing for Hull, this hard-working right-sided forward was unable to break the Linton Brown - Dean Windass attacking partnership in 1994-95 and was released at the end of the season.
Grimsby T (From trainee on 6/12/89) FL 15+36/5 FLC 2+2/1 FAC 1+2/1 Others 2+4
Scarborough (Loaned on 4/3/93) FL 2+1
Hull C (Signed on 26/7/93) FL 34+15 FLC 1 FAC 2+1/1 Others 3+1

HARKES John Andrew
Born: New Jersey, USA, 8 March 1967
Height: 5'10" Weight: 11.10
Club Honours: FLC '91
International Honours: USA
Returned after a successful World Cup campaign in his home country, but an injury early in 1994-95 kept him on the sidelines. An adaptable right-sided Derby player, either in defence or midfield, he has explosive shooting ability. Very much a stop-start season for him, due to a succession of niggling injuries which also kept him out of the USA's first visit to Wembley, John filled in at left-back in the second half of the campaign.
Sheffield Wed (£70,000 from North Carolina University on 3/10/90) F/PL 59+22/7 FLC 17/3 FAC 12+1/1 Others 7
Derby Co (Signed on 17/8/93) FL 60+6/2 FLC 5 Others 6/1

HARKNESS Steven (Steve)
Born: Carlisle, 27 August 1971
Height: 5'10" Weight: 11.2
International Honours: E: Yth
An aggressive, strong-tackling midfielder, who can also play at full-back if required, and both dependable and unspectacular, Steve has always played to the best of his ability, whenever called upon for Liverpool's first team. Had a period on loan at Southend last February, but was recalled to Anfield when the club were plagued by injury problems and performed well.

Carlisle U (From trainee on 23/3/89) FL 12+1
Liverpool (£75,000 on 17/7/89) F/PL 34+6/2 FLC 4+2 FAC 2 Others 4+2
Huddersfield T (Loaned on 24/9/93) FL 5 Others 1
Southend U (Loaned on 3/2/95) FL 6

HARMON Darren John
Born: Northampton, 30 January 1973
Height: 5'5" Weight: 9.12
Battling Northampton midfielder with 100 per-cent commitment. Small of stature, but with a "never-say-die" attitude, he is the club's penalty taker.
Notts Co (From trainee on 17/7/91)
Shrewsbury T (Free on 21/2/92) FL 1+5/2
Northampton T (Signed on 24/10/92) FL 76+13/12 FLC 2+1 FAC 5 Others 9/1

HARPER Alan
Born: Liverpool, 1 November 1960
Height: 5'8" Weight: 11.9
Club Honours: Div 1 '85, '87; CS '86, '87
International Honours: E: Yth
Signed from Luton prior to last season's start, as a player capable of slowing the pace and taking the heat out of situations, his great experience was rarely seen to best effect in a struggling Burnley side. Although an automatic choice, until injury sidelined him in February, he proved unable to regain his place for the run-in.
Liverpool (From trainee on 22/4/78)
Everton (£100,000 on 1/6/83) FL 103+24/4 FLC 17+2 FAC 10+8/1 Others 13+1
Sheffield Wed (£275,000 on 6/7/88) FL 32+3 FLC 1+1 FAC 1 Others 1
Manchester C (£150,000 on 15/12/89) FL 46+4/1 FLC 3/1 FAC 6 Others 3
Everton (£200,000 on 12/8/91) F/PL 45+6 FLC 5+1 FAC 2+1 Others 2
Luton T (Free on 13/9/83) FL 40+1/1 FAC 7
Burnley (Free on 11/8/94) FL 27 FLC 4 FAC 5

HARPER Steven (Steve) James
Born: Newcastle under Lyme, 3 February 1969
Height: 5'10" Weight: 11.5
Club Honours: Div 4 '92
Speedy Doncaster winger who scored nine goals, despite missing much of the 1994-95 season through a series of niggling injuries, Steve is often more of a provider rather than a taker of chances.
Port Vale (From trainee 29/6/87) FL 16+12/2 FLC 1+2 Others 1+1
Preston NE (Signed on 23/3/89) FL 57+20/10 FLC 1+1 FAC 1+2 Others 6+1/1
Burnley (Free on 23/7/91) FL 64+5/8 FLC 1+2 FAC 10/3 Others 8
Doncaster Rov (Free on 7/8/93) FL 56+8/11 FLC 2/1 FAC 3 Others 4

HARRIOTT Marvin Lee
Born: Dulwich, 20 April 1974
Height: 5'8" Weight: 11.6
International Honours: E: Yth; Sch
Bristol City right-back who has a useful turn of speed and is very quick to get forward when the occasion arises. Started last season in the first team but, following the change of manager in November, Marvin made just four more appearances. Will obviously be looking to get back into the side in 1995-96.
Oldham Ath (Free from West Ham U juniors on 3/4/92)

Barnsley (Free on 26/4/93)
Leyton Orient (Loaned on 1/10/93) FL 8 FAC 1
Bristol C (Free on 9/12/93) FL 36 FLC 1

HARRIS Mark Andrew
Born: Reading, 15 July 1963
Height: 6'3" Weight: 13.11
Club Honours: AMC '94
Last season saw "Chopper" sidelined from October with an achilles heel injury, having missed only 11 league games for Swansea prior to the start of 1994-95. Tall and dominant in defence, he is always dangerous in the opposing penalty area and has scored some vital goals for the "Swans".
Crystal Palace (£25,000 from Wokingham T on 29/2/88) FL 0+2
Burnley (Loaned on 7/8/87(FL 4 FLC 2
Swansea C (£22,500 on 22/9/89) FL 228/14 FLC 16/1 FAC 18/1 Others 26/2

HARRISON Garry Mark
Born: Daventry, 12 March 1975
Height: 5'9" Weight: 11.5
A striker turned midfielder, he made limited appearances at Northampton as a non-contract player last season and has recently been playing on loan to RC Warwick and Bashley.
Northampton T (Free from Aston Villa juniors on 16/12/93) FL 7 Others 0+1

HARRISON Gerald (Gerry) Randall
Born: Lambeth, 15 April 1972
Height: 5'10" Weight: 12.12
A versatile and combative player, Gerry signed for Burnley, at the beginning of last season, having been freed by Huddersfield. Seldom an automatic choice, he was capable of filling in at right-back, or in midfield, and scoring spectacular goals, as evidenced by his late winner against Luton.
Watford (From trainee on 18/12/89) FL 6+3 Others 1
Cardiff C (Loaned on 24/1/92) FL 10/1
Bristol C (Free on 23/7/91) FL 24+13/1 FLC 2+2 FAC 1 Others 4+1
Hereford U (Loaned on 19/11/93) FL 6 FAC 1 Others 1
Huddersfield T (Free on 24/3/94)
Burnley (Free on 5/8/94) FL 16+3/2 FLC 1+1 FAC 1

HARRISON Lee David
Born: Billericay, 12 September 1971
Height: 6'2" Weight: 12.0
Tall and athletic, Lee's first team outings in the Fulham goal in 1994-95 were limited by the consistency of Jim Stannard, but he showed that he is ready to stake his claim for a regular place.
Charlton Ath (From trainee on 3/7/90)
Fulham (Loaned on 18/11/91) Others 1
Gillingham (Loaned on 24/3/92) FL 2
Fulham (Free on 18/12/92) FL 6+1 FAC 1 Others 4

HARTENBERGER Uwe
Born: Lauterecken, Germany, 1 February 1968
Height: 6'1" Weight: 13.0
Has now spent two seasons with Reading since coming over from Germany, but his opportunities as a striker in 1994-95 were limited by the form of Jimmy Quinn, Stuart Lovell and Lee Nogan, and he was freed at the end of the campaign.
Reading £100,000 from Bayer Uerdingen on 30/9/93) FL 8+16/4 FAC 0+2 Others 3/1

HARTFIELD Charles (Charlie) Joseph
Born: Lambeth, 4 September 1971
Height: 6'0" Weight: 12.2
International Honours: E: Yth
Having joined Sheffield United as a left-back, Charlie has played the majority of his games for the club in central midfield, and has become a set-piece specialist. After starting last season out of the side, he gained a place in the side that was defeated in the Coca Cola Cup by Bolton and maintained his position until being ruled out by suspension following the FA Cup Third Round-tie against Manchester United. During this period he scored his first goal for the club with a rasping drive against Bristol City. On regaining his place in the first team, an accidental clash in a reserve game at Villa Park led to ligament damage, which ruled him out until this coming Christmas.
Arsenal (From trainee on 20/9/89)
Sheffield U (Free on 6/8/91) F/PL 44+10/1 FLC 2+1 FAC 4 Others 1

HARTSON John
Born: Swansea, 5 April 1975
Height: 6'1" Weight: 14.6
International Honours: W: 3; U21-5
Not sure of a regular place at Luton at the start of last season, he finished the campaign as a key member of the Arsenal side that reached the European Cup Winners Cup Final and was capped for Wales. Tall and strong, John is ideally suited to the role of central striker. Broke the British record fee for a teenage transfer when signing for the "Gunners" in January and impressed fairly early when standing in for the injured Alan Smith. Equally effective in the air, or on the ground, he has good first touch for such a big man.
Luton T (From trainee on 19/12/92) FL 32+22/11 FLC 0+1 FAC 3+3/2 Others 2
Arsenal (£2,500,000 on 13/1/95) PL 14+1/7 Others 6+1/1

HARVEY Lee Derek
Born: Harlow, 21 December 1966
Height: 5'11" Weight: 11.7
International Honours: E: Yth
Hard-working, right-sided Brentford midfielder. As consistent as usual, Lee unfortunately sustained a leg injury at Hull at the end of last January, which saw him miss the rest of the campaign. Despite the "Bees'" good run, the side missed his presence.
Leyton Orient (From apprentice on 5/12/84) FL 135+49/23 FLC 13+3/3 FAC 10+4/2 Others 19+4/3
Nottingham F (Free on 4/8/93) FL 0+2 FLC 0+1
Brentford (Free on 18/11/93) FL 47+4/6 FLC 4 FAC 3 Others 4

HARVEY Richard George
Born: Letchworth, 17 April 1969
Height: 5'9" Weight: 11.10
International Honours: E: Yth Sch
A steady left-back or, if necessary, a defensive left-sided midfielder, it was in the

latter position that Richard played for Luton against Barnsley last January. He would not have minded where he played that day - it was his first appearance since Easter 1993, having overcome appalling injury problems. A good tackler, who does not often get caught out, he is also able to deliver accurate crosses and has an exceptionally hard shot.
Luton T (From apprentice on 10/1/87) FL 100+17/3 FLC 6/1 FAC 6+2 Others 5
Blackpool (Loaned on 30/10/92) FL 4+1

HATHAWAY Ian Ashley
Born: Worsley, 22 August 1968
Height: 5'6" Weight: 11.4
Midfielder, cum winger. An enigmatic Torquay player, but a matchwinner on his day, Ian scored some wonderful goals last season and his crosses under pressure also created many chances for the strikers.
Mansfield T (£8,000 from Bedworth U on 8/2/89) FL 21+23/2 FLC 1+1 FAC 1 Others 3+1/1
Rotherham U (Signed on 22/3/91) FL 5+8/1 Others 0+1
Torquay U (Free on 30/7/93) FL 71+8/12 FLC 5 FAC 6/1 Others 3+3

HAWORTH Robert John
Born: Edgware, 21 November 1975
Height: 6'2" Weight: 12.12
Although Robert has shown himself to be a hard-working, persistent, and brave striker, in his handful of Fulham appearances, not only scoring himself, but in setting up opportunities for others, he was freed at the end of last season.
Fulham (From trainee on 15/7/94) FL 7+14/1 FLC 3+1/2 FAC 1+1 Others 1+1/2

HAWTHORNE Mark
Born: Glasgow, 31 October 1973
Height: 5'9" Weight: 10.12
Midfield player. A free transfer signing from Crystal Palace at the start of 1994-95, Mark came to Sheffield United on a non-contract basis and made his debut in the Anglo-Italian Cup, playing three games. Released towards the end of the year, he had further trials at Walsall and Torquay.
Crystal Palace (From juniors on 26/6/92)
Sheffield U (Free on 16/8/94) Others 3/1
Walsall (Free on 23/1/95)
Torquay U (Free on 23/3/95) FL 1+1

HAY Darren Andrew
Born: Hitchin, 17 December 1969
Height: 6'0" Weight: 13.0
A forward on the fringe of the Cambridge first team, Darran transferred to Woking in March 1995 - the team that he had scored for whilst on loan in the 1994 FA Trophy final.
Cambridge U (Free from Biggleswade T on 11/3/94) FL 7+22/3 FAC 4/1 Others 1+1/1

HAYES Martin
Born: Walthamstow, 21 March 1966
Height: 6'0" Weight: 12.4
Club Honours: Div 1 '89; FLC '87
International Honours: E: B-1; U21-3
A goalscorer at reserve team level for Swansea, Martin struggled to attain a consistency that merited a regular first team place in the starting line-up last season. Often played on the right-side of midfield, at

times, he showed excellent ball control reminiscent of his Arsenal days. Freed during the summer.

Arsenal (From apprentice on 2/11/83) FL 70+32/26 FLC 14+7/5 FAC 8+1/3 Others 0+2
Glasgow Celtic (£650,000 on 1/8/91) SL 3+4 SLC 3
Wimbledon (Loaned on 22/2/92) FL 1+1
Swansea C (Free on 6/1/93) FL 44+17/8 FLC 5+1 FAC 7+1 Others 10+7/7

HAYNES Junior Lloyd
Born: Croydon, 16 April 1976
Height: 5'8" Weight: 12.1

A former Tottenham YTS, Junior was dogged by injury during his first season at Barnet in 1994-95. Unable to demonstrate his true ability in a start-stop campaign, he was released during the summer.

Barnet (Free from Tottenham H juniors on 22/8/94) FL 2+4 FLC 1+1 Others 1

HAYRETTIN Hakan
Born: Enfield, 4 February 1970
Height: 5'9" Weight: 12.9

Joined Cambridge from Wycombe as an all purpose midfielder during the summer of 1994, but only managed three games before a knee injury kept him out for most of 1994-95. Released at the end of the season.

Leyton Orient (From trainee on 4/7/88)
Barnet (Free on 1/6/89) FL 0+6 FLC 0+1 FAC 1+2 Others 0+2
Torquay U (Loaned on 15/1/93) FL 3+1
Wycombe W (Free on 25/3/93) FL 15+4/1 FLC 2+2 FAC 2 Others 2
Cambridge U (Free on 26/8/94) FL 15+2 Others 1

HAYWARD Andrew (Andy) William
Born: Barnsley, 21 June 1970
Height: 6'0" Weight: 11.2

A late newcomer to the Football League, Andy had been a prolific scorer in non-league football when he made the step up to the full time scene and grabbed the opportunity with both hands. After previously playing as a central striker, he was used mainly wide on the right at Rotherham, becoming a regular.

Rotherham U (Free from Frickley Ath on 10/8/94) FL 33+4/6 FLC 1+1/1 FAC 2 Others 2

HAYWARD Steven (Steve) Lee
Born: Pelsall 8 September 1971
Height: 5'10" Weight: 11.7
International Honours: E: Yth

Having joined Carlisle from Derby last March, after protracted negotiations, his passing and creative play should be an asset to the club in the Second Division. Following a difficult debut in the AWS Northern Final at Rochdale, he soon earned a regular place in the side.

Derby Co (From juniors on 17/9/88) FL 15+11/1 FLC 0+2 FAC 1 Others 3+4
Carlisle U (£100.000 on 13/3/95) FL 9/2 Others 2

HAZARD Michael (Micky)
Born: Sunderland, 5 February 1960
Height: 5'7" Weight: 10.5
Club Honours: FAC '82; UEFAC '84

Now in the twilight of a career that, initially, was spent very much in the shadows of the illustrious Glenn Hoddle at Tottenham, Micky is now back with the team he first joined as a schoolboy in January 1975. A player who still has excellent skill, vision, and great ability on the ball in midfield, even if the legs are a little slower these days, he made 13 appearances for "Spurs" last season, ten of them as a sub, and was instrumental in the team's 6-3 Cola Cola first-leg victory over Watford.

Tottenham H (From apprentice on 2/2/78) FL 73+18/13 FLC 11+3/5 FAC 7+3/2 Others 23/3
Chelsea (£310,000 on 19/9/85) FL 78+3/9 FLC 7+3/1 FAC 4+2/1 Others 5+1/2
Portsmouth (£100,000 on 11/1/90) FL 8/1
Swindon T (£130,000 on 1/9/90) F/PL 112+7/17 FLC 12/1 FAC 7 Others 23+2
Tottenham H (£50,000 on 3/11/93) PL 15+13/2 FLC 1+1 FAC 2

HAZEL Desmond (Des) Lloyd
Born: Bradford, 15 July 1967
Height: 5'10" Weight: 11.1
Club Honours: Div 4 '89

Paul Heald

Barry Coombs
(Empics Sports Photo Agency)

Although signed by Chesterfield on last March's deadline day, the former Rotherham winger had to wait until the play-offs for his debut, where he made an immediate impact in giving much-needed width to the attack. It is to be hoped that his accurate passing and crisp crosses will get the "Spireites'" 1995-96 Second Division campaign off to a good start.
Sheffield Wed (From apprentice on 29/7/85) FL 5+1 FLC 1 Others 0+1
Grimsby T (Loaned on 23/10/86) FL 9/2
Rotherham U (£45,000 on 13/7/88) FL 204+34/29 FLC 17+1/3 FAC 17/1 Others 18/6
Chesterfield (Signed on 23/3/95) Others 2

HEALD Gregory (Greg) James
Born: Enfield, 26 September 1971
Height: 6'1" Weight: 12.8
Central defender, who can also play at full-back, he made an unconvincing start to last season, after making the transition from non-league soccer to Peterborough. However, the longer the season went the more improvement Greg showed and he could well turn out to be a shrewd investment.
Peterborough U (£35,000 from Enfield on 8/7/94) FL 27+2 FLC 1 Others 3/1

HEALD Paul Andrew
Born: Wath on Dearne, 20 September 1968
Height: 6'2" Weight: 12.5
Made a welcome return to the Orient team in 1994-95 after missing 18 months, apart from a short loan spell at Swindon, with back injuries. Safe, reliable and, at times, courageous and agile, he made very few mistakes in a difficult season for the club and was often the star performer. As the regular first choice, he missed out only when needing to rest a minor injury.
Sheffield U (From trainee on 30/6/87)
Leyton Orient (Signed on 2/12/88) FL 176 FLC 13 FAC 9 Others 21
Coventry C (Loaned on 10/3/92) PL 2
Swindon T (Loaned on 24/3/94) PL 1+1

HEANEY Neil Andrew
Born: Middlesbrough, 3 November 1971
Height: 5'9" Weight: 11.9
Club Honours: FAYC '88
International Honours: E: U21-4; Yth
Fast, skilful Southampton winger who can play on either flank and who loves to take on his full-back, Neil is most dangerous when cutting inside or running at defenders at speed. Can also go outside and gets in some good crosses. The possessor of a good shot, he scored a fair number of headed goals last season and was sometimes left on the bench to attack tiring defences later in the game.
Arsenal (From trainee on 14/11/89) F/PL 4+3 FLC 0+1
Hartlepool U (Loaned on 3/1/91) FL 2+1
Cambridge U (Loaned on 9/1/92) FL 9+4/2 FAC 2
Southampton (£300,000 on 22/3/94) PL 23+13/2 FLC 2+1 FAC 5/2

HEATH Adrian Paul
Born: Stoke, 11 January 1961
Height: 5'6" Weight: 10.1
Club Honours: Div 1 '85, '87; FAC '84; CS '84, '85, '86, '87
International Honours: E: U21-8 (UEFAC '82)

The most naturally talented player on Burnley's books, Adrian started last season up-front, but later moved back to a position just behind the two strikers. Although not prolific, he scored the goal of the season, a stunning turn-and-shoot effort which sealed an FA Cup win at Chester. A serious Achilles tendon injury ruled him out for the remaining months of the campaign, and his recovery will take some time yet.
Stoke C (From apprentice on 12/1/79) FL 94+1/16 FLC 9 FAC 4/1
Everton (£700,000 on 7/1/82) FL 206+20/17 FLC 33+2/11 FAC 24+5/6 Others 14+3/5 (£600,000 to Espanol on 15/11/88)
Aston Villa (£360,000 on 14/8/89) FL 8+1 FLC 1+1 FAC 0+1
Manchester C (£300,000 on 23/2/90) FL 58+17/4 FLC 7+1/2 FAC 2+1 Others 1+2
Stoke C (£50,000 on 27/3/92) FL 5+1 Others 3+1
Burnley (Free on 21/8/92) FL 105+6/29 FLC 7+1 FAC 12/6 Others 6

HEATHCOTE Michael (Mike)
Born: Kelloe, 10 September 1965
Height: 6'2" Weight: 12.5
Solid, reliable Cambridge defender in a young team, Mike was unfortunately sidelined by a pelvic injury in the first half of last season, but returned to bolster a young defence in January. Also used as a stand in centre-forward at the end of the campaign.
Sunderland (£15,000 from Spennymoor on 19/8/87) FL 6+3 Others 0+1
Halifax T (Loaned on 17/12/87) FL 7/1 FAC 1
York C (Loaned on 4/1/90) FL 3 Others 1
Shrewsbury T (£55,000 on 12/7/90) FL 43+1/6 FLC 6 FAC 5 Others 4
Cambridge U (£150,000 on 12/9/91) FL123+5/13 FLC 7/1 FAC 5+2/2 Others 7/2

Trevor Hebberd   Steve Morton
(Empics Sports Photo Agency)

HEBBERD Trevor Neal
Born: Alresford, 19 June 1958
Height: 6'0" Weight: 11.4
Club Honours: Div 3 '84, Div 2 '85; FLC '86
An experienced midfield man whose ability to read the game more than compensates for a lack of pace, he held Lincoln's middle line together on a number of occasions last

season, before being freed during the summer.
Southampton (From apprentice on 1/7/76) FL 69+28/7 FLC 9+1/3 FAC 4+3
Bolton W (Loaned on 21/9/81) FL 6
Leicester C (Loaned on 27/11/81) FL 4/1
Oxford U (Signed on 25/3/82) FL 260/37 FLC 37/3 FAC 17/1 Others 9/1
Derby Co (£150,000 on 17/8/88) FL 70+11/10 FLC 13/2 FAC 5/2 Others 7
Portsmouth (Free on 3/10/91) FL 1+3
Chesterfield (Free on 7/11/91) FL 67+7/1 FLC 7+1/1 FAC 2 Others 8/1
Lincoln C (Free on 12/8/94) FL 20+5 FLC 3 FAC 3 Others 2

HEGGS Carl Sydney
Born: Leicester, 11 October 1970
Height: 6'0" Weight: 11.10
A well built, strong-running, mobile forward, who is quick over short distances, Carl had very few opportunities at WBA last season, owing to the presence of Bob Taylor and Andy Hunt, and then Tony Rees, before going on loan to Bristol Rovers early in 1995.
West Bromwich A (£25,000 from Leicester U on 22/8/91) FL 13+27/3 FLC 2 FAC 0+1 Others 6+3/1
Bristol Rov (Loaned on 27/1/95) FL 2+3/1

HELDER Glenn
Born: Leiden, Holland, 28 October 1968
Height: 5'11" Weight: 11.7
International Honours: Holland
A Dutch international, Glen, who came to Highbury from Vitesse Arnhem last February, was George Graham's final signing for Arsenal before he was dismissed. Very quick and skilful, unfortunately, he was ineligible for the "Gunners'" European campaign and the best of him should be seen in 1995-96. As a very fast left-winger who can drive quality balls into the box and weigh in with his fair share of goals, his best should be worth waiting for.
Arsenal (£2,300,000 from Vitesse Arnhem on 14/2/95) PL 12+1

HELLIWELL Ian
Born: Rotherham, 7 November 1962
Height: 6'3" Weight: 13.12
Centre-forward who poses an aerial menace to most teams, Ian scored twice on his Stockport debut, while on loan from Rotherham. It was a performance which helped to persuade the then manager, Danny Bergara, to sign him permanently last February.
York C (£10,000 from Matlock T on 23/10/87) FL 158+2/40 FLC 8/1 FAC 5 Others 9+1/7
Scunthorpe U (£80,000 on 16/8/91) FL 78+2/22 FLC 8/5 FAC 4/2 Others 9/2
Rotherham U (£50,000 on 1/8/93) FL 47+5/4 FLC 4+1 FAC 1+2/1 Others 2+1/1
Stockport Co (Signed on 12/1/95) FL 17/4

HEMMINGS Anthony (Tony) George
Born: Burton, 21 September 1967
Height: 5'10" Weight: 12.10
Extremely quick Wycombe left-winger, cum centre-forward, whose total unpredictability created many openings for colleagues in 1994-95. Particularly dangerous on the break and the goals, when they came, were often spectacular.

Wycombe W (£25,000 from Northwich Victoria on 8/9/93) FL 28+18/12 FLC 1+3 FAC 2+2/1 Others 3+3/1

HENDERSON Damian Michael
Born: Leeds, 12 May 1973
Height: 6'2" Weight: 13.8

Big, strong, hard-running Scunthorpe attacker who, after failing to get the goals to justify his place, was loaned to both Hereford and Hartlepool in 1994-95. At Hartlepool, Damien impressed as both a central defender and striker, while showing an excellent touch. Given a free transfer at the end of the campaign, at this moment in time, he looks set to sign for the "Pool".

Leeds U (From trainee on 5/7/91)
Scarborough (Free on 1/8/93) FL 17/5 FLC 2 FAC 2 Others 3
Scunthorpe U (Free on 10/12/93) FL 31+6/4 FLC 2/1 FAC 1 Others 1
Hereford U (Loaned on 27/1/95) FL 5
Hartlepool U (Loaned on 6/3/95) FL 12/3

HENDON Ian Michael
Born: Ilford, 5 December 1971
Height: 6'1" Weight: 12.10
Club Honours: FAYC '90; CS '91
International Honours: E: U21-7; Yth

A strong Leyton Orient central defender who is useful in the air and also an excellent striker of the long ball, Ian enjoyed a good personal season in 1994-95, despite the "O's" lowly position, but his hopes of skippering them in the AWS at Wembley were dashed when they were despatched by Birmingham at the semi-final stage. However, he must have impressed City, who moved to sign him on loan on deadline transfer day with a view to a £65,000 permanent transfer being concluded at the end of the campaign. Made just four appearances for City and, at the time of going to press, is still registered as an Orient player.

Tottenham H (From trainee on 20/12/89) FL 0+4 FLC 1 Others 0+2
Portsmouth (Loaned on 16/1/92) FL 1+3
Leyton Orient (Loaned on 26/3/92) FL 5+1
Barnsley (Loaned on 17/3/93) FL 6
Leyton Orient (£50,000 on 9/8/93) FL 64+1/2 FLC 4 FAC 4 Others 9
Birmingham C (Loaned on 23/3/95) FL 4

John Hendrie
Barry Coombs
(Empics Sports Photo Agency)

HENDRIE John Grattan
Born: Lennoxtown, 24 October 1963
Height: 5'8" Weight: 12.3
Club Honours: Div 3 '85, Div 2 '90, Div 1 '95
International Honours: S: Yth

"One John Hendrie, there's only one John Hendrie", so chanted the adoring Middlesbrough fans as he scored two brilliant goals against Luton in the very last League game to be played at Ayresome Park, when "Boro" clinched promotion to the Premiership as Champions. A former Scottish Youth International, John, who has enjoyed enormous success since joining the club, is exhilaratingly fast up-front and strikes terror into the hearts of those who have to defend against him. Leading scorer for the "Boro" last season, he is above all else a great team man who has never delivered less than 100 per-cent effort. Yet another "Boro" player to be recognised by their fellow pro's when being elected to the PFA Award winning First Division side.

Coventry C (From apprentice on 18/5/81) FL 15+6/2 FLC 2
Hereford U (Loaned on 10/1/84) FL 6
Bradford C (Free on 2/7/84) FL 173/46 FLC 17/3 FAC 11/6 Others 11/4
Newcastle U (£500,000 on 17/6/88) FL 34/4 FLC 2/1 FAC 4 Others 3
Leeds U (£600,000 on 20/6/89) FL 22+5/5 FLC 1 FAC 1 Others 2
Middlesbrough (£550,000 on 5/7/90) F/PL 174+5/43 FLC 20/6 FAC 10+2/2 Others 6/3

HENDRY Edward Colin James
Born: Keith, 7 December 1965
Height: 6'1" Weight: 12.2
Club Honours: FMC '87; PL '95
International Honours: S: 11; B-1

Colin Hendry
Phil O'Brien
(Empics Sports Photo Agency)

The blond Scot, whose love for his adopted town of Blackburn is both fierce and genuine, produced the kind of performances in 1994-95 that will become legend as the club powered its way to the Premier League title. A big, imposing centre-half, his will to win and self belief saw him dominating the airways and throwing himself into every tackle like a human claymore. Towards the end of the campaign, as goals dried up, Colin returned to his buccaneering attacking ways and scored crucial goals at Aston Villa and Leeds. In short, he was the inspirational cornerstone that the Championship was built on and would have led Scotland on the 1995 close season tour of Japan had an ankle injury not required surgery. Selected for the PFA "PL Team of the Year" award.

Dundee (Signed from Islavale in 1983) SL 17+24/2 SC 2+3/1
Blackburn Rov (£30,000 on 11/3/87) FL 99+3/22 FLC 4 FAC 3 Others 13/1
Manchester C (£700,000 on 16/11/89) FL 57+6/5 FLC 4+1/1 FAC 5/2 Others 4/2
Blackburn Rov (£700,000 on 8/11/91) F/PL 127+5/9 FLC 16 FAC 9+1 Others 6

HENDRY John
Born: Glasgow, 6 January 1970
Height: 5'11" Weight: 10.6

Early last season, in an effort to keep John busy, Tottenham loaned their reserve striker out to Swansea. A skilful player, with great awareness and good touch, he scored seven goals from 12 starts and was greatly appreciated by "Swans'" supporters, who would loved to have kept him.

Dundee (Signed from Hillington YC in 1988-89) SL 0+2
Forfar Ath (Loaned on 1/2/90) SL 10/6

Tottenham H (£50,000 on 31/7/90) F/PL 5+12/5 FLC 0+2 FAC 0+1
Charlton Ath (Loaned on 27/2/92) FL 1+4/1
Swansea C (Loaned on 7/10/94) FL 8/2 Others 4/5

HENRY Liburd Algernon
Born: Dominica, 29 August 1967
Height: 5'11" Weight: 12.12
Joined Peterborough at the start of 1994-95 and proved to be a useful player in attack, where his speed was occasionally used to good effect. An experienced player, he was freed during the summer.
Colchester U (Signed on 28/4/86)
Watford (£20,000 from Leytonstone/Ilford, via Rainham T, on 20/11/87) FL 8+2/1 FLC 1 FAC 3 Others 1
Halifax T (Loaned on 1/9/88) FL 1+4
Maidstone U (£40,000 on 1/7/90) FL 61+6/9 FAC 3+1/1 Others 3
Gillingham (Free on 11/6/92) FL 37+5/2 FLC 4 FAC 2+1/1 Others 2/2
Peterborough U (Free on 16/8/94) FL 22+10/7 FLC 0+1 FAC 2/1 Others 2/2

HENRY Nicholas (Nicky) Ian
Born: Liverpool, 21 February 1969
Height: 5'6" Weight: 10.8
Club Honours: Div 2 '91
A tigerish player with an eye for goal and captain of Oldham, Nicky is acknowledged by the new manager, Graeme Sharp, as being the key man in midfield. Holds the ball up well and a good passer who is always available when team-mates are in trouble, he had a difficult season in 1994-95 as he struggled with injury and the loss of Mike Milligan to Norwich but, with a new contract and over 250 games under his belt, he will still be a force to be reckoned with.
Oldham Ath (From trainee on 6/7/87) F/PL 229+8/18 FLC 25+3/3 FAC 20 Others 4

HERBERT Craig Justin
Born: Coventry, 9 November 1975
Height: 5'10" Weight: 11.4
A strong-tackling centre-half with a confident approach who made his WBA debut v Luton (away) on the opening day of the 1994-95 campaign, having previously failed to make the breakthrough at Torquay. He remained a regular in the side until injury struck and thereafter was confined to reserve team football. Has the ability and could be one for the future.
West Bromwich A (Free from Torquay U juniors on 18/3/94) FL 8 FLC 2

HERRERA Roberto
Born: Torquay, 12 June 1970
Height: 5'7" Weight: 10.6
A flamboyant-looking full-back, whose pace and control have made him a firm favourite at Fulham, Roberto enjoys pushing forward, with his surging runs down the left-flank making him an extra attacker.
Queens Park R (From trainee on 1/3/88) FL 4+2 FLC 1+2 Others 1+1
Torquay U (Loaned on 17/3/92) FL 11
Torquay U (Loaned on 24/10/92) FL 5
Fulham (Signed on 29/10/93) FL 49+1/1 FLC 3 FAC 4 Others 4

HESKEY Emile William Ivanhoe
Born: Leicester, 11 January 1978
Height: 6'1" Weight: 13.0

Promising first year YTS striker who was thrown in at the deep end at Loftus Road when Leicester were ravaged by a flu epidemic, Emile aquitted himself with distinction and is one to watch out for.
Leicester C (Trainee) PL 1

HESSENTHALER Andrew (Andy)
Born: Dartford, 17 August 1975
Height: 5'7" Weight: 11.0
International Honours: E: SP-1
Terrier-like Watford midfielder, who patrolled the right-flank in 1994-95 and never knew when he was beaten, he also scored some useful long-range goals. In leading by example, Andy proved to be an inspirational captain.
Watford (£65,000 from Dagenham on 12/9/91) FL 165/11 FLC 13/1 FAC 5/2 Others 4

HEWITT James (Jamie) Robert
Born: Chesterfield, 17 May 1968
Height: 5'10" Weight: 10.8
Jamie stands 13th in Chesterfield's all-time list of League appearance-makers. Although he is usually found on the right-hand side of defence or midfield, his best position is just behind the back four, where his great ability to read a game comes into its own. Now in his second spell at the club, he was a vital cog in the team that won promotion to the Second Division, via the play-offs, last season.
Chesterfield (From trainee on 22/4/86) FL 240+9/14 FLC 10/1 FAC 8+1 Others 11+2
Doncaster Rov (Free on 1/8/92) FL 32+1 FLC 3+1/1 FAC 1 Others 3
Chesterfield (Signed on 8/10/93) FL 66+1/6 FLC 4 FAC 2 Others 8

HEWLETT Matthew Paul
Born: Bristol, 25 February 1976
Height: 6'2" Weight: 10.11
International Honours: E: Yth
Following a successful run in 1993-94, Matthew did not return to the Bristol City side until the end of last season, when he came on as a substitute at Millwall. It is to be hoped that the young midfielder will emerge again in the 1995-96 season.
Bristol C (From trainee on 12/8/93) FL 11+2 FLC 2

HICKS Stuart Jason
Born: Peterborough, 30 May 1967
Height: 6'1" Weight: 12.6
Widely travelled defensive strongman who joined Scarborough from Preston last February. Quickly settled in and impressed, before suffering a groin injury which sidelined him for the last nine matches of the season.
Peterborough U (From apprentice on 10/8/84)
Colchester U (Free from Wisbech on 24/3/88) FL 57+7 FLC 2 FAC 5/1 Others 5
Scunthorpe U (Free on 19/8/90) FL 67/1 FLC 4 FAC 4/1 Others 8
Doncaster Rov (Free on 10/8/92) FL 36 FLC 2 FAC 1 Others 2
Huddersfield T (Signed on 27/8/93) FL 20+2/1 FLC 3 FAC 3 Others 1
Preston NE (Signed on 24/3/94) FL 11+1 FLC 2 Others 1/1
Scarborough (Signed on 22/2/95) FL 6

HIGGINS David (Dave) Anthony
Born: Liverpool, 19 August 1961
Height: 6'0" Weight: 11.0
Club Honours: AMC '90
Found his first team opportunities at Tranmere limited in 1994-95, due to the emergence of John McGreal and Shaun Garnett as a central defensive pairing, but has nevertheless proved a dependable deputy when called upon. Is an excellent close marker and a fierce competitor.
Tranmere Rov (Free from Eagle FC on 22/8/83) FL 27+1 FAC 2 Others 5 (Free to South Liverpool during 1985 close season)
Tranmere Rov (Free from Caernarfon on 20/7/87) FL 278+2/10 FLC 25 FAC 17 Others 34

HIGNETT Craig John
Born: Prescot, 12 January 1970
Height: 5'9" Weight: 11.6
Club Honours: Div 1 '95
Ferocious Middlesbrough dead-ball specialist, who is very fast off the mark, Craig is a gutsy little midfielder whose exciting bursts of speed and runs down the wing result in many goals and scoring chances for his colleagues. Also delivers a superb long ball. His 26 FL games in 1994-95 entitled him to a First Division Championship medal.
Crewe Alex (Free from Liverpool juniors on 11/5/88) FL 108+13/42 FLC 9+1/4 FAC 11+1/8 Others 6+1/3
Middlesbrough (£500,000 on 27/11/92) F/PL 62+14/17 FLC 6+1/6 FAC 2 Others 5+1

HILEY Scott Patrick
Born: Plymouth, 27 September 1968
Height: 5'9" Weight: 10.4
Club Honours: Div 4 '90
Talented Birmingham right-back who takes the eye with dangerous forays down the flank. A stylish defender, sadly, much of his "Blues'" career has been blighted by injury and last season was no exception as he missed being involved in the club's "double". Out for most of the campaign with ligament trouble, Scott managed to get an occasional game towards the promotion run-in and looks to be fully fit for 1995-96.
Exeter C (From trainee on 4/8/86) FL 205+5/12 FLC 17 FAC 14 Others 16+2
Birmingham C (£100,000 on 12/3/93) FL 44 FLC 6 FAC 1 Others 1

Andy Hill
Paul Marriott
(Empics Sports Photo Agency)

HILL Andrew (Andy) Rowland
Born: Maltby, 20 January 1965
Height: 5'11" Weight: 12.0
International Honours: E: Yth

Again unlucky with injuries in 1994-95, Andy rarely seemed to get through a full game for Manchester City without suffering one. Although not a headline maker, when fully fit his contribution in midfield and at full-back was always significant in tidying up around the penalty area and going forward with the ball. His one wish must be for an injury free season in 1995-96.
Manchester U (From apprentice on 16/1/83)
Bury (Free on 4/7/84) FL 264+10 FLC 22/1 FAC 12 Others 19/1
Manchester C (£200,000 on 21/12/90) F/PL 91+7/6 FLC 11 FAC 2+1 Others 1

HILL Colin Frederick
Born: Uxbridge, 12 November 1963
Height: 5'11" Weight: 11.11
International Honours: NI: 8

Right-footed central defender. Was an early injury victim who re-established himself at Leicester after Brian Little's departure, to be installed as skipper by Mark McGhee. Missed a number of international opportunities due to illness or injury last season, but finally added to his tally of caps after a long absence during March.
Arsenal (From apprentice on 7/8/81) FL 46/1 FLC 4 FAC 1 (Free to Maritimo during 1986 close season)
Colchester U (Free on 30/10/87) FL 64+5 FLC 2 FAC 7/2 Others 3+1
Sheffield U (£85,000 on 1/8/89) FL 77+5/1 FLC 5 FAC 10+2 Others 3
Leicester C (£200,000 on 26/3/92) F/PL 110+1 FLC 6/1 FAC 6 Others 9

HILL Daniel Ronald
Born: Enfield, 1 October 1974
Height: 5'9" Weight: 11.2
International Honours: E: U21-3; Sch

Two-footed, skilful Tottenham midfielder with good touch and a passing ability that sees him spraying the ball all over the field. Made his first appearance last season as a sub in the Coca Cola Cup game against Watford, prior to playing in three PL games, one of them as a starter. Selected for England in the Toulon U21 tournament during the summer, Danny played in all three matches.
Tottenham H (From trainee on 9/9/92) PL 4+6 FLC 0+2

HILL David Michael
Born: Nottingham, 6 June 1966
Height: 5'9" Weight: 10.3

Hard working left-footed midfield player and Lincoln's free-kick specialist, David spent the early part of last season on loan at Chesterfield, but returned to win back his first team place in November. Released during the summer.
Scunthorpe U (From trainee on 15/2/85) FL 139+1/10 FLC 8/2 FAC 9/3 Others 8+2
Ipswich T (£80,000 on 29/7/88) FL 54+7 FLC 6+1 FAC 1 Others 3
Scunthorpe U (Loaned on 28/3/91) FL 8+1/1 Others 2/1
Scunthorpe U (£30,000 on 4/9/91) FL 55+1/6 FLC 4 FAC 2 Others 5
Lincoln C (Signed on 16/7/93) FL 52+6/6 FLC 3+1 FAC 5 Others 6/1
Chesterfield (Loaned on 22/8/94) FL 3

HILL Keith John
Born: Bolton, 17 May 1969
Height: 6'0" Weight: 11.3

Central defender who has pace, he is capable of playing right across the back four, making him a valuable squad player. Captained Plymouth in the absence of Steve Castle, but suffered from a few niggling injuries which truncated his season.
Blackburn Rov (From juniors on 9/5/87) F/PL 89+7/4 FLC 6/1 FAC 5+1 Others 3+2
Plymouth Arg (Signed on 23/9/92) FL 96+3/2 FLC 7 FAC 7 Others 7

David Hillier   Steve Morton
(Empics Sports Photo Agency)

HILLIER David
Born: Blackheath, 18 December 1969
Height: 5'10" Weight: 12.5
Club Honours: FAYC '88; Div 1 '91
International Honours: E: U21-1

Versatile two-footed Arsenal midfield player with an unflappable temperament, David has loads of stamina, is a strong tackler, and a youngster who always puts the team first. Always willing to take a penalty in a shoot-out situation, he had limited opportunities in 1994-95, with just 11 starts, mainly due to an influx of midfielders at the club and the good form of Ray Parlour.
Arsenal (From trainee on 11/2/88) F/PL 79+18/2 FLC 11+2 FAC 13+2 Others 5+4

HIMSWORTH Gary Paul
Born: Pickering, 19 December 1969
Height: 5'8" Weight: 10.6

After breaking his leg in February 1994, Gary made a full recovery and re-established himself in Darlington's first team in 1994-95. A skilful, tricky midfield player, with quick acceleration, he spent the latter part of last season overlapping from left-back with good effect.
York C (From trainee on 27/1/88) FL 74+14/8 FLC 5 Others 5+2

Scarborough (Free on 5/12/90) FL 83+9/6 FLC 7+2/1 FAC 1+1 Others 6+1
Darlington (Free on 16/7/93) FL 60+6/5 FLC 3+1 FAC 3 Others 6/4

HINCHCLIFFE Andrew (Andy) George
Born: Manchester, 5 February 1969
Height: 5'10" Weight: 12.10
Club Honours: FAC '95
International Honours: E: U21-1; Yth

Left-sided Everton defender who plays as an attacking full-back. Makes good use of possession by overlapping midfielders and managing to provide good telling crosses. Also uses his speed and agility to make important defensive tackles and is extremely useful in dead-ball situations, where his curling shots cause 'keepers great headaches. This element of his game was shown on numerous occasions in 1994-95, and it was his brilliant corner that set up the club's FA Cup semi-final win over "Spurs". Won his first major honour in the game, following the "Toffees'" great FA Cup Final victory over Manchester United.
Manchester C (From apprentice on 17/6/86) FL 107+5/8 FLC 11/1 FAC 12/1 Others 4/1
Everton (£800,000 on 17/7/90) F/PL 114+5/4 FLC 14+2 FAC 11/1 Others 4

Andy Hinchcliffe   Neal Simpson
(Empics Sports Photo Agency)

HIRST David Eric
Born: Cudworth, 7 December 1967
Height: 5'11" Weight: 12.5
Club Honours: FLC '91
International Honours: E: 3; B-3; U21-7; Yth

Yet another disappointing injury hit season for the fine Sheffield Wednesday striker. Started 1994-95 in the side and, following a quiet start, the goal that beat Manchester United seemed to get his career going again. Unfortunately, he was out injured for another spell straight away, although coming back well after Christmas. Still the crowd's favourite, he lifts everyone's spirits when fit and deserves a long injury free run.

Certainly, with his great balance, pace, and deadly left-foot, a place alongside Alan Shearer in the England side remains a distinct possibility in the near future.
Barnsley (From apprentice on 8/11/85) FL 26+2/9 FLC 1
Sheffield Wed (£200,000 on 11/8/86) F/PL 209+24/87 FLC 23+8/10 FAC 11+5/6 Others 8/5

HISLOP Neil (Shaka)
Born: London, 22 February 1969
Height: 6'6" Weight: 12.2
Club Honours: Div 2 '94
1994-95 was an outstanding season for Reading's giant goalkeeper, whose amazing reflexes and telescopic reach made him a target for many Premier clubs. Ever-present for the last two seasons, Shaka was the fans' choice as "Player of the Year", as well as being selected by his fellow professionals at the PFA awards night as being the First Division's leading 'keeper. Rejected the chance of honours with Trinidad & Tobago, in hoping to attract the attention of the England selectors.
Reading (Signed on 9/9/92) FL 104 FLC 10 FAC 3 Others 9

Shaka Hislop   Neal Simpson
(Empics Sports Photo Agency)

HITCHCOCK Kevin Joseph
Born: Canning Town, 5 October 1962
Height: 6'1" Weight: 12.2
Normally the substitute goalkeeper for Chelsea, when Dmitri Kharine was injured last season, Kevin stepped comfortably into the breach, making 15 starts in all, including four in the European Cup Winners Cup. Very agile and quick in coming for the ball, he also had to overcome a hernia operation in 1994-95. Proved his mettle in the 2-1 victory at Manchester City, with both sides staring at the relegation zone, when producing a series of tremendous saves that pushed the home side deeper into trouble.

Nottingham F (£15,000 from Barking on 4/8/83)
Mansfield T (£140,000 on 1/2/84) FL 182 FLC 12 FAC 10 Others 20
Chelsea (£250,000 on 25/3/88) F/PL 68+1 FLC 8 FAC 5 Others 13
Northampton T (Loaned on 28/12/90) FL 17 Others 1

HOBSON Gary
Born: Hull, 12 November 1972
Height: 6'1" Weight: 12.10
Although both are very left-footed, Gary developed a solid centre-back partnership for Hull with Rob Dewhurst last season. Strong and deceptively quick, having reached 100 League appearances in January, "Hobo" is now gaining the experience to back up his undoubted talent. Missed the final games of the campaign with a gashed shin. However, a bright future beckons.
Hull C (From trainee on 17/7/91) FL 107+6 FLC 10 FAC 1+1/1 Others 4+1

HOCKADAY David (Dave)
Born: Billingham, 9 November 1957
Height: 5'9" Weight: 11.2
Club Honours: Div 4 '86, Div 3 '94
Vastly experienced right-back and a hard tackler who, despite his years, is still one of the fittest players at Shrewsbury. Looks dangerous going forward and combines well with a wide man to whom he will provide a continual supply of telling balls. Unfortunately, an injury interrupted his season in 1994-95 and he was freed during the summer.
Blackpool (Signed from Billingham Synthonia on 15/7/75) FL 131+16/24 FLC 18+1 FAC 10+2/2
Swindon T (Free on 2/8/83) FL 227+18/6 FLC 21/2 FAC 18+2 Others 22/2
Hull C (£50,000 on 13/9/90) FL 72/2 FLC 4/1 FAC 2+1 Others 4
Stoke C (Loaned on 8/3/93) FL 7
Shrewsbury T (Free on 11/8/93) FL 46+2 FLC 6 FAC 4 Others 3

HODDLE Carl
Born: Harlow, 8 March 1967
Height: 6'0" Weight: 11.0
Brother of the brilliant Glenn, currently Chelsea's manager, Carl was an ever-present in the Barnet side last season, until injury and loan signings saw him lose his place. A thinking midfield playmaker who relies on his passing ability to open up opposing defences, he was released at the end of the campaign.
Tottenham H (From apprentice on 22/8/84)
Leyton Orient (£10,000 from Bishops Stortford on 24/7/89) FL 19+9/2 FLC 1 Others 2
Barnet (Free on 22/7/91) FL 80+12/3 FLC 11+1 FAC 6+1/1 Others 7+1

HODDLE Glenn
Born: Hayes, 27 October 1957
Height: 6'0" Weight: 11.6
Club Honours: FAC '81, '82
International Honours: E: 53; B-2; U21-12; Yth
Arguably the most gifted English player of the last decade, Glenn, the PFA "Young Player of the Year" in 1980, brought his career to an end on the final day of last season. He went out in style too, leading Chelsea as player-manager to a 2-1 victory

over Arsenal. With the ability to make accurate long passes from midfield better than anybody since Johnny Haynes, and the scorer of over 100 first class goals, many struck from long-range, he was chaired off the pitch. Prior to that, injury plagued like many of the other players, he started just three times. Will now concentrate on management and will be looking to put Chelsea back on the footballing map in a big way.
Tottenham H (From apprentice on 8/4/75) FL 371+7/88 FLC 44/10 FAC 47+1/11 Others 21+4/1 (£800,000 to Monaco on 1/7/87)
Swindon T (Free on 16/8/91) FL 63+1/1 FLC 6/1 FAC 1 Others 3+1/1
Chelsea (£75,000 on 15/7/93) PL 19+12/1 FLC 3 FAC 0+2 Others 0+3

HODGE John
Born: Skelmersdale, 1 April 1969
Height: 5'7" Weight: 11.3
Club Honours: AMC '94
In the two seasons John has been at Swansea he has become a firm favourite with the Vetch Field regulars, with his skilful, teasing wing play and excellent crossing ability. The only feature he will be disappointed in is his lack of consistency in front of goal.
Exeter C (Signed from Falmouth T on 12/9/91) FL 57+8/10 FLC 3/1 FAC 2 Others 8+2/1
Swansea C (Signed on 14/7/93) FL 43+18/9 FLC 4+2/1 FAC 5 Others 11+3

HODGE Martin John
Born: Southport, 4 February 1959
Height: 6'2" Weight: 14.2
Having started his career with Plymouth in 1977, he came back last season as goalkeeping cover for Alan Nicholls and played a number of games due to varying circumstances. Taking over the role of youth team manager, following the departure of Peter Shilton and subsequent promotion of Ian Bowyer, he is an excellent man to have around the squad.
Plymouth Arg (From apprentice on 1/2/77) FL 43 FLC 1 FAC 1
Everton (£135,000 on 1/7/79) FL 25 FAC 6
Preston NE (Loaned on 13/12/81) FL 28
Oldham Ath (Loaned on 22/7/82) FL 4
Gillingham (Loaned on 13/1/83) FL 4
Preston NE (Loaned on 27/2/83) FL 16
Sheffield Wed (£50,000 on 1/8/83) FL 197 FLC 24 FAC 25 Others 3
Leicester C (£250,000 on 31/8/88) FL 75 FLC 4 FAC 1 Others 1
Hartlepool U (Free on 7/8/91) FL 69 FLC 8 FAC 6 Others 6
Rochdale (Free on 12/7/93) FL 42 FLC 4 FAC 2 Others 1
Plymouth Arg (£10,000 on 10/8/94) FL 17 FLC 2 FAC 1

HODGE Stephen (Steve) Brian
Born: Nottingham, 25 October 1962
Height: 5'7" Weight: 10.3
Club Honours: FLC '89, '90; FMC '89; Div 1 '92
International Honours: E: 24; B-2; U21-8 (UEFAC '84)
Signed by Gerry Francis from Leeds, two days before the QPR managers' resignation, and following a loan spell at Derby, Steve played in 14 consecutive games before losing his place. However, throughout he

showed real class during what was a difficult time at QPR, both on and off the pitch. Recalled to the side at the end of the season, he provided much needed competition for the midfield places.

Nottingham F (From apprentice on 25/10/80) FL 122+1/30 FLC 10/2 FAC 6 Others 11/4
Aston Villa (£450,000 on 27/8/85) FL 53/12 FLC 12/3 FAC 4/1 Others 1
Tottenham H (£650,000 on 23/12/86) FL 44+1/7 FLC 2 FAC 7/2
Nottingham F (£550,000 on 17/8/88) FL 79+3/20 FLC 20+1/6 FAC 11+1/2 Others 9/2
Leeds U (£900,000 on 25/7/91) F/PL 28+26/10 FLC 4+3 FAC 2+1 Others 0+3
Derby Co (Loaned on 30/8/94) FL 10/2 Others 1/2
Queens Park R (£300,000 on 28/10/94) PL 15 FAC 1

HODGES Glyn Peter
Born: Streatham, 30 April 1963
Height: 6'0" Weight: 12.3
Club Honours: Div 4 '83
International Honours: W: 16; B-1; U21-5; Yth

Without doubt on his day one of the most skilful left-footed midfield players in the First Division. A torn calf ten minutes into Sheffield United's game against Sunderland last September led to a period of inactivity, and that, coupled with suspension, meant he only started 20 matches during the season. His forte is in crossing great early balls that give defenders all sorts of problems.

Wimbledon (From apprentice on 3/2/81) FL 200+32/49 FLC 14+2/3 FAC 13+2/2 Others 0+1
Newcastle U (£200,000 on 15/7/87) FL 7
Watford (£300,000 on 1/10/87) FL 82+4/15 FLC 5/2 FAC 8/1 Others 2_1/1
Crystal Palace (£410,000 on 16/7/90) FL 5+2 FLC 2+2/1
Sheffield U (£450,000 on 17/1/91) F/PL 101+24/16 FLC 4+1 FAC 12+1/3 Others 1

HODGES Kevin
Born: Bridport, 12 June 1960
Height: 5'8" Weight: 10.0

Torquay's right-sided midfielder, or defender, who, although approaching the end of a fine career, is still an example to any youngster. Released at the end of 1994-95.

Plymouth Arg (From apprentice on 2/3/78) FL 502+28/81 FLC 32+3 FAC 39/3 Others 9+2/2
Torquay U (Loaned on 21/1/92) FL 3
Torquay U (Free on 7/12/92) FL 48+17/4 FLC 2 FAC 2+2 Others 8/1

HODGES Lee Leslie
Born: Epping, 4 September 1973
Height: 5'9" Weight: 10.9
International Honours: E: Yth

A left-sided Barnet midfielder, signed from "Spurs" at the end of 1993-94, Lee, whose high workrate and good ball skills mark him out as a player to watch, weighed in with goals to back up the front two last season, and has become an integral member of the side.

Tottenham H (From trainee on 29/2/92) PL 0+4
Plymouth Arg (Loaned on 26/2/93) FL 6+1/2
Wycombe W (Loaned on 31/12/93) FL 2+2 FAC 1 Others 1
Barnet (Free on 31/5/94) FL 32+2/4 FLC 4 FAC 1/1 Others 2

HODGSON Douglas (Doug) John
Born: Frankston, Australia, 27 February 1969
Height: 6'2" Weight: 13.10

Signed from Australia, following an impressive performance against Sheffield United on their tour in the 1994 close season, the popular central defender has been very unlucky with injury. Following a Coca Cola Cup debut against Stockport, and two more first team appearances, he sustained a serious nose injury in training which necessitated several hospital stays and cut short his season. Returned home to Australia to recuperate and hopes to be fully fit in time for the new season.

Sheffield U (£30,000 from Heidelberg Alex on 22/7/94) FL 0+1 FLC 1 Others 1

HOGG Graeme James
Born: Aberdeen, 17 June 1964
Height: 6'1" Weight: 12.4
Club Honours: AIC '95
International Honours: S: U21-4

Signed from Hearts last January, Graeme has been a more than useful aquisition for Notts County. Strong in the air, and a good tackler, he brings a commanding presence to the centre of the club's defence, leading by example and organisational skills. If under pressure, clears his lines well, but never misses the opportunity to make a telling pass.

Manchester U (From apprentice on 1/6/82) FL 82+1/1 FLC 7+1 FAC 8 Others 12
West Bromwich A (Loaned on 3/11/87) FL 7 Others 1
Portsmouth (£150,000 on 25/8/88) FL 97+3/2 FLC 2 FAC 6 Others 2
Heart of Midlothian (£200,000 on 23/8/91) SL 49+8/3 SLC 5 SC 1/1 Others 4
Notts Co (£75,000 on 27/1/95) FL 17 Others 1

HOLDEN Ian Andrew (Andy)
Born: Flint, 14 September 1962
Height: 6'1" Weight: 13.2
International Honours: W: 1; U21-1

A very experienced, strong central defender, who is good in the air and likes to tackle, Andy thought his playing days were over when he took up the positions of team-coach and reserve team manager at Oldham. However, much to his surprise, he was recalled to play centre-half at Charlton last season during an injury crisis and, needless to say, disgraced nobody.

Chester C (£3,000 from Rhyl on 18/8/83) FL 100/17 FLC 8/1 FAC 2/2 Others 2
Wigan Ath £45,000 on 30/10/86) FL 48+1/4 FLC 3 FAC 7 Others 7
Oldham Ath (£130,000 on 12/1/89) FL 22/4 FAC 2

HOLDEN Richard (Rick) William
Born: Skipton, 9 September 1964
Height: 5'11" Weight: 12.7
Club Honours: Div 2 '91

A lively left-winger when on song, Rick lost his Oldham place to Mark Brennan, following the appointment of Graeme Sharp as manager. Still one of the best crossers in the game, his speciality is in picking the ball up deep and running at the full-back, thus giving himself the option of crossing early or going past his man.

Burnley (Free from Carnegie College on 27/3/86) FL 0+1
Halifax T (Free on 24/9/86) FL 66+1/12 FLC 2 FAC 7 Others 8
Watford (£125,000 on 24/3/88) FL 42/8 FLC 2 FAC 6/1 Others 3+1/1
Oldham Ath (£165,000 on 18/8/89) FL 125+4/19 FLC 15+1/4 FAC 13/2Others 3/1
Manchester C (£900,000 on 10/7/92) PL 49+1/3 FLC 3/1 FAC 5/1
Oldham Ath (£450,000 on 11/10/93) P/FL 46+14/9 FLC 3+2 FAC 7+1/1

HOLDSWORTH David Gary
Born: Walthamstow, 8 November 1968
Height: 6'1" Weight: 12.4
International Honours: E: U21-1; Yth

Polished Watford central defender, and the brother of Wimbledon's Dean, David was equally at home last season as part of an orthodox back four, or as one of three central defenders. The defence always looked more secure when he was playing and he also scored some useful goals from set-pieces.

Watford (From apprentice on 8/11/86) FL 223+8/9 FLC 18/2 FAC 12+1/1

HOLDSWORTH Dean Christopher
Born: Walthamstow, 8 November 1968
Height: 5'11" Weight: 11.13
Club Honours: Div 3 '92
International Honours: E: B-1

Started last season as Wimbledon's skipper, but suffered a loss of form due to injuries and transfer speculation, scoring just twice in the first 11 matches before being sidelined. Came back and hit form in December, with three goals in two games, but did not really show his best in 1994-95 and will be looking to rediscover his shooting boots this time round. A natural goalscorer, he will remain a threat to opposing defences with his shooting power and instinctive finishing.

Watford (From apprentice on 12/11/86) FL 2+14/3 Others 0+4
Carlisle U (Loaned on 11/2/88) FL 4/1
Port Vale (Loaned on 18/3/88) FL 6/2
Swansea C (Loaned on 25/8/88) FL 4+1/1
Brentford (Loaned on 13/10/88) FL 2+5/1
Brentford (£125,000 on 29/9/89) FL 106+4/53 FLC 7+1/6 FAC 6/7 Others 12+2/9
Wimbledon (£720,000 on 20/7/92) PL 103+3/43 FLC 10+1/5 FAC 6+3/3

HOLLAND Matthew (Matt) Rhys
Born: Bury, 11 April 1974
Height: 5'9" Weight: 11.4

Having arrived at Bournemouth initially on loan from West Ham last January, and impressing, the club signed him permanently in April. A left-sided midfielder, Matt looks comfortable on the ball, is a good passer, and always shows a lot of commitment in his play.

West Ham U (From trainee on 3/7/92)
Bournemouth (Signed on 27/1/95) FL 9+7/1

HOLLAND Paul
Born: Lincoln, 8 July 1973
Height: 5'11" Weight: 12.4
International Honours: E: U21-3

Right-footed Mansfield midfield player. Selection for the PFA Division Three team at the end of last season was fully justified, due to his all-round strengths, including hard-tackling, hard-running, aerial ability, goalscoring and a "never-say-die" attitude. Suffered a knee injury against Rochdale on 7 March and was expected to miss the remainder of the campaign, however, typically, he returned for the vital last few matches and went on to represent England in the Toulon U21 tournament during the summer.

Mansfield T (From juniors on 4/7/91) FL 149/25 FLC 11 FAC 7/3 Others 9

HOLLOWAY Ian Scott
Born: Kingswood, 12 March 1963
Height: 5'7" Weight: 10.0
Club Honours: Div 3 '90

A very consistent performer in the centre of QPR's midfield, alongside Simon Barker, where he began 1994-95, playing some excellent football. Unfortunately, an injury at the end of October disrupted his season, but he regained his place in January and rediscovered his form very quickly. An important player to QPR, his assists are just as valuable, as are his defensive qualities.

Bristol Rov (From apprentice on 18/3/81) FL 104+7/14 FLC 10/1 FAC 8/2 Others 5
Wimbledon (£35,000 on 18/7/85) FL 19/2 FLC 3 FAC 1
Brentford (£25,000 on 12/3/86) FL 27+3/2 FLC 2 FAC 3 Others 0+1
Torquay U (Loaned on 30/1/87) FL 5
Bristol Rov (£10,000 on 21/8/87) FL 179/26 FLC 5 FAC 10/1 Others 20/3
Queens Park R (£230,000 on 12/8/91) F/PL 104+16/3 FLC 10+1 FAC 6+1/1 Others 1+1

Ian Holloway   Neal Simpson
(Empics Sports Photo Agency)

HOLMES Matthew (Mattie) Jason
Born: Luton, 1 August 1969
Height: 5'7" Weight: 10.7

A dedicated West Ham midfielder, who always gives 100 per-cent, Mattie has a good left-foot and moves and passes well. Having been left out of the side during last February and early March, he regained his place against Southampton and played a large part in the final run-in when the "Hammers" lost only one game in the last 11. Actually scored his only goal of the season in a 3-0 win over Liverpool, thus ensuring Premiership survival.

Bournemouth (From trainee on 22/8/88) FL 105+9/8 FLC 7 FAC 8+2 Others 5

Cardiff C (Loaned on 23/3/89) FL 0+1
West Ham U (£40,000 on 19/8/92) F/PL 63+13/4 FLC 4 FAC 6 Others 3/1

Matthew Holmes   Paul Marriott
(Empics Sports Photo Agency)

HOLMES Paul
Born: Stocksbridge, 18 February 1968
Height: 5'10" Weight: 11.0

Bought as a right-back, but also adept on the right side of Everton's midfield, Paul is able to link up well and has a good turn of pace. Also looks at ease on the ball and is effective at cutting out opposition moves. Not able to gain a first team position during 1994-95, due to increased competition for places, he started just once.

Doncaster Rov (From apprentice on 24/2/86) FL 42+5/1 FAC 3+1/1 Others 1
Torquay U (£6,000 on 12/8/88) FL 127+11/4 FLC 9 FAC 9+2 Others 13+3
Birmingham C (£40,000 on 5/6/92) FL 12 FAC 1
Everton (£100,000 on 19/3/93) PL 20 FLC 4 FAC 1

HOLMES Steven (Steve) Peter
Born: Middlesbrough, 13 January 1971
Height: 6'2" Weight: 13.0

Central defender. Sound in defence, both in the air and on the ground and dangerous at set-pieces, Steve could easily have had a hat-trick on his Preston debut against Exeter last season. A great prospect for the future, as part of the learning process he was loaned to Hartlepool in March.

Lincoln C (From trainee on 17/7/89)
Preston NE (£10,000 from Guisborough T, via Gainsborough Trinity, on 14/3/94) FL 5/1 FAC 3 Others 3
Hartlepool U (Loaned on 10/3/95) FL 5/2

HOLSGROVE Paul
Born: Telford, 26 August 1969
Height: 6'1" Weight: 11.10

Signed at the start of last season on a free transfer from Millwall, Paul would have played many more games for Reading as a strong midfield player, but for breaking his leg against Bristol City in October. Returned to the side in January with the winner at Middlesbrough and continued to show a

wide range of passing skills, and to score some vital goals for the club. Son of John, the former Swindon and "Wolves'" player.

Aldershot (From trainee on 9/2/87) FL 0+3 Others 1 (Free to Wokingham T in 1990 close season)
Luton T (£25,000 on 1/1/91) FL 1+1 (Free to Heracles in November 1991)
Millwall (Free on 13/8/92) FL 3+8 FLC 0+1 FAC 0+1 Others 2
Reading (Free on 10/8/94) FL 23+1/3 FLC 2+2/1 FAC 1

HOMER Christopher (Chris)
Born: Stockton, 16 April 1977
Height: 5'9" Weight: 11.5

Second year Hartlepool YTS midfielder, and highly-rated by club coach, Billy Horner, Chris played his first ever game for the club last season after it had been announced that none of the trainees were to be offered pro contracts. However, following a re-think by new manager, Keith Houchen, it was decided that he had earned one.

Hartlepool U (Trainee) FL 1

HONE Mark Joseph
Born: Croydon, 21 August 1969
Height: 6'1" Weight: 12.0

Right-sided full-back whose conversion from non-league to First Division football with Southend last season was achieved with the minimum of fuss. Good in the air and an excellent tackler, Mark is also keen to get forward and supply crosses into the opposition's penalty area. Only a minor injury towards the end of the season prevented him from completing a full run of appearances.

Crystal Palace (From juniors on 3/11/85) FL 4 FLC 0+1
Southend U (£50,000 from Welling U on 11/8/94) FL 39+1 FLC 2 FAC 1

HONOUR Brian
Born: Horden, 16 February 1964
Height: 5'7" Weight: 12.5

Long-serving Hartlepool midfielder who played in the first two games of last season before a persistent knee injury forced him to retire from senior football. Briefly on the coaching staff, he later had spells with Spennymoor and Durham, before coming back to United in a coaching capacity.

Darlington (From apprentice on 26/2/82) FL 59+15/4 FLC 5/1 FAC 5 Others 2/2 (Free to Peterlee during 1984 close season)
Hartlepool U (Free on 6/2/85) FL 301+18/25 FLC 21+3/3 FAC 21+1/2 Others 19/6

HONOUR Christian (Chris) Robert
Born: Bristol, 5 June 1968
Height: 5'10" Weight: 12.2

Strong-running, hard-tackling defender, who can also play up front, Chris returned to Airdrie during the third week of his second month on loan at Cardiff last season, when it became clear that the Scottish club wanted £70,000 for him, rather than let him stay.

Bristol C (From apprentice on 4/7/86) FL 44+16/1 FLC 4+1 FAC 4 Others 3
Torquay U (Loaned on 21/11/86) FL 3
Hereford U (Loaned on 29/12/89) FL 2+1
Swansea C (Loaned on 23/1/91) FL 2 Others 2
Airdrie (Signed on 10/8/91) SL 90+3/5 SLC 5 SC 12 Others 4
Cardiff C (Loaned on 3/2/95) FL 10

HOOKER Jonathan (Jon) William
Born: London, 31 May 1973
Height: 5'7" Weight: 11.0
On trial from non-league Hertford Town, Jon played an AWS game for Gillingham against Brentford last November, before signing for the "Bees". An outside-left, he made just one substitute appearance in the League for Brentford.
Gillingham (On trial from Hertford T on 7/11/94) Others 1
Brentford (£5,000 from Hertford T on 14/11/94) FL 0+1

HOOPER Dean Raymond
Born: Harefield, 13 April 1971
Height: 5'11" Weight: 10.12
Pacy winger snapped up by Swindon from non-league football last March who, although impressing in five substitute appearances, has yet to start a game. Should not have too long a wait.
Swindon T (£15,000 from Hayes on 3/3/95) FL 0+4 FLC 0+1

HOOPER Michael (Mike) Dudley
Born: Bristol, 10 February 1964
Height: 6'2" Weight: 13.0
Club Honours: CS '86; FMC '86
Mike has had few opportunities in the Newcastle first team last season, due to illness and injury. However, he is a very experienced goalkeeper to have as cover and his time will come again. Called off the bench when Pavel Srnicek was sent off against "Spurs", his first piece of action was to face the resulting penalty from Jurgen Klinsman, which he saved.
Bristol C (Free from Mangotsfield on 8/11/83) FL 1 FAC 1 Others 1
Wrexham (Free on 8/2/85) FL 34 FLC 4
Liverpool (£40,000 on 25/10/85) F/PL 50+1 FLC 10 FAC 5 Others 6+1
Leicester C (Loaned on 21/9/90) FL 14 Others 1
Newcastle U (£550,000 on 23/9/93) PL 23+2 FLC 2 FAC 3

HOPE Christopher (Chris) Jonathan
Born: Sheffield, 14 November 1972
Height: 6'1" Weight: 12.2
A regular, although not automatic, first team member for Scunthorpe last season, he performs equally well at right-back or as a central defender. Good in the air and on the ground.
Nottingham F (Free from Darlington juniors on 23/8/90)
Scunthorpe U (£50,000 on 5/7/93) FL 59+6 FLC 2 FAC 6/1 Others 5

HOPKIN David
Born: Greenock, 21 August 1970
Height: 6'0" Weight: 13.0
A good man to have in reserve, David is a strong-running winger, cum midfielder, and occasional striker for Chelsea, whose sub appearances outweighed his starts in 1994-95. However, the figures should not be misread, as he was often used to shake the game up in its latter stages, especially when running at defenders. Strong in the air and a good early crosser.
Morton (Signed from Port Glasgow BC in 1989-90) SL 33+15/4 SLC 2/2 SC 2/1
Chelsea (£300,000 on 25/9/92) PL 21+19/1 FLC 0+1 FAC 3+2

HOPKINS Jeffrey (Jeff)
Born: Swansea, 14 April 1964
Height: 6'0" Weight: 12.12
Club Honours: Div 2 '94
International Honours: W: 16; U21-5; Yth
A very experienced Welsh international defender, Jeff played at full-back and centre-back for Reading during 1994-95, also skippering the team on many occasions. A dedicated professional who helps with the coaching of younger players and is a superb example to them, he missed much of the season through injury, but was back to his commanding best for the final run-in.
Fulham (From apprentice on 10/9/81) FL 213+6/4 FLC 26/2 FAC 12 Others 3
Crystal Palace (£240,000 on 17/8/88) FL 70/2 FLC 7/1 FAC 4/1 Others 12
Plymouth Arg (Loaned on 24/10/91) FL 8 Others 1
Bristol Rov (Free on 5/3/92) FL 4+2
Reading (Free on 13/7/92) FL 96+3/3 FLC 8+1/1 FAC 6+1 Others 6+2

Jeff Hopkins   Neal Simpson
(Empics Sports Photo Agency)

HOPPER Anthony (Tony)
Born: Carlisle, 31 May 1976
Height: 5'10" Weight: 11.13
Midfielder. Another local product who has emerged from Carlisle's youth ranks to make an occasional appearance in 1994-95, building on his FL debut of the previous season. Certainly one for the future.
Carlisle U (From trainee on 18/7/94) FL 3+3

HORLOCK Kevin
Born: Bexley, 1 November 1972
Height: 6'0" Weight: 12.0
International Honours: NI: 2
Equally at home in Swindon's midfield, or at left-back, Kevin has performed consistently well, especially since the arrival of Steve McMahon last December. This did not go unnoticed and culminated in his selection for a full Northern Ireland cap against Latvia in April.

West Ham U (From trainee on 1/7/91)
Swindon T (Free on 27/8/92) F/PL 79+11/2 FLC 7+1 FAC 5 Others 4

HORNE Barry
Born: St Asaph, 18 May 1962
Height: 5'10" Weight: 12.2
Club Honours: WC '86; FAC '95
International Honours: W: 49
Tenacious central midfielder who is a battler and ball-winner that every team requires. Has a great engine, which allows him to control Everton's play between the two penalty areas, but his main strength is his tigerish tackling. Formed the crucial backbone to Everton's midfield in 1994-95, a difficult season in which the club languished in the bottom half of the Premiership for much of the time. Due to the nature of his play, he inevitably missed matches, mainly due to ankle injuries, but brought much needed steel into the side on his returns. Having helped the club stave off relegation, Barry was delighted to get his hands on an FA Cup winners' medal, following the 1-0 victory over Manchester United at Wembley.
Wrexham (Free from Rhyl on 26/6/84) FL 136/17 FLC 10/1 FAC 7/2 Others 15/3
Portsmouth (£60,000 on 17/7/87) FL 66+4/7 FLC 3 FAC 6
Southampton (£700,000 on 22/3/89) FL 111+1/6 FLC 15+2/3 FAC 15/3 Others 7/1
Everton (£675,000 on 1/7/92) PL 93+4/2 FLC 10+1 FAC 7+1

HORNE Brian Simon
Born: Billericay, 5 October 1967
Height: 5'11" Weight: 12.4
Club Honours: Div 2 '88
International Honours: E: U21-5; Yth
A commanding goalkeeper who is not easily rushed, with Hartlepool having a difficult season in 1994-95, Brian was able to inspire confidence and lapses were rare. Had joined the club from Portsmouth in order to re-build his career, and must have been pleased that his first term at the Vic provided him with plenty of opportunities to impress the bigger sides.
Millwall (From apprentice on 10/10/85) FL 163 FLC 14 FAC 9 Others 10
Middlesbrough (Loaned on 28/8/92) FL 3+1
Stoke C (Loaned on 2/10/92) FL 1 FLC 1
Portsmouth (Free on 24/12/92) FL 3 Others 2
Hartlepool U (Free on 2/8/94) FL 41 FLC 3 FAC 1 Others 2

HORNER Philip Matthew
Born: Leeds, 10 November 1966
Height: 6'1" Weight: 12.7
International Honours: E: Yth
A Blackpool regular for the majority of last season, he was used in defence, where his height served him in good stead and, occasionally, as a midfielder who liked to get forward for the odd shot.
Leicester C (From apprentice on 15/11/84) FL 7+3 FLC 1 FAC 0+1
Rotherham U (Loaned on 27/3/86) FL 3+1
Halifax T (Free on 3/8/88) FL 70+2/4 FLC 6 FAC 6/2 Others 8/1
Blackpool (£40,000 on 14/9/90) FL 184+3/22 FLC 14 FAC 8 Others 18+1/1

HOTTIGER Marc

Born: Lausanne, Switzerland, 7 November 1967
Height: 5'10" Weight: 11.7
International Honours: Switzerland

Signed for Newcastle after performing for Switzerland in the 1994 USA World Cup, Marc must be considered one of the bargains of last season. Likes to get forward at every opportunity from his right-back spot, this he does with ease, due to his exceptional pace. Is also very comfortable on the ball and produces quality crosses. Scored a superb goal in the 2-1 FAC replay victory at Blackburn and another late in the game to earn a 1-1 draw at Chelsea. Was left out of the side mid-season for four games, having looked a little jaded, but returned as good as new.

Newcastle U (£520,000 on 4/8/94) PL 38/1 FLC 5 FAC 4/1 Others 4

Marc Hottiger   Steve Morton
(Empics Sports Photo Agency)

HOUCHEN Keith Morton

Born: Middlesbrough, 25 July 1960
Height: 6'2" Weight: 12.8
Club Honours: FAC '87

Experienced forward who can be well satisfied with his second term back at Hartlepool. In rediscovering his goalscoring boots in 1994-95, he was easily the leading marksman, and is now well within range of the club record. Appointed player-manager in April, his season was capped by him being voted "Player of the Year" by the supporters.

Hartlepool U (Free from Chesterfield juniors on 9/2/78) FL 160+10/65 FLC 8/1 FAC 4+1
Leyton Orient (£25,000 on 26/3/82) FL 74+2/20 FLC 3/1 FAC 3 Others 0+1
York C (£151,000 on 22/3/84) FL 56+11/19 FLC 6/3 FAC 9+2/3 Others 4/2
Scunthorpe U (£40,000 on 28/3/86) FL 9/3
Coventry C (£60,000 on 3/7/86) FL 43+11/7 FLC 2+1 FAC 5+1/5 Others 2+1
Hibernian (£100.000 on 29/3/89) SL 51+6/11 SLC 5/1 SC 6/4 Others 4/1
Port Vale (£100,000 on 9/8/91) FL 44+5/10 FLC 2+1/1 FAC 2 Others 1+1
Hartlepool U (Free on 1/8/93) FL 66/21 FLC 5/1 FAC 2 Others 3

HOUGHTON Raymond (Ray) James

Born: Glasgow, 9 January 1962
Height: 5'7" Weight: 10.10
Club Honours: FLC '86, '94; Div 1 '88, '90; CS '88, '90; FAC '89, '92
International Honours: Ei: 64

The last player to be transferred before the 1995 transfer deadline, having failed to find a place in new manager, Brian Little's Aston Villa side, Ray moved to Crystal Palace. A vastly experienced and industrious midfielder, who can unlock the best of defences and always makes himself available, he came to Palace just too late to save them from relegation. Scored the club's last goal in the Premiership and will be a prime mover in trying to get them back to the top flight. Still a regular for the Republic of Ireland.

West Ham U (From juniors on 5/7/79) FL 0+1
Fulham (Free on 7/7/82) FL 129/16 FLC 12/2 FAC 4/3
Oxford U (£147,000 on 13/9/85) FL 83/10 FLC 13/3 FAC 3 Others 6/1
Liverpool (£825,000 on 19/10/87) FL 147+6/28 FLC 14/3 FAC 26+1/4 Others 8/3
Aston Villa (£900,000 on 28/7/92) PL 83+12/6 FLC 11+2/2 FAC 7/2 Others 4+2/1
Crystal Palace (£300,000 on 23/3/95) PL 10/2 FAC 2

HOUGHTON Scott Aaron

Born: Hitchin, 22 October 1971
Height: 5'5" Weight: 11.5
Club Honours: FAYC '90
International Honours: E: Yth; Sch

Midfielder, cum winger, Scott is a crowd pleaser as he takes on defenders at speed and, from time-to-time, releases an unstoppable shot. As a Luton player, he impressed in pre-season friendlies for Walsall and eventually signed last September, making a goal for Kyle Lightbourne in the tenth minute of his debut against Northampton. Opened his own account ten days later at Colchester, and his nine goals during the season included two at Hartlepool, one of which screamed into the net from fully 30-yards.

Tottenham H (From trainee on 24/8/90) FL 0+10/2 FLC 0+2 Others 0+2
Ipswich T (Loaned on 26/3/91) FL 7+1/1
Gillingham (Loaned on 17/12/92) FL 3
Charlton Ath (Loaned on 26/2/93) FL 6
Luton T (Free on 10/8/93) FL 7+9/1 FLC 2+1 FAC 0+1 Others 2
Walsall (£20,000 on 2/9/94) FL 38/8 FAC 5/1 Others 2

HOULT Russell

Born: Leicester, 22 November 1972
Height: 6'3" Weight: 13.2

A loan signing from Leicester last February, as cover for the injuries which had affected Derby in terms of goalkeepers. Though inexperienced, Russell made a good start at the club, retaining his place to the end of the season. Excellent at crosses, where his height is a great asset, he was outstanding in the home game against Bristol City. Started 1994-95 with a similar spell on loan at Lincoln, where he played 16 games.

Leicester C (From trainee on 28/3/91) FL 10 FLC 3 Others 1
Lincoln C (Loaned on 27/8/91) FL 2 FLC 1
Bolton W (Loaned on 3/11/93) FL 3+1 Others 1
Lincoln C (Loaned on 12/8/94) FL 15 Others 1
Derby Co (Loaned on 17/2/95) FL 15

HOUSHAM Steven James

Born: Gainsborough, 24 February 1976
Height: 5'10" Weight: 11.8

In his first year as a professional at Scunthorpe, Steve came into the side at the end of last season and acquitted himself well at right-back. Can also operate as a central defender.

Scunthorpe U (From trainee on 23/12/93) FL 4 Others 0+1

HOVI Thomas Henning

Born: Norway, 15 January 1972
Height: 5'10" Weight: 11.3

Left-sided defender, or midfield player, Tom came to Charlton last season, initially on trial, and then on a month's loan from Norwegian First Division club, Hamarkameratene. Made two appearances as a substitute, but failed to impress, and returned to Norway.

Charlton Ath (Loaned from Hamarkameratene on 6/1/95) FL 0+2

HOWARD Jonathan

Born: Sheffield, 7 October 1971
Height: 5'10" Weight: 11.7

The former Rotherham forward became a full-time substitute in Chesterfield's push for the play-offs last season. Although preferring an old-fashioned centre-forward role, Jonathan's versatility in attack led to his becoming a valued squad member of the side that ultimately won promotion to the Second Division.

Rotherham U (From trainee on 10/7/90) FL 25+11/5 FLC 0+1 FAC 4/2 Others 3+1 (Free to Buxton on 11/11/94)
Chesterfield (Free on 9/12/94) FL 1+11/1 Others 2+1/2

HOWARD Terence (Terry)

Born: Stepney, 26 February 1966
Height: 6'1" Weight: 14.0
International Honours: E: Yth

Wycombe's bargain of last season, having being snapped up on a free from Leyton Orient in February. Strong on the ground, and in the air, his consistent performances quickly earned him a "Player of the Month" award.

Chelsea (From apprentice on 1/3/84) FL 6
Crystal Palace (Loaned on 9/1/86) FL 4
Chester C (Loaned on 23/1/87) FL 2 FAC 2
Leyton Orient (£10,000 on 19/3/87) FL 327+5/31 FLC 26/1 FAC 23+1/3 Others 29/1
Wycombe W (Free on 10/2/95) FL 20

HOWARTH Lee

Born: Bolton, 3 January 1968
Height: 6'1" Weight: 12.6

Consistent and reliable central defender who

had a fine season for Mansfield in 1994-95. A good header of the ball, he was dependable on either the right or left-hand side of central defence.

Peterborough U (Free from Chorley on 16/8/91) FL 56+6 FLC 8 FAC 3 Others 3+2/1
Mansfield T (£15,000 on 5/8/94) FL 39+1/2 FLC 5 FAC 3 Others 4

HOWELL David Christopher
Born: Hammersmith, 10 October 1958
Height: 6'0" Weight: 12.0
Club Honours: GMVC '86, '91; FAT '88
International Honours: E: SP-15

Having played a handful of games in Southend's central defence early in 1993-94, David joined his former manager, Barry Fry, as Birmingham's coach last October. All but retired, he was called out for two games over Christmas when Liam Daish was suspended and, despite not playing League football for well over a year, acquitted himself well.

Barnet (Signed from Enfield during 1990 close season) FL 57/3 FLC 2 FAC 7 Others 3
Southend U (Free on 15/7/93) FL 6 FLC 1 Others 2+2
Birmingham C (Free on 18/10/94) FL 2

David Howells   Neal Simpson
(Empics Sports Photo Agency)

HOWELLS David
Born: Guildford, 15 December 1967
Height: 5'11" Weight: 11.10
Club Honours: FAC '91; CS '91
International Honours: E: Yth

Given a new role last season as Gerry Francis positioned him in a defensive midfield position just in front of the back four, it proved invaluable as Tottenham's form improved dramatically. David, too, found his form and became a regular in the first team, consistently demonstrating his ability to pick up attackers from long-ball situations and man-to-man marking, thus reducing the space available to opponents between midfield and defence. His versatility was also proved as he showed great ability to finish as in the re-arranged Manchester City home game in April, when bringing the scores level with a well taken

goal that any striker would have been pleased with. "Spurs" went on to clinch victory through Jurgen Klinsmann, but only after he had seen two further efforts go wide.
Tottenham H (From apprentice on 28/1/85) F/PL 163+33/17 FLC 19+5/3 FAC 15+3/1 Others 7

HOWEY Lee Matthew
Born: Sunderland, 1 April 1969
Height: 6'2" Weight: 13.9

Sunderland's reserve centre-forward, who also played in central defence last season, he has a habit of scoring important goals when called upon and weighed in with a brace against Bristol City last December. The elder brother of Newcastle defender, Steve, Lee has made a fine recovery from a career threatening knee injury.
Sunderland (Free from Bishop Auckland on 25/3/93) FL 13+17/5 FLC 0+4 FAC 2+2/1 Others 0+1

HOWEY Stephen (Steve) Norman
Born: Sunderland, 26 October 1971
Height: 6'2" Weight: 11.9
Club Honours: Div 1 '93
International Honours: E: 1

Steve was a regular in central defence for Newcastle last season, where his speed, height, and skill, provide a formidable barrier. He also seemed to have shaken off the groin trouble that earlier halted his progress. His consistent performances forced him into the England squad and he made his full debut against Nigeria. Provides attacking options with his height at corners and free-kicks and his skill on the ball enables him to set-up attacks with penetrating passes. His big disappointment was in missing the vital FAC quarter-final-tie against Everton, due to suspension.
Newcastle U (From trainee on 11/12/89) F/PL 99+19/4 FLC 9+2/1 FAC 10+2 Others 8

HOY Kristian
Born: Doncaster, 27 April 1976
Height: 5'11" Weight: 12.7

A former Doncaster junior striker, now on non-contract terms at the club and, who is presently undergoing a course of business studies at college, Kris made his debut when coming on as a sub towards the end of last season.
Doncaster Rov (From juniors on 18/7/94) FL 0+1

HOYLAND Jamie William
Born: Sheffield, 23 January 1966
Height: 6'0" Weight: 12.8
International Honours: E: Yth

Normally regarded as a midfield player, Jamie made an outstanding debut for Burnley at Sunderland last October, having come on loan from Sheffield United, when standing in for the suspended Steve Davis in central defence. He was most effective in that role, often as part of a three-centre-back formation, though used equally as often within the defensive element in midfield. Also dangerous at set-pieces, and one of Burnley's most consistent performers of 1994-95, his initial loan transfer from Sheffield United was firmed up three weeks later. The son of Tommy who played for Sheffield United and Bradford City (1949-1962).

Manchester C (From apprentice on 12/11/83) FL 2 FLC 0+1/1
Bury (Free on 11/7/86) FL 169+3/35 FLC 14+1/5 FAC 6 Others 12/2
Sheffield U (£250,000 on 4/7/90) F/PL 72+17/6 FLC 5+3/1 FAC 2+2/1 Others 5/1
Bristol C (Loaned on 4/3/94) FL 6
Burnley (£130,000 on 14/10/94) FL 30/2 FAC 4

HOYLE Colin Roy
Born: Wirksworth, 15 January 1972
Height: 5'11" Weight: 12.3

Having been released by Bradford during the 1994 close season, Colin signed for Notts County and played in the first three games of the season before making way. Originally a right-back, who can play in midfield in a wide role and likes to go forward, he later had a spell on loan with Mansfield.
Arsenal (From trainee on 29/1/90)
Chesterfield (Loaned on 8/2/90) FL 3
Barnsley (Free on 1/7/90)
Bradford C (£25,000 on 28/8/92) FL 55+7/1 FLC 1 FAC 3+1 Others 4
Notts Co (Free on 6/8/94) FL 3 Others 1
Mansfield T (Loaned on 3/10/94) FL 4+1 FLC 2 Others 1

HUCKERBY Darren Carl
Born: Nottingham, 23 April 1976
Height: 5'11" Weight: 10.8

Speedy and enthusiastic Lincoln striker, who had come off the bench six times in 1993-94, he was given his full League debut in last season's Easter Monday match against local rivals, Scunthorpe.
Lincoln C From trainee on 14/7/93) FL 4+8/3

HUGHES Bryan
Born: Liverpool, 19 June 1976
Height: 5'10" Weight: 11.2
Club Honours: WC '95

The "Find of the Season" from the Wrexham youth factory, Brian is developing into a quality central or right-sided midfield player, and one of the club's major assets. Good first touch, awareness and a powerful shot, are just part of this promising youngster's make up. Even his "own goals" in 1994-95 were special. He is definitely one for the future and could well play at the very top level.
Wrexham (Trainee) FL 40+9/9 FLC 1 FAC 4/1 Others 12/2

HUGHES Ceri Morgan
Born: Pontypridd, 26 February 1971
Height: 5'10" Weight: 11.6
International Honours: W: 4; B-1; Yth

A hard-working, strong-tackling, attacking Luton midfielder, Ceri had an eventful start to last season in which just about everything happened to him. After missing the opening games due to an ankle injury, he recovered, played well, demanded a transfer, was sent off against Fulham in the Coca Cola Cup, and spent another period out of action. On returning to the side, he recaptured his best form before severely damaged knee ligaments in November effectively ended his season. An aggressive two-footed player, he could play at a higher level.
Luton T (From trainee on 1/7/89) FL 100+16/12 FLC 6 FAC 8/1 Others 3

HUGHES Darren John

Born: Prescot, 6 October 1965
Height: 5'11" Weight: 10.11
Club Honours: FAYC '84

An experienced left-back who arrived at Northampton from Port Vale as one of Ian Atkins' first signings, having missed the previous two seasons due to a serious injury. A player who likes to go forward, with the overlap his speciality, he is still retained by the club on a month-to-month contract.

Everton (From apprentice on 8/10/83) FL 3
Shrewsbury T (Free on 13/6/85) FL 34+3/1 FLC 5+1 FAC 1 Others 2
Brighton & Hove A (£35,000 on 30/9/86) FL 26/2 FAC 2 Others 1
Port Vale (£10,000 on 4/9/87) FL 183+1/4 FLC 12 FAC 14 Others 12
Northampton T (Signed on 12/1/95) FL 12+1

HUGHES David Robert

Born: St Albans, 30 December 1972
Height: 5'9" Weight: 11.5
International Honours: W: U21-1. E: Sch

Young Southampton forward who made good progress last season when forcing his way into the Welsh senior squad. Hard-working and skilful, he scored a goal against QPR with a falling volley worthy of "Le-Tiss" himself. This was followed by two more spectaculars against Luton and Manchester United, before a burst disc at the base of the spine ended his hopes of a first full cap.

Southampton (From juniors on 2/7/91) PL 2+12/2 FAC 0+4/1

HUGHES Ian

Born: Bangor, 2 August 1974
Height: 5'10" Weight: 11.5
International Honours: W: U21-11

An exceptionally talented Bury player who never appears flustered when in possession, Ian is the current Welsh U21 captain. His adaptability in that he can play either in defence or midfield, and is seen primarily as a utility player, meant that a regular spot in the side was not always forthcoming.

Bury (From trainee on 19/11/91) FL 81+12/1 FLC 5 FAC 5+2 Others 12+3/1

HUGHES Leslie Mark

Born: Wrexham, 1 November 1963
Height: 5'8" Weight: 12.5
Club Honours: FAC '85, '90, '94; ECWC '91; ESC '91; FLC '92; PL '93, '94; CS '93, '94
International Honours: W: 57; U21-5; Yth

PFA "Young Player of the Year" in 1985 and "Player of the Year" in 1989 and 1991, Mark is a wonderful striker, who is equally adept at receiving the ball in front, or with his back to goal. Also a lovely volleyer and a spectacular goalscorer. Had another outstanding season for Manchester United in 1994-95, despite constant speculation regarding his future, showing admirable courage when playing with a nagging injury in the early part of the campaign, and later becoming the main source of inspiration in attack, following Eric Cantona's ban. A shining example of his all-round commitment came in the Premiership game at Newcastle, when he suffered a serious injury while scoring in the "Reds'" 1-1 draw. The arrival of Andy Cole took some of the pressure off him as the partnership began to blossom and he signed a new two-year contract in February, much to the delight of manager, Alex Ferguson, and the United faithful. Stop Press: Surprisingly, in the light of the above, Mark was signed by Chelsea for a fee of around £1,500,000 during the summer.

Manchester U (From apprentice on 5/11/80) FL 85+4/37 FLC 5+1/4 FAC 10/4 Others 14+2/2 (£2,500,000 to Barcelona on 1/7/86)
Manchester U (£1,500,000 on 20/7/88) F/PL 251+5/82 FLC 32/12 FAC 34+1/13 Others 27+1/8

HUGHES Mark

Born: Port Talbot, 3 February 1962
Height: 6'0" Weight: 12.8
Club Honours: AMC '90

International Honours: W: Yth

Joined Shrewsbury prior to last season and was most influential when occupying a sweeping role rather than that of central defender, seeming to thrive on the toughest games. Having not always been chosen and suffering some injuries, he was rarely a regular, though.

Bristol Rov (From apprentice on 5/2/80) FL 73+1/3 FLC 1 FAC 9+1 Others 3/1
Torquay U (Loaned on 24/12/82) FL 9/1 FAC 3/1
Swansea C (Free on 30/7/84) FL 12
Bristol C (Signed on 7/2/85) FL 21+1 FLC 1 Others 3
Tranmere Rov (£3,000 on 19/9/85) FL 258+8/9 FLC 27/2 FAC 12+3 Others 36+1/1
Shrewsbury T (Free on 4/7/94) FL 18+2 FAC 1 Others 1

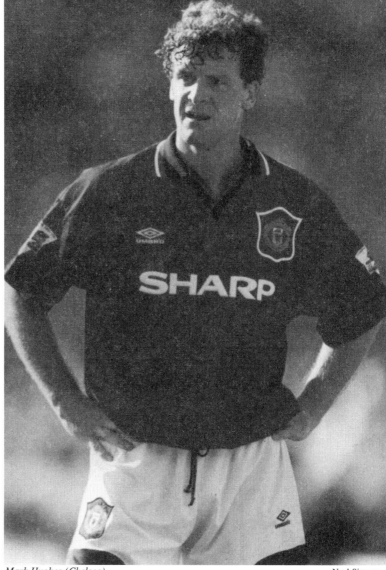

Mark Hughes (Chelsea)

Neal Simpson
(Empics Sports Photo Agency)

HUGHES Michael Eamonn
Born: Larne, 2 August 1971
Height: 5'6" Weight: 10.8
International Honours: NI: 26; U21-1; Yth; Sch

An attacking winger, who can play either side, but who is predominantly left-footed. Having transferred to Strasbourg from Manchester City during the 1992 close season, Michael arrived back in England on loan to West Ham last November, with a view to a permanent transfer. A player with great pace and the ability to beat defenders to get in telling crosses, he had several excellent games, but will be remembered by Manchester United fans as the man whose goal in the 1-1 draw at Upton Park denied them of the Premiership title. Currently, still on loan.

Manchester C (From trainee on 17/8/88) FL 25+1/1 FLC 5 FAC 1 Others 1 (£450,000 to RS Strasbourg in 1992 close season)
West Ham U (Loaned on 29/11/94) PL 15+2/2 FAC 2

HUGHES Stephen (Steve) John
Born: Reading, 18 September 1976
Height: 6'0" Weight: 12.12
Club Honours: FAYC '94
International Honours: E: Yth

Still an Arsenal trainee, Stephen, a left-sided midfield player, made his debut at Highbury against Aston Villa on Boxing Day last season. Substituted after 76 minutes in a game where many experienced players were out of sorts, the youngster will be all the better for the experience.

Arsenal (Trainee) PL 1

HULME Kevin
Born: Farnworth, 2 December 1967
Height: 5'10" Weight: 11.9

Known to everyone at Bury as "Reg", 1994-95 saw Kevin in his second spell with the "Shakers", having been signed during the summer from Doncaster. A forward with an all-action style, Kevin could certainly not be faulted for effort, but surprisingly failed to hit the target throughout the campaign.

Bury (£5,000 from Radcliffe Borough on 16/3/89) FL 82+28/21 FLC 4+3/2 FAC 4+1/1 Others 4+8/2
Chester C (Loaned on 26/10/89) FL 4
Doncaster Rov (£42,500 on 14/7/93) FL 33+1/8 FLC 2/1 FAC 1 Others 2
Bury (£42,500 on 11/8/94) FL 24+4 FLC 1 FAC 2 Others 2

HUMES Anthony (Tony)
Born: Blyth, 19 March 1966
Height: 5'11" Weight: 11.0

The Wrexham "Player of the Year" in promotion team of 1992-93, Tony has been unlucky with injuries since, which have often left him lacking match fitness and unable to produce a consistent run in the first team. Suspensions have not helped either. A tough-tackling centre-back, who can also play in midfield in an aggressive role, he excelled in the FA Cup-tie with Ipswich, his former club, and is a very useful utility player to have in the squad.

Ipswich T (From apprentice on 26/5/83) FL 107+13/10 FLC 6 FAC 4/1 Others 10/1
Wrexham (£40,000 on 27/3/92) FL 99+3/1 FLC 7 FAC 6 Others 10

HUMPHREY John
Born: Paddington, 31 January 1961
Height: 5'10" Weight: 10.13
Club Honours: FMC '91; Div 1 '94

Very experienced Crystal Palace right-back who can both defend and attack and, more often than not, clears his lines with accurate long passes. A grand servant of the club, and no stranger to relegation battles, John started last season in the reserves before getting the call to duty. Very popular with the supporters, he had made over 500 League appearances in a career that stretched back to 1979, prior to being released at the end of 1994-95.

Wolverhampton W (From apprentice on 14/2/79) FL 149/3 FLC 8 FAC 7
Charlton Ath (£60,000 on 22/7/85) FL 194/3 FLC 13 FAC 9 Others 15/1
Crystal Palace (£400,000 on 16/8/90) F/PL 153+7/2 FLC 23+2 FAC 8+1 Others 8+1
Reading (Loaned on 9/12/93) FL 8 Others 1

HUMPHRIES Mark
Born: Glasgow, 23 December 1971
Height: 5'11" Weight: 12.0

Tough-tackling Bristol City left-back. Defensively sound, with a good recovery rate, Mark moved to Ashton Gate from Leeds last October in order to get his first taste of English football. Played in three out of four games, following his FL debut, but failed to add to this total throughout the remaining six months of the campaign.

Aberdeen (Signed from Cove R on 30/5/90) SL 2
Leeds U (Free on 24/6/93)
Bristol C (Signed on 8/10/94) FL 4

HUNT Andrew (Andy)
Born: Thurrock, 9 June 1970
Height: 6'0" Weight: 12.0

A tall, rangy WBA player who seems to have the knack of being in the right place at the right time, he has formed a fine partnership with Bob Taylor. Andy broke a bone in his foot in December 1993 and took time to recover full-fitness. But once back he was the mainstay of the Albion front line and scored some important goals in 1994-95 as the team battled to stay clear of the relegation zone. Was a hat-trick hero in a 3-0 home win over Millwall last March.

Newcastle U (£150,000 from Kettering T on 29/1/91) FL 34+9/11 FLC 3/1 FAC 2/2 Others 3
West Bromwich A (£100,000 on 25/3/93) FL 77+7/34 FLC 3/1 FAC 3/1 Others 3/2

HUNT Jonathan Richard
Born: Camden, 2 November 1971
Height: 5'10" Weight: 12.3
Club Honours: Div 2 '95; AMC '95

Joined Birmingham from Southend, along with Gary Poole, as part of the deal that saw Dave Regis and Roger Willis going in the opposite direction last September. Made an immediate impression in midfield and had the honour of scoring "Blues'" first hat-trick for nine years against Peterborough in the Auto Windscreen Shield. Comfortable on the ball, with an eye for goal, Jon followed that up with another a few weeks later against Crewe. Unfortunately, damaged knee ligaments kept him out of the game for four months, but he was back in time to win

a Second Division Championship medal, having already participated in the AWS win at Wembley.

Barnet (From juniors in 1989-90) FL 12+21 FLC 1 FAC 0+1 Others 6+2
Southend U (Free on 20/7/93) FL 41+8/6 FLC 1+3 FAC 1 Others 6+1
Birmingham C (£50,000 on 16/9/94) FL 18+2/5 FAC 1 Others 3/3

HUNTER Barry Victor
Born: Coleraine, 18 November 1968
Height: 6'3" Weight: 12.0
Club Honours: WC '95
International Honours: NI: 1; B-2

Tall, slim and angular, and a Joey Jones look-alike, he was a "snip" signing for Wrexham after impressing for the Irish club, Crusaders. Holds the defence well and has fine distribution for a tall player, with a good awareness on what goes on around him. A good tackler, he is also a fine header of a ball, like his uncle, Alan Hunter, the former Ipswich and Northern Ireland International. His excellent displays last season saw him following Alan, his father Vic, and another member of his footballing family, Ian McFaul, into the full Northern Ireland side.

Wrexham (£50,000 from Crusaders on 20/8/93) FL 58+2/1 FLC 4 FAC 5 Others 13/1

HUNTER Alvin **Junior**
Born: Lambeth, 1 February 1975
Height: 5'7" Weight: 11.10

A second year Cambridge professional, this speedy winger broke into the side in 1994-95 after some impressive displays in the youth team and was later converted to right-back. Released by the club at the end of the season.

Cambridge U (From trainee on 19/5/93) FL 26+14 FLC 3 FAC 1+2 Others 1+2

HURDLE Augustus (Gus) Athel
Born: Kensington, 14 October 1973
Height: 5'8" Weight: 11.11

Steady Brentford right-back with a good turn of speed. Signed during the 1994 close season from non-league football, Gus had an impressive early run in the side, but made only a few appearances thereafter.

Fulham (From trainee on 3/7/92)
Brentford (Free from Dorchester T on 19/7/94) FL 7+2 FLC 2 FAC 0+1 Others 1

HURLOCK Terence (Terry) Alan
Born: Hackney, 22 September 1958
Height: 5'9" Weight: 13.2
Club Honours: Div 3 '86, Div 2 '88; SPD '91; SLC '91
International Honours: E: B-3

Brought in by Fulham to act as the midfield anchor, Terry proved he had lost none of his passing skills, although his competitive instincts brought him into frequent contact with the authorities in collecting a British record of 61 disciplinary points in 1994-95.

Brentford (£6,000 from Leytonstone/Ilford on 28/8/80) FL 220/18 FLC 17/2 FAC 17/4 Others 9
Reading (£82,000 on 20/2/86) FL 29 FLC 3 FAC 1 Others 2
Millwall (£95,000 on 12/2/87) FL 103+1/8 FLC 9/2 FAC 5 Others 5
Glasgow R (£325,000 on 1/9/90) SL 29/2 SLC 3+1 SC 2

Southampton (£400,000 on 9/9/91) F/PL 59+2 FLC 7 FAC 5 Others 6/1
Millwall (Free on 1/3/94) FL 13 Others 2
Fulham (Free on 21/7/94) FL 27/1 FLC 1+1 FAC 2 Others 2

Terry Hurlock   Tony Marshall
                          (Empics Sports Photo Agency)

HURST Glynn
Born: Barnsley, 17 January 1976
Height: 5'10" Weight: 11.6
Signed professional forms for Barnsley, his hometown club, during the 1994 close season, having earlier been a YTS with "Spurs'". Came as a defender but, after being given a run as a striker in the reserves, he forced himself into first team contention and made a couple of subs' appearances towards the end of the term.
Barnsley (Free from Tottenham H juniors on 13/7/94) FL 0+2

HURST Paul Michael
Born: Sheffield, 25 September 1974
Height: 5'7" Weight: 10.4
A diminutive utility player who once again, in 1994-95, demonstrated his willingness to turn out for Rotherham in any position. Having always given his utmost, no matter in which department of the team he has been asked to perform, Paul is the type of player whose attitude makes up for his lack of physical stature.
Rotherham U (From trainee on 12/8/93) FL 11+6 FAC 2/1 Others 3

HUTCHINGS Carl Emil
Born: Hammersmith, 24 September 1974
Height: 5'11" Weight: 11.0
Enthusiastic, right-footed Brentford player who does the simple things well. Started last season at left-back, before moving to his favourite central midfield role and later

converting to right-back, where he played as if he'd been there all his life.
Brentford (From trainee on 12/7/93) FL 58+10 FLC 5 FAC 3+1 Others 6+2

HUTCHINSON Ian Nicholas
Born: Stockton on Tees, 7 November 1972
Height: 5'9" Weight: 11.10
An intelligent midfielder who appeared for Gillingham on monthly contracts last season, on being released in February 1995 he linked up with one of his previous clubs, Halifax Town, in the Vauxhall Conference.
Halifax T (From trainee on 5/7/91) FL 7+1/1 Others 1
Gillingham (Free from Cork C, via Berwick R and Whitley Bay, on 16/8/94) FL 1+4 Others 2

HUTCHINSON Simon
Born: Sheffield, 24 September 1969
Height: 5'10" Weight: 12.9
Club Honours: GMVC '93; FAT '91, '93
International Honours: E: Sch
A direct Wycombe right-winger whose injury hit 1994-95 will be remembered for the cross which won the League match at Birmingham, Simon was released at the end of the season.
Manchester U (From trainee on 25/9/87)
Wycombe W (£7,000 from Eastwood T on 14/7/93) FL 2+10 FLC 0+2 FAC 7+3 Others 2

HUTCHISON Donald (Don)
Born: Gateshead, 9 May 1971
Height: 6'2" Weight: 11.4
A skilful midfielder, who likes coming forward to score goals, Don became the West Ham record signing when joining them from Liverpool last September. Took time to settle down, but came back to score vital goals in away victories at Arsenal and Aston Villa in March. And, in May, against his old Liverpool team-mates, he was very pleased to grab two goals in the 3-0 win. Nine League goals from 23 appearances was excellent form for a midfielder and "Hutch" will look to build on that in 1995-96.
Hartlepool U (From trainee on 20/3/90) FL 19+5/2 FLC 1+1 FAC 2 Others 1
Liverpool (£175,000 on 27/11/90) F/PL 33+12/7 FLC 7+1/2 FAC 1+2 Others 3+1/1
West Ham U (£1,500,000 on 30/8/94) PL 22+1/9 FLC 3/2 FAC 0+1

HUXFORD Richard John
Born: Scunthorpe, 25 July 1969
Height: 5'11" Weight: 12.2
Played three months on loan at Bradford last season before signing fully from Millwall, Richard performed equally well at either full-back or centre-half. A player who gives his all, he had the unhappy experience of being sent off twice against Bournemouth in the League.
Barnet (Signed from Kettering T on 6/8/92) FL 33/1 FLC 2 FAC 2 Others 2+1
Millwall (Free on 16/7/93) FL 25+7 FLC 1+1/1 FAC 1 Others 3
Birmingham C (Loaned on 21/2/94) FL 5
Bradford C (£50,000 on 7/10/94) FL 33/1 FAC 2 Others 3

HYDE Graham
Born: Doncaster, 10 November 1970
Height: 5'7" Weight: 11.7

An underrated player, Graham had another effective season at Sheffield Wednesday in 1994-95 and, despite not being weighty, showed up as a terrific tackler with plenty of energy to "battle" away in midfield. There was also significant improvement in his running with the ball and passing. Very popular with the fans, he also had his best-ever season for goalscoring as he looks to become an all-rounder.
Sheffield Wed (From trainee on 17/5/88) F/PL 83+21/7 FLC 14+2/2 FAC 8+5/1 Others 4/1

HYDE Micah Anthony
Born: Newham, 10 November 1974
Height: 5'9" Weight: 11.5
A talented Cambridge central midfielder, and a product of the youth team, Micah is a right-footed player with the kind of passing skills that make him a key playmaker in central midfield.
Cambridge U (From trainee on 19/5/93) FL 31+14/2 FLC 2 FAC 4+2 Others 2+1

HYDE Paul David
Born: Hayes, 7 April 1963
Height: 6'1" Weight: 15.5
Club Honours: GMVC '93; FAT '93
Extremely popular Wycombe 'keeper whose bravery and quick reflexes kept his side in many games last season. The only player ever-present in all competitions, his fierce commitment to the side is renowned.
Wycombe W (£15,000 from Hayes on 6/7/93) FL 88 FLC 6 FAC 11 Others 11

HYSON Matthew Alexander
Born: Stockton, 2 May 1976
Height: 6'3" Weight: 12.10
Ex-YTS player who was given a six month contract by Hartlepool in the 1994 close season. A tall forward, he did particularly well against Arsenal in the Coca Cola Cup, but otherwise got few opportunities and was released. Matty, keen to succeed, was tried as a central defender and also continued to train with the club.
Hartlepool U (From trainee on 8/7/94) FL 1+4 FLC 0+1

IGOE Samuel (Sammy) Gary
Born: Spelthorne, 30 September 1975
Height: 5'6" Weight: 9.10
A Portsmouth midfielder, Sammy made his FL debut when coming on for the last 20 minutes of the final game of last season, at home to Oldham, and will be hoping to be given further opportunities in 1995-96.
Portsmouth (From trainee on 15/2/94) FL 0+1

IMPEY Andrew (Andy) Rodney
Born: Hammersmith, 30 September 1971
Height: 5'8" Weight: 10.6
International Honours: E: U21-1
Without question, 1994-95 was his best season so far with some superb perform-ances for QPR, particularly on the favoured right-wing. Seems to enjoy playing against London teams, with his four goals coming against Tottenham, Arsenal, home and away, and West Ham. Missed just three games throughout and was rewarded with a call-up to Terry Venables' England get-

together in April, as well as being chosen by both QPR players and supporters as their "Player of the Year".

Queens Park R (£35,000 from Yeading on 14/6/90) F/PL 123+3/8 FLC 9+1/1 FAC 4+2/1 Others 0+2/1

Andy Impey   Neal Simpson
(Empics Sports Photo Agency)

INCE Paul Emerson Caryle
Born: Ilford, 21 October 1967
Height: 5'11" Weight: 11.7
Club Honours: CS '90, '93, '94; FAC '90, '94; ECW '91; ESC '91; FLC '92; PL '93, '94
International Honours: E: 16; B-1; U21-2; Yth

A Manchester United midfield bundle of energy, who is destructive when breaking up attacks and highly constructive on the counter-attack, Paul leads by example, and is capable of scoring spectacular goals. Had a memorable start to last season when he became the first recipient of the Bobby Moore Trophy for his outstanding performance in the 1994 FA Cup Final, a fitting tribute to a player who continues to show outstanding leadership qualities. His phenomenal workrate kept the "Reds" in contention for honours in 1994-95, and he was at his most inspiring "when the chips were down," giving a brilliant account of himself during United's short-lived European Cup campaign. The biggest testament that one can pay to Paul, is that he has helped the club to forget about Bryan Robson. Stop Press: A regular for England, along with Gary Pallister he was chosen by his fellow professionals for the PFA Divisional Award, prior to being transferred during the summer to Inter Milan in a deal worth £8 million, a move that stunned many of United's fans.

West Ham U (From apprentice on 18/7/85) FL 66+6/7 FLC 9/3 FAC 8+2/1 Others 4/1
Manchester U (£1,000,000 on 14/9/89) F/PL 203+3/24 FLC 23+1/2 FAC 26+1/1 Others 24/1

INGESSON Klas
Born: Odeshog, Sweden, 20 August 1968
Height: 6'2" Weight: 13.0
International Honours: Sweden

Joining Sheffield Wednesday in the wake of the World Cup, Klas has not really imposed himself on the English game since arriving last September. A tall, well-built central midfielder, his season was unfortunately interrupted by injury, a stomach strain also causing him to miss several games. However, with an injury free run behind him, he could yet make an impact. Is still a vital part of the Swedish international side's midfield.

Sheffield Wed (£800,000 from PSV Eindhoven on 1/9/94) PL 9+4/2 FLC 1 FAC 1

INGLETHORPE Alexander (Alex) Matthew
Born: Epsom, 14 November 1971
Height: 5'11" Weight: 11.6

On loan last season from Watford, Alex was the one that got away as far as Barnet were concerned. Signed in March, the centre-forward scored three goals in as many games, but the "Bees" could not afford to keep him and he returned to Vicarage Road, prior to moving to Leyton Orient during the summer.

Watford (From juniors on 1/7/90) FL 2+10/2 FLC 1+2 Others 1+1/1
Barnet (Loaned on 23/3/95) FL 5+1/3
Leyton Orient (Signed on 19/5/95)

INGRAM Stuart Denevan (Denny)
Born: Sunderland, 27 June 1976
Height: 5'10" Weight: 11.8

The most consistent of Hartlepool's youngsters, right-footed and primarily a midfielder, he seemed to visibly grow in confidence as the 1994-95 season progressed. Also became something of a utility player, wearing many different shirts, including those in all outfield defensive positions.

Hartlepool U (From trainee on 5/7/94) FL 48 FLC 3+1 FAC 1 Others 2

IORFA Dominic
Born: Lagos, Nigeria, 1 October 1968
Height: 6'1" Weight: 12.12
International Honours: Nigeria

Tall, gangly Southend forward whose 1994-95 season was interrupted by an injury received in August, resulting in an operation to repair ruptured knee ligaments. He made his comeback in January, but seemed unable to recapture the form that promised so much earlier. However, the blow was softened by a call-up to play for his native Nigeria.

Queens Park R (£145,000 from Royal Antwerp on 23/3/90) FL 1+7 FLC 1 (Signed for Galatasaray on 1/12/91)
Peterborough U (Free on 24/10/92) FL 27+33/9 FLC 2+1 FAC 2+2 Others 1/1
Southend U (£15,000 on 3/8/94) FL 4+4/1 FLC 2

IRELAND Simon Piers
Born: Barnstaple, 23 November 1971
Height: 5'11" Weight: 11.12
International Honours: E: Sch

Pacy right-sided wide player, who also appeared on the left-hand side for Mansfield

in a few matches last season, and who scored a vital goal against Leeds in the Coca Cola Cup. However, it was his ball-carrying abilities that often relieved pressure on the defence, which made him an important member of the side.

Huddersfield T (From juniors on 1/7/90) FL 10+9 FLC 1/1 FAC 0+1 Others 1+1
Wrexham (Loaned on 11/3/92) FL 2+3
Blackburn Rov (£200,000 on 3/11/92) PL 0+1
Mansfield T (£60,000 on 8/3/94) FL 46+3/6 FLC 5/1 FAC 4/1 Others 3

IRONS Kenneth (Kenny)
Born: Liverpool, 4 November 1970
Height: 5'10" Weight: 11.2

Tenacious and skilful midfielder who was at the heart of Tranmere's promotion challenge for much of the last campaign. Two-footed, with a powerful shot, he scored five goals from deep positions, but with a bit of luck could have doubled his tally. A strong runner with the ball, Kenny is likely to break into space to create danger for the opposition. Scored at both ends in the 4-2 victory over Portsmouth.

Tranmere Rov (From trainee on 9/11/89) FL 175+17/27 FLC 13+3/4 FAC 11+1/3 Others 28+3/3

IRONSIDE Ian
Born: Sheffield, 8 March 1964
Height: 6'2" Weight: 13.0

Confident and agile 'keeper, and an excellent shot-stopper, Ian is a former Scarborough "Player of the Year", who returned to the club from Stockport towards the end of last season. Always looked solid, as he helped his team climb off bottom rung in the Third Division, he is the son of Roy, who played for Rotherham and Barnsley (1956-1968).

Barnsley (From juniors on 17/9/82)
Scarborough (Free from North Ferriby U on 8/3/88) FL 88 FLC 2 FAC 2 Others 10
Middlesbrough (£80,000 on 15/8/91) F/PL 12+1 FLC 2
Scarborough (Loaned on 5/3/92) FL 7
Stockport Co (Signed on 23/9/93) FL 17+2 FAC 1 Others 1
Scarborough (Free on 23/3/95) FL 9

IRWIN Joseph Denis
Born: Cork, 31 October 1965
Height: 5'8" Weight: 11.0
Club Honours: CS '90, '93; ECWC '91; ESC '91; FLC '92; PL '93, '94; FAC '94
International Honours: Ei: 36; B-1; U21-3; Yth; Sch

A versatile full-back who can play on either side of Manchester United's defence, Denis is a lovely striker of the ball and a free-kick specialist. He also takes most of the right-sided corners. Once again, a model of consistency in 1994-95, he showed no sign of fatigue following a gruelling World Cup in America. The main highlights of his season came in the FA Cup, with spectacular goals against Wrexham and Crystal Palace, the latter game also establishing him as the club's new penalty king. Although his "quiet man" image makes him one of United's least high profile players, his overall contribution to the side is beyond reproach. Signed a new three year contract in April.

Leeds U (From apprentice on 3/11/83) FL 72/1 FLC 5 FAC 3 Others 2
Oldham Ath (From on 22/5/86) FL 166+1/4 FLC 19/3 FAC 13 Others 5
Manchester U (£625,000 on 20/6/90) F/PL 192+2/13 FLC 27+2 FAC 23/6 Others 21

JACKSON Christopher (Chris) Dean
Born: Barnsley, 16 January 1976
Height: 6'0" Weight: 12.0
International Honours: E: Yth; Sch

Chris had a mixed season in 1994-95. A prolific scorer from centre-forward at lower levels, he struggled to establish himself in the Barnsley first team, yet in November and December, because of injuries, he found himself getting an extended run. Overall, his play was good, but his contribution of only one goal meant that when injuries cleared he would return to the reserves.

Barnsley (From trainee on 19/1/93) FL 10+5/2 FLC 1+1 Others 0+1

JACKSON Matthew Alan
Born: Leeds, 19 October 1971
Height: 6'0" Weight: 12.12
Club Honours: FAC '95
International Honours: E: U21-10; Sch

Young Everton right-back whose first touch is excellent and who is able to work well with the midfielders to overlap and provide quality crosses. Also shows great maturity for his age when forcing attackers towards the touchline, thus holding the ball up to allow colleagues to recover. Played in the majority of Everton's games in 1994-95, only niggling ankle injuries occasionally keeping him out, and was a member of the side that won the FA Cup when beating Manchester United 1-0.

Luton T (From juniors on 4/7/90) FL 7+2 FLC 2 Others 0+1
Preston NE (Loaned on 27/3/91) FL 3+1 Others 1
Everton (£600,000 on 18/10/91) F/PL 118+6/4 FLC 8 FAC 12/2 Others 1

JACKSON Michael James
Born: Chester, 4 December 1973
Height: 5'11" Weight: 11.10
International Honours: E: Yth; Sch

Began and ended last season as Chris Lucketti's partner at the heart of the Bury defence. In between, Michael had a spell at right-back and performed well, but centre-half is his preferred position.

Crewe Alex (From trainee on 29/7/92) FL 5 FLC 1 FAC 1 Others 2
Bury (Free on 13/8/93) FL 61+2/2 FLC 4 FAC 2 Others 9

JACKSON Peter Allan
Born: Bradford, 6 April 1961
Height: 6'0" Weight: 13.6
Club Honours: Div 3 '85

Joined Chester, initially on loan from Huddersfield last October, before signing full terms. A vastly experienced central defender, who reads the game well, Peter has played on every FL ground except Molineux.

Bradford C (From apprentice on 7/4/79) FL 267+11/24 FLC 27/1 FAC 10+1 Others 4
Newcastle U (£250,000 on 23/10/86) FL 60/3 FLC 3 FAC 6 Others 3

Bradford C (£290,000 on 15/9/88) FL 55+3/5 FLC 7 FAC 4 Others 2
Huddersfield T (Free on 6/9/90) FL 152+3/3 FLC 11 FAC 13/1 Others 18/1
Chester C (Free on 29/9/94) FL 32/1 FAC 1 Others 1

JACOBS Wayne Graham
Born: Sheffield, 3 February 1969
Height: 5'9" Weight: 10.2

Had an outstanding first season at Bradford in 1994-95 as a very attack minded defender, taking many of the free-kicks and proving to be accurate with either foot.

Sheffield Wed (From apprentice on 3/1/87) FL 5+1 FLC 3 Others 1
Hull C (£27,000 on 25/3/88) FL 127+2/4 FLC 7 FAC 8 Others 6
Rotherham U (Free on 5/8/93) FL 40+2/2 FLC 4 FAC 1 Others 2
Bradford C (Free on 5/8/94) FL 38/1 FLC 4 FAC 1 Others 1

JAKUB Yanek (Joe)
Born: Falkirk, 7 December 1956
Height: 5'6" Weight: 9.6
Club Honours: Div 4 '92

An experienced and extremely popular left-back, Joe must have thought his League career was over when Chester released him at the end of 1993-94. However, after spending a short spell in non-league football with Colwyn Bay, he was recruited as a calming influence to a then young Wigan side. Stop Press: Joined the Preston Coaching staff, having been freed at the end of last season.

Burnley (From apprentice on 1/12/73) FL 42 FLC 2
Bury (£19,000 on 8/10/80) FL 262+3/27 FLC 16/4 FAC 21/2 Others 6
Chester C (Free from AZ 67 Almaar on 24/8/88) FL 42/1 FLC 4 FAC 2 Others 3
Burnley (£15,000 on 25/7/89) FL 161+2/8 FLC 9 FAC 19 Others 18/1
Chester C (Free on 13/8/93) FL 35+1 FLC 2 FAC 4 Others 4 (Free to Colwyn Bay during 1994 close season)
Wigan Ath (Free on 15/9/94) FL 16 FLC 2 FAC 2 Others 3+1

JAMES Anthony (Tony) Craig
Born: Sheffield, 27 June 1967
Height: 6'3" Weight: 13.8

Centre-half. Dominant and strong, and certainly not afraid to put a challenge in, Tony, having been released by Leicester during the summer, only played for Hereford in the early part of last season, due to a long-term back injury.

Lincoln C (£20,000 from Gainsborough Trinity on 22/8/88) FL 24+5 FLC 2 Others 0+1
Leicester C (£150,000 on 23/8/89) FL 79+28/10 FLC 6 FAC 2/1 Others 3+1
Hereford U (Free on 25/7/94) FL 18/2 FLC 4 FAC 1 Others 3/1

JAMES David Benjamin
Born: Welwyn Garden City, 1 August 1970
Height: 6'5" Weight: 14.5
Club Honours: FAYC '89; FLC '95
International Honours: E: B-1; U21-10; Yth

Still a young man, David has made Liverpool's number one jersey his own. A goalkeeper somewhat in the mould of his predecessor, Bruce Grobbelaar, he has the ability to produce saves of world class with his spectacular athleticism and his outgoing

personality makes him one of the game's true characters. One of two "Reds'" ever-presents in 1994-95, he also progressed to an England "B" cap when coming on for Kevin Pressman during the matcha gainst Eire in December.

Watford (From trainee on 1/7/88) FL 89 FLC 6 FAC 2 Others 1
Liverpool (£1,000,000 on 6/7/92) PL 84+1 FLC 9 FAC 8 Others 1

David James   Neal Simpson
(Empics Sports Photo Agency)

JAMES Julian Colin
Born: Tring, 22 March 1970
Height: 5'10" Weight: 11.10
International Honours: E: U21-2

Dependable Luton right-back, who is strong in the tackle, sound in the air and a good runner, he was an automatic choice throughout last season, missing games only through minor injuries or suspension. Prepared to go forward when necessary.

Luton T (From trainee on 1/7/88) FL 172+18/11 FLC 8+1 FAG 16+1 Others 8+1
Preston NE (Loaned on 12/9/91) FL 6

JAMES Martin Joseph
Born: Crosby, 18 May 1971
Height: 5'10" Weight: 11.7

After joining Rotherham in the 1994 close season as a left-winger, he was used as a full-back, following injuries to other players, and made such a success of his new defensive role that he stayed there for most of the season. His ability to get forward and help the attackers was particularly useful down the left-hand side and he will probably start 1995-96 at left-back.

Preston NE (From trainee on 19/7/89) FL 92+6/11 FLC 6 FAC 4 Others 8+1
Stockport Co (£50,000 on 16/3/93) FL 13+19 FLC 2 FAC 0+1 Others 0+2
Rotherham U (£50,000 on 3/8/94) FL 40 FLC 2 FAC 3 Others 3

JEFFERS John Joseph
Born: Liverpool, 5 October 1968
Height: 5'10" Weight: 10.10
International Honours: E: Sch

Jinking Port Vale left-winger who missed the majority of last season through injury and the arrival of Steve Guppy. The possessor of an excellent left-foot, John scored his one goal at Tranmere, a ground just yards from where he was living at the time. Had a spell on loan at Shrewsbury, but brought it to an end himself, hoping to prove

that he still has a future in the First Division.
Liverpool (From apprentice on 13/10/86)
Port Vale (£30,000 on 11/12/88) FL 147+33/10
FLC 8+1 FAC 13+2 Others 13+2/1
Shrewsbury T (Loaned on 6/1/95) FL 3/1 Others 2

JEFFREY Andrew (Andy) Samuel
Born: Bellshill, 15 January 1972
Height: 5'10" Weight: 12.7
After an impressive first season at Cambridge, Andy spent much of 1994-95 sidelined by a knee injury. Equally at home at right-back or in the sweeper role, he also has an eye for goal.
Leicester C (From trainee on 13/2/90)
Cambridge U (£8,500 from Cambridge C on 9/7/93) FL 72+6/2 FLC 4 FAC 5 Others 4

JEFFREY Michael (Mike) Richard
Born: Liverpool, 11 August 1971
Height: 5'11" Weight: 11.6
Can play in midfield or attack, but had very few opportunities for the Newcastle first team last season. Started at Maine Road against Manchester City in the Coca Cola Cup, where he marked the occasion by scoring with a left-foot volley in the 1-1 draw and also came on as a substitute in the away UEFA Cup-ties against Royal Antwerp and Athletic Bilbao.
Bolton W (From trainee on 9/2/89) FL 9+6 FLC 1+2 FAC 1 Others 2+1
Doncaster Rov (£20,000 on 5/3/92) FL 48+1/19 FLC 4 Others 2/1
Newcastle U (£60,000 on 4/10/93) PL 2 FLC 1/1 Others 0+2

JEMSON Nigel Bradley
Born: Hutton, 10 August 1969
Height: 5'10" Weight: 12.10
Club Honours: FLC '90
International Honours: E: U21-1
A striker with good first touch and a creator of opportunities around the box, Nigel, signed from Sheffield Wednesday last September, made very few appearances for his new club, Notts County, and was loaned out to Watford early in the New Year. Following that, he went on loan to Coventry in March with a view to a permanent transfer, but has yet to make the first team.
Preston NE (From trainee on 6/7/87) FL 28+4/8 FAC 2/1 Others 5+1/5
Nottingham F (£150,000 on 24/3/88) FL 45+2/13 FLC 9/4 FAC 3+1/3 Others 1
Bolton W Loaned on 23/12/88) FL 4+1
Preston NE (Loaned on 15/3/89) FL 6+3/2 Others 2/1
Sheffield Wed (£800,000 on 17/9/91) F/PL 26+25/9 FLC 3+4 FAC 3+3/1 Others 2+2/1
Grimsby T (Loaned on 10/9/93) FL 6/2 Others 1
Notts Co (£300,000 on 8/9/94) FL 5+6/1 FLC 1+1/1 Others 1
Watford (Loaned on 12/1/95) FL 3+1

JENKINS Iain
Born: Whiston, 24 November 1972
Height: 5'9" Weight: 11.10
Iain can play anywhere in defence, although his best position is undoubtedly at right-back, where he started most of last season's games for Chester. Is a skilful defender who also likes to join the attack.
Everton (From trainee on 4/6/91) PL 3+2 FLC 0+1
Bradford C (Loaned on 31/12/92) FL 6 Others 1

Chester C (Free on 13/8/93) FL 70+4 FLC 2+2 FAC 6 Others 7

JENKINS Stephen (Steve) Robert
Born: Merthyr, 16 July 1972
Height: 5'10" Weight: 10.9
Club Honours: AMC '94
International Honours: W: U21-2; Yth
One of the unsung heroes of the Swansea defence, churning out steady performances week in and week out, and a strong tackler, not many wingers go past him in wide positions. A former midfield player, originally given a free transfer by former manager, Terry Yorath, in 1991, Stephen has become a regular feature at full-back for the club over the last four seasons.
Swansea C (From trainee on 1/7/90) FL 140+10/1 FLC 10+1 FAC 10+1 Others 25

JENKINSON Leigh
Born: Thorne, 9 July 1969
Height: 6'0" Weight: 12.2
Left-sided Coventry midfielder, with a clever "step-over" trick, he has failed to set the world alight in his two years at the club. Got a chance at the start of last season due to injury to Peter Ndlovu and some excellent performances for the reserves. Had a run of eight games after the turn of the year, during which he scored a spectacular goal at Norwich, before suffering a hamstring injury against Chelsea.
Hull C (From trainee on 15/6/87) FL 95+35/13 FLC 7+2 FAC 6+1 Others 9+2/1
Rotherham U (Loaned on 13/9/90) FL 5+2
Coventry C (£300,000 on 12/3/93) PL 22+10/1 FLC 0+1 FAC 3
Birmingham C (Loaned on 1/11/93) FL 2+1

JENSEN John
Born: Copenhagen, Denmark, 3 May 1965
Height: 5'11" Weight: 12.4
Club Honours: FAC '93; ECWC '94
International Honours: Denmark (EC '92)
A strong and willing worker in Arsenal's midfield and one who enjoys the tackling side of the game, John finally scored that elusive first goal for the club during 1994-95, his third season at Highbury, against QPR. Fortunately recovered from the leg injury sustained while playing for Denmark v Hungary, which prevented his appearing for the "Gunners" against Palma in his native Copenhagen the previous term. Keeps his passing simple.
Arsenal (£1,100,000 from Brondby on 1/8/92) PL 80+3/1 FLC 9+1 FAC 6+1 Others 15

JEPSON Ronald (Ronnie) Francis
Born: Stoke, 12 May 1963
Height: 6'1" Weight: 13.2
A bargain buy from Exeter in 1993-94, "Rocket" Ron not only formed a deadly Huddersfield scoring partnership with Andy Booth last season, but his phenomenal work-rate and value to the team was immense. This was reflected when he was voted by both the players and supporters as their "Player of the Year", and received more match awards than anyone else at the club. Vital to Town's newly acquired First Division status, he wins the ball, holds up play, and passes with panache.

Port Vale (Free from Nantwich T on 23/3/89) FL 12+10 FLC 1+1 FAC 1+1
Peterborough U (Loaned on 25/1/90) FL 18/5
Preston NE (£80,000 on 12/2/91) FL 36+2/8 FLC 2 Others 3/4
Exeter C (£60,000 on 29/7/92) FL 51+3/21 FLC 6/2 FAC 3/1 Others 4/1
Huddersfield T (£80,000 on 7/12/93) FL 55+9/24 FLC 3+1/2 FAC 2/1 Others 6/1

Ronnie Jepson   Matthew Ashton
(Empics Sports Photo Agency)

JEWELL Paul
Born: Liverpool, 28 September 1964
Height: 5'8" Weight: 11.10
Carrying the obvious sobriquet of "Jimmy", Paul started last season off with a bang at Bradford, scoring ten goals in nine games, including two hat-tricks away from home. Can play either in midfield or up front.
Liverpool (From apprentice on 30/9/82)
Wigan Ath (£15,000 on 20/12/84) FL 117+20/35 FLC 5+2 FAC 9/5 Others 14+4/7
Bradford C (£80,000 on 21/7/88) FL 210+41/53 FLC 16+1/6 FAC 11+1/3 Others 8+1/1

Julian Joachim   Paul Marriott
(Empics Sports Photo Agency)

JOACHIM Julian Kevin
Born: Peterborough, 20 September 1974
Height: 5'6" Weight: 11.10
International Honours: E: U21-7; Yth
(UEFAC '93)

Right footed. Normally used on Leicester's right of midfield, or as a striker, he is an outstanding young talent yet to fully blossom. Added to his international reputation early last season, when notching the club's first Premiership goal in home defeat by Newcastle and starred with a brace in the home victory against Tottenham. Suffered a broken foot during training in the autumn, which was not diagnosed at first and was sidelined in December, but came back for the remaining two fixtures of the campaign.
Leicester C (From trainee on 15/9/92) F/PL 63+14/24 FLC 5+1/2 FAC 3/1 Others 4+2/2

JOBLING Kevin Andrew
Born: Sunderland, 1 January 1968
Height: 5'8" Weight: 12.0

Utility player, primarily right-footed. Although probably at his most effective in midfield, he appeared last season for Grimsby in defence, mainly at left-back. Made an impressive comeback, having spent over a year on the transfer list after struggling to hold his place, Paul is a strong tackler and useful distributor of the ball.
Leicester C (From apprentice on 9/1/86) FL 4+5 FAC 0+1 Others 3/2
Grimsby T (Signed on 19/2/88) FL 207+17/9 FLC 12+1 FAC 4+3/1 Others 5+4
Scunthorpe U (Loaned on 10/1/94) Others 1

JOBSON Richard Ian
Born: Holderness, 9 May 1963
Height: 6'1" Weight: 13.5
Club Honours: Div 2 '91
International Honours: E: B-1

Stalwart of the Oldham defence and a player Graham Taylor once described as being the most comfortable defender on the ball in the English game. Strong in the air, quick on the floor, and a joy to watch, Richard suffered a strange ankle injury last November and was out of the game for six months. Fit again now, what seemed fairly innocuous at first turned out to be a massive problem requiring two operations. Still good enough to win that elusive first England cap.
Watford (£22,000 from Burton A on 5/11/82) FL 26+2/4 FLC 2 FAC 0+1 Others 5+1
Hull C (£40,000 on 7/2/85) FL 219+2/17 FLC 12 FAC 13/1 Others 9
Oldham Ath (£460,000 on 30/8/90) F/PL 176+1/10 FLC 17/1 FAC 13 Others 2

JOHNROSE Leonard (Lenny)
Born: Preston, 29 November 1969
Height: 5'10" Weight: 12.0

A Bury midfielder who did not really establish himself last season, despite giving many encouraging performances, Lennie scored some useful goals, but made only one appearance after January.
Blackburn Rov (From trainee on 16/6/88) FL 20+22/11 FLC 2+1/1 FAC 0+3 Others 2
Preston NE (Loaned on 21/1/92) FL 1+2/1
Hartlepool U (Signed on 28/2/92) FL 59+7/11 FLC 5+1/4 FAC 5/1 Others 5
Bury (Signed on 7/12/93) FL 34+6/4 FLC 1+1 FAC 5/1 Others 5

JOHNSEN Erland
Born: Fredrikstad, Norway, 5 April 1967
Height: 6'1" Weight: 13.5
International Honours: Norway

Very consistent Chelsea centre-back who was greatly missed when occasionally unavailable last season. Having struck up an excellent partnership with another Scandinavian, Jacob Kjeldberg, at the heart of the defence, Erland had to play with a number of different men due to the latter's injury problems. Useful in the air and a confident passer out of defence, he was the club's joint "Player of the Year", along with Nigel Spackman, for 1994-95.
Chelsea (£306,000 from Bayern Munich on 6/12/89) F/PL 103+2/1 FLC 4 FAC 14 Others 9

JOHNSON Alan Keith
Born: Wigan, 19 February 1971
Height: 6'0" Weight: 12.0

A defender who featured as a left-sided midfield player and left-back for Lincoln during last season, he suffered a knee injury in February which required an operation and caused a lengthy lay-off.
Wigan Ath (From trainee on 1/4/89) FL 163+17/13 FLC 7+2/2 FAC 14+2/1 Others 14+3/3
Lincoln C (Signed on 15/2/94) FL 40+1 FLC 2 FAC 3 Others 2+1/1

JOHNSON Andrew James
Born: Bristol, 2 May 1974
Height: 6'0" Weight: 11.6
International Honours: E: Yth

A very quick defender, who can also play in midfield, Andy, along with Norwich, had a topsy-turvy time of it in 1994-95. Starting in eight games, he nearly scored after losing a boot in a challenge with Arsenal's Steve Bould on April Fools Day, having been sent off a few weeks earlier by a substitute referee for a foul he did not commit. That apart, his patience was sorely tested by a series of injuries, including a broken knee cap, which disrupted his season. Can only hope for better luck in 1995-96.
Norwich C (From trainee on 4/3/92) F/PL 9+4/1 FLC 2 FAC 1

JOHNSON David Alan
Born: Dinnington, 29 October 1970
Height: 6'2" Weight: 13.8

A skilful wide right-sided striker, who netted the winner for Lincoln against Crystal Palace in the first leg of the Coca Cola Cup-tie, he was later placed on the transfer list and missed last season's final matches after suffering a hamstring injury against Preston.
Sheffield Wed (From trainee on 1/7/89) FL 5+1
Hartlepool U (Loaned on 31/10/91) FL 7/2 FAC 2/1
Hartlepool U (Loaned on 20/11/92) FL 3 Others 2/1
Lincoln C (Signed on 20/8/93) FL 61+4/12 FLC 5+1/4 FAC 4/2 Others 7/2

JOHNSON Gavin
Born: Eye, 10 October 1970
Height: 5'11" Weight: 11.7
Club Honours: Div 2 '92

Flexible Ipswich player who can play anywhere down the left-flank - full-back and wide midfield - and has even turned out in central defence. Always comfortable when defending, although he has scored some

important, and spectacular, goals from midfield. Not a regular in 1994-95, he was released at the end of the season.
Ipswich T (From trainee on 1/3/89) F/PL 114+18/11 FLC 10+1/2 FAC 12/2 Others 3+1/1

JOHNSON Ian
Born: Sunderland, 1 September 1975
Height: 5'10" Weight: 11.8

A young forward with limited experience at Middlesbrough, he joined Bradford on non-contract terms towards the end of last season and played in two matches before being released.
Middlesbrough (From trainee on 14/1/94) FL 1+1 Others 0+1
Bradford C (Free on 30/1/95) FL 1+1

JOHNSON Marvin Anthony
Born: Wembley, 29 October 1968
Height: 5'11" Weight: 12.3

Primarily a central defender, but also able to operate as a left-back or in midfield, Marvin enjoyed his best ever season and was voted Luton's "Player of the Year" by his team-mates. Always enthusiastic, with a style the fans like, he has now become a more dependable performer and was ever-present during 1994-95.
Luton T (From apprentice on 12/11/86) FL 155+12/5 FLC 8+2 FAC 8+1 Others 8

JOHNSON Michael Owen
Born: Nottingham, 4 July 1973
Height: 5'11" Weight: 11.0
Club Honours: AIC '95

A Notts County central defender who played the odd game at left-back for the club last season, Michael is very pacy and quick off the mark. Very experienced for a 22-year-old, having close on 150 first team appearances under his belt and, with two good feet, his future seems assured.
Notts Co (From trainee on 9/7/91) FL 102+5 FLC 9 FAC 4 Others 15+1

JOHNSON Richard Mark
Born: Newcastle, Australia, 27 April 1974
Height: 5'10" Weight: 12.0

An aggressive, ball-winning Watford central midfielder, with a powerful shot, as "Wolves", among others, found out in 1994-95, as yet, he has not managed to hold down a regular place in the side.
Watford (From trainee on 11/5/92) FL 50+15/3 FLC 4+1 FAC 2 Others 0+1

JOHNSON Thomas (Tommy)
Born: Newcastle on Tyne, 15 January 1971
Height: 5'10" Weight: 11.2
International Honours: E: U21-7

Part of the deal that brought Gary Charles from Derby to Aston Villa last January, the young striker was quickly given his first taste of Premiership football. Prior to the move, he had scored seven goals in 14 FL games for County in 1994-95 but, in a Villa side that had begun to struggle, he found that kind of strike-rate too difficult to achieve. Renowned for jumping on half-chances in the area, a hat-trick against Wimbledon was his high spot, whilst a hamstring injury picked up in March, saw him struggling for fitness for the rest of the campaign.

Notts Co (From trainee on 19/1/89) FL 100+18/47 FLC 7+2/5 FAC 3+2/1 Others 14+3/4
Derby Co (£1,3000,000 on 12/3/92) FL 91+7/30 FLC 9+1/2 FAC 5/1 Others 16/8
Aston Villa (Signed on 6/1/95) PL 11+3/4 FAC 0+1

Tommy Johnson   Tony Marshall
(Empics Sports Photo Agency)

JONES Barry

Born: Prescot, 20 June 1970
Height: 5'11" Weight: 11.3
Club Honours: WC '95

Improving all the time with his consistent displays for Wrexham at right-back and in central defence, his distribution is now much better since his arrival from Liverpool. Latterly has been played in the centre of defence alongside Barry Hunter and, when pushed, admits he prefers this position. It has not gone unnoticed that the defence has a better balance about it following the switch, which could well become permanent in 1995-96.
Liverpool (Signed from Prescot T on 19/1/89) Others 0+1
Wrexham (Free on 10/7/92) FL 119/4 FLC 10/1 FAC 5 Others 16

JONES Cobi N'Gai

Born: Detroit, USA, 16 June 1970
Height: 5'7" Weight: 10.5
International Honours: USA

Small, skilful right-winger, who made a name for himself in the 1994 World Cup with the USA. After work permit difficulties he was given his Coventry debut at home to Leeds and made an instant impact, winning a penalty. Fast and direct, but a little lightweight, he scored the winner at home to Norwich and again at Palace in Phil Neal's final match in charge. Freed during the summer.
Coventry C (£300,000 from USSF on 8/9/94) PL 16+5/2 FLC 2+1 FAC 0+1

JONES Gary

Born: Huddersfield, 6 April 1969
Height: 6'1" Weight: 12.9

1994-95 saw Gary being told to "pack his bags" by Southend manager, Peter Taylor, before new manager, Steve Thompson, managed to find the form he had always promised. With seven goals in ten games from his central striking position, Gary's more supportive role was appreciated by the fans, as he helped lift the club out of the relegation area. Good at holding up the ball and bringing the midfield into attacks.
Doncaster Rov (Free from Rossington Main Colliery on 26/1/89) FL 10+10/2 FLC 1 (£8,500 to Grantham on 1/11/89)
Southend U (£25,000 from Boston U, via Kettering T, on 3/6/93) FL 33+14/14 FLC 1 FAC 1 Others 4+1/2
Lincoln C (Loaned on 17/9/93) FL 0+4/2 Others 0+1

JONES Gary Steven

Born: Chester, 10 May 1975
Height: 6'3" Weight: 13.5

A young giant who is equally at home at either centre-forward or centre-half, Gary has made his reputation for Tranmere up-front, deputising for the injured John Aldridge with a clutch of important goals. Deceptively faster than one would expect for his height and weight, he has good touch and shows signs of developing into a top-class striker. Scored 16 times for the first team and reserves during 1994-95.
Tranmere Rov (From trainee on 5/7/93) FL 8+17/5 FLC 0+1 FAC 1+1 Others 1+1

JONES Graeme Anthony

Born: Gateshead, 13 March 1970
Height: 6'0" Weight: 12.12

Excellent striker who ended last season as Doncaster's leading League goalscorer, despite missing many games through injury. Also scored in every other competition that Rovers played in during 1994-95, plus having the honour of being the first player in the country to register a goal in the Coca Cola Cup.
Doncaster Rov (£10,000 from Bridlington T on 2/8/93) FL 49+11/16 FLC 2+1/1 FAC 1+1/1 Others 3/1

JONES Keith Aubrey

Born: Dulwich, 14 October 1965
Height: 5'9" Weight: 10.11
International Honours: E: Yth; Sch

A competitive midfield player signed from Southend last September, Keith immediately came into the Charlton side, where he put in some solid performances and played exceptionally well in the televised game at The Hawthorns, being voted "Man of the Match". Predominantly right-footed, he tackles strongly and distributes the ball well, often joining the attacks. Captained the team on several occasions near the end of the season.
Chelsea (From apprentice on·16/8/83) FL 43+9/7 FLC 9+2/3 FAC 1 Others 4+1
Brentford (£40,000 on 3/9/87) FL 167+2/13 FLC 15/2 FAC 13/4 Others 16/1
Southend U (£175,000 on 21/10/91) FL 88+2/11 FLC 4 FAC 5 Others 9/1
Colchester U (Loaned on 8/10/93) FL 4 Others 1
Charlton Ath (£150,000 on 16/9/94) FL 31/1

JONES Lee

Born: Pontypridd, 9 August 1970
Height: 6'3" Weight: 14.4
Club Honours: AMC '94

A former Swansea youth player, and a giant of a goalkeeper, he rejoined the club from Welsh League club, AFC Porth, prior to the 1994 transfer deadline. Waited patiently in the wings last season as the regular substitute, making just two FL appearances, plus one in the Auto Windscreens Shield at Torquay.
Swansea C (£7,500 from AFC Porth on 24/3/94) FL 2 Others 1

JONES Philip Lee

Born: Wrexham, 29 May 1973
Height: 5'9" Weight: 10.5
International Honours: W: U21-12

A Liverpool striker who was bought ostensibly with an eye to the future in 1992, Lee finally made his club debut in 1994-95 with two subs' appearances. Scoring prolifically for the reserves last season, where he continues to learn his craft, his speed and first touch are his main attributes.
Wrexham (From trainee on 5/7/91) FL 24+15/10 FLC 2 FAC 1+2/1 Others 4+1/2
Liverpool (£300,000 on 12/3/92) PL 0+1 FLC 0+1
Crewe Alex Loaned on 3/9/93) FL 4+4/1

JONES Paul Steven

Born: Chirk, 18 April 1967
Height: 6'3" Weight: 13.10

Goalkeeper. Paul was Mike Stowell's patient deputy at Wolverhampton, being restricted to the AIC last season until Boxing Day, when he conceded four at Oldham. He settled down though, making a late penalty save to keep "Wolves" in the FA Cup at Sheffield, then stopped a couple more during the shoot-out in the replay and saved another against Middlesbrough.
Wolverhampton W (£40,000 from Kidderminster Harriers on 23/7/91) FL 25 FAC 5 Others 4

JONES Robert (Rob) Marc

Born: Wrexham, 5 November 1971
Height: 5'11" Weight: 11.0
Club Honours: FAC '92; FLC '95
International Honours: W: Sch. E: 8; U21-2; Yth

Rob had another season for both Liverpool and England in 1994-95, which has added to his growing reputation as an unspectacular, but extremely accomplished, right-back. Lethal in defence with his uncompromising tackling, he raids in much the same way as Phil Neal or Chris Lawler, in getting down the flank and setting up goals with powerful crosses. A solid performer who continues to learn his craft, he will surely become one of the all-time Liverpool greats. Elected by his fellow professionals to the PFA Award winning Premiership side.
Crewe Alex (From trainee on 20/12/88) FL 59+16/2 FLC 9 FAC 0+3 Others 3
Liverpool (£300,000 on 4/10/91) F/PL 127 FLC 15+1 FAC 20 Others 3

JONES Ryan Anthony

Born: Sheffield, 23 July 1973
Height: 6'1" Weight: 13.10
International Honours: W: 1; B-1; U21-4

Left-sided Sheffield Wednesday midfielder, who is strong in the tackle and possesses a great shot, Ryan had a disappointing time of it in 1994-95. Never really free from injury until the final month of the season, he found it difficult to build on his excellent form of 1993-94, which also saw him capped for Wales. Still a Welsh U21 regular, though, despite all his problems.

Sheffield Wed (From trainee on 18/6/91) PL 36+5/6 FLC 5+1 FAC 3/1

JONES Stephen (Steve) Gary
Born: Cambridge, 17 March 1970
Height: 6'0" Weight: 12.12

Signed from West Ham last October, Steve made his debut against Bradford and became Bournemouth's top-scorer in the 1994-95 season with nine goals. Strong and quick, with a penchant to run at defenders, his performances made him a favourite with the fans.

West Ham U (£22,000 from Billericay T on 16/11/92) PL 8+8/4 FAC 2+2/1 Others 1+1
Bournemouth (£150,000 on 21/10/94) FL 27+3/8 FAC 1/1 Others 1

JONES Steven
Born: Stockton, 31 January 1974
Height: 5'11" Weight: 12.2

Goalkeeper who spent almost all last season on the Hartlepool substitutes' bench and, with there being no reserve team, played few competitive games. However, he did become "Pool's" first ever substitute 'keeper to appear in a League game.

Hartlepool U (From trainee on 7/5/92) FL 38+1 FLC 1

JONES Thomas (Tommy)
Born: Aldershot, 7 October 1964
Height: 5'10" Weight: 11.7
Club Honours: Div 2 '94
International Honours: E: SP-1

Versatile player who can appear at full-back as well as in midfield, his progress at Reading has been disrupted by a series of injuries, including two broken legs. However, he enjoyed a long spell of first team action last season, proving to be an effective marker as well as an accurate distributor of the ball.

Aberdeen (£30,000 from Weymouth in 1987-88) SL 14+14/3 FAC 1+2
Swindon T (Signed on 27/9/88) FL 162+6/12 FLC 14+4 FAC 10 Others 11
Reading (£125,000 on 9/7/92) FL 50+8/2 FLC 3 FAC 3 Others 1

JONES Vincent (Vinny) Peter
Born: Watford, 5 January 1965
Height: 6'0" Weight: 11.12
Club Honours: FAC '88 DIV 2 '90
International Honours: W:

Tough-tackling central midfielder, who enjoyed a good season with Wimbledon in 1994-95, Vinny began to show some nice touches to go with his aggressive no-nonsense play. Leading by example, having been given the captain's armband early on in the campaign, he gained international recognition with Wales through his Grand-parentage and never let anyone down. Certainly added steel to the Welsh side, performing with both pride and passion, and had an excellent game against Germany.

Wimbledon (£10,000 from Weakstone on 20/11/86) FL 7/9 FLC 6+2 FAC 11+2/1 Others 3
Leeds U (£650,000 on 20/6/89) FL 44+2/5 FLC 2 FAC 1 Others 4
Sheffield U (£700,000 on 13/9/90) FL 35/2 FLC 4 FAC 1 Others 1
Chelsea (£575,000 on 30/8/91) F/PL 42/4 FLC 1 FAC 4/1 Others 5/2
Wimbledon (£700,000 on 10/9/92) F/PL 93/6 FLC 11/2 FAC 8

Vinnie Jones Barry Coombs
(Empics Sports Photo Agency)

JORDAN Scott Douglas
Born: Newcastle, 19 July 1975
Height: 5'10" Weight: 11.2
International Honours: E: Sch

A midfielder who shows quiet authority and whose chief assets are his composure and passing ability, he established himself in the York side during 1994-95, having played just one full game previously.

York C (From trainee on 21/10/92) FL 33+5/3 FAC 1 Others 1+1

JOSEPH Matthew (Matt) Nathan Adolphus
Born: Bethnal Green, 30 September 1972
Height: 5'7" Weight: 10.7

A former graduate of the Lilleshall School, Matt is a versatile right-footed Cambridge player who can perform in midfield, or at full-back, and can also get forward and score.

Arsenal (From trainee on 17/11/90)
Gillingham (Free on 7/12/92)
Cambridge U (Signed on 19/11/93) FL 66/4 FLC 2 FAC 4 Others 3

JOSEPH Roger Anthony
Born: Paddington, 24 December 1965
Height: 5'11" Weight: 11.10
International Honours: E: B-2

Wimbledon right-back with terrific pace and good at striking long balls in behind opposing full-backs, Roger found it difficult to establish himself last season, first with injuries, and then with heavy defensive competition barring his way. Having started only two matches prior to Christmas, he was loaned out to Millwall in March.

Rob Jones Neal Simpson
(Empics Sports Photo Agency)

Brentford (Free from Southall on 4/10/84) FL 103+1/2 FLC 7 FAC 1 Others 8
Wimbledon (£150,000 on 25/8/88) F/PL 155+7 FLC 17+2 FAC 11+1 Others 6
Millwall (Loaned on 2/3/95) FL 5

JOYCE Joseph (Joe) Patrick
Born: Consett, 18 March 1961
Height: 5'10" Weight: 11.6
Club Honours: Div 3 '95
Now occupying the role of player-coach at Carlisle, he still featured in half the club's League fixtures in 1994-95 and ended the season with a Third Division Championship medal. A solid and experienced defender, a facial injury at Barnet kept him out of the side for several weeks afterwards. He can play either at full-back or as a central defender.
Barnsley (From juniors on 14/11/79) FL 332+2/4 FLC 26+1/1 FAC 24/1 Others 3
Scunthorpe U (Free on 20/2/91) FL 91/2 FLC 5 Others 11
Carlisle U (Free on 5/8/93) FL 45+5 FLC 4+1 FAC 4+1 Others 9/1
Darlington (Loaned on 23/9/93) FL 4

JOYCE Warren Garton
Born: Oldham, 20 January 1965
Height: 5'9" Weight: 11.11
After the first half-dozen games of 1994-95, there was no place for the busy Warren in Burnley's midfield and he enjoyed the best of the season on loan at Hull, where he was the ideal replacement for the injured skipper, Greg Abbott.
Bolton W (From juniors on 23/6/82) FL 180+4/17 FLC 14+1/1 FAC 11/1 Others 11/2
Preston NR (£35,000 on 16/10/87) FL 170+7/34 FLC 8/2 FAC 6/1 Others 19/7
Plymouth Arg (£160,000 on 19/5/92) FL 28+2/3 FLC 6/1 FAC 2 Others 2
Burnley (£140,000 on 7/7/93) FL 23+4/4 FLC 4/1 FAC 4/1 Others 5/1
Hull C (Loaned on 20/1/95) FL 9/3

JULES Mark Anthony
Born: Bradford, 5 September 1971
Height: 5'10" Weight: 11.1
Mark struggled to maintain a role in Chesterfield's march to Wembley last season. A left-winger of no mean skill and ability, he found attacking opportunities few and far between, with John Duncan favouring a more direct style, and his games came mainly in an overlapping, left-back role.
Bradford C (From trainee on 3/7/90) FLC 0+1
Scarborough (Free on 14/8/91) FL 57+20/16 FLC 6+2/2 FAC 1+1 Others 6/4
Chesterfield (£40,000 on 21/5/93) FL 38+18/1 FLC 5+2/2 FAC 1+2 Others 4

JUPP Duncan Alan
Born: Haslemere, 25 January 1975
Height: 6'0" Weight: 12.0
International Honours: S: U21-8
Awarded another Scottish U21 cap in 1995, the young full-back is the one locally produced player of real quality to emerge at Fulham in recent years. Well built, fast, and a good reader of the game, his confidence is growing as he gains experience, although he needs to curb some of the more physical aspects of his play. At the end of last season,

he was elected by his fellow professionals to the PFA Third Division Award winning team.
Fulham (From trainee on 12/7/93) FL 66+3/2 FLC 7+1 FAC 4+1 Others 7+1

JURYEFF Ian Martin
Born: Gosport, 24 November 1962
Height: 5'11" Weight: 12.0
A Scunthorpe regular in first half of last season, but lost his place and moved to Farnborough Town. Playing up-front, he was adept at shielding the ball before laying it off and always had an eye for goal.
Southampton (From apprentice on 28/11/80) FL 0+2
Mansfield T (Loaned on 22/3/84) FL 12/5
Reading (Loaned on 12/11/84) FL 7/1 FAC 3/2
Leyton Orient (£5,000 on 15/2/85) FL 106+5/44 FLC 9/3 FAC 10/7 Others 9+1/6
Ipswich T (Loaned on 9/2/89) FL 0+2
Halifax T (£40,000 on 10/8/89) FL 15+2/7 FLC 3 FAC 2 Others 1/1
Hereford U (£50,000 on 14/12/89) FL 25+3/4 FLC 2
Halifax T (£50,000 on 14/9/90) FL 72/13 FLC 3/1 FAC 5/2 Others 4
Darlington (Free on 27/8/92) FL 26+8/6 FLC 1/1 FAC 1 Others 1
Scunthorpe U (Signed on 20/8/93) FL 41+3/13 FLC 2 FAC 5 Others 3

KAMARA Abdul Salam
Born: Southampton, 10 February 1974
Height: 5'9" Weight: 11.0
Released by Bristol City during the 1994 close season, this stocky inside-forward spent two months with Gillingham on trial before leaving in December. His only first team game was at Brentford in the AWS when, unable to get into the flow of things, he was replaced at half-time.
Bristol C (Signed on 2/3/93) FL 0+1
Gillingham (Free on 7/11/94) Others 1

KAMARA Christopher (Chris)
Born: Middlesbrough, 25 December 1957
Height: 6'1" Weight: 12.0
Club Honours: Div 4 '86, Div 2 '90
Out for three months with a broken toe, Chris is a vastly experienced midfielder who came to Bradford immediately prior to last season. He proved a leader who belied his 37 years and never stopped running. Also played at centre-half and is currently on non-contract terms.
Portsmouth (From apprentice on 1/1/76) FL 56+7/7 FLC 7/1 FAC 4/1
Swindon T (£20,000 on 10/8/77) FL 133+14/21 FLC 18+4/1 FAC 14/4
Portsmouth (£50,000 on 25/5/81) FL 11 FLC 3/1
Brentford (Signed on 28/10/81) FL 150+2/28 FLC 15/1 FAC 13/2 Others 7/1
Swindon T (£14,500 on 21/8/85) FL 86+1/6 FLC 9 FAC 5 Others 12+1
Stoke C (£27,500 on 4/7/88) FL 60/5 FLC 4/1 FAC 4 Others 3/1
Leeds U (150,000 on 29/1/90) FL 15+5/1 FLC 1+2 Others 1
Luton T (£150,000 on 1/11/91) FL 49 FLC 2 FAC 1 Others 2
Sheffield U (Loaned on 13/12/92) PL 6+2
Middlesbrough (Loaned on 19/2/93) PL 3+2
Sheffield U (Free on 26/6/93) PL 15+1 FAC 1
Bradford C (Free on 25/7/94) FL 22+1/3 FLC 3 FAC 2 Others 2/1

KANCHELSKIS Andrei
Born: Kirovograd, USSR, 23 January 1969
Height: 5'10" Weight: 12.4
Club Honours: ESC '91; FLC '92 PL '93, '94; CS '93, '94; FAC '94
International Honours: USSR
A very direct right-winger, Andrei uses his explosive pace to go past defenders to create good scoring opportunities for both him and his team-mates. Made a tremendous start to last season for Manchester United, scoring 12 goals, which included a memorable hat-trick against Manchester City at Old Trafford. But when a stomach strain laid him low, he found it difficult to regain his first-team place and his frustration led to a much publicised transfer request. Eventually, Andrei underwent surgery for his troublesome hernia, which effectively brought his season to an end. On his day, the talented Ukraine man has few rivals in the Premiership, and it would be a bitter blow if United were to lose a player of his standing.
Manchester U (£650,000 from Shakhtyor Donetsk on 26/3/91) F/PL 96+27/28 FLC 15+1/3 FAC 11+1/4 Others 10/1

KAVANAGH Graham Anthony
Born: Dublin, 3 December 1973
Height: 5'10" Weight: 12.11
International Honours: Ei: U21-8; Yth
Strong and fearless young Middlesbrough midfielder who displays superb ball control and passes with great accuracy, Graham has good positional sense and off the ball intelligence. 1994-95 was his best season since joining the club.
Middlesbrough (Signed from Home Farm on 16/8/91) F/PL 16+12/2 FLC 1 FAC 3+1/1 Others 7
Darlington (Loaned on 25/2/94) FL 5

KAVANAGH Jason Colin
Born: Meriden, 23 November 1971
Height: 5'9" Weight: 11.0
International Honours: E: Yth; Sch
An early student at the FA School of Excellence at the age of 16, Jason is a combative Derby right-back who can, when required, play alongside the centre-half. Made his 100th club appearance at Tranmere, but could only get a regular place in the second half of last season.
Derby Co (From trainee on 9/12/88) FL 66+24/1 FLC 2+2 FAC 6 Others 8+8

KEANE Roy Maurice
Born: Cork, 10 August 1971
Height: 5'10" Weight: 11.3
Club Honours: FMC '92; CS '93; PL '94; FAC '94
International Honours: Ei: 28; U21-4; Yth
Manchester United and Republic of Ireland midfield player, with plenty of stamina, who comes from deep positions to score vital goals, and a fierce competitor and excellent passer, Roy is always prepared to play his way out of trouble. Showed little sign of fatigue following a gruelling 1994 World Cup campaign in America and even put off an urgent hernia operation for the sake of United's cause. Although he played in a variety of roles in 1994-95, notably at right-back and in central defence, he eventually

Roy Keane

Neal Simpson
(Empics Sports Photo Agency)

settled in his more favoured role in central midfield. His commitment to United's cause remained as fearsome as ever and very few opponents got the better of him. A serious injury against Crystal Palace in the FA Cup semi-final replay appeared to have ended his season, but he made a remarkable recovery to play an important role in United's late attempt to claim the Premiership and FA Cup double.

Nottingham F (£10,000 from Cobh Ramblers on 12/6/90) F/PL 114/22 FLC 17/6 FAC 18/3 Others 5/2
Manchester U (£3,750,000 on 22/7/93) PL 57+5/7 FLC 7+1 FAC 12+1/1 Others 8/3

KEARTON Jason Brett
Born: Ipswich, Australia, 9 July 1969
Height: 6'1" Weight: 11.10
Club Honours: FAC '95

Noted for his command of the Everton 18 yard box, along with having a good pair of hands, shot-stopping, especially in one-to-one situations, is another major strength. Unlucky to be understudy to such a great goalkeeper as Neville Southall, this meant that Jason made just one appearance in 1994-95 but, as an unused sub in the sides' FA Cup Final win over Manchester United, he was entitled to a cup winners medal.

Everton (Free from Brisbane Lions on 31/10/88) PL 3+3 FLC 1 FAC 1
Stoke C (Loaned on 13/8/91) FL 16 Others 1
Blackpool (Loaned on 9/1/92) FL 14
Notts Co. (Loaned on 19/1/95) FL 10 Others 2

KEELEY John Henry
Born: Plaistow, 27 July 1961
Height: 6'1" Weight: 14.4

Began 1994-95 as Stockport's first choice goalkeeper, having proved both consistent and reliable for a number of teams down the years, eventually losing out to Ian Ironside and moving on to Peterborough. Three games and ten goals later, he signed for Chelmsford.

Southend U (From apprentice on 13/8/79) FL 63 FLC 4 FAC 5 Others 3 (Free to Chelmsford C during 1984 close season)
Brighton & Hove A (£5,000 on 23/8/86) FL 138 FLC 6 FAC 9 Others 7
Oldham Ath (£240,000 on 13/8/90) F/PL 2 FLC 1 Others 1
Oxford U (Loaned on 5/11/91) FL 6
Reading (Loaned on 6/2/92) FL 6
Chester C (Loaned on 28/8/92) FL 4
Colchester U (Free on 29/7/93) FL 15 FLC 2 FAC 1 Others 2 (Free to Chelmsford C on 19/3/94)
Stockport Co (Free on 24/3/94) FL 20 FLC 4 Others 3
Peterborough U (Free on 23/1/95) FL 3

KEEN Kevin Ian
Born: Amersham, 25 February 1967
Height: 5'6" Weight: 10.3
International Honours: E: Yth; Sch

As Lou Macari's record signing from "Wolves", his introduction into the Stoke first team in the key role on the right-hand side of midfield, was interrupted by a persistent ankle injury. A hardworker, who chases up and down the flank to support the attack and to assist his full-back, he struggled to find the net in 1994-95, his first season at the club.

West Ham U (From apprentice on 8/3/84) FL

187+32/21 FLC 21+1/5 FAC 15+7/1 Others 14+2/3
Wolverhampton W (£600,000 on 7/7/93) FL 37+5/7 FLC 2+1 FAC 5/1 Others 4/1
Stoke C (£300,000 on 19/10/94) FL 15+6/2

KEISTER John Edward Samuel
Born: Manchester, 11 November 1970
Height: 5'8" Weight: 11.0
International Honours: Sierra Leone U21

Tenacious, crowd-pleasing little Walsall midfielder. A great ball-winner with an eye for a goal, John regained his place in the side last season to play in several of the vital games during the Third Division promotion run-in.

Walsall (Free from Faweh FC on 18/9/83) FL 26+7/1 FAC 4 Others 0+1

KELLER Kasey
Born: Washington, USA, 27 November 1969
Height: 6'1" Weight: 13.7
International Honours: USA

Kasey, the current USA International goalie, has become one of the best shot-stoppers in English football since his arrival at Millwall. Served up many fine performances last season, highlighted by his penalty shoot-out save which won the FA Cup replay at Stamford Bridge. Right-footed, with very sharp reactions, he has survived the rigours of play in England at corners and crosses and is the stronger for it.

Millwall (Free from Portland University on 20/2/92) FL 134 FLC 11 FAC 7 Others 4

Alan Kelly   Tony Marshall
(Empics Sports Photo Agency)

KELLY Alan Thomas
Born: Preston, 11 August 1968
Height: 6'2" Weight: 12.5
International Honours: Ei: 10; B-1; U23-1; U21-1; Yth

Goalkeeper. Alan started 1994-95 in dispute with Sheffield United, and only played the first game of the season due to the suspension of Simon Tracey, who took over for the next five matches. With no transfer occurring, he signed a three year contract and regained his place as number one at the club, losing it only to international call-up or injury (a broken finger). Has progressed to first choice for the Republic of Ireland in

succession to Packy Bonner, a position earned by his undoubted ability and consistency that has established him as one of the top goalkeepers in the country.

Preston NE (From apprentice on 25/9/85) FL 142 FLC 1 FAC 8 Others 13
Sheffield U (£150,000 on 24/7/92) P/FL 99+2 FLC 6 FAC 9

KELLY Anthony (Tony) Gerald
Born: Prescot, 1 October 1964
Height: 5'10" Weight: 13.10
Club Honours: AMC '85

Released by Bolton during the 1994 close season, he had brief spells in midfield at Port Vale, Millwall and Wigan, before arriving at Peterborough. Showed great vision at London Road, when spraying accurate 40/50 yard passes around the ground, and was also used as a free-kick specialist.

Liverpool (From apprentice on 30/9/82)
Wigan Ath (Free from Prescot Cables on 4/1/84) FL 98+3/15 FLC 4/2 FAC 10/1 Others 12/4
Stoke C (£80,000 on 26/4/86) FL 33+3/4 FLC 2 FAC 5 Others 1
West Bromwich A (£60,000 on 13/7/87) FL 26/1 FLC 2 FAC 1 Others 1
Chester C (Loaned on 22/9/88) FL 5 FLC 2
Colchester U (Loaned on 24/10/88) FL 13/2 FAC 4 Others 3
Shrewsbury T (£30,000 on 28/1/89) FL 100+1/15 FLC 8/1 FAC 7/1 Others 4
Bolton W (£100,000 on 15/8/91) FL 103+3/5 FLC 9/2 FAC 15+3 Others 9/1
Port Vale (Free on 23/9/94) FL 3+1/1 FLC 1
Millwall (Free on 31/10/94) FL 1+1
Wigan Ath (Free on 25/11/94)
Peterborough U (Free on 9/12/94) FL 12+1/2

KELLY Nyrere Anthony (Tony)
Born: Meriden, 14 February 1966
Height: 5'9" Weight: 11.6

As a winger who can play on either flank and possessing incredible pace and ball control, when on song, Tony can change a game on his own. Unfortunately, niggling injuries saw him out of the Bury side more often than not last season.

Bristol C (Apprentice) FL 2+4/1
Stoke C (£20,000 from St Albans C, via Dulwich Hamlet, Cheshunt and Enfield, on 29/1/90) FL 33+25/5 FLC 5+4/3 Others 3+3
Hull C (Loaned on 30/1/92) FL 6/1
Cardiff C (Loaned on 30/10/92) FL 5/1
Bury (£10,000 on 17/9/93) FL 53+4/10 FLC 0+1 FAC 1+1 Others 8/3

KELLY David Thomas
Born: Birmingham, 25 November 1965
Height: 5'11" Weight: 11.3
Club Honours: Div '93
International Honours: Ei: 19; B-4; U23-1; U21-3

A hard-working Wolverhampton striker, he was already top-scorer when he got a hat-trick at Bristol City, but an uncharacteristically dangerous challenge saw him sent off at Millwall. The impending three-match suspension and the arrival of Don Goodman cast doubts over him, but he fought back with some sterling FA Cup performances, his goal against Leicester being a classic. He dummied a defender on the halfway line, passed neatly to Goodman, then ran in like a train to head the centre into the net. This made amends for the riot in midweek that had caused England's match in Dublin to be abandoned, the hosts being 1-0 up through David. He also played against Northern Ireland. A sub at Luton, he came on to score twice and finished top of both the appearances (54) and goalscoring (22) charts.

Walsall (Signed from Alvechurch on 21/12/83) FL 115+32/63 FLC 11+1/4 FAC 12+2/3 Others 14+3/10
West Ham U (£600,000 on 1/8/88) FL 29+12/7 FLC 11+3/5 FAC 6 Others 2+1/2
Leicester C (£300,000 on 22/3/90) FL 63+3/22 FLC 6/2 FAC 1 Others 2/1
Newcastle U (£250,000 on 4/12/91) FL 70/35 FLC 4/2 FAC 5/1 Others 4/1
Wolverhampton W (£750,000 on 23/6/93) FL 73+5/26 FLC 5/2 FAC 11/6 Others 4/2

David Kelly　　　　Neal Simpson
(Empics Sports Photo Agency)

KELLY Garry
Born: Drogheda, 9 July 1974
Height: 5'9" Weight: 11.0
International Honours: Ei: 14; EU2-3; Yth
Few people had heard of this youngster a year or so ago, but, following his performances at right-back for the Republic of Ireland, especially in the 1994 USA World Cup Finals, and his club, Leeds, he is now firmly established. A young player who goes from strength to strength, he was ever-present for the second successive season in 1994-95, producing numerous attacking displays of a remarkably high standard and consistency, his quick-silver speed and strength making him an exceptional man marker and defender. Automatic choice for both club and country, Garry should remain a permanent fixture for years to come.
Leeds U (Signed from Home Farm on 24/9/91) PL 84+2 FLC 4+1 FAC 7

KELLY Gary Alexander
Born: Preston, 3 August 1966
Height: 5'11" Weight: 12.3
Club Honours: FAYC '85
International Honours: Ei: B-1; U21-7
Rated by his fellow professionals as the Third Division "Goalkeeper of the Year" last season, the Bury custodian was in outstanding form throughout the campaign,

keeping an incredible 25 clean sheets. Despite his lack of height, he handled crosses comfortably and yet again proved an excellent shot-stopper as the "Shakers'" defence was at its meanest for over 70 years. The brother of the Republic's 'keeper, Alan, and son of a former Preston goalie, he has now clocked up over 250 appearances for the club.
Newcastle U (From apprentice on 20/6/84) FL 53 FLC 4 FAC 3 Others 2
Blackpool (Loaned on 7/10/88) FL 5
Bury (£60,000 on 5/10/89) FL 211 FLC 12 FAC 12 Others 27

KELLY Gavin John
Born: Beverley, 29 September 1968
Height: 6'1" Weight: 13.0
Began last season as Scarborough's first choice goalkeeper, having been signed from Bristol Rovers during the summer. Made 31 appearances for the club and gave a brilliant display against Middlesbrough in the Coca Cola Cup, before losing his place to Ian Ironside.
Hull C (From trainee on 9/5/87) FL 11 FLC 1 Others 1
Bristol Rov (Free on 1/7/90) FL 30 FAC 2
Scarborough (Free on 4/7/94) FL 24 FLC 4 FAC 3

KELLY Thomas (Tom) John
Born: Bellshill, 28 March 1964
Height: 5'10" Weight: 11.10
Inspirational, tough-tackling Torquay left-back, or left-sided midfield player, he is probably happier at the back, but is always willing to play anywhere.
Hartlepool U (Free from Queen of the South on 14/8/85) FL 14+1 FLC 2 Others 1
Torquay U (Free on 16/7/86) FL 116+4 FLC 7+1 FAC 7+1 Others 16
York C (Free on 1/7/89) FL 35/2 FLC 4 FAC 1 Others 3/1
Exeter C (£15,000 on 22/3/90) FL 76+12/9 FLC 5/1 FAC 5 Others 6
Torquay U (Free on 14/1/93) 83+3/8 FLC 3 FAC 6 Others 5

KENNA Jeffrey (Jeff) Jude
Born: Dublin, 27 August 1970
Height: 5'11" Weight: 11.7
International Honours: Ei: 3; B-1; U21-8
On the fringe of the Republic of Ireland side, Jeff, a 24-year-old Southampton full-back, was a shock signing for Blackburn a week before last March's transfer deadline. Initially, Jeff played at left-back, with Graham Le Saux moving upfield, but was later switched to wide right, wide left, and finally to right-back. Understandably, he found it difficult to fit into the team, but was a willing tackler, showed the capacity to slot a nice through ball and came up with a crucial goal against Crystal Palace. Just a few games short of a Championship medal, he made his international debut against Portugal in April.
Southampton (From trainee on 25/4/89) F/PL 100+6/9 FLC 4 FAC 10+1 Others 3
Blackburn Rov (£1,500,000 on 15/3/95) PL 9/1

KENNEDY Andrew (Andy) John
Born: Stirling, 8 October 1964
Height: 6'1" Weight: 11.10

International Honours: S: Yth
A tall centre-forward, with good touch, Andy came to Gillingham last September, having been released by Brighton. Just a couple of subs' appearances and a month later he left, and is thought to be now playing his football in the Far East.
Glasgow R (Signed from Sauchie Ath in 1983-84) SL 12+3/3 SLC 1+1 SC 3/1
Birmingham C (£50,000 on 28/3/85) FL 51+25/18 FLC 8/2 FAC 2 Others 1
Sheffield U (Loaned on 20/3/87) FL 8+1/1
Blackburn Rov (£50,000 on 2/6/88) FL 49+10/23 FLC 4 FAC 3/1 Others 4+1/3
Watford (£60,000 on 1/8/90) 17+8/4 FLC 2/1 FAC 0+1 Others 1
Bolton W (Loaned on 24/10/91) FL 1
Brighton & Hove A (£40,000 on 22/9/92) FL 34+8/10 FLC 3/1 FAC 6/4 Others 2+1/1
Gillingham (Free on 9/9/94) FL 0+2

Mark Kennedy　　　　Barry Coombs
(Empics Sports Photo Agency)

KENNEDY Mark
Born: Dublin, 15 May 1976
Height: 5'11" Weight: 11.9
International Honours: Ei: U21-4; Yth
Initially a central striker at Millwall, he is a highly talented left-footed player who benefited by being given a wide attacking role by Mick McCarthy last season. Very good ball control and exceptional talent at beating one or more defenders with a quick body swerve, his tremendous run and shot sealed Millwall's 2-0 win at Highbury in the FA Cup replay. Having made his debut for the Republic at U21 level, Mark joined Liverpool in March and was soon given the opportunity to shine at Anfield.
Millwall (From trainee on 6/5/92) FL 37+6/9 FLC 6+1/2 FAC 3+1/1
Liverpool (£1,500,000 on 21/3/95) PL 4+2

KENNY William (Billy) Aidan
Born: Liverpool, 19 September 1973
Height: 5'9" Weight: 11.4
International Honours: E: U21-1

A young midfielder with two good feet, who can switch play well by the use of long raking passes, Billy joined Oldham from Everton last August at the bequest of the PFA, following his well publicised problems off the park. Settling down well, he worked his way into the team where he made four appearances, before his contract was mutually terminated.

Everton (From trainee on 18/6/92) PL 16+1/1 FLC 4 FAC 2
Oldham Ath (Free on 26/8/94) FL 4

KENT Kevin John
Born: Stoke, 19 March 1965
Height: 5'8" Weight: 11.0
Club Honours: AMC '87, '93

Normally operates on the right-side of the Port Vale midfield, but can also play on the left and at right-back. Always gives everything and was a regular in the first dozen games in 1994-95, prior to being left out during a bad run of results. Suffered a broken hand at Tranmere after fighting his way back and scored the winning goal against Derby, before breaking his knee-cap and almost bringing his season to an end.

West Bromwich A (From apprentice on 31/12/82) FL 1+1
Newport Co (Free on 9/7/84) FL 23+10/1 FLC 2 FAC 0+1 Others 3+1/1
Mansfield T (Free on 15/8/85) FL 223+6/36 FLC 10/2 FAC 13/4 Others 21+2/4
Port Vale (£80,000 on 22/3/91) FL 87+27/7 FLC 9 FAC 2 Others 7+5

KENWORTHY Jonathan (Jon) Raymond
Born: St Asaph, 18 August 1974
Height: 5'8" Weight: 10.6
International Honours: W: U21-4; Yth

Due to the consistency of Tranmere's first choice wingers, Pat Nevin and John Morrissey, Jon was unable to force his way into the side on a regular basis last season, but, nevertheless, he made a contribution with his neat skills and willingness to chase back and tackle. Essentially right-sided, he scored some spectacular goals in the Pontins League and now awaits his opportunity to do likewise in the first team.

Tranmere Rov (From trainee on 14/7/93) FL 14+8/2 FLC 3 Others 1+2

KEOWN Martin Raymond
Born: Oxford, 24 July 1966
Height: 6'1" Weight: 12.4
International Honours: E: 11; B-1; U21-8; Yth

Probably the best man marker in the country and used in the past with great effect by England to contain the threat of Dutchman, Ruud Gullit. A central defender, now back with Arsenal the club he started with, Martin is a commanding player who reads the game well and is versatile enough to be used at full-back or in midfield. Scored his first ever goal for the "Gunners" at Nottingham Forest last season.

Arsenal (From apprentice on 2/2/84) FL 22 FAC 5
Brighton & Hove A (Loaned on 15/2/85) FL 21+2/1 FLC 2/1 Others 2/1
Aston Villa (£200,000 on 9/6/86) FL 109+3/3 FLC 12+1 FAC 6 Others 2
Everton (£750,000 on 7/8/89) F/PL 92+4 FLC 11 FAC 12+1 Others 6
Arsenal (£2,000,000 on 4/2/93) PL 62+18/1 FLC 6+2 FAC 3+2 Others 9+5

KERNAGHAN Alan Nigel
Born: Otley, 25 April 1967
Height: 6'1" Weight: 13.0
International Honours: Ei: 13

A two month spell on loan at Bolton right at the beginning of last season, saw him return to Maine Road, both his confidence and consistency renewed. Back in the Premiership with Manchester City, he produced some sterling performances alongside Keith Curle at the heart of the defence, before becoming the anchor man in midfield. An excellent clubman, and by now back to his best, he was a vital cog in the club's successful effort to stave off the threat of relegation. Twice selected for Eire, Alan played in the notorious abandoned game against England.

Middlesbrough (From apprentice on 8/3/85) F/PL 172+40/16 FLC 22+7/1 FAC 7+4/3 Others 14+2/2
Charlton Ath (Loaned on 17/1/91) FL 13
Manchester C (£1,600,000 on 20/9/93) PL 41+5/1 FLC 7 FAC 5/1
Bolton W (Loaned on 18/8/94) FL 9+2

KERR David William
Born: Dumfries, 6 September 1974
Height: 5'11" Weight: 11.2

Played just two Premiership games for Manchester City in 1994-95, filling in at full-back, mainly due to injuries to more senior players. A strong tackler, who can also play in midfield and thrives on a competitive atmosphere, David spent the rest of the season in the reserves where he was constantly on the brink of being elevated to the first team.

Manchester C (From trainee on 10/9/91) PL 4+1

KERR Dylan
Born: Valetta, Malta, 14 January 1967
Height: 5'9" Weight: 11.4
Club Honours: Div 2 '94

Reading left-back who enjoys making runs forward and has a powerful shot which has brought him some spectacular goals. A regular in the side until the final month of last season, Dylan lost his place to Michael Gilkes' pace as Reading re-organised their defensive system. Enjoys great rapport with the fans on the South Bank and may well come to the notice of the Maltese selectors.

Sheffield Wed (From juniors on 1/9/84)
Leeds U (Free from Arcadia Shepherds on 8/2/89) F/PL 6+7 FLC 2 FAC 1 Others 0+4
Doncaster Rov (Loaned on 22/8/91) FL 7/1
Blackpool (Loaned on 31/12/91) FL 12/1 Others 1
Reading (£75,000 on 15/7/93) FL 80+1/3 FLC 8 FAC 2 Others 3+1

KERR John Joseph
Born: Toronto, Canada, 6 March 1965
Height: 5'8" Weight: 11.5
International Honours: USA

Despite his birthplace, John is a current USA International, playing against both Saudia Arabia and Uruguay and scoring against the latter in a 2-2 draw. Right-footed, with his main asset his pace, he was unfortunate to suffer a groin strain which affected his form. Scored a hat-trick for Millwall last season when he came on as a sub against Derby County. Released at the end of 1994-95.

Portsmouth (Signed from Harrow Borough on 17/8/87) FL 2+2 FLC 0+1 Others 1
Peterborough U (Loaned on 11/12/87) FL 10/1 Others 1
Millwall (Signed from Chertsey T, via Washington Stars, Wycombe W and San Sourine, on 26/2/93) FL 21+22/8 FLC 2 Others 1+2

KERR Paul Andrew
Born: Portsmouth, 9 June 1964
Height: 5'8" Weight: 11.11
Club Honours: AMC '95

Released by Port Vale early last season, Paul joined Wycombe as a non-contract forward, scoring a dramatic late winner in his only League appearance at Blackpool in November. No longer with the club.

Aston Villa (From apprentice on 18/5/82) FL 16+8/3 FLC 5+1/2 FAC 2/1 Others 0+2
Middlesbrough (£50,000 on 7/1/87) FL 114+11/13 FLC 10/1 FAC 9+2/3 Others 13+3/1
Millwall (£100,000 on 28/3/91) FL 42+2/14 FLC 2 FAC 2/1 Others 3
Port Vale (£200,000 on 10/7/92) FL 58+5/15 FLC 4 FAC 4/1 Others 12+1/4
Leicester C (Loaned on 24/3/94) FL 4+3/2
Wycombe W (Free on 19/10/94) FL 0+1/1 Others 1

KERR James Stewart
Born: Bellshill, 13 November 1974
Height: 6'2" Weight: 13.0
International Honours: S: U21-10

Brighton manager, Liam Brady, returned to his previous club, Glasgow Celtic, for the loan services of goalkeeper, Stewart, who was very impressive during his brief stay at the Goldstone.

Glasgow Celtic (From juniors on 27/5/93)
Brighton & Hove A (Loaned on 1/11/94) FL 2

KERSLAKE David
Born: Stepney, 19 June 1966
Height: 5'8" Weight: 11.0
International Honours: E: U21-1; Yth; Sch

A right-back with good pace who began last season making 16 first team appearances for Tottenham up until mid-November, before losing his place to Dean Austin as the club struggled to keep goals out. Appearing in the first team against Southampton in April, David showed great ability in running forward and delivering quality crosses. Can also play in midfield and is excellent when getting down the line to deliver quality crosses to the forwards.

Queens Park R (From apprentice on 1/6/83) FL 38+20/6 FLC 6+2/4 FAC 2+2 Others 2+2
Swindon T (£110,000 on 24/11/89) FL 133+2/1 FLC 12 FAC 8 Others 10
Leeds U (£500,000 on 11/3/93) PL 8
Tottenham H (£450,000 on 24/9/93) PL 32+3 FLC 5 FAC 1+1

KEY Lance William
Born: Kettering, 13 May 1968
Height: 6'2" Weight: 14.6

Goalkeeper. Finally made his debut for Sheffield Wednesday in 1994-95, when coming on for Kevin Pressman at Gillingham, where his first task was to pick the ball out of the net following a penalty. He went on to make several excellent saves in helping "Owls" to a narrow victory. Still unable to establish himself at Hillsborough, being in the wings to Chris Woods and Pressman, Lance had a spell on loan at

Oxford early in 1995, before returning to the reserves.

Sheffield Wed (£10,000 from Histon on 14/4/90) FAC 0+1
Oldham Ath (Loaned on 12/10/93) PL 2
Oxford U (Loaned on 26/1/95) FL 6

Dmitri Kharine Steve Morton
(Empics Sports Photo Agency)

KHARINE Dmitri Victorvitch
Born: Moscow, Russia, 16 August 1968
Height: 6'2" Weight: 12.4
International Honours: Russia

Steady and reliable, with good hands, on his day, Chelsea's shot-stopping Russian inter-national goalie is as good as anyone in the Premiership. Unfortunate with injuries last season, after being carried off against West Ham, he missed several crucial games before coming back on a more regular basis towards the end of the campaign. Still a year left of his contract, Dmitri was the star of "Blues'" European Cup Winners Cup win at Viktoria Zizkov, including a penalty save and the follow-up.

Chelsea (£200,000 from CSKA Moscow on 22/12/92) PL 76 FLC 6 FAC 11 Others 4

Ryan Kidd Steve Morton
(Empics Sports Photo Agency)

KIDD Ryan Andrew
Born: Radcliffe, 6 October 1971
Height: 5'11" Weight: 10.0

Predominantly left-footed Preston defender at centre-half or full-back, Ryan added consistency to his undoubted talent last season. A strong tackler and header, his positional sense has benefited greatly from having a settled place alongside the experienced David Moyes.

Port Vale (From trainee on 12/7/90) FL 1 FLC 0+2 Others 0+1
Preston NE (Free on 15/7/92) FL 80+3/4 FLC 3 FAC 4 Others 5

KIELY Dean Laurence
Born: Salford, 10 October 1970
Height: 6'1" Weight: 11.8
International Honours: E: Yth

Popular York goalkeeper who continued his rapport with the City fans, Dean was again ever-present last season, having not missed a senior game since December 1992. As always, he showed fine form, although occasionally causing alarm when venturing outside the penalty area.

Coventry C (From trainee on 30/10/87)
York C (Signed on 9/3/90) FL 170 FLC 6 FAC 4 Others 13

KILCLINE Brian
Born: Nottingham, 7 May 1962
Height: 6'2" Weight: 12.0
Club Honours: FAC '87; Div 1 '93
International Honours: E: U21-2

Giant Swindon central defender who made just a handful of appearances last season, following firstly the departure of Adrian Whitbread and then the injury to Shaun Taylor. But after the club's Coca Cola Cup victory over Derby - Steve McMahon's first match in charge - Brian disappeared from the scene and spent the remainder of the campaign training with the youth squad, before going to Walsall on trial in April.

Notts Co (From apprentice on 1/4/80) FL 156+2/9 FLC 16/1 FAC 10/2
Coventry C (£60,000 on 11/6/84) FL 173/28 FLC 16+1/4 FAC 15/3 Others 8
Oldham Ath (£400,000 on 1/8/91) FL 8 FLC 2
Newcastle U (£250,000 on 19/2/92) F/PL 20+12 FLC 3+2 FAC 1+2 Others 5
Swindon T (£90,000 on 20/1/94) P/FL 16+1 FLC 3 Others 4

KILFORD Ian Anthony
Born: Bristol, 6 October 1973
Height: 5'10" Weight: 10.5

A graceful midfield player who is comfort-able on the ball, Ian joined Wigan at the start of last season on a permanent basis after a successful loan spell from Nottingham Forest. As an attacking player he scored five FL goals when joining up in attack, with the promise of more to come.

Nottingham F (From trainee on 3/4/91) FL 0+1
Wigan Ath (Loaned on 23/12/93) FL 7+1/3 FAC 0+1
Wigan Ath (Free on 13/7/94) FL 35/5 FLC 4 FAC 2/1 Others 3/1

KIMBLE Alan Frank
Born: Dagenham, 6 August 1966
Height: 5'10" Weight: 12.4
Club Honours: Div 3 '91

Troubled by injury, Alan came back into the

Wimbledon side against Manchester United last August, before succumbing again just seven matches later. Returned to the team in December and once again made the left-back slot his own, his searching long free-kicks and crosses giving the "Dons" a consistent outlet down the left-hand side. Also a long-throw expert.

Charlton Ath (From juniors on 8/8/84) FL 6
Exeter C (Loaned on 23/8/85) FL 1 FLC 6
Cambridge U (Free on 22/8/86) FL 295+4/24 FLC 23+1 FAC 29/1 Others 22
Wimbledon (£175,000 on 27/7/93) PL 40 FLC 5 FAC 3

KING Philip (Phil) Geoffrey
Born: Bristol, 28 December 1967
Height: 5'8" Weight: 11.9
Club Honours: FLC '91
International Honours: E: B-1

An attacking full-back who is very composed on the ball, if the occasion demands, Phil can be used on either flank or as an extra forward with his ability to deliver telling passes and crosses. Signed by Aston Villa from Sheffield Wednesday prior to the start of last season, he soon formed an excellent left-sided partnership with Steve Staunton, especially on the overlap, but struggled to feature in the side·following the re-appearance of Shaun Teale in December. Scored the penalty winner against Inter Milan in the UEFA Cup.

Exeter C (From apprentice on 7/1/85) FL 24+3 FLC 1 Others 1+2
Torquay U (£3,000 on 14/7/86) FL 24/3 FLC 2 FAC 1 Others 2
Swindon T (£155,000 on 6/2/87) FL 112+4/4 FLC 11 FAC 5 Others 13
Sheffield Wed (£400,000 on 30/11/89) F/PL 124+5/2 FLC 17 FAC 9 Others 4
Notts Co (Loaned on 22/10/93) FL 6 Others 2
Aston Villa (£250,000 on 1/8/94) PL 13+3 FLC 3 Others 4

KINSELLA Mark Anthony
Born: Dublin, 12 August 1972
Height: 5'9" Weight: 11.8
Club Honours: GMVC '92; FAT '92
International Honours: Ei: U21-8

Skilful and combative Colchester mid-fielder, who always gets his share of goals, he can also play sweeper with equal success and even filled in at full-back when injuries and suspensions hit. The only ever-present for United last season, this former Eire U21 cap seems to have been at Layer Road for ages.

Colchester U (Free from Home Farm on 18/8/89) FL 123+1/20 FLC 6/1 FAC 10/1 Others 3+1/2

KIRBY Ryan Mark
Born: Redbridge, 6 September 1974
Height: 5'11" Weight: 12.0

One of Doncaster's success stories of 1994-95, this young full-back, who joined the club on a free transfer, having been released by Arsenal during the summer, came on as a substitute at Hereford on the opening day of the season, and held his place for the remainder of the campaign. Keen to go forward and sure in the tackle, he is definitely a player to look out for in the future.

Arsenal (From trainee on 6/7/93)
Doncaster Rov (Free on 6/7/94) FL 41+1 FLC 0+1 FAC 1 Others 3

KIRKHAM Peter Jonathan
Born: Newcastle, 28 October 1974
Height: 6'0" Weight: 11.4

A ball playing winger, who shows great skill, Peter was unable to establish a first team place at Darlington with any regularity last season.
Darlington (Free from Newcastle U juniors on 3/9/93) FL 5+8 FAC 0+2 Others 0+1

KITCHEN David Edward **(Sam)**
Born: Rintein, Germany, 11 June 1967
Height: 5'9" Weight: 11.0

This defender had limited opportunities in the Doncaster first team last season, due largely to the consistent performances of Russ Wilcox and the now departed Chris Swailes. Although given a taste of League action towards the end of 1994-95, following the departure of Swailes on deadline day, he left at the end of the campaign to join Gateshead.
Leyton Orient (Signed from Frickley Ath on 6/8/92) FL 35+8/1 FLC 2 FAC 4 Others 3+1
Doncaster Rov (Free on 10/2/94) FL 21+1/1 FLC 1 Others 1

KITE Philip (Phil) David
Born: Bristol, 26 October 1962
Height: 6'1" Weight: 14.7
International Honours: E: Yth; Sch

A very experienced goalkeeper, Phil signed for Bristol City during the 1994 close season as cover for Keith Welch, playing just two games during the season when the latter was injured. Although performing well in both games, he was granted a free transfer during the summer as it was felt that young Wayne Brown, still only a trainee, was ready to take over the cover position.
Bristol Rov (From apprentice on 31/10/80) FL 96 FLC 12 FAC 8 Others 2
Southampton (£50,000 on 16/8/84) FL 4 Others 1
Middlesbrough (Loaned on 27/3/86) FL 2
Gillingham (Free on 7/2/87) FL 70 FLC 5 FAC 4 Others 10
Bournemouth (£20,000 on 16/8/89) FL 7 FLC 1
Sheffield U (£25,000 on 10/8/90) FL 11 FLC 5 FAC 1 Others 1
Mansfield T (Loaned on 21/11/91) FL 11 Others 1
Plymouth Arg (Loaned on 9/9/92) FL 2
Rotherham U (Loaned on 24/10/92) FL 1
Crewe Alex (Loaned on 27/11/92) FL 5 FAC 1 Others 2
Stockport Co (Loaned on 25/3/93) FL 5
Cardiff C (Free on 1/7/93) FL 17+1 FLC 2 FAC 0+1 Others 2
Bristol C (Free on 11/8/94) FL 2

KITSON Paul
Born: Peterlee, 9 January 1971
Height: 5'11" Weight: 10.12
International Honours: E: U21-7

Paul's on-off move from Derby was finally completed last September when Newcastle got their man. As a striker, he is brave, with two good feet and excellent heading ability, and is also able to hold the ball up to bring other players into the game. All this, coupled with pace and a tremendous work-rate, make him a handful for any defender. Highlights of his season include a hat-trick

in the 3-0 home FAC-tie against Swansea and his first goal for the club in the Coca Cola Cup at home to Manchester United. Missed four games after damaging ankle ligaments against Wimbledon and the final four of the campaign, following a neck injury sustained in training.
Leicester C (From trainee on 15/12/88) FL 39+11/6 FLC 5/3 FAC 1+1/1 Others 5/1
Derby Co (£1,300,000 on 11/3/92) FL 105/36 FLC 7/3 FAC 5/1 Others 13+1/9
Newcastle U (£2,250,000 on 24/9/94) PL 24+2/8 FLC 3/1 FAC 4+1/3

KIWOMYA Andrew (Andy) Derek
Born: Huddersfield, 1 October 1967
Height: 5'9" Weight: 10.10
International Honours: E: Yth

Left-sided Scunthorpe forward who was recruited from non-league Halifax last March, thus resurrecting his professional career after a lengthy spell away from the game through injury. His main attribute is his pace, just like his younger brother, Chris, and he delighted the fans with his desire to run at defenders. Still at the club as a non-contract player.
Barnsley (From apprentice on 16/7/85) FL 1
Sheffield Wed (£5,000 on 7/10/86)
Dundee (Free in 1992-93) SL 11+10/1 SC 0+1
Rotherham U (Free on 1/10/93) FL 4+3 FLC 0+1 Others 0+2 (Free to Halifax during 1994 close season)
Scunthorpe U (Free on 23/3/93) FL 9/3

KIWOMYA Christopher (Chris) Mark
Born: Huddersfield, 2 December 1969
Height: 5'9" Weight: 11.0
Club Honours: Div 2 '92

An athletic striker with great pace, Chris's main asset is his turn of speed that enables him to set in behind defences and run onto balls played in "over the top" of the defence. With Ipswich up until last January, and playing in a side that was always going to find it difficult to remain in the top flight, "out of the blue" he was transferred to Arsenal. Still to settle at Highbury, he scored vital goals in successive February games to keep the "Gunners" just above the relegation zone.
Ipswich T (From trainee on 31/3/87) F/PL 197+28/51 FLC 14+1/8 FAC 14/2 Others 5+1/3
Arsenal (£1,500,000 on 13/1/95) PL 5+9/3 Others 1+2

KJELDBJERG Jakob
Born: Denmark, 21 October 1969
Height: 6'2" Weight: 13.8
International Honours: Denmark

Unfortunate with injuries last season, Chelsea's Danish international central defender was out on six separate occasions, being just one of a dozen or more squad members sidelined at the same time, on occasion. Glenn Hoddle's first signing for the club was absent for all but one of the European Cup Winners Cup games and made only 29 starts in all, having just got a good partnership going with Erland Johnsen. A cultured player, and good in the air, he was sadly missed.
Chelsea (£400,000 from Silkeborg on 13/8/93) PL 52/2 FLC 6 FAC 6+1 Others 1

KLINSMANN Jurgen
Born: Geopingen, Germany, 30 July 1964
Height: 6'2" Weight: 12.13
International Honours: West Germany/ Germany

Signed from Monaco at the beginning of last August, this German international striker of amazing ability in the air, on the ground, and in the creation of goalscoring opportunities, began last season as he meant to go on, scoring on his Tottenham debut in the 4-3 victory against Sheffield Wednesday. His enthusiasm and ability to create and hit goals from the most unlikely of positions soon won him praise from all corners of the game, as he scored seven in his first seven appearances, and became a hero at White Hart Lane. The sheer workrate demonstrated by him injected enthusiasm to his colleagues, while his superb finishing was demonstrated at its best with goals against Everton in Tottenham's 2-1 victory and in the 3-1 win over Sheffield Wednesday, among others too numerous to mention here. An outstanding individual who works hard for his team, whose flair, enthusiasm, and enjoyment of the game, has made him one of the most outstanding players in the Premier League, he was voted the Football Writers' "Player of the Year" in March and elected by his fellow professionals to the PFA Award winning Premier League team. It is ironic that Jurgen, who took responsibility as penalty taker, should go on to miss two late in the season, meaning a draw instead of victory for "Spurs" on both occasions. Nonetheless, his outstanding contribution to the Tottenham team will go down in history, alongside the likes of Glenn Hoddle and Gary Lineker. Stop Press: With a contractual opt-out clause in place, the German surprised his vast legion of English fans when going home to sign for Bayern Munich during the summer. However, following the Premiership signings of the equally world class Ruud Gullit (Chelsea) and Dennis Bergkamp (Arsenal) this summer, the void appears to have been more than adequately filled.
Tottenham H (£2,000,000 from Monaco on 1/8/94) PL 41/20 FLC 3/4 FAC 6/5

KNIGHT Alan Edward
Born: Balham, 3 July 1961
Height: 6'1" Weight: 13.1
Club Honours: Div 3 '83
International Honours: E: U21-2; Yth

An experienced goalkeeper with good reflexes who commands the area, 1994-95 was his 18th season in football and he again maintained a high level of consistency to keep Portsmouth in many games. Lost his place for a couple of matches to on loan, Jimmy Glass, in March, but soon regained it. During the season, he passed 550 league games and 650 total games, but was also dismissed for the first time in his career against Leicester in the FA Cup.
Portsmouth (From apprentice on 12/3/79) FL 578 FLC 48 FAC 34 Others 21

KNILL Alan Richard
Born: Slough, 8 October 1964
Height: 6'2" Weight: 11.7
Club Honours: WC '89
International Honours: W: 1; Yth

On-field Scunthorpe captain, he is a lanky central defender whose sterling displays have earned him many "Man of the Match" awards. Always dangerous at set-pieces, he shrugged off several bad knocks in 1994-95 for the team's cause.
Southampton (From apprentice on 14/10/82)
Halifax T (Free on 13/7/84) FL 118/6 FLC 6 FAC 6 Others 6
Swansea C (£15,000 on 14/8/87) FL 89/3 FLC 4 FAC 5 Others 7
Bury (£95,000 on 18/8/89) FL 141+3/8 FLC 7 FAC 8/1 Others 14+1/1
Cardiff C (Loaned on 24/9/93) FL 4
Scunthorpe U (Signed on 5/11/93) FL 64/5 FLC 2 FAC 8 Others 4

KNOTT Gareth Raymond
Born: Blackwood, 19 January 1976
Height: 5'11" Weight: 11.4
International Honours: W: Yth

Stylish left-winger with plenty of pace and at his best when going at defenders. Not having been blooded in the Premiership with Tottenham, he went on loan to Third Division Gillingham last February and impressed. Incidentally, his wages were paid thanks to the generosity of the "Gills'" Supporters' Club.
Tottenham H (From trainee on 1/7/94)
Gillingham (Loaned on 17/2/95) FL 5

KNOWLES Darren Thomas
Born: Sheffield, 8 October 1970
Height: 5'6" Weight: 10.1

Scarborough's "Mr Consistency", has been a near ever-present over the past two seasons, after successfully reverting to the right-back role from midfield. Darren was voted the club's "Away Player of the Year" last season by the travelling supporters.
Sheffield U (From trainee on 1/7/89)
Stockport Co (£3,000 on 14/9/89) FL 51+12 FLC 2+4 Others 14+1
Scarborough (Free on 4/8/93) FL 81/1 FLC 6 FAC 7 Others 4

KRISTENSEN Bjorn
Born: Malling, Denmark, 10 October 1963
Height: 6'1" Weight: 12.5
International Honours: Denmark

A strong Portsmouth midfielder who packs a powerful shot from distance, "Benny" failed to hold down a regular place in the team and was left to play just a bit-part in the proceedings, before being freed during the summer.
Newcastle U (£250,000 from Aarhus on 21/3/89) FL 69+11/4 FLC 3 FAC 6 Others 8/1/1
Bristol C (Loaned on 20/11/92) FL 4
Portsmouth (£120,000 on 19/3/93) FL 56+15/1 FLC 8+1/1 FAC 3 Others 6+1/2

KUBICKI Dariusz
Born: Warsaw, Poland, 6 June 1963
Height: 5'10" Weight: 11.7
International Honours: Poland

Polish international full-back who established himself as a crowd favourite at Sunderland in 1994-95 with a series of solid, consistent displays, Dariusz links well with the midfield and attack, but is still searching for that elusive first goal. Mainly operating at right-back, although he can play on the opposite flank as well, he was Mick Buxton's first signing and was ever-present last season.
Aston Villa (£200,000 from Legia Warsaw on 28/8/91) F/PL 24+1 FLC 3 FAC 4+1 Others 1
Sunderland (£100,000 on 4/3/94) FL 61 FLC 2 FAC 3

KUHL Martin
Born: Frimley, 10 January 1965
Height: 5'11" Weight: 11.3

A surprise Bristol City signing from Derby last December. A defensive midfielder with two good feet, Martin was bought primarily to anchor down and provide stability to the club's midfield. Not unnaturally, he took a little time to settle down before showing his value, especially in a side trying to battle its way out of the relegation zone. However, much will be expected of him in 1995-96.
Birmingham C (From apprentice on 13/1/83) FL 103+8/5 FLC 13 FAC 8/1 Others 1+1/1
Sheffield U (Signed on 20/3/87) FL 38/4 FLC 2 FAC 1 Others 1
Watford (Signed on 19/2/88) FL 4
Portsmouth (£125,000 on 30/9/88) FL 146+11/27 FLC 11/1 FAC 13 Others 3
Derby Co (£650,000 on 26/9/92) FL 68/1 FLC 6 FAC 6 Others 4/1
Notts Co (Loaned on 9/9/94) FL 2
Bristol C (£330,000 on 30/12/94) FL 17+1 FAC 2

KYDD Michael Robert
Born: Milton Keynes, 21 May 1977
Height: 5'8" Weight: 12.10

Made an impressive start to his career in Cambridge's midfield last March, making his full FL debut and scoring a week later at Bristol Rovers. Shows good skill on the ball.
Cambridge U (From trainee on 18/5/95) FL 10+9/1

LAIGHT Ellis Stanley
Born: Birmingham, 30 June 1976
Height: 5'10" Weight: 11.2

A first year Torquay pro, chances were limited in 1994-95, due to recovery from a broken leg. However, he showed good late season form without much luck in front of goal.
Torquay U (Trainee) FL 4+7 Others 0+2/1

LAKE Michael (Mike) Charles
Born: Manchester, 16 November 1966
Height: 6'1 " Weight: 12.11
International Honours: E: SP-2

Tall and ungainly, Mike is a "Bits-and-Pieces" type of central midfield player who forges the link between defence and attack. The Wrexham fans' "favourite" when initially signed, he disappointed in 1993-94, and an injury early in 1994-95 that prevented him taking any further part in the proceedings, saw him released at the end of the season.
Sheffield U (£60,000 from Macclesfield T on 11/10/89) FL 19+16/4 FLC 3+2 FAC 5/1 Others 1
Wrexham (£60,000 on 26/11/92) FL 56+2/6 FLC 3 FAC 1 Others 6

LAKIN Barry
Born: Dartford, 19 September 1973
Height: 5'9" Weight: 12.6

An attacking Orient midfielder, who has the ability to win the ball and then produce long runs deep into the opponents' territory to set up chances for colleagues. Also possesses a hard shot. Unfortunately, he was sidelined for much of last season with an ankle injury.
Leyton Orient (From trainee on 6/7/92) FL 36+10/2 FLC 4 FAC 2+2/1 Others 2+1

Barry Lakin   Mattew Ashton
(Empics Sports Photo Agency)

LAMBERT Christopher James (Jimmy)
Born: Henley, 14 September 1973
Height: 5'7" Weight: 10.4

Another graduate of Reading's youth policy, Jimmy made a spectacular debut in the side shortly after leaving school. However, with opportunities scarce in 1994-95, there were only glimpses of the exciting dribbling skills which earned him a month's loan at Blackburn Rovers, his isolated appearances being mainly as a substitute, although there was a late equaliser against Grimsby.
Reading (From juniors on 3/7/92) FL 13+31/4 FLC 0+1 FAC 4 Others 2+3/1

LAMPKIN Kevin
Born: Liverpool, 20 December 1972
Height: 5'10" Weight: 11.8

Ball-winning, hard-tackling, and spoiling Mansfield midfield player who missed the first half of last season due to a toe injury, which received surgery. Performed a vital role within the framework of a team that reached the Third Division play-offs.
Liverpool (From trainee on 17/5/91)
Huddersfield T (Free on 1/7/92) FL 13 FLC 1
Mansfield T (Free on 18/2/94) FL 33+3/3 FAC 1 Others 1+1

LAMPTEY Nii Odartey
Born: Accra, Ghana, 10 December 1974
Height: 5'5" Weight: 10.7
International Honours: Ghana

Signed by Aston Villa from Belgian football during the 1994 close season, the young Ghanaian international striker was rarely given an opportunity, making just three starts during the campaign. Very quick and nimble, when he did play, Nii showed excellent balance and control, along with two good feet. No longer with the club, he joined the Italian side, Udinese, at the end of 1994-95.

Aston Villa (£1,000,000 from Anderlecht on 3/8/94) PL 1+5 FLC 2+1/3

LANCASHIRE Graham
Born: Blackpool, 19 October 1972
Height: 5'10" Weight: 11.12
Club Honours: Div 4 '92

Signed last season from Burnley, Graham took some time to settle into the Preston first team, before losing his place through injury. A 100 per-cent trier, who was unlucky in front of goal, which seemed to affect his confidence, he is obviously talented and will hopefully come good in 1995-96.

Burnley (From trainee on 1/7/91) FL 11+20/8 FLC 1+1 FAC 2+2/1 Others 2+4
Halifax T (Loaned on 20/11/92) FL 2 Others 1+1
Chester C (Loaned on 21/1/94) FL 10+1/7
Preston NE (£55,000 on 23/12/94) FL 9+8 Others 1

LANCASTER David
Born: Preston, 8 September 1961
Height: 6'3" Weight: 14.0

Joining Bury from non-league Halifax last March as forward cover, David made only a handful of appearances due to the return from injury of both Mark Carter and John Paskin.

Blackpool (Free from Colne Dynamoes on 15/8/90) FL 7+1/1 FLC 2 Others 0+1
Chesterfield (Loaned on 26/2/91) FL 12/4
Chesterfield (£70,000 on 27/8/91) FL 66+3/16 FLC 5/3 FAC 2 Others 6/3
Rochdale (Free on 5/7/93) FL 37+3/14 FLC 4/1 FAC 2 Others 1 (Free to Halifax T on 20/7/94)
Bury (Free on 12/3/95) FL 3+2/1

LANDON Richard John
Born: Worthing, 22 March 1970
Height: 6'0" Weight: 12.2

A centre-forward who was in and out of the Plymouth team last term, he is predominantly right-footed, has an eye for goal, and is one of the team's leading scorers. Possibly hasn't fully made the transition from non-league to professional football, although there have been plenty of enquiries about his availability.

Plymouth Arg (£30,000 from Bedworth U on 26/1/94) FL 21+9/12 FLC 0+1 FAC 0+1 Others 4

LANGE Anthony (Tony) Stephen
Born: West Ham, 10 December 1964
Height: 6'1" Weight: 12.9

A confident WBA goalkeeper, good when coming for high balls, he took over from the injured Stuart Naylor for a time during 1994-95 and produced some excellent performances, before being freed at the end of the season.

Charlton Ath (From apprentice on 15/12/82) FL 12 Others 1
Aldershot (Loaned on 22/8/85) FL 7
Aldershot (Free on 7/7/86) FL 125 FLC 5 FAC 10 Others 16
Wolverhampton W (£150,000 on 13/7/89) FL 8 FLC 2
Aldershot (Loaned on 23/11/90) FL 2 Others 1
Torquay U (Loaned on 12/9/91) FL 1
West Bromwich A (Free on 12/8/92) FL 45+3 FLC 3 FAC 1 Others 7

LANGFORD Timothy (Tim)
Born: Kingswinford, 12 September 1965
Height: 5'6" Weight: 11.13

Nimble Wycombe striker who started just one game in 1994-95, after a season interrupted by injury, he was freed during the summer.

Wycombe W (£15,000 from Telford on 19/3/93) FL 19+16/8 FLC 1+2/1 FAC 2+2/1 Others 3+3/3

LAUNDERS Brian Terence
Born: Dublin, 8 January 1976
Height: 5'10" Weight: 11.12
International Honours: Ei: U21-5; Yth

One of several Irish lads at Crystal Palace, and having already been capped by the Republic of Ireland at U21 level a week or so earlier, Brian made his PL debut against Chelsea last September. A forward of whom much is expected in the future, apart from the Chelsea match, he twice came off the bench during the season and will be looking for further opportunities in 1995-96.

Crystal Palace (Signed on 2/9/93) PL 1+1 FLC 0+1

LAVIN Gerard
Born: Corby, 5 February 1974
Height: 5'8" Weight: 10.8
International Honours: S: U21-7

Consistent, tigerish Watford defender, who last season added a calmer temperament to his already considerable skills, he now seems settled at right-back, although also effective in midfield. Gerard is currently a regular at Scottish U21 level.

Watford (From trainee on 11/5/92) FL 105+5/3 FLC 9/1 FAC 6 Others 2+1

LAW Brian John
Born: Merthyr Tydfil, 1 January 1970
Height: 6'2" Weight: 11.12
International Honours: W: 1; U21-1; Yth; Sch

A central defender, Brian was forced to retire in 1992 but later realised the tendon injury was standing up well to arduous hobbies such as climbing and trekking and decided to try again. Wolverhampton gave him a trial, but had to pay £34,000 to the insurers for compensation he had received and £100,000 to his old club, QPR. It all seemed good business when he made his debut last December, forming a good, although temporary, partnership with John De Wolf. Later, he was called up by the Welsh squad in Bulgaria, and got back in the "Wolves" team when De Wolf's season came to an end.

Queens Park R (From trainee on 15/8/87) FL 19+1 FLC 2+1 FAC 3 Others 1
Wolverhampton W (£134,000 on 23/12/94) FL 17 FAC 6

LAW Marcus William
Born: Coventry, 28 September 1975
Height: 5'11" Weight: 12.0

Goalkeeper. An unused sub on four occasions in 1993-94, Marcus signed professional forms for Bristol Rovers during the 1994 close season. Made his FL debut at Brentford last October in place of the

injured Brian Parkin, and had a difficult time of it as the home club scored twice in the opening four minutes on their way to a 3-0 victory. Played once more, before being allowed to join non-league Stafford Rangers on a free transfer in March, following a spell at Yeovil.

Bristol Rov (From trainee on 13/7/94) FL 2

LAW Nicholas (Nicky)
Born: Greenwich, 8 September 1961
Height: 6'0" Weight: 13.5
International Honours: E: Sch

Chesterfield's captain and an inspirational leader by example, who is curiously nicknamed "Herman the German" by the fans, Nicky's experience has been a boon to the centre of the defence; his attitude, too, has been exemplary, in playing out last season despite two leg injuries. An enthusiastic player, he relished the challenge of the play-offs, as the club regained their Second Division status after a gap of six years, and his long, raking crosses from the right, plus his trademark long-throw, added much to the attack, too.

Arsenal (From apprentice on 17/7/79)
Barnsley (Free on 4/8/81) FL 113+1/1 FLC 5 FAC 6
Blackpool (Free on 28/8/85) FL 64+2/1 FLC 2 FAC 2 Others 3
Plymouth Arg (£40,000 on 12/3/87) FL 37+1/5 FLC 2 FAC 2 Others 0+1
Notts Co (£70,000 on 17/6/88) FL 44+3/4 FLC 4 FAC 1 Others 4
Scarborough (Loaned on 10/11/89) FL 12 FLC 1
Rotherham U (£35,000 on 1/8/90) FL 126+2/4 FLC 12/1 FAC 12 Others 7
Chesterfield (Signed on 8/10/93) FL 66/3 FLC 1 FAC 1 Others 6/2

LAWFORD Craig Brian
Born: Dewsbury, 25 November 1972
Height: 5'10" Weight: 11.0

Scored five times in six pre-season games to secure a contract last August, following his release by Bradford, so adding to Hull's connections with the Valley Paraders. Craig had a regular berth on the left-side of midfield in the first half of 1994-95 and enjoyed another goals purple patch in October, hitting three in four games. Fractured a bone in his left foot when Bradford visited Hull last Easter.

Bradford C (From trainee on 2/7/91) FL 13+7/1 FLC 3 FAC 1+1 Others 1+1
Hull C (Free on 5/8/94) FL 25+6/3 FLC 2 FAC 1 Others 2

LAWRENCE James (Jamie) Hubert
Born: Balham, 8 March 1970
Height: 5'10" Weight:12.3

After impressing in the lower reaches with Doncaster, Jamie signed for Leicester last January and quickly established himself as a full squad member. A tricky right-winger, with a distinctive hairstyle, he scored his first goal in the topsy-turvy April Fools Day defeat at the hands of Wimbledon. A player to watch out for.

Sunderland (Signed from Cowes on 15/10/93) FL 2+2 FLC 0+1
Doncaster Rov (£20,000 on 17/3/94) FL 16+9/3 FLC 2 FAC 1 Others 3
Leicester C (£125,000 on 6/1/95) PL 9+8/1

LAWS Brian
Born: Wallsend, 14 October 1961
Height: 5'8" Weight: 11.0
Club Honours: Div 3 '82; FLC '89, '90;
FMC '89
International Honours: E: B

Although joining Grimsby as the manager last December, having been freed by Nottingham Forest, he appeared as a substitute on a regular basis, before making his full debut at Port Vale late in the season. During his few appearances in defence and midfield as an aggressive tackler, with an ability to run at defences, his Premier League pedigree shone through and his goal on his full debut must rank amongst the best of the season.
Burnley (From apprentice on 19/10/79) FL 125/12 FLC 14/2 FAC 15/1
Huddersfield T (£10,000 on 26/8/83) FL 56/1 FLC 7 FAC 3
Middlesbrough (£30,000 on 15/3/85) FL 103+5/12 FLC 6+1/2 FAC 8+1 Others 6+1
Nottingham F (£120,000 on 7/7/88) F/PL 136+11/4 FLC 28+4 FAC 16+2/1 Others 11+1
Grimsby T (Free on 1/12/94) FL 6+10/1.

LAWTON Craig Thomas
Born: Mancot, 5 January 1972
Height: 5'8" Weight: 10.3
International Honours: W: B-1; U21-1;
Yth; Sch

Diminutive Port Vale midfielder who appeared for the Welsh U21 side as an over-age player before making his League debut last season. That came as a substitute for the last two minutes at Watford on New Years Eve, but any further first team ambitions ended in March when he suffered a broken leg in a reserve game.
Manchester U (From trainee on 1/7/90)
Port Vale (Free on 2/8/94) FL 0+1

LEABURN Carl Winston
Born: Lewisham, 30 March 1969
Height: 6'3" Weight: 13.0
International Honours: E: Yth

Tall Charlton striker who missed the early part of 1994-95 with knee ligament damage and several games mid-season with a torn hamstring. Not a prolific scorer, his main strengths are his heading power, particularly at corners and set-pieces, and an ability to hold the ball up and lay it off. Has a very long-throw.
Charlton Ath (From apprentice on 22/4/87) FL 185+39/33 FLC 11/3 FAC 13+2/3 Others 7+5/4
Northampton T (Loaned on 22/3/90) FL 9

LEADBITTER Christopher (Chris) Jonathan
Born: Middlesbrough, 17 October 1967
Height: 5'9" Weight: 10.6
Club Honours: Div 3 '91

A predominantly left-footed player whose favourite position in the Bournemouth set-up is in central midfield, although he has also played at left-back, Chris is a particularly tigerish tackler with a fierce left-foot. Freed during the summer.
Grimsby T (From apprentice on 4/9/85)
Hereford U (Free on 21/8/86) FL 32+4/1 FLC 2 FAC 2 Others 3
Cambridge U (Free on 2/8/88) FL 144+32/18 FLC 12/3 FAC 16+2/3 Others 11+2/1
Bournemouth (£25,000 on 16/8/93) FL 45+9/3 FLC 6+1 FAC 5 Others 2

LEANING Andrew (Andy) John
Born: Howden, 18 May 1963
Height: 6'0" Weight: 13.0

Performed goalkeeping heroics in Lincoln's cup matches in 1994-95, but could only gain a place in the League side last November after Russell Hoult returned to Leicester. Unfortunate to suffer a nasty back injury at Wigan, which put him out of action for several matches.
York C (Free from Rowntree Mackintosh on 1/7/85) FL 69 FLC 4 FAC 8 Others 5
Sheffield U (Free on 28/5/87) FL 21 FLC 2 FAC 2
Bristol C (£12,000 on 27/9/88) FL 75 FLC 5 FAC 7 Others 2
Lincoln C (Free on 24/3/94) FL 29 FLC 4 FAC 3 Others 2

LE BIHAN Neil Ernest
Born: Croydon, 14 March 1976
Height: 5'11" Weight: 12.13

Not offered a pro contract by Tottenham, Neil came to Peterborough during the 1994 close season, having been a trainee at White Hart Lane since July 1992. Immediately showed fine control and vision and, with experience, he looks likely to become more than useful. Always seemed to have plenty of time on the ball - the hallmark of a good player.
Peterborough U (Free from Tottenham H juniors on 13/7/94) FL 3+1

LEE Christopher (Chris)
Born: Halifax, 18 June 1971
Height: 5'10" Weight: 11.10

The son of Hull's assistant manager, Jeff, Chris is a tireless worker who can fill the midfield role of winning and giving. Right-footed, he has the adaptability to play in defence. Has a potent attacking weapon with his flick-ons from near post corners.
Bradford C (From trainee on 1/7/89)
Rochdale (Free on 14/6/90) FL 24+2/2 FLC 4/1 FAC 2 Others 3
Scarborough (Free on 14/3/91) FL 75+3/3 FLC 11/2 FAC 2 Others 4
Hull C (Free on 30/7/93) FL 79+9/4 FLC 2/1 FAC 1+1 Others 3

LEE David John
Born: Kingswood, 26 November 1969
Height: 6'3" Weight: 13.12
Club Honours: Div 2 '89
International Honours: E: U21-10; Yth

Versatile Chelsea player who can perform with equal ability in the centre of the defence, in midfield, or up front. With two good feet and a footballing brain, David will bring the ball out of defence rather than just clear his lines. Having overcome injuries and having had a long spell in the reserves, he came into the "Blues'" defence towards the end of last season in place of the unavailable Jacob Kjeldberg, and did well. Had a great game at Manchester United when the home side failed to claim three points, and hopes to build on that performance in 1995-96.
Chelsea (From trainee on 1/7/88) F/PL 88+30/9 FLC 12+4/1 FAC 3+4 Others 6+2/1
Reading (Loaned on 30/1/92) FL 5/5
Plymouth Arg (Loaned on 26/3/92) FL 9/1
Portsmouth (Loaned on 12/8/94) FL 4+1

LEE David Mark
Born: Blackburn, 5 November 1967
Height: 5'7" Weight: 11.0

One of the most exciting wingers in the League on his day, David scored what was perhaps his best goal for Bolton against Norwich in the quarter-finals of the Coca Cola Cup against Norwich at Burnden. In the space of 30 yards he got past three defenders to blast the winner and earn the club a game against Swindon Town. Unfortunately, he broke three bones in his foot in the play-off with "Wolves", an injury that kept him out of the final against Reading.
Bury (From juniors on 8/8/86) FL 203+5/35 FLC 15/1 FAC 6 Others 19+1/4
Southampton (£350,000 on 27/8/91) F/PL 11+9 FAC 0+1 Others 1+1
Bolton W (£300,000 on 2/11/92) FL 102+10/14 FLC 12/2 FAC 11+1 Others 8+1/1

David Lee (Bolton)   Barrington Coombs
(Empics Sports Photo Agency)

LEE Jason Benedict
Born: Forest Gate, 9 May 1971
Height: 6'3" Weight: 13.8

Extremely popular with the Nottingham Forest fans, and recognisable anywhere by his haircut, Jason built a reputation in 1994-95 when regularly coming on as a substitute striker for the last ten minutes or so of a game, often at the expense of Bryan Roy. A player who always gives 100 per-cent, and who is very fast, he will be remembered for scoring in the 2-2 draw against Tottenham after chasing a lost cause.
Charlton Ath (From trainee on 2/6/89) FL 0+1 Others 0+2
Stockport Co (Loaned on 6/2/91) FL 2
Lincoln C (£35,000 on 1/3/91) FL 86+7/21 FLC 6 FAC 2+1/1 Others 4
Southend U (Signed on 6/8/93) FL 18+6/3 FLC 1 FAC 1 Others 5+3/3
Nottingham F (£200,000 on 4/3/94) F/PL 15+20/5 FLC 0+2

Jason Lee Steve Morton
(Empics Sports Photo Agency)

LEE Robert Martin
Born: West Ham, 1 February 1966
Height: 5'10" Weight: 11.6
Club Honours: Div 1 '93
International Honours: E: 2; B-1; U21-2

Started last season for Newcastle in superb style, with 11 goals from the same number of games. This form forced him into the full England set-up, where he made a scoring debut in the 1-1 draw against Romania, following it up with his second cap in the 1-0 defeat of Nigeria. Strong and skilful on the ball, he links defence with attack perfectly and is also good in the air, as well as having a strong shot in either foot. Among many excellent strikes, his brilliant equaliser in the FAC against Blackburn was seen nationwide on BBC, when he skipped past two challenges on the left, cut inside and smashed a right-foot shot past Tim Flowers. Niggling injuries, mainly to his groin, forced him to miss several games, disrupting his season, slightly.

Charlton Ath (Free from Hornchurch on 12/7/83) FL 274+24/59 FLC 16+3/1 FAC 14/2 Others 10+2/3
Newcastle U (£700,00 on 22/9/92) F/PL 112/26 FLC 8/2 FAC 11/3 Others 3/4

LEGG Andrew (Andy)
Born: Neath, 28 July 1966
Height: 5'8" Weight: 10.7
Club Honours: WC '89, '91; AIC '95

In the Guinness Book of Records as having the longest throw in League football, being measured at 49 metres, Andy normally plays on the left-wing for Notts County, but was pressed into full-back service last season in an emergency. A good tackler, passer, and crosser of the ball, he is also the club's corner-kick specialist.

Swansea C (Signed from Britton Ferry on 12/8/88) FL 155+8/29 FLC 9+1 FAC 16/4 Others 15+3/5
Notts Co (£275,000 on 23/7/93) FL 61+3/5 FLC 7 FAC 4+1 Others 10+1/4

LENNON Neil Francis
Born: Lurgan, 25 June 1971
Height: 5'9" Weight: 12.4
International Honours: NI: 2; B-2; U23-1; U21-1

A really important member of the Crewe midfield, Neil, easily recognised by his red hair, has been capped by Northern Ireland at several levels. His consistency also saw him elected by his fellow professionals, both in 1994 and 1995, to the teams that won the PFA Divisional Awards.

Manchester C (From trainee on 26/8/89) FL 1
Crewe Alex (Free on 9/8/90) FL 117+5/13 FLC 4+1 FAC 7/1 Others 12+1

LEONARD Mark Anthony
Born: St Helens, 27 September 1962
Height: 5'11" Weight: 11.10

An unselfish old fashioned target man, and a wonderful team player, who performed with distinction in a sole striking role, Mark was Graham Barrow's first signing for Wigan when he was recruited from Chester during the 1994 close season.

Everton (Signed from Witton A on 24/2/82)
Tranmere Rov (Loaned on 24/3/83) FL 6+1
Crewe Alex (Free on 1/6/83) FL 51+3/15 FLC 4/2 FAC 2 Others 3+1
Stockport Co (Free on 13/2/85) FL 73/23 FLC 5/2 FAC 1 Others 2/3
Bradford C (£40,000 on 27/9/86) FL 120+37/29 FLC 13+5/6 FAC 6+3/1 Others 6+5/3
Rochdale (Signed on 27/3/92) FL 9/1
Preston NE (£50,000 on 13/8/92) FL 19+3/1 FLC 2
Chester C (Free on 13/8/93) FL 28+4/8 FLC 2 FAC 3/1 Others 3
Wigan Ath (Signed on 15/9/94) FL 28+1/5 FAC 2/1 Others 4/2

Graham Le Saux Neal Simpson
(Empics Sports Photo Agency)

LEONHARDSEN Oyvind
Born: Norway, 17 August 1970
Height: 5'10" Weight: 11.13
International Honours: Norway

Norwegian international signed on loan by Wimbledon until the end of 1994-95, with a view to a permanent £650,000 transfer, Oyvind proved to be a skilful, versatile midfield performer, with an eye for goal, and "busy bee" qualities rather like Ray Houghton. Scoring in the 90th minute on his debut against Aston Villa to give the "Dons" a 4-3 win, he featured in the majority of games from that moment on. Has adjusted well to the English game and it now remains to be seen whether the transfer becomes permanent. Very popular with the fans.
Wimbledon (Loaned from Rosenborg on 8/11/94) PL 18+2/4 FAC 3/1

LE SAUX Graham Pierre
Born: Harrow, 17 October 1968
Height: 5'10" Weight: 11.2
Club Honours: PL '95
International Honours: E: 10; B-2; U21-4

As the current England left-back, and a regular in the Blackburn side, his form was such that his deputy, Alan Wright, willingly transferred to Aston Villa last season. A passionate enthusiast, who is capable of going forward with great flair and the ability to beat an opponent, Graham brought diversity to the attack and, at the same time, enhanced his reputation in defence. Quick off the mark and even quicker to spot danger, he was seldom beaten for speed and had a ready eye for an interception and, like Colin Hendry alongside him, he developed a rare capacity for smothering attacks. Contributed three goals in all, with two glorious swerving free-kicks against Manchester City and West Ham, and a stunning volley at home to Arsenal. His season ended with a well deserved Championship medal and election to the PFA "PL Team of the Year".
Chelsea (Free from St Paul's, Jersey, on 9/12/87) F/PL 77+13/8 FLC 7+6/1 FAC 7+1 Others 8+1
Blackburn Rov (Signed on 25/3/93) PL 88+1/5 FLC 8 FAC 6 Others 3

LESLIE Steven
Born: Dumfries, 6 February 1976
Height: 5'4" Weight: 10.7

A diminutive and industrious midfielder, who was initially attracted to Stoke by Lou Macari, he made two subs' appearances in 1994-95, and looks likely to make the grade in a central midfield role during the next couple of seasons.
Stoke C (Signed on 20/3/93) FL 0+1 Others 0+1

LESTER Jack William
Born: Sheffield, 8 October 1975
Height: 5'10" Weight: 11.2

A right-footed striker, Jack has proved himself to be a fast and, accurate goalscorer for Grimsby at Pontins Division Two level and showed great promise on his occasional first team outings last season.
Grimsby T (From juniors on 8/7/94) FL 1+6 FLC 0+1 FAC 0+1

LE TISSIER Matthew Paul
Born: Guernsey, 14 October 1968
Height: 6'0" Weight: 11.10
International Honours: E: 6; B-5; Yth

Whether scoring stunning goals or making them with passes no other player would seemingly be capable of, he is surely the most naturally gifted individual in the Premier League. Needs only one moment to turn a game and usually that moment involves some sublime ball skill which alone is worth the admission charge. Of many spectacular goals for Southampton last season, one could select 35 yard efforts at Ewood Park and Villa Park, and a deadly accurate free-kick in the return game against Villa. Many are scored from the edge of the penalty area with an almost arrogant ease, indicating the little time he needs to assess situations. Played his first full game for England against Romania in October 1994, but has yet to prove himself at International Level and needs to be given an extended run in the side in order to do so. Matthew, the PFA "Young Player of the Year" for 1990, added to that honour when he was elected by his fellow professionals to the PL team at the recent PFA Awards Dinner.
Southampton (From apprentice on 17/10/86) F/PL 262+30/120 FLC 26+6/18 FAC 23+1/11 Others 11+1/9

LEVER Mark
Born: Beverley, 29 March 1970
Height: 6'3" Weight: 13.5

A right-footed central defender, he is yet another of the excellent group of young players to come up through Grimsby's youth scheme. Strong in the tackle, and in the air, he was the lynchpin of the defence for the greater part of last season, owing to the absence and eventual departure of veteran, Paul Futcher.
Grimsby T (From trainee on 9/8/88) FL 213+6/7 FLC 16+1 FAC 10+1 Others 9

LEWIS Michael (Mickey)
Born: Birmingham, 15 February 1965
Height: 5'8" Weight: 10.6
International Honours: E: Yth

Very committed midfielder who comes with a 100 per-cent guarantee. A ball-winner, rather than creator, goalscoring is not his strong point either, but he did score one of Oxford's goals of last season - his first for three years! Hard work and strong, fair challenges are his speciality.
West Bromwich A (From apprentice on 18/2/82) FL 22+2 FLC 4+1 FAC 4
Derby Co (£25,000 on 16/11/84) FL 37+6/1 FLC 2 FAC 0+1 Others 4
Oxford U (Signed on 25/8/88) FL 271+10/7 FLC 15+2 FAC 12+1 Others 11+1

LEWIS Neil Anthony
Born: Wolverhampton, 28 June 1974
Height: 5'7" Weight: 10.9

A talented left-sided youngster who can operate either as full-back or in midfield, he had an outstanding spell early last season when he regularly tormented defences. Lost some confidence as Leicester's performances faltered and found it hard to hold down a regular place. Could blossom into a star of the future, though.
Leicester C (From trainee on 9/7/92) F/PL 39+8 FLC 4 FAC 2 Others 2

Matt Le Tissier

Tony Morton
(Empics Sports Photo Agency)

LIBURD Richard John
Born: Nottingham, 26 September 1973
Height: 5'9" Weight: 11.1
A right-back who joined Bradford from Middlesbrough prior to the start of 1994-95, he played only 11 games before being forced out for 17 weeks with a hip muscle injury. Came back in a couple of reserve matches, but was again injured and missed the rest of the season.
Middlesbrough (£20,000 from Eastwood T on 25/3/93) FL 41/1 FLC 4 FAC 2 Others 5
Bradford C (£200,000 on 2l/7/94) FL 9/1 FLC 2

LIDDELL Andrew Mark
Born: Leeds, 28 June 1973
Height: 5'8" Weight: 10.5
International Honours: S: U21-5
Centre-forward. A fringe player at Barnsley for a couple of seasons, up to his breakthrough last November, he had made more substitutional appearances than actual starts in his career. His eye for a goal has always been apparent and some of his finishing has been of the top order and, despite not scoring until November, he ended the season in the teens. Also selected for the Scottish U21 side on a number of occasions.
Barnsley (From trainee on 6/7/91) FL 58+25/16 FLC 3+1/1 FAC 2+1 Others 2+1

LIDDLE Craig George
Born: Chester le Street, 21 October 1971
Height: 5'11" Weight: 12.7
Dependable young Middlesbrough central defender with tremendous heading ability. Fearless and brave in the tackle, with two Anglo Italian Cup appearances to his credit in 1994-95, Craig made his League debut against Tranmere in the final game of last season.
Middlesbrough (Free from Blyth Spartans on 12/7/94) FL 1 Others 2

LIGHTBOURNE Kyle Lavince
Born: Bermuda, 29 September 1968
Height: 6'2" Weight: 11.0
International Honours: Bermuda
Tall, elegant Walsall forward who shows delightful skill on the ball and can finish with either head or feet. Kyle's striking rate was a revelation in 1994-95, his 27 from 52 games, including a hat-trick against Fulham in September, saw him in third place to Barnet's Dougie Freedman in the Third Division goalscoring charts. And, at the PFA Awards Ceremony, he was elected by his fellow professionals for the divisional team. Also an ever-present for the club in the Endsleigh League.
Scarborough (Signed on 11/12/92) FL 11+8/3 FLC 1 Others 0+1
Walsall (Free on 17/9/93) FL 76+1/30 FLC 4/1 FAC 9/5 Others 3

LIGHTFOOT Christopher (Chris) Ian
Born: Penketh, 1 April 1970
Height: 6'2" Weight: 13.6
Although originally a central defender, Chris has recently played for Chester in midfield. A good strong player, with good passing ability, he was unfortunate to miss a

number of games during last season due to an ankle injury.
Chester C (From trainee on 11/7/88) FL 263+14/32 FLC 15+2/1 FAC 16+2/1 Others 14+2/5

LILLIS Jason Warren
Born: Chatham, 1 October 1969
Height: 5'11" Weight: 11.10
Centre-forward. After joining Cambridge from Walsall as a non-contract player last September, and scoring both goals at Peterborough, he was allowed to move to Dover on loan in March.
Gillingham (From trainee on 5/10/87) FL 15+14/3 FLC 2+2/2 FAC 2/1 Others 2+1/1 (Free to Jaro in April 1989)
Maidstone U (Free on 28/7/89) FL 57+18/18 FLC 4+1 FAC 2 Others 3+5 (Free to Sittingbourne on 22/7/92)
Carlisle U (Loaned on 28/2/91) FL 4/1
Walsall (Free on 15/10/93) FL 14+11/6 FLC 0+1 Others 0+1
Cambridge U (Free on 15/9/94) FL 14+5/4 FAC 3+1/2 Others 2+1/2

LILWALL Stephen
Born: Solihull, 15 February 1970
Height: 5'10" Weight: 12.0
Bandy-legged WBA full-back with a useful left-foot, Steve is strong in the tackle, has sound heading ability, good positional sense, and loves to overlap. Lost his place in the side to Paul Edwards and when Paul Agnew arrived at The Hawthorns he became third choice in his position, prior to being freed during the summer.
West Bromwich A (£75,000 from Kidderminster Harriers on 7/6/92) FL 71+2 FLC 3 FAC 4 Others 6

LIMBER Nicholas
Born: Doncaster, 23 January 1974
Height: 5'10" Weight: 11.0
Young Doncaster defender, or midfielder, whose 1994-95 was virtually written off due to a serious back injury. He failed to feature in the first team at League level and, indeed, his appearances were limited to just two early games in the Coca Cola Cup, prior to him being released at the end of the season.
Doncaster Rov (From trainee on 3/1/92) FL 13/1 Others 1+1/1
Manchester C (£75,000 on 24/1/92)
Peterborough U (Loaned on 9/10/92) FL 2
Doncaster Rov (Free on 3/3/94) FL 3+1 FLC 2

LIMPAR Anders Erik
Born: Solna, Sweden, 24 August 1965
Height: 5'8" Weight: 11.5
Club Honours: Div 1 '91; FAC '95
International Honours: Sweden
A Swedish international left-winger, Anders is extremely skilful and quick, runs well with the ball, and invites defenders to commit themselves before changing direction and dancing past them. Likes to get to the by-line and pin-point crosses to forwards, or to maze his way through into the penalty area. Having moved to Everton from Arsenal in March 1994, initially knee injuries kept his outings down to a premium, but under Joe Royle last season his style has been incorporated into the team's game plan. This has resulted in sound performances, where his undeniable skill as a provider have shone

through, especially in the FA Cup Final win over Manchester United.
Arsenal (£1,000,000 from Cremonese on 6/8/90) F/PL 76+20/17 FLC 9 FAC 7/2 Others 4/1
Everton (£1,600,000 on 24/3/94) PL 28+8/2 FAC 5+1/1

LINDSEY Scott
Born: Walsall, 4 May 1972
Height: 5'9" Weight: 11.10
Son of the former Gillingham right-back, Keith, he is a chip off the old block in the same position and for the same club. Strong in the tackle, and with an appetite to get forward, he was given a one year contract at the start of last season and ended the term as a regular member of the first team squad.
Gillingham (Free from Bridlington T on 28/7/94) FL 11+1 Others 1

LING Martin
Born: West Ham, 15 July 1966
Height: 5'8" Weight: 10.2
Experienced Swindon performer who has given good value for money since his arrival at the County Ground four years ago. In that time, he has rarely filled other than a midfield role, but has donned many different shirts - adding the numbers three and nine to his collection in 1994-95. Not renowned as a goalscorer, he found the net just three times during the season, but all earned his side points.
Exeter C (From apprentice on 13/1/84) FL 109+8/14 FLC 8 FAC 4 Others 5
Swindon T (£25,000 on 14/7/86) FL 2 FLC 1+1
Southend U (£15,000 on 16/10/86) FL 126+12/31 FLC 8/2 FAC 7/1 Others ll+l/3
Mansfield T (Loaned on 24/1/91) FL 3
Swindon T (£15,000 on 28/3/91) F/PL 120+14/10 FLC 11+1/1 FAC 8 Others 9+1

LINGER Paul Hayden
Born: Stepney, 20 December 1974
Height: 5'8" Weight: 10.1
Charlton midfield player, who made his full FL debut against Millwall at the New Den last season after several substitute outings, he likes to get forward and is capable of scoring goals as he has done regularly for the reserve team. Has a nice touch and is an accurate passer of the ball.
Charlton Ath (From trainee on 1/7/93) FL 3+12 Others 0+3

LINIGHAN Andrew (Andy)
Born: Hartlepool, 18 June 1962
Height: 6'3" Weight: 13.10
Club Honours: FLC '93; FAC '93; ECWC '94
International Honours: E: B-4
From a footballing family, father, Brian, played for Darlington and brothers, David and Brian, currently turn out for Ipswich and Sheffield Wednesday, respectively. As a dependable and experienced centre-back with Arsenal, his opportunities were somewhat limited last season, due to the club's strength in depth, but he is a good man to be able to call on in an emergency. Very good when hitting long diagonal balls out of defence.
Hartlepool U (Free from Smiths Dock on 19/9/80) FL 110/4 FLC 7+1/1 FAC 8 Others 1/1
Leeds U (£20,000 on 15/5/84) FL 66/3 FLC 6/1 FAC 2 Others 2

Oldham Ath (£65,000 on 17/1/86) FL 87/6 FLC 8/2 FAC 3 Others 4
Norwich C (£350,000 on 4/3/88) FL 86/8 FLC 6 FAC 10 Others 4
Arsenal (£1,250,000 on 4/7/90) F/PL 74+15/4 FLC 11+1/1 FAC 12+1/1 Others 7+1/1

LINIGHAN David
Born: Hartlepool, 9 January 1965
Height: 6'2" Weight: 12.6
Club Honours: Div 2 '92

Ipswich central defender, who is commanding in the air, and now into his eighth season at the club, David began last season on a weekly contract and lost the captaincy as a result. Recovered the armband following many consistent displays in a beleaguered defence, holding it together on more than one occasion. Scored his first ever cup goal for the club at Wrexham in the FA Cup reverse.
Hartlepool U (From juniors on 3/3/82) FL 84+7/5 FLC 3+1/1 FAC 3 Others 1
Derby Co (£25,000 on 11/8/86)
Shrewsbury T (£30,000 on 4/12/86) FL 65/1 FLC 5 FAC 3 Others 1
Ipswich T (£300,000 on 23/6/88) F/PL 273+2/12 FLC 20 FAC 18/1 Others 10

LINTON Desmond (Des) Martin
Born: Birmingham, 5 September 1971
Height: 6'1" Weight: 11.13

A tall, rangy full-back or left-sided midfield player, he started last season as a regular Luton squad member, but a hamstring and then a torn stomach muscle kept him out for long periods. Capable of carrying the ball on long runs as well as winning it, he will be looking to avoid injuries in 1995-96 in order to resurrect his career.
Leicester C (From trainee on 9/1/90) FL 6+5 FLC 0+1 Others 1
Luton T (Signed on 22/10/91) FL 56+10/1 FLC 3+1 FAC 7 Others 3

LITTLEJOHN Adrian Sylvester
Born: Wolverhampton, 26 September 1970
Height: 5'9" Weight: 10.5
International Honours: E: Sch

Sheffield United forward player possessing lightening pace. With the acquisition of Nathan Blake, he found first team opportunities limited last season, managing only nine full League appearances, but is too good a player to remain in the reserve side for long.
Walsall (Free from West Bromwich A juniors on 24/5/89) FL 26+18/1 FLC 2+1 FAC 1+1 Others 4+1
Sheffield U (Free on 6/8/91) F/PL 44+25/12 FLC 5+1 FAC 3+2/1 Others 2/1

LIVETT Simon Robert
Born: Plaistow 8 January 1969
Height: 5'10" Weight: 12.9

Midfielder. Unable to command a first team place at Cambridge in 1994-95, Simon spent some time on loan at Dagenham & Redbridge and then Dover, before being released at the end of the season.
West Ham U (From trainee on 23/1/87) FL 1 FAC 0+1 Others 1
Leyton Orient (Free on 10/8/92) FL 16+8 FLC 2 FAC 2 Others 1/1
Cambridge U (Signed on 1/10/93) FL 12 FLC 1 FAC 3 Others 2

LIVINGSTONE Stephen (Steve)
Born: Middlesbrough, 8 September 1969
Height: 6'1" Weight: 12.7

A right-footed, hard-working striker, who is strong and physical in the old "centre-forward" mould, he is good in the air and adds deft touches to a sense of awareness in the box. A lengthy spell of injury limited his opportunities for Grimsby last season, but on his return to the side in early March, he showed that his eye for a goal has not deserted him.
Coventry C (From trainee on 16/7/86) FL 17+14/5 FLC 8+2/10 Others 0+1
Blackburn Rov (£450,000 on 17/1/91) F/PL 25+5/10 FLC 2 FAC 1/1
Chelsea (£350,000 on 23/3/93) PL 0+1
Port Vale (Loaned on 3/9/93) FL 4+1
Grimsby T (£140,000 on 29/10/93) FL 56+5/11 FLC 2 FAC 1

LLEWELLYN Andrew (Andy) David
Born: Bristol, 26 February 1966
Height: 5'7" Weight: 11.4
International Honours: E: Yth

Released by Bristol City after ten years service, Andy joined Hereford on a monthly contract last October, making only a handful of starts at right-back, before being freed in January.
Bristol C (From apprentice on 13//3/84) FL 291+10/3 FLC 20 FAC 23 Others 26+2
Exeter C (Loaned on 10/3/94) FL 15
Hereford U (Free on 7/10/94) FL 3+1 FAC 1+1 Others 1

LLOYD Kevin Gareth
Born: Llanidloes, 26 September 1970
Height: 6'0" Weight: 12.1

Signed last November from non-league Caersws, Kevin quickly made the Hereford left-back spot his own. Strong and reliable, he is a player who enjoys going forward, hence a couple of goals.
Hereford U (Free from Caersws on 7/11/94) FL 24/3 Others 3

LOCK Anthony (Tony) Charles
Born: Harlow, 3 September 1976
Height: 5'11" Weight: 11.0

A prolific scorer from midfield for the Colchester youth team, and a final year YTS lad, Tony opened his first team account when coming on as substitute against Exeter last season after injuries and suspensions had depleted the ranks. Turned pro in April.
Colchester U (From trainee on 18/4/95) FL 0+3/1

LOCKE Adam Spencer
Born: Croydon, 20 August 1970
Height: 5'11" Weight: 12.7

Played at Colchester during a month on loan in 1993-94, but has really made his mark since joining from Southend permanently last autumn. A skilful midfielder who excels in running at opponents, and did not look out of place against Premiership opposition, Adam can also fill in at right-back if required. His abilities were sadly missed through injury as the play-off challenge faded away.
Crystal Palace (From trainee on 21/6/88)
Southend U (Free on 6/8/90) FL 56+17/4 FLC 5 FAC 2+1 Others 6+1

Colchester U (Loaned on 8/10/93) FL 4 Others 1
Colchester U (Free on 23/9/94) FL 20+2/1 FAC 4 Others 2

LOGAN Richard Anthony
Born: Barnsley, 24 May 1969
Height: 6'1" Weight: 13.3

A recruit from non-league soccer, and originally a bricklayer, Richard's long-throw set-pieces have become a feature of Huddersfield's play. Assured of a place in Town's history as a Wembley scorer in the 1993-94 Autoglass Trophy, he plays a central midfield ball-winning role.
Huddersfield T (Free from Gainsborough Trinity on 15/11/93) FL 33+10/1 FLC 3 FAC 1 Others 9

LOMAS Andrew (Andy) James
Born: Hartlepool, 26 April 1965
Height: 6'2" Weight: 13.5

Goalkeeper. Signed on loan to cover an injury to Jon Sheffield, he made just two appearances for Cambridge before moving to Rushden Diamonds on a more permanent basis.
Cambridge U (Loaned from Stevenage Borough on 17/3/95) FL 2

LOMAS Stephen (Steve) Martin
Born: Hanover, Germany, 18 January 1974
Height: 6'0" Weight: 11.10
International Honours: NI: 6; B-1; Yth

Selected for Manchester City at home to Everton early in 1994-95, Steve was in contention right up to the January Coca Cola match against Crystal Palace when he fractured a shin bone and, at the same time, swallowed his tongue. Prior to that disaster, the youngster had gained two more international caps for Northern Ireland against Portugal and Austria. Predominately a midfielder with lovely touches, who can really pass the ball, he can be used in a number of utility roles and is a great clubman.
Manchester C (From trainee on 22/1/91) PL 35+10/2 FLC 10/2 FAC 2+1

Steve Lomas   Neal Simpson
(Empics Sports Photo Agency)

127

LORMOR Anthony (Tony)
Born: Ashington, 29 October 1970
Height: 6'0" Weight: 12.3

Probably the free transfer find of 1994-95, Tony joined Chesterfield from Peterborough last December, having earlier been released by Lincoln, after injury had threatened his career. From his debut, the club went 21 games unbeaten, such was his impact, and he scored the first play-off goal at Wembley as the "Spireites" ultimately rejoined the Second Division. A tall, rangy centre-forward in the traditional mould, his persistence and pace upset many defences and made him an immediate crowd favourite.

Newcastle U (From trainee on 25/2/88) FL 6+2/3
Lincoln C (£25,000 on 29/1/90) FL 90+10/30 FLC 1+2/3 FAC 4/2 Others 6
Peterborough U (Free on 4/7/94) FL 2+3 FAC 1 Others 1+1
Chesterfield (Free on 23/12/94) FL 23/10 Others 3/2

Tony Lormor   Steve Morton
(Empics Sports Photo Agency)

LOSS Colin Paul
Born: Brentwood, 15 August 1973
Height: 5'11" Weight: 11.4

Bristol City midfield player. Signed from non-league football towards the end of 1993-94, Colin broke into the first team early last season, making four starts, but following the 1-0 Coca Cola Cup defeat at the hands of Notts County he disappeared from senior contention and was released during the summer.

Derby Co (Free from Norwich C juniors on 20/11/91)
Bristol C (£12,000 from Gresley Rov, via Derry C, on 21/3/94) FL 3+2 FLC 1

LOVELL Stuart Andrew
Born: Sydney, Australia, 9 January 1972
Height: 5'10" Weight: 11.0
Club Honours: Div 2 '94

Another to come through Reading's excellent youth policy, Stuart has become a regular and dynamic goalscorer, forging successful partnerships, firstly with Jimmy Quinn and, more recently, with Lee Nogan. Missed several games through hamstring

injuries last season, but finished the campaign as the club's leading goalscorer in FL matches. Although he likes to smack the ball at goal, he works hard to set up chances for his team-mates too.

Reading (From trainee on 13/7/90) FL 124+27/45 FLC 9/3 FAC 5+5/2 Others 7+3/2

LOWE David Anthony
Born: Liverpool, 30 August 1965
Height: 5'10" Weight: 11.4
Club Honours: AMC '85; Div 2 '92
International Honours: E: U21-2; Yth

Fiery character who scored a class goal in the Leicester victory over Tottenham, which was voted the club's "Goal of the Season", and a brave one to defeat Arsenal. Lost his place as a striker midway through last season, but made a comeback in a midfield role under Mark McGhee, registering two late strikes in the dramatic draw at Villa Park. Always likely to score his share of goals, particularly from inside the six yard box, he finished second in the "Foxes'" goalscoring charts, despite only appearing in two thirds of the games.

Wigan Ath (From apprentice on 1/6/83) FL 179+9/40 FLC 8 FAC 16+1/4 Others 18/9
Ipswich T (£80,000 on 26/6/87) FL 121+13/37 FLC 10/2 FAC 3 Others 10+2/6
Port Vale (Loaned on 19/3/92) FL 8+1/2
Leicester C (£250,000 on 13/7/92) F/PL 57+19/19 FLC 0+3/1 FAC 1+2 Others 3
Port Vale (Loaned on 18/2/94) FL 18+1/5

LOWE Kenneth (Kenny)
Born: Sedgefield, 6 November 1961
Height: 6'1" Weight: 11.4
Club Honours: FAT '90

Once described as the "Glenn Hoddle of non-league football", and Barry Fry's first signing for Birmingham, Kenny had a disappointing time of it in 1994-95. Loaned out to Carlisle in August, he returned to the City side just before Christmas, only to suffer a serious knee injury which sidelined him for the rest of the campaign.

Hartlepool U (From apprentice on 14/11/78) FL 50+4/3 FLC 1+1 FAC 2 Others 1 (Free to Billingham during 1984 close season)
Scarborough (Free from Barrow, via Spearwood, Australia, Gateshead and Morecambe, on 15/1/88) FL 4 (Free to Barrow in April 1989)
Barnet (£40,000 on 1/3/91) FL 55+17/5 FLC 2+1 FAC 5 Others 4
Stoke C (Free on 5/8/93) FL 3+6 FLC 2 Others 2
Birmingham C (£75,000 on 17/12/93) FL 14+5/3 FLC 0+1 FAC 3+1 Others 2+1
Carlisle U (Loaned on 22/9/94) FL 1+1

LOWTHORPE Adam
Born: Hull, 7 August 1975
Height: 5'7" Weight: 10.6

The former Hull junior team captain, and widely regarded as the best young prospect at the club, Adam's progress in 1994-95 was hampered by a worrying succession of injuries. A "natural" right-back, who also looks comfortable at left-back despite his slight frame, he is a tigerish tackler and is always keen to go forward.

Hull C (From trainee on 2/7/93) FL 24+1 FLC 1 Others 0+1

LUCAS Richard
Born: Chapeltown, 22 September 1970
Height: 5'10" Weight: 11.4

An extremely versatile, hard-tackling player who, although being predominantly left-footed and defensive, can play in a number of positions, including both full-back slots, right across midfield, and even up-front on occasion. Due to competition for places at Preston last season, Richard had a spell on loan with Lincoln in October before being released in April and, at the time of going to press, he had yet to find another club.

Sheffield U (From trainee on 1/7/89) FL 8+2 FAC 1 Others 0+1
Preston NE (£40,000 on 24/12/92) FL 47+3 FAC 4 Others 4+1
Lincoln C (Loaned on 14/10/94) FL 4 Others 2

LUCKETTI Christopher (Chris) James
Born: Littleborough, 28 September 1971
Height: 6'0" Weight: 12.1

Voted Bury's "Player of the Year" last season, Chris showed himself to be a solid central defender, commanding in the air and seemingly first to every ball on the ground. Always joined the attack for set-pieces, his presence creating many chances for others, and scored four useful goals himself. Is the jewel in the "Shakers'" crown right now.

Rochdale (Trainee) FL 1
Stockport Co (Free on 23/8/90)
Halifax T (Free on 12/7/91) FL 73+5/2 FLC 2/1 FAC 2 Others 4
Bury (£50,000 on 1/10/93) FL 66/4 FLC 2 FAC 6/1 Others 10

LUDDEN Dominic James
Born: Basildon, 30 March 1974
Height: 5'9" Weight: 11.0
International Honours: E: Sch

A left-back signing for Watford during the 1994 close season, he was unfortunately injured early on in 1994-95 and had only limited opportunities. Particularly impressive going forward, Dominic will come again.

Leyton Orient (From trainee on 6/7/92) FL 50+8/1 FLC 1 FAC 0+1 Others 6/1
Watford (£100,000 on 7/8/94) FL 1

John Lukic   Paul Marriott
(Empics Sports Photo Agency)

LUKIC Jovan (John)
Born: Chesterfield, 11 December 1960
Height: 6'4" Weight: 13.7
Club Honours: Div 1 '89, '92; FLC '87; CS '89, '92
International Honours: E: B-1; EU21-7; Yth

A hugely experienced Leeds' goalkeeper, in 1995, John celebrated the 20th anniversary of his initial signing date and, at the same time, re-established himself as the club's number one with a series of consistent displays. Has superb reflexes for such a big man and, in producing a stream of excellent and spectacular saves, he looked to be different class after his confidence had returned. Along with Garry Kelly, he was ever-present in 1994-95.

Leeds U (From apprentice on 16/12/78) FL 146 FLC 7 FAC 9 Others 3
Arsenal (£50,000 on 25/7/83) FL 223 FLC 32 FAC 21 Others 4
Leeds U (£1,000,000 on 14/6/90) F/PL 181 FLC 16 FAC 14 Others 11

LUND Gary James
Born: Grimsby, 13 September 1964
Height: 5'11" Weight: 11.0
International Honours: E: U21-1; Yth

A player fast approaching 100 goals for Notts County, Gary is a hard-running striker who shoots on sight of the goal and has a flair for holding up play, notably from throw-ins, until support is at hand. Played sporadically last season and spent a period on loan at Hull as cover for the injured Linton Brown, following up an earlier spell.

Grimsby T (From juniors on 27/7/83) FL 47+13/24 FLC 6+2/1 FAC 4/5 Others 2/1
Lincoln C (Free on 22/8/86) FL 41+3/13 FLC 4/1 FAC 1/1 Others 3/1
Notts Co (£40,000 on 17/6/87) FL 223+25/62 FLC 15+2/5 FAC 13+3/4 Others 28+6/8
Hull C (Loaned on 14/8/92) FL 11/3
Hull C (Loaned on 23/3/95) FL 11/3

LYDIATE Jason Lee
Born: Manchester, 29 October 1971
Height: 5'11" Weight: 12.3

Started last season in the Bolton defence, mainly at right-back, before being ousted by Scott Green. Unable to get back into the side, Jason was transferred to Blackpool in March and impressed immediately with his strength, speed and aerial ability. Looks to be a bargain signing for the "Pool".

Manchester U (From trainee on 1/7/90)
Bolton W (Free on 19/3/92) FL 29+1 FLC 4 FAC 2 Others 1
Blackpool (£75,000 on 3/3/95) FL 11

LYNCH Christopher (Chris) John
Born: Middlesbrough, 18 November 1974
Height: 6'0" Weight: 11.0

Useful midfielder or defender. Began last season well for Hartlepool, scoring an important winning goal against Darlington. However, unable to hold a regular first team place, in mid-season he was one of three players informed that they could leave the club. Chose to play on and, under Keith Houchen, he finished 1994-95 back in the first team squad, with the offer of a three month contract.

Hartlepool U (From trainee on 2/8/93) FL 25+6/1 FLC 2+1

Tommy Lynch

Matthew Ashton
(Empics Sports Photo Agency)

LYNCH Thomas (Tommy) Michael
Born: Limerick, 10 October 1964
Height: 6'0" Weight: 12.6
Club Honours: Div 3 '94

Left-back. Firm crowd favourite at Shrewsbury who gives his utmost every game with his hard-tackling and no-nonsense defending. Always looks happy to move forward and, with a strong shot at dead-ball situations, Tommy is equally at home in central defence, being a powerful header of the ball. For a defender, he rarely finds himself in trouble with referees.

Sunderland (£20,000 from Limerick on 11/8/88) FL 4 Others 1
Shrewsbury T (£20,000 on 16/1/90) FL 198+11/11 FLC 14 FAC 12 Others 15+1/1

LYNE Neil George Francis
Born: Leicester, 4 April 1970
Height: 6'1 " Weight: 12.2
Forward. Signed from Cambridge during the

1994 close season, Neil is one of the fastest players at Hereford, who looks good when taking defenders on and is very skilful with the ball at his feet. Took a while to get into the side, but appears to be a regular now.

Nottingham F (Signed from Leicester U on 16/8/89) FLC 0+1
Walsall (Loaned on 22/3/90) FL 6+1
Shrewsbury T (Loaned on 14/3/91) FL 16/6
Shrewsbury T (Signed on 11/7/91) FL 61+3/11 FLC 6/2 FAC 3/2 Others 3
Cambridge U (£75,000 on 15/1/93) FL 5+12
Chesterfield (Loaned on 24/9/93) FL 3/1
Chesterfield (Loaned on 24/3/94) FL 2+1
Hereford U (Free on 27/7/94) FL 27+4/1 FAC 2 Others 4/1

LYONS Andrew (Andy)
Born: Blackpool, 19 October 1966
Height: 5'10" Weight: 11.0

A lively Wigan left-winger who can not only score goals, but creates many others for his fellow strikers, Andy has proved an excellent signing since arriving from Crewe

Gary Mabbutt
Steve Morton
(Empics Sports Photo Agency)

two years ago. After topping the goal-scoring charts in 1993-94, he repeated the dose last season with 15 in the League.

Crewe Alex (£15,000 from Fleetwood T on 26/10/92) FL 7+4/2 FLC 1/1 Others 1+1
Wigan Ath (Signed on 1/10/93) FL 65/26 FLC 3 FAC 4 Others 4

LYTTLE Desmond (Des)

Born: Wolverhampton, 24 September 1971
Height: 5'9" Weight: 12.0

Possibly the most improved player in the Nottingham Forest side, Des won the critics over in 1994-95 with consistently sound displays. In making the right-back spot his own, he proved to be a good tackler and not adverse to the overlap, building up an excellent understanding with Steve Stone down the flank. Ever-present, apart from suspension, two of his best performances came in the games against Manchester United, which saw Ryan Giggs subbed on both occasions.

Leicester C (From trainee on 1/9/90)
Swansea C (£12,500 from Worcester C on 9/7/92) FL 46/1 FLC 2 FAC 5 Others 5
Nottingham F (£375,000 on 27/7/93) F/PL 75/1 FLC 10 FAC 4 Others 1

MABBUTT Gary Vincent

Born: Bristol, 23 August 1961
Height: 5'10" Weight: 12.9
Club Honours: UEFA '84; FAC '91; CS '91
International Honours: E: 16; B-9; U21-7; Yth

Gary, in his 13th season at Tottenham, once again established himself as a first team regular last September in the 6-3 victory over Watford in the Coca Cola Cup. His enthusiasm and sheer presence in the club's back four, with his tremendous ability in the air, began to steady a very unsettled defence which continued to be a decisive factor throughout the remainder of the campaign. Along with his consistency in defending the Tottenham goal, he was also keen to demonstrate his ability to score goals, as in the 4-1 victory over Sunderland in the FA Cup. Seems to enjoy his football more and more as seasons pass and is a firm favourite at White Hart Lane.

Bristol Rov (From apprentice on 9/1/79) FL 122+9/10 FLC 10/1 FAC 5+1/1
Tottenham H (£105,000 on 11/8/82) F/PL 417+16/27 FLC 56+2/2 FAC 39+2/3 Others 29+4/4

McALLISTER Gary

Born: Motherwell, 25 December 1964
Height: 6'1" Weight: 11.5
Club Honours: S Div 1 '85; Div 1 '92; CS '92
International Honours: S: 33; B-2; U21-1

Captain of both club and country, and widely regarded as one of the best midfield playmakers in Britain, Gary is the driving force behind most of Leeds' attacking moves, using great all-round vision and specialising in long diagonal passes to switch the play and wrong foot defenders. Tony Yeboah, in particular, benefited from chances created by Gary in 1994-95. Scorer of spectacular goals himself, his form is a major influence on Leeds' performances, emphasised none more so than last season. Was also the subject of great interest from Glasgow Rangers, a bid of £2,500,000 being turned down. For Leeds' fans, it is hard to imagine him away from Elland Road.

Motherwell (Signed from Fir Park BC in 1981) SL 52+7/6 SLC 3+1 SC 7/2
Leicester C (£125,000 on 15/8/85) FL 199+2/47 FLC 14+1/3 FAC 5/2 Others 4
Leeds U (£1,000,000 on 2/7/90) F/PL 194+1/26 FLC 18/3 FAC 18/3 Others 10/3

McAREE Rodney (Rod) Joseph

Born: Dungannon, 19 August 1974
Height: 5'7" Weight: 10.9
International Honours: NI: Yth

Signed from Liverpool during the 1994 close season, Rod got an early start with Bristol City, making his FL debut on the opening day. An attacking midfielder who likes to be involved and is constructive when in possession, despite five more starts, he was given a free transfer during the summer.

Liverpool (From trainee on 21/8/91)
Bristol C (Free on 26/7/94) FL 4+2 FLC 2

Gary McAllister
Neal Simpson
(Empics Sports Photo Agency)

McATEER Jason Wynn

Born: Birkenhead, 18 June 1971
Height: 5'9" Weight: 11.5
International Honours: Ei: 14; B-1

Suffered during the early part of last season when it was obvious that he had not sufficiently recovered from his exploits in the World Cup Finals with the Republic. Manager, Bruce Rioch, rested him for a spell, before he bounced back with his usual

Jason McAteer

Steve Morton
(Empics Sports Photo Agency)

midfield gusto that continues to attract the attention of a number of large clubs, and netted Bolton's important play-off goal against "Wolves" at Molineux. Selected for the PFA Division One side by his fellow professionals, Jason will be in the Premiership in 1995-96, following the club's play-off victory over Reading.

Bolton W (Signed from Marine on 22/1/92) FL 105+5/8 FLC 11/2 FAC 11/3 Others 8+1/2

McAULEY Sean
Born: Sheffield, 23 June 1972
Height: 6'0" Weight: 11.7
International Honours: S: U21-1
This skilful, attacking midfielder joined Chesterfield on loan from St Johnstone last November and scored in his only full League appearance. Despite showing promise, he was released after an injury and the arrival of Phil Robinson had reduced his opportunities.

Manchester U (From trainee on 1/7/90)
St Johnstone (Signed on 22/4/92) SL 52+2 SLC 3 SC 3
Chesterfield (Loaned on 4/11/94) FL 1/1 FAC 1+1 Others 2

MACAULEY Steven (Steve) Roy
Born: Lytham, 4 March 1969
Height: 6'1" Weight: 12.0
Club Honours: FAYC '86

The lynchpin at the heart of the Crewe defence who, since coming from non-league football, has made the number five spot his own. Now captaining the side, Steve inspires confidence and became the supporters' "Player of the Year" in May 1995. A very useful player to have around in dead-ball situations, with excellent heading ability.

Manchester C (From trainee on 5/11/87)
Crewe Alex (£25,000 from Fleetwood T on 24/3/92) FL 94/11 FLC 6 FAC 5 Others 10/2

McCALL Stephen (Steve) Harold
Born: Carlisle, 15 October 1960
Height: 5'11" Weight: 11.3
Club Honours: UEFAC '81
International Honours: E: B-1; U21-6; Yth

Out for most of last season through injury, he is an extremely talented midfielder with a "sweet" left-foot, who reads the game very well, and his guile and passing were sorely missed from the Plymouth midfield. Took over the role of player-manager, following Peter Shilton's departure, but later resigned the role to concentrate on playing.

Ipswich T (From apprentice on 5/10/78) FL 249+8/7 FLC 29 FAC 23+1/1 Others 18+1/3
Sheffield Wed (£300,000 on 3/6/87) FL 21+8/2 FLC 2+3 FAC 1 Others 0+1
Carlisle U (Loaned on 8/2/90) FL 6
Plymouth Arg (£25,000 on 26/3/92) FL 95+1/4 FLC 5 FAC 6 Others 6

McCARTHY Alan James
Born: Wandsworth, 11 January 1972
Height: 5'11" Weight: 12.10
International Honours: EY-1. W: U21-3

A left-footed QPR central defender who is very calm and good at bringing the ball out of defence, he made just two appearances for the first team last season, both as substitute. Will be pushing for a more permanent place in 1995-96.

Queens Park R (From trainee on 8/12/89) F/PL 8+3 FAC 0+1 Others 1
Watford (Loaned on 26/11/93) FL 8+1
Plymouth Arg (Loaned on 11/2/94) FL 1+1

McCARTHY Anthony (Tony) Paul
Born: Dublin, 9 November 1969
Height: 6'1" Weight: 12.10
International Honours: Ei: U21-5

Tall centre-half who joined Colchester from Millwall in March 1995, having earlier been on loan at Crewe, he immediately helped to shore up a defence hard hit by injuries and suspensions. Outstanding on his debut against Exeter, it is expected that he will score his share of goals from set pieces.

Millwall (£100,000 from Shelbourne on 25/6/92) FL 20+4/1 FLC 3
Crewe Alex (Loaned on 9/12/94) FL 2
Colchester U (Free on 17/3/95) FL 10/1

131

McCARTHY Jonathan (Jon) David
Born: Middlesbrough, 18 August 1970
Height: 5'9" Weight: 11.0
Very skilful and exciting York performer, who was at his most dangerous in 1994-95 when operating wide on the right-wing, his electrifying pace and sheer persistence caused problems for most Second Division defences. Voted "Clubman of the Year" for the second time in four seasons.
Hartlepool U (From juniors on 7/11/87) FL 0+1 (Free to Shepshed Charterhouse in March 1989)
York C (Free on 22/3/90) FL 198+1/31 FLC 8/1 FAC 11/3 Others 15/3

McCARTHY Paul Jason
Born: Cork, 4 August 1971
Height: 6'0" Weight: 13.6
International Honours: Ei: U21-10
A Brighton central defender, who continues to improve and mature, Paul had a six match absence early last season, due to an ankle injury, but returned to the fray to have a very consistent campaign, full of solid defensive displays. Good in the air, and a strong tackler, he is a wholehearted player.
Brighton & Hove A (From trainee on 26/4/89) FL 147+1/5 FLC 9/1 FAC 98 Others 10

McCARTHY Sean Casey
Born: Bridgend, 12 September 1967
Height: 6'1" Weight: 12.5
International Honours: W: B-1; Sch
Top-scorer for Oldham in 1994-95, with 18 goals, Sean is a striker who never stops trying and never gives up. Disappointed to miss out on a place in the Republic of Ireland's World Cup squad, he proved more than a match for the First Division's centre-backs. Is a player who need continually watching.
Swansea C (Signed from Bridgend T on 22/10/85) FL 76+15/25 FLC 4+1/3 FAC 5+2/4 Others 9+1/6
Plymouth Arg (£50,000 on 18/8/88) FL 67+3/19 FLC 7/5 FAC 3/1 Others 0+1/1
Bradford C (£250,000 on 4/7/90) FL 127+4/60 FLC 10+2/10 FAC 8/2 Others 8+1/7
Oldham Ath (£500,000 on 3/12/93) P/FL 54+5/22 FLC 4 FAC 1

McCLAIR Brian John
Born: Belshill, 8 December 1963
Height: 5'10" Weight" 12.13
Club Honours: SC '85; SPD '86; FAC '90, '94; CS '90, '94; ECWC '91; ESC '91; FLC '91; PL '93, '94
International Honours: S: 30; B-1; U21-8
Brian is a wonderful team player, who is equally adept in Manchester United's midfield, or as part of the strike-force, and always makes himself available by timing his runs to perfection. A regular scorer for the club, most of his goals come on the blind side of defenders, his re-emerging first team career was one of the main highlights of United's season. His canny skills and remarkable vision gave the side that extra dimension and, although he only scored eight goals in all competitions, he made many more for his team-mates through his unselfish play. Perhaps his greatest contribution came in the FA Cup, with fine strikes against Wrexham and Leeds.
Motherwell (Free from Aston Villa juniors on

1/8/81) SL 33+7/15 SLC 9+1/4 SC 2/1
Glasgow Celtic (£100,000 on 1/7/83) SL 129+16/99 SLC 19+1/9 SC 14+4/11 Others 13+2/3
Manchester U (£850,000 on 30/7/87) F/PL 278+23/85 FLC 40+1/19 FAC 35+4/14 Others 23/7

McCREERY David
Born: Belfast, 16 September 1957
Height: 5'6" Weight: 10.7
Club Honours: FAC '77
International Honours: NI: 67; U21-1; Yth; Sch
Appointed Hartlepool's player-manager last October, this vastly experienced midfielder made only occasional first team appearances. Although he had some success when leading by example, there was criticism that he did not play himself enough. Realistically, he had enough problems as manager, without having to be a player as well. Left the club by mutual consent in April.
Manchester U (From apprentice on 1/10/74) FL 48+39/7 FLC 4/1 FAC 1
Queens Park R (£200,000 on 16/8/79) FL 56+1/4 FLC 8/1 FAC 1+1 (£125,000 to Tulsa Roughnecks in March 1981)
Newcastle U (£80,000 on 4/10/82) FL 237+6/2 FLC 15 FAC 10+1 Others 1 (Free to Sweden on 1/6/89)
Heart of Midlothian (Free in September 1989) SL 24+5 SLC 3 SC 3 Others 1
Hartlepool U (Free on 17/8/91) FL 27+3 FLC 2+1 FAC 3
Carlisle U (Signed on 3/10/92) FL 25+10 FLC 0+1 FAC 3 Others 1
Hartlepool U (Signed on 20/10/94) FL 7+2 FAC 1

McDERMOTT John
Born: Middlesbrough, 3 February 1969
Height: 5'7" Weight: 10.6
Since the departure of Paul Agnew, John is now Grimsby's senior professional. Surprisingly fast for a defender, he is a strong tackler who provides excellent service for the front runners and is not adverse in going forward with the ball. A very consistent player who, when fit, has dominated the right-back position for almost eight seasons.
Grimsby T (From trainee on 1/6/87) FL 233+13/4 FLC 17+1 FAC 16+1 Others 11

McDONALD Alan
Born: Belfast, 12 October 1963
Height: 6'2" Weight: 12.7
International Honours: NI: 50; Yth; Sch
Strong-tackling defender who is very good in the air and a real threat from set-pieces in the opposing box, when creating goals rather than scoring. As captain of QPR and Northern Ireland, he has had yet another season of high consistency, missing just three games.
Queens Park R (From apprentice on 12/8/81) F/PL 332+5/10 FLC 38/2 FAC 28/1 Others 5
Charlton Ath (Loaned on 24/3/83) FL 9

MacDONALD David Hugh
Born: Dublin, 2 January 1971
Height: 5'10" Weight: 11.0
International Honours: Ei: B; U21-2; Yth
Tough, strong-tackling, no-nonsense Barnet right-back who likes to break forward. Showing his ability to adapt for the team last season, David also filled in at left-back when the occasion arose. Also showed a

willingness to use the ball from deep positions, with long passes into the channels.
Tottenham H (From trainee on 5/8/88) PL 2
Gillingham (Loaned on 27/9/90) FL 10 Others 2
Bradford C (Loaned on 28/8/92) FL 7
Reading (Loaned on 6/3/93) FL 11
Peterborough U (Free on 13/8/93) FL 28+1 FLC 4 FAC 2 Others 1
Barnet (Free on 24/3/94) FL 45 FLC 4 FAC 2 Others 2

McDONALD Neil Raymond
Born: Wallsend, 2 November 1965
Height: 5'11" Weight: 11.4
International Honours: E: U21-5; Yth; Sch
Signed from Oldham during the 1994 close season, Neil suffered a broken leg in only his second League game for Bolton, against Bristol City at Burnden Park. Recovered to play a part in the club's end of season run-in, only to suffer again when he was sent off in the play-off semi-final against "Wolves" at Molineux. Has played in both full-back and midfield positions for Wanderers.
Newcastle U (From apprentice on 19/2/83) FL 163+17/24 FLC 12/3 FAC 10+1/1 Others 3
Everton (£525,000 on 3/8/88) FL 76+14/4 FLC 7/3 FAC 17 Others 10+1
Oldham Ath (£500,000 on 1/10/91) F/PL 19+5/1 FLC3 FAC2
Bolton W (Free on 20/7/94) FL 4 Others 2

McDONALD Paul Thomas
Born: Motherwell, 20 April 1968
Height: 5'7" Weight: 9.5
Club Honours: S Div 1 '88; B&QC '92, '93
A speedy winger who gave many good displays for Southampton's reserves, but made only two sub appearances for the first team last season, he was transfer listed in March.
Hamilton Academical (Signed from Merry Street BC on 30/6/86) SL 187+28/26 SLC 8+2/2 SC 8+1 Others 8/3
Southampton (£75,000 on 8/6/93) PL 0+2

McDOUGALD David Eugene **Junior**
Born: Texas, USA, 12 January 1975
Height: 5'11" Weight: 10.12
International Honours: E: Sch
Junior can be pleased with his first season at Brighton. A hard-working striker, with good pace and full of running, who deserved better service on occasions, he seemed to lose confidence in mid-term and was replaced by on loan striker, Ade Akinbiyi, but bounced back well to reach a creditable goal tally.
Tottenham H (From apprentice on 12/7/93)
Brighton & Hove A (Signed on 12/5/94) FL 37+4/10 FLC 6/2 FAC 1 Others 2/1

McELHATTON Michael
Born: Kerry, 16 April 1975
Height: 6'1" Weight: 12.8
After making his Bournemouth debut against Wigan late in 1993-94, Michael established himself in the first team squad last season, playing mainly in the centre of midfield and occasionally in defence.
Bournemouth (From trainee on 5/7/93) FL 19+19/2 FLC 3 FAC 0+2/1

McFARLANE Andrew (Andy) Antonie
Born: Wolverhampton, 30 November 1966
Height: 6'3" Weight: 13.8
Club Honours: AMC '94
Swansea's Wembley goal scoring hero made a surprise comeback in the FA Cup-tie against Middlesbrough at the Vetch Field last season, his first game after recovering from a back operation in the summer. Tall and awkward in attack, he was unable to score goals consistently, and, after nearly joining Stockport on transfer deadline day, had a trial period with Sheffield United.
Portsmouth (£20,000 from Cradley Heath on 20/11/90) FL 0+2
Swansea C (£20,000 on 6/8/92) FL 33+22/8 FLC 3/1 FAC 0+6 Others 7+4/5

McGARRIGLE Kevin
Born: Newcastle, 9 April 1977
Height: 5'11" Weight: 11.4
Young Brighton central defender who was drafted into the side at the beginning of last March when the manager opted for a more defensive 5-3-2 formation. Very composed, he is highly-rated at the Goldstone.
Brighton & Hove A (From trainee on 21/7/94) FL 17+1

McGAVIN Steven (Steve) James
Born: North Walsham, 24 January 1969
Height: 5'10" Weight: 10.10
Club Honours: GMVC '92; FAT '92; Div 2 '95
Record Wycombe signing from Birmingham last March, Steve proved to be a skilful two-footed forward who created several goals. Possesses a hard shot and is very dangerous when cutting in from the wing.
Colchester U (£10,000 from Sudbury T on 28/7/92) FL 55+3/17 FLC 2 FAC 6/2 Others 4
Birmingham C (£150,000 on 7/1/94) FL 16+7/2 FLC 1+1/1 FAC 3+1/2 Others 1+3
Wycombe W (£175,000 on 20/3/95) FL 12/2

McGHEE David Christopher
Born: Worthing, 19 June 1976
Height: 5'10" Weight: 11.4
Speedy Brentford striker. Spent the second half of last season as a regular substitute and scored his first goal at Bristol Rovers in the last League game of the campaign.
Brentford (From trainee on 15/7/94) FL 1+6/1

McGINLEY John
Born: Inverness, 8 April 1964
Height: 5'9" Weight: 11.6
International Honours: S: 9; B-1
Bolton's leading striker, with 22 goals in 49 first team appearances last season, John struck the 100th FL goal of his career at one of his former clubs, Millwall, to earn Wanderers a 1-0 win in March. Suffered from a couple of lean spells, but was there when it mattered, hitting the winner in the Coca Cola Cup semi-final against Swindon and two more in the play-off second-leg against "Wolves", to earn Wembley visits. A regular for Scotland, as they strive to qualify for the next years European Championships, he will be playing Premiership football this season, following the club's promotion, via the play-offs.
Shrewsbury T (Signed from Elgin C on 22/2/89) FL 58+2/27 FLC 4 FAC 1/2 Others 3/2

Bury (£175,000 on 11/7/90) FL 16+9/9 FLC 1 FAC 1 Others 1+1
Millwall (£80,000 on 21/1/91) FL 27+7/10 FLC 2+1 FAC 2 Others 2/1
Bolton W (£125,000 on 30/9/92) FL 104+6/57 FLC 10+1/5 FAC 14/8 Others 11/7

John McGinley   Tony Marshall
(Empics Sports Photo Agency)

McGLASHAN John
Born: Dundee, 3 June 1967
Height: 6'1" Weight: 13.3
Signed from Peterborough early last season, he made his debut for Rotherham in December and celebrated it with a goal from the midfield position, which he made his own for the remainder of 1994-95. With hardwork the hallmark of his usual whole-hearted performances, John is another player who is good in the air and an asset at set-pieces.
Montrose (Signed from Dundee Violet in 1988-89) SL 67+1/11 SLC 2 SC 4
Millwall (£50,000 on 22/8/90) FL 9+7 FAC 0+1 Others 1
Fulham (Loaned on 11/12/92) FL 5/1 Others 1
Cambridge U (Loaned on 15/1/93) FL 0+1
Peterborough U (£75,000 on 27/1/93) FL 44+2/3 FLC 4+1/1 FAC 1 Others 2/1
Rotherham U (Free on 4/11/94) FL 27/3

McGLEISH Scott
Born: Barnet, 10 February 1974
Height: 5'10" Weight: 11.7
A pacy striker or right-winger signed from Edgware Town in the 1994 close season, Scott performed well in the reserves and made several substitute appearances for the Charlton first team after making his debut at Port Vale last October. Went on loan to Leyton Orient in March for a month and scored his first senior goal, before being freed during the summer.

Charlton Ath (Free from Edgware T on 24/5/94) FL 0+6
Leyton Orient (Loaned on 10/3/95) FL 4+2/1 Others 1/1

McGOLDRICK Edward (Eddie) John
Born: Islington, 30 April 1965
Height: 5'10" Weight: 11.7
Club Honours: Div 4 '87; FMC '91; ECWC '94
International Honours: Ei: 15; B-1
Useful Arsenal utility player who can fill in at full-back, in midfield, and as a sweeper. Originally a winger, he is at his best in a wide attacking role where his pace can take him past opposing defenders to get in good early crosses. Made just 13 starts in 1994-95, as he battled away to hold down a regular place.
Northampton T (£10,000 from Nuneaton Borough on 23/8/86) FL 97+10/9 FLC 9 FAC 6+1/1 Others 7/1
Crystal Palace (£200,000 on 10/1/89) FL 139+8/11 FLC 21+1/2 FAC 5 Others 13+2/3
Arsenal (£1,000,000 on 18/6/93) PL 32+5 FLC 7+2 FAC 1+1 Others 4+4/1

McGORRY Brian Paul
Born: Liverpool, 16 April 1970
Height: 5'10" Weight: 12.8
Industrious Peterborough midfielder who can be a match winner on occasion, Brian started 34 games last season, and with more experience could be a highly coveted player.
Bournemouth (£30,000 from Weymouth on 13/8/91) FL 56+5/11 FLC 7 FAC 7+3/2 Others 5/1
Peterborough U (£60,000 on 10/2/94) FL 44+8/6 FLC 0+2 FAC 2 Others 2

McGOWAN Gavin Gregory
Born: London, 16 January 1976
Height: 5'10" Weight: 11.4
Club Honours: FAYC '94
International Honours: E: Yth; Sch
Given two substitute appearances for Arsenal in 1992-93, while still a trainee, young Gavin finally started in the Premiership side at Chelsea in the last match of 1994-95. A player of whom much is expected, he can play at right-back, as a central defender, or in midfield, with equal aplomb.
Arsenal (From trainee on 1/7/94) PL 1+2

McGRATH Lloyd Anthony
Born: Birmingham, 24 February 1965
Height: 5'9" Weight: 11.0
Club Honours: FAC '87
International Honours: E: U21-1; Yth
A tough-tackling Portsmouth midfielder, Lloyd was signed on a free transfer after leaving Coventry in the summer of 1994. On his arrival, he immediately found a place in the team to shore up a lightweight midfield, but injured his leg against Millwall in March and was ruled out for the rest of the season.
Coventry C (From apprentice on 31/12/82) F/PL 200+14/4 FLC 22/1 FAC 16 Others 6 (Free to Hong Kong during 1994 close season)
Portsmouth (Free on 13/10/94) FL 15+3 FLC 1 FAC 2

McGRATH Paul
Born: Ealing, 4 December 1959
Height: 6'0" Weight: 14.0

Club Honours: FAC '85; FLC '94

International Honours: Ei: 76

Inspirational Aston Villa central defender, who is an excellent reader of the game and consistent to a fault, Paul, the PFA "Player of the Year" for 1993, continued to prove he was one of the best around last season. Strong in the air and good on the ground, he missed very few games, despite his well known knee problems, and continued to pass the ball around even when the side were struggling near the bottom of the Premiership. Still one of the first names on Jack Charlton's Republic team sheet, it would be difficult to imagine the international side and Villa without him.

Manchester U (f30,000 from St Patricks on 30/4/82) FL 159+4/12 FLC 13/2 FAC 15+2/2 Others 9

Aston Villa (£400,000 on 3/8/89) F/PL 219+4/7 FLC 24/1 FAC 20 Others 15

Paul McGrath Neal Simpson
(Empics Sports Photo Agency)

McGREAL John

Born: Liverpool, 2 June 1972

Height: 5'11" Weight: 10.11

The jewel in Tranmere's defensive crown. At times it is hard to believe he has only played 60 odd first team games, such is his composure and authority, and with many of the big clubs casting envious eyes in his direction, Rovers face a battle to hang on to their prized possession. As a youngster, his idol was Alan Hansen - and it shows. Cool, calm, and effective, he always looks to use the ball thoughtfully. Won "Player of the Year" awards from supporters, local radio, and newspapers last season.

Tranmere Rov (From trainee on 3/7/90) FL 59+2/1 FLC 5 FAC 2 Others 7+2

McGREGOR Mark Dale Thomas

Born: Chester, 16 February 1977

Height: 5'11" Weight: 10.12

A second year Wrexham YTS player who can perform anywhere in the back four, he earned the plaudits of the club's coaching staff for his assured displays as captain of the youth side before his introduction to first team football. Closes opponents down well and looks to have a good future.

Wrexham (Trainee) FL 1

McGREGOR Paul Anthony

Born: Liverpool, 17 December 1974

Height: 5'10" Weight: 10.4

Young Nottingham Forest striker who has yet to start a game, but who made 11 substitute appearances last season in a wide right position, normally as a straight replacement for Steve Stone, or in a reshuffle when Bryan Roy came off. A prolific goalscorer and record breaker in the Forest youth side, Paul is both sharp and quick, and most definitely a player you will be hearing plenty about in the future.

Nottingham F (From trainee on 13/12/91) F/PL 0+11/1 Others 0+1

McGUCKIN Thomas Ian

Born: Middlesbrough, 24 April 1973

Height: 6'2" Weight: 12.2

Big Hartlepool central defender who has long attracted interest from bigger clubs, despite reputedly having a £200,000 price tag. Quick for a big man, he turned in many solid performances in 1994-95, with his aggressive style of play. Seemed more settled after signing a new 18 month contract in mid-season and was later rewarded with the captaincy in succession to Phil Gilchrist.

Hartlepool U (From trainee on 20/6/91) FL 86+4/6 FLC 8 FAC 3 Others 5

McKEARNEY David Jonathan

Born: Crosby, 20 June 1968

Height: 5'10" Weight: 11.2

Playing in midfield, or at left-back, with good vision, and excellent passing ability, David is one of several players at Wigan brought by ex-manager, Kenny Swain, from his old club Crewe. Scored five League goals last season, before being released during the summer.

Bolton W (Signed from Prescot Cables on 23/11/87)

Crewe Alex (Free from Northwich Victoria on 13/10/89) FL 95+13/12 FLC 10+1 FAC 10/4 Others 14+2/2

Wigan Ath (Free on 19/7/93) FL 45+4/9 FLC 2+1 FAC 5/l Others 4/1

McKENZIE Christopher (Chris)

Born: Northampton, 14 May 1972

Height: 6'0" Weight: 12.6

Top non-league 'keeper, who signed for Hereford prior to the start of last season, Chris finally gained a place in the side around Christmas time. Young, agile, and brave, he was one of United's outstanding players in 1994-95.

Hereford U (£15,000 from Corby on 20/7/94) FL 21+1 Others 1

McKOP Henry George

Born: Bulawayo, Zimbabwe, 8 July 1967

Height: 5'11" Weight: 12.0

International Honours: Zimbabwe

Despite gaining over 50 caps for Zimbabwe, the most recent being last April, Henry has yet to make his mark at Bristol City, with just one subs' appearance in 1994-95. However, in the reserve side he turned in many excellent displays in central defence, especially towards the end of the campaign when the ground was harder and more suited to his style of play.

Bristol C (Signed from Bonner SC on 2/2/94) FL 2+3

McLAREN Ross

Born: Edinburgh, 14 April 1962

Height: 5'10" Weight: 12.12

Club Honours: WC '85; Div 2 '87

Appointed Swindon reserve team-coach at the commencement of 1994-95, although still registered as a player, Ross made four appearances during an injury crisis in November. Last season was his 15th as a pro and, at his best, a very underrated midfielder, or central defender, who was both adept at breaking up opponents' attacks and setting up counter moves.

Shrewsbury T (Free from Glasgow Rangers juniors on 15/8/80) FL 158+3/18 FLC 11/3 FAC 7+1/1

Derby Co (£67,000 on 11/7/85) FL 113+9/4 FLC 13/1 FAC 9 Others 5

Swindon T (£165,000 on 4/8/88) F/PL 195+2/9 FLC 21/2 FAC 11 Others 16/1

McLEAN Ian

Born: Paisley, 18 August 1966

Height: 6'2" Weight: 13.2

International Honours: Canada

Central defender. Despite several spells out, due to various injuries, Ian managed to make his full international debut for Canada last January and later made a further appearance for the country he emigrated to as a youngster. However, unable to add further full League appearances to his Bristol Rovers' tally, he spent two separate loan periods at Cardiff during the season.

Bristol Rov (Signed from Metroford on 15/9/93) FL 17+11/2 Others 2+2/1

Cardiff C (Loaned on 9/9/94) FL 3

Cardiff C (Loaned on 21/12/94) FL 1

McLEARY Alan Terence

Born: Lambeth, 6 October 1964

Height: 6'0" Weight: 11.9

Club Honours: FLT '83; Div 2 '88

International Honours: E: B-2; U21-1; Yth

Vastly experienced right-footed central defender who started last season as Charlton's club captain, but lost his place in the side midway through the campaign. Reads the game well and strong in the air, Alan was recalled for one game against his old club, Millwall, towards the end of the campaign, but with the central defensive partnership of Richard Rufus and Stuart Balmer playing so well, was unable to keep his place and was freed during the summer.

Millwall (From apprentice on 12/10/81) FL 289+18/5 FLC 16+1 FAC 24+1/2 Others 22+1/2

Sheffield U (Loaned on 23/7/92) PL 3

Wimbledon (Loaned on 16/10/92) PL 4 FLC 2

Charlton Ath (Free on 27/5/93) FL 66/3 FLC 2 FAC 6 Others 3

McLOUGHLIN Alan Francis

Born: Manchester, 20 April 1967

Height: 5'8" Weight: 10.0

International Honours: Ei: 17; B-3

Skilful Portsmouth midfielder with good passing ability and awareness, Alan started

1994-95 indifferently, but the arrival of Terry Fenwick seemed to relight his charges as he scored in two of the new manager's first three games. Representing Eire at both full and "B" level during the season, he would hope to be in their squad for Euro '96 if they qualify.

Manchester U (From apprentice on 25/4/85)
Swindon T (Free on 15/8/86) FL 101+5/19 FLC 11+3/5 FAC 4+2 Others 10/1
Torquay U (Loaned on 13/3/87) FL 21+3/4
Southampton (£1,000,000 on 13/12/90) FL 22+2/1 FLC 0+1 FAC 4 Others 1
Aston Villa (Loaned on 30/9/91) Others 1
Portsmouth (£400,000 on 17/2/92) FL 133+3/23 FLC 14/3 FAC 6+1/5 Others 9/1

McMAHON Gerard Joseph
Born: Belfast, 29 December 1973
Height: 5'11" Weight: 11.6
International Honours: NI: 3; B; U21-2

Signed by Barnet last October on a three month loan basis from Tottenham, Gerard formed an exciting Barnet partnership with Dougie Freedman, as he foraged forward from wide positions. A skilful player, with plenty of pace, he left a big hole at Underhill when "Spurs" recalled him in January. Having made his PL debut, and impressing, his good form saw him rewarded by Northern Ireland with three full caps at the end of the season.

Tottenham H (£100,000 from Glenavon on 31/7/92) PL 2
Barnet (Loaned on 20/10/94) FL 10/2 FAC 2/1 Others 1

McMAHON Samuel (Sam) Keiron
Born: Newark, 10 February 1976
Height: 5'7" Weight: 11.5

In making a long overdue debut from the Leicester bench against Wimbledon, and nearly scoring with a fierce long-range drive, he proved to be a classy young midfielder who could well come to the fore in 1995-96.

Leicester C (From trainee on 10/7/94) PL 0+1

McMAHON Stephen (Steve)
Born: Liverpool, 20 August 1961
Height: 5'9" Weight: 12.1
Club Honours: Div 1 '86, '88, '90; FAC '86, '89; CS '86, '88, '89
International Honours: E: 17; B-2; U21-6

Arrived from Manchester City to take over as player-manager at Swindon last November and soon discovered the added pressures of management, being sent off on his debut at Southend. His return lasted just 16 minutes, before he was led off with a broken arm! The trials and tribulations were far from over as Town slid down the League table with alarming speed and he had to suffer the final ignominy of relegation from the dugout, following a further dismissal on 5 April.

Everton (From apprentice on 29/8/79) FL 99+1/11 FLC 11/3 FAC 9
Aston Villa (£175,000 on 20/5/83) FL 74+1/7 FLC 9 FAC 3 Others 4
Liverpool (£375,000 on 12/9/85) FL 202+2/29 FLC 27/13 FAC 30/7 Others 16/1
Manchester C (£900,000 on 24/12/91) F/PL 83+4/1 FLC 8 FAC 3
Swindon T (Free on 1/12/94) FL 16+1

Steve McManaman

Barrington Coombs
(Empics Sports Photo Agency)

McMANAMAN Steven (Steve)
Born: Bootle, 11 February 1972
Height: 5'11" Weight: 10.2
Club Honours: FAC '92; FLC '95
International Honours: E: 3; U21-7; Yth

A player with the ability to "ghost" past defenders in keeping with the old-fashioned wingers, after a poor season by his own standards in 1993-94, Steve once again brought notice of his skills to fans throughout the country in 1994-95. His silky runs and ability to find the net were never more in evidence than in the Coca Cola Cup Final against Bolton, when his two goals won the trophy for Liverpool. Earlier in his career, he was accused of drifting in-and-out of games, but he since became more consistent throughout the duration of a season, his excellent form gaining him England honours.

Liverpool (From trainee on 19/2/90) F/PL 122+11/18 FLC 19+1/7 FAC 18+1/3 Others 11/1

McMILLAN Lyndon Andre (Andy)
Born: Bloemfontein, South Africa, 22 June 1968

Height: 5'10" Weight: 10.13

Although his form was a little up-and-down at times last season, and he lost his regular York position at right-back for a while, Andy generally continued to be a polished and unhurried defender. Scored a rare goal in the win against Cambridge in April, only his third in nearly 300 games for the club.

York C (Signed on 17/10/87) FL 254+12/3 FLC 11 FAC 12 Others 18

McMINN Kevin (Ted) Clifton
Born: Castle Douglas, 28 September 1962
Height: 5'11" Weight: 11.2
Club Honours: SLC '86

Equally at home on the left or right-flank, Ted is a winger in the traditional sense, at his best when beating defenders by trickery rather than speed. Still able to turn a game for Burnley, he was a particularly lethal weapon when coming on as a substitute.

Queen of the South (Signed from Glenafton Ath on 1/1/82) SL 56+6/5 SLC 4+2 SC 1
Glasgow R (£50,000 on 1/10/84) SL 37+26/4 SLC 4+2/2 Others 2+3 (£225,000 to Seville on 5/2/88)

Derby Co (£300,000 on 5/2/88) FL 108+15/9 FLC 11/3 FAC 6+1/1 Others 12/1
Birmingham C (£115,000 on 28/7/93) FL 19+3 FLC 1+1 FAC 1 Others 1
Burnley (Signed on 5/4/94) FL 31+5/3 FLC 3 FAC 1+2 Others 3

McNALLY Bernard Anthony
Born: Shrewsbury, 17 February 1963
Height: 5'7" Weight: 11.2
International Honours: NI-5

An industrious midfielder, always busy and wanting the ball, he enjoys a battle in the centre of the park, but was never able to hold down a regular place in WBA's first team last season, owing to injury and the presence of so many other players of similar style. Indeed, he also suffered injury problems which kept him out of action for the last four weeks of the campaign, prior to being released during the summer.
Shrewsbury T (From apprentice on 19/2/81) FL 278+4/23 FLC 22/3 FAC 13 Others 1
West Bromwich A (£385,000 on 27/7/89) FL 137+19/10 FLC 8+1/1 FAC 11/2 Others 12+1/1

McNAMARA Brett
Born: Newark, 8 July 1972
Height: 6'0" Weight: 11.5

Signed for Northampton early last season from non-league football, but has been unable to break into the first team on a regular basis. Was a prolific scorer for the reserves and for Corby, where he spent most of 1994-95 on loan, before being released at the end of the season.
Northampton T (Free from Stamford on 23/8/94) FL 0+1 Others 1

McNIVEN Scott Andrew
Born: Leeds, 27 May 1978
Height: 5'10" Weight: 10.6

When making his FL debut at Barnsley in a 1-1 draw, while still a trainee last season, the 16-year-old became the second youngest player ever to don an Oldham shirt. Son of the former Leeds star, David, with a twin brother, David, junior, also on "Latics'" books, Scott is a talented left-back with a big future ahead of him.
Oldham Ath (Trainee) FL 1

McPHAIL John
Born: Dundee, 7 December 1955
Height: 6'0" Weight: 12.3
Club Honours: Div '82, '84, Div 3 '88

Dismissed as Hartlepool's manager last September, surprisingly he was then offered a playing contract. There was an uneasy alliance with David McCreery but, at the age of 39, and still supremely fit, John gave a good account of himself in his few appearances a
nd became the second oldest player ever to play League football for the club, before leaving in March.
Dundee (Signed from St Columba's in 1971) SL 64+4 SLC 11 SC 5
Sheffield U (£30,000 on 18/1/79) FL 135/7 FLC 9 FAC 8/1
York C (Free on 3/2/83) FL 141+1/24 FLC 10/3 FAC 16/1 Others 5/1
Bristol C (£14,000 on 18/7/86) FL 26/1 FAC 5 Others 6
Sunderland (£23,000 on 31/7/87) FL 130/22 FLC 10 FAC 5 Others 8
Hartlepool U (Signed on 16/9/90) FL 159+4/4 FLC 7/1 FAC 10 Others 9

McPHERSON Keith Anthony
Born: Greenwich, 11 September 1963
Height: 5'11" Weight: 11.0
Club Honours: FAYC '81; Div 4 '87, Div 2 '94

Strong, commanding centre-back who captained Reading to the Division Two Championship in 1993-94, Keith failed to get into the Division One side last season until Adrian Williams was injured in October. Played a vital role in Reading's defensive system as the club moved towards the play-off places and was back to his best by the end of the term.
West Ham U (From apprentice on 12/9/81) FL 1
Cambridge U (Loaned on 30/9/85) FL 11/1
Northampton T (£15,000 on 23/1/86) FL 182/8 FLC 9/1 FAC 12 Others 13
Reading (Signed on 24/8/90) FL 172+5/6 FLC 10+1 FAC 10+1 Others 9+1

McROBERT Lee Peter
Born: Bromley, 4 October 1972
Height: 5'8" Weight: 10.0

Fresh from non-league football, this talented midfielder was immediately thrust into action with Millwall, due to the club's injury status, and scored with his first touch on his full debut at the Den against Charlton with a left-footed half volley.
Millwall (£35,000 from Sittingbourne on 17/2/95) FL 4+3/1

Gary McSwegan Paul Marriott
(Empics Sports Photo Agency)

McSWEGAN Gary
Born: Glasgow, 24 September 1970
Height: 5'8" Weight: 10.9
Club Honours: SC '93

Out-and-out Notts County striker who, since coming south from Glasgow Rangers, has been hampered by hamstring problems. With good feet, a hard shot, and a penchant to shoot on sight, Gary would score many more goals if he could only manage a full season. When playing, he is the side's natural penalty taker.
Glasgow R (From juniors in 1986) SL 9+9/4 SLC 1 SC 0+2 Others 0+3/1
Notts Co (£400,000 on 13/7/93) FL 47+12/21 FLC 6/3 FAC 4+1/1 Others 6/1

MADDEN Lawrence (Lawrie) David
Born: London, 28 September 1955
Height 5'11" Weight: 13.1
Club Honours: AMC '91

Lawrie's playing career was given an unexpected extension in 1994-95, after early-season injuries to Chesterfield's regular central defenders, and he proved to be a powerful deputy, using all his 20 years' experience in the game to calm the defence when needed. His career as a football journalist took off, too, with Sky Sports and the Sheffield Star.
Mansfield T (Free from Arsenal on 1/3/75) FL 9+1 FLC 2 FAC 2
Charlton Ath (Free from Manchester University on 4/3/78) FL 109+4/7 FLC 4+2 FAC 8
Millwall (£10,000 on 25/3/82) FL 44+3/2 FLC 2 FAC 1
Sheffield Wed (Free on 24/8/83) FL 200+12/2 FLC 26+2/3 FAC 20+1 Others 5
Leicester C (Loaned on 17/1/91) FL 3
Wolverhampton W (Free on 15/8/91) FL 62+5/1 FLC 4 FAC 3 Others 2
Darlington (Free on 3/9/93) FL 5 Others 1
Chesterfield (Free on 4/10/93) FL 36/1 FLC 2 FAC 1 Others 1

MADDISON Lee Robert
Born: Bristol, 5 October 1972
Height: 5'11" Weight: 12.4

After being injured in the opening game of last season, Lee found it difficult to regain his Bristol Rovers' place from Andy Gurney. A strong-tackling left-back, he uses his height well in defensive positions.
Bristol Rov (From trainee on 18/7/91) FL 68+5 FLC 4 FAC 2 Others 6+1

Neil Maddison Paul Marriott
(Empics Sports Photo Agency)

MADDISON Neil Stanley
Born: Darlington, 2 October 1969
Height: 5'9" Weight: 11.8

Neil's determined and forceful style is the perfect foil to the skills of Matt Le Tissier and Jim Magilton in Southampton's midfield. An under-appreciated player, who can also play up-front if required, his workrate was badly missed when he was out of the side through injury last season. Always runs well off the ball and gets into the penalty often enough to score the occasional goal.

Southampton (From trainee on 14/4/88) F/PL 117+13/16 FLC 5+2 FAC 7+3 Others 1

MADDIX Daniel (Danny) Shawn
Born: Ashford, 11 October 1967
Height: 5'11" Weight: 11.0

After two years out of the game with a serious injury, Danny made his QPR comeback as a substitute at Old Trafford on the opening day of last season and played his first full game in the televised match at Nottingham Forest where he performed superbly. Made his next start, again in a televised game, against West Ham and kept his place alongside Alan McDonald at the heart of the QPR defence for the remainder of the campaign.

Tottenham H (From apprentice on 25/7/85)
Southend U (Loaned on 1/11/86) FL 2
Queens Park R (Free on 23/7/87) F/PL 143+23/7 FLC 15/2 FAC 18/2 Others 2+3

MAGEE Kevin
Born: Bangour, 10 April 1971
Height: 5'10" Weight: 11.4

A lightning fast Preston left-winger, Kevin can hit telling crosses from a flat-out run and his speed and acceleration are often rewarded by some heavy marking. Having recovered from three broken legs, he made 15 appearances last season and, at times, looked to be getting back to his best, before being released during the summer.

Partick Thistle (Signed from Armadale Thistle on 12/8/91) SL 0+11 SC 1
Preston NE (£25,000 on 5/5/93) FL 19+2/1 Others 1

Jim Magilton   Neal Simpson
(Empics Sports Photo Agency)

MAGILTON Jim
Born: Belfast, 6 May 1969
Height: 5'10" Weight: 12.7
International Honours: NI: 29; U23-1; U21-1

A much improved player, and an ever-present last season, Jim is now an essential part of the Southampton midfield. Usually on hand to receive the ball played out of

defence, he is the link with the attack and weighed in with his share of goals, including winners against Arsenal and Tottenham. One of Alan Ball's best signings, he looks like being a fixture in the side for the foreseeable future and is a regular member of the Northern Ireland International team.

Liverpool (From apprentice on 14/5/86)
Oxford U (£100,000 on 3/10/90) FL 150/34 FLC 9/1 FAC 8/4 Others 6/3
Southampton (£600,000 on 11/2/94) PL 57/6 FLC 3 FAC 5/1

MAIL David
Born: Bristol, 12 September 1962
Height: 5'11" Weight: 11.12
Club Honours: FMC '87

Became Hull's most senior squad member following Steve Moran's retirement. After recovering from a knee injury, picked up in the autumn, the uncomplicated central defender remained out of the first team spotlight and was transfer listed last March. However, after a brief trial at Mansfield Town, he received a surprise recall, before being freed during the Summer.

Aston Villa (From apprentice on 15/7/80)
Blackburn Rov (Free on 4/1/82) FL 200+6/4 FLC 12+1 FAC 12 Others 17
Hull C (£160,000 on 3/8/90) FL 140+10/2 FLC 5 FAC 4 Others 9+1

MAKEL Lee Robert
Born: Sunderland, 11 January 1973
Height: 5'10" Weight: 9.10

A constructive Blackburn midfield player, who is a confident passer excelling at one-twos and always looking to split opposing defences, Lee failed to make a first team impact last season, apart from a call from the subs' bench in a European match. Underwent surgery after the turn of the year, he returned in sparkling form with the reserves.

Newcastle U (From trainee on 11/2/91) FL 6+6/1 FLC 1 Others 0+1
Blackburn Rov (£160,000 on 20/7/92) PL 1+2 FLC 0+3 Others 0+1

MAKIN Christopher Gregory
Born: Manchester, 8 May 1973
Height: 5'10" Weight: 11.2
International Honours: E: U21-5; Yth; Sch

Young Oldham full-back with two good feet, who can play on either flank and also in midfield, Chris has a good "engine" and pressures opponents into errors. Following the arrival of Ian Snodin from Everton last January, although making way initially, he was back in the side by the end of the season. Is an England U21 international.

Oldham Ath (From trainee on 2/11/91) F/PL 54+1/2 FLC 5 FAC 9
Wigan Ath (Loaned on 28/8/92) FL 14+1/2

MALKIN Christopher (Chris) Greg
Born: Hoylake, 4 June 1967
Height: 6'3" Weight: 12.0
Club Honours: AMC '90

Many of John Aldridge's goals are down to the unselfish hard work of Chris Malkin, whose pace and tireless effort have been instrumental in Tranmere's success. Though not regarded as a prolific scorer, he nevertheless, contributed 19 goals in 1994-

95 - his best tally for five seasons - though all but one, at Millwall, came on home soil. Has now played over 300 matches for the club, scoring 75 goals.

Tranmere Rov (Free from Stork AFC on 27/7/87) FL 184+48/60 FLC 20+5/6 FAC 9+4/3 Others 26+7/7

Chris Malkin   Barry Coombs
(Empics Sports Photo Agency)

MANN Neil
Born: Nottingham, 19 November 1972
Height: 5'10" Weight: 12.1

Neil is the son of Arthur, the WBA assistant manager, and has exceeded all expectations in his first season as a full-time pro at Hull. Predominantly left-footed, but can also put his right to good effect, this midfielder has the valuable quality - and confidence - to carry the ball and go past an opponent. A shoulder injury ruled him out of the final run-in, but he is definitely one to watch.

Grimsby T (Free from Notts Co juniors on 6/9/90)
Hull C (Free from Grantham T, via Spalding, on 30/7/93) FL 31+5/2 FLC 1+2 FAC 1 Others 2+1

MANUEL William (Billy) Albert James
Born: Hackney, 28 June 1969
Height: 5'10" Weight: 12.8
Club Honours: Div 3 '92

A non-contract player, he was released by Brentford at the start of last season, spending little over a month at Peterborough, before moving on to Brentford. Arriving back at London Road in February, Billy proved to be a fiery, terrier-like midfielder who quickly proved to be a good man to have on your side.

Tottenham H (From trainee on 28/7/87)
Gillingham (Signed on 10/2/89) FL 74+13/5 FLC 2 FAC 3 Others 5
Brentford (£60,000 on 14/6/91) FL 83+11/1 FLC 7+1/1 FAC 4 Others 8+2
Peterborough U (Free on 16/9/94)
Cambridge U (Free on 28/10/94) FL 10 FAC 2
Peterborough U (Free on 28/2/95) FL 14/1

MARDENBOROUGH Stephen (Steve) Alexander
Born: Birmingham, 11 September 1964
Height: 5'7" Weight: 11.9
Club Honours: GMVC '90; Div 4 '91

Widely travelled winger who is both fast and aggressive, Steve came to Scarborough on trial last February, after being released by Lincoln. Signing on non-contract terms, coincidentally, he made his one and only appearance when coming on in the 82nd minute of a 1-1 draw against his old club.

Coventry C (From apprentice on 6/8/82)
Wolverhampton W (Free on 20/9/83) FL 9/1 FLC 0+1 FAC 0+1
Cambridge U (Loaned on 23/2/84) FL 6
Swansea C (Free on 30/7/84) FL 32+4/7 FLC 2 FAC 2 Others 3+1
Newport Co (Free on 19/7/85) FL 50+14/11 FLC 4+1 FAC 5+1/1 Others 2+1/1
Cardiff C (Free on 27/3/87) FL 18+14/1 FLC 1 FAC 0+1 Others 1+1
Hereford U (Free on 28/7/88) FL 20+7 FLC 2 FAC 1 Others 1+1 (Free to IFK Ostersund on 1/7/89)
Darlington (Free from Cheltenham T on 6/7/90) FL 79+27/18 FLC 2+5/1 FAC 3+1 Others 2/1
Lincoln C (£10,000 on 12/7/93) FL 14+7/2 FLC 2 FAC 0+1 Others 1+1
Scarborough (Free on 1/2/95) FL 0+1

MARDON Paul Jonathan
Born: Bristol, 14 September 1969
Height: 6'0" Weight: 11.10

Became WBA's most expensive defender ever when he moved the five miles from St Andrews to The Hawthorns in 1993. A strong, dominant player, very powerful in the air, sound and capable on the ground, with a fair bit of pace, Paul can also play at right-back and in midfield. He was in tremendous form throughout 1994-95, forming a fine partnership with Paul Raven until suffering a severe facial injury in the away game at Grimsby in late March, which caused him to miss the remainder of the campaign.

Bristol C (From trainee on 29/1/88) FL 29+13 FLC 3+3/1 Others 1
Doncaster Rov (Loaned on 13/9/90) FL 3
Birmingham C (£115,000 on 16/8/91) FL 54+10/1 FLC ll+1 FAC 1 Others 3
West Bromwich A (£400,000 on 18/11/93) FL 49+1/2 FAC 2

MARGINSON Karl Kevin
Born: Manchester, 11 November 1970
Height: 6'0" Weight: 11.0

Karl is a left-footed player who featured in Rotherham's midfield, but with his appearances still in single figures in 1994-95, he moved on loan to GM Vauxhall Conference side, Macclesfield Town, in the closing stages of the season, before being released.

Rotherham U (£15,000 from Ashton U on 25/3/93) FL 11+4/1 FLC 1 FAC 1 Others 2/1

MARPLES Christopher (Chris)
Born: Chesterfield, 3 August 1964
Height: 6'0" Weight: 13.3
Club Honours: Div 4 '85

One of the few footballers of recent times to have played county cricket, Chris's return to the Chesterfield side last season saw him back to his best form when, in a typically brave incident, he suffered a double fracture of the leg diving at the feet of an advancing forward. A decisive commander of his penalty area, who punches well to clear danger, he was released at the end of 1994-95 to concentrate on cricket.

Chesterfield (Free from Goole T on 21/3/84) FL 84 FAC 5 Others 5
Stockport Co (Signed on 25/3/87) FL 57 FLC 2 FAC 4 Others 2
York C (£28,000 on 12/7/88) FL 138 FLC 10 FAC 9 Others 9
Scunthorpe U (Loaned on 14/2/92) FL 1
Chesterfield (Free on 17/12/92) FL 57 FLC 4 FAC 3 Others 2

MARQUIS Paul Raymond
Born: Enfield, 29 August 1972
Height: 6'1" Weight: 11.12

Classy Doncaster defender who missed virtually all of 1994-95 with a shoulder injury that was slow in healing. One full game and an appearance as a substitute, summed up his involvement when he should have been establishing himself in the Rovers' first team.

West Ham U (From trainee on 1/7/91) PL 0+1
Doncaster Rov (Free on 10/3/94) FL 10+1

MARRIOTT Andrew (Andy)
Born: Sutton in Ashfield, 11 October 1970
Height: 6'0" Weight: 12.6
Club Honours: Div 4 '92; FMC '92; WC '95
International Honours: E: U21-1; Yth; Sch

A superb shot-stopper who covers his angles well, he has the make-up to become a top flight 'keeper and was often the difference between Wrexham winning or losing in 1994-95. Many will not forget his point-blank save against Ipswich Town in injury time in a hurry, and he was the club's only ever-present last season.

Arsenal (From trainee on 22/10/88)
Nottingham F (£50,000 on 20/6/89) F/PL 11 FLC 1 Others 1
West Bromwich A (Loaned on 6/9/89) FL 3
Blackburn Rov (Loaned on 29/12/89) FL 2
Colchester U (Loaned on 21/3/90) FL 10
Burnley (Loaned on 29/8/91) FL 15 Others 2
Wrexham (£200,000 on 8/10/93) FL 82 FLC 4 FAC 6 Others 14

MARROWS Dean
Born: Sutton in Ashfield, 30 September 1975
Height: 5'9" Weight: 11.7

A former Mansfield trainee, but not offered pro terms, Dean, a full-back, made one sub's appearance as a non-contract player for the club last season.

Mansfield T (From trainee on 5/1/95) Others 0+1

MARSDEN Christopher (Chris)
Born: Sheffield, 3 January 1969
Height: 5'11" Weight: 10.12

Signed from Wolverhampton last November, Chris scored on his Notts County debut against Venezia in the Anglo-Italian Cup but, for various reasons, managed only six more starts in 1994-95. A midfielder who links up well with the forwards, as you would expect, he is a good passer of the ball.

Sheffield U (From apprentice on 6/1/87) FL 13+3/1 FLC 1 Others 1
Huddersfield T (Signed on 15/7/88) FL 113+8/9 FLC 15+1 FAC 6+2 Others 10
Coventry C (Loaned on 2/11/93) PL 5+2
Wolverhampton W (£250,000 on 11/1/94) FL 8 FAC 3
Notts Co (£250,000 on 15/11/94) FL 7 Others 1/1

MARSH Christopher (Chris) Jonathan
Born: Sedgley, 14 January 1970
Height: 6'0" Weight: 12.10

Enjoyed his best season yet for Walsall in 1994-95, as he captained the side to promotion from the Third Division and scored 12 first team goals, including an unforgettable one from a narrow angle that came so close to putting Leeds out of the FA Cup. A splendidly versatile player, he is at his best as an attacking midfielder, bursting through from a wide position.

Walsall (From trainee on 11/7/88) FL 165+30/19 FLC 11+2/1 FAC 16+1/1 Others 11+1/3

Andy Marriott   Neal Simpson
(Empics Sports Photo Agency)

Mike Marsh   Steve Morton
(Empics Sports Photo Agency)

Chris Marsh

Barry Coombs
(Empics Sports Photo Agency)

MARSH Michael (Mike) Andrew
Born: Liverpool, 21 July 1969
Height: 5'8" Weight: 10.14
Club Honours: FAC '92

Signed from West Ham last Christmas after months of speculation, the slight midfielder took time to settle at Coventry. A skilful player with a good first touch, he was played up-front after Ron Atkinson arrived, scoring in successive home wins over West Ham and Leicester, before being dropped from the side.

Liverpool (Free from Kirby T on 21/8/87) F/PL 42+27/2 FLC 10+1/3 FAC 6+2 Others 12+1/1
West Ham U (Signed on 17/9/93) PL 46+3/1 FLC 6 FAC 6/1
Coventry C (£450,000 on 30/12/94) PL 15/2 FAC 4

MARSH Simon Thomas Peter
Born: Ealing, 29 January 1977
Height: 5'11" Weight: 11.2

Promoted from the youth team into the Oxford first team after injuries to others last season, Simon did well enough to earn a professional contract. A left-back, he gave some accomplished displays and could go far. Much used on taking set-pieces.

Oxford U (From trainee on 22/11/94) FL 8 FLC 2 FAC 1 Others 2

MARSHALL Andrew (Andy) John
Born: Bury St Edmunds, 14 April 1975
Height: 6'2" Weight: 12.7
International Honours: E: U21-1

Promising young Norwich goalkeeper who, like Bryan Gunn, is good on crosses and commands the penalty area like a veteran. Called into senior action for the first time last December, following the injury to Gunn, he gave many excellent displays throughout the rest of the season and was even named March's "Goalkeeper of the Month" by a certain football magazine. One save he made from Coventry's Dion Dublin being likened to that of Gordon Banks' from Pele in the 1970 World Cup Finals. Most definitely one for the future, Andy was selected for the England U21 side in the Toulon tournament and made the first goal with a long kick up-field in a 2-0 win over Malaysia.

Norwich C (From trainee on 6/7/93) PL 20+1 FLC 1 FAC 2+1

MARSHALL Daniel John
Born: Newark, 18 December 1975
Height: 5'10" Weight: 11.5

An ex-Notts County trainee midfielder, Daniel joined Chesterfield last August after a successful pre-season trial, but made only one first team appearance as a substitute,

before being freed at the end of 1994-95.

Chesterfield (Free from Notts Co juniors on 12/8/94) FL 0+1

MARSHALL Dwight Wayne
Born: Jamaica, WI, 3 October 1965
Height: 5'11" Weight: 11.8

A right-sided striker who likes to play wide, often taking the ball across the back four rather than down the wing, he became top-scorer at Luton after signing in the 1994 close season from Plymouth. Started the campaign on the subs' bench, but quickly impressed with his blistering pace on the ball and gained a regular place in the starting line-up, notching a hat-trick against Swindon last February. Although Dwight was back on the bench by the end of 1994-95, in one way or another he had been involved in almost every game.

Plymouth Arg (£35,000 from Grays Athletic on 9/8/91) FL 93+6/27 FLC 8/1 FAC 7+2/4 Others 7+1/4
Middlesbrough (Loaned on 25/3/93) PL 0+3
Luton T (£150,000 on 15/7/94) FL 36+9/11 FLC 1+1/1 FAC 4/1

MARSHALL Ian Paul
Born: Liverpool, 20 March 1966
Height: 6'1" Weight: 12.12
Club Honours: CS '86; Div 2 '91

A player who is equally at home up-front, or in central defence, but who prefers to lead the Ipswich attack, Ian is predominantly right-footed and good in the air. The 1994-95 season was surely one that he will want to forget as he was beset by injuries for most of the time. After receiving a head injury in the second game, he then injured a hip in training and, on coming back and regaining his first team place, he then broke his elbow at Newcastle in November. The break did not heal properly and had to be put back in plaster before he returned in February. Able to put a run together towards the end of the campaign and had his best game against his former club, Everton.

Everton (From apprentice on 23/3/84) FL 9+6/1 FLC 1+1/1 Others 7
Oldham Ath (£100,000 on 24/3/88) F/PL 165+5/36 FLC 17 FAC 14/3 Others 2+1/1
Ipswich T (£750,000 on 9/8/93) PL 42+5/13 FLC 3/2 FAC 5/3

MARSHALL John Philip
Born: Balham, 18 August 1964
Height: 5'9" Weight: 11.4

This long-serving Fulham player was desperately unlucky to break a leg towards the end of last season. Either in midfield, or defence, he can be relied on to produce a thoroughly professional display. John is the all-rounder needed in the modern game, who can pass, tackle, cross and mark and, as his pace slows, he compensates by intelligent reading of the play.

Fulham (From apprentice on 20/8/82) FL 379+16/29 FLC 33/2 FAC 17+1/3 Others 20/2

MARSHALL Lee Alan
Born: Nottingham, 1 August 1975
Height: 5'9" Weight: 9.12

Unable to make his mark at Nottingham Forest, the young midfielder was released and joined Stockport immediately prior to last March's transfer deadline. Comfortable on the ball, as are most Forest products, Lee made his FL debut in the final game of the season.

Nottingham F (From trainee on 3/8/92)
Stockport Co (Free on 20/3/95) FL 1

MARSHALL Scott Roderick
Born: Islington, 1 May 1973
Height: 6'1" Weight: 12.5
International Honours: S: U21-2; Yth; Sch

An Arsenal central defender who has yet to play in the Premiership, Scott was loaned to Sheffield United last August as cover for the injured Paul Beesley. Very good in the air, he formed a steady partnership with Brian Gayle, not missing a FL game during his three month stint, before returning to Highbury. Already a Scottish international at schoolboy and youth levels, his form at Bramall Lane saw him rewarded with two U21 caps towards the end of the year.

Arsenal (From trainee on 18/3/91) PL 2
Rotherham U (Loaned on 3/12/93) FL 10/1 Others 1
Sheffield U (Loaned on 25/8/94) FL 17

MARTIN Alvin Edward
Born: Bootle, 29 July 1958
Height: 6'1" Weight: 13.9
Club Honours: FAC '80; Div 2 '81

International Honours: E: 17; B-2; Yth

Experienced West Ham centre-half, who reads the game well and is very good in the air, Alvin had a brilliant game against Nottingham Forest last December, when stifling the threat of Stan Collymore. There was no joy, however, in January, when he was unfairly dismissed by referee Danson in the home encounter with Sheffield Wednesday but, following video evidence, the decision was turned around. Was a regular in the side until a hamstring injury gained at Coventry forced him to miss the rest of the season.

West Ham U (From apprentice on 1/7/76) F/PL 452+3/27 FLC 69/6 FAC 39 Others 16/1

MARTIN David
Born: East Ham, 25 April 1963
Height: 6'1" Weight: 12.2
Club Honours: FAYC '79; FLT '83; FAT '92 (On loan at Colchester U)
International Honours: E: Yth

Bristol City missed the services of this tough, aggressive midfield player during the first half of last season, due to injury. Having recovered, David was loaned to Northampton in February, playing seven games, before being recalled and appearing in three of the last four matches of the campaign.

Millwall (From apprentice on 10/5/80) FL 131+9/6 FLC 10+2/3 FAC 7/1 Others 4/1
Wimbledon (£35,000 on 14/9/84) FL 30+5/3 FLC 21 FAC 2+1
Southend U (Free on 23/8/86) FL 212+9/19 FLC 25/4 FAC 9+1 Others 10+1/3
Bristol C (Free on 19/7/93) FL 36+2/1 FAC 5 Others 2
Northampton T (Loaned on 13/2/95) FL 7/1

MARTIN Dean Stacey
Born: Halifax, 9 September 1967
Height: 5'11" Weight: 11.10

Midfield player, or forward, who signed on loan from Scunthorpe last January, he made a permanent move to Rochdale just before the transfer deadline, replacing the injured Shaun Reid.

Halifax T (From apprentice on 10/9/85) FL 149+4/7 FLC 7 FAC 10 Others 12/3
Scunthorpe U (Free on 8/7/91) FL 100+6/7 FLC 8/1 FAC 7 Others 13+1/1
Rochdale (Free on 13/1/95) FL 12+3

MARTIN Eliot James
Born: Plumstead, 27 September 1972
Height: 5'7" Weight: 10.2

Eliot returned to Gillingham in March 1995, having left Priestfield the previous summer. Despite trials with various League clubs, this young left-back signed for non-league Chelmsford in October 1994 and impressed sufficiently to make the return journey.

Gillingham (From trainee on 13/5/91) FL 52+1/1 FLC 2 FAC 4 Others 4 (Freed during 1994 close season)
Gillingham (Free from Chelmsford C on 23/3/95) FL 7

MARTIN Jae Andrew
Born: London, 5 February 1976
Height: 5'11" Weight: 12.4

Southend player who promised much, but failed to deliver on his few first-team

appearances, Jae was released on a free transfer last April. Earlier in the season, he had been on loan at Orient where he made an excellent impression as a speedy right-winger.

Southend U (From trainee on 7/5/93) FL 1+7 FLC 1+1 Others 0+1
Leyton Orient (Loaned on 9/9/94) FL 1+3 Others 1

MARTIN Kevin
Born: Bromsgrove, 26 June 1976
Height: 6'0" Weight: 12.8

Scarborough YTS goalkeeper who gained his first taste of senior action last season and showed much promise. Kept clean sheets in both FA Cup first round-ties against Chesterfield, and ended 1994-95 as the club's "Young Player of the Year".

Scarborough (Trainee) FL 3 FAC 2 Others 1

MARTIN Lee Brendon
Born: Huddersfield, 9 September 1968
Height: 6'0" Weight: 13.0

Blackpool's "Player of the Year" in 1993-94, Lee lost his place in goal to Les Sealey at the beginning of last season. However, by late September he was back between the sticks performing as consistently as ever, and Sealey moved on.

Huddersfield T (From trainee on 1/7/87) FL 54 FAC 4 Others 5
Blackpool (Free on 31/7/92) FL 98 FLC 8 FAC 4 Others 7

Nigel Martyn — Paul Marriott
(Empics Sports Photo Agency)

MARTYN Antony Nigel
Born: St Austell, 11 August 1966
Height: 6'2" Weight: 14.0
Club Honours: Div 3 '90, FMC '91; Div 1 '94
International Honours: E: 3; B-6; U21-11

Commanding Crystal Palace goalkeeper. Had another magnificent season in 1994-95, following a troubled summer, which included a hernia operation. Recovering in time to be present for the first Premiership match, Nigel and the club were on the wrong end of a 6-1 scoreline as Liverpool ran amok. Had a brilliant run after that, conceding just 29 goals with 13 clean sheets to his name, before a broken index finger brought an end to 150 consecutive first team appearances. Not out of the England reckoning, he is very agile for a big man and stands up well, always presenting an imposing figure to the opposition.

Bristol Rov (Free from St Blazey on 6/8/87) FL 101 FLC 6 FAC 6 Others 11
Crystal Palace (£1,000,000 on 21/11/89) F/PL 226 FLC 32 FAC 20 Others 16

Philomen Masinga Paul Marriott
(Empics Sports Photo Agency)

MASINGA Philomen Raul
Born: South Africa, 28 June 1969
Height: 6'2" Weight: 12.0
Striker. Struggled to come to terms with the pace and strengths of the English game initially, having previously played as a part-timer, he came on as a sub for Leeds at West Ham on the opening day of last season, remaining for the next seven games and scoring against Chelsea, before being rested until the turn of the year. Came back to lift a side that was struggling for goals, with two at Arsenal, a nine minute extra-time hat-trick that sent Walsall crashing out of the FA Cup, another two against QPR and the Fourth Round FA Cup winner against Oldham. However, following a difficult match at Manchester United that saw Leeds dumped out of the FA Cup, he was dropped from the side.
Leeds U (£275,000 from Marmelodo Sundown on 3/8/94) PL 15+7/5 FLC 1 FAC 2+2/4

MASKELL Craig Dell
Born: Aldershot, 10 April 1968
Height: 5'10" Weight: 11.4
Forward. Had little opportunity at Southampton last season and, with recent signings, would look to have little future at the Dell, although scoring plenty of goals for the reserves.
Southampton (From apprentice on 15/4/86) FL 2+4/1
Huddersfield T (£20,000 on 31/5/88) FL 86+1/43 FLC 6/4 FAC 8/3 Others 7/4
Reading (f250,000 on 7/8/90) FL 60+12/26 FLC 2 FAC 5+1 Others 1
Swindon T (£225,000 on 9/7/92) F/PL 40+7/22 FLC 3+1/1 FAC 2+1 Others 4+1/4
Southampton (£250,000 on 7/2/94) PL 8+8/1 FAC 1

MASON Paul David
Born: Liverpool, 3 September 1963
Height: 5'8" Weight: 12.1
Club Honours: SLC '90; SC '90
Predominantly right-footed Ipswich man who can play anywhere in midfield, although preferring one of the wide positions, and possesses a powerful shot in either foot. Had a mixed season in 1994-95, starting well, but later being sidelined with a foot injury for several weeks. Scored the first two goals in the 3-2 defeat of Manchester United, his second being outstanding when, after cutting in from the right, he curled in a left-foot shot into the top corner. Restored to the side virtually at the end of the season, he made both goals against Coventry with determined runs down the flanks.
Aberdeen (£200,000 from FC Groningen on 1/8/88) SL 138+20/27 SLC 13+2/8 SC 11+1/1 Others 7/1
Ipswich T (£400,000 on 18/6/93) PL 37+6/6 FLC 3/1 FAC 2+2

MASSEY Stuart Anthony
Born: Crawley, 17 November 1964
Height: 5'11 " Weight: 11.8
Signed from Crystal Palace in the summer of 1994, he was a regular on the right-side of Oxford's midfield until mid-November, when suffering a hernia. This put Stuart out of action for four months before a return was attempted and, following further setbacks, he has not appeared much since then. Is a determined and useful member of the squad, who can also produce good quality crosses.
Crystal Palace (£20,000 from Sutton U on 17/7/92) F/PL 1+1 Others 1
Oxford U (Free on 5/7/94) FL 20+2 FLC 4/1 FAC 1 Others 1

MASTERS Neil Bradley
Born: Ballymena, 25 May 1972
Height: 6'1" Weight: 13.3
Left-back. Neil began last season with a knee problem and then had to endure a hernia operation. A thigh strain added to his woe and he was restricted to two appearances for Wolverhampton as a sub in December, before finally starting three games in April, when he then suffered from a sore back!
Bournemouth (From trainee on 31/8/90) FL 37+1/2 FLC 4/1 FAC 5+2/1 Others 1
Wolverhampton W (£600,000 on 22/12/93) FL 7+2

MATHIE Alexander (Alex)
Born: Bathgate, 20 December 1968
Height: 5'10" Weight: 10.7
Unable to break into the Newcastle side on a regular basis, Alex moved to Ipswich last February. As an attacking player with tremendous ball skills, who has the control to beat players, both on the inside and the outside, he scored on his debut against Southampton. Another facet of his play is the ability to hold the ball up and bring others into the game.
Glasgow Celtic (From juniors on 15/5/87) SL 7+4 SC 1 Others 0+1
Morton (£100,000 on 1/8/91) SL 73+1/31 SLC 2/1 SC 5/3 Others 7/9
Port Vale (Loaned on 30/3/93) FL 0+3

Newcastle U (£285,000 on 30/7/93) PL 3+22/4 FLC 5+2
Ipswich T (£500,000 on 24/2/95) PL 13/2

MATTEO Dominic
Born: Dumfries, 28 April 1974
Height: 6'1" Weight: 11.8
International Honours: E: U21-3; Yth
Liverpool left-back with good skills, who is good on the overlap and brings added height to a defensive situation when required. Continued to make progress in the reserve side last season and was loaned out to Sunderland in March in an effort to gain further experience.
Liverpool (From trainee on 27/5/92) PL 13+5 FLC 2 FAC 1
Sunderland (Loaned on 28/3/95) FL 1

MATTHEW Damian
Born: Islington, 23 September 1970
Height: 5'11" Weight" 10.10
Club Honours: Div 1 '94
International Honours: E: U21-9
Former Crystal Palace manager, Alan Smith's first signing for a fee, Damien had a disappointing time in 1994-95, failing to make the breakthrough that had been expected of him. As a creative midfielder, with great stamina, he made just four starts, having his best game at Liverpool in the Coca Cola Cup, but, in the main, was confined to the reserves.
Chelsea (From trainee on 13/6/89) F/PL 13+8 FLC 5 Others 1
Luton T (Loaned on 25/9/92) FL 3+2 Others 1
Crystal Palace (£150,000 on 11/2/94) F/PL 13+3/1 FLC 1 FAC 1

MATTHEWS Neil
Born: Grimsby, 19 September 1966
Height: 5'11" Weight: 12.0
A wholehearted wide forward or midfield player, who was in-and-out of Lincoln's first team last season, he spent January on loan at promotion contenders, Bury, before being released during the summer.
Grimsby T (From apprentice on 25/9/84) FL 9+3
Scunthorpe U (Loaned on 9/11/85) FL 1
Halifax T (Loaned on 10/10/86) FL 9/2
Bolton W (Loaned on 23/3/87) FL 1
Halifax T (Free on 20/8/87) FL 99+6/29 FLC 4 FAC 10/1 Others 9+2/5
Stockport Co (£70,000 on 3/7/90) FL 27+16/15 FLC 1+1 FAC 0+1 Others 1
Halifax T (Loaned on 25/9/91) FL 3
Lincoln C (£20,000 on 17/12/92) FL 69+14/20 FLC 2/1 FAC 4 Others 4+3/1
Bury (Loaned on 23/12/94) FL 2/1

MATTHEWS Neil Peter
Born: Manchester, 3 December 1967
Height: 6'0" Weight: 11.7
Club Honours: Div 3 '93
International Honours: NI: B-1; U21-1; Yth
Again hit by injuries, Peter played some sterling games for Rochdale in the AWS Trophy when standing in at centre-half for the cup-tied Peter Valentine. Prior to signing for a club in China last March, he had the honour of being "Dale's" first international representative of any kind for 75 years when turning out for Northern Ireland "B".
Blackpool (From apprentice on 12/12/85) FL 67+9/1 FLC 7 FAC 1 Others 4+2

Cardiff C (£25,000 on 13/9/90) FL 48+4/1 FLC 3 FAC 3 Others 4 (Signed for Songdal in May 1992)
Cardiff C (Free on 4/12/92) FL 12+2/1 FAC 1 Others 1
Rochdale (Free on 5/7/93) FL 15+4 FLC 1 FAC 1 Others 6

MATTHEWS Robert (Rob) David
Born: Slough, 14 October 1970
Height: 6'0" Weight: 12.5
International Honours: E: Sch
With good control skills and a goalscoring record to match, there was some surprise expressed when Notts County allowed Rob to join Luton just before last season's transfer deadline. Although injured on his debut, when coming on as a sub against Millwall, he adds individual flair and attacking power down the left-flank.
Notts Co (Free from Loughborough University on 26/3/92) FL 23+20/11 FLC 0+2 FAC 3+2/2 Others 4+3
Luton T (£80,000 on 17/3/95) FL 6+5

MATTHEWSON Trevor
Born: Sheffield, 12 February 1963
Height: 6'1" Weight: 12.5
Club Honours: GMVC '88; AMC '91
Signed from Preston last September, having earlier been released by Birmingham, Trevor went immediately into the Bury side at centre-half, where he became a member of the meanest defence in the country. Unfortunately lost his place through injury at Christmas.
Sheffield Wed (From apprentice on 12/2/81) FL 3 FAC 2
Newport Co (Free on 15/10/83) FL 73+2 FLC 2 FAC 7 Others 6
Stockport Co (Free on 27/9/85) FL 79+1 FLC 3 FAC 2 Others 3
Lincoln C (£13,000 on 1/8/87) FL 43/2 FLC 3 FAC 3 Others 2
Birmingham C (£45,000 on 3/8/89) FL 167+1/12 FLC 11 FAC 8 Others 16/1
Preston NE (Signed on 20/8/93) FL 12/1 FLC 1 Others 1
Bury (£10,000 on 2/9/94) FL 18 FAC 4 Others 4

MATTISON Paul Andrew
Born: Wakefield, 24 April 1973
Height: 5'10" Weight: 11.5
Joining Darlington after impressing in pre-season games, Paul went straight into the first team at the beginning of 1994-95. A direct and pacy winger, he played in the first few games before settling into the reserve side.
Darlington (Free from Ferrybridge Amateurs on 12/8/94) FL 4+6 FLC 1

MAUGE Ronald (Ronnie) Carlton
Born: Islington, 10 March 1969
Height: 5'10" Weight: 10.6
A Bury midfield player of undoubted talent, Ronnie made only 22 first team starts last season, as he struggled to find the kind of form everybody at the club knows he is capable of. Is bound to come back with a bang.
Charlton Ath (From trainee on 22/7/87)
Fulham (Free on 21/9/88) FL 47+3/2 FLC 4 FAC 1 Others 2
Bury (£40,000 on 30/7/90) FL 92+16/10 FLC 8+2/2 FAC 8/2 Others 10+2
Manchester C (Loaned on 26/9/91) Others 0+1

MAXFIELD Scott
Born: Doncaster, 13 July 1976
Height: 5'8" Weight: 10.7
A former Doncaster junior, this promising young full-back was given his chance towards the end of last season and looked a terrific prospect.
Doncaster Rov (From trainee on 8/7/94) FL 10

MAY Andrew (Andy) Michael Peter
Born: Bury, 26 February 1964
Height: 5'8" Weight: 11.0
International Honours: E: U21-1
Another Millwall player who was sidelined by a series of injuries in 1994-95, such as calf strains and achilles tendon, Andy, a vastly experienced central midfielder who usually supports the back four, was freed at the end of the season.
Manchester C (From apprentice on 1/3/82) FL 141+9/8 FLC 10 FAC 6 Others 7+1
Huddersfield T (£36,000 on 13/7/87) FL 112+2/5 FLC 5 FAC 10/1 Others 8
Bolton W (Loaned on 24/3/88) FL 9+1/2
Bristol C (£90,000 on 7/8/90) FL 88+2/4 FLC 5 FAC 4/1 Others 2/1
Millwall (Signed on 18/6/92) FL 49+5/1 FLC 3 FAC 2

MAY David
Born: Oldham, 24 June 1970
Height: 6'0" Weight: 11.4
Club Honours: CS '94
Strong Manchester United central defender who has excellent positional sense and is very quick off the mark. Also good in the air and a useful passer of the ball, David made a satisfactory start to his United career last season, following his big-money transfer from Blackburn. Initially used as a stop-gap replacement for Paul Parker, his form suffered as a result, but on the few occasions that he played in the centre of defence he looked a different proposition, and all three of his first team goals came from that position. Although his season ended in injury, he did enough to suggest that he will be challenging Steve Bruce for that elusive number four shirt this coming season.
Blackburn Rov (From trainee on 16/6/88) F/PL 123/3 FLC 12+1/2 FAC 10/1 Others 5
Manchester U (£1,400,000 on 1/7/94) PL 15+4/2 FLC 2/1 FAC 1 Others 5

MEADE Rafael Joseph
Born: London, 22 November 1962
Height: 5'10" Weight: 11.9
Forward. Given a two month contract by Brighton at the start of last season, he came on as substitute on three occasions but was then released. Subsequently played in local non-league soccer and is currently with Beazer Homes Premier side, Crawley.
Arsenal (From apprentice on 9/6/80) FL 25+16/14 FLC 3/1 FAC 1 (Signed for Sporting Lisbon on 1/7/85)
Dundee U (Signed in August 1988) SL 8+3/4 SLC 1+1/1 SC 3+1/1 Others 3+1/1
Luton T (Signed on 21/3/89) FL 2+2 (Signed for Odense in August 1989)
Ipswich T (On trial on 5/1/90) FL 0+1
Plymouth Arg (Free on 10/1/91) FL 2+3
Brighton & Hove A (Free on 28/9/91) FL 35+5/9 FLC 2/2 FAC 2/2 Others 2 (Free to Hong Kong during 1992 close season)
Brighton & Hove A (Free from Dover on 25/7/94) FL 0+3

MEAKER Michael John
Born: Greenford, 18 August 1971
Height: 5'11" Weight: 11.5
International Honours: W: U21-2
Made ten full appearances for QPR last season, when coming into the side to cover for injuries and produced some exciting performances on either wing. Scored the fourth goal in the 4-0 FA Cup victory over Aylesbury and is very good at cutting in from the left and shooting with his favoured right-foot.
Queens Park R (From trainee on 7/2/90) F/PL 21+13/1 FLC 2/1 FAC 1 Others 2+1/1
Plymouth Arg (Loaned on 20/11/91) FL 4 Others 1

MEAN Scott James
Born: Crawley, 13 December 1973
Height: 5'11" Weight: 11.11
Last season, Scott established himself in centre of Bournemouth's midfield, showing good distribution skills and having the ability to make some good runs. Also scored some important goals, none more so than against Brentford and Shrewsbury in the last two games of the 1994-95 season that ensured the club's Second Division survival.
Bournemouth (From trainee on 10/8/92) FL 39+21/8 FLC 4+1 FAC 2 Others 4

MEARA James (Jim) Stephen
Born: Hammersmith, 7 October 1972
Height: 5'7" Weight: 10.6
Club Honours: FAYC '89
Stylish midfielder who can often create goal opportunities with subtle passes, he never really cemented his place in Doncaster's first team last season, despite playing in a third of the league games, following his move from Watford the previous July.
Watford (From trainee on 30/4/91) FL 1+1
Doncaster Rov (Free on 15/7/94) FL 14+1/1 FLC 1 FAC 1 Others 1

MEASHAM Ian
Born: Barnsley 14 December 1964
Height: 5'11" Weight: 11.1
Club Honours: Div 4 '92
Completed a miraculous recovery from a broken neck suffered 15 months ago, when he played for Doncaster in the last League game of the 1994-95 season at Wigan. A classy full-back, his cool and cultured play in defence had been sadly missed up until then.
Huddersfield T (From apprentice on 16/12/82) FL 17
Lincoln C (Loaned on 18/10/85) FL 6
Rochdale (Loaned on 21/3/86) FL 12
Cambridge U (Free on 8/8/86) FL 46 FLC 6 FAC 3 Others 2
Burnley (Free on 10/11/88) FL 181+1/2 FLC 8 FAC 19 Others 19
Doncaster Rov (Signed on 16/9/93) FL 22 FAC 2 Others 2

MEGSON Gary John
Born: Manchester, 2 May 1959
Height: 5'10" Weight: 11.6
Having made his FL debut as long ago as 1977-78, and as Norwich's assistant manager, Gary played just once in 1994-95. Called into the City midfield for the "six pointer" at Filbert Street in April, there was

to be no happy ending, however, with Leicester taking the points. Appointed care-taker manager for the remaining five games, following John Deehan's resignation, he then had to preside over the club's fall from grace after nine years in the top flight, prior to being released at the end of the season.

Plymouth Arg (From apprentice on 1/5/77) FL 78/10 FLC 9 FAC 5
Everton (£250,000 on 18/12/79) FL 20+2/2 FAC 3/1
Sheffield Wed (£130,000 on 7/8/81) FL 123/13 FLC 13/2 FAC 12/5
Nottingham F (£175,000 on 28/8/84)
Newcastle U (£130,000 on 21/11/84) FL 21+3/1 FLC 1+1 FAC 2/1
Sheffield Wed (£60,000 on 20/12/85) FL 107+3/12 FLC 10 FAC 15/1 Others 3
Manchester C (£250,000 on 12/1/89) FL 78+4/2 FLC 5 FAC 7+1 Others 2
Norwich C (Free on 1/7/92) PL 42+4/1 FLC 1 FAC 4 Others 2+1

MEHEW David Stephen
Born: Camberley, 29 October 1967
Height: 5'11" Weight: 12.0
Club Honours: Div 3 '90

Goalscoring midfielder nicknamed "Boris", due to his resemblance to the tennis star, Boris Becker. Freed by Bristol Rovers during the 1994 close season, David followed his former coach, Kenny Hibbitt, to Walsall but, after just ten starts, he was released by the latter's successor, Chris Nicholl.

Bristol Rov (Free from Leeds U juniors on 11/7/85) FL 195+27/63 FLC 11/2 FAC 8+1/1 Others 16+3/4
Exeter C (Loaned on 24/3/94) FL 5+2
Walsall (Free on 30/7/94) FL 6+7 FLC 3+1 FAC 0+2 Others 1

MELLON Michael Joseph
Born: Paisley, 18 March 1972
Height: 5'8" Weight: 11.3

A skilful midfielder who came to Blackpool from West Bromwich Albion last November, he made an immediate impres-sion on the locals with his tremendous work-rate. Will also be remembered for scoring two goals in a remarkable 5-2 victory over Plymouth.

Bristol C (From trainee on 6/12/89) FL 26+9/1 FLC 3 FAC 1+1 Others 5+3
West Bromwich A (£75,000 on 11/2/93) FL 38+7/6 FLC 3+2 FAC 0+1 Others 6/1
Blackpool (£50,000 on 23/11/94) FL 26/4

MELVILLE Andrew (Andy) Roger
Born: Swansea, 29 November 1968
Height: 6'1" Weight: 12.6
Club Honours: WC '89
International Honours: W: 24; B-1; U21-2

A Welsh international centre-half, Andy had an indifferent season in 1994-95, losing his Sunderland place in Peter Reid's reign to Richard Ord. Powerful in the air, he is particularly dangerous at set-plays and his last-gasp goal at Roker against Stoke in March was one of the best celebrated strikes of the season. He is a player who always looks to use the ball intelligently from defence.

Swansea C (From trainee on 25/7/86) FL 165+10/22 FLC 10 FAC 14+1/5 Others 13/2

Oxford U (£275,000 on 23/7/90) FL 135/13 FLC 12/1 FAC 6 Others 6/1
Sunderland (Signed on 9/8/93) FL 80/5 FLC 7 FAC 5 Others 2

MENDONCA Clive Paul
Born: Islington, 9 September 1968
Height: 5'10" Weight: 12.6

This right-footed striker's ability to take on and beat opposing defenders, his tireless running to create space for his team-mates and his lightning reaction in front of goal, have earned him the soubriquet "Super-Clive", from Grimsby supporters. A per-sistent thigh injury and the after effects of a road accident limited his appearances last season and there is no doubt that his absence during the vital "run-in" was largely responsible for the side fading from contention for a place in the divisional play-offs.

Sheffield U (From apprentice on 10/9/86) FL 8+5/4 FLC 0+1 Others 1
Doncaster Rov (Loaned on 26/2/88) FL 2
Rotherham U (£35,000 on 25/3/88) FL 71+13/27 FLC 5+2/1 FAC 4+1/2 Others 4+2/1
Sheffield U (£110,000 on 1/8/91) FL 4+6/1 FLC 0+2 Others 0+1
Grimsby T (Loaned on 9/1/92) FL 10/3
Grimsby T (£85,000 on 13/8/92) FL 98+5/35 FLC 8+1/2 FAC 7/2 Others 2/1

MERCER William (Billy)
Born: Liverpool, 22 May 1969
Height: 6'2" Weight: 13.5

Goalkeeper who guested for Sheffield United on the 1994 close season tour of Australia and became back-up to Alan Kelly, when signed from Rotherham. Made his debut in the home win over Derby when Kelly was on international duty and was immaculate. Continued as second-string, with two further appearances, until joining Nottingham Forest on loan in March, without getting a game until the end of the season.

Liverpool (From trainee on 21/8/87)
Rotherham U (Signed on 16/2/89) FL 104 FLC 12 FAC 12 Others 10
Sheffield U (Signed on 12/10/94) FL 3

MERSON Paul Charles
Born: Harlesden, 20 March 1968
Height: 6'0" Weight: 12.10
Club Honours: Div 1 '89, '91; FLC '93; FAC '93; ECWC '94
International Honours: E: 14; B-3; U21-4; Yth

Came back from his well publicised personal problems far leaner and in superb form for Arsenal last season. Supremely

Paul Merson

Steve Morton
(Empics Sports Photo Agency)

143

gifted, with his close control he can play wide or up-front and, on occasion, in central midfield. An exciting player with an explosive finish, Paul favours his right-foot and will regulrly come off the left-flank looking to get in a shot. 1995-96 could well see the former PFA "Young Player of the Year" (1989) back at his very best.

Arsenal (From apprentice on 1/12/85) F/PL 219+38/67 FLC 26+2/8 FAC 23+3/4 Others 16+1/3
Brentford (Loaned on 22/1/87) FL 6+1 Others 1+1

MEYER Adrian Michael
Born: Yate, 22 September 1970
Height: 6'0" Weight: 14.0
Strong Scarborough centre-back, and the club's longest serving player, having progressed through the youth and reserve sides. A powerful header of the ball, he made just 20 starts in 1994-95, having been unfortunate with injuries over the past couple of years. Son of Barrie Meyer, the famous cricket umpire.

Scarborough (From trainee on 10/6/89) FL 114/9 FLC 12 FAC 4+1 Others 4+1/1

MICKLEWHITE Gary
Born: Southwark, 21 March 1961
Height: 5'7" Weight: 10.4
Club Honours: Div 2 '83, Div '87
An industrious midfielder who brings a bit of class to Gillingham, Gary turned in some impressive performances during the latter part of last season. Was appointed player-coach when Neil Smillie was put in charge of team affairs.

Manchester U (From apprentice on 23/3/78)
Queens Park R (Free on 4/7/79) FL 97+9/11 FLC 12+1/5 FAC 4+2/1 Others 1+1
Derby Co (£90,000 on 26/2/85) FL 223+17/31 FLC 23+3/2 FAC 8+3/4 Others 8+3/6
Gillingham (Free on 22/7/93) FL 61+3/3 FLC 4 FAC 6/1 Others 1+1

MIDGLEY Craig Steven
Born: Bradford, 24 June 1976
Height: 5'8" Weight: 10.13
A midfield player who was yet another product of the Bradford youth set-up given a first team opportunity in 1994-95. Still a trainee.

Bradford C (Trainee) FL 0+3 Others 1

MIKE Adrian (Adie) Roosevelt
Born: Manchester, 16 November 1973
Height: 6'0" Weight: 11.9
International Honours: E: Yth; Sch
Very quick, well built Manchester City striker who spent seven weeks during the 1994 English close season on loan to Swedish club, Linkoping, as part of a rehabilitation programme, he ultimately played less than a handful of senior games in 1994-95. Consistently on the fringe of first team soccer and a squad member, Adie will be looking for a good start in 1995-96.

Manchester C (From trainee on 15/7/92) F/PL 5+11/2 FLC 1+1 FAC 0+1
Bury (Loaned on 25/3/93) FL 5+2/1

MIKLOSKO Ludek (Ludo)
Born: Ostrava, Czechoslovakia, 9 December 1961
Height: 6'5" Weight: 14.0
International Honours: Czechoslovakia
Giant West Ham goalkeeper whose consistent displays have made him a great favourite at Upton Park. His courage and bravery was recognised at Leeds last December when he suffered a terrible eye injury and then took a crushing blow in the ribs, but still managed to play on. Had a brilliant match against Chelsea in the Coca Cola Cup and in the final game of the campaign, made three incredible saves to deny Manchester United the Premier League title. Set a new goalkeeping record at the club, when ever-present for the third season running.

West Ham U (£300,000 from Banik Ostrava on 19/2/90) F/PL 230 FLC 17 FAC 20 Others 8

Ludek Miklosko   Phil O'Brien
(Empics Sports Photo Agency)

MILLAR William Paul
Born: Belfast, 16 November 1966
Height: 6'2" Weight: 12.7
Club Honours: IC '86; Div 3 '93
Cardiff central midfielder and a free-kick specialist. Although goals were few and far between in 1994-95, he scored with two 40 yard volleys in back-to-back games against Swansea and Birmingham.

Port Vale (£35,000 from Portadown on 29/12/88) FL 19+21/5 FAC 0+2 Others 1+1
Hereford U (Loaned on 11/10/90) FL 5/2
Cardiff C (£20,000 on 21/8/91) FL 91+29/17 FLC 7+1/1 FAC 8+1/1 Others 13+2/3

MILLEN Keith Derek
Born: Croydon, 26 September 1966
Height: 6'1" Weight: 12.0
Club Honours: Div 3 '92
Underrated Watford central defender who broke into the first team on a regular basis last October and was thereafter the model of consistency, especially when playing alongside Colin Foster and David Holdsworth in a three man central defence.

Brentford (From apprentice on 7/8/84) FL 301+4/17 FLC 26/2 FAC 18/1 Others 30+1
Watford (Signed on 22/3/94) FL 41/1 FLC 1 FAC 5

MILLER Allan John
Born: Epping, 29 March 1970
Height: 6'3" Weight: 14.6
Club Honours: FAYC '88; ECWC '94; Div 1 '95
International Honours: E: U21-4; Yth
Fearless and agile Middlesbrough goalie in the best traditions of his position, who is technically faultless in reflexes and angles. Now seen as an inspirational 1994 close season buy, by "Robbo", as "cover" for the redoubtable Stephen Pears, Alan is without doubt, one of the reasons why "Boro" ran out clear First Division Champions, after winning the number one spot exclusively for himself.

Arsenal (From trainee on 5/5/88) PL 6+2
Plymouth Arg (Loaned on 24/11/88) FL 13 FAC 2
West Bromwich A (Loaned on 15/8/91) FL 3
Birmingham C (Loaned on 19/12/91) FL 15 Others 1
Middlesbrough (£500,000 on 12/8/94) FL 41 FLC 1 FAC 2 Others 2

MILLER David Brian
Born: Burnley, 8 January 1964
Height: 5'11" Weight: 11.12
The son of Brian, the former Burnley and England defender, David, who signed last September from Stockport, proved to be a good positional central defender whose steady and reliable performances helped Wigan climb up the table. An experienced campaigner, he has played all his football in the North-West and celebrated 300 FL appearances during the season.

Burnley (From apprentice on 11/1/82) FL 27+5/3 FLC 2 FAC 1 Others 2+1
Crewe Alex (Loaned on 18/3/83) FL 3
Tranmere Rov (Free on 16/7/85) FL 25+4/1 FLC 1 FAC 4 Others 2/1 (Free to Colne Dynamoes during 1986 close season)
Preston NE (Free on 18/12/86) FL 50+8/2 FLC 6 FAC 0+2 Others 7+2
Burnley (Loaned on 16/2/89) FL 4
Carlisle U (£30,000 on 14/9/89) FL 108+1/7 FLC 6 FAC 4 Others 7
Stockport Co (£25,000 on 31/3/92) FL 72+9/1 FLC 6 FAC 5+2 Others 12+2
Wigan Ath (Signed on 6/10/94) FL 31/3 FAC 2 Others 3

MILLER Kevin
Born: Falmouth, 15 March 1969
Height: 6'1" Weight: 13.0
Club Honours: Div 4 '90
In his first season with Watford, having been signed from Birmingham during the summer of 1994, Kevin emerged as one of the best goalkeepers outside the Premiership, breaking a 46-year-old club record by keeping a clean sheet for nine consecutive matches from 2 January to 21 February. Athletic and a good shot-stopper, he enjoyed the total confidence of his defenders.

Exeter C (Free from Newquay on 9/3/89) FL 163 FLC 7 FAC 12 Others 18
Birmingham C (£250,000 on 14/5/93) FL 24 FLC 4 Others 2
Watford (£250,000 on 7/8/94) FL 44 FLC 3 FAC 4

MILLER Paul Anthony
Born: Woking, 31 January 1968
Height: 6'0" Weight: 11.7

A quality striker who enjoyed many seasons with Wimbledon, where he developed into a determined, skilful and brave attacker, he has also played on occasions in Bristol Rovers' midfield. In 1994-95, it was Paul's scoring contribution that ensured the club enjoyed a remarkable season, his four goal haul against Bath City in the FA Cup was a personal highlight, while one at Crewe in the play-offs ensured a Wembley place.

Wimbledon (From Yeovil T on 12/8/87) F/PL 65+15/10 FLC 3+3 FAC 3 Others 1
Newport Co (Loaned on 20/10/87) FL 6/2
Bristol C (Loaned on 11/1/90) FL 0+3 Others 2
Bristol Rov (£100,000 on 16/8/94) FL 41+1/16 FLC 2 FAC 4/4 Others 6/2

MILLETT Michael Paul
Born: Billinge, 22 September 1977
Height: 5'10" Weight: 11.0
International Honours: E: Yth

Playing in midfield, Michael, who is a good competitor, and a strong tackler, was rewarded with three appearances in Wigan's first team after making impressive performances at junior level. Now a professional, he also represented England at youth level in 1994-95.

Wigan Ath (From trainee on 1/10/94) FL 1+2

MILLIGAN Michael (Mike) Joseph
Born: Manchester, 20 February 1967
Height: 5'8" Weight: 11.0
International Honours: Ei: 1; B-2; U21-1

An all-action player, who really gets to grips with problems and a good man to have in your side, he joined Norwich during the 1994 close season from Oldham. A prime component in midfield as City reached the upper echelons of the Premiership last Christmas, he cut a disconsolate figure at Manchester Airport having been left out of the side that lost to Bolton in the Coca Cola quarter-finals. His greatest challenge at the club has yet to come, following relegation to the First Division.

Oldham Ath (From apprentice on 2/3/85) FL 161+1/17 FLC 19+1/1 FAC 12/1 Others 4
Everton (£1,000,000 on 24/8/90) FL 16+1/1 FLC 0+1 FAC 1 Others 4+1/1
Oldham Ath (£600,000 on 17/7/91) F/PL 117/6 FLC 11/1 FAC 9 Others 1/1
Norwich C (£800,000 on 27/6/94) PL 25+1/2 FLC 4 FAC 3

MILLS Gary Roland
Born: Northampton, 11 November 1961
Height: 5'9" Weight: 11.10
Club Honours: EC '80; AIC '95
International Honours: E: U21-2; Yth; Sch

The son of former pro, Roley, at school Gary represented England both at soccer and rugby, but ultimately followed his father into League football. Signed from Leicester last September, for his second spell at Notts County, he came into the side at right-back, before moving over to the other flank on the return of Chris Short. Can play both the tackling and passing game, and occasionally captained County when Phil Turner was out injured.

Nottingham F (From apprentice on 13/11/78) FL 113+23/12 FLC 16+5/3 FAC 5 Others 7+3
Derby Co (Loaned on 13/10/82) FL 18/2 FLC 2 FAC 3

Notts Co (Signed on 14/8/87) FL 75/8 FLC 6/1 FAC 5 Others 10
Leicester C (Signed on 2/3/89) F/PL 195+5/16 FLC 9+1/1 FAC 7 Others 15
Notts Co (£50,000 on 26/9/94) FL 33+1 FLC 3 FAC 2 Others 4/1

MILLS Rowan Lee
Born: Mexborough, 10 July 1970
Height: 6'1" Weight: 12.11
Signed from Wolverhampton last February to add some height and power up-front, he made his Derby debut against Bolton and scored a spectacular late solo goal, brushing off several challenges before driving home. Full of enthusiasm, Lee hit two in the memorable 4-2 victory at Middlesbrough, and is set to become a firm favourite with the crowd.

Wolverhampton W (Signed from Stocksbridge on 9/12/92) FL 12+13/2 FLC 1 FAC 3+1/1 Others 3/1
Derby Co (£400,000 on 24/2/95) FL 16/7

MILNER Andrew (Andy) John
Born: Kendal, 10 February 1967
Height: 6'0" Weight: 11.0
Chester forward with great speed, who loves to take defenders on, Andy came to the club from Rochdale during the 1994 close season. Skilful on the ball, he can play either wide on the right, or up-front as a central striker.

Manchester C (Signed from Netherfield on 24/1/89)
Rochdale (£20,000 on 18/1/90) FL 103+24/25 FLC 9+4/5 FAC 6+2/1 Others 4/2
Chester C (Free on 12/8/94) FL 32+4/8 FLC 1+1 FAC 1+1/1 Others 1

MILSOM Paul Jason
Born: Bristol, 5 October 1974
Height: 5'10" Weight: 13.4
Young striker of limited experience. Having made his debut for Bristol City in 1993-94, Paul was unable to build on that last season and was freed, immediately signing as a non-contract player for Cardiff. So far his few appearances have been as a sub, but he will not be deterred.

Bristol C (From trainee on 7/7/93) FL 1+2
Cardiff C (Free on 23/3/95) FL 1+2 Others 1

MILTON Simon Charles
Born: Fulham, 23 August 1963
Height: 5'10" Weight: 11.0
Club Honours: Div 2 '92
Ipswich right-winger who is capable of scoring explosive goals, after pushing up from midfield, and who has a relatively good scoring record. Missed most of last season through injury, netting only twice from 21 appearances. Strangely enough, both goals were in League games against Wimbledon and earned Town a point on both occasions.

Ipswich T (£5,500 from Bury T on 17/7/87) F/PL 168+33/39 FLC 11+3/2 FAC 8/1 Others 10+1/3
Exeter C (Loaned on 1/11/87) FL 2/3 Others 1
Torquay U (Loaned on 1/3/88) FL 4/1

MIMMS Robert (Bobby) Andrew
Born: York, 12 October 1963
Height: 6'2" Weight: 12.10
Club Honours: Div 1 '87; CS '86, '87

International Honours: E: U21-3
Very experienced Blackburn reserve goalkeeper. Extremely agile for such a big man, Bobby ably demonstrated why the deputy 'keeper is so prized, when he came on against Leeds last season after Tim Flowers had been sent off. Despite the team being down to ten men, he was soundness itself until beaten by a late penalty. Following that, he had the rare opportunity of playing three consecutive games until Flowers was able to resume.

Halifax T (From apprentice on 5/8/81)
Rotherham U (£15,000 on 6/11/81) FL 83 FLC 7 FAC 3 Others 1
Everton (£150,000 on 30/5/85) FL 29 FLC 2 FAC 2 Others 4
Notts Co (Loaned on 13/3/86) FL 2 Others 1
Sunderland (Loaned on 11/12/86) FL 4
Blackburn Rov (Loaned on 23/1/87) FL 6
Manchester C (Loaned on 24/9/87) FL 3
Tottenham H (£325,000 on 25/2/88) FL 37 FLC 5 FAC 2
Aberdeen (Loaned on 16/2/90) SL 6 SC 2
Blackburn Rov (£250,000 on 22/12/90) F/PL 125+1 FLC 14 FAC 9 Others 4

MINETT Jason
Born: Peterborough, 12 August 1971
Height: 5'10" Weight: 10.2
A defender who was converted effortlessly from midfield last season, Jason was freed by Exeter during the summer.

Norwich C (From trainee on 4/7/89) F/PL 0+3
Exeter C (Free on 19/3/93) FL 83+5/3 FLC 4 FAC 6 Others 7/2

Scott Minto   Steve Morton
(Empics Sports Photo Agency)

MINTO Scott Christopher
Born: Heswall, 6 August 1971
Height: 5'9" Weight: 10.7
International Honours: E: U21-6; Yth

Charlton's young England U21 left-back joined Premier League side, Chelsea, during the 1994 close season, with a view to enhancing his prospects at full international level. Bearing that in mind, Scott suffered a disappointing campaign, often struggling with a long-term ankle injury and only starting in 27 games. However, he showed enough promise as a naturally left-sided player who was not adverse to joining up with the attack on occasion. Is undoubtedly a player with a future.

Charlton Ath (From trainee on 2/2/89) FL 171+9/7 FLC 8/2 FAC 8+2 Others 7/1
Chelsea (£775,000 on 28/5/94) PL 19 FAC 3 Others 5+1

MINTON Jeffrey (Jeff) Simon Thompson
Born: Hackney, 28 December 1973
Height: 5'5" Weight: 11.7

Another young man who progressed well with Brighton during in his first full season in 1994-95. A stocky, two-footed, busy midfield player, he did a great man-to-man marking job on Leicester's Mark Draper in the two legged Coca Cola Cup-tie when Brighton beat their Premiership opponents 3-0 on aggregate. Also liked to get forward, and possessing a good shot, he scored his first goal for the "Seagulls" at Hull.

Tottenham H (From trainee on 11/1/92) FL 2/1 FLC 0+1
Brighton & Hove A (Free on 25/7/94) FL 37+2/5 FLC 5 FAC 1 Others 1

MISON Michael
Born: London, 8 November 1975
Height: 6'3" Weight: 13.2

Another of Fulham's juniors to make the grade in 1994-95, Michael is a tall, gangling midfield playmaker whose superficial clumsiness masks considerable skill. As he matures, and builds up physical strength, he could develop into an exciting and creative player.

Fulham (From trainee on 15/7/94) FL 18+10/1 FLC 3 FAC 3 Others 2+1/1

MITCHELL David (Dave) Stewart
Born: Glasgow, 13 June 1962
Height: 6'0" Weight: 12.7
International Honours: Australia

Returning to England with Millwall last October, Dave is a right-footed striker, full of running and good in the air. Did well early on, but a nagging ankle injury decided him to look for a coaching position in Malaysia.

Glasgow R (Signed from Cologne during 1983 close season) SL 18+8/6 SLC 6+5/3 SC 2+1/1 Others 2+3/4 (Signed for Feyenoord in 1985)
Chelsea (£200,000 on 6/1/89) FL 7 Others 1
Newcastle U (Loaned on 8/1/91) FL 2/1
Swindon T (£30,000 on 26/7/91) FL 61+7/16 FLC 4/4 FAC 4/2 Others 4/3 (£25,000 to Altay Izmir during 1993 close season)
Millwall (£100,000 on 14/10/93) FL 49+6/16 FLC 3+1/1 FAC 6 Others 2

MITCHELL Graham Lee
Born: Shipley, 16 February 1968
Height: 6'0" Weight: 11.4

Signed by Bradford as part of the deal that took Lee Sinnott to Huddersfield last December, he came into the side at centre-half and looked very comfortable on the ball, with good passing skills.

Huddersfield T (From trainee on 16/6/86) FL 235+9/2 FLC 13+2/1 FAC 27/1 Others 24/1
Bournemouth (Loaned on 24/12/93) FL 4
Bradford C (Signed on 23/12/94) FL 26

MITCHELL Neil Nicholas
Born: Lytham, 7 November 1974
Height: 5'6" Weight: 10.0
International Honours: E: Yth

Striker with an eye for goal, who shows much promise, and has benefited from having an extended run for Blackpool.

Blackpool (From trainee on 28/11/92) FL 39+28/8 FLC 0+3 FAC 2+1/1 Others 5+1/1

Nicky Mohan   Matthew Ashton
(Empics Sports Photo Agency)

MOHAN Nicholas (Nicky)
Born: Middlesbrough, 6 October 1970
Height: 6'0" Weight: 11.10

Right-footed central defender, who was a 1994 summer signing for Leicester from his home town club, he battled hard at the heart of a beleaguered defence, without ever being able to stem the tide of goals against. Occasionally displaced as formations changed, but always fought back to recapture his place.

Middlesbrough (From juniors on 18/11/87) F/PL 93+6/4 FLC 11 FAC 9+1 Others 11
Hull C (Loaned on 26/9/92) FL 5/1
Leicester C (£330,000 on 7/7/94) PL 23 FLC 2 FAC 1

MOLBY Jan
Born: Kolding, Jutland, 4 July 1963
Height: 6'1" Weight: 13.8
Club Honours: Div 1 '86, '90; FAC '86, '92; CS '86; FLC '95
International Honours: Denmark

Injured for much of 1994-95, although looking as calm and as elegant of old whenever he was called upon by Liverpool, his usefulness is most apparent in the reserves where he can assist the development of younger players. A midfielder with wonderful touch and vision, he started 14

games last season and still posed problems with his super passing skills. Continues to be dangerous at set-pieces.

Liverpool (£575,000 from Ajax on 24/8/84) F/PL 195+23/4 FLC 25+3/9 FAC 24+4/4 Others 16+2/4

Jan Molby   Neal Simpson
(Empics Sports Photo Agency)

MONCUR John Frederick
Born: Stepney, 22 September 1966
Height: 5'7" Weight: 9.10

John, a skilful midfielder, was signed by West Ham during the 1994 close season from Swindon. An excellent passer of the ball and, although not a recognised goal-scorer, he had good efforts that counted in away victories at Aston Villa and Chelsea. Saved his best displays, however, for the big games against "Spurs" and Manchester United, where his running with the ball caused all sorts of problems for the opposition.

Tottenham H (From apprentice on 22/8/84) FL 10+11/1 FLC 1+2
Doncaster Rov (Loaned on 25/9/86) FL 4
Cambridge U (Loaned on 27/3/87) FL 3+1
Portsmouth (Loaned on 22/3/89) FL 7
Brentford (Loaned on 19/10/89) FL 5/1 Others 1
Ipswich T (Loaned on 24/10/91) FL 5+1
Swindon T (£80,000 on 30/3/92) F/PL 53+5/5 FLC 4 FAC 1 Others 4/1
West Ham U (£900,000 on 24/6/94) PL 30/2 FLC 3/1 FAC 2

John Moncur   Matthew Ashton
(Empics Sports Photo Agency)

MONINGTON Mark David
Born: Bilsthorpe, 21 October 1970
Height: 6'1" Weight: 13.0

Signed from Burnley last November, Mark was the first major signing of the new management team at Rotherham and soon became the rock on which the defence was to be built, having a telling influence on other defenders. He reads the game very well and brought a good positional sense to the team, while netting a couple of vital goals in the process.

Burnley (From juniors on 23/3/89) FL 65+19/5 FLC 5 FAC 4+1/1 Others 4+2
Rotherham U (Signed on 28/11/94) FL 25/2

MONKOU Kenneth John
Born: Surinam, 29 November 1964
Height: 6'0" Weight: 12.9
Club Honours: FMC '90
International Honours: Holland U21

If Matt Le Tissier is the spirit of Southampton, then Ken Monkou is the heart. At the centre of the defence, he used his great experience to help a basically young side through a difficult season in 1994-95. Strong in the air and in the tackle, his clearances are not always elegant, but invariably effective, and if he finds his way into too many referees' notebooks, this is usually the result of mistimed, rather than vindictive tackles.

Chelsea (£100,000 from Feyenoord on 2/3/89) FL 92+2/2 FLC 12 FAC 3 Others 10
Southampton (£750,000 on 21/8/92) PL 99/6 FLC 6 FAC 7/1

Ken Monkou   Tony Marshall
(Empics Sports Photo Agency)

MOODY Paul
Born: Portsmouth, 13 June 1967
Height: 6'3" Weight: 12.6

1994-95 was Paul's first full season at Oxford and he started the campaign in great form, scoring 19 times by mid-November.

However, a series of niggling injuries and family matters set him back, but he returned to form in March. Scored a series of spectacular goals, both with head and boot, and, despite missing three penalties, was still top-scorer by a long way.

Southampton (£50,000 from Waterlooville on 15/7/91) F/PL 7+5 FLC 1 FAC 0+1
Reading (Loaned on 9/12/92) FL 5/1 Others 1
Oxford U (£60,000 on 19/2/94) FL 49+7/29 FLC 4/1 FAC 1 Others 1/2

Paul Moody   Barrington Coombs
(Empics Sports Photo Agency)

MOONEY Thomas (Tommy) John
Born: Middlesbrough, 11 August 1971
Height: 5'11" Weight: 12.6

Buccaneering left-sided forward who generally proved a handful for defenders, he joined Watford from Southend prior to last season, having been on loan earlier. Became a great favourite with the home crowd and was unfortunate to be out of action for several months with knee injuries.

Aston Villa (From trainee on 23/11/89)
Scarborough (Free on 1/8/90) FL 96+11/30 FLC 11+2/8 FAC 3 Others 6/2
Southend U (£100,000 on 12/7/93) FL 9+5/5 FLC 1+1 Others 2+3
Watford (Signed on 17/3/94) FL 39/5 FLC 4/1 FAC 1+1

MOORE Alan
Born: Dublin, 25 November 1974
Height: 5'10" Weight: 10.7
Club Honours: Div 1 '95
International Honours: Ei: U21-3; Yth

Another highly rated young Middlesbrough prospect, Alan, who scored two goals on his debut against Notts County in the opening game of 1993-94, is a quick witted winger, possessing the ability to run at defences. He is also armed with the ability to strike and score goals from any angle or opportunity. Won a First Division Championship medal in 1994-95, a season that saw his good play rewarded by the Republic of Ireland at U21 level.

Middlesbrough (From trainee on 5/12/91) F/PL 77+4/14 FLC 6/1 FAC 2+1/2 Others 3+1

Alan Moore   Neal Simpson
(Empics Sports Photo Agency)

MOORE Darren Mark
Born: Birmingham, 22 April 1974
Height: 6'2" Weight: 12.0

Torquay central defender who had a difficult season in 1994-95, he is good enough to come through even stronger than before. His huge physique belies a good touch when on the ball.

Torquay U (From trainee on 18/11/92) FL 102+1/7 FLC 6 FAC 7/2 Others 8/2

MOORE Ian Ronald
Born: Birkenhead, 26 August 1976
Height: 5'11" Weight: 11.0
International Honours: E: Yth

The son of Tranmere coach, Ronnie, Ian will certainly remember the 1994-95 season, having made his first team debut in Italy at Atalanta and his League debut at WBA, as well as becoming number one striker for the England youth side. Scored a hat-trick on his England debut v Denmark and struck the winning goal in Hungary to add to his haul of 26 in Rovers' various other teams.

Tranmere Rov (From trainee on 6/7/94) FL 0+1 Others 0+1

MOORE Kevin Thomas
Born: Grimsby, 29 April 1958
Height: 5'11" Weight: 12.2
Club Honours: Div 3 '80; FLC '82
International Honours: E: Sch

A 1994 close season signing for Fulham, having been released by Southampton, despite his age, Kevin is remarkably fit and retains an obvious enthusiasm for the game. Strong in the air, the trademark of a central defender, he gave some wholehearted performances and also found time to get forward to score some vital goals.

Grimsby T (From juniors on 1/7/76) FL 397+3/27 FLC 41/3 FAC 25/3 Others 2

147

Oldham Ath (£100,000 on 20/2/87) FL 13/1 Others 2
Southampton (£125,000 on 3/8/87) F/PL 144+4/10 FLC 19+1/2 FAC 12 Others 5/1
Bristol Rov (Loaned on 9/1/92) FL 7
Bristol Rov (Loaned on 17/10/92) FL 4/1
Fulham (Free on 28/7/94) FL 31/3 FLC 4/2 FAC 4 Others 2

MOORE Neil
Born: Liverpool, 21 September 1972
Height: 6'1" Weight: 12.3
Young Everton centre-back who uses his height to good effect by getting up well to clear danger. Strong in the tackle, with good distribution, he began to fulfill the potential suggested of him regularly in the reserve set-up last season, which resulted in him making the first team squad and challenging seriously for one of the defensive places. Played five games on loan at Oldham in February and impressed.
Everton (From trainee on 4/6/91) PL 4+1 FLC 0+1
Blackpool (Loaned on 9/9/94) FL 7 Others 1
Oldham Ath (Loaned on 16/2/95) FL 5

MORAH Olisa (Ollie) Henry
Born: Islington, 3 September 1972
Height: 6'2" Weight: 13.7
International Honours: E: Yth; Sch
Signed by Cambridge during the 1994 close season, this quick, strong, right-footed striker unfortunately suffered from shin splints, which restricted his first team appearances in 1994-95, before being loaned out to Torquay.
Tottenham H (From trainee on 17/8/91)
Hereford U (Loaned on 20/11/91) FL 0+2
Swindon T (Free on 13/11/92)
Cambridge U (£50,000 from Sutton U on 8/6/94) FL 8+6/2 FLC 1+1 Others 0+1
Torquay U (Loaned on 23/3/95) FL 2

Jamie Moralee   Paul Marriott
(Empics Sports Photo Agency)

MORALEE Jamie David
Born: Wandsworth, 2 December 1971
Height: 5'11" Weight: 11.0

Signed for Watford as an out-and-out striker from Millwall before the start of last season and, although proving a cultured player, Jamie had a disappointing goal return, something he will be looking to remedy in 1995-96.
Crystal Palace (From trainee on 3/7/90) FL 2+4
Millwall (Free on 3/9/92) FL 56+11/19 FLC 3+1/1 FAC 1 Others 3+1
Watford (£450,000 on 13/7/94) FL 23+1/4 FLC 4 FAC 3

MORAN Paul
Born: Enfield, 22 May 1968
Height: 5'10" Weight: 11.12
Once thought to have a great future in the game as a forward, Paul joined Peterborough during the 1994 close season from "Spurs", having been a pro at White Hart Lane for close on nine years. Unfortunately, his appearances with his new club were limited due to injury.
Tottenham H (From apprentice on 15/7/85) F/PL 14+22/2 FLC 1+6 FAC 3+1 Others 0+1
Portsmouth (Loaned on 11/1/89) FL 3
Leicester C (Loaned on 2/11/89) FL 10/1
Newcastle U (Loaned on 14/2/91) FL 1
Southend U (Loaned on 21/3/91) FL 1
Peterborough U (Free on 8/7/94) FL 5+2 FLC 2 FAC 1 Others 1

MORENO Jaime
Born: Bolivia, 19 January 1974
Height: 5'10" Weight: 11.9
Club Honours: Div 1 '95
International Honours: Bolivia
Having represented Bolivia in the 1994 World Cup in the USA, Jamie impressed the Middlesbrough management team enough for them to sign him. A deceptive striker with a great turn of speed, and a good dribbler, he is adapting very well to the differences between the game as it is played here and back home in Bolivia and is maturing brilliantly. His 14 FL appearances in 1994-95 entitled him to a First Division Championship medal.
Middlesbrough (£250,000 from Blooming on 20/9/94) FL 6+8/2 FLC 1 Others 3/1

MORGAN James (Jamie)
Born: Lincoln, 11 September 1975
Height: 5'11" Weight: 11.0
A young Plymouth midfielder, who filled in for Steve Castle in 1994-95, he covers a lot of the pitch but is still very inexperienced. Due to be released at the end of the season.
Plymouth Arg (From trainee on 29/6/94) FL 9+2 FLC 0+1 Others 1

MORGAN Phillip Jonathan
Born: Stoke, 18 December 1974
Height: 6'1" Weight: 13.0
International Honours: E: Yth; Sch
Young Ipswich goalkeeper who is very brave and an excellent shot stopper. Having waited in the wings since turning pro in the 1993 close season, Phillip finally made his debut at Leicester in 1994-95 after a number of occasions spent on the bench, prior to being released during the summer.
Ipswich T (From trainee on 1/7/93) PL 1

MORGAN Simon Charles
Born: Birmingham, 5 September 1966
Height: 5'10" Weight: 11.7

International Honours: E: U21-2
A fierce competitor, and inspirational leader, and the obvious choice as Fulham's captain, Simon is a natural defender who was switched into midfield in 1994-95. In this new role, he was able to push forward and finished as the club's second highest goalscorer. Also ever-present last season.
Leicester C (From apprentice on 15/11/84) FL 147+13/3 FLC 14/1 FAC 4+1 Others 3
Fulham (£100,000 on 12/10/90) FL 182+4/27 FLC 12 FAC 9/1 Others 10/2

MORGAN Stephen (Steve) Alphonso
Born: Oldham, 19 September 1968
Height: 5'11" Weight: 13.0
International Honours: E: Yth
Tall, well built left-back, who also played a handful of games in the centre of the Coventry defence when injuries and suspension took their toll last season, Steve lost his place to David Burrows in March. Unfortunately, he suffered a back injury soon afterwards.
Blackpool (From apprentice on 12/8/86) FL 135+9/10 FLC 13/2 FAC 16/1 Others 10+1
Plymouth Arg (£115,000 on 16/7/90) FL 120+1/6 FLC 7 FAC 6 Others 5
Coventry C (£110,000 on 14/7/93) PL 65+3/2 FLC 5/3 FAC 5

Steve Morgan   Matthew Ashton
(Empics Sports Photo Agency)

MORGAN Trevor James
Born: Forest Gate, 30 September 1956
Height: 6'2" Weight: 13.4
Exeter's assistant manager and a non-contract player, Trevor was used as an emergency forward when suspensions and injuries deemed necessary in 1994-95. A bustling player, he held the ball up well to allow others to join the play and weighed in with two goals. Great for morale in the dressing room.
Bournemouth (£3,000 from Leytonstone/Ilford on 2/9/80) FL 53/13 FLC 2 FAC 2 Others 3
Mansfield T (£10,000 on 2/11/81) FL 12/6 FAC 1
Bournemouth (£10,000 on 9/3/82) FL 88/33 FLC 6/3 FAC 6/1 Others 1/1
Bristol C (£12,000 on 2/3/84) FL 32/8 FLC 4/3 FAC 1
Exeter C (Free on 30/11/84) FL 30/9 FLC 2 Others 2
Bristol Rov (£15,000 on 19/9/85) FL 54+1/24 FLC 2 FAC 6/3 Others 4

Bristol C (£16,000 on 23/1/87) FL 19/8
Bolton W (£30,000 on 25/6/87) FL 65+12/17 FLC 2/2 FAC 4 Others 7/1
Colchester U (Signed on 27/10/89) FL 31+1/12 FAC 2 Others 2 (Free to Happy Valley, Hong Kong in May 1990)
Exeter C (Free on 9/11/90) FL 14+3/3 FAC 1 Others 3 (Free to Hong Kong during 1991 close season)
Birmingham C (Free on 13/8/93) FL 0+1 Others 1 (Free to Hong Kong in December 1993)
Exeter C (Free on 9/9/94) FL 4+5/1 FAC 1+1/1 Others 0+1

MORLEY Trevor William
Born: Nottingham, 20 March 1961
Height: 5'11" Weight: 12.1
Club Honours: Div 4 '87
International Honours: E: SP-6

Experienced West Ham striker who holds the ball up well and is an excellent target man. Failed to gain a regular place in the side in 1994-95, due to early season injuries, plus the emergence of Jeroen Boere. With his contract due to expire at the end of June 1995, it is unsure at this moment in time as to his future at Upton Park.
Northampton T (£20,000 from Nuneaton Borough on 21/6/85) FL 107+39 FLC 10/4 FAC 6/2 Others 7
Manchester C (£175,000 on 22/1/88) FL 69+3/18 FLC 7/3 FAC 1 Others 2
West Ham U (£500,000 on 28/12/89) F/PL 159+19/57 FLC 10+1/5 FAC 14+5/7 Others 5+1/1

MORRIS Andrew (Andy) Dean
Born: Sheffield, 17 November 1967
Height: 6'4" Weight: 15.7

Andy made a steady comeback in 1994-95, after successive knee injuries and, at 6'4", presented an intimidating presence in Chesterfield's attack. Possessing a skilful ground game, with good close control, he is an awkward man to knock off the ball and his mazy dribbles are a delight. A member of the side that won promotion to the Second Division, as he regains fitness and pace, he will become even more of an asset.
Rotherham U (From juniors on 29/7/85) FL 0+7 FLC 0+1
Chesterfield (Signed on 12/1/88) FL 189+29/46 FLC 15/8 FAC 9+1/3 Others 14+4/3
Exeter C (Loaned on 4/3/92) FL 4+3/2

MORRIS Christopher (Chris) Barry
Born: Newquay, 24 December 1963
Height: 5'10" Weight: 11.6
Club Honours: SPD '88; SC '88, '89; Div '95
International Honours: E: Sch. Ei:35

Middlesbrough defender or midfielder, Chris is happiest in the full-back position of either flank. Unique in having represented England at schoolboy level and the Republic of Ireland at full level, he is a determined professional who fights hard to win every ball. Overlapping well and accurate in the pass, his 15 FL appearances in 1994-95 entitled him to a First Division Championship medal.
Sheffield Wed (Signed on 1/10/82) FL 61+13/1 FLC 5+5/1 FAC 7+5
Glasgow Celtic (£125,000 on 10/8/87) SL 157+6/8 SLC 16+1 SC 22/1 Others 9
Middlesbrough (Signed on 14/8/92) F/PL 50+5/1 FLC 6 FAC 4 Others 4/1

MORRIS Mark John
Born: Morden, 26 September 1962
Height: 6'1" Weight: 13.8
Club Honours: Div 4 '83

A centre-back who is strong in the air, Mark likes to push forward at set pieces and scored four goals for Bournemouth last season. As the club captain, he is a player you can rely on and one who always gives 100 per-cent.
Wimbledon (From apprentice on 26/9/80) FL 167+1/9 FLC 11 FAC 11 Others 1+1
Aldershot (Loaned on 5/9/85) FL 14 FAC 1
Watford (£35,000 on 21/7/87) FL 41/1 FLC 5/1 FAC 7
Sheffield U (£175,000 on 11/7/89) FL 53+3/3 FLC 5 FAC 5 Others 2
Bournemouth (£100,000 on 31/7/91) FL 162/7 FLC 11/1 FAC 14/1 Others 7

MORRIS Stephen (Steve)
Born: Liverpool, 13 May 1976
Height: 5'9" Weight: 10.7
Club Honours: WC '95

A short, pacy, enthusiastic, attacking player who shows keen awareness, he was released by Liverpool during the 1994 close season, but to date has had limited opportunities at Wrexham. Good on the ground, in the air, and in front of goal, any raw edges should be ironed out with more experience.
Wrexham (Free from Liverpool juniors on 5/9/94) FL 10+2/2 Others 3+1

MORRISON Andrew (Andy) Charles
Born: Inverness, 30 July 1970
Height: 5'11" Weight: 12.0

Never given many opportunities to shine at Blackburn, he became Blackpool's record signing when switching clubs last December. Although he came as a defender, he was mainly used in midfield where his resolute tackling and commitment were seen to good effect.
Plymouth Arg (From trainee on 6/7/88) FL 105+8/6 FLC 10+1/1 FAC 6 Others 2+1
Blackburn Rov (£500,000 on 5/8/93) PL 1+4 FAC 1
Blackpool (£245,000 on 9/12/94) FL 18

MORRISON David Ellis
Born: Waltham Forest, 30 November 1974
Height: 5'11" Weight: 12.5

An exciting young prospect who came to Peterborough from non-league football, David has not yet fulfilled the potential he showed at the beginning of last season when used as a wide attacking player. In time, however, could turn out to be a very sound investment for the future.
Peterborough U (£30,000 from Chelmsford C on 12/5/94) FL 34+8/8 FLC 1/1 FAC 0+1 Others 2

MORRISSEY John Joseph
Born: Liverpool, 8 March 1965
Height: 5'8" Weight: 11.9
International Honours: E: Yth

Often sacrificed for tactical reasons away from home, Tranmere without Johnny weaving and jinking his way down the right-touchline was like champagne without bubbles - you instinctively knew there was something missing. A naturally gifted winger, who makes more chances for others

than he ever scores himself, John, in his 11th season, is now well on his way to 500 appearances for the club.
Everton (From apprentice on 10/3/83) FL 1 Others 0+1
Wolverhampton W (Free on 2/8/85) FL 5+5/1 FLC 1
Tranmere Rov (£8,000 on 2/10/85) FL 335+27/47 FLC 29+2 FAC 25+1/5 Others 39+3/6

MORROW Stephen (Steve) Joseph
Born: Belfast, 2 July 1970
Height: 6'0" Weight: 11.3
Club Honours: FAYC '88; FLC '93; ECEC '94
International Honours: NI: 17; U21-3; Yth; Sch

Left-footed Arsenal midfielder, cum defender. Played a number of games last season, frequently in a midfield holding role, and scored a rare goal in the Coca Cola Cup against Sheffield Wednesday, the same team and the same competition he had suffered a freak accident against in 1992-93. A left-sided player, Steve normally fills in for Nigel Winterburn, if required, although preferring a place in central defence.
Arsenal (From trainee on 5/5/88) F/PL 31+13/1 FLC 6+2/2 FAC 3+2 Others 1+4
Reading (Loaned on 16/1/91) FL 10
Watford (Loaned on 14/8/91) FL 7+1 Others 1
Reading (Loaned on 30/10/91) FL 3
Barnet (Loaned on 4/3/92) FL 1

MORTIMER Paul Henry
Born: Kensington, 8 May 1968
Height: 5'11" Weight: 11.3
International Honours: E: U21-2

Extremely talented left-sided Charlton midfield player who loves to run at defences and is capable of scoring outstanding individual goals, with two such efforts last season coming against Bristol City and "Wolves". Played several games at left-back, performing well, he is now in his second spell at the club. Unfortunate to sustain a ruptured achilles tendon during the final week of the campaign.
Charlton Ath (Free from Farnborough T on 22/9/87) FL 108+5/17 FLC 4+1 FAC 8 Others 3+1
Aston Villa (£350,000 on 24/7/91) FL 10+2/1 FLC 2
Crystal Palace (£500,000 on 18/10/91) F/PL 18+4/2 FLC 1 FAC 1 Others 3
Brentford (Loaned on 22/1/93) FL 6 Others 2
Charlton Ath (£200,000 on 5/7/94) FL 26/4 FAC 1

MORTON Neil
Born: Congleton, 21 December 1968
Height: 5'9" Weight: 10.7

Live-wire Wigan striker, with good control, Neil's first team appearances slowed appreciably last season, following the appointment of manager, Graham Barrow. Allowed to join non-league Altrincham in November, he played a major part in their shock FA Cup victory over his former club.
Crewe Alex (From trainee on 25/9/87) FL 18+13/1 FLC 0+3 FAC 0+1 Others 0+2
Chester C (£50,000 from Northwich Victoria on 5/10/90) FL 63+32/13 FLC 2+2 FAC 2+4 Others 6+1/2
Wigan Ath (Free on 9/7/93) FL 41+7/5 FLC 5+1/1 FAC 2/1 Others 3

MOSES Adrian Paul
Born: Doncaster, 4 May 1975
Height: 6'1" Weight: 12.5
Adrian, by a quirk of nature, had to make his first team debut for Barnsley in 1994-95 twice. The strong central-defender made his initial start against Middlesbrough, but because of the conditions the match was abandoned at half-time and his full debut officially came a week later in an FA Cup-tie against Aston Villa, with John Fashanu leading the line. His opportunities were limited last season, because of the form of the first choice defenders, but he will have learnt much from his experience.
Barnsley (From juniors on 2/7/93) FL 3+1 FAC 1

MOSS David Albert
Born: Doncaster, 15 November 1968
Height: 6'2" Weight: 13.7
The tall midfielder, or centre-forward, is one of two semi-pros in Chesterfield's regular first team, but is no less a player for that. Good in the air, hard-working, and with a powerful shot, his ability to play well in two positions, perversely, reduced his opportunities in either of them last term.
Doncaster Rov (Signed from Boston U on 10/3/93) FL 18/5 FLC 2 Others 0+1
Chesterfield (Free on 8/10/93) FL 53+5/16 FLC 2/1 FAC 2+1 Others 3

MOSS Neil Graham
Born: New Milton, 10 May 1975
Height: 6'1" Weight: 12.11
Although only 18-years-old, Neil became Bournemouth's first team goalie between the departure of Vince Bartram to Arsenal and the signing of Ian Andrews last season. Currently the reserve 'keeper at the club, he still has a promising future ahead of him.
Bournemouth (From trainee on 29/1/93) FL 14+1 FLC 1 FAC 0+1

MOULDEN Paul Anthony
Born: Farnworth, 6 September 1967
Height: 5'7" Weight: 10.9
Club Honours: FAYC '86; Div 2 '91
International Honours: E: Yth; Sch
A striker who twists and turns well around the box, Paul was signed by Huddersfield from Birmingham just before last March's transfer deadline, initially as cover for the injured Ronnie Jepson. However, having been limited to just two substitute appearances, one of them against his old club, he has now been released.
Manchester C (From apprentice on 7/9/84) FL 48+16/18 FLC 5+1/4 FAC 2+3/1 Others 3+1/3
Bournemouth (£160,000 on 2/8/89) FL 32/13 FLC 4 FAC 0+1 Others 1
Oldham Ath (£225,000 on 23/3/90) F/PL 17+21/4 FLC 2+1/1
Brighton & Hove A (Loaned on 14/8/92) FL 11/5
Birmingham C (£150,000 on 12/3/93) FL 18+2/5 FLC 1+1 Others 1
Huddersfield T (Free on 23/3/95) FL 0+2

MOUNTFIELD Derek Neal
Born: Liverpool, 22 November 1962
Height: 6'0" Weight: 13.6
Club Honours: FAC '84; CS '84, '85; Div 1 '85, '87, Div 3 '95; ECWC '85
International Honours: E: B-1; U21-1
A player who has already scaled the heights of the game, notably with Everton, a Third Division Championship medal and another Wembley appearance added a further chapter to his career. His experience and organisational ability were key factors in what proved to be the meanest defence in the Carlisle's history, especially away from home. Recognised with the award of "Away Player of the Year" by the supporters, he also scored the vital away goal in the AWS Northern Final at Rochdale.
Tranmere Rov (From apprentice on 4/11/80) FL 26/1 FLC 2 FAC I
Everton (£30,000 on 2/6/82) FL 100+6/19 FLC 16/3 FAC 17/2 Others 14+1/1
Aston Villa (£450,000 on 6/6/88) FL 88+2/9 FLC 13/2 FAC 6/1 Others 11/5
Wolverhampton W (£150,000 on 7/11/91) FL 79+4/4 FLC 4/1 FAC 2 Others 2
Carlisle U (Free on 3/8/94) FL 30+1/3 FLC 3+1 FAC 4/1 Others 6/1

Derek Mountfield   Matthew Ashton
(Empics Sports Photo Agency)

MOYES David William
Born: Blythswood, 25 April 1963
Height: 6'1" Weight: 11.5
Club Honours: SPL '82; AMC '86
Preston's captain and coach, David is a quality player, whose influence extends far beyond his central defensive role. A strong tackler and header, especially in opposing boxes at set-pieces, he is as important to Preston on the training pitch as on match-days where he is very consistent indeed.
Glasgow Celtic (From juniors in 1980) SL 19+5 SLC 7+1 Others 2+1
Cambridge U (Free on 28/10/83) FL 79/1 FLC 3 FAC I Others 3
Bristol C (£10,000 on 10/10/85) FL 83/3 FLC 6 FAC 5 Others 5
Shrewsbury T (£30,000 on 30/10/87) FL 91+5/11 FLC 4 FAC 3/1 Others 5
Dunfermline Ath (Signed on 1/8/90) SL 105/13 SLC 7/1 SC 5
Hamilton Academical (Signed in August 1993) SL 5
Preston NE (Free on 20/9/93) FL 67/8 FLC 2/1 FAC 7/1 Others 10/1

MUDD Paul Andrew
Born: Hull, 13 November 1970
Height: 5'9" Weight: 11.4
International Honours: E: Sch
Consistently sound displays during 1994-95 enhanced the left-back's popularity with the Scunthorpe fans, who appreciated him as a good tackler who worked the flank well, prior to him being surprisingly released during the summer.
Hull C (From trainee on 1/7/89) FL 1
Scarborough (£5,000 on 25/7/90) FL 95+3/2 FLC 10 FAC 3 Others 6
Scunthorpe U (Free on 26/7/93) FL 66+2/4 FLC 4 FAC 8 Others 5

MUGGLETON Carl David
Born: Leicester, 13 September 1968
Height: 6'1" Weight: 12.7
International Honours: E: U21-1
Signed after Lou Macari's departure from Celtic saw him made available, he soon settled into the Stoke side and reaffirmed himself as an excellent shot-stopper, highlighted by his record of saving penalties. His save against David Preece of Luton last October meant that only one penalty had been scored against him in seven previous attempts. A stomach muscle injury forced him to miss much of the second half of the season.
Leicester C (From apprentice on 17/9/86) FL 46 FAC 3 Others 5
Chesterfield (Loaned on 10/9/87) FL 17 Others 2
Blackpool (Loaned on 1/2/88) FL 2
Hartlepool U (Loaned on 28/10/88) FL 8 Others 2
Stockport Co (Loaned on 1/3/90) FL 4
Stoke C (Loaned on 13/8/93) FL 6 FLC 1 Others 2
Glasgow Celtic (£150,000 on 11/1/94) SL 12 SC 1
Stoke C (£150,000 on 21/7/94) FL 24 FLC 3 Others 4

MUIR Ian James
Born: Coventry, 5 May 1963
Height: 5'8" Weight: 11.0
Club Honours: AMC '90
International Honours: E: Yth; Sch
Tranmere's leading all-time scorer - with 180 goals - again had to play second fiddle to John Aldridge for most of last season, but really came into his own when "Aldo" got injured. Though he suffered with a niggling groin strain for most of the campaign, Ian responded to the challenge with ten FL and FA Cup goals before injury struck again. A skilful penalty box poacher, he is now in his testimonial season with the club.
Queens Park R (From apprentice on 3/9/80) FL 2/2
Burnley (Loaned on 8/10/82) FL 1+1/1
Birmingham C (Free on 27/8/83) FL 1 FLC 1
Brighton & Hove A (Free on 15/2/84) FL 3+1
Swindon T (Loaned on 28/1/85) FL 2 Others 1
Tranmere Rov (Free on 26/7/85) FL 283+31/141 FLC 22+3/6 FAC 17+1/14 Others 29+7/19

MULLIGAN James (Jimmy)
Born: Dublin, 22 April 1974
Height: 5'5" Weight: 10.0
Bury right-winger whose season was wrecked in 1994-95 through bad luck and injury. Having been sidelined himself, on recovering, and waiting patiently for an opportunity to play, twice he found himself injured yet again within 30 minutes of

coming onto the pitch. Must hope for a change in fortune in 1995-96.
Stoke C (From trainee on 7/7/92)
Bury (Loaned on 5/11/93) FL 2+1/1 Others 1
Bury (£15,000 on 5/7/94) FL 9+6/2 FLC 2/1 FAC 0+2 Others 1+1

MULLIN John
Born: Bury, 11 August 1975
Height: 6'0" Weight: 11.5
Overlooked for half of last season, while Burnley sought the magic formula up-front, the star of the 1993-94 successful youth side almost became an instant hero, but narrowly failed to score what could have been a late FA Cup winner against Liverpool. John was perhaps unfortunate that his only extended first team run coincided with the team's worst bout of form.
Burnley (From trainee on 18/8/92) FL 7+11/2 FAC 2

MUNDAY Stuart Clifford
Born: Newham, 28 September 1972
Height: 5'11" Weight: 11.0
First choice right-back for Brighton at the start of last season, he was unfortunate to be out for three weeks with an ankle injury which gave Peter Smith his chance to impress. Stuart had a memorable match at Leicester when he scored a great goal from 30 yards to put Albion well on the way to victory. Can also play in midfield and has a good long throw-in.
Brighton & Hove A (From trainee on 6/7/90) FL 72+14/4 FLC 6+1/1 FAC 2+1 Others 6+1

MUNDEE Denny William John
Born: Swindon, 10 October 1968
Height: 5'10" Weight: 11.0
Versatile right-footed player who gives Brentford 100 per-cent commitment. Started last season as a regular substitute, but broke into the side in a midfield role, first as deputy for the injured Paul Smith and then Lee Harvey. Known for his stinging shot and "shuffle", he scored some vital goals, including a long-distance screamer against Crewe.
Swindon T (Free from Queens Park R juniors on 21/8/86)
Bournemouth (Free on 29/3/88) FL 76+24/6 FLC 3+2 FAC 9+2/4 Others 5+1/2
Torquay U (Loaned on 7/9/89) FL 9
Brentford (Free on 12/8/93) FL 59+19/16 FLC 0+3 FAC 3 Others 5+3/2

MUNGALL Steven (Steve) Henry
Born: Bellshill, 22 May 1958
Height: 5'8" Weight: 11.5
Club Honours: AMC '90
Even though he is now 37-years-old, few players can match Steve for sheer enthusiasm and commitment to the cause of Tranmere. The club's longest serving player, he still managed 36 outings in the 1994-95 season, and only Ray Mathias has played more games for Rovers. Though usually utilised at full-back, he even had a few games in midfield and scored at Swindon in a 2-2 draw. A great servant to the club, he also coaches the youth team.
Motherwell (Signed from Chapelhall in 1976) SL 14+6 SLC 11+2 SC 14+1

Tranmere Rov (Free on 3/7/79) FL 475+30/14 FLC 32+3/2 FAC 30+1 Others 43+2/1

MUNRO Stuart
Born: Falkirk, 15 September 1962
Height: 5'8" Weight: 10.5
Club Honours: SPD '87, '89, '90, '91; SLC '87, '88, '89, '91
Has proved to be an excellent signing for Bristol City, his tenacious tackling and "never-say-die" spirit at left-back, or in central defence, having added much steel to the rearguard. Earlier last season, it appeared he might be losing favour, but with Joe Jordan's return as manager, he missed just one match after being restored to the side at Sunderland in December.
St Mirren (From Bo'ness U in 1980) SL 1
Alloa (Signed during 1982 close season) SL 58+2/6 SLC 14/1 SC 2/1
Glasgow R (Signed in February 1984) SL 173+6/3 SLC 21+1 SC 13+2 Others 19+1
Blackburn Rov (£350,000 on 12/8/91) FL 1
Bristol C (Free on 4/2/93) FL 88+3 FLC 3 FAC 8 Others 1/1

MURPHY Daniel (Danny) Benjamin
Born: Chester, 18 March 1977
Height: 5'9" Weight: 10.8
International Honours: E: Yth; Sch
The youngest player in the Crewe side last season, and capped at Schoolboy and U18 level for England, Danny is a midfield player. Captained the 1994-95 Youth side and, at the same time, made his own contribution to the first team. A player of great potential.
Crewe Alex (From trainee on 21/3/94) FL 25+22/7 FLC 1 Others 6+2/1

MURPHY James (Jamie) Anthony
Born: Manchester, 25 February 1973
Height: 6'1" Weight: 13.10
Used mainly as a utility player, who played the odd game both in defence and attack for Blackpool last season, Jamie did not figure as much as he would have wished following a summer operation.
Blackpool (From juniors on 23/8/90) FL 48+7/1 FLC 4/1 FAC 3 Others 2+3

MURPHY John James
Born: Whiston, 18 October 1976
Height: 6'1" Weight: 14.0
Chester youngster who came through the club's youth policy to make his FL debut last season, James is a tall central striker with a great deal of promise. Still a trainee.
Chester C (Trainee) FL 0+5 FAC 0+1 Others 1+1

MURPHY Matthew Simon
Born: Northampton, 20 August 1971
Height: 5'10" Weight: 11.5
Although making his debut for Oxford two seasons ago, Matt's career was kick-started in November 1994 at Brentford. Since then he has chipped in with a good number of goals, advancing from midfield, just behind the strikers. Was earlier given a free transfer, but won his way back into the side with a series of good displays.
Oxford U (£20,000 from Corby T on 12/2/93) FL 19+5/7 Others 1+2/1

MURPHY Michael John
Born: Slough, 5 May 1977
Height: 5'10" Weight: 10.6
Made his Reading first-team debut against Bristol City last October as a substitute for Uwe Hartenberger, just nine days after leaving school in Slough and signing pro forms. Having joined the club's Centre of Excellence as a 12-year-old, Michael progressed through the youth scheme, showing much promise in midfield or as front player. Exceptionally hard-working, he has great awareness in and around the penalty area.
Reading (From juniors on 8/10/94) FL 0+1

MURPHY Shaun Peter
Born: Sydney, Australia, 5 November 1970
Height: 6'1" Weight: 12.0
Club Honours: AIC '95
Notts County central defender and the supporters' "Player of the Year" for 1994-95, Shaun is a no-nonsense tackler, who is good in the air and on the ground, and who clears his lines well. Performed consistently well after taking over the number five shirt from Dean Yates last December, well enough to allow the latter to move to Derby. Proud to have an Irish father and an Indian mother.
Notts Co (Signed from Perth Italia on 4/9/92) FL 45+9/2 FLC 2+2 FAC 3 Others 6+1/1

MURRAY Edwin (Eddie) John
Born: Ilford, 31 August 1973
Height: 5'11" Weight: 12.0
Left-sided Swindon defender who performed exceptionally well on stepping up from the Combination side, following Paul Bodin's enforced absence last season. Made just a handful of appearances and featured in both Coca Cola Cup semi-final legs against Bolton.
Swindon T (From trainee on 9/7/91) FL 4+3 FLC 2 FAC 1+1

MURRAY Paul
Born: Carlisle, 31 August 1976
Height: 5'8" Weight: 10.5
International Honours: E: Yth
Defender/midfielder. A local born player of great potential, who made his England U18 debut during last season, international duties and injuries restricted his appearances for Carlisle during the campaign. That apart, he is a highly promising prospect.
Carlisle U (From trainee on 14/6/94) FL 10+3 Others 2+1

MURRAY Robert (Rob) James
Born: Hammersmith, 21 October 1974
Height: 5'11" Weight: 11.7
Initially a striker, but converted to a defender by Bournemouth last Christmas, Rob is comfortable as a full-back, although most effective as a centre-back. Showing fine distribution and looking good when coming forward with the ball, he has also developed the skills of tackling and heading that are important to a defender.
Bournemouth (From trainee on 11/1/93) FL 38+38/8 FLC 0+5 FAC 0+2 Others 0+4/2

MURRAY Shaun
Born: Newcastle, 7 December 1970
Height: 5'8" Weight: 11.2
International Honours: E: Yth
Signed from Scarborough at the beginning of 1994-95, Shaun turned out for Bradford on the left-side of midfield, although occasionally switching to the right. Made a great impression at Valley Parade, becoming one of the fans' favourite players.
Tottenham H (From trainee on 10/12/87)
Portsmouth (£100,000 on 12/6/89) FL 21+13/1 FLC 2+1/1 FAC 1+3 Others 2+2
Scarborough (Signed on 1/11/93) FL 29/5 FAC 2 Others 2
Bradford C (£200,000 on 11/8/94) FL 38+3/5 FLC 3/1 FAC 2 Others 2/1

MURTY Graeme Stuart
Born: Middlesbrough, 13 November 1974
Height: 5'10" Weight: 11.2
Another of York's promising youngsters, Graeme greatly impressed when having an extended run in the first team in the second half of last season. A skilful, pacy player, he proved capable of operating on the right or left-side of midfield.
York C (From trainee on 23/3/93) FL 19+3/2 Others 1

Paul Musselwhite   Neal Simpson
(Empics Sports Photo Agency)

MUSSELWHITE Paul Stephen
Born: Portsmouth, 22 December 1968
Height: 6'2" Weight: 12.9
Club Honours: AMC '93
Tall, commanding goalkeeper who took his number of consecutive appearances for Port Vale to 161 in helping the club establish itself in the First Division. An excellent shot-stopper, who made some important saves, his personal highlights included keeping two clean sheets against the club that released him as a youngster, Portsmouth, and in the local derby victory at Stoke.

Portsmouth (From apprentice on 1/12/86)
Scunthorpe U (Free on 21/3/88) FL 132 FLC 11 FAC 7 Others 13
Port Vale (£20,000 on 30/7/92) FL 131 FLC 6 FAC 11 Others 13

MUSTOE Robin (Robbie)
Born: Witney, 28 August 1968
Height: 5'11" Weight: 11.12
Club Honours: Div 1 '95
Signed from Oxford in July 1990, Robbie is a tenacious midfielder who never delivers less than 100 per-cent effort for Middlesbrough. A seasoned professional, he is always to be found in the "thick" of the action, and played a major role in "Boro's" success last season, in winning a First Division Championship medal.
Oxford U (From juniors on 2/7/86) FL 78+13/10 FLC 2 FAC 2 Others 3
Middlesbrough (£375,000 on 5/7/90) F/PL 150+9/12 FLC 21+1/6 FAC 10 Others 12+1/1

Andy Mutch   Paul Marriott
(Empics Sports Photo Agency)

MUTCH Andrew (Andy) Todd
Born: Liverpool, 28 December 1963
Height: 5'10" Weight: 11.3
Club Honours: Div 4 '88, Div 3 '89; AMC '88
International Honours: E: B-3; U21-1
Steve Bull's former strike partner at Molineux had a frustrating campaign at Swindon in 1994-95, with two-thirds of his appearances coming off the substitutes' bench. Andy was kept out of the picture, firstly by Keith Scott, then by the arrival of Peter Thorne, and finally by a niggling groin injury. In between, there were glimpses of the old scoring flair, including two goals in Town's Coca Cola Cup quarter-final win over Millwall.
Wolverhampton W (Signed from Southport on 25/2/86) FL 277+12/97 FLC 14/4 FAC 11+1/1 Others 23/4
Swindon T (£250,000 on 16/8/93) F/PL 34+16/6 FLC 6+1/3 FAC 4/1 Others 3/2

MUTCHELL Robert David
Born: Solihull, 2 January 1974
Height: 5'10" Weight: 11.2

Another left-sided Barnet full-back, he was used sparingly by the manager in 1994-95, but always performed well when called on. Released before the end of the season.
Oxford U (From trainee on 3/7/92)
Barnet (Free on 17/12/93) FL 21+1 FAC 2+1

MYALL Stuart Thomas
Born: Eastbourne, 12 November 1974
Height: 5'10" Weight: 12.12
It seemed his career at Brighton was over when transfer listed last September, but he worked hard and beat a weight problem. His performances in the reserves earned a recall to the first team and removal from the transfer list. Some fine displays in midfield followed, showing some neat football and good passing ability. Another long-throw specialist.
Brighton & Hove A (From trainee on 9/7/93) FL 42+5/2 FLC 2 Others 2

MYERS Andrew (Andy) John
Born: Hounslow, 3 November 1973
Height: 5'8" Weight: 9.10
International Honours: E: U21-3; Yth
Called up by Chelsea during their ongoing injury crisis last season, Andy proved to be a hard-tackling and enthusiastic player. His favourite position would have to be at left-back, or along the left-side of midfield, but he was happy to play anywhere in the best interests of the club. Having won youth caps earlier in his career, he played in all three matches for England during the Toulon U21 tournament in June and would hope to build on those performances in 1995-96.
Chelsea (From trainee on 25/7/91) F/PL 27+6/1 FLC 1+1 FAC 6 Others 3

NARBETT Jonathan (Jon) Velelzer
Born: Birmingham, 21 November 1968
Height: 5'11" Weight: 12.3
The former Hereford midfielder returned from Kalmar of Sweden last November, and was turning out for Merthyr Tydfil at the time of joining Chesterfield a month later. Although an experienced player, Jon made just two starts as cover.
Shrewsbury T (From apprentice on 19/9/86) FL 20+6/3 FLC 4 FAC 1
Hereford U (£30,000 on 6/10/88) FL 148+1/31 FLC 8/1 FAC 10/2 Others 14/3
Oxford U (£65,000 on 7/7/92) FL 13+2 FLC 1 FAC 2 Others 2+1 (Free to Kalmar FF on 30/3/94)
Chesterfield (Free from Merthyr Tydfil on 23/12/94) FL 2+1

NAYLOR Anthony (Tony) Joseph
Born: Manchester, 29 March 1967
Height: 5'5" Weight: 9.0
Small, nippy Port Vale striker who caused endless problems for big opposing defenders with his pace in 1994-95, in what was his first season at that level. Marked his debut with a goal at Bristol Rovers in the Coca Cola Cup and went on to score at around once every three games to become the main strike partner for Martin Foyle.
Crewe Alex (£20,000 from Droylsden on 22/3/90) FL 104+18/45 FLC 7+2/5 FAC 9/7 Others 12/9
Port Vale (£150,000 on 18/7/94) FL 29+4/9 FLC 3/1

NAYLOR Dominic John

Born: Watford, 12 August 1970
Height: 5'10" Weight: 11.7
Club Honours: FAYC '89

A combative left-back, with a completely wholehearted approach to tackling, he played in nearly all Plymouth's games last season. Pushing forward effectively, with plenty of crosses, Dominic has become a force from dead-ball situations with his left-foot and scored a great goal against Exeter.

Watford (From trainee on 20/9/88)
Halifax T (Loaned on 6/12/89) FL 5+1/1 Others 1+1 (Free to Hong Kong in October 1990)
Barnet (Free on 12/8/91) FL 50+1 FLC 2 FAC 5/1 Others 4
Plymouth Arg (Free on 16/7/93) FL 84+1 FLC 2 FAC 8 Others 4+1/1

NAYLOR Glenn

Born: Howden, 11 August 1972
Height: 5'10" Weight: 11.10

Although making his York debut back in 1990-91, Glenn again failed to fully establish himself last season. Still a skilful forward, however, he came second in the goalscoring charts behind Paul Barnes with 11.

York C (From trainee on 5/3/90) FL 58+27/23 FLC 2+2 FAC 4+1/2 Others 3+4

NAYLOR Stuart William

Born: Wetherby, 6 December 1962
Height: 6'4" Weight: 12.10
International Honours: E: B-3; Yth

Tall, strong, commanding WBA goalkeeper and a very good shot-stopper, Stuart produced the best form of his career during 1994-95 after overcoming a minor injury problem (back trouble). Awarded a Testimonial at Albion this coming season.

Lincoln C (Free from Yorkshire Amateurs on 19/6/80) FL 49 FLC 4 FAC 2 Others 6
Peterborough U (Loaned on 23/2/83) FL 8
Crewe Alex (Loaned on 6/10/83) FL 55 FLC 2 FAC 2 Others 3
West Bromwich A (£100,000 on 18/2/86) FL 327+1 FLC 18 FAC 12 Others 15

NDAH George Ehialimolisa

Born: Dulwich, 23 December 1974
Height: 6'1" Weight: 10.0

Tall, Skilful Crystal Palace winger. Although George had his best season to date in 1994-95, making ten first team starts, with John Salako now fully recovered, he was unable to hold down a regular place. That aside, he scored his first ever League goal in the home fixture against Leicester and followed it up with the last minute winner that knocked Watford out of the FA Cup. Is sure to get a regular spot soon.

Crystal Palace (From trainee on 10/8/92) F/PL 9+17/1 FLC 6+3/1 FAC 1+1/1 Others 1+1

NDLOVU Peter

Born: Buluwayo, Zimbabwe, 25 February 1973
Height: 5'8" Weight: 10.2
International Honours: Zimbabwe

The most exciting player on Coventry's books, Peter had an up and down season in 1994-95, but always generated a buzz when he got the ball. A knee injury meant he didn't start a League game until the last

Saturday in October, when he set up the late winner against Manchester City. Injured again at Hillsborough, he returned for the cup replay at WBA and his winning goal won the "Goal of the Month" award. After playing a few games up-front under Phil Neal, Big Ron played him on the left-side and got results. A goal in each of his first two games, against West Ham and Leicester was followed by a hat-trick at Anfield, the first by a visiting player there for 33 years. His third goal was a classic, bemusing Ruddock before thundering a right-foot shot low into the corner. Another classic clinched victory at home to Wednesday, when he raced half the length of the pitch before sending Chris Woods the wrong way. Peter is definitely a prize asset and the fans would revolt if he was sold.

Coventry C (£10,000 from Highlanders on 16/8/91) F/PL 104+21/31 FLC 6/1 FAC 5/2 Others 0+1

NEILL Warren Anthony

Born: Acton, 21 November 1962
Height: 5'10" Weight: 12.5
Club Honours: Div 2 '83
International Honours: E: Sch

A right-back who likes to attack where possible Having played in the opening eight games of last season for Portsmouth, he missed the next two months due to an injured back, before re-appearing in the 4-1 home defeat by Sunderland and announced his retirement soon after.

Queens Park R (From apprentice on 3/9/80) FL 177+4/3 FLC 18+1/1 FAC 11+1/2 Others 3/1
Portsmouth (£110,000 on 28/7/88) FL 216+2/2 FLC 20/1 FAC 14 Others 8

NEILSON Alan Bruce

Born: Wegburg, Germany, 26 September 1972
Height: 5'11" Weight: 12.4
International Honours: W: 4; B-1; U21-7

A reliable central defender who reads the game well and is composed on the ball. Although he played for Wales last season, he had very few opportunities at club level, starting only six games for Newcastle. Highlight of the season was at Maine Road where he headed a right-wing cross back into the area for Mike Jeffrey to volley home in the Coca Cola Cup 1-1 draw. Stop Press: Signed by Sunderland for a fee of £300,000 during the summer.

Newcastle U (From trainee on 11/2/91) F/PL 35+7/1 FLC 4 Others 4

NELSON Garry Paul

Born: Braintree, 16 January 1961
Height: 5'10" Weight: 11.10
Club Honours: Div 4 '81

Hard working Charlton striker who can also play on left side of midfield, his workrate belies his age. Started 1994-95 well, scoring eight goals before the end of November. His best performance was in the Coca Cola Cup-tie at Swindon where he struck twice, as he did three days later at Notts County. Unfortunately, Garry's season was ended at Bristol City in early March, when he sustained ankle and knee ligament damage after a bad tackle late in the game.

Southend U (From juniors on 9/7/79) FL 106+23/17 FLC 3+1/1 FAC 6+2
Swindon T (£10,000 on 17/8/83) FL 78+1/7 FLC 4/1 FAC 5 Others 5/1
Plymouth Arg (£15,000 on 12/7/85) FL 71+3/20 FLC 4 FAC 7/2 Others 3
Brighton & Hove A (£80,000 on 17/7/87) FL 132+12/46 FLC 7 FAC 7/6 Others 8/6
Notts Co (Loaned on 8/11/90) FL 0+2
Charlton Ath (£50,000 on 16/8/91) FL 135+20/34 FLC 12+1/2 FAC 7+1/1 Others 6

NETHERCOTT Stuart David

Born: Ilford, 21 March 1973
Height: 5'9" Weight: 12.4
International Honours: E: U21-8

A competitive central defender, Stuart's early appearances last season suited the rather cavalier approach Tottenham adopted in their early games, his ability to deliver long balls from the back four ensuring the club's ability to attack. But, as problems began in keeping goals out, he was replaced as first choice by Gary Mabbutt. His great strength in the air was amply demonstrated by the tremendous goal that rounded off Tottenham's 3-0 victory over Altrincham in the FA Cup.

Tottenham H (From trainee on 17/8/91) PL 20+12 FAC 3+2/1
Maidstone U (Loaned on 5/9/91) FL 13/1 Others 1
Barnet (Loaned on 13/2/92) FL 3

NEVILLE Gary Alexander

Born: Bury, 18 February 1975
Height: 5'10" Weight: 11.7
Club Honours: FAYC '92
International Honours: E: 2; U21-3; Yth (UEFAC '93)

Excellent in the tackle and commanding in the air, Gary is a naturally gifted Manchester United defender, who can play in central defence, or at right-back. Also possesses a long-throw capability. Showed great composure as he helped to solve Alex Ferguson's problem right-back spot, the main highlight of his season coming in the FA Cup when he provided the throw-in that enabled Gary Pallister to keep United in the competition against Crystal Palace. Looks certain to have a bright future, having recently made his England debut against Japan in the Umbro Cup.

Manchester U (From trainee on 29/1/93) PL 17+2 FLC 2+1 FAC 4 Others 1+3

NEVILLE Philip John

Born: Bury, 21 January 1977
Height: 5'11" Weight: 12.0
Club Honours: FAYC '95
International Honours: E: Yth

Good in the air and excellent in the tackle, Phil was the other member of the Neville clan to make a big impression for Manchester United in 1994-95. Made his first team debut against Manchester City at Maine Road, giving a polished performance at left-back, and looks to have a bright future.

Manchester U (Trainee) PL 1+1 FAC 1

NEVIN Patrick (Pat) Kevin Francis Michael

Born: Glasgow, 6 September 1963
Height: 5'6" Weight: 11.9
Club Honours: S Div 2 '82, Div 2 '84; FMC '86

International Honours: S: 25; B-3; U21-5; Yth
The current PFA Chairman, Pat continues to maintain his reputation as one of the most dangerous forwards in the First Division, the type of player opposing defenders hate playing against with his ability to run with the ball seemingly tied to his nimble feet. Although his five goal tally last season disappointed him, his overall contribution to Tranmere's (and indeed Scotland's) attacking ideas, particularly at Prenton Park, more than compensated. Off the field he has been a fine ambassador both for the club and the PFA in what has been a difficult season for the game.

Clyde (Signed from Gartcosh in 1981) SL 60+13/17 SLC 5+3 SC 10/3
Chelsea (£95,000 on 14/7/83) FL 190+3/36 FLC 25+1/5 FAC 8+1/1 Others 13/4
Everton (£925,000 on 13/7/88) FL 81+28/16 FLC 10+1/2 FLC 12+6/2 Others 9+3/1
Tranmere Rov (Loaned on 4/3/92) FL 8 Others 9+3/1
Tranmere Rov (£300,000 on 18/8/92) FL 132/25 FLC 13/5 FAC 6/2 Others 14/2

NEWELL Michael (Mike) Colin
Born: Liverpool, 27 January 1965
Height: 6'0" Weight: 11.0
Club Honours: AMC '85; PL '95
International Honours: E: B-2; U21-4

Blackburn striker with a high workrate, a physical presence, and a capacity to pull opposing defences wide. It was a frustrating year for Mike, who started 1994-95 still recovering from injuries sustained at the end of 1993-94. When he did come back, however, the SAS partnership was well established and, although Kenny Dalglish kept him in the picture as a substitute, he found that the team's style had changed somewhat. Still very much a squad member, two starts and ten substitutions were enough to reward him with a Championship medal, as the club won the title for the first time since 1913-14.

Crewe Alex (Free from Liverpool juniors on 28/9/83) FL 3
Wigan Ath (Free on 31/10/83) FL 64+8/25 FLC 6/1 FAC 8/6 Others 5+1/3
Luton T (£100,000 on 9/1/86) FL 62+1/18 FAC 5/1
Leicester C (£350,000 on 16/9/87) FL 81/21 FLC 9/5 FAC 2 Others 4
Everton (£1,100,000 on 27/7/89) FL 48+20/15 FLC 7+3/4 FAC 6+4 Others 6/2
Blackburn Rov (£1,100,000 on 15/11/91) F/PL 87+13/25 FLC 10+2/7 FAC 7+2/6 Others 3/2

NEWELL Paul Clayton
Born: Woolwich, 23 February 1969
Height: 6'1" Weight: 12.8

Started last season as Barnet's second choice goalkeeper, having earlier been freed by Colchester, but waited for his chance and ended the year as the club's number one. Is a good shot-stopper who will continue to improve with more starts under his belt.

Southend U (From trainee on 17/6/87) FL 15 FAC 2 Others 1
Leyton Orient (£5,000 on 6/8/90) FL 61 FLC 3 FAC 3 Others 4
Colchester U (Loaned on 12/8/92) FL 14 FLC 2
Barnet (Free on 26/7/94) FL 15 Others 1

NEWHOUSE Aidan Robert
Born: Wallasey, 23 May 1972
Height: 6'1" Weight: 13.5
International Honours: E: Yth

Wimbledon striker with two good feet and equal ability on the ball, Aidan is at his best when getting into wide positions. Has never really fitted in with the "Dons" and, unable to get an opportunity with them last season, he partnered Gerry Creaney in a spell on loan at Portsmouth, contributing well in six games.

Chester C (From trainee on 1/7/89) FL 29+15/6 FLC 5+1 FAC 0+2 Others 2+3/1
Wimbledon (£100,000 on 22/2/90) F/PL 7+16/2 FLC 1+1 FAC 2 Others 0+1
Port Vale (Loaned on 21/1/94) FL 0+2 FAC 0+1
Portsmouth (Loaned on 2/12/94) FL 6/1

NEWLAND Raymond (Ray) James
Born: Liverpool, 19 July 1971
Height: 6'3" Weight: 13.10

Goalkeeper. Having made his League debut for Chester against Huddersfield in August 1994, after signing from Plymouth during the summer, Ray was mainly employed to understudy Dave Felgate.

Plymouth Arg (Free from St Helens on 3/7/92) FL 25+1 FLC 1 FAC 2
Chester C (Free on 18/7/94) FL 9+1 Others 1

NEWMAN Richard (Ricki) Adrian
Born: Guildford, 5 August 1970
Height: 5'9" Weight: 10.7

Ricki, one of Alan Smith's first youngsters from his youth team coaching days, became a Crystal Palace first team regular last season, scoring spectacularly against Coventry and Ipswich, and the best of the lot, a brilliant volley against Leicester, after the club had gone nine games without a goal. A busy midfielder, he is expected to go a long way in the game.

Crystal Palace (From juniors on 22/1/88) F/PL 43+5/3 FLC 5 FAC 5+2 Others 2
Maidstone U (Loaned on 28/2/92) FL 9+1/1

NEWMAN Robert (Rob) Nigel
Born: Bradford on Avon, 13 December 1963
Height: 6'2" Weight: 12.0
Club Honours: AMC '86

A utility player who can play in midfield, at centre-back, or at full-back, following a spate of injuries at Norwich last season, Rob was even pressed into service as a striker on several occasions. Proved to be no "mug" in that role either, having a remarkable Coca Cola Cup game against Tranmere, scoring once, narrowly missing twice, and making two goals to turn a 2-0 deficit into a 4-2 win. One of the club's free-kick specialists, and reputed to have the hardest shot in English football after winning a Wembley dead-ball (timed at 85 mph) competition, he will relish next season's challenge.

Bristol C (From apprentice on 5/10/81) FL 382+12/52 FLC 29+1/2 FAC 27/2 Others 33/5
Norwich C (£600,000 on 15/7/91) F/PL 112+11/12 FLC 17+1/2 FAC 11/1 Others 7

NEWSOME Jonathan (Jon)
Born: Sheffield, 6 September 1970
Height: 6'2" Weight: 13.11
Club Honours: Div 1 '92

Following his big money move from Leeds during the 1994 close season, Jon soon became an integral part of the Norwich set-up, eventually captaining the side. A scrupulously fair, tough-tackling central defender, who can play equally well at full-back, very few strikers bettered him in 1994-95 and he consistently gained top marks for his performances in various football magazines. Having signed a three year contract, the fans will be looking for him to lead the club back to the top flight at the first time of asking. Voted Norwich's "Player of the Year".

Sheffield Wed (From trainee on 1/7/89) FL 6+1 FLC 3
Leeds U (£150,000 on 11/6/91) F/PL 62+14/3 FLC 3 FAC 3+1 Others 5
Norwich C (£1,000,000 on 30/6/94) PL 35/3 FLC 4 FAC 4

Jon Newsome Neal Simpson
(Empics Sports Photo Agency)

NEWSON Mark Joseph
Born: Stepney, 7 December 1960
Height: 5'11" Weight: 12.0
Club Honours: Div 3 '87
International Honours: E: SP-5

Another wholehearted Barnet player. Normally a centre-half, Mark was used right across the back four to plug gaps caused by injury during 1994-95, prior to being released at the end of the season.

Charlton Ath (From apprentice on 15/12/78)
Bournemouth (Free from Maidstone U on 24/5/85) FL 172+5/23 FLC 12/2 FAC 11/2 Others 4+1
Fulham (£125,000 on 28/2/90) FL 98+4/4 FLC 3 FAC 4+1 Others 8
Barnet (Free on 9/8/93) FL 58+1/4 FLC 5 FAC 5 Others 2

NEWTON Edward (Eddie) John Ikem
Born: Hammersmith, 13 December 1971
Height: 5'11" Weight: 11.2
International Honours: E: U21-2; Yth

Young Chelsea midfielder who could still go all the way. With two good feet, Eddie is versatile enough to play in a number of different positions, but is most effective when surging forward from midfield.

Unfortunately, he was yet another victim of the injury crisis at the club last season and made fewer appearances than would have normally been expected of him. On his day, a very good player.

Chelsea (From trainee on 17/5/90) F/PL 87+14/7 FLC 11+1/1 FAC 7+2 Others 5
Cardiff C (Loaned on 23/1/92) FL 18/4

NEWTON Shaun O'Neill
Born: Camberwell, 20 August 1975
Height: 5'8" Weight: 10.4

One of the best prospects at Charlton, and primarily a right-sided midfield player, he is exciting on the ball and has a great burst of speed. Was used mainly in a defensive role last season, particularly as a right-back where he coped well. Has the ability to be a great player.

Charlton Ath (From trainee on 1/7/93) FL 23+24/2 FLC 4 FAC 0+1 Others 2+1

NICHOLLS Alan
Born: Birmingham, 28 August 1973
Height: 5'11" Weight: 12.0
International Honours: E: U21-1

Although a supremely talented goalkeeper, he suffered a little from the new rulings which saw him sent off twice last season, but is a good communicater who lets the Plymouth defence know what he expects from them. Sure to improve further.

Plymouth Arg (£5,000 from Cheltenham T on 1/8/93) FL 64+1 FLC 1 FAC 7 Others 6

NICHOLLS Ryan Rhys
Born: Cardiff, 10 May 1973
Height: 5'9" Weight: 12.0
International Honours: W: Sch

A midfielder who was released by Leeds last season and joined Cardiff on a non-contract basis, he made an encouraging debut against Blackpool before picking up an injury at the end of January. As a youngster at Leeds, he was seen as an excellent dribbler and passer of the ball, but prone to injury.

Leeds U (From trainee on 5/7/91)
Cardiff C (Free on 5/1/95) FL 6+6/2

NICHOLSON Maximillian (Max)
Born: Leeds, 3 October 1971
Height: 5'10" Weight: 11.8

Left-sided midfield player whose strength is going forward to attack defenders, he started 1994-95 with Torquay, before joining Scunthorpe in November as a non-contract player. Is a good squad member, if not a first team regular.

Doncaster Rov (From trainee on 27/6/90) FL 23+4/2 FAC 0+1 Others 0+2
Hereford U (Free on 16/5/92) FL 52+11/7 FLC 4+1 FAC 4 Others 4
Torquay U (Free on 9/9/94) FL 1
Scunthorpe U (Free on 18/11/94) FL 14+1/4

NICHOLSON Shane Michael
Born: Newark, 3 June 1970
Height: 5'10" Weight: 11.0
Club Honours: GMVC '88

A versatile left-sided Derby player who, though preferring the left-back spot, can also play effectively in midfield. Perhaps his greatest threat is an ability to strike 30-yard shots on target. Off the field incidents led to

him being put on the transfer list last September, though after overcoming these and a viral illness, he reclaimed his place in November until a knee injury sidelined him in March.

Lincoln C (From trainee on 19/7/88) FL 122+11/6 FLC 8+3 FAC 6/1 Others 7+1
Derby Co (£100,000 on 22/4/92) FL 54/1 FLC 1 FAC 3/1 Others 5

NICOL Stephen (Steve)
Born: Irvine, 11 December 1961
Height: 5'10" Weight: 12.0
Club Honours: Div 1 '84, '86, '88, '90; FAC '86, '89, '92; EC '84; CS '89
International Honours: S: 27; U21-14

Took over the number ten shirt at Notts County after arriving from Liverpool last January, wearing it in both defence and midfield. A former Scottish international with more than 450 first team appearances for the "Reds", Steve has always been recognised as a versatile player who can carry his competitiveness and skill to any position. Became part of the club's management team, alongside Wayne Jones, for the last seven games of the season.

Ayr U (From juniors in 1979) SL 68+2/7 SLC 16/1 SC 3
Liverpool (£300,000 on 26/10/81) F/PL 328+15/36 FLC 42/4 FAC 50/3 Others 32+2/3
Notts Co (Free on 20/1/95) FL 19 Others 2/1

NIJHOLT Luc
Born: Amsterdam, Holland, 29 July 1961
Height: 5'11" Weight: 11.8
Club Honours: SC '91

Vastly experienced midfielder, now reaching the "veteran" stage after performing at the highest level across Europe, in Scotland, and in England, Luc's influence on the fast emerging youngsters at Swindon was more than apparent in 1994-95. Strong in the tackle, with an excellent left-foot, he has a good business head off the field too, and speaks five languages.

Motherwell (£125,000 from Basle OB on 1/8/90) SL 91+5/5 SLC 6 SC 1+1 Others 2
Swindon T (£175,000 on 20/7/93) F/PL 64+1/1 FLC 14 FAC 11/2 Others 5

NILSEN Roger
Born: Tromso, Norway, 8 August 1969
Height: 5'9" Weight: 12.0
International Honours: Norway

Versatile left-sided Sheffield United defender who has appeared at full-back, centre-back, and sweeper for the "Blades", but mainly in the centre for his country. After starting last season as first choice left-back, injury in the game against Port Vale led to a spell out of the team. He returned to put in strong performances both in the centre and at full-back, although still searching for that first goal for the club, despite many long-range attempts.

Sheffield U (£550,000 from Viking Stavanger on 2/11/93) P/FL 54+1 FLC 1 FAC 1+1

NIXON Eric Walter
Born: Manchester, 4 October 1962
Height: 6'4" Weight: 14.3
Club Honours: AMC '90

Goalkeeper. Last season ended for Eric as it

started, with him watching from the sidelines. But in between, Tranmere's big number one produced some virtuoso performances which did much to propel the club into the promotion pack. Tall and dominating, with as safe a pair of hands as anyone in the League, he chalked up 14 clean sheets during the campaign.

Manchester C (£1,000 from Curzon Ashton on 10/12/83) FL 58 FLC 8 FAC 10 Others 8
Wolverhampton W (Loaned on 29/8/86) FL 16
Bradford C (Loaned on 28/11/86) FL 3
Southampton (Loaned on 23/12/86) FL 4
Carlisle U (Loaned on 23/1/87) FL 16
Tranmere Rov (£60,000 on 24/3/88) FL 316 FLC 34 FAC 18 Others 45+1

Eric Nixon   Barrington Coombs
(Empics Sports Photo Agency)

NOGAN Kurt
Born: Cardiff, 9 September 1970
Height: 5'11" Weight: 12.7
International Honours: W: U21-2

A natural goalscorer who started last season in cracking form for Brighton with 12 goals in 15 games. Unaccountably, the goals suddenly dried up and he failed to add to his tally in the next 20 games. Sidelined with a hairline fracture of the shoulder, Brighton sold him to Burnley after acquiring the services of John Byrne.

Luton T (From trainee on 11/7/89) FL 17+16/3 FLC 1+3/1 Others 1+1
Peterborough U (Free on 30/9/92) Others 0+1
Brighton & Hove A (Free on 17/10/92) FL 97/49 FLC 10/7 FAC 5/4 Others 7/4
Burnley (£250,000 on 24/4/95) FL 11+4/3

NOGAN Lee Martin
Born: Cardiff, 21 May 1969
Height: 5'10" Weight: 11.0
International Honours: W: 1; B-1; U21-1

Signed by Reading player-managers, Jimmy Quinn and Mick Gooding, from Watford last January, for a fee equalling the club's record, Lee proved to be a shrewd investment, forming a prolific striking partnership with Stuart Lovell. Took a time to settle into the side, but his goalscoring

155

feats, including a spectacular opener at Wembley in the play-off final, earned him a recall to the Welsh squad.

Oxford U (From trainee on 25/3/87) FL 57+7/10 FLC 4+1 FAC 2+1/1 Others 4+1/1
Brentford (Loaned on 25/3/87) FL 10+1/2
Southend U (Loaned on 17/9/87) FL 6/1 FLC 2 Others 1/1
Watford (£350,000 on 12/12/91) FL 97+8/26 FLC 5+2/3 FAC 2/1 Others 1+2
Southend U (Loaned on 17/3/94) FL 4+1
Reading (£250,000 on 12/1/95) FL 18+2/10 Others 3/2

NOLAN Ian Robert
Born: Liverpool, 9 July 1970
Height: 6'0" Weight: 11.10

A Sheffield Wednesday signing from Tranmere at the start of 1994-95, Ian had a steady season, showing much improvement in the second half and ending the campaign as the club's only ever-present. Although playing the majority of his games at left-back, his stronger side would seem to be his right, and he also looks more comfortable in an attacking role than a defensive one. The bitter-sweet highlight of his season came when scoring his first goal for the club at Liverpool, the team he supported as a boy.

Preston NE (From trainee on 31/8/88)
Tranmere Rov (£10,000 from Marine, via Northwich Victoria, on 2/8/91) FL 87+1/1 FLC 10/1 FAC 7 Others 9
Sheffield Wed (£1,500,000 on 17/8/94) PL 42/3 FLC 4 FAC 3

NORBURY Michael (Mickey) Shaun
Born: Hemsworth, 22 January 1969
Height: 6'0" Weight: 12.0

Striker. Failed to find the net for weeks after his transfer from Preston last November, but broke his duck in tremendous fashion with a hat-trick in Doncaster's 5-0 win at Scunthorpe in April. Appeared to grow in confidence as the season drew to a close.

Scarborough (Signed from Ossett T on 30/12/89)
Cambridge U (Signed from Bridlington T, via Ossett T, on 13/2/92) FL 11+15/3 Others 1+2
Preston NE (£32,500 on 23/12/92) FL 32+10/13 FLC 1+1 FAC 0+3 Others 3+1/1
Doncaster Rov (£30,000 on 21/11/94) FL 17+5/5 Others 1

NORFOLK Lee Richard
Born: Dunedin, New Zealand, 17 October 1975
Height: 5'10" Weight: 11.3

Right-footed Ipswich midfield player who plays with great determination, Lee made his debut last season as a substitute against Southampton and created the second goal with a perfect cross for Lee Chapman to head home.

Ipswich T (From trainee on 1/7//94) PL 1+2

NORMAN Anthony (Tony) Joseph
Born: Deeside, 24 February 1958
Height: 6'2" Weight: 12.8
International Honours: W: 5; B-1

Long-serving goalkeeper who reclaimed his Sunderland first team place from Alec Chamberlain last February, he is both brave and agile, and occasional mistakes are easily outweighed by his outstanding contributions to some vital victories. At the age of 37,

Tony was freed last summer.

Burnley (From juniors on 1/8/76)
Hull C (£30,000 on 14/2/80) FL 372 FLC 22 FAC 26 Others 13
Sunderland (Signed on 29/12/88) FL 198 FLC 8 FAC 14 Others 7

NORRIS Stephen (Steve) Mark
Born: Coventry, 22 September 1961
Height: 5'10" Weight: 10.10
International Honours: E: SP-1

A goal poacher, plain and simple, and very effective, Steve's experience was helpful in the development of Kevin Davies, but his absence from the side at a time when Chesterfield were struggling to find the net was mystifying to his fans. Went on loan to Scarborough last December, before finishing the season at VS Rugby.

Scarborough (£46,000 from Telford U on 25/7/88) FL 35+10/13 FLC 9/2 FAC 1 Others 3+1/1
Notts Co (Loaned on 8/11/89) FL 0+1
Carlisle U (£40,000 on 28/12/89) FL 21+8/5 FLC 0+2
Halifax T (Signed on 5/10/90) FL 56/35 FLC 2/1 FAC 5/2 Others 3/1
Chesterfield (£33,000 on 16/1/92) FL 84+13/43 FLC 10+1/6 FAC 3 Others 3+1/1
Scarborough (Loaned on 23/12/94) FL 8/4

NORTON David Wayne
Born: Cannock, 3 March 1965
Height: 5'7" Weight: 11.3
International Honours: E: Yth

Skilful Northampton full-back, with the ability to take on and beat opponents, he was signed from Hull last August. Likes to overlap and is an accurate crosser of the ball, who can also play in midfield.

Aston Villa (From apprentice on 23/3/83) FL 42+2/2 FLC 8 FAC 2+1 Others 2
Notts Co (£30,000 on 24/8/88) FL 22+5/1 FLC 3+1 Others 4+1
Rochdale (Loaned on 18/10//90) FL 9 Others 2
Hull C (Loaned on 10/1/91) FL 15
Hull C (£80,000 on 16/8/91) FL 134/5 FLC 7 FAC 7/1 Others 9/1
Northampton T (£25,000 on 15/8/94) FL 36+2 FLC 2 FAC 1 Others 1

NORTON Paul Stuart
Born: Middlesbrough, 15 October 1975
Height: 5'7" Weight: 11.8

Young Middlesbrough defensive, left-sided midfielder, and a local product, Paul made just one sub appearance in the Anglo-Italian Cup last season, before being released.

Middlesbrough (From trainee on 15/7/93) Others 0+1

NOTEMAN Kevin Simon
Born: Preston, 15 October 1969
Height: 5'10" Weight: 11.12

A left-hand wide player, who on his day can be match-winner, Kevin played 27 full FL games for Mansfield last season to help the club reach the play-offs. Surprisingly released at the end of 1994-95.

Leeds U (From trainee on 13/6/88) FL 0+1 Others 1
Doncaster Rov (£10,000 on 10/11/89) FL 105+1/20 FLC 4/1 FAC 5+1/2 Others 11/1
Mansfield T (£25,000 on 27/3/92) FL 77+18/15 FLC 7/1 FAC 3 Others 5+1

NTAMARK Charles (Charlie) Batmbog
Born: Paddington, 22 July 1964
Height: 5'8" Weight: 11.12

International Honours: Cameroon

Outstanding Walsall utility player whose ball skills, although most frequently seen in midfield or as a flank-attacker, can also be used to good effect in defence. As a key member of the side that were promoted to the Second Division last season, Charlie scored his first goal for two years in a vital win at Mansfield.

Walsall (Free from Borehamwood on 22/8/90) FL 186+10/11 FLC 13+1/1 FAC 14 Others 15/1

NUGENT Kevin Patrick
Born: Edmonton, 10 April 1969
Height: 6'1" Weight: 12.4
International Honours: Ei: Yth

An extremely hard-working centre-forward, with good close control, who leads the line well and brings players into the game with his passing ability. Predominantly right-footed, Kevin failed to score his normal quota of goals last season for Plymouth, but is still very valuable to the team, even if underrated. A big player who wins his fair share of headers, he is at his best alongside a speedy partner.

Leyton Orient (From trainee on 8/7/87) FL 86+8/20 FLC 9+3/6 FAC 9/3 Others 9+1/1
Plymouth Arg (£200,000 on 23/3/92) FL 120+5/31 FLC 9/2 FAC 10/3 Others 4+3

NYAMAH Kofi
Born: Islington, 20 June 1975
Height: 5'8" Weight: 10.12

Loaned to Stevenage Borough last December, Kofi, a quick left-footed forward who was on the fringe of Cambridge side at the time, returned for the final two months of the season before being released.

Cambridge U (From trainee on 19/5/93) FL 9+14/2 FLC 0+2 FAC 3+1/1 Others 4

OAKES Michael Christian
Born: Northwich, 30 October 1973
Height: 6'1" Weight: 12.6
International Honours: E: U21-5

Young Aston Villa goalkeeper with loads of potential and with five England U21 caps to his credit, apart from one Coca Cola Cup appearance last season on his first team debut for the club, he had to wait in the wings behind Mark Bosnich and Nigel Spink. The son of Alan, the former Manchester City wing-half and club appearance record holder, further opportunities should not be too long in coming.

Aston Villa (From juniors on 16/7/91) FLC 1
Scarborough (Loaned on 26/11/93) FL 1 Others 1

OAKES Scott John
Born: Leicester, 5 August 1972
Height: 5'10" Weight: 11.4

Although mainly known for his wing play, Scott has played as a striker, midfielder and full-back. In fact, in many of his games he will play all these roles at different times. He continued to be Luton's most exciting player, often beating an opponent to create openings and providing excellent passes. Also possesses a good shot and is a free-kick specialist. Is the son of a member of the famous pop-group, Showaddywaddy.

Leicester C (From trainee on 9/5/90) FL 1+2 Others 1
Luton T (Signed on 22/10/91) FL 110+34/24 FLC 3+3/1 FAC 11+2/5 Others 0+3

OAKLEY Matthew
Born: Peterborough, 17 August 1977
Height: 5'10" Weight: 11.0

Young right-sided Southampton midfielder who made his PL debut when coming on for Simon Charlton in a 0-0 draw at Everton last May. Offered a pro contract for this coming season, Matthew is a good passer with plenty of vision and possesses a very long-throw indeed.

Southampton (Trainee) PL 0+1

OATWAY Anthony (Charlie)
Born: Hammersmith, 28 November 1973
Height: 5'7" Weight: 10.10

A non-league signing for Cardiff during the summer of 1994, Charlie made a strong impact in midfield during pre-season friendlies, with his terrior-like workrate. An instant hit with the fans, he was unfortunate to be involved in a non-football related problem that saw him out of the game for several months.

Cardiff C (Free from Yeading on 4/8/94) FL 27+3 FLC 2/1 FAC 1 Others 3+1

O'BRIEN Liam Francis
Born: Dublin, 5 September 1964
Height: 6'1" Weight: 11.10
Club Honours: Div 1 '93
International Honours: Ei: 11; Yth

Skilful playmaker who has been at the fulcrum of Tranmere's promotion bids during the past two seasons. A gifted player with wonderful touch and vision, Liam can spray the ball long or short, quicken the tempo, or slow it down according to need. Earned a recall to the Eire squad for the abandoned England match after missing out on World Cup '94. Rover's dead-ball specialist, though he failed to net from such a situation during 1994-95.

Manchester U (£60,000 from Shamrock Rov on 14/10/86) FL 16+15/2 FLC 1+2 FAC 0+2
Newcastle U (£250,000 on 15/11/88) F/PL 131+20/19 FLC 9/1 FAC 12+2/1 Others 9+2/1
Tranmere Rov (£300,000 on 21/1/94) FL 55/2 FLC 7 FAC 3/1 Others 5+1

O'CONNELL Brendan
Born: Lambeth, 12 November 1966
Height: 5'10" Weight: 10.9

Playing for Barnsley in his usual position just behind the front two for the first part of last season, because of the emergence of Martin Bullock he moved into more of a holding role and his form improved immeasurably. Whether playing well or not he never gives less than 100 per-cent.

Portsmouth (From apprentice on 1/7/85)
Exeter C (Free on 4/8/86) FL 73+8/19 FLC 3+1/2 FAC 3 Others 4
Burnley (Free on 1/7/88) FL 62+2/17 FLC 6/3 FAC 3/1 Others 5/2
Huddersfield T (Loaned on 30/11/89) FL 11/1
Barnsley (£50,000 on 23/3/90) FL 192+23/34 FLC 10+1/1 FAC 12/1 Others 7+1/2

O'CONNOR Mark Andrew
Born: Southend, 10 March 1963
Height: 5'7" Weight: 10.2

Club Honours: Div 3 '87

Now in his second spell with Bournemouth, although Mark is more used to playing in midfield he began the 1994-95 season at left-back, starting 15 games. Later made two further appearances as a substitute, before being freed during the summer.

Queens Park R (From apprentice on 1/6/80) FL 2+1
Exeter C (Loaned on 7/10/83) FL 38/1 FAC 2/1 Others 3/1
Bristol Rov (£20,000 on 13/8/84) FL 79+1/10 FLC 8/1 FAC 7/1 Others 4/1
Bournemouth (£25,000 on 27/3/86) FL 115+13/12 FLC 5+3 FAC 7 Others 4+1
Gillingham (£70,000 on 15/12/89) FL 107+9/8 FLC 8 FAC 7+1 Others 6+2/1
Bournemouth (Free on 5/7/93) FL 56+2/3 FLC 7+1 FAC 4 Others 1

O'CONNOR Martyn John
Born: Walsall, 10 December 1967
Height: 5'8" Weight: 10.8

Skilful Walsall midfield operator with delicate touches and explosive finishing power. Apart from a calming influence on the side, Martyn became a regular scorer last season and his coolness from the penalty spot also proved a vital factor, not only in the successful promotion run, but also in taking the third round FA Cup replay into extra-time at Leeds. Aside from all that, recognition also came in the shape of election to the PFA Award winning Third Division team.

Crystal Palace (£25,000 from Bromsgrove Rov on 26/6/92) FL 2 Others 1+1
Walsall (Loaned on 24/3/93) FL 10/1 Others 2/1
Walsall (£40,000 on 14/2/94) FL 53/12 FLC 4/1 FAC 5/1 Others 1

O'DRISCOLL Sean Michael
Born: Wolverhampton, 1 July 1957
Height: 5'8" Weight: 11.3
Club Honours: AMC '84; Div 3 '87
International Honours: Ei: 3

Due to Bournemouth having such a small squad at the start of last season, Sean, by now the club physio, found himself making 14 appearances at right-back, taking his total for the club to 511. Took charge of the youth side in December, before being freed in the summer.

Fulham (£12,000 from Alvechurch on 26/11/79) FL 141+7/13 FLC 12+1 FAC 11+1
Bournemouth (£6,000 on 16/2/84) FL 409+14/19 FLC 32+1/1 FAC 31/1 Others 24/3

OGDEN Neil
Born: Billinge, 29 November 1975
Height: 5'10" Weight: 10.4

Local YTS discovery who made his Wigan debut as a 17-year-old at the end of 1992-93. Since then, however, Paul, a left-winger with a cultured left-foot, has been restricted by injuries, making just one substitute appearance last season.

Wigan Ath (From trainee on 18/3/94) FL 1+4 FAC 0+1

OGRIZOVIC Steven (Steve)
Born: Mansfield, 12 September 1957
Height: 6'5" Weight: 15.0
Club Honours: FAC '87

The Big Man goes on and on. "Oggy" reached 400 League appearances for Coventry last season and again displayed a high level of consistency, only missing five games because of a foot infection in March, before tragically breaking his ankle at Northampton in a friendly and not being available for the last four matches. Looked as good as ever and gave great individual performances in home games against Newcastle, when he stopped everything the "Magpies" threw at him including an Andy Cole penalty, Manchester City, and Sheffield Wednesday, when he superbly saved a David Hirst thunderbolt from close range. Voted "Player of the Year" by the London branch of the Supporters' Club.

Chesterfield (Signed from ONRYC on 28/7/77) FL 16 FLC 2
Liverpool (£70,000 on 18/11/77) FL 4 Others 1
Shrewsbury T (£70,000 on 11/8/82) FL 84 FLC 7 FAC 5
Coventry C (£72,000 on 22/6/84) F/PL 415/1 FLC 40 FAC 25 Others 11

O'HAGEN Daniel (Danny) Alexander Nicholas
Born: Truro, 24 April 1976
Height: 6'0" Weight: 11.5

A young centre-forward who turned pro during the 1994 close season, he scored his first League goal for Plymouth at Stockport last October.

Plymouth Arg (From trainee on 29/6/94) FL 1+2/1 Others 1

O'HALLORAN Keith James
Born: Dublin, 10 November 1975
Height: 5'9" Weight: 12.3
International Honours: Ei: Yth

Very brave and determined young Middlesbrough player, who is equally at home at full-back or in midfield.Given a couple of starts last season, Keith proved to be fast off the mark and strong in the tackle, with good heading ability.

Middlesbrough (Signed from Cherry Orchard on 6/9/94) FL 1 Others 1

O'KANE John Andrew
Born: Nottingham, 15 November 1974
Height: 5'10" Weight: 11.5
Club Honours: FAYC '92

Son of Liam, the first team coach at Nottingham Forest, John is an excellent right-back, who is good in the air and likes to get forward to join the attack. Was yet another member of Manchester United's excellent youth side to make his mark in 1994-95 and is a natural athlete who seems to have an excellent future ahead of him.

Manchester U (From trainee on 29/1/93) FLC 1+1 FAC 1

OKORIE Chima Ephraim
Born: Nigeria, 8 October 1968
Height: 5'10" Weight: 12.8
International Honours: Nigeria

Striker. Made a good start to 1994-95 with Torquay, but found it more and more difficult to adapt to the physical requirements of Third Division football and was released at the end of the campaign.

Peterborough U (Signed on 14/9/93) FL 1/1
Grimsby T (Free on 22/9/93) FL 0+5 FLC 0+1/1
Torquay U (Free on 22/3/94) FL 32+4/6 FLC 4 FAC 3+1/1 Others 3

OLDFIELD David Charles
Born: Perth, Australia, 30 May 1968
Height: 5'11" Weight: 12.2
International Honours: E: U21-1

A hard-running midfielder who regained his Leicester place last October, he was always likely to pop up with a stunning goal, but was dogged by inconsistency. Operated as an emergency striker at the turn of the year, before being loaned out to Millwall.
Luton T (From apprentice on 16/5/86) FL 21+8/4 FLC 4+2/2 FAC 0+1 Others 2+1/2
Manchester C (£600,000 on 14/3/89) FL 18+8/6 FLC 2+1/2 Others 0+1/1
Leicester C (£150,000 on 12/1/90) F/PL 163+25/26 FLC 10+2/1 FAC 7/3 Others 11+3/2
Millwall (Loaned on 24/2/95) FL 16+1/6

OLIVER Darren
Born: Liverpool, 1 November 1971
Height: 5'8" Weight: 10.5

Rochdale left-back who spent much of the term in the reserves in 1994-95, his run of games in mid-season was ended by suspension due to an unfortunate sending off for handling a ·goal bound shot. Released during the summer.
Bolton W (From trainee on 8/5/90) FL 3 FLC 1
Peterborough U (Loaned on 4/10/93) FLC 1/1
Rochdale (£30,000 on 8/10/93) FL 22+6 FAC 1 Others 1

OLIVER Gavin Ronald
Born: Felling, 6 September 1962
Height: 6'0" Weight: 12.10

Looking forward to his testimonial, over the years at Bradford, Gavin has played at right-back, centre-half and in midfield. A popular and well respected figure, he unfortunately missed the final months of last season with an achilles tendon injury, before being released during the summer.
Sheffield Wed (From apprentice on 7/8/80) FL 14+6 FLC 2+3 FAC 2+1
Tranmere Rov (Loaned on 14/1/83) FL 17/1
Brighton & Hove ·A (Loaned on 12/8/85) FL 15+1 Others 1
Bradford C (£20,000 on 22/11/85) FL 308+5/9 FLC 29+1/2 FAC 16 Others 22

OLIVER Keith
Born: South Shields, 15 January 1976
Height: 5'8" Weight: 10.3

Tenacious young Hartlepool midfielder. Disastrously sent off on his full League debut in 1994-95, in subsequent games, Keith looked a fine prospect, playing an important role in front of the defence with the responsibility of closing down the opposition's attack. Out of the side for a lengthy spell with a knee ligament injury, he now looks to be fully recovered.
Hartlepool U (From trainee on 5/7/94) FL 18+1 FLC 4 Others 2

OLIVER Michael
Born: Cleveland, 2 August 1975
Height: 5'10" Weight: 12.4

A hard-tackling Stockport midfielder, Michael was picked up from Middlesbrough in the 1994 close season after winning their "Young Player of the Year" award. Although failing to make an immediate impact in 1994-95, his performances towards the end of the term suggested that he would soon become a regular.

Middlesbrough (From trainee on 19/8/92) Others 0+1
Stockport Co (£15,000 on 7/7/94) FL 10+3

OLSSON Paul
Born: Hull, 24 December 1965
Height: 5'8" Weight: 10.11

The only Darlington ever-present last season, this vastly experienced midfield player contributed five goals on his runs forward from the central part of the field that he covers comprehensively during a game.
Hull C (From apprentice on 7/1/84) Others 1/1
Exeter C (Free on 13/3/87) FL 38+5/2 FLC 2 FAC 0+1
Scarborough (Free on 17/8/88) FL 34+14/5 FLC 5+1 FAC 2 Others 8
Hartlepool U (£5,000 on 26/12/89) FL 162+9/13 FLC 11+2 FAC 10 Others 11+1/2
Darlington (Free on 1/7/94) FL 42/4 FAC 2 Others 3/1

O'NEILL Keith Padre
Born: Dublin, 16 February 1976
Height: 6'2" Weight: 12.7
International Honours: Ei: Yth

Right-back, cum midfielder, with a propensity to going forward. Made his Norwich debut last season as a substitute at Southampton, having played just 40 youth and reserve matches for the club, when replacing Rob Newman after 54 minutes. Has grown nine inches in the last four years and looks to be a "good 'un".
Norwich C (From trainee on 1/7/94) PL 0+1

ONUORA Ifem (Iffy)
Born: Glasgow, 28 July 1967
Height: 5'10" Weight: 11.10

Signed from Huddersfield during the summer of 1994, Iffy sustained a toe injury in a pre-season game for Mansfield, which subsequently required an operation and forced him out of first team action, initially as a substitute, until February. As a central striker, he caused problems for opposition defenders with his pace and aggression, scoring a hat-trick within a seven minute period against Lincoln and helping the club into the play-offs.
Huddersfield T (Signed from British Universities on 28/7/89) FL 115+50/30 FLC 10+6/4 FAC 11+3/3 Others 13+3/3
Mansfield T (Free on 20/7/94) FL 10+4/7 Others 1

Udo Onwere Steve Morton
(Empics Sports Photo Agency)

ONWERE Udo Alozie
Born: Hammersmith, 9 November 1971
Height: 6'0" Weight: 11.3

Hard-tackling midfield man who signed for Lincoln from Fulham prior to last season starting, he quickly became a popular figure with the fans, but spent much of the campaign on the injury list, following a cartilage operation.
Fulham (From trainee on 11/7/90) FL 66+19/7 FLC 4+2 FAC 1+1 Others 9
Lincoln C (Free on 12/8/94) FL 7+1 FLC 3 Others 1

ORD Richard John
Born: Murton, 3 March 1970
Height: 6'2" Weight: 12.8
International Honours: E: U21-3

A tall Sunderland central defender, Richard finally looks like realising the potential he showed as a teenager, having been restored to the side towards the end of 1994-95 by Peter Reid. The new manager emphasised that Richard was his first choice centre-back, a show of confidence that produced immediate results. Dominant in the air, a good tackler, and surprisingly skilful for such a big man, he can look forward to building on his England U21 caps.
Sunderland (From trainee on 14/7/87) FL 136+18/4 FLC 11+5 FAC 7+1/1 Others 5+1
York C (Loaned on 22/2/90) FL 3

O'REGAN Kieran Michael
Born: Cork, 9 November 1963
Height: 5'8" Weight: 10.12
International Honours: Ei: 4; Yth

Experienced international right-back or central midfielder with a heart of gold, he never shirks a tackle. Injuries interrupted his WBA performances in 1994-95, and he was freed at the end of the season.
Brighton & Hove A (Signed from Tramore Ath on 9/4/83) FL 69+17/2 FLC 6+1 FAC 3 Others 2+1/1
Swindon T (Free on 12/8/87) FL 23+3/1 FLC 5+1 FAC 2+1 Others 3/1
Huddersfield T (Signed on 4/8/88) FL 187+12/25 FLC 15+1/1 FAC 16+1/3 Others 20+1/3
West Bromwich A (£25,000 on 8/7/93) FL 36+9/2 FLC 3+1 FAC 2 Others 3

O'RIORDAN Donald (Don) Joseph
Born: Dublin, 14 May 1957
Height: 5'11" Weight: 12.0
International Honours: Ei: U21-1

Torquay's manager who doubled up in a number of positions in 1994-95, in defence, sweeping up or in midfield, Don is still one of the best players at Torquay and is still capable of hitting the killer 30 or 40 yard ball.
Derby Co (From apprentice on 1/5/75) FL 2+4/1 FLC 0+1 (£30,000 to Tulsa Roughnecks in February 1978)
Doncaster Rov (Loaned on 21/1/78) FL 2
Preston NE (£30,000 on 13/10/78) FL 153+5/8 FLC 10 FAC 8/1
Carlisle U (£30,000 on 8/8/83) FL 84/18 FLC 4 FAC 4
Middlesbrough (£55,000 on 8/8/85) FL 41/2 FLC 2 FAC 1/1 Others 2/1
Grimsby T (Free on 22/8/86) FL 86/14 FLC 6 FAC 6 Others 3
Notts Co (£16,000 on 13/7/88) FL 102+7/5 FLC 5+1/1 FAC 6/2 Others 16+2/1
Mansfield T (Loaned on 28/9/89) FL 6
Torquay U (Free on 12/2/93) FL 70+1/3 FLC 2 FAC 5 Others 3

ORLYGSSON Thorvaldur (Toddy)
Born: Odense, Iceland, 2 August 1966
Height: 5'11" Weight: 10.13
International Honours: Iceland

"Toddy" arrived at the Victoria Ground from Nottingham Forest in the summer of 1993, after predominantly being used as a right-winger, but at Stoke he found his best position in a more central midfield role. A hit with the fans in 1994-95, with his penetrating runs into the heart of the opposition defence, he also enjoyed dead-ball situations, having a good record from the penalty spot.
Nottingham F (£175,000 from KA Akureyri on 9/12/89) F/PL 31+6/2 FLC 5+1/2 FAC 1 Others 0+1
Stoke C (Free on 5/8/93) FL 80+3/18 FLC 7/1 FAC 6/1 Others 6/1

ORMONDROYD Ian
Born: Bradford, 22 September 1964
Height: 6'4" Weight: 13.9

Awkward looking, lanky forward who is often used on the left-side of the Leicester midfield. Netted from an impossible angle in the home win over Arsenal for his first Premiership strike, only for it to be deleted by the panel who decided it was an "own goal", prior to rediscovering his shooting boots with a vengeance when on loan at Hull last January. Playing under his former Bradford boss, Terry Dolan, his goals did much to keep the "Tigers" in the race for the play-offs, before he was recalled to Filbert Street in April to cover an emergency injury crisis.
Bradford C (Signed from Thackley on 6/9/85) FL 72+15/20 FLC 12+2/4 FAC 7/2 Others 7+2/1
Oldham Ath (Loaned on 27/3/87) FL 8+2/1
Aston Villa (£600,000 on 2/2/89) FL 41+15/6 FLC 4+2/2 FAC 5/2 Others 6+1
Derby Co (£350,000 on 19/9/91) FL 25/8 FLC 3 FAC 3/1
Leicester C (Signed on 11/3/92) F/PL 67+10/7 FLC 6/2 FAC 1+1 Others 11/3
Hull C (Loaned on 27/1/95) FL 10/6

ORMSBY Brendan Thomas
Born: Birmingham, 1 October 1960
Height: 5'11" Weight: 11.3
International Honours: E: Yth; Sch

Experienced centre-back and true competitor, Brendan joined Wigan in August 1994 on a non-contract basis, following a spell in charge of the Irish side, Waterford. A former playing colleague of Kenny Swain, he left the club following the manager's departure.
Aston Villa (From apprentice on 1/10/78) FL 115+2/4 FLC 11+1/2 FAC 3+1 Others 7/1
Leeds U (£65,000 on 28/2/86) FL 46/5 FLC 1 FAC 6/1 Others 6/1
Shrewsbury T (Loaned on 18/1/90) FL 1
Doncaster Rov (Free on 25/7/90) FL 78/7 FLC 3 FAC 4 Others 2
Scarborough (Free on 3/8/92) FL 15+1/1 FLC 1 Others 1 (Free to Waterford on 1/5/93)
Wigan Ath (Free on 12/8/94) FL 2

OSBORN Simon Edward
Born: Croydon, 19 January 1972
Height: 5'10" Weight: 11.4

One of the bargain buys of last season, arriving at Reading for just £90,000 from Crystal Palace, Simon proved to be a revelation with penetrative passing and the ability to score spectacular volleyed goals from long-range. Another who missed a large chunk of the campaign with a knee injury, he had returned to his creative best as he guided the club towards the play-offs.
Crystal Palace (From trainee on 3/1/90) F/PL 47+8/5 FLC 11/1 FAC 2 Others 1+3
Reading (£90,000 on 17/8/94) FL 31+1/5 FLC 4 Others 3

O'SHEA Daniel (Danny) Edward
Born: Kennington, 26 March 1963
Height: 6'0" Weight: 12.8
Club Honours: Div 3 '91

Predominantly a right-footed central defender, Danny also played in midfield during 1994-95 as a steadying influence on a young Cambridge side, before moving to Northampton as player-coach last March.
Arsenal (From apprentice on 23/12/80) FL 6 FLC 3
Charlton Ath (Loaned on 23/2/84) FL 9
Exeter C (Free on 24/8/84) FL 45/2 FLC 2 FAC 2 Others 2
Southend U (£5,000 on 9/8/85) FL 116+2/12 FLC 8 FAC 5+1 Others 6
Cambridge U (Free on 18/8/89) FL 186+17/1 FLC 18+1 FAC 15+3 Others 12+2/1
Northampton T (Free on 23/3/95) FL 7/1

O'SULLIVAN Wayne St John
Born: Akrotiri, Cyprus, 25 February 1974
Height: 5'11" Weight: 11.2

Slightly built midfielder who can also fill the right-back berth. Came through Swindon's ranks under the watchful eye of ex-Town full-back, John Trollope, and could secure a similar future for himself, having made over 30 appearances during 1994-95, in what could best be described as a turbulent season.
Swindon T (From trainee on 1/5/93) FL 22+8 FLC 5 FAC 0+2 Others 3

Ricky Otto   Ross Kinnaird
(Empics Sports Photo Agency)

OTTO Ricky
Born: Hackney, 9 November 1967
Height: 5'10" Weight: 10.10
Club Honours: Div 2 '95; AMC '95

Another signing from Southend, Ricky began his Birmingham career last December in bizarre fashion, when scoring at both ends. Renowned for his dazzling displays down the "Shrimpers'" left-wing and some spectacular goals, he has yet to fully settle at St Andrews. Still a successful season though, with a Second Division Championship medal to go with the one from the Auto Windscreen Shield victory over Carlisle.
Leyton Orient (Free from Haringey Borough on 7/11/90) FL 41+15/13 FLC 3 FAC 2+1 Others 5+1/2
Southend U (£100,000 on 9/7/93) FL 63+1/17 FLC 3 FAC 1 Others 8/2
Birmingham C (£800,000 on 19/12/94) FL 18+6/4 FAC 2/1 Others 5/1

OVENDALE Mark John
Born: Leicester, 22 November 1973
Height: 6'3" Weight: 13.2

Signed from Wisbech, last season, he is a tall commanding 'keeper who is still learning his trade. Will be remembered for saving a penalty for Northampton on his home debut against Barnet in the AWS competition. Released during the summer.
Northampton T (Free from Wisbech on 15/8/94) FL 6 Others 2

Vince Overson   Barry Coombs
(Empics Sports Photo Agency)

OVERSON Vincent (Vince) David
Born: Kettering, 15 May 1962
Height: 6'0" Weight: 13.0
Club Honours: Div 3 '82, Div 2 '93; AMC '91, '92
International Honours: E: Yth

An essentially right-footed central defender, Vince started last season in the Stoke side, but then fell out of favour with manager Joe Jordan, before regaining his place and the captaincy when Lou Macari returned to the manager's chair. A strong, uncompromising centre-half, his battling qualities, particularly in the air, are his strong point.
Burnley (From apprentice on 16/11/79) FL 207+4/6 FLC 9/1 FAC 19 Others 10
Birmingham C (Free on 11/6/86) FL 179+3/3 FLC 11+1 FAC 8 Others 11/1
Stoke C (£55,000 on 29/8/91) FL 149+3/6 FLC 10/1 FAC 10 Others 21

OWEN Gareth
Born: Chester, 21 October 1971
Height: 5'8" Weight: 11.4
Club Honours: WC '95
International Honours: W: U21-8

Aggressive, skilful central midfield player, Wrexham's Welsh U21 International remains something of an enigma as it was the opinion of many that he would have been playing in the Premier League by now. His "forte", are long defence splitting passes and a strong shot. Many fans would like to see him in a more forward midfield role where he is most effective, foraging through defences and creating chances for himself and team-mates.

Wrexham (From trainee on 6/7/90) FL 151+21/18 FLC 5+1 FAC 12+3 Others 26

OWERS Gary
Born: Newcastle, 3 October 1968
Height: 5'11" Weight: 11.10
Club Honours: Div 3 '88

Transferred from Sunderland to Bristol City last December in a deal that saw Martin Scott go in the opposite direction, this dynamic, two-footed midfield general supplied much needed drive to a club already in the relegation zone. Reckoned by many to be City's outstanding player, it is to be hoped he continues in this vein in the forthcoming campaign, as such performances are going to be needed if they are to return to the First Division at the first time of asking.

Sunderland (From apprentice on 8/10/86) FL 259+9/25 FLC 27+1/1 FAC 10+2 Others 11+1/1
Bristol C (£250,000 on 23/12/94) FL 21/2 FAC 3

Mixu Paatelainen   Barrington Coombs
(Empics Sports Photo Agency)

PAATELAINEN Mika (Mixu) Matti
Born: Helsinki, Finland, 3 February 1967
Height: 6'0" Weight: 13.11
International Honours: Finland

A regular in Finland's attack, Mixu came to Bolton from Aberdeen in July 1994 and quickly got off the mark with two goals on his FL debut during an opening day 3-3 draw at Grimsby. Although not the fastest player in the club, he has proved to be more than a handful for opponents, and created many a goal to supplement the 15 that he

netted during last season, including the third in the 4-3 First Division play-off victory over Reading.

Dundee U (Signed from Valkeakosken in October 1987) SL 101+32/33 SLC 7+2/5 SC 20+1/8 Others 8+1/1
Aberdeen (Signed on 31/3/92) SL 53+22/23 SLC 6/3 SC 7+1/1 Others 3/1
Bolton W (£300,000 on 29/7/94) FL 43+1/12 FLC 7+1/2 FAC 1 Others 3/1

PACK Leonard (Lenny) John
Born: Salisbury, 27 September 1976
Height: 5'10" Weight: 12.9

Another Cambridge trainee to make his debut in 1994-95, this sturdy, hard-tackling, right-sided midfielder started against Leyton Orient in March, showing great enthusiasm and promise. Although his registration has been retained by the club, he was released at the end of the season.

Cambridge U (Trainee) FL 3

PAGE Donald (Don) Richard
Born: Manchester, 18 January 1964
Height: 5'10" Weight: 11.2

A Chester signing from Doncaster, prior to the start of 1994-95, Don showed that he could play anywhere up-front. Pacy, and able to hold the ball up well, he scored five League goals last season prior to being released.

Wigan Ath (Signed from Runcorn on 23/3/89) FL 62+12/15 FLC 5/2 FAC 5/2 Others 4+2/3
Rotherham U (Signed on 16/8/91) FL 40+15/13 FLC 2+2 FAC 3/2 Others 1+2/1
Rochdale (Loaned on 17/2/93) FL 3+1/1
Doncaster Rov (Signed on 17/11/93) FL 18+4/4
Chester C (Free on 29/7/94) FL 22+8/5 FLC 2/1 FAC 2/1 Others 3/2

PAGE Robert John
Born: Llwynpia, 3 September 1974
Height: 6'0" Weight: 11.8
International Honours: W: U21-5

A first year Watford professional, his opportunities in 1994-95 were limited by the consistent form of David Holdsworth and company. Particularly strong in the air, and having now been recognised by Wales at U21 level, Robert will be looking to claim a regular place in the side this coming season.

Watford (From trainee on 19/4/93) FL 8+1 FAC 0+1

PAINTER Peter Robert
Born: Wigan, 26 January 1971
Height: 5'10" Weight: 11.0

Darlington's leading scorer in 1993-94, Robbie was troubled by injury towards the end of last season and finished with only nine goals. A hard worker, he never gives up chasing through balls in attack.

Chester C (From trainee on 1/7/88) FL 58+26/8 FLC 2+2 FAC 7+1/3 Others 3+3
Maidstone U (£30,000 on 16/8/91) FL 27+3/5 FLC 2 FAC 1+1 Others 0+2
Burnley (£25,000 on 27/3/92) FL 16+10/2 FLC 2 FAC 1
Darlington (Signed on 16/9/93) FL 69+5/20 FLC 2 FAC 3/1 Others 5/2

PALLISTER Gary Andrew
Born: Ramsgate, 30 June 1965
Height: 6'4" Weight: 13.0
Club Honours: FAC '90, '94; CS '90, '93, '94; ECWC '91; ESC '91; FLC '92; PL '93, '94

International Honours: E: 18; B-9

PFA "Player of the Year" in 1992 and elected to the award winning PL team this year, Gary is a magnificent central defender, who is a tower of strength in the air and possesses a good turn of pace on the ground. A superb reader of the game, he has excellent timing in the tackle and again looked a "class act" in the centre of Manchester United's defence, missing just one match last season. His partnership with Steve Bruce remained one of the strongest in the Premiership and gave the "Reds" that look of invulnerability, while his presence at set-pieces always caused a threat and two headed goals in the FA Cup semi-final against Crystal Palace helped the club to Wembley. Certain to feature in England's plans for the European Championships.

Middlesbrough (Free from Billingham on 7/11/84) FL 156/5 FLC 10 FAC 10/1 Others 13
Darlington (Loaned on 18/10/85) FL 7
Manchester U (£2,300,000 on 29/8/89) F/PL 233+3/8 FLC 34 FAC 31/1 Others 27+1/1

Carlton Palmer   Laurence Griffiths
(Empics Sports Photo Agency)

PALMER Carlton Lloyd
Born: Rowley Regis, 5 December 1965
Height: 6'2" Weight: 11.10
International Honours: E: 18; B-5; U21-4

Became Leeds' main pre-season signing when joining the club from Sheffield Wednesday in June 1994, having been persuaded by manager, Howard Wilkinson, that his future lay at centre-half and not in midfield. Carlton immediately impressed with his authority and composure under pressure, timing his tackles and interceptions well. At the turn of the year, after a run of poor results, he reverted to a deep-lying midfield position and was as consistent as ever. An excellent club player, the only games he missed were through suspension.

West Bromwich A (From apprentice on 21/12/84) FL 114+7/4 FLC 7+1/1 FAC 4 Others 6
Sheffield Wed (£750,000 on 23/2/89) F/PL 204+1/14 FLC 31/1 FAC 18/2 Others 8+1/1
Leeds U (£2,600,000 on 30/6/94) PL 39/3 FLC 2 FAC 3/1

PALMER Charles (Charlie) Anthony
Born: Aylesbury, 10 July 1963
Height: 5'11" Weight: 12.5

A cool centre-back, and a calming influence on fellow defenders, Charlie signed for Walsall in time to make his debut on the opening day of last season at Fulham and missed just three games, as he took his tally of FL appearances past the 300 mark.

Watford (From apprentice on 13/7/81) FL 10/1 FLC 2 Others 4
Derby Co (Free on 12/7/84) FL 51/2 FLC 7 FAC 1 Others 2
Hull C (£32,000 on 13/2/87) FL 69+1/1 FLC 3 FAC 3 Others 2
Notts Co (£25,000 on 15/2/89) FL 178+4/7 FLC 9 FAC 10 Others 19/2
Walsall (Free on 30/7/94) FL 39/2 FLC 4 FAC 5 Others 2

PALMER Lee James
Born: Croydon, 19 September 1970
Height: 6'0" Weight: 13.0

As the longest serving player on Gillingham's books he failed to gain a regular first team place last season, but impressed in the reserves with his performances at centre-half, instead of his usual left-back position. In March 1995, he joined Beazer Homes side Sittingbourne on loan for the rest of the season, before being freed during the summer.

Gillingham (From trainee on 28/7/89) FL 109+11/5 FLC 7+1 FAC 7+1 Others 8

PALMER Stephen (Steve) Leonard
Born: Brighton, 31 March 1968
Height: 6'1" Weight: 12.7
Club Honours: Div 2 '92

Right-footed Ipswich midfield player, more of a grafter than a creator, and an excellent man marker. One of four Town players with a university degree, Steve began last season on the substitutes' bench for the first five games without ever coming on. Made his first appearance in the 3-2 defeat of Manchester United and was instrumental in the victory, getting in amongst United's midfield and visibly upsetting them. In the second half of the campaign, he played in central defence for the reserves and was given a couple of first team appearances in the same role.

Ipswich T (Free from Cambridge University on 1/8/89) F/PL 82+24/2 FLC 3 FAC 8+3/1 Others 3+2

PARDEW Alan Scott
Born: Wimbledon, 18 July 1961
Height: 5'11" Weight: 11.0

Vastly experienced right-sided Charlton attacking midfield player who likes to get into the opposition's penalty area, Alan put in some solid performances, particularly towards the end of the season. Freed during the summer.

Crystal Palace (£7,000 from Yeovil T on 17/3/87) FL 111+17/8 FLC 9+3/1 FAC 8/1 Others 20/2
Charlton Ath (Free on 21/11/91) FL 98+6/24 FLC 3+1 FAC 9+1/1 Others 6/1

PARKER Garry Stuart
Born: Oxford, 7 September 1965
Height: 5'8" Weight: 11.0
Club Honours: FLC '89, '90; ESC '89

International Honours: E: B-1; U21-6; Yth

Signed for Leicester last February, having last played for Villa on 19 December, Garry is a right-footed central midfielder who will prove invaluable to City's promotion campaign in 1995-96. Turned in a classy performance on his debut in the FA Cup defeat at "Wolves" and acted as skipper during a flu crisis in March. Scored his first goal to earn victory over Norwich in April - City's first home win for over four months and an even better one in the final fixture at the Dell. More and more influential as the season wore on.

Luton T (From apprentice on 5/5/83) FL 31+11/3 FLC 1+3/1 FAC 6+2
Hull C (£72,000 on 21/2/86) FL 82+2/8 FLC 5 FAC 4 Others 2/1
Nottingham F (£260,000 on 24/3/88) FL 99+4/17 FLC 22+1/4 FAC 16/5 Others 9/3
Aston Villa (£650,000 on 29/11/91) F/PL 91+4/13 FLC 12 FAC 10/1 Others 0+2
Leicester C (£300,000 on 10/2/95) PL 14/2 FAC 1

PARKER Paul Andrew
Born: West Ham, 4 April 1964
Height: 5'7" Weight: 10.8
Club Honours: FLC '92; PL '93, '94; CS '93; FAC '94
International Honours: E: 19; B-3; U21-8; Yth

Paul is a duel purpose Manchester United defender who can play in central defence or at right-back. Remarkable in the air for his size, he has plenty of pace and a fast recovery rate, and reads the game well, which allows him plenty of time on the ball. In 1994-95, his season unfortunately came to a premature end in October, following surgery on his right-ankle. While Paul's main priority will be in helping United to further honours in 1995-96, he will also be eager to regain his place in the England side for the forthcoming European Championships.

Fulham (From apprentice on 15/4/82) FL 140+13/2 FLC 16/1 FAC 11 Others 2
Queens Park R (£300,000 on 18/6/87) FL 121+4/1 FLC 14 FAC 16 Others 5
Manchester U (£2,000,000 on 8/8/91) F/PL 95+4/1 FLC 14 FAC 13 Others 8+2

PARKIN Brian
Born: Birkenhead, 12 October 1965
Height: 6'3" Weight: 14.7
Club Honours: Div 3 '90

Bristol Rovers' goalkeeper who is considered by many to be one of the best outside the Premier League. A fine shot-stopper with good reflexes, his confidence increased as he kept 18 clean sheets during 1994-95. Very consistent, Brian has completed almost six seasons with the club, having arrived as part of the £1 million transfer deal which took Nigel Martyn to Crystal Palace in November 1989.

Oldham Ath (From juniors on 31/3/83) FL 6 FLC 2
Crewe Alex (Free on 30/11/84) FL 98 FLC 7 FAC 2 Others 6
Crystal Palace (Free on 1/7/88) FL 20 FLC 3 Others 2
Bristol Rov (Free on 11/11/89) FL 221 FLC 11 FAC 12 Others 21

PARKIN Stephen (Steve) John
Born: Mansfield, 7 November 1965
Height: 5'6" Weight: 11.7
International Honours: E: U21-5; Yth; Sch

Mansfield captain and central midfield player. A keen tackler, and a well disciplined performer, Steve helps to give the team formation and shape. Missed the majority of the first half of the 1994-95 season with a groin injury, but was a driving force in the club's march to the Third Division play-offs.

Stoke C (From apprentice on 12/11/83) FL 104+9/5 FLC 9 FAC 9 Others 6
West Bromwich A (£190,000 on 16/6/89) FL 44+4/2 FLC 3 Others 2+1
Mansfield T (Free on 16/7/92) FL 59+2/2 FLC 4 FAC 3+1 Others 5+1

PARKINSON Gary Anthony
Born: Thornaby, 10 January 1968
Height: 5"10" Weight: 11.6

An automatic selection at right-back for Burnley last season, Gary continued to prove he was a capable defender. His last-minute equaliser at Grimsby, scored from the left-back position after running half the length of the field, was one of 1994-95's most memorable goals.

Middlesbrough (Free from Everton juniors on 17/1/86) FL 194+8/5 FLC 20/1 FAC 17/1 Others 19
Southend U (Loaned on 10/10/92) FL 6
Bolton W (Free on 2/3/93) FL 1+2 Others 4
Burnley (Signed on 27/1/94) FL 62+1/3 FLC 4 FAC 5 Others 3/1

PARKINSON Joseph (Joe) Simon
Born: Eccles, 11 June 1971
Height: 5'8" Weight: 12.2
Club Honours: FAC '95

A lively Everton central midfield player, his main attributes are his excellent skill and a competitive nature. Unusual for him to give the ball away, Joe has a cool head for one so young and uses it effectively, with accurate passes. Last season he progressed well by taking his chance in the first team and performing admirably to become an automatic choice, winning an FA Cup winners' medal, following the club's 1-0 victory over Manchester United.

Wigan Ath (From trainee on 1/4/89) FL 115+4/6 FLC 11/1 FAC 9 Others 8
Bournemouth (£35,000 on 1/7/93) FL 30/1 FLC 4/1 FAC 4 Others 1
Everton (£250,000 on 24/3/94) PL 32+2 FLC 2 FAC 6/1

PARKINSON Philip (Phil) John
Born: Chorley, 1 December 1967
Height: 6'0" Weight: 11.6
Club Honours: Div 2 '94

Combative and abrasive Reading midfield player, whose determination and will-to-win did so much for the team in its advance from Division Two to the Division One play-offs. Excels at the man-to-man marking job, but also shows great flair and vision in his own play. Having also filled in at centre-back in emergencies, Phil is a highly valued member of the squad.

Southampton (From apprentice on 7/12/85)
Bury (£12,000 on 8/3/88) FL 133+12/5 FLC 6+1 FAC 4/1 Others 13/1
Reading (£37,500 on 10/7/92) FL 105+7/7 FLC 9/1 FAC 6/1 Others 4+2

PARKINSON Stuart George
Born: Fleetwood, 18 February 1976
Height: 5'8" Weight: 10.0

A first year pro and a promising winger with pace and skill, who top-scored for Blackpool's reserves last term, he came off the bench for his first team debut against Brentford on 25 March.

Blackpool (From trainee on 18/7/94) FL 0+1

PARLOUR Raymond (Ray)
Born: Romford, 7 March 1973
Height: 5'10" Weight: 11.12
Club Honours: FLC '93
International Honours: E: U21-12

An Arsenal midfielder who has come on in leaps and bounds over the past couple of seasons, towards the latter stages of 1994-95, Ray impressed as an integral part of the club's engine room, having an especially fine game against Real Zaragoza in the European Cup Winners Cup Final. Maturing on the right-side of midfield, he operates between both penalty areas and looks set to fill the void left when Michael Thomas departed for Liverpool. Also has an impressive range of passing skills.

Arsenal (From trainee on 6/3/91) F/PL 64+20/4 FLC 10+1 FAC 9/1 Others 7+2

PARRIS George Michael
Born: Ilford, 11 September 1964
Height: 5'9" Weight: 12.7
International Honours: E: Sch

An all-action Birmingham midfield player, who had previously impressed the fans with his determination and battling qualities, George was sadly forced out of the side by injury. Unable to regain his place, due to the form of Mark Ward, he spent much of last season on loan at Brentford, Bristol City and Brighton, prior to being released during the summer.

West Ham U (From apprentice on 9/9/82) FL 211+28/12 FLC 27+3/1 FAC 21/4 Others 7+1/1
Birmingham C (£150,000 on 12/3/93) FL 36+3/1 FLC 2 FAC 1
Brentford (Loaned on 8/8/94) FL 5 FLC 2/1
Bristol C (Loaned on 1/12/94) FL 6
Brighton & Hove A (Loaned on 9/2/95) FL 18/2

PARRISH Sean
Born: Wrexham, 14 March 1972
Height: 5'10" Weight: 11.0

Energetic midfielder whose first season at Doncaster in 1994-95, after signing from Telford in the summer, was marred by a series of injuries. However, he did enough in 25 League games to suggest he has much to offer Rovers with his hard-running, hard-tackling style of play.

Shrewsbury T (From trainee on 12/7/90) FL 1+2/1 FLC 1 Others 3 (Free to Telford during 1992 close season)
Doncaster Rov (£20,000 on 28/5/94) FL 25/3 FLC 1+1 FAC 1 Others 2

PARSLEY Neil Robert
Born: Liverpool, 25 April 1966
Height: 5'9" Weight: 10.12

A WBA player who can occupy the right-back berth, or even a central-defensive position, he had a rather disappointing 1994-95, and was freed during the summer.

Leeds U (£20,000 from Witton A on 8/11/88)
Chester C (Loaned on 13/12/89) FL 6 Others 1
Huddersfield T (Free on 25/7/90) FL 55+2 FLC 6/1 FAC 6 Others 6
Doncaster Rov (Loaned on 20/2/91) FL 2+1
West Bromwich A (£25,000 on 9/9/93) FL 38+5 FLC 3 FAC 1 Others 1

PARTNER Andrew (Andy) Neil
Born: Colchester, 21 October 1974
Height: 6'4" Weight: 13.6

Young Colchester centre-half whose bad luck with injuries continued in 1994-95, when a serious knee injury sustained in August ended his season prematurely just when a regular run in the first team seemed possible.

Colchester U (From trainee on 24/6/93) FL 1+1 Others 1

PARTRIDGE Scott Malcolm
Born: Grimsby, 13 October 1974
Height: 5'9" Weight: 10.9

Son of the former Grimsby favourite, Malcolm, Bristol City's Scott could well develop into an exciting forward if he is able to get a consistent run in the side. A skilful, two-footed player, who reminds you of an old-fashioned inside-forward, he was mainly used from the bench last season as a means of injecting fresh legs to take on tired defenders. Should become a regular in 1995-96.

Bradford C (From trainee on 10/7/92) FL 0+5 FLC 1+1
Bristol C (Free on 18/2/94) FL 21+21/6 FLC 1 FAC 1+2

PASCOE Colin James
Born: Port Talbot, 9 April 1965
Height: 5'10" Weight: 12.0
Club Honours: WC '83; AMC '94
International Honours: W: 10; U21-4; Yth

Energetic and skilful in midfield, Colin showed a high level of fitness in 1994-95 after recovering from a cartilage operation the previous summer. Despite missing almost 20 matches in mid-season, his return to first team duty coincided with Swansea's late surge for a play-off place. On the fringe of being recalled to the Welsh side, he excelled in midfield, showing a consistency that proved he could still play in a higher standard of football.

Swansea C (From apprentice on 12/4/83) FL 167+7/39 FLC 11/3 FAC 9/2 Others 7/1
Sunderland (£70,000 on 25/3/88) FL 116+10/22 FLC 12/3 FAC 4+2 Others 5
Swansea C (Loaned on 24/7/92) FL 15/4 FLC 2
Swansea C (£70,000 on 1/8/93) FL 63+5/10 FLC 7+1/2 FAC 2 Others 12/3

PASCOE Jason
Born: Mansfield, 15 February 1970
Height: 5'11" Weight: 11.11

Full-back who had his first taste of league football last season having earlier joined Northampton from non-league circles. Made only limited appearances before being freed during the summer.

Northampton T (Free from Clipstone Colliery on 19/6/94) FL 11+4 FLC 1 FAC 1 Others 2

PASKIN John William
Born: Capetown, South Africa, 1 February 1962
Height: 5'11" Weight: 12.2

Signed from Wrexham during the close season, John was a big hit with Bury supporters in 1994-95, as he showed an ability to hold the ball upfield and bring team-mates into the game. An ideal foil for the prolific goalscoring types such as Mark Carter and Phil Stant, he also managed to grab himself ten goals in 22 starts. Later on in the campaign, he was used more as a second-half substitute, but once on the field there always seemed to be an extra dimension to the "Shakers'" play.

West Bromwich A (Free from K.V. Kortrijk on 27/8/88) FL 14+11/5 FLC 1 FAC 0+2
Wolverhampton W (£75,000 on 26/6/89) FL 21+13/3 FLC 2+1 FAC 2 Others 0+1
Stockport C (Loaned on 11/9/91) FL 3+2/1
Birmingham C (Loaned on 21/11/91) FL 8+2/3 FLC 0+1
Shrewsbury T (Loaned on 13/2/92) FL 1
Wrexham (Signed on 21/2/92) FL 28+23/11 FLC 1+3/3 Others 3+2/2
Bury (Free on 22/7/94) FL 15+11/8 FLC 1 FAC 3/1 Others 3+3/1

PATERSON Scott
Born: Aberdeen, 13 May 1972
Height: 5'11" Weight: 11.9

A promising young midfielder with skill on the ball and good passing ability. Freed by Liverpool, Scott signed for Bristol City during the 1994 close season and made a number of promising appearances during 1994-95. Much is expected from him this coming term.

Liverpool (£15,000 from Cove R on 19/3/92)
Bristol C (Free on 4/7/94) FL 2+1 FLC 1

PATES Colin George
Born: Carshalton, 10 August 1961
Height: 6'0" Weight: 13.0
Club Honours: Div 2 '84; FMC '86
International Honours: E: Yth (UEFAYC '80)

Unspectacular, left-footed, good in the air, calm and unflappable, he played for Brighton last season either at left-back or as a central defender, his last appearance being in the home match against Peterborough. Unfortunately, his League career came to a premature end, due to a knee injury, and he is now playing for Crawley in the Beazer Homes Premier League.

Chelsea (From apprentice on 19/7/99) FL 280+1/10 FLC 32 FAC 20 Others 13
Charlton Ath (£430,000 on 26/10/88) FL 37+1 FLC 3 FAC 3
Arsenal (£500,000 on 22/1/90) F/PL 12+9 FLC 2 Others 2/1
Brighton & Hove A (Loaned on 28/2/91) FL 17 Others 3
Brighton & Hove A (Free on 11/8/93) FL 49+1 FLC 8 FAC 2 Others 0+1

PATMORE Warren James
Born: Kingsbury, 14 August 1971
Height: 6'2" Weight: 13.7

Tall, well built forward, who has been in and out of League football, he spent most of last season on loan in Ireland, before being released by Northampton in February.

Cambridge U (Signed from Northwood on 25/3/92) FL 1
Millwall (Free on 27/8/93) FL 0+1
Northampton T (Free on 9/12/93) FL 12+9/2

PATTERSON Darren James
Born: Belfast, 15 October 1969
Height: 6'2" Weight: 11.10
International Honours: NI: 8; B; U21; Yth
After spending two seasons in the Crystal Palace reserve side, Darren was finally given his chance at Norwich last August, following the Liverpool mauling. A Northern Ireland international, who can play at right-back, or in central defence, and is a strong tackler, he came into the team in place of Darren Pitcher and impressed. Added to his collection of caps during 1994-95.
West Bromwich A (From trainee on 5/7/88)
Wigan Ath (Free on 17/4/89) FL 69+28/6 FLC 7+1/3 FAC 5+4/1 Others 7
Crystal Palace (£225,000 on 1/7/92) PL 22/1 FLC 4 FAC 6

PATTERSON Gary
Born: Newcastle, 27 November 1972
Height: 6'1" Weight: 12.5
Club Honours: Div 3 '94
In his second season of League football, Gary was a Shrewsbury regular until his surprise sale to Wycombe last December. A busy player, who liked to support the forwards at Town, following his move, he became noted for some strong central midfield performances.
Notts Co (From trainee on 17/7/91)
Shrewsbury T (Free on 2/7/93) FL 52+5/2 FLC 5 FAC 4 Others 3
Wycombe W (£75,000 on 9/12/94) FL 9+4/1

PATTERSON Mark
Born: Leeds, 13 September 1968
Height: 5'10" Weight: 11.5
Plymouth right-back with plenty of pace and tenacity, who exhibits good control and tackling ability. A most dangerous attacker when he goes forward, using his speed to take on players, he has the ability to supply good crosses from the flank and scores some terrific goals. Played consistently throughout last season, although suffering from a few niggling injuries.
Carlisle U (From trainee on 30/8/86) FL 19+3 FLC 4 Others 1
Derby Co (£60,000 on 10/11/87) FL 41+10/3 FLC 5+2 FAC 4 Others 5+1/2
Plymouth Arg (£85,000 on 23/7/93) FL 78+1/3 FLC 2 FAC 6 Others 5

PATTERSON Mark Andrew
Born: Darwen, 24 May 1965
Height: 5'6" Weight: 11.4
Club Honours: FMC '87
A fiery little Bolton midfielder who bounced back into the side on three occasions during last season, his three goals all earned vital 1-0 victories against Millwall, Port Vale and Bristol City, respectively. Unfortunately injured in the final League game against Burnley, he missed the First Division play-offs but, following the club's 4-3 win over Reading, he can look forward to PL football this coming season.
Blackburn Rov (From apprentice on 1/5/83) FL 89+12/20 FLC 4/1 FAC 3+1 Others 2+4/1
Preston NE (£20,000 on 15/6/88) FL 54+1/19 FLC 4 FAC 4 Others 7/2
Bury (Signed on 1/2/90) FL 42/10 FLC 2 FAC 1 Others 4
Bolton W (£65,000 on 10/1/91) FL 146+7/10 FLC 11+3/1 FAC 17/1 Others 9

PAUL Martin Leighton
Born: Whalley, 2 February 1975
Height: 5'11" Weight: 11.8
Young striker who has graduated through Bristol Rovers' youth trainee scheme. A regular reserve team player for the past three seasons, Paul made his full League debut for Rovers in the opening match of 1994-95 at Peterborough, but had few other first team opportunities to build on.
Bristol Rov (From trainee on 19/7/93) FL 2+7 Others 2+1

PAYNE Derek Richard
Born: Edgware, 26 April 1967
Height: 5'6" Weight: 10.8
Signed for Watford from Southend during the 1994 close season and, as the smallest member of a pint-sized midfield, he proved to be both tenacious in the tackle and skilful on the ball.
Barnet (£12,000 from Hayes on 22/7/91) FL 50+1/6 FLC 2 FAC 2 Others 3+1
Southend U (Free on 15/7/93) FL 32+3 FLC 2 FAC 1 Others 8/1
Watford (Signed on 21/7/94) FL 24 FLC 3 Others 2

PAYNE Ian Neil
Born: Crawley, 19 January 1977
Height: 5'9" Weight: 10.2
International Honours: W: Yth
A young Plymouth full-back with plenty of talent, he made his debut on the opening day of last season while still a trainee.
Plymouth Arg (Trainee) FL 1 FLC 1

Andy Payton   Matthew Ashton
(Empics Sports Photo Agency)

PAYTON Andrew (Andy) Paul
Born: Whalley, 3 October 1967
Height: 5'9" Weight: 10.6
Striker. After scoring twice for Barnsley early last season, Andy went through the longest drought of his career. It ended in spectacular fashion with a hat-trick against Grimsby and, as his form came back, his finishing inside the penalty box was second to none.
Hull C (From apprentice on 29/7/85) FL 116+28/55 FLC 9+2/1 FAC 8 Others 3/1
Middlesbrough (£750,000 on 22/11/91) FL 8+11/3 FAC 1+3

Glasgow Celtic (Signed on 14/8/92) SL 20+16/15 SLC 3+2/5 SC 1+1 Others 3
Barnsley (Signed on 25/11/93) FL 63+5/24 FLC 4 FAC 5/1

PAZ Charquero **Adrian**
Born: Montevideo, Uruguay, 9 September 1968
Height: 5'11" Weight: 11.10
International Honours: Uruguay
A right-sided Ipswich player, more suited to a wide role, rather than that of a central striker, Adrian possesses great ability on the ball and is often able to beat opponents with ease. Signing for Town last September, he took time to settle to the English game and had the additional burden of being expected to score the goals that would carry them up the table. Made his debut against Manchester United where he learnt the harsh realities of close marking, before being substituted because of an injury, and had what was probably his best game for the club against Liverpool at Portman Road, scoring his side's only goal and running Phil Babb ragged. Will not feature in the Endsleigh First Division in 1995-96 and as the season drew to a close he was back home in his native country negotiating for a new club.
Ipswich T (£900,000 from Penarol on 22/9/94) PL 13+4/1

PEACOCK Darren
Born: Bristol, 3 February 1968
Height: 6'2" Weight: 12.6
Club Honours: WC '90
A tough-tackling central defender, he not only wins the ball but has enough ability to be constructive as well. Very consistent for Newcastle last season, showing total commitment every game, he was also very dangerous at set-pieces as he showed in the home game against Leicester, when he flicked on a near post corner for Philippe Albert to volley in. Had two spells on the sidelines with injury, missing three games with a groin strain and two games with influenza, which caused him to lose a stone in weight.
Newport Co (From apprentice on 11/2/86) FL 24+4 FLC 2 FAC 1 Others 1+1
Hereford U (Free on 23/3/89) FL 56+3/4 FLC 6 FAC 6/1 Others 6
Queens Park R (£200,000 on 22/12/90) F/PL 123+3/6 FLC 12/1 FAC 3 Others 2
Newcastle U (£2,700,000 on 24/3/94) PL 44/1 FLC 4 FAC 5 Others 4

PEACOCK Gavin Keith
Born: Eltham, 18 November 1967
Height: 5'8" Weight: 11.5
Club Honours: Div 1 '93
International Honours: E: Yth; Sch
Son of the former Charlton player, Keith, and a pro for over ten years, Gavin captained Chelsea in Dennis Wise's absence last season. At the same time, he also took over the latter's wide role, which would account for his strike-rate being down on the previous season, although on the reverse side of the coin he got in some great crosses which ultimately resulted in goals. Is at his best operating behind the front two, where

his ability to play one-twos often take him into good scoring positions.

Queens Park R (From apprentice on 19/11/84) FL 7+10/1 FAC 0+1
Gillingham (£40,000 on 5/10/87) FL 69+1/11 FLC 4 FAC 2 Others 5/1
Bournemouth (£250,000 on 16/8/89) FL 56/8 FLC 6 FAC 2 Others 2
Newcastle U (£150,000 on 30/11/90) FL 102+3/35 FLC 6/5 FAC 6/2 Others 3/4
Chelsea (£1,250,000 on 12/8/93) PL 75/12 FLC 5/1 FAC 11/7 Others 7

Gavin Peacock   Barrington Coombs
(Empics Sports Photo Agency)

PEACOCK Lee Anthony
Born: Paisley, 9 October 1976
Height: 6'0" Weight: 12.8
International Honours: S: Yth

Forward. A Scottish U18 international and another player to have come through the Youth team, Lee made a number of appearances for Carlisle towards the end of last season.

Carlisle U (From trainee on 10/3/95) FL 2+6

PEACOCK Richard John
Born: Sheffield, 29 October 1972
Height: 5'10" Weight: 10.9

Like Neil Mann, Richard made remarkable progress at Hull in his first full-time season. Takes the eye as an orthodox winger (usually on the right, but has been used to good effect on the left), he has worked very hard on his defensive duties. Not scared to take his man on, he has also weighed in with his fair share of goals - noticeably the winner in the exciting Boxing Day "derby" against Huddersfield.

Hull C (Signed from Sheffield FC on 14/10/93) FL 32+16/6 FLC 2/1 FAC 1 Others 2

PEAKE Jason William
Born: Leicester, 29 September 1971
Height: 5'9" Weight: 11.5

Classy left-sided midfielder, who became a key member of the Rochdale side in 1994-95, ending the campaign at left-back. Scored one of the goals of the season with a 30 yard floater against the wind to equalize against runaway leaders, Carlisle.

Leicester C (From trainee on 9/1/90) FL 4+4/1 Others 1+1
Hartlepool U (Loaned on 13/2/92) FL 5+1/1
Halifax T (Free on 26/8/92) FL 32+1/1 FAC 1 Others 2
Rochdale (Signed on 23/3/94) FL 46+3/2 FLC 1 FAC 1 Others 5

PEAKE Trevor
Born: Nuneaton, 10 February 1957
Height: 6'0" Weight: 12.9
Club Honours: FAC '87
International Honours: E: SP-2

Now in his 39th year, Trevor had another outstanding campaign at the heart of the Luton defence in 1994-95. As captain, he instils confidence as he sweeps up and generally organises the defence, and what he lacks in pace he makes up for in positional sense, rarely getting caught out. Ever-present for the first time for 12 seasons, he ended the season with the fans "Player of the Year award", having won it in each of the previous three seasons.

Lincoln C (£27,500 from Nuneaton Borough on 15/6/79) FL 171/7 FLC 16/2 FAC 7
Coventry C (£100,000 on 6/7/83) FL 277+1/6 FLC 30 FAC 17/1 Others 10
Luton T (£100,000 on 27/8/91) FL 160 FLC 7 FAC 13 Others 3

PEARCE Andrew (Andy) John
Born: Bradford on Avon, 20 April 1966
Height: 6'4" Weight: 14.6

A tall, imposing Sheffield Wednesday centre-back, Andy failed to consolidate his fine form of 1993-94, in which he dominated the club's back-line. In 1994-95, he lacked confidence at times and was not included at the start. However, after forcing his way back into contention, he established himself once again and, at his best, he is a straightforward, honest, and reliable defender.

Coventry C (£15,000 from Halesowen T on 14/5/90) F/PL 68+3/4 FLC 6 FAC 3 Others 1
Sheffield Wed (£500,000 on 24/6/93) PL 63+3/3 FLC 10+1/1 FAC 6+1

PEARCE Ian Anthony
Born: Bury St Edmonds, 7 May 1974
Height: 6'1" Weight: 12.4
Club Honours: PL '95
International Honours: E: U21-2; Yth

Versatile Blackburn player who can perform in defence and attack. Started last season as a substitute, but after giving a fine display against Barcelona's Romario in November, Rovers decided to play him alongside Colin Hendry in a central defensive role. With careful positioning, precise and measured tackling, and the ability to compete with anyone in the air, Ian made the position his own and, at the end of the club's most successful campaign since 1913-14, he had won a Championship medal and gained his first England U21 cap in the match against Eire.

Chelsea (From juniors on 1/8/91) F/PL 0+4 Others 0+1
Blackburn Rov (£300,000 on 4/10/93) PL 23+10/1 FLC 0+3/1 FAC 1+2 Others 1+1

PEARCE Stuart
Born: Hammersmith, 24 April 1962
Height: 5'10" Weight: 13.0

Club Honours: FLC '89, '90; FMC '89, '92
International Honours: E: 59; U21-1

Now in his 11th season at Nottingham Forest, Stuart yet again proved in 1994-95, that he is probably the most popular player ever to turn out for the club, and enjoyed being recalled for the England side that played Romania last October. Still the most formidable of left-backs, in maintaining the strength and power which enables him to burst out of defence, and still a penalty and free-kick specialist, as in the past, he never gave much away at the back with his no-nonsense tackling. Continues to be an inspirational club captain.

Coventry C (£25,000 from Wealdstone on 20/10/83) FL 52/4 FAC 2
Nottingham F (£200,000 on 3/6/85) F/PL 337/55 FLC 57/9 FAC 31/7 Others 16/6

Stuart Pearce   Tony Marshall
(Empics Sports Photo Agency)

PEARCEY Jason
Born: Leamington, 23 July 1971
Height: 6'1" Weight: 13.5

Signed from Mansfield last November, initially as cover for Paul Crichton in the Grimsby goal, he was given three games at the end of the season to allow him First Division experience. Proved to be a more than capable deputy, being strong in his box, and showing lightning reflexes that kept Town in the game in his sole home appearance, against "Wolves".

Mansfield T (From trainee on 18/7/89) FL 77 FLC 5 FAC 2 Others 7
Grimsby T (Signed on 15/11/94) FL 3

PEARS Richard James
Born: Exeter, 16 July 1976
Height: 6'0" Weight: 12.6

Forward with a quick turn of speed and another graduate from Exeter's youth team, Richard's chances were limited last season due to injury and lack of chances. Will be looking to make the breakthrough in 1995-96.

Exeter C (From trainee on 7/7/94) FL 18+12/2 FLC 1+1 Others 0+1

PEARS Stephen (Steve)
Born: Brandon, 22 January 1962
Height: 6'0" Weight: 13.12

A fearless goalie, blessed with brilliant agility and anticipation, Steve is now quite rightly enjoying his testimonial year, knowing that his many fine displays between the posts have assisted Middlesbrough to many distinguished achievements. Unfortunately, injured both calves at the start of 1994-95, he gave way to new signing, Allan Miller, and, on coming back to the side, a recurrence of the earlier injury, saw him playing second fiddle to the former Arsenal man, prior to being released at the end of the season.

Manchester U (From apprentice on 25/1/79) FL 4 FLC 1
Middlesbrough (Loaned on 1/11/83) FL 12 FAC 2
Middlesbrough (£80,000 on 9/7/85) F/PL 327 FLC 32 FAC 23 Others 28

PEARSON John Stewart
Born: Sheffield, 1 September 1963
Height: 6'2" Weight: 14.0
International Honours: E: Yth

Freed by Barnsley during the 1994 close season, this much travelled striker had spells with both Carlisle and Mansfield, before arriving at Cardiff early in the New Year. Although not scoring many goals, he worked hard as a target man to ensure plenty of possession and showed that he had not lost the knack of being able to bring others into the game. Given a free transfer at the end of 1994-95.

Sheffield Wed (From apprentice on 18/5/81) FL 64+41/24 FLC 7+3/1 FAC 8+5/2
Charlton Ath (£100,000 on 20/5/85) FL 52+9/15 FLC 3+3 FAC 1 Others 4/1
Leeds U (£70,000 on 15/1/87) FL 51+48/12 FLC 5+4 FAC 5+5 Others 6+3
Rotherham U (Loaned on 28/3/91) FL 11/5
Barnsley (£135,000 on 8/7/91) FL 29+3/4 FLC 3/1 FAC 0+3 Others 2
Hull C (Loaned on 9/1/92) FL 15 Others 2/1
Carlisle U (Free on 9/8/93) FL 5+3 Others 1
Mansfield T (Free on 18/11/94) FL 0+2 FAC 1+1
Cardiff C (Free on 27/1/95) FL 12

PEARSON Nigel Graham
Born: Nottingham, 21 August 1963
Height: 6'1" Weight: 14.0
Club Honours: FLC '91; Div 1 '95

Justified, both his transfer fee and his new managers' faith when he joined Middlesbrough's promotion push at the start of the 1994-95 season from Sheffield Wednesday. Making his debut as team captain on the opening match of the season, Nigel got the club off to a dream start, winning 2-0. His aerial ball-winning qualities and ability to control the midfield areas had an inspirational effect on the rest of the team and, despite having to overcome the setback of suffering two broken legs in recent years, is currently playing the best football of his illustrious career. He is a brilliant tactician whose outstanding heading ability breaks up many dangerous opposition attacks and sets up counter attacking situations for his strikers and his experience and coolness under extreme

pressure have earned him the ultimate accolade from his legion of fans, that of "Captain Fantastic". The First Division Championship medal was a just reward for all the effort.

Shrewsbury T (£5,000 from Heanor T on 12/11/81) FL 153/5 FLC 19 FAC 6 Others 3
Sheffield Wed (£250,000 on 16/10/87) F/PL 176+4/14 FLC 17+2/5 FAC 15/1 Others 10
Middlesbrough (£500,000 on 19/7/94) FL 33/3 FAC 2

PEEL Nathan James
Born: Blackburn, 17 May 1972
Height: 6'1" Weight: 12.7

Like John Mullin, Nathan seemed destined not to feature in Jimmy Mullen's many striking permutations, and his 1994-95 season at Burnley was restricted to a few substitute appearances. Loaned to Rotherham on transfer deadline day, he immediately became a firm favourite with the fans when scoring three times in his first four games.

Preston NE (From trainee on 9/7/90) FL 1+9/1 FLC 1 Others 1+1
Sheffield U (£50,000 on 1/8/91) FL 0+1
Halifax T (Loaned on 3/2/93) FL 3
Burnley (£60,000 on 24/9/93) FL 4+12/2 FLC 1 FAC 0+3 Others 0+2
Rotherham U (Loaned on 23/3/95) FL 9/4

PEER Dean
Born: Stourbridge, 8 August 1969
Height: 6'2" Weight: 12.0
Club Honours: AMC '91

A busy Walsall midfielder with tremendous stamina and a regular goalscorer, Dean lost his place soon after the arrival of new manager, Chris Nicholl, last autumn, and was released at the end of the season. Still only 26, there would seem to be plenty of good football left in the tank.

Birmingham C (From trainee on 9/7/87) FL 106+14/8 FLC 14+1/3 FAC 3+1 Others 10+1/1
Mansfield T (Loaned on 18/12/92) FL 10 Others 1
Walsall (Free on 16/11/93) FL 41+4/8 FLC 2 FAC 4+2 Others 3

PEJIC Melvin (Mel)
Born: Newcastle under Lyne, 27 April 1959
Height: 5'9" Weight: 11.0
Club Honours: WC '90

A strong-tackling, rugged central defender, or full-back, although not a regular at Wrexham these days, he will always come in and do a good job. Having served the club well, Mel has been given a new 12 month contract with wider responsibilities, such as assisting with coaching duties.

Stoke C (From juniors on 22/7/77) FL 1
Hereford U (Free on 13/6/80) FL 404+8/14 FLC 23+2/3 FAC 20+1/3 Others 26+1
Wrexham (£7,000 on 9/1/92) FL 103+3/3 FLC 7/1 FAC 3 Others 8

PEMBERTON John Matthew
Born: Oldham, 18 November 1964
Height: 5'11" Weight: 12.3

After operating mainly in the reserves, including a spell as a striker and scoring a hat-trick against Sunderland, John came into the Leeds' starting line-up for the game at Arsenal and, having shared in the impressive victory, stayed on the right-side of the defence for the remainder of last

season. An extremely quick and aggressive tackler, who provided the perfect foil to David Wetherall in the centre of the defence, he gave a string of consistent performances, including the shackling of Andy Cole on more than one occasion.

Rochdale (Free from Chadderton on 26/9/84) FL 1
Crewe Alex (Free on 29/3/85) FL 116+5/1 FLC 7/1 FAC 3 Others 7
Crystal Palace (£80,000 on 24/3/88) FL 76+2/2 FLC 6+1 FAC 8 Others 12
Sheffield U (£300,000 on 27/7/90) F/PL 67+1 FLC 4 FAC 4 Others 1
Leeds U (£250,000 on 12/11/93) PL 28+8 FLC 0+1 FAC 4

John Pemberton   Neal Simpson
(Empics Sports Photo Agency)

PEMBRIDGE Mark Anthony
Born: Merthyr Tydfil, 29 November 1970
Height: 5'7" Weight: 11.1
International Honours: W: 11; B-1; U21-1

Predominantly left-footed, the Welsh international midfielder started off at Derby last season with three goals in the first five games, including a spectacular free-kick on the opening day at Barnsley. At Southend, in November, Mark sustained a knee ligament injury which would keep him sidelined until March, during which time there was some transfer speculation involving him. Was disappointed to lose his regular place in the Welsh team, but with four goals in his first five games after injury, including a last minute 20-yarder at Grimsby, he proved to be back to his best.

Luton T (From trainee on 1/7/89) FL 60/6 FLC 2 FAC 4 Others 4
Derby Co (£1,250,000 on 2/6/92) FL 108+2/28 FLC 9/1 FAC 6/3 Others 15/5

PENDER John Patrick
Born: Luton, 19 November 1963
Height: 6'0" Weight: 12.3
Club Honours: Div 4 '92
International Honours: Ei: U21-12; Yth

The arrival of Mark Winstanley at Burnley seemed to signal the end of the former skipper's place in the first team line-up last season but, in any event, he spent the first few months sidelined with a heel injury. His few appearances, either as stand-in for the suspended Steve Davis, or as part of a five man defence, suggested that his commanding presence in the centre was still very much intact.

Wolverhampton W (From apprentice on 8/11/81) FL 115+2/3 FLC 5 FAC 7/1
Charlton Ath (£35,000 on 23/7/85) FL 41 FLC 1 FAC 1 Others 2/1
Bristol C (£50,000 on 30/10/87) FL 83/3 FLC 11 FAC 8 Others 12
Burnley (£70,000 on 18/10/90) FL 170/8 FLC 10/1 FAC 17/1 Others 21/1

PENNEY David Mark
Born: Wakefield, 17 August 1964
Height: 5'10" Weight: 12.0
Club Honours: WC '91

David signed a contract with Swansea in the 1994 close season, following his transfer from Oxford, having spent the last month of 1993-94 at the Vetch Field on loan. An experienced, determined midfielder, his explosive long-range shooting ability brought a new dimension to the "Swans'" midfield but, unfortunately, he missed the last month of the season with hernia problems, which neccessitated an operation.

Derby Co (£1,500 from Pontefract on 26/9/85) FL 6+13 FLC 2+3/1 FAC 1/1 Others 1+3/1
Oxford U (£175,000 on 23/6/89) FL 76+34/15 FLC 10+1 FAC 2+2/1 Others 3+1
Swansea C (Loaned on 28/3/91) FL 12/3
Swansea C (£20,000 on 24/3/94) FL 40+6/7 FLC 3+1/2 FAC 5/1 Others 8

PENNOCK Adrian Barry
Born: Ipswich, 27 March 1971
Height: 5'11" Weight: 12.1

Adrian spent the majority of 1994-95 in midfield for Bournemouth, but in previous seasons has played both there and at right-back and, on occasions, as a centre-back, looking equally capable in all these positions. Predominantly a right-sided player, he scored some important goals during the campaign.

Norwich C (From trainee on 4/7/89) FL 1
Bournemouth (£30,000 on 14/8/92) FL 114/9 FLC 6 FAC 9/1 Others 5

PENNOCK Anthony (Tony)
Born: Swansea, 10 April 1971
Height: 5'11" Weight: 10.9

Another Hereford newcomer during the 1994 close season, Tony was first choice goalkeeper up until Christmas, when losing his place to Chris McKenzie. Although competent, with all-round ability and good attitude, with the latter showing such good form he was given a free transfer at the end of 1994-95.

Stockport Co (Free from Clydach U on 20/8/90)
Wigan Ath (Loaned on 28/12/90) FL 2 FAC 2
Wigan Ath (Free on 5/6/91) FL 8 FAC 1 Others 2
Hereford U (Free on 25/7/94) FL 13+2 FLC 2 FAC 2 Others 3

PENRICE Gary Kenneth
Born: Bristol, 23 March 1964
Height: 5'7" Weight: 10.0

Involved in the first eight games of last season, Gary scored both QPR goals in the

2-2 home draw with Coventry, until being recalled to the substitutes' bench. Came on against Manchester City and his old club, Aston Villa, and scored late goals in both matches, before minor injuries ruled him out until late February. An excellent finisher with great vision, he is a creator of many chances for his team-mates.

Bristol Rov (Free from Mangotsfield on 6/11/84) FL 186+2/54 FLC 11/3 FAC 11/7 Others 13+2/2
Watford (£500,000 on 14/11/89) FL 41+2/18 FAC 4/1 Others 1/1
Aston Villa (£1,000,000 on 8/3/91) FL 14+6/1
Queens Park R (£625,000 on 29/10/91) F/PL 55+24/20 FLC 5+2/2 FAC 2+2/1 Others 1

Gary Penrice   Neal Simpson
(Empics Sports Photo Agency)

PEPPER Colin **Nigel**
Born: Rotherham, 25 April 1968
Height: 5'10" Weight: 11.6

A hard-tackling and hard-working York midfield player, Nigel showed consistently fine form in 1994-95, until missing the closing weeks of the season through injury.

Rotherham U (From apprentice on 26/4/86) FL 35+10/1 FLC 1/1 FAC 1+1 Others 3+3
York C (Free on 18/7/90) FL 158+8/19 FLC 8+1/1 FAC 8/1 Others 11+1

PERIFIMOU Christopher (Chris) James
Born: Enfield, 27 November 1975
Height: 5'8" Weight: 12.2

Yet to turn pro and still an Orient YTS, he found the going tough on his first team debut away to Cardiff last season and was substituted. However, Barry Hearn's policy of developing local youngsters will ensure that he gets further opportunities to impress.

Leyton Orient (Trainee) FL 3+1

PERKINS Christopher (Chris) Peter
Born: Nottingham, 9 January 1974
Height: 5'11" Weight: 10.9

Chris filled in for a number of defensive and

midfield positions at Chesterfield last season, usually on the left, but has yet to stamp out one as his own. A good reader of the game, with a well-timed tackle, his development holds great promise for the future.

Mansfield T (From trainee on 19/11/92) FL 3+5 Others 0+1
Chesterfield (Free on 15/7/94) FL 17+1 FLC 1/1 FAC 2 Others 3+2

PERKINS Declan Oliver
Born: Ilford, 17 October 1975
Height: 5'11" Weight: 12.4
International Honours: Ei: U21-3

Declan came through the Southend junior ranks to make his first-team debut during the 1994-95 season. A strong winger, with good close control, he looks like having a long future ahead of him in the game and has already won international honours for the Republic of Ireland U21 side. Brother of the actress, Louise Lombard.

Southend U (From trainee on 27/5/94) FL 1+5

PERRETT Darren John
Born: Cardiff, 29 December 1969
Height: 5'8" Weight: 11.6

A regular goalscorer at reserve team level, Darren made regular appearances as a substitute in 1994-95 for Swansea, scoring the quickest ever hat-trick in the club's history in the Welsh Cup game against Rhyl. With injuries affecting his first team appearances last season, at times, he displayed good ball control and exceptional pace on the left-flank.

Swansea C (Free from Cheltenham T on 9/7/93) FL 11+15/1 FLC 2 FAC 1+1 Others 4+1/4

PERRY Christopher (Chris) John
Born: Carshalton, 20 April 1975
Height: 5'8" Weight: 11.1

Came on in leaps and bounds at Wimbledon in 1994-95 to gain acclaim as one of the Premiership's most promising young defenders. Used sparingly in the first half of the season, this tough, young central defender was almost a regular from then on. Reads the game well for a youngster, Chris has plenty of pace and is a good, competitive tackler.

Wimbledon (From trainee on 2/7/91) PL 17+7 FLC 2 FAC 3

PERRY Jason
Born: Newport, 2 April 1970
Height: 5'11" Weight: 10.4
Club Honours: WC '92, '93; Div 3 '93
International Honours: W: 1; B-1; U21-3; Yth

At last began to show Cardiff fans some of the form that won him a Welsh cap, when producing many dominant displays at left-back last season. On numerous occasions it was his commanding presence alone that held the defence together.

Cardiff C (From trainee on 21/8/87) FL 230+2/5 FLC 16 FAC 13+1 Others 20+1

PESCHISOLIDO Paolo (Paul) Pasquale
Born: Scarborough, Canada, 25 May 1971
Height: 5'4" Weight: 10.5
International Honours: Canada

Transferred to Stoke in a swop deal that saw Dave Regis move in the other direction last August, he is a diminutive striker, who uses his pace in the heart of opposing defences. Maintained a good scoring ratio, which underlined his popularity with the Stoke fans, despite having a number of strike partners.

Birmingham C (£25,000 from Toronto Blizzards on 11/11/92) FL 37+6/16 FLC 2/1 FAC 0+1 Others 1+1
Stoke C (£400,000 on 1/8/94) FL 39+1/13 FLC 3/2 FAC 2 Others 3+1

PETERS Mark
Born: St Asaph, 6 July 1972
Height: 6'0" Weight: 11.3
International Honours: W: B-1; U21-3
Sturdy central Mansfield defender. Signed from Peterborough last September, Mark proved to be an excellent header of the ball and a strong tackler, but missed too many matches through suspension. An integral part of the side that reached the Third Division play-offs, he should be a force this coming season.

Manchester C (From trainee on 5/7/90)
Norwich C (Free on 2/9/92)
Peterborough U (Free on 10/8/93) FL 17+2 FLC 2 Others 2
Mansfield T (Free on 30/9/94) FL 25+1/4 FLC 2 FAC 2 Others 4

PETERS Robert (Rob) Anthony
Born: Kensington, 18 May 1971
Height: 5'8" Weight: 11.6
After leaving Brentford last November, Rob joined Carlisle on a non-contract basis and featured in a number of matches in mid-season. A talented ball player, he just failed to find the net on several occasions.

Brentford (From trainee on 6/7/89) FL 16+14/1 FLC 2+3/1 FAC 1 Others 3+3
Carlisle U (Free on 23/11/94) FL 5+3 FAC 0+1 Others 1+2

PETHICK Robert (Robbie) John
Born: Tavistock, 8 September 1970
Height: 5'10" Weight: 11.7
An attacking Portsmouth right-back with good passing ability, Robbie made leaps-and-bounds last season after making his debut during the 1993-94 season. Confident when coming forward, and a good crosser, he formed an effective right-sided partnership with "Preki", which resulted in a number of goals being set up by the pair of them.

Portsmouth (£30,000 from Weymouth on 1/10/93) FL 53+9/1 FLC 5+2 FAC 2 Others 3+1

PETRESCU Daniel (Dan) Vasile
Born: Romania, 22 December 1967
Height: 5'8" Weight: 11.0
International Honours: Romania
Highly skilled player who came to Sheffield Wednesday last season, via Italy, after his great World Cup experience with Romania in the summer. With his country, Dan plays in the right-back area with freedom to attack, but at Wednesday he has appeared in a number of positions without ever being given an extended run in any one of them. The great majority of fans appreciate him though, and would always have him in the side, preferably in midfield, where his skill

on the ball and an eye for a goal could flourish.

Sheffield Wed (£1,250,000 from Genoa on 6/8/94) PL 20+9/3 FLC 2 FAC 0+2

PETTERSON Andrew (Andy) Keith
Born: Freemantle, Australia, 26 September 1969
Height: 6'2" Weight: 14.12
Signed for Charlton in the 1994 close season as goalkeeping cover for Mike Salmon, he missed his chance of an early debut due to a bout of shingles in September, before making his first appearance against Swindon. Failed to establish himself in the side, and was allowed to go on loan to Bradford in December, being recalled a month later. Made a couple of appearances towards the end of the season, but is currently third choice 'keeper at the club.

Luton T (Signed on 30/12/88) FL 16+3 FLC 2 Others 2
Ipswich T (Loaned on 26/3/93) PL 1
Charlton Ath (£85,000 on 15/7/94) FL 8+1 FLC 2
Bradford C (Loaned on 8/12/94) FL 3

PETTINGER Paul Allen
Born: Sheffield, 1 October 1975
Height: 6'1" Weight: 13.4
Club Honours: FAYC '93
International Honours: E: Yth; Sch
Yet to make his debut for Leeds, the former England schools and youth international goalkeeper, known for his good technique and reflex saves, had a spell on loan at Torquay last season. With Ashley Bayes out injured, Paul stepped in to make three appearances before returning to Elland Road.

Leeds U (From trainee on 16/10/92)
Torquay U (Loaned on 23/12/94) FL 3

PEVERELL Nicholas (Nicky) John
Born: Middlesbrough, 28 April 1973
Height: 5'11" Weight: 11.10
Came back into English soccer last season on trial with Hartlepool, having been in Hong Kong, but quickly moved on to York. After impressing with the City reserves, Nicky appeared in the senior side, mainly as a substitute, and showed a great deal of promise, especially in his ability to hold the ball up in attack.

Middlesbrough (From trainee on 3/7/91)
Hartlepool U (Free on 27/11/92) FL 14+21/3 FAC 1+2/1 Others 1+2 (Free to Hong Kong during 1994 close season)
Hartlepool U (Free on 16/12/94) FL 0+1
York C (Free on 3/2/95) FL 2+7/1

PHELAN Michael (Mike) Christopher
Born: Nelson, 24 September 1962
Height: 5'10" Weight: 12.0
Club Honours: Div 3 '82, Div 2 '86; FAC '90; CS '90; ECWC '91 FLC '92; PL '93
International Honours: E: 1; Yth
Competent, hard-working WBA midfielder who had heaps of experience behind him when he moved to The Hawthorns from Manchester United during the summer of 1994. Had a mixed 1994-95 season, suffering from loss of form and injury, although he did produce some enterprising performances from time to time.

Burnley (From apprentice on 29/7/80) FL 166+2/9 FLC 16/2 FAC 16 Others 8/2
Norwich C (£60,000 on 13/7/85) FL 155+1/9 FLC 14 FAC 11/1 Others 13
Manchester U (£750,000 on 1/7/89) F/PL 88+14/2 FLC 14+2 FAC 10/1 Others 15+3
West Bromwich A (Free on 11/7/94) FL 17+3 FLC 2

PHELAN Terence (Terry) Michael
Born: Manchester, 16 March 1967
Height: 5'8" Weight: 10.0
Club Honours: FAYC '88
International Honours: Ei: 26; B-2; U23-1; U21-1; Yth
A very fast Manchester City left-back who loves to run at defenders, Terry had an up-and-down season in 1994-95, suffering injuries and a loss of form as the club struggled to hold onto its Premiership place. Came back in spirited fashion, though, against Ipswich on a sodden pitch, giving a superb performance that stood him out from the rest and continued to excel right through to the end of the campaign. Played for Eire in the abandoned international against England, along with Niall Quinn and Alan Kernaghan.

Leeds U (From apprentice on 3/8/84) FL 12+2 FLC 3 Others 2
Swansea C (Free on 30/7/86) FL 45 FLC 4 FAC 5 Others 3
Wimbledon (£100,000 on 29/7/87) FL 155+4/1 FLC 13+2 FAC 16/2 Others 8
Manchester C (£2,500,000 on 25/8/92) PL 93+1/2 FLC 10 FAC 8/1

PHILLIPS David Owen
Born: Wegburg, Germany, 29 July 1963
Height: 5'10" Weight: 11.2
Club Honours: FAC '87
International Honours: W: 59; U21-4; Yth
The most versatile member of the Nottingham Forest side, throughout his worthy career, David has played in every position except goal. Well known for his diagonal passing, he is comfortable in possession, with two good feet, and remains an excellent striker of the ball. Started last season on the wide right of midfield, until Steve Stone developed, before settling in to the defensive anchor man slot. Scored his only goal in 1994-95 on the last day of the campaign at Wimbledon.

Plymouth Arg (From apprentice on 3/8/81) FL 65+8/15 FLC 2+1 FAC 12+1 Others 4/1
Manchester C (£65,000 on 23/8/84) FL 81/13 FLC 8 FAC 5 Others 5/3
Coventry C (£150,000 on 5/6/86) FL 93+7/8 FLC 8 FAC 9/1 Others 5+1/2
Norwich C (£525,000 on 31/7/89) F/PL 152/18 FLC 12 FAC 14/1 Others 8/1
Nottingham F (Signed on 20/8/93) F/PL 78+3/5 FLC 11 FAC 4 Others 1

PHILLIPS Gary Christopher
Born: St Albans, 20 September 1961
Height: 5'11" Weight: 14.5
Club Honours: GMVC '91
International Honours: E: SP-1
Long serving Barnet goalkeeper who ended his testimonial season in 1994-95 sitting on the bench. Always interesting to watch, Gary could pull out top drawer saves just when required. Rejected a reduced terms

contract, but will stay on at the club as the community officer for the time being.

West Bromwich A (Free from Brighton & Hove A juniors on 27/6/79)
Brentford (£5,000 from Barnet on 7/12/84) FL 143 FLC 8 FAC 5 Others 15
Reading (Signed on 25/8/88) FL 24 FAC 7 Others 3
Hereford U (Loaned on 1/9/89) FL 6
Barnet (£12,500 on 1/12/89) FL 117 FLC 10 FAC 9 Others 7

PHILLIPS James (Jimmy) Neil
Born: Bolton, 8 February 1966
Height: 6'0" Weight: 12.7

The consistent left-back was the only player to appear in every Bolton first class game throughout 1994-95, a season that ultimately saw the club reach the Premiership, via the play-offs. Never spectacular, he does not need to be, but gets forward well to support the attack. His only goal came from a left-footed thunderbolt, during the 5-1 defeat of "Wolves" in February.

Bolton W (From apprentice on 1/8/83) FL 103+5/2 FLC 8 FAC 7 Others 14
Glasgow R (£95,000 on 27/3/87) SL 19+6 SLC 4 Others 4
Oxford U (£110,000 on 26/8/88) FL 79/8 FLC 3 FAC 4 Others 2/1
Middlesbrough (£250,000 on 15/3/90) F/PL 139/6 FLC 16 FAC 10 Others 5/2
Bolton W (£250,000 on 20/7/93) FL 87+1/1 FLC 12 FAC 8 Others 9/2

PHILLIPS Kevin
Born: Hitchin, 25 July 1973
Height: 5'7" Weight: 11.0

Signed from non-League, Baldock, just before last Christmas, Kevin was given an early chance at Watford because of injuries. Proved an instant success, scoring in five of his first six matches. Small and slight, he demonstrated a priceless knack for keeping his head in the area and netting decisive late goals.

Watford (£10,000 from Baldock on 19/12/94) FL 15+1/9

PHILLIPS Marcus Stuart
Born: Trowbridge, 17 October 1973
Height: 5'10" Weight: 11.4

A Swindon midfield player with two good feet and strong shooting ability who can wrong foot defenders to set up an attack, Marcus made just one substitute appearance in the Anglo-Italian Cup last season, prior to being released in March.

Swindon T (From trainee on 1/5/93) FLC 0+1 Others 0+1

PHILLIPS Martin John
Born: Exeter, 13 March 1976
Height: 5'6" Weight: 9.4

Exeter winger with fantastic close control and skill, left-footed "Buster" can turn defenders inside out. Had a host of clubs eyeing his talents, with Southampton having a bid for him rejected last season, after previous manager, Alan Ball, who nurtured him, had said he would become a £10 million player.

Exeter C (From trainee on 4/7/94) FL 25+14/2 FLC 1+1 FAC 1+2 Others 0+5

PHILLIPS Wayne
Born: Bangor, 15 December 1970
Height: 5'10" Weight: 11.2
International Honours: W: B-1

A central midfielder who often plays just in front of the Wrexham defence, where he can also perform, Wayne is a determined, battling player who likes to get forward. Suffered an ankle injury early on in 1994-95, which restricted his first team appearances for the side thereafter.

Wrexham (From trainee on 23/8/89) FL 101+16/5 FLC 12 FAC 6+2/1 Others 13+5/1

PHILLISKIRK Anthony (Tony)
Born: Sunderland, 10 February 1965
Height: 6'1" Weight: 11.2
International Honours: E: Sch

Tony was not fully fit until the tail-end of last season, when he returned to Burnley's first team and made two of the goals in the home game against Derby. Always a maker as well as a taker, he needs a run in the side to re-establish his claim to be the scorer Burnley badly needed in 1994-95.

Sheffield U (From juniors on 16/8/83) FL 62+18/20 FLC 4+1/1 FAC 5/1 Others 3+2
Rotherham U (Loaned on 16/10/86) FL 6/1
Oldham Ath (£25,000 on 13/7/88) FL 3+7/1 FLC 0+2/1 Others 1
Preston NE (Signed on 10/2/89) FL 13+1/6
Bolton W (£50,000 on 22/6/89) FL 139+2/52 FLC 18/12 FAC 10/7 Others 13/5
Peterborough U (£85,000 on 17/10/92) FL 37+6/15 FLC 2/1 FAC 4/1 Others 2/1
Burnley (£80,000 on 21/1/94) FL 26+6/8 FLC 1+1

PHILPOTT Lee
Born: Barnet, 21 February 1970
Height: 5'9" Weight: 11.8
Club Honours: Div 3 '91

Left-sided midfielder with a reputation as a good crosser, Lee turned in some fine performances during the early months of last season, when he enjoyed his best spell since moving to Leicester. Occasionally used as an emergency left-back, he was less regular after Mark McGhee arrived.

Peterborough U (From trainee on 17/7/86) FL 1+3 FAC 0+1 Others 0+2
Cambridge U (Free on 31/5/89) FL 118+16/17 FLC 10/1 FAC 19/3 Others 15/2
Leicester C (£350,000 on 24/11/92) F/PL 56+13/3 FLC 2+1 FAC 4+2 Others 4+1

PICK Gary Mark
Born: Leicester, 9 July 1971
Height: 5'8" Weight: 11.8

Signed on a free from Stoke in the summer of 1994, Gary failed to get an extended run at Hereford last season. However, as a strong, hard-tackling ball-winner, he may get an extended run in 1995-96.

Stoke C (Signed from Leicester U on 19/8/92)
Hereford U (Free on 28/6/94) FL 23+6/2 FLC 3+1 FAC 1+1/1 Others 3

PICKERING Albert (Ally) Gary
Born: Manchester, 22 June 1967
Height: 5'11" Weight: 11.1

A solid Coventry right-back who is better going forward than defending, Ally won a place when Brian Borrows was injured early last season and performed well, creating a lot of chances with good crosses. He was

retained until John Salako got the better of him in the 1-4 Palace drubbing, but came back at Christmas when Borrows moved to centre-back, giving some solid performances.

Rotherham U (£18,500 from Buxton on 2/2/90) FL 87+1/2 FLC 6 FAC 9 Others 7
Coventry C (£80,000 on 27/10/93) PL 28+7 FLC 3 FAC 2

Ally Pickering   Paul Marriott
(Empics Sports Photo Agency)

PIKE Christopher (Chris)
Born: Cardiff, 19 October 1961
Height: 6'2" Weight: 12.7
Club Honours: WC '92, '93; Div 3 '93

The bargain of the season, so far as Gillingham were concerned, when he moved from Hereford in September 1994. Strong in the air and, for such a big fellow, mobile on the ground, he suffered towards the end of the campaign with injuries which resulted in him playing only one game per week. In all competitions, Chris notched up nearly 20 goals, and in April 1995, scored the 100th League goal of his career.

Fulham (Free from Barry T on 14/3/85) FL 32+10/4 FLC 3+1/1 Others 3/1
Cardiff C (Loaned on 12/12/86) FL 6/2 FAC 3/1
Cardiff C (Free on 1/8/89) FL 134+14/65 FLC 6+2/2 FAC 5+2/2 Others 9/2
Hereford U (Free on 9/7/93) FL 36+2/18 FLC 3+1 FAC 2/1 Others 2+1
Gillingham (£15,000 on 30/9/94) FL 26+1/13 FAC 4/4 Others 2/1

PIKE Martin Russell
Born: South Shields, 21 October 1964
Height: 5'10" Weight: 11.7

Martin joined Rotherham from Fulham, prior to the start of 1994-95, but his debut was delayed when he picked up an injury in pre-season training. After getting over that, he suffered an achilles problem which restricted his appearances to just seven.

West Bromwich A (From apprentice on 26/10/82)
Peterborough U (Free on 18/8/83) FL 119+7/8 FLC 8 FAC 10 Others 5/1

Sheffield U (£20,000 on 22/8/86) FL 127+2/5 FLC 10 FAC 12 Others 5+1
Tranmere Rov (Loaned on 10/11/89) FL 2 FLC 2 FAC 1
Bolton W (Loaned on 14/12/89) FL 5/1 Others 1
Fulham (£65,000 on 8/2/90) FL 187+3/14 FLC 10 FAC 5/1 Others 12/2
Rotherham U (Free on 3/8/94) FL 7

PILKINGTON Kevin William
Born: Hitchin, 8 March 1974
Height: 6'0" Weight: 12.6
Club Honours: FAYC '92
International Honours: E: Sch

Competent young Manchester United goalkeeper who comes out for crosses, stands up well, and also possesses an excellent kick. Made his PL debut when coming on for Peter Schmeichel against Crystal Palace last November and showed much presence when making a series of fine saves. Looks to have a bright future.
Manchester U (From trainee on 6/7/92) PL 0+1

PITCHER Darren Edward
Born: Stepney, 12 October 1969
Height: 5'9" Weight: 12.2
International Honours: E: Sch

A surprise Crystal Palace signing from Charlton during the 1994 close season, Darren came in a deal that saw David Whyte and Paul Mortimer going in the opposite direction. Made his debut in the first game of 1994-95 and, following a period in the reserves, came back into the midfield where he remained for the rest of the campaign. Was an ever-present in the club's run to the FA Cup semi-finals.
Charlton Ath (From trainee on 12/1/88) FL 170+3/8 FLC 11 FAC 12/3 Others 8
Crystal Palace (£700,000 on 5/7/94) PL 21+4 FLC 3/1 FAC 8/1

PITCHER Geoffrey (Geoff)
Born: Sutton, 15 August 1975
Height: 5'7" Weight: 11.2

A junior partner in the deal that took Jamie Moralee to Watford from Millwall during the summer of 1994, he was given a first team chance at the end of last season and scored on his debut against his old team. Aggressive and determined, Geoff plays on the right side of midfield.
Millwall (From trainee on 18/3/93)
Watford (Signed on 13/7/94) FL 2+2/1

PITMAN Jamie Roy
Born: Trowbridge, 6 January 1976
Height: 5'6" Weight: 10.8

Blond Swindon midfielder and former YTS, Jamie followed in Wayne O'Sullivan's footsteps to break into Town's first team. Made his FL bow against Portsmouth last April and impressed enough to be given two further opportunities to stake a claim for a regular place in 1995-96.
Swindon T (From trainee on 8/7/94) FL 2+1

PLATNAUER Nicholas (Nicky) Robert
Born: Leicester, 10 June 1961
Height: 5'11" Weight: 12.10
Club Honours: WC '88

A much travelled left-back who joined Lincoln from Mansfield early last season, he lost his first team place in October. Since

then, however, he was involved in coaching City's reserves and assisting manager, Sam Ellis, prior to being freed during the summer.
Bristol Rov (Free from Bedford T on 4/8/82) FL 21+3/7 FLC 1/1 FAC 0+1
Coventry C (£50,000 on 26/8/83) FL 38+6/6 FLC 5 FAC 4
Birmingham C (£60,000 on 14/12/84) FL 23+5/2 FLC 3 FAC 5
Reading (Loaned on 30/1/86) FL 7 Others 1
Cardiff C (Free on 26/9/86) FL 110+5/6 FLC 6/2 FAC 9 Others 12
Notts Co (£50,000 on 1/8/89) FL 57/1 FLC 6 FAC 1 Others 10
Port Vale (Loaned on 18/1/91) FL 14 FAC 1
Leicester C (Free on 19/7/91) FL 32+3 FLC 4+1 Others 2
Scunthorpe U (Free on 8/3/93) FL 14/2
Mansfield T (Free on 12/8/93) FL 25 FLC 2 FAC 1 Others 4
Lincoln C (Free on 1/2/94) FL 26 FLC 4

POINTON Neil Geoffrey
Born: Warsop, 28 November 1964
Height: 5'10" Weight: 11.0
Club Honours: Div 1 '87; CS '87

A very experienced Oldham left-back who likes to push forward at every opportunity to deliver telling crosses, Neil can also score valuable goals. Sound in defence, he put in consistent performances throughout last season, only missing games when injured. When he does get injured, however, he makes a proper job of it; a 16 inch gash from the game against Port Vale was quite the worst the physio had ever seen. Possesses one of the longest throw-ins in the game.
Scunthorpe U (From apprentice on 10/8/82) FL 159/6 FLC 9/1 FAC 13 Others 4
Everton (£75,000 on 8/11/85) FL 95+7/5 FLC 6+2 FAC 16+2 Others 9+3
Manchester C (£600,000 on 17/7/90) FL 74/2 FLC 8 FAC 4 Others 4
Oldham Ath (£600,000 on 10/7/92) P/FL 89+2/3 FLC 5 FAC 7+1/2

POLLITT Michael Francis
Born: Farnworth, 24 September 1972
Height: 6'3" Weight: 14.11

Big framed Darlington goalkeeper who was signed from Lincoln just before the start of the last campaign, he missed only two games all season, while managing to keep 15 clean sheets with his aerial dominance and reflex shot-stopping ability.
Manchester U (From trainee on 1/7/90)
Bury (Free on 10/7/91)
Lincoln C (Free on 1/12/92) FL 57 FLC 5 FAC 2 Others 4
Darlington (Free on 11/8/94) FL 40 FLC 2 FAC 2 Others 3

POLLOCK Jamie
Born: Stockton, 16 February 1974
Height: 5'11" Weight: 14.0
Club Honours: Div 1 '95
International Honours: E: U21-1; Yth

Brilliant young Middlesbrough prospect, who is an aggressive and determined midfielder, Jamie was born within a stones throw of Ayresome Park in nearby Stockton on Tees. Proud to have been able to make such a valuable contribution to "Boro's" promotional victory year in 1994-95, his good form saw him capped by England at U21 level and elected by his fellow

professionals to the PFA Award winning First Division team.
Middlesbrough (From trainee on 18/12/91) F/PL 113+11/17 FLC 11+2/1 FAC 10+1 Others 4+1

POLSTON John David
Born: Walthamstow, 10 June 1968
Height: 5'11" Weight: 11.3
International Honours: E: Yth

A centre-back, who is strong in the air and on the ground, he formed an excellent partnership last season with Jon Newsome at the heart of the Norwich defence. Nearly always overworked in a dire season for the club, his ball-winning ability firmly kept "Spurs'" Jurgen Klinsman under control, while he was absent from the club's two biggest defeats, 5-0 at Everton and 5-1 at Arsenal. That tells you much about a player, who, despite needing a hernia operation, continued right up until the final game.
Tottenham H (From apprentice on 16/7/85) FL 17+7/1 FLC 3+1
Norwich C (£250,000 on 24/7/90) F/PL 139+3/6 FLC 11+1/2 FAC 15+1 Others 9/1

POOLE Gary John
Born: Stratford, 11 September 1967
Height: 6'0" Weight: 11.0
Club Honours: GMVC '91; Div 2 '95; AMC '95

After joining Birmingham with Jon Hunt last September, in the deal that took Dave Regis and Roger Willis to Southend, Gary appeared mainly at right-back, although he can play in midfield if required. Strong in the tackle and devastating on the overlap, it was seldom that an opposing winger got the better of him, and he was one of four Birmingham players who were elected for the divisional award at the PFA annual dinner. In a very successful season for the club, he appeared at Wembley in the Auto Windscreen victory and won a Second Division Championship medal as City gained promotion.
Tottenham H (From juniors on 15/7/85)
Cambridge U (Free on 14/8/87) FL 42+1 FLC 2 FAC 2 Others 3
Barnet (£3,000 on 1/3/89) FL 39+1/2 FLC 2 FAC 7 Others 26/1
Plymouth Arg (Free on 5/6/92) FL 39/5 FLC 6/2 FAC 2 Others 0+1
Southend U (£350,000 on 9/7/93) FL 43+1/2 FLC 2 FAC 1 Others 6
Birmingham C (£50,000 on 16/9/94) FL 34/1 FAC 5 Others 7/1

POOLE Kevin
Born: Bromsgrove, 21 July 1963
Height: 5'10" Weight: 11.11

Had an outstanding season between the sticks and was in no way to blame for Leicester's poor showing in 1994-95. Enhanced his reputation as a shot-stopper, showing good judgement on crosses, and frequently turned in star performances for the team, as at Tottenham. Deservedly voted "Player of the Season" by the supporters.
Aston Villa (From apprentice on 26/6/81) FL 28 FLC 2 FAC 1 Others 1
Northampton T (Loaned on 8/11/84) FL 3
Middlesbrough (Signed on 27/8/87) FL 34 FLC 4 FAC 2 Others 2
Hartlepool U (Loaned on 27/3/91) FL 12
Leicester C (£40,000 on 30/7/91) F/PL 111 FLC 6 FAC 6 Others 9

Kevin Poole   Paul Marriott
(Empics Sports Photo Agency)

POOM Mart
Born: Tallin, Estonia, 3 February 1972
Height: 6'4" Weight: 13.6
International Honours: Estonia

A good all-round goalkeeper who, despite his size, is extremely agile and a good shot-stopper, Mart signed for Portsmouth in August 1994, but due to an injury and also the consistency of veteran, Alan Knight, he has rarely had the opportunity to show himself. Despite this, he has remained Estonia's number one and played against the likes of Italy and Croatia during the season.
Portsmouth (£200,000 from FC Will on 4/8/94) FLC 2

POPESCU Gica Gheorghe
Born: Calafat, Romania, 9 October 1967
Height: 6'2" Weight: 12.7
International Honours: Romania

Having joined Tottenham last September, shortly after fellow Romanian international, Illie Dumitrescu, Gica seemed a little in awe of the English game in his first two matches, but soon overcame this with a goal in his third appearance of the season in the 2-1 victory over Wimbledon. He continually added flair to the midfield, demonstrating a great individual skill and the ability to instigate forward movements by attacking the opponents goal, while his awareness of the game and those around him helped provide a vital link between the back four and the attack. Making his London "derby" debut against Arsenal in January, he made a beautiful surging run through the centre of the field to score the goal that was to secure a Tottenham victory, having, ironically, passed a late fitness test after suffering from a virus! He ably demonstrated with his goal against Newcastle last December, that he gave some of his best performances when there was a need to rise to the occasion. Signed by Barcelona on 13 May for £2.8 million.
Tottenham H (£2,900,000 from PSV Eindhoven on 16/9/94) PL 23/3 FLC 2 FAC 3

PORIC Adem
Born: London, 22 April 1973
Height: 5'9" Weight: 11.13

Stocky, compact Sheffield Wednesday midfield player who, although born in England, was signed from an Australian club. Adem has made himself a valuable member of the "Owls'" reserve side as he continues to look for an opportunity to break-through into the first team, only making sparse senior appearances in 1994-95.
Sheffield Wed (£60,000 from St George's Budapest on 1/10/93) PL 3+7 FLC 0+2

PORTER Andrew (Andy) Michael
Born: Holmes Chapel, 17 September 1968
Height: 5'9" Weight: 11.2
Club Honours: AMC '93

Hard-tackling Port Vale midfield player who was one of the mainstays of the team throughout the season. Only missed two games, both through suspension, and the one time he was relegated to the subs' bench he was called upon after just six minutes! Achieved a personal best in the goalscoring stakes with three.
Port Vale (From trainee on 29/6/87) FL 197+30/7 FLC 14 FAC 11+4/2 Others 19+1

Andy Porter   Paul Marriott
(Empics Sports Photo Agency)

PORTER Gary Michael
Born: Sunderland, 6 March 1966
Height: 5'6" Weight: 10.6
Club Honours: FAYC '82
International Honours: E: U21-12; Yth

Classy Watford midfield player with a wonderfully cultured left-foot, and a dead-ball specialist, he played competently at left-back in 1994-95, missing just five matches all season.

Watford (From apprentice on 6/3/84) FL 328+37/46 FLC 26+2/4 FAC 25+2/3 Others 12+1/2

POTTER Graham Stephen
Born: Solihull, 20 May 1975
Height: 5'11" Weight: 11.0
International Honours: E: Yth

Still to emerge into the Stoke first team as a regular, following his move from Birmingham in December 1993, he is a stylish and composed left-back who can be seen to advantage when breaking forward down the left when the team plays a five man defence. Clearly a player with potential to fulfill the high expectations, his first team chances in 1994-95 were limited due to the consistency of Lee Sandford and the adaptability of John Butler.
Birmingham C (From trainee on 1/7/92) FL 23+2/2 FAC 1 Others 6
Wycombe W (Loaned on 17/9/93) FL 2+1 FLC 1 Others 1
Stoke C (£75,000 on 20/12/93) FL 3+1 FLC 0+1 FAC 2

Steve Potts   Barry Coombs
(Empics Sports Photo Agency)

POTTS Steven (Steve) John
Born: Hartford, USA, 7 May 1967
Height: 5'8" Weight: 10.5
International Honours: E: Yth

West Ham captain and a key centre-back, Steve is the epitome of consistency. Small for a defender, he makes up for that in his interceptions and pace, and was outstanding in almost every game throughout last season. It was therefore no surprise when he was named as "Hammer of the Year", an honour he richly deserved. Also ever-present in 1994-95.
West Ham U (From apprentice on 11/5/84) F/PL 268+10/1 FLC 27+7 FAC 31 Others 14+1

POUNDER Anthony (Tony) Mark
Born: Yeovil, 11 March 1966
Height: 5'9" Weight: 11.4

Signed from Weymouth last September,

Tony proved he could play on either left or right-wing for Hereford. Very pacy, with good ball skills, he loves to take full-backs on and, as a determined challenger, is always prepared to help the defence out. Surprisingly given a free transfer at the end of the season.

Bristol Rov (Signed from Weymouth on 24/7/90) FL 102+11/10 FLC 4 FAC 3+1 Others 5/2 (Free to Weymouth during 1994 close season)
Hereford U (Free on 2/9/94) FL 23+5/2 FLC 1 FAC 1+1 Others 1+1

POVEY Neil Andrew
Born: Birmingham, 26 June 1977
Height: 5'8" Weight: 10.0
A second year YTS, Neil is the cream of the crop of young Torquay players. Immediately looked at home in the first team last season, with good passing and movement off the ball. Due to be given a full contract.

Torquay U (Trainee) FL 5+3

POWELL Christopher (Chris) George Robin
Born: Lambeth, 8 September 1969
Height: 5'8" Weight: 10.13
Southend club captain, Chris proved himself to be one of the best left-backs outside the Premiership with his cultured performances throughout last season. Comfortable on either foot, his unflappability under pressure resulted in many enquiries from top clubs. What really gives him the time and space to play in the manner he does is his exceptional reading of the game and positional sense, while his excellent disciplinary record makes him the ideal captain.

Crystal Palace (From trainee on 24/12/87) FL 2+1 FLC 0+1 Others 0+1
Aldershot (Loaned on 11/1/90) FL 11
Southend U (Free on 30/8/90) FL 219+2/3 FLC 11 FAC 7 Others 17

POWELL Darryl Anthony
Born: Lambeth, 15 November 1971
Height: 6'0" Weight: 12.3
Gangling forward/midfielder who is a good left-footed passer and strong in the tackle, Darryl produced his best season for Portsmouth so far in terms of consistency and appearances, and showed enormous improvement in the mature way he played. Was unfortunate to receive a four match ban in February for picking up too many disciplinary points, but gave total commitment throughout the season.

Portsmouth (From trainee on 22/12/88) FL 83+49/16 FLC 11+3/3 FAC 10 Others 9+5/4

POWER Lee Michael
Born: Lewisham, 30 June 1972
Height: 5'11" Weight: 11.2
International Honours: Ei: B-1; U21-11; Yth
Signed by Bradford in 1993-94, Lee played just two full games before being struck down with a mysterious illness. Returned to the side last October, but has yet to get back to his full playing potential. Spent a month on loan at Millwall without making an appearance, due to injury.

Norwich C (From trainee on 6/7/90) F/PL 28+16/10 FLC 1 FAC 0+1 Others 0+2
Charlton Ath (Loaned on 4/12/92) FL 5
Sunderland (Loaned on 13/8/93) FL 1+2 FLC 2/1

Portsmouth (Loaned on 15/10/93) FL 1+1 Others 1
Bradford C (£200,000 on 8/3/94) FL 14+16/5 FLC 0+2 FAC 0+2/1 Others 1+1/1

PREECE Andrew (Andy) Paul
Born: Evesham, 27 March 1967
Height: 6'1" Weight: 12.0
With Chris Armstrong at Wrexham, where the pair formed a deadly strike partnership, Andy arrived at Crystal Palace, via Stockport, during the 1994 close season. Although signed as reserve cover, he made his debut in the opening match of 1994-95 and found himself the club's top-scorer, come November. Looked a more than useful player, but eventually lost his place following a barren spell for Palace that took in four games without a goal. Stop Press: Signed for Blackpool during the summer in a deal worth £200,000.

Northampton T (From Evesham on 31/8/88) FL 0+1 FLC 0+1 Others 0+1 (Free to Worcester C during 1989 close season)
Wrexham (Free on 22/3/90) FL 44+7/7 FLC 5+1/1 FAC 1/2 Others 5/1
Stockport Co (£10,000 on 18/12/91) FL 89+8/42 FLC 2+1 FAC 7/3 Others 12+2/9
Crystal Palace (£350,000 on 23/6/94) PL 17+3/4 FLC 4+2/1 FAC 2+3

PREECE David William
Born: Bridgnorth, 28 May, 1963
Height: 5'6" Weight: 11.6
Club Honours: FLC '88
International Honours: E: B-3
Diminutive player, now in 11th year with Luton, he is a lively midfielder who is always in the thick of the action and regularly wins "Man of the Match" awards. Mainly operating down the left-side, David acts as an extra attacker, carrying the ball to the forwards and joining in the assault. A tenacious ball-winner, with the ability to dribble and an excellent passer, he also scores occasional goals.

Walsall (From apprentice on 22/7/80) FL 107+4/5 FLC 18/5 FAC 6/1 Others 1
Luton T (£150,000 on 6/12/84) FL 328+8/21 FLC 23/3 FAC 27/2 Others 8+1/1

PREECE Roger
Born: Much Wenlock, 9 June 1969
Height: 5'8" Weight: 10.11
Terrier-like Chester player, used mainly in an attacking midfield role last season, Roger is a good passer of the ball with tremendous enthusiasm for the game. Also, a crowd pleaser who never knows when to give up.

Wrexham (Free from Coventry C juniors on 15/8/86) FL 89+21/12 FLC 2+1 FAC 5 Others 8+1/1
Chester C (Free on 14/8/90) FL 164+5/4 FLC 10 FAC 8/1 Others 11

PREEDY Philip (Phil)
Born: Hereford, 20 November 1975
Height: 5'10" Weight: 10.8
Left-sided Hereford utility player, who filled in at full-back or in midfield up until last Christmas, but has not figured since. Skilful and pacy, with good control, he will come again.

Hereford U (From trainee on 13/7/94) FL 24+5/1 FLC 4 FAC 2 Others 1/1

PRESSLEY Steven
Born: Elgin, 11 October 1973
Height: 6'0" Weight: 11.0
International Honours: S: U21-20
A highly rated young Coventry defender, who has been described as "the new Richard Gough", Steven was signed as a replacement for Phil Babb from Glasgow Rangers last October. Suspension cost him a place when Ron Atkinson took over, but he came back at Easter and again began to look an excellent prospect. Captain of the Scottish U21 side and an excellent prospect for the future, his strong points are his speed and aerial ability.

Glasgow R (Free from Inverkeithing BC on 2/8/90) SL 25+7/1 SLC 3 SC 1+1 Others 1+1
Coventry C (£630,000 on 19/10/94) PL 18+1/1 FAC 3

PRESSMAN Kevin Paul
Born: Fareham, 6 November 1967
Height: 6'1" Weight: 14.2
International Honours: E: B-3; U21-1; Yth; Sch
Sheffield Wednesday goalkeeper with good reflexes and a great left-foot clearance, vital with the new back-pass rule, he had a rather up-and-down season in 1994-95. Started off as England's third choice 'keeper and ended it losing not only his international ranking, but also his club place to Chris Woods. Despite this, Kevin played well for most of the time, although having his confidence jolted following two sendings off at Gillingham and Blackburn. However, he showed the gritty side to his character when scoring in the penalty shoot-out at "Wolves".

Sheffield Wed (From apprentice on 7/11/85) F/PL 128 FLC 21 FAC 7 Others 4
Stoke C (Loaned on 10/3/92) FL 4 Others 2

PRICE Ryan
Born: Coven, 13 March 1970
Height: 6'4" Weight: 14.0
Club Honours: AMC '95
International Honours: E: SP-1
Goalkeeper. Joined Birmingham from Stafford immediately prior to the start of 1994-95 as understudy to Ian Bennett, having long been recognised as one of the best young 'keepers outside the League. Although he only made one appearance in the AWS, he sat on the bench for all other first team games and actually won a medal as an unused sub when City defeated Carlisle at Wembley in the Auto Windscreen Shield.

Birmingham C (£20,000 from Stafford R on 9/8/94) Others 1

PRIEST Christopher (Chris)
Born: Leigh, 18 October 1973
Height: 5'10" Weight: 10.10
Signed from Everton during last season after a spell on loan, Chris is a midfielder with good ball skills, who looks to have a good future in the game. Made his League debut for Chester against Brighton in September.

Everton (From trainee on 1/6/92)
Chester C (Loaned on 9/9/94) FL 11/1 Others 2
Chester C (Free on 11/1/94) FL 11+2

PRIMUS Linvoy Stephen
Born: Forest Gate, 14 September 1973
Height: 6'0" Weight: 14.0
A Barnet free transfer signing from Charlton during the summer of 1994, Linvoy eventually proved to be a classy centre-half with good pace and tackling ability. Took a while to settle at Underhill before becoming one of last season's real successes, his confident and assured play was often the difference between winning and losing.
Charlton Ath (From trainee on 14/8/92) FL 4 FLC 0+1 Others 0+1
Barnet (Free on 18/7/94) FL 39 FLC 3+1 FAC 2 Others 2

PRIOR Spencer Justin
Born: Southend, 22 April 1971
Height: 6'3" Weight: 12.10
Norwich central defender who is powerful, good in the air, and has great mobility. A manager's dream, Spencer can always be relied upon in a crisis. With competition for places fierce at City last season, his career was somewhat curtailed by the arrival of Jon Newsome but, during an injury crisis, he came in for six successive matches and performed so admirably that the skipper was hardly missed. As a young player, he will continue to improve.
Southend U (From trainee on 22/5/89) FL 135/3 FLC 9 FAC 5 Others 7/1
Norwich C (£200,000 on 24/6/93) PL 25+5 FLC 4/1 FAC 0+1 Others 2

PRITCHARD David Michael
Born: Wolverhampton, 27 May 1972
Height: 5'8" Weight: 11.4
Strong and very determined Bristol Rovers' right-back. Signed by Rovers towards the end of the 1993-94 season, having earlier been discarded by West Bromwich Albion, he has fully grasped his second opportunity in full-time football and quickly made himself one of the supporters' favourite players with his strong tackling and whole-hearted effort.
Bristol Rov (£15,000 from Telford on 25/2/94) FL 54 FLC 2 FAC 3 Others 6

PROCTOR Mark Gerard
Born: Middlesbrough, 30 January 1961
Height: 5'10" Weight: 11.4
International Honours: E: U21-4; Yth
Released at the end of 1994-95 season, Mark was expected to enter football management during the summer. Dogged by injury for much of the campaign, he nevertheless led Tranmere reserves by example and proved an inspiration to the younger players. Played just one game in the first team.
Middlesbrough (From apprentice on 14/9/78) FL 107+2/12 FLC 6/1 FAC 10/1
Nottingham F (£440,000 on 4/8/81) FL 60+4/5 FLC 10/3 FAC 2/1
Sunderland (£115,000 on 18/3/83) FL 115+2/19 FLC 13/2 FAC 6 Others 2/2
Sheffield Wed (£275,000 on 3/9/87) FL 59/4 FLC 1 FAC 6/1 Others 3
Middlesbrough (£300,000 on 23/3/89) F/PL 101+19/6 FLC 7+2 FAC 4+3 Others 11+1
Tranmere Rov (Free on 15/3/93) FL 31/1 FLC 1 FAC 1 Others 2+1/1

PROKAS Richard
Born: Penrith, 22 January 1976
Height: 5'8" Weight: 11.4
Club Honours: Div 3 '95
Made his League debut for Carlisle at Torquay last August and kept his place almost throughout the campaign. A grafting midfield player, with an unspectacular style, he progressed enormously, and ended his first season as a professional with a Third Division Championship medal and a Wembley appearance.
Carlisle U (From trainee on 18/7/94) FL 37+2/1 FLC 3 FAC 3 Others 7

PRUDHOE Mark
Born: Washington, 8 November 1963
Height: 6'0" Weight: 13.0
Club Honours: GMVC '90; Div 4 '91
A frustrating last season for the ever popular goalie, who has proved to be a good shot-stopper and entertainer, his first team chances at Stoke were limited by the summer signing of Carl Muggleton and a return from injury of Ronnie Sinclair. Had loan spells at Peterborough and Liverpool (non-playing) and, although there was much talk that both would lead to full transfers, nothing materialised.
Sunderland (From apprentice on 11/9/81) FL 7
Hartlepool U (Loaned on 4/11/83) FL 3
Birmingham C (£22,000 on 24/9/84) FL 1 FLC 4
Walsall (£22,000 on 27/2/86) FL 26 FLC 4 FAC 1
Doncaster Rov (Loaned on 11/12/86) FL 5
Grimsby T (Loaned on 26/3/87) FL 8
Hartlepool U (Loaned on 29/8/87) FL 13
Bristol C (Loaned on 6/11/87) FL 3 Others 2
Carlisle U (£10,000 on 11/12/87) FL 34 FLC 2
Darlington (£10,000 on 16/3/89) FL 146 FLC 8 FAC 9 Others 6
Stoke C (£120,000 on 24/6/93) FL 30 FLC 3 FAC 2 Others 3
Peterborough U (Loaned on 30/9/94) FL 6

PUGH David
Born: Liverpool, 19 September 1964
Height: 5'10" Weight: 11.0
Signed from Chester prior to the start of last season, David proved an inspirational Bury captain after being appointed in October, following an injury to Mark Carter, and ended the campaign as the only ever-present. He certainly led by example, creating many chances from his left-wing berth and scoring 18 goals to finish the club's leading scorer. Always to be seen encouraging his team-mates, in scoring one and making the other, he was involved in both semi-final play-off goals that took Bury to Wembley.
Chester C (£35,000 from Runcorn on 21/7/89) FL 168+11/23 FLC 13 FAC 11+1 Others 9
Bury (£22,500 on 3/8/94) FL 42/16 FLC 1 FAC 4 Others 7/2

PUGH Stephen (Steve)
Born: Bangor, 27 November 1973
Height: 5'10" Weight: 11.0
International Honours: W: U21-2; Yth
Another Welsh U21 cap at Wrexham, he has had very limited opportunities due mainly to the Gary Bennett/Steve Watkin strike partnership. Steve is a very pacy player who lays the ball off well and shows improvement in awareness but, unfortunately

injuries seem to be hampering his progress. However, he still looks good for the future.
Wrexham (From trainee on 3/7/92) FL 3+8 FAC 0+2 Others 1

PURSE Darren John
Born: London, 14 February 1977
Height: 6'0" Weight: 12.4
Having made his debut for Orient the previous season, Darren captured a regular place in 1994-95. As an enthusiastic centre-back, he is good in the air and a robust tackler. Started with his first League goal in the opening match and went on to score several more, although he was less successful when asked to play as an emergency striker. Has already attracted interest from leading clubs, and at 18-years-of-age a bright future can be safely predicted. Surprisingly appointed captain towards the end of the season, following Ian Hendon's departure, thus becoming the youngest skipper in the four senior Leagues.
Leyton Orient (From trainee on 22/2/94) FL 39+4/3 FLC 2 FAC 1 Others 7/2

PUTNEY Trevor Anthony
Born: Harold Hill, 9 April 1960
Height: 5'9" Weight: 11.11
Experienced midfielder who joined Colchester on a free fransfer last August, after two loan spells from Leyton Orient, he made a great impact initially, before suffering from illness and injury as the season wore on. Freed at the end of the season, Trevor was due to retire from football to take up a position in the city.
Ipswich T (Signed from Brentwood & Warley on 19/9/80) FL 94+9/8 FLC 15/1 FAC 9
Norwich C (Signed on 13/6/86) FL 76+6/9 FLC 8/1 Others 6
Middlesbrough (£300,000 on 14/8/89) FL 45+3/1 FLC 5 FAC 2 Others 5
Watford (£150,000 on 15/8/91) FL 42+10/2 FLC 8 FAC 2 Others 3
Leyton Orient (£40,000 on 29/7/93) FL 20+2/2 FLC 2 FAC 2 Others 1+1
Colchester U (Free on 26/8/94) FL 28/2

PUTTNAM David Paul
Born: Leicester, 3 February 1967
Height: 5'10" Weight: 11.9
A skilful, tricky left-sided Lincoln midfield player, who spent much of last season out injured, he eventually returned to fitness in the spring, following a series of operations.
Leicester C (£8,000 from Leicester U on 9/2/89) FL 4+3 FLC 0+1
Lincoln C (£35,000 on 21/1/90) FL 156+16/20 FLC 12+1/1 FAC 4 Others 8+1

QUIGLEY Michael (Mike) Anthony
Born: Manchester, 2 October 1970
Height: 5'7" Weight: 9.13
This hard-working Manchester City midfield player, unable to get a game with his home-town club, was loaned out to Wrexham early in 1995. Arriving at the Racecourse when the Second Division side were going through a bad patch, he was soon back at Maine Road, prior to being released at the end of the season.
Manchester C (From trainee on 1/7/89) F/PL 3+9 Others 1
Wrexham (Loaned on 17/2/95) FL 4

QUINN James (Jimmy) Martin
Born: Belfast, 18 November 1959
Height: 6'0" Weight: 11.6
Club Honours: Div 2 '94
International Honours: NI: 44; B-1

A vastly experienced player who became Reading's most capped international in 1994-95 and, who now totals 44 appearances for Northern Ireland, Jimmy was appointed joint player-manager with Mick Gooding last December. Not as regular a first-team player or goalscorer as formerly, he scored the last goal of the domestic season in the play-off final at Wembley and had his contract as manager extended until the end of 1995-96.
Swindon T (£10,000 from Oswestry on 31/12/81) FL 34+15/10 FLC 1+1 FAC 5+3/6 Others 1/2
Blackburn Rov (£32,000 on 15/8/84) FL 58+13/17 FLC 6+1/2 FAC 4/3 Others 2/1
Swindon T (£50,000 on 19/12/86) FL 61+3/30 FLC 6/8 FAC 5 Others 10+1/5
Leicester C (£210,000 on 20/6/88) FL 13+18/6 FLC 2+1 FAC 0+1 Others 0/1
Bradford C (Signed on 17/3/89) FL 35/14 FLC 2/1 Others 1
West Ham U (£320,000 on 30/12/89) FL 34+13/18 FLC 3/1 FAC 4+2/2 Others 1
Bournemouth (£40,000 on 5/8/91) FL 43/19 FLC 4/2 FAC 5/2 Others 2/1
Reading (£55,000 on 27/7/92) FL 119+4/57 FLC 9/7 FAC 7/3 Others 7+3/6

QUINN Stephen James (Jimmy)
Born: Coventry, 15 December 1974
Height: 6'2" Weight: 11.11
International Honours: NI: B-1; U21; Yth

This promising young Blackpool striker who was recognised by Northern Ireland at "B" level in 1993-94, continued to improve. Has the pace to unsettle defences, but with more steadiness in front of goal, his goal-rate could increase dramatically.
Birmingham C (Trainee) FL 1+3
Blackpool (£25,000 on 5/7/93) FL 38+17/10 FLC 2+4/2 FAC 0+2 Others 2
Stockport Co (Loaned on 4/3/94) FL 0+1

QUINN Michael (Mick)
Born: Liverpool, 2 May 1962
Height: 5'9" Weight: 13.0

Mick had a frustrating time in 1994-95. Started the first three Coventry games, but struggled to make an impact, and in the third he was dismissed. He did not play first team football again until the Christmas period when he appeared as substitute three times, again without success. Loaned out to first Plymouth and then Watford, before being released by the club at the end of the season.
Wigan Ath (Free from Derby Co juniors on 27/9/79) FL 56+13/19 FLC 5/1 FAC 3/1
Stockport Co (Free on 6/7/82) FL 62+1/39 FLC 5/2 FAC 2
Oldham Ath (£52,000 on 31/1/84) FL 78+2/34 FLC 4/2 FAC 2/1
Portsmouth (£150,000 on 14/3/86) FL 115+6/54 FLC 7/6 FAC 7/7 Others 4/1
Newcastle U (£680,000 on 18/8/89) FL 110+5/59 FLC 7 FAC 7/4 Others 8+1/8
Coventry C (£250,000 on 19/11/92) FL 57+7/25 FLC 1+1/1 FAC 1+1
Plymouth Arg (Loaned on 16/11/94) FL 3
Watford (Loaned on 16/3/95) FL 4+1

QUINN Niall John
Born: Dublin, 6 October 1966
Height: 6'4" Weight: 12.4

Club Honours: FLC '87
International Honours: Ei: 50; B-2; U23-1; U21-5; Yth

Not only a target man who is one of today's finest headers, but a regular goalscorer himself, Niall made a quiet start to last season after returning to the Manchester City side from injury. Having appeared as a sub on several occasions, he started against Norwich with a goal and, for the first time teamed up with Uwe Rossler, complimenting each other well. Finished the last quarter of the campaign as a "super sub", with the odd game being turned round by the decision to bring him on for the second-half. Still first choice for the Republic of Ireland.
Arsenal (From juniors on 30/11/83) FL 59+8/14 FLC 14+2/4 FAC 8+2/2 Others 0+1
Manchester C (£800,000 on 21/3/90) F/PL 159+12/58 FLC 17+2/6 FAC 9+3/2 Others 3/1

Niall Quinn   Paul Marriott
(Empics Sports Photo Agency)

QUY Andrew John
Born: Harlow, 4 July 1976
Height: 6'0" Weight: 13.1

Beginning last season as Derby's third choice 'keeper, the former "Spurs'" apprentice suddenly found himself, through Martin Taylor's injury, as the first team substitute and then, two games later, coming on for Steve Sutton after his injury. Took his chance well and certainly impressed, keeping his place on the bench for the rest of the campaign.
Derby Co (Free from Tottenham H juniors on 12/7/94) FLC 0+1

RADEBE Lucas
Born: Johannesburg, South Africa, 12 April 1969
Height: 6'0" Weight: 11.8

Having signed for Leeds early last season and joining up with fellow South African, Philomen Masinga, at Elland Road, it was not until mid-November that he played his first full game. Showing some nice touches,

he looked very comfortable on the ball, whether operating in midfield or defence, until suffering torn cruciate ligaments in his knee at Coventry in March, an injury that could keep him out of the game for quite a while.
Leeds U (£250,000 from Kaizer Chiefs on 5/9/94) PL 9+3 FLC 0+1 FAC 1+1

RADOSAVLJEVIC Predrag (Preki)
Born: Belgrade, Yugoslavia, 24 June 1963
Height: 5'11" Weight: 12.10

A classy winger with a strong left-foot, great close control and skill, Preki started 1994-95 badly when he broke his arm during the pre-season. It was not until he had played a handful of games that he finally showed his form for Portsmouth. Left-footed, he plays predominantly on the right-hand side and scores most of his goals when cutting into the area.
Everton (£100,000 from St Louis Storms on 28/8/92) PL 22+24/4 FLC 2+4 FAC 1
Portsmouth (£100,000 on 27/7/94) FL 30+10/5 FLC 2+1 FAC 2/2

RAE Alexander (Alex) Scott
Born: Glasgow, 30 September 1969
Height: 5'9" Weight: 11.8
International Honours: S: B-1; U21-9

From his attacking midfield role, Alex was Millwall's leading goalscorer in League games last season. Right-footed, he hit some spectacular goals and used his skill skills to create shooting opportunities for others. A hard tackler and a very good passer, he was recently capped by Scotland at "B" level and was elected by his fellow professionals to the PFA Award winning First Division side.
Falkirk (Free from Bishopbriggs in 1987) SL 71+12/20 SLC 5/1 SC 2+1
Millwall (£100,000 on 20/8/90) FL 168+13/50 FLC 11+2 FAC 11/4 Others 10/1

RAMAGE Andrew (Andy) William
Born: Barking, 3 October 1974
Height: 5'11" Weight: 12.2

Hard-working Gillingham midfielder, who was mainly on the fringe of a first team place in 1994-95, he scored his first ever League goal in the 3-1 defeat of Northampton last February. Freed during the summer.
Gillingham (Free from Leyton Orient juniors on 18/11/93) FL 8+5/1 Others 0+2

RAMAGE Craig Darren
Born: Derby, 30 March 1970
Height: 5'9" Weight: 11.8
International Honours: E: U21-2

Prodigiously talented Watford midfielder who is at his best when playing just behind the front two. Excellent skills on the ball, good vision and an eye for goal are his main assets.
Derby Co (From trainee on 20/7/88) FL 33+9/4 FLC 6+1/2 FAC 3+1/1 Others 0+3
Wigan Ath (Loaned on 16/2/89) FL 10/2 Others 0+1
Watford (£90,000 on 21/2/94) FL 55+2/9 FLC 4/2 FAC 5

RAMMELL Andrew (Andy) Victor
Born: Nuneaton, 10 February 1967
Height: 5'10" Weight: 11.7

Last season started in fine style for Andy, with a double that saw off Derby on the opening day and established him as Barnsley's first choice striker. A knee injury then restricted his appearances and, with the emergence of Andy Liddell, he returned to fitness to have to wait for his chance. Is still Barnsley's most powerful forward.

Manchester U (£40,000 from Atherstone U on 26/9/89)
Barnsley (£100,000 on 14/9/90) FL 138+27/40 FLC 10+2 FAC 11+1/4 Others 8/1

RAMSEY Paul Christopher
Born: Londonderry, 3 September 1962
Height: 5'11" Weight: 13.0
Club Honours: Div 3 '93; WC '92, '93
International Honours: NI: 14

Having been at Cardiff in the early '90s, this constructive midfielder arrived back at Ninian Park on loan last season, following a disappointing spell in Scottish football. Stayed for three months but, despite some gritty performances, he never really captured his earlier form.

Leicester C (From apprentice on 11/4/80) FL 278+12/13 FLC 19/1 FAC 9+1/1 Others 2+1
Cardiff C (£100,000 on 23/8/91) FL 69/7 FLC 2 FAC 2 Others 7/1
St Johnstone (Signed on 8/10/93) SL 22 SLC 2 SC 4
Cardiff C (Loaned on 4/11/94) FL 11 FAC 1 Others 3

RANDALL Adrian John
Born: Amesbury, 10 November 1968
Height: 5'11" Weight: 11.0
Club Honours: Div 4 '92
International Honours: E: Yth

Ever since his arrival at Burnley, Adrian has promised much. However, it was only during the second half of last season that his adventurous midfield play and threatening forward runs were finally allied to a new awareness of the team's needs. If his recent form is maintained, he is capable of being devastating in the Second Division.

Bournemouth (From apprentice on 2/9/86) FL 3 Others 1+2
Aldershot (Signed on 15/9/88) FL 102+5/12 FLC 3 FAC 11/3 Others 10/2
Burnley (£40,000 on 12/12/91) FL 93+17/8 FLC 4 FAC 7+3 Others 2

RANKINE Simon Mark
Born: Doncaster, 30 September 1969
Height: 5'10" Weight: 11.8

A hard-working player, who prefers midfield yet wore Wolverhampton's number nine shirt for the first away match last season when Steve Bull was injured. Lined up alongside Bull in October, before having a spell at right-back later in the autumn. Remained a utility player until the closing stages of the campaign, when he had a fine spell in his favoured right-sided midfield role.

Doncaster Rov (From trainee on 4/7/88) FL 160+4/20 FLC 8+1/1 FAC 8/2 Others 14/2
Wolverhampton W (£70,000 on 31/1/92) FL 85+15/1 FLC 3+1 FAC 11+1 Others 7+2

RATCLIFFE Kevin
Born: Mancot, 12 November 1960
Height: 6'0" Weight: 13.6
Club Honours: CS '84, '87; FAC '84; Div 1 '85, '87; ECWC '85
International Honours: W: 59; U21-2; Yth; Sch

Arriving at Chester from Derby during the 1994 close season, Kevin is a vastly experienced defender, who is also the club coach. Mainly at centre-back, although making most of his appearances during the season at left-back, he also had a spell as caretaker-manager towards the end of the campaign.

Everton (From apprentice on 18/11/78) FL 356+3/2 FLC 46 FAC 57 Others 31+1
Dundee (Loaned on 1/8/92) SL 4
Cardiff C (Free on 12/8/93) FL 25/1 FLC 1 Others 3
Derby Co (Free on 20/1/94) FL 6
Chester C (Free on 19/7/94) FL 23 FLC 2 FAC 1 Others 2+1

RATCLIFFE Simon
Born: Urmston, 8 February 1967
Height: 5'11" Weight: 11.9
Club Honours: Div 3 '92
International Honours: E: Yth; Sch

A right-footed midfield ball-winner with a good shot, and consistently reliable, Simon had another steady season in Brentford's engine room during 1994-95. Played in both play-off fixtures as the "Bees" failed at the final hurdle, having finished as Second Division runners-up.

Manchester U (From apprentice on 13/2/85)
Norwich C (£40,000 on 16/6/87) FL 6+3 FLC 2
Brentford (£100,000 on 13/1/89) FL 197+17/14 FLC 13+3 FAC 9+1 Others 26+2/2

RATTLE Jonathan (Jon) Paul
Born: Melton, 22 July 1976
Height: 5'9" Weight: 12.6

This versatile, left-footed, former Cambridge youth team defender, having already played seven matches in 1994-95, was allowed to move to Stevenage Borough on loan last February in order to gain first team experience.

Cambridge U (From trainee on 24/5/94) FL 6 FLC 1

RAVEN Paul Duncan
Born: Salisbury, 28 July 1970
Height: 6'1" Weight: 12.1
International Honours: E: Sch

A classy defender, smart and competent on the ground, he is also confident and strong in the air, as well as being always a danger at set-pieces, having scored some fine goals from dead-ball situations. Paul can compete with the fastest attackers around and was in good form for WBA throughout 1994-95, playing with confidence and determination alongside Paul Mardon.

Doncaster Rov (From juniors on 6/6/88) FL 52/4 FLC 2 FAC 5 Others 2
West Bromwich A (£100,000 on 23/3/89) FL 135+4/9 FLC 7 FAC 6/2 Others 9
Doncaster Rov (Loaned on 27/11/91) FL 7

RAVENSCROFT Craig Anthony
Born: London, 20 December 1974
Height: 5'6" Weight: 9.7

Diminutive Brentford front man, or outside-right, with plenty of pace. Had little opportunity to shine in 1994-95, making just two first team appearances.

Brentford (From trainee on 27/7/93) FL 5+3/1 Others 1+2

RAYNOR Paul James
Born: Nottingham, 29 April 1966
Height: 5'8" Weight: 11.12
Club Honours: WC '89, '91

Undoubtedly the most skilful ball-player with either foot on the Preston staff, he plays all along the front line, but generally out wide is his best position. Missed just nine matches in 1994-95.

Nottingham F (From apprentice on 2/4/84) FL 3 FLC 1
Bristol Rov (Loaned on 28/3/85) FL 7+1
Huddersfield T (Free on 15/8/85) FL 38+12/9 FLC 3 FAC 2+1 Others 1
Swansea C (Free on 27/3/87) FL 170+21/27 FLC 11+1/3 FAC 8+1/1 Others 15+1/3
Wrexham (Loaned on 17/10/88) FL 6
Cambridge U (Free on 10/3/92) FL 46+3/2 FLC 5 FAC 1 Others 2+1/1
Preston NE (£36,000 on 23/7/93) FL 70+7/9 FLC 3+1 FAC 7/1 Others 10/2

READ Paul Colin
Born: Harlow, 25 September 1973
Height: 5'11" Weight: 12.6
International Honours: E: Sch

Yet to play a first team match for Arsenal, Paul joined Leyton Orient on loan after scoring 22 goals in 24 games for the "Gunners'" reserve side. Although unable to reproduce that scoring rate, he strengthened "O's" front line and was a major influence in most of their attacking moves.

Arsenal (From trainee on 11/10/91)
Leyton Orient (Loaned on 10/3/95) FL 11 Others 1

READY Karl
Born: Neath, 14 August 1972
Height: 6'1" Weight: 12.2
International Honours: W: B-1; U21-5

Very good defender who can play anywhere across the back four, he was involved in the QPR first team squad for most of last season, either as a substitute or playing in defence as cover for injuries. His performances have beeen good enough to warrant his inclusion in the Welsh national squad.

Queens Park R (From trainee on 13/8/90) F/PL 33+6/2 FLC 0+2

REDDISH Shane
Born: Bolsover, 5 May 1971
Height: 5'10" Weight: 11.10

An aggressive player who was well known to Hartlepool manager, David McCreery, when signed from Carlisle United last November, having had an earlier spell on loan at Chesterfield. A useful addition to the staff, as a midfielder he showed great awareness in going forward, but then, as a defender, he proved to be a great success at right-back.

Mansfield T (From trainee on 25/7/89)
Doncaster Rov (Free on 7/2/90) FL 51+9/3 FLC 1 FAC 2 Others 2
Carlisle U (Free on 7/7/93) FL 35+2/1 FLC 3 FAC 3+1 Others 7+2
Chesterfield (Loaned on 30/9/94) FL 2+1
Hartlepool U (Free on 18/11/94) FL 23

REDFEARN Neil David
Born: Dewsbury, 20 June 1965
Height: 5'10" Weight: 12.4
Club Honours: Div 2 '91

A permanent fixture at Barnsley for the last three seasons in central midfield, Neil continued to score regularly in 1994-95 and his goals, particularly before the New Year, kept the club in the promotion race. His ability to regularly knock them in from 30 yards was an added threat. Injury ended a run of 156 consecutive League appearances and because of the form of the team he had to wait when he returned to fitness. He remains an integral member of the team, however.
Bolton W (Free from Nottingham F juniors on 23/6/82) FL 35/1 FLC 2 FAC 4
Lincoln C (£8,250 on 23/3/84) FL 96+4/13 FLC 4 FAC 3/1 Others 7
Doncaster Rov (Signed on 22/8/86) FL 46/14 FLC 2 FAC 3/1 Others 2
Crystal Palace (£100,000 on 31/7/87) FL 57/10 FLC 6 FAC 1 Others 1
Watford (£150,000 on 21/11/88) FL 22+2/3 FLC 1 FAC 6/3 Others 5/1
Oldham Ath (£150,000 on 12/1/90) FL 56+6/16 FLC 3/1 FAC 7+1/3 Others 1
Barnsley (£150,000 on 5/9/91) FL 164+3/30 FLC 11/3 FAC 10/2 Others 5

Jamie Redknapp　　　Neal Simpson
(Empics Sports Photo Agency)

REDKNAPP Jamie Frank
Born: Barton, 25 June 1973
Height: 5'11" Weight: 11.8
Club Honours: FLC '95
International Honours: E: B-1; U21-13; Yth; Sch

From a footballing family, father, Harry, is the West Ham manager, Jamie was playing with a ball almost before he could walk. A Liverpool midfielder, with all-round ability and a very good passer of the ball, on his day, he is a player of consummate ability, and strong in the tackle. Will continue to get better as he gains experience and has already graduated to the latest full England squad.

Bournemouth (From trainee on 27/6/90) FL 6+7 FLC 3 FAC 3 Others 2
Liverpool (£350,000 on 15/1/91) F/PL 97+14/10 FLC 18/3 FAC 11/1 Others 5+1

REDMOND Stephen (Steve)
Born: Liverpool, 2 November 1967
Height: 5'11" Weight: 12.7
Club Honours: FAYC '86
International Honours: E: U21-14; Yth

Oldham central defender who reads situations well from the back and is a sweet striker of the ball. Having previously vied with Craig Fleming for the responsibility of forming a defensive partnership with Richard Jobson, following the former's injury, Steve made the place his own in 1994-95 and had his best season so far, winning both the club's and supporters' "Player of the Year" awards.
Manchester C (From apprentice on 3/12/84) FL 231+4/7 FLC 24 FAC 17 Others 11
Oldham Ath (£300,000 on 10/7/92) P/FL 102+5/1 FLC 12 FAC 4+2

REECE Andrew (Andy) John
Born: Shrewsbury, 5 September 1962
Height: 5'11" Weight: 12.0
Club Honours: Div 3 '90

Hereford free-kick specialist with a strong and hard, although fair, tackle, Andy enjoys being in the centre of midfield, but can play equally well in defence. A great clubman, when in midfield, he has an eye for goal.
Bristol Rov (Signed from Dudley T on 11/8/87) FL 230+9/17 FLC 11+1 FAC 10+2/3 Others 21/3
Walsall (Loaned on 20/11/92) FL 9/1 Others 3
Walsall (Loaned on 12/8/93) FL 6 FLC 2
Hereford U (Signed on 5/11/93) FL 63+2/5 FLC 3 FAC 4 Others 6/2

REECE Paul John
Born: Nottingham, 16 July 1968
Height: 5'10" Weight: 12.7
Club Honours: AIC '95

Brave, shot-stopping goalkeeper. Joining Notts County from Oxford before last season got underway, Paul impressed as Steve Cherry's number two and always gave a good account of himself when called upon.
Stoke C (From apprentice on 18/7/86) FL 2 (Free to Kettering T during 1987 close season)
Grimsby T (£10,000 on 18/7/88) FL 54 FLC 3 FAC 5 Others 4
Doncaster Rov (Free on 25/9/92) FL 1
Oxford U (Free on 2/10/92) FL 39 FLC 3 FAC 2 Others 1
Notts Co (Free on 2/8/94) FL 11 FLC 1 Others 2+1

REED Adam Maurice
Born: Bishop Auckland, 18 February 1975
Height: 6'0" Weight: 12.0

Tremendous young Darlington prospect who established himself firmly in the heart of the defence last season after coming through the youth ranks. Excellent anticipation and strength in the air are qualities that should see him play at a higher level.
Darlington (From trainee on 16/7/93) FL 45+7/1 FLC 1+1 FAC 1 Others 3

REED Ian Paul
Born: Lichfield, 4 September 1975
Height: 5'9" Weight: 10.10

Young Shrewsbury midfielder, and a first year professional, Ian made his FL debut in the latter stages of last season and is one to follow for the future.
Shrewsbury T (From trainee on 4/7/94) FL 1+3

John Reed　　　Tony Marshall
(Empics Sports Photo Agency)

REED John Paul
Born: Rotherham, 27 August 1972
Height: 5'8" Weight: 10.7

Right-sided Sheffield United midfielder who makes up for his slight frame with skilful dribbling and accurate crossing. After beginning 1994-95 as a fringe player, he made several appearances in the first team until a serious cruciate ligament injury against Charlton, on his recall to the team, curtailed his season.
Sheffield U (From trainee on 3/7/90) FL 11+2/2 FLC 1 Others 1/1
Scarborough (Loaned on 10/1/91) FL 14/6
Scarborough (Loaned on 26/9/91) FL 5+1 FLC 1
Darlington (Loaned on 19/3/93) FL 8+2/2
Mansfield T (Loaned on 23/9/93) FL 12+1/2 FAC 1 Others 3/2

REES Anthony (Tony) Andrew
Born: Merthyr Tydfil, 1 August 1964
Height: 5'9" Weight: 11.13
Club Honours: FAYC '80
International Honours: W: 1; B-1; U21-3; Yth; Sch

Tony was Alan Buckley's initial signing for WBA, but had a disastrous first game for the "Baggies", being injured and substituted after 11 minutes with a hamstring problem against Notts County, just 48 hours after arriving at The Hawthorns from Grimsby last November. He returned to first team action early in the New Year and did well alongside both Bob Taylor and Andy Hunt.
Aston Villa (From apprentice on 1/8/82)
Birmingham C (Free on 1/7/83) FL 75+20/12 FLC 7+1/2 FAC 5/2 Others 1+2
Peterborough U (Loaned on 1/10/85) FL 5/2
Shrewsbury T (Loaned on 1/3/86) FL 1+1
Barnsley (Signed on 1/3/88) FL 27+4/3 FLC 2 FAC 0+1 Others 1
Grimsby T (Signed on 17/8/89) FL 124+17/33 FLC 11+2/1 FAC 8+1 Others 5/3
West Bromwich A (£30,000 on 25/11/94) FL 8+6/2 FAC 2

REES Jason Mark
Born: Aberdare, 22 December 1969
Height: 5'5" Weight: 10.2
International Honours: W: 1; U21-3; B1;
Yth

Battling Portsmouth midfielder, although slightly built, for most of last season he was a bit-part player, but on the arrival of new manager, Terry Fenwick, and various suspensions, he managed to get a look-in. Scored on his full debut against Millwall with a 25 yard shot past Kasey Keller.

Luton T (From trainee on 1/7/88) FL 59+23 FLC 3+2 FAC 2+1 Others 5+1/2
Mansfield T (Loaned on 23/12/93) FL 15/1 Others 1
Portsmouth (Free on 18/7/94) FL 14+5/1 FLC 0+1 FAC 0+1

REEVE James (Jamie) Michael
Born: Weymouth, 26 November 1975
Height: 6'1" Weight: 11.7

A striker who started three games last season for Bournemouth and made four further appearances as a substitute, he was transferred to Hereford in March, where he came off the bench five more times before being freed in the summer.

Bournemouth (From trainee on 14/7/94) FL 2+5 FLC 1+1 Others 0+1
Hereford U (Free on 23/3/95) FL 0+5

REEVES Alan
Born: Birkenhead, 19 November 1967
Height: 6'0" Weight: 12.0

Signed from Rochdale last September as the direct replacement for John Scales, despite having a few disciplinary problems, he adjusted to the Premiership well and was automatic choice for Wimbledon at centre-half for most of the season. A strong tackler with good leadership qualities, Alan can distribute the ball well and is an excellent header. Looks to be a good long-term bet.

Norwich C (Signed from Heswall on 20/9/88)
Gillingham (Loaned on 9/2/89) FL 18
Chester C (£10,000 on 18/8/89) FL 31+9/2 FLC 1+1 FAC 3 Others 3
Rochdale (Free on 2/7/91) FL 119+2/9 FLC 12/1 FAC 6 Others 5
Wimbledon (£300,000 on 6/9/94) PL 31/3 FAC 2

REEVES David Edward
Born: Birkenhead, 19 November 1967
Height: 6'0" Weight: 11.7
Club Honours: Div 3 '95

The only Carlisle ever-present in a total of 58 FL and cup matches played by the club last season, after Simon Davey's departure he became club captain and with his work rate and unselfish style led the team very much from the front. As Carlisle's top-scorer and the first player for over a decade to net over 20 League goals in a season for the club, he was deservedly nominated for the PFA Select side in Division Three for the second season running. Also won a Third Division Championship medal.

Sheffield Wed (Free from Heswall on 6/8/88) FL 8+9/2 FLC 1+1/1 FAC 1+1 Others 0+1
Scunthorpe U (Loaned on 17/12/86) FL 3+1/2
Scunthorpe U (Loaned on 1/10/87) FL 6/4
Burnley (Loaned on 20/11/87) FL 16/8 Others 2/1
Bolton W (£80,000 on 17/8/89) FL 111+23/29 FLC 14+1/1 FAC 8+5/5 Others 9+2/7
Notts Co (£80,000 on 25/3/93) FL 9+4/2 FLC 1+1
Carlisle U (Signed on 1/10/93) FL 76/33 FLC 4/2 FAC 8/3 Others 16/4

David Reeves   Mike Egerton
(Empics Sports Photo Agency)

REGIS Cyrille
Born: French Guyana, 9 February 1958
Height: 6'0" Weight: 13.7
Club Honours: FAC '87
International Honours: E: 5; B3; U21-6

Popular Wycombe forward whose nine goals in the first 17 games of 1994-95 was a major factor in the side's good start to the season. Never really recovered his striking form after a mid-season injury, but was still excellent in the target man role. In the record books as the club's oldest player, and a former PFA "Young Player of the Year" (1979), Cyrille was released during the summer.

West Bromwich A (£5,000 from Hayes on 1/5/77) FL 233+4/82 FLC 27+1/16 FAC 25/10 Others 10/4
Coventry C (£250,000 on 11/10/84) FL 231+7/47 FLC 24/12 FAC 15+1/3 Others 4
Aston Villa (Free on 2/7/91) F/PL 46+6/12 FLC 3+1 FAC 5+2
Wolverhampton W (Free on 3/8/93) FL 8+11/2 FAC 1+2 Others 1
Wycombe W (Free on 12/8/94) FL 30+5/9 FLC 2/1 FAC 1

REGIS David (Dave)
Born: Paddington, 3 March 1964
Height: 6'3" Weight: 13.0
Club Honours: Div 2 '93

A cartilage operation last November put paid to three months of Dave's first season with Southend, having joined the club from Birmingham in September. A brave, diving headed winner in the televised game against Derby made him a very popular player and his running strength and aerial abilities showed him to be the perfect foil for the smaller Andy Thomson. Further injuries unfortunately saw him miss the final part of the campaign.

Notts Co (£25,000 from Barnet on 28/9/90) FL 31+15/15 FLC 0+2 Others 6/2
Plymouth Arg (£200,000 on 7/11/91) FL 28+3/4 FLC 2/3 FAC 1

Bournemouth (Loaned on 13/8/92) FL 6/2
Stoke C (£100,000 on 23/10/92) FL 49+14/15 FLC 2/1 FAC 4+1/2 Others 7+1/2
Birmingham C (£200,00 on 1/8/94) FL 4+2/2 FLC 1
Southend U (Signed on 16/9/94) FL 9/1

REID Nicholas (Nicky) Scott
Born: Urmston, 30 October 1960
Height: 5'10" Weight: 12.5
International Honours: E: U21-6

Hard-running Wycombe central midfielder with good passing ability, whose 1994-95 was marred by injury, allowing him only four starts. A very experienced player, having represented England at U21 level earlier in his career, he was released at the end of the season.

Manchester C (From apprentice on 4/11/78) FL 211+5/2 FLC 20 FAC 17 Others 6
Blackburn Rov (Free on 10/7/87) FL 160+14/9 FLC 13 FAC 6+2 Others 13+1/1
Bristol C (Loaned on 17/9/92) FL 3+1 Others 1
West Bromwich A (Free on 7/11/92) FL 13+7 FAC 2+1 Others 2+1/1
Wycombe W (Free on 4/3/94) FL 6+2 FAC 0+1 Others 5

REID Paul Robert
Born: Oldbury, 19 January 1968
Height: 5'9" Weight: 10.8

A left-winger who tackles well from midfield, and yet another ex-Bradford player at Huddersfield, although signed before last season started, he was a consistent selection throughout 1994-95 and was appointed team captain. Almost ever-present, an injury at the end of the campaign curtailed his appearance in the play-offs.

Leicester C (From apprentice on 9/1/86) FL 140+4/22/1 FLC 13/4 FAC 5+1 Others 6+2
Bradford C (Loaned on 19/3/92) FL 7
Bradford C (£25,000 on 27/7/92) FL 80+2/15 FLC 3/2 FAC 3 Others 5/1
Huddersfield T (Signed on 20/5/94) FL 42/6 FLC 3/1 FAC 2 Others 1

REID Peter
Born: Huyton, 20 June 1956
Height: 5'8" Weight: 10.8
Club Honours: Div 2 '78, Div 1 '85, '87; FAC '84; CS '84, '85, '87; ECWC '85
International Honours: E: 13; U21-6

A former England midfielder and elder brother of Rochdale's Shaun, Peter signed for Bury on a non-contract basis during the 1994 close season, having been freed by Notts County. Unfortunately, a hamstring injury 17 minutes into the opening game ended his campaign, but that was enough to give the former PFA "Player of the Year" (1985) the distinction of being the club's oldest participant at the age of 38. Left to become Sunderland's manager in March, just in time to mastermind their First Division survival.

Bolton W (From apprentice on 1/5/74) FL 223+3/23 FLC 18+1/1 FAC 17/1
Everton (£60,000 on 22/12/82) FL 155+4/8 FLC 23+2/1 FAC 35/3 Others 15/1
Queens Park R (Free on 9/2/89) FL 29/1 FLC 2+1
Manchester C (Free on 15/12/89) FL 90+13/1 FLC 3+1 FAC 7/1
Southampton (Free on 1/10/93) PL 7 FLC 1
Notts Co (Free on 2/2/94) FL 5
Bury (Free on 8/7/94) FL 1 Others 1

REID Shaun
Born: Huyton, 13 October 1965
Height: 5'8" Weight: 11.10
Rochdale's midfield dynamo, his combative style, like that of elder brother, Peter, earned him his club nickname of "The Terminator", as every time he was knocked down he just got up again. Even playing on with two cracked ribs, he was eventually put out of action by a knee-injury.
Rochdale (From apprentice on 20/9/83) FL 126+7/4 FLC 10/2 FAC 5/1 Others 11
Preston NE (Loaned on 12/12/85) FL 3
York C (£32,500 on 23/12/88) FL 104+2/7 FLC 7 FAC 4 Others 5/1
Rochdale (Free on 16/8/92) FL 106+1/10 FLC 8 FAC 5/1 Others 8+1/2

REINELT Robert (Robbie) Squire
Born: Loughton, 11 March 1974
Height: 5'10" Weight: 11.13
A striker who joined Colchester in March 1995 in the exchange deal which took Steve Brown to Gillingham, Robbie had already scored twice for Gillingham at Layer Road last season, once in the League and also against Heybridge Swifts in the FA Cup. Had to wait a while for his full debut, but appearances as a substitute hinted at his ability.
Aldershot (Trainee) FL 3+2
Gillingham (Free from Wivenhoe T on 19/3/93) FL 34+18/5 FLC 3/1 FAC 5+2/2 Others 5
Colchester U (Signed on 22/3/95) FL 2+3

RENNIE David
Born: Edinburgh, 29 August 1964
Height: 6'0" Weight: 12.0
International Honours: S: Yth;
The balding Coventry midfielder, cum defender, had a contrasting season in 1994-95. Roundly booed by City fans during the Villa home defeat in August for a pass which led to Villa's winner, he ended the season as one of the key members of a defence which gave little away. Never at ease in a midfield anchor role, he stepped in for the injured David Busst and Steven Pressley and played consistently well at centre-back. With excellent timing, good in the air and tigerish in the tackle, he was singled out on more than one occasion for praise from Ron Atkinson.
Leicester C (From apprentice on 18/5/82) FL 21/1 FLC 2
Leeds U (£50,000 on 17/1/86) FL 95+6/5 FLC 7 FAC 7/1 Others 4/1
Bristol C (£175,000 on 31/7/89) FL 101+3/8 FLC 8 FAC 9 Others 5
Birmingham C (£120,000 on 20/2/92) FL 32+3/4 FLC 1 Others 1
Coventry C (£100,000 on 11/3/93) PL 71/1 FLC 5 FAC 3+1

RENNIE Paul Andrew
Born: Nantwich, 26 October 1971
Height: 5'10" Weight: 11.7
A steady player either at right-back, or in the centre of defence, and another former Crewe player at Wigan. The scorer of a spectacular goal in the Coca Cola Cup victory over his former team last season, he was given a free transfer at the end of 1994-95.
Crewe Alex (Trainee) FL 1+1
Stoke C (£20,000 on 11/5/90) FL 4 FAC 1 Others 0+1
Wigan Ath (Signed on 9/8/93) FL 36+4/3 FLC 5+1/1 FAC 4 Others 3

RICE Gary James
Born: Zambia, 25 September 1975
Height: 5'9" Weight: 11.6
Left-footed Gary stepped up from the Exeter reserve side on several occasions last season and was found more than able, before being surprisingly freed during the summer.
Exeter C (From trainee on 7/7/94) FL 5+5 FLC 1 Others 1

RICHARDS Dean Ivor
Born: Bradford, 9 June 1974
Height: 6'0" Weight: 12.0
International Honours: E: U21-3
Brilliant Bradford centre-half and captain, "Deano" missed ten games with a foot injury before moving to Wolverhampton on transfer deadline day on loan until the end of the season, with a view to a permanent signing. Having represented the Endsleigh League against the Italian League, prior to being elected by his fellow professionals for the PFA Award winning Second Division side, and then winning three U21 caps for England, his move to "Wolves" was firmed up during the summer, a reported £1,850,000 changing hands.
Bradford C (From trainee on 10/7/92) FL 82+4/4 FLC 7/1 FAC 4/1 Others 3+2
Wolverhampton W (Loaned on 25/3/95) FL 10/2 Others 2

RICHARDSON Barry
Born: Wallsend, 5 August 1969
Height: 6'1" Weight: 12.1
Pony-tailed goalkeeper, "Bar-ee" was an immediate hit with the Preston fans last season, although his confident play was sometimes overshadowed by too much faith in his dribbling skills. Commanding in his area, Barry lost his place to John Vaughan in mid-season through injury.
Sunderland (From trainee on 20/5/88)
Scarborough (Free on 21/3/89)
Scarborough (Free from Seaham Red Star on 3/8/89) FL 30 FAC 1 Others 1
Stockport Co (Free on 16/8/91)
Northampton T (Free on 10/9/91) FL 96 FLC 4 FAC 5 Others 8
Preston NE (£20,000 on 25/7/94) FL 17 FLC 2 FAC 3 Others 1

RICHARDSON Jonathan (Jon) Derek
Born: Nottingham, 29 August 1975
Height: 6'0" Weight: 12.0
Promising young defender who became first choice for Exeter last season, Jon is good in the air and rarely caught for speed. Built up a good understanding with Mark Came and already catching the eye of scouts, he looks good for 1995-96.
Exeter C (From trainee on 7/7/94) FL 42+3/1 FLC 1 FAC 2 Others 3

RICHARDSON Kevin
Born: Newcastle, 4 December 1962
Height: 5'7" Weight: 11.7
Club Honours: FAC '84; CS '84, '86; Div 1 '85, '89; ECWC '85; FLC '94
International Honours: E: 1
Very experienced, much travelled midfielder, who is a great competitor and decisive tackler, Kevin was Ron Atkinson's first acquisition as Coventry manager. He made an instant impression by doing the simple things right, in making space for himself, holding the ball up well and using it to good effect. While not captaining the side, his ability in that area was put to good use as City fought hard to remain in the Premiership.
Everton (From apprentice on 8/12/80) FL 95+14/16 FLC 10+3/3 FAC 13/1 Others 7+2
Watford (£225,000 on 4/9/86) FL 39/2 FLC 3 FAC 7 Others 1
Arsenal (£200,000 on 26/8/87) FL 88+8/5 FLC 13+3/2 FAC 9/1 Others 3 (£750,000 to Real Sociedad on 1/7/90)
Aston Villa (£450,000 on 6/8/91) F/PL 142+1/13 FLC 15/3 FAC 12 Others 10
Coventry C (£300,000 on 16/2/95) PL 14

Kevin Richardson   Mike Egerton
(Empics Sports Photo Agency)

RICHARDSON Lee James
Born: Halifax, 12 March 1969
Height: 5'10" Weight: 11.0
A strong, tricky Oldham midfield player who packs a lethal shot and has an eye for goal, Lee came to the club immediately prior to the start of last season from Aberdeen. Scored seven times during the campaign, almost all spectacularly, but for one reason or another was unable to stake a regular place. Incidentally, he started his career as current team-mate, Rick Holden's boot boy at Halifax.
Halifax T (From trainee on 6/7/87) FL 43+13/2 FLC 4 FAC 4+2 Others 6
Watford (£175,000 on 9/2/89) FL 40+1/1 FLC 1+1 FAC 1
Blackburn Rov (£250,000 on 15/8/90) FL 50+12/3 FLC 1 Others 2+2
Aberdeen (Signed on 16/9/92) SL 59+5/6 SLC 2/1 SC 8/2 Others 3/1
Oldham Ath (£300,000 on 12/8/94) FL 28+2/6 FLC 2/1 FAC 2

RICHARDSON Neil Thomas
Born: Sunderland, 3 March 1968
Height: 5'10" Weight: 13.5
A player who is equally at ease in either the

backline or midfield, Neil found himself playing most of his games in midfield in 1994-95. Probably the best passer of a ball at Rotherham, he is another player whose attitude is exemplary and is a superb example to all those around him.
Rotherham U (Signed from Brandon U on 18/8/89) FL 94+8/4 FLC 8+1 FAC 4+1 Others 4+1

RICHARDSON Nicholas (Nick) John
Born: Halifax, 11 April 1967
Height: 6'1" Weight: 12.6
Club Honours: Div 3 '93; WC '93

Gave many adventurous midfield performances in the Cardiff cause last season, apart from having loan spells with both Wrexham and Chester, and is one of the few players at the club who would command a fee if he moved on.
Halifax T (Free from Emley on 15/11/88) FL 89+12/17 FLC 6+4/2 FAC 2+1/1 Others 6/1
Cardiff C (£35,000 on 13/8/92) FL 106+5/13 FLC 4 FAC 6 Others 12+2/2
Wrexham (Loaned on 21/10/94) FL 4/2
Chester C (Loaned on 16/12/94) FL 6/1

RICHARDSON Paul
Born: Durham, 22 July 1977
Height: 5'8" Weight: 11.1

Given a subs' opportunity in the Anglo-Italian Cup by Middlesbrough last season, Paul is a highly regarded young striker, who is fast accurate and powerful. Still a trainee.
Middlesbrough (Trainee) Others 0+1

RICKERS Paul Steven
Born: Leeds, 9 May 1975
Height: 5'10" Weight: 11.0

Right-sided Oldham midfield player with excellent stamina and skill to match. Comfortable in possession, and always busy, Paul made his FL debut in 1994-95, winning two "Man of the Match" awards from four games and chipping in with a very important goal in the 3-1 win over Bolton. A bright future is predicted.
Oldham Ath (From trainee on 16/7/93) FL 4/1

RIDEOUT Paul David
Born: Bournemouth, 14 August 1964
Height: 5'11" Weight: 12.2
Club Honours: FAC '95
International Honours: E: U21-5; Yth; Sch

Mobile Everton striker who is terrier-like in his pursuit of possession, hurrying opponents into mistakes, before distributing the ball simply and looking to get into an unmarked area. Possesses tremendous chest control, is a good header of the ball, especially with flick-ons, and generates much power to send bullet headers goalwards from crosses. Began slowly in 1994-95, with niggling injuries often keeping him out of contention. However, in the latter stages of the campaign, he hit a rich vein of form while partnering Duncan Ferguson, and capped the year by scoring the winning goal in the FA Cup Final victory over Manchester United.
Swindon T (From apprentice on 15/8/81) FL 90+5/38 FLC 3/2 FAC 7/1
Aston Villa (£200,000 on 1/6/83) FL 50+4/19 FLC 4+2/3 FAC 1+1 Others 1 (£400,000 to Bari on 1/7/85)

Southampton (£430,000 on 5/7/88) FL 68+7/19 FLC 13/2 FAC 5+2 Others 1
Swindon T (Loaned on 28/3/91) FL 9/1
Notts Co (£250,000 on 16/9/91) FL 9+2/3 FLC 2 FAC 1 Others 2
Glasgow R (£500,000 on 10/1/92) FL 7+5/1 FLC 0+1 FAC 1
Everton (£500,000 on 14/8/92) PL 63+14/23 FLC 8+1/2 FAC 7/3

RIDGEWAY Ian David
Born: Reading, 28 December 1975
Height: 5'8" Weight: 10.6

A Notts County first year pro, Ian was given his chance at the end of last season, when coming off the bench for Michael Galloway in the 73rd minute in the penultimate game at Swindon. Plays on the right-side of midfield where he can get forward to deliver good early crosses.
Notts Co (From trainee on 15/7/94) FL 0+1

RIEPER Marc
Born: Rodoure, Denmark, 5 June 1968
Height: 6'4" Weight: 14.2
International Honours: Denmark

A tall, stylish Danish international, Marc was initially signed on loan from Brondby last December. Took some time to settle into the pace of the English game, but an injury to Alvin Martin gave him a regular place in the West Ham side, and he quickly proved to be an outstanding central defender of real quality. Scored his only goal against Blackburn and, at the same time, kept the twin threat of Chris Sutton and Alan Shearer quiet. Signed on a permanent basis before the Manchester United match, he promptly played a major part in denying United the Championship.
West Ham U (£500,000 from Brondby on 8/12/94) PL 17+4/1

RIGBY Anthony (Tony) Angelo
Born: Ormskirk, 10 August 1972
Height: 5'7" Weight: 10.8

Stocky, skilful Bury midfielder who enjoys the attacking game and often conjures up spectacular goals, one of which against Preston in the Third Division play-offs last season ensured the club's first ever Wembley visit. Capable of producing the unexpected, Tony was given a free role later on in the campaign where his talents really flourished.
Crewe Alex (From trainee on 16/5/90)
Bury (Free from Burscough, via Lancaster C, on 6/1/93) FL 78+6/11 FLC 2/1 FAC 4+2/1 Others 11+1/2

RIMMER Neil
Born: Liverpool, 13 November 1967
Height: 5'6" Weight: 10.3
International Honours: E: Yth; Sch

The longest serving player at Wigan, and club captain, Neill's performances last season were rewarded when winning the shareholders and supporters' "Player of the Year" award. A great midfield competitor, strong tackler, and a ball-winner, he thankfully recovered from a serious injury to make his 50th FL appearance for the club during the campaign.
Everton (From apprentice on 14/4/84) FL 0+1

Ipswich T (Free on 13/8/85) FL 19+3/3 FLC 3 Others 1+1
Wigan Ath (Free on 4/7/88) FL 157+3/10 FLC 14/1 FAC 9/2 Others 14/2

RIMMER Stuart Alan
Born: Southport, 12 October 1964
Height: 5'7" Weight: 11.0
International Honours: E: Yth

Chester's record goalscorer, and a forward with a great deal of speed, Stuart spent most of last season at the club on a week-to-week basis, before signing a new contract in February. During that period he had loan spells at Rochdale and Preston. Is a skilful player and a handful for defenders.
Everton (From apprentice on 15/10/82) FL 3
Chester C (£10,000 on 17/1/85) FL 110+4/67 FLC 6/6 FAC 4+3 Others 11+1/3
Watford (£205,000 on 18/3/88) FL 10/1 FLC 0+1/1
Notts Co (£200,000 on 10/11/88) FL 3+1/2 FAC 2 Others 3
Walsall (£150,000 on 2/2/89) FL 85+3/31 FLC 6/4 FAC 5/2 Others 7/7
Barnsley (£150,000 on 5/3/91) FL 10+5/1 Others 1
Chester C (£150,000 on 15/8/91) FL 135+12/43 FLC 9/3 FAC 6+2 Others 6+2/1
Rochdale (Loaned on 2/9/94) FL 3
Preston NE (Loaned on 5/12/94) FL 0+2

Stuart Ripley   Neal Simpson
(Empics Sports Photo Agency)

RIPLEY Stuart Edward
Born: Middlesbrough, 20 November 1967
Height: 5'11" Weight: 12.6
Club Honours: PL '95
International Honours: E: 1; U21-8; Yth

Blond-haired Blackburn right-winger who is good on the ball and has the ability to use his pace to go past defenders to get telling crosses in from the by-line. In a season where he missed only six PL games in winning a Championship medal, Stuart somewhat surprisingly failed to get on the scoresheet in 1994-95. However, his great strength has always been in providing chances for others, and a capacity to drop deep to prevent opponents building up attacks was another key factor in the club's success, as was his ability to hold-up the ball played out of defence until colleagues could could arrive.

Middlesbrough (From apprentice on 23/12/85) FL 210+39/26 FLC 21+2/3 FAC 17+1/1 Others 20+1/1
Bolton W (Loaned on 18/2/86) FL 5/1 Others 0+1
Blackburn Rov (£1,300,000 on 20/7/92) PL 114+3/11 FLC 15 FAC 9/2 Others 3

RITCHIE Andrew (Andy) Timothy
Born: Manchester, 28 November 1960
Height: 5'10" Weight: 11.10
Club Honours: Div 2 '91
International Honours: E: U21-1; Yth; Sch

As a striker, Andy matured with age and is recognised as being one of the most skilful players ever to pull on an Oldham shirt. At his best, he had the ability to draw away from defenders to get into great scoring positions and also to run off the ball well. His phenomenal scoring record speaks for itself and even in 1994-95, a season at the end of which he was awarded a free transfer, 13 goals in 28 starts was good by any standard. However, "time waiteth for no man" and, at the age of 35, it was time for him to move on to pastures new.

Manchester U (From apprentice on 5/12/77) FL 26+7/13 FLC 3+2 FAC 3+1
Brighton & Hove A (£500,000 on 17/10/80) FL 82+7/23 FLC 3+1/1 FAC 9/2
Leeds U (£150,000 on 25/3/83) FL 127+9/40 FLC 11/3 FAC 9/1 Others 2+1
Oldham Ath (£50,000 on 14/8/87) F/PL 187+30/82 FLC 18+2/18 FAC 8+2/4 Others 3

RITCHIE Paul Michael
Born: St Andrews, 25 January 1969
Height: 5'11" Weight: 12.0
Club Honours: S Div 2 '90

Returned to Gillingham for his second loan spell in two years last September. A strong-running Dundee inside-forward, although scoring a goal in six starts, he failed to make a lasting impression and went back to Scotland.

Dundee (Free from Kirkcaldy YMCA in 1986-87)
Brechin C (Loaned in March 1988) SL 7+1/3
Brechin C (Signed in December 1988) SL 101+17/42 SLC 4/3 SC 5/4 Others 2/2
Dundee (Signed on 29/2/92) SL 30+12/6 SLC 1 SC 1
Gillingham (Loaned on 5/2/93) FL 6/3
Gillingham (Loaned on 9/9/94) FL 5/1 Others 1

RIX Graham
Born: Doncaster, 23 October 1857
Height: 5'9" Weight: 11.0
Club Honours: FAC '79
International Honours: E: 17; B-3; U21-7

Became Chelsea's oldest debutant when coming on as a 90th minute substitute in the first leg of the European Cup Winners Cup against Viktoria Zizkov last September. In the return, again due to the three foreigners in a side ruling, Graham actually started. Never out of place, he showed some super touches, allied to a brilliant ability to read the game from a wide role. Before being pressed into action, he had joined the club from Dundee during the 1994 close season as the youth team coach.

Arsenal (From apprentice on 13/1/75) FL 338+13/41 FLC 45+2/2 FAC 42+2/6 Others 21/1 (Free to SM Caen on 22/6/88)
Brentford (Loaned on 23/12/87) FL 6
Dundee (Signed from Le Havre on 31/7/92) SL 12+2/2 SLC 2
Chelsea (Free on 26/5/94) PL 0+1 Others 1+2

ROBERTS Andrew (Andy) James
Born: Dartford, 20 March 1974
Height: 5'10" Weight: 13.0
Club Honours: FAYC '91
International Honours: E: U21-3

A product of the Millwall youth policy, Andy is now firmly established as a regular first team member who can play with equal skill at centre-back or in midfield. Right-footed, with good positional sense, his sound displays last season were rewarded with an England U21 cap against Eire in Dublin. Took over the Millwall captaincy while Keith Stevens was out injured.

Millwall (From trainee on 29/10/91) FL 132+6/5 FLC 12/2 FAC 7 Others 4/1

ROBERTS Anthony (Tony) Mark
Born: Holyhead, 4 August 1969
Height: 6'0" Weight: 12.0
International Honours: W: 1; B1; U21-2; Yth

Started last season as first choice QPR 'keeper, but lost his place after 12 games. Returning to the first team on New Years' Eve at Highbury, he performed superbly to help Rangers to a famous 3-1 victory over Arsenal and kept his place for the remainder of the season with some solid displays. Currently the Welsh number two.

Queens Park R (From trainee on 24/7/87) F/PL 94 FLC 7 FAC 6+1 Others 2

ROBERTS Benjamin (Ben) James
Born: Bishop Auckland, 22 June 1975
Height: 6'1" Weight: 12.11

An all-round sportsman and aspiring young Middlesbrough goalkeeper, Ben represents his home town in the Durham cricket league. On the football field, his ability to cover angles, coupled to outstanding reflexes, make him a natural shot-stopper.

Middlesbrough (From trainee on 24/3/93) Others 1

ROBERTS Daniel (Danny)
Born: Chelmsford, 12 November 1975
Height: 5'8" Weight: 11.11

Young Colchester midfielder or winger who made a couple of first team appearances early last season, but found opportunities limited as more experienced players joined the club. A player with pace and an eye for goal, he was freed during the summer.

Colchester U (From trainee on 10/7/94) FLC 1+1

ROBERTS Darren Anthony
Born: Birmingham, 12 October 1969
Height: 6'0" Weight: 12.4

The former Wolverhampton forward found himself at Chesterfield during the 1994 close season after negotiating his release from Doncaster, having been there only a matter of days, following a change in management. A strong runner, and a persis-

tent 90-minute man, Darren's campaign never quite took off at Saltergate, and he played out much of the second half of it on loan at Telford.

Wolverhampton W (£20,000 from Burton A on 23/4/92) FL 12+9/5 FLC 0+1 Others 1+1
Hereford U (Loaned on 18/3/94) FL 5+1/5
Doncaster Rov (Free on 6/7/94)
Chesterfield (Free on 18/7/94) FL 4+7/1 FLC 2 Others 1+1/1

ROBERTS Glyn Shane
Born: Ipswich, 19 October 1974
Height: 5'11" Weight: 12.2

Used as a substitute on just two occasions for Rotherham in 1994-95, Glyn always worked hard in the midfield for the reserves where he occasionally also filled in at the back. Went for a spell on loan to Buxton.

Rotherham U (Free from Norwich C juniors on 5/8/93) FL 11+5/1

Iwan Roberts   Paul Marriott
(Empics Sports Photo Agency)

ROBERTS Iwan Wyn
Born: Bangor, 26 June 1968
Height: 6'3" Weight: 12.6
International Honours: W: 7; Yth

Brave striker who led the Leicester line for most of last season and always gave 100 per-cent, he scored a Monday night brace to rescue a point against Coventry and regularly found the net to top City's goalscoring charts. Linked up with Joachim during the early months, then subsequently with Mark Robins, and was a regular choice for the Welsh squad, despite fierce competition. Suffered a bad toe injury in March, but was soon back in action. Thrives on quality crosses and will make an impact in Division One next season.

Watford (From trainee on 4/7/88) FL 40+23/9 FLC 6+2/3 FAC 1+6 Others 5
Huddersfield T (£275,000 on 2/8/90) FL 141+1/50 FLC 13+1/6 FAC 12/4 Others 14/8
Leicester C (£100,000 on 25/11/93) F/PL 58+5/22 FLC 2 FAC 3/2 Others 1

ROBERTSON Alexander (Sandy)
Born: Edinburgh, 26 April 1971
Height: 5'9" Weight: 10.7
Club Honours: SPL '91
International Honours: S: U21-1

Young Scottish midfielder, who finally broke through to the Coventry first team last season after some excellent reserve performances brought him to notice, he came on as a sub against QPR and showed some nice touches, but has yet to live up to his earlier promise.

Glasgow R (From trainee on 29/2/88) SL 11+15/1 SLC 0+1 SC 1 Others 0+2
Coventry C (£250,000 on 4/1/94) PL 0+4

ROBERTSON John Nicholas
Born: Liverpool, 8 January 1974
Height: 6'2" Weight: 12.8

Tough-tackling Wigan central defender who is very strong in the air. Made his 100th League appearance for the club in 1994-95, his third season as a professional, and his "never-say-die" approach to the game was recognised by his fellow colleagues who voted him as the players' "Player of the Year".

Wigan Ath (From trainee on 6/7/92) FL 94+4/3 FLC 10 FAC 6+1 Others 8+1

ROBINS Mark Gordon
Born: Ashton under Lyne, 22 December 1969
Height: 5'8" Weight: 10.10
Club Honours: FAC '90; ECWC '91; ESC '91
International Honours: E: U21-6

Out of favour at Norwich, Mark, in signing for Leicester last January, became the club's second million pound signing. A right-footed, skilful striker, who always looks to play his team-mates into position, he showed that he had lost none of his predatory instincts when scoring a dramatic winner in appalling conditions at Manchester City on his debut. Sure to be a force in Division One in 1995-96.

Manchester U (From apprentice on 23/12/86) FL 19+29/11 FLC 0+7/2 FAC 4+4/3 Others 4+3/1
Norwich C (£800,000 on 14/8/92) PL 57+10/20 FLC 6+3/1 Others 1+1
Leicester C (£1,000,000 on 16/1/95) PL 16+1/5 FAC 2

ROBINSON Jamie
Born: Liverpool, 26 February 1972
Height: 6'1" Weight: 12.3
Club Honours: Div 3 '95

Defender/midfielder. Something of a utility player, who appeared in several positions during the last campaign, he was often used by Carlisle as a substitute where he stuck manfully to his appointed tasks. Won a Third Division Championship medal.

Liverpool (From trainee on 4/6/90)
Barnsley (Free on 17/7/92) FL 8+1 Others 3
Carlisle U (Signed on 28/1/94) FL 22+8/2 FAC 1 Others 5+4/1

ROBINSON John Robert Campbell
Born: Bulawayo, Rhodesia, 29 August 1971
Height: 5'10" Weight: 11.2
International Honours: W: U21-5

Tricky Charlton winger who can play on either side, though predominantly right-footed, John has a good burst of speed, likes to run at players, and is a good crosser of the ball. Had limited appearances in the side last season, but played well when called upon, either to replace Mark Robson, or when the team required two wingers.

Brighton & Hove A (From trainee on 21/4/89) FL 57+5/6 FLC 5/1 FAC 2+1 Others 1+2/2
Charlton Ath (£75,000 on 15/9/92) FL 58+5/6 FLC 1+1 FAC 4+1 Others 2

ROBINSON Leslie (Les)
Born: Shirebrook, 1 March 1967
Height: 5'8" Weight: 11.1

Deservedly Oxford's "Player of the Year", Les was an ever-present in all of United's games in the right-back spot last season. Steady and reliable, tackling and distribution are his strong points and he is always willing to get into attacking positions.

Mansfield T (Free from Chesterfield juniors on 6/10/84) FL 11+4 Others 1
Stockport Co (Signed on 27/11/86) FL 67/3 FLC 2 FAC 4 Others 4
Doncaster Rov (£10,000 on 24/3/88) FL 82/12 FLC 4 FAC 5 Others 5/1
Oxford U (£150,000 on 19/3/90) FL 167+2/2 FLC 14/1 FAC 8+1 Others 9

ROBINSON Spencer Liam
Born: Bradford, 29 December 1965
Height: 5'7" Weight: 11.5

Starting last season as half of a diminutive Burnley strike force, alongside Adrian Heath, having been signed from Bristol City during the summer, Liam retained his place until February, before becoming an often effective regular substitute. Unable to regain the scoring rate he had achieved earlier in his career at Bury, he could never be accused of giving up the struggle.

Huddersfield T (Free from Nottingham F juniors on 5/1/84) FL 17+4/2
Tranmere Rov (Loaned on 18/12/85) FL 4/3
Bury (£60,000 on 8/7/86) FL 248+14/89 FLC 17+3/6 FAC 9/1 Others 24/4
Bristol C (£130,000 on 14/7/93) FL 31+10/4 FLC 2/1 FAC 5 Others 1
Burnley (£250,000 on 26/7/94) FL 29+10/7 FLC 4/2 FAC 5/1

ROBINSON Mark James
Born: Rochdale, 21 November 1968
Height: 5'9" Weight: 10.6

Briefly Swindon's costliest import at £600,000 from Newcastle in July 1994, Mark took a little time to settle in at right-back, before becoming the only Town player to reach 40 League appearances for the season and only suspension cost him a place in the crucial Coca Cola Cup semi-final second leg-tie at Bolton. Very consistent, he later slotted in to a central defensive role quite comfortably.

West Bromwich A (From apprentice on 10/1/87) FL 2 FLC 0+1
Barnsley (Free on 23/6/87) FL 117+20/6 FLC 7+2 FAC 7+1 Others 3+2/1
Newcastle U (£450,000 on 9/3/93) F/PL 14+11 FAC 1
Swindon T (£600,000 on 22/7/94) FL 40 FLC 7 FAC 2 Others 4

ROBINSON Matthew Richard
Born: Exeter, 23 December 1974
Height: 5'11" Weight: 10.8

Left-sided Southampton midfielder. A player with nice touches who can make runs that often take him into the opposing penalty area for scoring chances, he made his PL debut last season when coming on for Simon Charlton at the Dell against Sheffield Wednesday. We should hear more of him in 1995-96.

Southampton (From trainee on 1/7/93) PL 0+1

ROBINSON Phillip (Phil) John
Born: Stafford, 6 January 1967
Height: 5'10" Weight: 10.7
Club Honours: Div 4 '88, Div 3 '89; AMC '88, '91

The playmaker in Chesterfield's midfield, Phil's arrival from Huddersfield last December had an immediate impact on the team, with his strength in the tackle and awareness of play always providing options for others. A good passer, too, he also weighed in with some valuable goals, including the second in a 2-0 play-off win at Wembley that saw the club promoted to the Second Division.

Aston Villa (From apprentice on 8/1/85) FL 2+1/1
Wolverhampton W (£5,000 on 3/7/87) FL 63+8/8 FLC 6 FAC 3/1 Others 8+2
Notts Co (£67,500 on 18/8/89) FL 65+1/5 FLC 6/1 FAC 1+1 Others 9+1
Birmingham C (Loaned on 18/3/91) FL 9 Others 2+1
Huddersfield T (Signed on 1/9/92) FL 74+1/5 FLC 4 FAC 8/1 Others 8
Northampton T (Loaned on 2/9/94) FL 14 FLC 1 FAC 1 Others 2
Chesterfield (Signed on 9/12/94) FL 22/8 Others 3/2

ROBINSON Ronald (Ronnie)
Born: Sunderland, 22 October 1966
Height: 5'9" Weight: 11.5

Solid left-footed defender who linked up well with Mark Gavin down the Exeter flank last season, Ronnie has a powerful shot and likes to have a crack at free-kicks. Freed during the summer, due to the club's financial position.

Ipswich T (Free from SC Vaux on 6/11/84)
Leeds U (Free on 22/11/85) FL 27
Doncaster Rov (£5,000 on 25/2/87) FL 76+2/5 FLC 6 FAC 5 Others 3
West Bromwich A (£80,000 on 22/3/89) FL 1
Rotherham U (£40,000 on 18/8/89) FL 86/2 FLC 9/1 FAC 6 Others 7/1
Peterborough U (Free on 10/12/91) FL 44+3 FLC 3 FAC 3 Others 10
Exeter C (£25,000 on 24/7/93) FL 37+2/1 FLC 4 FAC 2+1 Others 3+1
Huddersfield T (Loaned on 13/1/94) FL 2

ROBINSON Stephen
Born: Lisburn, 10 December 1974
Height: 5'8" Weight: 10.7
International Honours: NI: B; U21-6; Yth; Sch

Signed from "Spurs" early last season, along with Neil Young, Steve made his debut for Bournemouth against Bradford. Started for the club up-front, but in the second half of the season he moved to the midfield, where his excellent workrate and support of the front players established him in a midfield role.

Tottenham H (From trainee on 27/1/93) PL 1+1
Bournemouth (Free on 20/10/94) FL 30+2/5 FAC 2 Others 1

ROBINSON Steven Eli
Born: Nottingham, 17 January 1975
Height: 5'4" Weight: 10.11

Young Birmingham player with a promising future ahead of him. Came into the side last season due to injuries and suspensions, showing great enthusiasm, strong-running, and crisp-tackling, in six starts from midfield. Eventually made way for more experienced players during the promotion run-in, but it should not be too long before he is holding down a regular place.

Birmingham C (From trainee on 9/6/93) FL 5+1 Others 1

ROBSON Bryan
Born: Witton Gilbert, 11 January 1957
Height: 5'11" Weight: 12.6
Club Honours: CS '83, '93; FAC '83, '85, '90; ECWC '91; PL '93, '94; Div 1 '95
International Honours: E: 90; B-3; U21-7; Yth

Brian was sensationally appointed player-manager of Middlesbrough in the summer of 1994. The faithful Ayresome followers couldn't believe that such a high profile "signing" had been achieved, and "Robbo's" arrival gave the whole of the Teesside area a massive boost. The rookie manager made it clear from the start that his aim was to win promotion to the Premiership and stay there and assembled around himself a team of the highest calibre back-room boy's, including professionals like Viv Anderson (assistant manager), John Pickering (first team coach), Gordon McQueen (reserve team coach), Bob Ward and Tommy Johnson (physios). He also bought shrewdly in the transfer market, bringing in players who were to prove inspirational in the long and hard fought campaign to the top of the First Division, with Nigel Pearson (team captain), proving to be the most inspirational of all. Most importantly, to the elation of the long suffering fans, he played himself. His greatest accolade must come from that his players who, to a man, insist that his presence on the pitch and his ability to stop the game and control the midfield, inspired all of them to greater efforts. He won immortal fame, so far as the fans are concerned, when "Boro" gained promotion as Champions to the Premiership at his first attempt.

West Bromwich A (From apprentice on 1/8/74) FL 194+4/39 FLC 17+1/2 FAC 10+2/2 Others 12/3
Manchester U (£1,500,000 on 5/10/81) F/PL 326+19/74 FLC 50+1/5 FAC 33+2/10 Others 32+2/11
Middlesbrough (Free on 1/5/94) FL 21+1/1

ROBSON Gary
Born: Chester le Street, 6 July 1965
Height: 5'7" Weight: 10.12

A strong-tackling Bradford midfielder, who had his share of niggly injuries last season, he took over the captaincy in March. Is the younger brother of Bryan, the former England captain.

West Bromwich A (From apprentice on 5/5/83) FL 184+34/28 FLC 12+2 FAC 10+2/3 Others 7+5/3
Bradford C (Free on 16/7/93) FL 68+1/3 FLC 7 FAC 2 Others 1

ROBSON Mark Andrew
Born: Newham, 22 May 1969
Height: 5'7" Weight: 10.2

Fast and busy Charlton winger who can play on either wing, although predominantly left-footed, he likes to take on defenders and often switches wings several times during games. An excellent crosser of the ball, Mark gets to the line and cuts the ball back for the oncoming strikers. Can score goals and got the winner at Grimsby last September, but his main strength is in creating chances for others.

Exeter C (From apprentice on 17/12/86) FL 26/7 FAC 2 Others 2
Tottenham H (£50,000 on 17/7/87) FL 3+5 FLC 1
Reading (Loaned on 24/3/88) FL 5+2
Watford (Loaned on 5/10/89) FL 1
Plymouth Arg (Loaned on 22/12/89) FL 7
Exeter C (Loaned on 3/1/92) FL 7+1/1 Others 3/1
West Ham U (Free on 14/8/92) F/PL 42+5/8 FLC 2 FAC 2/1 Others 4+1
Charlton Ath (£125,000 on 17/11/93) FL 60+3/5 FLC 2 FAC 7/1 Others 1

ROCASTLE David Carlyle
Born: Lewisham, 2 May 1967
Height: 5'9" Weight: 11.1
Club Honours: FLC '87; Div 1 '89, '91
International Honours: E: 14; B-2; U21-14

Skilful right-sided Chelsea player, having been signed from Manchester City just in time for the start of 1994-95, David's ability to find space and read the game well were obviously part of the reason why Glenn Hoddle felt it necessary to bring him to Stamford Bridge. On occasion, showed up as a good tackler, but found it difficult to establish a rhythm in a side struggling with injuries from one game to the next. Is yet another player at the club capable of scoring spectacular goals.

Arsenal (From apprentice on 31/12/84) FL 204+14/24 FLC 32+1/6 FAC 18+2/4 Others 9
Leeds U (£2,000,000 on 4/8/92) PL 17+8/2 FLC 0+3 FAC 0+3 Others 2+1
Manchester C (£2,000,000 on 22/12/93) PL 21/2 FAC 2
Chelsea (£1,250,000 on 12/8/94) PL 26+2 FLC 3/1 Others 7+1/1

ROCHE David
Born: Newcastle, 13 December 1970
Height: 5'11" Weight: 12.1

An aggressive midfielder, David started last September for Doncaster, following an ankle injury, and was a regular prior to being transferred to Southend on transfer deadline day. Arguably the best passer at his former club, at Roots Hall he has yet to make his full debut.

Newcastle U (From trainee on 30/8/88) FL 23+13 FLC 2 FAC 1 Others 1+2
Peterborough U (Loaned on 8/1/93) FL 4
Doncaster Rov (Signed on 1/10/93) FL 49+1/8 FAC 1 Others 3/1
Southend U (£55,000 on 23/3/95) FL 0+4

ROCKETT Jason
Born: London, 26 September 1969
Height: 5'11" Weight: 11.5

One of Scarborough's most consistent players over the past couple of years, Jason is a strong, dominant central defender who

attracted the attention of several higher division clubs in 1994-95. Looks set for a bright future in the game.

Rotherham U (Signed on 25/3/92)
Scarborough (Free on 4/8/93) FL 60+1 FLC 4 FAC 5 Others 3

RODGER Graham
Born: Glasgow, 1 April 1967
Height: 6'2" Weight: 11.13
Club Honours: FAC '87
International Honours: E: U21-4

Exceptionally strong in the air and very useful in the box during set-pieces, the plethora of fine central defenders at Grimsby, together with a long spell of injury, limited his appearances. However, the departure of Paul Futcher, and injuries to Mark Lever and Peter Handyside, enabled him to re-establish himself in the number five shirt during the latter half of last season.

Wolverhampton W (Apprentice) FL 1
Coventry C (Free on 18/2/85) FL 31+5/2 FLC 3+1 FAC 1+1 Others 0+1
Luton T (£150,000 on 1/8/89) FL 27+1/2 FLC 2 Others 3
Grimsby T (£135,000 on 8/1/92) FL 83+8/9 FLC 3 FAC 5 Others 2

RODGER Simon Lee
Born: Shoreham, 3 October 1971
Height: 5'9" Weight: 10.13
Club Honours: Div 1 '94

Hard-working left-sided Crystal Palace midfield player who likes to take the ball forward while looking for attacking options. A regular in the club's 1993-94 promotion campaign, Simon, after playing in the opening four Premiership games, was unlucky to sustain a back injury which finished his season.

Crystal Palace (£1,000 from Bognor Regis T on 2/7/90) F/PL 83+8/5 FLC 14 FAC 2+1 Others 2+1

RODGERSON Ian
Born: Hereford, 9 April 1966
Height: 5'8" Weight: 10.7

Another frustrating season for right-sided midfielder Ian, who has spent two years at Sunderland either in the reserves or on the treatment table, before being freed during the summer.

Hereford U (From juniors on 3/7/85) FL 95+5/6 FLC 7 FAC 4 Others 7+1
Cardiff C (£35,000 on 3/8/88) FL 98+1/4 FLC 8 FAC 10 Others 6+1
Birmingham C (£50,000 on 4/12/90) FL 87+8/13 FLC 7+1/2 FAC 2 Others 11/1
Sunderland (£140,000 on 23/7/93) FL 5+5

RODWELL Anthony (Tony)
Born: Southport, 26 August 1962
Height: 5'11" Weight: 11.2

Skilful and experienced winger, and an excellent crosser of the ball, Tony signed from Blackpool last December. Did well for Scarborough but, following a change of manager, he later had a loan spell with Wigan.

Blackpool (Free from Colne Dynamoes on 15/8/90) FL 137+5/17 FLC 13+1 FAC 8 Others 16+1/4
Scarborough (£10,000 on 5/12/94) FL 6+2/1 FAC 2
Wigan Ath (Loaned on 20/1/95) FL 5/1

ROGAN Anthony (Anton) Gerard Patrick
Born: Belfast, 25 March 1966
Height: 5'11" Weight: 12.6
Club Honours: SPD '88; SC '88, '89
International Honours: NI: 17

Anton suffered a stop-go season for Oxford in 1994-95, missing through injury, coupled with games both at full-back and also in the centre-back spot, before being released during the summer.
Glasgow Celtic (Signed from Distillery on 9/5/86) SL 115+12/4 SLC 12+1 SC 18/1 Others 8
Sunderland (£350,000 on 4/10/91) FL 45+1/1 FLC 1 FAC 8 Others 2
Oxford U (Signed on 9/8/93) FL 56+2/3 FLC 4 FAC 4 Others 2

ROGERS Darren John
Born: Birmingham, 9 April 1970
Height: 5'9" Weight: 11.2

Skilful, speedy left-flank defender, who is equally happy in the centre of defence, Darren signed for Walsall during the 1994 close season, having been released by Birmingham. Lost his place when Colin Gibson arrived, but proved to be a more than useful squad member during the promotion run-in.
West Bromwich A (From trainee on 5/7/88) FL 7+7/1 FAC 0+1 Others 1/1
Birmingham C (Free on 1/7/92) FL 15+3 FLC 2 FAC 0+1 Others 5
Wycombe W (Loaned on 5/11/93) FL 0+1 Others 1
Walsall (Free on 19/7/94) FL 20+7 FLC 4 FAC 1+2 Others 2

ROGERS Lee Julian
Born: Doncaster, 28 October 1966
Height: 5'11" Weight: 12.1

"Nobby" enters his testimonial season of 1995-96 as Chesterfield's first-choice left-back; solid, rock-like and utterly reliable. In 1994-95, his game continued to improve, with his attacking forays down the wings and wicked free-kicks being welcome diversions. Justly voted "Players' Player of the Year" last season, and an excellent example to any aspiring professional, he missed few games as the club were promoted to the Second Division.
Doncaster Rov (From trainee on 27/7/84) Others 1
Chesterfield (Free on 29/8/86) FL 274+19/1 FLC 15+1 FAC 10+1 Others 25+1

ROGERS Paul Anthony
Born: Portsmouth, 21 March 1965
Height: 6'0" Weight: 11.13
International Honours: E: SP-6

A gritty and combative Sheffield United midfielder, he only missed two matches for the club throughout last season. His solid running for 90 minutes was a feature of his game and he is now a fixture in the side, following his move from non-league football.
Sheffield U (£35,000 from Sutton U on 29/1/92) F/PL 107+2/10 FLC 7/1 FAC 4 Others 1

ROSARIO Robert Michael
Born: Hammersmith, 4 March 1966
Height: 6'3" Weight: 13.12
International Honours: E: U21-4; Yth

Nottingham Forest striker who is strong in the air and shields the ball well in setting up

chances for others, especially the mid-fielders. Injured in 1993-94, Robert only managed a single sub's appearance last season before having an operation to repair the cruciate ligament damage to his right-knee. Now in the process of recovering, he has gone to America to play during the summer season, with a view to being match fit in time for the coming season.
Norwich C (Free from Hillingdon Borough on 23/12/83) FL 115+11/18 FLC 11/3 FAC 13+1/3 Others 8+1/5
Wolverhampton W (Loaned on 13/12/85) FL 2/1 Others 2
Coventry C (£600,000 on 27/3/91) F/PL 54+5/8 FLC 3+1/2 FAC 3 Others 1
Nottingham F (£400,000 on 2/3/93) F/PL 25+2/3 FLC 1 Others 2

ROSCOE Andrew Ronald
Born: Liverpool, 4 June 1973
Height: 5'11" Weight: 12.0

A player who featured on the left-hand side of midfield, he had two spells on loan with Rotherham, before he joined them from Bolton last season on a full-time basis and giving the team the balance they had been missing. He can take defenders on and has a good turn of speed.
Bolton W (Free from Liverpool juniors on 17/7/91) FL 2+1 Others 1+1
Rotherham U (Loaned on 27/10/94)
Rotherham U (£70,000 on 22/12/94) FL 31/4

ROSENTHAL Ronny
Born: Haifa, Israel, 11 October 1963
Height: 5'10" Weight: 12.0
Club Honours: CS '90
International Honours: Israel

Inevitably, Ronny, despite his contribution in the Premiership games of last season, will continue to be acclaimed for his outstanding hat-trick achieved in the FA Cup fifth round replay against Southampton in March. After being brought on by Gerry Francis, with Tottenham 2-0 down, he was to begin an individual performance which brought praise from all corners of the English game, with three outstanding goals, including two from well outside the area which left Bruce Grobbelar stunned and began a "Spurs'" revival. Naturally a striker, he also showed the ability to get himself into defensive positions when clearing off the line in the 1-1 draw with Crystal Palace at Selhurst Park in April. His pace and willingness to run at opposing defences remain his greatest assets.
Liverpool (Loaned from Standard Liege on 22/3/90) FL 5+3/7
Liverpool (£1,000,000 on 29/6/90) F/PL 27+39/14 FLC 2+7/1 FAC 5+3 Others 2+4
Tottenham H (£250,000 on 26/1/94) PL 25+10/2 FLC 1 FAC 2+2/4

ROSS Michael (Mickey) Patrick
Born: Southampton, 2 September 1971
Height: 5'7" Weight: 9.13

A quick centre-forward picked up by Plymouth from local rivals Exeter, he appeared to be an ideal partner for Kevin Nugent, with his pace and his constant harrying of defenders. Scored two goals on his full debut against Bournemouth, but missed a number of games through injury.

Portsmouth (From trainee on 30/12/88) FL 0+4 FAC 0+1 Others 2+3
Exeter C (£60,000 on 1/8/93) FL 27+1/9 FLC 4 FAC 3/1 Others 2+1
Plymouth Arg (Free on 22/11/94) FL 11+6 FAC 1/2

Uwe Rosler   Paul Marriott
(Empics Sports Photo Agency)

ROSLER Uwe
Born: Attenburg, Germany, 15 November 1968
Height: 6'0" Weight: 12.4
International Honours: East Germany

An exciting and most skilful striker, his Manchester City partnership with Paul Walsh was a revelation throughout the first half of 1994-95, a season that often saw him compared by the press to fellow German, Jurgen Klinsman. Scored some electrifying goals and netted four in the FA Cup replay against Notts County, the highest cup haul by a City player since Johnny Hart achieved the same tally in 1953. Although the club struggled on occasion, Uwe did not, having a style of play all of his own, and with the right support and consistency he will continue to captivate Premiership audiences.
Manchester C (£750,000 from Dynamo Dresden on 2/3/94) PL 41+2/20 FLC 3+1/2 FAC 4/5

ROWBOTHAM Darren
Born: Cardiff, 22 October 1966
Height: 5'10" Weight: 11.5
Club Honours: Div 4 '90
International Honours: W: Yth

Enjoys playing in a striker's role for Crewe, and always on the lookout for openings, Darren scored his 100th League and cup goal in 1994-95. Surprisingly released at the end of the season, having participated in 27 first team games.
Plymouth Arg (From juniors on 7/11/84) FL 22+24/2 FLC 1 FAC 0+3/1 Others 1+1

Exeter C (Signed on 31/10/87) FL 110+8/47 FLC 11/6 FAC 8/5 Others 5/1
Torquay U (£25,000 on 13/9/91) FL 14/3 FAC 3/1 Others 2
Birmingham C (£20,000 on 2/1/92) FL 31+5/6 FLC 0+1 Others 3+1
Mansfield T (Loaned on 18/12/92) FL 4
Hereford U (Loaned on 25/3/93) FL 8/2
Crewe Alex (Free on 6/7/93) FL 59+2/21 FLC 1/1 FAC 4/3 Others 6+2/1

ROWE Rodney Carl
Born: Huddersfield, 30 July 1975
Height: 5'8" Weight: 12.8
Pacy Huddersfield player who plays on the right-side of midfield. Despite breaking into the first team in 1993-94, Rodney failed to claim a regular place last season, being limited to reserve matches and was loaned out, first to Scarborough, and then to Bury, before returning to Leeds Road.
Huddersfield T (From trainee on 12/7/93) FL 7+6/1 FAC 3/1 Others 3/1
Scarborough (Loaned on 11/8/94) FL 10+4/1 FLC 4/1
Bury (Loaned on 20/3/95) FL 1+2

ROWETT Gary
Born: Bromsgrove, 6 March 1974
Height: 6'0" Weight: 12.0
Everton central midfielder who likes to support the forwards with late runs into the opposing penalty area. On the edge of the first team, Gary played twice last season, before going on loan to Blackpool in January and starring in 17 matches for the "Seasiders". A good tackler who rarely gives the ball away, and has an impressive goal tally for a non-forward in the reserve side, he could still get a break in the Premiership.
Cambridge U (From trainee on 10/9/91) FL 51+12/9 FLC 7/1 FAC 5+2 Others 5/3
Everton (£200,000 on 21/5/94) PL 2+2
Blackpool (Loaned on 23/1/95) FL 17

ROWLAND Keith
Born: Portadown, 1 September 1971
Height: 5'10" Weight: 10.0
International Honours: NI: 3; B-1; Yth
Young West Ham full-back who possesses a good left foot and is able to cross the ball with perfection. Only made 12 League appearances last season, due to the fine form of Julian Dicks, but is currently a member of the Northern Ireland squad, having won three caps this past summer.
Bournemouth (From trainee on 2/10/89) FL 65+7/2 FLC 5 FAC 8 Others 3
Coventry C (Loaned on 8/1/93) PL 0+2
West Ham U (£110,000 on 6/8/93) PL 27+8/2 FLC 3 FAC 4

ROY Bryan Edward
Born: Amsterdam, Holland, 12 February 1970
Height: 5'10" Weight: 10.8
International Honours: Holland
Nottingham Forest's record signing was a personal triumph for manager, Frank Clark, who was quoted at the time as saying: "There is no doubt about Bryan being a world class player and the fact that he has agreed to join us is a remarkable coup on our part". How right he was. The Dutch international star set Forest alight on occasion

last season, with skilful runs into the heart of the opposition's defence, and formed a good understanding with Stan Collymore. Fast, tricky, two-footed, with great balance, his crosses from the wide left also gave the team an extra dimension. Although getting bogged down on heavy pitches, that was a small price to pay for his great talent.
Nottingham F (£2,500,000 from Foggia on 4/8/94) PL 37/13 FLC 4/1 FAC 2

ROYCE Simon Ernest
Born: Forest Gate, 9 September 1971
Height: 6'1" Weight: 12.0
Simon made the Southend goalkeeper's jersey his own when Steve Thompson was made caretaker manager towards the end of last season, his instinctive reflex saves being

exceptional, along with a strong punch and good handling. With his kicking improving all the time, the new season should be a good one for him.
Southend U (£10,000 from Heybridge Swifts on 15/10/91) FL 21+2 FLC 2 FAC 1 Others 1

RUDDOCK Neil
Born: Wandsworth, 9 May 1968
Height: 6'2" Weight: 12.0
Club Honours: FLC '95
International Honours: E: 1; B-1; U21-4; Yth
Neil's fierce tackling and height in the heart of the Liverpool defence was one of the main reasons for Liverpool's success last season. Although taking a little time to settle in and become acquainted with the club's way of doing things, he is now a player in

Bryan Roy

Neal Simpson
(Empics Sports Photo Agency)

the mould of Ron Yeats. Has learned to curb his temper, being a much better player for it, and provides much needed stability to the back-line. Won his first full cap for England against Nigeria in November and will be looking to build on that in 1995-96.

Millwall (From apprentice on 3/3/86) Others 3+1/1
Tottenham H (£50,000 on 14/4/86) FL 7+2 FAC 1+1/1
Millwall (£300,000 on 29/6/88) FL 0+2/1 FLC 2/3 Others 1+1
Southampton (£250,000 on 13/2/89) FL 100+7/9 FLC 14+1/1 FAC 10/3 Others 6
Tottenham H (£750,000 on 29/7/92) PL 38/3 FLC 4 FAC 5
Liverpool (£2,500,000 on 22/7/93) PL 76/5 FLC 13/1 FAC 9

Neil Ruddock   Neal Simpson
(Empics Sports Photo Agency)

RUFUS Marvin Marcell
Born: Lewisham, 11 September 1976
Height: 5'8" Weight: 11.0
Introduced to the Leyton Orient midfield at the end of last season, and with the club committed to a youth development policy, this lively YTS youngster can expect further opportunities in 1995-96.
Leyton Orient (Trainee) FL 5+2

RUFUS Richard Raymond
Born: Lewisham, 12 January 1975
Height: 6'1" Weight: 11.2
Tall central defender who came into the Charlton side last October as a substitute at Derby and made his full debut three days later against Sunderland, immediately making an impact with his tackling, heading ability, and distribution. Exceptionally fast for a central defender, he looks unbeatable at times, but recovers well should he make a mistake, which is rare. Voted "Player of the Year" by the supporters and already in the England U21 squad, Richard should go all the way.
Charlton Ath (From trainee on 1/7/93) FL 27+1

RUSH David
Born: Sunderland, 15 May 1971
Height: 5'10" Weight: 10.3
"Rushie", a nippy striker, joined Oxford from Sunderland in September 1994 and was an instant hit with the fans, scoring a last minute winner (playing as substitute). Remained the regular bench warmer for half the season, but took the chance of a regular game on John Byrne's departure and weighed in with some important goals.
Sunderland (Free from Notts Co juniors on 21/7/89) FL 40+19/12 FLC 1+1 FAC 9/1 Others 1+1
Hartlepool U (Loaned on 15/8/91) FL 8/2
Peterborough U (Loaned on 27/10/93) FL 2+2/1 FLC 1/1
Cambridge U (Loaned on 12/9/94) FL 2
Oxford U (£100,000 on 23/9/94) FL 22+12/9 FLC 0+1 FAC 0+1 Others 3+1

Ian Rush   Neal Simpson
(Empics Sports Photo Agency)

RUSH Ian James
Born: St Asaph, 20 October 1961
Height: 6'0" Weight: 12.6
Club Honours: Div 1 '82, '83, '84, '86, '90; FLC '81, '82, '83, '84, '95; FAC '86, '89, '92; EC '84
International Honours: W: 71; U21-2; Sch
The PFA "Young Player of the Year" in 1983 and "Player of the Year" in 1984, Ian continued to set the standards for other strikers to follow in 1994-95. Relishing the Liverpool captaincy, and continuing to score goals, he also found the time to coach young Robbie Fowler and create chances for other players. He is much more than just an out-and-out goalscorer, and proves it by chasing and harrying like a player ten years younger. Has won it all, but continues to have the hunger to want to go on winning.

Chester C (From apprentice on 25/9/79) FL 33+1/14 FAC 5/3
Liverpool (£300,000 on 1/5/80) FL 182/109 FLC 38/21 FAC 22/20 Others 31+1/17 (£3,200,000 to Juventus on 1/7/86)
Liverpool (Loaned on 1/7/86) FL 42/30 FLC 9/4 FAC 3 Others 3/6
Liverpool (£2,800,000 on 23/8/88) F/PL 214+12/85 FLC 29/22 FAC 30+2/18 Others 14/7

RUSH Matthew James
Born: Hackney, 6 August 1971
Height: 5'11" Weight: 12.10
International Honours: Ei: U21-3
A West Ham right-winger with excellent pace and two good feet, who can also score goals, as he proved in successive games against "Spurs" and Southampton last season. Linking up well with full-back Tim Breacker, Matthew will threaten many defences in 1995-96 as he gains in experience.
West Ham U (From trainee on 24/3/90) F/PL 29+19/5 FLC 4 Others 2+1
Cambridge U (Loaned on 12/3/93) FL 4+6
Swansea C (Loaned on 10/1/94) FL 13 Others 4

RUSSELL Alexander (Alex) John
Born: Crosby, 17 March 1973
Height: 5'8" Weight: 11.7
Young Rochdale midfielder, and son of former Southport stalwart, Alex, he impressed in his few first team outings last season, especially on his full debut against Blackpool.
Rochdale (£4,000 from Burscough on 11/7/94) FL 2+5/1 Others 1+2

RUSSELL Craig Stewart
Born: South Shields, 4 February 1974
Height: 5'10" Weight: 12.0
Powerfully built young striker, who is still striving with determination to establish himself as a regular first choice at Sunderland, he possesses great pace and packs a powerful left-foot shot. Although not a vintage season for Craig, 1994-95 will no doubt hold some fair memories for him, including two goals away at Middlesbrough in September and a last minute winner at Roker against Sheffield United, after coming off the bench.
Sunderland (From trainee on 1/7/92) FL 58+19/14 FLC 3/1 FAC 3+2/1 Others 2

RUSSELL Kevin John
Born: Brighton, 6 December 1966
Height: 5'9" Weight: 10.12
Club Honours: Div 2 '93
International Honours: E: Yth
Starting last season at Bournemouth, before joining Notts County in February, Kevin showed himself to be a forward who does much running off the ball and one who is always looking to harry defenders into mistakes. Could be an ideal foil for Devon White.
Portsmouth (Free from Brighton & Hove A juniors on 9/10/84) FL 3+1/1 FLC 0+1 FAC 0+1 Others 1+1
Wrexham (£10,000 on 17/7/87) FL 84/43 FLC 4/1 FAC 4 Others 8/3
Leicester C (£175,000 on 20/6/89) FL 24+19/10 FLC 0+1 FAC 1 Others 5/2
Peterborough U (Loaned on 6/9/90) FL 7/3
Cardiff C (Loaned on 17/1/91) FL 3

Hereford U (Loaned on 7/11/91) FL 3/1 Others 1/1
Stoke C (Loaned on 2/1/92) FL 5/1
Stoke C (£95,000 on 16/7/92) FL 30+10/5 FLC 3 FAC 2 Others 4+1/1
Burnley (£150,000 on 28/6/93) FL 26+2/6 FLC 4/1 FAC 4 Others 1/1
Bournemouth (£125,000 on 3/3/94) FL 30/1 FLC 3/1 FAC 2/1
Notts Co (£60,000 on 24/2/95) FL 9+2

RUSSELL Lee Edward
Born: Southampton, 3 September 1969
Height: 5'11" Weight: 12.0
Solid Portsmouth defender who is capable of playing in midfield with a good left-foot and solid in the air, Lee was yet again "Mr Reliable", but failed to get a real opportunity in the first team. When he did come in he more than held his own and never really let the side down. Unlucky with injuries, otherwise he would have made more appearances, he also had a period on loan with Bournemouth early in 1994-95.
Portsmouth (From trainee on 12/7/88) FL 60+16/1 FLC 2+1 FAC 3+2 Others 5+2
Bournemouth (Loaned on 9/9/94) FL 3

RUSSELL Wayne Leonard
Born: Cardiff, 29 November 1967
Height: 6'2" Weight: 13.7
Made his Burnley first team debut, following Marlon Beresford's sending off at Oldham last season, and later enjoyed a brief run as first choice 'keeper, his best display being against Liverpool in the FA Cup, a performance that gave a clear indication of his ability.
Burnley (Signed from Ebbw Vale on 28/10/93) FL 6+2 FAC 1

RUST Nicholas (Nicky) Charles Irwin
Born: Cambridge, 25 September 1974
Height: 6'0" Weight: 13.1
International Honours: E: Sch
A young Brighton goalkeeper who, overall, had a fine season in 1994-95. Reliable and a good shot-stopper, he demonstrated his bravery when he played with an injured elbow for two games, before undergoing surgery once a replacement had been found. Achieved five consecutive clean sheets between 25 February and 15 March 1995.
Brighton & Hove A (Free from Arsenal juniors on 9/7/93) FL 90 FLC 10 FAC 2 Others 4

RUTHERFORD Jonathan Paul
Born: Sunderland, 23 February 1967
Height: 5'9" Weight: 11.0
Was a regular scorer in the Scottish lower reaches, before joining Scarborough from Meadowbank Thistle last September. A ligament injury prevented him from establishing himself, and he moved to Berwick Rangers for £12,000 just three months later.
Newcastle U (From apprentice on 4/7/85)
Alloa (Free during 1987 close season) SL 38/15 SLC 1/1 SC 1
Falkirk (Signed in September 1988) SL 47+21/18 SLC 1+2 SC 2/1 Others 1
Meadowbank (Signed on 10/10/92) SL 59/17 SLC 1 SC 2/2 Others 6/2
Scarborough (£15,000 on 9/9/94) FL 6+2/1 FAC 2+1 Others 1

RYAN Darren Thomas
Born: Oswestry, 3 July 1972
Height: 5'10" Weight: 11.0
Forward. top-scorer for Rochdale's reserve side with two hat-tricks, after being in-and-out of the side, he gained a regular place towards the end of last season and responded with a couple of goals.
Shrewsbury T (From trainee on 23/10/90) FL 3+1 Others 0+1
Chester C (Free on 14/8/92) FL 5+12/2 FLC 2 FAC 1+1/1 Others 1+1
Stockport Co (Signed on 25/1/93) FL 29+7/6 FLC 2/1 FAC 1+1 Others 5+1
Rochdale (Free on 21/7/94) FL 15+10/2 FLC 1+1 FAC 0+1 Others 1+4

RYAN Keith James
Born: Northampton, 25 June 1970
Height: 5'11" Weight: 12.8
Club Honours: FAT '91, '93; GMVC '93
Extremely popular Wycombe central midfielder with remarkable ball-winning ability and the scorer of some valuable goals. An injury last January ruled him out for the rest of the season, his absence being a prime reason for the side's faltering form.
Wycombe W (Signed from Berkhamsted in 1989-90) FL 66/5 FLC 6/1 FAC 6+3/3 Others 10+1

Keith Ryan   Barry Coombs
(Empics Sports Photo Agency)

RYAN Vaughan William
Born: Pimlico, 2 September 1968
Height: 5'8" Weight: 10.12
An aggressive, defensive left-sided midfielder, he was used at the start of last season to bring extra muscle to the Orient team, especially in away matches. Hernia problems then sidelined him, before he was freed during the summer.
Wimbledon (From apprentice on 22/8/86) FL 67+15/3 FLC 7 FAC 1 Others 7+1
Sheffield U (Loaned on 11/1/89) FL 2+1 Others 1
Leyton Orient (Signed on 14/8/92) FL 40+4 FLC 2+1 FAC 3 Others 1

RYDER Stuart Henry
Born: Sutton Coldfield, 6 November 1973
Height: 6'0" Weight: 12.1
International Honours: E: U21-2
An unflappable, steady, and commanding young player, whose style has been likened to that of former Liverpool star, Alan Hansen, he was struck down by glandular fever in March 1994. Returned last September and, in the course of 36 games in Walsall's run to promotion, played as both a flank and central defender and snatched five goals, one of them a match-winner against Torquay. Recognised at U21 level by England at the end of last season, Stuart was twice capped during the Toulon tournament, against Brazil and France.
Walsall (From trainee on 16/7/92) FL 74+10/5 FLC 3+1 FAC 8 Others 4+1

SALAKO John Akin
Born: Nigeria, 11 February 1969
Height: 5'10" Weight: 11.0
Club Honours: FMC '91; Div '94
International Honours: E: 5
Crystal Palace left-winger who overcame a bad injury to both re-establish and then put himself back into contention for an England place, when selected for the "B" squad last December. A player with great pace and skill, and capable of unlocking the tightest of defences, John showed that he was back to his very best when scoring two goals in a game that saw Palace win at Arsenal for the first time in their history. Has been awarded a testimonial for next season.
Crystal Palace (From apprentice on 3/11/86) F/PL 172+43/22 FLC 19+5/5 FAC 20/4 Others 11+3/2
Swansea C (Loaned on 14/8/89) FL 13/3 Others 2/1

John Salako   Steve Morton
(Empics Sports Photo Agency)

SALE Mark David
Born: Burton on Trent, 27 February 1972
Height: 6'5" Weight: 13.8

Missed four months of last season through hernia and toe injuries, having started as Preston's first choice centre-forward, without completely winning over the fans, despite scoring. A good dribbler for his height.
Stoke C (From trainee on 10/7/90) FL 0+2
Cambridge U (Free on 31/7/91)
Birmingham C (Signed on 26/3/92) FL 11+10 FLC 2/1 Others 3+1/2
Torquay U (£10,000 on 5/3/93) FL 30+14/8 FLC 1 FAC 2/1 Others 3+1
Preston NE (£20,000 on 26/7/94) FL 10+3/6 FLC 1+1 FAC 0+1 Others 4

SALMON Michael (Mike) Bernard
Born: Leyland, 14 July 1964
Height: 6'2" Weight: 12.12
An experienced Charlton goalkeeper who suffered several injuries last season, Mike is confident on crosses and a reasonable shot-stopper. Injured his hand against Barnsley in the second match, and then dislocated a finger on the other hand, before requiring a knee operation. Regained his first team place in December, but in early April he sustained a groin injury at Burnley, which again kept him out of the side.
Blackburn Rov (From juniors on 16/10/81) FL 1
Chester C (Loaned on 18/10/82) FL 16 FAC 2
Stockport Co (Free on 3/8/83) FL 118 FLC 10 FAC 3 Others 3
Bolton W (Free on 31/7/86) FL 26 FLC 2 FAC 4 Others 4
Wrexham (£18,000 on 7/3/87) FL 100 FLC 4 FAC 4 Others 9
Charlton Ath (£100,000 on 6/7/89) FL 87 FLC 3 FAC 5 Others 6

SAMPSON Ian
Born: Wakefield, 14 November 1968
Height: 6'2" Weight: 12.8
A Northampton 1994 close season signing from Sunderland, having spent a period on loan at the club, he is now the club's vice-captain. Playing in the centre of the defence, he is good in the air and likes to go forward and, above all, is consistent. The only ever-present player for Town in 1994-95.
Sunderland (Signed from Goole T on 13/11/90) FL 13+4/1 FLC 1 FAC 0+2 Others 0+1
Northampton T (Loaned on 8/12/93) FL 8
Northampton T (Free on 5/8/94) FL 42/2 FLC 2 FAC 1 Others 3

SAMWAYS Mark
Born: Doncaster, 11 November 1968
Height: 6'0" Weight: 11.12
Ever-improving Scunthorpe goalkeeper and often the unsung hero when "Man of the Match" votes are concerned. A good shot-stopper, he gave consistently good performances in 1994-95 and made excellent saves at vital times. Has greatly improved on handling and crosses and was the club's only ever-present last season.
Doncaster Rov (From trainee on 20/8/87) FL 121 FLC 3 FAC 4 Others 10
Scunthorpe U (Signed on 26/3/92) FL 122 FLC 6 FAC 10 Others 13

SAMWAYS Vincent (Vinny)
Born: Bethnal Green, 27 October 1968
Height: 5'8" Weight: 11.0
Club Honours: FAC '91; CS '91
International Honours: E: U21-5; Yth

Everton midfielder who can play in any position across the centre, although preferring a dictating central role. Has the stamina to support attacks and, in the next minute, to be making last ditch tackles in his own penalty area. With the skill to make the ball do the work, and an ability to maintain possession, he is always looking to get into goalscoring positions. Bought from Tottenham by Mike Walker during the summer of 1994, Vinny was unable to hold down a regular position following the subsequent change of management, coupled with constant knee injuries, and made just 16 starts.
Tottenham H (From apprentice on 9/11/85) F/PL 165+28/11 FLC 27+4/4 FAC 15+1/2 Others 7+1
Everton (£2,200,000 on 2/8/94) PL 14+5/1 FLC 2/1

SANDEMAN Bradley Robert
Born: Northampton, 24 February 1970
Height: 5'10" Weight: 10.8
Attacking right-back who was a regular in the Port Vale team, apart from an 11 game spell in mid-season when he was left out after a poor run of results. He returned all the better and added an extra dimension to the attack with his forays down the right.
Northampton T (From trainee on 14/7/88) FL 28+30/3 FLC 2+3 FAC 2 Others 6+1
Maidstone U (£10,000 on 22/2/91) FL 55+2/8 FLC 1 FAC 2 Others 2
Port Vale (Free on 14/8/92) FL 61+7/1 FLC 5+1 FAC 3+1 Others 2

SANDFORD Lee Robert
Born: Basingstoke, 22 April 1968
Height: 6'1" Weight: 12.2
Club Honours: AMC '92; Div 2 '93
International Honours: E: Yth
Originally signed by Alan Ball as an all purpose defender or midfielder, Lee has made the left-back role his own, and with a strong left-foot, he has built up a sound understanding with a succession of left-sided midfielders at Stoke. His adaptability also runs to a central defensive role where, either as a sweeper or in a conventional marking situation, he is sound, both on the ground and in the air.
Portsmouth (From apprentice on 4/12/85) FL 66+6/1 FLC 11 FAC 4 Others 2+1
Stoke C (£140,000 on 22/12/89) FL 109+3/8 FLC 16 FAC 14/2 Others 27/4

SANSAM Christian (Chris)
Born: Hull, 26 December 1975
Height: 5'11" Weight: 11.0
Showed good form at junior level for Scunthorpe, but hasn't managed, as yet, to prove himself when called into the senior side. A front-runner, whose pace can make up for lack of physical strength, he looks to come good in 1995-96.
Scunthorpe U (From trainee on 23/12/93) FL 8+8 FAC 2+1 Others 0+3

SANSOM Kenneth (Kenny) Graham
Born: Camberwell, 26 September 1958
Height: 5'6" Weight: 11.8
Club Honours: FAYC '77; Div 2 '79; FLC '87
International Honours: E: 86; B-2; U21-8; Yth; Sch

A former England left-back, with nearly 100 caps to his name, Kenny came to Watford early last season as a non-contract player and assistant manager. Although he was usually to be found on the bench, he proved to be a more than useful stand-in when required.
Crystal Palace (From apprentice on 1/12/75) FL 172/3 FLC 11 FAC 17/1
Arsenal (£955,000 on 14/8/80) FL 314/6 FLC 48 FAC 26 Others 6
Newcastle U (£300,000 on 24/12/88) FL 20 FAC 4
Queens Park R (£300,000 on 8/6/89) FL 64 FLC 7 FAC 10/2 Others 1
Coventry C (£100,000 on 22/3/91) FL 51 FLC 2 FAC 2
Everton (Signed on 4/2/93) FL 6+1/1
Brentford (Free on 25/3/93) FL 8 (After being freed during 1993 close season, he signed for Chertsey T on 7/12/94)
Watford (Free on 11/8/94) FL 1

SANSOME Paul Eric
Born: New Addington, 6 October 1961
Height: 6'0" Weight: 13.8
Club Honours: FLT '83
Although first choice Southend goalkeeper for many seasons, Paul lost his place during the relegation dog-fight at the end of the 1994-95 season. His reflex saves are still a joy to watch and he proved an exceptional last line of defence on so many occasions last season. His experience will still be invaluable in years to come.
Millwall (Free from Crystal Palace juniors on 18/4/80) FL 156 FLC 12 FAC 13 Others 9
Southend U (£40,000 on 24/3/88) FL 305 FLC 18 FAC 8 Others 16

Dean Saunders   Neal Simpson
(Empics Sports Photo Agency)

SAUNDERS Dean Nicholas
Born: Swansea, 21 June 1964
Height: 5'8" Weight: 10.6
Club Honours: FAC '92; FLC '94
International Honours: W: 49
One of three Aston Villa players with a top-class footballing pedigree, his dad, Roy, played for Liverpool and Swansea between 1948 and 1963, Dean is a real "chip off the old block". A quick-silver striker, with an

explosive finish, he also has a talent in dragging defenders out of position with his unselfish running off the ball, and is an industrious player who always gives 100 per-cent. Top-scored for Villa in 1994-95, a difficult season for the club, his efforts were rewarded when voted the fans' "Player of the Year". Scored a brilliant goal for Wales against Germany in April.

Swansea C (From apprentice on 24/6/82) FL 42+7/12 FLC 2+1 FAC 1 Others 1+1
Cardiff C (Loaned on 29/3/85) FL 3+1
Brighton & Hove A (Free on 7/8/85) FL 66+6/21 FLC 4 FAC 7/5 Others 3
Oxford U (£60,000 on 12/3/87) FL 57+2/22 FLC 9+1/8 FAC 2/2 Others 2/1
Derby Co (£1,000,000 on 28/10/88) FL 106/42 FLC 12/10 FAC 6 Others 7/5
Liverpool (£2,900,000 on 19/7/91) F/PL 42/11 FLC 5/2 FAC 8/2 Others 6/10
Aston Villa (£2,300,000 on 10/9/92) PL 111+1/37 FLC 15/7 FAC 9/4 Others 8/1

SAVAGE David (Dave) Thomas Patrick
Born: Dublin, 30 July 1973
Height: 6'1" Weight: 12.7
International Honours: Ei: U21-2

Another of the younger players to grab a first team chance at Millwall last season because of injuries to senior men, Dave is a wide right attacking midfielder or forward. Skilful, with a mazy dribble and neat ball control, he had an outstanding debut for Eire against England at under 21 level.

Millwall (£15,000 from Longford T on 27/5/94) FL 31+6/2 FLC 5 FAC 2+2/1

SAVAGE Robert (Rob) William
Born: Wrexham, 18 October 1974
Height: 5'11" Weight: 10.7
Club Honours: FAYC '92
International Honours: W: U21-3; Yth; Sch

This former Manchester United player has only just completed his first season with Crewe, but in that time has earned himself three caps in the Welsh U21 side. Few League outings as yet, but he is young enough to make the transition into the first team on a regular basis.

Manchester U (From trainee on 5/7/93)
Crewe Alex (Free on 22/7/94) FL 5+1/2

SAVILLE Andrew (Andy) Victor
Born: Hull, 12 December 1964
Height: 6'0" Weight: 12.0

An instant success as a striker when first coming to Birmingham in 1993-94, with the heavy competition for forward positions he has since faded out of the picture and made only five starts last season. However, when loaned out to Burnley in December, Andy made an instant impression with a goal in a 5-1 win against Southend, before returning to St Andrews.

Hull C (Signed on 23/9/83) FL 74+27/18 FLC 6/1 FAC 3+2/1 Others 4+2
Walsall (£100,000 on 23/3/89) FL 28+10/5 FLC 2 Others 1+1
Barnsley (£80,000 on 9/3/90) FL 71+11/21 FLC 5+1 FAC 2+1 Others 4/1
Hartlepool U (£60,000 on 13/3/92) FL 37/13 FLC 4/1 FAC 4/5 Others 3/1
Birmingham C (£155,000 on 22/3/93) FL 51+8/17 FLC 4/1 FAC 1 Others 1
Burnley (Loaned on 30/12/94) FL 3+1/1 FAC 1

SCAIFE Nicholas
Born: Middlesbrough, 14 May 1975
Height: 6'2" Weight: 11.0

Tall midfielder who came out of non-league soccer last March. Has already been given a first team opportunity at York and, as a strong, hard-tackling player, he could have a bright future.

York C (Signed from Whitby T on 4/3/95) FL 0+1

John Scales   Neal Simpson
(Empics Sports Photo Agency)

SCALES John Robert
Born: Harrogate, 4 July 1966
Height: 6'2" Weight: 12.7
Club Honours: FAC '88; FLC '95
International Honours: E: 3; B-1

A 1994 summer signing from Wimbledon, John was the perfect foil for Neil Ruddock in Liverpool's defence last season. An equally effective and determined tackler, he used his height to great effect in the defence and proved there is more to his game than simply preventing the opposition from scoring, when bringing the ball out from defence to set up penetrating attacks. His good play was rewarded when capped for England.

Bristol Rov (Free from Leeds U juniors on 11/7/85) FL 68+4/2 FLC 3 FAC 6 Others 3+1
Wimbledon (£70,000 on 16/7/87) F/PL 235+5/11 FLC 18+1 FAC 20+1 Others 7+1/4
Liverpool (£3,500,000 on 2/9/94) PL 35/2 FLC 7/1 FAC 7

SCARGILL Wayne
Born: Barnsley, 30 April 1968
Height: 5'10" Weight: 11.9

Played one game in the League for Bradford at right-back before transferring to Emley of the Unibond Premier League last November.

Bradford C (Free from Frickley Ath on 4/11/93) FL 1

SCHMEICHEL Peter Boleslaw
Born: Glodsone, Denmark, 18 November 1968
Height: 6'4" Weight: 14.0

Club Honours: ESC '91; FLC '92; PL '93, '94; FAC '94; CS '93, '94
International Honours: Denmark (UEFAC '92)

A top-class international goalkeeper with outstanding presence, Peter is extremely agile and very fast off his line. Also capable of setting up attacks with long, accurate throws. His value to Manchester United in 1994-95 was immense. When he suffered a disabling back injury against Crystal Palace in November, his absence from the side coincided with shattering defeats by Barcelona and Gothenburg in the European Cup, and the loss of United's unbeaten home record to Nottingham Forest, after not conceding a goal in the Premiership for 1,135 minutes. Once recovered, he continued to give the side that air of invulnerability, with a succession of magnificent performances. Perhaps the best example of his commitment came in the FA Cup Final when he led a series of sorties on the Everton goal in a vain attempt to salvage the game. One leading bookmaker had offered odds of 25/1 on Peter scoring. He certainly tried!

Manchester U (£550,000 from Brondby on 12/8/91) F/PL 154 FLC 16 FAC 20 Others 14

Peter Schmeichel   Phil O'Brien
(Empics Sports Photo Agency)

SCHOFIELD John David
Born: Barnsley, 16 May 1965
Height: 5'11" Weight: 11.3

Tidy midfielder who arrived at Doncaster from Lincoln last November and whose hard work often went unnoticed by the supporters. Sharp in the tackle, and a good distributor of the ball, he is also capable of shooting from distance to good effect.

Lincoln C (Free from Gainsborough Trinity on 10/11/88) FL 221+10/11 FLC 15/4 FAC 5+2 Others 13+1
Doncaster Rov (Free on 18/11/94) FL 25+2/1

SCHOLES Paul
Born: Salford, 16 November 1974
Height: 5'6" Weight: 10.8
International Honours: E: Yth (UEFAC '93)

A very talented midfield player who can also play up front for Manchester United, Paul possesses a tremendous attitude and can score "cheeky" goals. He also plays a magnificent through-ball. His emergence from the youth side to first team action was one of the highlights of last season, having appeared to have solved United's search for a goalscorer when he netted two against Port Vale in the Coca Cola Cup and three in the Premiership. Although the signing of Andy Cole and a new contract for Mark Hughes may limit his progress, his excellent attitude, and eye for a goal, will keep him in regular contention in 1995-96.

Manchester U (From trainee on 29/1/93) PL 6+11/5 FLC 3/2 FAC 1+2 Others 0+2

Stefan Schwarz   Steve Morton
(Empics Sports Photo Agency)

SCHWARZ Stefan Hans
Born: Kulladal, Sweden, 18 May 1969
Height: 5'10" Weight: 12.6
International Honours: Sweden

An excellent midfield all-rounder, Stefan signed for Arsenal in May 1994, before going on to impress for Sweden in the USA World Cup. Has a venomous left-foot at dead-ball situations, scoring the all-important late goal in Genoa during the "Gunners'" European Cup Winners Cup campaign. Sometimes compared to Bryan Robson, he is also a strong tackler, who, when in possession, picks his passes well.

Arsenal (£1,750,000 from Benfica on 31/5/94) PL 34/2 FLC 4 FAC 1 Others 10/2

SCOTT Andrew (Andy)
Born: Epsom, 2 August 1972
Height: 6'1" Weight: 11.5

A pacy left-sided player who is equally at home in defence or attack. Having joined Sheffield United as a striker, in his first match at left-back in 1994-95, he scored two goals in the Anglo-Italian Cup and followed that up with a stunner against Stockport in the Coca Cola Cup. Unfortunately, in the next round, it was his tragic last minute own goal which cost United the game. Appears to have fully recovered from the glandular fever which affected him the previous season and was used with success as a late substitute, when his searing pace stretched defences.

Sheffield U (£50,000 from Sutton U on 1/12/92) P/FL 31+23/5 FLC 2/1 FAC 1+1 Others 3+1/3

SCOTT Andrew (Andy) Michael
Born: Manchester, 27 June 1975
Height: 6'0" Weight: 12.11

Former Blackburn left-back, who is both pacy and constructive, Andy joined Cardiff last August, playing 15 games before going out of contention due to injury.

Blackburn Rov (From trainee on 4/1/93)
Cardiff C (Free on 9/8/94) FL 13/1 FAC 1 Others 1

SCOTT Keith
Born: London, 10 June 1967
Height: 6'3" Weight: 13.4
Club Honours: GMVC '93; FAT '93

A target man with excellent aerial ability, and having already scored 12 goals from 32 games for Swindon in 1994-95, he signed for Stoke in December with a view to forming an effective strike partnership with Paul Peschisolido. However, when the goals failed to arrive, he ended the season both frustrated and out of favour.

Lincoln C (Free from Leicester U on 22/3/90) FL 7+9/2 FLC 0+1 Others 1+1
Wycombe W (£30,000 during 1991 close season) FL 15/10 FLC 4/2 FAC 8/1 Others 10/2
Swindon T (£300,000 on 18/11/93) P/FL 43+8/12 FLC 5/3 Others 3/1
Stoke C (£300,000 on 30/12/94) FL 16+2/3 FAC 2/1

SCOTT Kevin Watson
Born: Easington, 17 December 1966
Height: 6'2" Weight: 11.6
Club Honours: FAYC '85; Div 1 '93

Formerly Newcastle's longest serving central defender, Kevin appeared only four times for Tottenham last season, unable to demonstrate his strength in the air and the ability to play a vital role in set-pieces which had made him a favourite at St James' Park. However, a three month spell on loan at Port Vale gave him something to play for, in helping their back-line considerably as the club climbed away from the relegation zone.

Newcastle U (From apprentice on 19/12/84) F/PL 227/8 FLC 18 FAC 15+1/1 Others 12+1/2
Tottenham H (£850,000 on 1/2/94) PL 16/1
Port Vale (Loaned on 13/1/95) FL 17/1

SCOTT Martin
Born: Sheffield, 7 January 1968
Height: 5'9" Weight: 11.0
Club Honours: Div 4 '89

Left-back who looks to have been an outstanding purchase by Mick Buxton, he was signed from Bristol City last December and quickly won the Sunderland crowd over with his powerful tackling ability and his willingness to join up with the attack. His overall defensive awareness and pace meant that Sunderland finally solved a positional problem that had been evident for a number of seasons.

Rotherham U (From apprentice on 10/1/86) FL 93+1/3 FLC 11/2 FAC 7+2 Others 7/2
Bristol C (£200,000 on 5/12/90) FL 171/14 FLC 10/1 FAC 10 Others 8/1
Sunderland (£750,000 on 23/12/94) FL 24 FAC 3

Martin Scott   Barry Coombs
(Empics Sports Photo Agency)

SCOTT Peter Reginald
Born: Notting Hill, 1 October 1963
Height: 5'8" Weight: 11.0

Made Barnet's captain at the start of last season, this experienced central midfielder lead from the front and provided the strong platform on which the attack could build. A really good pro.

Fulham (From apprentice on 2/10/81) FL 268+9/27 FLC 18+2/6 FAC 9/1 Others 15
Bournemouth (Free on 14/8/92) FL 9+1 FLC 2 FAC 1 Others 0+1
Barnet (Free on 4/11/93) FL 53+5/2 FLC 2+2 FAC 6 Others 2

SCOTT Richard Paul
Born: Dudley, 29 September 1974
Height: 5'9" Weight: 10.10

Right-sided midfield player, who is also able to play in defence, he arrived at Shrewsbury from Birmingham last March. Looked happier in his own half, but did score a spectacular goal, his first in the League against Brighton and seemed to gain in confidence with every game.

Birmingham C (From trainee on 17/5/93) FL 11+1 FLC 3+1 Others 3
Shrewsbury T (Signed on 22/3/95) FL 17+1/1

SCOTT Robert (Rob)
Born: Epsom, 15 August 1973
Height: 6'1" Weight: 11.4

A midfield player and younger brother of Andy, he followed him from non-league football to Sheffield United. After a successful debut in the Anglo-Italian Cup, Rob made one substitute appearance in the Coca Cola Cup against Bolton and came off the bench in a FL game at Swindon, before going on loan to Scarborough for further experience. Unfortunately, torn ankle ligaments brought his season to a premature end after an impressive start with several goals.

Sheffield U (£20,000 from Sutton U on 1/8/93) FL 0+1 FLC 0+1 Others 2+1
Scarborough (Loaned on 22/3/95) FL 8/3

SCULLY Anthony (Tony) Derek Thomas
Born: Dublin, 12 June 1976
Height: 5'7" Weight: 11.12
International Honours: Ei: U21-2

Left-winger. Yet to make his debut for Crystal Palace, having come through the club's junior ranks and currently starring in the reserve side, Tony was loaned to Bournemouth last October in order to gain League experience. Showed much promise and shortly afterwards gained selection for the Republic of Ireland U21 side, later becoming a regular in the squad.

Crystal Palace (From trainee on 2/12/93)
Bournemouth (Loaned on 14/10/94) FL 6+4 Others 2

SCULLY Patrick (Pat) Joseph
Born: Dublin, 23 June 1970
Height: 6'1" Weight: 12.7
International Honours: Ei: 1; B-3; U23-1; U21-9

Firmly established as Huddersfield's first choice centre-back, proving consistent throughout last season, Pat won a well publicised bet with manager, Neil Warnock, when scoring his solitary FL goal. Also had a foot in the opening goal against Bristol Rovers in the Second Division play-off final at Wembley, where a 2-1 win saw Town promoted.

Arsenal (From trainee on 16/9/87)
Preston NE (Loaned on 7/9/89) FL 13/1 Others 1
Northampton T (Loaned on 23/8/90) FL 15 Others 1
Southend U (£100,000 on 8/1/91) FL 114+1/6 FLC 3 FAC 4 Others 5
Huddersfield T (Free on 24/3/94) FL 49/1 FLC 4/1 FAC 2 Others 6

SEABURY Kevin
Born: Shrewsbury, 24 November 1973
Height: 5'9" Weight: 11.6

A local Shrewsbury right-back, who established himself in the side last season with confident displays of sound defending and good use of the ball, he looked just at home in midfield and even central defence. With greater experience, Kevin should cement a place in every starting line-up.

Shrewsbury T (From trainee on 6/7/92) FL 27+4 Others 2+1

SEAGRAVES Mark
Born: Bootle, 22 October 1966
Height: 6'0" Weight: 13.4
International Honours: E: Yth; Sch

Unable to force his way into the Bolton team until last March, when he replaced the injured Simon Coleman, Mark, a solid and reliable defender, was part of a defence that conceded only three goals in ten League games during that spell. Earned a Coca Cola Cup runners-up medal, before losing his place in the side to Gudni Bergsson for the final run-in, including the ultimately successful First Division play-off victories. Stop Press: Signed by Swindon for a fee of £300,000 during the summer.

Liverpool (From apprentice on 4/11/83) FLC 1 FAC 1
Norwich C (Loaned on 21/11/86) FL 3
Manchester C (£100,000 on 25/9/87) FL 36+6 FLC 3 FAC 3 Others 2
Bolton W (£100,000 on 24/9/90) FL 152+5/7 FLC 8 FAC 17/1 Others 13/1

SEAL David
Born: Sydney, Australia, 26 January 1972
Height: 5'11" Weight: 12.4

A prolific scorer in Belgian football (47 goals in 31 games), David joined Bristol City last October, following trials at West Ham and Norwich. After impressing in the reserves, with six goals in two games, he made his debut against Millwall, but when failing to find the net in ten matches, five of them as a sub, he went back to the reserves. Has undoubted ability in front of goal, as 22 successful reserve team strikes would testify and it is hoped that 1995-96 will see the best of this enthusiastic player.

Bristol C (£80,000 from Eendracht Aalst on 7/10/94) FL 5+4 FAC 0+1

SEALEY Leslie (Les) Jesse
Born: Bethnal Green, 29 September 1957
Height: 6'0" Weight: 11.6
Club Honours: FAC '90; ECWC '91; CS '90

Brave and agile goalkeeper who is recognised for his last ditch saves. Very experienced, he was freed by Manchester United during the 1994 close season and signed for Blackpool. Joined West Ham last November, having made nine appearances for the "Seasiders", when the Premiership side required a deputy 'keeper, due to Ian Feuer being relatively inexperienced. Although Les played in 12 reserve games, with Ludek Miklosko ever-present, he was not required for first team duty.

Coventry C (From apprentice on 1/3/76) FL 158 FLC 11 FAC 5
Luton T (£100,000 on 3/8/83) FL 207 FLC 21 FAC 28 Others 3
Plymouth Arg (Loaned on 5/10/84) FL 6
Manchester U (Loaned on 21/3/90) FL 2 FAC 1
Manchester U (Free on 6/6/90) FL 31 FLC 8 FAC 3 Others 9
Aston Villa (Free on 19/7/91) FL 18 FAC 4 Others 2
Coventry C (Loaned on 25/3/92) FL 2
Birmingham C (Loaned on 2/10/92) FL 12 Others 3
Manchester U (Free on 6/1/93) FLC 1 FAC 0+1
Blackpool (Free on 18/7/94) FL 7 FLC 2
West Ham U (Free on 28/11/94)

SEAMAN David Andrew
Born: Rotherham, 19 September 1963
Height: 6'2" Weight: 14.10
Club Honours: Div 1 '91; FAC '93; FLC '93; ECWC '94
International Honours: E: 17; B-6; U21-10

Arsenal and England's goalkeeper, David is unflappable and reliable, stands up really well, and has great hands. Always on his toes, when he is brought into action he can make difficult saves look easy and inspires confidence in the defence. A hero for the "Gunners" last season, especially when playing with a broken rib in the European Cup Winners Cup against Auxerre and Sampdoria, he received international acclaim for his penalty shoot-out performance in Genoa that took the club into the final for the second year running. In the

final, with just seconds left on the clock against Real Zaragoza, it took the goal of a lifetime to beat him; Nayim's 45 yarder from the right-flank doing the trick. Broke an ankle during the 1995 close season trip to China.

Leeds U (From apprentice on 22/9/81)
Peterborough U (£4,000 on 13/8/82) FL 91 FLC 10 FAC 5
Birmingham C (£100,000 on 5/10/84) FL 75 FLC 4 FAC 5
Queens Park R (£225,000 on 7/8/86) FL 141 FLC 13 FAC 17 Others 4
Arsenal (£1,300,000 on 18/5/90) F/PL 189 FLC 21 FAC 28 Others 26

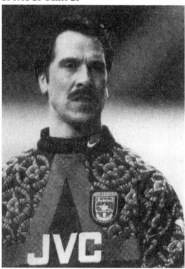

David Seaman — Neal Simpson (Empics Sports Photo Agency)

SEARLE Damon Peter
Born: Cardiff, 26 October 1971
Height: 5'11" Weight: 10.4
Club Honours: WC '92, '93; Div 3 '93
International Honours: W: 1; B-1; U21-6; Yth

Cardiff left-back. After making a shaky start to 1994-95, he improved steadily and by the end of the season was back to the kind of form that had him knocking on the Welsh selectors' doors some 12 months earlier.

Cardiff C (From trainee on 20/8/90) FL 191+2/2 FLC 5/1 FAC 11 Others 26

SEDGEMORE Benjamin (Ben) Redwood
Born: Wolverhampton, 5 August 1975
Height: 5'10" Weight: 13.11

Birmingham midfield player. Yet to make an appearance for City, he was loaned out to Northampton last December, making his FL debut at Colchester on Boxing Day. On the field for 12 minutes, he suffered damaged ligaments as the result of a bad tackle and has been sidelined ever since.

Birmingham C (From trainee on 17/5/93)
Northampton T (Loaned on 22/12/94) FL 1

SEDGLEY Stephen (Steve) Philip
Born: Enfield, 26 May 1968
Height: 6'1" Weight: 12.6
Club Honours: FAC '91; CS '91
International Honours: E: U21-11

Became Ipswich's first £1 million player, when signing from Tottenham in the 1994 close season and proved to be most versatile, at home in defence, or midfield, and scoring his fair share of goals. Last season started badly when a shin injury forced him to delay his debut, which finally came in the local derby against Norwich. He took some time to settle into the side, before being given the captaincy when George Burley arrived. However, after heavy defeats at Manchester United and Tottenham in March, he spent the rest of the campaign on the sidelines.

Coventry C (From apprentice on 2/6/86) FL 81+3/3 FLC 9/2 FAC 2+2 Others 5+1
Tottenham H (£750,000 on 28/7/89) F/PL 147+17/8 FLC 24+3/1 FAC 22+1/1 Others 5+3
Ipswich T (£1,000,000 on 15/6/94) PL 26/4 FLC 2 FAC 1

SEGERS Johannes (Hans)
Born: Eindhoven, Holland, 30 October 1961
Height: 5'11" Weight: 12.7
Goalkeeper. A key factor in Wimbledon's winning or losing games in 1994-95, his saves, often inspirational, were, on occasion, the only difference between the two sides. An athletic 'keeper, Hans was an ever-present until being replaced by long-time understudy, Neil Sullivan, in early March but, due to the latter's good form, he was unable to regain his place in the side.

Nottingham F (£50,000 from PSV Eindhoven on 14/8/84) FL 58 FLC 4 FAC 5
Stoke C (Loaned on 13/2/87) FL 1
Sheffield U (Loaned on 19/11/87) FL 10 Others 1
Dunfermline Ath (Loaned on 1/3/88) SL 4
Wimbledon (£180,000 on 28/9/88) F/PL 262+1 FLC 26 FAC 22 Others 7

Scott Sellars   Neal Simpson
(Empics Sports Photo Agency)

SELLARS Scott
Born: Sheffield, 27 November 1965
Height: 5'8" Weight: 10.0
Club Honours: FMC '87; Div 1 '93
International Honours: E: U21-3

A time very much to forget for the skilful left-sided midfield player, Scott only managed to play 19 first team games for Newcastle last season before a knee ligament injury, which required surgery, put him out of the game until 1995-96. The pick of few highlights was the goal he scored in the away UEFA Cup match against Royal Antwerp and the perfect left-footed cross he produced in the home match versus Sheffield Wednesday, for Andy Cole to tap in from close range. One of the most underrated players in the team.

Leeds U (From apprentice on 25/7/83) FL 72+4/12 FLC 4/1 FAC 4 Others 2/1
Blackburn Rov (£20,000 on 28/7/86) FL 194+8/35 FLC 12/3 FAC 11/1 Others 20/2
Leeds U (£800,000 on 1/7/92) PL 6+1 FLC 1+1 Others 1
Newcastle U (£700,000 on 9/3/93) F/PL 54+1/5 FLC 4+1/1 FAC 3 Others 4/1

SELLEY Ian
Born: Chertsey, 14 June 1974
Height: 5'9" Weight: 10.1
Club Honours: FLC '93; FAC '93; ECWC '94
International Honours: E: U21-3; Sch
Skilful Arsenal midfield player with vision, who is also a good tackler. Rated second only to Martin Keown in the man-to-man marking role, the season ended cruelly for him when sustaining a broken leg at Highbury against Leicester last February. Sure to be back before too long.

Arsenal (From trainee on 6/5/92) PL 35+5 FLC 5+1 FAC 3 Others 8+2/2

SEMPLE Ryan
Born: Derry, 2 July 1977
Height: 5'10" Weight: 12.0
Young attacking right-sided Peterborough midfielder. Still a trainee, Ryan was given a run-out in the Football League side last season, playing in two matches and impressing with some nice touches and passing skills.

Peterborough U (Trainee) FL 1+1

SERTORI Mark Anthony
Born: Manchester, 1 September 1967
Height: 6'3" Weight: 13.4
Club Honours: GMVC '88
A fringe player who did not manage to force his way into the Bury side last season, he made just three starts as an emergency centre-forward, before going back to his regular central defensive position in the reserves.

Stockport Co (Signed on 7/2/87) FL 3+1 FLC 1
Lincoln C (Free on 1/7/88) FL 43+7/9 FLC 6 FAC 4/1 Others 5/2
Wrexham (£30,000 on 9/2/90) FL 106+4/3 FLC 8+1 FAC 6 Others 9+1
Bury (Free on 22/7/94) FL 0+2 FAC 2 Others 1+1/1

SHAIL Mark Edward David
Born: Sandviken, Sweden, 15 October 1966
Height: 6'1" Weight: 13.3
International Honours: E: SP-1

Since joining Bristol City in March 1993, Mark has been an almost permanent member of the first team. Good in the air in both areas, and more than capable on the ground, he has proved that the step-up from non-league soccer to the Football League is not too great. Captained the side last season and, despite the club being relegated, he still formed a formidable central defensive barrier with Matt Bryant as the goals against column testified.

Bristol C (£45,000 from Yeovil on 25/3/93) FL 75+3/4 FLC 4 FAC 8/1 Others 1

SHAKESPEARE Craig Robert
Born: Birmingham, 26 October 1963
Height: 5'10" Weight: 12.5

Primarily right-footed, but with a strong left-foot, he is probably most effective at the centre of midfield, but also at home on either flank. Unfortunately, a long spell of injury kept him out of the Grimsby side last season.

Walsall (From apprentice on 5/11/81) FL 276+6/15 FLC 16/2 FAC 16 Others 2/1
Sheffield Wed (£300,000 on 19/6/89) FL 15+2 FLC 3/1 Others 0+1
West Bromwich A (£275,000 on 8/2/90) FL 104+8/12 FLC 6/1 FAC 5/2 Others 5/1
Grimsby T (£115,000 on 14/7/93) FL 37+15/3 FLC 4+1 FAC 1+2 Others 0+1

SHARP Graeme Marshall
Born: Glasgow, 16 October 1960
Height: 6'1" Weight: 11.8
Club Honours: CS '84, '87; FAC '84; Div 1 '85, '87; ECWC '85
International Honours: S: 12; U21-1

Graeme only made ten appearances for Oldham last season, three of which were after taking on the managerial position vacated by Joe Royle when he moved to Everton. His skill is undoubted, but a back problem means that he will be donning the manager's tracksuit more often than a playing shirt. In his prime, he was a striker who was difficult to get the better of and always looking to bring his team-mates into the game.

Dumbarton (Free from Eastercraigs in 1978) SL 37+3/17 SLC 2 SC 3/2
Everton (£125,000 on 4/4/80) FL 306+16/111 FLC 46+2/15 FAC 52+2/20 Others 21+1/11
Oldham Ath (£500,000 on 17/7/91) F/PL 103+6/31 FLC 12+1/4 FAC 11+1/2 Others 1

SHARP Kevin Phillip
Born: Canada, 19 September 1974
Height: 5'9" Weight: 10.7
Club Honours: FAYC '93
International Honours: E: Yth (UEFAYC '93); Sch

A very promising left-back, Kevin is a player with excellent technique, who can provide telling passes and strong running. Following the arrival of Nigel Worthington at Leeds last season, he struggled to make the first team, as the latter proved to be a capable deputy for Tony Dorigo. However, at the end of the campaign, he came off the bench twice for Rod Wallace in the last three matches and settled in easily, producing polished performances.

Leeds U (£60,000 from Auxerre on 20/10/92) PL 11+5

SHARP Raymond (Ray)
Born: Stirling, 16 November 1969
Height: 5'11" Weight: 12.5
Club Honours: S Div 1 '89
International Honours: S: U21-4

An experienced Scottish left-back, he settled down well in English football at Preston following his transfer from Dunfermline last October. Calm and assured in possession, Ray overlaps well on his flank, is quick in recovery and a strong and determined tackler, who uses his height to good effect.
Dunfermline Ath (Signed from Gairdoch U on 18/8/86) SL 144+7/1 SLC 4+3 SC 7 Others 2+1/1
Preston NE (Signed on 5/10/94) FL 21 FAC 3 Others 1

Lee Sharpe   Neal Simpson
(Empics Sports Photo Agency)

SHARPE Lee Stuart
Born: Halesowen, 27 May 1971
Height: 5'11" Weight: 11.4
Club Honours: ECWC '91; FLC '92; PL '93, '94; FAC '94; CS '94
International Honours: E: 8; B-1; U21-8

The PFA "Young Player of the Year" for 1991 and an England international, Lee is a very skilful Manchester United player who can operate in central midfield, on the wing, or at left-back. Possesses great balance and, excellent when taking defenders on, he is now firmly established at United's leading assist player. Began last season in out-standing form, making his mark on the European stage with two goals against Barcelona and Gothenburg. But when he suffered damaged ankle ligaments and a stress fracture to his foot, United's European Cup ambitions faded fast. Once recovered, his versatility gave the "Reds" more options than most, and his eye for a goal was an invaluable asset.
Torquay U (From trainee on 31/5/88) FL 9+5/3 Others 2+3
Manchester U (£185,000 on 10/6/88) F/PL 139+23/17 FLC 13+8/9 FAC 18+5/1 Others 16+2/3

SHARPE Richard
Born: Wokingham, 14 January 1967
Height: 5'11" Weight: 11.7

Striker. The all-time record scorer in American college soccer, he joined Rochdale on trial in 1994-95 and stayed until the start of the new USA season. After breaking into the side, he proved a useful partner for Steve Whitehall.
Rochdale (On trial from Cocoa Expos (USA) on 5/10/94) FL 9+7/2 FAC 0+1 Others 6/1

SHAW Graham Paul
Born: Stoke, 7 June 1967
Height: 5'8" Weight: 10.5
Club Honours: Div 2 '93

Striker. Started 1994-95 with Stoke, before having a spell on loan at Plymouth in August and eventually joining Rochdale on transfer deadline day in March. Acquired to try and increase "Dale's" scoring power, he replaced Ray Sharpe on the latter's return to America, but four games later he joined the club's list of injured strikers.
Stoke C (From apprentice on 10/6/85) FL 83+16/18 FLC 7/2 FAC 2+4/1 Others 3+2/2
Preston NE (£70,000 on 24/7/89) FL 113+8/29 FLC 5/6 FAC 5/1 Others 13/6
Stoke C (£70,000 on 12/8/92) FL 23+13/5 FLC 2+1/1 FAC 2+1 Others 2+4
Plymouth Arg (Loaned on 26/8/94) FL 6
Rochdale (Free on 23/3/95) FL 4

SHAW Paul
Born: Burnham, 4 September 1973
Height: 5'11" Weight: 12.4
International Honours: E: Yth

The most successful of the various strikers brought in by Burnley during last season, Paul was quick, skilful, and had an eye for goal, as he proved with four strikes in his first five appearances. His spell on loan from Arsenal was extended to the end of the campaign as he continued to keep Burnley's expensive forwards out of the side.
Arsenal (From trainee on 18/9/91) PL 0+1
Burnley (Loaned on 23/3/95) FL 8+1/4

SHAW Richard Edward
Born: Brentford, 11 September 1968
Height: 5'9" Weight: 11.5
Club Honours: FMC '91; Div 1 '94

After missing the Liverpool mauling on the opening day of last season, Richard was ever-present from thereon, forming an excellent partnership with Chris Coleman in the centre of Crystal Palace's defence. Not the tallest of defenders, but an excellent reader of the game and a tough tackler, he can mark man-for-man if required, perform equally well at full-back, and is very comfortable on the ball. Although relegated from the Premiership the club had an excellent goals against record, better than seventh placed Tottenham, for which much of the credit must go to the man who was ultimately voted the fans' "Player of the Year".
Crystal Palace (From apprentice on 4/9/86) F/PL 178+14/3 FLC 24+2 FAC 18 Others 12+1
Hull C (Loaned on 14/12/89) FL 4

SHAW Simon Robert
Born: Middlesbrough, 21 September 1973
Height: 6'0" Weight: 12.0

Another of Darlington's home grown youngsters, Simon has now completed three

years at the club, playing mainly in midfield. Graceful and a good passer of the ball, he only re-appeared towards the end of last season, at right-back.
Darlington (From trainee on 14/8/92) FL 46+20/6 FLC 2+1 FAC 1 Others 2+1

SHEARER Alan
Born: Newcastle, 13 August 1970
Height: 5'11" Weight: 11.3
Club Honours: PL '95
International Honours: E: 17; B-1; U21-12; Yth

Superlatives are the only coin suitable for the man who was voted the PFA "Footballer of the Year" and also won a PFA Divisional Award. Not only did he equal the Premiership scoring record of 34 goals as an ever-present, but he brought to Blackburn a determination to rise to the occasion and overcome all obstacles. In all aspects of the game he was supreme, finishing with either head or foot, acting as a target man who is too strong to knock off the ball, or dropping back to tackle as hard as any defender. In short, he inspired all around him and his performance when playing on his own up-field for 88 minutes against Leeds was the definitive version of a striker's art. Like all Rovers' players, Alan knew what had to be done to win the Premiership and was prepared to do whatever it took, hence the Championship medal. Needless to say, he was an England regular.
Southampton (From trainee on 14/4/88) FL 105+13/23 FLC 16+2/11 FAC 11+3/4 Others 8/5
Blackburn Rov (£3,600,000 on 24/7/92) PL 97+6/81 FLC 12/9 FAC 6/2 Others 2/1

SHEARER Lee Sean
Born: Southend, 23 October 1977
Height: 6'3" Weight: 12.0

Tall Leyton Orient central defender, and still a trainee, who impressed in a couple of outings at the end of last season, Lee is bound to get further opportunities following Barry Hearn's statement that the club's youth players should be given every chance.
Leyton Orient (Trainee) FL 2

SHEARER Peter Andrew
Born: Coventry, 4 February 1967
Height: 6'0" Weight: 11.6
Club Honours: Div 2 '95; AMC '95
International Honours: E: SP-1

Now in his second spell at Birmingham, Peter proved any doubters wrong with some powerful displays on the left-side of midfield last season, while winning Second Division and Auto Windscreen medals. Contributing several important goals, and playing to great effect, it was said that he was the first name on Barry Fry's teamsheet every week. Sadly, he suffered a serious achilles tendon injury in the Brighton game at the end of April and is likely to be absent for a considerable time.
Birmingham C (From apprentice on 5/2/85) FL 2+2 FLC 1/1
Rochdale (Free on 4/8/86) FL 1 FLC 1/2 (Free to Nuneaton Borough in November 1986)
Bournemouth (£18,000 from Cheltenham T on 9/3/89) FL 76+9/10 FLC 6/1 FAC 5/1 Others 2+1/1

Birmingham C (£75,000 on 5/1/94) FL 22+3/7 FLC 2 FAC 2/2 Others 4/3

SHEFFIELD Jonathan (Jon)
Born: Bedworth, 1 February 1969
Height: 5'11" Weight: 12.10

With his first team opportunities limited at Cambridge last season, an injury to John Filan saw him recalled from a spell on loan at Hereford. Athletic and agile, he gave many impressive displays and was often the difference between United winning or losing.

Norwich C (From apprentice on 16/2/87) FL 1
Aldershot (Loaned on 22/9/89) FL 11 Others 1
Aldershot (Loaned on 21/8/90) FL 15 Others 1
Cambridge U (Free on 18/3/91) FL 56 FLC 3 FAC 4 Others 6
Colchester U (Loaned on 23/12/93) FL 6
Swindon T (Loaned on 28/1/94) PL 2
Hereford U (Loaned on 15/9/94) FL 8 FLC 2

SHELTON Gary
Born: Nottingham, 21 March 1958
Height: 5'7" Weight: 10.12
International Honours: E: U21-1

Skilful midfielder who brought a great deal of experience to Chester last season, after signing from Bristol City during the summer. A good ball-player, who reads the game well, he missed the opening matches of the season with an ankle injury, but soon became one of the play-makers of the team.

Walsall (From apprentice on 1/3/76) FL 12+12 FLC 0+1 FAC 2+2/1
Aston Villa (£80,000 on 18/1/78) FL 24/7 FLC 2+1/1
Notts Co (Loaned on 13/3/80) FL 8
Sheffield Wed (£50,000 on 25/3/82) FL 195+3/18 FLC 19/3 FAC 23+1/3 Others 1
Oxford U (£150,000 on 24/7/87) FL 60+5/1 FLC 7+1/2 FAC 5 Others 1
Bristol C (Signed on 24/8/89) FL 149+1/24 FLC 12 FAC 9 Others 9/3
Rochdale (Loaned on 9/2/94) FL 3
Chester C (Free on 22/7/94) FL 31+2/2 FAC 2 Others 2/2

SHERIDAN Darren Stephen
Born: Manchester, 8 December 1967
Height: 5'6" Weight: 10.12

Because of an injury crisis at Barnsley last season, Darren, who had been a reserve midfield player, was pressed into the wing-back position on the left-hand side. Taking over in early October, he became so successful that he only missed one more game (through suspension). Accurate passing became his hallmark and he twice found the net while supporting the attack.

Barnsley (£10,000 from Winsford U on 12/8/93) FL 37+3 FAC 1 Others 1+1

SHERIDAN John Joseph
Born: Stretford, 1 October 1964
Height: 5'9" Weight: 10.8
Club Honours: FLC '91
International Honours: Ei: 32; B-1; U23-1; U21-2; Yth

Surprisingly quiet for Sheffield Wednesday in 1994-95, after his World Cup displays for Eire in the summer, he is at his best when producing defence splitting passes. Still neat and tidy in his midfield promptings, and a fine player to watch from the stands, possessing great technique, John will

certainly be looking to increase his scoring rate in 1995-96.

Leeds U (Free from Manchester C juniors on 2/3/82) FL 225+5/47 FLC 14/3 FAC 11+1/1 Others 11/1
Nottingham F (£650,000 on 3/8/89) FLC 1
Sheffield Wed (£500,000 on 3/11/89) F/PL 174+4/25 FLC 24/3 FAC 17+1/3 Others 4/2

John Sheridan   Phil O'Brien
(Empics Sports Photo Agency)

SHERINGHAM Edward (Teddy) Paul
Born: Highams Park, 2 April 1966
Height: 5'11" Weight: 12.5
Club Honours: Div 2 '88; FMC '92
International Honours: E: 9; B-; U21-1; Yth

Teddy enjoyed another good season at Tottenham in 1994-95, enforcing his ability to score and create fine goals. His presence in the opposing 18 yard box and his terrific ability to volley precisely from long crosses and corners resulted in many goals of good calibre, not least his hat-trick against Newcastle in December. The link-up of Darren Anderton's corners and his ability to create space to strike was a combination that many defenders dreaded and he consistently proved that, despite having to contend with the world class Jurgen Klinsmann, he was still a very reliable source of goals, demonstrating his versatility both in the air and on the ground. Continued to find scoring for England a problem but, nonetheless, gave some notable performances, in particular, the draw with Uruguay at Wembley in March.

Millwall (From apprentice on 19/1/84) FL 205+15/93 FLC 16+1/8 FAC 12/5 Others 11+2/5
Aldershot (Loaned on 1/2/85) FL 4+1 Others 1
Nottingham F (£2,000,000 on 23/7/91) FL 42/14 FLC 10/5 FAC 4/2 Others 6/2
Tottenham H (£2,100,000 on 28/8/92) PL 96+3/54 FLC 8/3 FAC 11/8

SHERLOCK Paul Graeme
Born: Wigan, 17 November 1973
Height: 5'10" Weight: 11.5

Signed from Notts County last March, Paul came into the Mansfield side as a left-sided midfielder, playing in the final two FL

matches and making a subs' appearance in the losing play-off game at Chesterfield. Captain of the reserves at County, he scored the first team's "Goal of the Season" on the opening day, a thundering 30-yard volley against Portsmouth.

Notts Co (From trainee on 1/7/92) FL 8+4/1 FLC 1 FAC 2 Others 2+1
Mansfield T (£15,000 on 23/3/95) FL 1+1 Others 0+1

SHERON Michael (Mike) Nigel
Born: Liverpool, 11 January 1972
Height: 5'9" Weight: 11.3
International Honours: E: U21-11

Transferred from Manchester City to Norwich at the beginning of last season, Mike was probably unaware that he faced a difficult time ahead of him. Scored twice in an exciting win over Coventry, but it took him until the end of the year to have an extended run in the side and his partnership with Ashley Ward flourished only briefly. As a striker, with both vision and skill, fitness problems hampered him throughout the season, a recurring hamstring injury restricting his appearances and hindering his form. 1995-96 should see him back at his best.

Manchester C (From trainee on 5/7/90) F/PL 82+18/24 FLC 9+1/1 FAC 5+3/3 Others 1
Bury (Loaned on 28/3/91) FL 1+4/1 Others 2
Norwich C (£1,000,000 on 26/8/94) PL 17+4/1 FLC 4/1 FAC 4/2

SHERWOOD Stephen (Steve)
Born: Selby, 10 December 1953
Height: 6'4" Weight: 14.7
Club Honours: Div 4 '78

An experienced 'keeper who signed from Grimsby shortly before last March's transfer deadline on a non-contract basis, Steve was quickly called into action for Lincoln after Andy Leaning was injured at Wigan in early April. No longer with the club.

Chelsea (From apprentice on 1/7/71) FL 16 FLC 1
Millwall (Loaned on 1/10/73) FL 1
Brentford (Loaned on 1/1/74) FL 62 FLC 2 FAC 2
Watford (£4,000 on 1/11/76) FL 211/1 FLC 23 FAC 23 Others 6
Grimsby T (Free on 6/7/87) FL 183 FLC 12 FAC 9 Others 8
Northampton T (Free on 30/7/93) FL 15+1 FLC 1 FAC 1 Others 2
Grimsby T (Free on 12/8/94)
Lincoln C (Free on 22/3/95) FL 6+1

SHERWOOD Timothy (Tim) Alan
Born: St Albans, 6 February 1969
Height: 6'0" Weight: 11.6
Club Honours: PL '95
International Honours: E: B-1; U21-4; Yth

Tim's Blackburn career enjoyed such a transformation in 1994-95 that by the end of the season he was not only collecting the Premiership trophy as club captain, but was also called up for the England squad. A fluid midfielder who controlled play by making himself available and transferring possession quickly, both long and short, his defensive duties consisted of closing down opponents and placing himself between them and the goal. Although possessing the ability to get into the penalty area, his responsibility to the side did not permit him to do this on a regular basis. Being elected to the PFA PL Team and on the short list for the "Player of the Year" award, were among his many successes.

Watford (From trainee on 7/2/87) FL 23+9/2 FLC 4+1 FAC 9 Others 4+1
Norwich C (£175,000 on 18/7/89) FL 66+5/10 FLC 7/1 FAC 4 Others 5+1/2
Blackburn Rov (£500,000 on 12/2/92) F/PL 121+5/11 FLC 14 FAC 8+1/1 Others 3

Tim Sherwood   Neal Simpson
                    (Empics Sports Photo Agency)

SHILTON Peter Leslie
Born: Leicester, 18 September 1949
Height: 6'0" Weight: 14.2
Club Honours: Div 2 '71, Div 1 '78; CS '78; EC '79, '80; ESC '79; FLC '79
International Honours: E: 125; U23-3; Yth; Sch

A famous international goalie, Peter holds the English appearance record with 125 caps to his name, and has only recently been surpassed, as the most capped in his position throughout the world of football, by the Swedish number one, Thomas Ravelli. Dismissed as Plymouth manager last season, amid much publicity, he amazingly came back as a player, first with Wimbledon (no first team appearances) and then with Bolton, a month later in March. Signed as cover for Jim Branagan and Aidan Davison, he became the oldest man ever to play for the club when coming on as a sub in a 1-1 draw at Stoke and, holding his place for the play-off semi-final first-leg at "Wolves", he produced a sterling display in a narrow defeat. An OBE and an MBE, and a former PFA "Player of the Year" (1978), he won the PFA Merit Award for services to football in 1990.

Leicester C (From apprentice on 1/9/66) FL 286/1 FLC 20 FAC 30
Stoke C (£300,000 on 1/11/74) FL 110 FLC 4 FAC 7
Nottingham F (£270,000 on 15/9/77) FL 202 FLC 26 FAC 18 Others 26
Southampton (£325,000 on 28/8/82) FL 188 FLC 28 FAC 17 Others 9
Derby Co (£90,000 on 7/7/87) FL 175 FLC 18 FAC 10 Others 8
Plymouth Arg (Free on 5/3/92) FL 34 FLC 6 FAC 1 Others 2
Wimbledon (Free on 10/2/95)
Bolton W (Free on 11/3/95) FL 0+1 Others 1

SHILTON Samuel (Sam) Roger
Born: Nottingham, 21 July 1978
Height: 5'10" Weight: 10.0
A tricky left-winger and the son of the former manager, Peter, he made his full debut against Brighton as the youngest player ever to play for Plymouth at 16 years, four months, and 12 days. Still a trainee.
Plymouth Arg (Trainee) FL 1+1 FAC 0+1

SHIPPERLEY Neil Jason
Born: Chatham, 30 October 1974
Height: 6'1" Weight: 13.12
International Honours: E: U21-4
A Southampton club record fee was needed to bring Neil from Chelsea last Janaury and that money looks to have been well spent. He brought much needed height and mobility to the forward line and, if his goals are not spectacular, they show a good eye for an opportunity. Leading the line well and providing good distribution, his all-round game continued to improve. Neil made a goalscoring return to the England U21 side in March.
Chelsea (From trainee on 24/9/92) PL 26+11/7 FLC 4+2/1 FAC 3/1 Others 2
Watford (Loaned on 7/12/94) FL 5+1/1
Southampton (£1,250,000 on 6/1/95) PL 19/4 FAC 4/2

SHIRTLIFF Peter Andrew
Born: Hoyland, 6 April 1961
Height: 6'2" Weight: 12.10
Club Honours: FLC '91
An experienced defender, Peter is noted for his reliability, and played in Wolverhampton's first 18 games last season, except for the trip to Venice. Tendonitis eventually led to him being left out against Forest and his problems lingered on until he had surgery in December, being out for around four months in all. On his return he resumed the captaincy from John De Wolf, as the club battled for a play-off place.
Sheffield Wed (From apprentice on 31/10/78) FL 188/4 FLC 17+1 FAC 17+1/1
Charlton Ath (£125,000 on 6/8/86) FL 102+1/7 FLC 10 FAC 5 Others 7/2
Sheffield Wed (£500,000 on 26/7/89) F/PL 104/4 FLC 18/1 FAC 9/2 Others 4
Wolverhampton W (£250,000 on 18/8/93) FL 65+2 FLC 4 FAC 7 Others 5

SHORT Christian (Chris) Mark
Born: Munster, Germany, 9 May 1970
Height: 5'10" Weight: 12.2
Club Honours: AIC '95
Excellent Notts County defender, who is predominantly a right-back, but who can also play in central defence. Strong in the tackle, and good when going forward, Chris, the brother of Derby's Craig, was out for a year with a stamina sapping illness and had a spell on loan at Huddersfield last December in a bid to regain his fitness. Came back into the County side for the final 14 games of the season.
Scarborough (Free from Pickering T on 11/7/88) FL 42+1/1 FLC 5 FAC 1 Others 3+1
Notts Co (£100,000 on 5/9/90) FL 77+15/2 FLC 5 FAC 4+1 Others 7/1
Huddersfield T (Loaned on 23/12/94) FL 6 Others 1

SHORT Craig Jonathan
Born: Bridlington, 25 June 1968
Height: 6'0" Weight: 11.4
International Honours: E: Sch
At one point in time Britain's most expensive defender, Craig added a great deal more aggression to his defending last season. Very dangerous at set-pieces and setting up chances for the Derby forwards, he scored his first goal in over a year against Oldham, followed by a terrific 25 yard volley against Charlton. Gave an outstanding performance in the home win over Bolton, but missed the end of the campaign through suspension, after being sent off at Burnley. Elected by his fellow professionals at the PFA Awards' Night as the best centre-half in the First Division.
Scarborough (Free from Pickering T on 15/10/87) FL 61+2/7 FLC 6 FAC 2 Others 7/1
Notts Co (£100,000 on 27/7/89) FL 128/6 FLC 6/1 FAC 8/1 Others 16/2
Derby Co (£2,500,000 on 18/9/82) FL 118/9 FLC 11 FAC 7/4 Others 7

SHOTTON Malcolm
Born: Newcastle, 16 February 1957
Height: 6'1" Weight: 12.7
Club Honours: Div 3 '84, Div 2 '85; FLC '88
A much travelled defender, he rejoined Barnsley in the 1994 close season as a non-contract player and reserve team coach, but due to a centre-half crisis in mid-season he was forced back into service. Became the oldest man to score for Barnsley when, after his 38th birthday, he netted against Sunderland. His forceful play enabled the club to maintain their promotion push right to the very end.
Leicester C (From apprentice on 1/2/75)
Oxford U (£15,000 from Nuneaton Borough on 19/5/80) FL 262+1/12 FLC 41+1/2 FAC 21/1 Others 6
Portsmouth (£70,000 on 28/8/87) FL 10 FLC 2
Huddersfield T (£20,000 on 16/2/88) FL 16/1 FLC 2
Barnsley (Signed on 9/9/88) FL 64+2/6 FLC 2 FAC 3+1 Others 2
Hull C (£35,000 on 28/2/90) FL 58+1/2 FLC 2 FAC 4 Others 3
Ayr U (Free on 4/9/92) SL 73/3 SLC 1 SC 3 Others 6
Barnsley (Free on 20/7/94) FL 8/1

SHOWLER Paul
Born: Doncaster, 10 October 1966
Height: 5'10" Weight: 11.6
International Honours: E: SP-2
An ex-policeman, hence the nickname PC, Paul is a left-sided midfield player, who had his fair share of injuries last season. Takes all the corners at Bradford and is a good crosser of the ball.
Barnet (Free from Altrincham T on 15/8/91) FL 69+2/12 FLC 2 FAC 3+1/1 Others 7
Bradford C (Free on 4/8/93) FL 43+12/7 FLC 3+1/1 FAC 3 Others 2+1

SHUTT Carl Steven
Born: Sheffield, 10 October 1961
Height: 5'10" Weight: 11.13
Club Honours: Div 2 '90; Div 1 '92
A midfielder who can also play up front, being attack minded, he signed for Bradford

last September after spending a month on loan from Birmingham. A very experienced player, he is now in the twilight of a career that has taken in football at the highest level.

Sheffield Wed (Free from Spalding on 13/5/85) FL 36+4/16 FLC 3/1 FAC 4+1/4
Bristol C (£55,000 on 30/10/87) FL 39+7/10 FLC 5+2/4 FAC 7+1/4 Others 10+1/4
Leeds U (£50,000 on 23/3/89) F/PL 46+33/17 FLC 6+2/2 FAC 10/1 Others 4+5/4
Birmingham C (£50,000 on 23/8/93) FL 18+8/4 FLC 3
Manchester C (Loaned on 31/12/93) PL 5+1
Bradford C (£75,000 on 11/8/94) FL 28+4/4 FLC 4/1 FAC 1+1 Others 2

SIGURDSSON Larus Orri
Born: Akureyri, Iceland, 4 June 1973
Height: 6'0" Weight: 11.5
International Honours: Iceland; U21; Yth
Having been introduced to Stoke last season, he was an instant hit after a short trial. An outstanding prospect, who turned out to be the find of the season, he is quick, good in the air, and with his man-to-man marking skills, he seems likely to make enormous progress in the English game.
Stoke C (£150,000 on 21/10/94) FL 22+2/1 FAC 0+1

SIMMONDS Daniel (Denny) Brian
Born: Eastbourne, 17 December 1972
Height: 5'11" Weight: 11.7
A young Brighton reserve defender, he had the occasional run out with the first eleven early last season, prior to being released during the summer.
Brighton & Hove A (From trainee on 9/7/93) FL 8+10 FLC 1+1 Others 2+1

SIMPKIN Darren Spencer
Born: Walsall, 24 March 1970
Height: 6'0" Weight: 12.0
Right-back. Joined Shrewsbury last December from "Wolves", but sustained an ankle injury on his debut at Brighton, which sidelined him for six games. Found it difficult to regain his form, although his strong-tackling should eventually become an asset to the team.
Wolverhampton W (£10,000 from Blakenhall on 3/12/91) FL 14+1 FLC 1
Shrewsbury T (£36,000 on 20/12/94) FL 10+2

SIMPSON Elliott David
Born: Fulford, 1 July 1976
Height: 5'10" Weight: 10.10
A former York trainee, and a naturally left-sided defender, he turned pro with the club prior to the start of 1994-95 and made one senior appearance early in the season. Freed during the summer.
York C (From trainee on 11/6/94) FL 1

SIMPSON Fitzroy
Born: Bradford on Avon, 26 February 1970
Height: 5'7" Weight: 10.4
Not in contention for a Manchester City place at the start of last season, Fitzroy was loaned out to Bristol City and played four games, before returning to Maine Road to fight for further first team opportunities. Recognised as a hard-running left-winger with a powerful shot, he was seen more

regularly towards the end of 1994-95 in a creative midfield role, where his contribution and workrate stood out as a member of the side that fought its way out of the relegation zone.
Swindon T (From trainee on 6/7/88) FL 78+27/9 FLC 15+2/1 FAC 2+1 Others 3+2
Manchester C (£500,000 on 6/3/92) F/PL 58+13/4 FLC 5+1 FAC 4+1
Bristol C (Loaned on 16/9/94) FL 4

SIMPSON Michael
Born: Nottingham, 28 February 1974
Height: 5'9" Weight: 10.8
Club Honours: AIC '95
Relatively inexperienced Notts County midfielder, who is seen by the club as the natural replacement for Mark Draper. A mainly right-sided midfielder, with a good repertoire of passing skills, including long balls for the wingers to run on to, Michael impressed enough to be selected for the Endsleigh League side that played in Italy last season. Good with free-kicks and corners.
Notts Co (From trainee on 1/7/92) FL 20+5/3 FLC 2+1 Others 4+3

SIMPSON Paul David
Born: Carlisle, 26 July 1966
Height: 5'6" Weight: 11.3
International Honours: E: U21-5; Yth
An old-fashioned left-winger, cum striker, Paul had a highly consistent season in 1994-95 as Derby's most dangerous forward. With an ability to accurately cross a ball on the run, or hit in a troublesome corner, after the injury to Mark Pembridge he took most of the free-kicks around the box and scored a Brazilian-like effort as part of a second-half hat-trick against Portsmouth in January, which won "Goal of the Month" on ITV. Also the team's regular penalty taker, he was given something of a free role from March onwards, which he relished.
Manchester C (From apprentice on 4/8/83) FL 99+22/18 FLC 10+1/2 FAC 10+2/4 Others 8+3
Oxford U (£200,000 on 31/10/88) FL 138+6/43 FLC 10/3 FAC 9/2 Others 5/2
Derby Co (£500,000 on 20/2/92) FL 112+15/36 FLC 8+1/4 FAC 3+1 Others 14+2/2

SINCLAIR Frank Mohammed
Born: Lambeth, 3 December 1971
Height: 5'8" Weight: 11.2
A player who can turn out for Chelsea either at left-back, or in central defence, where he gets great leverage for someone of his height. Frank's other assets include exceptional pace and a general enthusiasm for the game, always giving 100 per-cent effort. While those around him were struggling with injuries, he missed very few games and scored some valuable goals, including the first of the season for the club and two in the European Cup Winners Cup. Once finding his rightful place in the side, he could move up a gear.
Chelsea (From trainee on 17/5/90) F/PL 114/4 FLC 11/1 FAC 12/1 Others 7/2
West Bromwich A (Loaned on 12/12/91) FL 6/1

SINCLAIR Ronald (Ronnie) McDonald
Born: Stirling, 19 November 1964
Height: 5'9" Weight: 11.12

Club Honours: Div 2 '93
International Honours: S: Yth; Sch
Small for a goalkeeper, he came back in 1994-95 after effectively being out of the Stoke first team for more than a season following a serious knee injury. An excellent shot-stopper, his bravery and consistency served the team well during a difficult second half of the campaign, with Ronnie producing heroics behind a solid defence.
Nottingham F (From apprentice on 30/10/82)
Wrexham (Loaned on 1/3/84) FL 11 Others 1
Leeds U (£10,000 on 27/6/86) FL 8 FLC 1
Halifax T (Loaned on 1/3/87) FL 4
Halifax T (Loaned on 23/12/88) FL 10 Others 1
Bristol C (Free on 1/9/89) FL 44 FLC 3 FAC 5 Others 3
Walsall (Loaned on 5/9/91) FL 10 Others 1
Stoke C (£25,000 on 21/11/91) FL 77+2 FLC 2 FAC 4 Others 9

SINCLAIR Trevor Lloyd
Born: Dulwich, 2 March 1973
Height: 5'10" Weight: 11.2
International Honours: E: U21-12; Yth
Turned in some excellent performances throughout last season for both QPR and the England U21 side, scoring five goals for both. Injury and a bout of tonsillitis kept him sidelined for a number of games mid-season, but he was back in the side by early March and scored a tremendous winner at Coventry in April, his first away goal of the season. His performances were rewarded with a call-up to Terry Venables' full England squad get-together in April.
Blackpool (From trainee on 21/8/90) FL 84+28/15 FLC 8 FAC 6+1 Others 8+5/1
Queens Park R (£600,000 on 12/8/93) PL 62+3/8 FLC 6/2 FAC 2

SINNOTT Lee
Born: Pelsall, 12 July 1965
Height: 6'1" Weight: 12.7
International Honours: E: U21-1; Yth
Signed last December from local rivals Bradford, in the deal which also saw Lee Duxbury arrive at Huddersfield and Graham Mitchell go in the opposite direction, Lee established himself immediately in the centre of defence with Pat Scully. A key player in promotion to the First Division, via the play-offs, he took over the captaincy in the absence of Paul Reid.
Walsall (From apprentice on 16/11/82) FL 40/2 FLC 3 FAC 4
Watford (£100,000 on 15/9/83) FL 71+7/2 FLC 6 FAC 11
Bradford C (£130,000 on 23/7/87) FL 173/6 FLC 19 FAC 9 Others 12/1
Crystal Palace (£300,000 on 8/8/91) F/PL 53+2 FLC 9+1 FAC 1 Others 2
Bradford C (Signed on 9/12/93) FL 34/1 FLC 2 FAC 2 Others 2
Huddersfield T (£105,000 on 23/12/94) FL 25/1 Others 3

SINTON Andrew (Andy)
Born: Newcastle, 19 March 1966
Height: 5'7" Weight: 10.7
International Honours: E: 12; B-3; Sch
Had a most frustrating time of it in 1994-95, being unable to get a decent run in the Sheffield Wednesday side due to suffering a

Trevor Sinclair

Laurence Griffiths
(Empics Sports Photo Agency)

whole range of injuries. When he was fit he played on the wide left-side but, unfortunately, just when his form was about to return, he would pick up another injury which cost him his place in the England set-up. At his best, he is the ideal wide player with a good footballing brain who will often play the ball early, hoping to getting it back.
Cambridge U (From apprentice on 13/4/83) FL 90+3/13 FLC 6/1 FAC 3 Others 2/1
Brentford (£25,000 on 13/12/85) FL 149/28 FLC 8/3 FAC 11/1 Others 14/2
Queens Park R (£350,000 on 23/3/89) F/PL 160/22 FLC 14 FAC 13/2 Others 3/1
Sheffield Wed (£2,750,000 on 19/8/93) PL 47+3/3 FLC 10 FAC 4

SKEDD Anthony (Tony) Stuart
Born: Hartlepool, 19 May 1975
Height: 5'5" Weight: 10.0
Diminutive Hartlepool midfielder who can also play as a left-sided defender. Having received much praise the previous season, he worked hard in 1994-95 to try and win a regular first team place. Unfortunately, his tough-tackling style of play continually got him into trouble. A popular player, it must have been a hard decision for Keith Houchen to release him in the 1995 close season.
Hartlepool U (From trainee on 18/10/93) FL 39+7/1 FLC 1+1 FAC 1+1

SKELLY Richard Brian
Born: Norwich, 24 March 1972
Height: 5'11" Weight: 11.7
A skilful left-back with excellent ball control, he has found it hard to hold down a first team position at Northampton since coming out of non-league football during the 1994 close season.
Cambridge U (On trial from Newmarket T on 14/1/94) FL 2
Northampton T (Free on 19/6/94) FL 3 Others 2

SKELTON Aaron Matthew
Born: Welwyn Garden City, 22 November 1974
Height: 5'10" Weight: 11.5
This young defensive left-sided or central midfielder returned to action with Luton last season, after missing the whole of 1993-94 through injury. An attack minded player and an enthusiastic tackler, he was in the starting line-up for the opening game, thereby making his league debut and a steady performance saw him retain a squad place until the arrival of Gary Waddock. Further injuries held back his progress, but he remains very much in Luton's future plans.
Luton T (From trainee on 16/12/92) FL 3+2 FLC 0+1

SKINNER Craig Richard
Born: Heywood, 21 October 1970
Height: 5'10" Weight: 11.0
Normally on the right-side of the Plymouth midfield, in 1994-95 he featured as a centre-forward. Went through a purple patch in the middle of the season where he showed his best form since arriving at Home Park. Has plenty of pace and on his day is a very tricky player.
Blackburn Rov (From trainee on 13/6/89) FL 11+5 FLC 0+1 FAC 1 Others 3/1
Plymouth Arg (Signed on 21/8/92) FL 42+11/3 FLC 4 FAC 5+2/1 Others 3+1

SKINNER Justin
Born: Hounslow, 30 January 1969
Height: 6'0" Weight: 12.0
Bristol Rovers' record buy in August 1991 from Fulham. Justin is an accurate passer with good vision and much of the club's creative play revolves around his central role in midfield. Composed on the ball, he was very involved in set-pieces last season, using his skill and judgement to great effect in opposing penalty areas.
Fulham (From apprentice on 17/11/86) FL 111+24/23 FLC 10+1/4 FAC 5+1 Others 10+1/1
Bristol Rov (£130,000 on 27/8/91) FL 118+3/10 FLC 7 FAC 7 Others 11+1/2

SKINNER Justin James
Born: Dorking, 17 September 1972
Height: 5'8" Weight: 10.12
An enthusiastic Wimbledon left-back who tackles well and impresses with good long diagonal passes out of defence, Justin had a spell on loan at Wycombe last season, filling in for the injured David Titterton.
Wimbledon (From trainee on 2/7/91) PL 1
Bournemouth (Loaned on 7/3/94) FL 16
Wycombe W (Loaned on 26/8/94) FL 4+1

SKIVERTON Terence (Terry) John
Born: Mile End, 26 June 1975
Height: 6'0" Weight: 12.6
Right-back signed by Wycombe on loan from Chelsea for the final three months of last season, his young years betrayed some very mature and composed performances. Useful in the air, Terry might well end up as a centre-back, but regardless, he looks to have a good future ahead of him.
Chelsea (From trainee on 19/5/93)
Wycombe W (Loaned on 17/2/95) FL 8+2

SLATER Robert (Robbie) David
Born: Skelmersdale, 22 November 1964
Height: 5'11" Weight: 12.7
Club Honours: PL '95
International Honours: Australia

A red-headed midfielder, who was born in Ormskirk but had emigrated to Australia as a child, he went to play for Lens from where Blackburn signed him last season when it was apparent that David Batty's injuries would take longer to heal than had first been thought. Robbie slotted in easily, impressing with his mobile, harassing style, and his strong-running on the ball. Later used as a deputy on both wings, with his most crucial performance coming at Coventry when he was brought off the bench to play wide on the left to help the club claw back from a goal behind, he was good value for his Championship medal.

Blackburn Rov (£300,000 from Lens on 4/8/94) PL 12+6 FLC 1 FAC 1 Others 2

SLATER Stuart Ian
Born: Sudbury, 27 March 1969
Height: 5'7" Weight: 10.5
International Honours: E: B-2; U21-3

Versatile Ipswich forward who can play in midfield or on the wing, Stuart is at his best when given a free role, having the ability to take on defenders and leave them in his wake. Started last season brightly enough, before injuring his hip in mid-October. Returning in the New Year for the defeat of Leicester, he impressed new manager, George Burley, and gained a regular place in the side until a calf injury forced him to miss the last four games.

West Ham U (From apprentice on 2/4/87) FL 134+7/11 FLC 16+1/2 FAC 16/3 Others 5/2
Glasgow Celtic (£1,500,000 on 14/8/92) SL 40+3/3 SLC 3+2 SC 3 Others 4
Ipswich T (£750,000 on 30/9/93) PL 50+5/2 FLC 4 FAC 6

SLAVEN Bernard (Bernie) Joseph
Born: Paisley, 13 November 1960
Height: 5'10" Weight: 10.10
Club Honours: AMC '93
International Honours: Ei: 6

Proven goalscorer and Irish international whose possible Darlington appearances last season were halved through injury, Bernie scored his 200th first team goal at Fulham in February, but claimed only seven all season while operating wide on the left. Freed during the summer.

Morton (Signed from Rutherglen Glencairn in 1980) SL 11+11/1 SC 2
Airdrie (Signed during 1983 close season) SL 2 SLC 3+1
Queen of the South (Signed in November 1983) SL 2
Albion Rov (Signed in April 1984) SL 42/27 SLC 2/3 SC 1
Middlesbrough (£25,000 on 10/10/85) F/PL 286+21/118 FLC 26+2/10 FAC 16+3/4 Others 27/14
Port Vale (Free on 19/3/93) FL 29+4/9 FLC 2/1 FAC 2+2/1 Others 7/2
Darlington (Free on 23/2/94) FL 35+2/7 FLC 2/1 FAC 2/1 Others 0+1

SLAWSON Stephen Michael
Born: Nottingham, 13 November 1972
Height: 6'0" Weight: 12.6

Notts County striker with good shooting ability, especially from the left-foot. Made only one subs' appearance last season, and had a spell on loan at Shrewsbury, but goals remained sparse. Another County player whose contract expired during the summer and who was given a free transfer.

Notts Co (From trainee on 9/7/91) FL 16+22/4 FLC 1+1 FAC 0+3 Others 3+3/1
Burnley (Loaned on 12/2/93) FL 5/2
Shrewsbury T (Loaned on 31/10/94) FL 6 Others 0+1

SLINN Kevin Paul
Born: Northampton, 2 September 1974
Height: 5'11" Weight: 11.0

A forward who joined Stockport from Watford during the 1994 season on a monthly contract, he left last March after failing to secure a regular place in the team.

Watford (From trainee on 9/4/93)
Stockport Co (Free on 8/7/94) FL 2+2/1 FLC 0+1 Others 1

SLOAN Scott
Born: Wallsend, 14 December 1967
Height: 5'10" Weight: 11.6

Hartlepool striker signed from Falkirk in the 1994 close season. Began the season well, but was unlucky with a knee ligament injury early on. Subsequently, he completely lost his goal touch, although he continued to work hard alongside Keith Houchen.

Berwick R (Signed from Ponteland in 1988) SL 58+3/20 SLC 2/2 SC 4/1
Newcastle U (£75,000 on 31/7/90) FL 11+5/1 FAC 1 Others 1
Falkirk (£50,000 on 8/11/91) SL 49+15/11 SLC 6/2 SC 3+1/4 Others 3+1/2
Cambridge U (Loaned on 25/2/94) FL 4/1
Hartlepool U (Free on 12/8/94) FL 26+3/2 FLC 2+1 FAC 0+1 Others 1

SMALL Bryan
Born: Birmingham, 15 November 1971
Height: 5'9" Weight: 11.9
International Honours: E: U21-7; Yth

A left-back, who can also alternate in midfield, Bryan is strong with plenty of pace and is a player who likes to get forward at every opportunity. However, with tough competition for places from men like Steve Staunton and Phil King, he struggled to feature in the Aston Villa side last season, making just five appearances. Still one for the future though and excellent in a man-to-man marker role.

Aston Villa (From trainee on 9/7/90) F/PL 31+5 FLC 2 FAC 2+1 Others 4
Birmingham C (Loaned on 9/9/94) FL 3

SMART Allan Andrew Colin
Born: Perth, 8 July 1975
Height: 6'2" Weight: 11.0

Preston's find of last season. A strong, aggressive and determined centre-forward, Alan has a powerful shot in either foot, is good in the air and possesses a clever footballing brain. Still learning about the game, following his transfer from Scotland, his talent and keeness has established an instant rapport with the crowd.

Preston NE (£15,000 from Caledonian Thistle on 22/11/94) FL 17+2/6 FAC 2/1 Others 1

SMILLIE Neil
Born: Barnsley, 19 July 1958
Height: 5'6" Weight: 10.7
Club Honours: FMC '88; Div 3 '92

Ball playing Gillingham winger, who missed a large majority of last season through injuries, he was appointed caretaker manager when Mike Flanagan left at the beginning of March 1995.

Crystal Palace (From apprentice on 1/10/75) FL 71+12/7 FLC 7 FAC 7/1
Brentford (Loaned on 1/1/77) FL 3
Brighton & Hove A (Signed on 9/8/82) FL 62+13/2 FLC 2 FAC 8+1/1
Watford (£100,000 on 24/6/85) FL 10+6/3 FLC 1 FAC 2/1
Reading (Free on 4/12/86) FL 38+1 FLC 3 Others 5+1/2
Brentford (Free on 15/8/88) FL 163+9/18 FLC 21 FAC 12/1 Others 18+1/3
Gillingham (Free on 26/7/93) FL 53/3 FLC 2 FAC 4 Others 1

SMITH Alan Martin
Born: Bromsgrove, 21 November 1962
Height: 6'3" Weight: 12.0
Club Honours: Div 1 '89, '91; FLC '93; FAC '93; ECWC '94
International Honours: E: 13; B-4; SP-3

Unselfish Arsenal striker who has proved to be an excellent clubman over the years, especially when acting as a foil for others. Following his euphoric winner against Parma, which brought the European Cup Winners Cup to Highbury in 1993-94, Alan's season came to an abrupt halt when he suffered an ankle injury in the home fixture against QPR last December. Initially, it was thought he would be back before the end of the campaign, something that did not happen, and Arsenal fans must now hope he will be fit in time for 1995-96.

Leicester C (£22,000 from Alvechurch on 14/6/82) FL 190+10/76 FLC 8+1/4 FAC 8/4
Arsenal (£800,000 on 26/3/87) F/PL 242+22/86 FLC 36+2/16 FAC 23+3/6 Others 20+2/7

SMITH Anthony (Tony)
Born: Sunderland, 21 September 1971
Height: 5'10" Weight: 11.4
International Honours: E: Yth

Left-back who can also operate effectively at centre-half. Made his first appearance for Sunderland last season since a serious leg injury that had halted his progress in August 1993 but, in facing an uphill battle for places following the arrival of Martin Scott, he was released during the summer.

Sunderland (From trainee on 31/7/90) FL 19+1 FLC 5
Hartlepool U (Loaned on 6/1/92) FL 4+1 Others 2

SMITH David
Born: Stonehouse, 29 March 1968
Height: 5'8" Weight: 10.7
International Honours: E: U21-10

A competent, hard-working, left-sided WBA midfield player with fair speed and adequate all-round ability, it was anticipated that David would add width and competitiveness to Albion's play. However, he struggled to get into the side on a regular basis in 1994-95 and hopes for better luck this time round.

Coventry C (From apprentice on 7/7/86) F/PL 144+10/19 FLC 17 FAC 6 Others 4+1
Bournemouth (Loaned on 8/1/93) FL 1
Birmingham C (Signed on 12/3/93) FL 35+3/3 FLC 4 FAC 0+1 Others 1
West Bromwich A (£90,000 on 31/1/94) FL 34+6 FLC 1 FAC 0+2

SMITH David (Dave) Christopher
Born: Liverpool, 26 December 1970
Height: 5'9" Weight: 11.2

Dave became a regular in the Oxford midfield after joining from Norwich in the summer of 1994, playing in the first 50 games, before suffering a knee injury which kept him out for all but the final match of last season. An unselfish player, yet to score, who clears up behind the others.
Norwich C (From trainee on 4/7/89) F/PL 13+5 FAC 2+1 Others 1+1
Oxford U (£100,000 on 5/7/94) FL 41+1 FLC 4 FAC 1 Others 4

SMITH Dean
Born: West Bromwich, 19 March 1971
Height: 6'1" Weight: 12.0

Centre-half. Signed from Walsall during the 1994 close season, having broken Hereford's record transfer fee, he immediately took over as the skipper. An excellent leader and anchor man, his appointment played great dividends, especially in the second half of the campaign. Deadly from free-kicks, Dean is equally effective either on the ground or in the air.
Walsall (From trainee on 1/7/89) FL 137+5/2 FLC 10 FAC 4 Others 10
Hereford U (£75,000 on 17/6/94) FL 35/3 FLC 4 FAC 2 Others 3+1/1

SMITH Gary Neil
Born: Harlow, 3 December 1968
Height: 5'10" Weight: 12.9

Midfield player. Having spent a year recovering from a broken leg, Gary was almost immediately hit with a damaged ankle as 1994-95 got underway. Unable to get back into the Barnet side, he was released by the club at the end of the season.
Fulham (From apprentice on 12/8/86) FL 0+1
Colchester U (Free on 12/9/87) FL 11 Others 1 (Free to Enfield during 1988 close season)
Barnet (Free from Wycombe W, via Wycombe W, on 10/8/93) FL 11+2 FLC 2 FAC 0+1 Others 1

SMITH James (Jamie) Jade Anthony
Born: Birmingham, 17 September 1974
Height: 5'6" Weight: 10.8

A quick, attacking Wolverhampton right-back, who is skilful on the ball and whose good pre-season form made him a surprise choice on the opening day of 1994-95. His rise to stardom even saw him in the England U21 squad, but by November he needed a rest. Returned for four games in December, although he was out of the team when he represented the Endsleigh League, who beat their Italian counterparts 3-2. Another brief spell ended with him being sent off in the local derby cauldron of the Hawthorns.
Wolverhampton W (From trainee on 7/6/93) FL 24+1 FLC 3 FAC 1 Others 2

SMITH Mark Alexander
Born: Glasgow, 16 December 1964
Height: 5'9" Weight: 10.4
Club Honours: S Div 1 '89

Troubled by injury for much of last season, Mark only had a decent run in the Shrewsbury team at the end of 1994-95 . A left-winger who is speedy on the ball and happy to take defenders on, he also makes telling runs, often cutting in to the middle with good effect. Scored his first goal for two years in April, before being freed during the summer.
Queens Park R (Signed from Gairdoch U in 1983-84) SL 71+11/7 SLC 1 SC 3+1
Glasgow Celtic (Signed on 6/6/86) SL 3+3 SLC 2
Dunfermline Ath (Signed in October 1987) SL 48+5/6 SLC 3+1 SC 4+2/1
Hamilton Academical (Loaned in September 1989) SL 5/1
Stoke C (Loaned on 15/2/90) FL 2
Nottingham F (£75,000 on 27/3/90)
Reading (Loaned on 27/12/90) FL 3
Mansfield T (Loaned on 21/3/91) FL 6+1
Shrewsbury T (£25,000 on 13/8/91) FL 64+14/4 FLC 5 FAC 3+1/1 Others 4+2

SMITH Mark Allen
Born: Birmingham, 2 January 1973
Height: 6'1" Weight: 13.9

Had been the number one 'keeper after joining Crewe from Nottingham Forest, but lost his place in the side to Mark Gayle during last season. Mark will undoubtedly work hard to regain his first team spot in 1995-96.
Nottingham F (From trainee on 7/2/91)
Crewe Alex (Free on 24/2/93) FL 61+2 FLC 4 FAC 5 Others 10

SMITH Mark Cyril
Born: Sheffield, 16 December 1961
Height: 5'9" Weight: 12.2

Left-sided Scunthorpe midfield man, with good close control, who likes to run at defenders, he also gets back to provide defensive cover. Made 31 starts for the club last season, before being released during the summer.
Sheffield U (From juniors on 14/8/80)
Scunthorpe U (On trial from Kettering T, via Worksop T and Gainsborough Trinity, on 23/9/85) FL 0+1
Rochdale (Free on 15/7/88) FL 26+1/7 FLC 2 FAC 2 Others 2
Huddersfield T (£50,000 on 10/2/89) FL 85+11/11 FLC 5 FAC 5+1/1 Others 5/1
Grimsby T (£55,000 on 21/3/91) FL 37+40/4 FLC 2+3 FAC 1+3 Others 2+1
Scunthorpe U (£20,000 on 14/7/93) FL 50+12/8 FLC 4 FAC 6+1 Others 6

SMITH Martin Geoffrey
Born: Sunderland, 13 November 1974
Height: 5'11" Weight: 12.0
International Honours: E: U21-1

Considered to be the jewel in the crown at Sunderland, Martin is a left-sided striker, or midfielder, who made his debut for the England U21 side last season at Newcastle and looks to have a great future. Has the ability to go past defenders with ease, possesses a powerful shot, and is no slouch in the air. Whether or not Sunderland can resist the interests of other clubs and hang on to Martin remains to be seen.
Sunderland (From trainee on 9/9/92) FL 60+4/18 FLC 2+1 FAC 6/1

SMITH Neil James
Born: Lambeth, 30 September 1971
Height: 5'9" Weight: 12.0
Club Honours: FAYC '90

Tough-tackling Gillingham midfielder, who started last season on a weekly contract after refusing new terms, he came back into the side, where his "never-say-die" spirit soon spread to his team-mates.
Tottenham H (From trainee on 24/7/90)
Gillingham (£40,000 on 17/10/91) FL 126+8/8 FLC 7 FAC 12/2 Others 7/2

SMITH Nicholas (Nick) Leslie
Born: Berkeley, 28 January 1969
Height: 5'7" Weight: 10.0
Club Honours: GMVC '92; FAT '92

Freed by Colchester, Nick signed for Wycombe during the 1994 close season, but was released and joined Sudbury Town, prior to 1994-95 getting underway. Equally at home in midfield or the defence, and an excellent crosser of the ball, Nick had another taste of League soccer on loan at Northampton in January, before returning to the Suffolk non-league side.
Southend U (From trainee on 9/7/87) FL 49+11/6 FLC 0+2 FAC 2+2 Others 4+2
Colchester U (Free on 1/6/90) FL 71+10/4 FLC 4 FAC 8 Others 3
Wycombe W (Free on 21/7/94)
Northampton T (Loaned from Sudbury T on 27/1/95) FL 6/1

SMITH Paul Michael
Born: Rotherham, 9 November 1964
Height: 5'10" Weight: 11.10
Club Honours: GMVC '88

Right-sided midfielder or defender, and Lincoln's longest serving player, Paul spent a lengthy period on loan at Kettering in the early part of last season, but regained his first team place on his return. Released during the summer.
Sheffield U (From apprentice on 11/11/82) FL 29+7/1 FAC 2 Others 1
Stockport Co (Loaned on 16/8/85) FL 7/5 FLC 2/1
Port Vale (Signed on 31/7/86) FL 42+2/7 FLC 5/1 FAC 2 Others 3/1
Lincoln C (Signed on 1/8/87) FL 219+13/27 FLC 10+2 FAC 6+2/1 Others 11

SMITH Paul William
Born: East Ham, 18 September 1971
Height: 5'11" Weight: 14.0

Right-footed Brentford central midfielder. A perceptive passer, who also makes strong runs into the penalty area, Paul had an excellent start to last season until missing two months through injury. Took a while to regain form, but ended the campaign in style.
Southend U (From trainee on 16/3/90) FL 18+2/1 Others 0+1
Brentford (Free on 6/8/93) FL 67/6 FLC 4/1 FAC 4 Others 7/1

SMITH Peter John
Born: Stone, 12 July 1969
Height: 6'1" Weight: 12.7

Brighton's find of last season. Signed on a one year contract, Peter had an early first team chance at right-back, due to injuries.

Although inexperienced, he greatly impressed with his enthusiasm, firm tackling and electrifying pace down the right-flank.

Brighton & Hove A (Free from Alma Swanley on 8/8/94) FL 35+3/1 FLC 4+1 FAC 1 Others 1

SMITH Richard Geoffrey
Born: Lutterworth, 3 October 1970
Height: 5'11" Weight: 12.4

Right-footed central defender, with a prodigious long-throw, who only figured spasmodically for Leicester during last season, suffering from injury problems, before being diagnosed as having a hernia. Always a wholehearted performer.

Leicester C (From trainee on 15/12/88) F/PL 81+16/1 FLC 4 FAC 5/1 Others 12
Cambridge U (Loaned on 6/9/89) FL 4 FLC 1

SMITH Scott David
Born: Christchurch, New Zealand, 6 March 1975
Height: 5'8" Weight: 11.6

Scott was restricted to just a handful of first team appearances for Rotherham in 1994-95, but was a virtual ever-present in the reserve team, displaying the kind of form which showed him to be a right-back for the future.

Rotherham U (From trainee on 1/10/93) FL 10+1 FAC 2 Others 0+1

SMITH Gareth **Shaun**
Born: Leeds, 9 April 1971
Height: 5'10" Weight: 11.0

A left-sided player, who normally occupied the number two spot in the Crewe side last season, he is very mobile and a player to be feared from dead-ball situations. Also, he is more than a little useful when it comes to taking penalties.

Halifax T (From trainee on 1/7/89) FL 6+1 Others 1 (Free to Emley in May 1991)
Crewe Alex (Free on 31/12/91) FL 118+10/19 FLC 3+1 FAC 5/2 Others 14+1/1

SNEEKES Richard
Born: Amsterdam, Holland, 30 October 1968
Height: 5'11" Weight: 12.2

Signed from Fortuna Sittard at the start of last season, Richard became well known in the English game for his powerful shot, which brought him some spectacular goals for Bolton. The Dutchman grabbed eight during the campaign, two of them coming in the Wanderers' 2-1 win at Charlton, both from long-range. The Burnden crowd now shout "shoot!" whenever he gets the ball. Unfortunately, missed the final month of the season through injury, thus being unavailable for the side that eventually reached the Premiership, via the play-offs.

Bolton W (£200,000 from Fortuna Sittard on 12/8/94) FL 37+1/6 FLC 7+1/1 FAC 1/1

SNODIN Glyn
Born: Rotherham, 14 February 1960
Height: 5'6" Weight: 10.5

Started last season as Barnsley's first choice left-back, but injury again wrecked his season and the emergence of Darren Sheridan kept him in the reserves. Granted a free transfer during the summer.

Doncaster Rov (From apprentice on 1/10/77) FL 288+21/61 FLC 12+2/1 FAC 15/1 Others 5/1
Sheffield Wed (£115,000 on 19/6/85) FL 51+8/1 FLC 3+1 FAC 9 Others 1
Leeds U (£135,000 on 31/7/87) FL 83+11/10 FLC 9+1/3 FAC 5+2 Others 4
Oldham Ath (Loaned on 15/8/91) FL 8/1 FLC 1
Rotherham U (Loaned on 28/2/92) FL 3
Heart of Midlothian (Free on 31/3/92) SL 20+14 SLC 0+2 SC 2+1/1 Others 2+1/1
Barnsley (Free on 23/7/93) FL 18+7 FLC 3

SNODIN Ian
Born: Rotherham, 15 August 1963
Height: 5'7" Weight: 11.0
Club Honours: Div 1 '87
International Honours: E: B-2; U21-4; Yth

An accomplished right-sided player who looks comfortable either defending or further forward, Ian, the brother of Barnsley's Glyn, left Everton bound for Oldham last January, following a spell earlier in the season on loan at Sunderland. Very experienced, with over 400 first team appearances under his belt, he took up the right-back spot almost immediately and showed he had lost none of his old touches.

Doncaster Rov (From apprentice on 18/8/80) FL 181+7/25 FLC 9/1 FAC 11+1/1 Others 3
Leeds U (£200,000 on 22/5/85) FL 51/6 FLC 3/2 FAC 1
Everton (£840,000 on 16/1/87) F/PL 142+6/3 FLC 19+4/2 FAC 26/2 Others 3
Sunderland (Loaned on 13/10/94) FL 6
Oldham Ath (Free on 9/1/95) FL 17

SOLOMAN Jason Rafael
Born: Welwyn Garden City, 6 October 1970
Height: 6'0" Weight: 12.2
Club Honours: FAYC '89
International Honours: E: Yth

March 1995 signing from Watford, he displayed impressive strength and no little skill in Wycombe's central midfield. Earlier in the season he had been on loan at Peterborough.

Watford (From trainee on 9/12/88) FL 79+21/5 FLC 9/1 FAC 1 Others 5+1
Peterborough U (Loaned on 13/1/95) FL 4
Wycombe W (Free on 17/3/95) FL 5+1

SOMMER Juergen Petersen
Born: New York, USA, 27 February 1969
Height: 6'4" Weight: 15.12
International Honours: USA

As one of the tallest goalies in British soccer, Juergen is hard to beat. At times a brilliant shot-stopper and impregnable in the air, he saved Luton on a number of occasions in 1994-95. The highlight of his season came at Wembley in September when he made his international debut for the USA against England, coming on as a substitute. He went on to play against Saudi Arabia and Uruguay, but the latter game cost him his club place when young Kelvin Davis took the opportunity with both hands.

Luton T (Signed on 5/9/91) FL 80 FLC 4 FAC 11 Others 2
Brighton & Hove A (Loaned on 13/11/91) FL 1
Torquay U (Loaned on 31/10/92) FL 10 Others 1

SOUTHALL Neville
Born: Llandudno, 16 September 1958
Height: 6'1" Weight: 13.0
Club Honours: FAC '84, '95; CS '84, '85;

Div 1 '85, '87; ECW '85
International Honours: W: 81

Undoubtedly one of the top 'keepers in the Premiership, Neville's main qualities are his lightning reflexes, the ability to make himself big when challenging a striker and, most importantly, his great consistency. Began 1994-95, his 13th year with Everton, by continuing to provide an extremely solid rearguard, relentlessly turning in inspired performances, and calling on his experience at both domestic and international levels. His season ended on the highest possible note with an incredible display of saves in the FA Cup Final, which helped Everton lift the trophy.

Bury (£6,000 from Winsford U on 14/6/80) FL 39 FAC 5
Everton (£150,000 on 13/7/81) F/PL 494 FLC 60 FAC 64 Others 32
Port Vale (Loaned on 27/1/83) FL 9

Neville Southall   Neal Simpson
(Empics Sports Photo Agency)

SOUTHALL Leslie **Nicholas** (Nicky)
Born: Stockton, 28 January 1972
Height: 5'10" Weight: 11.4

Attacking midfielder, and still a youngster, but now Hartlepool's longest-serving player. Early in 1994-95, he was out with a foot injury, but came back to have another good season, impressing with skilful runs down the left-wing. Scored fewer goals, but against Colchester recorded his first ever hat-trick and the "Pool" will struggle to keep him free from the clutches of bigger clubs.

Hartlepool U (Free from Darlington juniors on 21/2/91) FL118+20/24 FLC 6+1/3 FAC 4+4 Others 6+2

SOUTHGATE Gareth
Born: Watford, 3 September 1970
Height: 5'10" Weight: 11.12
Club Honours: Div 1 '94

Athletic, hard-working midfielder with two good feet, who can also play at full-back, and who is always ready to support his team-mates when they need a passing option. As the Crystal Palace captain and only ever-present last season, he led by example, and right up until the final whistle of the last game was still trying desperately to motivate all around him as the club spiralled towards the First Division. Stop Press: Signed by Aston Villa for a fee of £2,500,000 during the summer.

Crystal Palace (From trainee on 17/1/89) F/PL 148+4/15 FLC 23+1/7 FAC 9 Others 6

SPACKMAN Nigel James
Born: Romsey, 2 December 1960
Height: 6'1" Weight: 12.4
Club Honours: Div 2 '84, Div 1 '88; FMC '86; SPD '90, '91, '92; SLC '91; SC '92

At the age of 34, Nigel was a revelation for Chelsea last season, especially in the European Cup Winners Cup, where he was able to put his foot on the ball and encourage the youngsters in the side. As the midfield anchor man and a consistent ball-winner, fetcher and carrier, along with Erland Johnsen, he was the club's "Player of the Year", an honour well deserved.

Bournemouth (Free from Andover on 8/5/80) FL 118+1/10 FLC 5 FAC 7
Chelsea (£40,000 on 20/6/83) FL 139+2/12 FLC 22+1 FAC 8/1 Others 7/1
Liverpool (£400,000 on 24/2/87) FL 39+12 FLC 6+1 FAC 5
Queens Park R (£500,000 on 2/2/89) FL 27+2/1 FLC 2/1 Others 2
Glasgow R (£500,000 on 30/11/89) SL 100/1 SLC 10 SC 9 Others 5
Chelsea (£485,000 on 8/9/92) PL 47+4 FLC 4 FAC 6 Others 7

SPEARING Anthony (Tony)
Born: Romford, 7 October 1964
Height: 5'6" Weight: 11.10

Tough-tackling Peterborough full-back with a "never-say-die" spirit, he always gives 100 per-cent. Has tremendous enthusiasm and is a great clubman.

Norwich C (From apprentice on 11/10/82) FL 67+2 FLC 5 FAC 4 Others 4
Stoke C (Loaned on 1/11/84) FL 9
Oxford U (Loaned on 1/2/85) FL 5
Leicester C (£100,000 on 12/7/88) FL 71+2/1 FLC 2+1 FAC 1 Others 2
Plymouth Arg (Free on 1/7/91) FL 35 FLC 6 FAC 1 Others 2+1
Peterborough U (Free on 21/1/93) FL 85+4/1 FLC 4 FAC 2+1 Others 5

SPEED Gary Andrew
Born: Mancot, 8 September 1969
Height: 5'11" Weight: 10.12
Club Honours: Div 2 '90, Div 1 '92; CS '92
International Honours: W: 31; U21-3; Yth

A Leeds' clubman in every sense of the word, Gary is a great competitor who never gives less than 100 per-cent for both club and country. This was highlighted none more so than at the beginning of the year when, by his own admission, "he was struggling". However, he kept battling away to rediscover both touch and form. Not so effective operating in deep central midfield, as when used in an attacking left-sided role last season, he can also play in defence, create and defend well, is powerful in the air at either end and has a superlative left-foot.

Leeds U (From trainee on 13/6/88) F/PL 202+17/37 FLC 18+1/8 FAC 17/4 Others 10+3/1

SPENCER John
Born: Glasgow, 11 November 1970
Height: 5'7" Weight: 9.10
International Honours: S: 4; U21-3

A skilful and quick-silver striker, who turns defenders to get his shots in, John made a great start for Chelsea in 1994-95 when scoring twice at Leeds on his seasonal debut. The "Blues" were actually 2-0 down at one stage, before Dennis Wise put them back into the game from the spot. Then John struck, with goals in the 61st and 83rd minute, the winner squirming through an unsighted 'keeper's legs. There was more to come. In November, away to Austria Vienna in the European Cup Winners Cup, he scored one of the goals of the season, running from his own penalty area to round the goalie to give Chelsea the tie on away goals. Another who missed games intermittently through injury, he still ended the campaign as the club's leading PL scorer. Awarded his first Scottish cap against Russia in November.

Glasgow R (From juniors in 1986) SL 7+6/2 SLC 2 Others 1+1/1
Morton (Loaned on 4/3/89) FL 4/1
Chelsea (£450,000 on 1/8/92) PL 52+19/23 FLC 1+4 FAC 8+4/3 Others 4+1/1

John Spencer   Steve Morton
(Empics Sports Photo Agency)

SPINK Dean Peter
Born: Birmingham, 22 January 1967
Height: 5'11" Weight: 13.8
Club Honours: Div 3 '94

Centre-forward. Strong, tireless and very hard working, the Shrewsbury captain never gives up. A lack of continuous service from the flanks robbed him of many goalscoring opportunities in 1994-95, which made his haul even more creditable. A good target man and equally effective on the ground as in the air.

Aston Villa (£30,000 from Halesowen T on 1/7/89)
Scarborough (Loaned on 20/11/89) FL 3/2 Others 1
Bury (Loaned on 1/2/90) FL 6/1
Shrewsbury T (£75,000 on 15/3/90) FL 173+25/44 FLC 16+2/1 FAC 13+1/3 Others 10+1/3

SPINK Nigel Philip
Born: Chelmsford, 8 August 1958
Height: 6'2" Weight: 14.6
Club Honours: EC '82; ESC '82; FLC '94
International Honours: E: 1; B-2

Commanding Aston Villa goalkeeper whose huge build helps him dominate his penalty area, and a quick thinker, Nigel can turn defence into attack with accurate throws or long right-footed clearances. The most experienced player on the staff, having been at Villa Park since the beginning of 1977, his strong presence is always felt, even when on the subs' bench and, although Mark Bosnich is the first choice 'keeper these days, he is an ideal man to be able to call upon in an emergency.

Aston Villa (£4,000 from Chelmsford C on 1/1/77) F/PL 357+2 FLC 45 FAC 28 Others 25+1

SPOONER Nicholas (Nicky) Michael
Born: Manchester, 5 June 1971
Height: 5'10" Weight: 11.9

Troubled by injury throughout his career, 1994-95 proved to be no different for this gutsy defender. Having forced his way into the Bolton side that defeated Ipswich at Burnden in the Coca Cola Cup, he then suffered a broken leg in the next game at Burnley and was out for the rest of the season.

Bolton W (From trainee on 12/7/89) FL 22+1/1 FLC 2 FAC 3 Others 0+1

SPOONER Stephen (Steve) Alan
Born: Sutton, 25 January 1961
Height: 5'11" Weight: 12.0
Club Honours: Div 4 '85

Another midfielder who didn't quite make the hoped-for impact at Chesterfield last season, despite the great promise shown in an earlier spell at the club, Steve was released in December and joined Rushden & Diamonds.

Derby Co (From apprentice on 5/12/78) FL 7+1
Halifax T (Free on 4/12/81) FL 71+1/13 FLC 2 FAC 1
Chesterfield (Free on 14/7/83) FL 89+4/14 FLC 7+1 FAC 3+2 Others 3/1
Hereford U (£7,000 on 1/8/86) FL 84/19 FLC 5/1 FAC 4/1 Others 8/1
York C (£29,000 on 12/7/88) FL 72/11 FLC 6/3 FAC 1 Others 4/1
Rotherham U (£45,000 on 18/7/90) FL 15+4/1 FLC 4 FAC 3 Others 2
Mansfield T (Signed on 22/3/91) FL 55+3/3 FLC 3/1 FAC 1 Others 4
Blackpool (Free on 5/2/93) FL 2
Chesterfield (Free on 22/10/93) FL 11+1 FLC 3

SQUIRES James (Jamie) Alexander
Born: Preston, 15 November 1975
Height: 6'1" Weight: 12.3

Potentially a big star of the future, in central defence, Jamie was loaned to Stafford Rangers last season and experience gained there showed on his return to the Preston first team.

Preston NE (From trainee on 26/4/94) FL 15 Others 1

SRNICEK Pavel
Born: Ostrava, Czechoslovakia, 10 March 1968
Height: 6'2" Weight: 14.9
Club Honours: Div 1 '93
International Honours: Czechoslovakia

One of the most popular players at Newcastle, having a great relationship with the supporters, last season started disastrously, with his sending off at Leicester causing him to miss one match due to suspension. However, as a 'keeper with great shot-stopping ability, he recently signed a new contract, having convinced Kevin Keegan of his worth. In fact, his performances, especially at Manchester United, Liverpool and Chelsea, have undoubtedly placed him into the top-class bracket. Highlights of the season must include his selection as first choice for the Czech Republic and the unbelievable save he made in the last minute in the 2-1 home win against Nottingham Forest, when he foiled Stan Collymore after the striker had actually got past him in the box.

Newcastle U (£350,000 from Banik Ostrava on 5/2/91) F/PL 111 FLC 8 FAC 9 Others 10

STABB Christopher (Chris) John
Born: Bradford, 12 October 1976
Height: 5'9" Weight: 11.12

Still a trainee, Chris is the reserve team captain at Bradford and usually plays in the middle of the defence. Another player who would appear to have a fine future, he made one appearance for the first team last season.

Bradford C (Trainee) FL 1

STALLARD Mark
Born: Derby, 24 October 1974
Height: 6'0" Weight: 12.6
International Honours: E: Yth

Bustling right-footed striker who, unable to force his way into the Derby side in front of the more recognised strikers, agreed to a loan period at Third Division Fulham last September. This gave him valuable first team experience which he put to good use on his return in October, when teaming up with Tommy Johnson, before losing his place to new signing, Lee Mills, after sustaining a leg injury. Scored a memorable header in the away win at "Wolves".

Derby Co (From trainee on 6/11/91) FL 16+8/2 FLC 1+1/1 FAC 2+1 Others 3/2
Fulham (Loaned on 23/9/94) FL 4/3

STAMP Philip Lawrence
Born: Middlesbrough, 12 December 1975
Height: 5'10" Weight: 12.3
International Honours: E: Yth

Hard-running, strong-tackling, determined and exciting young midfielder, whose gutsy performances and intelligent running off the ball have ensured that his progress through the Middlesbrough ranks is assured.

Middlesbrough (From trainee on 4/2/93) FL 9+4 FLC 2 FAC 1 Others 5+1

STAMPS Scott
Born: Birmingham, 20 March 1975
Height: 5'11" Weight: 11.0

Torquay left-back who is a good passer of the ball. Probably under-achieved in 1994-95, but still has the capacity to become a very good player.

Torquay U (From trainee on 6/7/93) FL 30+3/1 FLC 2 FAC 1 Others 1

STANCLIFFE Paul Ian
Born: Sheffield, 5 May 1958
Height: 6'2" Weight: 12.13
Club Honours: Div 3 '81

Veteran York central defender who was called up for first team duty in an emergency last season after deciding to concentrate on coaching duties. Incidentally, his last game was against Rotherham - the club he started his career with 20 years earlier - in an FA Cup first round replay. Currently assistant to York manager, Alan Little.

Rotherham U (From apprentice on 1/3/76) FL 285/8 FLC 10 FAC 22/2
Sheffield U (Signed on 16/8/83) FL 278/12 FLC 21/4 FAC 25/3 Others 13
Rotherham U (Loaned on 10/9/90) FL 5 FLC 1
Wolverhampton W (Free on 8/11/90) FL 17 FAC 1 Others 2
York C (Free on 15/7/91) FL 89+2/3 FLC 2 FAC 3 Others 7

STANISLAUS Roger Edmund Philbert
Born: Hammersmith, 2 November 1968
Height: 5'9" Weight: 12.6

Starting last season as Bury's left-back before being replaced by Stuart Bimson, he continued in the side as a makeshift right-back. A skilful player, who loves to join in the attack, he would make a more than useful winger.

Arsenal (From apprentice on 31/7/86)
Brentford (Free on 18/9/87) FL 109+2/4 FLC 8/1 FAC 7 Others 9
Bury (£90,000 on 30/7/90) FL 167+9/5 FLC 9/1 FAC 10/1 Others 21

STANNARD James (Jim) David
Born: Harold Hill, 6 October 1962
Height: 6'2" Weight: 14.12

Fulham's longest-serving professional, Jim now holds the club's goalkeeping appearances record. Despite his size, he is remarkably agile, and there are few better shot-stoppers at this level. A character, his bravery and acrobatics have made him a firm favourite with the supporters over the years.

Fulham (Signed from Ford U on 5/6/80) FL 41 FLC 3 FAC 1
Southend U (Loaned on 17/9/84) FL 6
Charlton Ath (Loaned on 1/2/85) FL 1
Southend U (£12,000 on 28/3/85) FL 103 FLC 6 FAC 4 Others 5
Fulham (£50,000 on 14/8/87) FL 348/1 FLC 22 FAC 13 Others 18

STANT Phillip (Phil) Richard
Born: Bolton, 13 October 1962
Height: 6'1" Weight: 12.7
Club Honours: Div 3 '93; WC '93

Signed from Cardiff last January, Phil proved a tremendous acquisition, as his 13 goals in 19 FL starts, catapulted a Bury side in a slump to a team just a whisker away from promotion. Known as "Corporal Stant", a throwback to his days as a regular soldier, interestingly enough, he had produced identical figures earlier in 1994-95 with the Welsh side.

Reading (Signed from Camberley on 19/8/82) FL 3+1/2
Hereford U (Free from Army on 25/11/86) FL 83+6/38 FLC 3/2 FAC 3/2 Others 11/7
Notts Co (£175,000 on 18/7/89) FL 14+8/6 FLC 2/1 FAC 0+1 Others 3+2

Blackpool (Loaned on 5/9/90) FL 12/5
Huddersfield T (Loaned on 3/1/91) FL 5/1
Lincoln C (Loaned on 22/11/90) FL 4
Fulham (£60,000 on 8/2/91) FL 19/5 Others 1
Mansfield T (£50,000 on 1/8/91) FL 56+1/32 FLC 4/1 FAC 2 Others 2
Cardiff C (£100,000 on 4/12/92) FL 77+2/34 FLC 2/2 FAC 6+1/4 Others 10/3
Mansfield T (Loaned on 12/8/93) FL 4/1 FLC 1/1
Bury (£90,000 on 27/1/95) FL 19+1/13 Others 3

STAPLETON Francis (Frank) Anthony
Born: Dublin, 10 July 1956
Height: 6'0" Weight: 13.0
Club Honours: FAC '79, '83, '85
International Honours: Ei: 71

Vastly experienced former Republic of Ireland international striker, having made his FL debut with Arsenal over 21 years ago, Frank was released by Bradford early last season. Joining Brighton on a non-contract basis, he appeared in an Albion shirt during an all too brief stay at the club, before moving on.

Arsenal (From apprentice on 1/9/73) FL 223+2/75 FLC 26/14 FAC 32/15 Others 15/4
Manchester U (£900,000 on 28/8/81) FL 204+19/60 FLC 26+1/6 FAC 21/7 Others 19+1/5 (Signed for Ajax on 1/8/87)
Derby Co (Loaned on 18/3/88) FL 10/1
Blackburn Rov (Free from Le Havre on 11/8/89) FL 80+1/13 FLC 5/1 FAC 4/1 Others 3
Aldershot (Free on 15/9/91)
Huddersfield T (Free on 28/10/91) FL 5 FLC 0+1 FAC 1/1 Others 1
Bradford C (Free on 11/12/91) FL 49+19/2 FLC 1+2 Others 1+1
Brighton & Hove A (Free on 1/11/94) FL 1+1

STAPLETON Simon John
Born: Oxford, 10 December 1968
Height: 6'0" Weight: 13.0
Club Honours: FAT '91; GMVC '93
International Honours: E: SP-1

Versatile two-footed player who appeared for Wycombe in 1994-95, mainly as a left-sided midfielder. A hard tackler, he has the ability to run past opponents.

Portsmouth (From apprentice on 16/12/86)
Bristol Rov (Free on 19/7/88) FL 4+1 FLC 1 FAC 1 Others 1
Wycombe W (Free on 1/8/89) FL 45+3/3 FLC 3 FAC 12+1/3 Others 4

STARBUCK Philip (Phil) Michael
Born: Nottingham, 24 November 1968
Height: 5'10" Weight: 10.13

Signed from Huddersfield last October, Phil was played by Sheffield United mainly wide on the right, although versatile enough to perform almost anywhere. The spell away from striking meant he could only manage one goal throughout the season for his new club, and was substituted on many occasions when a change of tactics was required. Unfortunately, his season was cut short by the need for an operation on his feet.

Nottingham F (From apprentice on 19/8/86) FL 9+27/2 FLC 1+3 FAC 2+5 Others 0+4
Birmingham C (Loaned on 7/3/88) FL 3
Hereford U (Loaned on 19/2/90) FL 6 Others 1
Blackburn Rov (Loaned on 6/9/90) FL 5+1/1
Huddersfield T (Free on 17/8/91) FL 120+17/36 FLC 13+2/4 FAC 5+1 Others 16+3/7
Sheffield U (£150,000 on 28/10/94) FL 20+3/1 FAC 0+1

STARK Wayne Robert
Born: Derby, 14 October 1976
Height: 5'11" Weight: 11.13
Forward. Still a trainee, Wayne made just one full appearance for Mansfield in the Auto Windscreen Shield last season.
Mansfield T (Trainee) FL 0+1 Others 1

STATHAM Brian
Born: Zimbabwe, 21 May 1969
Height: 5'8" Weight: 11.0
Club Honours: Div 3 '92
International Honours: E: U21-3; Yth
Fast moving, right-footed Brentford defender, who is good in the air despite his lack of inches. Missing the start of last season, before regaining his right-back spot, Brian later became a regular substitute. However, after coming on and impressing, he then had an excellent run as the midfield anchorman, prior to finishing the campaign at right-back.
Tottenham H (From trainee on 3/8/87) FL 20+4 FLC 2 FAC 0+1
Reading (Loaned on 28/3/91) FL 8
Bournemouth (Loaned on 20/11/91) FL 2 Others 1
Brentford (£70,000 on 16/1/92) FL 120+10/1 FLC 8 FAC 4 Others 14

STATHAM Mark Andrew
Born: Barnsley, 11 November 1975
Height: 6'2" Weight: 12.2
Self-assured young goalkeeper who is very agile and a good shot-stopper, Mark celebrated his Wigan first team debut in 1994-95 by winning the sponsor's "Man of the Match" award in a AWS game against Blackpool. A free transfer from Nottingham Forest, along with Ian Kilford, during the 1994 close season, he also appeared twice in FL matches.
Nottingham F (From trainee on 22/3/93)
Wigan Ath (Free on 13/7/94) FL 1+1 Others 0+1

Steve Staunton   Neal Simpson
(Empics Sports Photo Agency)

STAUNTON Stephen (Steve)
Born: Dundalk, 19 January 1969
Height: 5'11" Weight: 11.2
Club Honours: FAC '89; CS '89; Div 1 '90; FLC '94
International Honours: Ei: 59; U21-4
An Aston Villa and Republic of Ireland regular who is comfortable at left-back or on the left-side of midfield, Steve is a good linking player between defence and attack for both club and country. Commencing last season as an attacking left-back, but progressively moving forward into a midfield role, he was unfortunate to be out of action during the last two months of the year with a knee tendon injury and, after coming back, thankfully shook off a hamstring strain towards the end of the campaign. Recognition of his strong leadership came when he was offered the captain's armband and subsequently maintained it in a difficult season.
Liverpool (£20,000 from Dundalk on 2/9/86) FL 55+10 FLC 6+2/4 FAC 14+2/1 Others 1/1
Bradford C (Loaned on 13/11/87) FL 7+1 FLC 2 Others 1
Aston Villa (£1,100,000 on 7/8/91) F/PL 137+1/13 FLC 14 FAC 12 Others 6

STEELE Timothy (Tim) Wesley
Born: Coventry, 1 December 1967
Height: 5'9" Weight: 11.0
Hard-working Hereford winger who can play on either flank and deliver excellent crosses into the area. Signed from Bradford during the summer, he had very limited opportunities with United last season, due to a number of injuries.
Shrewsbury T (From apprentice on 7/12/85) FL 41+20/5 FLC 3+1/1 Others 1+1
Wolverhampton W (£80,000 on 22/2/89) FL 53+22/7 FLC 5/3 FAC 1 Others 4
Stoke C (Loaned on 20/2/92) FL 7/1
Bradford C (Free on 16/7/93) FL 8+3 FLC 2+1/1
Hereford U (Free on 14/1/94) FL 24+1/2 FLC 2 FAC 1 Others 1

STEIN Mark Earl Sean
Born: Capetown, South Africa, 28 January 1966
Height: 5'6" Weight: 10.0
Club Honours: FLC '88; AMC '92; Div 2 '93
International Honours: E: Yth
A natural goalscorer who "sniffs" out chances and then puts them away, Mark scored an average of two in every three PL games for Chelsea in 1993-94, but was unable to match that last season, mainly due to a wide range of injuries which continually set him back. However, there were promising signs that a successful strike partnership could be formed with Paul Furlong. From a footballing family, he has two other brothers, Brian (Luton) and Eddie (Barnet), who have played League football.
Luton T (From juniors on 31/1/84) FL 41+13/19 FLC 4+1 FAC 9/3 Others 3/1
Aldershot (Loaned on 29/1/86) FL 2/1
Queens Park R (£300,000 on 26/8/88) FL 20+13/4 FLC 4/2 FAC 2+1/1 Others 4
Oxford U (Signed on 15/9/89) FL 72+10/18 FLC 4 FAC 2+1 Others 3
Stoke C (£100,000 on 15/9/91) FL 94/50 FLC 8/8 FAC 4 Others 17/10
Chelsea (£1,500,000 on 28/10/93) PL 39+3/16 FAC 9/2 Others 2+1/2

STEPHENSON Paul
Born: Wallsend, 2 January 1968
Height: 5'10" Weight: 12.12
International Honours: E: Yth
A right-footed Brentford winger who can play on either flank, Paul was a regular in the side until he suffered a double fracture of the skull at Bradford last November. Having amazingly returned to the first team, less than three months later, he was ever-present from then to the end of the season.
Newcastle U (From apprentice on 2/1/86) FL 58+3/1 FLC 3+1 FAC 2 Others 2
Millwall (£300,000 on 10/11/88) FL 81+17/6 FLC 3/1 FAC 9/2 Others 8/1
Gillingham (Loaned on 21/11/92) FL 12/2 Others 2
Brentford (£30,000 on 4/3/93) FL 70/2 FLC 6/1 FAC 1+1 Others 5

STERLING Worrell Ricardo
Born: Bethnal Green, 8 June 1965
Height: 5'7" Weight: 11.0
Club Honours: FAYC '82
A very experienced Bristol Rovers' professional, and an ever-present last season, Worrell has played in over 350 League matches and has been a popular player at every club he has served. A tricky right-winger, who can supply accurate crosses and provide a hard-working display in every match, his defensive contribution to deny opponents is readily accepted by his playing colleagues as a real asset.
Watford (From apprentice on 10/6/83) FL 82+12/14 FLC 7+2/1 FAC 18/2 Others 0+1
Peterborough U (£70,000 on 23/3/89) FL 190+3/29 FLC 15/3 FAC 14/5 Others 14/2
Bristol Rov (£140,000 on 29/7/93) FL 89/6 FLC 4/1 FAC 5 Others 9

STEVENS Michael **Gary**
Born: Barrow, 27 March 1963
Height: 5'11" Weight: 12.7
Club Honours: FAC '84; Div 1 '85, '87; ECWC '85; CS '84, '85; SPD '89, '90, '91, '92, '93, '94; SLC '89, '91, '94; SC '92
International Honours: E: 46; B-1; U21-8; Yth
Signed from Glasgow Rangers in October 1994, after a month's loan, for a Tranmere club record, the former England full-back proved yet another of John King's astute buys. King later described him as a "Rolls Royce". Vastly experienced, Gary initially slotted into his old right-back spot, but was then moved to left-back and, in an emergency, centre-back, all without complaint. Still the model professional, he likes to overlap.
Everton (From apprentice on 8/4/81) FL 207+1/8 FLC 30/1 FAC 39/3 Others 10
Glasgow R (£1,000,000 on 19/7/88) SL 186+1/8 SLC 22 SC 22/1 Others 14
Tranmere Rov (£350,000 on 22/9/94) FL 37/1 FLC 3 FAC 3 Others 4

STEVENS Ian David
Born: Malta, 21 October 1966
Height: 5'9" Weight: 12.0
Club Honours: AMC '89
Having come to Shrewsbury from Bury during the 1994 close season, Ian played up-front, both in the middle and on the right. Fast on the ball and showing good control, he has a strong shot at distance and, despite a lack of height, good heading ability.

Mark Stein

Neal Simpson
(Empics Sports Photo Agency)

Preston NE (From apprentice on 22/11/84) FL 9+2/2 Others 1
Stockport Co (Free on 27/10/86) FL 1+1 FAC 0+1 Others 0+1 (Free to Lancaster C on 27/11/86)
Bolton W (Free on 25/3/87) FL 26+21/7 FLC 1+2 FAC 4/2 Others 3+1
Bury (Free on 3/7/91) FL 100+10/38 FLC 3+1 FAC 2+2 Others 7+1/2
Shrewsbury T (£20,000 on 11/8/94) FL 26+12/8 FLC 0+1 FAC 1 Others 2+1/4

STEVENS Keith Henry
Born: Merton, 21 June 1964
Height: 6'0" Weight: 12.0
Club Honours: FLT '83; Div 2 '88

Millwall's longest-serving player, Keith always gives his utmost to the cause and is a club captain who leads by example. A hard-tackling, right-footed central defender, he was forced to miss the first part of last season through a back injury and it was no coincidence that his return saw an upsurge in the club's fortunes. On 14 January 1995, against Sheffield United at the Den, Keith reached second place in Millwall's all-time FL appearance charts.
Millwall (From apprentice on 23/6/81) FL 403+7/7 FLC 31/1 FAC 28 Others 29

STEWART William Marcus
Born: Bristol, 7 November 1972
Height: 5'10" Weight: 11.0
International Honours: E: Sch

A talented Bristol Rovers' striker who has now matured into a player who will surely play at the highest level one day. Confident on the ball, Marcus has added a good goalscoring rate to his fine performances and broke a 39-year club record of scoring in nine consecutive matches during last season. An excellent performance at Wembley in the play-off final against Huddersfield, culminated in a superb goal, taking his season's tally to 23.
Bristol Rov (From trainee on 18/7/91) FL 93+34/36 FLC 7/1 FAC 6+1/3 Others 9+1/9

STEWART Paul Andrew
Born: Manchester, 7 October 1964
Height: 5'11" Weight: 11.10
Club Honours: FAC '91; CS '91; Div 1 '94
International Honours: E: 3; B-5; U21-1; Yth

Still not figuring in Liverpool's plans, Paul was loaned out to Wolverhampton and Burnley last season. The bustling midfielder, cum forward, made his debut for "Wolves" on the day that the great Billy Wright died. He had his moments during an injury prone stay, before going to Turf Moor. At Burnley, it was even worse, with a sending off and several bookings making a difficult task in a struggling team even more trying. Strong and powerful, and with a lot to offer, even at the age of 30, Paul needs the challenge of regular first team football.
Blackpool (From apprentice on 13/10/81) FL 188+13/56 FLC 11/3 FAC 7/2 Others 6/1
Manchester C (£200,000 on 19/3/87) FL 51/26 FLC 6/2 FAC 4/1 Others 2/1
Tottenham H (£1,700,000 on 21/6/88) FL 126+5/28 FLC 23/7 FAC 9/2 Others 9
Liverpool (£2,300,000 on 29/7/92) PL 28+4/1 FLC 6 FAC 1 Others 3/2
Crystal Palace (Loaned on 24/1/94) FL 18/3

Wolverhampton W (Loaned on 2/9/94) FL 5+3/2 Others 2
Burnley (Loaned on 8/2/95) FL 6

STEWART William (Billy) Ian
Born: Liverpool, 1 January 1965
Height: 6'2" Weight: 14.7

An experienced goalkeeper who joined Northampton during the 1994 close season, Billy was a regular until the arrival of Andy Woodman. Unable to win his place back, he was loaned out to Chesterfield, as cover for Andy Beasley, immediately prior to the transfer deadline and made four great point-blank saves on his debut. Not too many players will make their second full appearance for a Third Division club at Wembley, but that was his good fortune. And, as the hero of a 2-0 play-off win over Bury that saw Chesterfield reach the Second Division, it was the stuff that dreams are made of. Released by the "Cobblers" at the end of the season.
Liverpool (From apprentice on 5/1/83)
Wigan Ath (Free on 2/7/84) FL 14 Others 1
Chester C (Free on 11/8/86) FL 272 FLC 21 FAC 19 Others 20
Northampton T (Free on 4/7/94) FL 26+1 FLC 2 FAC 1 Others 1
Chesterfield (Loaned on 17/3/95) FL 1 Others 1+1

STIMSON Mark
Born: Plaistow, 27 December 1967
Height: 5'11" Weight: 11.0

Left-sided Portsmouth defender who is good going forward, he had an injury plagued 1994-95, which included having an operation on his back to correct a problem. Still to find his real position, he was tried at left-back and in midfield by Jim Smith during the course of last season.
Tottenham H (From apprentice on 15/7/85) FL 1+1
Leyton Orient (Loaned on 15/3/88) FL 10
Gillingham (Loaned on 19/1/89) FL 18
Newcastle U (£200,000 on 16/6/89) FL 82+4/2 FLC 5 FAC 7/1 Others 6
Portsmouth (Loaned on 10/12/92) FL 3+1
Portsmouth (£100,000 on 23/7/93) FL 43+1/1 FLC 9/1 FAC 2 Others 3

STOCKWELL Michael (Micky) Thomas
Born: Chelmsford, 14 February 1965
Height: 5'6" Weight: 10.13
Club Honours: Div 2 '92

Ipswich utility player who is equally at home at full-back, in midfield, or as a striker, and always gives 100 per-cent, wherever he plays. His appearances last season were curtailed by injury. First of all he was laid low by a groin strain and then damaged knee ligaments in a training accident, which required surgery to put right. Originally thought to be out for the rest of the season, Micky recovered well and returned to the side in April. Had his testimonial at the start of the season when former Town manager, Bobby Robson, brought his FC Porto side to Portman Road.
Ipswich T (From apprentice on 17/12/82) F/PL 299+16/20 FLC 23+3/2 FAC 18+3/1 Others 16+2/1

STOKER Gareth
Born: Bishop Auckland, 22 February 1973
Height: 5'9" Weight: 10.10

Late season signing for Hereford in 1994-95, Gareth played in midfield. A robust and determined lightweight, he made ten appearances and looks to have settled in.
Hull C (Free from Leeds U juniors on 13/9/91) FL 24+6/2 FLC 3 FAC 2+1 Others 0+2 (Released during 1993 close season)
Hereford U (Signed on 16/3/95) FL 10

Gareth Stoker   Matthew Ashton
(Empics Sports Photo Agency)

STOKES Dean Anthony
Born: Birmingham, 23 May 1970
Height: 5'9" Weight: 10.5

Port Vale left-back who spent nearly all of last season on the sidelines with an ankle injury, Dean was called up for the first team in March, having played just two reserve games in 12 months, but returned to the "stiffs" two matches later with Allen Tankard fit again. Very good defensively, he will be hoping for better luck next time around.
Port Vale (Signed from Halesowen T on 15/1/93) FL 24 FAC 3 Others 1

STONE Steven (Steve) Brian
Born: Gateshead, 20 August 1971
Height: 5'9" Weight: 12.7

Nicknamed "Bulldog", having recovered from three broken legs during his time at Nottingham Forest, Steve is a player who will run for ever for the good of the team. Originally a central midfielder, he has never looked back since being converted to a wide right position. Had a great session in the Premiership in 1994-95 and must surely be on the verge of international honours of some kind.
Nottingham F (From trainee on 20/5/89) F/PL 97+2/11 FLC 9+1 FAC 2 Others 4

STONEMAN Paul
Born: Tynemouth, 26 February 1973
Height: 6'1" Weight: 13.0

Central defender who had a spell on loan at Colchester as defensive cover last Christmas and scored a vital goal during his stay. With chances limited after suspensions had been served, he returned to Blackpool, before

being freed during the summer.
Blackpool (From trainee on 26/7/91) FL 38+5 FLC 5 FAC 3 Others 3
Colchester U (Loaned on 23/12/94) FL 3/1

STORER Stuart John
Born: Rugby, 16 January 1967
Height: 5'11" Weight: 11.8
Club Honours: AMC '89

Right-winger with turbo charged heels, who can leave defenders trailing, Stuart rarely puts in a poor cross. Popular with the Exeter crowd, unfortunately for them, he left for Brighton last March, partly in order to help the financial position of the club.
Mansfield T (Juniors) FL 0+1
Birmingham C (Free from VS Rugby on 18/7/84) FL 5+3 FLC 1
Everton (Signed on 6/3/87)
Wigan Ath (Loaned on 23/7/87) FL 9+3 FLC 4
Bolton W (£25,000 on 24/12/87) FL 95+28/12 FLC 9+2 FAC 7+3/2 Others 16+5/1
Exeter C (£25,000 on 25/3/93) FL 75+2/8 FLC 4/1 FAC 4+1/1 Others 6
Brighton & Hove A (£15,000 on 2/3/95) FL 2/1

STOWELL Michael (Mike)
Born: Preston, 19 April 1965
Height: 6'2" Weight: 11.10

Goalkeeper. Apart from when rested, he was a Wolverhampton ever-present up to last Christmas. His superb shot-stopping ability, often literally saved the side and after conceding two in five games in September he won the Wilkinson Sword "Protector of the Month" award for Division One. He won it again in March, when he also kept "Wolves" in the FA Cup with a great reaction save in the last minute of the quarter-final, before letting in four in the replay.
Preston NE (Free from Leyland Motors on 14/2/85)
Everton (Free on 12/12/85) Others 1
Chester C (Loaned on 3/9/87) FL 14 Others 2
York C (Loaned on 24/12/87) FL 6
Manchester C (Loaned on 2/2/88) FL 14 FAC 1
Port Vale (Loaned on 21/10/88) FL 7 Others 1
Wolverhampton W (Loaned on 17/3/89) FL 7
Preston NE (Loaned on 8/2/90) FL 7
Wolverhampton W (£250,000 on 28/6/90) FL 194 FLC 12 FAC 9 Others 9

STRACHAN Gordon David
Born: Edinburgh, 9 February 1957
Height: 5'6" Weight: 10.8
Club Honours: SPD '80, '84; SC '82, '83, '84; ECWC '83; ESC '83; FAC '85; Div 2 '90, Div 1 '92; CS '92
International Honours: S: 50; U21-1; Yth

Having made only seven first team appearances for Leeds, in January 1995, Gordon announced that the end of a marvellous career had finally arrived. He had intended to quit at the end of the season but brought the deadline forward, in showing the same strength of character and decisiveness that had long been the hallmark of his many performances. Following that, surprisingly and, somewhat "out of the blue", he joined Coventry as Ron Atkinson's assistant and extended his playing career to aid a side struggling in the Premiership danger zone. At his best, in midfield, Gordon had brilliant football brain, saw openings quickly, rarely ever gave the ball

away and displayed a steely determination to win at all times. That spirit will stand City in good stead.
Dundee (From juniors in 1971) SL 56+13/13 SLC 10+1/1 SC 7/1
Aberdeen (£50,000 on 1/11/77) SL 175+8/55 SLC 43+3/20 SC 25/7 Others 30+4/7
Manchester U (£500,000 on 13/8/84) FL 155+5/33 FLC 12+1/1 FAC 22/2 Others 10+2/3
Leeds U (£300,000 on 23/3/89) F/PL 188+9/37 FLC 19/3 FAC 14/2 Others 14+1/3
Coventry C (Free on 22/3/95) PL 5

STREET Daniel Charles
Born: Cardiff, 20 March 1976
Height: 5'8" Weight: 10.6

A young Cardiff defender who came into the side at left-back last season and had a difficult debut in the Coca Cola Cup defeat at Torquay, he was freed during the summer.
Cardiff C (From trainee on 4/7/94) FLC 1

STRODDER Gary John
Born: Cleckheaton, 1 April 1965
Height: 6'1" Weight: 13.3

Sturdy, solid and determined centre-back, a real rugged, no-nonsense defender who clears his lines well. Lacks a bit of pace, but gives nothing less than 100 per-cent for WBA every time he takes the field. Was a reserve for most of 1994-95 because of the fine form shown by Paul Raven, Paul Mardon and Daryl Burgess, but when Mardon was injured he stepped into the vacant centre-half position and did an excellent job alongside Raven.
Lincoln C (From apprentice on 8/4/83) FL 122+10/6 FLC 7+1 FAC 2+1 Others 5+1
West Ham U (Signed on 20/3/87) FL 59+6/2 FLC 8 FAC 4+2 Others 2
West Bromwich A (£190,000 on 22/8/90) FL 123+17/8 FLC 8+1 FAC 7/1 Others 10

STRONG Gregory (Greg)
Born: Bolton, 5 September 1975
Height: 6'2" Weight: 11.12
International Honours: E: Yth; Sch

Former trainee, and in his third season as a professional at Wigan, Greg is a strong left-footed defender, who is equally adept in the centre or at left-back. Has a great first touch of the ball.
Wigan Ath (From trainee on 1/10/92) FL 28+7/3 FLC 5 FAC 1 Others 3+1

STRONG Steven George
Born: Watford, 15 March 1978
Height: 5'7" Weight: 11.2

A versatile Bournemouth YTS who played in attack and defence for the club's reserves in 1994-95, Steve made his first team debut when coming off the subs' bench for the final two minutes of the last match of the season.
Bournemouth (Trainee) FL 0+1

STUART Graham Charles
Born: Tooting, 24 October 1970
Height: 5'8" Weight: 11.6
Club Honours: FAC '95
International Honours: E: U21-5; Yth; Sch

Right-sided Everton midfielder who likes to play in the old fashioned outside-right position. With a tremendous turn of pace, good control, and the use of both feet,

Graham is difficult to dispossess. Also links up well with defenders to pick the ball up deep and whip in early crosses. Although taking time to settle, after joining from Chelsea, he began to show his true form in 1994-95, having an excellent game in the 4-1 FA Cup semi-final win over "Spurs", scoring the second goal, and being a member of the side that lifted the trophy after defeating Manchester United.
Chelsea (From trainee on 15/6/89) F/PL 70+17/14 FLC 11/2 FAC 5+2/1 Others 3+2/1
Everton (£850,000 on 19/8/93) PL 46+12/6 FLC 4/1 FAC 4+3/2

STUART Jamie Christopher
Born: Southwark, 15 October 1976
Height: 5'10" Weight: 10.7
International Honours: E: Yth

A young left-sided defender or midfielder, Jamie made his Charlton debut at left-back in front of the TV cameras at West Bromwich Albion last February and performed well. Strong in the tackle, he also has good distribution and is very self assured. Could make the position his own, if continuing to play with the same confidence.
Charlton Ath (From trainee on 18/1/95) FL 12

STUART Mark Richard
Born: Chiswick, 15 December 1966
Height: 5'10" Weight: 11.3

A tricky left-winger or midfield man, the goalscoring touch which had made him Rochdale's joint leading scorer in 1993-94 deserted him somewhat last term, but he remained the side's specialist from dead-ball situations.
Charlton Ath (From juniors on 3/7/84) FL 89+18/28 FLC 7+3/2 FAC 1/1 Others 9+1
Plymouth Arg (£150,000 on 4/11/88) FL 55+2/11 FLC 4 FAC 3 Others 2/1
Ipswich T (£80,000 on 22/3/90) FL 5/2
Bradford C (£80,000 on 3/8/90) FL 22+7/5 FLC 6/1 FAC 0+1 Others 1+1
Huddersfield T (Free on 30/10/92) FL 9+6/3 FAC 2 Others 4/1
Rochdale (Free on 5/7/93) FL 67+6/15 FLC 5+1/1 FAC 3/1 Others 3+3/1

STUBBS Alan
Born: Liverpool, 6 October 1971
Height: 6'2" Weight: 13.10
International Honours: E: B-1

As Bolton's team captain, Alan continued to show his class throughout 1994-95 with some sterling central defensive displays. Allied to this, was an ability to spray accurate passes all over the field, a feature of his play that brought him to the attention of Premiership clubs. Missed six weeks due to a broken collar bone in the early part of the season, but, once recovered, he became a permanent fixture in the side, making his 200th Bolton appearance in the Coca Cola Cup defeat of Norwich and leading Wanderers to the Premiership, via the play-offs. Elected by his fellow professionals to the PFA Award winning First Division team, he can take great satisfaction from his performances in a memorable season.
Bolton W (From trainee on 24/7/90) FL 157+20/5 FLC 20/4 FAC 14+3/2 Others 12+1

STURGESS Paul Christopher
Born: Dartford, 4 August 1975
Height: 5'11" Weight: 12.5
Strong left-footed Charlton defender who likes to get forward, Paul improved dramatically from the first few games of last season, when he struggled to find his form, and was ever-present until sustaining an ankle injury against Southend on Boxing Day. Unfortunately, there was no early return and he was out for virtually the rest of the season.
Charlton Ath (From trainee on 1/7/93) FL 29+6 FLC 2 Others 5

STURRIDGE Dean Constantine
Born: Birmingham, 26 July 1973
Height: 5'7" Weight: 10.10
Right-sided striker who, after a pre-season hamstring injury, came on for Derby as a substitute to score early in 1994-95 at Millwall. However, unable to break into the side on a regular basis, he went on loan to Torquay as part of the deal that brought Paul Trollope to the Baseball Ground and impressed during his spell there. Noted for his pace, on his return, injuries allowed him a short spell up-front.
Derby Co (From trainee on 1/7/91) FL 16+7/1 FLC 0+1 Others 2+1
Torquay U (Loaned on 16/12/94) FL 10/5

STURRIDGE Simon Andrew
Born: Birmingham, 9 December 1969
Height: 5'5" Weight: 10.7
Club Honours: AMC '91
A frustrating 1994-95 for the diminutive striker. Simon would clearly have benefited from an extended run in the Stoke first team, but his chances were limited, despite a hatful of goals in the reserve side. His frustrations deepened when, in March, after his goalscoring return to the first team, he suffered a fractured cheekbone which brought a premature end to his season.
Birmingham C (From trainee on 8/7/88) FL 129+21/30 FLC 10+4/1 FAC 8/2 Others 14/5
Stoke C (£75,000 on 24/9/93) FL 7+14/1 FLC 1 FAC 1+3 Others 3+3

SUCKLING Perry John
Born: Leyton, 12 October 1965
Height: 6'1" Weight: 11.2
International Honours: E: U21-10; Yth
Having been signed from Watford in July 1994, Perry spent much of last season at Doncaster as second choice goalkeeper to Dean Williams, but let no-one down when called into action, as his record of just seven goals conceded in nine games would imply.
Coventry C (From apprentice on 19/10/83) FL 27 FLC 2
Manchester C (Signed on 5/6/86) FL 39 FLC 3 FAC 1 Others 3
Crystal Palace (£100,000 on 14/1/88) FL 59 FLC 4 FAC 1 Others 7
West Ham U (Loaned on 15/12/89) FL 6
Brentford (Loaned on 11/10/91) FL 8 Others 1
Watford (Free on 13/7/92) FL 39 FLC 4 FAC 1 Others 2
Doncaster Rov (Free on 8/7/94) FL 9 FLC 1

SULLIVAN Neil
Born: Sutton, 24 February 1970
Height: 6'0" Weight: 12.1

Finally got an extended run in the Wimbledon side last March, after Hans Segers made way, and put in some excellent performances, keeping three clean sheets in his first three outings. Brave and not afraid to come for crosses, Neil proved more than capable but, unfortunately, in the last game of the season at home to Nottingham Forest, he was carried off with a suspected broken leg following a collision with Jason Lee.
Wimbledon (From trainee on 26/7/88) F/PL 15+1
Crystal Palace (Loaned on 1/5/92) FL 1

Nicky Summerbee   Paul Marriott
(Empics Sports Photo Agency)

SUMMERBEE Nicholas (Nicky) John
Born: Altrincham, 26 August 1971
Height: 5'8" Weight: 11.8
International Honours: E: B-1; U21-3
The son of former Manchester City favourite, Mike, Nicky made a promising start for City in 1994-95, having arrived from Swindon during the close season in return for a large fee. A right-back, who can double as a winger, his forte is in getting forward to produce telling crosses and in many ways has a style reminiscent to that of his father. Had an exciting run-in to the end of the season, crossing from either wing with successful results and greatly contributing to the team pulling away from prospective relegation. Scored his first City goal at home to Liverpool.
Swindon T (From trainee on 20/7/89) F/PL 89+23/6 FLC 9+1/3 FAC 2+4 Others 7/1
Manchester C (£1,500,000 on 24/6/94) PL 39+2/1 FLC 6/2 FAC 4

SUMMERFIELD Kevin
Born: Walsall, 7 January 1959
Height: 5'11" Weight: 11.0
Club Honours: FAYC '76; Div 3 '94
International Honours: E: Yth
Having reached the twilight of his playing career, Kevin is spending more time with the Shrewsbury youth team these days, but still showed good control and thoughtful passing ability last season. A midfielder, who likes

to get into the opposing box to support the attack, he also filled in for central defenders when required.
West Bromwich A (From apprentice on 1/1/77) FL 5+4/4 FLC 2
Birmingham C (Free on 31/5/82) FL 2+3/1 FLC 1 FAC 1+1/1
Walsall (Free on 14/12/82) FL 42+12/17 FLC 5+2/2 FAC 1
Cardiff C (Free on 6/7/84) FL 10/1 FLC 2
Plymouth Arg (Free on 21/12/84) FL 118+21/26 FLC 6+1/3 FAC 13/4 Others 4/1
Exeter C (Loaned on 22/3/90) FL 4
Shrewsbury T (Free on 10/10/90) FL 140+22/22 FLC 13+1/7 FAC 11+1/1 Others 8

SUNDERLAND Jonathan (Jon) Paul
Born: Newcastle, 2 November 1975
Height: 5'11" Weight: 11.9
A first year pro who made his debut as a sub for Blackpool against Wycombe in November, he is a speedy winger who can also play in midfield.
Blackpool (From trainee on 18/7/94) FL 0+2 Others 0+1

SUNLEY Mark
Born: Guisborough, 11 August 1972
Height: 6'1" Weight: 12.7
Primarily a central defender, although his one appearance in 1994-95 was at full-back, Mark was signed by Hartlepool on a non-contract basis from non-league, Halifax.
Middlesbrough (From trainee on 4/10/89)
Millwall (Free on 16/2/91)
Darlington (Free on 21/1/92) FL 34+1 Others 3+1 (Free to Halifax T during 1994 close season)
Hartlepool U (Free on 27/2/95) FL 1+1

SUSSEX Andrew (Andy) Robert
Born: Enfield, 23 November 1964
Height: 6'0" Weight: 11.6
Andy finally found his niche under Southend caretaker-manager, Steve Thompson, after many seasons in the shadows. Tall and strong, his midfield generalship proved a key element in the club's successful fight against relegation during 1994-95, the partnership with Ronnie Whelan showing his passing skills to great effect.
Leyton Orient (From apprentice on 25/11/82) FL 126+18/17 FLC 7+1/2 FAC 8/1 Others 5+3
Crewe Alex (£16,000 on 23/6/88) FL 86+16/24 FLC 10/6 FAC 7+1/4 Others 5/2
Southend U (£100,000 on 4/7/91) FL 62+12/14 FLC 6 FAC 2+1 Others 3+1/1

SUTCH Daryl
Born: Beccles, 11 September 1971
Height: 5'11" Weight: 10.12
International Honours: E: U21-4; Yth
An attacking midfielder and a good passer of the ball, Daryl had a frustrating time in 1994-95 in trying to establish himself at Norwich, following a niggling groin injury and bouts of illness. Repaid the manager's faith with some fine performances in mid-season as he vied with Neil Adams for the wide right flank position. Later became the perennial substitute, before being recalled by the caretaker manager, Gary Megson, as the season drew to a close.
Norwich C (From trainee on 6/7/90) F/PL 42+26/3 FLC 6+3 FAC 4+1 Others 2+3

SUTTON Christopher (Chris) Roy
Born: Nottingham, 10 March 1973
Height: 6'2" Weight: 12.1
Club Honours: PL '95
International Honours: E: B-2; U21-8

A 1994 close season signing for Blackburn, Chris had the added handicap of becoming England's most expensive footballer. However, if that created pressure then it did not show and he only had to wait for the third game of the campaign against Coventry to score his first hat-trick. For a time, he actually outscored Alan Shearer, as the SAS became the premier strike force around and, at his best, proved to be an awkward opponent who could take the ball and turn, and had the confidence to go forward for a shot. His style had many similarities to that of Shearer's, so much so, that their routes had to be carefully worked out in order for them to feed off each other. But, when the time came for grinding out results, Chris was willing to sacrifice his goals for the good of the team, be it dropping back into midfield, or even into central defence when the going got really rough. The Championship medal was worth it of course and while there were clamours for his inclusion in the international side, which were ignored in the short term, Chris was deemed good enough by his fellow professionals to be elected for the PFA PL Team Award. Father Mike played for Norwich in the 1960s.
Norwich C (From trainee on 2/7/91) F/PL 89+13/35 FLC 8+1/3 FAC 10/5 Others 6
Blackburn Rov (£5,000,000 on 13/7/94) PL 40/15 FLC 4/3 FAC 2/2 Others 2/1

Chris Sutton   Barry Coombs
(Empics Sports Photo Agency)

SUTTON Stephen (Steve) John
Born: Hartington, 16 April 1961
Height: 6'1" Weight: 14.0
Club Honours: FLC '89, '90; FMC '89

The experienced former Forest 'keeper (but lifelong Derby supporter) started as regular back-up to Martin Taylor last August until the latter's injury at Southend gave him his chance again. A wonderful reflex save at home to Charlton showed he had lost none of the ability that had earned him honours at Forest. Kept a record five consecutive clean sheets in League matches pre-Xmas, prior to a 1-3 defeat at Tranmere, though, even in that game, he managed to save a penalty. Injury led to his being replaced by loan 'keeper, Russell Hoult.
Nottingham F (From apprentice on 16/4/79) FL 199 FLC 33 FAC 14 Others 11
Mansfield T (Loaned on 10/3/81) FL 8
Derby Co (Loaned on 25/1/85) FL 14
Coventry C (Loaned on 1/2/91) FL 1
Luton T (Loaned on 28/11/91) FL 14
Derby Co (£300,000 on 6/3/92) FL 54+1 FLC 6 FAC 3 Others 11

SUTTON Wayne Frank
Born: Derby, 1 October 1975
Height: 6'0" Weight: 13.2

Another of the highly-rated players coming through from the Derby youth set-up, the right-footed central defender, cum midfielder, was entrusted with his debut in the FAC-tie at Everton. A fine tackler, Wayne will hopefully maintain his progress.
Derby Co (From trainee on 27/10/92) FL 3+3 FAC 1

SWAILES Christopher (Chris) William
Born: Gateshead, 19 October 1970
Height: 6'2" Weight: 12.11

Tall, right-sided defender who is quicker than he looks, Chris returned to Ipswich, via Peterborough, Birmingham and Doncaster, on transfer deadline day last March for a second spell, having earlier been at Portman Road in the club's youth and reserve team. Made his debut against Aston Villa and conceded an unfortunate own goal in the last minute.
Ipswich T (From trainee on 23/5/89)
Peterborough U (£10,000 on 28/3/91)
Birmingham C (Free from Boston U on 26/3/92)
Doncaster Rov (Free from Guisborough on 27/10/93) FL 49 FLC 2/1 FAC 1 Others 2
Ipswich T (£225,000 on 23/3/95) PL 4

SWALES Stephen (Steve) Colin
Born: Whitby, 26 December 1973
Height: 5'8" Weight: 10.0

Promising young left-back who graduated through the ranks at Scarborough to become a regular first teamer over the past couple of seasons. Has the ability to progress to a higher level of the game and was probably Scarborough's most "saleable" asset in 1994-95.
Scarborough (From trainee on 3/8/92) FL 51+3/1 FAC 5 Others 3

SWAN Peter Harold
Born: Leeds, 28 September 1966
Height: 6'2" Weight: 12.0
Club Honours: AMC '93

Plymouth's record signing had a topsy-turvy first season. A very strong and capable defender, who can also play up front, he was made captain on his arrival, but later lost the arm band. Although

showing good ability in the air, getting plenty of distance on his clearances, he lacked consistency after not completely settling in the area. However, his end of season form showed his undoubted ability, especially at this level.
Leeds U (From trainee on 6/8/84) FL 43+6/11 FLC 3/2 FAC 3 Others 1+2
Hull C (£200,000 on 23/3/89) FL 76+4/24 FLC 2+3/1 FAC 2 Others 1
Port Vale (£300,000 on 16/8/91) FL 105+6/5 FLC 6 FAC 9/1 Others 12/1
Plymouth Arg (£300,000 on 22/7/94) FL 24+3/2 FLC 2/1 FAC 2

SWANN Gary
Born: York, 11 April 1962
Height: 5'9" Weight: 11.2

Vastly experienced Scarborough midfielder who was previously with local rivals, York. Could always be relied on to give 100 percent effort and was the match-winner in "Boro's" FA Cup victory over Port Vale, before being released last March.
Hull C (From apprentice on 17/5/80) FL 176+10/9 FLC 9+1 FAC 11/1 Others 10
Preston NE (£10,000 on 27/11/86) FL 194+5/37 FLC 11+1/4 FAC 12/1 Others 27/5
York C (Free on 12/6/92) FL 82/4 FLC 4 FAC 1 Others 8/2
Scarborough (Free on 12/8/94) FL 24+3/3 FLC 2 FAC 5/1 Others 1

SWEENEY Paul Martin
Born: Glasgow, 10 January 1965
Height: 5'8" Weight: 11.5

Hartlepool defender signed on a week-to-week contract in the 1994 close season. Keen to get back into senior football, he slimmed down in his attempts to win a regular first team place, but was not successful, and returned to play for Gateshead.
Raith Rov (Signed from St Kentigerns Academy in 1981) SL 198+6/8 SLC 5+1 SC 16
Newcastle U (Signed on 22/3/89) FL 28+8 FLC 2+1 FAC 3 Others 3
St Johnstone (£100,000 on 8/3/91) SL 10 SC 1 (Free to Gateshead on 9/8/93)
Hartlepool U (Free on 12/8/94) FL 1 FLC 1

SYMONS Christopher (Kit) Jeremiah
Born: Basingstoke, 8 March 1971
Height: 6'2" Weight: 13.0
International Honours: W: 18; B-1; U21-2; Yth

Strong Portsmouth defender with all-round ability, the Welsh international had a good season in 1994-95, and continued to be the subject of much discussion regarding expensive transfers to Premier League clubs. As club captain he formed an effective partnership with Guy Butters on the latter's belated inclusion in the first team, and led by example.
Portsmouth (From trainee on 30/12/88) FL 160/10 FLC 19 FAC 10 Others 13+1/1

TAGGART Gerald (Gerry) Paul
Born: Belfast, 18 October 1970
Height: 6'1" Weight: 13.4
International Honours: NI: 35; U21-1; Yth

Central defender. The cornerstone of the Barnsley team last season, his immense presence was always apparent. Physically very strong, he relished the challenges thrown down and, as a regular in the Northern Ireland team, he is setting a club record for internationals that is going to be hard to beat. Always a big threat from set pieces, he will probably concede that he didn't score enough, although he was always picked up by the opposition's number one defender.

Manchester C (From trainee on 1/7/89) FL 10+2/1 Others 1
Barnsley (£75,000 on 10/1/90) FL 209+3/16 FLC 15/1 FAC 14/2 Others 6/1

TAIT Michael (Mick) Paul
Born: 30 September 1956
Height: 5'11" Weight: 12.5
Club Honours: Div 3 '83, Div 4 '91; FMC '88

Experienced Hartlepool defender/midfielder who was re-signed by caretaker manager, Billy Horner, last September, after a short spell with Gretna. Aged 38, his whole-hearted approach to the game was an example to the younger players, with his uncompromising performances belying his advanced years. Unfortunately, he had two lengthy spells out of the side with torn hamstrings. Appointed player-coach in April.

Oxford U (From apprentice on 8/10/74) FL 61+3/23 FLC 2+1/1 FAC 2
Carlisle U (£65,000 on 3/2/77) FL 101+5/20 FLC 7 FAC 7/2
Hull C (£150,000 on 6/9/79) FL 29+4/3 FAC 1/1
Portsmouth (£100,000 on 11/6/80) FL 228+12/30 FLC 23+1/1 FAC 13/1 Others 2+1
Reading (£50,000 on 1/9/87) FL 98+1/10 FLC 9/2 FAC 16 Others 9/3
Darlington (Free on 3/8/90) FL 79/2 FLC 5 FAC 4 Others 3
Hartlepool U (Free on 31/7/92) FL 60+1/1 FLC 5/1 FAC 2 (Free to Gretna during 1994 close season)
Hartlepool U (Free on 9/9/94) FL 20 FLC 1

TAIT Paul
Born: Newcastle, 24 October 1974
Height: 6'1" Weight: 11.0

Arrived at Wigan from Everton at the start of last season, having an impressive scoring record with the "Toffees'" youth side. Paul, a centre-forward who is strong and direct, was restricted to just a few appearances due to injuries, but has been offered a further three month contract.

Everton (From trainee on 8/7/93)
Wigan Ath (Free on 22/7/94) FL 1+4

TAIT Paul Ronald
Born: Sutton Coldfield, 31 July 1971
Height: 6'1" Weight: 10.10
Club Honours: Div 2 '95; AMC '95

Once described as "the new Trevor Francis", his progress at Birmingham has been held up by a series of injuries, including one that kept him out of the game for over a year and, at times, threatened his career. Has fought back well from adversity and could still make a major impact in the game. Formerly a striker, but now operating in midfield, Paul will be remembered for scoring two winning goals last season. One of them was enough to bring the Auto Windscreen trophy to St Andrews, while the other, at Huddersfield, saw City crowned Second Division Champions.

Birmingham C (From trainee on 2/8/88) FL 95+22/11 FLC 9 FAC 5+2 Others 12+4/4

Paul Tait (Birmingham)   Barry Coombs
(Empics Sports Photo Agency)

TALBOT Stuart
Born: Birmingham, 14 June 1973
Height: 5'10" Weight: 11.0

Powerful Port Vale midfield player who was given his chance in the first team for the final two games of last season. Made a goal in his first game at Charlton and put himself about quite well.

Port Vale (Signed from Moor Green on 10/8/94) FL 2

Steve Talboys   Matthew Ashton
(Empics Sports Photo Agency)

TALBOYS Steven (Steve) John
Born: Bristol, 18 September 1966
Height: 5'10" Weight: 11.6

In and out of the Wimbledon side during the opening months of last season, Steve scored his first goal for the club at home to "Spurs", before injury kept him in the background. A left-winger, with plenty of stamina and skill, he is also adept at crossing or getting into good shooting positions.

Wimbledon (£10,000 from Gloucester C on 10/1/92) PL 16+5/1 FLC 1+1 FAC 0+1

TANKARD Allen John
Born: Islington, 21 May 1969
Height: 5'10" Weight: 11.7

Attacking Port Vale left-back with a sharp turn of pace. Only missed seven games during the whole of last season, all through injury, and played when not fully fit against Tranmere on live TV, producing a blistering 25 yard shot for the opening goal! Improved as the season went on and is now one of the crowd's favourites.

Southampton (From apprentice on 27/5/87) FL 5 Others 2
Wigan Ath (Free on 4/7/88) FL 205+4/4 FLC 15/1 FAC 13 Others 20
Port Vale (£87,500 on 26/7/93) FL 61+4/1 FLC 6 FAC 4/1 Others 3

TANNER Adam David
Born: Maldon, 25 October 1973
Height: 6'0" Weight: 12.1

Ipswich central midfield player with good vision and good passing ability, and who possesses a powerful shot, Adam made his belated debut against Leicester last season and scored with a low volley - a goal that won him the "Goal of the Season" award from the supporters. He also scored the goal that secured the club's first ever victory at Anfield.

Ipswich T (From trainee on 13/7/92) PL 9+1/2 FAC 1

TARICCO Mauricio Ricardo
Born: Buenos Aires, Argentine, 10 March 1973
Height: 5'9" Weight: 11.7

A versatile Ipswich player who can play at full-back, or in midfield, with a preference for the right-side, Mauricio has an Italian father and therefore can play without a work permit under EEC rules. He can also speak English quite well. Having signed from Argentinos last September, he made his debut in the home leg of the Coca Coca Cup-tie against Bolton, who fielded two wingers. It was a tough baptism and, while he appeared to be uncomfortable defensively, he made some penetrating passes when going forward. Did not appear in the first team again.

Ipswich T (£175,000 from Argentinos on 9/9/94) FLC 1

TAYLOR Gareth Keith
Born: Weston super Mare, 25 February 1973
Height: 6'2" Weight: 12.5
International Honours: W: U21-6

Having made a remarkable recovery from a career threatening knee injury, Gareth has also made rapid strides in developing into an effective targetman and goalscorer. Good in the air, his close control and physical presence in opponents' penalty areas was a significant factor in Bristol Rovers' successes in 1994-95. A regular member of the Welsh U21 team, in fact, he scored his first ever senior goal in international football.

Bristol Rov (Free from Southampton juniors on 29/7/91) FL 24+16/2 FLC 0+1 FAC 1+1 Others 5

TAYLOR **Ian** Kenneth
Born: Birmingham, 4 June 1968
Height: 6'1" Weight: 12.4
Club Honours: AMC '93

An attacking midfielder with an eye for a goal, Ian was transferred from Port Vale to Sheffield Wednesday, prior to the start of last season and then, having made just 11 starts for the "Owls", and less than six months later, moved to Aston Villa (the club he supported as a boy) as part of the deal that saw Guy Whittingham travelling in the other direction. Scored on his home debut against Chelsea and showed plenty of stamina. At his best, he is comfortable on the ball and a good tackler.

Port Vale (£15,000 from Moor Green on 13/7/92) FL 83/28 FLC 4/2 FAC 6/1 Others 13/4
Sheffield Wed (£1,000,000 on 12/7/94) PL 9+5/1 FLC 2+2/1
Aston Villa (£1,000,000 on 21/12/94) PL 22/1 FAC 2

TAYLOR **Jamie** Lee
Born: Bury, 11 January 1977
Height: 5'6" Weight: 9.12

Teenage Rochdale striker, and the sensation of the previous campaign, he was limited to a handful of appearances in 1994-95, despite scoring the winner on his first outing of the season.

Rochdale (From trainee on 12/1/94) FL 2+17/1 FLC 0+1 Others 1+2/1

TAYLOR **John** Patrick
Born: Norwich, 24 October 1964
Height: 6'2" Weight: 11.2
Club Honours: Div 3 '91

Tall, willowy Luton striker with an excellent goalscoring record at Cambridge and Bristol Rovers, John signed in March from Bradford, where he had scored his 100th FL goal just a month earlier. Good in the air, and an intelligent player prepared to help with defensive duties when under pressure, the club will be looking to him and Dwight Marshall as their strike force in 1995-96.

Colchester U (From juniors on 17/12/82)
Cambridge U (Signed from Sudbury T on 24/8/88) FL 139+21/46 FLC 9+2/2 FAC 21/10 Others 12+2/2
Bristol Rov (Signed on 28/3/92) FL 91+4/44 FLC 4/1 FAC 3 Others 5
Bradford C (£300,000 on 5/7/94) FL 35+1/11 FLC 4/2 FAC 2 Others 3
Luton T (£200,000 on 23/3/95) FL 9/3

TAYLOR **Mark** Simon
Born: Saltburn, 8 November 1974
Height: 6'2" Weight: 13.10

A left-sided central defender, or left-back, Mark was another Middlesbrough ex-junior who represented the first team squad last season, when playing three games in the Anglo-Italian Cup. Released by "Boro" at the end of 1994-95, he had earlier had a spell on loan at Darlington.

Middlesbrough (From trainee on 29/3/93) Others 3+1
Darlington (Loaned on 28/10/94) FL 8 Others 2

TAYLOR **Peter** Mark Richard
Born: Hartlepool, 20 November 1964
Height: 5'7" Weight: 10.8

Never really made his mark at Wrexham as a wide midfield player, but showed up much better when pushed into a central attacking role. Retired from playing at the beginning of 1995, due to persistent injuries, but has been undergoing a "physio" course for which he has now qualified, hence his nickname "The Doc".

Hartlepool U (Signed on 16/8/82) FL 42+5/4 FLC 0+1 FAC 2/1 Others 2
Crewe Alex (Loaned on 23/12/85) FL 3
Blackpool (Free on 28/8/86) FL 104+15/43 FLC 6+3/1 FAC 8/2 Others 9+3/1
Cardiff C (Loaned on 21/12/90) FL 6/3
Wrexham (£30,000 on 24/3/92) FL 50+11/9 FLC 4+1 FAC 1 Others 2

TAYLOR **Robert** Mark
Born: Birmingham, 22 February 1966
Height: 5'8" Weight: 11.8

Bob Taylor (WBA)

Club Honours: Div 3 '94

Midfielder Mark had an outstanding season at Shrewsbury in 1994-95. Resilient, and a good tackler, he took players on and was very effective going forward on the right. Is able to pinpoint crosses from the edge of the box and is a creator and provider, rather than a scorer, even though he has a strong shot.

Walsall (From trainee on 24/7/84) FL 100+13/4 FLC 7+1 FAC 3+4 Others 10
Sheffield Wed (£50,000 on 22/6/89) FL 8+1 FLC 2
Shrewsbury T (£70,000 on 13/9/91) FL 175/13 FLC 11 FAC 9 Others 9/1

TAYLOR **Martin** James
Born: Tamworth, 9 December 1966
Height: 5'11" Weight: 12.4

First choice Derby goalkeeper as 1994-95 unfolded, ahead of the more experienced Steve Sutton, Martin started in excellent form, allowing defenders in front of him the chance to settle down. Highly regarded for

Barry Coombs
(Empics Sports Photo Agency)

his ability on the ground and at saving penalties, after 77 consecutive appearances in the first team he had the misfortune to break his right-leg at Southend in a challenge with striker, Dave Regis, and played no further part in the campaign.

Derby Co (Signed from Mile Oak Rov on 2/7/86) FL 94 FLC 7 FAC 4 Others 11
Carlisle U (Loaned on 23/9/87) FL 10 FLC 1 FAC 1 Others 2
Scunthorpe U (Loaned on 17/12/87) FL 8

TAYLOR Robert (Bob)
Born: Horden, 3 February 1967
Height: 5'10" Weight: 12.0

Star man at WBA where his supreme marksmanship has made him a cult figure. Strong and powerful, both on the ground and in the air, he went through a thin time midway through 1994-95 when he suffered a hamstring injury and loss of form, and failed to score for almost four months. However, he bounced back in style with an important brace at Portsmouth and a stunning header in the 2-0 home win over "Wolves", before again suffering injury late on in the season. The subject of several big money transfer bids from Premiership clubs, he vowed to see out the 1994-95 campaign with Albion.

Leeds U (Free from Horden Colliery on 27/3/86) FL 33+9/9 FLC 5+1/3 FAC 1 Others 4+1/1
Bristol C (£175,000 on 23/3/89) FL 96+10/50 FLC 6+1/2 FAC 9+1/5 Others 3/1
West Bromwich A (£300,000 on 31/1/92) FL 145+4/67 FLC 7/2 FAC 5+1/3 Others 11+1/5

TAYLOR Robert Anthony
Born: Norwich, 30 April 1971
Height: 6'1" Weight: 13.8

Tall Brentford striker and an excellent target man, with deft flicks and passes, plus a good shot in either foot. Scored 25 goals last season, including a fantastic lob against Cambridge and a marvellous shot on the turn in mid-air against Stockport. Only one goal came from his head, all the rest being converted by his feet. Also made many of Nicky Forster's goals, as the pair set up an excellent strike partnership that almost took the club back to the First Division.

Norwich C (From trainee on 26/3/90)
Leyton Orient (Loaned on 28/3/91) FL 0+3/1
Birmingham C (Signed on 31/8/91)
Leyton Orient (Free on 21/10/91) FL 54+19/20 FLC 1+1 FAC 2+1 Others 2+1
Brentford (£100,000 on 24/3/94) FL 48/25 FLC 4/1 FAC 2/1 Others 4

TAYLOR Scott Dean
Born: Portsmouth, 28 November 1970
Height: 5'10" Weight: 11.0
Club Honours: Div 2 '94

Yet another to progress through Reading's youth policy, and the youngest player ever to complete 200 first team games for the club. Much improved during last season, and the scorer of some vital goals, many after coming on as substitute, Scott shows great pace, loves to take players on, and can make electrifying runs from midfield.

Reading (From trainee on 22/6/89) FL 164+43/24 FLC 7+5/1 FAC 11+2/3 Others 12+4/1

TAYLOR Scott James
Born: Chertsey, 5 May 1976
Height: 5'10" Weight: 11.4

Signed by Millwall from non-league Staines last February, this right-footed striker made a surprise entry into League football just ten days later, when summoned from the stands after Dave Savage was injured in a pre-match warm up.

Millwall (£15,000 from Staines on 8/2/95) FL 1+5

TAYLOR Shaun
Born: Plymouth, 26 March 1963
Height: 6'1" Weight: 12.8
Club Honours: Div 4 '90

Began 1994-95 at Swindon in dispute over his contract, but ended it as "Player of the Year". Defenders do not come any braver than this quietly spoken Devonian, who often puts his head where others fear to tread! A broken arm, sustained at Middlesbrough at the end of October, kept him out of action for seven weeks, but he was soon back and later reclaimed the captain's arm-band.

Exeter C (Free from Bideford T on 10/12/86) FL 200/16 FLC 12 FAC 9 Others 12
Swindon T (£200,000 on 26/7/91) F/PL 167/23 FLC 17/2 FAC 8 Others 7/1

TEALE Shaun
Born: Southport, 10 March 1964
Height: 6'0" Weight: 13.7
Club Honours: FLC '94
International Honours: E: SP-1

Combative Aston Villa central defender who is strong in the air and composed on the ground. Had a difficult start to last season, but managed to regain his place in the side soon after the introduction of new manager, Brian Little. Often employed in a three man central defence, Shaun produced good performances throughout the second half of the campaign as Villa fought to survive relegation.

Bournemouth (£50,000 from Weymouth on 22/1/89) FL 99+1/4 FLC 8 FAC 5/1 Others 3
Aston Villa (£300,000 on 25/7/91) F/PL 146+1/2 FLC 15/3 FAC 13 Others 6

Scot Taylor

Steve Morton
(Empics Sports Photo Agency)

TELFER Paul Norman
Born: Edinburgh, 21 October 1971
Height: 5'9" Weight: 11.6
International Honours: S: U21-3

An attacking Luton midfielder, more at home on the right, but able to play on either side, he experienced his best ever season in 1994-95, both scoring and making goals. His contribution to the team grew, especially after he was omitted from one game by the manager. Paul, who is developing into the all-round player, went on to become one of the most influential members of the team, his aggressive ball-winning and good distribution, allied to tremendous shooting ability. Has also been played at right-back with success. Stop Press: Signed for Coventry in a deal expected to cost City around £1.5 million.
Luton T (From trainee on 7/11/88) FL 136+8/19 FLC 5 FAC 14/2 Others 2/1

THACKERAY Andrew (Andy) John
Born: Huddersfield, 13 February 1968
Height: 5'9" Weight: 11.0
Club Honours: FAYC '86

An experienced and reliable right-back, and captain of Rochdale, Andy enjoys the overlap, although being equally firm at the back. And consistent to a tee, in missing just one game last season, he made his 100th FL appearance at Scunthorpe on New Year's Eve.
Manchester C (From juniors on 15/2/86)
Huddersfield T (Free on 1/8/86) FL 2 Others 0+1
Newport Co (£5,000 on 27/3/87) FL 53+1/4 FLC 3+1 FAC 1 Others 2+1/1
Wrexham (£5,000 on 20/7/88) FL 139+13/14 FLC 10/1 FAC 6 Others 13+2
Rochdale (£15,000 on 15/7/92) FL 117+2/13 FLC 8 FAC 5 Others 8+2/2

Ben Thatcher   Steve Morton
(Empics Sports Photo Agency)

THATCHER Benjamin (Ben) David
Born: Swindon, 30 November 1975
Height: 5'10" Weight: 11.10
International Honours: E: Yth; Sch

A left-back who graduated through youth ranks and the Lilleshall School of Excellence, he can also play in the heart of the Millwall defence with equal aplomb. Scored his first League goal in the local derby against Charlton at the Den last season, a 30 yard volley which flew past the 'keeper. Proof that his tough tackling displays were being noticed, came in the shape of a call-up for England's U21 squad. Elected by his fellow professionals to the PFA Award winning First Division side.
Millwall (From trainee on 8/6/92) FL 46+2/1 FLC 4 FAC 5 Others 1

THEW Lee
Born: Sunderland, 23 October 1974
Height: 5'10" Weight: 11.5

A young midfield player who has yet to win a regular place in Doncaster's first team, although finding himself a regular fixture in the squad last season, he was freed at the end of 1994-95.
Doncaster Rov (From trainee on 3/8/93) FL 21+11/2 FLC 1 FAC 0+2 Others 2/1

THIRLBY Anthony Dennis
Born: Berlin, Germany, 4 March 1976
Height: 5'10" Weight: 11.5
International Honours: NI: Yth

A creative Exeter midfield teenager who supplies the forwards, Anthony is now into his third season of regular football. One to watch out for.
Exeter C (From trainee on 4/7/94) FL 27+10/1 FLC 2+1 Others 1

THOMAS Anthony (Tony)
Born: Liverpool, 12 July 1971
Height: 5'11" Weight: 12.5
Club Honours: AMC '90

One of the unluckiest players around, Tony was again struck down by injury early last season, but bounced back to recover his best form, marauding down the right and whipping crosses in. A powerfully built and strong-tackling full-back, he has been unsettled at Tranmere for some time and has been on the transfer list for the past 12 months. However, as yet, no one has matched Rovers' £1 million valuation.
Tranmere Rov (From trainee on 1/2/89) FL 195+1/12 FLC 18+1/1 FAC 5 Others 26/1

THOMAS David John
Born: Caerphilly, 26 September 1975
Height: 5'10" Weight: 11.7

David made his full Swansea debut against Bournemouth at the Vetch Field last April after a couple of substitute appearances for the first team. As top goalscorer for the reserves he showed some excellent touches, plus an ability to handle the aggressive style of Second Division football. Currently on non-contract terms.
Swansea C (From trainee on 25/7/94) FL 2+2 Others 0+3/1

THOMAS Geoffrey (Geoff) Robert
Born: Manchester, 5 August 1964
Height: 6'1" Weight: 12.0
Club Honours: FMC '91
International Honours: E: 9; B-3

Wolverhampton's midfield dynamo who can help his team in all areas of the field. After a long lay-off, he played in the first five fixtures of 1994-95, requiring a tidying up operation before having nine games in the autumn. However, his knee was still not strong enough to cope with the rigours of the modern game and he had a dismal time against Middlesbrough in February, although really looking the part in another comeback, scoring versus Watford. Sadly, he limped off well before the end, with another cartilage operation needed.
Rochdale (Free from Littleborough on 13/8/82) FL 10+1/1 Others 0+1
Crewe Alex (Free on 22/3/84) FL 120+5/20 FLC 8 FAC 2 Others 2+1
Crystal Palace (£50,000 on 8/6/87) F/PL 192+3/26 FLC 24/3 FAC 13+1/2 Others 15+1/4
Wolverhampton W (£800,000 on 18/6/93) FL 21+1/5 FLC 1 Others 4

THOMAS Glen Andrew
Born: Hackney, 6 October 1967
Height: 6'1" Weight: 11.0

Playing at left-back or centre-back for Barnet, he helped in the ultimately unsuccessful push for a play-off place in 1994-95 and, with a few more games under his belt, the fans should see him at his best this coming season.
Fulham (From apprentice on 9/10/85) FL 246+5/6 FLC 21 FAC 8 Others 14+1
Peterborough U (Free on 4/11/94) FL 6+2 FAC 0+1 Others 2
Barnet (Free on 23/3/95) FL 6+1

THOMAS Martin Russell
Born: Lymington, 12 September 1973
Height: 5'8" Weight: 10.8

Since joining Fulham during the 1994 close season, Martin has been dogged by a series of niggling injuries. When he was fit, however, his pace, control, and crossing down the right-flank gave the team an extra dimension. Still only in his early 20s, he is an exciting prospect.
Southampton (From trainee on 19/6/92)
Leyton Orient (Free on 24/3/94) FL 5/2
Fulham (Free on 21/7/94) FL 21+2/3 FLC 1 Others 1

THOMAS Michael Lauriston
Born: Lambeth, 24 August 1967
Height: 5'10" Weight: 12.4
Club Honours: FLC '87, 95; Div 1 '89, '91; CS '91; FAC '92
International Honours: E: 2; B-5; U21-12; Yth; Sch

A midfield player with great stamina, Michael always impresses those in the know with great runs, both on and off the ball. Also has the ability to turn up in the opposition's penalty area to score at vital moments. 1994-95 was a somewhat disappointing season as he failed to gain a regular place in the Liverpool team. But, as a valued member of the squad, his powerful running from midfield could again prove useful this coming season.
Arsenal (From apprentice on 31/12/84) FL 149+14/24 FLC 21+2/5 FAC 14+3/1 Others 5+2/1
Portsmouth (Loaned on 30/12/86) FL 3
Liverpool (£1,500,000 on 16/12/91) F/PL 39+16/4 FLC 2+2 FAC 9+1/2 Others 2

THOMAS Mitchell Anthony
Born: Luton, 2 October 1964
Height: 6'0" Weight: 12.0
International Honours: E: B-1; U21-3; Yth
Primarily a left-sided defensive or midfield player, Luton also used Mitchell at right-back and in central midfield last season. Extremely adventurous with the overlap, he is still a hard man to pass. While his somewhat awkward style can lead to free-kicks or penalties, he offsets that with his strength in the air and his total commitment to the game.
Luton T (From apprentice on 27/8/82) FL 106+1/1 FLC 5 FAC 18
Tottenham H (£233,000 on 7/7/86) FL 136+21/6 FLC 28+1/1 FAC 12/1
West Ham U (£525,000 on 7/8/91) FL 37+1/3 FLC 5 FAC 4 Others 2
Luton T (Free on 12/11/93) FL 50+6/1 FAC 4

THOMAS Roderick (Rod) Clive
Born: Brent, 10 October 1970
Height: 5'6" Weight: 10.6
Club Honours: FAYC '89; Div 3 '95
International Honours: E: U21-1; Yth; Sch

A mercurial forward who, on his day, is the most exciting player at Carlisle. The possessor of immense ability as a ball player, Rod loves taking on defenders and his spell at the club has revived a promising career that appeared to have gone into the doldrums. As a goalscorer last season, he was especially effective in AWS matches with five in seven appearances. Also won a Third Division Championship medal.
Watford (From trainee on 3/5/88) FL 63+21/9 FLC 3+2 FAC 0+1 Others 3+1
Gillingham (Loaned on 27/3/92) FL 8/1 Others 1
Carlisle U (Free on 12/7/93) FL 73+1/15 FLC 6/1 FAC 8 Others 16/7

THOMAS Scott Lee
Born: Bury, 30 October 1974
Height: 5'11" Weight: 11.4
A promising Manchester City youngster who can perform equally well, either as a right-winger, or at full-back. Skilful with the ball, Scott likes to take defenders on when

Alan Thompson　　　Steve Morton
(Empics Sports Photo Agency)

Rod Thomas　　　Tony Marshall
(Empics Sports Photo Agency)

going direct for goal and his potential was recognised last season with a couple of subs' appearances in the Premiership.
Manchester C (From trainee on 26/3/92) PL 0+2

THOMPSON Alan
Born: Newcastle, 22 December 1973
Height: 6'0" Weight: 12.8
International Honours: E: U21-1; Yth
The Bolton winger produced his most consistent form to date in 1994-95, with his trusty left-foot causing opposing defences immeasurable problems and earning him recognition with the England U21 squad. Saved his best performances, however, for the TV cameras, winning "Man of the Match" awards at Millwall and in the play-off final against Reading, the game that saw the club go back to the top flight for the first time since 1979-80. In the Coca Cola Cup

Final he had the satisfaction of scoring the best goal of the game and then went on to score winners in two League matches against Swindon and West Bromwich Albion.
Newcastle U (From trainee on 11/3/91) FL 13+3 FAC 1 Others 3
Bolton W (£250,000 on 22/7/93) FL 53+11/13 FLC 11+1/2 FAC 3+1/1 Others 7+1/1

THOMPSON Andrew (Andy) Richard
Born: Cannock, 9 November 1967
Height: 5'4" Weight: 10.6
Club Honours: Div 4 '88, Div 3 '89; AMC '88
A nippy Wolverhampton left-back, he had scored seven penalties, including two in one match, by the end of last November. Had a hernia operation at the start of December, but returned two months later with some

tenacious tackling as though he had never been away. Fourteen of his 45 appearances had been in cup-ties when he was injured again, suffering ruptured ankle ligaments.

West Bromwich A (From apprentice on 16/11/85) FL 18+6/1 FLC 0+1 FAC 2 Others 1+1
Wolverhampton W (£35,000 on 21/11/86) FL 285+14/35 FLC 14 FAC 16/1 Others 32/1

THOMPSON David George
Born: Ashington, 20 November 1968
Height: 6'3" Weight: 12.7
Central defender. Started last season at Brentford, before moving to Blackpool in

mid-season and eventually joining Cambridge on transfer deadline day. Good in the air, his move to United coincided with a bolstering of the defence and only two defeats in seven games.

Millwall (From apprentice on 26/11/86) FL 88+9/6 FLC 4 FAC 4/1 Others 6
Bristol C (Signed on 18/6/92) FL 17 FLC 4 Others 5+1
Brentford (Free on 1/2/94) FL 9+1/1
Blackpool (Signed on 9/9/94) FL 17 FAC 1 Others 2
Cambridge U (Free on 23/3/95) FL 7

THOMPSON David (Dave) Stephen
Born: Manchester, 27 May 1962

Height: 5'11" Weight: 12.10
A former Rochdale favourite outside-right, he re-signed at the beginning of last season and quickly settled down, with his wing play helping the club to an excellent start.

Rochdale (Free from Withington on 26/9/81) FL 147+8/13 FLC 7 FAC 7+1 Others 6
Notts Co (Signed on 22/8/86) FL 52+3/8 FLC 3+1 FAC 3 Others 2
Wigan Ath (£35,000 on 20/10/87) FL 107+1/14 FLC 5/2 FAC 3+1 Others 6/1
Preston NE (£77,500 on 1/8/90) FL 39+7/4 FLC 1+1 Others 3+1
Chester C (Free on 14/8/92) FL 70+10/9 FLC 4 FAC 5 Others 4
Rochdale (£6,000 on 8/8/94) FL 38+2/6 FLC 2 Others 7

THOMPSON Garry Linsey
Born: Birmingham, 7 October 1959
Height: 6'2" Weight: 13.3
Club Honours: FMC '91
International Honours: E: U21-6
A tall, well-built striker, who experienced the higher echelons of football before joining Northampton from Cardiff last February. Mainly used as a target man, with good aerial strengths and hard to knock off the ball, he quickly got among the goals for the "Cobblers".

Coventry C (From apprentice on 29/6/77) FL 127+7/38 FLC 12+1/7 FAC 11/4
West Bromwich A (£225,000 on 17/2/83) FL 91/39 FLC 9/5 FAC 5/1
Sheffield Wed (£450,000 on 12/8/85) FL 35+1/7 FLC 2+1/1·FAC 5/1
Aston Villa (£450,000 on 5/6/86) FL 56+4/17 FLC 6/2 FAC 4 Others 3
Watford (£325,000 on 24/12/88) FL 24+10/8 FLC 0+1 FAC 7+1
Crystal Palace (£200,000 on 24/3/90) FL 17+3/3 FLC 0+1/1 Others 0+1
Queens Park R (£125,000 on 19/8/91) F/PL 10+9/1 FLC 3+2/3 Others 1
Cardiff C (Free on 15/7/93) FL 39+4/5 FLC 2 FAC 5+2/1 Others 6+3/3
Northampton T (Signed on 10/2/95) FL 15/4

THOMPSON Neil
Born: Beverley, 2 October 1963
Height: 5'11" Weight: 13.7
Club Honours: GMVC '87; Div 2 '92
International Honours: E: SP-4

Attacking Ipswich left-back who loves to join up with his strikers, and has an extremely powerful shot, Neil can also play in midfield. His other attributes include strong tackling, a penchant for in-swinging corners and a long-throw. After missing the first half of 1994-95 with a knee injury, sustained in the pre-season build-up, he only got back into the side when Tony Vaughan was injured, by which time Town were virtually relegated.

Hull C (Free from Nottingham F juniors on 28/11/81) FL 29+2
Scarborough (Free on 1/8/83) FL 87/15 FLC 8/1 FAC 4 Others 9/1
Ipswich T (£100,000 on 9/6/89) F/PL 194+7/18 FLC 14+1/1 FAC 17/1 Others 8/2

THOMPSON Niall Joseph
Born: Birmingham, 16 April 1974
Height: 6'0" Weight: 12.0
Striker. Initially at Colchester on non-contract terms, Niall took his chance when it came and was rewarded with a professional

Dave Thompson (Rochdale)
Matthew Ashton
(Empics Sports Photo Agency)

contract. Became an instant favourite with two goals in five minutes at Scunthorpe, after coming on as substitute at 3-2 down, then repeated the feat at Gillingham with two goals in two minutes for another United victory! Surprisingly freed during the summer.
Crystal Palace (From juniors on 16/7/92)
Colchester U (Free from Hong Kong on 4/11/94) FL 5+8/5 FAC 0+1

THOMPSON Paul Derek Zetland
Born: Newcastle, 17 April 1973
Height: 5'11" Weight: 11.10
Young Hartlepool player, who had some success as a forward, before injuries to others meant he was tried in midfield. With this switch, his fitness improved and he became a more all-round player, and was a regular first teamer for most of last season, before unluckily being sidelined with an ankle injury late on. Many supporters will be surprised that he was not retained.
Hartlepool U (Signed on 22/10/91) FL 44+12/9 FLC 4+1/1 FAC 1 Others 1+1

THOMPSON Simon Lee
Born: Sheffield, 27 February 1970
Height: 5'10" Weight: 10.6
A versatile player, Simon is capable of operating at full-back, or as an orthodox winger. Having given Scarborough splendid service since being signed from Rotherham, he was released at the end of last season.
Rotherham U (From trainee on 1/7/88) FL 12+16 FLC 2+2 FAC 4+2 Others 1+3/1
Scarborough (£5,000 on 24/12/91) FL 99+9/6 FLC 12 FAC 4+1 Others 6+1

THOMPSON Stephen (Steve) James
Born: Plymouth, 12 January 1963
Height: 5'8" Weight: 11.1
Club Honours: GMVC '93; FAT '93
International Honours: E: SP-1
Skilful and pacy Wycombe midfielder with good close control, Steve likes to run at defenders and shoot from a distance. Niggling injuries reduced his appearances last season.
Bristol C (From juniors on 31/7/81) FL 10+2/1 FLC 3 FAC 0+1
Torquay U (Free on 1/2/83) FL 0+1 (Free to Saltash U in March 1983)
Wycombe W (£15,000 from Slough T in February 1992) FL 41+21/3 FLC 5/1 FAC 5+2/1 Others 7+1/2

THOMPSON Steven (Steve) James
Born: Oldham, 2 November 1964
Height: 5'10" Weight: 12.0
Club Honours: AMC '89
A right-footed midfield playmaker, he looked to have been displaced by Mark Draper at Leicester last season, but won his place back, alongside the record signing, before transferring to Burnley in February and taking over the role previously filled by John Deary. Steve arrived too late to save the sinking ship, but his early performances were impressive, and the side was weaker for his absence, following an Achilles tendon injury towards the end of the campaign.
Bolton W (From apprentice on 4/11/82) FL 329+6/49 FLC 27/2 FAC 21/4 Others 39/2
Luton T (£180,000 on 13/8/91) FL 5 FLC 2

Leicester C (Signed on 22/10/91) F/PL 121+6/18 FLC 6/2 FAC 8/1 Others 11+3/4
Burnley (£200,000 on 24/2/95) FL 12

THOMPSTONE Ian Philip
Born: Bury, 17 January 1971
Height: 6'0" Weight: 11.3
Big and solid, with a powerful shot, Ian performed on the right-side of Scunthorpe's midfield last season, although preferring the right-back position. Can also play up-front. Making more appearances from the bench than he started, he was released during the summer.
Manchester C (From trainee on 1/9/89) FL 0+1/1
Oldham Ath (Free on 25/5/90)

Exeter C (Free on 23/1/92) FL 15/3
Halifax T (Free on 14/7/92) FL 31/9 FLC 1+1 FAC 1 Others 2
Scunthorpe U (£15,000 on 25/3/93) FL 47+13/8 FLC 2 FAC 4+2/1 Others 2

THOMSEN Claus
Born: Aarhus, Denmark, 31 May 1970
Height: 6'3" Weight: 13.6
International Honours: Denmark
A tall midfielder with good aerial ability, Claus generates much excitement with penetrating runs and can play up-front if required. Yet another player who had to postpone his Ipswich debut in 1994-95, this time because of a hernia operation, he

Steve Thompson (Wycombe)

Barry Coombs
(Empics Sports Photo Agency)

eventually made his first start in the Coca Cola Cup-tie against Bolton and proved his mettle in the 3-2 defeat, when setting up the first goal. Found it quite hard to adjust to the pace of the English game, but possesses plenty of skill and deft touches. Played in a central midfield role towards the end of the season and made his full international debut for Denmark in April.

Ipswich T (£250,000 from Aarhus on 15/6/94) PL 31+2/5 FLC 2 FAC 1

THOMSON Andrew (Andy)

Born: Motherwell, 1 April 1971
Height: 5'10" Weight: 9.7

A small and nippy forward, and a very good footballer, Andy proved himself with Southend after moving down from Scotland for a substantial fee during the 1994 close season. A knee injury hampered him during the early part of last season, but he developed and began taking chances regularly. His neat lay-offs and running off the ball make him a difficult opponent to mark.

Queen of the South (Free from Jerviston BC on 28/7/89) SL 133+12/93 SLC 8/3 SC 6+3/5 Others 7+1/7
Southend U (£250,000 on 4/7/94) FL 35+4/11 FLC 1 FAC 1

THOMSON Andrew John

Born: Swindon, 28 March 1974
Height: 6'3" Weight: 12.0

After making his League debut in Swindon's final Premiership game in May 1994, much was expected of this powerfully built central defender. And, with the swift departure of Adrian Whitbread, the way was left clear. Scored his first senior goal in a Coca Cola Cup-tie at Brighton, but his Christmas present for the visit to Stoke was a substitutes' shirt and he was rarely given a first team opportunity after that.

Swindon T (From trainee on 1/5/93) P/FL 21+1 FLC 5/1 Others 3

THORN Andrew (Andy) Charles

Born: Carshalton, 12 November 1966
Height: 6'0" Weight: 11.5
Club Honours: FAC '88
International Honours: E: U21-5

Rejoined Wimbledon last October after finding himself out of favour at Crystal Palace, following a long spell out injured. A dogged central defender, who enjoys a "battle", and is strong in the air in both penalty areas, he soon established himself as a regular at his old club. Now having a new lease of life, Andy did not have to move far, with both Palace and Wimbledon sharing Selhurst Park.

Wimbledon (From apprentice on 13/11/84) FL 106+1/2 FLC 7 FAC 9 Others 1
Newcastle U (£850,000 on 1/8/88) FL 36/2 FLC 4/1 Others 3
Crystal Palace (£650,000 on 5/12/89) F/PL 128/3 FLC 19/4 FAC 10 Others 11
Wimbledon (Free on 5/10/94) PL 22+1/1 FLC 1 FAC 3

THORNBER Stephen (Steve) John

Born: Dewsbury, 11 October 1965
Height: 5'10" Weight: 11.2
Club Honours: WC '89

A left-footed player used in central midfield for Scunthorpe, he was always busy and always involved in 1994-95, often making good runs into attacking positions. Also a good tackler.

Halifax T (From juniors on 24/1/83) FL 94+10/4 FLC 3+1/1 FAC 9/1 Others 11
Swansea C (£10,000 on 23/8/88) FL 98+19/6 FLC 7/3 FAC 9+2/1 Others 8+3
Blackpool (Free on 13/8/92) FL 21+3 FLC 3 Others 1
Scunthorpe U (Free on 12/7/93) FL 57+4/7 FLC 2 FAC 3+1 Others 3

THORNE Peter Lee

Born: Manchester, 21 June 1973
Height: 6'0" Weight: 12.3

Signed last January, Peter emerged from the shadows of Alan Shearer and Chris Sutton at Blackburn to become an instant "hit" at Swindon. Grabbed two goals in his first full appearance, at Burnley, and another two a week later in Town's first-leg Coca Cola Cup semi-final. Has all the attributes of a natural goalscorer and, at only 22, is an exciting prospect for the future.

Blackburn Rov (From trainee on 20/6/91) Others 0+1
Wigan Ath (Loaned on 11/3/94) FL 10+1
Swindon T (£225,000 on 18/1/95) FL 20+1/9 FLC 2/2 FAC 0+1

THORNLEY Timothy (Tim) James

Born: Leicester, 3 March 1977
Height: 5'9" Weight: 11.0

A young Torquay trainee goalkeeper, Tim made a 90th minute substitution appearance at Hereford last season, when replacing the injured Ashley Bayes.

Torquay U (Trainee) FL 0+1

THORPE Anthony (Tony) Lee

Born: Leicester, 10 April 1974
Height: 5'9" Weight: 12.0

A central or left-sided attacking midfielder, Tony was not able to build on the progress made in 1993-94 and break into Luton's first team on a regular basis last season, but is still a reliable player who backs up well and has a firm shot. Played well for the reserves in 1994-95 and was unfortunate to be out with injury at a time in the season when a first team place was available.

Luton T (Free from Leicester C juniors on 18/8/92) FL 4+14/1 FAC 1+2/1

THORPE Jeffrey (Jeff) Roger

Born: Cockermouth, 17 November 1972
Height: 5'10" Weight: 12.8
Club Honours: Div 3 '95

Having missed the whole of 1993-94 with back trouble, his return to the Carlisle side last season was often in the role of substitute as he gradually returned to full fitness. The possessor of great pace, his finest moment came at Scunthorpe where he netted twice in the dying minutes to snatch victory from the jaws of defeat. Is yet another representative of the cadre of locally developed talent to emerge in recent years at the club. His 28 FL games, 21 of them as a sub, brought him a Third Division Championship medal.

Carlisle U (From trainee on 2/7/91) FL 64+33/5 FLC 6+3 FAC 3+2 Others 5+6/1

THORPE Lee Anthony

Born: Wolverhampton, 14 December 1975
Height: 6'1" Weight: 12.4

Another first year Blackpool pro who shows much promise, Lee is a striker who should not have to wait too long to prove his worth on a regular basis.

Blackpool (From trainee on 18/7/94) FL 0+2

THORSVEDT Erik

Born: Stavanger, Norway, 28 October 1962
Height: 6'3" Weight: 14.4
Club Honours: FAC '91; CS '91
International Honours: Norway

A goalkeeper of great ability who, due to injury and the superb form of Ian Walker, appeared only twice for Tottenham last season. Agile, and with a great build, Erik seems to fill the goal, being a shot-stopper of the highest order and safe on crosses. He continues to be the Norwegian international side's first choice, however, while having to take his place on the bench as Walker goes from strength to strength.

Tottenham H (£400,000 from Borussia Moenchengladbach on 22/12/88) F/PL 171+2 FLC 25 FAC 14 Others 7

TIERNEY Francis

Born: Liverpool, 10 September 1975
Height: 5'10" Weight: 11.0
International Honours: E: Sch; Yth

A wide player, and naturally right-footed, Francis operated on either flank last season, being confident and quick to get the ball under control. He is another of Crewe's youngsters who could go a long way in the game. Stop Press: Signed for Liverpool during the summer for a fee of £700,000.

Crewe Alex (From trainee on 22/3/93) FL 17+12/5 FLC 2 FAC 0+2 Others 4+2/2

TILER Carl

Born: Sheffield, 11 February 1970
Height: 6'4" Weight: 13.0
International Honours: E: U21-13

A tall, left-footed Nottingham Forest central defender, who uses his height to good advantage in both penalty areas and, who is calm and reliable on the ground, Carl took over a lot of extra responsibility in the side following Des Walker's departure in August 1992. Although temporarily deputising for Colin Cooper last season, since unfortunately suffering an ankle injury at the end of 1992-93, he has played only three first team games, plus two more on loan at Swindon last November.

Barnsley (From trainee on 2/8/88) FL 67+4/3 FLC 4 FAC 4+1 Others 3+1
Nottingham F (£1,400,000 on 30/5/91) F/PL 67+2/1 FLC 10+1 FAC 6 Others 1
Swindon T (Loaned on 18/11/94) FL 2

TILLSON Andrew (Andy)

Born: Huntingdon, 30 June 1966
Height: 6'2" Weight: 12.10

Bristol Rovers' record transfer signing, Andy was appointed club captain for 1994-95 and his leadership qualities proved excellent. Comfortable on the ball, his heading and passing ability contributed much to the club's successful season. Celebrated the end of the campaign as Rovers' "Player of the Year".

Grimsby T (Free from Kettering T on 14/7/88) FL 104+1/5 FLC 8 FAC 10 Others 5
Queens Park R (£400,000 on 21/12/90) FL 27+2/2 FLC 2 Others 1
Grimsby T (Loaned on 15/9/92) FL 4 Others 1
Bristol Rov (£370,000 on 7/11/92) FL 81+1/2 FLC 4/1 FAC 5 Others 7

TILSON Stephen (Steve) Brian
Born: Wickford, 27 July 1966
Height: 5'11" Weight: 12.6
Steve showed some of his best ever Southend form during the 1994-95 relegation battle under Steve Thompson, giving much needed skill and commitment to the midfield. The development of his right foot made him even more useful to the team, and he scored what he described as his "best-ever-goal" in the 4-2 defeat of Stoke. Intelligent passing and strong tackling helped Steve gain an automatic first team shirt by the end of the campaign.
Southend U (Signed from Witham T on 7/2/89) FL 149+34/22 FLC 6+1 FAC 3 Others 10+1/3
Brentford (Loaned on 16/9/93) FL 2

TIMONS Christopher (Chris) Brian
Born: Nottingham, 8 December 1974
Height: 6'1" Weight: 12.6
As a right-side Mansfield central defender, who made a few appearances last season, Chris was unable to hold down a regular place in the side.
Mansfield T (Signed from Clipstone Colliery on 1/2/94) FL 19+3/1 FLC 0+1Others 2+1

TINKLER Mark Roland
Born: Bishop Auckland, 24 October 1974
Height: 6'0" Weight: 11.4
Club Honours: FAYC '93
International Honours: E: Yth (UEFAC '93); Sch
The former skipper of Leeds' most successful youth team, Mark came back from a badly broken leg last season and did well when called into the side on rare occasions as cover for injuries, operating mainly in central midfield. Showing good vision and ball control, and always looking to get forward, he safely came through an horrific tackle at Sheffield Wednesday, which, thankfully, resulted in no further damage. Most definitely one to watch out for.
Leeds U (From trainee on 29/11/91) PL 8+5

TINNION Brian
Born: Stanley, 23 February 1968
Height: 5'11" Weight: 11.5
Left-sided Bristol City player who can perform either at full-back or in defence. Following an outstanding campaign in 1993-94, his form dipped following an injury sustained during the Gloucestershire Cup match against Bristol Rovers, prior to the commencement of 1994-95. His mobility appeared restricted throughout the season and it must be hoped that the summer respite will see him back on song.
Newcastle U (From apprentice on 26/2/86) FL 30+2/2 FLC 5 Others 1+1
Bradford C (£150,000 on 9/3/89) FL 137+8/22 FLC 12/1 FAC 9/4 Others 7+1/2
Bristol C (£180,000 on 23/3/93) FL 84+3/9 FLC 4 FAC 8/3

TISDALE Paul Robert
Born: Malta, 14 January 1973
Height: 5'9" Weight: 10.9
International Honours: E: Sch
Made just nine sub appearances in Southampton's midfield last season, but looks to have a promising career ahead of him. Played almost the whole game as sub for Neil Maddison in the vital 2-0 win at Chelsea and is sure to get further opportunities in 1995-96.
Southampton (From juniors on 5/6/91) PL 0+7 FLC 0+1 FAC 0+1
Northampton T (Loaned on 12/3/92) FL 5

TITTERTON David Stewart
Born: Warwick, 25 September 1971
Height: 5'11" Weight: 13.10
International Honours: E: Yth
Gutsy Wycombe left-back with good passing ability, his 1994-95 season was cut short by injury after just two games and he was freed during the summer.
Coventry C (From trainee on 24/5/90) FL 0+2 FLC 1
Hereford U (£8,000 on 12/9/91) FL 39+12/1 FAC 2+2 Others 4+1
Wycombe W (Free on 12/8/93) FL 15+4/1 FLC 3 Others 4+1

TODD Andrew (Andy) John James
Born: Derby, 21 September 1974
Height: 5'9" Weight: 12.3
Strong young Middlesbrough defender with the highest credentials as the son of former England star, Colin, Andy is an ambitious and enthusiastic player whose ball distribution is superb. Powerful in the air and strong with either foot, and having represented the club at every level, at the end of last season, he was on loan at Swindon as makeweight in the Jan Aage Fjortoft transfer.
Middlesbrough (From trainee on 6/3/92) FL 7+1 FLC 1+1 Others 5
Swindon T (Loaned on 27/2/95) FL 13

TODD Lee
Born: Hartlepool, 7 March 1972
Height: 5'5" Weight: 10.3
Full-back, who is equally at home on the right or left, after being converted from a winger, his all-action style and chirpy character have made him a big favourite with Stockport fans.
Stockport Co (Free from Hartlepool U juniors on 23/7/90) FL 133+9/2 FLC 10+1 FAC 9/2 Others 24+1

TODD Mark Kenneth
Born: Belfast, 4 December 1967
Height: 5'7" Weight: 10.2
International Honours: NI: U23-1
Mark was another player who had to show enormous courage in forcing his way back into first team contention for Rotherham in 1994-95, after having a long spell out of the game through injury. Battling back well, hopefully he will look back at the campaign as one which helped to resurrect his career.
Manchester U (From apprentice on 7/8/85)
Sheffield U (Free on 1/7/87) FL 62+8/5 FLC 5+1 FAC 10+1/1 Others 5+1
Wolverhampton W (Loaned on 14/3/91) FL 6+1
Rotherham U (£35,000 on 11/9/91) FL 60+4/7 FLC 5/2 FAC 3 Others 2/1

TOLSON Neil
Born: Walsall, 25 October 1973
Height: 6'1" Weight: 12.4
Centre-forward. Neil struggled for Bradford at the beginning of last season and later had a period on loan at Chester. However, when John Taylor was transferred, he got back in the side and scored two goals in three games, before suffering a knee injury and missing the last eight games of the campaign.
Walsall (From trainee on 17/12/91) FL 3+6/1 FAC 0+1/1 Others 1+2
Oldham Ath (£150,000 on 24/3/92) PL 0+3
Bradford C (Signed on 2/12/93) FL 20+12/4 FLC 0+3 FAC 1/1 Others 1+1/2
Chester C (Loaned on 6/1/95) FL 3+1

TOMAN James Andrew (Andy)
Born: Northallerton, 7 March 1962
Height: 5'10" Weight: 11.7
Club Honours: GMVC '90; Div 4 '91
Seasoned and skilful Scarborough midfielder whose biggest attribute is his tremendous passing ability. Has great experience in the lower divisions, but was unfortunately blighted by hernia and injury problems over the past season.
Lincoln C (£10,000 from Bishop Auckland on 16/8/85) FL 21+3/4 FLC 2 Others 0+1 (Free to Bishop Auckland during 1986 close season)
Hartlepool U (£6,000 on 23/1/87) FL 112/28 FLC 4 FAC 9/4 Others 7
Darlington (£40,000 on 1/8/89) FL 108+7/10 FLC 8 FAC 8/2 Others 6/3
Scarborough (Loaned on 25/2/93) FL 6
Scunthorpe U (Free on 20/8/93) FL 15/5 FLC 1 FAC 2/1 Others 1
Scarborough (Free on 10/12/93) FL 21+8/1 FLC 1 FAC 3/1 Others 1

TOMLINSON Graeme Murdoch
Born: Keighley, 10 December 1975
Height: 5'9" Weight: 11.7
An excellent young striker, who is quick off the mark, with excellent awareness, Graeme is remarkably good in the air for his size and capable of scoring brilliant goals. Was signed by Manchester United manager, Alex Ferguson, after impressing in Bradford's City's 2-0 second round Youth Cup victory over United in 1994. Made his first team debut last season as a substitute in the Coca Cola Cup against Port Vale, showing some excellent touches, and has the potential to go right to the top.
Bradford C (Trainee) FL 12+5/6 FAC 0+1
Manchester U (£100,000 on 12/7/94) FLC 0+2

TOMLINSON Michael (Micky) Lloyd
Born: Lambeth, 15 September 1972
Height: 5'9" Weight: 10.7
Tricky right-winger who can also play inside, and who possesses a good turn of pace, Micky began to hit his best form at the latter end of last season, thus coinciding with Barnet's upturn in fortunes.
Leyton Orient (From trainee on 5/7/91) FL 7+7/1 FLC 4/1 FAC 1 Others 0+1
Barnet (Free on 21/3/94) FL 31+7/1 FLC 3 FAC 0+2 Others 0+2

TOMLINSON Paul
Born: Brierley Hill, 22 February 1964
Height: 6'2" Weight: 13.12

Arguably one of the best goalies outside of the Premier League, "Tommo" broke two long-standing Bradford goalkeeping records last season. Firstly, on 2 November, he attained 71 clean sheets and later, on 25 February, he reached 284 FL appearances. The latter record had stood since 1928-29 and Paul looks to extend that considerably.

Sheffield U (Free from Middlewood on 1/6/83) FL 37 FLC 1 FAC 5 Others 3
Birmingham C (Loaned on 20/3/87) FL 11
Bradford C (£47,500 on 23/6/87) FL 293 FLC 28 FAC 15 Others 14

TORFASON Gudmundur (Gunnar)
Born: West Mann Isles, 13 December 1961
Height: 6'1" Weight: 13.2
International Honours: Iceland

Striker. Signed by Doncaster Rovers during the 1994 close season, having been freed by St Johnstone, Gunnar showed himself to be a once talented player nearing the end of his career. At times, there were excellent touches from both feet but, after just six appearances, he was released.

St Mirren (Signed from RSC Genk during 1989 close season) SL 74+2/24 SLC 3/1 SC 8/2
St Johnstone (Signed on 11/8/92) SL 30+9/9 SLC 4/1 SC 0+4
Doncaster Rov (Free on 28/7/94) FL 1+3 FLC 1+1/1

TORPEY Stephen David James
Born: Islington, 8 December 1970
Height: 6'3" Weight: 14.3
Club Honours: AMC '94

Playing for Swansea as a solitary striker for most of last season, he battled hard up-front and showed a tremendous willingness to hard work. Although outnumbered for most of the time, he finished as the club's leading goalscorer with 19.

Millwall (From trainee on 14/2/89) FL 3+4 FLC 0+1
Bradford C (£70,000 on 21/11/90) FL 86+10/22 FLC 6 FAC 2+1 Others 8/6
Swansea C (£80,000 on 3/8/93) FL 73+8/20 FLC 6+1/1 FAC 7/4 Others 10+3/4

TOTTEN Alexander (Alex) Reginald
Born: Southampton, 1 October 1976
Height: 5'7" Weight: 10.7

Left-sided Portsmouth defender who likes going forward from full-back, Alex broke into the first team last season while still a trainee, but signed professional forms soon after. Following that, he made fleeting appearances when "Pompey" had injuries in defence.

Portsmouth (From trainee on 23/11/94) FL 3+1

TOWN David Edward
Born: Bournemouth, 9 December 1976
Height: 5'8" Weight: 11.7

Striker. A prolific scorer for Bournemouth's youth and reserve sides last season, he made several appearances as a substitute while still a trainee, in gaining experience as a member of the first team squad. Now a professional.

Bournemouth (From trainee on 11/4/95) FL 0+6 FLC 0+1

TOWNSEND Andrew (Andy) David
Born: Maidstone, 27 July 1963
Height: 5'11" Weight: 12.7
Club Honours: FLC '94
International Honours: Ei: 54; B-1

The driving force of the Aston Villa engine-room, and a regular for the Republic of Ireland, Andy combines hard work with a shrewd tactical view of the game. Plays on the left-side of midfield and possesses an accurate and incisive passing ability, allied to strong-tackling and an explosive long-range shot. Only missed a handful of games in 1994-95 and, following the arrival of Ian Taylor, took up a more defensive role. Given the captaincy whenever Steve Staunton was absent.

Southampton (£35,000 from Weymouth on 15/1/85) FL 77+6/5 FLC 7+1 FAC 2+3 Others 3+2
Norwich C (£300,000 on 31/8/88) FL 66+5/8 FLC 3+1 FAC 10/2 Others 3
Chelsea (£1,200,000 on 5/7/90) F/PL 110/12 FLC 17/7 FAC 7 Others 4
Aston Villa (£2,100,000 on 26/7/93) PL 64/4 FLC 10/1 FAC 5 Others 8/1

TRACEY Simon Peter
Born: Woolwich, 9 December 1967
Height: 6'0" Weight: 13.0

Goalkeeper. Started last season as first choice at Sheffield United, until losing his place to Alan Kelly through injury. Following Kelly's signing of a new contract, at Sheffield United, his first team opportunities there were limited, and he spent a period on loan at Manchester City, playing three PL games, to assist them over an injury crisis. Later on, he had another spell on loan, this time at Norwich, with a view to a permanent transfer, but when that came to nothing, Simon ended the season as number two to Kelly back at the Lane.

Wimbledon (From apprentice on 3/2/86) FL 1 Others 1
Sheffield U (£7,500 on 19/10/88) F/PL 141+2 FLC 7 FAC 10 Others 7
Manchester C (Loaned on 27/10/94) PL 3
Norwich C (Loaned on 31/12/94) PL 1 FAC 2

TREBBLE Neil David
Born: Hitchin, 16 February 1969
Height: 6'3" Weight: 12.10

Big, strong Scarborough striker, with good heading ability, Neil joined the club on loan from Preston in the latter part of last season. Influential in helping "Boro" climb away from the bottom of the Third Division, before moving to them on a more permanent basis.

Scunthorpe U (Free from Stevenage Borough on 8/7/93) FL 8+6/2 FLC 0+1 FAC 1 Others 1+1
Preston NE (Free on 18/7/94) FL 8+11/4 FLC 1 FAC 2+1 Others 2/1
Scarborough (Signed on 20/2/95) FL 15/3

TREVITT Simon
Born: Dewsbury, 20 December 1967
Height: 5'11" Weight: 11.10

As a home-grown product who has made over 200 FL appearances for Huddersfield, Simon puts in many quality crosses from his position as an overlapping right-back. Unfortunate with injury problems last season, his appearances were somewhat restricted.

Huddersfield T (From apprentice on 16/6/86) FL 212+13/3 FLC 21/1 FAC 13 Others 19+1

TRINDER Jason Lee
Born: Leicester, 3 March 1970
Height: 5'11" Weight: 14.2

Originally with Grimsby, Jason came to Mansfield last November from non-league circles. Signed as goalkeeping cover for Darren Ward, in seven matches used, including three from the bench, he never let the side down.

Grimsby T (Signed on 23/12/92)
Mansfield T (Free from Oadby T on 18/11/94) FL 4+3

TROLLOPE Paul Jonathan
Born: Swindon, 3 June 1972
Height: 6'0" Weight: 12.2

Son of the former Swindon Town star, John, the holder of the club's appearance record, Paul is a combative central midfielder who arrived at Derby on loan last December from Torquay. Having settled in immediately, the deal was made permanent and he has proved to be a useful goalscorer and an important link between defence and attack, preferring to play the ball along the ground, than kick-and-rush tactics.

Swindon T (From trainee on 23/12/89)
Torquay U (Free on 26/3/92) FL 103+3/16 FLC 9+1/1 FAC 7 Others 8+1
Derby Co (£100,000 on 16/12/94) FL 23+1/4

TROTT Dean
Born: Barnsley, 13 May 1967
Height: 6'2" Weight: 14.0

Stocky and well built, good in the air and able to hold the ball up well, he is a target man rather than an out-and-out striker. Unfortunate to miss a lot of last season through injury, he was released by Northampton during the summer, having joined the club from Boston in June 1994.

Northampton T (Free from Boston U on 10/6/94) FL 20+2/4 FLC 2 FAC 1 Others 1

TROTT Robin Francis
Born: Orpington, 17 August 1974
Height: 6'1" Weight: 11.4

Gillingham centre-half or left-back, who deputised for injuries and suspensions at the club last season, he never let the side down before being freed during the summer.

Gillingham (From trainee on 19/5/93) FL 8+2 Others 1+1

TUCK Stuart Gary
Born: Brighton, 1 October 1974
Height: 5'11" Weight: 11.2

A versatile left-footed youngster who was used by Brighton either at left-back or as a central defender, he proved to be a whole-hearted player. Yet to have an extended run in the side.

Brighton & Hove A (From trainee on 9/7/93) FL 23+11 FLC 3 FAC 1 Others 3+1

TUCKER Adrian John
Born: Merthyr Tydfil, 26 September 1976
Height: 5'10" Weight: 11.0
International Honours: W: Yth

A promising second year Torquay YTS goalkeeper, Adrian was called off the bench following Ashley Bayes' sending off after 43 minutes of last December's FA Cup replay against Enfield. The non-league

side's winner came 11 minutes later, with no blame being attached to the youngster.
Torquay U (Trainee) FAC 0+1

TURNBULL Lee Mark
Born: Stockton, 27 September 1967
Height: 6'0" Weight: 13.0

A strong target man, he scored two goals for Wycombe as a sub early last season, but only really found his scoring form when on loan at Scunthorpe towards the end of the campaign.
Middlesbrough (From trainee on 7/9/85) FL 8+8/4 FLC 0+1 Others 1+1/1
Aston Villa (Signed on 24/8/87)
Doncaster Rov (£17,500 on 3/11/87) FL 108+15/21 FLC 3+1/2 FAC 5+1 Others 9+1/2
Chesterfield (£35,000 on 14/2/91) FL 80+7/26 FLC 2+3/1 FAC 3/1 Others 5
Doncaster Rov (Signed on 8/10/93) FL 10+1/1 FAC 2 Others 1
Wycombe W (£20,000 on 21/1/94) FL 8+3/1 FLC 0+1/1 FAC 1 Others 1
Scunthorpe U (Loaned on 6/3/95) FL 10/3

TURNER Andrew (Andy) Peter
Born: Woolwich, 28 March 1975
Height: 5'9" Weight: 11.0
International Honours: Ei: U21-4. E: Yth; Sch

Very quick and skilful Tottenham left-winger who has a great left-foot and is capable of producing excellent crosses, Andy was loaned out to Wycombe and Doncaster last season.
Tottenham H (From trainee on 8/4/92) PL 8+12/3 FLC 0+2/1 FAC 0+1
Wycombe W (Loaned on 26/8/94) FL 3+1
Doncaster Rov (Loaned on 10/10/94) FL 4/1 Others 1/1

TURNER Christopher (Chris) Robert
Born: Sheffield, 15 September 1958
Height: 5'10" Weight: 11.11
Club Honours: FLC '91
International Honours: E: Yth

One of the most experienced 'keepers in the Endsleigh League, Chris concentrated on his role as joint-manager at Orient with John Sitton and was content to play second fiddle to the reliable Paul Heald. He did not make his first appearance until last March when he was beaten twice in the away defeat at Hull. Freed at the end of the season after losing his job as joint-manager.
Sheffield Wed (From apprentice on 1/8/76) FL 91 FLC 11 FAC 13
Lincoln C (Loaned on 6/10/78) FL 5
Sunderland (£80,000 on 4/7/79) FL 195 FLC 21 FAC 7
Manchester U (£275,000 on 15/8/85) FL 64 FLC 7 FAC 8 Others 2
Sheffield Wed (£175,000 on 12/9/88) FL 75 FLC 6 FAC 8 Others 1
Leeds U (Loaned on 15/11/89) FL 2
Leyton Orient (£75,000 on 25/10/91) FL 58 FLC 4 FAC 6 Others 4

TURNER Graham Mark
Born: Bebbington, 4 October 1972
Height: 6'0" Weight: 11.1

The son of Graham, Mark is a midfielder who relies on skill and neat passing technique. At Northampton since coming from "Wolves" in the 1994 close season, he has had limited experience to date.

Wolverhampton W (Signed from Paget R on 2/7/91) FL 1
Northampton T (Free on 1/7/94) FL 2+2 Others 1

TURNER Philip (Phil)
Born: Sheffield, 12 February 1962
Height: 5'8" Weight: 11.0
Club Honours: AIC '95

Notts County club captain, and a player who has been to Wembley four times, Phil is an experienced midfielder, having made nearly 300 appearances since March 1989, despite being held back by injuries. Can play in either a defensive, or attacking role, whatever suits the club's needs at the time, being a good passer. A great clubman, he is also County's corner specialist.
Lincoln C (From apprentice on 5/2/80) FL 239+2/19 FLC 19 FAC 12/1 Others 5
Grimsby T (Signed on 22/8/86) FL 62/7 FLC 6 FAC 6 Others 3/1
Leicester C (£42,000 on 19/2/88) FL 18+6/2 FLC 1+1 FAC 1
Notts Co (£125,000 on 3/3/89) FL 211+14/15 FLC 14+3 FAC 13/3 Others 33+1/3

TURNER Robert (Robbie) Peter
Born: Ripon, 18 September 1966
Height: 6'3" Weight: 14.1

A no-nonsense, versatile Exeter player who, although able to operate as a central defender, is mainly used as a target man up-front where he is most effective at flicking balls onto oncoming players. Suffered badly from injuries last season, having had a back operation and not featuring in the side since November.
Huddersfield T (From apprentice on 19/9/84) FL 0+1 FLC 1
Cardiff C (Free on 19/7/85) FL 34+5/8 FLC 3/1 FAC 1 Others 1
Hartlepool U (Loaned on 2/10/86) FL 7/1
Bristol Rov (Free on 31/12/86) FL 19+7/2 FLC 2 Others 0+1
Wimbledon (£15,000 on 17/12/87) FL 2+8 FLC 1+1 FAC 0+1/1 Others 3+1/1
Bristol C (£45,000 on 27/1/89) FL 45+7/12 FAC 7/3 Others 2
Plymouth Arg (£150,000 on 23/7/90) FL 66/17 FLC 5/1 FAC 3 Others 3/1
Notts Co (£90,000 on 21/11/92) FL 7+1/1 FAC 1 Others 1
Shrewsbury T (Loaned on 25/3/93) FL 9
Exeter C (Free on 4/2/94) FL 32+1/4 FLC 1/1 FAC 1 Others 2/1

TUTILL Stephen (Steve) Alan
Born: York, 1 October 1969
Height: 6'0" Weight: 11.0
International Honours: E: Sch

Local lad who always gives 100 per-cent commitment to York, both on and off the field, Steve is a hard-tackling and commanding central defender. Captained the side in 1994-95 and was a virtual ever-present.
York C (From trainee on 27/1/88) FL 253+6/6 FLC 14 FAC 14 Others 16+3/1

TUTTLE David Philip
Born: Reading, 6 February 1972
Height: 6'1" Weight: 12.10
Club Honours: FAYC '90
International Honours: E: Yth

Sheffield United centre-back. Following his cruciate ligament injury towards the end of 1993-94, he was not expected to be back in contention for a first team place last season.

However, due to the loss of Brian Gayle, and his faster than expected recovery, David made a successful return against his home-town club. Appeared five more times before the season came to a close.
Tottenham H (From trainee on 8/2/90) F/PL 10+3 FLC 3+1 Others 1/1
Peterborough U (Loaned on 21/1/93) FL 7
Sheffield U (£350,000 on 1/8/93) P/FL 37 FLC 1 FAC 1

TWIDDY Christopher (Chris)
Born: Pontypridd, 19 January 1976
Height: 5'10" Weight: 11.2
International Honours: W: U21-4; Yth

An out-and-out winger who came into the Plymouth side through the absence of Paul Dalton, he proved a very talented young player, with good close control and pace, and performed well until getting injured. Also forced himself into the Welsh U21 team.
Plymouth Arg (From trainee on 29/6/94) FL 13+2/1 FLC 0+1 FAC 1 Others 2

TYLER Mark Richard
Born: Norwich, 2 April 1977
Height: 6'0" Weight: 12.9
International Honours: E: Yth

Fine young Peterborough goalkeeper who should go on to better things, he started last season as a trainee, before turning pro in December. Although making only limited appearances to date, Mark has already shown very good handling and shot-stopping skills.
Peterborough U (From trainee on 7/12/94) FL 4+1 Others 2

ULLATHORNE Robert
Born: Wakefield, 11 October 1971
Height: 5'8" Weight: 10.7
International Honours: E: Yth

A left-back who can play anywhere down the left side, Robert had an impressive early run of games for Norwich in 1994-95, as he looked to make the position his own. Unfortunately, a cracked rib saw him miss six matches, before enjoying another run in the side prior to being sent off in the FA Cup at Grimsby. Finished the campaign in the first team and his goal at West Ham saw him become one of City's 17 goalscorers of the season, a tally that had not been previously exceeded since 1908-09.
Norwich C (From trainee on 6/7/90) F/PL 60+5/7 FLC 5+1 FAC 6+1 Others 1

UNSWORTH David Gerald
Born: Chorley, 16 October 1973
Height: 6'2" Weight: 13.0
Club Honours: FAC '95
International Honours: E: 1; U21-5; Yth

Strong and athletic Everton central defender who uses his pace to scupper attacks and is very competitive in aerial battles. Technically an excellent all-round defender who is able to shadow and regularly rob forwards, he manages to recover situations that appear lost. Made a tremendous impression during 1994-95, taking his chance in the first team, then never looking back. After gaining rave reports in the media, David capped the season with both a FA

David Unsworth

Neal Simpson
(Empics Sports Photo Agency)

Cup winners' medal and an England cap during the summer.

Everton (From trainee on 25/6/92) F/PL 48+3/4 FLC 3+1 FAC 5

VALENTINE Peter
Born: Huddersfield, 16 April 1963
Height: 5'10" Weight: 12.0

Very experienced centre-half who was bought in from Carlisle to replace the departed Alan Reeves, he played a large part in Rochdale's recovery from a mid-season slump in form.

Huddersfield T (From apprentice on 16/4/81) FL 19/1 FLC 2 FAC 1
Bolton W (Free on 18/7/83) FL 66+2/1 FLC 4 FAC 4 Others 5
Bury (Free on 23/7/85) FL 314+5/16 FLC 28/3 FAC 17/1 Others 23+1
Carlisle U (£10,000 on 18/8/93) FL 27+2/2 FLC 3 Others 4/1
Rochdale (£15,000 on 18/11/94) FL 27/2

VAN BLERK Jason
Born: Sydney, Australia, 16 March 1968
Height: 6'1" Weight: 12.8
International Honours: Australia

Australian international who signed for Millwall early last season. As a left-footed full-back, with good all-round skills, he also fitted in well on the left-side of midfield when needed, where his attacking runs and well flighted crosses resulted in a number of "assists". Two broken ribs unfortunately put him out of action for a couple of months.

Millwall (£300,000 from Go Ahead on 8/9/94) FL 24+3/1 FLC 2 FAC 5

VAN DEN HAUWE Patrick (Pat) William Roger
Born: Dendermonde, Belgium, 16 December 1960
Height: 5'11" Weight: 12.0
Club Honours: CS '85, '91; Div 1 '85, '87; ECWC '85; FAC '91

International Honours: W: 13

Although a proven, solid and reliable left-sided defender, hamstring injuries and personal problems restricted his number of games at the heart of the Millwall defence last season and he was released from his contract in January.

Birmingham C (From apprentice on 2/8/78) FL 119+4/1 FLC 12 FAC 5
Everton (£100,000 on 24/9/84) FL 134+1/2 FLC 20 FAC 30/1 Others 14+1
Tottenham H (£575,000 on 25/8/89) F/PL 110+6 FLC 16 FAC 7 Others 7
Millwall (Free on 9/9/93) FL 27 FLC 5 FAC 1 Others 3

VAN DER LAAN Robertus (Robin) Petrus
Born: Schiedam, Holland, 5 September 1968
Height: 5'10" Weight: 12.0
Club Honours: AMC '93

Imposing Port Vale midfield player who had a superb second half for last season. Strong-tackling, with a good engine, his height in the air at set pieces is more than useful at both ends of the pitch. Appeared in every game until relegation was mathematically avoided, despite carrying an injury.

Port Vale (£80,000 from Wageningen on 21/2/91) FL 154+22/24 FLC 11+1/1 FAC 9+1/1 Others 11+1/1

VAN HEUSDEN Arjan
Born: Alphen, Holland, 11 December 1972
Height: 6'4" Weight: 12.0

Tall, commanding goalkeeper who had to wait virtually all of last season before being given his chance in the final two games. Had an excellent debut at Charlton, making some good saves to put pressure on the club's number one, Paul Musselwhite.

Port Vale (£4,500 from Noordwijk on 15/8/94) FL 2

VARADI Imre
Born: Paddington, 8 July 1959
Height: 5'8" Weight: 11.2
Club Honours: Div 2 '90

After topping Rotherham's scoring charts in 1993-94, Imre was unable to have the same impact the next time round and was mainly used as a substitute, before being freed last May.

Sheffield U (Free from Letchworth on 1/4/78) FL 6+4/4 FAC 2
Everton (£80,000 on 1/3/79) FL 22+4/6 FAC 6+1/1 Others 0+2
Newcastle U (£100,000 on 27/8/81) FL 81/39 FLC 4/1 FAC 5/2
Sheffield Wed (£150,000 on 26/8/83) FL 72+4/33 FLC 11/2 FAC 7/5
West Bromwich A (£285,000 on 19/7/85) FL 30+2/9 FLC 5/4 FAC 2 Others 2
Manchester C (£50,000 on 17/10/86) FL 56+9/26 FLC 4+2/2 FAC 6+1/1 Others 2+1/2
Sheffield Wed (£50,000 on 30/9/88) FL 14+8/3 FLC 1+1/1 FAC 2/2 Others 1
Leeds U (£50,000 on 8/2/90) F/PL 21+5/5 FLC 1 Others 1+1/1
Luton T (Loaned on 26/3/92) FL 5+1/1
Oxford U (Loaned on 21/1/93) FL 3+2
Rotherham U (Free on 5/3/93) FL 55+12/25 FLC 5/2 FAC 2+1 Others 2+2/1

VAUGHAN Anthony (Tony) John
Born: Manchester, 11 October 1975
Height: 6'1" Weight: 11.2

A defender who can play at full-back, or in

central defence, Tony made his debut for Ipswich at left-back at Chelsea and had started to stake a regular claim when he injured a knee badly at Manchester City last February, which ended his season. Recovering well, and currently ahead of schedule, he is a player around whom fans think a future Town side could be built.

Ipswich T (From trainee on 1/7/94) PL 10 FAC 1

VAUGHAN John
Born: Isleworth, 26 June 1964
Height: 5'10" Weight: 13.1
Club Honours: Div 3 '91

A 1994 close season signing, John took over as Preston's regular 'keeper in mid-term and proved to be a reliable player. His lack of inches has not proved to be a handicap and he pulled off some remarkable reflex saves, as well as handling safely.

West Ham U (From apprentice on 30/6/82)
Charlton Ath (Loaned on 11/3/85) FL 5
Bristol Rov (Loaned on 5/9/85) FL 6
Wrexham (Loaned on 23/10/85) FL 4
Bristol C (Loaned on 4/3/86) FL 2
Fulham (£12,500 on 21/8/86) FL 44 FLC 4 FAC 4 Others 3
Bristol C (Loaned on 21/1/88) FL 3
Cambridge U (Free on 6/6/88) FL 178 FLC 13 FAC 24 Others 16
Charlton Ath (Free on 5/8/93) FL 5+1 FAC 2 Others 1+1
Preston NE (Free on 26/7/94) FL 25+1 Others 3

VEART Thomas **Carl**
Born: Whyalla, Australia, 21 May 1970
Height: 5'11" Weight: 12.8
International Honours: Australia

A striker signed by Sheffield United, following their Australian tour in the 1994 close season, he had previously had a trial at Everton. Not expected to immediately challenge for a first team place, an impressive string of displays saw him become a regular first team member with 11 goals to his credit. He also had a spell in midfield during a period of injuries at the club. A full Australian International, Carl played in their World Cup campaign, and in all their other matches last season.

Sheffield U (£250,000 from Adelaide C on 22/7/94) FL 30+9/11 FLC 1 FAC 1 Others 2

VENISON Barry
Born: Consett, 16 August 1964
Height: 5'10" Weight: 11.12
Club Honours: CS '86, '88, '89, '90; ESC '86; Div 1 '88, '90, '93; FAC '89
International Honours: E :2; U21-10; Yth

Is a most valued member of the Newcastle side, capable of performing at a consistently high level, either at right-back, centre-half, or in midfield. Whereby his good form was rewarded last season when he won his first international caps for England against USA and Uruguay, he had the misfortune to suffer a bad hamstring injury in the home match against Liverpool, which caused him to miss 12 matches. Apart from international call-ups, the main highlight of the campaign was his first goal for the club in the 3-1 home win against Aston Villa, when he hit an unstoppable 20 yard right-foot shot, which flew into the roof of the net, giving Bosnich no chance. Missed the last five matches of the campaign with a back injury.

Sunderland (From apprentice on 20/1/82) FL 169+4/2 FLC 21 FAC 7+1 Others 3/1
Liverpool (£200,000 on 31/7/86) FL 103+7/1 FLC 14+3 FAC 16+5 Others 6+4/2
Newcastle U (£250,000 on 31/7/92) F/PL 108+1/1 FLC 9 FAC 11 Others 4

VENUS Mark
Born: Hartlepool, 6 April 1967
Height: 6'0" Weight: 11.8
Club Honours: Div 3 '89

A versatile player, he can play at left-back, in central defence or in midfield, and always runs his heart out for Wolverhampton. He lashed in an equaliser at Sunderland, then scored three in four games last October,

enjoying a 30 match run until coming on as sub at Hillsborough. By April he had worn nine different shirt numbers in 1994-95, numbers one and nine being the exceptions!

Hartlepool U (From juniors on 22/3/85) FL 4 Others 0+1
Leicester C (Free on 6/9/85) FL 58+3/1 FLC 3 FAC 2 Others 2+1
Wolverhampton W (£40,000 on 23/3/88) FL 216+9/7 FLC 12+1 FAC 12+1 Others 17/2

VERVEER Etienne
Born: Surinam, 22 September 1967
Height: 5'11" Weight: 11.12

Nicknamed "ET", Millwall's flying Dutchman was unable to win his place back in the side last season, even though back to full

Mark Venus

Paul Marriott
(Empics Sports Photo Agency)

fitness after being out for the whole of 1992-93, and was loaned out to Bradford. A midfielder, with strength and speed going forward, he played just nine games for the "Bantams" before being injured and returning to London. Back at the Den, he was released immediately prior to the campaign ending.

Millwall (£100,000 from Chur on 13/12/91) FL 46+10/7 FLC 3/1 FAC 3/1 Others 2/1
Bradford C (Loaned on 6/2/95) FL 9/1

VICK Lee
Born: Cardiff, 8 January 1978
Height: 5'9" Weight: 10.3

Still a trainee, Lee made an encouraging debut in Cardiff's home defeat against York last March, but took some heavy knocks in his next game and was rested.

Cardiff C (Trainee) FL 2

VICKERS Stephen (Steve)
Born: Bishop Auckland, 13 October 1967
Height: 6'1" Weight: 12.9
Club Honours: AMC '90; Div 1 '95

A local boy who slipped through the net of local scouts when signing for Tranmere, he returned "home" after being signed by Lennie Lawrence to assist Middlesbrough for a thrust return to the big-time in 1993-94. Recognised as another important reason for "Boro's" resurgence to the Premiership as First Division Champions, Steve is a central defender, who displays the most consummate of skills in his position on every outing.

Tranmere Rov (Signed from Spennymoor U on 11/9/85) FL 310+1/11 FLC 20+1/5 FAC 19/3 Others 36/1
Middlesbrough (£700,000 on 3/12/93) FL 69+1/6 FLC 3 FAC 4 Others 2

VINCENT Jamie Roy
Born: London, 18 June 1975
Height: 5'10" Weight: 11.8

A talented Crystal Palace left-back, Jamie had a spell on loan at Bournemouth last October where he made his FL debut and teamed up with Tony Scully, another young "Eagle" at the club on a temporary basis. A regular in the Palace reserve side, and cover for Dean Gordon, his first appearance for the club should not be too long in coming.

Crystal Palace (From trainee on 13/7/93)
Bournemouth (Loaned on 18/11/94) FL 8

VINNICOMBE Christopher (Chris)
Born: Exeter, 20 October 1970
Height: 5'9" Weight: 10.4
Club Honours: SPD '91
International Honours: E: U21-12

Signed from Glasgow Rangers in the 1994 close season, Chris immediately looked the most accomplished left-back at Burnley for some time, as effective going forward as at the back. A broken jaw sustained in an incident at Reading kept him out of the side for four months, but he returned looking as solid as before and could be one of the classiest defenders in next season's Second Division.

Exeter C (From trainee on 1/7/89) FL 35+4/1 FLC 5/1 Others 2

Glasgow R (£150,000 on 3/11/89) SL 14+9/1 SLC 1+2 Others 1
Burnley (£200,000 on 30/6/94) FL 29/1 FLC 3

VIVEASH Adrian Lee
Born: Swindon, 30 September 1969
Height: 6'1" Weight: 11.9

Could not have had a worse start to last season, suffering a broken leg on a pre-season trip to Cyprus. Having recovered, and unable to secure a place in Swindon's senior side, Adrian went on loan to Reading, where he made six appearances for the "Royals", before being hastily recalled, following the Ian Culverhouse injury. Performed exceptionally well on the left-side of the back four in the two months that remained.

Swindon T (From trainee on 14/7/88) FL 51+3/3 FLC 6+1 FAC 0+1 Others 2
Reading (Loaned on 4/1/93) FL 5 Others 1/1
Reading (Loaned on 20/1/95) FL 6

VONK Michel Christian
Born: Alkmaar, Holland, 28 October 1968
Height: 6'2" Weight: 12.2

Started last season playing in the centre of the Manchester City defence alongside Keith Curle, but was eventually kept out of the side, firstly by injuries and then by the improved form of Alan Kernaghan. Not the most elegant of defenders, Michel can be used to good effect, however, as a man marker against many of today's leading strikers and will always be a danger from set pieces, especially at corners.

Manchester C (£500.000 from SVV Dordrecht on 11/3/92) F/PL 87+4/3 FLC 3+2/1 FAC 6+1/1

WADDLE Christopher (Chris) Roland
Born: Felling, 14 December 1960
Height: 6'0" Weight: 11.5
International Honours: E: 62; U21-1

Carried a long-term injury over into 1994-95 which kept him out the Sheffield Wednesday side until just before Christmas. Once again, however, Chris showed all the old skill and guile that has defenders backing off when he runs at them. A great favourite with the fans, and a player with charismatic appeal, memories of his famous England penalty miss must have come flooding back in the club's FA Cup penalty shoot-out at "Wolves", when he again failed from the spot. Time is not on his side anymore, but there are still few better sights on a football pitch than Chris in full flight.

Newcastle U (£1,000 from Tow Law on 28/7/80) FL 169+1/46 FLC 8/2 FAC 12/4
Tottenham H (£590,000 on 1/7/85) FL 137+1/33 FLC 21/4 FAC 14/5 Others 4 (£4,250,000 to Marseilles on 1/7/89)
Sheffield Wed (£1,000,000 on 1/7/92) PL 71+6/8 FLC 15 FAC 11+1/3 Others 3+1/1

WADDOCK Gary Patrick
Born: Kingsbury, 17 March 1962
Height: 5'10" Weight: 11.12
Club Honours: Div 2 '83
International Honours: Ei: 21; B-2; U23-1; U21-1

Arrived at Luton on loan from Bristol Rovers last September and stayed for the rest of the season. Very much a defensive

midfielder, who wins the ball with ferocious tackling and distributes quickly and accurately, his career was all but over as long ago as 1985 when a serious injury seemingly forced him out of the game for ever. That he ever came back, shows the kind of inspirational qualities he can bring to a game.

Queens Park R (From apprentice on 26/7/79) FL 191+12/8 FLC 14 FAC 14 Others 1 (Free to Charleroi in December 1987)
Millwall (£130,000 on 16/8/89) FL 51+7/2 FLC 5+1 FAC 5 Others 3/1
Queens Park R (Free on 20/12/91)
Swindon T (Loaned on 19/3/92) FL 5+1
Bristol Rov (£100,000 on 7/11/92) FL 71/1 FLC 2 FAC 2 Others 2
Luton T (Free on 9/9/94) FL 40/1 FAC 1

WADE Shaun Peter
Born: Stoke, 22 September 1969
Height: 5'10" Weight: 13.8

Central striker. Arrived at Stoke from Newcastle Town last October on a non-contract basis and became an instant hit with his aggressive play up-front. A bricklayer by trade, he was quickly given his chance in the first team by Lou Macari, but sadly, damaged his knee in a reserve match and needed cruciate ligament surgery. Hopefully, he will fully recover to pick up where he left off.

Stoke C (Free from Newcastle T on 28/10/94) FL 0+1

WALKER Alan
Born: Mossley, 17 December 1959
Height: 6'1" Weight: 12.2
Club Honours: FAT '83; Div 2 '88

Ended last season with more stitches than a football. Always going in where it hurts, it was a surprise to see the popular Barnet centre-back freed in March to join non-league, Sittingbourne.

Stockport Co (Signed on 23/8/78)
Lincoln C (£50,000 from Telford U on 14/10/83) FL 74+1/4 FLC 2 FAC 5/1 Others 4/2
Millwall (£32,500 on 30/7/85) FL 92/8 FLC 7/3 FAC 9/1 Others 6/1
Gillingham (£50,000 on 25/3/88) FL 150+1/7 FLC 8/2 FAC 5/3 Others 6/3
Plymouth Arg (Free on 3/9/92) FL 2/1
Mansfield T (Free 16/9/92) FL 22/1 FAC 1 Others 1
Barnet (Free on 9/8/93) FL 59/2 FLC 5/1 FAC 6 Others 3/1

WALKER Desmond (Des) Sinclair
Born: Hackney, 26 November 1965
Height: 5'11" Weight: 11.9
Club Honours: FLC '89, '90; FMC '89, '92
International Honours: E: 59; U21-7

A quiet and unassuming character, Des had another excellent season as the cover player for Sheffield Wednesday in 1994-95 and could consider himself unlucky not to have been involved with the England set-up. Fast, steady, and a great reader of situations as they develop, apart from one minor hiccup, he was invaluable to the "Owls'" cause and, as the club captain, remains a great influence on all those around him.

Nottingham F (From apprentice on 2/12/83) FL 259+5/1 FLC 40 FAC 27 Others 14 (£1,500,000 to Sampodoria on 1/8/92)
Sheffield Wed (£2,700,000 on 22/7/93) PL 80 FLC 10 FAC 7

Chris Waddle

Tony Marshall
(Empics Sports Photo Agency)

Des Walker   Paul Marriott
(Empics Sports Photo Agency)

WALKER Ian Michael
Born: Watford, 31 October 1971
Height: 6'1" Weight: 11.9
Club Honours: FAYC '90; CS '91
International Honours: E: U21-9; B-; Yth

Ian's season blossomed after the appointment of Gerry Francis as Tottenham's new manager last November. Early season problems often saw him as the last hope in what was a very disorganised defence, although the score lines seldom reflected his goalkeeping performances. Lost his place for two matches in October, but came back to achieve his first clean sheet against Chelsea, and later notched up no less than six consecutive clean sheets between mid-December and early January. On many occasions, "Spurs" were saved from conceding more goals by his agility and quick reflexes, capped with an ability to read the game well and organise the defence. It was these skills that earned him a call-up to the full England squad on their ill-fated visit to Dublin for the friendly against the Republic of Ireland.
Tottenham H (From trainee on 4/12/89) F/PL 87+1 FLC 6 FAC 8 Others 2
Oxford U (Loaned on 31/8/90) FL 2 FLC 1

Ian Walker   Tony Marshall
(Empics Sports Photo Agency)

WALKER James Barry
Born: Nottingham, 9 July 1973
Height: 5'11" Weight: 11.8
Brave and adventurous Walsall goalkeeper, known as "Whacker" because of his hefty kicking upfield, James made only rare appearances in 1994-95, due to the fine form of Trevor Wood. However, with Wood indisposed, he was back for the last vital match when the club clinched promotion to the Second Division at Bury.
Notts Co (From trainee on 9/7/91)
Walsall (Free on 4/8/93) FL 34+1 FAC 4 Others 1

WALKER Keith Cameron
Born: Edinburgh, 17 April 1966
Height: 6'0" Weight: 12.8
Keith has constantly battled to overcome injuries since arriving in South Wales and his start to last season was delayed owing to a third hernia operation. Originally a midfielder, he is a very popular player at Swansea, with his tackling at the heart of the defence, plus an ability to hit his front runners with long-range passes.
Stirling A (Signed from ICI in 1984) SL 82+9/17 SLC 5/3 SC 5/2
St Mirren (Signed during 1987 close season) SL 41+2/6 SLC 3 SC 1 Others 3
Swansea C (£80,000 on 23/11/89) FL 159+7/5 FLC 6 FAC 16/1 Others 18

WALKER Raymond (Ray)
Born: North Shields, 28 September 1963
Height: 5'10" Weight: 12.0
Club Honours: FAYC '80
International Honours: E: Yth
Skilful Port Vale midfield player who returned in 1994-95, having being injured for over 12 months, only to again have his appearances curtailed. A spell on loan at Cambridge helped him to get fully fit but, after just eight games in a Vale shirt, he was on the sidelines again. Came back for a further ten matches before suffering a leg injury at Burnley. Inspires players around him when he plays and Vale tended to get better results the more he is in the side.
Aston Villa (From apprentice on 26/9/81) FL 15+8 FLC 2+1 FAC 2
Port Vale (Loaned on 7/9/84) FL 15/1
Port Vale (£12,000 on 5/8/86) FL 292+7/33 FLC 16+1/1 FAC 22/3 Others 19/3
Cambridge U (Loaned on 23/9/94) FL 5 Others 2

WALKER Richard Neil
Born: Derby, 9 November 1971
Height: 6'0" Weight: 12.0
Notts County central defender who has good aerial ability in both penalty areas. Played in the final game of last season, having been out with a back injury since being substituted at Southend at the beginning of November, and following a spell on loan with Mansfield. A good tackler, with fair distribution, Richard can also play at left-back and would prove a capable deputy for Graeme Hogg and Shaun Murphy, if required.
Notts Co (From trainee on 3/7/90) FL 39+1/4 FLC 6 Others 5+1
Mansfield T (Loaned on 23/3/95) FL 4

WALLACE David (Danny) Lloyd
Born: Greenwich, 21 January 1964
Height: 5'4" Weight: 10.4

Club Honours: CS '90; ECWC '91
International Honours: E: 1; U21-14 (UEFAC '84); Yth
A winger with two good feet, and extremely quick off the mark, Danny runs straight at defenders in order to commit them. Unable to hold down a regular place at Birmingham, he signed for Wycombe last March and in his solitary appearance as a sub showed traces of his explosive pace, before being released at the end of the season.
Southampton (From apprentice on 25/1/82) FL 238+15/64 FLC 36/6 FAC 21+1/4 Others 10+2/5
Manchester U (£1,200.000 on 18/9/89) F/PL 36+11/6 FLC 4+3/2 FAC 7+2/2 Others 6+2
Millwall (Loaned on 25/3/93) FL 3
Birmingham C (£250,000 on 15/10/93) FL 12+4/2 FLC 1+1 Others 0+1
Wycombe W (Free on 22/3/95) FL 0+1

WALLACE Michael
Born: Farnworth, 5 October 1970
Height: 5'8" Weight: 11.10
International Honours: E: Yth
Versatile player who initially came to Stockport as a winger, he has since been transformed into a useful left-sided midfielder or left-back, making 26 starts last season. Freed during the summer.
Manchester C (From trainee on 1/7/89)
Stockport Co (Free on 30/9/92) FL 65+5/5 FLC 2+2 FAC 4+1/1 Others 10+3/1

WALLACE Raymond (Ray) George
Born: Greenwich, 2 October 1969
Height: 5'6" Weight: 10.2
International Honours: E: U21-4
Perhaps the least known of the Wallace brothers, Ray joined Stoke in the 1994 close season from Leeds. A man who can play either at full-back or in midfield, no-one would ever question his commitment, enthusiasm and workrate. At the turn of the year he was loaned out to Hull, who may well have made the move permanent if their financial circumstances had allowed.
Southampton (From trainee on 21/4/88) FL 33+2 FLC 8 FAC 2 Others 2
Leeds U (£100,000 on 8/7/91) F/PL 5+2
Swansea C (Loaned on 20/3/92) FL 2
Reading (Loaned on 11/3/94) FL 3
Stoke C (Free on 11/8/94) FL 16+4/1 FLC 1 FAC 1 Others 6
Hull C (Loaned on 16/12/94) FL 7

WALLACE Rodney (Rod) Seymour
Born: Greenwich, 2 October 1969
Height: 5'7" Weight: 10.1
Club Honours: Div 1 '92; CS '92
International Honours: E: B-2; U21-11
Having finished the previous season as Leeds' top-scorer, Rod began 1994-95 in a much deeper and wider position. On his day, one of the most exciting strikers in the Premier, he appeared to struggle for form after the switch but, following a period out of the side, plus the arrival of Tony Yeboah, things got better. His current spell and partnership with Yeboah looks to be working well and immediately prior to the transfer deadline, manager, Howard Wilkinson, turned down a £1,500,000 Southampton bid for his services.

Rod Wallace

Neal Simpson
(Empics Sports Photo Agency)

Southampton (From trainee on 19/4/88) FL 111+17/45 FLC 18+1/6 FAC 10/3 Others 3+1/2
Leeds U (£1,600,000 on 7/6/91) F/PL 129+6/39 FLC 8/3 FAC 5+4 Others 1+3/1

WALLING Dean Anthony
Born: Leeds, 17 April 1969
Height: 6'0" Weight: 10.8
Club Honours: Div 3 '95

A former striker turned central defender, who not only received the Carlisle "Player of the Year" award, after winning a Third Division Championship medal, but became the third member of the side to be chosen for the PFA Selection last season. A fine header of the ball, and a whole hearted performer who clearly benefited from partnering Derek Mountfield at the heart of the defence, he was very popular with the supporters for both his defensive attributes and his aerial ability at set piece moves which brought a number of goals throughout the campaign.

Rochdale (Free from Leeds U juniors on 30/7/87) FL 43+22/8 FLC 3 FAC 0+1 Others 1+1 (Free to Guiseley during 1990 close season)
Carlisle U (Free on 1/7/91) FL 135+6/17 FLC 11/1 FAC 9+1/1 Others 21/3

WALSH Alan
Born: Hartlepool, 9 December 1956
Height: 6'0" Weight: 12.8
Club Honours: AMC '86

Another vastly experienced Hartlepool player, he was signed in September by caretaker manager, Billy Horner, after previously being player-coach with Taunton Town. Once a prolific goalscorer, but now aged 37 and a full-back, he made a great debut for his hometown club, in scoring from a penalty. Later out of favour with manager, David McCreery, he was released in February to join Bath City.
Middlesbrough (Signed from Horden Colliery on 24/12/76) FL 0+3
Darlington (Signed on 20/10/78) FL 245+6/90 FLC 12/7 FAC 14+1/6

Bristol C (£18,000 on 16/8/84) FL 215+3/77 FLC 21/8 FAC 18/3 Others 10/11 (Released in August 1989)
Walsall (Free from Besiktas on 3/10/91) FL 4 Others 1
Huddersfield T (Free on 18/12/91) FL 0+4 FAC 0+1
Shrewsbury T (Free on 30/1/92) FL 2
Cardiff C (Free on 18/3/92) FL 1 (Released during 1992 close season)
Hartlepool U (Free from Taunton T on 16/9/94) FL 4/1 FLC 2 FAC 1 Others 2

WALSH Colin David
Born: Hamilton, 22 July 1962
Height: 5'9" Weight: 11.0
International Honours: S; U21-5; Yth

Charlton's longest serving player, Colin is a gifted midfielder with a sweet left-foot. Still a very effective player, who is able to hold up the ball and switch play with an accurate long pass, his shooting power is phenomenal and he is very dangerous at set-pieces. Scored an excellent goal against "Wolves" late last season.
Nottingham F (From apprentice on 16/8/79) FL 115+24/32 FLC 8+5 FAC 9+2/2 Others 12/3
Charlton Ath (£125,000 on 11/9/86) FL 218+18/21 FLC 16/4 FAC 11+2 Others 17/5
Peterborough U (Loaned on 2/2/89) FL 5/1
Middlesbrough (Loaned on 17/1/91) FL 10+3/1 FAC 1

WALSH Gary
Born: Wigan, 21 March 1968
Height: 6'3" Weight: 14.0
Club Honours: ECWC '91; ESC '91; FAC '94
International Honours: E; U21-2

Tall, commanding Manchester United goalkeeper with good, safe hands and excellent distribution skills. Once again, Gary proved to be an admirable deputy for Peter Schmeichel in 1994-95, showing great maturity with every successive first team outing. And although he had to weather the turmoil surrounding United's early European Cup exit, his confidence remained largely unaffected.
Manchester U (From juniors on 25/4/85) F/PL 49+1 FLC 7 Others 6
Airdrie (Loaned on 11/8/88) SL 3 SLC 1
Oldham Ath (Loaned on 19/11/93) PL 6

WALSH Michael Shane
Born: Rotherham, 5 August 1977
Height: 6'0" Weight: 12.4

A young Scunthorpe left-back who showed so much promise as a second year YTS that he was drafted into the first team, making three appearances at the end of last season. Still a trainee.
Scunthorpe U (Trainee) FL 3

WALSH Paul Anthony
Born: Plumstead, 1 October 1962
Height: 5'8" Weight: 10.4
Club Honours: Div 1 '86; FAC '91; CS '91
International Honours: E; 5; U21-7; Yth

Made a tremendous start to 1994-95, thriving on knockdowns and crosses from either wing to power in 11 goals for Manchester City before the end of November. Throughout an up-and-down season, Paul made a terrific contribution to City, not only with his goals, but also with his ability to create openings for others, his workrate and generally inspirational play.

Paul Walsh

Paul Marriott
(Empics Sports Photo Agency)

A natural left-footed central defender, although operating as striker during last season, Leicester's Wembley hero suffered another serious injury setback, when twisting his knee after only two games. A brief comeback in November only confirmed the extent of the ligament damage and ruled him out of first team action for the rest of the campaign.

Wigan Ath (From juniors on 11/9/82) FL 123+3/4 FLC 7 FAC 6 Others 10+2
Leicester C (£100,000 on 24/6/86) F/PL 248+2/41 FLC 21/3 FAC 7 Others 19/4

WALTERS Mark Everton
Born: Birmingham, 2 June 1964
Height: 5'9" Weight: 11.5
Club Honours: FAYC '80; ESC '82; SPD '89, '90, '91; SLC '89, '91; FAC '92
International Honours: E: 1; B-1; U21-9; Yth; Sch

Skilful, speedy left-winger, with good balance, Mark commits defenders by running at them and can go both ways. Currently a Liverpool squad player, he only made the occasional appearance in 1994-95. However, as an experienced wide player, he is a good man to have up your sleeve in an emergency.

Aston Villa (From apprentice on 18/5/82) FL 168+13/39 FLC 20+1/6 FAC 11+1/1 Others 7+3/2
Glasgow R (£500,000 on 31/12/87) SL 101+5/32 SLC 13/11 SC 14/6 Others 10/2
Liverpool (£1,250,000 on 13/8/91) F/PL 58+36/14 FLC 10+2/4 FAC 6+3 Others 8+1/1
Stoke C (Loaned on 24/3/94) FL 9/2
Wolverhampton W (Loaned on 9/9/94) FL 11/3

WALTERS Steven (Steve) Paul
Born: Plymouth, 9 January 1972
Height: 5'10" Weight: 11.8
International Honours: E: Yth; Sch

Still the youngest player to appear for Crewe, Steve, a good tackler who reads the game well, made most of his appearances on the right-hand side of midfield. Not a regular in 1994-95 and, following just nine starts, he joined Northwich Victoria in December.

Crewe Alex (From trainee on 2/3/89) FL 135+11/10 FLC 13+2 FAC 11+1/2 Others 15

WALTON David Lee
Born: Bedlington, 10 April 1973
Height: 6'2" Weight: 13.4
Club Honours: Div 3 '94

Central defender who is a strong, determined mainstay of the Shrewsbury defence, he seemed to thrive on the more difficult opponent and games in 1994-95. A very hard worker, who hates to lose, he gets forward well for set pieces and occasionally finds himself supporting the attack. Also scored some important goals.

Sheffield U (Free from Ashington on 15/5/91)
Shrewsbury T (Signed on 5/11/93) FL 63/8 FLC 2 FAC 3/1 Others 1

WANLESS Paul Steven
Born: Banbury, 14 December 1973
Height: 6'1" Weight: 13.4

Paul is a skilful player who will play anywhere with the same enthusiasm and never gives the opposition time on the ball.

Despite his small stature and his age, his tight ball control and speed continue to make him a difficult man to mark and it would be a surprise if he was not in the thick of it again in 1995-96. Incidentally, he was the PFA "Young Player of the Year" in 1984.

Charlton Ath (From apprentice on 2/10/79) FL 85+2/24 FLC 9/6 FAC 4/1
Luton T (£400,000 on 26/7/82) FL 80/24 FLC 5/1 FAC 4/3
Liverpool (£700,000 on 21/5/84) FL 63+14/25 FLC 10+2/4 FAC 6+2/3 Others 13+2/5
Tottenham H (£500,000 on 16/2/88) FL 84+44/19 FLC 9+6/2 FAC 4+4 Others 1+3
Queens Park R (Loaned on 16/9/91) FL 2
Portsmouth (£400,000 on 3/6/92) FL 67+6/14 FLC 7+1/4 FAC 3 Others 6+1/3
Manchester C (£750,000 on 10/3/94) PL 50/16 FLC 6/2 FAC 3/1

WALSH Steven (Steve)
Born: Preston, 3 November 1964
Height: 6'2" Weight: 11.10
Club Honours: AMC '85

In 1994-95, he performed for Oxford in defence, midfield and up-front, making just four starts, before being released at the end of the season.

Oxford U (From trainee on 3/12/91) FL 12+20 FLC 0+3/1 Others 2+2

WARBURTON Raymond (Ray)
Born: Rotherham, 7 October 1967
Height: 6'0" Weight: 11.5
Central defender and club captain, who was signed from York during the 1994 close season, he is good in the air, tackles well on the ground and scored some crucial goals for Northampton last season. Incidentally, he is the most expensive player the club have bought during the past five years.

Rotherham U (From apprentice on 5/10/85) FL 3+1 FAC 2 Others 2
York C (Free on 8/8/89) FL 86+4/9 FLC 8/1 FAC 6/1 Others 7
Northampton T (£35,000 on 4/2/94) FL 56/4 FLC 2 FAC 1 Others 3/1

Ashley Ward   Neal Simpson
(Empics Sports Photo Agency)

WARD Ashley Stuart
Born: Manchester, 24 November 1970
Height: 6'1" Weight: 12.4
Striker. Prior to signing for Norwich last December, Ashley, who netted ten goals in his last six games for Crewe, had survived two broken legs and a bad back injury to finally come good. Scored a double against Chelsea, followed by four more in his next nine games and showed excellent back-to-the-goal control. Looks an excellent buy for City.

Manchester C (From trainee on 5/8/89) FL 0+1 FAC 0+2
Wrexham (Loaned on 10/1/91) FL 4/2 Others 1
Leicester C (£80,000 on 30/7/91) FL 2+8 FLC 2+1 FAC 0+1 Others 0+1
Blackpool (Loaned on 21/11/92) FL 2/1
Crewe Alex (£80,000 on 1/12/92) FL 58+3/25 FLC 4/2 FAC 2/4 Others 7/5
Norwich C (£500,000 on 8/12/94) PL 25/8

WARD Darren
Born: Worksop, 11 May 1974
Height: 5'11" Weight: 12.9

Outstanding Mansfield goalkeeper who had a fine season in 1994-95 and was included in the Wales U21 squad. Injured during the match at Scunthorpe, he did not appear for the second half and, although starting the next seven matches, did not complete two of them. Was then rested for three games until the problem had cleared. Made several outstanding saves during a campaign that led the club to the play-offs and, although conceding numerous goals, it was mainly due to the team's attacking policy.

Mansfield T (From trainee on 27/7/92) FL 81 FLC 5 FAC 5 Others 6

WARD Gavin John
Born: Sutton Coldfield, 30 June 1970
Height: 6'4" Weight: 12.12
Club Honours: Div 3 '93; WC '93
Goalkeeper. Performed well for Leicester when called upon, but found it impossible to displace the in-form Kevin Poole between the sticks. Enjoyed a rare substitute appearance in the FA Cup defeat against "Wolves", where he turned in an outstanding second-half display.

Shrewsbury T (Free from Aston Villa juniors on 26/9/88)
West Bromwich A (Free on 18/9/89)
Cardiff C (Free on 5/10/89) FL 58+1 FAC 1 Others 7
Leicester C (£175,000 on 16/7/93) F/PL 38 FLC 3 FAC 0+1 Others 4

WARD Mark William
Born: Huyton, 10 October 1962
Height: 5'5" Weight: 10.0
Club Honours: Div 2 '95; AMC '95
International Honours: E: SP-1
Joining Birmingham as player-coach last August, having been on loan from Everton towards the end of 1993-94, Mark proved extremely influential in "Blues'" run of success, as a tigerish and tenacious, sweet passing midfielder. After winning Second Division and Auto Windscreen medals, he was named by his fellow professionals at the PFA awards night as the division's leading player in his position. Takes the club's penalties and is also deadly at free-kicks.

Everton (From apprentice on 5/9/80)
Oldham Ath (£10,000 from Northwich Victoria on 19/7/83) FL 84/12 FLC 5 FAC 3
West Ham U (£250,000 on 15/8/85) FL 163+2/12 FLC 20+1/2 FAC 17 Others 6
Manchester C (£1,000,000 on 29/12/89) FL 55/14 FLC 3 FAC 6 Others 3/2
Everton (£1,100,000 on 12/8/91) F/PL 82+1/6 FLC 6/1 FAC 4 Others 1
Birmingham C (£500,000 on 24/3/94) FL 50/4 FLC 3 FAC 4 Others 7/1

WARD Mitchum (Mitch) David
Born: Sheffield, 19 June 1971
Height: 5'8" Weight: 10.7
Local-born, right-sided midfield player, or full-back, who started last season for Sheffield United in explosive style, with two goals in the opening day win over Watford. Sustained a broken nose in the Anglo-Italian Cup and, having won back his first team place towards the end of the campaign, was seriously injured in the defeat at Notts County, suffering a punctured lung and a broken rib.

Sheffield U (From trainee on 1/7/89) F/PL 59+13/5 FLC 3+3/1 FAC 4+2/2 Others 2+1/1
Crewe Alex (Loaned on 1/11/90) FL 4/1 FAC 1/1 Others 2

WARD Peter
Born: Durham, 15 October 1964
Height: 5'10" Weight: 11.7
Skilful and hard-tackling Stockport midfielder, with a "wicked" left-foot from set-pieces, his 1994-95 season was troubled by injury. Formerly the club captain.

Huddersfield T (Signed from Chester le Street on 7/1/87) FL 24+13/2 FLC 1+1 FAC 2 Others 1
Rochdale (Free on 20/7/89) FL 83+1/10 FLC 5 FAC 7/1 Others 5
Stockport Co (Signed on 6/6/91) FL 140+2/10 FLC 8/1 FAC 7 Others 26/6

WARE Paul David
Born: Congleton, 7 November 1970
Height: 5'9" Weight: 11.5
Club Honours: Div 2 '93
Hard-working Stockport midfielder who signed from Stoke early in 1994-95. In failing to secure a regular place, he became a more than useful squad member.

Stoke C (From trainee on 15/11/88) FL 92+23/10 FLC 7+1 FAC 4+1 Others 12+2/4
Stockport Co (Signed on 8/9/94) FL 16+3/1 FLC 1+1 FAC 1 Others 1

WARHURST Paul
Born: Stockport, 26 September 1969
Height: 6'1" Weight: 12.10
Club Honours: PL '95
International Honours: E: U21-8
Son of Roy, the former star of the '40s and '50s, Paul, in recovering from a broken leg, took some time to regain his fitness in 1994-95, but eventually became a Blackburn regular, although he never had a regular role. After looking the obvious replacement for the injured David Batty, his versatility led him to being switched to right-back, to the centre of the defence, and even wide on the left. At his best when breaking up attacks with such nonchalance that he gave himself the time to hit the ball into crucial areas, he scored a wonderful goal against Manchester United in October with a finely judged chip over the 'keeper. However, his hopes of being involved in the Championship run-in, although he ultimately gained a winners' medal, were cruelly terminated when he broke his other leg on the training ground.

Manchester C (From trainee on 1/7/88)
Oldham Ath (£10,000 on 27/10/88) FL 60+7/2 FLC 8 FAC 5+4 Others 2
Sheffield Wed (£750,000 on 17/7/91) F/PL 60+6/6 FLC 9/4 FAC 7+1/5 Others 5/3
Blackburn Rov (£2,700,000 on 17/8/93) PL 24+12/2 FLC 5 FAC 2 Others 0+1

WARK John
Born: Glasgow, 4 August 1957
Height: 5'10" Weight: 12.10
Club Honours: FAYC '75; FAC '78; UEFAC '81; SC '86; Div 2 '92
International Honours: S: 29; U21-8
The PFA "Player of the Year" as long ago as 1981, the evergreen Scot is now in his third spell at Ipswich, and back where he started - central defence. Predominantly right-footed,

age is no longer on his side, but he more than makes up for that in experience and excellent positional play. A consistent performer again last season, he prevented more heavier defeats on occasions. Does not score as many goals these days, but is still the club's regular penalty taker, netting three times from the spot. John combined his playing duties in 1994-95 with coaching the first team, firstly with Paul Goddard, under the eye of John Lyall, and latterly with George Burley and Dale Roberts.

Ipswich T (From apprentice on 1/8/74) FL 295+1/94 FLC 24+1/12 FAC 36+1/12 Others 25/18
Liverpool (£450,000 on 10/3/84) FL 64+6/28 FLC 6+4/3 FAC 11+2/6 Others 13+2/5
Ipswich T (£100,000 on 4/1/88) FL 87+2/23 FLC 4 FAC 3 Others 9/2
Middlesbrough (£50,000 on 23/8/90) FL 31+1/2 FLC 5 FAC 2 Others 1
Ipswich T (Free on 21/9/91) F/PL 136+2/16 FLC 12+1 FAC 14/2 Others 3

WARNER Robert (Robbie) Mark
Born: Stratford on Avon, 20 April 1977
Height: 5'8" Weight: 10.10
A former Hereford youth team player who was given his first team chance against Exeter last season. Robbie, a keen, tough-tackler, quickly made the right-back spot his own, before breaking a leg a few games from the end of the campaign, an injury that will keep him out until 1996.
Hereford U (From trainee on 17/1/95) FL 15+1

WARNER Vance
Born: Leeds, 3 September 1974
Height: 6'0" Weight: 11.12
A big, strong right-sided central defender who is good in the air and tough in the tackle, Vance made his PL debut at home to Crystal Palace last season and looked very much at ease. Definitely one for the future.
Nottingham F (From trainee on 3/9/74) FL 2 FLC 1

WARREN Lee Anthony
Born: Manchester, 28 February 1969
Height: 6'0" Weight: 11.10
Signed from Hull during the summer of 1994, Lee is a midfield player who rarely featured in Doncaster's first team picture until late last season when he finally won a regular place in the Rovers "engine room".
Leeds U (From trainee on 27/7/87)
Rochdale (Free on 28/10/87) FL 31/1 FAC 1 Others 2
Hull C (£100,000 on 25/8/88) FL 141+12/1 FLC 2 FAC 5+1 Others 3+2/1
Lincoln C (Loaned on 20/9/90) FL 2+1/1
Doncaster Rov (Free on 21/7/94) FL 10+4/2 Others 0+1

WARREN Mark Wayne
Born: Clapton, 12 November 1974
Height: 5'9" Weight: 10.5
International Honours: E: Yth
Having missed the previous season with injury, Warren was determined to enjoy 1994-95 and he certainly succeeded. In February, when playing for Orient as an emergency striker, he scored a hat-trick against Peterborough - his first ever League goals, having scored against Shrewsbury in the AWS competition a few days earlier.

Normally a tough-tackling central mid-fielder, with attacking instincts, and a tireless worker, he showed a more mature attitude throughout the season and drew interest from several Premier and First Division clubs.
Leyton Orient (From trainee on 6/7/92) FL 43+9/3 FLC 2 Others 6+4/1

WASSALL Darren Paul
Born: Birmingham, 27 June 1968
Height: 5'11" Weight: 12.3
Club Honours: FMC '92
Derby centre-back and a specialist in man-to-man marking, he started off 1994-95 as a regular alongside Craig Short, until replaced by Paul Williams. Disappointed, he had a transfer request in mid-October temporarily turned down, but showed a commendable attitude in the reserves and filled in competently at right-back when required.
Nottingham F (From apprentice on 1/6/86) FL 17+10 FLC 6+2 FAC 3+1 Others 4+2/1
Hereford U (Loaned on 23/10/87) FL 5 FAC 1 Others 1
Bury (Loaned on 2/3/89) FL 7/1
Derby Co (£600,000 on 15/6/92) FL 74+7 FLC 8 FAC 4 Others 11

WATKIN Stephen (Steve)
Born: Wrexham, 16 June 1971
Height: 5'10" Weight: 11.0
Club Honours: WC '95
International Honours: W: B-2
Holds the ball up excellently for his Wrexham colleagues and shows good control. Although his goals tally dried up in 1994-95, and at times he seemed to lack confidence, an in-form Steve Watkin is a player who leads the line very well.
Wrexham (From juniors on 24/7/89) FL 127+15/40 FLC 8+1/3 FAC 9+2/8 Others 14+5/4

WATKISS Stuart Paul
Born: Wolverhampton, 8 May 1966
Height: 6'2" Weight: 13.7
Commanding Walsall central defender and a useful goalsnatcher when going forward. Missed only three games in 1993-94, but last season was rarely selected. However, the new manager, Chris Nicholl, did bring him back for the FA Cup replay at Leeds in which he played his part in taking the tie into extra-time.
Wolverhampton W (From trainee on 13/7/84) FL 2
Crewe Alex (Free on 28/2/86) FL 3
Walsall (Free from Rushall Olympic on 5/8/93) FL 46+1/2 FLC 6/1 FAC 4 Others 2

WATSON Alexander (Alex) Francis
Born: Liverpool, 5 April 1968
Height: 6'0" Weight: 11.9
Club Honours: CS '88
International Honours: E: Yth
An experienced centre-back, Alex is very strong in the air and a hard tackler who can move forward at set pieces to great effect. Lost his place at Bournemouth after the emergence of Rob Murray as a centre-back, but will be pushing him hard to regain his place in the side this coming season.
Liverpool (From apprentice on 18/5/85) FL 3+1 FLC 1+1 FAC 1+1 Others 1
Derby Co (Loaned on 30/8/90) FL 5
Bournemouth (£150,000 on 18/1/91) FL 145+6/5 FLC 14/1 FAC 12/1 Others 5

WATSON Andrew (Andy) Anthony
Born: Leeds, 1 April 1967
Height: 5'9" Weight: 11.2
Club Honours: WC '91
A striker with a good goalscoring record, Andy formed a splendid partnership at Blackpool in 1994-95 with Tony Ellis. Unfortunate to miss part of the season with injuries, he soon got back among the goals and has the knack of being in the right place in the right time.
Halifax T (Free from Harrogate T on 23/8/88) FL 75+8/15 FLC 5+1/2 FAC 6/1 Others 7/1
Swansea C (£40,000 on 31/7/90) FL 9+5/1 FLC 0+1 Others 1+1
Carlisle U (£30,000 on 19/9/91) FL 55+1/22 FLC 4/5 FAC 3 Others 1/1
Blackpool (£55,000 on 5/2/93) FL 74+14/37 FLC 6/5 FAC 2 Others 3/1

WATSON David (Dave)
Born: Liverpool, 20 November 1961
Height: 6'0" Weight: 13.0
Club Honours: FLC '85; Div 2 '86; Div 1 '87; CS '87; FAC '95
International Honours: E: 12; U21-7 (UEFAC '84)
Everton central defender of the traditional mould, Dave uses his height to great effect while both clearing his lines and attacking the opposition's goal. Recognised for his tough-tackling and unrivalled profession-alism, he sticks to his task regardless of the opponent. Often looks for the simple pass, but equally has an eye for picking out well placed colleagues. Continuing in a typical skipper's role in 1994-95, as the bedrock of the "Toffee's" defence, his consistent performances were achieved even though recurring back problems hampered the latter part of his season. Capped another solid year in great style by lifting the FA Cup, the biggest prize of them all, following the club's 1-0 victory over Manchester United.
Liverpool (From juniors on 25/5/79)
Norwich C (£100,000 on 29/11/80) FL 212/11 FLC 21/3 FAC 18/1
Everton (£900,000 on 22/8/86) F/PL 304+2/21 FLC 34/6 FAC 38/5 Others 14/3

WATSON David Neil
Born: Barnsley, 10 November 1973
Height: 6'0" Weight: 12.0
International Honours: E: U21-4
David had a fine season for Barnsley in 1994-95, and his shot-stopping was second to none. Anyone who saw the double save, near the end of the Newcastle match, will never forget it. Included in the Endsleigh League team which beat its Italian counter-parts, he was also a regular member of the England U21 side and was the number one choice for his club all season, missing only a handful of games because of a stomach injury.
Barnsley (From trainee on 4/7/92) FL 51 FLC 6 FAC 1 Others 1

WATSON Gordon William George
Born: Sidcup, 20 March 1971
Height: 6'0" Weight: 12.9
International Honours: E: U21-1
Signed by Southampton from Sheffield Wednesday, 90 seconds before last season's transfer deadline, Gordon scored the last

Dave Watson (Everton)

Neal Simpson
(Empics Sports Photo Agency)

minute goal which won the game against Newcastle on his home debut and then the winner against QPR. Looks to be forming a useful partnership up-front with Neil Shipperley, which promises to improve when he regains full match fitness.

Charlton Ath (From trainee on 5/4/89) FL 20+11/7 FLC 2/1 FAC 0+1 Others 1+1
Sheffield Wed (£250,000 on 20/2/91) F/PL 29+37/15 FLC 6+5/3 FAC 5+2/2 Others 2+2/1
Southampton (£1,200,000 on 17/3/95) PL 12/3

WATSON Kevin Edward
Born: Hackney, 3 January 1974
Height: 5'9" Weight: 10.6

A skilful central midfielder with good touch, and a passer, Kevin played his football away from Tottenham in 1994-95. Loaned out last December to Bristol City, he made a couple of appearances before finishing the season off at Barnet, where he impressed in a creative role tailor made for his abilities.

Tottenham H (From trainee on 15/5/92) PL 4+1 FLC 1+1/1 FAC 0+1
Brentford (Loaned on 24/3/94) FL 2+1
Bristol C (Loaned on 2/12/94) FL 1+1
Barnet (Loaned on 16/2/95) FL 13

WATSON Mark Stewart
Born: Vancouver, Canada, 8 September 1970
Height: 6'0" Weight: 12.6
International Honours: Canada

Having been given a good run for Watford midway through 1993-94, he looked forward to holding down a regular slot in central defence last season. However, although given opportunities, Mark again failed to command a first team place and was freed during the summer.

Watford (Signed on 19/11/93) FL 18 FAC 1+2

WATSON Paul Douglas
Born: Hastings, 4 January 1975
Height: 5'8" Weight: 10.10

A youngster with a big future, if 1994-95 was anything to go by. Equally at home in the left-back position or on the left of midfield, he is regarded as Gillingham's corner and free-kick taker and was a virtual ever-present during the season.

Gillingham (From trainee on 8/12/92) FL 54/2 FLC 4 FAC 4 Others 3+3

WATSON Stephen (Steve) Craig
Born: North Shields, 1 April 1974
Height: 6'0" Weight: 12.7
International Honours: E: U21-11; Yth

Played in midfield when selected, but since the beginning of 1995 he has mainly been on the Newcastle substitutes' bench. A versatile player, he has also been a regular at right-back for the England U21 side. Strong in the tackle as well as being skilful and fast, he also scored several goals, the best being a superb individual effort in the UEFA Cup match in Belgium against Royal Antwerp. One of the highlights of the season, and his career so far, was being selected for the England U21 side against Eire on his home ground, St James Park. Being a "Geordie", this was a very special night and was watched by a crowd of over 26,000.

Newcastle U (From trainee on 6/4/91) F/PL 97+16/7 FLC 6+1 FAC 7+2 Others 4+3/1

WATSON Thomas (Tommy) Robert
Born: Liverpool, 29 September 1969
Height: 5'8" Weight: 11.6

A strong physical player, with a mean streak and a good footballing brain, he is perhaps unfortunate in having had to compete for the right-sided Grimsby midfield spot with Gary Childs, which limited his first team opportunities in 1994-95.

Grimsby T (From trainee on 12/7/88) FL 134+36/24 FLC 9+5/4 FAC 3 Others 8+2

WATTS Grant Steven
Born: Croydon, 5 November 1973
Height: 6'0" Weight: 11.2

Signing a monthly contract for Gillingham in September 1994, after being released by Crystal Palace and unsuccessfully trialing at Sheffield United, he made just a handful of first team appearances. In December 1995 it was reported he was playing for non-league, Sutton United.

Crystal Palace (From trainee on 26/6/92) PL 2+2 FLC 3+1/2
Sheffield U (Free on 17/8/94)
Gillingham (Free on 2/9/94) FL 2+1 Others 0+1

WDOWCZYK Dariusz
Born: Warsaw, Poland, 21 September 1962
Height: 5'11" Weight: 11.11
International Honours: Poland

Former captain of the Polish national side, and a bargain free transfer from Glasgow Celtic during the 1994 close season, Dariusz added style and elegance to Reading's defence during the campaign, as well as a touch of steel. His long raking passes, especially off his left foot, set up many attacks and proved him to still be a player of true international class.

Glasgow Celtic (£400,000 from Legia on 17/11/89) SL 112+4/4 SLC 11 SC 13/2 Others 6+1
Reading (Free on 12/8/94) FL 37+1 FLC 2 FAC 1 Others 3

Steve Watson

Steve Morton
(Empics Sports Photo Agency)

WEBB Matthew Leslie
Born: Bristol, 24 September 1976
Height: 5'9" Weight: 10.2

A young Birmingham midfielder who showed great promise in "Blues'" reserves last season. Given a taste of first team action as a sub against Swansea, he did well enough to suggest that he could be pushing for a first team spot in 1995-96. Still a trainee.
Birmingham C (Trainee) FL 0+1

WEBB Neil John
Born: Reading, 30 July 1963
Height: 6'1" Weight: 13.7
Club Honours: Div 3 '83; FLC '89, '92; FMC '89; FAC '90; ECWC '91; ESC '91
International Honours: E: 26; B-4; U21-3; Yth

A gifted former England international midfielder with great vision, at his best Neil could open up the opposition with defence splitting passes and score goals that put many forwards to shame. Having returned to Nottingham Forest, he played just once in 1994-95, when coming on as a sub in the Premiership, before being loaned to Swindon last October in a bid to regain match fitness, prior to being freed in the summer.
Reading (From apprentice on 14/11/80) FL 65+7/22 FLC 2+2 FAC 2
Portsmouth (£83,000 on 29/7/82) FL 123/34 FLC 9/3 FAC 6/1
Nottingham F (£250,000 on 3/6/85) FL 146/47 FLC 21/4 FAC 13/2 Others 6/4
Manchester U (£1,500,000 on 24/7/89) F/PL 70+5/8 FLC 14/1 FAC 9/1 Others 12/1
Nottingham F (£800,000 on 23/11/92) F/PL 26+4/3 FLC 2+3/1 FAC 6+1/2 Others 1
Swindon T (Loaned on 7/10/94) FL 5+1

WEBBER Damian John
Born: Rustington, 8 October 1968
Height: 6'4" Weight: 14.0

A right-footed central defender, he joined Millwall from Bogner Regis Town at the height of the injury crisis last season and showed exceptional poise and confidence when thrust into League football.
Millwall (Signed from Bognor Regis on 27/10/94) FL 19+3/2 FLC 1+1 FAC 1+2

WEBSTER Kenneth (Kenny) Darren
Born: London, 2 March 1973
Height: 5'8" Weight: 13.2
International Honours: E: Yth

An enthusiastic right-back who can also play in the centre of the defence, Kenny was freed by Arsenal during the 1994 close season and signed for Peterborough. Given a run-out in a couple of AWS matches, although showing himself to be a firm tackler and possessing a powerful right-foot, he was released in January and joined non-league, Stevenage Borough.
Arsenal (From trainee on 8/3/91)
Peterborough U (Free on 2/7/94) Others 2

WEBSTER Simon Paul
Born: Hinckley, 20 January 1964
Height: 6'0" Weight: 12.0

After two painful years recovering from a broken leg, it was good to see the central defender coming on as a substitute in each of West Ham's last four Premier League games of 1994-95. Having earlier played seven games on loan at Oldham, to prove his fitness, this determined player can now look forward to the coming season in order to show the West Ham fans what they have been missing.

Tottenham H (From apprentice on 1/12/81) FL 2+1
Exeter C (Loaned on 10/11/83) FL 26 Others 3
Huddersfield T (£15,000 on 21/2/85) FL 118/4 FLC 7 FAC 7 Others 2
Sheffield U (£35,000 on 18/3/88) FL 26+11/3

FLC 5 FAC 5+1 Others 3+1
Charlton Ath (£50,000 on 16/8/90) FL 127/7 FLC 7 FAC 6 Others 3
West Ham U (£525,000 on 30/6/93) PL 0+5
Oldham Ath (Loaned on 24/3/95) FL 7

WEGERLE Roy Connon
Born: Pretoria, South Africa, 19 March 1964
Height: 5'11" Weight: 11.0
International Honours: USA

A frustrating last season, which started with him on the Coventry bench, his best period was probably when Dion Dublin was first signed and Roy scored three in four games. On his good days a very exciting striker, at all times he remained the fans' favourite because of his ability to produce something out of the ordinary to brighten up a dull game. Appeared to be out for the season after a bad knee injury in the FA Cup replay at Norwich, but after some intensive treatment in the States he returned for Easter.

Chelsea (£100,000 from Tampa Bay Rowdies on 21/7/86) FL 15+8/3 FAC 1+1/1 Others 2+1
Swindon T (Loaned on 24/3/88) FL 7/1
Luton T (£75,000 on 27/7/88) FL 39+6/10 FLC 10/8 FAC 1 Others 2+1
Queens Park R (£1,000,000 on 14/12/89) FL 71+4/29 FLC 5/1 FAC 11/1 Others 1
Blackburn Rov (£1,000,000 on 6/3/92) F/PL 20+14/6 FLC 3+3/4 FAC 4+1/2
Coventry C (£1,000,000 on 23/3/93) PL 46+7/9 FLC 5/1 FAC 3+2/1

WELCH Keith James
Born: Bolton, 3 October 1968
Height: 6'2" Weight: 12.5

A goalkeeper very much in the David Seaman mould, it took him a while to win over the Bristol City fans after his transfer from Rochdale. It was the change in the back-pass rule that wrought the transformation, as Keith proved to be an accomplished player with the ball at his feet, and his form as a shot-stopper improved to such an extent that he kept 25 clean sheets in 1993-94. Although the club were relegated last season, he still performed well in difficult circumstances.

Rochdale (Free from Bolton W juniors on 3/3/87) FL 205 FLC 12 FAC 10 Others 12
Bristol C (£200,000 on 25/7/91) FL 160 FLC 10 FAC 9 Others 8

WELLS David Peter
Born: Portsmouth, 29 December 1977
Height: 6'1" Weight: 13.0
International Honours: NI: Yth

Thrown in at the deep end at the beginning of last season as Bournemouth's goal-keeping understudy to Neil Moss, although only 16 and still a YTS, David made one appearance when coming on as sub against Wrexham. As the youth team 'keeper, the experience of being involved in the first team set-up can only have benefited him.

Bournemouth (Trainee) FL 0+1

WELLS Mark Anthony
Born: Leicester, 15 October 1971
Height: 5'9" Weight: 10.10

Tough-tackling and tenacious left-sided player who impressed in patches with Scarborough last term, having joined them during the 1994 close season from Huddersfield. Unfortunately, Mark missed several matches through injury, but always gave total commitment.

Notts Co (From trainee on 3/7/90) FL 0+2 Others 0+1
Huddersfield T (Free on 9/8/93) FL 21+1/4 FLC 4 FAC 3 Others 2+1
Scarborough (Free on 21/7/94) FL 16+2/1 FAC 4 Others 1

WELSH Stephen (Steve)
Born: Glasgow, 19 April 1968
Height: 6'0" Weight: 12.0

A fine clubman whose performances in the heart of the Peterborough defence last

Roy Wegerle

Tony Marshall
(Empics Sports Photo Agency)

season did not meet his usual high standards, he transferred to Partick Thistle for £40,000 on 23 December 1994. Word from north of the border is that Steve appears to have had a new lease of life.

Cambridge U (Free from Wimborne T on 22/6/90) FL 0+1 Others 2
Peterborough U (Free on 8/8/91) FL 146/2 FLC 20 FAC 8 Others 13

WEST Colin
Born: Wallsend, 13 November 1962
Height: 6'1" Weight: 13.2

Possesses virtually all the attributes of a good striker - powerful shot, strong in the air, a ball-winner and creating chances for colleagues, as well as scoring regularly himself. Once again he topped Orient's scoring charts, despite missing a chunk of both the middle and end of 1994-95 through injury. Scored a hat-trick against Fulham in the AWS competition, but saw his dream of a Wembley appearance disappear when the club went down 2-4, on aggregate, to Birmingham in the Southern Final.

Sunderland (From apprentice on 9/7/80) FL 88+14/21 FLC 13+4/5 FAC 3+1/2
Watford (£115,000 on 28/3/85) FL 45/20 FLC 2+1 FAC 8/3
Glasgow R (£180,000 on 23/5/86) SL 4+6/2 SLC 2/1 SC 0+1 Others 0+2
Sheffield Wed (£150,000 on 7/9/87) FL 40+5/8 FLC 6/3 FAC 6/1 Others 3/1
West Bromwich A (Signed on 24/2/89) FL 64+9/22 FLC 2 FAC 4/1 Others 2/1
Port Vale (Loaned on 1/11/91) FL 5/1
Swansea C (Free on 5/8/92) FL 29+4/12 FLC 0+1 FAC 5/2 Others 3+2/1
Leyton Orient (Free on 26/7/93) FL 69+4/23 FLC 2 FAC 4/1 Others 8/4

WEST Dean
Born: Morley, 5 December 1972
Height: 5'10" Weight: 11.7

A right-sided midfield player or full-back, who is extremely popular with Lincoln's supporters, Dean is known for his whole-hearted approach and an ability to get forward into goalscoring positions.

Lincoln C (From trainee on 17/8/91) FL 86+25/19 FLC 9/1 FAC 5/1 Others 5+2/1

WEST Paul Darrell
Born: Wolverhampton, 17 June 1970
Height: 5'11" Weight: 11.0

Paul's playing time at Wigan in 1994-95 was restricted to the opening game of the campaign, when he picked up a serious knee ligament injury. A defender who can play at full-back, or as a sweeper, he was released at the end of the season.

Port Vale (Signed from Alcester T on 15/2/91)
Bradford C (Free on 3/7/92)
Wigan Ath (Free on 10/9/93) FL 2+1 FLC 1

WESTLEY Shane Lee Mark
Born: Canterbury, 16 June 1965
Height: 6'2" Weight: 13.8

A tall, commanding Brentford centre-half, Shane had limited opportunities in 1994-95. Unable to dislodge the Jamie Bates/Barry Ashby defensive partnership, he spent a month on loan at Southend, prior to being released at the end of the season.

Charlton Ath (From apprentice on 8/6/83) FL 8 FAC 1

Southend U (£15,000 on 1/3/85) FL 142+2/10 FLC 10+1/1 FAC 5 Others 7/1
Wolverhampton W (£150,000 on 19/6/89) FL 48+2/1 FLC 5/1 Others 2
Brentford (£100,000 on 30/10//92) FL 61+3/1 FLC 5/2 FAC 5 Others 6
Southend U (Loaned on 3/2/95) FL 4+1

WETHERALL David
Born: Sheffield, 14 March 1971
Height: 6'2" Weight: 13.8
International Honours: E: Sch

Leeds' defender with a bright future in the game, he made fine progress in 1994-95 and is quickly maturing into an all-rounder. Indeed, he seemed to reserve his best performances in matches where up against big target men, such as John Fashanu and Lee Chapman. A keen competitor and very good in the air, David is dangerous at set-pieces and scored some vital goals, notably in games against Walsall and Manchester United. Looks to have a bright future.

Sheffield Wed (From trainee on 1/7/89)
Leeds U (£125,000 on 15/7/91) F/PL 82+2/5 FLC 5 FAC 8+2/3

WHALLEY Gareth
Born: Manchester, 19 December 1973
Height: 5'10" Weight: 11.6

Yet another of the talented youngsters to have come through Crewe's YT scheme,

Noel Whelan

Phil O'Brien
(Empics Sports Photo Agency)

although basically a midfield player he has also played at full-back. Always looking to use the ball effectively, Gareth is not a prolific scorer, but helps to create openings for others in the side.

Crewe Alex (From trainee on 29/7/92) FL 78+6/3 FLC 4+1 FAC 7+1/3 Others 14/2

WHALLEY David Neil
Born: Prescot, 29 October 1965
Height: 6'0" Weight: 12.6
A tough-tackling midfielder and good passer, Neil never fully realised his potential after signing for Preston and unable to claim a regular place last season, he returned to non-league football with Altrincham on deadline day.
Preston NE (£25,000 from Warrington T on 2/3/93) FL 45+5/1 FLC 4 FAC 2+2 Others 6+1

WHELAN Noel
Born: Leeds, 30 December 1974
Height: 6'2" Weight: 11.3
Club Honours: FAYC '93
International Honours: E: U21-2; Yth (UEFAC '93)
Nicknamed "Snowy", Noel is a versatile Leeds' forward who invariably covers plenty of ground in his quest for goals. Coming off the bench to score a fortuitous last minute winner against Arsenal, after deceiving David Seaman with a long-range effort, he went on to score seven in his first 14 games in 1994-95. And, as the leading Leeds' scorer for most of the season, he also grabbed the winner for England against Eire on his full U21 debut. Excellent in the air, with super skills on the ground, he was unfortunate to miss several club games towards the end of the campaign when suffering a hairline fracture of the foot. A name to remember, though.
Leeds U (From trainee on 5/3/93) PL 25+15/7 FLC 3/1 FAC 2

WHELAN Philip (Phil) James
Born: Stockport, 7 March 1972
Height: 6'4" Weight: 14.1
International Honours: E: U21-4
Tall central defender with surprising pace for his size, who is dangerous at corners, Phil made a promising start to Ipswich's Second Division Championship winning season, but in suffering an horrendous ankle injury in the last home match of 1993-94, he was not expected to play until 1995 at the earliest. However, in making good progress in his recovery, Phil was back in the first team last November. Made just 12 starts before being transferred to Middlesbrough on transfer deadline day. Still to make his debut for his new club, following a registration mix-up.
Ipswich T (From juniors on 2/7/90) F/PL 76+6/2 FLC 6+1 FAC 3+1 Others 1
Middlesbrough (£300,000 on 3/3/95)

WHELAN Ronald (Ronnie) Andrew
Born: Dublin, 25 September 1961
Height: 5'9" Weight: 11.0
Club Honours: Div 1 '82, '83, '84, '86, '88, '90; FLC '82, '83, '84; EC '84; FAC '86, '89
International Honours: Ei: 53; U21-1; B-1
An inspiration to all around him, Ronnie's

arrival at Southend last September coincided with a distinct upturn in form and, when a groin operation caused him to miss five weeks during January and February, the team's form slumped. His passing and leadership qualities are there for all to see and his help in bringing on the likes of Julian Hails and Steve Tilson, along with his influential midfield partnership with Andy Sussex, saw the club to relegation safety with two matches to spare.
Liverpool (Free from Home Farm on 1/10/79) F/PL 351+11/46 FLC 46+4/14 FAC 40+1/7 Others 38+2/6
Southend U (Free on 9/9/94) FL 33/1 FAC 1

WHELAN Spencer Randall
Born: Liverpool, 17 September 1971
Height: 6'2" Weight: 13.0
A central defender with tremendous pace, Spencer missed a huge chunk of last season, due to a broken leg sustained at Plymouth in September. Returned to the Chester side in February and was ever-present, scoring his first ever League goal against Wycombe in April. Still only 23-years-of-age, with a good future ahead of him.
Chester C (Free from Liverpool juniors on 3/4/90) FL 108+8/1 FLC 6+1/1 FAC 5+1 Others 2+1

WHITBREAD Adrian Richard
Born: Epping, 22 October 1971
Height: 6'2" Weight: 11.8
Originally with Leyton Orient, Adrian spent a season with Swindon before coming back to London's East-End with West Ham in the 1994 close season, as part of the deal that took Joey Beauchamp in the opposite direction. Unfortunately hampered by injuries, the young centre-half only played in a handful of first team games, and will be looking for the opportunity of a successful run in the side this coming season.
Leyton Orient (From trainee on 13/11/89) FL 125/2 FLC 10+1 FAC 9+1 Others 8
Swindon T (£500,000 on 29/7/93) P/FL 35+1/1 FAC 2
West Ham U (£650,000 on 17/8/94) PL 3+5 FLC 2+1

WHISTON Peter Michael
Born: Widnes, 4 January 1968
Height: 6'0" Weight: 11.6
Reserve Southampton defender who made only one sub appearance last season after his summer signing from Exeter, and that a 1-5 defeat at Newcastle! Bought to provide defensive cover, it remains to be seen whether he will come good in the Premiership.
Plymouth Arg (Signed on 17/12/87) FL 4+6 FAC 1 Others 1
Torquay U (Free on 21/3/90) FL 39+1/1 FLC 5/1 FAC 1 Others 6
Exeter C (£25,000 on 13/9/91) FL 85/7 FLC 7 FAC 10 Others 10/1
Southampton (£30,000 on 10/8/94) PL 0+1

WHITE Alan
Born: Darlington, 22 March 1976
Height: 6'1" Weight: 13.2
Middlesbrough centre-back who is equally

at home at full-back. Strong, solid, remarkably fast, a good distributor and powerful in the air, Alan made his only appearance for the club in a Anglo-Italian Cup game last season.
Middlesbrough (From trainee on 8/7/94) Others 1

WHITE David
Born: Manchester, 30 October 1967
Height: 6'1" Weight: 12.9
International Honours: E: 1; B-2; U21-6; Yth
A player who has unfortunately suffered a string of niggling injuries while at Leeds, David again looked impressive, before being sidelined after the Manchester United game last September. On returning to the side, while vying with Rod Wallace for a place, he showed good form in a wide-right midfield position, scoring excellent long-range efforts against Crystal Palace and Wimbledon. At Manchester City, he had proved to be one of the most exciting forwards of the modern game, running at defences and scoring from prodigious distances and acute angles, and it is felt that he will only be seen at his best at Leeds if being able to settle into an injury free season.
Manchester C (From apprentice on 7/11/85) F/PL 273+12/79 FLC 24+2/11 FAC 22/4 Others 9/2
Leeds U (£2,000,000 on 22/12/93) PL 27+11/8 FAC 6/1

WHITE Devon Winston
Born: Nottingham, 2 March 1964
Height: 6'3" Weight: 14.0
Club Honours: Div 3 '90; AIC '95
Big, strong striker with good aerial power on the far post, and a player who can provide goals for others from timely knockdowns. Signed from QPR last December, Devon quickly established himself in the Notts County side, scoring in three consecutive games in April, including one of the goals that beat Ascoli in the Anglo-Italian Cup Final at Wembley.
Lincoln C (From Arnold Kingswell on 14/12/84) FL 21+8/4 Others 2+1/2 (Free to Boston U in October 1986)
Bristol Rov (Free on 21/8/87) FL 190+12/53 FLC 9/2 FAC 10/3 Others 19/2
Cambridge U (£100,000 on 28/3/92) FL 15+7/4 FLC 4/1 FAC 1 Others 1/1
Queens Park R (£100,000 on 26/1/93) PL 16+10/9 FLC 1+1
Notts Co (£110,000 on 23/12/94) FL 16+4/7 FAC 2/1 Others 3/1

WHITE Jason Gregory
Born: Meriden, 19 October 1971
Height: 6'2" Weight: 12.0
Bustling Scarborough striker who leads the forward line with great distinction, being very skilful on the ball and capable of beating defenders for pace. Was a popular choice as Scarborough's "Player of the Year" last season.
Derby Co (From trainee on 4/7/90)
Scunthorpe U (Free on 6/9/91) FL 44+24/16 FLC 2 FAC 3+3/1 Others 4+4/1
Darlington (Loaned on 20/8/93) FL 4/1
Scarborough (Free on 10/12/93) FL 60+3/20 FLC 2+1 FAC 5/1 Others 1

WHITE Stephen (Steve) James
Born: Chipping Sodbury, 2 January 1959
Height: 5'10" Weight: 11.4
Club Honours: Div 2 '82
Hereford's top-scorer last season, having come on a free from Swindon, he found himself on his own up-front in most games. Lively and dangerous in the box, Steve is good at holding the ball up until help arrives.
Bristol Rov (Free from Mangotsfield on 11/7/77) FL 46+4/20 FLC 2/1 FAC 3/3
Luton T (£200,000 on 24/12/79) FL 63+9/25 FLC 3+1/1 FAC 2+1
Charlton Ath (£150,000 on 30/7/82) FL 29/12 FLC 2
Lincoln C (Loaned on 28/1/83) FL 2+1
Luton T (Loaned on 24/2/83) FL 4
Bristol Rov (£45,000 on 26/8/83) FL 89+12/24 FLC 8/2 FAC 7+1/2 Others 5+2/1
Swindon T (Free on 8/7/86) F/PL 200+44/83 FLC 21+8/11 FAC 9+2/2 Others 22+6/15
Hereford U (Free on 26/8/94) FL 31+5/14 FLC 3/2 FAC 2/1 Others 3+1/1

WHITE Thomas (Tom) Matthew
Born: Bristol, 26 January 1976
Height: 6'1" Weight: 13.6
A former Bristol Rovers' YTS, Tom made his League debut with four league appearances in 1994-95, his first season as a full-time professional. Deputising for the injured Billy Clark, he proved to be a commanding central defender who will challenge strongly for a regular first team place in the future.
Bristol Rov (From trainee on 13/7/94) FL 4

WHITEHALL Steven (Steve) Christopher
Born: Bromborough, 8 December 1966
Height: 5'9" Weight: 10.11
Strong-running forward player and crowd favourite at Rochdale, who had to shoulder most of the goalscoring burden in 1994-95. Nearly sold to Chesterfield in mid-season, he became one of the very few players to have netted 50 senior goals for "Dale" and was an ever-present, if you allow for one sub appearance.
Rochdale (£20,000 from Southport on 23/7/91) FL 139+18/46 FLC 7+3/3 FAC 7+2/2 Others 11+1/7

WHITEHEAD Philip Matthew
Born: Halifax, 17 December 1969
Height: 6'3" Weight: 13.7
Started 1994-95 as Oxford's first choice goalkeeper, he was missed after suffering a broken finger in mid-season. Regaining his place when fit again, Phil continued to prove himself to be a good shot-stopper who controls his area well. He also uses his height to good advantage when taking crosses.
Halifax T (From trainee on 1/7/88) FL 42 FLC 2 FAC 4 Others 4
Barnsley (£60,000 on 9/3/90) FL 16
Halifax T (Loaned on 7/3/91) FL 9
Scunthorpe U (Loaned on 29/11/91) FL 8 Others 2
Scunthorpe U (Loaned on 4/9/92) FL 8 FLC 2
Bradford C (Loaned on 19/11/92) FL 6 Others 4
Oxford U (£75,000 on 1/11/93) FL 77 FLC 4 FAC 5 Others 1

WHITEHOUSE Dane Lee
Born: Sheffield, 14 October 1970

Height: 5'9" Weight: 10.12
Another local-born player who is equally at home anywhere on the left-side, although he prefers a midfield role. Scored a hat-trick in the Coca Cola Cup game at Stockport and became Sheffield United's recognised penalty taker. Always enthusiastic, he is proud to play for the club he has supported since the age of 12.
Sheffield U (From trainee on 1/7//89) F/PL 121+25/25 FLC 9+1/4 FAC 11+3/1 Others 3/2

Mike Whitlow   Tony Marshall
(Empics Sports Photo Agency)

WHITLOW Michael (Mike) William
Born: Northwich, 13 January 1968
Height: 5'11" Weight: 11.6
Club Honours: Div 2 '90, Div 1 '92
Dependable Leicester left-back, who grabbed a rare goal to earn an unlikely point at Old Trafford last season. Missed a handful of games due to injuries, but was always one of the first names on the teamsheet when fit.
Leeds U (£10,000 from Witton A on 11/11/88) FL 62+15/4 FLC 4+1 FAC 1+4 Others 9
Leicester C (£250,000 on 27/3/92) F/PL 86+2/5 FLC 4/1 FAC 5 Others 11

WHITNEY Jonathan (Jon) David
Born: Nantwich, 23 December 1970
Height: 5'10" Weight: 12.3
A very able, hard-tackling Huddersfield left-back whose progress in 1994-95 was cut short by a knee ligament injury suffered the previous seeason. Limited to a handful of reserve appearances, he was loaned to Wigan in March, playing 12 games in a bid to recover full fitness. Interestingly, it was Jon's second spell at the club, having been there as a trainee.
Huddersfield T (£10,000 from Winsford on 21/10/93) FL 14 Others 4/1
Wigan Ath (Loaned on 17/3/95) FL 12

WHITTAKER Stuart
Born: Liverpool, 2 January 1975
Height: 5'7" Weight: 9.6

Exciting Bolton winger who was a regular in the Pontin's Central League Championship winning side in 1994-95. With first team opportunities limited, due to the form of Alan Thompson and David Lee, he will have to bide his time.
Bolton W (Free from Liverpool juniors on 14/5/93) FL 2+1

WHITTINGHAM Guy
Born: Evesham, 10 November 1964
Height: 5'10" Weight: 11.12
Not able to gain a regular place in the Aston Villa line-up, Guy moved to Sheffield Wednesday last December in exchange for Ian Taylor, plus cash, and made an immediate impact. In supplying pace and enthusiasm so badly missing up-front until then from "Owls'" front-line, two goals in two matches set an impossible standard. Although playing well, but lacking goals, he found himself on the bench until fighting his way back again.
Portsmouth (Free from Yeovil on 9/6/89) FL 149+11/88 FLC 7+2/3 FAC 7+3/10 Others 9/3
Aston Villa (£1,200,000 on 1/8/93) PL 17+8/5 FLC 4+1/1 Others 2+1
Wolverhampton W (Loaned on 28/2/94) FL 13/8 FAC 1
Sheffield Wed (£700,000 on 21/12/94) PL 16+5/9 FAC 2+1

WHITTINGTON Craig
Born: Brighton, 3 September 1970
Height: 5'11" Weight: 12.4
Signed from Scarborough at the beginning of last season as a striker, Craig has yet to make his mark on the Huddersfield first team, having been restricted to just one first team appearance. Loaned out to Rochdale last November, as a player with pace and good in the air, he could be a key member of the First Division squad.
Scarborough (£50,000 from Crawley on 19/11/93) FL 26+1/10 Others 1
Huddersfield T (Signed on 12/8/94) FL 1
Rochdale (Loaned on 25/11/94) FL 1

WHITTON Stephen (Steve) Paul
Born: East Ham, 4 December 1960
Height: 6'1" Weight: 13.7
Club Honours: Div 2 '92
Colchester player-coach whose experience, strength, vision and touch, aided an otherwise very young front line throughout last season. Scored two outstanding long-distance goals (at Darlington and against Yeading in the FA Cup), plus a stunning volley at Northampton, and showed he can still play at the top level. Recovered from missing penalties in each of the first two games to become a supporters' favourite.
Coventry C (From apprentice on 15/9/78) FL 64+10/21 FLC 3+2 FAC 3/2
West Ham U (£175,000 on 11/7/83) FL 35+4/6 FLC 6/2 FAC 1
Birmingham C (Loaned on 31/1/86) FL 8/2
Birmingham C (£60,000 on 28/8/86) FL 94+1/28 FLC 7+1/4 FAC 5 Others 3/1
Sheffield Wed (£275,000 on 3/3/89) FL 22+10/4 FLC 3/4 FAC 0+1 Others 0+1
Ipswich T (£150,000 on 11/1/91) F/PL 80+8/15 FLC 7+1/2 FAC 8+1/2 Others 4
Colchester U (£10,000 on 24/3/94) FL 44/12 FLC 2 FAC 4/2 Others 2

WHYTE Christopher (Chris) Anderson
Born: Islington, 2 September 1961
Height: 6'1" Weight: 13.0
Club Honours: Div 1 '92, Div 2 '95
International Honours: E: U21-4

Strong in the air and timely with interceptions on the ground, Chris regained his best form in the centre of Birmingham's defence last season. Unfortunately, an eye injury confined him to the sidelines and by the time he recovered, the Liam Daish and Dave Barnett partnership had taken shape. However, not to be outdone, he switched to left-back and turned in several impressive performances on his way to a Second Division Championship medal.

Arsenal (From apprentice on 24/12/79) FL 86+4/8 FLC 14 FAC 5 Others 3+1 (Free to Los Angeles Lazers during 1986 close season)
Crystal Palace (Loaned on 23/8/84) FL 13 FLC 4
West Bromwich A (Free on 25/8/88) FL 83+1/7 FLC 5/2 FAC 5 Others 2
Leeds U (£400,000 on 18/6/90) F/PL 113/5 FLC 14+1/1 FAC 8 Others 11
Birmingham C (£250,000 on 12/8/93) FL 64/1 FLC 7 FAC 4 Others 4+1

WHYTE David Antony
Born: Greenwich, 20 April 1971
Height: 5'9" Weight: 10.7
Club Honours: Div 1 '94

A striker who has been an immediate success since signing for Charlton in the summer of 1994, he scored in his first game and continued to do so throughout the campaign on a regular basis. Fast, with a powerful right-foot, David claimed several spectacular goals amongst his haul and became the first Charlton player for 14 years to record over 20 in a season. Appears to have a great future in the game.

Crystal Palace (Free from Greenwich Borough on 15/2/89) FL 17+10/4 FLC 5+2/2 FAC 0+1 Others 0+3/1
Charlton Ath (Loaned on 26/3/92) FL 7+1/2
Charlton Ath (£450,000 on 5/7/94) FL 36+2/19 FLC 2/2 FAC 1

WHYTE Derek
Born: Glasgow, 31 August 1968
Height: 5'11" Weight: 12.12
Club Honours: SPD '88; SC '88, '89; Div 1 '95
International Honours: S: 8; B-2; SU21-9; Yth; Sch

Having joined Middlesbrough in August 1992 (with Chris Morris) for what was then a club record signing of £950,000, Derek has proved to be a brilliant central defender, who is more than capable of filling any defensive position. Voted the most improved player in "Boro's" First Division Championship year of 1994-95, winning, in the process, many "Man of the Match" awards, and even more, admirers, friends, and well-wishers.

Glasgow Celtic (From juniors in 1985) SL 211+5/7 SLC 18+1 SC 26 Others 15/1
Middlesbrough (Signed on 1/8/92) F/PL 112+1/2 FLC 8 FAC 1+1 Others 6

WIDDRINGTON Thomas (Tommy)
Born: Newcastle, 1 October 1971
Height: 5'8" Weight: 11.1

Former midfielder, now playing as a sweeper, or just in front of the Southampton back four, Tommy covers the midfield players who are making forward runs. A gritty hard-tackler, who is always trying hard to the end of every game, surprisingly, he is often the one taken off when more forward power is needed.

Southampton (From trainee on 10/5/90) F/PL 47+7/1 FLC 1+1 FAC 7
Wigan Ath (Loaned on 12/9/91) FL 5+1 FLC 2

WIGG Nathan Marlow
Born: Newport, 27 September 1974
Height: 5'9" Weight: 10.5

Another of Cardiff's young midfielders, Nathan improved immensely as last season progressed and relished the battles for points on the run-in. Was one of the club's few successes in a poor season.

Cardiff C (From trainee on 4/8/93) FL 26+12/1 FAC 0+1 Others 7+3

Jason Wilcox

Steve Morton
(Empics Sports Photo Agency)

233

WILCOX Jason Malcolm
Born: Farnworth, 15 July 1971
Height: 5'10" Weight: 11.6
Club Honours: PL '95
International Honours: E: B-1

A vital piece of the Blackburn jigsaw in 1994-95, Jason missed the run-in to the club's most important season in living memory through injury, a blow that was only softened when he ultimately won a Championship medal. The team badly missed the width he brought to the left-side, his capacity to make long runs and deliver wicked oblique balls to the strikers, along with his workrate in getting back to aid Graham Le Saux. The moment in question came at Tottenham in February, when he sustained cruciate ligament injuries that, despite a brief attempt to return, required surgery. A bitter pill to swallow for a man who had recently been invited to England squad sessions after being capped at "B" level!

Blackburn Rov (From trainee on 13/6/89) F/PL 138+12/19 FLC 13+1/1 FAC 11/1 Others 5

WILCOX Russell (Russ)
Born: Hemsworth, 25 March 1964
Height: 6'0" Weight: 11.10
Club Honours: Div 4 '87
International Honours: E: SP-3

Central defender and skipper of Doncaster's team, Russ was a commanding figure at the heart of Rovers' defence last season, being voted the supporters' "Player of the Year" for the second year running. Was also elected into the PFA Third Division team for 1994-95 by his fellow professionals.

Doncaster Rov (Apprentice) FL 1
Northampton T (£15,000 from Frickley Ath on 30/6/86) FL 137+1/9 FLC 6 FAC 10 Others 8/1
Hull C (£120,000 on 6/8/90) FL 92+8/7 FLC 5 FAC 5/1 Others 5+1
Doncaster Rov (£60,000 on 30/7/93) FL 77/6 FLC 3/1 FAC 3 Others 3

WILDER Christopher (Chris) John
Born: Stocksbridge, 23 September 1967
Height: 5'11" Weight: 10.10

As skipper of Rotherham, Chris almost went through last season without having missed a game. He showed that he could support his forwards whenever the occasion arose, getting up from his right-back position as often as possible. The most reliable defender at the club, he also displayed a talent with free-kicks from the edge of opposing penalty areas.

Southampton (From apprentice on 26/9/85)
Sheffield U (Free on 20/8/86) FL 89+4/1 FLC 8+1 FAC 7 Others 3
Walsall (Loaned on 2/11/89) FL 4 FAC 1 Others 2
Charlton Ath (Loaned on 12/10/90) FL 1
Charlton Ath (Loaned on 28/11/91) FL 2
Leyton Orient (Loaned on 27/2/92) FL 16/1 Others 1
Rotherham U (£50,000 on 30/7/92) FL 111+3/11 FLC 7 FAC 5+1/1 Others 5+1

WILKIE Glen Alan
Born: Stepney, 22 January 1977
Height: 5'10" Weight: 12.4

Teenage midfielder. Made his Orient debut as a sub last December, whilst still a YTS boy, and four days after signing pro forms he

made a cracking full debut against Cambridge. A busy player, he is on the brink of a regular squad place in 1995-96

Leyton Orient (From trainee on 17/3/95) FL 10+1

WILKIN Kevin
Born: Cambridge, 1 October 1967
Height: 6'0" Weight: 12.6

A striker, who has been with Northampton since 1990, he has missed a large part of that time following two serious injuries, one keeping him out for a whole season. His goals come through being at the right place at the right time. Released at the end of last season.

Northampton T (£10,000 from Cambridge C on 22/8/90) FL 67+11/11 FLC 5+1/2 FAC 4/2 Others 3+1

WILKINS Dean Mark
Born: Hillingdon, 12 July 1962
Height: 5'10" Weight: 12.4

Stylish Brighton midfield player who is a good passer of the ball and dangerous at dead ball situations, he has, however, been troubled by injuries and unable to maintain consistent form. Brother of Ray.

Queens Park R (From apprentice on 17/5/80) FL 1+5 FLC 1
Brighton & Hove A (Free on 4/8/83) FL 2 FAC 1 (Freed during 1984 close season)
Leyton Orient (Loaned on 22/3/84) FL 10
Brighton & Hove A (Free from PEC Zwolle on 28/7/87) FL 264+11/22 FLC 20/3 FAC 15+1 Others 18/3

WILKINS Raymond (Ray) Colin
Born: Hillingdon, 14 September 1956
Height: 5'8" Weight: 11.2
Club Honours: FAC '83; SPD '90
International Honours: E: 84; U23-2; U21-1; Yth; Sch

Returned to QPR as player-manager in November 1994, having made just one appearance for Crystal Palace in 1994-95 before a broken foot ruled him out. Still a very stylish midfield playmaker, Ray restricted himself to just one full appearance at Chelsea and one as a substitute in the blue and white hoops at Southampton. Awarded an MBE in last year's Honours List.

Chelsea (From apprentice on 1/10/73) FL 176+3/30 FLC 6+1/2 FAC 10+1/2
Manchester U (£825,000 on 1/8/79) FL 158+2/7 FLC 14+1/1 FAC 10/1 Others 9/1 (£1,500,000 to AC Milan on 1/7/84)
Glasgow R (£250,000 from Paris St Germain on 1/11/87) SL 69+1/2 SLC 10/1 SC 8+1 Others 7
Queens Park R (Free on 30/11/89) F/PL 153+1/7 FLC 13 FAC 13/2 Others 2/1
Crystal Palace (Free on 26/5/94) PL 1
Queens Park R (Free on 17/11/94) PL 1+1

WILKINS Richard John
Born: Lambeth, 28 May 1965
Height: 6'0" Weight: 11.6
Club Honours: Div 3 '91

Having signed from Cambridge during the 1994 close season, Richard became a highly respected and regular member of the Hereford team. As a competent, pacy and skilful right-sided midfielder, he also has the ability to deliver long-throws into the opposition's box.

Colchester U (Free from Haverhill Rov on

20/11/86) FL 150+2/22 FLC 6 FAC 7+2/4 Others 9+3/3
Cambridge U (£65,000 on 25/7/90) FL 79+2/7 FLC 6 FAC 8+1 Others 9
Hereford U (Free on 20/7/94) FL 34+1/2 FLC 4 FAC 2 Others 2

WILKINSON Paul
Born: Louth, 30 October 1964
Height: 6'1" Weight: 12.4
Club Honours: CS '86; Div 1 '87, '95
International Honours: E: U21-4

Fearless Middlesbrough front-runner, who struck up a great partnership with John Hendrie and every other forward with whom he played with last season, "Wilko" has long perfected the skill of knocking-on glancing headers for his striking partners to take advantage of. In last season's First Division Championship success, he was the epitome of guts and hard working endeavour, and his heroic displays, coupled with the injuries he suffered beyond the call of normal duty, saw his "stock" rise even further.

Grimsby T (From apprentice on 8/11/82) FL 69+2/27 FLC 10/5 FAC 4+2/1
Everton (£250,000 on 28/3/85) FL 19+12/7 FLC 3+1/7 FAC 3/1 Others 6+2/1
Nottingham F (£200,000 on 26/3/87) FL 32+2/5 FLC 3/1 FAC 4+1/1/2 Others 1
Watford (£300,000 on 16/8/88) FL 133+1/52 FLC 4/1 FAC 8+1 Others 8/3
Middlesbrough (£550,000 on 16/8/91) F/PL 159+4/12 FLC 16/8 FAC 11/5 Others 5+1/4

WILKINSON Stephen (Steve) John
Born: Lincoln, 1 September 1968
Height: 6'0" Weight: 11.2

An impressive and talented two-footed Mansfield striker, who played the occasional game in midfield, Steve had a marvellous season in 1994-95 and was named the club's "Player of the Year". A pacy performer, he played consistently well throughout the campaign and made considerable efforts to improve his all-round games in order to benefit the team. Scored a hat-trick against Chesterfield.

Leicester C (From apprentice on 6/9/86) FL 5+4/1 FAC 1
Crewe Alex (Loaned on 8/9/88) FL 3+2/2
Mansfield T (£80,000 on 2/10/89) FL 214+18/83 FLC 13+1/4 FAC 10+1/2 Others 17/1

WILLIAMS Adrian
Born: Reading, 16 August 1971
Height: 6'2" Weight: 12.6
Club Honours: Div 2 '94
International Honours: W: 5

The first player to progress from Reading's Centre of Excellence to full international level, he is now a regular member of the Welsh squad. As club captain, and a powerful and dominant centre-back sought by many Premier clubs, Adrian had a long spell out last season with a neck injury, but returned to score some important goals, including one at Wembley. Has played in every position, including goalkeeper, for the club's first team.

Reading (From trainee on 4/3/89) FL 160+5/12 FLC 14/1 FAC 14/2 Others 14/2

WILLIAMS Andrew (Andy)
Born: Birmingham, 29 July 1962
Height: 6'0" Weight: 11.10
Club Honours: Div 2 '90

Like his fellow Rotherham midfielder, Shaun Goodwin, Andy was enjoying an excellent spell of form when he sustained the knee injury at the end of November which was to keep him out for the rest of last season. Freed during the summer.

Coventry C (£20,000 from Solihull Borough on 24/7/85) FL 3+6 Others 0+1
Rotherham U (Signed on 16/10/86) FL 87/13 FLC 8 FAC 6 Others 5/2
Leeds U (£175,000 on 11/11/88) FL 25+21/3 FLC 3+3 FAC 2 Others 5+2/2
Port Vale (Loaned on 11/12/91) FL 5
Notts Co (£115,000 on 4/2/92) FL 32+7/2 FLC 3 FAC 1
Huddersfield T (Loaned on 13/9/93) FL 4+2
Rotherham U (Signed on 21/10/93) FL 51/2 FLC 2 FAC 3 Others 4

WILLIAMS Carey

Born: Sheffield, 22 February 1972
Height: 6'2" Weight: 12.11

Forward. Having joined Rotherham in the 1994 close season, Carey made just four appearances as a substitute, prior to being released during the summer.

Rotherham U (Free from Denaby U on 3/8/94) FL 0+2 FLC 0+2

WILLIAMS Carl Junior

Born: Cambridge, 14 January 1977
Height: 5'8" Weight: 12.10

Another product of Fulham's juniors and still a YTS player, Carl had one substitute outing in 1994-95 (at Colchester in the AWS). Small, but thick set, he is a competitive right-sided midfielder who loves to get forward and go for goal.

Fulham (Trainee) Others 0+1

WILLIAMS Christopher (Chris) John

Born: Neath, 21 September 1976
Height: 5'11" Weight: 11.0
International Honours: W: Yth

Limited to a single start and four substitute outings in 1994-95, when the squad was depleted, this young Hereford centre-forward was given a free transfer by the club at the end of the season.

Hereford U (From trainee on 16/9/94) FL 1+3 FLC 1 FAC 0+1 Others 0+1

WILLIAMS Darren

Born: Middlesbrough, 28 April 1977
Height: 5'10" Weight: 10.10

Promising young midfielder, cum striker, and still a trainee, Darren came on as sub for his York debut in 1994-95.

York C (Trainee) FL 0+1

WILLIAMS David Peter

Born: Liverpool, 18 September 1968
Height: 6'0" Weight: 12.0

Goalkeeper. Signed from Burnley early last season, he gave many superb performances for Cardiff and was undoubtedly the club's "Player of the Year". Unfortunately, his season came to a premature end when breaking his ribs in the Welsh Cup against Swansea.

Oldham Ath (From trainee on 15/8/87)
Burnley (Signed on 23/3/88) FL 24 FLC 2 Others 2
Rochdale (Loaned on 2/9/91) FL 6 FLC 1
Cardiff C (Free on 12/8/94) FL 40 FLC 2 FAC 1 Others 8

WILLIAMS Dean Anton

Born: Hampstead, 14 November 1970
Height: 6'1" Weight: 13.0

Centre-forward. Having been released by Brentford at the end of 1993-94, and subsequently playing for Stevenage Borough in the Conference, Dean had trials with Doncaster on a non-contract basis last September. However, after being substituted at half-time in his one and only appearance, he signed for non-league Aylesbury.

Cambridge U (Trainee) FL 1 FLC 0+1
Brentford (£14,000 from St Albans C, via Hemel Hempstead, Chesham U & Wokingham T, on 28/7/93) FL 2+1/1 (Free to Stevenage Borough on 12/5/94)
Doncaster Rov (Free on 22/9/94) FL 1

WILLIAMS Dean Paul

Born: Lichfield, 5 January 1972
Height: 6'0" Weight: 12.8

Excellent Doncaster goalkeeper who occupied the 'keepers jersey for the majority of last season with some distinction. Agile and a good shot stopper, Dean, who came from Brentford on a free transfer in the summer of 1994, shows all the attributes of a top class goalie.

Birmingham C (From trainee on 11/7/90) FL 4 FAC 1 (Free to Tamworth in March 1992)
Brentford (£2,000 on 8/8/93) FL 6+1
Doncaster Rov (Free on 12/8/94) FL 33+2 FLC 1 FAC 1 Others 3

WILLIAMS Gareth James

Born: Isle of Wight, 12 March 1967
Height: 5'10" Weight: 11.8

A much travelled striker, and a convert to midfield, who was released by Barnsley early into last season after recovering from an operation in the summer. Given trials at both Wolverhampton and Bournemouth, where he appeared in the first team, he quickly moved on to Northampton, but found his chances limited, making just 17 starts.

Aston Villa (£30,000 from Gosport Borough on 9/1/88) FL 6+6 FLC 0+1 FAC 2 Others 0+1
Barnsley (£200,000 on 6/8/91) FL 23+11/6 FLC 1 FAC 1+1 Others 1+1
Hull C (Loaned on 17/9/92) FL 4
Hull C (Loaned on 6/1/94) FL 16/2
Wolverhampton W (Free on 23/8/94)
Bournemouth (Free on 16/9/94) FL 0+1
Northampton T (Free on 27/9/94) FL 13+2 FAC 1 Others 3

WILLIAMS David Geraint

Born: Treorchy, 5 January 1962
Height: 5'7" Weight: 10.6
Club Honours: Div 2 '87
International Honours: W: 12; U21-2; Yth

Tenacious, hard-tackling Ipswich midfielder who is always in the thick of things, George, as he is known by, began last season as club captain, but missed three games because of injury just after Christmas. Restored to the side, but not the captaincy, he was at his best when hurrying opponents into losing possession. Scored his first ever goal for the club in the 2-0 win over Leeds, when he fired home from Bontcho Guentchev's cross.

Bristol Rov (From apprentice on 12/1/80) FL 138+3/8 FLC 14 FAC 9+2/2 Others 5
Derby Co (£40,000 on 29/3/85) FL 276+1/9 FLC 26+1/1 FAC 17 Others 11
Ipswich T (£650,000 on 1/7/92) PL 109/1 FLC 9+1 FAC 9

WILLIAMS John Nelson

Born: Birmingham, 11 May 1968
Height: 6'2" Weight: 12.4

The speedy Coventry winger, cum striker, made six brief and sporadic appearances as substitute in 1994-95, before making the starting line-up at Forest last Easter. Loaned out to Notts County, Stoke and Swansea with some success, his pace and ability to get past his man are his prime assets.

Swansea C (£5,000 from Cradley T on 19/8/91) FL 36+3/11 FLC 2+1 FAC 3 Others 1
Coventry C (£250,000 on 1/7/92) PL 66+14/11 FLC 4 FAC 2
Swansea C (Loaned on 2/7/94) FL 6+1/2
Notts Co (Loaned on 7/10/94) FL 3+2/2
Stoke C (Loaned on 23/12/94) FL 1+3

WILLIAMS Lee

Born: Birmingham, 3 February 1973
Height: 5'7" Weight: 11.13
International Honours: E: Yth; Sch

Peterborough player who is equally at home in midfield, or at full-back, and is both skilful and industrious, Lee is also a good reader of the game.

Aston Villa (From trainee on 26/1/91)
Shrewsbury T (Loaned on 8/11/92) FL 2+1 FAC 1+1/1 Others 2
Peterborough U (Signed on 23/3/94) FL 51+7/1 FLC 1+1 FAC 2/1 Others 2

WILLIAMS Marc Lloyd

Born: Bangor, 8 February 1973
Height: 5'10" Weight: 10.12

A striker with a big goalscoring reputation in non-league soccer, Marc was signed by Stockport last March and made his FL debut when coming on at Rotherham for Matthew Bound in the 81st minute of the final game of last season.

Stockport Co (£10,000 from Bangor on 23/3/95) FL 0+1

WILLIAMS Mark Stuart

Born: Hyde, 28 September 1970
Height: 6'0" Weight: 13.0
Club Honours: Div 3 '94

Consistent Shrewsbury central defender who quietly gets on with the task, Mark is a strong header of the ball and likes to get forward at set pieces. His effectiveness is highlighted by his unobtrusiveness.

Shrewsbury T (Free from Newtown on 27/3/92) FL 96+7/3 FLC 7+1 FAC 6 Others 6/1

WILLIAMS Martin Keith

Born: Luton, 12 July 1973
Height: 5'9" Weight: 11.2

Fast, attacking Luton midfielder who had very few opportunities in 1994-95, he was most unlucky to break his nose in a reserve match when in line for a first team recall last January. A few late sub appearances was all he could muster and he spent a spell on loan at Colchester, before being granted a free transfer at the end of the season.

Luton T (Free from Leicester C juniors on 13/9/91) FL 12+28/2 FLC 1 FAC 0+1 Others 2+1
Colchester U (Loaned on 9/3/95) FL 3

WILLIAMS Michael (Mike) Anthony
Born: Bradford, 21 November 1969
Height: 5'10" Weight: 11.6
Starting 1994-95 in Sheffield Wednesday's reserve side, and having played very few senior games, he was finally given the call towards the end of the season and kept his place. Right-sided, with pace, and good ability on the ball, Mike, like several others on the staff, would prefer a more central role, but it is the wide position that he looks best suited to. Needs to build on last season's performances to fully realise his potential.
Sheffield Wed (Free from Maltby Colliery on 13/2/91) F/PL 14+3/11 FLC 1+1 Others 1
Halifax T (Loaned on 18/12/92) FL 9/1

WILLIAMS Michael John
Born: Mansfield, 3 November 1976
Height: 5'11" Weight: 10.12
Still a trainee, Mansfield introduced this young midfield player as a sub towards the end of last season and have high hopes of him.
Mansfield T (Trainee) FL 0+1

WILLIAMS Paul Andrew
Born: Sheffield, 8 September 1963
Height: 6'3" Weight: 14.6
International Honours: NI: 1; Yth
Tall Rochdale striker who made an excellent start to last season with five goals in the first 11 games. Briefly filled in at the back after Alan Reeves' departure and even substituted in goal, but was then ruled out by a long-term injury.
Preston NE (Free from Nuneaton Borough on 18/12/86) FL 1 Others 1
Carlisle U (Free on 17/7/87)
Newport Co (Free on 12/8/87) FL 26/3 FLC 2 Others 2
Sheffield U (£17,000 on 7/3/88) FL 6+2 Others 2+1
Hartlepool U (Free on 10/10/89) FL 7+1 FAC 1 Others 1
Stockport Co (Free on 23/8/90) FL 24/14 FLC 2/1 Others 3/1
West Bromwich A (£250,000 on 28/3/91) FL 26+18/5 FLC 1+1 FAC 1+2/1 Others 1+2/1
Coventry C (Loaned on 23/10/92) PL 1+1
Stockport Co (£25,000 on 12/1/93) FL 6+10/3 Others 5/1
Rochdale (Free on 5/11/93) FL 21+4/7 FLC 1 FAC 1 Others 2

WILLIAMS Paul Anthony
Born: Stratford, 16 August 1965
Height: 5'7" Weight: 10.3
Club Honours: FLC '91; Div 1 '94
International Honours: E: U21-4
Crystal Palace striker with tremendous pace. A player who, at his best, seems to come alive in the penalty area, Paul never really figured in Alan Smith's plans last season, managing only four appearances and, early in the New Year, was loaned out to first Sunderland, then Birmingham.
Charlton Ath (£12,000 from Woodford T on 23/2/87) FL 74+8/23 FLC 6/3 FAC 6+1/3
Brentford (Loaned on 20/10/87) FL 7/3 Others 1/3
Sheffield Wed (£700,000 on 15/8/90) F/PL

78+15/25 FLC 10+3/3 FAC 3+2 Others 3
Crystal Palace (Signed on 11/9/92) F/PL 38+8/7 FLC 4+1 Others 2/2
Sunderland (Loaned on 19/1/95) FL 3
Birmingham C (Loaned on 13/3/95) FL 8+3 Others 1/1

Paul Williams (Derby) Neal Simpson
(Empics Sports Photo Agency)

WILLIAMS Paul Darren
Born: Burton, 26 March 1971
Height: 5'11" Weight: 12.0
International Honours: E: U21-6
Inspirational Derby central defender, cum midfielder, who was injured after the opening game of last season at Barnsley, his return in mid-September coincided with an improved defensive record as he formed a solid partnership with Craig Short. His determination to succeed was best demonstrated by his crucial Coca Cola Cup goal against Reading, when bursting through several penalty box challenges to shoot home. After the transfer of Gordon Cowans to "Wolves", he was appointed team captain.
Derby Co (From trainee on 13/7/89) FL 153+7/26 FLC 10+2/2 FAC 8/3 Others 14+1/2
Lincoln C (Loaned on 9/11/89) FL 3 FAC 2 Others 1

WILLIAMS Paul Leslie
Born: Liverpool, 25 September 1970
Height: 6'0" Weight: 11.0
Finally getting into the Doncaster first team picture towards the end of last season, after 18 months out of the game with a viral complaint, Paul showed himself to be a hard-running midfielder, who loves to get forward in support of the attack.
Sunderland (From trainee on 21/7/89) FL 6+4 FLC 1 Others 2
Swansea C (Loaned on 28/3/91) FL 12/1
Doncaster Rov (Free on 14/7/93) FL 6+2

WILLIAMS Paul Richard Curtis
Born: Leicester, 11 September 1969
Height: 5'7" Weight: 10.7

Played just seven times for Coventry last season, as cover for Steve Morgan and was twice loaned out to Huddersfield, initially to stand-in for the injured Tom Cowan in November and, again in March, when the same player was suspended. Proving something of a lucky talisman, Town losing only once during his time there, it is probable that he would have been signed permanently were the club not already well served in the left-back position.
Leicester C (From trainee on 1/7/88)
Stockport Co (Free on 5/7/89) FL 61+9/4 FLC 3 FAC 4 Others 7+5/1
Coventry C (£150,000 on 12/8/93) PL 8+6 FLC 1+1 FAC 3
West Bromwich A (Loaned on 19/11/93) FL 5
Huddersfield T (Loaned on 17/11/94)
Huddersfield T (Loaned on 17/3/95) FL 9 Others 1

WILLIAMS Scott John
Born: Bangor, 7 August 1974
Height: 6'0" Weight: 11.0
International Honours: W: U21-5
Beginning to stake a claim for a regular Wrexham first team place, Scott is tall for a midfield player, but is very composed and has a cool head, with good distribution. A regular in the Welsh U21 team managed by Brian Flynn and Joey Jones, he was praised by his manager towards the end of the season for his defensive central midfield qualities.
Wrexham (From trainee on 2/7/93) FL 20+5 FLC 1 Others 2+2

WILLIAMS Steven (Steve) David
Born: Cardigan, 16 October 1974
Height: 6'3" Weight: 12.12
As his Cardiff namesake, a goalie, Steve made a rather edgy start to last season and spent most of his time on the bench. He came good, however, when brought on as a substitute in the Welsh Cup semi-final and saved a Steve Torpey penalty.
Cardiff C (Free from Coventry C juniors on 13/8/93) FL 24 FAC 1 Others 5+1

WILLIAMS Steven (Steve) Robert
Born: Sheffield, 3 November 1975
Height: 6'1" Weight: 11.7
Promising young Lincoln striker who had the misfortune to suffer torn ankle ligaments just 13 minutes into his first full League game last season, he eventually recovered fitness and came back to net the equaliser in the 3-3 home draw with Scunthorpe.
Lincoln C (From trainee on 11/6/94) FL 7+7/2 FAC 0+1 Others 0+2

WILLIAMSON Daniel (Danny) Alan
Born: West Ham, 5 December 1973
Height: 5'11" Weight: 12.3
A young local born West Ham midfielder, who is being tipped for a big future, Danny had an outstanding game in the 2-1 win at Leicester and ended last season with four appearances to his credit. Should become a regular with experience.
West Ham U (From trainee on 3/7/92) PL 6+1/1
Doncaster Rov (Loaned on 8/10/93) FL 10+3/1 FAC 2/2 Others 1

WILLIS James (Jimmy) Anthony
Born: Liverpool, 12 July 1968
Height: 6'0" Weight: 12.4
Club Honours: GMVC '90

Popular right-footed Leicester central defender who suffered the ignominity of scoring own goals in successive fixtures against QPR and Wimbledon, he finally got on the scoresheet at the right end in the return fixture with the "Dons", followed by a superb strike to earn a point against Chelsea. Always gave 100 per-cent, alongside a variety of partners.
Halifax T (Free from Blackburn Rov juniors on 21/8/86)
Stockport Co (Free on 30/12/87) FL 10
Darlington (£12,000 on 24/3/88) FL 90/6 FLC 5 FAC 5 Others 6/1
Leicester C (£100,000 on 20/12/91) F/PL 47+1/3 FLC 3 FAC 4 Others 5+1
Bradford C (Loaned on 26/3/92) FL 9/1

WILLIS Roger Christopher
Born: Sheffield, 17 June 1967
Height: 6'2" Weight: 12.0
Club Honours: GMVC '91

"Harry" joined Southend from Birmingham last September and immediately showed his good passing and crossing abilities, allied to excellent heading. A knee injury forced him to miss out on the end of season relegation battle, but he will be remembered for his 90th minute equalising goal in a 2-2 draw at Notts County, after Southend had played for 60 minutes with nine men.
Grimsby T (Signed on 20/7/89) FL 1+8 FLC 0+1
Barnet (£10,000 on 1/8/90) FL 39+5/13 FLC 2 FAC 5+1/3 Others 1+4/1
Watford (£175,000 on 6/10/92) FL 30+6/2 FAC 1
Birmingham C (£150,000 on 31/12/93) FL 12+7/5 FAC 0+1
Southend U (Signed on 16/9/94) FL 21/4 FAC 1

WILMOT Rhys James
Born: Newport, 21 February 1962
Height: 6'1" Weight: 12.0
International Honours: W: U21-6; Sch

An experienced goalkeeper of many years standing, Rhys finally got the opportunity to come back to the top flight, after ten years away, when transferring from Grimsby to Crystal Palace, immediately prior to the start of last season, as cover for Nigel Martyn. Given ten minutes at Nottingham Forest, after Martyn was injured, he came into the side for the next six weeks, including the losing FA Cup semi-final replay against Manchester United. Reliable, and without frills, at no stage did he let the club down.
Arsenal (From apprentice on 8/2/80) FL 8 FLC 1
Hereford U (Loaned on 18/3/83) FL 9
Leyton Orient (Loaned on 27/5/84) FL 46 FLC 4 FAC 4 Others 3
Swansea C (Loaned on 26/8/88) FL 16
Plymouth Arg (£100,000 on 23/2/89) FL 133 FLC 8 FAC 2 Others 4
Grimsby T (£87,500 on 1/7/92) FL 33 FLC 4 FAC 4 Others 2
Crystal Palace (£80,000 on 9/8/94) PL 5+1 FAC 1

WILSON Clive Euclid Aklana
Born: Manchester, 13 November 1961
Height: 5'7" Weight: 10.0
Club Honours: Div 2 '89

Very experienced QPR defender, who is just as capable in midfield, and who is widely thought of as the best uncapped left-back in the Premiership. Excellent at getting forward and a superb crosser of the ball, last season started off disastrously for him at Old Trafford when he was sent off after just seven minutes, a victim of the new FIFA directives to referees. Scored four goals, including a last minute penalty against Millwall in the FA Cup Fifth Round to ensure a 1-0 victory. Stop Press: Joined Tottenham on a free transfer.
Manchester C (From juniors on 8/12/79) FL 107+2/9 FLC 9/2 FAC 2 Others 5
Chester C (Loaned on 16/9/82) FL 21/2
Chelsea (£250,000 on 19/3/87) FL 68+13/5 FLC 3+3 FAC 4 Others 10+2
Queens Park R (£450,000 on 4/7/90) F/PL 170+2/12 FLC 16/1 FAC 8/1 Others 2+1

WILSON Daniel (Danny) Joseph
Born: Wigan, 1 January 1960
Height: 5'7" Weight: 10.3
Club Honours: FLC '88, '89
International Honours: NI: 25

His influence on Barnsley, both as manager and player, was unbelievable in 1994-95. On the pitch, apart from having a fine season in midfield as a player where his passing at times was a joy to watch, he cajoled the rest of the team into the football playing unit he wanted. Barnsley were poorer for not having him in the side, when injured or suspended.
Bury (Free from Wigan Ath on 21/9/77) FL 87+3/8 FLC 4 FAC 11/2
Chesterfield (£100,000 on 22/7/80) FL 100/13 FLC 8/1 FAC 9/1
Nottingham F (£50,000 on 24/1/83) FL 9+1/1 Others 0+1
Scunthorpe U (Loaned on 7/10/83) FL 6/3
Brighton & Hove A (£100,000 on 30/11/83) FL 132+3/33 FLC 7/3 FAC 10/1 Others 3/2
Luton T (£150,000 on 16/7/87) FL 110/24 FLC 20/3 FAC 8/2 Others 4
Sheffield Wed (£200,000 on 8/8/90) F/PL 91+7/11 FLC 22/2 FAC 9+1 Others 5+2/1
Barnsley (£200,000 on 1/7/93) FL 77/2 FLC 6 FAC 5 Others 1

WILSON Eugene (Gus) Anthony
Born: Manchester, 11 April 1963
Height: 5'11" Weight: 11.8

A player who can perform across the defence, Gus is more effective for Crewe when adopting the sweeper role. Played fewer games than normal during 1994-95 and was released at the end of the season.
Crewe Alex (Free from Runcorn on 31/7/91) FL 112+3 FLC 11+1 FAC 12 Others 16+2

WILSON Kevin James
Born: Banbury, 18 April 1961
Height: 5'7" Weight: 10.10
Club Honours: Div 2 '89; FMC '90
International Honours: NI: 42

Skilful ball-player with determination and staying power, who has proved his ability to both make and score goals at every level. Joined Walsall as player-coach from Notts County prior to the start of last season and two goals on his home debut set the tone for a magnificent season, in which his goal tally of 23 was the highest of a long career. For good measure, Kevin was capped by Northern Ireland for the 41st time and was an ever-present for the club in the Endsleigh League.

Derby Co (£20,000 from Banbury U on 21/12/79) FL 106+16/30 FLC 8+3/8 FAC 8/3
Ipswich T (£100,000 on 5/1/85) FL 94+4/34 FLC 8/8 FAC 10/3 Others 7/4
Chelsea (£335,000 on 25/6/87) FL 124+28/42 FLC 10+2/4 FAC 7+1/1 Others 14+5/8
Notts Co (£225,000 on 27/3/92) FL 58+11/3 FLC 3+1 FAC 2 Others 5+1
Bradford C (Loaned on 13/1/94) FL 5
Walsall (Free on 4/8/94) FL 42/16 FLC 4/2 FAC 4/3 Others 2

WILSON Paul Adam
Born: Maidstone, 22 February 1977
Height: 5'8" Weight: 11.0

An inside-forward of stocky build, he made his FL debut for Gillingham when coming on as a sub in the 3-0 defeat at Scunthorpe last season. Still a YTS at the time, Paul finished as top-scorer for the club's South-Eastern Counties side.
Gillingham (From trainee on 25/4/95) FL 0+2

WILSON Paul Anthony
Born: Bradford, 2 August 1968
Height: 5'10" Weight: 10.6

A hard-tackling left-back, Paul came to York from Burnley last November, following a spell on loan. Initially, he showed fine form and, on a couple of occasions, also impressed in the centre of defence, before a lean period towards the end of the season saw him lose his place in the side.
Huddersfield T (From apprentice on 12/6/86) FL 15 FLC 1
Norwich C (£30,000 on 23/7/87)
Northampton T (£30,000 on 12/2/88) FL 132+4/9/6 FLC 10/1 FAC 7 Others 6+3
Halifax T (£30,000 on 19/12/91) FL 45/7 FLC 2 FAC 1 Others 2
Burnley (Signed on 1/2/93) FL 31 FAC 0+1
York C (Signed on 6/10/94) FL 21+1 FAC 2 Others 1

WILSON Paul Robert
Born: Forest Gate, 26 September 1964
Height: 5'9" Weight: 10.11
Club Honours: GMVC '91

Struggled to find a roll in the team early last season but, eventually, was the main reason Barnet made a late push for promotion. Is a real powerhouse in the centre of midfield when the chips are down.
Barnet (Signed from Barking on 1/3/88) FL 101+3/7 FLC 6 FAC 14+1 Others 6+2

WILSON Stephen (Steve) Lee
Born: Hull, 24 April 1974
Height: 5'10" Weight: 10.7

Hull have no worries when Alan Fettis goes off on international duty, as Steve is a more than able deputy. Indeed, he retained the number one shirt from last October to the end of January. Good reflexes and anticipation, he cuts a willowy figure but, with age and experience, he is developing a stronger frame.
Hull C (From trainee on 13/7/92) FL 40 FLC 23 FAC 3 Others 5

WINDASS Dean
Born: Hull, 1 April 1969
Height: 5'9" Weight: 12.3

Hull's captain during Greg Abbott's lengthy absence, Dean is an outstanding all-round performer. Usually partnering Linton Brown in attack, he is equally adept in centre-midfield or his preferred "free" role behind the front two where he is given license to display his full range of talents. Two-footed (favouring his right), the charismatic local hero is certainly more than capable of playing at a higher level.

Hull C (Free from North Ferriby U on 24/10/91) FL 157+3/53 FLC 7/1 FAC 6 Others 9/2

WINSTANLEY Mark Andrew
Born: St Helens, 22 January 1968
Height: 6'1" Weight: 12.4
Club Honours: AMC '89

An experienced and dependable centre-back for ten years with Bolton, he slotted easily into Burnley's defence alongside Steve Davis, after signing for the club last August. Very much the traditional defensive centre-half, Mark scored twice when Burnley won at Millwall in September.

Bolton W (From trainee on 22/7/86) FL 215+5/3 FLC 19+1 FAC 19 Others 26/3
Burnley (Signed on 5/8/94) FL 44/2 FLC 4 FAC 5

WINSTONE Simon John
Born: Bristol, 4 October 1974
Height: 5'7" Weight: 10.7

Released by Stoke during the 1994 close season without making a first team appearance, the young left-sided defender joined Torquay as a non-contract player. Specifically on trial, he appeared twice early on, prior to moving back to the Midlands with Telford.

Stoke C (From trainee on 12/7/93)
Torquay U (Free on 30/9/94) FL 1+1

WINTERBURN Nigel
Born: Nuneaton, 11 December 1963
Height: 5'10" Weight: 11.4
Club Honours: Div 1 '89, '91; FAC '93; FLC '93; ECWC '94
International Honours: E: 2; B-3; U21-1; Yth

Strong-tackling Arsenal left-back who, like his partner, Lee Dixon, missed just three PL games last season. Also like his team-mate, he loves getting forward to supply crosses to the front men, and relishes quick one-twos that take him clear of the opposition. An ever-present in the "Gunners'" European campaign and noted for his ability to throw the ball into the danger zone, his excellent left-foot allows him to play both short and long balls with accuracy.

Birmingham C (From apprentice on 14/8/81)
Wimbledon (Free on 22/9/83) FL 164+1/8 FLC 13 FAC 12 Others 2
Arsenal (£407,000 on 26/5/87) F/PL 271+1/5 FLC 35/3 FAC 30 Others 30

WISE Dennis Frank
Born: Kensington, 15 December 1966
Height: 5'6" Weight: 9.5
Club Honours: FAC '88
International Honours: E: 8; B-3; U21-1

Dennis' brilliant form for Chelsea last season, ultimately saw him in a starring role for Terry Venables' England side against Nigeria, having earlier been recalled for the Romanian game. When making nearly 50 passes during the match, it was later confirmed that 95 per-cent of them had been accurate; a fabulous statistic for an international match. One on the best dead-ball experts in the country, he normally operates in a wide-right role, delivering superb crosses that can be bent either way to confuse goalies. Lost his England place following a well documented off the field incident, and then picked up an injury to his right leg that necessitated an operation in the final week of a campaign that had somewhat soured. A "bubbly" character, he is sure to come back in positive fashion.

Wimbledon (Free from Southampton juniors on 28/3/85) FL 127+8/27 FLC 14 FAC 11/3 Others 5
Chelsea (£1,600,000 on 3/7/90) F/PL 150+2/27 FLC 19/6 FAC 11/2 Others 10/3

WITHE Christopher (Chris)
Born: Liverpool, 25 September 1962
Height: 5'10" Weight: 11.12
Club Honours: Div 3 '85, '94

A consistent left-back, with a keeness to get forward and play some decisive balls into the box, he scored his first goal for Shrewsbury last New Years day at Huddersfield and his celebration "Crow Dance", since seen on Gay Meadow for the same reason, was breathtaking!

Newcastle U (From apprentice on 10/10/80) FL 2
Bradford C (Free on 1/6/83) FL 141+2/2 FLC 14 FAC 7 Others 6
Notts Co (£50,000 on 2/10/87) FL 80/3 FLC 4 FAC 5 Others 12/1
Bury (£40,000 on 31/7/89) FL 22+9/1 FLC 2+2 Others 0+3
Chester C (Loaned on 18/10/90) FL 2
Mansfield T (Signed on 24/1/91) FL 75+1/5 FLC 4 FAC 1 Others 2
Shrewsbury T (Free on 11/8/93) FL 50+7/2 FLC 5+2 FAC 2 Others 2+1

WITSCHGE Richard
Born: Amsterdam, Holland, 20 September 1969
Height: 6'0" Weight: 11.7
International Honours: Holland

With the 1995 transfer deadline rapidly approaching, and Blackburn aware that they would be without Jason Wilcox for the rest of the season, they moved to sign the former Dutch international on loan from Bordeaux. A left-sided midfielder, comfortable in possession, and a threat from dead-ball situations, Richard made his PL debut at West Ham but, apart from showing a penchant for hard-tackling, he was never in the game as an attacking force and returned to France soon after.

Blackburn Rov (Loaned from Bordeaux on 23/3/95) PL 1

WITTER Anthony (Tony) Junior
Born: London, 12 August 1965
Height: 6'1" Weight: 13.0

Signed for Millwall last December after a period on loan in the centre of the defence, Tony can use either foot, has a very fast turn of pace and is cool and calm under pressure. Showed great form in the FA Cup-ties against Arsenal and Chelsea.

Crystal Palace (£10,000 from Grays Ath on 24/10/90)
Queens Park R (£125,000 on 19/8/91) PL 1
Plymouth Arg (Loaned on 9/1/92) FL 3/1

Reading (Loaned on 11/2/94) FL 4
Millwall (£100,000 on 14/10/94)·FL 26+1/1 FLC 1 FAC 5

WOAN Ian Simon
Born: Heswall, 14 December 1967
Height: 5'10" Weight: 12.4

Another Nottingham Forest man who has had more than his fair share of injury problems, Ian is a talented left-footer who can play anywhere down the left-flank. With a wide range of passing skills and good touch, he can chip or drive balls in, whatever the fancy. Came back into the side last October, following Kingsley Black contacting a virus, and remained, playing his part in the club's rise to third place in the Premiership.

Nottingham F (£80,000 from Runcorn on 14/3/90) F/PL 114+8/21 FLC 10+2/1 FAC 10+1/1 Others 5/1

WOOD Paul Anthony
Born: Saltburn, 1 November 1964
Height: 5'9" Weight: 11.3

Portsmouth forward/midfielder. Paul missed the start of last season following an ankle operation, but came back to play in a handful of games prior to Christmas, before getting injured again. In his second spell with the club he showed some bright form.

Portsmouth (From apprentice on 3/11/82) FL 25+22/6 FLC 5+3/1 FAC 2 Others 2+2/3
Brighton & Hove A (£40,000 on 28/8/87) FL 77+15/8 FLC 4 FAC 2+2 Others 5
Sheffield U (£90,000 on 9/2/90) FL 19+9/3 FLC 1 Others 1
Bournemouth (Loaned on 31/1/91) FL 20+1
Bournemouth (£40,000 on 3/10/91) FL 73+5/18 FLC 1+1 FAC 13/2 Others 5/2
Portsmouth (Signed on 18/2/94) FL 12+5/2 FAC 1

WOOD Stephen (Steve) Alan
Born: Bracknell, 2 February 1963
Height: 6'0" Weight: 12.7
Club Honours: Div 3 '86, Div 2 '88

Steve will have been disappointed with the 1994-95 season, as he suffered from one injury after the other, making just three starts (and only one finish). A centre-back with a wealth of experience, which Oxford sadly missed, he joined the club during the 1994 close season from Southampton.

Reading (From apprentice on 19/2/81) FL 216+3/9 FLC 10 FAC 15 Others 4
Millwall (£80,000 on 17/6/87) FL 108+2 FLC 10 FAC 10 Others 3+1
Southampton (£400,000 on 9/10/91) F/PL 46 FLC 1+1 FAC 3/1 Others 4
Oxford U (Free on 20/7/94) FL 2 Others 1

WOOD Trevor John
Born: Jersey, 3 November 1968
Height: 6'0" Weight: 12.6

A free signing from Port Vale during the 1994 close season, he proved to be a brave, alert and agile goalkeeper for Walsall, with good hands. Seventeen clean sheets in 50 games gives some indication of his value to the team and his consistency was a major contribution to Walsall gaining automatic promotion from Division Three. To cap a fine season, his excellent displays saw him called into the Republic of Ireland squad.

Brighton & Hove A (From apprentice on 7/11/86)

Port Vale (Free on 8/7/88) FL 42 FLC 4 FAC 2 Others 2
Walsall (Free on 18/7/94) FL 39 FLC 4 FAC 5 Others 2

WOODMAN Andrew (Andy) John
Born: Camberwell, 11 August 1971
Height: 6'1" Weight: 12.4
Goalkeeper. Cool, in command of his area, and excellent with crosses, Andy joined Northampton from Exeter last March. Never really settled in the west country due to suspension and the form of Peter Fox.
Crystal Palace (From trainee on 1/7/89)
Exeter C (Free on 4/7/94) FL 6 FLC 1 FAC 1 Others 2
Northampton T (Free on 10/3/95) FL 10

WOODS Christopher (Chris) Charles Eric
Born: Boston, 14 November 1959
Height: 6'2" Weight: 13.5
Club Honours: Div 2 '86; FLC '78, '85; SPD '87, '89, '90, '91; SLC '87, '89, '91
International Honours: E: 43; U21-6; Yth
A goalkeeper who has had a bad time with injuries over the past two years, losing both his Sheffield Wednesday and England places, at one stage last season, Chris thought he would have to leave Hillsborough in order to get a game. However, towards the end of 1994-95, he regained his jersey following the 1-7 drubbing at the hands of Nottingham Forest. Taking full advantage of the opportunity, he played really well and has recently signed a new contract.
Nottingham F (From apprentice on 1/12/76) FLC 7
Queens Park R (£250,000 on 4/7/79) FL 63 FLC 8 FAC 1
Norwich C (£225,000 on 12/3/81) FL 216 FLC 26 FAC 19 Others 6
Glasgow R (£600,000 on 2/7/86) SL 173 SLC 21 SC 15 Others 21
Sheffield Wed (£1,200,000 on 15/8/91) F/PL 98+1 FLC 13 FAC 10 Others 5

WOODS Neil Stephen
Born: Bradford, 30 July 1966
Height: 6'0" Weight: 12.11
A right-footed play-maker who is particularly adept at holding, shielding and laying off the ball. Very fast in the box, with quick reactions in front of goal, his absence during the vital run-in period, together with that of Clive Mendonca, was largely responsible for Grimsby fading from a challenge for a play-off spot.
Doncaster Rov (From apprentice on 31/8/83) FL 55+10/16 FLC 4/1 FAC 5+2/3
Glasgow R (£120,000 on 22/12/86) SL 0+3
Ipswich T (£120,000 on 3/8/87) FL 15+12/5 Others 4/1
Bradford C (Signed on 1/3/90) FL 13+1/2
Grimsby T (£82,000 on 23/8/90) FL 129+30/38 FLC 9+1/1 FAC 3 Others 7/1

WOODS Raymond (Ray) Guy
Born: Birkenhead, 7 June 1965
Height: 5'11" Weight: 10.0
Troubled by injury and illness last season, Ray was unable to obtain a continuous run in the side. A right-winger who takes on defences and crosses well into the box, the best of him is yet to be seen at Shrewsbury.
Tranmere Rov (From apprentice on 8/6/83) FL 9+5/2 FLC 1 Others 0+1 (Free to Bangor C in November 1984)

Wigan Ath (Free from Colne Dynamoes, via Northwich Victoria, Runcorn and Caernarfon, on 1/3/89) FL 25+3/3 FLC 2 FAC 4/1 Others 2
Coventry C (£200,000 on 30/1/91) FL 21/1 FLC 1 FAC 0+1
Wigan Ath (Loaned on 8/1/93) FL 12+1 Others 4/3
Shrewsbury T (Free on 23/3/94) FL 22+6/1 FLC 1 FAC 1 Others 2

WOODSFORD Jamie Marcus
Born: Ipswich, 9 November 1976
Height: 5'11" Weight: 11.10
International Honours: E: Yth
Reserve and youth team striker who made a first team debut for Luton as a substitute in a 1-0 away win against Port Vale last September, he continued to score regularly for the minor teams and was called up for England youth team training in October. Very much a name for the future.
Luton T (From trainee on 3/3/95) FL 1+6

WOODWARD Andrew (Andy) Stephen
Born: Stockport, 23 September 1973
Height: 5'11" Weight: 11.0
Unable to hold down a regular place at Crewe, with just two subs' appearances in 1994-95, Andy moved to Bury last March and, after just ten first team games, found himself playing at Wembley in the Third Division play-off final. A right-back, when coming to Gigg Lane he joined a back four with an average age of 22.
Crewe Alex (From trainee on 29/7/92) FL 9+11 FLC 2 Others 0+3
Bury (Signed on 13/3/95) FL 8 Others 3

WORBOYS Gavin Anthony
Born: Doncaster, 14 July 1974
Height: 6'2" Weight: 12.0
Young striker signed from Notts County last November, Gavin started at Darlington with five goals in his first four games. Strong in the air, with good skill on the ground, he ended as top-scorer with 11 goals, only two of those at home.
Doncaster Rov (From trainee on 1/4/92) FL 6+1/2
Notts Co (£100,000 on 1/5/92)
Exeter C (Loaned on 6/12/93) FL 4/1 Others 1/1
Darlington (Free on 1/11/94) FL 24+3/6 FAC 2/2 Others 2/3

WORRALL Benjamin (Ben) Joseph
Born: Swindon, 7 December 1975
Height: 5'4" Weight: 9.10
International Honours: E: Yth
A tiny, terrier-like Swindon midfield player, Ben started his first FL game for Town on the final day of last season at Wolverhampton, following two promising substitute displays.
Swindon T (From trainee on 8/7/94) FL 1+2

WORTHINGTON Nigel
Born: Ballymena, 4 November 1961
Height: 5'10" Weight: 12.6
Club Honours: FLC '91
International Honours: NI: 58; Yth
Signed by Leeds' manager, Howard Wilkinson, during the 1994 close season, for the third time in his career, this experienced left-sided player came to the club primarily as defensive and midfield cover. However, following an injury to Tony Dorigo, Nigel

made the left-back spot his own for the first 17 games and did well, before going back to the bench on the former's return to the side. An excellent squad member, when further called upon, he performed admirably and showed he has lost none of the old vigour.
Notts Co (£100,000 from Ballymena on 1/7/81) FL 62+5/4 FLC 11 FAC 4
Sheffield Wed (£125,000 on 6/2/84) F/PL 334+4/12 FLC 41/1 FAC 29 Others 9/1
Leeds U (£325,000 on 4/7/94) PL 21+6/1 FLC 2 FAC 3+1

WOTTON Paul Anthony
Born: Plymouth, 17 August 1977
Height: 5'11" Weight: 11.1
A young trainee midfielder who was undoubtedly the find of last season for Plymouth, he came into the team due to the injury list and remained in the squad on merit. Covers a lot of ground and has good passing ability and is certainly one for the future.
Plymouth Arg (Trainee) FL 5+2

WRACK Darren
Born: Cleethorpes, 5 May 1976
Height: 5'9" Weight: 11.10
Lively right-footed Derby winger who started off last season in the reserves. Injuries in the squad led to his eventual promotion to the subs' bench, from where he made his debut at Sunderland on New Year's Eve and, though not yet able to claim a regular place, his enthusiasm and ability to get wide and cross bodes well for his future. Scored with a well struck shot against Bristol City, his first goal for the club.
Derby Co (From trainee on 12/7/94) FL 2+14/1 FAC 0+1

WRIGHT Alan Geoffrey
Born: Ashton under Lyne, 28 September 1971
Height: 5'4" Weight: 9.4
International Honours: E: U21-2; Yth; Sch
Left-back who has the assets of a winger, with good control and excellent crossing ability. Having recovered from a hernia operation, and unable to oust Graham Le Saux from a Blackburn side riding high, Alan moved to Aston Villa just before last March's transfer deadline. One of the smallest defensive players around, something that has never held him back, he immediately settled in to an overlapping role down the left-flank with Steve Staunton.
Blackpool (From trainee on 13/4/89) FL 91+7 FLC 10+2 FAC 8 Others 11+2
Blackburn Rov (£400,000 on 25/10/91) F/PL 67+7/1 FLC 8 FAC 5+1 Others 3
Aston Villa (£1,000,000 on 10/3/95) PL 8

WRIGHT Ian Edward
Born: Woolwich, 3 November 1963
Height: 5'10" Weight: 11.8
Club Honours: FMC '91; FLC '93; FAC '93
International Honours: E: 20; B-3
Prolific Arsenal and England live-wire striker with electric pace. Scored 30 goals last season for the "Gunners", including nine in the European Cup Winners Cup, when he hit the target in every round apart from the Final. An invaluable player at club

level, especially in a side that looks to turn defence into attack and to hit the front men quickly, Ian is that rare commodity of being a scorer of great goals, as well as being a great goalscorer. And with tremendous self belief in his ability to take on defences up-and-down the country, even at 31-years-of-age he shows no signs of slowing down.
Crystal Palace (Free from Greenwich Borough on 2/8/85) FL 206+19/89 FLC 19/9 FAC 9+2/3 Others 19+3/16
Arsenal (£2,500,000 on 24/9/91) F/PL 129+2/80 FLC 18/16 FAC 12/11 Others 18/14

WRIGHT Ian Matthew
Born: Lichfield, 10 March 1972
Height: 6'1" Weight: 12.4

Central defender. Having failed to establish himself at Stoke, Ian found the same problem at Bristol Rovers when trying to displace Andy Tillson and Billy Clark. A good passer, suffering several injuries did not help his cause last season and he must hope for a trouble free 1995-96.
Stoke C (From trainee on 11/7/90) FL 6 FLC 1+1 Others 1
Bristol Rov (Signed on 23/9/93) FL 35+1/2 FAC 1 Others 3

WRIGHT Jermaine Malaki
Born: Greenwich, 21 October 1975
Height: 5'9" Weight: 10.13
International Honours: E: Yth

As a young right-winger, having failed to appear for the Millwall first team, he transferred to Wolverhampton at the end of last year. Made his debut as a sub and wasted no time at all in whipping in dangerous crosses.
Millwall (From trainee on 27/11/92)
Wolverhampton W (£60,000 on 29/12/94) FL 0+6 Others 0+1

WRIGHT Jonathan (Jon)
Born: Belfast, 24 November 1975
Height: 5'8" Weight: 11.0
International Honours: NI: B-1; Yth

Promising young Norwich right-back, and a

Ian Wright (Arsenal)

Steve Morton
(Empics Sports Photo Agency)

Northern Ireland youth international, Jon was included in the national "B" side to play Scotland last February. He had earlier made his City debut as a 74th minute substitute at Aston Villa, following an injury to Carl Bradshaw, and retained his place in the team that faced QPR a week later, before being forced off the field with a knee injury. However, the talented first year professional had regained his fitness by the end of the season, having performed consistently well in the reserves. Is very sound defensively and could have a good future.

Norwich C (From trainee on 1/7/94) PL 1+1

WRIGHT Mark

Born: Dorchester, 1 August 1963
Height: 6'3" Weight: 12.11
Club Honours: FAC '92
International Honours: E: 45; U21-4

Liverpool central defender and former England international. Following the signings of John Scales and Phil Babb, Mark spent most of last season in the reserves, making just six appearances for the first team. At his best, he was a player who always seemed to have plenty of time on the ball, was an accurate passer, and could attack the ball in the air at both ends of the field with relish. Now that Anfield is flush with centre-backs, he could provide more than useful service for any number of clubs in League football.

Oxford U (From juniors on 26/8/80) FL 8+2 FAC 1
Southampton (£80,000 on 25/3/82) FL 170/7 FLC 25/2 FAC 17/1 Others 10/1
Derby Co (£760,000 on 27/8/87) FL 144/10 FLC 15 FAC 5 Others 7
Liverpool (£2,200,000 on 15/7/91) F/PL 89+2/3 FLC 8+2 FAC 9 Others 8

WRIGHT Mark Andrew

Born: Manchester, 29 January 1970
Height: 5'11" Weight: 10.12

In 1994-95, his second season with Wigan, Mark showed himself to be a strong left-footed full-back, who enjoyed playing in an overlapping role. His appearances, however, were restricted following Graham Barrow's new signings and he was released at the end of the campaign.

Everton (From trainee on 10/6/88) FL 1
Blackpool (Loaned on 23/8/90) FL 3
Huddersfield T (Free on 21/3/91) FL 25+7/1 FLC 3 FAC 4+2 Others 1+3
Wigan Ath (Free on 25/11/93) FL 27+3/1 FLC 2 FAC 3 Others 1

WRIGHT Richard Ian

Born: Ipswich, 5 November 1977
Height: 6'2" Weight: 13.0
International Honours: E: Sch

Left-footed goalkeeper whose size belies his age, Richard made his Ipswich debut at home to Coventry last May and kept a clean sheet - only the third Ipswich had achieved all season. After making two wonderful saves from Dion Dublin, he kept his place for the remaining two fixtures and did enough to convince the fans that the long-term goalkeeping position is in safe hands.

Ipswich T (From trainee on 2/1/95) PL 3

WRIGHT Thomas (Tommy) Elliott

Born: Dunfermline, 10 January 1966
Height: 5'7" Weight: 11.4
International Honours: S: U21-1; Yth

A fast and tricky little winger, Tommy always gives 100 per-cent effort with gutsy performances, typical of his Fifeshire background. Surprisingly, in the light of his end of the previous season form, he only made one League start for Middlesbrough in 1994-95, prior to being released during the summer.

Leeds U (From apprentice on 15/1/83) FL 73+8/24 FLC 3+2/1 FAC 4/3
Oldham Ath (£80,000 on 24/10/86) FL 110+2/3 FLC 7+1/2 FAC 3/2 Others 3
Leicester C (£350,000 on 14/8/89) FL 122+7/22 FLC 7+1 FAC 4 Others 10/7
Middlesbrough (£650,000 on 1/7/92) F/PL 44+9/5 FLC 3+1 FAC 3/1 Others 5+1

WYATT Michael James

Born: Bristol, 12 September 1974
Height: 5'10" Weight: 11.3

Forward. Together with Matthew Hewlett, Michael was once heralded as the future of Bristol City, having come through the club's junior ranks in style. After making just one start last season, he was given a free transfer during the summer. Still has much ability and could yet make his mark with another League side.

Bristol C (From trainee on 7/7/93) FL 9+4 FLC 2 Others 1

YALLOP Frank Walter

Born: Watford, 4 April 1964
Height: 5'11" Weight: 12.0
International: E: Yth. Canada

Right-footed Ipswich full-back who has also played for Town in central defence, Frank currently performs the duties of sweeper for his chosen national side, Canada. Very experienced, he likes to get forward to support his attackers and possesses a strong shot. After a couple of seasons on the fringe of the first team scene, 1994-95 saw him back as a regular, missing only one game, and filling a variety of roles.

Ipswich T (From apprentice on 5/1/82) F/PL 286+23/7 FLC 22+2/1 FAC 14+2 Others 21+2

YATES Dean Richard

Born: Leicester, 26 October 1967
Height: 6'1" Weight: 12.0
Club Honours: AIC '95
International Honours: E: U21-5

A vastly experienced centre-back, Dean was signed from Notts County last January to team up again with Craig Short at Derby, after a long spell out of the game through injury. More a sweeper than a marker, he formed, initially, a three-man defensive unit with Short and Paul Williams, allowing greater freedom for the wide players in the side. However, he aggravated an old knee injury in April and missed the rest of the season.

Notts Co (From apprentice on 14/6/85) FL 312+2/3 FLC 24 FAC 20 Others 36/4
Derby Co (£350,000 on 26/1/95) FL 11/1

YATES Stephen (Steve)

Born: Bristol, 29 January 1970
Height: 5'11" Weight: 11.0
Club Honours: Div 3 '90

Began 1994-95 as partner to Alan McDonald in the heart of the QPR defence and really impressed after an unsettled first season. Kept his place until injury forced him out in December and for the remainder of the campaign he was used as substitute and playing across the back four when covering injuries. Scored his first goal for QPR at Aston Villa in a 1-2 defeat.

Bristol Rov (From trainee on 1/7/88) FL 196+1 FLC 9 FAC 11 Others 21
Queens Park R (£650,000 on 16/8/93) PL 49+3/1 FLC 3 FAC 2

YEBOAH Anthony

Born: Ghana, 6 June 1966
Height: 5'10" Weight: 13.11

Leeds' manager, Howard Wilkinson, had been determined to bring a world class striker to Elland Road last season and ultimately settled on Tony. Coming from the German Bundesliga, in a deal shrouded in mystery and red tape, some parts of the media reported it as being a one year loan worth £800,000, a rumour discounted by the club. On a footballing front, though, what a difference he made, scoring ten goals in his first ten games and becoming an instant cult hero and Carling "Player of the Month" for March. Quick and strong, and rarely missing the target, his goals were the focal point in the club's quest for Europe and included a superb first-half hat-trick against Ipswich. It has now been confirmed that he is remaining at Elland Road.

Leeds U (£3,400,000 from Eintracht Frankfurt on 5/1/95) PL 16+2/13 FAC 0+2/1

YORKE Dwight

Born: Canaan, Tobago, 3 November 1971
Height: 5'10" Weight: 11.12
International Honours: Trinidad & Tobago

Versatile Aston Villa forward who is capable of playing on either flank or up-front as an out-and-out striker. With a good left-foot, plenty of speed and balance, and excellent close control, after an in-and-out start to 1994-95, Dwight managed to secure a regular place at the turn of the year, eventually becoming a valuable member of the side. Made just one appearance for Trinidad and Tobago last season, after receiving permission to miss the Pan-American tournament in March because he did not wish to endanger his place at Villa.

Aston Villa (£120,000 from Signal Hill on 19/12/89) F/PL 92+36/27 FLC 9+2/1 FAC 13+2/7 Others 1/1

YOUDS Edward (Eddie) Paul

Born: Liverpool, 3 May 1970
Height: 6'1" Weight: 13.0

After experiencing an up-and-down season with Ipswich, Eddie signed for Bradford last March, having spent six weeks on loan at Valley Parade. A very strong and robust utility player, he appeared for Bradford at full-back, centre-half and in midfield and created a good impression.

Everton (From trainee on 10/6/88) FL 5+3 FLC 0+1 Others 1

Cardiff C (Loaned on 29/12/89) FL 0+1 FAC 0+1
Wrexham (Loaned on 8/2/90) FL 20/2
Ipswich T (£250,000 on 15/11/91) F/PL 38+12/1
FLC 1+2 FAC 5+1
Bradford C (£175,000 on 2/1/95) FL 17/3

YOUNG Eric
Born: Singapore, 25 March 1960
Height: 6'3" Weight: 12.6
Club Honours: FAC '88; FMC '91; Div 1
'94

Anthony Yeboah

Neal Simpson
(Empics Sports Photo Agency)

International Honours: W: 20
The oldest member of the Crystal Palace
side and out of favour since the first game of
last season, Eric was recalled in March
when Chris Coleman was suspended. A
solid, hard-tackling central defender, he kept
his place for the remaining 17 games of the
campaign and proved he was still a difficult
obstacle to pass. Is the most capped player,
while at the club, in Palace's history, with 19
Welsh appearances to his credit.
Brighton & Hove A (£10,000 from Slough T on
1/11/82) FL 126/10 FLC 8 FAC 11/1 Others 2
Wimbledon (£70,000 on 29/7/87) FL 96+3/9 FLC
12 FAC 6+1/1 Others 7
Crystal Palace (£850,000 on 15/8/90) F/PL
161/15 FLC 25/1 FAC 10 Others 8/1

YOUNG Neil Anthony
Born: Harlow, 31 August 1973
Height: 5'8" Weight: 10.5
Signed from "Spurs" early last season, Neil
made his debut for Bournemouth against
Brentford in October. A quick, solid,
predominantly right-sided player, who spent
most of the season at right-back, towards the
end of the campaign he was used more as a
sweeper. An excellent tackler, and cool
under pressure, he likes to go forward and
can provide good crosses and support to the
front players.
Tottenham H (From trainee on 17/8/91)
Bournemouth (Free on 11/10/94) FL 32 FAC 2
Others 2

YOUNG Roy Edmund
Born: Romsey, 28 October 1973
Height: 5'9" Weight: 10.6
Striker. Left Stockport last February after
making one brief substitute appearance,
while on loan from Poole Town, and was
immediately snapped up by Aldershot of the
Diadora First Division.
Portsmouth (From trainee on 9/7/92)
Stockport Co (Loaned from Poole T on 2/1/95)
Others 0+1

YOUNG Scott
Born: Pontypridd, 14 January 1976
Height: 6'1" Weight: 12.0
Central defender. Still only a youngster,
despite making his Cardiff debut in 1993-
94, Scott performed well last season when
required.
Cardiff C (From trainee on 4/7/94) FL 18+10
FLC 1 Others 4+3/1

YOUNG Stuart Rodney
Born: Hull, 16 December 1972
Height: 5'11" Weight: 12.0
Busy, strong-running attacker, who started
last season with Scarborough, before joining
Scunthorpe as a non-contract player in
December, he is always keen to be in the
action and thus takes a fair amount of stick
from defenders. Makes the runs to create
space for others
Hull C (Free from Arsenal juniors on 11/7/91) FL
11+8/2 FLC 1/1 FAC 2 Others 1+1
Northampton T (Free on 5/2/93) FL 7+1/2
Scarborough (Free on 4/8/93) FL 28+13/10 FLC
3+2/1 FAC 3+1/1 Others 3
Scunthorpe U (Free on 23/12/94) FL 12+2/2

FA Carling Premiership and Endsleigh League Clubs : Summary of Appearances and Goals for 1994-95

ARSENAL (PREM)

	P/FL	FLC	FAC	Others
Adams	27/3	4/1	0+1	10
Bartram	11	0+1		
Bould	30+1	5	1	7+1/2
Campbell	19+4/4	5/1	1+1	3+2
Carter	2+1			
Clarke	0+1			
Davis	3+1/1	2		
Dickov	4+5	2+2/3		
Dixon	39/1	5	2	11
Flatts	1+2		0+1	
Hartson	14+1/7			6+1/1
Helder	12+1			
Hillier	5+4	2	2	2+3
Hughes	1			
Jensen	24/1	1+1	2	6
Keown	24+7/1	3+2	1+1	5+1
Kiwomya	5+9/3			1+2
Linighan	13+7/2	2	2	3
McGoldrick	9+2	3+2		1+1
McGowan	1			
Merson	24/4	2/1		9+1/2
Morrow	11+4/1	1+1/1	1	0+4
Parlour	22+8	5	2	7+2
Schwarz	34/2	4	1	10/2
Seaman	31	6	2	11
Selley	10+3	3		3/1
Shaw	0+1			
Smith	17+2/2	3/1	1	4/1
Winterburn	39	5	2	11
Wright	30+1/18	3/3	2	11/9

ASTON VILLA (PREM)

	P/FL	FLC	FAC	Others
Atkinson	11+5/3	2/3		3/1
Barrett	24+1	3	2	4
Boden	0+1			
Bosnich	30	3	1	
Carr	0+2			
Charles	14+2			
Ehiogu	38+1/3	3	2	4/1
Farrell		2		
Fashanu	11+2/3		2	1
Fenton	7+10/2	1+2		
Houghton	19+7/1	2		3+1/1
Johnson	11+3/4		0+1	
King	13+3	3		4
Lamptey	1+5	2+1/3		
McGrath	36+4	3	2	4
Oakes		1		
Parker	12+2/1	4		0+2
Richardson	18+1			4
Saunders	39/15	3/1	2/1	4
Small	5			
Spink	12+1		1	4
Staunton	34+1/5	2	2	4
Taylor	22/1		2	
Teale	28	2	2	
Townsend	32/1	2/1	2	4
Whittingham	4+3/2	2+1/1		1+1
Wright	8			
Yorke	33+4/6	4/1	2/1	

BARNET (DIV 3)

	P/FL	FLC	FAC	Others
Adams	2+2			
Alexander	2+2	0+1		0+1
Brady	0+1			

	P/FL	FLC	FAC	Others
Carmichael	2+1			
Cooper G.	1			
Cooper M.	32+2/11	2+1/2	2/2	1/1
Freedman	42/24	4/5	2	2
Gale	25+2/2	4		1
Gibson	4+8/1			
Hamlet	3			
Haynes	2+4	1+1		1
Hoddle	26+4	4	2	2
Hodges	32+2/4	4	1/1	2
Inglethorpe	5+1/3			
McDonald	35	4	2	2
McMahon	10/2		2/1	1
Mutchell	7+1		0+1	
Newell	15			1
Newson	29+1/2	3	2	2
Phillips	27	4	2	1
Primus	39	3+1	2	2
Scott	23+5	2+2	2	2
Smith	3+1			
Thomas	6+1			
Tomlinson	21+6/1	3	0+2	0+2
Walker	21/1	2	2	1
Watson	13			
Wilson	35+1/3	4	1+1	1+1

BARNSLEY (DIV 1)

	P/FL	FLC	FAC	Others
Archdeacon	6+3/1			
Bishop	7+1	4		
Bullock	17+12		0+1	
Butler	9			
Davis	34+2/2	2	1	
Eaden	44+1/1	3	1	
Fleming	46	4	1	
Hurst	0+2			
Jackson	7+1/1	1		
Liddell	31+8/13	0+1	1	
Moses	3+1		1	
O'Connell	44+1/7	4	1	
Payton	38+5/12	4	1	
Rammell	17+7/7	3+1	0+1	
Redfearn	37+2/11	4/2	1	
Sheridan	35/2		1	
Shotton	8/1			
Snodin	11+3	3		
Taggart	41/3	4/1		
Watson	37	4	1	
Wilson	34/2	4	1	

BIRMINGHAM CITY (DIV 2)

	P/FL	FLC	FAC	Others
Barnett	31	1	5	8
Bass		1		
Bennett	46	4	5	7
Bodley	3			
Bull	10/6			2/1
Claridge	41+1/20	3/1	5	7/4
Cooper	26/1	1	3+1/1	4+1
Daish	37/3	3/1	5	7
Desouza	4+4	2		1
Doherty	3+5	1	0+1	0+2
Dominguez	12+18/3	1+2	2+1	2+2/1
Donowa	21+10/9	3	5/1	5+1/1
Dryden	3	1		
Estevez				1
Frain	6+1	2	1	1
Francis	15/8			3/1
Harding	5+1	3		

	P/FL	FLC	FAC	Others
Hendon	4			
Hiley	9	2		
Howell	2			
Hunt	18+2/5		1	3/3
Lowe	4+3/2	0+1	2+1	2+1
McGavin	10+5/1	1+1/1	3+1/2	1+3
Moulden		0+1		
Otto	18+6/4		2/1	5/1
Parris	1+1/1			
Poole	34/1		5	7/1
Price				1
Regis	4+2/2	1		
Robinson	5+1			1
Saville	3+7	1/1		1
Scott	5	3		2
Shearer	20+3/7	2	2/2	4/3
Small	3			
Tait	18+7/4	1	2+1	2+3/3
Wallace	4+2/1	1+1		0+1
Ward	41/3	3	4	7/1
Webb	0+1			
Whyte	31/1	3	3	3+1
Williams	8+3			1/1
Willis	1+2			

BLACKBURN ROVERS (PREM)

	P/FL	FLC	FAC	Others
Atkins	30+4/6	3	2	2+1
Batty	4+1			
Berg	40/1	4	2	3
Flowers	39	4	2	3
Gale	15	2		3
Gallacher	1/1			
Hendry	38/4	4	2	3
Kenna	9/1			
Le Saux	39/3	4	2	3
Makel				0+1
Mimms	3+1			
Newell	2+10	0+1	0+2	
Pearce	22+6	0+1	1	1+1
Ripley	36+1	4	1	3
Shearer	42/34	3/2	2	2/1
Sherwood	38/6	3	1	3
Slater	12+6	1	1	2
Sutton	40/15	4/3	2/2	2/1
Thorne				0+1
Warhurst	20+7/2	4	2	0+1
Wilcox	27/5	4/1	2	3
Witschge	1			
Wright	4+1		0+1	

BLACKPOOL (DIV 2)

	P/FL	FLC	FAC	Others
Bamber	2	1+1		
Beech	25+3/2	1	1	1
Bonner	9+8			0+1
Bradshaw	26/1		1	1
Briggs	1	1		
Brown	28+3/5	2/1	1	2
Burke	23	2	1	2
Capleton	8+2			
Cook	4+2			
Darton	18			
Davies	1			
Ellis	40/18	2/1	1	1
Gibson	1+1	2		
Gore	3+1	2		
Gouck	35+4/2	0+2		1
Griffiths	12+2/1	2	1	1

	P/FL	FLC	FAC	Others
Horner	33+1/2	2	1	2
Lydiate	11			
Martin	31		1	2
Mellon	26/4			
Mitchell	25+5/4		1	2/1
Moore	7			1
Morrison	18			
Murphy	6/1			
Parkinson	0+1			
Quinn	37+4/8	1+1/1	0+1	2
Rodwell	7+2	2		1
Rowett	17			
Sealey	7	2		
Stoneman	4			
Sunderland	0+2			0+1
Thompson	17		1	2
Thorpe	0+1			
Watson	24+9/15		1	1

BOLTON WANDERERS (DIV 1)

	P/FL	FLC	FAC	Others
Bergsson	8	0+1		3
Branagan	43	8	1	2
Coleman	22/4	4	1	
Coyle	8+11/5	2+1	1	2+1/1
Davison	3+1			
De Freitas	7+6/2	0+3		0+2/2
Dreyer	1+1			1+1
Fisher	10+1	2		
Green	26+5/1	6	1	3
Kelly	4			
Kernaghan	9+2			
Lee	35+4/4	8/2	0+1	1
Lydiate	17+1	3		
McAteer	41+2/5	7/2	1	3/1
McDonald	4			2
McGinlay	34+3/16	7+1/4	1	3/2
Paatelainen	43+1/12	7+1/2	1	3/1
Patterson	23+3/3	2+2	1	
Phillips	46/1	8	1	3
Seagraves	13	2		
Shilton	0+1			1
Sneekes	37+1/6	7+1/1	1/1	
Spooner	1	1		
Stubbs	37+2/1	6/1	1	3
Thompson	34+3/7	8/2	0+1	3
Whittaker	0+1			

BOURNEMOUTH (DIV 2)

	P/FL	FLC	FAC	Others
Adekola		0+1		
Andrews	38	3	2	2
Aspinall	8+1/4	4		1
Barfoot	0+2	0+1		
Beardsmore	43/3	4	2	2
Brissett	24+1			
Brooks	1			
Chivers	5		1	1+1
Cotterill	8/1	2/2		
Ferrett	0+1			
Fletcher	37+3/6	4		1
Holland	9+7/1			
Jones	27+3/8		1/1	1
Leadbitter	25+2/3	4	2	1
McElhatton	13+14/2	3	0+2/1	
Mean	32+8/7	2+1	2	2
Morris	38/3	1	2/1	2
Moss	8	1		
Murray	28+3	0+2	0+2	0+2/1
O'Connor	11+2	4		
O'Driscoll	10	4		
Pennock	31/5		2	2
Reeve	2+5	1+1		0+1

	P/FL	FLC	FAC	Others
Robinson	30+2/5		2	1
Russell K.	13	3/1	2/1	
Russell L.	3			
Scully	6+4			2
Strong	0+1			
Town	0+5	0+1		
Vincent	8			
Watson	16+6	4	2	2
Wells	0+1			
Williams	0+1			
Young	32		2	2

BRADFORD CITY (DIV 2)

	P/FL	FLC	FAC	Others
Benn	8+2	3		1
Bowling	6		0+1	
Dow	5			
Duxbury	19+1	3+1/1	2	3
Grayston	3			1
Hamilton	23+7/1	1	1	1
Huxford	33/1		2	3
Jacobs	38/1	4	1	1
Jewell	32+6/14	4	1	2
Johnson	1+1			
Kamara	22+1/3	3	2	2/1
Liburd	9/1	2		
Midgley	0+3			1
Mitchell	26			
Murray	38+3/5	3/1	2	2/1
Oliver	11	1	1	3
Petterson	3			
Power	12+15/3	0+2	0+2/1	1+1/1
Richards	30/1	3/1	1/1	1
Robson	22+1/1	3		
Scargill	1			
Showler	17+6/2		1	1+1
Shutt	28+4/4	4/1	1+1	2
Sinnott	16/1	2	2	2
Stabb	1			
Taylor	35+1/11	4/2	2	3
Tolson	4+6/2	0+3	1/1	0+1/1
Tomlinson	37	4	2	3
Verveer	9/1			
Youds	17/3			

BRENTFORD (DIV 2)

	P/FL	FLC	FAC	Others
Abrahams	7+3/3			1
Annon	9+1/1		1/1	1+1/1
Ansah	2+1/1			2/1
Asaba				1/1
Ashby	40/1	3	2	5
Bailey	6/3			
Bates	38/2	2	1	4
Benjamin	1	0+1		
Dearden	43	4	2	5
Fernandes	3+1			0+1
Forster	46/24	4	2	4+1/2
Grainger	36+1/7	2	2/1	5/2
Harvey	24+1/2	4	2	2
Hooker	0+1			
Hurdle	7+2	2	0+1	1
Hutchings	38+1	4	1+1	2+2
McGhee	1+6/1			
Mundee	22+17/5	0+1	1	3+1
Parris	5	2/1		
Ratcliffe	24+1/1	0+1		3
Ravenscroft	1			0+1
Smith	35/3	4/1	2	3
Statham	26+10	2	2	4
Stephenson	34/2	4/1		3
Taylor	43/23	4/1	2/1	4
Westley	15+1	3	2	2

BRIGHTON & HOVE ALBION (DIV 2)

	P/FL	FLC	FAC	Others
Akinbiyi	7/4			
Andrews	0+5	0+1	0+1	0+1
Bissett	12/1	4		2
Byrne J.	14/4			
Byrne P.	8/1			
Case	9	2		
Chamberlain	12+7/2	3/1	1	1
Chapman	38+2/4	5	1	1
Codner	21+2/4	4+2	1/1	1
Foster	38	5		
Fox M.	4+5/1			1
Fox S.	1+1			
Funnell	0+1	0+1		0+1
Kerr				
McCarthy	37/2	4/1	1	2
McDougald	37+4/10	6/2	1	2/1
McGarrigle	16+1			
Meade	0+3			
Minton	37+2/5	5	1	1
Munday	18+13/2	2+1/1	0+1	2
Myall	23+4/2			
Nogan	26/7	6/5	1	2
Parris	18/2			
Pates	15+1	5	1	0+1
Rust	44	6	1	2
Simmonds	2+2	0+1		2
Smith	35+3/1	4+1	1	1
Stapleton	1+1			
Storer	2/1			
Tuck	18+5	2	1	2
Wilkins	11+3	3		

BRISTOL CITY (DIV 1)

	P/FL	FLC	FAC	Others
Allison	37/13		3	
Baird	28+9/6	1	2/1	
Bent	40+1/6	2	3/1	
Brown	0+1	0+2		
Bryant	37/3	2	3	
Dryden	15+4/1		0+1	
Edwards	29+1	2	1+1	
Flatts	4+2			
Fleck	10/1			
Fowler	10+3	0+1		
Hansen	29		3	
Harriott	19	1		
Hewlett	0+1			
Humphries	4			
Kite	2			
Kuhl	17/1		2	
Loss	3+2	1		
McAree	4+2	2		
McKop	0+1			
Martin	3+1			
Munro	29+2	1	3	
Owers	21/2		3	
Parris	6			
Partridge	14+19/2	1	1+2	
Paterson	2+1	1		
Scott	18/2	2		
Seal	5+4		0+1	
Shail	37+1/2	2	3	
Simpson	4			
Tinnion	33+2/2	2	3/1	
Watson	1+1			
Welch	44	2	3	
Wyatt	1+2			

BRISTOL ROVERS (DIV 2)

	P/FL	FLC	FAC	Others
Archer	32+10/6	2	3+1	4+2
Browning	31+10/1	1	3	3+2
Channing	35+5/2	2	3	4+1
Clark	42/6	2	4	7

	P/FL	FLC	FAC	Others
Collett	4			1
Davis	0+2			
Gurney	35+3/1	1	4	7
Hardyman	1+4		1+1	1
Heggs	2+3/1			
Law	2			
McLean	0+1			0+1
Maddison	12+2	1		1+1
Miller	41+1/16	2	4/4	6/2
Parkin	40	2	4	6
Paul	2+3			2+1
Pritchard	43	2	3	6
Skinner	38/2	2	3	6+1/1
Sterling	46/1	2	4	6
Stewart	26+1/15	2/1	3/3	5/4
Taylor	23+16/12	0+1	1+1	5
Tillson	40/2	2/1	4	6
Waddock	1			
White	4			
Wright	6+1/1			1

BURNLEY (DIV 1)

	P/FL	FLC	FAC	Others
Armstrong	4			
Beresford	40	4	4	
Brass	2+3			
Davis	43/7	4	4	
Deary	12+4/1	1+2	1+1/1	
Dowell	5	1	2	
Eyres	38+1/8	2	5/2	
Francis	0+2		0+1	
Gayle	7+7/3	1+1/1	1+1/1	
Harper	27	4	5	
Harrison	16+3/2	1+1	1	
Heath	21+6	4	3/2	
Hoyland	30/2		4	
Joyce	4+1	2/1		
Lancashire	0+1	1+1		
McMinn	17+5	3	1+2	
Mullin	6+6/1		2	
Nogan	11+4/3			
Parkinson	42+1/2	4	5	
Peel	0+3		0+1	
Pender	5			
Philliskirk	7+6/1	1+1		
Randall	32/1		5/1	
Robinson	29+10/7	4/2	5/1	
Russell	6+2		1	
Saville	3+1/1		1	
Shaw	8+1/4			
Stewart	6			
Thompson	12			
Vinnicombe	29/1	3		
Winstanley	44/2	4	5	

BURY (DIV 3)

	P/FL	FLC	FAC	Others
Bimson	19			2
Bracey	4+2		1	
Carter	21+5/14	2/1	2	5+1
Cross	11+1	2	4	1
Daws	30+4/2		4	6+2
Desouza	2+1			
Hughes	19+4/1	1	2+2	3+3
Hulme	24+4	1	2	2
Jackson	24/2	2	1	6
Johnrose	23+3/4		5/1	5
Kelly A.	19+3/3	0+1	1+1	5/2
Kelly G.	38	2	4	8
Lancaster	3+2/1			
Lucketti	39/3	2	5/1	8

	P/FL	FLC	FAC	Others
Matthews	2/1			
Matthewson	18		4	4
Mauge	14+4	2	3	3
Mulligan	9+6/2	2/1	0+2	1+1
Paskin	15+11/8	1	3/1	3+3/1
Pugh	42/16	1	4	7/2
Reid	1			1
Rigby	24+6/2	1/1	3+2/1	5+1/2
Rowe	1+2			
Sertori	0+2		2	1+1/1
Stanislaus	33	2	5/1	6
Stant	19+1/13			3
Woodward	8			3

CAMBRIDGE UNITED (DIV 2)

	P/FL	FLC	FAC	Others
Barrick	44/1	2/1	4/1	3
Butler	35+2/14	1+1	4/4	3
Campbell D.	1			
Campbell J.	12			
Corazzin	45+1/19	2	4	3/2
Craddock	38	2/1	3	3
Danzey	7+4			1
Elad	2+1	0+1		
Filan	16	2		2
Fowler	12+4		1+1	1+1
Granville	11+5/2	1	0+1	1+1
Hay	7+19/3		4/1	1+1/1
Hayrettin	15+2			1
Heathcote	24/1	2	1	
Hunter	23+3	2	1+2	1+1
Hyde	18+9	2	4	1
Jeffrey	25+3/2		2	1
Joseph	39/2	2	4	3
Kyd	10+9/1			
Lillis	14+5/4		3+1/2	2+1/2
Livett	2			
Lomas	2			
Manuel	10		2	
Morah	8+6/2	1+1		0+1
Nyamah	5+4		0+1	1
Pack	3			
O'Shea	30+1	2	3	2
Rattle	6	1		
Rush	2			
Sheffield	28		4	1
Thompson	7			
Walker	5			2

CARDIFF CITY (DIV 2)

	P/FL	FLC	FAC	Others
Adams	4+2			2+1
Aizlewood	17/2	1	0+1	7/1
Baddeley	33+3/1		1	11
Bird	7+12/3	2		6/1
Brazil	26+4/1	2		6+2/1
Dale	33+2/5	1+1	1	7+1/9
Evans D.A.	4+8			1+2
Evans T.	7	2	1	1
Fereday	26+1/1	1		4
Griffith	31+7/3	1	1	8+2/1
Honour	10			
McLean	4			
Millar	25+10/7	1+1	1	8/2
Milsom	1+2			1
Nicholls	6+6/2			
Oatway	27+3	2/1	1	3+1
Pearson	12			
Perry	34/1	1	1	7
Ramsey	11		1	3
Richardson	32+1/4	2		5+2/1
Scott	13/1		1	1

	P/FL	FLC	FAC	Others
Searle	32			10
Stant	19/13	2/2	1	4
Street		1		
Thompson	11+2		0+1	4+1/2
Vick	2			
Wigg	18+1/1			7+1
Williams D.	40	2	1	8
Williams S.	6			3+1
Young	15+7	1		4+3/1

CARLISLE UNITED (DIV 3)

	P/FL	FLC	FAC	Others
Arnold	1+3	0+1	0+1	1/1
Aspinall	6+1/1			
Caig	40	4	4	7
Conway	24/6		4/2	7/1
Currie	38/4	3+1	3/1	7/4
Davey	25/4	4	4/1	5
Delap	2+1			
Edmondson	36+2/2	4	4	8
Elliott	2+1			1
Gallimore	40/5	4	4	8/1
Hayward	9/2			2
Hopper	2+3			
Joyce	17+4	4	0+1	1
Lowe	1+1			
Mountfield	30+1/3	3+1	4/1	6/1
Murray	2+3			1+1
Peacock	2+5			
Pearson	0+1			
Peters	5+3		0+1	1+2
Prokas	37+2/1	3	3	7
Reddish	2	1		
Reeves	42/21	4/2	4/2	8
Robinson	6+8/1		1	1+4
Thomas	36/6	4	4	7/5
Thorpe	7+21/4	0+3	1+2	1+5
Valentine	9	2		1
Walling	41/7	4/1	4/1	8

CHARLTON ATHLETIC (DIV 1)

	P/FL	FLC	FAC	Others
Ammann	18+1			
Balmer	28+1/2	2		
Bennett	9+5		1	
Bowyer	5	0+1		
Brown	42/3	2	1	
Chandler	1/1			
Chapple	21/2	2	1	
Garland	6+4	2		
Grant	14+12/6	0+1		
Hovi	0+2			
Jones	31/1			
Leaburn	22+5/3		1	
Linger	3+5			
McGleish	0+6			
McLeary	22		1	
Mortimer	26/4		1	
Nelson	21+6/7	2/2	0+1	
Newton	10+16	2		
Pardew	22+2/3		0+1	
Petterson	8+1	2		
Robinson	16+5/3		1	
Robson	40/3	2	1	
Rufus	27+1			
Salmon	20		1	
Stuart	12			
Sturgess	23	2		
Walsh	23+5/1	2	1	
Whyte	36+2/19	2/2	1	

CHELSEA (PREM)

	P/FL	FLC	FAC	Others
Barness	10+2	1		2+1
Burley	16+9/2		1+1	1
Clarke	29	2	3	5
Furlong	30+6/10	2	1	7/3
Hall	4	1		1+1
Hitchcock	11+1			4
Hoddle	3+9			0+3
Hopkin	7+8/1	0+1		
Johnsen	33	3	2	8
Kharine	31	3	3	4
Kjeldberg	23/1	3	2	1
Lee	9+5	0+2	1	1+1
Minto	19		3	5+1
Myers	9+1			2
Newton	22+8/1	2+1	0+2	5
Peacock	38/4	3/1	3/1	7
Rix	0+1			1+2
Rocastle	26+2	3/1		7+1/1
Shipperley	6+4/2	2+1		2
Sinclair	35/3	2	3/1	7/2
Spackman	36	2	3	7
Spencer	26+3/11	1	3/1	4+1/1
Stein	21+3/3		3/1	2+1/2
Wise	18+1	3	2	5/1

Steve Clarke (Chelsea)   Paul Marriott
(Empics Sports Photo Agency)

CHESTER CITY (DIV 2)

	P/FL	FLC	FAC	Others
Alsford	32+3/1	1	2	2
Anthrobus	7			
Aunger	1+4			
Bishop	16+3/4	2	1	0+1
Burnham	22+2	2	1	2
Chambers	6+7/1	1/1		2
Felgate	37+1	2	2	2
Flitcroft	20+12	1	2	2
Gardiner	2+1			
Hackett	30+5/5		2	2
Jackson	32/1		1	1
Jenkins	40	2	2	3
Lightfoot	26+2/3		1	2
Milner	32+4/8	1+1	1+1/1	1
Murphy	0+5		0+1	1+1

	P/FL	FLC	FAC	Others
Newland	9+1			1
Page	22+8/5	2/1	2/1	3/2
Preece	42+1/2	2	2	3
Priest	22+2/1			2
Ratcliffe	23	2	1	2+1
Richardson	6/1			
Rimmer	22+3/2	2	0+1	0+1
Shelton	31+2/2		2	2/2
Tolson	3+1			
Whelan	23/1	2/1		

CHESTERFIELD (DIV 3)

	P/FL	FLC	FAC	Others
Beasley	20+1	1		5
Bibbo	0+1			
Carr	35/2	4	2	5
Cheetham	5	2/1		0+1
Curtis	39+1/2	4/1	2	4
Davies	41/11	3/1	1	3+2/1
Dyche	22		2	3
Fairclough	12+1	3	2	3
Hazel				2
Hewitt	38/3	4	1	6
Hill	3			
Howard	1+11/1			2+1/2
Jules	10+13	1+2/1	1+1	2
Law	35/1	2		4/2
Lormor	23/10			3/2
McAuley	1/1		1+1	2
Madden	10/1	1		1
Marples	21	3	2	
Marshall	0+1			
Morris	21+5/6	2/1	1+1	4
Moss	27+5/10	2/1	1+1	3
Narbett	2+1			
Norris	5+2/3	2+1/1	2	1
Perkins	17+1	1/1	2	3+2
Reddish	2+1			
Roberts	4+7/1	2		1+1/1
Robinson	22/8			3/2
Rogers	39	4	2	5
Spooner	6+1	3		
Stewart	1			1+1

COLCHESTER UNITED (DIV 3)

	P/FL	FLC	FAC	Others
Abrahams	20+8/2	2	4/2	2/2
Allen	0+2			
Allpress	3+8	2		
Asaba	9+3/2			
Betts	34+1/2		4	2
Brown	26+2/6	2	4	2
Burley	5+2	0+1		0+1
Caesar	39/1	2	4	2
Cawley	23/2		4	2
Cheesewright	23	1	3	2
Cheetham	8+1/1			
Culling	2	1		
Dalli	1			
Davis	4	1		
Dennis	32+1/2	2	1+3	2
Emberson	19+1	1	1	
English	33/2	2	4/1	2
Fry	24+9/8	1	1+1	0+1
Gibbs	8+1			
Kinsella	42/6	2	4/1	2/1
Lock	0+3/1			
Locke	20+2/1		4	2
McCarthy	10/1			
Partner	0+1			

	P/FL	FLC	FAC	Others
Putney	28/2		2	
Reinelt	2+3			
Roberts		1+1		
Stoneman	3/1			
Thompson	5+8/5		0+1	
Whitton	36/10	2	4/2	2
Williams	3			

COVENTRY CITY (PREM)

	P/FL	FLC	FAC	Others
Babb	3			
Boland	9+3	1		
Borrows	33+2	1	4	
Burrows	11			
Busst	20/2	3		
Cook	33+1/3	3	3	
Darby	27+2	3/1	1+2	
Dublin	31/13	3/2	4/1	
Filan	2			
Flynn	32/4	3/1	2	
Gillespie	2+1	1		
Gould	7			
Hall	2+3			
Jenkinson	10+1/1		3	
Jones	16+5/2	2+1	0+1	
Marsh	15/2		4	
Morgan	26+2	2	4	
Ndlovu	28+2/11	1	3/2	
Ogrizovic	33	3	4	
Pickering	27+4	3	2	
Pressley	18+1/1		3	
Quinn	3+3			
Rennie	28	2	3	
Richardson	14			
Robertson	0+1			
Strachan	5			
Wegerle	21+5/3	2/1	2+2/1	
Williams J.	1+6			
Williams P.	5	2		

CREWE ALEXANDRA (DIV 2)

	P/FL	FLC	FAC	Others
Adebola	25+5/7	0+1	1	4/2
Annon	1			
Barr	29+5/2	2		6
Booty	44/2	2	2	7
Clarkson	19+4/6			2+2
Collier	3+2	1		0+2
Collins	38+2/11		2	6/1
Edwards	8+9/2			0+1
Gardiner	9+2			1+1
Garvey	22+6/3	1+1/1	2/1	4
Gayle	24+1			4
Lennon	31/6		2	6
Macauley	43/4	2	2	5/1
McCarthy	2			
Murphy	20+15/5	1		5
Rowbotham	20+1/6	1	1/2	2+2/1
Savage	5+1/2			
Smith M.	22+2	2	2	3
Smith S.	45/8	1	2/1	6
Tierney	13+7/4	2		3+1
Walters	8+3/1	1		
Ward	16/8	2/1	2/4	3/3
Whalley	40/1	2	2	7/2
Wilson	20+1	1	2	3+1
Woodward	0+2			

CRYSTAL PALACE (PREM)

	P/FL	FLC	FAC	Others
Armstrong	40/8	5/5	6/5	
Bowry	13+5	3		
Coleman	35/1	7	6/1	

	P/FL	FLC	FAC	Others
Cox	1+10		1+1	
Dowie	15/4		6/4	
Dyer	7+9/1	1+2/1	1+2	
Gordon	38+3/2	7/1	5+1/1	
Houghton	10/2		2	
Humphrey	19+2	4	3+1	
Launders	1+1	0+1		
Martyn	37	7	7	
Matthew	2+2	1	1	
Ndah	5+7/1	4	1+1/1	
Newman	32+3/3	5	4+2	
Patterson	22/1	4	6	
Pitcher	21+4	3/1	8/1	
Preece	17+3/4	4+2/1	2+3	
Rodger	4			
Salako	39/4	7/1	8/2	
Shaw	41	7	8	
Southgate	42/3	7/2	8	
Wilkins	1			
Williams	2+2			
Wilmot	5+1		1	
Young	13	1	4	

DARLINGTON (DIV 3)

	P/FL	FLC	FAC	Others
Appleby	35+1/1	2	1	3/1
Banks	39/1	2	2	3
Blake	3+6			
Bolton	1+1			
Chapman	19+14/2	0+1	1	2
Collier	2			
Crosby	35	2	2	2
Cross	13	2/1		1
Gaughan	39+2/8	2	2	3
Gregan	22+3/2	1	1	2+1
Himsworth	32+6/2	1+1	2	3/3
Kirkham	3+1		0+1	0+1
Mattison	4+6	1		
Olsson	42/4	2	2	3/1
Painter	34+4/9	2	2	2
Pollitt	40	2	2	3
Reed	34+4/1	1	1	2
Shaw	9+3/1			
Slaven	24+2/5	2/1	2/1	0+1
Taylor	8			2
Worboys	24+3/6		2/2	2/3

DERBY COUNTY (DIV 1)

	P/FL	FLC	FAC	Others
Ashbee	1			
Boden	4+2			
Carsley	22+1/2	3+1	1	3
Charles	18/2	3		4
Cooper	0+1			0+1
Cowans	17	3		2+1
Davies	1+1			0+1
Forsyth	21+1	3	0+1	1
Gabbiadini	30+2/11	3/2	1	2
Harkes	29+4	3		2
Hayward	3			1
Hodge	10/2			1/2
Hoult	15			
Johnson	14/7	4		1/2
Kavanagh	20+5/1	1+1	1	0+4
Kitson	8/2			1/4
Kuhl	9	1		2
Mills	16/7			
Nicholson	15	1	1	4
Pembridge	27/9	2		2/1
Quy	0+1			
Short	37/3	4	1	2
Simpson	37+5/8	2+1/1	1	3

	P/FL	FLC	FAC	Others
Stallard	13+3/2	1+1/1	1	2/1
Sturridge	7+5/1	0+1		2+1
Sutton S.	19+1	2	1	2
Sutton W.	3+3		1	
Taylor	12	2		2
Trollope	23+1/4			
Wassall	25+7	2	1	3
Williams	37/3	4/1	1	2/1
Wrack	2+14/1		0+1	
Yates	11/1			

DONCASTER ROVERS (DIV 3)

	P/FL	FLC	FAC	Others
Brabin	27+1/8	2	1	2
Bryan	5/1			
Donaldson	7+2/2	2		0+1
Finlay	6+2/1	1+1		0+1
Hackett	39/2	2	1	3
Harper	31+2/9		1	2
Hoy	0+1			
Jones	25+7/12	1/1	0+1/1	2/1
Kirby	41+1	0+1	1	3
Kitchen	7+1	1		1
Lawrence	14+2/2	2	1	3
Limber		2		
Marquis	1+1			
Maxfield	10			
Meara	14+1/1	1	1	1
Measham	1			
Norbury	17+5/5			1
Parrish	25/3	1+1	1	2
Roche	19+1/3		1	2
Schofield	25+2/1			
Suckling	9	1		
Swailes	32	2/1	1	2
Thew	15+6/1	1	0+1	2/1
Torfason	1+3	1+1/1		
Turner	4/1			1/1
Warren	10+4/2			0+1
Wilcox	37/4	1	1	3
Williams D. A.	1			
Williams D. P.	33+2	1	1	3
Williams P.	6+1			

EVERTON (PREM)

	P/FL	FLC	FAC	Others
Ablett	26/3		4	
Amokachi	17+1/4	2	0+2/2	
Angell	3+1	0+1		
Barlow	7+4/2		2+1	
Barrett	17			
Burrows	19	2	2	
Cottee	3			
Durrant	4+1			
Ebbrell	26		3	
Ferguson	22+1/7	1	3+1/1	
Grant	1+4			
Hinchcliffe	28+1/2	2	5/1	
Holmes	1			
Horne	31		5	
Jackson	26+3	1	6/2	
Kearton	1			
Limpar	19+8/2		5+1/1	
Parkinson	32+2	2	6/1	
Rideout	25+4/14	1+1	5/2	
Rowett	2			
Samways	14+5/1	2/1		
Snodin	2+1	1+1		
Southall	41	2	6	
Stuart	20+8/3	2/1	3+2/2	
Unsworth	37+1/3	2	5	
Watson	38/2	2/1	6/1	

EXETER CITY (DIV 3)

	P/FL	FLC	FAC	Others
Anderson	21/1	1		1
Bailey	14/2	2	1	3
Barrett	4			
Bellotti	1+1		0+1	
Brown	32+5/1	1+1	2	3/1
Came	32/1	2	1	1
Cecere	27+1/11	2/1	1/1	3/2
Cooper D.	14			
Cooper M.	31+9/6	1	2	4/1
Coughlin	23+2		2	2
Daniels	6+1	1	1	2
Fox	31	1	1	2
Gavin	37/2	2	2	3
Hare				1
Minett	38/2	1	2	4/1
Morgan	4+5/1		1+1/1	0+1
Pears	12+7/1	1+1		0+1
Phillips	18+6/2	1		0+2
Rice	5+5	1		1
Richardson	38/1	1	2	3
Robinson	16+1		1+1	2
Ross	1			0+1
Storer	21+2/2		1+1	4
Thirlby	20+7/1	2		1
Turner	10+1/1	1/1	1	2/1
Woodman	6	1	1	2

FULHAM (DIV 3)

	P/FL	FLC	FAC	Others
Adams	18+3/7	1	2/4	2/1
Angus	21+2			2
Bartley	1	1		
Bedrossian	3	0+1		
Blake	34+1/3	2/1	4/1	3
Bolt	2			
Brazil	30+2/7	4	2	2
Cork	11+4/3	3	4/1	
Cusack	26+1/7		2	2/1
Ferney	5+2			
Finnigan	7+4		1	1
Gregory	0+1			
Hails	6+2/1	0+1		1
Hamill	18+5/5		0+2/2	0+1
Harrison	6+1		1	1
Haworth	3+7	3+1/2	1+1	1+1/2
Herrera	26+1	3	4	2
Hurlock	27/1	1+1	2	2
Jupp	35+1/2	4	3+1	2+1
Marshall	25+2/3	4	4	2
Mison	17+7/1	3	3	2/1
Moore	31/3	4/2	4	2
Morgan	42/10	4	4/1	3
Stallard	4/3			
Stannard	36	4	3	2
Thomas G.	7	2		
Thomas M.	21+2/3	1		1
Williams				0+1

GILLINGHAM (DIV 3)

	P/FL	FLC	FAC	Others
Arnott	24+4/2	0+2	4	2
Baker	7+1/2	2		
Banks	38		4	1
Barrett	4	2		2
Bodley	6+1			1
Brown	8/1			
Butler	31+2/2	2	3	2
Carpenter	26+3		4	3/1
Dunne	35/1	2	1	1
Foster	27+2/8	2	3	1
Freeman	0+2			

	P/FL	FLC	FAC	Others
Green	37/1	2	4	1
Hooker				1
Hutchinson	1+4			2
Kamara				1
Kennedy	0+2			
Knott	5			
Lindsey	11+1			1
Martin	7			
Micklewhite	33+2/2	2	4	1+1
Palmer	10/1	2		2
Pike	26+1/13		4/4	2/1
Ramage	8+5/1			0+2
Reinelt	18+9/4	2	3+1/2	3
Ritchie	5/1			1
Smillie	15/1		3	1
Smith	32+2/1	2	3	1
Trott	7+2			1
Watson	39/2	2	4	2
Watts	2+1			0+1
Wilson	0+2			

GRIMSBY TOWN (DIV 1)

	P/FL	FLC	FAC	Others
Agnew	7+4	1+1		
Childs	18+7/4	1	1	
Crichton	43	2	1	
Croft	44/1	2	1	
Dobbin	35+3/2			
Fickling	1			
Forrester	7+2/1			
Futcher	6+1	2		
Gilbert	40/6	2/1	1	
Groves	46/5	2/1	1	
Handyside	34+1		1	
Jobling	37+1/1	1		
Laws	6+10/1			
Lester	1+6	0+1	0+1	
Lever	31	2		
Livingstone	29+5/8	2		
McDermott	8+4		1	
Mendonca	21+1/11	2	1	
Pearcey	3			
Rodger	20+1/1		1	
Shakespeare	16+3/3	2	1	
Watson	20+1/3	1		
Woods	33+4/14	0+1	1	

HARTLEPOOL UNITED (DIV 3)

	P/FL	FLC	FAC	Others
Ainsley	14+1/1	2	1	2
Burgess	11	2		
Cook	22+2			
Daughtry	14+1			
Foster	4/1			2
Garrett	0+1			
Gilchrist	23	4	1	2
Gourlay	0+1			
Halliday	19+9/5	2+1	1	1
Henderson	12/3			
Holmes	5/2			
Homer	1			
Honour	1	1		
Horne	41	3	1	2
Houchen	32/13	4/1	1	2
Hyson	1+4	0+1		
Ingram	35	3+1	1	2
Jones	1+1	1		
Lynch	8+3/1	2+1		
McCreery	7+2		1	
McGuckin	34/3	4	1	2
MacPhail	6			
Oliver	18	4		2
Peverell	0+1			

	P/FL	FLC	FAC	Others
Reddish	23			
Skedd	17+6/1	1+1	0+1	
Sloan	26+3/2	2+1	0+1	1
Southall	37/6	2/2	1	2
Sunley	1+1			
Sweeney	1	1		
Tait	20	1		
Thompson	24+4/4	3+1/1	1	0+1
Walsh	4/1	2	1	2

HEREFORD UNITED (DIV 3)

	P/FL	FLC	FAC	Others
Brough	16+2/1			0+2
Brownrigg	8			1
Clark	17+1	3		2
Clarke	3+2	0+1		
Cross	24+4/6	4	2	2+1/1
Davies	26+2/1	1+2	1	2
Davis	1			
Downs	2+1	1		
Eversham	3+2			
Farrington	0+1			
Fishlock	12+2	1		2
Gonzaque	2+1			1
Gregory	2			1
Hall	0+1			
Henderson	5			
James	18/2	4	1	3/1
Llewellyn	3+1		1+1	1
Lloyd	24/3			3
Lyne	27+4/1		2	4/1
McKenzie	21+1			1
Pennock	13+2	2	2	3
Pick	23+6/2	3+1	1+1/1	3
Pike	2+2	1+1		0+1
Pounder	23+5/2	1	1+1	1+1
Preedy	15+1/1	4	2	1/1
Reece	35+2/4	3	2	4/2
Reeve	0+5			
Sheffield	8	2		
Smith	35/3	4	2	3+1/1
Steele	4+1	2	1	1
Stoker	10			
Warner	15+1			
White	31+5/14	3/2	2/1	3+1/1
Wilkins	34+1/2	4	2	2
Williams	0+2	1	0+1	0+1

HUDDERSFIELD TOWN (DIV 2)

	P/FL	FLC	FAC	Others
Baldry	8+3	2		0+2/1
Billy	30+7/2	3+1	2	6+1/2
Blackwell	3+1	0+1	1	3
Booth	45+1/26	4	2/1	5+1/3
Bullock	39/6	3	2/1	3
Clayton	0+2		0+1	4/2
Collins	2+2			1+1
Cowan	37/2	4	2	5
Crosby	16+3/4	1	1	5+2/1
Dunn	13+26/5	1+2	0+2/1	4+3/1
Duxbury	26/2			3
Dyson	23+5/2	4		1+2
Francis	43	4	1	4
Gray	5			3
Jepson	36+5/19	3+1/2	2/1	6/1
Logan	24+3/1	3	1	3
Mitchell	11+1		2	3/1
Moulden	0+2			
Reid	42/6	3/1	2	1
Scully	38/1	4/1	2	5
Short	6			1
Sinnott	25/1			3
Starbuck	4+5/1	3		2/1

	P/FL	FLC	FAC	Others
Trevitt	20+1	2	2	5
Whittington	1			
Williams	9			1

HULL CITY (DIV 2)

	P/FL	FLC	FAC	Others
Abbott	22+4/2	1	0+1	1+1
Allison	11+2			1
Atkinson	7+2/1	0+2		1
Brown	32+1/14	2	1	
Cox	5/1			
Dakin	19+2/1	1+1	1	1
Dewhurst	41/8	2	1	2
Edeson	0+3			
Fettis	27+1/2	2		
Fewings	0+2			
Graham	39	2	1	2
Hargreaves	13+8	1	0+1	2
Hobson	35+1	2	1	1
Joyce	9/3			
Lawford	25+6/3	2	1	2
Lee	42+3/1	1/1	1	2
Lowthorpe	21+1	1		
Lund	11/3			
Mail	10+4			1
Mann	29+2/2	1+1	1	1+1
Ormondroyd	10/6			
Peacock	28+9/5	2/1	1	2
Wallace	7			
Wilson	20		1	2
Windass	43+1/17	2	1	1

IPSWICH TOWN (PREM)

	P/FL	FLC	FAC	Others
Baker	2		1	
Chapman	9+7/1			
Cotterell	0+2	0+1		
Ellis	1			
Forrest	36	2		
Gregory D.	0+1			
Gregory N.	1+2			
Guentchev	11+5/1	2		
Johnson	14+3	2		
Kiwomya	13+2/3	0+1	1	
Linighan	31+1	1	1/1	
Marshall	14+4/3			
Mason	19+2/3		1	
Mathie	13/2			
Milton	19+6/2	1		
Morgan	1			
Norfolk	1+2			
Palmer	10+2	1		
Paz	13+4/1			
Sedgley	26/4	2	1	
Slater	22+5/1	2	1	
Stockwell	14+1			
Swailes	4			
Tanner	9+1/2		1	
Taricco		1		
Thompson	9+1			
Thomsen	31+2/5	2	1	
Vaughan	10		1	
Wark	26/4	2		
Whelan	12+1		1	
Williams	38/1	2		
Wright	3			
Yallop	41/1	2	1	
Youds	9+1			

LEEDS UNITED (PREM)

	P/FL	FLC	FAC	Others
Couzens	2+2			
Deane	33+2/9	1+1	3/1	
Dorigo	28	0+1	1	

	P/FL	FLC	FAC	Others
Fairclough	1+4	2		
Kelly	42	2	4	
Lukic	42	2	4	
McAllister	41/6	2	4	
Masinga	15+7/5	1	2+2/4	
Palmer	39/3	2	3/1	
Pemberton	22+5	0+1	4	
Radebe	9+3	0+1	1+1	
Sharp	0+2			
Speed	39/3	2	4	
Strachan	5+1	1		
Tinkler	3			
Wallace	30+2/4	2	2+1	
Wetherall	38/3	1	4/2	
Whelan	18+5/7	2	2	
White	18+5/3		3/1	
Worthington	21+6/1	2	3+1	
Yeboah	16+2/13		0+2/1	

LEICESTER CITY (PREM)

	P/FL	FLC	FAC	Others
Agnew	7+4	1+1	1	
Blake	26+4/3	2		
Carey	11+1			
Carr	12+1/1			
Draper	39/5	2	2	
Galloway	4+1		1	
Gee	3+4/2			
Grayson	34	2	3	
Heskey	1			
Hill	24		3	
Joachim	11+4/3	2		
Lawrence	9+8/1			
Lewis	13+3	2	1	
Lowe	19+10/8	0+1	0+1	
McMahon	0+1			
Mills	1			
Mohan	23	2	1	
Oldfield	8+6/1	0+1	1/1	
Ormondroyd	6			
Parker	14/2		1	
Philpott	19+4	2	2+1	
Poole	36	2	3	
Roberts	32+5/9	2	3/2	
Robins	16+1/5		2	
Smith	10+2		1	
Thompson	16+3		3	
Walsh	5			
Ward	6		0+1	
Whitlow	28/2	1	3	
Willis	29/2	2	2	

LEYTON ORIENT (DIV 2)

	P/FL	FLC	FAC	Others
Austin	39/2	2	2	6
Barnett	15+12	2	2	2+2
Barry	5+1			
Bellamy	32		2	5
Bogie	28+3/2	2	2	5+1
Brooks	8+1		0+1	3/1
Carter	25+4	0+1	2/1	5+1
Cockerill	32+1/4	2/1	2	6
Dempsey	43/1	2	1+1	5/1
Gray	13+12/3	0+2	1/1	0+1
Hague	17+1/1			2+1
Heald	45	2	2	7
Hendon	29	2	1	6
Howard	27/1	1	2	5
Lakin	17+5	2	0+2	1+1
McGleish	4+2/1			1/1
Martin	1+3			1
Perifimou	3+1			

	P/FL	FLC	FAC	Others
Purse	37+1/3	2	1	7/2
Putney				1
Read	11			1
Rufus	5+2			
Ryan	6+1			
Shearer	2			
Turner	1			
Warren	24+7/3	1		3+4/1
West	27+3/9	2	2/1	5/4
Wilkie	10+1			

LINCOLN CITY (DIV 3)

	P/FL	FLC	FAC	Others
Bannister	25+4/7	2	1+1/1	1
Brown	39/3	4	3	3
Carbon	30+3/7	2/1	3	1+2
Daley	19+1/4	2+1	1	2+1/1
Daws	20+6/7		1+1	1
Dixon	17+1		0+1	1
Foley	15+1	1	2	2
Greenall	39/3	4	3/1	2
Hebberd	20+5	3	3	2
Hill	25+1/3		3	2
Hoult	15			1
Huckerby	4+2/2			
Johnson A.	24+1	2	3	2+1/1
Johnson D.	23+1/4	3/2	2/1	2
Leaning	21	4	3	2
Lucas	4			2
Matthews	17+6/2		2	1+1
Onwere	7+1	3		1
Platnauer	13	4		
Puttnam	8+9/4	2+1		1
Schofield	12/1	4/2		1
Sherwood	6+1			
Smith	15+2	0+1		
West	41/6	4/1	3	3/1
Williams	3+3/1			

LIVERPOOL (PREM)

	P/FL	FLC	FAC	Others
Babb	33+1	7	6	
Barnes	38/7	6	6/2	
Bjornebye	31	7	5+1	
Clough	3+7	1/1		
Fowler	42/25	8/4	7/2	
Harkness	8/1			
James	42	8	7	
Jones P.L.	0+1	0+1		
Jones R.	31	8	7	
Kennedy	4+2			
McManaman	40/7	8/2	7	
Matteo	2+5		1	
Molby	12+2/2	2		
Nicol	4	1		
Redknapp	36+5/3	8/2	6/1	
Ruddock	37/2	8	7	
Rush	36/12	7/6	7/1	
Scales	35/2	7/1	7	
Thomas	16+7	1+2	2+1	
Walters	7+11	1	2+2	
Wright	5+1			

LUTON TOWN (DIV 1)

	P/FL	FLC	FAC	Others
Adcock	0+2		0+1	
Allen	4			
Biggins	6+1/1		2/1	
Chenery			1	
Davis	9			
Dixon	23+6/7	2	2+1	
Greene	7+1	2		

	P/FL	FLC	FAC	Others
Hartson	11+9/5		1/1	
Harvey	9+3/1			
Houghton	1	1		
Hughes	8+1/2	2	1	
James	42/3	2	2	
Johnson	46/1	2	4	
Linton	5+5	1+1		
Marshall	36+9/11	1+1/1	4/1	
Matthews	6+5			
Oakes	37+6/9	1+1/1	3	
Peake	46	2	4	
Preece	42/4	2	4	
Skelton	3+2	0+1		
Sommer	37	2	4	
Taylor	9/3			
Telfer	45+1/9	2	4	
Thomas	33+3		4	
Thorpe	0+4		0+1	
Waddock	40/1		4	
Williams	0+2		0+1	
Woodsford	1+6			

MANCHESTER CITY (PREM)

	P/FL	FLC	FAC	Others
Beagrie	33+4/2	6/1	4/1	
Brightwell D.	9	1+1	3+1/1	
Brightwell I.	29+1	5	4	
Burridge	3+1			
Coton	21+1	1	1	
Curle	31/2	3/1	3	
Dibble	15+1	5	3	
Edghill	14	3		
Flitcroft	37/5	5	4	
Foster	9+2	1+1	1+1	
Gaudino	17+3/3	1+1	3/1	
Griffiths	0+2	0+1		
Hill	10+3	3		
Kernaghan	18+4/1	2	3	
Kerr	2			
Lomas	18+2/2	6/1	1	
McMahon	6+1	1		
Mike	1+1		0+1	
Phelan	26+1	3	1	
Quinn	24+11/8	4+2/2	1+3	
Rosler	29+2/15	3+1/2	4/5	
Simpson	10+6/2		0+1	
Summerbee	39+2/1	6/2	4	
Thomas	0+2			
Tracey	3			
Vonk	19+2	1+1	1	
Walsh	39/12	6/2	3/1	

MANCHESTER UNITED (PREM)

	P/FL	FLC	FAC	Others
Beckham	2+2	3	1+1	1/1
Bruce	35/2	1	5/2	6+2
Butt	11+11/1	3	3+1	5+1
Cantona	21/12		1/1	3/1
Casper		1		
Cole	17+1/12			
Davies	3+2	3		2/1
Giggs	29/1		6+1/1	4/2
Gillespie	3+6/1	3		
Hughes	33+1/8		5/2	6/2
Ince	36/5		6	6/1
Irwin	40/2	2	7/4	5
Kanchelskis	25+5/14		2+1	6/1
Keane	23+2/2	1	6+1	4/1
McClair	35+5/5	3/1	7/2	3
May	15+4/2	2/1	1	5
Neville G.	16+2	2+1	4	1+1
Neville P.	1+1		1	

	P/FL	FLC	FAC	Others
O'Kane		1+1	1	
Pallister	42/2	2	7/1	7
Parker	1+1			2+1
Pilkington	0+1			
Schmeichel	32		7	4
Scholes	6+11/5	3/2	1+2	0+2
Sharpe	26+2/3	0+2	6+1/1	4/2
Tomlinson		0+2		
Walsh	10	3		3

MANSFIELD TOWN (DIV 3)

	P/FL	FLC	FAC	Others
Alexander	0+2			0+1/2
Aspinall	13+7	3	2+1/1	2
Baraclough	36/3	5	4	3
Boothroyd	35+1	5	4	3
Campbell	3/1		2	
Castledine	3+7	0+1		1
Clifford	1			
Donaldson	4/6		1/1	
Doolan	21+3/1	2	2	1+1
Elad	0+2			
Fleming	2	0+1		
Frain	4+2	1		
Hadley	28+11/14	3+2	3/1	3/1
Holland	33/9	5	4/3	3
Howarth	39+1/2	5	3	4
Hoyle	4+1	2		1
Ireland	38+2/5	5/1	4/1	3
Lampkin	22+1/2		1	1+1
Marrows				0+1
Noteman	27+5/6	5	2	2
Onoura	10+4/7			1
Parkin	22/1	2	1+1	2
Pearcey	3			1
Pearson	0+2		1+1	
Peters	25+1/4	2	2	4
Sherlock	1+1			0+1
Stark				1
Timons	4+2	0+1		2
Trinder	4+3			
Walker	4			
Ward	35	5	4	3
Wilkinson	41/22	5/3	4	3
Williams	0+1			

MIDDLESBROUGH (DIV 1)

	P/FL	FLC	FAC	Others
Anderson	2			
Barron				2+1
Blackmore	26+4/2	1		1
Byrne				1
Cox	39+1/1	2+1		2
Fjortoft	8/3			
Fleming	21	3	2	1
Freestone	0+1			
Fuchs	13+2/9			
Hendrie	37+2/15	2/1	2/1	
Hignett	19+7/8	2+1/1	1	1
Kavanagh	5+2		1	2
Liddle	1			2
Miller	41	1	2	2
Moore	35+2/4	2/1	1+1/1	2
Moreno	6+8/2	1		3/1
Morris	14+1	1	2	3/1
Mustoe	24+3/3	2/1	2	2
Norton				0+1
O'Halloran	1			1
Pears	5	2		1
Pearson	33/3		2	
Pollock	41/6	3/1	2	1
Richardson				0+1
Roberts				1

	P/FL	FLC	FAC	Others
Robson	21+1/1			
Stamp	1+2			4
Taylor				3
Todd	5	1		3
Vickers	44/3	3	2	2
White				1
Whyte	36/1	3	1	1
Wilkinson	27+4/9	3/3	2	0+1
Wright	1	1+1		4

Jamie Pollock (Middlesbrough)
Neal Simpson
(Empics Sports Photo Agency)

MILLWALL (DIV 1)

	P/FL	FLC	FAC	Others
Beard	24+7/1	2+1	4/1	
Beckford	6+3			
Berry	4+5	1/2		
Cadette	12+4/4	2/1	1	
Carter	2	0+1		
Chapman	4+8	0+1		
Connor	1			
Cunningham	15	2		
Dawes	12+2	2+1	4	
Dixon	9/4			
Edwards	3+1		3+1	
Forbes	0+1			
Goodman	15/8	3/2		
Huxford	0+1			
Joseph	5			
Keller	44	5	5	
Kelly	1+1			
Kennedy	28+2/5	5/2	3+1/1	
Kerr	7+7/3	1		
McCarthy	12	3		
McRobert	4+3/1			
May	14+2		1	
Mitchell	23+5/7	3+1/1	5	
Oldfield	16+1/6			
Rae	38/10	4	4	
Roberts	44/3	5	5	
Savage	31+6/2	5	2+2/1	
Stevens	20	2	3	
Taylor	1+5			
Thatcher	38+2/1	4	4	

	P/FL	FLC	FAC	Others
Van Blerk	24+3/1	2	5	
Van den Hauwe	4	2		
Webber	19+3/2	1+1	1+2	
Witter	26+1/1	1	5	

NEWCASTLE UNITED (PREM)

	P/FL	FLC	FAC	Others
Albert	17/2	4/1		4
Allen	0+1			
Beardsley	34/13	3	3	4/2
Beresford	33	5	4/1	4
Bracewell	13+3	0+1	3	
Clark	9+10/1	3	2/1	1+2
Cole	18/9	5/2	1	3/4
Elliott	10+4/2		3+1	
Fox	40/10	2/1	5	4/1
Gillespie	15+2/2		3/2	
Guppy		0+1		
Hooper	4+2			
Hottiger	38/1	5	4/1	4
Howey	29+1/1	3	4	3
Jeffrey		1/1		0+2
Kitson	24+2/8	3/1	4+1/3	
Lee	35/9	2	4/1	3/4
Matthie	3+6/1	1+2		
Neilson	5+1	1		
Peacock	35/1	4	5	4
Sellars	12	3		4/1
Srnicek	38	5	5	4
Venison	28/1	2	5	1
Watson	22+5/4	3+1	0+1	1+2/1

NORTHAMPTON TOWN (DIV 3)

	P/FL	FLC	FAC	Others
Aldridge	18+9/7	1	0+1	2/2
Bell	12/1	1		
Brown	23/4			
Burns	16+1/2			
Byrne	2	1		
Cahill	5+3/1			1+2
Colkin	28+5/1	1	1	1
Curtis	13	2		1+1
Daniels	5+3			
Flounders	2			
Grayson	34+4/8	2	1	3/2
Harmon	26+7/4	2	1	3/1
Harrison	5			0+1
Hughes	12+1			
MacNamara	0+1			1
Martin	7/1			
Norton	36+2	2	1	1
O'Shea	7/1			
Ovendale	6			2
Pascoe	11+4	1	1	2
Patmore	1+3			
Robinson	14	1	1	2
Sampson	42/2	2	1	3
Sedgmore	1			
Skelly	3			2
Smith	6/1			
Stewart	26+1	2	1	1
Thompson	15/4			
Trott	20+2/4	2	1	1
Turner	2+2			1
Warburton	39/3	2	1	3/1
Wilkin	2+2	0+1		0+1
Williams	13+2		1	3
Woodman	10			

NORWICH CITY (PREM)

	P/FL	FLC	FAC	Others
Adams	23+10/3	6/1	3	
Akinbiyi	6+7	0+1	1+2	
Bowen	34+2/2	5	3	

	P/FL	FLC	FAC	Others
Bradshaw	25+1/1	2/1	1	
Crook	33+1	4+2	2/1	
Cureton	9+8/4	0+1	0+2	
Eadie	22+4/2	6/1	4/1	
Ekoku	5+1	1		
Goss	19+6/2	3+3	1+2	
Gunn	21	5		
Johnson	6+1	1	1	
Marshall	20+1	1	2+1	
Megson	1			
Milligan	25+1/2	4	3	
Newman	23+9/1	5+1/1	3	
Newsome	35/3	4	4	
O'Neill	0+1			
Polston	38	5/2	3	
Prior	12+5	3/1	0+1	
Robins	14+3/4	3+1		
Sheron	17+4/1	4/1	4/2	
Sutch	20+10/1	3+1	4	
Tracey	1		2	
Ullathorne	27/2	1+1	4	
Ward	25/8			
Wright	1+1			

NOTTINGHAM FOREST (PREM)

	P/FL	FLC	FAC	Others
Black	5+5/2	2		
Bohinen	30+4/6	4	1/1	
Bull	1/1		0+1	
Chettle	41	4	2	
Collymore	37/22	4/2	2/1	
Cooper	35/1	4	1	
Crossley	42	4	2	
Gemmill	19/1	1	2/1	
Haaland	18+2/1	0+1	1	
Lee	5+17/3	0+2		
Lyttle	38	4	2	
McGregor	0+11/1			
Pearce	36/8	3/2	1	
Phillips	38/1	4	2	
Rosario	0+1			
Roy	37/13	4/1	2	
Stone	41/5	4	2	
Tiler	3		1	
Warner	1			
Webb			0+1	
Woan	35+2/5	2+1	1	

NOTTS COUNTY (DIV 1)

	P/FL	FLC	FAC	Others
Agana	25+6/3	3+1/1		6/2
Butler	20	2	2	3
Cherry	25	3	2	3
Cox	3			0+1
Daniel	5			1
Devlin	37+3/9	4/1	2	5+1/2
Emenalo	7			3+1
Forsyth	7			
Gallagher	7			2+1
Galloway	6+1			
Hogg	17			1
Hoyle	3			1
Jemson	5+6/1	1+1/1		1
Johnson	27+4	4	2	4+1
Kearton	10			2
Kuhl	2			
Legg	32+2/3	4	2	4+1/1
Lund	17+6/5	3/2	0+1	3
McSwegan	19+3/6	3/2	2/1	1
Marsden	7			1/1
Matthews	11+7/3	0+2	2/2	3+2
Mills	33+1	3	2	4/1

	P/FL	FLC	FAC	Others
Murphy	31+4	2+1	2	5+1/1
Nicol	19			2/1
Reece	11	1		2+1
Ridgeway	0+1			
Russell	9+2			
Sherlock	2+3/1	1		1
Short	11+2			1
Simpson	15+4/2	1		3+1
Slawson	0+1			
Turner	37+1/1	4	2	7/1
Walker	6+1	1		1
White	16+4/7		2/1	3/1
Williams	3+2/2			
Yates	21	4		4

OLDHAM ATHLETIC (DIV 1)

	P/FL	FLC	FAC	Others
Banger	20+8/3	2	1	
Barlow	2			
Beckford	0+3		0+2	
Beresford	0+2			
Bernard	16+1/2	2		
Brennan	34+6/1	3+1	2	
Eyre	3+5/1	0+2		
Fleming	5			
Gerrard	42	3	2	
Graham	29+3/2	4	2	
Halle	40/5	4	2/2	
Hallworth	4+2	1		
Henry	33+1/2	4	2	
Holden A.	1			
Holden R.	18+13/3	1+2	0+1	
Jobson	20	4		
Kenny	4			
McCarthy	35+4/18	4	1	
McNiven	1			
Makin	28/1	3	2	
Moore	5			
Pointon	32	1	2	
Redmond	43	4	2	
Richardson	28+2/6	2/1	2	
Rickers	4/1			
Ritchie	25+8/12	2+1/1	1	
Sharp	10+2/3	0+1	1/1	
Snodin	17			
Webster	7			

Paul Bernard (Oldham)   Neal Simpson
(Empics Sports Photo Agency)

OXFORD UNITED (DIV 2)

	P/FL	FLC	FAC	Others
Allen	32+4/2	4		2
Butters	3/1			1
Byrne	25/10	4	1	2
Carter	3+1			
Collins	3		1	1
Cusack	0+2			
Deegan	2			3
Dobson	5			
Druce	9+10/3	0+2		2
Dyer	32+6/1	3/1	1	3
Elliott	45/5	4	1	3
Ford M.	15+3	4/1		1
Ford R.	20+3/2		1	3/1
Gilchrist	18/1			
Key	6			
Lewis	30+9/1	1+1		3
Marsh	8	2	1	2
Massey	20+2	4/1	1	1
Moody	34+7/21	4/1	1	1/2
Murphy	17+5/7			1+2/1
Robinson	46	4/1	1	4
Rogan	27+2/1	2		1
Rush	22+12/9	0+1	0+1	3+1
Smith	41+1	4	1	4
Wanless	3+7			1+1
Whitehead	38	4	1	1
Wood	2			1

PETERBOROUGH UNITED (DIV 2)

	P/FL	FLC	FAC	Others
Ashley	27	2	2	
Barber	5			
Breen	43+1/1	2	2	3/1
Brissett	4+1	1	0+1	1+1/1
Charlery	44/16	2	1/2	2/1
Clark	32	2	2	0+1
Cooksey	12	2	2	1
Dunphy	0+2			
Ebdon	35/6	2	2	3
Farrell	25+8/8	2	1	1
Feuer	16			
Furnell	4+4			
Gordon	6/1			
Heald	27+2	1		3/1
Henry	22+10/7	0+1	2/1	2/2
Keeley	3			
Kelly	12+1/2			
Le Bihan	3+1			
Lormor	2+3		1	1+1
McGorry	30+4/3	0+2	2	2
Manuel	14/1			
Moran	5+2	2	1	1
Morrison	34+8/8	1/1	0+1	2
Prudhoe	6			
Semple	1+1			
Soloman	4			
Spearing	31+2		2	3
Thomas	6+2		0+1	2
Tyler	4+1			2
Webster				2
Welsh	14	2		
Williams	35+5/1	1+1	2/1	2

PLYMOUTH ARGYLE (DIV 2)

	P/FL	FLC	FAC	Others
Barber	4		1	
Barlow	40+2/2	2	3	2
Bradshaw	5+1/1	1		
Burnett	25+7/1	1	3	2
Castle	23+3/3	1/1		
Comyn	30	2	2	2

PORTSMOUTH - ROCHDALE

	P/FL	FLC	FAC	Others
Crocker	3+2			
Dalton	23+3/4	1		
Dawe	3+1			
Dungey	3+1			
Edworthy	24+3/1	2	3	1+1
Evans	12+11/4	2	2+1	1
Gee	6			
Hill	32+2/1	2	1	2
Hodge	17	2	1	
Landon	18+6/7	0+1	0+1	2
McCall	7			
Morgan	6+2	0+1		1
Naylor	42		3	2/1
Nicholls	26+1		2	2
Nugent	34+3/6	2	3	0+1
O'Hagan	1+2/1			1
Patterson	37+1/3		3	1
Payne	1	1		
Quinn	3			
Ross	11+6		1/2	
Shaw	6			
Shilton	1+1		0+1	
Skinner	21+3/2	1	2/1	1+1
Swan	24+3/2	2/1	2	
Twiddy	13+2/1	0+1	1	2
Wotton	5+2			

PORTSMOUTH (DIV 1)

	P/FL	FLC	FAC	Others
Awford	3+1	1		
Burton	5+2/2	0+1		
Butters	24		2	
Creaney	39/18	4/3	2/1	
Daniel	17+5	2+1	2	
Dobson	14	3		
Doling	2+3/1			
Durnin	8+8/2	0+1		
Flahaven			0+1	
Gittens	37+1	5	2	
Glass	3			
Hall	30+13/5	4+1/1		
Igoe	0+1			
Knight	43	3	2	
Kristensen	15+10	2+1/1	1	
Lee	4+1			
McGrath	15+3	1	2	
McLoughlin	36+2/6	5	0+1	
Neill	7	2		
Newhouse	6/1			
Pethick	39+5/1	4+1	2	
Poom		2		
Powell	34/5	5/3	2	
Radosavljevic	30+10/5	2+1	2/2	
Rees	14+5/1	0+1	0+1	
Russell	18+1		1	
Stimson	15	5/1		
Symons	40/4	5	1	
Totten	3+1			
Wood	5/1		1	

PORT VALE (DIV 1)

	P/FL	FLC	FAC	Others
Allon	10+9/7	0+1	2/1	
Aspin	37	1	2	
Billing	6			
Bogie	7+2/2			
Burke	4+11/2	1+2	0+2	
Burndred	1			
Corden	0+1			
Foyle	40+2/16	4/1	2/3	
Glover D.	28+1	4	2/1	
Glover L.	21+7/4	4/3	0+2	
Griffiths	20	3	2/1	

	P/FL	FLC	FAC	Others
Guppy	25+2/2		1	
Jeffers	6+4/1		1	
Kelly	3+1/1	1		
Kent	19+4/2	4		
Lawton	0+1			
Musselwhite	44	4	2	
Naylor	29+4/9	3/1		
Porter	43+1/3	4	2	
Sandeman	37	4		
Scott	17/1			
Stokes	3			
Talbot	2			
Tankard	39/1	4	2	
Van der Laan	43+1/5	3+1	2	
Van Heusden	2			
Walker	20+3/1	0+1	2	

PRESTON NORTH END (DIV 3)

	P/FL	FLC	FAC	Others
Ainsworth	16/1	1	1	1+1
Atkinson	8+7/1			
Beckham	4+1/2			
Bryson	41/5	1+1	3	4
Carmichael	7+3/3			
Cartwright	25+11/1	2	3	2+2
Conroy	22+3/10	1+1	3/1	0+2
Davey	13/3			2
Emerson	1+1		0+2	
Fensome	42	2/1	3	4
Fleming	20+7/2	2	0+1	3+1
Hicks	8	2		
Holmes	5/1		3	3
Kidd	32/3	2		1
Lancashire	9+8			1
Magee	14/1			1
Moyes	38/4	2/1	3	4
Raynor	34+4/3	1+1	3	4
Richardson	17	2	3	1
Rimmer	0+2			
Sale	10+3/6	1+1	0+1	4
Sharp	21		3	1
Smart	17+2/6		2/1	1
Squires	11			1
Trebble	8+11/4	1	2+1	2/1
Vaughan	25+1			3
Whalley	14+1/1	2	1+1	1+1

QUEENS PARK RANGERS (PREM)

	P/FL	FLC	FAC	Others
Allen	2+3/2	1/1	0+1	
Bardsley	30	3	4	
Barker	37/4	3	4	
Brevett	17+2		1	
Dichio	4+5/3	1	1	
Dykstra	11	1		
Ferdinand	37/24	2/1	3/1	
Gallen	31+6/10	1+1/1	4/1	
Hodge	15		1	
Holloway	28+3/1	3	3+1	
Impey	40/3	2	4/1	
McCarthy	0+2			
McDonald	39/1	3	4	
Maddix	21+6/1		4/1	
Meaker	7+1	1	2/1	
Penrice	9+10/3	1+1/1	0+1	
Ready	11+2/1	0+1		
Roberts	31	2	4	
Sinclair	32+1/4	3/1	1	
White	1			
Wilkins	1+1			
Wilson	36/2	3/1	3/1	
Yates	22+1/1	3	1	

READING (DIV 1)

	P/FL	FLC	FAC	Others
Barnard	3+1			
Bernal	33	3	1	3
Carey	0+2			
Gilkes	37+3/8	2	1	3
Gooding	37+2	4	1	3
Hartenberger	8+7/2		0+1	
Hislop	46	4	1	3
Holsgrove	23+1/3	2+2/1		
Hopkins	20+1	3+1/1	0+1	0+2
Jones	18+2/1		1	
Kerr	35+1/1	4		
Lambert	3+8/1			
Lovell	25+5/11	4/1	1	3/2
McPherson	19+4	0+1		3
Murphy	0+1			
Nogan	18+2/10			3/2
Osborn	31+1/5	4		3
Parkinson	25+6	3	1	
Quinn	31+4/5	4/4	1	0+2/1
Taylor	31+13/8	1+2	1/1	3
Viveash	6			
Wdowczyk	37+1	2	1	3
Williams	20+2/2	4		3/1

Simon Osborn (Reading)   Neal Simpson
(Empics Sports Photo Agency)

ROCHDALE (DIV 3)

	P/FL	FLC	FAC	Others
Bayliss	1			
Bowden	6+5	1		
Butler	39/3	1	1	7
Clarke	24	2		3
Deary	17/1			3
Dickens	4			1
Doyle	7+4		1	2
Dunford	2		1	
Formby	27+1	2	1	7
Gray	12			3
Hall	5+4/1	1+1		1+2
Martin	12+3			
Matthews	10+3	1	1	6

	P/FL	FLC	FAC	Others
Oliver	8+1			
Peake	36+3/2	1	1	5
Reeves	5	2		
Reid	27+1/3	2	1	6/2
Rimmer	3			
Russell	2+5/1			1+2
Ryan	15+10/2	1+1	0+1	1+4
Sharpe	9+7/2		0+1	6/1
Shaw	4			
Stuart	26+5/2	1+1	1	2+3/1
Taylor	1+8			0+2/1
Thackeray	41/3	2	1	7
Thompson	38+2/6	2		7
Valentine	27/2			
Whitehall	41+1/10	2/1	1	7/6
Whittington	1			
Williams	12+2/5	1	1	2

ROTHERHAM UNITED (DIV 2)

	P/FL	FLC	FAC	Others
Ayrton				1
Breckin	41/2	1	3	3
Brien	16+1	2	3	3
Clarke	45		3	3
Davison	19+2/4		2/3	2
Dolby	0+2		1	1
Farrelly	9+1/2			
Foran	3			
Goater	45/19	1	3/3	3/3
Goodwin	10/3	2		1
Hayward	33+4/6	1+1/1	2	2
Hazel	16+5	2		1
Helliwell	10+2/1	1	0+2/1	1/1
Hurst	8+5		2/1	1
James	40	2	3	3
McGlashan	27/3			
Marginson	5+3/1		1	1
Mercer	1	2		
Monington	25/2			
Peel	9/4			
Pike	7			
Richardson	23+2	1	2	1
Roberts	0+2			
Roscoe	31/4			
Smith	3+1		2	0+1
Todd	12+2	1		1/1
Varadi	6+11/2	2/1	1+1	0+2
Wilder	45/1	2	3	3
Williams A.	17	2	2	2
Williams C.	0+2	0+2		

SCARBOROUGH (DIV 3)

	P/FL	FLC	FAC	Others
Blackstone	11+2	4/2	0+2	
Calvert	26+4/2	4	0+1	0+1
Charles	40/5	4/1	5	1/1
D'Auria	31+3/7	1+2	3+1	1
Davis	22+1/2	0+1	4	1
Dunphy	10	2		
Ford	6			
Foreman	10+4/1	2		
Griffiths	5/1			
Hicks	6			
Ironside	9			
Kelly	24	4	3	
Knowles	39	4	5	1
Mardenborough	0+1			
Martin	3		2	1
Meyer	13	4	3	
Norris	8/4			

	P/FL	FLC	FAC	Others
Rockett	27	2	3	1
Rodwell	6+2/1		2	
Rowe	10+4/1	4/1		
Rutherford	6+2/1		2+1	
Scott	8/3			
Swales	21/1		3	
Swann	24+3/3	2	5/1	1
Thompson	14+2/1	3	2+1	0+1
Toman	9+7	1	3/1	1
Trebble	15/3			
Wells	16+2/1		4	1
White	36+3/11	2+1	5/1	1
Young	7+6/1	1+2/1	1+1	

SCUNTHORPE UNITED (DIV 3)

	P/FL	FLC	FAC	Others
Alexander	38+2/4	2	4/1	2/1
Bradley	24+1/2	2	4	2
Bullimore	34+1/6	2/1	4/1	2/1
Carmichael	9+11/2	0+1	0+3/1	1
Eli	0+2			
Eyre	9/8			
Ford	38/2	2	4	1
Goodacre	1+4	0+1		2
Gregory	10/7			
Henderson	16+1/3	2/1	1	1
Hope	22+2		2/1	1
Housham	4			0+1
Juryeff	21/8	2	4	
Kiwomya	9/3			
Knill	39/4	2	4	2
Martin	0+5	1		0+1
Mudd	35/1	2	4	1
Nicholson	14+1/4			
Samways	42	2	4	2
Sansam	4+2		2+1	0+2
Smith	24+8/2	2	3	2
Thompstone	8+11/1		1+2/1	1
Thornber	36+1/5	1	3	2
Turnbull	10/3			
Walsh	3			
Young	12+2/2			

SHEFFIELD UNITED (DIV 1)

	P/FL	FLC	FAC	Others
Anthony	0+1			2
Battersby				2+1/1
Beesley	26+1/2	1		
Bibbo				2
Black	8+3/2			
Blake	28+7/17	2+1/1	1	1
Blount	4+1			2
Carr				1/1
Davidson	1			2
Davison	1+2/1			2
Fickling		1+1		3
Flo	25+7/6	2/2	0+1	
Foran	4/1	1		0+1
Foreman				1+2
Gage	40/5	2	1	1
Gannon	12	1+1		2/1
Gayle	35/1	2	1	
Hartfield	23+2/1	1	1	1
Hawthorne				3/1
Hodges	20+5/4		1	1
Hodgson	0+1	1		1
Hoyland	0+2	2		3
Kelly	38	3	1	
Littlejohn	9+7/1	1+1		1/1
Marshall	17			
Mercer	3			
Nilsen	33	1	1	

	P/FL	FLC	FAC	Others
Reed	11+1/2	1		1/1
Rogers	44/4	2	1	1
Scott A.	18+19/4	2/1	1	3+1/3
Scott R.	0+1	0+1		2+1
Starbuck	20+3/1		0+1	
Tracey	5			2
Tuttle	6			
Veart	30+9/11	1	1	2
Ward	10+4/2	2		2/1
Whitehouse	35+4/7	3/3	1	

SHEFFIELD WEDNESDAY (PREM)

	P/FL	FLC	FAC	Others
Atherton	41/1	4	3	
Bart-Williams	32+6/2	4/2	3	
Bright	33+4/11	3	3/2	
Briscoe	6			
Coleman	1			
Donaldson	0+1			
Hirst	13+2/3	1+1		
Hyde	33+2/5	4/1	3	
Ingesson	9+4/2	1	1	
Jones	3+2	0+1		
Key			0+1	
Nolan	42/3	4	3	
Pearce	34	4	3	
Petrescu	20+9/3	2	0+2	
Poric	1+3			
Pressman	34	4	3	
Sheridan	34+2/1	4	2+1	
Sinton	22+3	4	1	
Taylor	9+5/1	2+2/1		
Waddle	20+5/4		3/1	
Walker	38	2	3	
Watson	5+18/2	2+1	0+1	
Whittingham	16+5/9		2+1	
Williams	8+2/1			
Woods	8+1			

SHREWSBURY TOWN (DIV 2)

	P/FL	FLC	FAC	Others
Brown	9/3	2		
Clarke T.	15+1			
Clarke W.	26+5/11	2/1		1
Currie	15+2/2			
Edwards	31	2	1	3
Evans	27+5/5			2
Harford	3+3			
Hockaday	16	2	1	2
Hughes	18+2		1	1
Jeffers	3/1			2
Lynch	34/1	2		2+1
Patterson	17+1/1	2	1	1
Reed	1+3			
Scott	7+1/1			
Seabury	27+3			1+1
Simkin	10+2			
Slawson	6			0+1
Smith	10+7/2			1
Spink	36+3/11	2/1	1/1	3/1
Stevens	26+12/8	0+1	1	2+1/4
Summerfield	14+4	0+1	1	1
Taylor	44/2	2	1	3
Walton	36/3			1
Williams	33+2/1		1	3/1
Withe	27+4/2	1+1	1	2
Woods	15+4	1	1	2

SOUTHAMPTON (PREM)

	P/FL	FLC	FAC	Others
Allen	11	2		
Banger	4/2			
Beasant	12+1			
Benali	32+3	3	4	

	P/FL	FLC	FAC	Others
Bennett		0+1		
Charlton	25/1	2+1	1	
Dodd	24+2/2	1	3	
Dowie	17/5	3		
Ekelund	15+2/5	2+1		
Grobbelaar	30	3	5	
Hall	36+1/4	2	4	
Heaney	21+13/2	2+1	5/2	
Hughes	2+10/2		0+4/1	
Kenna	28	2	5	
Le Tissier	41/20	3/5	5/5	
McDonald	0+2			
Maddison	35/3	2	4	
Magilton	42/6	3	5/1	
Maskell	2+4		1	
Monkou	31/1	2	4/1	
Oakley	0+1			
Robinson	0+1			
Shipperley	19/4		4/2	
Tisdale	0+7	0+1	0+1	
Watson	12/3			
Whiston	0+1			
Widdrington	23+5	1	5	

SOUTHEND UNITED (DIV 1)

	P/FL	FLC	FAC	Others
Ansah	7+2		1	
Battersby	6+2/1			
Bodley	12			
Bressington	19+1/2	1	1	
Chapman	1/1			
Davidson		0+1		
Dublin	40/2	2	1	
Edwards	42+2/3	1		
Foot	2+1			
Forrester	3+2			
Gridelet	26+3/4		1	
Hails	20+6/2			
Harkness	6			
Hone	39+1	2	1	
Hunt	5+2	1+1		
Iorfa	4+4/1	2		
Jones G.	19+6/11			
Jones K.	7	2		
Martin	0+4	1+1		
Otto	19/4	1		
Perkins	1+5			
Poole	5+1	2		
Powell	44	2	1	
Regis	9/1			
Roche	0+4			
Royce	13	2		
Sansome	33		1	
Sussex	14+1/1	1		
Thomson	35+4/11	1	1	
Tilson	17+9/2	1	1	
Westley	4+1			
Whelan	33/1		1	
Willis	21/4		1	

STOCKPORT COUNTY (DIV 2)

	P/FL	FLC	FAC	Others
Armstrong	40+5/14	3/1	0+1	2
Beaumont	33+5/2	0+1/1	1	2
Bound	14		1	2/1
Brock		1		
Brown	1			
Chalk	24+9/6	3/1	1	1+1
Connelly	37+2	4	1	1
Davenport	3+3/1			
Dickins	11+1			
Dinning	38+2/1	2	0+1	2/1

	P/FL	FLC	FAC	Others
Eckhardt	26+1/1	4	1	1
Edwards	18+1			2
Emerson	1+2	2/1		
Flynn	43/2	4	1	2
Frain	2			
Francis	16+1/12	4/1		
Gannon	43+2/7	4	1	1+1
Graham	5+6/2			
Helliwell	17/4			
Ironside	7+1		1	
Keeley	10	4		
Marshall	1			
Miller	0+3	1		
Oliver	10+3			
Slinn	2+2/1	0+1		1
Todd	37/2	4		2
Wallace	24+1/2	0+2	1	1+1/1
Ward	27+1/3	3/1	1	1/1
Ware	16+3/1	1+1	1	1
Williams	0+1			
Young				0+1

STOKE CITY (DIV 1)

	P/FL	FLC	FAC	Others
Allen	17/1			2
Andrade	2+2/1			
Beckford	2+2			1
Beeston	15+1/1	1		1
Biggins	8+9/2	1+1		3+1/2
Butler	38+3	3	2	4+1/2
Carruthers	26+6/5	3	0+1	4+2/3
Clark	5			1/1
Clarkson	15+3	1	2	3+1
Cranson	37/1	3	2	5
Downing	16	2	1	3+2
Dreyer	16+2/2	2		3
Gayle	1+3			2
Gleghorn	44+2/7	3/1	2	6/1
Keen	15+6/2			
Leslie	0+1			0+1
Muggleton	24	3		4
Orlygsson	38/7	3/1	2	1
Overson	33+2	1	2	5
Peschisolido	39+1/13	3/2	2	3+1
Potter	1	0+1		
Sandford	34+1/1	3	2	6/1
Scott	16+2/3		2/1	
Shaw	1+2			0+1
Sigurdsson	22+1/1		0+1	
Sinclair	22+2		2	2
Sturridge	2+6/1		0+1	1+1
Wade	0+1			
Wallace	16+4/1	1	1	6
Williams	1+3			

SUNDERLAND (DIV 1)

	P/FL	FLC	FAC	Others
Agnew	16/2			
Angell	8			
Armstrong	10+5/1		3/2	
Atkinson	16+1		1	
Ball	42/2	2	2	
Bennett	19+1	1	3	
Brodie	1+7			
Chamberlain	17+1		3	
Cunnington	3+5			
Ferguson	23	1	3	
Goodman	17+1/3	2		
Gray Martin	17+5	1	0+1	
Gray Michael	10+6	0+1	0+1	
Gray P.	41+1/12	2/1	3/2	
Howey	6+9/2	0+1	1+1	

	P/FL	FLC	FAC	Others
Kubicki	46	2	3	
Matteo	1			
Melville	36/3	2	2	
Norman	29	2		
Ord	33	2		
Owers	18+1/1	2		
Rodgerson	3+3			
Russell	28+10/5	2/1	3/1	
Scott	24		3	
Smith A.	0+1			
Smith M.	33+2/10	1+1	3	
Snodin	6			
Williams	3			

SWANSEA CITY (DIV 2)

	P/FL	FLC	FAC	Others
Ampadu	36+8/6	3+1	3/1	7/1
Barnhouse	4		1	1
Basham	13		5	7
Bowen	25+6/5	3+1	2	6+2/5
Burns	3+2		0+1	
Chapple	4+5/2		2+1	4+1
Clode	33/1	4	1	3
Coates	0+5			
Cook	1			1
Cornforth	32+1/3	4	5	7/1
Edwards	9			1+1
Ford	46/3	4	5/2	9
Freestone	44+1/1	4	5	9
Harris	14	4/1		2
Hayes	14+10/4	1+1	3+1	4+6/5
Hendry	8/2			4/5
Hodge	38+6/7	3+1/1	5	9
Jenkins	42	4	4	9
Jones	2			1
McFarlane	1+2		0+2	1+1/2
Pascoe	32+3/5	3+1/1		5/1
Penney	29+6/5	3+1/2	5/1	8
Perrett	3+12	1	0+1	1+1/3
Thomas	2+2			0+3/1
Torpey	37+4/11	3	5/2	5+1/3
Walker	28		4	6
Williams	6+1/2			

SWINDON TOWN (DIV 1)

	P/FL	FLC	FAC	Others
Beauchamp	38+4/3	7+1	2	4
Berkley	0+1	0+1		2+1
Bodin	25/6	6	1	2
Culverhouse	9	1	2	
Digby	39	6		2+1
Drysdale	1			
Fenwick	2			
Fjortoft	36/15	8/9	2/1	1+1
Gooden	13+3/2	1		0+1
Hammond	7	2	2	2
Hamon	2+3/1		0+1	0+2/1
Hooper	0+4	0+1		
Horlock	34+4/1	5		4
Kilcline	6+1	3		4
Ling	31+5/3	6+1	2	3+1
MacLaren	3			1
McMahon	16+1			
Murray	4+2	2	1	
Mutch	7+13	3+1/2	2	3/2
Nijholt	35	8	2/1	3
O'Sullivan	22+8	5	0+2	2
Phillips				0+1
Pitman	2+1			
Robinson	40	7	2	4
Scott	21+3/8	5/3		3/1
Taylor	37/4	5	2	1